Principles of Human Neuropsychology

Principles of Human Neuropsychology

G. Dennis Rains

Kutztown University of Pennsylvania

Boston   Burr Ridge, IL   Dubuque, IA   Madison, WI   New York
San Francisco   St. Louis   Bangkok   Bogotá   Caracas   Kuala Lumpur
Lisbon   London   Madrid   Mexico City   Milan   Montreal   New Delhi
Santiago   Seoul   Singapore   Sydney   Taipei   Toronto

McGraw-Hill Higher Education

A Division of The **McGraw-Hill** *Companies*

1 2 3 4 5 6 7 8 9 0 DOC/DOC 0 9 8 7 6 5 4 3 2 1

Library of Congress Cataloging-in-Publication Data

Rains, G. Dennis
    Principles of human neuropsychology / G. Dennis Rains
      p. cm.
    Includes bibliographical references and index.
    ISBN 1-55934-623-X
     1. Neuropsychology.   I. Title.

    QP360   .R34 2001
    612.8—dc21   2001031489

Sponsoring editor, Ken King; developmental editor, Kathleen Engelberg; production editor, Melissa Williams; manuscript editor, Beverley J. DeWitt; design manager and cover designer, Jean Mailander; text designer, Michael Remener; art editor, Robin Mouat; manufacturing manager, Randy Hurst. The text was set in 9/12 Palatino by Thompson Type, Inc. and printed on acid-free 45# Scholarly Matte by R. R. Donnelley & Sons Inc.

Cover Images: The cover shows four self-portraits made by the German artist Anton Räderscheidt in the months following a stroke that damaged his right parietal lobe. In the first painting, done 2 months after the stroke (upper left), he omitted the left half of the face and everything else on the left side. This is characteristic of his pervasive neglect of the left side of space during this period, despite his preserved visual acuity. Over the next several months he gradually recovered his ability. This is evidenced by the progressively more detailed depiction of the left side of the face and the left background in the portraits done 3.5 months (upper right), 6 months (lower left), and 9 months (lower right) after his stroke. Unilateral neglect of space is discussed in chapter 7.

Text, photo, and illustration credits appear on a continuation of the copyright page, pages 547–551.

www.mhhe.com

To three who inspired me:

    Gregg Rains, to be curious about the wonders of the universe

    Rita Rains, to recognize the compass of my reaching

    Mary Rains, to grasp the meaning of it all

Preface

I wrote this book because I wanted my students to have access to an account of neuropsychology that was at once clear and in-depth. I wanted them to experience the sense of wonder that I have felt since I first became captivated by this field 25 years ago. It seemed to me that the way to do this was to create a text that, without overwhelming the student, would provide sufficient detail and depth of treatment to kindle a sense of wonder and to whet the appetite for further forays into this at-once most mysterious and most intimate of all domains of science. An in-depth treatment achieves this end, it seems to me, by paradoxically making the material *easier* to grasp by offering deeper explanation. And, of course, a by-product of a deeper understanding is the even more exciting revelation of the questions that remain to be answered. The search for ways to achieve these ends has guided the writing of this book.

The other guiding principle has been the essential unity of knowledge and, particularly in a domain as fraught with difficult problems as neuropsychology, the necessity of integrating insights gleaned from widely disparate levels of analysis. Although the continually expanding breadth of the neurosciences demands that any single book focus its attention, adhering to the perspective of a single level of analysis runs the risk of providing only a two-dimensional view of brain-behavior relationships. One of my central objectives has been to provide the reader with the in-depth view that is possible when the attempt is made to integrate the perspectives afforded by different disciplines and the data derived from different levels of analysis. One of the most exciting results of this integrative attempt is the often stunning degree to which findings derived from different levels

of analysis inform and illuminate each other, and I have tried to share this excitement with my readers. We have moved far beyond the time when the reports of different levels of analysis seem like the isolated reports of the many blind men feeling different parts of the proverbial elephant; we are beginning to integrate different levels of understanding into a coherent representation of the animal itself.

The book is divided into three major sections: The Foundations (chapters 1–5), Neuropsychology of Major Functional Systems (6–12), and Application of Neuropsychology to Broad Functional Domains (13–15). It ends with an Epilogue.

Part I: Foundations

The first three chapters of this text approach neuropsychology from three different levels. Chapter 1 provides an overview of neuropsychology in the context of its historical development. In addition to serving as a general introduction to the field, this chapter offers insights into the processes underlying the development of our understanding of brain-behavior relationships. These processes are always at work in any evolving field. A consideration of their influence in the past sheds light on how future developments are likely to unfold.

Chapter 2, Neural Mechanisms at the Molecular and Cellular Levels, approaches the function of the nervous system at the micro level. This has great intrinsic interest because much has been learned in recent years about events at these levels. The chapter's examination of the ways in which neurons interact also provides insight into the integrative function of the nervous system as a whole. The discussion of recently elucidated neuronal mechanisms of simple forms of learning in relatively uncomplicated organisms that concludes the chapter serves as an example of how the principles derived from investigations into processes at the micro level can be applied to psychological functions on a more molar level. In doing this, it also previews the kinds of explanation of other cognitive processes that may be possible in the future.

Chapter 3, Introduction to the Structure and Function of the Nervous System, introduces the basic structures of the nervous system and discusses general aspects of their function. In addition to providing information that is critical for understanding material in subsequent chapters, this chapter surveys the relationship between gross anatomical structures and behavior.

Chapter 4, Methods in Neuropsychology, provides information about how insight into and understanding of brain-behavior relationships is achieved. The answers to our questions are inextricable from the methods we use to ask them. A thorough grounding in and appreciation of methodology is thus essential to an understanding of the current state of neuropsychology and its probable future directions. The methods reviewed in this chapter range from the most recent advances in PET, fMRI, and magnetoencephalography to classical methods employed to study the effect of cerebral lesions on behavior and psychological functioning. An emphasis is placed on the importance—or rather, the necessity—of applying a wide range of methods in our attempts to approach an integrated understanding of the relationship between brain and behavior.

Chapter 5, The Visual System as a Model of Nervous System Functioning, integrates the levels of analysis and approach addressed in the first four chapters. It does this by examining the most completely understood system of the brain, the visual system, at a number of different levels. Knowledge in this area has been expanding at an ever-increasing pace in recent years as new techniques and research strategies have been aimed at unlocking the mysteries of the visual brain. This chapter focuses on recent findings at a variety of levels, from the study of the individual neuron and small populations of neurons, to the anatomical microstructure of the visual cortex, and the gross anatomy of the visual system. The combination of these levels of approach reveals the elegant segregation—both anatomical and functional—inherent in the magnocellular and parvocellular streams, as well as the remarkable localization of specific visual function within selected regions of the extrastriate cortex.

In addition to providing information about the neuropsychology of an important and relatively well understood functional system, chapter 5 also provides a model of how several different levels of analysis can be integrated into a comprehensive understanding. In doing this, it serves as a preview of the kind of understanding of other brain systems that will some day be achieved and that is already in the process of evolving.

Part II: Neuropsychology of Major Functional Systems

The seven chapters of Part II (chapters 6–12) address the major domains of higher functioning: language, spatial processing, visual recognition, voluntary action, memory, emotion, and the higher-order regulation of behavior by the prefrontal cortex.

Language, perhaps the most exclusively human function, is also the first functional domain to be localized in specific regions of the cerebral cortex—a discovery that ushered in the modern era of neuropsychology. Chapter 6 surveys the investigation of the neural basis of language from Broca's classical findings to the use of recently developed functional imaging techniques that have revealed areas of brain involved in relatively complex linguistic processes, such as word generation. These recent findings have suggested an unexpected modularity of function in the neural mechanisms underlying language.

Analogously, chapter 7's survey of spatial processing emphasizes how the insights revealed by early lesion studies have been extended by such findings as the recent discovery of single cells in the hippocampus that fire when an animal is in a specific location and location-specific attention-enhanced cells in monkey parietal cortex. This extension of classical findings implicating these two regions in aspects of spatial processing to findings on the level of the single neuron suggests that we may be approaching an integrated understanding of spatial processing, an understanding nourished by data from widely disparate levels of analysis. Also highly illuminating is recent work indicating that the same structures mediating visual perceptual processing may also underlie visual imagery and that the two hemispheres are specialized with regard to the ways in which they process images. These were unexpected findings, and they hold promise for further understanding of the relationship between visual perception and visual thought processes.

The recurring theme of attempts to achieve understanding through the convergence of findings from disparate levels of analysis also pervades the remaining chapters in part II. In chapter 8, we examine visual agnosia, first identifying problems with classical theories of visual recognition and then examining how recent theories attempt to resolve these problems. In particular, recent massively parallel constraint-satisfaction models of object recognition are reviewed, as are the most recent neurobiologically based conceptualizations of visual agnosia. These constitute two explanatory approaches based on widely different levels of analysis. For the present, the possibility of integrating the two approaches into a unified understanding remains remote, although a satisfactory account of visual recognition will eventually have to draw on data and conceptualizations from the levels of explanation addressed by both of these theories.

The leitmotif of understanding through converging levels of analysis also pervades the remaining chapters dealing with the major functional systems. In the discussion of voluntary action (chapter 9), data from classical studies on the effect of cerebral lesions on movement are interfaced with current advances in the neurophysiology of movement. For example, the recent use of studies simultaneously recording from more than 100 single neurons in the motor cortex has revealed a stunning distribution of function in that region, a distribution that helps to explain the extremely high correlation between actual and intended movement in persons without brain lesions and the disruption of that correlation after lesions of motor cortex. Analogously, as we see in chapter 10, single-unit recording in prefrontal cortex has revealed neurons that are intimately involved in the neural processes underlying spatial working memory. This discovery of individual neuronal activity correlated with memory processes is among the most exciting recent advances in the understanding of the neural basis of higher cognitive processes.

Although sometimes neglected in accounts of brain-behavior relationships, emotion is clearly an important, if enigmatic, domain of psychological functioning. In the examination of emotion in chapter 11, we first discuss classical theories of the relationship between brain and emotion and then proceed to see how these have been superseded by more recent advances. In particular, recent investigations into the neural basis of learned fear have not only provided further support for the notion that the amygdala plays a central role in emotional response, they have also made significant progress in elucidating the neural mechanisms through which the amygdala exercises this role.

As one explores each of the major functional domains, one must eventually confront the problem of the highest level of control within that domain, a level frequently referred to as executive function. Although there is a separate chapter on executive function (chapter 12), the text also addresses the problem of executive function within each chapter, in the context of the domain under consideration. This allows the reader to view executive function in the context of the functions that are its tangible manifestations, rather than presenting it as a rarefied function isolated from specific functional domains.

Chapter 12 examines aspects of prefrontal cortex and the higher-order regulation of behavior. Humans suffer an extremely broad range of symptoms after prefrontal lesions, and these are reviewed in some detail with an eye toward bringing some conceptual coherence to their apparently bewildering range. The latter part of this chapter considers the hypothesis that the essence of prefrontal function is the guidance of behavior by representational knowledge. True to the theme of converging levels of analysis, this discussion focuses on recent advances in devising an animal model of prefrontal function This makes possible investigations on the anatomical, physiological, and behavioral levels that would not be possible with human subjects. The data from human subjects with prefrontal lesions, taken together with those derived from the animal models, emphasize once again how different levels of analysis inform each other. This approach also makes possible the beginning of a coherent picture of the neural basis of prefrontal function.

Part III: The Application of Neuropsychology to Broad Behavioral Domains: Psychopathology, Developmental Neuropsychology, and Recovery of Function

The three chapters in part III address areas of application of neuropsychology: psychopathology, developmental neuropsychology, and recovery of function. Currently there is a great deal of investigative work in the neuropsychology of psychopathology (chapter 13), particularly schizophrenia. In this disorder—or, more aptly, this spectrum of disorders—a wide range of neurobiological correlates have been identified. Of particular interest are recent findings of specific metabolic abnormalities in prefrontal cortex during tasks, such as the Wisconsin Card Sorting Test, that tap the functional capacity of this area. This combination of functional imaging and neuropsychological measures appears to be an extremely promising research strategy for future attempts to elucidate biological factors in schizophrenia as well as other psychiatric disorders.

The chapter on developmental neuropsychology (chapter 14), in addition to reviewing the almost miraculous events involved in the development of the nervous system, focuses on recent attempts to infer the course of development of different brain systems from the course of development of function. From this perspective, chapter 14 reviews recent work in the development of visual function, executive function, and language. It also surveys recent

advances in our understanding of developmental abnormalities, both those in which considerable progress in understanding the cause has been made and those in which causal factors remain obscure.

Chapter 15 considers recovery of function, including the factors that affect recovery and the neural mechanisms that have been shown to underlie it. Particular attention is paid to the development of therapeutic approaches to the consequences of brain lesions. Of special interest are recent advances in the development of compensatory interventions, such as strategies that utilize intact implicit memory in severely amnesic patients to enhance their capacity for adaptive functioning.

Epilogue

Finally, the Epilogue considers philosophical issues in neuropsychology, particularly the issue of whether psychological and behavioral processes can be reduced to more micro levels. It presents a case for the possibility of such reduction. More generally, the chapter provides a broad context for considering issues in the relationship between brain and behavior that are implicit in earlier discussions. In addition, the Epilogue is intended to provide a more formal argument for what has been a central theme of this book: the virtue, if not the necessity, of striving for an understanding of brain-behavior relationships derived from the integration of different (and often seemingly incommensurable) levels of analysis. This is an understanding that to date has been most fully realized in our current understanding of the visual system. Yet, as the pages of this book testify, it is a goal toward which progress is being made in all domains of functioning.

Pedagogical Features

Each chapter begins with a chapter outline to help orient the reader and ends with a summary that touches on the central content of the chapter. Captions are often extensive, supplementing descriptions in the body of the text. Major terms are boldfaced and defined both in the context of the discussion and in a glossary at the end of the book.

Complete references to cited studies will hopefully encourage students to embark on the direct exploration of published research, an endeavor always rewarded by more intimate understanding.

Supplementary Materials

There is a student web site for the book at www. mhhe.com/rains. Matt Heinly, one of my former students, who possesses an intense passion for neuropsychology, helped develop the web site. Matt's ability to locate interesting web sites is matched only by his ability to locate restaurants that serve the finest and largest steaks. The web site also includes review questions and key terms and definitions for each chapter.

Melvyn King of the State University of New York at Cortland and Debra Clark, a neuropsychologist in private practice, have prepared a test bank that includes multiple-choice, fill-in, true-false, and essay questions for all chapters.

Acknowledgments

A project of this magnitude is the product of many influences going far back in time. While it is impossible to mention all of the early influences, I mention some of them here. Thomas McDonald of St. John's College inspired a love of intellectual exploration and adventure that has never left me. Many at Cornell University were inspiring and guiding during my time as a graduate student there, including Barbara Finlay, Ulrick Neisser, Frank Keil, Eleanor Gibson, and J. J. Gibson. During my neuropsychology internship, at Upstate Medical Center in Syracuse, I was able to learn from John Wolf, who had an exuberant passion for brain dissection and neurological diagnosis, even at 6 a.m.

During my years in Montreal, Frank Greene, at the McGill University Reading Centre, was helpful and supportive in many ways. In the process of conducting my thesis research at the Montreal Neurological Institute, I had the good fortune to work with a number of extraordinarily talented people who were also passionate about neuropsychology. I shared an office with Gus Buchtel, always encourag-

ing and energizing, as were Gabriel Leonard, Enda McGovern, and Laughlin Taylor. I spent many hours in dialogue with Michael Patrides, whose love of all things neuropsychological is contagious and whose energy for conversation about the mysteries of the brain is inexhaustible. I feel deep gratitude to Brenda Milner, my thesis advisor, who made work in Montreal possible and whose indefatigable passion for neuropsychology and impeccable investigation of its mysteries has served as an inspiration for me, as it does for so many throughout the world. I also owe an enormous debt of gratitude to all the patients in Montreal, and later at Friends Hospital in Philadelphia, from whom I have learned so much.

I would like to thank the following reviewers for their valuable suggestions: Gary G. Berntson, Ohio State University; Erin D. Bigler, Brigham Young University; Sarah Creem, University of Utah; Philip S. Fastenau, Indiana University–Purdue University, Indianapolis; Gary Groth-Marnat, Cal Poly, San Luis Obispo; Phillip J. Holcomb, Tufts University; Stephen W. Keifer, Kansas State University; John P. Kline, Eastern Washington University; Charles Long, University of Memphis; Mark E. McCourt, North Dakota State University; James D. Rose, University of Wyoming; Paula K. Schear, University of Cincinnati; Michael J. Selby, California State University, San Luis Obispo; Robert Solso, Ohio State University; and Joseph E. Steinmetz, Indiana University.

I would not have begun writing this book in earnest had it not been for the loving persistence of Ray Conlon and Anne Conlon who, in the first hours of 1995, insisted that we leave the kitchen table, go into my study, and write a cover letter to prospective publishers to introduce the early draft chapters I had composed at that point. Frank Graham, my sponsoring editor, was encouraging and constructively challenging throughout the writing process and into the early stages of production, before his retirement. Ken King, who took up the torch from Frank, had many excellent ideas that made the book a better one. Beverley DeWitt did wonderful copyediting, respecting my voice, while finding and fixing all problems. Rennie Evans and Robin Mouat did a superb job with the art, flexibly modifying early versions of figures until they were just right.

The book's production editors, Deneen Sedlack, Carla Kirschenbaum, and Melissa Williams, all guided the production expertly and were a delight to work with, as were all the other members of the Mayfield and McGraw-Hill team.

Thanks to my wife, Mary, and my two sons, Brendan and Jesse, for their encouragement and for their tolerance during what must have felt like an interminable process. More than they can ever know, they gave me the courage and the purpose to write this book.

Brief Contents

PART I: Foundations

CHAPTER 1   The Historical Development of Neuropsychology   1
CHAPTER 2   Neural Mechanisms at the Molecular and Cellular Levels   18
CHAPTER 3   Introduction to the Structure and Function of the Central Nervous System   45
CHAPTER 4   Methods in Neuropsychology   72
CHAPTER 5   The Visual System as a Model of Nervous System Functioning   93

PART II: Neuropsychology of Major Functional Systems

CHAPTER 6   Language   128
CHAPTER 7   Spatial Processing   157
CHAPTER 8   Visual Recognition   194
CHAPTER 9   Voluntary Action   226
CHAPTER 10   Memory Systems   255
CHAPTER 11   Emotion   302
CHAPTER 12   The Prefrontal Cortex and the Higher-Order Regulation of Behavior   339

PART III: The Application of Neuropsychology to Broad Behavioral Domains

CHAPTER 13   Psychopathology   379
CHAPTER 14   Developmental Neuropsychology   411
CHAPTER 15   Recovery of Function   442

Epilogue   456
Glossary   465
Bibliography   509
Credits   547
Index   553

Contents

Preface   vii

PART I: Foundations

CHAPTER 1   The Historical Development of Neuropsychology   1

Early Attempts at Understanding the Brain   2
The Brain Hypothesis   2
The Problem of Localization of Function   5

The Beginnings of Modern Neuropsychology: Broca   8
Antecedents to Broca: Gall and Bouillaud   8
The Case of "Tan"   9
The Concept of Hemispheric Dominance: The Left Hemisphere and Language   9
The Discovery of the Motor Cortex: Fritsch and Hitzig   10

Further Discoveries: Wernicke   10
Wernicke's Discovery of Receptive Aphasia   10
The Concept of Sequential Processing   10
The Disconnection Syndrome Hypothesis   11
The Concept of Complementary Hemispheric Specialization:
*   The Role of the Right Hemisphere   11*
An Example of a Disconnection Syndrome: Alexia Without Agraphia   12

Localization Versus Holism   13
The Limits of Localization: The Mapmakers   13
Reconciliation of the Holist and Localizationist Views: Hughlings-Jackson's Concept
*   of Hierarchy   13*
Bias and Preconception in Early-20th-Century Neuropsychology   15

The Psychometric Approach to Neuropsychology   15
Group Studies and Statistical Analysis   16
The Continuing Role of the Case Study   16

Recent Findings   16

Summary   17

CHAPTER 2 Neural Mechanisms at the Molecular
            and Cellular Levels   18

The Adaptive Significance of the Nervous System   19

The Capacity for Modulation: The Neuron and the Synapse   19

Discovery of the Neuron and the Synapse   20
General Components of the Neuron   20
Glia   21
Overview of Events at the Synapse   22

Neural Activity at the Molecular and Cellular Levels   23

Physical Forces Underlying Ion Movement   24
Membrane Resting Potential   25
Effects of Neurotransmitter Release on the Postsynaptic Membrane   27
Integration of Input at the Axon Hillock   27
The Action Potential   29
Saltatory Conduction   30
Neurotransmitter Release   31
Mechanisms for Clearing Neurotransmitter After Neuron Firing   33
Responses to Neurotransmitter-Receptor Binding   35

Neuronal Mechanisms of Learning   37

Habituation and Sensitization in Aplysia: *Examples of Presynaptic Modulation*
  of Neuronal Activity   37
Classical Conditioning   39
Long-Term Potentiation   41

**Two Exceptions to General Rules: Receptor Potentials and Electrical
  Transmission   42**

Receptor Potentials: Transduction Without Action Potentials   42
Electrical Transmission: Communication Between Neurons Without
  Chemical Synapses   42

Summary   44

CHAPTER 3 Introduction to the Structure and Function
            of the Central Nervous System   45

General Terminology   45

An Overview of the Central Nervous System   47

The Central and Peripheral Nervous Systems   47
Major Divisions of the Brain   48
The Meninges   48
The Cerebral Ventricles   49
Gray Matter and White Matter   50

The Forebrain 51
The Cerebral Cortex 51
The Basal Ganglia 60
The Limbic System 61
The Diencephalon 63

The Brain Stem 66
The Midbrain 67
The Hindbrain 68

The Cerebellum 68

The Spinal Cord 69

Summary 70

CHAPTER 4 Methods in Neuropsychology 72

Anatomical Methods 73
Identifying Anatomical Connections 73
Structural Imaging Methods 74

Methods Measuring Function 76
Functional Imaging Methods 78
Neurophysiological Methods 80

Lesion Methods 83
Dissociation of Function 83
Interpretation of Single and Double Dissociation 84
Associated Impairments 84
*Dissociations as a Window on the Structure of Cognition
    and on Localization of Function 85*
Limits on the Interpretation of Dissociations 85
Further Thoughts on the Logic of Dissociation and Association 86

Commissurotomy 86

The Sodium Amobarbital Test 89
Hemispheric Specialization and Handedness 89
*Use of the Sodium Amobarbital Test in the Neurosurgical Management
    of Focal Seizures 89*
The Testing Procedure 90

Studies of People With Behavioral and Cognitive Abnormalities 90

Studies of Normal People: Laterality Studies 91

Summary 92

CHAPTER 5 The Visual System as a Model of Nervous System
          Functioning   93

The Classical Sequential-Hierarchical View of the Visual Brain   94

**An Overview of Recent Advances in the Understanding of Central
  Visual Processing   94**

The Retina   95
The General Organization of the Retina   95
The Photoreceptors   96
Biochemistry of Phototransduction   97
Neural Processing Within the Retina   98

Retinofugal Projections   104
The Lateral Geniculate Nucleus of the Thalamus   107
An Overview of Cortical Areas Mediating Vision   109
Projections From the LGN to the Visual Cortex   109

Specialization Within Cortex Devoted to Vision   110
The Parvocellular-Blob Channel   110
The Parvocellular-Interblob Channel   116
The Magnocellular-V5 Channel and the Magnocellular-V3 Channel   118

**The Microanatomy of the Visual Cortex and the Concept of Modular
  Organization   120**

**The Problem of Integration and the Construction of a Representation
  of the Visual World   124**

Summary   127

PART II: Neuropsychology of Major Functional Systems

CHAPTER 6 Language   128

Characteristics of Language   129

The Development of Language in Children: Nature Versus Nurture   130

Language Disorders: The Concept of Aphasia   131
Broca's Aphasia   132
Wernicke's Aphasia   134
Global Aphasia   135
The Transcortical Aphasias   135
Other Central Language Disorders   136

The Disconnection Syndrome Hypothesis Applied to Language Disorders   136

Major Components of Language Function   138
Auditory Word Comprehension   138
Word Retrieval   141
Sentence Comprehension and Production   142
Speech Production   143
Acquired Reading Impairment   146
Spelling   148
Writing   150

Further Theoretical Considerations   150

The Right Hemisphere and Language   151

Hemispheric Anatomical Asymmetries   153

The Evolution of Human Language   154

Summary   155

CHAPTER 7 Spatial Processing   157

General Considerations   158
Problems in the Neuropsychology of Spatial Processing   158
Types of Spatial Behavior   159
Early Empirical Studies   160

Body Space   160
Body Surface   160
Joint and Muscle Sense   161

Egocentric Space   161
Visual Disorientation   161
Visual Localization   162
Neural Correlates of Visual Disorientation and Impairment in Visual Localization   162

Allocentric Space   164
Spatial Analysis   165
Search for the Mechanisms Underlying Spatial Behavior   166
Perception of Relative Spatial Location   167
Orientation Discrimination   167
Complex Spatial Tasks   167
Topographical Orientation and Memory   168
The Two-Pathway Hypothesis for Object Recognition and Spatial Processing   170

The Role of the Hippocampus in Spatial Processing   171
Unit Recording Studies   172
Lesion Studies   172
Neuroethological Studies   174

Neglect of One Side of Space   176
Neglect as a Disorder of Attention   177
Neglect as a Disruption of the Internal Representation of Space   182

Spatial Thinking and Mental Imagery   184
Electrophysiological Studies   185
Imaging Studies   185
Lesion Studies   186
Hemispheric Specialization for Imagery   187
Implications for Our Initial Questions About Imagery   188

The Role of the Frontal Lobes in Spatial Processing   188

Summary   190

CHAPTER 8 Visual Recognition   194

A Case of Visual Agnosia   195

Disorders of Visual Recognition   196
Early Attempts at Understanding   196
Partial Cortical Blindness   198
Apperceptive Agnosia   199
Associative Agnosia   203
Summary of the Classical View of Visual Agnosia   206

Problems With the Classical Model   207
Perceptual Impairment in Associative Agnosia   207
Significance of the Apperceptive-Associative Distinction   211
Perceptual Impairment in Prosopagnosia and Pure Alexia   211
The Problem of Category-Specific Impairments in Visual Recognition   212

Theories of Visual Agnosia   214
Disconnection Model   215
Symbolic Search Model   216
Massively Parallel Constraint-Satisfaction Models of Object Recognition   217
A Neurobiologically Based Conceptualization of Visual Agnosia   220

Restoration of Sight in Adulthood After Early Onset of Blindness   223

Summary   224

CHAPTER 9 Voluntary Action   226

Voluntary Movement   227

The Components of Voluntary Movement   227
Dimensions of Regulation of Movement   227
Levels of Regulation of Movement   228

Elementary Disorders of Movement   228

An Overview of Higher-Order Control of Movement   229

The Motor Cortex   230
Defining the Motor Cortex   230
Characteristics of Single Neurons in M1   230
How M1 Neurons Code Movement   233
Sensory Input to M1 Neurons   234

The Premotor and Supplementary Motor Areas   235
Anatomical Considerations   235
Stimulation and Lesion Studies   236
Neuroimaging Evidence of Area 6's Role in Planning Movement Sequences   237
Single Cell Recording   238

The Cerebellum   238
Anatomical Considerations   239
Lesion Studies   240

The Basal Ganglia   240
Anatomical Considerations   240
The Effects of Basal Ganglia Lesions   241
The Contribution of the Basal Ganglia to Movement   242

Apraxia and the Left Parietal Cortex   243
Early Conceptualizations of Apraxia   243
Liepmann's Classification of the Apraxias   244
A More Theoretically Neutral Approach to Apraxia   245
The Role of the Left Hemisphere in the Control of Voluntary Movement   250

Other Movement-Related Functions of Parietal Cortex   251

The Prefrontal Cortex   251

Summary   252

CHAPTER 10 Memory Systems   255

An Overview of Normal Memory   257
Categorizing Memory in Terms of What Is Remembered   257

Categorizing Memory in Terms of Capacity and Duration   258
Component Processes of Memory   260
The Relationship Between Memory and Other Domains of Cognition   261

Medial Temporal-Lobe Amnesia and the Consolidation Hypothesis   261
Patient H. M.   261
Some Implications of H. M.'s Memory Impairment   264

Memory Impairment After Unilateral Temporal-Lobe Lesions   265
*Complementary Specialization of Memory Function for the Left and Right
    Temporal Lobes*   265
*The Roles of Medial Temporal-Lobe Structures and Lateral Temporal Cortex
    in Memory*   265

**The Critical Structures Involved in Memory Loss After
    Temporal-Lobe Lesions   268**
H M.'s Lesions   268
Discrepancy Between Findings in Animals and Humans   268
Apparent Resolution of the Discrepancy   269
Search for the Critical Structures Involved in Recognition Memory   269
Some Conflicting Findings   270
The Importance of Medial-Temporal Cortex   270

Diencephalic Amnesia   271
Korsakoff's Disease   271
Other Causes of Diencephalic Amnesia   273
The Relationship Between Medial-Temporal and Diencephalic Amnesia   273

Where in the Memory Process Is the Impairment?   274
Registration/Encoding   274
Consolidation/Storage/Maintenance   274
Retrieval   275

Preserved Aspects of Memory in Amnesia   275
Motor Learning   276
Perceptual Learning   277
Classical Conditioning   277
Cognitive Skill Learning   278
Priming   279

Episodic Memory and Semantic Memory   281
Global Amnesia   282
Selective Impairment of Episodic Memory   282
Selective Impairment of Semantic Memory   282

Short-Term/Working Memory Impairment   283
Short-Term Memory   283

Working Memory   284
The Frontal Lobes and Working Memory   285

Conceptualization of Multiple Memory Systems   290

The Neural Substrate of Long-Term Memory   291

Lashley's Search for the Engram   291
Evidence That Long-Term Memory Is Stored in the Cortex   292
*Hippocampal Binding of Different Memory Elements as an Integral Component
  in Explicit Memory   294*
Storage of Implicit Memory   295
Protein Synthesis and the Structural Plasticity Underlying Long-Term Memory   295
So Where Is Memory Stored?   296

Further Consideration of the Role of the Frontal Lobes in Memory   296

The Frontal Lobes and Organization   297
Impairment in Metamemory   298

Summary   298

CHAPTER 11 Emotion   302

Theories of the Relationship Between Brain and Emotion   305

The James-Lange Theory of Emotion   305
The Cannon-Bard Theory   306
Importance of the Hypothalamus for Emotion   306
The Papez Circuit   308
The Klüver-Bucy Syndrome   310
The Concept of the Limbic System   312

The Neural Basis of Learned Fear as a Model System   316

Advantages of Studying Fear   316
Fear Conditioning   316
Critical Structures for Conditioned Fear   316
*The Amygdala: Interface Between Information About the World and
  Emotional Response   321*
The Interspecies Generality of the Amygdala's Role in Fear Conditioning   321

Emotional Memory   323

Emotional Memory and Memory of Emotion   323
Brain Systems Mediating Emotional Memory and Memory of Emotion   323

The Cortex and Emotion   324

The Cortex and Mood   324
The Cortex and the Perception and Interpretation of Emotion   325
The Cortex and Emotional Expression   327
The Temporal Lobes and Emotion   328

The Interaction of Cortex and Amygdala in the Higher-Order Mediation of Emotion   329
Amygdala Influences on Cortex   330
Integration of Cortex and Amygdala   332

Emotion and Conscious Experience   335
Requirements for the Conscious Experience of Emotion   336
Thoughts and Feelings   336

Summary   337

CHAPTER 12   The Prefrontal Cortex and the Higher-Order Regulation of Behavior   339

Toward a Working Model of Prefrontal Cortex Function   340
The Essence of Intelligence   340
Phineas Gage: A Case of the Disruption of Goal-Directed Behavior   340
Anatomical Considerations   342
Problems in the Interpretation of Deficits Following Prefrontal Lesions   345
A Working Model of Prefrontal Function   345

Impairment in Function After Prefrontal Lesions in Humans   347
Emotion and Motivation   347
Social Behavior   348
Memory   349
General Intelligence   350
Language   350
Inventiveness, Ideational Fluency, and Divergent Thinking   351
Abstract and Conceptual Thinking   352
Executive Function: Planning and the Goal-Directed Organization of Behavior   353
The Channeling of Drive Into Goal-Directed Behavior: Inhibiting the Disruptive Effect of Impulsive Behavior   358
Goal-Directed Behavior and Environmental Stimuli   358
Integrating Goal-Directed Behavior With Its Consequences   359
Prefrontal Syndromes   362

Theories of Prefrontal Function   363
An Animal Model of Prefrontal Function   364
Breakdown in the Guidance of Behavior by Representational Knowledge as the Essence of Impairment in Delayed Response   366
Specialization of the Principal Sulcus for Visuospatial Delayed Response in the Monkey   367
Other Prefrontal Subsystems   373
The Problem of Integration in Prefrontal Cortex   377

Summary   377

PART III: The Application of Neuropsychology to Broad Behavioral Domains

CHAPTER 13 Psychopathology   379

What Is Psychopathology?   380

The Schizophrenic Disorders   382

Description   383
The Hypothesis of Multiple Etiologies of Schizophrenia   383
Genetic Factors   384
The Dopamine Hypothesis of Schizophrenia   384
Gross Structural Abnormalities   385
Microstructural Abnormalities   388
Abnormalities Revealed by Functional Imaging   389
Neurological Abnormalities in Schizophrenia   391
Neuropsychological Functioning in Schizophrenia   392
The Hypothesis That Prefrontal Dysfunction Underlies Schizophrenia   393

Mood Disorders   394

Major Depressive Disorder   394
Seasonal Affective Disorder   397
Bipolar Disorder   397

Anxiety Disorders   398

General Neurochemical Factors   398
Simple Phobias   399
Generalized Anxiety Disorder   399
Panic Disorder   399
Obsessive-Compulsive Disorder   400

Sociopathy   400

Dementing Diseases   401

Alzheimer's Disease: A Cortical Dementia   401
Subcortical Dementias   405

Unsolved Problems   407

The Heterogeneity of Diagnostic Categories   407
Invalid Findings   407
Inferring Cause Based on the Effective Treatment of Symptoms   408
Disentangling Cause and Effect   408
Levels of Explanation   408

Summary   409

CHAPTER 14 Developmental Neuropsychology   411

Development of the Brain   412

Induction   412
Neuroblast Proliferation   413
Cell Migration   413
Axonal Growth   416
Dendritic Growth   417
The Formation of Connections and the Contribution of the Environment   417
Myelination   420

Brain Development and the Development of Higher-Order Function   420

Development of Visual Acuity   421
Development of Control of Visual Orienting   422
Development of Executive Function   422
Language Development   425

Known Causes of Developmental Abnormality   427

Inherited Disorders   428
Chromosomal Disorders   428
Structural Abnormalities   428
Prematurity and Low Birth Weight   428
Infection   429
Toxin-Related Damage   429
Nutritional Disorders   429
Anoxic Episodes   429
Traumatic Brain Injury and Focal Cerebral Abnormality   429

Developmental Disorders of Unknown Cause   430

Learning Disorders   430
Attention Deficit Disorder   435
Autism   438

Summary   440

CHAPTER 15 Recovery of Function   442

The Effects of Brain Damage   442

Cellular Effects   443
Physiological Effects   443

Functional Recovery After Brain Damage   444

Factors Affecting Recovery of Function   444
Age at Time of Lesion as a Factor in Recovery   445

Neural Mechanisms of Recovery of Function   449
Rerouting   449
Sprouting   449
Denervation Supersensitivity   449
The Neural Basis of Cerebral Reorganization   450

Therapeutic Approaches to the Consequences of Brain Lesions   451
Rehabilitation   451
Pharmacological Treatments   454
Brain Tissue Transplantation   454

Summary   455

Epilogue   456

Skepticism About the Possibility of a Unified Theory of Mind-Brain   456
The Mind-Brain Problem   456
Substance Dualism   457
Property Dualism   458
Functionalism   459

The Possibility of Intertheoretic Reduction and a Unified Theory of Mind-Brain   460
Intertheoretic Reduction   460
The Inadequacy of Folk Psychology as a Criterion for the Possibility of Reduction   462

Where Are We Now and Where Are We Going?   464

Glossary   465
Bibliography   509
Credits   547
Index   553

CHAPTER 1

The Historical Development of Neuropsychology

EARLY ATTEMPTS AT UNDERSTANDING THE BRAIN
  The Brain Hypothesis
  The Problem of Localization of Function
THE BEGINNINGS OF MODERN NEUROPSYCHOLOGY: BROCA
  Antecedents to Broca: Gall and Bouillaud
  The Case of "Tan"
  The Concept of Hemispheric Dominance:
    The Left Hemisphere and Language
  The Discovery of the Motor Cortex: Fritsch and Hitzig
FURTHER DISCOVERIES: WERNICKE
  Wernicke's Discovery of Receptive Aphasia
  The Concept of Sequential Processing
  The Disconnection Syndrome Hypothesis
  The Concept of Complementary Hemispheric
    Specialization: The Role of the Right Hemisphere

An Example of a Disconnection Syndrome:
    Alexia Without Agraphia
LOCALIZATION VERSUS HOLISM
  The Limits of Localization: The Mapmakers
  Reconciliation of the Holist and Localizationist
    Views: Hughlings-Jackson's Concept of Hierarchy
  Bias and Preconception in Early-20th-Century
    Neuropsychology
THE PSYCHOMETRIC APPROACH TO NEUROPSYCHOLOGY
  Group Studies and Statistical Analysis
  The Continuing Role of the Case Study
RECENT FINDINGS
SUMMARY

In 1882, French neurologist Joseph Jules Dejarine reported an unusual case. His patient, a successful businessman, had awakened one morning to find he had lost the ability to read. He could speak and understand language, he could see, and he could write, yet he could not read, not even what he himself had written. (He could, however, read by touching raised letters.) A few days later, on awakening, the man found that he had also lost the ability to write.

What could cause such a puzzling syndrome? The answer to this question, discovered only post-mortem, provided evidence for an important hypothesis about the nervous system in the 19th century—the hypothesis that different areas of the brain are specialized for different functions and that, if connections between areas are disrupted, distinct capabilities are lost. The early history of neuropsychology is marked by individual cases like this one, each contributing some important piece to the puzzle of how the brain works. In this chapter we consider the history of neuropsychology, from the earliest human attempts at understanding how behavior is controlled to the most recent findings about the organization of the brain.

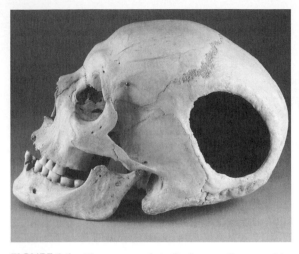

FIGURE 1.1   The trepanned skull of a man discovered in a cave in France in 1854. The skull is from the collection of the Musée de l'Homme, Paris. *(From Finger, 1994, p. 4)*

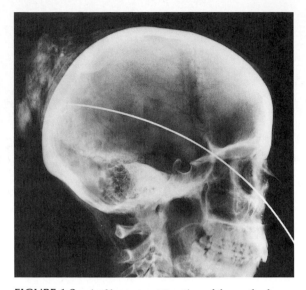

FIGURE 1.2   An X-ray reconstruction of the method believed to have been used by the ancient Egyptians to drain the contents of the skull during the embalming process. *(From Fleming et al., 1980, p. 32)*

EARLY ATTEMPTS AT UNDERSTANDING THE BRAIN

The Brain Hypothesis

As we consider the history of neuropsychology, one of the first concepts we encounter is the **brain hypothesis,** the idea that the brain is the biological organ that controls and directs behavior. It may seem strange to think of this as a hypothesis because today we take it as a given. Yet throughout history, a variety of organs have been identified as the center of thinking and feeling. The residues of some of these notions survive in our language when, for example, we speak of the heart as the seat of compassion or the guts as the source of courage.

The beginnings of human speculation about the relationship between the body and the mind are lost in the mists of prehistory. It is known that in prehistoric times **trepanning,** the surgical opening of the skull (now termed **craniotomy**), was a widespread practice (Figure 1.1). Because many trepanned skulls show signs of healing around the wound, we may infer that patients frequently survived the procedure. Although we do not have direct information regarding why these procedures were performed, it seems almost certain that they represent primitive attempts at neurosurgery—and thus an appreciation of the importance of the brain to the functioning of the body.

THE EGYPTIANS   The ancient Egyptians have left hints about their regard for the brain in their burial practices. As part of their elaborate process of mummification, they removed organs from the body and either preserved them, if they were considered important for the afterlife, or discarded them, if they were considered unimportant. The heart, liver, spleen, and other organs were carefully removed and stored in separate jars. In contrast, the brain was simply discarded. It is believed that the embalmers got rid of the brain by inserting a metal rod into the cranial cavity through the nose and swishing the rod around until the already soft tissue liquefied and drained out through the nose (Figure 1.2).

Ironically, the same culture is the source of the earliest recorded observation of the relationship between the brain and behavior. The Edwin Smith Surgical Papyrus, dating probably from the second millennium B.C., contains descriptions of several medical cases. One of them (Figure 1.3) describes a man who

Title
IV 5

FIGURE 1.3   A portion of the Edwin Smith Surgical Papyrus. *(From Breasted, 1930, pp. 203, 205)*

Examination
IV 5–7

Diagnosis
IV 7–9

sustained a severe wound on the left side of his head and thereafter demonstrated a skewing of the left eye and a left-foot drag:

> [Title] INSTRUCTIONS CONCERNING A SMASH IN HIS SKULL UNDER THE SKIN OF THE HEAD [Examination] If thou examineth a man having a smash of his skull, under the skin of his head, while there is nothing at all upon it, thou shouldst palpate his wound. Shouldst thou find that there is a swelling protruding on the outside of the smash which is in his skull, while his eye is askew because of it, on the side of him having that injury which is in his skull; (and) he walks shuffling with his sole, on the side of him having that injury which is in his skull, [Diagnosis] thou shouldst accord him one whom something entering from outside has smitten. . . . an ailment not to be treated. (Breasted, 1930, pp. 203–206)

It is so commonplace to find impairment in the movement of the limbs following head injury that it may be difficult to appreciate the importance of this observation. What we have here is nothing less than the first record of an observation supporting the notion that the brain somehow controls the rest of the body, the first recorded step toward the development of knowledge about the relationship between brain and behavior.

It is interesting that this first description of a relationship between brain and behavior is misleading. The impairments are **ipsilateral** to the lesion (same side) rather than **contralateral** (opposite side) as we now expect based on our current understanding that the left side of the brain controls the right side of the body and vice versa. This discrepancy may be explained, however, by what is now known as a **contra coup effect.** When there is a blow to the head, the brain, floating in cerebrospinal fluid, is often bruised as it is thrust against the opposite side of the skull. This injury to the opposite side of the brain could cause impairment on the same side of the body as the blow to the head. Regardless of the details, however, this observation remains the first recorded evidence that could serve as support for the brain hypothesis, although the Egyptian observer did not take that theoretical leap.

THE GREEKS   The ancient Greeks were divided in their opinions about the brain. In the 5th century B.C. Alcmaeon of Croton proposed that the brain was the "seat of the soul," and in the 4th century B.C. Plato made a similar proposal, arguing that the head was the part of the body closest to the heavens and therefore the most likely to contain the most divine organ. In contrast, Empedocles, in the 5th century B.C., proposed that the heart was the seat of the soul, and Aristotle, a century later, agreed with him. Aristotle reasoned that the brain, with its elaborate network of blood vessels and its position near the surface of the body, served to cool the blood. The heart, he argued, being an active and central structure, was more suitable as the organ of thinking and feeling. This is a bold example of the pitfalls of rationalism, reasoning that is not subjected to the critique imposed by experimental testing. As we shall see shortly, this would not be the last instance in the history of neuropsychology when unfounded conclusions about the biological basis of behavior would be generated by a rationalist approach.

Hippocrates (460–377 B.C.), that most astute observer of disease, subscribed to the brain hypothesis. In one of the most famous passages ascribed to him we read:

> And men ought to know that from nothing else but thence (from the brain) come joys, delights, laughter and sports, and sorrows, griefs, despondency, and lamentations. . . . And by the same organ we become mad and delirious, and fears and terrors assail us, some by night, and some by day, and dreams and untimely wanderings, and cares that are not suitable, and ignorance of present circumstances, desuetude, and unskilfulness. All these things we endure from the brain, when it is not healthy, but is more hot, more cold, more moist, or more dry than natural, or when it suffers any other preternatural and unusual affection. And we become mad from humidity (of the brain). (Adams, 1939, p. 366)

Hippocrates must have based these conclusions in part on his recorded observations that persons with wounds to the head also suffered paralysis, seizures, and speech impairments. In fact, Hippocrates' observations could have led him to further discoveries about the brain. He had seen people with injury to the left side of the head and seizures on the right side of the body, evidence for the contralateral relationship between brain and body. He had also seen people who had speech impairments together with seizures on the right side of the body. From these two observations, he could have inferred left-hemisphere specialization for language. But the world would have to wait for more than two millennia before this relationship was conceptualized and then empirically established by the French surgeon Paul Broca in the 19th century.

The Problem of Localization of Function

GALEN AND THE VENTRICULAR HYPOTHESIS In Roman times the brain hypothesis became widely accepted. The great Roman physician Galen (129–ca. 199) adhered to this view. The question then arose of where in the brain various psychological functions (such as perception, memory, and thinking) take place. This question is referred to as the problem of **localization of function.** Galen believed that the cerebral ventricles, fluid-filled cavities deep within the brain, were the structures in which thinking and other psychological processes were localized, and this idea held on through the Middle Ages. In the 4th century, Nemesius elaborated on this **ventricular hypothesis,** assigning different psychological processes to locations within different ventricles. The idea was maintained for centuries, into the Renaissance, being embraced even by Leonardo da Vinci (1452–1519), as shown in Figure 1.4. Employing what we might regard today as an information processing approach, Nemesius stated that the ventricle, *cellula phantastica,* closest to the sense organs was the seat of perception. That ventricle then flowed into the next ventricle, *cellula logistica,* the seat of reasoning and cognition, which, in turn, flowed into the *cellula memoralis,* the seat of memory. Ventricles were also used to explain the mechanism of more elementary behaviors. For example, muscles were conceptualized as moving when filled with fluid from the cerebral ventricles. These often-elaborate ventricular theories were extremely popular for more than a thousand years. The only thing that these theories lacked

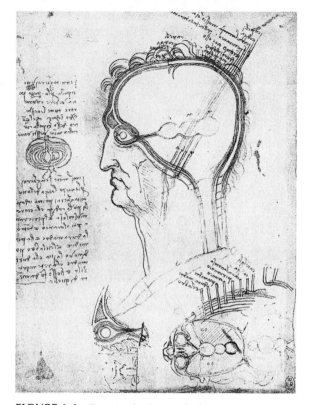

FIGURE 1.4   Drawing by Leonardo da Vinci showing the structure of the brain as conceptualized in the Renaissance. *(From Luria, 1966)*

was a shred of empirical support, a limitation that continued to characterize theories of brain-behavior relationships until well into the 19th century.

PROBLEMS IN VISUALIZING THE STRUCTURE OF THE BRAIN   Even the study of the *structure* of the brain, which would seem to be more straightforward than the study of its function, lagged far behind the study of other organs of the body. This is exemplified by the da Vinci drawing shown in Figure 1.4. In that figure, Leonardo depicts the ventricles as a linear sequence of compartments. One could make a case that this depiction connotes a certain conceptual accuracy in that the ventricles develop embryologically through the folding and enlargement of the primordial neural tube and in that the ventricles are all interconnected, with cerebrospinal fluid circulating in a directed path through them. Yet the spatial configuration of the ventricles in Leonardo's drawing is

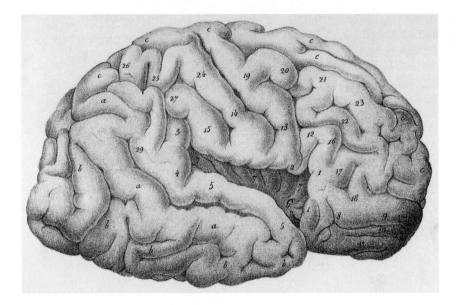

FIGURE 1.5   Rolando's drawing of the cerebral cortex. *(From McHenry, 1969, p. 145)*

shockingly inaccurate, particularly for an artistic genius who was generally so unremitting in his search for knowledge and so meticulous in his depictions of human anatomy. This is not unique to Leonardo, however. Other Renaissance artists portrayed the ventricles in fantastically complex patterns that are only vaguely related to their actual form.

Depictions of the cortical gyri and sulci (discussed in chapter 3) that form the convoluted surface of the cerebral hemispheres fared no better. Renaissance artists, failing to discern regularities in the pattern of these convolutions, drew seemingly random patterns. It was not until the early 19th century that Luigi Rolando provided an accurate depiction of the general pattern of cortical gyri and sulci (Figure 1.5).

Why did depiction of the brain lag so far behind that of other organs? The answer is not entirely clear, but several reasons can be suggested. First of all, there were technical considerations, such as the relative inaccessibility of the brain within its protective skull and the low density of fresh brain tissue, which causes its shape to distort rapidly after dissection (anatomical specimens are typically treated with chemicals to make them harder and more durable.) There were also widespread taboos against human dissection, which limited the ability of scientists to gain firsthand knowledge of the organ. It is likely, however, that these technical factors do not tell the whole story. Psychological factors were probably also at work, particularly the tendency of people to describe and depict what they expect to see rather than what they actually see. For some reason the human brain's attempts to depict itself have proved to be particularly vulnerable to distortion. This problem, more generally, has continually plagued our attempts to understand ourselves, as the history of psychology makes so clear.

THE MIND-BODY PROBLEM   One of the oldest issues in philosophy is implicit in the brain hypothesis and the problem of localization of function: How are mind and body related? How are subjective experience and biological function related? These questions are usually referred to as the **mind-body problem,** a problem that continues to baffle and stimulate the human mind.

Philosophically, there are a number of possible solutions to this perennial problem, each of which continues to find its adherents. One can believe that only one sphere is real, a belief known as **monism.** Within monism one may hold the belief either that the single sphere is physical (**materialism**) or that it is spiritual (**idealism**). Alternatively, one may posit that there are two spheres or modes of reality (**dualism**). Within dualism there are various positions one may take regarding the relationship between the two spheres and the degree and nature of their interaction.

The French philosopher René Descartes (1596–1650) was an important exponent of the dualistic view. He asserted that there is brain and there is mind; the two are independent of each other, but they interact. He even went so far as to specify the organ that mediated this interaction, the pineal gland. For Descartes, no localization of function beyond this bold assertion was meaningful because the mind was not localized, indeed, was not in space at all.

Such a view is in stark contrast with the localizationist views typified by the medieval ventricular hypotheses. We shall see that Descartes's dualism had an important influence on subsequent theories of brain function. In particular, his view that mind is not localized encouraged those who did view the brain as the substrate, or base, of behavior but who did not believe that functions were localized in particular parts of the brain to adopt a position called **holism.** That position held that the whole brain mediates all functioning and that particular functions are not localized within the brain. The debate over how the brain functions continues to this day, although modern conceptions represent an integration of these two views. But we are getting ahead of ourselves.

PHRENOLOGY: A SPECULATIVE THEORY OF LOCALIZATION   One of the most emphatic and least defensible theories of localization of function is represented by **phrenology** (Figure 1.6), developed by Franz Josef Gall (1758–1828) and Johann Casper Spurzheim (1776–1832). This attempt to relate specific brain regions to particular faculties, or functions, was enormously flawed. As is now well known, the bumps and protrusions on the skull, which Gall and Spurzheim assumed to be indicators of the size of underlying gyri, are in fact unrelated to the structure of the brain. The psychological side of phrenology was equally flawed. The faculty psychology that served as phrenology's conceptual framework was vague and had no basis in empirical evidence. The results of phrenology's attempts to relate skull features that are unrelated to brain structure to psychological faculties that are without precise definition or empirical basis were necessarily products of the imagination, and

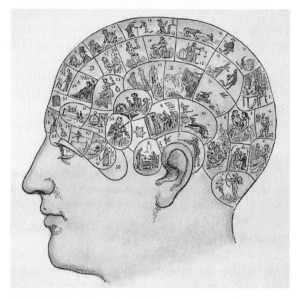

FIGURE 1.6   Phrenological diagram produced by Spurzheim in 1825. *(From Finger, 1994, p. 33)*

phrenology never attained wide academic recognition. Nevertheless, it is sobering to note that during its peak popularity, this thoroughly flawed methodology supported 19 journals. Obviously, many people were taking this work seriously. It would not be the last time in the history of neuroscience that an unsubstantiated body of opinions would generate such enormous interest and influence.

For all its flaws, phrenology did advance the idea of localization of function in the brain and spawned the first truly experimental work on the brain. Ironically, but perhaps not completely unexpectedly, this experimental work was motivated by a holistic reaction against phrenology rather than by an attempt to validate it.

FLOURENS'S ATTEMPT AT AN EXPERIMENTALLY BASED HOLISM   Marie-Jean-Pierre Flourens (1794–1867) was one of the first to study the brain by making experimental lesions in animals. (**Lesion** is a general term meaning "damage" or "disease." Making lesions in the brains of animals and studying their effects is the oldest and still one of the most fruitful methods in neuropsychology.) Dedicating his book to Descartes, the most extreme anti-localizationist, Flourens argued that there is no specialization of function within the **cortex** (the outer layer of the brain). He reported that when he made lesions in the cortex of animals, the resulting impairment of function was related not to the site of damage, but only to the amount of tissue destroyed.

Flourens was testing rather basic function in animals with relatively little cortex—typically, chickens, pigeons, rodents, and other small animals. It is not altogether surprising, therefore, that he did not find specific deficits related to the location of his cortical lesions. In any case, his position was to be definitively disproved by important discoveries later in the 19th century, which we discuss shortly.

A modified form of Flourens's position survived into modern times, however. In the 1950s, on the basis of a series of experiments with rats and other animals, Karl Lashley (1890–1952) espoused a very similar position. Lashley argued that, with the exception of the sensory and motor areas, all parts of the cortex contribute equally to complex functions such as maze learning, a concept he referred to as **equipotentiality.** He further concluded that the magnitude of the deficit was related to the extent of the damage to the cortex, a concept he termed **mass action.** There was, however, a critical flaw in his argument. He measured the effect of his lesions by subjecting his animals to very complex tasks (maze learning) and measuring their performance using gross measures that were too global to permit detection of specific impairment related to damage in specific cortical regions.

A metaphor may help illustrate this point. Suppose that we are using a complex and global measure of economic success such as gross national product (GNP). Suppose that one year this measure dips sharply after a major strike in the automotive industry and then drops an equal amount the next year after major crop failures. This does not entitle us to conclude that automobile factories and farms perform the same function. The GNP (and, by analogy, Lashley's complex tasks) is simply not sensitive enough to indicate which specific disruptions caused the effect.

We now know that particular areas of the cortex are specialized for particular functions and, further,

as we shall see in chapter 5, that there is subspecialization of function even within areas of the brain devoted to a single modality, such as vision. Moreover, as we will see in subsequent chapters, there is reason to believe that there is an analogous localization of function within all areas of cortex. This is true even of frontal cortex, an area that mediates extremely complex functions.

Flourens's and Lashley's error is highly instructive. It alerts us to the fact that testing that taps specific functions is more likely to reveal specialization of function, whereas measures of global function are unlikely to do so. This principle has important implications for the design of both experimental investigations and clinical assessment instruments.

THE BEGINNINGS OF MODERN NEUROPSYCHOLOGY: BROCA

Let us return now to the middle of the 19th century and what may be considered the beginning of modern neuropsychology: the first substantial empirical evidence for localization of function within the human brain. This evidence was put forward by the French surgeon Paul Broca (1824–1880) in 1865, but there were some important antecedents to his work.

Antecedents to Broca: Gall and Bouillaud

In the early years of the 19th century, Franz Gall, in one of his few empirical studies, reported the case of a soldier who sustained a knife wound to the left eye that penetrated the skull and who subsequently suffered an impairment in language. Possibly based on this case or similar cases, the French physician Jean Baptiste Bouillaud (1796–1881) in 1825 speculated that language might be represented in the anterior portion of the human brain. He went further, speculating that the left-hemisphere specialization for motor dexterity presumably underlying right-handedness might also extend to the specialized movements involved in speech. Subsequently, in 1861, Ernest Auburtin, Bouillaud's son-in-law, presented a talk before the Anthropological Society of Paris, attended by its founder, Paul Broca, in which he reported a case of a man who was unable to speak after pressure was applied to the exposed anterior region of his brain.

The Case of "Tan"

Shortly after hearing this talk, Broca became aware of a patient named Leborgne who was unable to speak more than a few words. It could be shown that this patient understood language and that he was not demented because he responded accurately to questions that could be answered through gestures, such as his age. It could also be shown that the muscles required for speech were not paralyzed or otherwise inoperative because he could reproduce individual speech sounds (phonemes), such as *ba* and *ga,* upon request. What was disrupted in this patient was the ability to rapidly combine these individual phonemes to produce coordinated speech. Instead, his verbal output was radically reduced to a few short fragments, one of which, "Tan," he repeated so often that it became his nickname.

Not long after Broca's examination, Leborgne died. Broca, taking the opportunity to examine Leborgne's brain, discovered what he described as a lesion in the left frontal lobe. As it turns out, Leborgne's brain was preserved, and, after being lost for some years during World War II, it turned up in a Paris museum. Figure 1.7 is a photograph of Leborgne's brain.

The Concept of Hemispheric Dominance: The Left Hemisphere and Language

At first Broca interpreted this finding of a lesion in the left frontal lobe as consistent with Bouillaud's idea that language is represented in the anterior part of the brain. As Broca went on to study a number of patients with language impairments similar to Leborgne's, he noted that in each instance in which he was able to study the brain post-mortem he found a lesion in the *left* frontal lobe. Finally, in 1865, after studying a number of cases, Broca concluded that the left hemisphere is *dominant* for language or, as he put it, "*nous parlons avec l'hemisphere gauche*" ("we speak with our left hemisphere").

After Broca's discovery, the son of a French physician by the name of Marc Dax stated that his father had collected a number of cases with symptoms similar to those of Broca and had also discovered the association between this disorder and damage to the left hemisphere. According to his son, the elder Dax

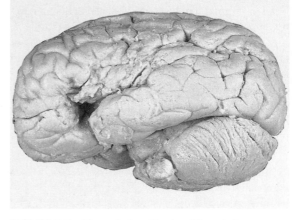

FIGURE 1.7 The embalmed brain of Broca's famous patient Leborgne. *(From Corsi, 1991, p. 217)*

had reported his findings at a conference in 1836 but had never published them. Documentation of the presentation was never found and it remains uncertain whether Dax or Broca was the first to discover this association.

Nevertheless, as Joynt (1964) points out, whoever first reported data supporting the idea that language is represented in the left hemisphere, the credit for describing the syndrome of impaired language production in the absence of impairment in the peripheral mechanisms of speech goes to Broca. In addition, Broca understood the implication of the fact that all the patients he studied with this syndrome had lesions in the left hemisphere, an implication embodied in the concept of **cerebral dominance for language.** In this concept we have what may be considered the beginning of modern neuropsychology. Broca had demonstrated the existence of a central (i.e., not peripheral) language impairment that is now generally referred to as **aphasia** (although Broca himself suggested the term *aphemia*). Furthermore, Broca demonstrated that the critical lesion was localized within a specific area of the left hemisphere, namely, the inferior and posterior part of the anterior region of the cortex, an area that came to be known as **Broca's area** (Figure 1.8). In doing so, he provided the first solid empirical support for what today is referred to as **intrahemispheric specialization of function,** specialization of function within one

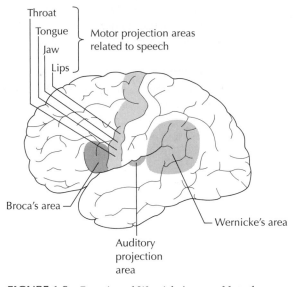

Throat
Tongue
Jaw
Lips

Motor projection areas
related to speech

Broca's area

Wernicke's area

Auditory
projection
area

FIGURE 1.8   Broca's and Wernicke's areas. Note the proximity of Broca's area to the cortical regions that control the speech muscles and the proximity of Wernicke's area to the primary auditory cortex. *(From H. Gleitman, 1995)*

hemisphere. We will see that much of the history of neuropsychology has to do with the development and delineation of these concepts.

The Discovery of the Motor Cortex: Fritsch and Hitzig

In 1870, five years after Broca's seminal discovery, a very different kind of investigation, carried out in Germany, further revealed specialization of function in the cerebral cortex. Studying the exposed brain of a dog, Gustav Fritsch (1838–1929) and Eduard Hitzig (1838–1909) discovered that stimulation of a specific region of cortex resulted in movement of the contralateral limbs. They had thus discovered that not only "higher" functions such as language were represented in the cerebral cortex but also seemingly less complex behaviors, simple movements. The area of cortex devoted to movement was called the **motor cortex.** This was an important discovery, both because it furthered the idea of functional specialization of the cortex and because it suggested that the cortex was not reserved solely for "higher," "associative" function. Both these

ideas received further support from the subsequent discovery of regions of the cortex specialized for somatosensory, auditory, and visual functions.

FURTHER DISCOVERIES: WERNICKE

Wernicke's Discovery of Receptive Aphasia

In 1874 another extremely important discovery was made. The German neurologist Carl Wernicke (1848–1904) described a different type of aphasia. Whereas Broca had described an aphasia (which came to be known as Broca's aphasia) involving impaired speech production, Wernicke described patients who were severely impaired in their ability to comprehend language. Unlike patients with Broca's aphasia, these patients were not impaired in the ability to coordinate the production of words, although the combination of correctly articulated words that they produced often didn't make sense. They spoke in a kind of "word salad" that obscured their underlying meaning. The lesion associated with this disorder was in the left *posterior* cortex (see Figure 1.8). This area came to be known as **Wernicke's area.**

The Concept of Sequential Processing

We will have more to say about both Broca's and Wernicke's aphasia in chapter 6. At this point, however, let us simply appreciate the importance of the discoveries these two pioneers made. In demonstrating that both types of aphasia are associated with damage to the left hemisphere, the findings of both Broca and Wernicke support the concept of hemispheric dominance. In addition, taken together, these findings show that different lesions within the left hemisphere produce different impairments in language, thus further supporting the idea of intrahemispheric specialization of function.

The work of Broca and Wernicke also supports the notion that language function is composed of a number of functions that, under certain conditions, can be separated or dissociated from one another. Wernicke thought of this in terms of a kind of **sequential processing** (Figure 1.9). According to his view, verbal auditory input was processed by the auditory

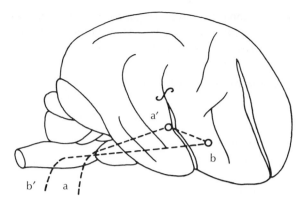

FIGURE 1.9   Wernicke's notion of the sequential processing of language in the cerebral cortex. *(From Wernicke, 1874)*

system (*a* in Figure 1.9) and then relayed to Wernicke's area (*a'*), which mediated the transformation or translation of the auditory representations of words into meaning. He conceptualized Wernicke's area as also mediating the reverse process, the transformation of meaning into some kind of verbal representation. This representation was then relayed to Broca's area (*b*), where the coordination of the peripheral motor mechanisms for speech (muscles, tongue, vocal chords, etc.) was organized. The motor cortex then activated the necessary speech mechanisms (*b'*), resulting in spoken language.

Wernicke believed that this conceptualization accounted for the disorders that followed damage to Broca's area and Wernicke's area. He went further, however, predicting the disorder that would occur after damage to the nerve fibers connecting these two areas: Such a lesion would impair the repetition of heard speech while leaving speech production and comprehension relatively intact, he proposed. Wernicke was later able to substantiate this hypothesis through the study of cases of people with such damage, patients exhibiting a syndrome that he termed **conduction aphasia.**

The Disconnection Syndrome Hypothesis

Wernicke had introduced an approach that conceptualized the cortex as comprising areas or centers, each of which mediates one in a series of relatively discrete

processes and which act together to make complex processes possible. He further argued that disorders could be understood either as the result of damage to these centers (e.g., Broca's or Wernicke's aphasia) or as a result of disruption of the connections between these centers (e.g., conduction aphasia). Disorders that are understood in terms of disconnections between centers became known as **disconnection syndromes.** In the latter part of the 19th century, this approach became a very popular way of theorizing about the nervous system. More recently, in the 1960s, this approach was reemphasized and reinvigorated by the work of the neurologist Norman Geschwind.

The Concept of Complementary Hemispheric Specialization: The Role of the Right Hemisphere

We will examine another example of the explanatory power of the disconnection approach in the next section of this chapter. Before we do this, however, let's consider the right hemisphere of the brain. We have seen that the concept of cerebral dominance for language developed out of the empirical finding that aphasic patients were found to have damage within the left but not the right hemisphere. (For the moment we are considering only right-handed people; we will consider the more complicated situation of left-handers later.) The implication of the idea of left-hemisphere dominance was obvious: The left hemisphere mediates language, a critically important function, and the right hemisphere, because it does not participate in this function, is therefore somehow inferior or ancillary. The concept of left-hemisphere dominance survived into the middle of the 20th century and is still sometimes heard as a kind of shorthand term to specify the hemisphere in which language is represented.

Since the 1950s, however, there has been an evolving appreciation that the right hemisphere is also specialized, but for functions that are not linguistic, such as perceptual and spatial processing. This evolving awareness that the right hemisphere is also the site of specialized functioning is reflected in the supplanting of the concept of cerebral dominance by the more accurate concept of complementary specialization of the two cerebral hemispheres or, more briefly, **hemispheric specialization** or **hemispheric functional asymmetry.** This reconceptualization was slow to emerge, considering that evidence for the functional specialization of the right hemisphere had been accumulating for a long time. As early as 1874, the year of Wernicke's seminal findings, the English neurologist John Hughlings-Jackson (1835–1911), whose hypotheses are often astonishingly modern, proposed that the right hemisphere is specialized for visual imagery. This was an astute speculation, and, although it has proved to be not entirely accurate, it nevertheless captures, in a metaphorical way, the notion of the importance of the right hemisphere for visual-perceptual processing.

By the beginning of the 20th century there was substantial evidence of right-hemisphere specialization for certain processes, yet the concept of left-hemisphere dominance held on for some time. As we will see when we address the function of the right hemisphere in later chapters, there were reasons for the tenacity of this concept. These include the fact that the functioning for which the left hemisphere is specialized (e.g., language) is more discrete and more precisely definable (and therefore more identifiable) than the functions for which the right hemisphere is specialized (e.g., visual perception and spatial processing). In addition, there is evidence that the left hemisphere is more specialized for verbal processes than the right hemisphere is for the processes for which it is specialized. We will explore these points further in chapter 7.

An Example of a Disconnection Syndrome: Alexia Without Agraphia

Having emphasized the importance of the concept of complementary functional specialization of the two cerebral hemispheres—the idea that both hemispheres are specialized for different functions—let's return to the disconnection syndrome approach and demonstrate how explanatory it can be. Again consider the case reported by the French neurologist Joseph Jules Dejarine in 1882 with which we began this chapter. As you will recall, Dejarine's patient first suffered from an **alexia** without **agraphia,** that is, he could not read but he could write. Subsequently, he

also lost the ability to write. On the face of it, this is a peculiar pattern of impairment and preservation of function. What kind of a brain lesion could produce such a baffling syndrome? In attempting to answer this question we are aided by the fact that the patient was blind in his right visual field. We shall discuss this disorder, termed a right hemianopia, in detail in a later chapter. At this point we will simply note that it is often associated with abnormality in the left posterior part of the brain (the occipital lobes). However, that damage alone would not account for the reading deficit, because most persons with a hemianopia can read quite well once they have adjusted to the visual field deficit. So the lesion must have included other parts of the brain as well. Furthermore, the subsequent loss of writing suggests the presence of yet another lesion.

So what did Dejarine find when he examined this patient's brain post-mortem? There was a lesion, secondary to a stroke, in the left occipital cortex, as we surmised. In addition, this lesion extended to include the posterior portion of the corpus callosum. The **corpus callosum** is a massive bundle of fibers connecting regions of the cortex of one hemisphere with homologous (i.e., corresponding) regions of the other hemisphere. As one might expect, the regions of the cortex that particular callosal fibers interconnect correspond to the position of those fibers along the anterior-posterior axis of the corpus callosum. In accordance with this general principle, the **splenium** of the corpus callosum transfers information from the right occipital region to the left hemisphere and vice versa. Because the left occipital cortex and the splenium were affected by lesions in Dejarine's patient, the language areas in the left hemisphere were deprived of any direct visual input. This patient's inability to read suggests that such direct input is necessary for reading. In contrast, Dejarine's patient could write because output from Wernicke's area was able to gain access to the motor cortex. (He could, incidentally, read by touching raised letters because, analogously, somatosensory input [sensory information about the body] from the fingers could gain access to Wernicke's area.)

The lesion that we have described so far accounts for this patient's alexia without agraphia. But how can we understand the subsequent loss of the ability to write? The explanation of this later development turns out also to be highly instructive. Dejarine found a second, more recent lesion in an area called the angular gyrus, just superior to Wernicke's area, in the left hemisphere (see Figure 1.8). From this we can infer that this area is necessary for the translation of verbal images (from Wernicke's area) into a form that can be utilized by the motor cortex in writing. We will see in chapter 6 that this region is also necessary for the translation of visual verbal material into a form that can be used by Wernicke's area for understanding, that is, for reading. This is shown by the fact that damage to the angular gyrus results in an inability to read (acquired alexia).

But we are anticipating our discussion of language. In the present context let us simply appreciate the explanatory power of the disconnection syndrome approach in furthering the understanding of impairments following brain abnormality. As we continue to examine neuropsychological syndromes in subsequent chapters, we will see that this approach, initiated by Wernicke, was utilized fruitfully by his contemporaries, including his student Hugo Liepmann (1863–1925) in Liepmann's analysis of **apraxia,** disorders of learned movement. Although the disconnection syndrome approach has some important limitations, which we shall discuss later, it continues to be a useful perspective from which to view the effects of cerebral lesions on behavior.

LOCALIZATION VERSUS HOLISM

The Limits of Localization: The Mapmakers

We have seen that the problem of localization of function, the extent to which specific functions can be localized in specific regions of the cortex, was an area of intense controversy in the period before Broca's seminal discovery. During that period, views as divergent as those of Flourens and those of Gall and Spurzheim stared uncompromisingly at one another. One might think that the dawn of an empirical neuropsychology in the mid-19th century and the specific finding of Broca, Fritsch and Hitzig, Wernicke, and others would have settled the matter in favor of the localizationist position. But the controversy continued in modified form and continues today. In the

late 19th and early 20th centuries a strong form of the localizationist position was espoused by the so-called mapmakers. These were theorists who used the general conceptual framework we saw in Wernicke's account of conduction aphasia and Dejarine's account of alexia without agraphia to explain a multitude of disorders in terms of the disruption of "centers" and the pathways connecting them.

As these explanations became more detailed and elaborate, they also became more speculative and divorced from empirical data. In particular, centers mediating highly specific cognitive functions were proposed, often in the absence of supporting evidence. In reaction to this, a forceful antilocalizationist position began to reemerge. The extreme form of this position is exemplified by the work of Friedrich Goltz (1834–1902) who, after making large and even complete lesions of the cortex of dogs, observed only a general decrease in function proportional to the size of the lesion but not related to its location. This led him to a holistic view of cortical functioning similar to the earlier view of Flourens. Even Broca's findings were criticized. Pierre Marie (1906), in his paper bearing the bold and provocative title "The Third Left Frontal Convolution Plays No Particular Role in the Function of Language," argued that the area of damaged cortex associated with Broca's aphasia extended beyond the area identified by Broca, into the posterior left hemisphere. Basing his conclusions on his own examination of the brain of Broca's patient "Tan," Marie insisted that Broca had no basis for inferring the existence of a speech "center."

Reconciliation of the Holist and Localizationist Views: Hughlings-Jackson's Concept of Hierarchy

There were positions more moderate than either of these extremes. Freud, in one of his last forays into neurology before becoming totally immersed in psychoanalysis, adopted a surprisingly modern view. In his book *On Aphasia* (Freud, 1893/1953) he criticized the speculative theorizing of the mapmakers without throwing out altogether the notion of localization of function. Perhaps one of the most useful approaches to this problem, however, was that espoused by Hughlings-Jackson. He conceptualized the brain as having many levels of control that are organized hierarchically. A metaphor that illustrates this notion, and to which I return often in my attempts to understand the human brain, is one of social organization and structure. In the context of our present discussion of hierarchical control by various levels of the nervous system, consider the organization of the executive branch of the federal government. There is the president at the top, and then the cabinet secretaries, assistant secretaries, deputy assistant secretaries, division heads, middle managers, section leaders, and so on. If the president were to become nonfunctional for some reason (I will resist the temptation to embellish this metaphor with a specific example), the Department of Defense, say, would not stop functioning. In fact, it might take some time for the impact to be felt, although it eventually surely would be, perhaps in the form of a change in the size of the defense budget. Or the effect might be immediate, in the case of the Commander in Chief's not decisively ordering the deployment of troops in a particular situation. Yet the president's nonfunctionality would probably not disrupt the day-to-day activities of military bases and aircraft carriers.

As we go further down the hierarchy (secretary of defense, chairman of the joint chiefs of staff, highest-ranking generals) the effect of nonfunction becomes more specific, disrupting particular actions. Dysfunction at even lower levels results in very visible but limited, specific problems (e.g., particular vehicles are not repaired or a particular gate is not guarded). Of course, if the dysfunction at low levels is widespread (e.g., all of the combat troops get sick), this would drastically impair the functioning of the armed forces. Note, also, as one descends the hierarchy, responses become more predictable and stereotyped (e.g., motor pool personnel fill the fuel tanks of vehicles and check the oil; MPs ask arrivals at a checkpoint for identification papers).

What does the metaphor of hierarchical function tell us about the brain? If we conceptualize the brain as being organized in an analogous manner, the metaphor helps us understand many phenomena. Goltz's dogs, who were able to engage in a variety of motor functions after removal of the entire cerebral cortex, but with diminished "will" and "intelligence," are analogous to the armed forces deprived of their highest levels of command. Many details are still in place, but the execution of complicated behaviors that require particular intelligence and strategic planning is disrupted.

We will return to this and related social metaphors often as we attempt to understand the behavioral and cognitive effects of cortical damage. This is because the brain is really much more like a social organization than like a machine. If one of various important components of a complicated machine is broken, the machine is likely to simply not work. Although an expert mechanic might be able to infer from the disrupted performance of the machine what is wrong, the machine isn't doing anything like what it was intended to do (assuming the problem is major). In contrast, if a major sector of society is dysfunctional (e.g., no new cars are produced or imported), the social structure will experience the impact, yet it will not stop working altogether. It will move to compensate. People will walk, buy bicycles, carpool, take public transportation, take better care of their cars, live nearer their jobs, or make some other adaptation. All of this may make society less efficient, but it will continue to function, albeit in an impaired manner. The same thing happens as a result of lesions to the cerebral cortex.

HIERARCHY AS AN EVOLUTIONARY DEVELOPMENT   Hughlings-Jackson viewed the development of hierarchical organization as one of the legacies of the process of evolution. According to this view, the complexity of hierarchical organization of the nervous system of a given species is related to that species' level of evolutionary development. The nervous system of simple creatures, like the jellyfish, will respond with a stereotyped reflex to the presence of food, regardless of other environmental events. In contrast, for the hungry cheetah, higher levels of neural organization will inhibit lower centers (that organize and activate his rapid predatory chase) until he has gotten close enough to his prey to have a good chance of overtaking it during the brief period when he has maximum speed available.

BRAIN DAMAGE AS A REVERSAL OF EVOLUTIONARY DEVELOPMENT   In the context of this understanding of brain function as hierarchically organized, Hughlings-Jackson conceptualized the effects of lesions to higher brain levels as a reversal of the evolutionary development of this organization, a process he termed **dissolution.** With higher levels of control disrupted, lower levels exert poorly modulated control—just as in the absence of higher levels of command, the whims and impulses of local sergeants are no longer regulated and their responses to events go unchecked. Hughlings-Jackson's concept of dissolution is thus a framework for understanding the effects of brain lesions.

For example, consider the so-called release symptoms, sometimes seen after cortical lesions. **Release symptoms** take the form of the reemergence, the disinhibition, of infantile reflexes that had long since left the individual's repertory, after damage to higher brain centers that normally inhibit those reflexes. One of these, the rooting reflex (turning the head toward a stimulus that has just touched the cheek), is a useful prewired mechanism that helps newborns find the nipple. It disappears after infancy but may reappear in adulthood, after years of absence, as a consequence of extensive frontal-lobe damage.

Bias and Preconception in Early-20th-Century Neuropsychology

The history of science is full of examples of empirical findings that were misinterpreted or even ignored because they did not conform to the prevailing theoretical constructs of the time, only to be recognized later as touchstones for deeper understanding. The history of neuropsychology is no exception to this tendency. For example, early in the 20th century, reports of specific impairment in color vision following cortical lesions were dismissed by many because they contradicted the prevailing view of the cortex as the site of "higher-order" processing. It is now clear that central color blindness is indeed a real phenomenon, and, as we will see in chapter 5, the study of this disorder has revealed much about how the brain is organized.

The critique of visual agnosia put forth by the German neurologist Eberhard Bay provides another example of how preconceptions can blind us to the truth. **Visual agnosia** is defined as impairment in visual object recognition not due to primary sensory impairment. Bay's critique challenged the validity of this concept. He argued that the visual-object-recognition impairments seen after cerebral lesions are due, not to a disruption of cortical processing, but, instead, to elementary visual impairments. Bay amassed evidence of subtle visual impairment in patients identified as agnosic to support his view. Although healthy skepticism is an indispensable component of scientific inquiry, it can also be used to shield our biases and preconceptions from data that are inconsistent with them. This happened in the case of agnosia. The subtle sensory impairments that Bay and others were detecting in patients with agnosia, though real, were not sufficiently severe to account for the magnitude of their object recognition impairments. Nevertheless, Bay's bias against the existence of a central disorder of object recognition prevented him from appreciating this disproportion.

Now that the existence of visual agnosia has been well established, we can look back on Bay's critique more sanguinely. Perhaps by stimulating investigations that definitively demonstrated that associated sensory deficits could not account for these patients' object recognition impairment, Bay's critique constituted a necessary phase of skepticism, which ultimately served the heuristic purpose of firmly establishing the validity of visual agnosia as a specific higher-order impairment.

THE PSYCHOMETRIC APPROACH TO NEUROPSYCHOLOGY

As we have already seen, much has been learned from the case study approach, and there undoubtedly remains much that the in-depth study of single individuals is uniquely capable of revealing. Nevertheless, one of the most important developments in neuropsychology was the application of the psychometric approach to neuropsychological investigation.

Group Studies and Statistical Analysis

The use of group studies, beginning in the late 1940s and early 1950s, added another dimension to the understanding of brain-behavior relationships. In particular, group studies allowed the formation of control groups to more clearly reveal the nature of the impairments associated with a particular lesion. In addition, the use of statistical procedures in group studies made quantitative definitions of impairment possible and thus enhanced the sensitivity of specific tests to the presence of impairment. For example, in assessing sensory thresholds after cortical lesions, one can define impairment in an individual in terms of performance below a certain level of the control group, say below the first percentile. One can also define a group as impaired if, using inferential statistics, the probability of that group's being drawn from the same population as the control group is below a certain level, say .01.

Thus, group studies and the statistical analyses they make possible have had an enormous impact on neuropsychology. By permitting precise quantification of the probability that a group with a particular lesion or condition is performing at a lower level than a control group on a particular task, they contribute to our understanding of the cerebral organization of psychological processes. Further, by providing a measure of the probability that a particular individual's performance is below that of a control group, group studies provide a basis for making inferences regarding the presence of cognitive impairment and associated cerebral abnormality in that individual (Reitan & Davison, 1974). This, in turn, provides a basis for clinical neuropsychological assessment, a set of procedures that can be highly useful in diagnosis and rehabilitation (Lezak, 1995).

The Continuing Role of the Case Study

Although the use of group studies is an enormous advance, group studies have not rendered the single case study obsolete. Single case studies remain of vital importance for several reasons. First, some disorders are so rare that assembling a group of cases would take many years. In addition, when one is studying a disorder so severe that it can be detected without statistical methods (such as agnosia and aphasia), the study of a single subject provides a vivid and detailed description of the impairment that is often lost in the analysis of group data. Moreover, a series of case studies provides information that is easily lost in the course of group analysis about variability of symptom pictures across individuals who share some symptoms or common areas of cerebral abnormality. For example, as we will see in chapter 6, there is considerable variability in the profile of impairments seen in patients with receptive aphasia. Some have virtually no language comprehension; others have some residual capacity to understand language. Similarly, there is significant variability across patients in the symptom picture seen after lesions to Broca's area. This variability is obscured or even lost in data that express function in terms of group averages. Thus, although often informative, analyses yielding generalities about groups run the risk of obscuring individual differences and providing an overgeneralized appraisal of the effects of particular lesions.

Finally, group studies present an additional problem: Groups defined on the basis of site of lesion (e.g., left posterior cortex) may in fact comprise subjects with widely varying lesion sites. This heterogeneity is likely to result in considerable variability in symptom pictures, which may lead to erroneous interpretations of the role of the presumably identified area or may even result in so much "noise" that the data are completely uninterpretable.

RECENT FINDINGS

We will end our discussion of historical aspects of neuropsychology with a few words about the impact of recent findings. Although evidence supporting two concepts—parallel distributed processing and modular organization in the visual cortex (concepts we will discuss in detail in chapter 5)—began to emerge more than 20 years ago, their implications are still being digested by students of the brain. Briefly, the concept of **parallel distributed processing** has emerged from the developing awareness that the neural activity mediating a specific psychological process rarely follows a sequential path through the nervous system, as had long been assumed. Rather, this activity is often distributed in parallel over many networks of neurons located in different brain regions.

Modular organization refers to the finding that specific aspects of cognitive processing are represented in different specialized brain regions. In visual processing, for example, color, form, and movement have each been shown to be represented in different, specialized cortical areas within cortical regions that had long been considered to be devoted only to higher-order perceptual processing. (See chapter 5 for a more detailed discussion.)

These findings are so different from the classical views of brain organization that they radically alter older hypotheses of how the brain works. According to the classical sequential models, elementary functions, such as the perception of color or movement, are mediated by areas of cortex receiving initial input from sensory centers (**primary sensory cortex**), whereas higher-order functions, such as object recognition, are mediated by cortical areas further downstream (**association cortex**). However, these sequential models, with their hypothesized segregation of elementary and complex processes, seem to require radical revision in the face of recent findings. As our discussion of vision in chapter 5 will make clear, we can no longer simply postulate that "elementary" processing goes on in the primary sensory cortex, from which it is transferred to association cortex for higher-order processing. Indeed, the parallel nature of cortical processing and the specialization of visual function within diverse areas of cortex force us to

consider the possibility that some familiar and seemingly basic conceptualizations, such as the distinction between elementary and higher-order processing, might reflect serious misunderstandings of how the brain is organized.

SUMMARY

In this chapter we have considered the historical development of neuropsychology. Our historical survey revealed that erroneous ideas about the relationship between brain and behavior can remain widely accepted for long periods. One example is the theory that the cerebral ventricles are the seat of cognition. Despite the absence of supporting empirical evidence, this theory prevailed from Roman times to the Renaissance. By the same token, a historical perspective also emphasizes how long it took for some now-seemingly-obvious principles to be discovered. Perhaps the most stunning example of this is the fact that it was not until the mid-19th century that localization of function within the cerebral cortex and the specialization of the left hemisphere for language were firmly established, even though these discoveries were not dependent on the development of specific technical advances.

Understanding the history of neuropsychology has yet another benefit. The issues embedded in many historical controversies, such as holism versus localization, continue to reemerge in contemporary contexts. An awareness of the historical antecedents of current controversies helps place them in perspective and provides a framework for possible resolutions.

CHAPTER 2

Neural Mechanisms at the Molecular and Cellular Levels

THE ADAPTIVE SIGNIFICANCE OF THE NERVOUS SYSTEM

THE CAPACITY FOR MODULATION: THE NEURON AND THE SYNAPSE
Discovery of the Neuron and the Synapse
General Components of the Neuron
Glia
Overview of Events at the Synapse

NEURAL ACTIVITY AT THE MOLECULAR AND CELLULAR LEVELS
Physical Forces Underlying Ion Movement
Membrane Resting Potential
Effects of Neurotransmitter Release on the Postsynaptic Membrane
Integration of Input at the Axon Hillock
The Action Potential
Saltatory Conduction

Neurotransmitter Release
Mechanisms for Clearing Neurotransmitter After Neuron Firing
Responses to Neurotransmitter-Receptor Binding

NEURONAL MECHANISMS OF LEARNING
Habituation and Sensitization in *Aplysia:* Examples of Presynaptic Modulation of Neuronal Activity
Classical Conditioning
Long-Term Potentiation

TWO EXCEPTIONS TO GENERAL RULES: RECEPTOR POTENTIALS AND ELECTRICAL TRANSMISSION
Receptor Potentials: Transmission Without Action Potentials
Electrical Transmission: Communication Between Neurons Without Chemical Synapses

SUMMARY

❖ ❖ ❖

In this chapter we look at the nervous system in microcosm, focusing on the individual nerve cell and especially on the individual synapse. Researchers have come to understand some of the complex electrochemical mechanisms that not only permit communication from one nerve cell to the next but also allow communication to be modified depending on circumstances. It is these mechanisms that permit higher organisms—in particular, human beings—to go beyond reflexes and engage in the highly complex behaviors required for

survival and success in complicated physical and social environments.

To understand these mechanisms we consider first the nature of the nerve cell membrane and the factors and forces influencing the movement of ions across it. We then look at how the activity of multiple synapses, situated at thousands of different positions on the cell membrane of a receiving neuron, are summed and integrated to cause the nerve cell to fire and release neurotransmitters, affecting other neurons. We then consider the types of neurotransmitters, the processes by which they bind to receptors, and additional factors that influence their effects. Finally, we will examine how some aspects of learning and memory are beginning to be understood in terms of processes at the neuronal level.

By looking at the processes occurring at the molecular and cellular levels we can get some idea of the kind of decision making that goes on in the nervous system as a whole. As we will see, these processes allow the system to code, or represent, enormous complexity.

THE ADAPTIVE SIGNIFICANCE OF THE NERVOUS SYSTEM

The mammalian nervous system is the product of millions of years of evolution. What are the aspects of this system that make it so highly adaptive? One answer is that the nervous system makes possible communication and coordination among the enormous number of cells that make up the bodies of large animals. To appreciate the advantages of a nervous system, one only has to compare organisms that possess one with organisms that do not, as William James does in this passage from *Principles of Psychology:*

> If I begin chopping the foot of a tree, its branches are unmoved by my act, and its leaves murmur as peacefully as ever in the wind. If, on the contrary, I do violence to the foot of a fellow man, the rest of his body instantly responds to the aggression by movements of alarm or defense. (James, 1890/1950, vol. 1, p. 12)

But the possibility of rapid and coordinated communication is only part of the story. The complex mammalian nervous system is the foundation for the flexibility of response that characterizes intelligent organisms. It is not the rapid but inevitable reflex response, for all its speed, that provides the basis for intelligence. Rather, it is the capacity to respond or not respond depending on other factors, such as the nature of the situation, its similarity or dissimilarity to past situations, and its potential meaning for the future of the organism. To understand this capacity of our nervous system for **modulation**—the capacity to respond flexibly to our environment, taking into account a complex array of factors—we must examine the nervous system at the micro level, considering the individual nerve cell and connections between nerve cells.

THE CAPACITY FOR MODULATION: THE NEURON AND THE SYNAPSE

The central nervous system is made up of a vast number of individual nerve cells, known as neurons. In humans this number reaches approximately 100 billion. (Some estimates are an order of magnitude higher or lower.) Of this number, few are **primary sensory neurons,** the first link in the afferent chain between **sensory receptors** (the first neurons to register the presence of stimuli) and the brain. This is partly because in the somatosensory system the cell bodies of most primary sensory neurons are located in ganglia that lie outside the central nervous system. Further, there are only about 3 million **motor neurons,** which leave the spinal cord to directly activate skeletal muscle. All the other cells in the human central nervous system are positioned between primary sensory neurons and motor neurons. It has been estimated (Nauta & Feirtag, 1979) that 99.98% of the neurons in the mammalian central nervous system are **interneurons,** neurons neither directly receiving information from the environment nor directly causing muscle contraction. Interneurons have the less direct but critically important function of providing a basis for the modulatory processes that make complex behavior possible. Whether we respond to someone who has just stepped on our toe with an angry snarl, a polite "excuse me," an abrupt punch in the nose, or a flirtatious smile depends on a host of factors that are weighed by neurons between the sensory neurons in our toe and the motor neurons that bring about our eventual response.

Simple animals have no such sophisticated capacity to regulate their response to stimuli. This is why we call them "simple." An example is the jellyfish, which has a nervous system composed of two layers of neurons. This kind of nervous system has been called a "doorbell" nervous system (Nauta & Feirtag, 1979), and with good reason. When a stimulus of adequate intensity impinges upon a sensory neuron of the jellyfish, the motor neuron connected with it always responds. There is no mechanism by which the jellyfish can respond differently depending on whether it's the class bully at the door or an attractive member of the opposite sex.

Discovery of the Neuron and the Synapse

At the turn of the 20th century an important debate was going on in neurobiology. The issue was whether the nervous system was composed of an interconnected net of tissue or of individual cells (neurons) with spaces between them. The former hypothesis was known as the **reticular hypothesis** (from the Latin *reticulum,* "net"). According to this theory, the nervous system was conceived as a continuous network of tissue that constituted an exception to the general rule that living tissue is made up of individual units or cells (cell theory). In contrast, the **neuron hypothesis** (sometimes called the **neuron doctrine**) held that the nervous system was made up of individual cells that were in close proximity to each other but did not form a continuous structure.

By the early 20th century, the neuron hypothesis became dominant, although the reticular hypothesis had had eminent proponents. One of these was Camillo Golgi, an Italian biologist who discovered the cell staining technique that bears his name and that continues to be in wide use today. This stain, which has been called the single most important advance in neuroanatomical methodology after the microscope itself (Hubel, 1979), makes possible the visualization of individual neurons with all their branches. It is able to do this because, for some unknown reason, it stains only about 1% of the neurons with which it comes in contact. Ironically, it was his meticulous observations of Golgi-stained neurons that led the Spanish biologist Santiago Ramón y Cajal to gather strong histological evidence in support of the neuron hypothesis and against Golgi's connectionist theory. It took several decades of additional research and the development of new techniques, including electron microscopy, to finally resolve the issue in favor of the neuron hypothesis.

Before the issue had been finally resolved, the British physiologist Sir Charles Sherrington proposed the concept of a narrow gap between neurons, which he called a **synapse,** on behavioral rather than anatomical grounds. He proposed this concept to account for his observation that when several mild electric shocks, each too weak to elicit a reflex when presented alone, are presented sequentially with an interval of less than 1 second between them, a reflex is elicited. This suggested to Sherrington that a kind of summation process was at work at the crossover point between neurons. It is now known that each stimulation is accompanied by release of small molecules called **neurotransmitters** into the synapse and that these effects are cumulative. Further evidence for this hypothesis came from the demonstration by Otto Loewi in 1920 that the vagus nerve secreted a substance that slowed heart rate. Loewi called this substance "vagus stuff" and it has since been identified as acetylcholine, now known to be the major excitatory neurotransmitter at the junction between motor neuron and muscle, but here exerting an inhibitory effect on heart rate.

These and other converging lines of evidence supporting the synapse hypothesis, including extensive physiological investigations, were dramatically corroborated by findings made possible with the development of electron microscopy. This made visualization of the synapse possible, and it was found to be a truly narrow gap: about 20–40 nanometers (a nanometer [nm] is 10^{-9} meter). Despite its miniscule size, the synapse turns out to have enormous implications for the workings of the nervous system. It means that the influence of a neuron on its neighbor can be modified by events that take place within the synapse. This, in turn, is part of the mechanism by which one portion of the nervous system is sensitive to a myriad of influences from other parts of the system. Let's take a look at how the system works at the level of the individual cell.

General Components of the Neuron

Neurons come in many different shapes and sizes, taking on wonderfully diverse forms in different parts of the nervous system. Figure 2.1 shows a

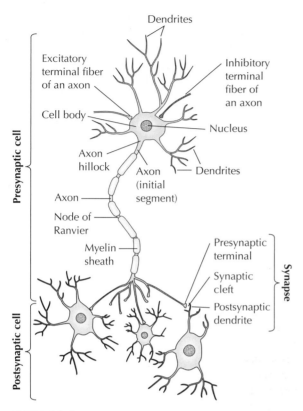

FIGURE 2.1   A schematic view of a typical neuron. The cell body contains a nucleus that holds the genetic material of the cell. Two types of processes extend from the cell body, the dendrites and the axon. The dendrites are the major receiving surface of the neuron, although input from other neurons also arrives at the cell body. The axon conducts the action potential, the cell's signal, to the next neuron. The axon hillock is the point at which the action potential is initiated. Many neurons are insulated by a myelin sheath that is periodically interrupted by nodes of Ranvier. Branches of one axon (the presynaptic terminal) transmit signals to another neuron (the postsynaptic dendrite) at a site called the synapse. *(From Kandel, Schwartz, & Jessell, 1995, p. 22)*

next neuron. The length of the axon varies greatly; it may be microscopic, or, in the case of the neurons whose axons extend from the cortex to the caudal region of the spinal cord in large animals, the axon may extend many feet. The axon is not responsible for the sensitivity of the system to diverse influences. Rather, it has the critical, if prosaic, role of transmitting signals from one structure to another. Once the portion of the axon near the cell body is activated, the signal simply travels its length, without modification or modulation, until it reaches the end of the axon, termed the **axon terminal** or **bouton.** The axon terminal is branched, though less extensively than the dendrite, so that a single axon can make functional contact with hundreds of dendritic sites on many other neurons. Although transmission of signals down the axon may be a prosaic process, it is obviously essential for the communication of information between neurons.

Glia

In addition to neurons, the central and peripheral nervous systems contain many cells called **neuroglia,** also called simply **glia** (from the Greek for "glue"). These cells obtained their name because they appeared to have some role in supporting the structure of the brain. Glial cells are numerous; in the brain they outnumber neurons. The main types of glia are microglia, astrocytes, and oligodendrocytes in the central nervous system and Schwann cells in the peripheral nervous system (Figure 2.2). Glia in the central nervous system provide structural and nutritive support for neurons. In addition, each type of glia performs specific functions. **Microglia,** taking the form of small, irregularly shaped cells, invade and remove damaged tissue. **Astrocytes** are large star-shaped cells that surround the brain's vasculature, forming a barrier that protects the brain by allowing only certain molecules to pass into it from the general circulation. This is the **blood-brain barrier,** a critical mechanism for the preservation of the physiological integrity of the brain.

Glia have not been shown to transmit or store information directly. However, they do perform a critical function that is more directly related to the focus

schematic view of a typical neuron. The **cell body** (or **soma**) contains the **nucleus** and many of the various **organelles** that are critical for the functioning of the cell. Radiating from the cell body are thin tubes, called **neurites.** Each neuron has two kinds of neurites: the highly branched **dendrite,** which receives signals, and an **axon,** which passes signals on to the

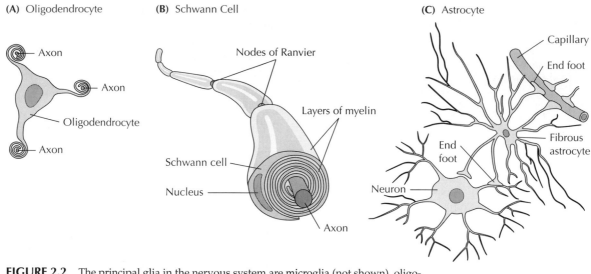

(A) Oligodendrocyte

(B) Schwann Cell

(C) Astrocyte

Axon

Axon

Oligodendrocyte

Axon

Nodes of Ranvier

Layers of myelin

Schwann cell

Nucleus

Axon

Capillary

End foot

End
foot

Fibrous
astrocyte

Neuron

FIGURE 2.2   The principal glia in the nervous system are microglia (not shown), oligodendrocytes, and astrocytes in the central nervous system and Schwann cells in the peripheral nervous system. (*A*) A single oligodendrocyte forms myelin sheaths around
many axons. (*B*) Schwann cells form the myelin sheaths that insulate neurons in the peripheral nervous system. They form segments of myelin sheath about 1 mm long with
intervals of bare axon, known as nodes of Ranvier, between the segments of myelin.
(*C*) Star-shaped astrocytes have broad end-feet that put them in contact both with capillaries and with neurons. They play a central role in the formation of the blood-brain barrier. *(From Kandel et al., 1995, p. 28)*

of the present chapter. In the course of development,
oligodendrocytes (in the central nervous system) and
Schwann cells (in the peripheral nervous system)
wrap their cell membranes around the axons of some
neurons, surrounding the axon with a concentrically
layered covering called **myelin** (see Figure 2.2). There
are periodic gaps in this covering, called **nodes of
Ranvier,** after the French anatomist Louis Antoine
Ranvier, who first described them. Myelin enhances
the speed of transmission of signals down the axon.
The importance of this process is evidenced by the
debilitating effects of demyelinating diseases, such as
multiple sclerosis, that interfere with the enhancing
effect of myelin. Multiple sclerosis severely disrupts
the function of affected parts of the nervous system,
leading to progressively severe symptoms and, ultimately, death. We will discuss the mechanism by
which myelin enhances the speed of axonal transmission in a later section, after we have discussed the
mechanism of neuronal transmission itself.

Overview of Events at the Synapse

To understand the complexities and nuances of neuronal transmission, we must direct our attention to
the two ends of the neuron. Let's begin at the axon
terminal. Here we find **synaptic vesicles** (membrane-
bound spheres) filled with small molecules called
neurotransmitters (Figure 2.3). When an impulse
traveling down the axon reaches the axon terminal,
it causes these synaptic vesicles to merge with the
presynaptic membrane and dump their contents
into the synapse. The neurotransmitter then diffuses
across the synaptic space and comes in contact with
a **receptor,** a specialized protein molecule or molecule complex on the **postsynaptic membrane** (i.e.,
the membrane of the receiving neuron), which recognizes and binds the neurotransmitter. Recognition
and binding are biochemical events whereby the
neurotransmitter, by virtue of its spatial and electrostatic configuration, is bound to a specific molecule

Dendrite

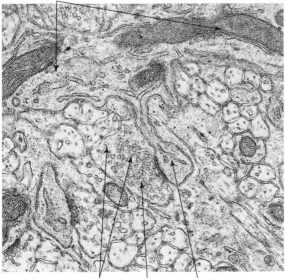

Synaptic   Axon   Dendritic
vesicles   spine

FIGURE 2.3   The synapse. The presynaptic part of the synapse is filled with round synaptic vesicles in which neurotransmitter is stored. The dendrite, the postsynaptic part of the synapse, crosses the top of the field. At the middle of the field the dendrite emits a downward branch called a dendritic spine, the left side of which makes contact with the axon. Dendritic spines increase the surface area of the dendrite, allowing a greater number of synapses to be established. The cleft is about 20 nm in width. Note that the synaptic membrane is darker, thicker, and more distinct than the other parts of the cell membrane. *(From Nauta & Feirtag, 1986, p. 7)*

(the receptor) that matches that configuration. Most neurotransmitters bind to receptors on the dendritic membrane; however, there are also receptors on the cell body and the axon terminal.[1] When the neurotransmitter binds to a receptor, important events are

set in motion in the receiving neuron. Before we consider these events, however, we'll focus our attention on the cell membrane because it is the properties of the cell membrane that underlie the molecular events involved in synaptic transmission.

NEURAL ACTIVITY AT THE MOLECULAR AND CELLULAR LEVELS

Like all other cells in the body, the neuron consists of cytoplasm bounded by a cell membrane. In the neuron, the membrane is composed of a double layer of lipid molecules (**lipid bilayer**) with membrane-spanning proteins embedded in it (Figure 2.4). The biophysics of the membrane's lipid bilayer makes it highly impermeable to fluid within the cell (**intracellular fluid** or **cytoplasm**), fluid outside the cell (**extracellular fluid**), and to **ions** (charged atoms or molecules) in solution in these fluids. Nevertheless, under certain conditions ions are able to pass through the cell membrane. This is accomplished by proteins that span the membrane's width, forming channels that regulate the **permeability** or **conductance** of the membrane to specific ions. Some of these protein ion channels, called **resting channels,** are open during the resting state of the neuron and allow the passive flow of particular ions across the membrane. As a general rule, channel proteins alter the membrane's conductance to a particular ion by changing their **conformational state** (i.e., their spatial configuration), a process called **gating.** The gating of some channels occurs in response to the binding of a specific neurotransmitter to postsynaptic receptors (**transmitter-gated channels** or **ligand-gated channels**). The gating of other channels is a response to changes in voltage (**voltage-gated channels**). Thus, channels differ both with regard to the factors controlling their gating and the particular ion to which they are selective. As we will see, it is these properties of the membrane ion channels that underlie the complexity of neuronal events.

Another much less common type of transmission also occurs across synapses. **Gap junction channels** (also called **electrical synapses**) utilize structural connections between two neurons to create direct current flow between them rather than using current

---

1. Synapses are often named in terms of the part of the transmitting neuron that is presynaptic followed by the parts of the receiving neuron that is postsynaptic. In additional to the most conventional axodendritic synapses, there are also axosomatic and axoaxonal synapses. Other combinations are also seen in the nervous system, though less frequently.

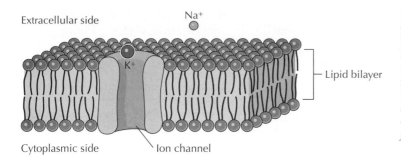

Extracellular side   Na⁺

K⁺

— Lipid bilayer

Cytoplasmic side   Ion channel

FIGURE 2.4 Phospholipids and glyco-proteins form the self-sealing lipid bilayers that are the basis for all cellular membranes. The lipid bilayer is extremely impermeable to the fluid around it (mostly water) and to ions in solution in that fluid. Ion channels are membrane-spanning proteins that allow one or another type of ion to pass through. *(Adapted from Kandel et al., 1995, pp. 116, 117)*

changes to trigger the release of neurotransmitter. We will have more to say about electrical synapses at the end of this chapter.

Physical Forces Underlying Ion Movement

Let's now consider the neuron when it is not being stimulated by neurotransmitter, the neuron in its resting state. The movement of ions through ion channels in the neuron membrane underlies the resting state of the neuron and many of the events involved in neural transmission. We therefore must first examine the factors that influence the movement of ions across biological membranes: conductance, diffusion force, and electrostatic force. Conductance refers to the extent to which a membrane, under specific conditions, has channels that are open to the passage of a particular ion. The qualification "under specific conditions" is necessary because the conductance of the neuronal membrane to a particular ion varies enormously, depending on the state of its transmitter-gated and voltage-gated channels. Obviously conductance is a limiting factor; there may be strong forces directing an ion to move across a membrane, yet that movement may not occur (or may be very limited) if there are no (or very few) membrane channels available for the passage of that ion.

The other two forces regulating ion movement are diffusion force and electrostatic force. **Diffusion force,** a force that tends to equalize the concentration of a particular molecule, is illustrated by the dispersal of a drop of ink introduced into a glass of water. The basic principle involved in **electrostatic force** is that like charges repel and opposites attract. Thus, if we have

negatively charged molecules in a beaker of water and we add some positively charged molecules, the two will be attracted to each other. But what happens if a membrane separates the two halves of the beaker? Let's say that there are negatively charged molecules (anions) on the left side of the beaker, but these molecules are too large to pass through the membrane. On the right side there are positively charged ions (cations), and these molecules are small enough to pass through the membrane (Figure 2.5). What will happen? The positively charged ions will be attracted to the negatively charged molecules, and some of them will pass across the membrane and enter the left side of the beaker. As this happens, however, the concentration of positively charged ions on the left side will rise and eventually reach a concentration greater than that on the right side. (We are assuming that the negatively charged molecules on the left have a high collective negative charge so that the net charge of the left side remains negative despite the inflow of positively charged ions).

As the concentration of positively charged ions on the left side begins to exceed that on the right, the two forces—diffusion force and electrostatic force—drive the positively charged ions in opposite directions. Diffusion force pushes the ions to the right side, the area of lower concentration. Electrostatic force pulls the ions to the left side, the negatively charged side. At some point diffusion force and electrostatic force will be equal, and a balance between movement of the particular ion into the left and right compartments will be achieved (Figure 2.6). This is called **electrochemical equilibrium,** and the difference in charge between two compartments at which

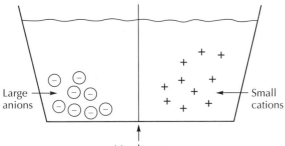

FIGURE 2.5   A beaker with a membrane that is permeable to positive ions but not to the larger, negative ions. In this situation positively charged ions will move to the left side of the beaker.

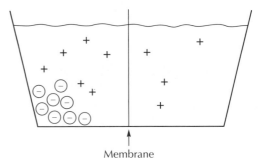

FIGURE 2.6   As the concentration of positive ions on the left side of the beaker exceeds the concentration on the right side, diffusion force will drive the cations to the right side and electrostatic force will drive the cations to the left side. When the magnitude of movement in the two directions is balanced, electrochemical equilibrium will be achieved.

point a particular type of ion would achieve electrochemical equilibrium is referred to as the **equilibrium potential** for that ion.

Membrane Resting Potential

What does this example have to do with our neuron? It turns out that the intracellular fluid of the neuron has some of the properties of the left-hand side of our beaker and the extracellular fluid has properties similar to the right-hand side of the beaker.

THE ROLE OF POTASSIUM IONS   Within the dendrite and the cell body are large, negatively charged proteins that are too large to pass through the membrane and out of the cell. At the same time, the membrane is permeable to positively charged potassium ions (K^+). Thus, as in our beaker, K^+ ions are drawn into the cell by electrostatic force. The concentration of K^+ inside the cell rises until it exceeds the concentration outside the cell to such an extent that electrostatic force drawing K^+ into the cell balances diffusion force pushing K^+ out of the cell. It so happens that when this equilibrium is achieved, the inside of the neuron is negative relative to the outside at a magnitude of –75 millivolts (mV). This is the K^+ equilibrium potential. The **resting potential,** the membrane potential when the membrane is at rest (not firing), is very close to this value, but a little less negative (about –65 mV). What is the reason for this discrepancy?

THE ROLE OF SODIUM IONS   In glial cells, the **membrane potential,** the difference in charge between the inside and the outside of the cell, can be accounted for entirely in terms of the K^+ equilibrium potential (Figure 2.7). However, in neurons the resting potential has a more complicated molecular basis. As we have seen, because the resting membrane has highest conductance for K^+, the K^+ electrochemical equilibrium is the most important factor contributing to the maintenance of the resting potential. Nevertheless, the resting membrane is also permeable to two other ions: sodium (Na^+) and chloride (Cl^-). We saw that there is a higher concentration of K^+ inside the neuron than outside; Na^+, on the other hand, is more highly concentrated outside than inside. This means that both diffusion force and electrostatic force tend to drive Na^+ into the neuron. However, there are very few open Na^+ channels in the resting membrane; this low conductance means that only a small influx of Na^+ occurs despite the magnitude of the forces driving it. This small inward leak of Na^+ does have an effect, however: It reduces the membrane potential, making it less negative than the K^+ equilibrium potential. This **depolarization** causes a slight efflux (outward movement) of K^+ at a rate that just balances the inward leak of Na^+. This steady state is achieved at about –65 mV, a polarization somewhat less negative than the K^+ equilibrium potential (Figure 2.8).

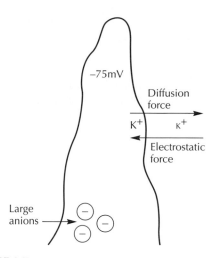

FIGURE 2.7   The molecular basis of the membrane potential in glial cells. In glia the membrane is almost exclusively permeable to K$^+$, and the membrane potential is therefore determined by the K$^+$ equilibrium potential.

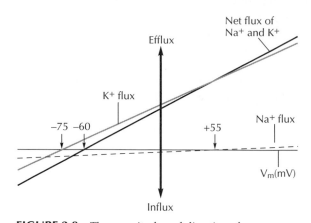

FIGURE 2.8   The magnitude and direction of movement of K$^+$ and Na$^+$ at different membrane potentials (mV) when the membrane is in the resting state. In addition to electrostatic force and diffusion force, the conductance of the membrane in the resting state to different ions (mediated by resting channels) is a major determinant of ion flow. At the resting potential of −65 mV, K$^+$ efflux is equal to Na$^+$ influx. The lines represent flux curves for K$^+$, Na$^+$, and the net K$^+$ and Na$^+$ flux. The steeper K$^+$ flux curve reflects the fact that the resting membrane has a higher conductance for K$^+$ than for Na$^+$. Changes in the conductance of the membrane for a particular ion, caused by the activation of transmitter-gated or voltage-gated channels, alter the flux of that ion. This change would be reflected by a change in the slope of that ion's flux curve, increased conductance being represented by a flux curve that has a steeper slope and decreased conductance being represented by a flux curve with a less steep slope. Change in membrane conductance for a particular ion does not affect that ion's equilibrium potential (the point at which the flux curve intersects the abscissa in this figure). By changing the slope of the flux curve of a particular ion while keeping its point of intersection with the abscissa constant, one can get a sense of the net change in the dynamics of ion flow resulting from a change in the conductance of that ion. (*After Kandel et al., 1995, p. 138*)

THE SODIUM-POTASSIUM PUMP   We have seen that in the resting state the membrane has a slight conductance to Na$^+$, resulting in a slow leak of sodium into the neuron due to both diffusion force and electrostatic force. As the neuron becomes slightly depolarized (less negative), this results in a compensating efflux of K$^+$ that just balances the Na$^+$ influx and, so, maintains the resting potential. This exchange presents a problem, however. Over time it would lead to the running down of the extracellular-intracellular concentration differences of each of these two ions, eventually resulting in the abolition of the resting potential.

To explain how the system prevents this outcome, we have to introduce the concept of a metabolic pump. Thus far we have been talking about the movement of ions across membranes in response to diffusion force, electrostatic force, and the conductance of the membrane. Sometimes, however, an ion is actively transported across a membrane in a direction that defies these factors. Such transport requires elaborate biochemical mechanisms that consume metabolic energy, the source of which is the energy released by the chemical breakdown of adenosine triphosphate (ATP). These mechanisms are referred to as **metabolic pumps** because they actively transport ions across membranes in the direction opposite to that dictated by electrochemical forces.

The metabolic pump that solves our present problem is called the **sodium-potassium pump.** This pump transports Na$^+$ out of the cell and K$^+$ into the cell. As is the case with all metabolic pumps, the sodium-potassium pump requires the expenditure of metabolic energy. This metabolically expensive pump maintains the steady state underlying the resting potential of the membrane. In fact, much of the energy expended by the brain is used to maintain the concentration gradients of K^+ and Na^+ that underlie the membrane's resting potential. Neurons use a lot of energy just maintaining a state of *readiness* for activity.

In summary, in the resting state, the neuronal membrane is most permeable to K^+, and the K^+ equilibrium potential of -75 mV is thus the major determinant of the resting potential. The resting membrane is, however, also slightly permeable to Na^+, and the electrochemical forces driving this ion into the cell result in a slow inward leak of Na^+. This is compensated for by a small outward flow of K^+. The net effect is to bring the resting potential to -65 mV, a level that is less negative than the K^+ equilibrium potential of -75 mV.

Effects of Neurotransmitter Release on the Postsynaptic Membrane

Now the stage is set for the events that are triggered by the binding of neurotransmitter to receptors in the postsynaptic membrane. Binding of neurotransmitter produces a profound change in the ion channels of the postsynaptic membrane. Whereas the conductance of the resting membrane is highly favorable to K^+ relative to Na^+, the binding of a transmitter to a receptor that is excitatory sets in motion a chain of biochemical events that will result in the opening of additional Na^+ channels. This change in permeability is brief and local, but while it is in effect, diffusion and electrostatic forces cause an influx of Na^+. This influx of positively charged ions creates a graded and transient decrease in the electrical potential between the inside and outside of the cell at a small area of the membrane such that there is a depolarization of several millivolts. Each instance of such a depolarization is called an **excitatory postsynaptic potential,** or **EPSP.** As this happens, the depolarizing effect of the Na^+ influx increases the rate of efflux of K^+ (because the electrostatic force keeping K^+ inside has been diminished), and the resting potential is rapidly reestablished (see Figure 2.8).

To add a further important dimension, some neurotransmitters bind to receptors that exert an inhibitory effect on the neuron. The most common mechanism of inhibition is the opening of additional chloride (Cl^-) channels. While the resting potential is in effect, there are few open Cl^- channels, and there is little flow of Cl^- across the membrane even though its high extracellular concentration would drive it into the neuron if it were allowed to pass. However, the opening of Cl^- channels by an inhibitory neurotransmitter results in an influx of Cl^- and an increase of the negativity inside the neuron (i.e., **hyperpolarization**). This is called an **inhibitory postsynaptic potential,** or **IPSP.** Alternatively, an IPSP can be caused by an increase in the K^+ conductance of the resting membrane. The opening of additional K^+ channels will result in an increased efflux of this ion as it moves in the direction of establishing its equilibrium potential of -75 mV, a value that we have seen is more negative than the resting potential.

Each of these inhibitory mechanisms is exemplified by the action of **gamma-aminobutyric acid (GABA),** a major inhibitory transmitter in the central nervous system. When GABA binds to the GABA-A receptor, it initiates inhibition by opening Cl^- channels. In contrast, when GABA binds to the GABA-B receptor, it initiates inhibition by increasing the resting membrane's K^+ conductance. In both cases—and in all cases of inhibition involving the binding of a neurotransmitter to a postsynaptic receptor—the result is an IPSP. IPSPs work in opposition to the EPSPs that we discussed previously.

At the neuromuscular junction, inhibition plays no important role. Excitatory inputs to muscle are simply summed until the threshold of muscle activation is reached. In contrast, inhibition plays a critical role in the central nervous system. In particular, the system often codes information in terms of a *decrease* in neuron firing frequency below the sluggish baseline rate characteristic of neurons that are not receiving input. By eliminating elements within the baseline firing sequence, inhibition can result in intricate patterns of neural firing, a process sometimes referred to as the *sculpting role of inhibition* (Figure 2.9).

Integration of Input at the Axon Hillock

Now that we have considered the effect on the membrane potential of the binding of a single neurotransmitter, let's consider the immensely more complicated pattern of events taking place over the whole

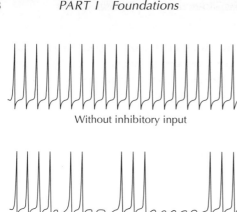

Without inhibitory input

With inhibitory input

↑
IPSP

FIGURE 2.9   A neural firing pattern activated by inhibiting portions of the baseline firing sequence, a process referred to as the sculpting effect of inhibition. *(Adapted from Kandel et al., 1995, p. 221)*

dendrite and cell body. On average, each dendrite receives input from more than 1,000 axons. (This means, incidentally, that the human brain has somewhere on the order of from 100 trillion to 1,000 trillion synapses, depending upon which estimate of the number of neurons in the human brain we use.)

These thousand incoming synapses, some excitatory and some inhibitory, occur at various places on the dendrite, the cell body, and even the axon. Some synapses are far away from the cell body, at the ends of long dendritic branches. Others occur on the cell body, some close to the junction between the cell body and the axon. At any given time there is a particular pattern of local depolarizations (EPSPs) and hyperpolarizations (IPSPs) across the surface of the dendrite and the cell body. Many of these will have a life of milliseconds and then be gone without a trace, never to make their mark on the system as a whole. Others will contribute to the initiation of an action potential in neurons that they depolarize. How does this pattern result in the firing of the neuron?

The **axon hillock** ("little hill") is the part of the neuron that forms the junction between the cell body and the axon (see Figure 2.1). This portion of the neuron has the lowest threshold for the triggering of an **action potential,** the process whereby a signal is com-

municated down the length of the axon. When the axon hillock is depolarized to –55 mV, an action potential is initiated. This is in marked contrast to dendrites and cell bodies, which may have thresholds as distant from the resting potential as –35 mV. The mechanism underlying the axon hillock's function as a trigger zone is its very high density of voltage-gated Na^+ channels. Thus, as the potential at the axon hillock approaches threshold depolarization, an active opening of a large number of voltage-gated Na^+ channels is initiated, leading to a massive influx of Na^+. We will see shortly that this is the beginning of the positive feedback process that is the action potential.

Before we examine the action potential, let's consider further the significance of the axon hillock as the trigger zone that integrates the input being received by the neuron. This integrative process means that the influence of the many EPSPs and IPSPs impinging on a given neuron is weighted, with those arriving at synapses closest to the axon hillock having a greater influence than those arriving at points on dendritic processes (branches) far away from the axon hillock. It's interesting to note that many of the inhibitory inputs to neurons take the form of axosomatic synapses. By synapsing on the cell body (and thus relatively near the axon hillock), these inhibitory inputs have a much greater influence over whether or not the cell will fire than do synapses located on dendritic sites, more distant from the axon hillock.

The effects of different synaptic potentials occurring at different places on the neuronal membrane are summed at the axon hillock trigger zone, a process known as **spatial summation.** The extent of spread of a given postsynaptic potential across the postsynaptic membrane is a function of a number of characteristics of a membrane. At any particular point in time and under specific conditions, these characteristics are quantified in terms of the **length constant** of that membrane. Thus, a large length constant signifies relatively less decrease in depolarizing (or hyperpolarizing) current as it spreads passively.

The effects of different synaptic potentials occurring at different times are also integrated at the axon hillock trigger zone. EPSPs separated from each other by sufficient time will each dissipate without further effect. On the other hand, EPSPs occurring closer together in time have a cumulative effect, a process referred to as **temporal summation.** As with spatial summation, temporal summation is in part a function of particular membrane characteristics, in this case the relative duration of a synaptic potential. This is referred to as the **time constant** of a membrane, with a large time constant indicating relatively longer duration. Together, spatial and temporal summation make possible the integration of input arriving at different parts of the neuron at different points in time (over a brief time interval, on the order of fractions of a millisecond). When the processes of spatial and temporal summation yield a threshold potential at the axon hillock, an action potential is initiated; when they fail to do so, the ongoing postsynaptic potentials dissipate without influencing other parts of the nervous system.

A military metaphor will help dramatize these two factors. Imagine an island with many narrow peninsulas jutting into the sea. The island is being defended by a limited number of troops (the tendency for the resting potential to be reestablished following an EPSP) with a headquarters (the axon hillock) on one long arm of the island. Imagine, further, that the island is being invaded by paratroopers (EPSPs), but at the same time reinforcing defenders (IPSPs) are also parachuting in. The effectiveness of the invading army, as individual troops parachute in, will depend upon a number of factors including (a) the extent to which they arrive within a narrow time window so that they are not individually picked off by the defending troops (temporal summation), (b) the number and location (relative to the defending headquarters) of arriving invaders at any point in time (spatial summation), and (c) the extent to which invaders are countered by incoming defending paratroopers (the algebraic sum of EPSPs and IPSPs).

We thus have a mechanism whereby different spatial and temporal patterns of excitatory and inhibitory input exert varying effects on the activity of a particular neuron. Within any given narrow window of time, the end result of any particular pattern of inhibitory and excitatory influences on a neuron is expressed in digital form: The neuron either fires or it

does not.[2] Thus, all nervous system activity, from the coding of physical stimuli to commands for action, are ultimately expressed in terms of the frequency and pattern of occurrence of action potentials.

The Action Potential

The EPSPs and IPSPs that we have been discussing are collectively referred to as **electrotonic potentials,** a term intended to emphasize that these graded changes in membrane potential are the result of passive ion fluxes in response to the opening of specific membrane channels following the binding of neurotransmitter. In contrast, if the axon hillock reaches **threshold potential,** an entirely different process is set in motion. In response to threshold depolarization, Na^+ channels open and K^+ channels close. Sodium, driven by its equilibrium potential of +55 mV, rushes in. This Na^+ influx results in a reversal of membrane potential, such that the inside is now positive relative to the outside at the level of about 40 mV. This voltage change sets in motion a positive feedback process whereby the change in potential of neighboring portions of the axon opens that portion's Na^+ channels, resulting in Na^+ influx, change in potential of neighboring portions, the opening of Na^+ channels on that portion of the membrane, Na^+ influx, and so on. This is the action potential, a kind of chain reaction that causes a wave of increased Na^+ conductance and a resulting change in membrane potential to travel down the axon. The word *propagation* is frequently used to describe the movement of the action potential down the axon, probably because this word captures the self-generating nature of the positive feedback mechanism underlying that movement.

Notice that the propagation of the action potential involves the opening of Na^+ channels in response to changes in membrane potential. As was mentioned earlier, membrane channels that open or close

---

2. However, we will see shortly that this statement requires some modification because variations in calcium (Ca^{2+}) influx at the axon terminal, regulated by axoaxonal synaptic connections, modulate the quantity of neurotransmitter released in response to an action potential.

in response to changes in voltage are referred to as voltage-gated channels. These contrast with resting channels, which underlie the resting potential, and transmitter-gated channels, like those responsible for EPSPs and IPSPs initiated by the binding of a neuro-transmitter.

The fact that voltage-gated K^+ channels close as the Na^+ channels open ensures that the depolarization caused by the Na^+ influx is not immediately negated by a compensatory K^+ efflux; this closure is, therefore, a necessary condition for the action potential. How-ever, after the Na^+ influx there is an abrupt closing and inactivation of Na^+ channels. During this inacti-vation period, the Na^+ channels will not open even if conditions for their opening are otherwise favorable. Then, as the Na^+ channels are reactivated (i.e., as their potential for opening if conditions are favorable re-turns), there is also a reopening of K^+ channels. This reopening creates more open K^+ channels than during the membrane's resting state. The membrane's en-hanced conductance for K^+ then causes a massive ef-flux of K^+, as it is driven out of the neuron both by virtue of its higher intracellular concentration and be-cause the inside of the neuron is positively charged. The net result is the rapid reestablishment of the rest-ing potential, after a brief hyperpolarization, known as the **afterpotential.** The afterpotential is caused by the fact that the additional K^+ channels remain open for a brief period after the reestablishment of the resting po-tential, resulting in further efflux of K^+ (Figure 2.10).

In the milliseconds before the resting potential is reestablished, there is a period of time during which a new action potential cannot be initiated, no matter how great the depolarization at the axon hillock. This time period corresponds to the time period during which the Na^+ channels are inactivated and is called the **absolute refractory period.** Moreover, during the period immediately following, when additional K^+ channels are open, the efflux of K^+ results in the hy-perpolarizing afterpotential noted earlier. This makes the initiation of an action potential more difficult, both because of the hyperpolarized state of the axon and because the effect of any Na^+ influx tends to be offset by an immediate compensatory K^+ efflux. This is the **relative refractory period.** During this period the neuron has an elevated threshold for firing (i.e., it

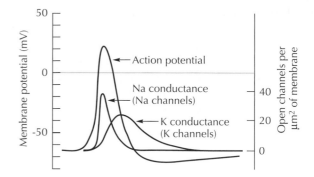

FIGURE 2.10   The sequential opening and closing of voltage-gated Na^+ and K^+ channels underlying the action potential. *(After Kandel et al., 1995, p. 168)*

requires a greater depolarization at the axon hillock). These factors limit the maximum firing frequency of a neuron to about 1,200 impulses per second.

Saltatory Conduction

As mentioned in an earlier section, axons that are wrapped in myelin transmit their signal at higher speeds than do those that are not myelinated. Speed of axonal transmission is an important factor, particu-larly in large animals in which some axons may be several meters in length. Now that we have discussed the propagation of the action potential down the axon, the process that takes place in unmyelinated axons, we are in a position to examine how myelin enhances the speed and efficiency of this transmission.

The continual reactivation of an action potential in unmyelinated axons is necessary because without this constant activation of Na^+ influx, low membrane resistance in these axons would lead to rapid dis-sipation of current flow down the axon core. Myeli-nation increases the resistance of the membrane dramatically, so that when an action potential is trig-gered at the axon hillock, the inward current that flows through the membrane at this point is avail-able to create a flow of current down the core of the axon. This flow is more rapid than the continual propagation of the action potential that takes place in unmyelinated axons. It is also more metabolically efficient because the reduced magnitude of Na^+ in-flux (and consequential counterbalancing K^+ efflux) does not make as high demands on the metabolically expensive sodium-potassium pump.

Despite the high resistance of the axonal membrane, the spread of current down the axon core would eventually dissipate if it were not for the interruptions in the myelin sheath at the nodes of Ranvier. These unmyelinated patches of membrane have a high density of voltage-gated Na^+ channels, thus generating an intense Na^+ inward current when the depolarizing current moving down the axon core reaches the node. The regular distribution of nodes of Ranvier along the axon (about every 1–2 mm) thus constantly renews the intensity of the depolarizing current as it moves down the axon core, preventing it from dying out before reaching the axon terminal. The term **saltatory conduction** (from the Latin *saltare*, "to leap") comes from the fact that as the current approaches a node of Ranvier it slows down, speeding up again as it passes back into myelinated axon. This leads to a jumping or leaping pattern of current flow down the axon.

Neurotransmitter Release

The propagated action potential eventually travels the length of the axon and reaches the axon terminal. Depolarization of the axon terminal activates the opening of voltage-gated calcium (Ca^{2+}) channels. Because Ca^{2+} has a higher concentration outside the neuron, a large electrochemical driving force thrusts Ca^{2+} into the cell. This influx of Ca^{2+} is necessary for the release of neurotransmitter at the axon terminal; much of the time delay between the onset of depolarization at the axon terminal and the release of neurotransmitter is due to the time required for the opening of voltage-gated Ca^{2+} channels. The mechanism by which Ca^{2+} influx contributes to the release of neurotransmitter is not completely understood. However, it is known that the Ca^{2+} influx plays a critical role in the merging of the synaptic vesicles (each containing several tens of thousands of neurotransmitter molecules) with regions (called **active zones**) of the presynaptic membrane where neurotransmitter will eventually be released. Calcium is also known to be involved in the subsequent release of neurotransmitter into the synaptic cleft, a process referred to as *exocytosis*. Thus, Ca^{2+} influx at the axon

terminal is a critical component in the mechanism by which the action potential, as it arrives at the axon terminal, initiates the release of neurotransmitter into the synapse.

The greater the Ca^{2+} influx, the larger the number of synaptic vesicles releasing their contents. The magnitude of Ca^{2+} influx is in turn influenced by excitatory and inhibitory axoaxonal inputs that determine the number of voltage-gated Ca^{2+} channels opening in response to an action potential. Inputs to the axon terminal that reduce Ca^{2+} influx result in **presynaptic inhibition,** and inputs that increase the influx of Ca^{2+} result in **presynaptic facilitation.** (As illustrated in Figure 2.11, these presynaptic modulations of transmitter release are to be distinguished from the postsynaptic inhibition and excitation discussed earlier.) This Ca^{2+}-mediated modulation of the quantity of neurotransmitter released in response to an action potential means that the effect of an action potential is not strictly digital, although an action potential per se is a stereotyped, all-or-none phenomenon. In addition to the decrease in Ca^{2+} influx due to the closing of specific voltage-gated Ca^{2+} channels in presynaptic inhibition, any other factor that decreases Ca^{2+} influx will reduce the amount of neurotransmitter released in response to an action potential. These include a decrease in the extracellular Ca^{2+} concentration and an increase in the concentration of Ca^{2+} binding agents.

In addition to factors decreasing Ca^{2+} influx, neurotransmitter release may be reduced by many other factors. To give a few examples, the drug reserpine, used to control high blood pressure, interferes with neurotransmitter release by inhibiting the storage of catecholamines in synaptic vesicles, thus rendering them unavailable for release. Botulin, produced by the bacterium *Clostridium botulinum* in improperly preserved food, is a highly active neurotoxin that inhibits the release of acetylcholine. This results in the serious type of food poisoning called botulism. Also, tetanus toxin, another bacterially generated agent, produces tetanus by blocking the release of GABA. Because GABA is an inhibitory neurotransmitter, it is not surprising that many of the symptoms of tetanus, including muscle spasms, hyperreflexia, and seizures, stem from disinhibition.

(A) Postsynaptic Excitation or Inhibition   **(B)** Presynaptic Facilitation or Inhibition

FIGURE 2.11   (*A*) In postsynaptic excitation (or inhibition), the EPSP (or IPSP) caused by the release of transmitter by neuron 1 results in a depolarization (or hyperpolarization) of the postsynaptic membrane of neuron 2, which, in turn, increases (or decreases) the probability that neuron 2 will fire. (*B*) In presynaptic facilitation (or inhibition), release of neurotransmitter by neuron 3, at an axoaxonal synapse with neuron 1, increases (or decreases) Ca^{2+} influx at the axon terminal of neuron 1 in response to the arrival of an action potential. This will result in an enhancement (or inhibition) of neurotransmitter release by neuron 1, which, in turn, will affect the probability that neuron 2 will fire.

Other agents achieve their effects by facilitating neurotransmitter release. For example, amphetamine enhances catecholamine release. More dramatically, the venom of the black widow spider causes such an immediate and intense release of acetylcholine as to rapidly deplete the neurotransmitter. Because acetylcholine is the neurotransmitter at the neuromuscular junction, including the intercostal muscles essential for breathing, the result is life threatening.

There are two general categories of neurotransmitters: small molecule transmitters and neuroactive peptides (also called neuropeptides).

SMALL MOLECULE NEUROTRANSMITTERS   In the vertebrate nervous system, nine small molecules have been positively identified as neurotransmitters, although many others have been found that are candidates for this status. Four of the established neurotransmitters, **dopamine, epinephrine, norepineph-**rine, and **serotonin,** are **monoamines,** molecules that have a single amine (NH_2). Three are amino acids: **glutamate, aspartate,** and **glycine.** One, gamma-aminobutyric acid (GABA), is formed by removal of a carboxyl group from glutamate. The ninth neurotransmitter is **acetylcholine,** found at the junction between motor neuron and muscle and the first neurotransmitter to be identified.

Because a particular receptor is selective with regard to the neurotransmitter that it binds, neurotransmitters with only slightly different chemical structures have very different sites of action. To take but one example: Dopamine and norepinephrine, despite the similarity of their chemical structures (Figure 2.12), bind to different receptors.

NEUROPEPTIDES   Peptides are short chains of amino acids. More than 50 peptides have been shown to be pharmacologically active in nerve cells. Collec-

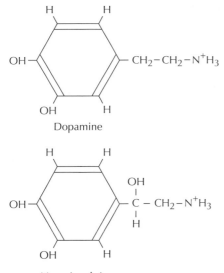

FIGURE 2.12   Dopamine and norepinephrine, two monoamine neurotransmitters. Because they bind to different receptors, they have very different sites of action, despite the similarity of their structure. *(From Nauta & Feirtag, 1986, p. 26)*

tively called **neuropeptides,** they are involved in the mediation of various neurobiological processes, ranging from pain perception to response to stress. Although a single neuron generally does not release more than one small molecule transmitter, a principle referred to as **Dale's law,** a small molecule transmitter and a neuropeptide may both be released by the same neuron, a situation termed **cotransmission.** In cotransmission the two released substances usually exert a synergistic effect—that is, they enhance each other's effect—although opposing effects are also seen. An example of a synergistic effect is the co-release of acetylcholine and calcitonin gene-related peptide (CGRP) from spinal motor neurons. CGRP increases the force of the muscle contraction activated by acetylcholine via an energy-releasing phosphory-lation in the muscle.

Unlike the small molecule transmitters, which are synthesized in the axon terminal, neuropeptides are synthesized only in the cell body and must be transported in secretory granules to the axon terminal for release. In this respect they resemble hormones. Neuropeptides also resemble hormones in that their effects are typically longer lasting than those mediated

by small molecule neurotransmitters. This suggests that they may be involved in long-term processes such as learning and memory.

Mechanisms for Clearing Neurotransmitter After Neuron Firing

ENZYMATIC DEGRADATION OF NEUROTRANSMITTER   One of the problems the nervous system faces is that of clearing neurotransmitter away from the synapse so that the effect of neurotransmitter release can have a decisive end point, thus sharpening the signal. One mechanism for accomplishing this is passive diffusion of neurotransmitter out of the synaptic cleft. However, passive diffusion presents another problem: Movement of transmitter away from its immediate target on the postsynaptic membrane compromises the specificity of its effect. One solution to this problem, seen particularly in acetylcholine systems, is the use of **degrading enzymes,** which destroy neurotransmitter that diffuses away from the postsynaptic membrane. The action of degrading enzymes localizes the area on the postsynaptic membrane accessible to the transmitter and confines its effect to a more discrete time frame, creating a kind of punctuation.

In the acetylcholine system, the major degrading enzyme is acetylcholinesterase. This enzyme is inhibited by the drug physostigmine, and, because disruption of cerebral acetylcholine activity is seen in Alzheimer's disease, it was hoped that physostigmine might lessen the symptoms of the disease. Unfortunately, despite the logic of the treatment, this has not proved to be the case.

Another example of drugs that block the enzymatic breakdown of neurotransmitter is the class of antidepressants called the **monoamine oxidase inhibitors.** These drugs enhance brain levels of monoamines by inhibiting monoamine oxidase, an enzyme that normally degrades them.

REUPTAKE   Another mechanism for regulating the quantity of neurotransmitter in the synapse is **reuptake,** the reabsorption of transmitter across the presynaptic membrane. This mechanism recycles unused or recently bound transmitter, thereby conserving both the metabolic energy and chemical precursors required for synthesis of these molecules. In addition, like other mechanisms that clear neurotransmitter from the synapse, reuptake modulates the impact of neurotransmitter release on the postsynaptic membrane.

As one would expect, drugs that block the reuptake of a neurotransmitter tend to enhance the availability of that neurotransmitter for binding to postsynaptic receptors and thereby potentiate its short-term effect. Examples are cocaine and amphetamine, both of which block the reuptake of norepinephrine. The short-term potentiating effect of these reuptake blockers is followed by a period of diminished neurotransmitter availability, as the prevention of reuptake depletes stores of neurotransmitter in presynaptic terminals. This accounts for the period of central nervous system (CNS) depression that follows the activating effect of these drugs.

Tricyclic antidepressants, such as imipramine, are also reuptake inhibitors, achieving their effect at least partly through blocking the reuptake of norepinephrine and serotonin. More recently, fluoxetine (Prozac) and other drugs that selectively inhibit serotonin reuptake (called **selective serotonin reuptake inhibitors**) have been shown to have significant antidepressant effects.

AUTORECEPTORS The quantity of neurotransmitter in the synapse is also regulated by **autoreceptors** on the presynaptic membrane. When the synaptic cleft is already saturated, neurotransmitters bind to these autoreceptors, providing feedback about the neurotransmitter's synaptic concentration and inhibiting further release. LSD is an example of a molecule that mimics serotonin at its autoreceptors and thereby slows the release of serotonin. Figure 2.13 summarizes these and other processes occurring at the synapse.[3]

We mentioned earlier that the action of neuropeptides is typically longer lasting than that of small

---

3. In general, any drug that opposes the action of a neurotransmitter is called an *antagonist* for that particular neurotransmitter, and any drug that facilitates the effect of a neurotransmitter is called an *agonist.* Thus, curare is an acetylcholine antagonist, whereas physostigmine is an acetylcholine agonist.

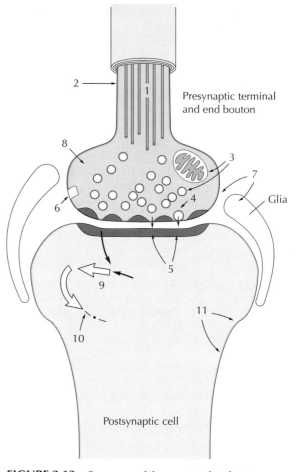

FIGURE 2.13 Summary of the events related to transmission at the chemical synapse. (*1*) Axons transport enzymes and precursors needed for synthesis of transmitter agents, vesicles, etc. (*2*) Action potential is propagated down the axon to the axon terminal. (*3*) Transmitter is synthesized and stored in vesicles. (*4*) Presynaptic terminal is depolarized, causing influx of Ca^{2+}, which leads vesicles to fuse with release sites on the presynaptic membrane and dump neurotransmitter into the synaptic cleft. (*5*) Transmitter binds to receptor molecules in the postsynaptic membrane, initiating postsynaptic potential. (*6*) Transmitter binds to an autoreceptor in the bouton membrane. (*7*) Degrading enzyme inactivates excess neurotransmitter, preventing it from passing beyond the synaptic cleft. (*8*) Reuptake of transmitter dampens synaptic action and saves transmitter for subsequent transmission. (*9*) Second messenger is released into postsynaptic neuron by certain transmitter-receptor combinations. (*10*) Enzyme inactivates second messenger. (*11*) Postsynaptic potentials spread passively over dendrites. (*From Rosenzweig & Leiman, 1982, p. 158*)

molecule transmitters. One of the factors contributing to the relatively prolonged effect of neuropeptides is their slow removal from the synapse. Another important mechanism of their long-lasting effect is the utilization of second messenger systems, discussed in the next section.

Responses to Neurotransmitter-Receptor Binding

The binding of a transmitter to a receptor sets in motion events that, aside from the fact that the binding is necessary to initiate them, are otherwise independent of the transmitter. Just as the effect of a key depends upon the lock that it opens, so the effect of a neurotransmitter depends upon the receptor to which it binds and the events initiated by that binding.

The critical importance of the events set in motion by receptor binding accounts for how the same transmitter can have opposite effects (excitatory or inhibitory) when it binds to different types of receptors. An example of this is the binding of acetylcholine to receptors (called nicotinic receptors) at the neuromuscular junction and its binding to receptors (called muscarinic receptors) in smooth muscle innervated by the parasympathetic nervous system. At nicotinic receptors, binding of acetylcholine is excitatory, causing movement. In contrast, in the parasympathetic nervous system, binding of acetylcholine to muscarinic receptors is inhibitory. Even within a single neuron, different receptors to the same neurotransmitter may initiate opposite effects. The importance of the events initiated by receptor binding also accounts for why the three amino acid neurotransmitters (glutamate, aspartate, and glycine), so ubiquitous in biological systems, often have no direct effect on neurons, serving instead as humble building blocks waiting to be incorporated into proteins. In neural tissue with no postsynaptic receptors for these molecules, they have no possibility of exhibiting their potential neurotransmitter function.

RECEPTOR BLOCKERS   Before we examine in more detail the effects of transmitter binding, let's consider an important factor that limits this critical first step in the sequence of events: molecules that block the binding of a neurotransmitter to its receptors. **Receptor blockers** are drugs that diminish the effectiveness of a neurotransmitter by competing for binding sites at its receptors. Because binding of a neurotransmitter to its receptor initiates all of the postsynaptic processes that eventually determine whether a neuron fires, any process that competes with this binding process will clearly have a major impact on neuronal activity. An example of a drug that utilizes this mechanism is curare, which blocks nicotinic acetylcholine receptors at the neuromuscular junction. Originally used as an arrow poison in South America, curare causes muscular paralysis and death by suffocation. Less active forms of the drug are used to control muscle spasms that occur in diseases such as tetanus and to prevent muscle spasms during shock treatments.

Muscarinic acetylcholine receptors at neuromuscular junctions in the parasympathetic nervous system are blocked by atropine, making this drug useful to eye specialists, who use it to inhibit muscles that normally constrict the pupil (a parasympathetically mediated process) in order to better visualize the retina. Another example of receptor blocking drugs is the class of medications called the **phenothiazines,** which block dopamine receptors and reduce the magnitude and frequency of psychotic symptoms in some schizophrenic patients. This has led to the **dopamine theory of schizophrenia,** the idea that schizophrenia is caused by dopamine overactivity. Although it is highly doubtful that the cause of schizophrenia is so simple, the effect of dopamine blockers on psychotic symptoms may be an important piece in the puzzle this devastating disease poses. We will discuss this further in chapter 13.

Let's now look at what happens when a transmitter binds to a receptor. There are two general categories of response, one involving gating and the other involving second messengers.

GATING   In many cases the bound receptor directly changes the gating of an ion channel in the postsynaptic membrane. These receptors, known as **ionotropic receptors,** work relatively fast (milliseconds) and often involve neural circuits that directly mediate behavior, such as those activating skeletal muscle. The opening of Na^+ channels that initiates EPSPs as well as the opening of Cl^- channels that produces IPSPs are both examples of gating that is directly mediated by a receptor. In many cases the gating effect of receptor binding is accomplished via a change in the conformation (shape) of a single large membrane protein.

SECOND MESSENGERS   The other general category of response that can occur when a transmitter binds to a receptor includes the activation of a second molecule, termed a **second messenger.** Several different second messengers have been identified, but perhaps the best understood is cyclic adenosine monophosphate (cAMP). These molecules indirectly alter the gating of membrane channels through the initiation of a sequence of biochemical events that can have far-reaching and long-lasting effects on the metabolic state of the neuron. The effect of activation of these receptors, termed **metabotropic receptors,** contrasts dramatically with the effects of ionotropic receptor binding. Whereas ionotropic receptor binding results in rapid and direct gating of ion channels within milliseconds, metabotropic receptor activation produces effects that are slower in onset (hundreds of milliseconds to seconds) and longer lasting (seconds or even minutes). Moreover, in contrast to the direct and localized effect of ionotropic receptor binding, a second messenger can move intracellularly to affect distant parts of the cell. Examples of receptors mediating ionotropic and metabotropic mechanisms of action are the GABA-A and GABA-B receptors, already discussed in the context of mechanisms of postsynaptic inhibition. GABA-A receptors are ionotropic: In response to the binding of GABA, they directly open Cl^- channels. GABA-B receptors are metabotropic: When GABA binds to them, it activates a second messenger, which sets in motion a series of biochemical processes that result in the opening of additional K^+ channels.

Although speed of onset and temporal and spatial specificity are often critically important in neuron functioning (as, for example, at the neuromuscular junction), the long-lasting and potentially diffuse effect of second messengers on ion channels has cer-

tain advantages. In particular, second messengers provide a mechanism for the relatively long-term modulation of neuron excitability. For example, a neuropeptide-mediated second messenger has been identified that initiates an excitatory postsynaptic potential lasting 10 minutes, in marked contrast to the typical directly gated EPSP, which lasts only a few milliseconds. In addition, second messengers can alter the biochemical and metabolic state of the neuron. For example, a second messenger can alter the effectiveness of a receptor, including its own activating receptor, thereby altering the intensity and duration of the neuron's response to neurotransmitter released by neighboring neurons.

The effect of second messengers is not, however, confined to the modification of existing proteins. Even more dramatically, second messengers can initiate the synthesis of new proteins. Second messengers do this by activating transcriptional proteins that alter the neuron's genetic expression by binding to regulatory regions of the gene and affecting the rate at which the gene transcribes messenger RNA. This is a powerful and versatile mechanism, strikingly similar to that seen in hormones. It affords the possibility of long-lasting structural and metabolic changes within the neuron that may last for days or even longer. There is in fact evidence that second-messenger activation of gene expression contributes importantly to the structural and metabolic changes underlying neuronal development and long-term memory.

The activity of second messengers can be affected by a number of agents. For example, nicotine and certain heavy metals, including lead, block the activation, by norepinephrine, of the synthesis of cAMP. Caffeine, found in coffee and tea, enhances the effect of second messengers by inhibiting their enzymatic inactivation.

In the next section we examine some of the biochemical and structural mechanisms that underlie relatively simple forms of learning, including habituation, sensitization, and classical conditioning. This will give us a chance to see some of the mechanisms that we have been discussing in action. It will also illustrate how effective these mechanisms can be in initiating and maintaining changes in the response characteristics of neurons.

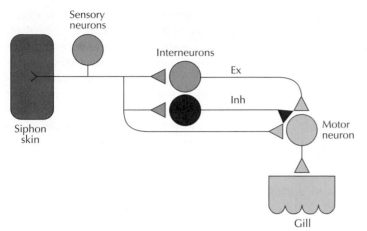

FIGURE 2.14   Simplified circuit showing the key elements involved in the gill-withdrawal reflex and its habituation in *Aplysia californica.* Sensory neurons, the cell bodies of which are situated in the abdominal ganglia, innervate the siphon skin. These sensory neurons use gluta-mate as their neurotransmitter and terminate on motor neurons that innervate the gill. They also terminate on excitatory (*Ex*) and inhibitory (*Inh*) interneurons that synapse on the motor neurons. Only one of each type of neuron is shown here. If the siphon is stimulated repeatedly, the result is a decrease in synaptic transmission between sensory and motor neurons and be-tween excitatory interneurons and motor neurons. *(From Kandel et al., 1995, p. 669)*

NEURONAL MECHANISMS OF LEARNING

Habituation and Sensitization in *Aplysia:* Examples of Presynaptic Modulation of Neuronal Activity

The relative simplicity of the nervous system of the marine snail *Aplysia californica* makes it a useful model for understanding neural mechanisms. What we know about the neural basis of some simple learning processes in *Aplysia* illustrates many of the mechanisms discussed in the previous sections of this chapter. We now briefly review some of these mechanisms.

HABITUATION   In **habituation,** the simplest form of learning, an organism learns to decrease or com-pletely suppress a response to a recurring neutral stimulus (i.e., a stimulus that is neither rewarding nor harmful). For example, if the siphon skin of *Aplysia* is mildly stimulated with a novel stimulus, the animal will energetically withdraw its gill. This is called the gill-withdrawal reflex. After repeated siphon stimu-lation, the intensity of this withdrawal response will be greatly reduced or even eliminated altogether. This is habituation of the gill-withdrawal reflex. Habitua-tion has two forms, short term and long term. For ex-ample, in response to approximately 10 stimulations of the siphon, reduction in gill withdrawal may last for about 10 minutes. This is **short-term habituation.**

A larger number of stimulations over a longer period of time will result in **long-term habituation,** lasting days or weeks.

Kandel and his colleagues (Castellucci, Carew, & Kandel, 1978; Hawkins, Kandel, & Siegelbaum, 1993) have worked out the circuitry for the gill-withdrawal reflex in *Aplysia.* Sensory neurons receiving input from the siphon make monosynaptic connections with motor neurons activating the gill. In addition, sensory neurons from the siphon send input to in-hibitory and excitatory interneurons, which then in-nervate the gill motor neurons (Figure 2.14). Studies by Kandel and his colleagues have revealed compo-nents of the mechanism of short-term habituation in this circuit. They have shown that this effect involves the modification of activity in the axon terminals of the sensory neurons and the excitatory interneurons that innervate the motor neurons. More specifically, during habituation there is a decrease in the release of glutamate, the neurotransmitter released by ter-minals of sensory neurons and interneurons that nor-mally activate the motor neurons, causing gill with-drawal. This decrease in glutamate release is due, at least in part, to the inactivation of Ca^{2+} channels in the presynaptic membrane. Recall that the magni-tude of influx of Ca^{2+} at the axon terminal influences the amount of neurotransmitter released in response to an action potential. Habituation is also associated with a decrease in the ability of transmitter vesicles to move to active zones of the presynaptic membrane so that they can be available to release their contents into the synapse. Although it is not known how repeated stimulation causes these presynaptic changes, it is clear that they are components of the mechanism of short-term habituation.

Interestingly, long-term habituation involves gene activation that results in structural changes in these connections. Electron microscopy studies comparing habituated and nonhabituated animals have revealed that after long-term habituation the average number of synaptic connections that the branching synaptic terminals of each sensory neuron make with motor neurons is reduced by as much as one third. In addition, the proportion of sensory axon terminals with active zones (regions at which neurotransmitter can be released) is significantly reduced (Castellucci et al., 1978).

Although our understanding of the mechanism of habituation in *Aplysia* is not complete, what we do know is illuminating. Particularly interesting are two implications of this mechanism. First, it demonstrates that even in this simplest of all forms of learning, several different kinds of neurons are involved: sensory neurons and excitatory interneurons. Thus, even in the habituation of a simple reflex, the changes in the functional strength of synaptic connections are not restricted to one neural site but are distributed to several. We will see in later chapters that the idea of **distributed representation** is widely employed in theories of the neural mechanisms of complex cognitive functioning, such as visual recognition and spatial processing, functions for which the neural mechanism remains highly speculative. It is therefore striking to find that it applies to those relatively simple neural mechanisms for which we do have a reasonably good understanding.

A second important aspect of this mechanism is that it does not depend on neurons that are specialized for learning. Instead, the neural changes underlying habituation of the gill-withdrawal reflex in *Aplysia* involve changes in the neurons that are components of the gill-withdrawal reflex itself.

SENSITIZATION   In habituation, repeated stimulation of sensory neurons can lead to the inhibition of events at their synaptic terminals that would normally result in activation of the motor neurons with which they synapse. In **sensitization,** the vigorousness of a response to a neutral stimulus is increased when it is preceded by a noxious (painful) stimulus. For example, if a strong shock is delivered to the tail of *Aplysia*, subsequent stimulation of the siphon will result in a more vigorous gill-withdrawal reflex. The circuit involved in this process is shown in Figure 2.15.

Kandel and his colleagues have shown that the mechanism of sensitization of the gill-withdrawal reflex in *Aplysia* involves the presynaptic facilitation of sensory neurons. They found that shock to the tail stimulates interneurons, which, for reasons that will become clear in a moment, are called **facilitating interneurons.** These facilitating interneurons synapse on the axon terminals of sensory neurons that receive input from the siphon skin and that, in turn, synapse on (a) motor neurons activating gill withdrawal and on (b) other interneurons that synapse on these motor neurons (see Figure 2.15). As we saw earlier, such axoaxonal connections allow one neuron to modify the activity of a second neuron by influencing events at the second neuron's axon terminal. In this case, in response to tail shock, the facilitating interneurons release serotonin. This binds to the sensory neuron axon terminal and sets in motion a biochemical cascade that ultimately causes an increased influx of Ca^{2+} into the axon terminal and a resulting increase in the level of neurotransmitter released.

As with habituation, sensitization may be either short term or long term, depending upon the number and magnitude of prior noxious stimulations. Also, like long-term habituation, long-term sensitization involves structural changes mediated by gene activation. These changes parallel those seen in long-term habituation but are in the opposite direction. They include an increase in the average number of synaptic connections each sensory neuron forms with motor neurons and a corresponding growth in the dendrites of motor neurons to accommodate this increased input. There is also an increase in the proportion of sensory neuron axon terminals with active zones. These structural changes are not seen after short-term sensitization.

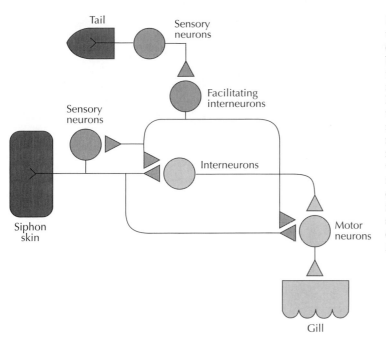

FIGURE 2.15 The reflex involving gill withdrawal after siphon skin stimulation is enhanced if siphon stimulation is preceded by the application of noxious stimuli to the tail. This sensitization of the gill-withdrawal reflex in *Aplysia* involves this circuit: Stimulation of the tail activates sensory neurons, which, in turn, activate facilitating interneurons. The facilitating interneurons are so named because they enhance the release of neurotransmitter by sensory neurons innervating the siphon skin and synapsing on motor neurons and on interneurons that connect with motor neurons. The facilitating interneurons do this by forming axoaxonal synapses with sensory neurons. This is an example of presynaptic facilitation. *(From Kandel et al., 1995, p. 672)*

Classical Conditioning

There is very little specificity in sensitization. In this process different noxious stimuli enhance the organism's response to a variety of neutral stimuli applied to different parts of the body. What is more, there is a wide range of time intervals between noxious stimulus and neutral stimulus that are compatible with the establishment of sensitization. In contrast, classical conditioning is a highly specific process. The establishment of a conditioned response requires that the onset of a particular neutral stimulus repeatedly precede the onset of a particular unconditioned stimulus at a specific time interval (about 0.5 sec). Thus, rather than having one stimulus enhance response to a variety of subsequent stimuli, as in sensitization, in classical conditioning the organism learns to associate one specific stimulus with another. When a **neutral stimulus** (one that does not produce a particular response) repeatedly precedes an **unconditioned stimulus** (a stimulus that naturally causes a particular response, called an **unconditioned response**), the previously neutral stimulus alone will become a trigger for a response identical to (or similar to) the unconditioned response. When this happens, the previously neutral stimulus is called a **conditioned stimulus** and the response it evokes is called a **conditioned response.**

Despite these differences, sensitization and classical conditioning appear to share some common cellular mechanisms in *Aplysia*. Let's consider conditioning of the gill-withdrawal reflex, where a shock to the tail is the unconditioned stimulus, mantle shelf stimulation is the conditioned stimulus, and gill withdrawal is the unconditioned and, eventually, the conditioned response. Thus, if shock to the tail is preceded over several trials by mild stimulation of the mantle shelf, mantle shelf stimulation will come to evoke vigorous gill withdrawal. Once again, the relative simplicity of *Aplysia*'s nervous system has made it possible to identify the circuitry involved in the conditioning of this gill-withdrawal reflex (Figure 2.16). As in sensitization, in conditioning of the gill-withdrawal reflex interneurons receiving input from sensory neurons innervating the tail form axoaxonal synapses with sensory neurons that carry input from the mantle shelf; the firing of

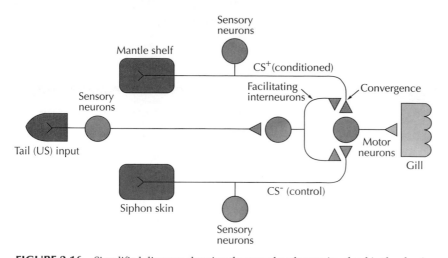

FIGURE 2.16   Simplified diagram showing the neural pathways involved in the classical conditioning of the gill-withdrawal reflex in *Aplysia*. In this example the conditioned stimulus (CS⁺) is mantle stimulation, and the unconditioned stimulus (US) is shock to the tail. Siphon stimulation is a control condition (CS⁻) not paired with shock to the tail. A shock to the tail activates facilitating interneurons that terminate on the axon terminals of sensory neurons from the mantle shelf and the siphon. The process of presynaptic facilitation enhances release of neurotransmitter by these sensory neurons. This is the mechanism of sensitization. If the mantle shelf sensory neuron is activated (CS⁺) just before the shock to the tail (US), this greatly enhances presynaptic facilitation of the mantle shelf sensory neuron axon terminal, but not sensory activation, such as that arising from siphon skin stimulation, that is not paired with the US. This is the mechanism of classical conditioning. The dependence of the facilitating interneuron-mediated presynaptic facilitation on the activity of the sensory neuron accounts for the requirement that the CS⁺ must just precede the US for conditioning to occur. It also accounts for the specificity of the CS⁺ and the US. These characteristics differentiate classical conditioning from sensitization. *(From Kandel et al., 1995, p. 678)*

these interneurons causes presynaptic facilitation of the sensory neuron transmitting input from the mantle shelf. The interneurons do this by releasing serotonin, leading to enhanced release of glutamate by sensory-neuron axon terminals synapsing with motor neurons. So far this is just like the mechanism of presynaptic facilitation seen in sensitization.

However, the mechanism of conditioning has an additional component that is very different from those seen in sensitization. In conditioning, presynaptic facilitation is greatly amplified if the conditioned stimulus (stimulation of the mantle shelf) produces action potentials in the sensory neurons just before the onset of the unconditioned stimulus (shock to the tail). Thus, the magnitude of presynap-

tic facilitation is *dependent upon the activity of the sensory neurons receiving the facilitation,* a phenomenon termed **activity-dependent presynaptic facilitation.**

The dependence of the magnitude of presynaptic facilitation on the activity level of the neuron being facilitated accounts for the associative component of classical conditioning, although it does not entirely explain how the conditioned stimulus alone eventually evokes a conditioned response. This probably entails structural and/or biochemical changes over time. What we do know about the cellular mechanisms underlying classical conditioning in *Aplysia* indicates that these mechanisms share similarities with those mechanisms thought to underlie sensitization. In both processes, presynaptic facilitation of sensory

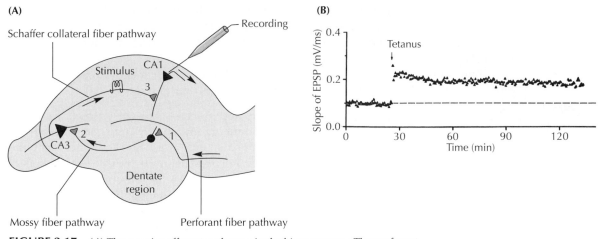

FIGURE 2.17   (*A*) Three major afferent pathways in the hippocampus. The perforant fiber pathway carries input from the subiculum to granule cells in the dentate gyrus. Axons of granule cells form the mossy fiber pathway, which synapses on pyramidal cells in the CA3 region of the hippocampus. Axons of pyramidal cells in CA3 form two branches, one of which, the Schaffer collateral fiber pathway, projects to pyramidal cells in the CA1 region. (*B*) Long-term potentiation in a cell in the CA1 region of the hippocampus. The graph shows the slope of EPSPs, a measure of the efficiency of synaptic transmission, in a CA1 neuron in response to test stimuli applied to the Schaffer collateral fiber pathway every 10 seconds. After recording for 30 minutes to establish a baseline, two 1-second trains of stimuli at 100 impulses per second, separated by a 20-second interval, were applied to the Schaffer collaterals. This resulted in a long-term potentiation (LTP) that lasted for several hours. (*From Kandel et al., 1995, p. 680*)

neurons is central (although, as we have seen, in conditioning, the magnitude of this facilitation is dependent on the timing of activity in the sensory neuron and the interneuron). The finding that in *Aplysia* classical conditioning appears to involve an elaboration of the mechanisms involved in sensitization suggests that, in at least certain instances, complex forms of learning may be built up from simpler forms.

Although it has not been discussed in detail here, it is important to realize that many steps in the biochemical mechanisms underlying habituation, sensitization, and conditioning in *Aplysia* have been worked out. This represents encouraging progress toward an understanding of the biochemical basis of learning.

Long-Term Potentiation

Thus far we have been considering very simple forms of learning in a very simple organism. Much

less is known about the mechanisms underlying learning in animals with more complex brains. Nevertheless, there have been some highly interesting studies of cells in the hippocampus of mammals, the activity of which is influenced by the prior activity of other neurons. Because the hippocampus is known to be important for memory, these findings may shed light on the neural mechanisms of memory in higher animals.

The circuitry of the hippocampus has been worked out in some detail and is shown schematically in Figure 2.17A. Axons forming the perforant fiber pathway carry input from the subiculum to granule cells in the dentate gyrus. The axons of these cells, forming the mossy fiber pathway, synapse on pyramidal cells in the CA3 region of the hippocampus (*CA* stands for *cornu Ammonis*, Latin for "Ammon's horn"). The Schaffer collateral fiber pathway, made up of axons of cells in CA3, projects to region CA1. It has been possible to cut slices of hippocampus and study the physiological properties of connections in these brain slice preparations in vitro. (*In vitro*, literally "in glass," refers to the study of biological processes in a preparation outside of the animal. *In vivo*, literally "in life," refers to the study of biological processes in the intact animal.) In vivo studies of the physiological properties of hippocampal cells have also been carried out.

With this as background, let's consider some very interesting findings that have emerged from the study of cells in the CA1 region of the hippocampus. While recording from single neurons in CA1, investigators stimulated the fiber pathway projecting to these cells (the Schaffer collaterals) with a test stimulus that was not sufficiently strong to cause the CA1 cell to fire. Instead, the test stimulus produced an EPSP of a certain slope (a measure of synaptic efficiency) in the CA1 cell. Next, two brief high-frequency trains of stimuli, each called a **tetanic stimulation,** or simply a tetanus (from the Greek for "rigid"), were applied to the pathway. Following this, a test stimulus of the same magnitude as the first test stimulus was applied. Now the target neuron responded to the test stimulus with a steeper slope of depolarization than it did before the tetanus (Figure 2.17B). The neuron's response to the same magnitude of stimulation had increased; it had been potentiated. Although the high-frequency trains were short (on the order of seconds), the potentiation of CA1 cell response continued for hours. This phenomenon is called **long-term potentiation (LTP).** Although we are focusing on neurons in the CA1 region of the hippocampus, LTP is found in other hippocampal regions as well.

What is particularly interesting about LTP is that it represents a long-term change in the response of a neuron as a result of the brief stimulation of its afferent fibers. LTP is thus, in a real sense, a record, a memory, of that past activation. Particularly striking is the fact that tetanus that is well within physiological range (on the order of 100 impulses per second) can result in potentiation that lasts hours, days, or even weeks. This suggests that LTP plays a role in memory in the mammalian species in which it has been demonstrated to occur, although this has not been fully established.

TWO EXCEPTIONS TO GENERAL RULES: RECEPTOR POTENTIALS AND ELECTRICAL TRANSMISSION

Receptor Potentials: Transduction Without Action Potentials

Sensory receptors are the entry points for information coming into the nervous system. In vision, audition, somatosensory function, and vestibular function, physical energy is transduced (converted) into neural activity by the sensory receptors specialized for each of these modalities. In olfaction and taste, the organism registers the presence of molecules in its immediate environment. In each case, the sensory receptors carry out the initial stage in the coding of a physical stimulus.

Sensory receptors do not generate action potentials. Instead, they transduce physical stimuli impinging on sensory receptors into graded potentials, called **receptor potentials** or **generator potentials.** Like the incoming EPSPs and IPSPs on the dendrite and soma of a neuron, receptor potentials undergo spatial and temporal summation. The net effect of these graded depolarizations and hyperpolarizations of the sensory receptor is expressed as the graded release of neurotransmitter, rather than as an action potential, as is typically the case for neurons. The graded release of transmitter by the sensory receptors then induces action potentials in primary sensory neurons, the next neuron in the afferent chain.

Electrical Transmission: Communication Between Neurons Without Chemical Synapses

Earlier in this chapter we emphasized the advantages of chemical transmission in the nervous system. We have seen that it provides a mechanism for extraordinary flexibility. An input to a neuron may or may not contribute to the firing of that neuron, depending on a constellation of other factors. The synapse and the mechanisms associated with it provide the machinery for this sensitivity of the neuron to circumstances and contingencies. In addition, the synapse has other functional advantages. The fact

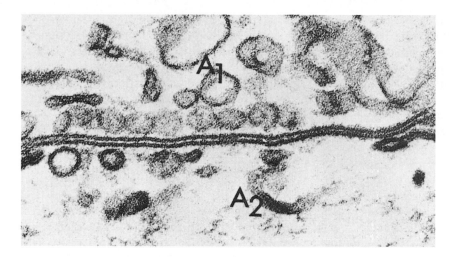

FIGURE 2.18   An electron micrograph of an electrical synapse in the crayfish. A_1 indicates the presynaptic neuron, and A_2 the postsynaptic neuron. *(From Rosenzweig & Leiman, 1982, p. 143)*

that many thousands of transmitter molecules are released in response to an action potential means that a relatively weak pattern of excitatory (or inhibitory) input, if it manages to trigger an action potential, can be amplified and have effects disproportionate to its absolute magnitude. Further, the fact that the mechanisms underlying synaptic transmission at a particular synapse can be modified over time in a way that leaves an enduring change on future events at that synapse makes plasticity within the system possible. Such plasticity, reflecting the prior experience of the system, almost certainly plays a central role in the neural changes underlying such processes as learning and memory.

Yet despite all these advantages of the chemical synapse, it turns out that some neurons have an entirely different mechanism of transmission, much like the interconnected net that Golgi erroneously argued characterized the whole nervous system. This is the **gap junction,** also called the **electrical synapse** (Figure 2.18). A gap junction consists of a set of extremely narrow (about 1.5 nm) tube-shaped bridging structures that essentially structurally connect two neurons (Figure 2.19). The virtual cytoplasmic continuity resulting from these connections allows for the direct transmission of ionic current generated by the action potential without the synaptic delay of 1–5 ms and without the opportunity for modulation by other factors that characterize transmission at the chemical synapse.

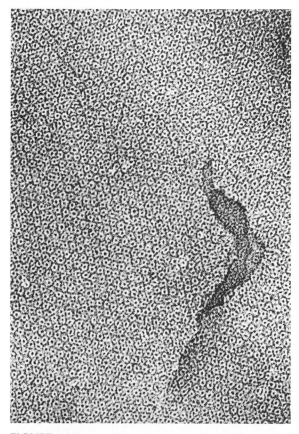

FIGURE 2.19   An electron micrograph showing, in cross section, an array of gap-junction channels forming structural connections between two neurons. *(From Kandel et al., 1995, p. 189)*

What function does this mechanism of direct ion flow between neurons serve? It makes possible the very rapid and synchronous firing of neighboring neurons, such as those mediating precise eye movement. Once the system has decided that the eyes should move, it is important that the neurons activating eye muscles deliver precise, synchronous, and unmodulated input. Gap junctions are also found in the motor neurons innervating cardiac muscle and in neurons activating escape and defense movement sequences in lower animals. Thus, gap junctions are found precisely in those neuronal connections where (a) speed and precision of response are of optimum importance and (b) sensitivity to a wide range of factors and the capacity for modulation and plasticity are not only not needed, but are actually disadvantageous. Gap junctions and the effects they mediate contrast strikingly with chemical synapses and their associated behaviors in terms of flexibility and plasticity. In this sense the gap junction is the exception that proves the rule; it highlights the characteristics of the vast majority of neuronal interconnections in the nervous system.

SUMMARY

From the discussion in this chapter we can get some idea of the enormous complexity of the factors that determine whether or not a particular neuron will fire. Each of the 100 billion to 1 trillion neurons in the human brain is influenced by an average of 1,000 other neurons, synapsing at various locations on its cell body and dendrites and firing varying temporal patterns. The results of spatial and temporal summation determine whether an action potential occurs. Once an action potential reaches the axon terminal, it initiates the release of neurotransmitter. The pattern of neurotransmitter release is further modulated by events at the synaptic terminal, the presynaptic membrane, the synapse, the postsynaptic membrane, and within the cytoplasm of the postsynaptic cell.

Here then—in the connection between two neurons within the span of milliseconds—we can get some idea of the enormous complexity of the human nervous system. This picture of the integrative processes carried out at the level of the single neuron represents in microcosm the task of decision making that confronts the entire nervous system. When we then consider the trillions of synapses within the human central nervous system and events at these synapses over time, the possibilities further expand, giving us some understanding of the capacity of the system to code or to represent tremendous complexity.

There is much more that could be said about all the processes involved at the level of the individual neuron; many brilliant scientists have spent their entire careers investigating the nervous system at this level of analysis. Let us, however, turn next to a consideration of the organization of groups of neurons on the molar level, the level of gross neuroanatomy. This will provide an additional framework for exploring the relationship between the human brain and the complex behaviors and cognitive processes that it mediates.

Introduction to the Structure and Function of the Central Nervous System

GENERAL TERMINOLOGY
AN OVERVIEW OF THE CENTRAL NERVOUS SYSTEM
  The Central and Peripheral Nervous Systems
  Major Divisions of the Brain
  The Meninges
  The Cerebral Ventricles
  Gray Matter and White Matter
THE FOREBRAIN
  The Cerebral Cortex
  The Basal Ganglia

  The Limbic System
  The Diencephalon
THE BRAIN STEM
  The Midbrain
  The Hindbrain
THE CEREBELLUM
THE SPINAL CORD
SUMMARY

❖ ❖ ❖

The human brain has been called the most complicated organization of matter in the known universe. Knowing the most important structures of the brain and their spatial relationships is important for understanding how the brain works. In addition, knowing how different structures are interconnected often provides valuable hints about how the activity of different brain areas is integrated to form a network that supports complex cognitive and emotional functions.

*This chapter presents some basic information about the major structures of the nervous system and their interconnections, an area of study called **neuroanatomy**. It also includes a general discussion of the relationship between structure and function, an area of investigation known as **functional neuroanatomy**.*

GENERAL TERMINOLOGY

To understand neuroanatomy, you will need to know some general terminology. Many of the terms in neuroanatomy are actually Greek or Latin words. It is

often useful to look up the literal translations of these words because many very imposing neuroanatomical terms end up having rather straightforward literal meanings. For example, the names of two structures in the brain, the substantia nigra and the locus ceruleus,

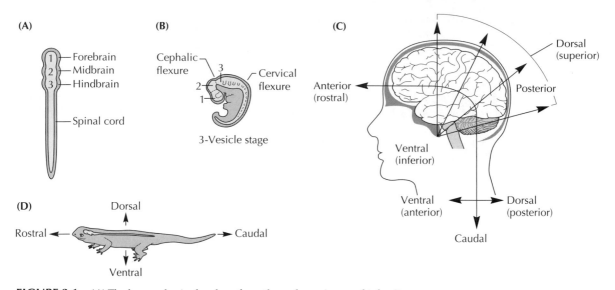

FIGURE 3.1   *(A)* The human brain develops from the embryonic neural tube, its rostral end giving rise to the brain and its caudal end becoming the spinal cord. *(B)* As it develops, the human nervous system flexes at the junction of the midbrain and the diencephalon. *(C)* Because of this flexure, the terms *dorsal* and *ventral* and the terms *anterior* and *posterior* refer to different directions when applied to the brain than to the brain stem and spinal cord. *(D)* In lower vertebrates the nervous system in organized in a straight line, and directional nomenclature is consistent throughout its length. *(From Kandel et al., 1995, p. 78)*

seemingly highly technical terms, translate from the Latin to "black stuff" and "blue place," respectively. Translating neuroanatomical terms makes them less mystifying and sometimes more memorable.

To find our way around the nervous system, we must first know some of the conventional terminology used in anatomy to indicate where a structure is located relative to other structures and relative to the whole brain. The most important terms are **superior** (above), **inferior** (below), **anterior** (front), **posterior** (behind), **lateral** (side), and **medial** (middle). With these six terms we can specify relative position within the three-dimensional framework of the brain and the body (Figure 3.1). Two or more of these terms can be combined to provide even more specific locations.

Although logically these terms are all we need to specify location in three dimensions, some additional terms are also used to denote relative location. Terminology differs to some extent when referring to the brain versus the brain stem and spinal cord. In the

brain, the superior/inferior axis is often referred to as the **dorsal/ventral** (literally "back" and "belly," respectively) axis, whereas in the brain stem and spinal cord, *dorsal* (or posterior) refers to the direction toward the back and *ventral* (or anterior) the direction toward the front. In addition, in the brain stem and spinal cord, the direction toward the brain is referred to as **rostral** ("beak"); the direction away from the brain is referred to as **caudal** ("tail") (see Figure 3.1).

These terms originated from the study of the anatomy of four-legged animals, such as dogs. In these animals, the head and brain are aligned with the central axis of the body, so the bottom parts of the brain have the same position relative to the upper parts of the brain as the belly of the animal has to its back. A similar relationship holds for the rostral/caudal areas of the body and the anterior/posterior axis of the brain. If you imagine that you are down on all fours looking straight ahead, the dorsal/ventral and rostral/caudal axes will make sense in a way that they don't when you imagine yourself standing. This is because over the course of evolution (and of individual development) the proliferation of the forebrain has caused the human brain to bend forward 90° relative to the central axis of the body (see Figure 3.1).

Because these terms indicate the location of structures relative to other structures, it is possible for a structure in the anterior portion of the brain to be posterior to a structure that is even further anterior, just as Greenland, north relative to most of the rest of the world, is south of the North Pole. In addition, these terms are used to denote different areas within a single structure. For example, the names of various areas within the thalamus, an egg-shaped structure, are derived from this nomenclature, as illustrated by the dorsomedial nucleus and the ventrolateral nucleus.

The terms **contralateral** (opposite side) and **ipsilateral** (same side), which we encountered in chapter 1, are used to designate the side of the body or brain on which a structure or connection occurs in relation to a reference point. For example, although about 90% of the fibers originating in the motor cortex of one cerebral hemisphere cross over to the contralateral side of the body, about 10% do not cross over and thus form ipsilateral connections. When structures or connections occur on both sides of the body, they are said to be **bilateral. Unilateral** refers to a structure or connection on only one side of the body.

The term **afferent** (from the Latin *ad + ferre*, "to carry inward"), encountered in chapter 1, refers to neural input feeding into a structure. Conversely, the term **efferent** (from the Latin *ex + ferre*, "to carry outward") denotes neural output leaving a structure. As with the other directional terms we have already discussed, these are relative terms. The same fiber tract will be efferent to one structure and afferent to another. For example, the fornix, an arching fiber tract deep within the base of the forebrain that conveys information from the hippocampus to the hypothalamus, is a hippocampal efferent and a hypothalamic afferent.

Finally, several terms are used to describe the different planes of anatomical section (cut) along which the brain can be dissected or visualized (Figure 3.2). These planes are typically seen in photographs and diagrams of the brain. **Sagittal** sections (from the Latin *sagitta*, "arrow") divide the brain into right and left parts. **Coronal** sections (from the Latin *coronalis*, "crown") divide the brain into anterior and posterior parts. These are also called **frontal** sections. By convention, sections in this plane are viewed from behind, so that the left side of the section is the left side of the brain. **Horizontal** (or **axial**) sections divide the brain into upper (superior) and lower (inferior) parts. Again, by convention, sections in this plane are typically viewed from above.

AN OVERVIEW OF THE CENTRAL NERVOUS SYSTEM

The Central and Peripheral Nervous Systems

The most basic structural subdivisions of the human nervous system are the **central nervous system (CNS)** and the **peripheral nervous system (PNS).** The central nervous system consists of the brain and spinal cord, and the peripheral nervous system consists of the sensory and motor nerves that are distributed throughout the body and that convey information to and from the brain (via 12 pairs of cranial nerves) and the spinal cord (via 31 pairs of spinal nerves). The peripheral nervous system is divided into the somatic nervous system and the autonomic nervous system. The **somatic nervous system** is the part of the PNS that innervates the skin, joints, and skeletal muscles. The **autonomic nervous system (ANS)** is the part of the PNS that innervates internal organs, blood vessels, and glands. Each of these systems has related motor and sensory components. The **somatic motor system** includes skeletal muscles and the parts of the nervous system that control them; the **somatosensory system** involves the senses of touch, temperature, pain, body position, and body movement. The autonomic nervous system also has a motor component, sending motor output to regulate and control the smooth muscles of internal organs, cardiac muscle, and glands (**autonomic motor**). The autonomic nervous system also includes sensory input from these internal structures that is used to monitor their status (**autonomic sensory**). The major sensory modalities other than touch (vision, audition, smell, and taste) are sometimes referred to as **special sensory.**

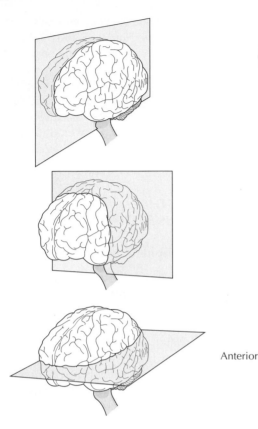

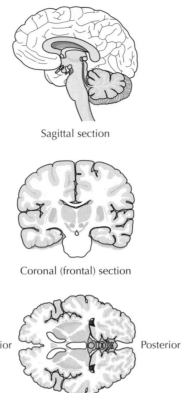

FIGURE 3.2   Terms used to describe the planes of section (cut) through the brain. *(From Rosenzweig & Leiman, 1989, p. 29)*

Sagittal section

Coronal (frontal) section

Anterior   Posterior

Horizontal (axial) section

Major Divisions of the Brain

The brain is divided into three parts: the **forebrain (prosencephalon)**, the **midbrain (mesencephalon)**, and the **hindbrain (rhombencephalon)** (Table 3.1 and Figure 3.3). The forebrain includes the **cerebral cortex, basal ganglia, limbic system** (together making up the **telencephalon**), and **diencephalon.** The midbrain and hindbrain together constitute the **brain stem,** with the hindbrain being further subdivided into the **pons** and **cerebellum (metencephalon)** and the **medulla oblongata (myelencephalon).** The medulla oblongata is often called simply the medulla.

In the course of evolution (and recapitulated in the course of individual human fetal development) these divisions developed from the enlargement of the rostral end of the primordial neural tube. In this process, the most rostral region expanded to become the forebrain, with its two subdivisions, the telen-

cephalon and the diencephalon, while more caudal regions expanded to become the hindbrain, with its two subdivisions, the pons (including the cerebellum) and the medulla. We consider each of these divisions in the remainder of this chapter, working from the most rostral to the most caudal, and end with a discussion of the spinal cord. First, however, we consider some general aspects of the brain.

The Meninges

The brain and the spinal cord are encased in three layers of protective membrane, the dura mater, the arachnoid, and the pia mater (Figure 3.4). These are collectively called the **meninges.** The outermost layer, the **dura mater** (Latin for "hard mother"), is a tough, inelastic membrane following the contour of the skull. Between the dura mater and the pia mater is the **arachnoid membrane** (Greek for "spider," re-

Table 3.1   Major Divisions of the Brain

Primitive Brain Divisions	Mammalian Brain Divisions	Regions of Human Brain	Alternative Terminology
Forebrain (prosencephalon)	Telencephalon	Neocortex Basal ganglia Lateral ventricles Limbic system	Forebrain
	Diencephalon	Thalamus Epithalamus Hypothalamus Pineal body Third ventricle	
Midbrain (mesencephalon)	Mesencephalon	Tectum Tegmentum Aqueduct of Sylvius	Brain stem
Hindbrain (rhombencephalon)	Metencephalon	Pons Cerebellum Fourth ventricle	
	Myelencephalon	Medulla oblongata Fourth ventricle	

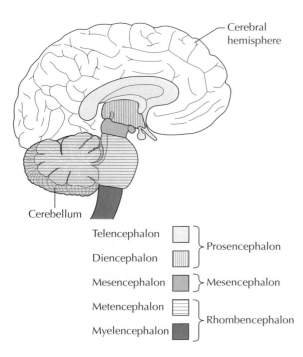

Cerebral hemisphere

Cerebellum

Telencephalon — ⬜ ⎤
Diencephalon — ▥ ⎦ Prosencephalon

Mesencephalon — ▦ } Mesencephalon

Metencephalon — ▤ ⎤
Myelencephalon — ⬛ ⎦ Rhombencephalon

◀ **FIGURE 3.3**   The major divisions of the human brain. *(From Kolb & Whishaw, 1996, p. 43)*

ferring to its weblike structure). This consists of two layers of fibrous and elastic tissue and does not follow the sulci and gyri of the cortex. Between the two layers of the arachnoid membrane is the **subarachnoid space,** a spongy structure containing **cerebrospinal fluid (CSF).** The innermost membrane, the **pia mater** (Latin for "pious mother"), adheres to the surface of the cortex, following the contours of its foldings and fissures.

The Cerebral Ventricles

The brain has four cavities filled with cerebrospinal fluid called **cerebral ventricles** (from the Latin for "stomach"). They are portions of the phylogenetically ancient neural canal that enlarged and changed their shape as a result of the massive expansion of

Skin
Bone
Dura mater
Arachnoid
membrane
Subarachnoid
space
Pia mater
Cortex

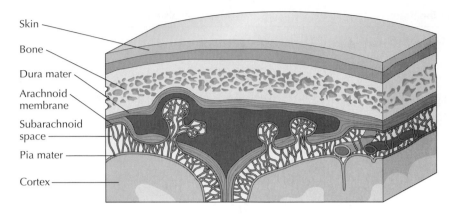

FIGURE 3.4 The membranes surrounding the brain, collectively termed the meninges. *(From Netter, 1974, p. 35)*

the forebrain in the course of evolution. This process has caused the ventricles to have a rather complicated shape (Figure 3.5).

There are two **lateral ventricles** (one in each hemisphere), the **third ventricle** in the diencephalon and the **fourth ventricle** in the hindbrain. Each ventricle contains a tuft of capillary vessels, called a **choroid plexus,** through which CSF enters the ventricles. Narrow channels connect all four ventricles, and CSF circulates through the lateral ventricles to the third and then to the fourth ventricle. From the fourth ventricle CSF leaves the ventricular system and circulates around the surface of the brain and spinal cord in the subarachnoid space. From there CSF is eventually absorbed into the venous circulation.

The brain is thus surrounded by CSF. This provides it with structural support (much as our body is supported by the water we swim in) and also with an added measure of protection from the effects of a blow to the head. If the circulation of CSF through the ventricles is blocked at one of the narrow channels that interconnect them, fluid builds up in front of the blockage. This condition, known as **hydrocephalus** (from the Greek for "water" + "brain"), is serious because as CSF accumulates it displaces and kills neighboring neurons.

Although, as mentioned in chapter 1, in medieval times the ventricles were thought to be directly involved in cognitive function, it is now recognized that there is no evidence that this is the case. They may, however, contain neuroactive molecules that exert some influence over brain function. In our dis-

cussions the cerebral ventricles will serve most often as descriptive reference points for location within the brain.

Gray Matter and White Matter

Parts of the central nervous system appear gray or white depending on the parts of the neuron that they contain (Figure 3.6). Where there is a concentration of cell bodies, the tissue appears gray. These areas, known as **gray matter,** have this color because the cell bodies contain the nucleus of the cell, which, in turn, contains darkly colored genetic material called chromatin. Gray matter is where almost all interactions between neurons take place, processes that underlie the complex functioning of the CNS.

Tissue containing axons, the extended part of the nerve cell, appears white because of the fatty myelin sheath surrounding each axon. As we saw in chapter 2, axons convey information from one area of the CNS to another. A large number of axons bundled together and conveying information from one region of gray matter to another is called a **tract** or **fiber tract** (from the Latin *tractus,* "extension" or "track").

The most elaborate concentration of cell bodies in the brain is arranged in a massive sheet, the **cerebral cortex.** In addition to the cortex, there are other concentrations of cell bodies in the central nervous system. Each of these is called a **nucleus** (plural, **nuclei**), not to be confused with the nucleus of an individual cell. The term nucleus is derived from the Latin word for "nut," reflecting the nutlike shape of many of

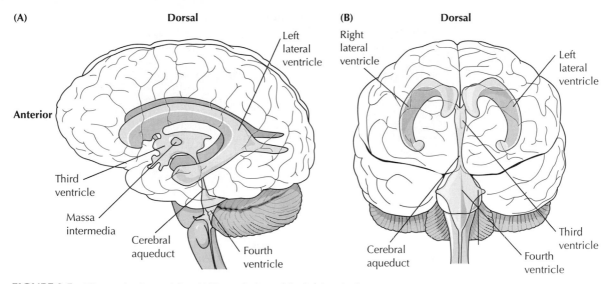

FIGURE 3.5 The cerebral ventricles. *(A)* Lateral view of the left hemisphere. *(B)* Frontal view. *(From Carlson, 1999, p. 63)*

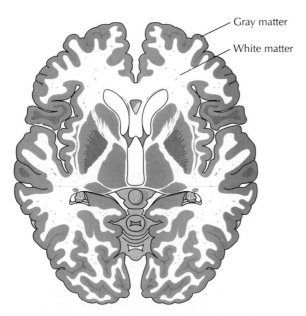

FIGURE 3.6 Horizontal section through the cerebral hemispheres showing gray matter and white matter. In addition to the cerebral cortex, the continuous enfolded sheet of gray matter on the surface of the cerebral hemispheres, this section also shows groups of gray-matter structures located deep within the hemispheres. *(From DeArmond, Fusco, & Dewey, 1974, p. 10)*

these clumps of cell bodies. Nuclei come in various sizes and shapes, ranging from the small and roughly spherical brain-stem nuclei (e.g., the abducens nucleus in the pons) to those that are relatively large and exotically shaped, such as the long, arching caudate nucleus in the forebrain.

Concentrations of cell bodies outside the central nervous system are called **ganglia** rather than nuclei. However, the inconsistent processes of naming and identifying structures have generated several exceptions to this general guideline. Thus, for example, a large and important group of gray-matter structures deep within the forebrain is collectively called the **basal ganglia.**

THE FOREBRAIN

The structures most identified with higher cognitive function are found in the forebrain. Foremost among these is the cerebral cortex.

The Cerebral Cortex

The cerebral cortex, forming the outer covering of the cerebral hemispheres (*cortex* comes from the Latin

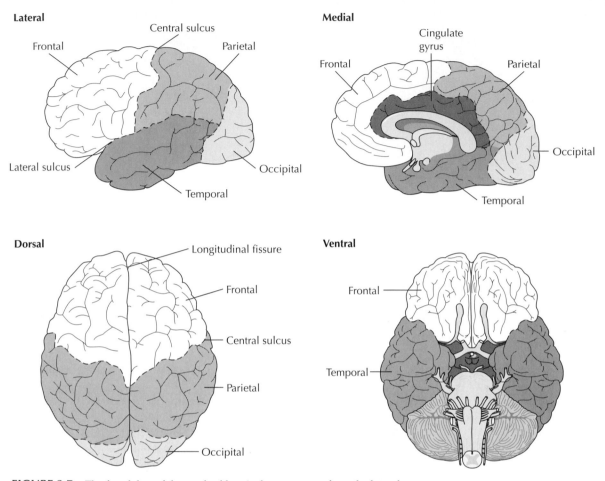

FIGURE 3.7   The four lobes of the cerebral hemispheres, as seen from the lateral, medial, dorsal, and ventral views. The central sulcus is the dividing line between the frontal and parietal lobes. The boundaries between the other three lobes are not precisely defined. Cortex in these border areas is often described in terms of the two adjacent lobes, thus generating such terms as parieto-occipital and parietotemporal. The cingulate gyrus (dark area on the medial surface) is usually identified specifically, rather than being classified as part of any of the four lobes. *(From Kolb & Whishaw, 1996, p. 52)*

word for "bark") is truly vast, particularly in humans, where it is estimated to contain 70% of all the neurons of the CNS. And if one considers that the medulla oblongata—with a diameter little more than that of a dime and a length of only a few inches—can mediate physiological functioning sufficient to sustain life, the relative enormity of the cerebral cortex, estimated to have an area of about 2,300 square centimeters (cm^2), can be appreciated.

THE FOUR LOBES   Each cerebral hemisphere is traditionally divided into four lobes: the **occipital, parietal, temporal,** and **frontal lobes** (Figure 3.7). These areas, taking their names simply from the bones of the skull that overlie them, were defined long before anything significant was known about the functional specialization of the cerebral cortex. Nevertheless, it turns out that these general areas are often useful in describing areas of the cortex that are

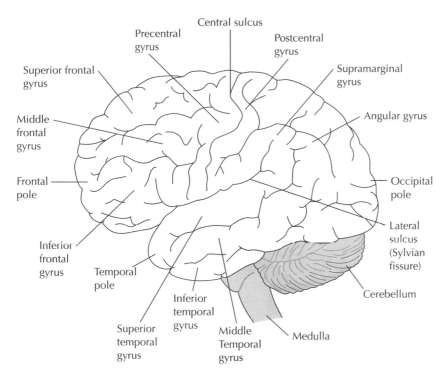

FIGURE 3.8 Lateral view of the left hemisphere, showing some major gyri and sulci. *(From DeArmond et al., 1974, p. 4)*

involved in particular behaviors. Because we will most often be considering functions mediated by the cortex, we will frequently use the names of these lobes to specify cortical location.

MAJOR CORTICAL FEATURES The characteristic folding of the cortex, which allows the enormous cortical surface to fit in the relatively small space enclosed by our skull, creates deep furrows or grooves on its surface. Each of these is called a **sulcus** (plural, **sulci**) and a few of the deeper ones are called **fissures.** Each outfolding is called a **gyrus** (plural, **gyri**). Some of the more important of these features, together with some major brain structures, are shown in Figures 3.8, 3.9, and 3.10.

THE LAYERED ORGANIZATION OF THE CORTEX The vast majority of cerebral cortex in humans has six layers: five layers of neurons and an outermost layer of fibers, termed the **plexiform layer.** This six-layered cortex, which appeared relatively late in evolution, is

called **neocortex.** It is also termed **isocortex** (from the Greek *iso*, meaning "same") because all of it is composed of six layers, although, as we will see shortly, the relative thickness of the different layers varies across the cortex. Areas of cortex with fewer than six layers are known as **allocortex** (from the Greek *allos*, meaning "other"). Allocortex has two major components, paleocortex and archicortex. **Paleocortex** includes olfactory cortex and has only two layers. **Archicortex** has only one layer and is found in areas of the hippocampus, including Ammon's horn and the dentate gyrus.

VARIATIONS IN CORTICAL LAYERS: CYTO-ARCHITECTONICS The relative thickness and cell composition of each of the six cortical layers varies across the neocortex, with different areas of the neocortex having characteristic patterns. The study of these patterns, called **cytoarchitectonics** (literally, "cell architecture"), was begun in the early 20th century. The two most widely accepted cytoarchitectonic

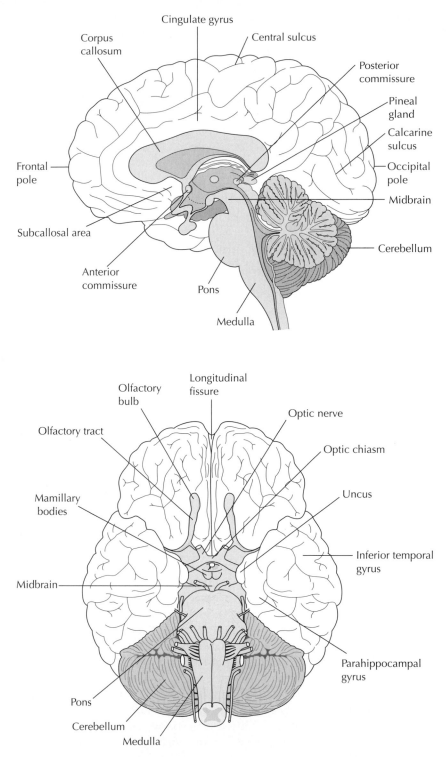

FIGURE 3.9   Medial view of the right hemisphere, showing some important gyri and sulci and the major divisions of the brain stem. *(From DeArmond et al., 1974, p. 8)*

FIGURE 3.10   Ventral view of the brain, showing some important cortical features and brain-stem structures. *(From DeArmond et al., 1974, p. 6)*

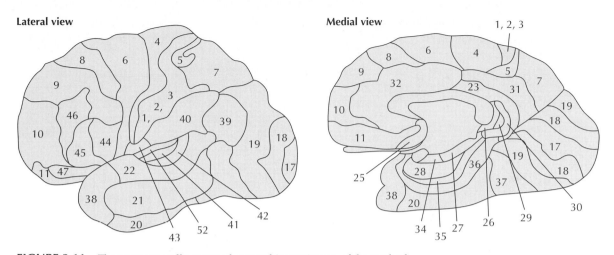

FIGURE 3.11 The most generally accepted cytoarchitectonic map of the cerebral cortex, developed by Korbinian Brodmann in 1909. *(From Nauta & Feirtag, 1986, p. 301)*

maps of the cortex are those developed by Korbinian Brodmann (Figure 3.11) and by von Economo and Koskinas. Brodmann's map is used most widely. The two systems have a fair amount of agreement, and yet they also differ significantly. This disagreement indicates that there is a significant amount of interpretation implicit in cytoarchitectonics, as there is in the development of any system of classification. The Brodmann numbering system is often used simply to identify a particular area of cortex, such as area 17 at the occipital pole of the cerebral hemispheres. It turns out that there is significant correspondence between areas defined by cytoarchitectonic studies and areas identified as having specialized function by other methods. Area 17, for example, turns out to be the primary visual cortex. This and other correspondences suggest that at least some of the areas defined by Brodmann are also areas specialized for particular psychological processes, although this is not always the case.

CORTICOCORTICAL FIBER CONNECTIONS   Let's now consider the interconnections between cortical areas, termed **corticocortical connections.** Some of these intracortical connections are short, the fibers taking a U-shaped course that connects adjacent gyri. Others are very long, connecting distant parts of the cortex within the same hemisphere **(ipsilateral cor-**

ticocortical fibers). Other long fibers connect **homotopic fields** (corresponding areas) in the right and left hemispheres **(cortical commissural fibers).**

Ipsilateral Corticocortical Fibers   Figure 3.12 shows the major ipsilateral corticocortical fibers including the **arcuate fasciculus,** the **uncinate fasciculus,** the **superior longitudinal fasciculus,** the **inferior longitudinal fasciculus,** the **cingulate fasciculus,** and the **superior occipitofrontal fasciculus.**

Commissural Fibers   The most prominent example of cortical commissural fibers, the fiber tracts connecting the left and right hemispheres, is the **corpus callosum** (Figure 3.12A; see also Figure 3.9). There are, however, other commissural fibers connecting the two hemispheres. These include the **anterior commissure** and the **posterior commissure** (see Figure 3.9). In chapter 1 we saw how knowledge of corticocortical connections can provide a conceptual framework for understanding patterns of cognitive impairment in terms of the disconnection of brain areas, that is, as disconnection syndromes.

FUNCTIONAL DIVISIONS OF THE CORTEX   The major functional divisions of the cerebral cortex are shown schematically in Figure 3.13. In this section we briefly review these divisions.

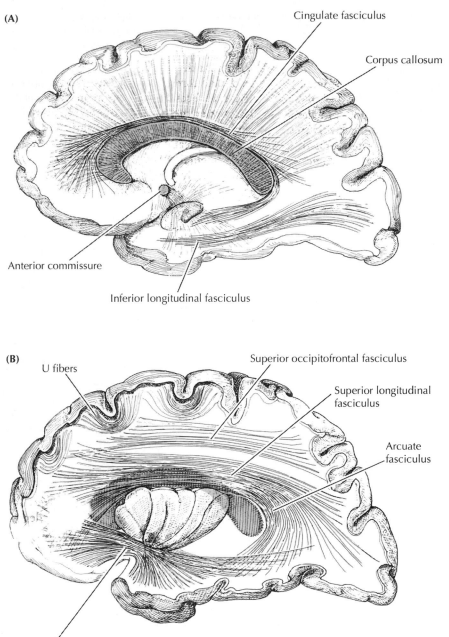

(A)

Cingulate fasciculus

Corpus callosum

Anterior commissure

Inferior longitudinal fasciculus

(B)   U fibers

Superior occipitofrontal fasciculus

Superior longitudinal
fasciculus

Arcuate
fasciculus

Uncinate fasciculus

FIGURE 3.12   Some major commissural fibers and ipsilateral corticocortical fibers linking neocortical areas. *(A)* A sagittal cut made near the midline showing the two most important commissural fibers linking the two hemispheres: the corpus callosum and the anterior commissure. *(B)* A more lateral sagittal cut showing the major ipsilateral corticocortical fibers. *(From Nauta & Feirtag, 1986, p. 304)*

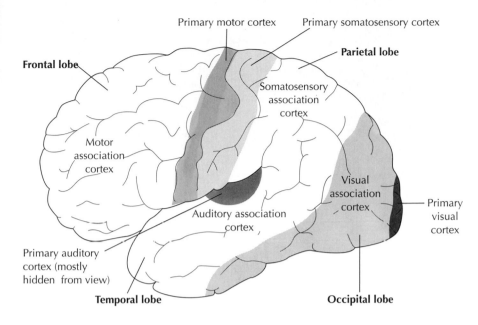

Primary motor cortex   Primary somatosensory cortex

Parietal lobe

Frontal lobe

Somatosensory association cortex

Motor association cortex

Visual association cortex

Primary visual cortex

Auditory association cortex

Primary auditory cortex (mostly hidden from view)

Temporal lobe   **Occipital lobe**

FIGURE 3.13 The main functional divisions of the cortex as seen from a lateral view. Note that most of the primary visual cortex is on the medial surface of each cerebral hemisphere, and so only the small lateral portion is visible in this figure. *(From Carlson, 1998, p. 69)*

Motor Cortex The frontal lobes play a major role in the planning and execution of movement. The **precentral gyrus,** just anterior to the **central sulcus,** is known as the **motor strip, motor cortex,** or **M1** and is involved in the execution of movement. Lesions of the motor cortex result in a loss of voluntary movement on the contralateral side of the body, a condition known as **hemiplegia.** Electrical stimulation of this cortex reveals a complete motor representation of the body on the precentral gyrus, the so-called **motor homunculus** ("little man"; Figure 3.14). Such mapping of a neural structure in terms of associated behaviors is called a **functional map.** There are many functional maps in the cortex and in other brain regions.

Just anterior to the motor cortex are the **premotor area,** on the lateral surface of the hemisphere, and the **supplementary motor area,** on the medial surface. These areas are involved in the coordination of sequences of movement. Frontal areas anterior to the premotor cortex, the **prefrontal cortex,** are involved in the higher-order control of movement, including planning and the modification of behavior in response to feedback about its consquences.

Somatosensory Cortex The **somatosensory cortex,** or **SI,** in the **postcentral gyrus** of each hemisphere receives sensory information from the contralateral side of the body about touch, pain, temperature, vibration, **proprioception** (body position), and **kinesthesis** (body movement). As with the motor cortex, there is an orderly mapping of the body surface represented on the postcentral gyrus, a mapping termed the **sensory homunculus.** Ventral to SI is the **secondary somatosensory cortex,** or **SII,** which receives input mainly from SI. Both SI and SII project to posterior parietal areas where higher-order somatosensory and spatial processing take place.

Information from sensory receptors in the body arrives at SI via two major systems, both relaying through the thalamus. The **spinothalamic system** conveys information about pain and temperature via a multisynaptic pathway, whereas the **lemniscal system** conveys more precise information about touch, proprioception, and movement via a more direct pathway. A comparison of the anatomy and function of these two systems exemplifies how different patterns of neuroanatomical interconnection underlie

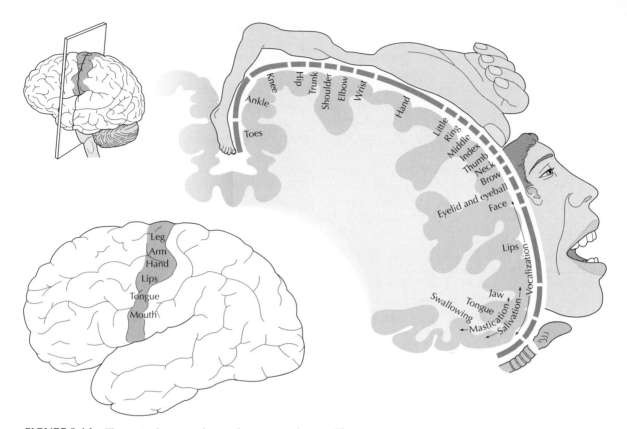

FIGURE 3.14   The motor homunculus on the precentral gyrus. The motor cortex can be seen in the lateral view of the cerebral cortex. *(From Netter, 1974, p. 68)*

specialization of function, a correspondence that we will find throughout the nervous system.

Visual Cortex   Visual information is conveyed from the retina to the **lateral geniculate nucleus** of the thalamus before being projected to the banks of the **calcarine sulcus** in the occipital lobes (see Figure 3.9). This route is called the **primary visual pathway,** and its initial cortical destination in the calcarine sulcus is known by several names, including the **primary visual cortex, V1,** and **striate cortex.** The last term is derived from the fact that a thin "thread" (Latin *stria*) of dark tissue is visible in layer IV of this cortical region. As we noted earlier, the primary visual cortex is also known by the area of Brodmann's cytoarchitectonic map corresponding to it: area 17.

The cortical visual system is organized analogously to the somatosensory system in that there is a contralateral relationship between the side (right-left) of the body that is stimulated (or, in the visual system, the side of space in which a stimulus appears) and the hemisphere to which the input is projected. Thus, stimuli from the right side of space (actually stimulating the left side of the retina because of right-left reversal caused by the lens of the eye) are projected to the left hemisphere. Therefore a lesion in the left visual cortex will result in a loss of vision in the right visual field, an impairment known as right **hemianopia** (literally, half-not-seeing).

The cortical visual system supports such critical functions as visual acuity, pattern vision, shape discrimination, and figure-ground discrimination.

Damage to the cortical visual system results in **cortical blindness.** This is experienced as complete blindness, just like that resulting from damage to the two eyes. These patients thus experience no knowledge of their immediate visual world. Nevertheless, unlike in blindness due to damage to the eyes, some residual visual functioning can be demonstrated in cortical blindness. We will discuss this residual function later in this chapter.

Surrounding V1 is cortex known as **extrastriate cortex** ("outside the striate"). It is also sometimes termed **prestriate cortex,** referring to the fact that it is anterior to the striate cortex, or **visual association cortex.** Literally dozens of visual areas have been discovered in extrastriate cortex, each with its own topographically organized map of visual space. These are specialized for the processing of specific aspects of the visual world. Some of these visual areas will be discussed in greater detail in chapter 5.

In addition to the primary visual pathways, there are several secondary visual pathways. The most important of these are the direct retinal projections to the superior colliculus in the midbrain, a structure involved in the mediation of visuomotor coordination. There are also direct retinal projections to the hypothalamus in the diencephalon, which are involved in the process of entrainment of light-dark activity cycles.

Auditory Cortex   The **primary auditory cortex (AI)** and the **auditory association cortex (AII)** surrounding it are located in **Heschl's gyrus** in the lower lip of the Sylvian fissure in each temporal lobe (see Figure 3.13). These regions of auditory cortex contain several orderly representations of sound frequency, known as **tonotopic maps,** and are important for the perception of such auditory properties as pitch, location, rhythm, and timbre.

As mentioned in chapter 1, input reaches the auditory cortex in an unusual way. As we have seen, in vision and somesthesis (body sense) there is an orderly contralateral relationship between the side of space from which a stimulus originates and the cerebral hemisphere to which input is projected. This exclusive contralaterality of direct input is not the case in the auditory system. Instead, efferents from the cochlear nucleus, the synaptic destination of the **auditory nerve,** cross the midline to form connections with the contralateral cochlear nucleus, as well as continuing ipsilaterally. These fibers course to the **superior olive** and then to the **inferior colliculus.** At each of these levels fibers also cross to the corresponding structure on the contralateral side of the brain stem. From the inferior colliculus these fibers reach the **medial geniculate nucleus** of the thalamus and from there project, via the **auditory radiations,** to the **auditory cortex** in the ipsilateral temporal lobe.

The result of all this crossing over at several levels of the auditory system is that each ear projects to both hemispheres and each hemisphere receives projections from both ears. This pattern of connectivity explains why damage to one auditory cortex does not produce noticeable impairment (as an analogous unilateral lesion in the visual or somatosensory cortex would), although, as we will see in chapter 4, special tests can detect a mild impairment in such cases. It also explains why **cortical deafness** (deafness due to cortical damage) is extremely rare. Such a condition would require damage to both auditory cortices. Because of the widely separated locations of the cortices in the right and left temporal lobes, such a pair of lesions is extremely rare, although cases of cortical deafness have been reported.

Olfactory Cortex   The cortical representation for smell is different from that of the three major sensory modalities just discussed. First, rather than being derived from the **transduction** of a specific form of energy into a pattern of neural impulses, as is the case in somesthesis, vision, and audition, olfactory input to cortex is derived from the coding of the presence of particular molecules in the environment of the organism. In addition, although input from each of the three major sensory modalities is relayed to the thalamus before reaching its respective primary cortical area, olfactory information gains access to the olfactory cortex on the ventral surface of the frontal lobes directly, without thalamic mediation. It has been suggested that the directness of this cortical input contributes to the emotional intensity so often associated with olfactory experience.

The Cortical Representation for Taste   The cortical representation for taste is the least understood of all cortical sensory areas. Its precise location is unclear, but it is thought to be in the upper lip of the Sylvian fissure. Like the three major sensory modalities, and unlike olfaction, information initially coded in taste buds on the tongue and on neighboring areas reaches its cortical destination after synapsing in the thalamus.

Association Cortex   **Association cortex** is traditionally defined as areas of cortex that do not mediate elementary sensory or motor function. This term connotes that elaborate associative or cognitive processes are mediated by these areas, including the higher-order processing of sensory information that underlies perception and the higher-order planning and organization underlying complex behavior. Although in some general sense this is accurate, it is now clear that specific areas within what had been termed association cortex have highly specialized functional roles. As a result, the sketchy notion of association cortex has given way to a more delineated picture of the contribution made by specific cortical areas to higher-order processing. For example, it is now clear that areas outside V1 and extrastriate cortex, in the parietal and temporal lobes, although not involved in the early stages of visual processing, are critical for the perception of specific aspects of the visual world. Similarly, prefrontal cortex, not directly involved in the execution or coordination of specific movements, is critical to the higher-order organization of action, including planning and the regulation of behavior in response to feedback about ongoing behavior. The language areas also exemplify the more specific identification of the functional characteristics of areas not involved in elementary sensory or motor processing.

LURIA'S MODEL OF SEQUENTIAL HIERARCHICAL CORTICAL PROCESSING   The Soviet neuropsychologist Aleksandr Luria (1902–1977) has proposed a model for cortical processing. Although in certain respects it is highly oversimplified, retaining, for example, the vague notion of association cortex, it nevertheless serves as a useful framework for thinking about cortical processing. According to Luria's model, each of the major primary sensory projection areas of the cortex (somatosensory, visual, and auditory) projects to a neighboring area of cortex for further processing. These areas are known as the **sensory association area** or **secondary sensory area** for the particular modality in question. For example, the visual association area is a ring of cortex on the lateral and medial surface of the hemisphere adjacent to the primary visual cortex in the occipital lobes. Whereas lesions in a primary sensory projection area are associated with impairments in elementary sensory function, such as visual acuity, lesions to sensory association areas result in impairments in higher-order perceptual processes that are termed **agnosias.** Agnosia can take different forms depending on the sensory modality affected and on other factors. We will consider visual agnosia in greater detail in chapters 5 and 8.

Luria's model goes on to propose that each of the modality-specific sensory association areas then projects to an area in the inferior parietal lobe, the **tertiary sensory area,** where the already highly processed information associated with each modality is integrated to yield a multimodal representation. From here information is projected to the **tertiary motor area** in the dorsolateral frontal cortex. Thus, dorsolateral frontal cortex receives input that is the product of extensive processing throughout the cerebral cortex. In terms of sensory processing, the dorsal region of the frontal lobes is, in the words of the neuroanatomist Walle Nauta, a "neocortical end of the line" (Nauta & Feirtag, 1986).

The frontal lobes then subject this highly processed sensory information to executive control in the form of superordinate motor organization such as planning. The specific behavioral manifestations of this superordinate organization are then implemented by the **secondary motor area,** which coordinates sequences of movements, and the primary motor area, which finally effects movement (Figure 3.15).

The Basal Ganglia

The **basal ganglia** are a group of subcortical gray-matter structures in the forebrain. The three main subdivisions of the basal ganglia are the **putamen,** the **globus pallidus,** and the **caudate nucleus** (Figure 3.16). The caudate and putamen are collectively called

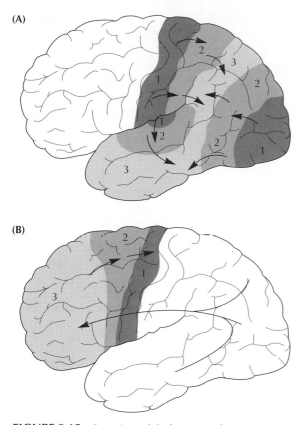

FIGURE 3.15 Luria's model of sequential processing in the cerebral cortex. *(A)* Information arriving at the primary sensory areas (dark shading) is processed and conveyed to secondary (medium shading) and tertiary (light shading) sensory areas for further perceptual and symbolic elaboration. *(B)* From the tertiary sensory area, information is then conveyed to the tertiary motor area (light shading) in the frontal lobes, which mediates higher-order motor processing such as planning and other forms of executive control. Specific motor sequences are then organized by the secondary motor area, (medium shading), which then sends this input on to the primary motor cortex (dark shading) for final implementation. *(From Kolb & Whishaw, 1996, p. 170 [based on information in Luria, 1973])*

the **neostriatum,** a term that reflects the fact that they are phylogenetically most recent and that they are structurally related, being connected by cell bridges. Together, the three structures are referred to as the **corpus striatum.** Because of their functional relationship with the corpus striatum, the **subthalamic nu-**

cleus and the **substantia nigra** are also generally considered to be components of the basal ganglia.

The caudate nucleus and the putamen are the major recipients of afferents to the corpus striatum. These afferents originate from areas throughout the cortex, including areas of cortex mediating motor function, and from the substantia nigra. The globus pallidus is the major source of efferents from the basal ganglia, projecting mainly to thalamic nuclei. These, in turn, project to motor cortex, premotor cortex, and prefrontal cortex. Thus, rather than being part of the stream from motor cortex to spinal cord that directly executes motor activity, the basal ganglia and their connections with the thalamus form a cortical-subcortical-cortical loop that appears to monitor and adjust motor activity. The regulatory role of the basal ganglia in motor function is also suggested by the fact that lesions to these structures frequently result in disorders that have unwanted movement as their major symptom. These are discussed in more detail in chapter 9. Some structures of the basal ganglia also have been shown to play a role in certain cognitive processes.

The Limbic System

In the 19th century Paul Broca called the cortical structures at the border between forebrain and brain stem *le grand lobe limbique*, the great limbic lobe (from the Latin *limbus*, meaning "border"). These structures include the **cingulate gyrus** (arching around the superior margin of the corpus callosum), the **subcallosal gyrus,** the **parahippocampal gyrus** (Figure 3.17), and the **hippocampus.**

In 1952 Paul MacLean hypothesized that a number of structures, including this cortical ring, constituted a functional system, which he named the **limbic system.** Although there is some disagreement about the basis for including a particular structure in this system, and even about the very validity of the limbic system concept (see chapter 11), structures traditionally considered to be part of the limbic system include, in addition to the cortical areas just mentioned, the **septum,** the **amygdala,** the **hypothalamus** (including its posterior portion, the **mamillary bodies**), and the **anterior nucleus** of the thalamus (Figure 3.18).

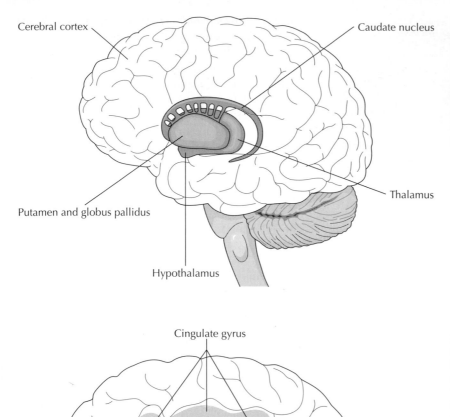

Cerebral cortex

Caudate nucleus

Putamen and globus pallidus

Thalamus

Hypothalamus

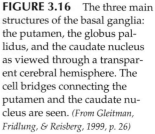

FIGURE 3.16   The three main structures of the basal ganglia: the putamen, the globus pallidus, and the caudate nucleus as viewed through a transparent cerebral hemisphere. The cell bridges connecting the putamen and the caudate nucleus are seen. *(From Gleitman, Fridlung, & Reisberg, 1999, p. 26)*

Cingulate gyrus

Frontal pole

Occipital pole

Subcallosal gyrus

Parahippocampal gyrus

FIGURE 3.17   Medial view of the right hemisphere, with the brain stem and cerebellum removed, showing limbic cortex. The hippocampus is hidden behind the parahippocampal gyrus. *(From Carlson, 1999, p. 69)*

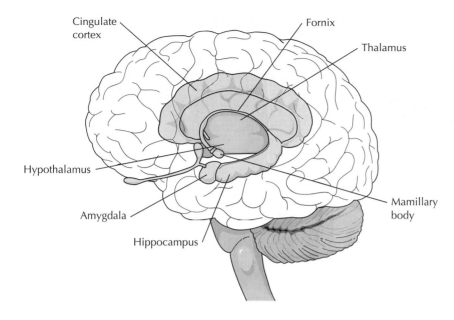

Cingulate cortex

Fornix

Thalamus

Hypothalamus

Mamillary body

Amygdala

Hippocampus

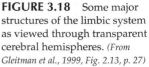

FIGURE 3.18   Some major structures of the limbic system as viewed through transparent cerebral hemispheres. *(From Gleitman et al., 1999, Fig. 2.13, p. 27)*

The limbic system receives three main sources of cortical input: (a) from posterior association cortex via the cingulate gyrus, hippocampus, and **fornix** (the pathway connecting the hippocampus with the mamillary bodies in the posterior hypothalamus); (b) from inferotemporal cortex via entorhinal cortex (the anterior portion of the parahippocampal gyrus) and hippocampus; and (c) from prefrontal cortex (Figure 3.19). Each of these sources of input carry information from association cortices, providing the limbic system with highly processed information about the environment.

There are three major sources of limbic efferents to cortex. The cingulate gyrus receives input from the mamillary bodies via the anterior thalamus. In addition, prefrontal cortex receives limbic input from the hypothalamus and from the amygdala (see Figure 3.19).

Limbic structures have been shown to be important in emotional function and in memory. The hypothalamus, in addition to its role in the regulation of autonomic and endocrine function, plays an important role in the regulation of emotional behavior, including rage behavior. In addition, the septum (and also parts of the hypothalamus) produces intense pleasure when electrically stimulated. The amygdala

is involved in emotional processing, particularly conditioned fear. It is also involved in social behavior.

Finally, although there is little evidence that the hippocampus is involved directly in emotion, the hippocampus is critical for normal memory. Bilateral damage to this structure results in a profound inability to remember anything new, a condition known as **anterograde amnesia.** It is not surprising that the same structures or system of structures might mediate both memory and emotion because these two domains of function are closely related.

The Diencephalon

The most important structures in the diencephalon are the thalamus and the hypothalamus (Figure 3.20). The word *thalamus* comes from the Greek for "inner room," presumably a reference to the fact that the thalamus is situated deep in the brain. Although it is usually referred to in the singular, as if there were only one, there are actually two thalami, one in each hemisphere. Each is an ovoid (roughly egg-shaped) group of nuclei, bordered laterally by the third ventricle, dorsally by the lateral ventricles, and laterally by the internal capsule (fibers from motor cortex to brain-stem nuclei and the spinal cord).

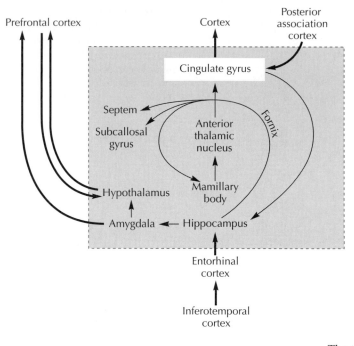

Prefrontal cortex

Cortex

Posterior association cortex

Cingulate gyrus

Septem

Subcallosal gyrus

Anterior thalamic nucleus

Fornix

Hypothalamus

Mamillary body

Amygdala ← Hippocampus

Entorhinal cortex

Inferotemporal cortex

FIGURE 3.19 Major connections within the limbic system and between the limbic system and other regions of the brain. Limbic structures are shown within the rectangle. Bold arrows indicate major sources of input to the limbic system and major targets of output from the limbic system. *(Adapted from Kandel et al., 1995, p. 606)*

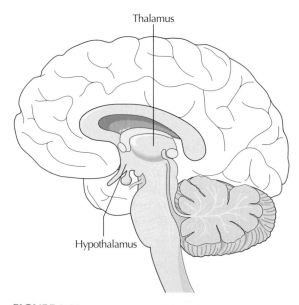

Thalamus

Hypothalamus

FIGURE 3.20 Medial view of the right hemisphere showing the medial surface of the right thalamus and, just below it, the right half of the hypothalamus. *(From DeArmond et al., 1974, p. 8)*

The thalamus contains many specific nuclei. Some of these are points where neurons carrying incoming sensory information from each sensory modality (except olfaction) synapse on their way to the cortex. Although these are sometimes referred to as relay nuclei, a great deal of processing takes place in these nuclei, so it would be a mistake to think of them as simply passing information on to the next link in the chain. The sensory input from each modality reaches a specific thalamic nucleus. These nuclei include the **lateral geniculate nucleus** (for vision), the **medial geniculate nucleus** (for audition), and specific nuclei for the relay of somatosensory input (Figure 3.21).

The thalamus also receives input from the basal ganglia, cerebellum, motor cortex, and medial temporal cortex and sends projections back to these areas. It thus serves as a pivotal structure in the formation of many cortical-subcortical-cortical loops that are involved in a broad range of functions. For example, returning connections from primary cortical sensory areas to the thalamus have been implicated in the modulation of thalamocortical input. In the motor domain, a loop involving motor cortex–basal ganglia–thalamus–motor cortex and a loop involving motor cortex–cerebellum–thalamus–motor

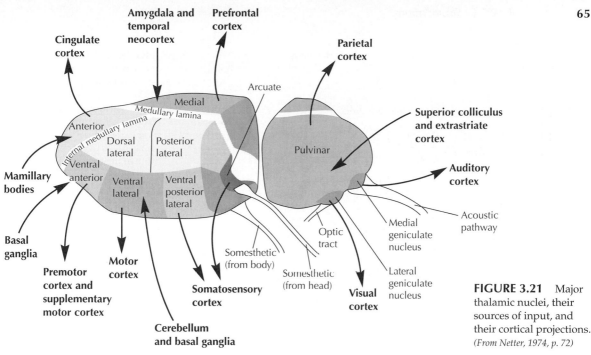

FIGURE 3.21 Major thalamic nuclei, their sources of input, and their cortical projections. *(From Netter, 1974, p. 72)*

cortex have been shown to be important in the control and regulation of movement. The thalamus is also involved in cognitive function, including language and memory.

The **hypothalamus,** true to its name, is located just below the thalamus, comprising the tissue forming lower walls of the third ventricle. This small and compact group of nuclei (Figure 3.22) is involved in an extremely broad range of functions. As we have already noted, the hypothalamus is a central component of the limbic system. In fact, Nauta has suggested that the limbic system should be defined as those structures that are in close synaptic contact with the hypothalamus (Nauta & Feirtag, 1986). It is thus critically involved in limbic-mediated emotional and motivational processes.

Structures sending input to the hypothalamus include limbic cortex, via the hippocampus and fornix, orbital (ventral) prefrontal cortex, the amygdala, and the reticular formation. Thus, the hypothalamus receives both highly processed input from the cortex and information from the internal environment. It also receives direct projections from the retina that are involved in hypothalamic control of circadian rhythms. Major hypothalamic output includes con-

nections to prefrontal cortex, the amygdala, the reticular formation, and the spinal cord. The fact that the hypothalamus receives input from and sends output to both higher cortical centers and lower brain stem and spinal centers suggests that it serves as an interface between these two neural domains, a notion that is consistent with the influence of the hypothalamus over both behavior and internal physiological state.

The influence of the hypothalamus on inner physiological state is most evident in its central role in the maintenance of **homeostasis,** the internal biological steady state that every living organism must constantly maintain in order to remain alive. It plays its role both by activating specific behaviors (such as drinking and eating) and by directly regulating physiological processes that maintain the integrity of the body's internal environment. Internal regulation is achieved partly through hypothalamic control of the autonomic nervous system, that division of the nervous system that controls smooth muscle, cardiac muscle, and glands. Thus, the hypothalamus may be thought of as the highest regulatory center of the autonomic nervous system. However, its control is far from absolute; it is influenced both by higher cortical centers processing information about the external

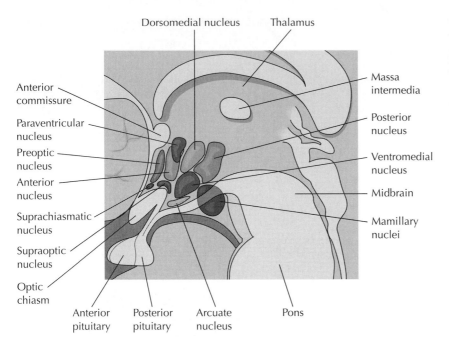

Dorsomedial nucleus — Thalamus

Anterior commissure

Paraventricular nucleus

Preoptic nucleus

Anterior nucleus

Suprachiasmatic nucleus

Supraoptic nucleus

Optic chiasm

Massa intermedia

Posterior nucleus

Ventromedial nucleus

Midbrain

Mamillary nuclei

Anterior pituitary   Posterior pituitary   Arcuate nucleus   Pons

FIGURE 3.22 Midsagittal view of the hypothalamus, showing some major hypothalamic nuclei and some neighboring structures. The optic chiasm is the point at which some fibers from each optic nerve cross over to the other side of the brain. *(From Netter, 1974, p. 76)*

environment and lower brain-stem centers participating in physiological regulation.

The other mechanism by which the hypothalamus exerts control over internal physiology is via regulation of endocrine function. Hormonal regulation of physiological function has certain advantages over neural mechanisms, particularly when slower, more diffuse, and more prolonged influence is required. The hypothalamus regulates endocrine function by controlling the release of hormones from the **anterior pituitary gland,** which protrudes from the base of the hypothalamus (see Figure 3.22). The anterior pituitary has been conceptualized as the "master gland" of the endocrine system in that it triggers the release of hormones by a number of endocrine glands, including the adrenal cortex, the thyroid gland, and the gonads. This anterior-pituitary regulation of endocrine function is, in turn, regulated by the hypothalamus. Interestingly, the hypothalamus achieves this regulation by secreting its own peptide hormones into a vascular portal system that delivers them directly to the anterior pituitary. The hypothalamus also monitors the consequences of this regulatory activity by assessing the levels of circulating hormones present in its blood supply.

Although the anterior pituitary gland is not part of the nervous system, the **posterior pituitary** is composed of axons of neurons whose cell bodies are in specific nuclei in the hypothalamus and whose axon terminals release hormones into the general circulation. These hormones include vasopressin (also called antidiuretic hormone), which regulates water retention, and oxytocin, which is involved in milk production and in uterine contractions. Thus, the hypothalamus is a gland, perhaps a startling conclusion until we realize the kinship between the release of neurotransmitter by neurons throughout the nervous system and the neurosecretory function of hypothalamic cells. As we saw in chapter 2, in a sense all neurons are secretory.

THE BRAIN STEM

The brain stem lies between the diencephalon and the spinal cord (Figure 3.23). It is composed of the midbrain (mesencephalon), the pons (metencephalon), and the medulla oblongata (myelencephalon). Much of the brain stem is primarily concerned with regulating and maintaining life-sustaining processes such as respiration, cardiac function, and homeosta-

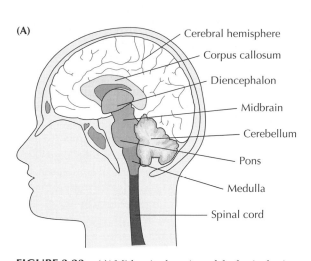

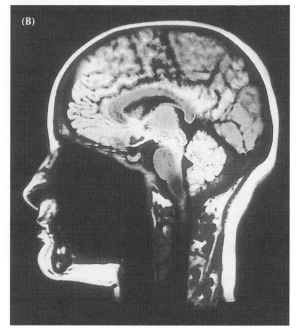

FIGURE 3.23   *(A)* Midsagittal section of the brain, brain stem, and spinal cord. *(B)* An MRI of the same structures in the living brain. *(From Kandel et al., 1995, p. 9)*

sis. It is also involved in the control of sleep and wakefulness, emotion, attention, and consciousness.

The brain stem contains groups of motor and sensory nuclei, as well as nuclei that exert a modulatory (regulatory) effect on higher brain centers by releasing specific neurotransmitters. An example of such a nucleus is the substantia nigra, a major site of dopamine synthesis. Axons projecting from this nucleus release dopamine at synapses in widespread areas of the anterior forebrain, including the basal ganglia and prefrontal cortex. In addition to its many nuclei, the brain stem has major ascending (sensory) and descending (motor) white-matter tracts running through it.

It may be tempting, in the context of considering higher-order brain function, to consider the brain stem as a simple conduit through which information flows back and forth between the forebrain and the spinal cord. This would be an error, however. As we have indicated, the brain stem plays a central role in the neural control of some extremely complex functions that are essential for survival and also participates in the regulation of a number of higher-order functions (Damasio, 1999).

The Midbrain

The midbrain lies between the diencephalon and the pons. The part of the midbrain dorsal to the cerebral aqueduct is called the **tectum** (Latin, "roof") and consists of two paired structures, the superior and inferior colliculi. The **tegmentum** (Latin, "covering") lies ventral to the aqueduct. The most ventral region of the midbrain contains larger fiber tracts carrying information from the forebrain to the spinal cord (the **corticospinal tract**) and from the forebrain to the brain stem (**corticobulbar tract**). Connections between the forebrain and the cerebellum, running in both directions, also pass through the midbrain.

The midbrain contains several structures involved with vision. These include the superior colliculus, which is involved in the mediation of visuomotor function. Earlier in this chapter we mentioned that patients with cortical blindness nevertheless have some preserved visual function. For example, they are able to accurately point to the location of a spot of light even though they have no conscious experience of seeing the stimulus. This paradoxical ability, which has been termed **blindsight** (Weiskrantz, 1986), may be mediated by the superior colliculus.

The midbrain is also the site of two of the three cranial nerve nuclei that control eye movement, the **occulomotor nucleus** and the **trochlear nucleus.** The **pupillary reflex** (constriction of the pupil of the eye in response to intense light) is mediated by a nucleus incorporated in the occulomotor nucleus. The pupillary reflex is tested to assess the integrity of midbrain structures in patients who are unconscious.

The inferior colliculus, an auditory relay, is located in the midbrain, just below the superior colliculus. The mesencephalic tegmentum contains a number of nuclei involved in motor function, including the red nucleus and the substantia nigra. Finally, the mesencephalic reticular formation, part of the diffuse set of nuclei extending from the lower medulla to the thalamus, takes up much of the midbrain. The reticular formation is involved in a number of functions, including arousal, autonomic regulation, and the regulation of pain.

The Hindbrain

The hindbrain (rhombencephalon) is made up of the pons (metencephalon) and the medulla (myelencephalon). The cerebellum is also considered to be part of the metencephalon, but it will be considered in a separate section.

PONS   The pons is composed of the pontine tegmental region, forming the floor of the fourth ventricle, and, more ventrally, a number of fiber tracts interspersed with pontine nuclei. In addition to the continuation of cortical projections to the brain stem and spinal cord, pontine fibers include massive connections between cortex and cerebellum, the **cerebellar peduncles** (Latin for "little feet"). Nuclei in the pons include those having auditory and **vestibular** (sense of head position and motion) function, as well as sensory and motor nuclei for the face and mouth. One of the three nuclei controlling the extraocular muscles of the eyes is also found in the pons. The pons also contains a large portion of the reticular formation.

MEDULLA   The medulla lies just caudal to the pons and rostral to the spinal cord. As the medulla

extends caudally, the fourth ventricle narrows and shifts ventrally until it becomes a narrow, centrally located tube as the medulla merges with the spinal cord. The medulla contains a number of important nuclei, fiber tracts, and the most caudal portion of the reticular formation.

At the dorsal edge of its rostral end, the medulla contains two pairs of large nuclei, the gracile nuclei and the cuneate nuclei, relay nuclei for the ascending lemniscal pathways, the somatosensory pathways carrying information about touch, body position sense, and kinesthesis from the spinal cord to the thalamus and then on to the cortical somatosensory area. In the ventral portion of its rostral part is the olivary complex, including the inferior and medial accessory olivary nuclei. This highly enfolded nucleus receives input from the cortex and the red nucleus and projects to the cerebellum. The medulla also contains several sensory nuclei, including those processing vestibular input and sensory input from the face, mouth, throat, and abdomen. The medulla also contains motor nuclei innervating the neck, tongue, and throat. Finally, motor nuclei in the medulla innervate organs of the body that are crucial for the maintenance of life, including the viscera, the heart, and muscles involved in respiration.

In the ventral medulla are found the continuations of the corticospinal motor projections. About halfway down the length of the medulla, 90% of the corticospinal fibers on each side cross over to the contralateral side. This point of crossover (**decussation**) is called the **pyramidal decussation.**

THE CEREBELLUM

Bulging out of the dorsal surface of the pons, the cerebellum is part of the hindbrain. However, its function is different from that of the brain-stem structures we have just discussed. Although the term *cerebellum* comes from the Latin for "little brain," it is actually a massive structure. The cerebellum overlies the dorsal surface of the brain at the level of the pons, forming the roof of the fourth ventricle and sitting on the massive cerebellar peduncles. The cerebellum has a cortex, the surface of which, because of its intricate infoldings, has an area equal to that of the cerebral cortex. In the depths of the cerebellum are

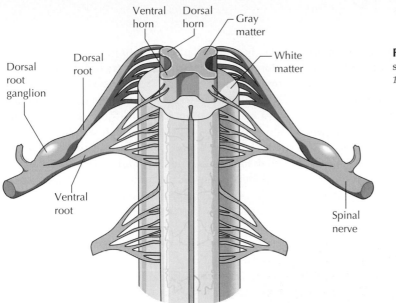

Ventral horn, Dorsal horn, Gray matter, White matter, Dorsal root, Dorsal root ganglion, Ventral root, Spinal nerve

FIGURE 3.24 Ventral view of a section of the spinal cord. *(From Netter, 1974, p. 52)*

four pairs of deep nuclei. Between the cortex and the deep nuclei is internal white matter.

Most input to the cerebellum reaches the cerebellar cortex via relays in the deep nuclei, although some arrives at the cortex directly. Cerebellar afferents bring information about the state of the body from sensory areas processing somatosensory, visual, auditory, and vestibular information. In addition, the cerebellum also receives afferents from structures involved in motor function, including the motor and premotor cortices.

Cerebellar output, almost entirely from the deep nuclei, projects, via the thalamus, to motor and premotor cortex. Cerebellar efferents also project to brain-stem nuclei that send descending projections to the spinal cord, and to the rhombencephalic reticular formation.

The multisensory and motor input to the cerebellum, together with its output to motor-related cortex and to spinal centers mediating posture and gait, suggest that the cerebellum plays a central role in the modulation, adjustment, and coordination of body movement on the basis of information about current body state and current and intended movement. This notion is supported by the fact that, despite the extensive sensory and motor input the cerebellum receives, lesions to the cerebellum do not cause sensory deficits or paralysis. Instead, cerebellar lesions cause disruptions in the maintenance of posture and in the

sequential coordination of movement on the side of the body ipsilateral to the lesion. (The ipsilateral effect is due to the fact that cerebellar efferents cross over to the other side of the brain stem, affecting brain-stem fibers that then themselves cross over again at the pyramidal decussation.) These disruptions are generally termed **cerebellar ataxia** (literally, "lack of order") and are exemplified by the disruption of the attempt to carry out a command, such as "extend your arm in front of you and then bring your finger to your nose." A patient with cerebellar ataxia who attempted this would evidence a marked instability of movement, with the hand increasingly lurching from side to side as the finger approached the nose.

THE SPINAL CORD

The **spinal cord** extends from the medulla, rostrally, to the **cauda equina** ("horse tail") caudally. Thirty-one pairs of **spinal nerves** leave the spinal cord, passing through small openings in the spinal column. The cauda equina is composed of the lowest spinal nerves as they continue to course caudally beyond the end of the spinal cord before leaving the spinal column.

In cross section the spinal cord has a butterfly-shaped center of gray matter, surrounded by white matter (Figure 3.24). The white matter consists of ascending somatosensory tracts, descending motor tracts, and intraspinal projection fibers connecting different regions within the spinal cord. On each side the gray matter is divided into a **ventral horn** and a **dorsal horn.** The ventral horn is the site of cell bodies of α motor neurons, the final link in the neuronal chain that activates muscle contraction. Axons of α motor neurons leave the spinal cord in the **ventral root.** The dorsal horn contains cell bodies of interneurons that convey input from primary somatosensory neurons to the brain and to motor neurons at the same and at other levels of the spinal cord. These latter pathways connecting somatosensory input with motor output are the basis for spinal reflexes. Axons of primary somatosensory neurons enter the spinal cord in the **dorsal root.** However, the cell bodies of these neurons are not in the dorsal horn, but remain outside the central nervous system in the **dorsal root ganglia.**

SUMMARY

There are several general terms that help us orient ourselves within the nervous system. *Anterior* (rostral) refers to the front, and *posterior* (caudal) refers to the back. *Superior* (dorsal) denotes the top or upper portion of a structure, and *inferior* (ventral) the bottom or underside. *Medial* refers to the middle, and *lateral* to the side. These terms are used to indicate the position of a structure relative to the whole brain and also relative to other structures.

The central nervous system consists of the brain and the spinal cord. The peripheral nervous system includes all of the sensory and motor nerves coursing through the body and conveying signals to and from the central nervous system.

The brain is traditionally divided into three parts: the forebrain (prosencephalon), the midbrain (mesencephalon), and the hindbrain (rhombencephalon). The forebrain includes the cerebral cortex, the basal ganglia, the lateral ventricles, and the limbic system. The cerebral cortex, the most highly evolved region of the human brain, is traditionally divided into four lobes: the occipital, parietal, temporal, and frontal. The surface of the cortex has many sulci and gyri that increase the area of cortex that can be contained in the limited volume of the skull. They also conve-

niently serve as landmarks for identifying cortical regions. Most cortex has six layers of cells, although a few regions have only one or two layers. Different cortical regions vary with respect to the thickness and cellular composition of these layers, and the study of this variation, called cytoarchitectonics, has yielded cortical maps that have turned out to be useful in identifying functional areas of the cortex.

Fibers tracts of varying length connect areas within each hemisphere and between the two hemispheres. Many patterns of cognitive impairment can be understood in terms of interruption of specific fiber tracts and the resulting disconnection of specific cortical regions.

Different cortical regions have been shown to be specialized for specific functions. These include the primary motor cortex and cortical areas that are specialized for the processing of elementary sensory information from each sensory modality. The term *association cortex* was long used to indicate cortex mediating higher-order processing. This concept has given way to a more delineated understanding of the specialized functions mediated by specific cortical regions outside the primary sensory and motor areas.

The basal ganglia are gray-matter structures located deep in the base of the forebrain. They are important for the regulation and control of movement. Structures within the basal ganglia have also been shown to play a role in some areas of cognition.

The limbic system includes a number of cortical and subcortical structures at the border between the forebrain and the brain stem. The limbic system serves as a useful term to describe structures involved in emotion, motivation, and the maintenance of homeostasis, although the validity of this concept has been questioned. Some structures within this system, including the hippocampus and the mamillary bodies, have been shown to be important for memory.

The diencephalon includes the thalamus and the hypothalamus. The thalamus receives information from each sensory modality (except olfaction) and conveys this information on to the respective primary cortical sensory area. The thalamus also receives input from the basal ganglia, cerebellum, and motor cortex and sends projections back to these areas. It thus serves as a central component in many cortical-subcortical-cortical loops. The hypothalamus is involved in an extremely broad range of functions, many of which have the goal of maintaining homeostasis, both through the regulation of behavior and the regulation of the body's internal state. The hypothalamus mediates control of the organism's internal state through the regulation of the autonomic nervous system and through the control of endocrine function.

The brain stem includes the midbrain, the pons, and the medulla. These structures contain groups of motor and sensory nuclei and neurons that exert a modulatory effect on higher brain centers. They also contain ascending and descending fiber tracts that mediate somatosensory and motor function. Many of the nuclei in the medulla mediate processes that are essential for life, such as cardiac function and blood pressure. For this reason, major lesions of the medulla often result in death.

The cerebellum plays a central role in the modulation and coordination of body movement on the basis of information about current body state and current and intended movement.

The spinal cord conveys motor commands from the brain to the muscles of the body via α motor neurons that leave the spinal cord in the ventral root. Axons of primary somatosensory neurons, conveying information about the body to the brain, enter the spinal cord in the dorsal root. The spinal cord also mediates many reflexes that allow for rapid and automatic responses to a variety of stimuli.

Now that we have surveyed the major structures of the central nervous system, we turn to a discussion of experimental methods in neuropsychology.

CHAPTER 4

Methods in Neuropsychology

ANATOMICAL METHODS
  Identifying Anatomical Connections
  Structural Imaging Methods
METHODS MEASURING FUNCTION
  Functional Imaging Methods
  Neurophysiological Methods
LESION METHODS
  Dissociation of Function
  Interpretation of Single and Double Dissociation
  Associated Impairments
  Dissociations as a Window on the Structure
    of Cognition and on Localization of Function
  Limits on the Interpretation of Dissociations

Further Thoughts on the Logic of Dissociation
    and Association
COMMISSUROTOMY
THE SODIUM AMOBARBITAL TEST
  Hemispheric Specialization and Handedness
  Use of the Sodium Amobarbital Test in the
    Neurosurgical Management of Focal Seizures
  The Testing Procedure
**STUDIES OF PEOPLE WITH BEHAVIORAL AND
  COGNITIVE ABNORMALITIES**
STUDIES OF NORMAL PEOPLE: LATERALITY STUDIES
SUMMARY

❖ ❖ ❖

We turn now to a consideration of the most important methods in neuropsychology, many of which we have already touched on in our earlier discussions. The data generated by these diverse methods are the soil out of which fruitful hypotheses, illuminating experiments, and novel theories are generated. It is therefore very important to understand the methods that are the basis for the inferences that experiments generate. Like the evil genie in the fairy tale who grants only the precise wish requesters ask for and not the wish they think they are making, nature answers precisely and only the question defined by the methodology of a particular ex-periment. This is not always the question we think we are asking.

In what follows we will consider (a) methods used to explore the nervous system's structures and its pathways of interconnection; (b) methods that measure functional aspects of the nervous system, such as level of glucose utilization or electrical activity; (c) lesion methods; (d) the study of patients who have undergone split-brain surgery; (e) the sodium amobarbital test; (f) the study of behavioral and cognitive abnormalities in people without detectable brain lesions; and (g) the study of normal human subjects.

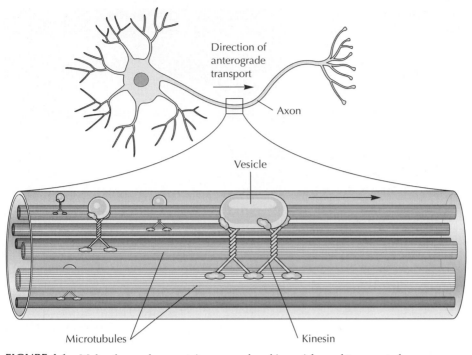

FIGURE 4.1   Molecules, such as proteins, are enclosed in vesicles and transported from their site of synthesis in the soma (cell body) to the axon terminal. The protein kinesin "walks" the vesicle down the microtubules. *(Adapted from Bear, Connors, & Paradiso, 1996, p. 38)*

ANATOMICAL METHODS

Identifying Anatomical Connections

We can identify structures within the nervous system in terms of their gross appearance. But in attempting to understand how the brain works, it is obviously useful to know as much as possible about the interconnections between different structures. Where a particular structure sends its efferents (output) and from where it receives its afferents (input) provide illuminating hints regarding the processes that it is mediating. In subsequent chapters we will see how useful information about anatomical connections can be in our attempts to understand brain-behavior relationships.

One way of determining the connections between structures is to trace the path of large **fiber tracts,** bundles of neurons stretching from one area of the nervous system to another. There are, however, obvi-ous limitations to this method; small fiber tracts will be undetected, and the precise origin and destination of those tracts that are visible will not be known. Fortunately there are some highly revealing methods that get around these problems.

TECHNIQUES USING AXOPLASMIC TRANSPORT
Axoplasmic transport is an active process whereby substances within a neuron are moved across its length. There are two types of axoplasmic transport. **Anterograde transport** conveys materials that are synthesized only in the cell body of the neuron, such as proteins, to the **axon terminal** (the transmitting end of the neuron). This process involves the storage of these materials in membrane-bound spherical spaces called **vesicles,** which then move down the length of the axon along **microtubules** (Figure 4.1). When a radioactive amino acid, such as proline, is injected into a particular region of the brain, it is taken up by the cell bodies of neurons in that region and then transported

to the axon terminals of those neurons. The animal is then sacrificed, and sections of the brain are placed next to a photographic plate so that the radioactivity within them exposes the film. This technique, known as **autoradiography,** detects the brain region or regions to which the injected region projects. There are two types of anterograde transport: slow (1–10 mm/day) and fast (up to 1,000 mm/day).

The second type of axoplasmic transport is called **retrograde transport,** and, as its name suggests, it moves substances in the opposite direction from that of anterograde transport, from the axon terminal to the cell body. The function of this direction of transport is not completely understood, but it is thought to provide a mechanism whereby information about the state of the axon terminal is communicated to the cell body, a kind of nervous system within the neuron, if you will. It so happens that there is an enzyme with the unlikely name of horseradish perioxidase (HRP) that is selectively taken up by axon terminals. It is then carried to the cell body by retrograde transport and can be visualized there. The horseradish perioxidase method thus complements methods utilizing anterograde transport by revealing the region or regions projecting *to* the injected area.

BIOCHEMICAL MICROARCHITECTURE   In our discussion of cortical visual areas in chapter 5 we will see that subregions within these areas can be defined in terms of their affinity for particular stains, cytochrome oxidase being one. Cytochrome oxidase is an enzyme that selectively binds to regions of relatively high metabolic activity; it therefore can serve to identify these regions. As we will see in chapter 5, regions defined by such a biochemical method can have distinctive physiological and anatomical characteristics, and the identification of these areas can therefore contribute to our understanding of the functional organization of the brain.

It is also possible, using sophisticated techniques, to stain tissue for the presence of particular neurotransmitters, the molecules released by axon terminals that activate neighboring neurons (see chapter 2). These techniques yield a description of major neurotransmitter pathways and systems within the brain.

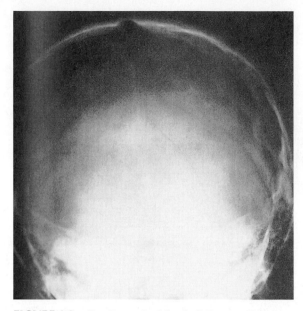

FIGURE 4.2   A radiograph of the skull. Because X rays are absorbed by bones and other tissues that absorb calcium, all structures appear light, and the differentiation of gray and white matter is not possible. *(From Kandel et al., 1995, p. 73)*

Structural Imaging Methods

There are a number of imaging techniques that can provide information about the structure of cerebral tissue. In addition, some imaging techniques provide a measure of the metabolic activity in different regions of the living brain; these techniques will be discussed in the next section. This is a rapidly developing area and one that has generated a great deal of excitement in recent years. Let us begin, however, with some of the more conventional techniques.

SKULL X RAY   The first radiological investigation of the brain consisted of simply x-raying the head (Figure 4.2). Although this reveals a good deal about the integrity of the skull (e.g., presence of fractures, etc.), it reveals little about the status of the brain tissue within. This is because the density of brain tissue does not vary greatly, so different parts of the brain absorb about the same quantity of X rays. This situation is analogous to shining a flashlight through a glass of water; no shadows emerge to hint at its inner

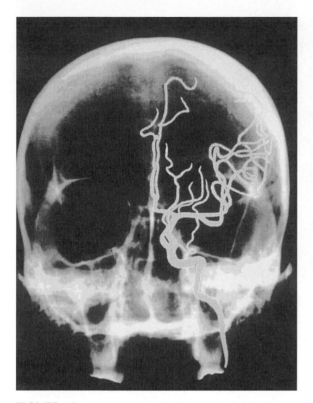

FIGURE 4.3   An angiogram in frontal view. The radio-paque dye injected into the internal carotid artery reveals the anterior and middle cerebral arteries. *(From Kandel et al., 1995, p. 73)*

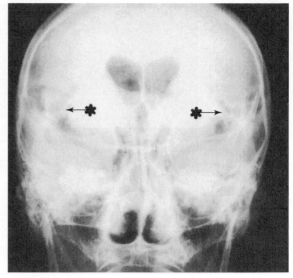

FIGURE 4.4   A pneumoencephalogram. The arrows with asterisks indicate air in the Sylvian fissure. *(From Kandel et al., 1995, p. 73)*

structure. So the problem became how to visualize structural differences (and changes) in an organ whose regions show little variation in their absorption of X rays.

CEREBRAL ANGIOGRAPHY AND PNEUMOEN-CEPHALOGRAPHY   Two early attempts to get around this problem were **angiography** (or arteriography) and **pneumoencephalography.** In the former procedure (Figure 4.3), a radiopaque (X-ray-absorbing) dye is injected into the cerebral circulation, making the vasculature (veins and arteries) visible on X ray. This allows the radiologist to infer the presence of structural changes in the brain (e.g., the presence of a tumor) by observing deviations from the normal spatial pattern

of the vasculature. The pneumoencephalogram, on the other hand, attempts to circumvent the virtually homogeneous density of the brain by draining the cerebral ventricles of cerebrospinal fluid and replacing it with air (Figure 4.4). This makes the ventricles less dense than the surrounding tissue, permitting detection of changes in their shape (due, for example, to the presence of cerebral atrophy or a tumor).

X-RAY COMPUTERIZED TOMOGRAPHY (CT) SCAN
In **computerized tomography (CT)** an X-ray beam is aimed through the head and then slowly rotated in an arc around the head to obtain a "shadow" of the brain from all angles (Figure 4.5). This information is then fed into a computer, which generates an image that depicts subtle changes in density and, in addition, generates an image of the brain in cross section. Initially the computer generates images of the brain in a series of horizontal sections (cuts); however, the computer can reconstruct the information to generate images of the brain in coronal and sagittal section as well. (See chapter 3 for a definition of the planes of these cuts.) This is a highly useful technique, one that revolution-

(A)

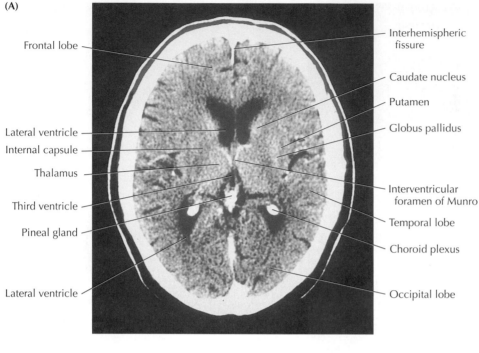

Frontal lobe

Interhemispheric fissure

Caudate nucleus

Putamen

Globus pallidus

Lateral ventricle

Internal capsule

Thalamus

Third ventricle

Pineal gland

Lateral ventricle

Interventricular foramen of Munro

Temporal lobe

Choroid plexus

Occipital lobe

(B)

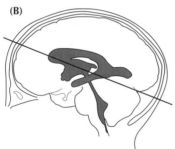

FIGURE 4.5   A CT scan in horizontal section passing through the cerebral hemispheres and diencephalon. *(From Kandel et al., 1995, p. 74)*

ized neuroradiology when it was introduced in the early 1970s.

MAGNETIC RESONANCE IMAGING (MRI)   This most recent development in imaging, **magnetic resonance imaging (MRI),** takes advantage of certain physical properties of hydrogen atoms. In particular, hydrogen atoms behave like spinning bar magnets in a magnetic field, and, in a high-magnitude magnetic field, they will line up in parallel. If radio waves are then bounced across these atoms, the waves will assume a characteristic pattern that is a function of the number of atoms present, which, in turn, is a function

of the density of the tissue. We have then a measure of tissue density that makes possible the formation of images that are far more sensitive to variations in tissue density than CT. The resolution of MRI is also significantly higher than that of CT (Figure 4.6).

METHODS MEASURING FUNCTION

The imaging techniques discussed so far reveal the structure of the brain. In this section we review methods that measure the brain's metabolic activity (functional imaging methods) or its electrical activity (neurophysiological methods).

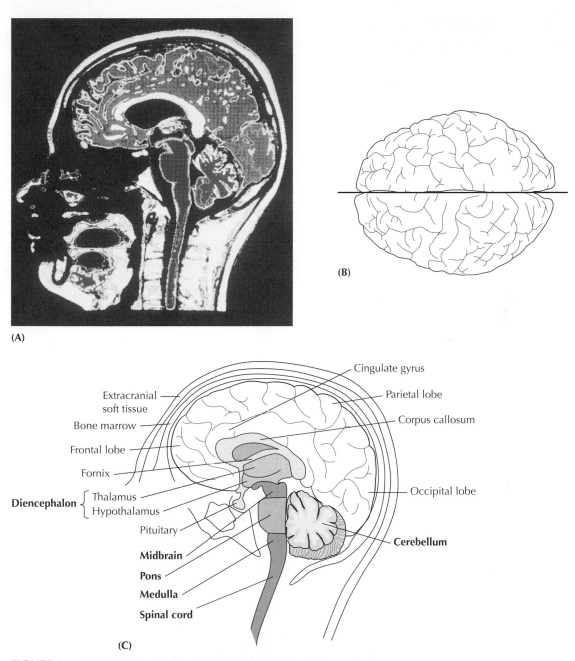

(A)

(B)

(C)

Cingulate gyrus

Parietal lobe

Corpus callosum

Occipital lobe

Cerebellum

Extracranial soft tissue

Bone marrow

Frontal lobe

Fornix

Diencephalon { Thalamus
              Hypothalamus

Pituitary

Midbrain

Pons

Medulla

Spinal cord

FIGURE 4.6   *(A)* An MRI scan of a midsagittal section through the cerebral hemispheres, corpus callosum, brain stem, and spinal cord. *(B)* A diagram showing the detail visible in the MRI scan. *(From Kandel et al., 1995, p. 80)*

Functional Imaging Methods

REGIONAL CEREBRAL BLOOD FLOW (rCBF)   The first reliable imaging method to measure cerebral functional activity was **regional cerebral blood flow (rCBF)**. In this method a radioactive isotope is inhaled or injected into the blood, and its distribution is then measured using a bank of sensors arranged systematically near the surface of the skull. The radioactive label thus is a marker for blood flow, which in turn is a correlate of brain metabolic activity. Using this method, it is in principle possible to visualize those brain areas that are most metabolically active during a particular activity. For example, when a subject is exposed to a visual stimulus, the occipital lobes in the posterior cortex (site of visual processing) show increased blood flow. Analogously, increased blood flow is seen in the motor cortex during movement and in the auditory cortex when a subject is exposed to sound. A subject who is speaking shows increased blood flow in Broca's area, and a subject attending to the meaning of words shows increased blood flow in Wernicke's area.

POSITRON EMISSION TOMOGRAPHY (PET)   Relative metabolic activity in the living animal or human can be measured by **positron emission tomography (PET)**. For this reason PET has been called in vivo functional autoradiography. One of its advantages is that it affords great versatility with regard to the atom or molecule being labeled.

The technology involved in PET is rather complicated, but, briefly stated, an unstable radioactive atom such as ^{15}O is injected into the subject. Within the brain this atom emits a positron, the antimatter equivalent of an electron. The positron travels a few millimeters before it loses kinetic energy and comes to rest. When this happens, the positron is attracted to a neighboring electron and, as they come together, they annihilate each other, releasing intense energy and two annihilation photons. These two photons leave the site of their creation in opposite directions at the speed of light. A ring of detectors surrounds the patient's head. These detectors are electronically coupled so that they record a radioactive event only when two detectors are struck simultaneously. This arrangement makes possible the precise measurement of the relative concentration of the labeled marker in different areas of the brain.

Using this technique, it can be shown that the primary sensory areas exhibit more metabolic activity during periods of stimulation. For example, when the eyes are open, the posterior occipital cortex shows a higher level of metabolic activity than when they are closed. In addition, a complex visual scene causes a different pattern of stimulation than either simple white light or the eyes-closed condition (Figure 4.7). Suppose, however, that we want to determine the pattern of brain activity associated with a complex cognitive process such as generating a verb that conveys the function of a heard noun (e.g., "cook" when the word "pot" is heard). This situation is complicated by the fact that many regions of the brain may be active during this task that are not directly related to word generation per se. These might include the auditory cortex, Wernicke's area, and Broca's area, among others.

Efforts to surmount this problem have centered on the **subtraction method,** a method developed by F. C. Donders in the 19th century and used extensively by Wilhelm Wundt and other structuralist psychologists, mostly in reaction-time experiments, during the early years of experimental psychology. When applied to PET studies, this method attempts to find a control task that is identical to the task under study except for one critical component. The record obtained during the control task is then subtracted from that obtained during the experimental task. We will see many examples of the use of the subtraction method in later discussions. For example, in chapter 5 we consider a PET study that attempts to identify in humans the area in the occipital cortex specialized for color vision. In this study the activity levels obtained when a subject viewed a black-and-white pattern were subtracted from the activity levels obtained while the same subject viewed a color pattern with the same spatial configuration. In that case the subtraction method yielded a rather precise localization of an area presumed to be specialized for color vision.

SINGLE PHOTON EMISSION COMPUTERIZED TOMOGRAPHY (SPECT)   Another technique, **single photon emission computerized tomography (SPECT),**

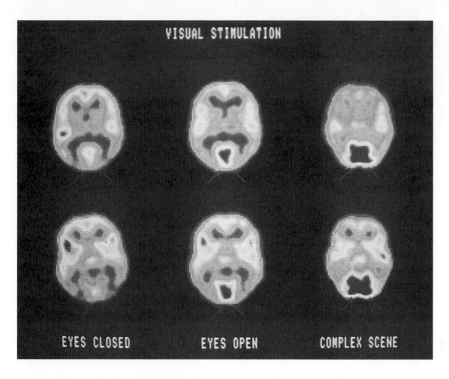

FIGURE 4.7 PET scans showing brain activation with *(A)* eyes closed, *(B)* eyes open viewing white light, and *(C)* eyes open viewing a complex scene. *(From Kandel et al., 1995, p. 76)*

makes use of the fact that certain commercially available tracers emit photons; this permits measurement of relative metabolic activity in a manner roughly analogous to PET. The advantage of this method is that these tracers are far less expensive than the isotopes used in PET, which, with extremely short half-lives, must be created in an on-site cyclotron. The negative characteristic of SPECT is that it has less spatial resolution than PET.

FUNCTIONAL MAGNETIC RESONANCE IMAGING (fMRI) We have seen that MRI provides high-resolution images that are sensitive to subtle variations in tissue density. MRI has yet another important feature: It is sensitive to the chemical environment of neural tissue. It is thus able to monitor function and, when employed in this way, is referred to as **functional MRI (fMRI).** Active neurons increase blood flow in their immediate neighborhood. The resulting increase in hemoglobin changes the magnetic properties of the blood, and this is detected

by fMRI. This technique has the advantage of not requiring injection of an isotope, decreasing both the risk to the patient and the expense of the procedure. In addition, because a structural image is obtained at the same time as the functional mapping, the accuracy of correlation between function and structure afforded by this method is greatly enhanced. Finally, fMRI has higher resolution than PET.

PROBLEMS IN INTERPRETING FUNCTIONAL IMAGING STUDIES Although functional imaging studies are highly informative, their interpretation can present problems. We look at three of these.

First, for all of the subtraction method's apparent plausibility, the interpretation of experiments using the method has some potential problems. Most important is the assumption that complex processes can be analyzed into one or more simple processes plus a process specific to the complex task. It was accumulating doubts about the validity of this additivity assumption that ultimately limited the usefulness of the subtraction method as an experimental paradigm in psychology, despite its prolific use by structural psychologists for several decades following its introduction by Donders.

To illustrate this problem, consider the study, which we discussed earlier in the section on PET, that attempted to identify the area specialized for color perception in human subjects. Underlying the use of the subtraction method in that experiment is the assumption that viewing the color pattern results in the same brain activity as that involved in the processing of form in the black-and-white pattern plus activity specific to color perception. It can be appreciated that this may in fact not be the case; the processing of form in the presence of color may involve brain structures and brain activity very different from the processing of form in the black-and-white condition.

A second problem in the interpretation of functional imaging studies arises from the fact that the time course of events that these methods directly measure is slow (on the order of minutes), whereas the neural events inferred from these direct measures take place over milliseconds. The low time resolution of these procedures raises the question of the extent to which these measures are assessing relatively long-term brain states rather than the specific correlates of distinct psychological processes.

Third, despite the clear correlation between sensory stimulation in a given modality and the activity level of cortical areas initially processing that information, an increase in the activity of an area during a *complex* task does not necessarily mean that that area is critical for the function in question. The change in activity may be an indirect effect of change in some other area or areas. This is a particularly important consideration when assessing the metabolic correlates of a relatively long-term state such as a psychiatric disorder. Abnormal metabolism in a given region does not necessarily indicate that the abnormality in that region is the cause of the disorder. The observed abnormality may instead be an epiphenomenon, a correlate of the effects of a primary abnormality in an entirely different area. Thus, although PET studies have provided promising insights into the cerebral metabolic correlates of psychological processes (and are likely to be even more useful in the future, as the methodology

is refined), one must interpret findings using this method with particular caution.

Neurophysiological Methods

In contrast to functional imaging methods, neurophysiological methods, which measure brain electrical activity, have the advantage of measuring neural events more directly and with a much higher time resolution. We consider several such methods in this section.

SINGLE-CELL RECORDING   **Single-cell recording** involves inserting an exceedingly small diameter electrode into a single neuron and then measuring changes in the cell's electrical potential. This results in a record of the cell's activity, its frequency of firing. As we will discuss in more detail in later chapters, when this activity is in response to sensory stimulation, we define a given cell's **receptive field** as that stimulus which causes the cell to fire maximally or minimally. Single-cell recording thus measures the activity of an individual cell at a particular time and within a particular environmental and/or behavioral context.

Although this approach has the disadvantage of assessing only a small proportion of cells in any given area of the brain, data derived from this method have been enormously illuminating. To take just one example, it is this method that revealed the presence of specialization and localization of sensory/perceptual processing within what had traditionally been known as association cortex, cortical areas in which such specialization and localization were thought to be completely absent. This discovery has caused some radical revisions in our views of cortical processing, which we discuss at greater length in chapter 5.

ELECTROENCEPHALOGRAPHY (EEG)   The **electroencephalogram (EEG),** invented by Hans Berger in the 1920s, is a measure of brain electrical activity derived from a bank of electrodes positioned on the scalp. Since the electrodes have the skull and other tissues between them and the brain, the signal is weak and represents the collective activity of a diffuse collection of neurons. Thus, EEG is a bit like putting a stethoscope up to the outer wall of a gymnasium and listening to the fluctuations of volume

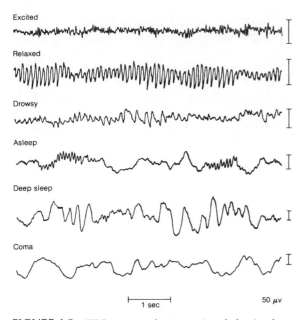

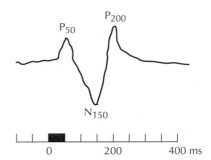

FIGURE 4.9   An ERP in the auditory cortex in response to auditory stimulation (blackened area). Note the two positive waves and the single negative wave, designated with their latency in milliseconds (ms).

FIGURE 4.8   EEG patterns during various behavioral states in humans. *(From Penfield & Jaspers, 1954 [in Kolb & Whishaw, 1996, p. 78])*

from the crowd within. This technique is useful for the detection and localization of seizure activity in the brain, and it has also been used to study such phenomena as sleep and the effect of drugs on brain activity. Some patterns of EEG activity characteristic of specific sleep stages and levels of consciousness are shown in Figure 4.8. Recently, there has been growing interest in using computerized methods to analyze EEG activity. These promising methods might make it possible to better quantify and localize EEG activity and may contribute to the further understanding of brain-behavior relationships.

EVENT-RELATED POTENTIALS (ERPs)   Event-related potentials (ERPs) are measurements of the brief change in EEG activity that occurs in a particular area of cortex after a specific event, such as the pattern of activity in the auditory cortex after the presentation of a tone. Investigators have also attempted to detect ERPs associated with more complex and differentiated stimuli, such as words and faces. Because the effect of such stimuli is difficult to detect, due to background neural activity, investigators using ERPs ex-

pose their subjects to repeated stimulus presentations and then compute the average response.

Typically, an ERP takes the form of a series of positive and negative waves that are designated P and N, respectively. Different positive and negative waves are often identified with the time in milliseconds between the onset of the stimulus and the peak's appearance (Figure 4.9). For example, a particular wave might be designated P_{150} or N_{300}. This technique is used clinically to assess the integrity of areas of the brain involved in a particular sensory modality, such as vision. For example, the response of brain areas involved in vision to a flashing light might be assessed. When used in this way, this method is sometimes referred to as **evoked potential.**

ELECTROCORTICOGRAPHY (ECo)   Electrocorticography (ECo) involves stimulating the exposed cortex of a patient during surgery with a low-voltage electrode. This is essentially a refinement of the procedure utilized by Fritsch and Hitzig in their discovery of the motor cortex in dogs in 1870. The American surgeon R. Bartholow first reported its use with humans in 1874, but the earliest systematic use of this procedure as a method for understanding brain-behavior relationships was the work of Wilder Penfield and his colleagues at the Montreal Neurological Institute. They used the procedure to identify specific areas of the cortex by assessing the functional effect of stimulation. This was necessary to allow Penfield to carry out a specially developed neurosurgical procedure for the relief of seizures. We must digress briefly to explain the procedure.

Most patients with cerebral seizures have reasonably good control when they use an appropriate anticonvulsant medication; this is one of the success stories of modern clinical pharmacology. Unfortunately, however, about 20% of patients are unable to achieve good control of their seizures even after many years of trials on all available medications. These patients may have 30 or more seizures each day, severely compromising the quality of their life and perhaps even being life-threatening.

Of those patients who cannot achieve significant help from available medications, about half benefit from the surgical procedure developed by Penfield. These are patients whose seizure focus (area from which the seizures originate) is in an area of cortex that can be surgically removed without producing an impairment worse than the seizure disorder. (Removing tissue from one of the language areas would, for example, produce such an impairment.) The 50% or so of patients with pharmacologically intractable epilepsy who do not benefit from this procedure are those with a seizure focus in one of the functionally critical cortical areas or those with seizures that originate in the brain stem. Using a range of refined assessment techniques (including electroencephalography, various radiological and other imaging methods, and neuropsychological assessment), it is possible to determine whether a particular patient has a cortical seizure focus and, if so, where in the cortex it is located.

Once it is determined that a candidate for this procedure has seizures that originate from a cortical focus and once the location of that focus is identified, the patient is brought to surgery to remove the epileptogenic (seizure-causing) area. When the cortex is exposed, however, the surgeon does not see the neat and tidy pattern of sulci and gyri typically depicted in neuroanatomy textbooks. Instead, what appears is the rich vasculature and membrane that overlie the cortex, rendering its pattern unrecognizable to even the most experienced neurosurgeon. It is at this point that cortical stimulation becomes indispensable. Using it, the surgeon can identify sensory, motor, and language areas based on the patient's response to stimulation. The patient must be awake to participate

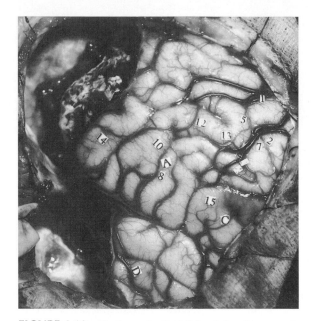

FIGURE 4.10   Photograph of a left frontal and temporal lobectomy at the time of surgery. The numbers indicate responses to electrical stimulation: for example, *14*, saying the months of the year interrupted; *15*, mistake in saying the days of the week forward, corrected after withdrawal of electrode. *(From Rasmussen & Milner, 1975, p. 241)*

in this procedure; the procedure is therefore performed under local anesthetic. Thus, if the surgeon's stimulating electrode elicits feeling in the arm, it may be inferred that the sensory cortex is being stimulated. Similarly, if a patient responds with a twitch of the hand, this identifies the motor cortex as the area of stimulation. Language areas can also be mapped out because stimulation to either will interrupt speech that is in progress (Figure 4.10).

Using this technique, the surgeon can identify major landmarks on the cortical surface and thereby find his or her bearings so that the previously identified epileptogenic area of cortex can be removed. As we will see, much can be learned about the brain from this technique, including the topographical organization (mapping of the body surface) of the motor and somatosensory cortices and the extent of the language areas. Perhaps the best-known result of this work is Penfield's report that the stimulation of certain cortical areas produced very vivid and realistic experiences that patients considered to be memories. We will have more to say about this and other work using this technique in subsequent chapters.

MAGNETOENCEPHALOGRAPHY (MEG)   A new technique, **magnetoencephalography (MEG),** also called magnetic source imaging, measures the small magnetic fields generated by the electrical currents of neurons. This technique appears to be promising.

In closing this section, we should note that advances in our understanding are most likely to be achieved through a combination of structural methods and functional methods. For example, those investigators using functional imaging methods (e.g., rCBF, PET, fMRI) are keenly aware of the need to more precisely localize areas of modified activity. This can be achieved by using concurrent measures of structure, such as MRI. In addition, these same investigators, aware of the problems inherent in the slow time course of their functional imaging techniques, are attempting to surmount this problem by using concurrent electrophysiological measures that have relatively rapid time resolution, such as EEG and MEG.

LESION METHODS

We have already seen how illuminating the study of the behavioral and cognitive effects of brain lesions—damage to the brain from whatever cause—can be for an understanding of how the brain works. The basic strategy in lesion studies with humans and with other animals is the same: the investigation of the effect of damage to a particular area. In lesion studies with lower animals, however, investigators can study the effects of precisely localized lesions. This allows for the explicit testing of hypotheses. In contrast, lesion studies in humans necessarily concern themselves with the effect of lesions that have already occurred through disease or trauma.

Despite this disadvantage, studies of lesions in humans have the advantage of allowing the assessment of functions that are specifically human or at least more developed in humans, such as language, problem solving, and planning. In addition, the effects of lesions in humans are sometimes more discernible because patients may be able to provide a phenomeno-

logical account of their altered experience. This is poignantly seen in a case study described by Oliver Sacks[1] of a painter with achromatopsia, color blindness due to cortical lesion. Sacks's patient complained despairingly about his achromatic world. Interestingly, because wavelength discrimination is retained in achromatopsia, the condition would be difficult to detect in other animals. Unless some specific experimental manipulations are employed, animals could perform discrimination learning tasks using their intact wavelength discrimination capacity. They would be unable to tell us about catastrophic change in their experience of color.

Dissociation of Function

There are two fundamental (and related) ways in which lesion methods (and other neuropsychological methods, for that matter) further our knowledge: by advancing analysis of the components of cognition and by providing evidence of localization of function. To explain, we must elaborate on a concept we have already mentioned: **dissociation of function.** This concept has at least two meanings. On the behavioral/cognitive level (knowing nothing about the particular lesion involved) dissociation of function denotes the finding that performance on one task is impaired while performance on a second is not. It is in this sense that functions or processes are said to be dissociable, or separable. This dissociation of function may be reciprocal: In some individuals function A is found to be impaired and B is not, whereas in other cases function B is impaired and A is not. On the other hand, it may not be reciprocal: In some instances function A is found to be impaired and B is not, but in no cases is impairment in function B seen

---

1. Oliver Sacks is a neurologist who has become widely known for his well-written case studies of patients with striking neurological and neuropsychological symptoms. He writes in a powerfully descriptive style that poignantly conveys a vivid impression of the disorders he studies. In addition, he possesses a broadly humanistic perspective from which he attempts to address all facets of neuropsychological impairment and to draw implications from these disorders for an understanding of the human condition in general.

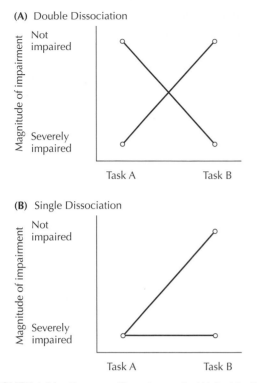

FIGURE 4.11 Patterns of impairment in *(A)* double dissociation and *(B)* single dissociation. Each line depicts the pattern of performance of one individual or group of individuals. *(From McCarthy & Warrington, 1990, p. 19)*

without impairment in function A. The first instance is referred to as **double dissociation,** and the second as **single dissociation** (Figure 4.11).

To take a simple example, deafness and blindness are doubly dissociable. Looking at a number of different cases, we find instances of one impairment in the absence of the other (although there are, of course, also cases in which they both are found). Similarly, Broca's aphasia and Wernicke's aphasia are doubly dissociable. In contrast, the inability to read visual material and blindness are singly dissociable. The inability to read may be seen in the presence of normal vision, but the ability to read visually presented words is not found together with blindness. To take another example, impaired ability to coordinate the fluent production of speech in Broca's aphasia and paralysis of the vocal musculature are singly

dissociable. Impairment in fluent speech production may be seen in the absence of impairment in movement of the vocal musculature (Broca's aphasia), but preservation of fluent speech production is not seen when the vocal musculature is paralyzed.

Interpretation of Single and Double Dissociation

If we consider the inferences that can be drawn from these two types of dissociation, we find that double dissociation provides evidence that two functions are relatively separate or independent (e.g., audition and vision; fluent speech and language comprehension). Single dissociation, on the other hand, indicates that the two functions are separate to some degree but that one of them is necessary for the other. This suggests a kind of hierarchical relationship between the two (e.g., the capacity to see words is necessary for reading visual material; the capacity to move the vocal musculature is necessary for fluent speech).

Of course, in the world of data, all is not so clearcut. The person with impaired visual acuity who is not totally blind can nevertheless read, though less rapidly. The person with partial paralysis of the vocal musculature still produces comprehensible speech, though slow and slurred. But this too is informative; it tells us that although the first function may be a prerequisite for the second, that second function is nevertheless relatively separate. This may be confirmed as we assess the second function by bypassing the impaired first function. Thus we find that people with acquired blindness are able to read raised letters that are sensed by the fingers and those with completely paralyzed speech musculature are able to express themselves linguistically by writing.

Associated Impairments

Just as dissociation of function indicates that the functions in question are to some degree separate and independent, so the consistent finding of **association** (consistent co-occurrence of two or more impairments) suggests that the behavioral or cognitive phenomena in question are a manifestation of one underlying process. For example, impaired speech comprehension and fluent but disrupted verbal output ("word salad") occur together in Wernicke's aphasia. This fact suggests that the disruption of a single underlying process is responsible for both impairments.

Dissociations as a Window on the Structure of Cognition and on Localization of Function

So far we have been talking as if we knew nothing about the lesions producing the impairments we are studying. This is often in fact the case, as, for example, in the study of children with dyslexia. It can be seen that if dissociations are found, we are in a position to understand something new about the nature of cognition, whether or not we know anything new about localization of function. In this way these methods contribute to an understanding of cognition, without necessarily revealing the regions of the brain mediating these processes. If we do have knowledge of the area in the brain that, when damaged, produces the impairment in question, this adds an additional dimension to our inquiry. Not only do we have the basis for making inferences about the structure of cognition, we also are in a position to say something about what parts of the brain are necessary for the mediation of certain functions. Dissociation that is informative in the context of localization of function takes one of two general forms. In single dissociation, a lesion in region X produces an impairment on task A but not task B, whereas a lesion in region Y does not produce an impairment in either task. In double dissociation, a lesion in region X produces impairment in task A but not impairment in task B, and a lesion in region Y produces impairment in task B but not task A.[2] Figure 4.12 illustrates these two forms of dissociation.

The finding of a single or a double dissociation is highly informative. It tells us that a particular observed impairment resulting from a specific lesion is not due to generalized, nonspecific brain dysfunc-

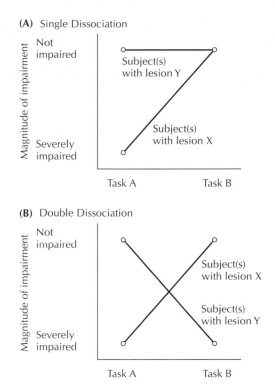

(A) Single Dissociation

(B) Double Dissociation

FIGURE 4.12 *(A)* Single dissociation and *(B)* double dissociation used to infer which cerebral areas are involved in the mediation of particular functions. *(From McCarthy & Warrington, 1990, p. 19)*

tion because the second lesion in another location does not produce the impairment. It also tells us that the lesion in question does not produce impairment in all tasks because relatively good performance is seen in the second task. Taken together, such findings provide important information about the relationship between particular brain regions and specific functions. It should be noted that a dissociation does not require completely normal performance on certain tasks. What is central to this method is the pattern of relative preservation and relative impairment.

Limits on the Interpretation of Dissociations

As with all scientific methodology, however, the process of making inferences from lesion data must be conducted with extreme care. The presence of a

---

2. An example of double dissociation is the finding that right parietal-lobe lesions produce impairment in spatial processing but not nonverbal memory, whereas right temporal-lobe lesions produce impairment in nonverbal memory but not spatial processing.

dissociation does not tell us that the impaired function is *localized* in the area of the lesion. It tells us only that the lesioned area is *necessary* for the function in question and that the other lesioned area, which did not produce the impairment, is not. Thus, other regions outside the area of either lesion, perhaps the entire rest of the brain, may also be involved in the normal processing of the function under consideration. In this sense the lesion method tells us something about which areas are involved in a particular function and which areas are not involved, but it does not tell us where in the brain the function is localized.

Adding to this conceptual limitation in determining localization of function is the technical problem of identifying the site of a lesion. Despite the development of the remarkable modern techniques for visualizing the brain discussed earlier, it is rarely possible to designate precisely the exact location of a lesion in the living brain. In addition, a lesion may exert temporary disruptive effects on neighboring tissue. This effect, termed **diaschisis,** may be due to swelling, bleeding, or other short-term pathological processes. Moreover, through the destruction of connections between neurons, a lesion may cause long-term disruptive effects in distant regions of the brain.

Further Thoughts on the Logic of Dissociation and Association

A few additional thoughts about the localizing implications of double dissociation and association may be useful at this point. In double dissociation each lesion-impairment pair serves as a control for the other. In this sense double dissociation is highly efficient: In the case of each of the two lesions we learn both that the region it has damaged is involved in a particular function and also that the region is not involved in some other function. There is another sense in which double dissociation is useful, however. Single dissociation leaves open the possibility that the critical lesion produced its effect, not because the area it disrupted is specifically involved in the particular function in question, but because that region of the brain is simply more important in some general sense. To draw on a social analogy, imagine that we shut down a town's power station and see that

school classes are disrupted; then in a "control" town we shut down a small gas station and see no associated disruption in the schools. It would clearly be an error to conclude on the basis of these data that power stations are specifically involved in education. They simply have a pervasive and general importance, whereas the single gas station does not.

The demonstration of a double dissociation reduces the likelihood that findings are due to such a nonspecific effect because each lesion has been shown to produce a specific and proportionately significant effect. To modify our metaphor, suppose we shut down the power plant in one town and all gas stations in the other town. Both will disrupt school, so school disruption is now understood to be a nonspecific effect. The double dissociation would be loss of electric power and loss of mobility of automobiles. These are both significant disruptions, and they are both specific. So we are on firmer grounds for inferring localization of function.

Finally, let us consider associated impairments further. We said earlier that failure to demonstrate dissociation between two functions suggests that they have one underlying mechanism. As you might expect, from the point of view of localization of function, the demonstration of association suggests that a single region is necessary for the different functions under consideration. On the other hand, when impairment in two functions usually but not always co-occurs, this demonstrates that the functions are in fact separable but that brain areas necessary for their mediation are in close proximity. We shall find that Wernicke's aphasia and apraxia, the impaired performance of learned movements in the absence of elementary motor impairment, are an example of two such frequently co-occurring but sometimes dissociable disorders. This has led to the hypothesis that a cortical area adjacent to Wernicke's area is critical for the execution of learned actions (see chapter 9).

COMMISSUROTOMY

Commissurotomy, or as it is sometimes called, **split-brain surgery,** involves the cutting of the corpus callosum, the band of fibers connecting the two hemispheres of the brain. As with the antiseizure surgery described earlier, the purpose is to control seizures, although in this case the rationale is different. Instead of removing the seizure focus, commissurotomy cuts the major fiber tracts between the two cerebral hemispheres in an attempt to limit the spread of seizures between the hemispheres and thereby reduce their severity.

This surgery, which began to be regularly conducted in the 1960s (although a number of patients had received a similar procedure in the 1930s), afforded the opportunity to study the effects of functionally separating the two hemispheres. Actually, "functional separation" is an overstatement because there are significant fiber tracts in addition to the corpus callosum that transmit certain types of information between the two hemispheres. Nevertheless, this procedure radically reduces the neural connections between the hemispheres and thereby affords the opportunity to investigate what each hemisphere is able to do in relative isolation.

Roger Sperry and his colleagues pioneered this work in the 1960s, and since then many investigators have conducted similar work. In the 1950s Sperry and Myers had conducted extensive work along these lines with other animals. By cutting the corpus callosum and the optic chiasm (not cut in human patients) in cats, Sperry and Myers showed that each hemisphere functioned independently on certain tasks. In the intact animal, input to one eye would be projected to both hemispheres because some of the fibers in the optic nerve would cross over to the contralateral hemisphere at the optic chiasm while others continued on to the ipsilateral hemisphere. Cutting the optic chiasm, the point where some of the fibers in the optic nerve cross over to the other side of the brain, confined input to one eye to the ipsilateral hemisphere. If such an animal also has a corpus callosum section, the functioning of each hemisphere can be tested by confining input to one eye.

Using this paradigm, Sperry and Myers were able to assess the independent functioning of the two hemispheres. For example, if one eye is covered, an animal with a section of the corpus callosum is able to learn a visual discrimination (e.g., the peanut is under the card with horizontal stripes). Then, if the covered eye is uncovered and the eye that had been exposed to the vi-

sual discrimination learning task is covered, the investigators showed that the animal demonstrated no learning and could actually be taught the opposite visual discrimination. Thus, the two hemispheres could be shown to have learned opposite discriminations and to retain these independently. These and other findings showed that after sectioning of the corpus callosum, learning and other cognitive processes could be confined to one cerebral hemisphere.

The potential usefulness of this method as a source of information about hemispheric specialization in humans would seem to be obvious. Research with humans presented certain technical difficulties, however. In particular, as has been mentioned, in humans the optic chiasm was not sectioned. Because of the way the eye and the brain are hooked up, a topic that we will consider in some detail in chapter 5, input from each eye projects to both hemispheres. Therefore, confining input to one hemisphere is not as simple as covering one eye. What is required is confining input to one visual field, because each visual field (left or right) projects to the contralateral hemisphere. In free vision such restriction is impossible because the movement of the head and eye ensures that a visual stimulus in a specific location in space will, in a brief period of time, appear in both the left and right visual fields.

These and other difficulties in confining sensory input to one hemisphere probably account for the fact that an earlier investigation of a series of patients who had undergone commissurotomy, carried out by the neurosurgeon Akelaitis in the 1930s, failed to yield evidence of behavioral deficits. This prompted some to suggest, not without a dash of humor, that this massive fiber bundle comprising 100 million axons merely served the structural function of mechanically keeping the two hemispheres from falling apart.

However, when commissurotomy again began to be used for therapeutic purposes in the 1960s, the prior work of Sperry and Myers with animals made it clear that some effects should be detectable. Based on this earlier work, Sperry and his colleagues were able to use techniques that would make these patients a highly fruitful source of insight into hemispheric specialization. For example, to restrict visual stimuli to one hemisphere, patients were exposed to tachistoscopically (rapidly) presented stimuli, each presented for 100 milliseconds or less, to one visual field only. Presentation time was thus too brief for subjects to move their heads or eyes and thereby place the stimulus in the opposite visual field. Using this and other ingenious techniques, Sperry showed, for example, that whereas a word flashed to the right visual field (i.e., left hemisphere) of a commissurotomy patient could be read aloud, words flashed to the left visual field (i.e., right hemisphere) could not.

Something analogous happens for stimuli presented through touch. An object that is out of sight and palpated by the right hand of a split-brain patient can be readily named. In contrast, an object palpated by the left hand cannot, although the left hand (right hemisphere) can be shown to have recognized the object if recognition is assessed by means that do not require verbal processing. For example, the left hand can pick out an object that it previously examined from a collection of objects. As one would expect, transfer between the hands is not possible in split-brain patients because the information from the somatosensory cortex of one hemisphere cannot be communicated across the corpus callosum to the somatosensory cortex of the other hemisphere.

In the case of audition the situation is more complicated because the connections from each ear to the cortex are both ipsilateral and contralateral. In other words, each ear projects to both hemispheres. Based on this anatomical fact, one would not expect effects analogous to those we have just discussed in vision and touch to apply to audition. In fact, if we simply present information to one or the other ear, no such effect is seen. For example, a split-brain patient can repeat words presented (through an earphone) to the left ear alone or the right ear alone. If, however, a commissurotomy patient is presented different verbal stimuli simultaneously to the two ears (a technique termed **dichotic listening**), an effect is found. Thus, when different words or numbers are presented to the two ears simultaneously, those presented to the right ear (contralateral to the left hemisphere) are reported, whereas those presented to the left ear are very seldom reported (Figure 4.13). This phenomenon is called **suppression;** it is as if the

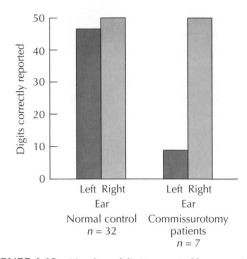

FIGURE 4.13   Number of digits reported by commissurotomy patients and normal control subjects in a dichotic listening task. *(From Milner, Taylor, & Sperry, 1968)*

right-ear input inhibits the recognition of simultaneous left-ear input. Suppression demonstrates that although the anatomy of the auditory system does not exhibit the manifest contralaterality seen in the visual and somatosensory systems, it nevertheless turns out that the contralateral connections are the most important in audition as well. We shall see shortly that a right-ear effect for verbal material is also seen in normal subjects, although the effect is much weaker than that seen in commissurotomy patients.

We will have much more to say about commissurotomy as we discuss particular abnormalities. Before we leave this discussion, however, let's consider the impact of commissurotomy on overall behavior. It might be expected that the two disconnected hemispheres would be in some kind of competition. There have been some silly dramatic plots written on this theme. In one of them a man found, to his distress, that his right hand wanted to murder his girlfriend but his left hand loved her. The story had an unhappy ending: His left hand was unsuccessful in using an ax to chop off his right hand and thus save his beloved, and the right hand's response to this foiled plan was not a kindly one.

TABLE 4.1   Language lateralization in right- and left-handed patients without early brain lesions as determined by the sodium amobarbital test.

Handedness	N	Hemisphere (%)		
		Left	Bilateral	Right
Right	140	96	0	4
Left	122	70	15	15

From Milner, Branch, & Rasmussen, 1964 (in McCarthy & Warrington, 1990, p. 8)

Table 4.2   The percentage of right-handed and left-handed patients with aphasia who had lesions in the left and in the right hemisphere.

Handedness	N	Side of Lesion (%)	
		Left	Right
Right	641	97	3
Left	82	65	35

From McCarthy & Warrington, 1990, p. 6

It turns out that commissurotomy patients do briefly experience something like this, although, thankfully, generally with less melodrama. A patient may find herself in a state of indecision as to what to wear as she selects one dress with her left hand and a different one with her right. Interestingly, this competition or incongruity is of brief duration, disappearing shortly after surgery. It is unclear how this happens. It may be that other interhemispheric connections mediate a high level of emotional and motivational coordination between the two hemispheres. In addition, to the extent that they remain independent, the two hemispheres must be like two individuals in an intimate relationship who, though separate, yet are highly sensitive to one another and modify their behavior accordingly.

THE SODIUM AMOBARBITAL TEST

The **sodium amobarbital test,** which has emerged out of the surgery for the relief of seizures that we have already discussed in some detail, creates a transient and reversible inactivation of one cerebral hemisphere. To explain its use, a brief digression is necessary. Up to this point we have been talking as if all persons had speech represented in the left hemisphere and spatial and other nonverbal functions in the right hemisphere. We already alluded to the fact that this is an oversimplification, and our consideration of the sodium amobarbital test provides a useful context to explain this further.

Hemispheric Specialization and Handedness

For right-handed individuals the assumption we have made is true in about 98% of cases. For left-handers the situation is different. About 70% of them have speech in the left hemisphere, as do the vast majority of right-handers. However, 15% have speech in the right hemisphere, and 15% have speech represented in both hemispheres (Table 4.1). These findings could be (and have been) inferred from the study of the relationship between side of cerebral lesion and onset of aphasia in right- and left-handers (Table 4.2). However, the sodium amobarbital test provides a more direct method of assessing this relationship, one that can be used to make this determination in people who are not aphasic.

Use of the Sodium Amobarbital Test in the Neurosurgical Management of Focal Seizures

Surgery for the relief of seizures involves the removal of an area of cortex that has been judged to be the origin of the seizures in a particular patient. It is critical that the surgeon not inflict an aphasia, a more debilitating disorder than the seizure disorder. The surgeon must know with the highest degree of certainty possible whether the area to be removed lies within the language hemisphere. If it does, then extreme care must be taken to avoid damage to the language areas. In contrast, if it is known that the area to be removed lies in the nonlanguage hemisphere, the surgeon can be less conservative in the removal, including all tissue that is suspected to be part of the seizure focus, without making special provision for sparing the language areas.

The Testing Procedure

The sodium amobarbital test was designed to address this need. In this test the barbiturate sodium amobarbital is injected into the internal carotid artery; from there it enters the cerebral circulation and passes into the ipsilateral middle cerebral artery. This causes the temporary anesthetization of that hemisphere. Just before the drug is injected, the patient is instructed to extend her arms and to wiggle her toes. After injection, as the drug takes effect, the patient suffers a hemiparesis (a severe weakness of one side of the body), such as one might experience after a stroke. During the 7 or so minutes that the drug is confined to one hemisphere, tests of various functions, particularly language functions, are conducted. As would be expected, if the language hemisphere has been injected, the patient manifests aphasic symptoms. In contrast, if the nonlanguage hemisphere has been injected, the patient will continue to understand and produce speech but will have difficulty with tasks that involve the nonlanguage hemisphere, such as copying geometric figures or remembering faces. After about 7 minutes, the drug circulates out of the hemisphere on the side of injection and enters the general circulation, and its effect on the brain rapidly tapers off. On the day following the first injection, the patient goes through the procedure again, but this time the internal carotid artery on the other side is injected and the effects of temporarily anesthetizing the other hemisphere are assessed. This serves to corroborate the findings of the first test and may provide additional information, such as evidence of bilateral speech representation.

The sodium amobarbital test thus serves the critical role of providing the surgeon with information about whether the intended removal is in the language hemisphere in patients, such as left-handers, in whom atypical speech representation is relatively likely. In addition, this test affords the opportunity to advance our understanding of hemispheric spe-

Table 4.3 Language lateralization in right- and left-handed patients as determined by the transient effects of administration of unilateral electroconvulsive therapy.

Handedness	N	Hemisphere (%)		
		Left	Bilateral	Right
Right	53	98	0	2
Left	30	70	6	23

From McCarthy & Warrington, 1990, p. 8

cialization. For example, it provides information about the relationship between hemispheric dominance for speech and handedness that corroborates and refines inferences derived from the transient effects of unilateral electroconvulsive shock (Table 4.3) and the effects of unilateral cerebral lesions (see Table 4.2). In the following chapters we will refer to reported results of the sodium amobarbital test in relation to a variety of topics.

STUDIES OF PEOPLE WITH BEHAVIORAL AND COGNITIVE ABNORMALITIES

In an earlier section we discussed the concept of dissociation of function and how informative such findings can be for an understanding of cognition, even when we have no information about a possible lesion. An example is a double dissociation seen among children with different kinds of reading disabilities who have no direct evidence of cerebral lesion. Among dyslexic children, some are able to read words by sound but not directly from the visual percept (i.e., sight reading). Such persons with **dyseidetic dyslexia** are thus able to sound out phonologically regular words and nonsense words but cannot read phonologically irregular words such as *yacht* or *ache*. In contrast, other persons show the opposite pattern: disrupted phonological decoding and intact sight reading (termed **dysphonetic dyslexia**). These persons are thus able to read irregular words but not unknown phonologically regular words or nonsense syllables. This double dissociation suggests that phonemic decoding and the decoding involved in sight reading are different and independent. We can draw inferences from such dissociations even though we do not know the sites of lesion in these dyslexic children or even if lesions are in fact present.

STUDIES OF NORMAL PEOPLE: LATERALITY STUDIES

Normal subjects obviously do not provide the possibility of studying hemispheric specialization afforded by patients with cerebral lesions or who have undergone commissurotomy. However, through the use of special techniques, the study of normal subjects can nevertheless extend our understanding of brain-behavior relationships. These studies, termed collectively **laterality studies,** generally take the form of presenting information in such a way that it reaches one hemisphere via more direct pathways (and hence slightly faster) than it reaches the other hemisphere and then measuring the resulting small differences in accuracy and/or speed of processing.

For example, if a visual stimulus—say, a word—is presented very briefly via a tachistoscope, it can be made to fall in only one visual field. It has been found that the subject's processing of that word (as assessed by the subject's simply reading it aloud or making some semantic decision about it) is slightly more accurate and more rapid (on the order of 100 ms) when it is presented to the right visual field. This difference is a function of the directness of anatomical connection between visual field and cerebral hemisphere. Information presented to the right visual field projects directly to the left (language) hemisphere, whereas information projected to the left visual field projects first to the right hemisphere and only gains access to the left hemisphere after crossing the corpus callosum.

In audition, as has already been pointed out, the anatomy of the auditory system renders the situation somewhat more complex. In contrast to the visual system, there is no obvious anatomical correspondence between the side of stimulus presentation and the hemisphere to which that input is most directly projected. Nevertheless, it has been demonstrated

that if information processed by the left hemisphere (e.g., numbers or words) is presented dichotically, slightly more items presented to the right ear (contralateral to the language hemisphere) are reported (see Figure 4.13). In contrast, when the dichotic task utilizes nonverbal material (e.g., music), which taps the specialized functioning of the right hemisphere, there is a slight left-ear advantage.

In touch, an analogous effect has been observed using what has been called **dichaptic** tasks. Thus, verbal material examined by touch has been reported to be slightly more efficiently processed when presented to the right hand, and spatial material examined by touch is slightly more efficiently processed when presented to the left hand. Dichaptic laterality effects are rather weak ones when compared with those emerging from tachistoscopic and dichotic studies.

All of these methods, tachistoscopic, dichotic, and dichaptic, which attempt to detect the effects of hemispheric specialization (hence the term *laterality*) in normal subjects, are widely employed because they are relatively inexpensive and because they do not require access to patients with cerebral lesions. Consequently, a vast literature has emerged, particularly for the dichotic listening method. These studies fall into two general categories depending on the type of question being addressed. One approach is to use tasks for which hemispheric specialization is well established (e.g., verbal: left hemisphere; spatial: right hemisphere) and then attempt to detect abnormalities in lateralization in particular populations, such as children with learning disabilities. An alternative approach investigates the nature of the specialization of the two hemispheres by assessing performance on different types of task by subjects in whom there is no reason to suspect anomalies of lateralization.

Much has been learned from these methods. However, as Robert Efron (1990) and others have pointed out, these techniques have some critical limitations. The effects found are very small, and, more important, the reliability of these measures is very low. For these reasons, studies using these techniques, particularly those attempting to infer anomalies in hemispheric representation in specific individuals or groups, must be interpreted with extreme caution.

SUMMARY

In this chapter we have considered some of the more important methods currently employed to investigate the relationship between brain and behavior. An understanding of the methods used in the study of the brain and its function is of enormous importance because it provides a basis for critically evaluating the reliability of emerging data and the validity and significance of theoretical inferences drawn from those data. Because neuropsychology is an interdisciplinary endeavor, it employs a wide range of methods. In line with this, our survey of methods has been extremely broad, ranging from techniques used to investigate the structure and function of single neurons, and even parts of neurons, to those measuring the structure and function of large areas of the brain. In addition, the study of patients with cerebral lesions, commissurotomy studies, sodium amobarbital studies, the study of people with behavioral and cognitive abnormalities, and studies of normal subjects all have made important contributions to our understanding of the relationship between brain and behavior.

The diversity of these methods springs from the varying levels of analysis that generate them. Each level investigates a different universe of phenomena, from the electrical activity of single neurons to the behavioral effects of focal brain lesions. Further, each level of analysis poses very different questions and yields very different answers, so much so that they are typically thought of as representing different disciplines. Yet most investigators share the assumption that all levels of analysis are united in the common goal of understanding the brain and that, in principle, all levels of analysis will ultimately be reducible to a basic fundamental level. In addition, as will be clear in the chapters that follow, inferences drawn from one level of analysis can stimulate and inform investigations at other levels.

These considerations suggest that approaching the understanding of brain-behavior relationships from a number of different levels will prove highly fruitful. In the next chapter we employ this multilevel approach in an examination of the visual system. More is known about vision than any other system of the brain, and it therefore serves as a model for how the convergence of a number of different levels of analysis on a specific problem can enhance our understanding. As we consider other, less well understood functional domains in the remainder of this book, we will again find that our understanding is enhanced when we are able to approach problems from a number of different levels of analysis.

CHAPTER 5

The Visual System as a Model of Nervous System Functioning

THE CLASSICAL SEQUENTIAL-HIERARCHICAL VIEW OF THE VISUAL BRAIN

AN OVERVIEW OF RECENT ADVANCES IN THE UNDERSTANDING OF CENTRAL VISUAL PROCESSING

THE RETINA
The General Organization of the Retina
The Photoreceptors
Biochemistry of Phototransduction
Neural Processing Within the Retina

RETINOFUGAL PROJECTIONS
The Lateral Geniculate Nucleus of the Thalamus
An Overview of Cortical Areas Mediating Vision

Projections From the LGN to the Visual Cortex

SPECIALIZATION WITHIN CORTEX DEVOTED TO VISION
The Parvocellular-Blob Channel
The Parvocellular-Interblob Channel
The Magnocellular-V5 Channel and the Magnocellular-V3 Channel

THE MICROANATOMY OF THE VISUAL CORTEX AND THE CONCEPT OF MODULAR ORGANIZATION

THE PROBLEM OF INTEGRATION AND THE CONSTRUCTION OF A REPRESENTATION OF THE VISUAL WORLD

SUMMARY

❖ ❖ ❖

In neuroscience, the most compelling examples of both progress toward reductionism (reducing complex phenomena to simpler, more basic terms) and the fruitful effects of the coevolution of different levels of analysis are seen in attempts to understand vision and the brain. We know more about vision than any other major brain process, and this knowledge is based on a confluence of data derived from a diverse range of methodological approaches, generated by many different levels of analysis. Thus, current understanding of the visual system serves as a model of a relatively advanced understanding of one domain of brain function and what that understanding tells us about the way the brain processes information. It also serves as an example of the power of a multidisciplinary and multilevel approach in achieving that understanding. Perhaps even more important, our current understanding of the visual system serves as a model for what the eventual reduction of perceptual processes to neural events may look like. As such, it is a kind of looking glass through which we can glimpse the level of understanding that will someday be available in other domains of cognition. At the same time, of course, it is also a harbinger of the new problems and questions that will be encountered as our understanding advances. It is in this spirit that we examine current knowledge of the visual system.

THE CLASSICAL SEQUENTIAL-HIERARCHICAL VIEW OF THE VISUAL BRAIN

Before discussing the visual system in detail, we need to make a few theoretical points and review some material from earlier chapters. Recent developments have caused a radical revision in our view of how the visual cortex is organized. As we have seen, it has been known since the late 19th century that the retinal surface is represented topographically in the occipital lobes (Brodmann's area 17). This area thus became known as the **primary visual cortex.** A neurologist of the time, Henschen, termed the primary visual cortex the "cortical retina," and it was assumed that, after elementary visual processing took place there, the results of this processing were then sent to the neighboring **visual association cortex** (Brodmann's areas 18 and 19). The term *association cortex* reflected the assumption that higher-order visual processing, including perception and object recognition, was achieved in this area. Thus processing within the cortex was seen as **sequential,** in the sense that there was a linear flow of information from one area to another, and **hierarchical,** meaning that processing becomes progressively more elaborate in later stages of the sequence.

This theoretical schema seemed to fit well with data indicating that, whereas lesions to the primary visual cortex result in blindness, damage to cortical areas surrounding the primary visual cortex, the "visual association cortex," produces disorders in the recognition of objects, without affecting the elementary components of vision. The latter condition is known as **visual agnosia.** We described this sequential, hierarchical schema of cortical processing in chapter 3. It is a model that had been widely accepted as late as the 1970s, as typified by its appearance in Aleksandr Luria's book *The Working Brain,* which appeared early in that decade (Luria, 1973). Discoveries since the early 1970s have, however, produced a powerful change in our conceptualization of the visual brain and, by extension, of cortical processing more generally.

AN OVERVIEW OF RECENT ADVANCES IN THE UNDERSTANDING OF CENTRAL VISUAL PROCESSING

The most important of these discoveries about the visual brain is that areas outside the primary visual cortex, far from being areas of undifferentiated "higher" functioning, are specialized for the processing of specific aspects of vision, such as color, movement, and form. This specialization of function along relatively elementary dimensions within cortex that was thought to be reserved for "associative" function was entirely unexpected. Furthermore, it was shown that, like the primary visual cortex (which is now most often termed **V1**), these areas of visual cortex outside but neighboring the primary visual cortex (which are collectively termed **extrastriate cortex** or **prestriate cortex**, meaning "outside or anterior to the striate or primary visual cortex") are also **retinotopically organized.** Retinotopic organization means that the retinal surface is mapped onto the cortical surface, although, as is the case in the somatosensory cortex, this mapping is somewhat distorted in that retinal locations with higher receptor density are mapped onto disproportionately larger cortical areas. In addition, it was found that many different extrastriate areas receive input directly from V1 and some also receive direct input from the principal subcortical structure projecting to the visual cortex, the lateral geniculate nucleus.

These discoveries seriously challenged earlier notions of sequential-hierarchical processing, suggesting instead that visual input is relayed in parallel to a number of centers, each of which is functionally specialized. This gave rise to the concepts of **parallel distributed processing** and **parallel hierarchical processing** in the visual cortex. Furthermore, anatomical investigations using a number of staining techniques revealed stunning correlations between anatomical subdivisions and specialization of function within visual areas of the cortex. Let us now consider the visual system in more detail. This will allow a fuller explanation of some of the concepts mentioned in this section, as well as providing a glimpse

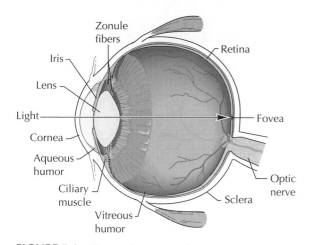

FIGURE 5.1   The eye in cross section. (*Adapted from Bear, Connors, & Paradiso, 1996, p. 216*)

into the workings of this important and relatively well understood system.

THE RETINA

The structures of the eye through which light passes on its way to the retina, including the cornea, aqueous humor, lens, and vitreous humor (Figure 5.1), have various functions but all contribute, directly or indirectly, to the formation of an image on the retina. It is the **retina,** the sheet of photoreceptors and their connecting neurons at the back of the eye, that is the site of the first stage in visual processing. The retina is unique among sensory surfaces in that it is actually part of the brain; that is, embryologically it is derived from a portion of the same neural ectoderm that gives rise to the rest of the brain. In the course of embryological development a portion of the neural ectoderm migrates to the periphery and then extends connecting links back to the rest of the brain. The retina is also a part of the brain by virtue of the fact that its synaptic organization, though relatively simple, is similar to that of other regions of the brain. This makes the retina a highly informative object of study, a touchstone, as it were, in our attempts to understand the synaptic organization underlying brain function. For this reason we consider the retina in some detail.

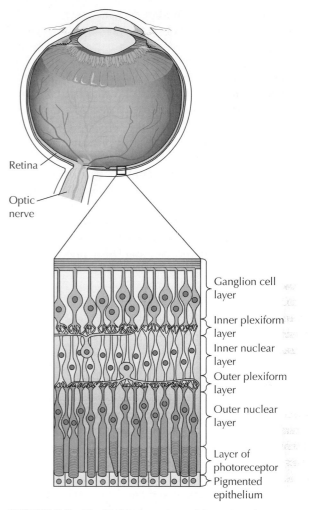

FIGURE 5.2   The laminar structure of the retina, showing its five layers. The figure also shows how light must pass through these layers to reach the photoreceptors, which are situated at the back of the retina. (*Adapted from Bear, Connors, & Paradiso, 1996, p. 222*)

The General Organization of the Retina

The retina has a very counterintuitive organization in that the **photoreceptors,** the first link in visual processing, are situated behind the neurons that connect them to the rest of the brain (Figure 5.2). This means that light has to pass through these neurons before it reaches the photoreceptors. At the back of the eye is the **pigmented epithelium.** This is a layer of cells in which the photoreceptors are embedded, which reduces distorting reflectance within the eye by absorbing any light not absorbed by the photoreceptors. Within the retina itself there are five layers, named with reference to the center of the eyeball. Three of these layers, the **outer nuclear layer** (composed of the photoreceptors), the **inner nuclear layer** (composed of **bipolar cells**) and the **ganglion cell layer,** together constitute the most direct path from the photoreceptors to the rest of the brain. Between the outer and inner nuclear layers is the **outer plexiform layer** (composed of **horizontal cells**), and between the inner nuclear layer and the ganglion cell layer is the **inner plexiform layer** (composed of **amacrine cells**). These plexiform layers play an important role in retinal processing.

The Photoreceptors

There are two categories of photoreceptors, **rods** and **cones.** Their general structure is similar. Rods, sensitive to dim light but not color, are found in the periphery of vision. Cones, less sensitive than rods to dim light, are sensitive to color and are found in central vision (Figure 5.3). There are actually three kinds of cones, each most sensitive to a particular wavelength of the **visible spectrum,** the band of the electromagnetic spectrum that humans are able to detect. The band of wavelengths that constitutes the visible spectrum is between 400 and 700 nm. Each of the three types of cones is maximally sensitive to one wavelength and less sensitive to a surrounding range of wavelengths (Figure 5.4). The optimal sensitivities are to 419 nm (blue), 531 nm (green), and 559 nm (red); these cones are called **B cones, G cones,** and **R cones,** respectively. In contrast, all rods are maximally sensitive to blue-green light (496 nm). As we have said, the three types of cones are important for color vision, whereas rods mediate an achromatic representation of the dimly lit world.

The wavelength to which a particular receptor is most sensitive depends upon the absorption characteristics of the **visual pigment** it contains. Visual pigment is a molecule found in a photoreceptor that changes its conformation when activated by specific

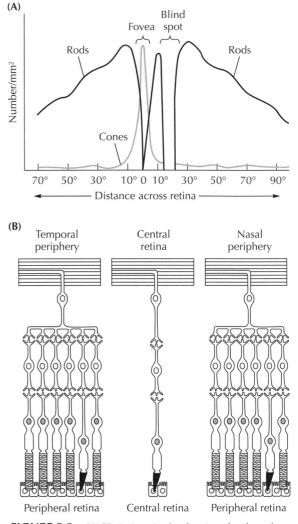

FIGURE 5.3   *(A)* Variations in the density of rods and cones in different regions of the retina. Cones, mediating high-resolution vision, are found mainly within 10° of the fovea. In contrast, rods, virtually absent from the fovea, are found mainly in the peripheral retina. *(B)* In the central retina a relatively small number of cones synapse directly onto a ganglion cell. In contrast, in the periphery many rods provide input to a single ganglion cell. This pattern of input enhances resolution in the fovea, the area of the retina mediating the highest visual acuity, and contributes to the high sensitivity of the peripheral retina to dim light. *(Adapted from Bear, Connors, & Paradiso, 1996, p. 224)*

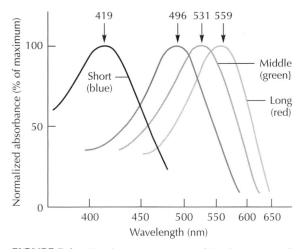

FIGURE 5.4   The absorption spectra of the three types of cones and of rods. The three types of cones respond maximally, but not exclusively, to short, middle, and long wavelengths. Note that light of any particular wavelength activates a unique pattern of absorption across the three cone types. The curve with peak absorption at 496 nm represents the absorption spectrum of rods. Because rods are the only receptors activated in dim light (scotopic vision), the coding of wavelength in terms of the relative activity of more than one receptor type (as takes place in bright light, i.e., in photopic vision) is not possible, and, therefore, vision is achromatic. *(Adapted from Kandel et al., 1995, p. 456)*

wavelengths of light. This is the only light-dependent step in vision, and it initiates the coding of light in the form of changes in receptor activity, a process termed **phototransduction.**

As mentioned, the critical process in the mediation of phototransduction in both rods and cones is the light-activated change in the conformation of the photoreceptor's visual pigment. We have also said that what underlies the specific response characteristics of rods and of each of the three different types of cones is the light-absorption profile that activates conformational change in their respective visual pigments. We turn now to the biochemical events underlying phototransduction.

Biochemistry of Phototransduction

The general nature of the processes involved in phototransduction is very similar in rods and cones, so let us consider the case of rods. Here the photopig-

ment is **rhodopsin,** composed of a non-light-absorbing component, **opsin,** and light-absorbing **retinal.** Retinal has several possible conformations.[1] The nonactivated cis form, present in darkness, is bound snugly to a site on the opsin molecule. This binding promotes the continual synthesis of **cyclic guanosine monophosphate (cGMP)** by the enzyme **guanylyl cyclase.** The resulting high levels of cGMP open membrane Na^+ channels, resulting in an influx of Na^+ (the so-called **dark current**) and the depolarization of the receptor to about -30 mV. Photoreceptors do not fire action potentials; instead, they code changes in illumination in terms of passive changes in membrane potential. Thus, the response of photoreceptors to darkness is a graded depolarization and a resulting graded increase in the release of the neurotransmitter glutamate at the receptor's synaptic terminal.

The presence of light causes a change in the conformation of retinal. This, in turn, changes the conformation of the opsin portion of rhodopsin, setting in motion a chain of biochemical processes, a biochemical cascade, which ultimately results in the hyperpolarization of the photoreceptor. The cascade nature of these processes serves the function of amplifying the effect of a stimulus, each step in the process multiplying the effect of the previous one. This process renders rods so sensitive that they can detect a single **photon** of light, the most elementary unit of light energy.

The biochemical mechanism of cone activation is similar to that seen in rods, except that the visual pigment in each of the three types of cone is different, resulting in the specific wavelength sensitivity profiles of the three cone types discussed earlier (see Figure 5.4). In the beginning of the 19th century Thomas Young proposed the idea that color vision is mediated by the activity of the three types of cones. This

---

1. Some molecules can have more than one potential spatial configuration (shape), even though each configuration contains the same number of atoms, in the same sequence. This is analogous to the way a particular tinker-toy structure can be made to have different shapes by rotating parts of the structure. The different configurations of a molecule, called conformations, often have different binding properties. Changes in the conformation of a molecule may therefore alter its biochemical properties in important ways.

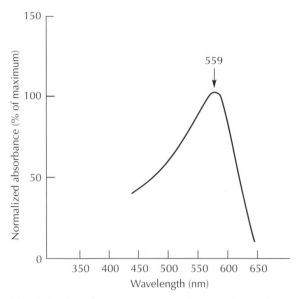

FIGURE 5.5   Absorption curve for R cones. The readout from any one cone type, taken alone, does not specify the wavelength of the ambient illumination. For example, if R cones absorb light at 50% of their maximum, this could be due to moderately intense red light or to more intense light of shorter or longer wavelength.

idea was championed some 50 years later by Hermann von Helmholtz and has come to be known as the **Young-Helmholtz trichromatic theory of color vision.** Although we will see that the trichromatic theory does not in fact account for color vision, its assertion that there are three types of cones, each most sensitive to a particular wavelength, is accurate. The existence of the three cone types posited by this theory was confirmed in the 1960s when the absorption characteristics of the three cone pigments were measured directly.

Interestingly, each cone type does not code wavelength in terms of a specific activity level corresponding to a particular wavelength; that is, each cone type does not send a unique signal to the rest of the nervous system that contains information about the specific wavelength of light that has activated it. This means that a single cone type cannot accurately represent the wavelengths of light impinging on the retina. For example, if R cones are activated such that they absorb, say, 50% of their maximum level of light, this

could be due to the presence of moderately intense red light. However, it could also be due to more intense light of shorter or longer wavelength (Figure 5.5). This accounts for why individuals with only one type of cone, a defect most frequently due to genetic abnormality, are colorblind. Their retinas are responding in a manner analogous to that of the normal retina in dim light, where only one type of receptor (rods) is activated. The resulting picture of the world, like normal vision in dim light, is achromatic. In normal vision the system codes wavelength in terms of the profile of relative activities of the three different cone types (see Figure 5.4). However, while this comparison of the output of the three cone types is a necessary component in color vision, it is not, as the trichromatic theory of color vision had proposed, sufficient for the perception of color. Rather, as we will see, it is only one component among many involved in the process.

Neural Processing Within the Retina

The photoreceptors, the rods and cones, are the only light-sensitive cells in the retina. The ganglion cells, which have their cell bodies in the retina and whose axons form the optic nerve and optic tract as they project to the lateral geniculate nucleus of the thalamus, are the only output from the retina to the rest of the brain. The importance of the processing carried out by the retina can be appreciated when we consider that there are about 120 million photoreceptors and only 1 million ganglion cells. Thus, the pattern of action potentials conducted by the optic nerve is the result of extensive processing within the retina. This processing is mediated by the bipolar cells, which link photoreceptors and ganglion cells; by the connections between photoreceptors and bipolar cells, formed by horizontal cells; and by the connections between bipolar cells and ganglion cells, formed by amacrine cells (see Figure 5.2). We turn now to an examination of the nature of this processing and its neural basis.

RECEPTIVE FIELDS   To proceed further it is necessary to introduce the concept of the **receptive field** of a neuron. As mentioned in chapter 4, this concept is derived from unit cell recording, the method in which a very small diameter electrode is inserted into a single neuron and the activity of that neuron is then recorded. Using this method one can investigate how the frequency of firing of a particular neuron varies as a function of different variables. Thus, in neurons within sensory systems, one can study how firing rate varies as a function of various stimulus characteristics. The receptive field of a particular neuron, then, is defined as the stimulus that produces the maximum (or in some cells the minimum) frequency of firing of that cell. It may at first seem strange that a reduction in the firing rate of a neuron below its baseline rate is also a way in which the nervous system codes information about stimuli, but this is in fact the case. As we saw in our earlier discussion of the role of inhibition (chapter 2), taking away is as effective a method of coding as adding.

Receptive fields of neurons were first discovered by Vernon Mountcastle is the 1950s in his investigation of the somatosensory cortex. Not long afterward Steven Kuffler discovered that retinal ganglion cells have receptive fields characterized by two concentric regions that work in opposition (Figure 5.6). There are two types of retinal ganglion cell receptive fields: **ON-center/OFF-surround** and **OFF-center/ON-surround.** ON-center/OFF-surround ganglion cells (often called simply ON-center) fire at their highest rate when the circular center of their visual field is illuminated and a donut-shaped area around it is not illuminated. In contrast, in response to the opposite pattern of illumination (i.e., a donut-shaped area of illumination), the cells fire minimally or not at all. The antagonistic relationship of center and surround means that if the center and surround are illuminated simultaneously, the firing rate of the neuron will be relatively low (see Figure 5.6). The same would be true when both portions are not illuminated. OFF-center/ON-surround ganglion cells have the opposite pattern from that just described.

Before we go further, it is necessary to introduce two terms. **Luminance,** quantified in units called **lumens,** is a measure of light intensity. A given surface will have more luminance when the intensity of the light illuminating it is high than when it is low, assuming that the wavelengths of the light source are held constant. (It is necessary to specify that the spectral composition of the light source be held constant because a given surface will reflect certain wavelengths more than others—and so varying spectral composition will vary luminance. We will have more to say about this later.) **Reflectance** is a measure of the fraction of the light illuminating a surface that the surface reflects. For a given surface, this varies as a function of the wavelength of the illuminating light, but not as a function of its intensity. In other words, if the wavelength of the illuminating light is held constant, the reflectance of a surface—the proportion of the light striking it that is reflected—is constant across varying illumination intensities.

Let's look further now at the receptive field characteristics of retinal ganglion cells. The antagonistic (ON-OFF) nature of their receptive fields means that these cells are sensitive to differences in light intensity reflected by different surfaces, rather than the absolute light intensity of reflected light from any given surface. In other words, these cells are sensitive to differences in the luminance of different surfaces (in uniform illumination, a function of their reflectance) rather than the absolute luminance of any particular surface. To see why this is the case, imagine that we have identified a ganglion cell with an ON-center/OFF-surround receptive field. Imagine, further, that in the ON-center area of the receptive field we present a white circle and in the OFF-surround area we present a gray donut. Next, we illuminate the concentric circles with varying intensities of light. In high illumination both the white circle and the gray donut will reflect more light than in low illumination. Thus, in high illumination, the white circle, falling in the ON-center of the receptive field, will tend to excite the cell more than it would in low illumination. However, in high illumination, the gray donut, falling on the OFF-surround, will tend to inhibit the cell more than it would in low illumination. The net effect is a constant firing of the cell across different intensities of illumination.

This sensitivity to reflectance rather than luminance is highly adaptive. In moving about and locating objects in our environment it is frequently critical to be able to identify differences in the reflectance of surfaces, particularly in low-intensity illumination and other conditions where color differences are minimal or absent. In contrast, the absolute level of

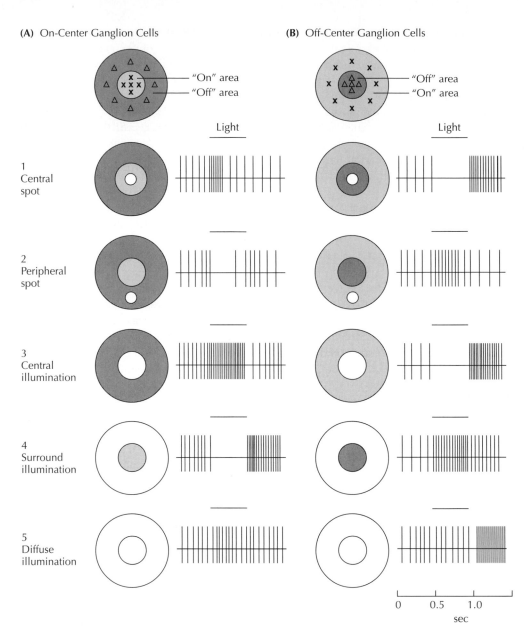

(A) On-Center Ganglion Cells

(B) Off-Center Ganglion Cells

"On" area
"Off" area

"Off" area
"On" area

Light

Light

1
Central
spot

2
Peripheral
spot

3
Central
illumination

4
Surround
illumination

5
Diffuse
illumination

0   0.5   1.0
sec

FIGURE 5.6   Retinal ganglion cells have circular receptive fields divided into a center and a surround. ON-center/OFF-surround cells are excited when illuminated in their center and inhibited when illuminated in their surround. OFF-center/ON-surround cells exhibit the opposite pattern. *(A)* ON-center cells respond maximally when *(3)* the center is illuminated and the surround is not and minimally in *(4)* the opposite illumination condition. Partial illumination of *(1)* center or *(2)* surround results in briefer excitation and inhibition, respectively. Diffuse illumination *(5)* or darkness (not shown) results in a weak level of excitation because the center and surround tend to cancel each other's effects. *(B)* The activity of OFF-center cells is inhibited when *(1, 3)* their center is illuminated and excited when *(2, 4)* their surround is illuminated. As in the ON-center cells, opposing effects on center and surround caused by diffuse illumination *(5)* and darkness (not shown) produce weak levels of excitation. *(Adapted from Kandel et al., 1995, p. 418)*

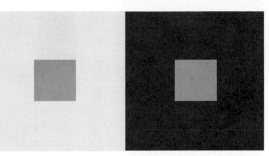

FIGURE 5.7 Although the central boxes are identical shades of gray, the left box appears darker because of the lighter border surrounding it. This distortion is an example of the visual system's emphasis on relative lightness. Lateral inhibition, one process underlying this phenomenon, is mediated at the neuronal level by the center-antagonistic surround receptive fields of retinal ganglion cells. *(Adapted from Bear, Connors, & Paradiso, 1996, p. 235)*

luminance of objects in the environment is of much less adaptive significance, as any wearer of sunglasses knows. An example of this emphasis on the relative reflectance of surfaces over their absolute luminance is dramatically illustrated by the distortion in perception of absolute luminance experienced in viewing Figure 5.7. Here the two central boxes actually have the same reflectance and, therefore, under the same conditions of illumination, the same luminance. However, in the process of emphasizing the contrast between the reflectance of the center square and the surround, the perceptual system distorts this fact, so that the gray square surrounded by the black background appears lighter than the gray square surrounded by the white background. Perception of lightness and darkness is relative, not absolute.

This feature of the system helps explain why the words on a page appear dark while the page appears light in both dim light and direct sunlight, even though in the latter condition the words are reflecting more light than the page reflects in dim light. This phenomenon, the perception of lightness and darkness on the basis of differences in the reflectance of surfaces across varying intensities of ambient illumination, is called **lightness constancy.** The fact that a retinal process—the center-antagonistic surround receptive field characteristics of retinal ganglion cells—contributes importantly to lightness constancy is an example of the

complex processing mediated by the retina. In the next section we consider some of the neural mechanisms underlying the center-antagonistic surround receptive field characteristics of retinal bipolar and ganglion cells.

THE NEURAL BASIS OF CENTER-ANTAGONISTIC SURROUND RECEPTIVE FIELDS: LATERAL INHIBITION The neural basis of the center-antagonistic surround receptive fields of retinal ganglion cells is the pattern of interconnections between photoreceptors and retinal ganglion cells mediated by bipolar, horizontal, and amacrine cells. Each photoreceptor is sensitive to the presence of light at a particular point in the visual field. Yet bipolar and ganglion cells, the next neurons down the line, are sensitive to concentric patterns of contrasting illumination impinging on a small circular patch of retina ranging from minutes of arc at the fovea to up to 5° in the periphery. How do the intervening neurons mediate this transformation of response characteristics?

Let's consider the bipolar cells, into which photoreceptors feed directly (**vertical pathways**) or indirectly, via horizontal cells (**lateral pathways**). Bipolar cells have receptive fields with center-antagonistic surround characteristics that are similar to those seen in ganglion cells. However, unlike ganglion cells, bipolar cells respond with a graded passive change in membrane potential, as do photoreceptors. If we consider first the relatively simple circuitry involved in the vertical pathway from the photoreceptors representing part of the center area of an ON-center receptive field in a bipolar cell, we find that the photoreceptors have an inhibitory input to their bipolar cell (Figure 5.8). Recall that the photoreceptor depolarizes in darkness and hyperpolarizes in light. Therefore, in the above connection, illumination of the photoreceptor would result in hyperpolarization of the receptor and a decrease in the release of its neurotransmitter (glutamate). Because this is an inhibitory connection, a decrease in neurotransmitter release would result in depolarization of the bipolar cell. As the bipolar cell, in turn, has an excitatory connection with the ganglion cell, the bipolar cell's depolarization tends to activate an action potential in the ganglion cell. In contrast, in darkness, the cone

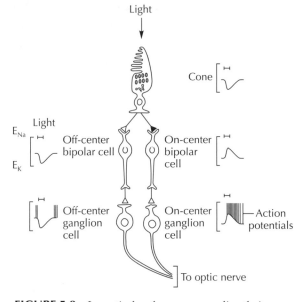

Light

Cone

E_Na

Light

Off-center
bipolar cell

On-center
bipolar
cell

E_K

Off-center
ganglion
cell

On-center
ganglion
cell

Action
potentials

To optic nerve

FIGURE 5.8   In vertical pathways a cone directly innervates the center portion of an OFF-center bipolar cell and an OFF-center retinal ganglion cell *(left)* and an ON-center bipolar cell and an ON-center retinal ganglion cell *(right)*. Each bipolar cell makes an excitatory connection *(open triangle)* with a retinal ganglion cell of the same type. The cone forms an excitatory synapse with OFF-center bipolar cells and an inhibitory synapse *(dark triangle)* with ON-center bipolar cells. The figure shows the effect of illumination on the two kinds of bipolar and ganglion cells. Upward curves (toward the Na+ equilibrium potential, E_{Na}) indicate depolarization, and downward curves (toward the K+ equilibrium potential, E_K) indicate hyperpolarization. It will be noted that in the innervation of the OFF-center bipolar cell the release of glutamate by the cone has an excitatory effect, whereas this transmitter has the opposite effect when it binds to the ON-center bipolar cell. This is yet another example of the general principle that the effect of a transmitter depends on the mechanisms set in motion by its binding to the postsynaptic receptors and not on the transmitter per se. *(Adapted from Kandel et al., 1995, p. 421)*

will depolarize, hyperpolarizing the ON-center bipolar cell and decreasing the probability that the ON-center ganglion cell will fire.

In the case of a vertical pathway from the receptors representing the center of an OFF-center bipolar cell the circuitry is similar except that the input to the bipolar cell is excitatory. Thus, illumination of the cone and its resulting hyperpolarization will hyperpolarize the bipolar cell and decrease the probability

of firing of the OFF-center ganglion cell. In darkness, on the other hand, the depolarized receptor will release more glutamate, resulting in depolarization of the OFF-center bipolar cell and an increase in the probability of firing of the OFF-center ganglion cell.

Now let's consider the somewhat more complicated circuitry mediating the entire center-surround receptive field of bipolar cells. Here we see the critical role of horizontal cells. Let us consider first the circuitry underlying the ON-center/OFF-surround receptive field (Figure 5.9A). We have already described the circuitry underlying the ON-center. Around the photoreceptors registering illumination in the receptive field's center is a ring of photoreceptors that constitute the first stage of processing of the OFF-surround. These feed, via lateral pathways, photoreceptors with vertical pathways to bipolar cells. The connections between photoreceptors and horizontal cells mediating the OFF-surround are excitatory, and the synapses between horizontal cells and photoreceptors mediating the ON-center are inhibitory (see Figure 5.9A). Thus, the illumination of OFF-surround receptors will result in the following chain of events: hyperpolarization of that receptor, a decrease in glutamate release, hyperpolarization of the horizontal cell, a decrease in inhibitory activation of the receptor within the ON center, depolarization of that receptor, release of glutamate, hyperpolarization of the bipolar cells, and decrease in firing of the ON-center ganglion cell. This runs counter to the effect of illuminating the receptive field's ON-center, which we discussed a moment ago. We thus have a schema of circuitry that accounts for the antagonistic effect of light impinging on both the center and the surround areas of an ON-center/OFF-surround receptive field. This involves one region inhibiting activity in an adjacent region, a process generally termed **lateral inhibition,** inhibition from the side. This mechanism is seen at many levels of the visual system. It can be seen that if the receptors in the surround are not illuminated, lateral inhibition will not take place, resulting in a chain of events that tends to depolarize the bipolar cell.

Figure 5.9B illustrates how this circuitry can account for the OFF-center/ON-surround receptive field. The reasoning here is similar. By considering these circuits under various possible combinations

(A)

Light on surround

(B)

Dark on surround

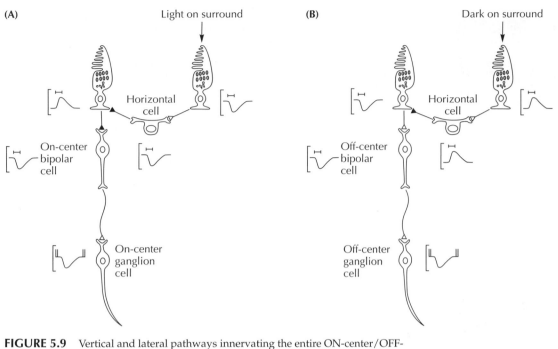

FIGURE 5.9   Vertical and lateral pathways innervating the entire ON-center/OFF-surround and OFF-center/ON-surround receptive field of retinal bipolar and ganglion cells. The cones in the area of the retina mediating the surround region of the receptive field form excitatory synapses *(open triangles)* with horizontal cells. Horizontal cells then form inhibitory synapses *(dark triangles)* with cones innervating the center region of the receptive field. *(A)* The circuitry of the ON-center/OFF-surround receptive field. In this situation the surround is illuminated, opposing the activation of the ON-center cell. The net effect is a hyperpolarization of the bipolar cell and a reduction in the firing rate of the ON-center ganglion cell. *(B)* The circuitry of the OFF-center receptive field. Again, the surround is in an illumination condition (darkness) that tends to hyperpolarize the bipolar cell and inhibit the firing of the OFF-center retinal ganglion cell. *(Adapted from Kandel et al., 1995, p. 422)*

of illumination and darkness in their center and surround, it can be seen that they account for their respective receptive field characteristics.

As already noted, the antagonistic effects of identical illumination on vertical and lateral pathways render retinal bipolar and ganglion cells most responsive to contrasting illumination within their receptive fields. This process sharpens vision by exaggerating differences in lightness, as illustrated by the phenomenon of **contrast enhancement.** In contrast enhancement a darker area that is next to a lighter area appears to have an even darker band along the common border, whereas the lighter area appears to have an even lighter band along the common border (Fig-

ure 5.10). These illusory bands, called **Mach bands** after their discoverer in the 19th century, result in part from processes of lateral inhibition within the retina.

TWO TYPES OF GANGLION CELLS   We have seen that the horizontal cells of the outer plexiform layer play a critical role in the circuitry underlying the center-antagonistic surround characteristics of bipolar cells and that these bipolar cells then synapse with retinal ganglion cells that have receptive fields with the same center-antagonistic surround characteristics. In addition, the characteristics of ganglion cell receptive fields is determined by the integrative action of all of the retinal cells distal to them, including those of

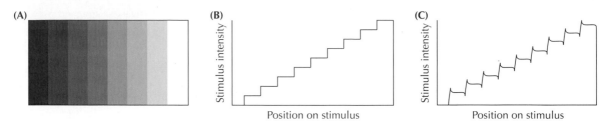

FIGURE 5.10   If a series of strips *(A)*, each of uniform light intensity *(B)*, is arranged in ascending brightness from left to right, each strip does not appear to be of uniform brightness. Instead, the left side of each strip (next to its darker neighbor) appears lighter, while the right side of each strip (next to its lighter neighbor) appears darker. These so-called Mach bands result in a perceived exaggeration of the contours that separate strips *(C)*. *(Adapted from H. Gleitman et al., 1999, p. 199)*

the inner and outer plexiform layers. As it turns out, these integrative processes result in two major functional types of retinal ganglion cell. These are termed **P ganglion cells** (from the Latin *parvo*, "small") and **M ganglion cells** (from *magno*, "large"). There are more P cells than M cells, the ratio being about 9:1.

These two types of ganglion cells have different receptive field characteristics. M ganglion cells have larger receptive fields (in part mediated by their larger and more extensively branched dendrites), are more sensitive to low contrast, are not sensitive to wavelength, and respond in transient bursts. They are believed to be sensitive to the gross features of stimuli. In contrast, the more numerous P cells have smaller receptive fields, respond with a sustained discharge, and are sensitive to wavelength. Most P ganglion cells are **color opponent,** and there are several types of color opponent cells (Figure 5.11). The most common type of color-coding cell within the retinal ganglion cells (and also among the lateral geniculate cells to which retinal ganglion cells project) is **concentric single-opponent cells.** In these cells, one type of cone (R or G) activates the center (exerting either an excitatory or an inhibitory effect on the ganglion cell), and the other type of cone has the opposite effect on the surround. In **concentric broadband cells,** R and G cones act together in each area of the receptive field but have opposite action in the two areas. **Coextensive single-opponent cells** have an undifferentiated receptive field (no center-surround organization) in which the action of B cones is opposed to the combined action of G and R cones.

The broadband (achromatic) ganglion cells can be either M type or P type, whereas both types of single-opponent cell are exclusively P type. The comparison of the functional characteristics of the M and P ganglion cells has led to the hypothesis that M cells are involved in the detection of large objects and the gross features of stimuli, whereas P cells are involved in the discrimination of more detailed aspects of form and of color. What is particularly revealing about the presence of these two retinal ganglion cell types is that they serve the same photoreceptors in parallel. In other words, a given group of photoreceptors projects to both types of retinal ganglion cell. The implications of this arrangement are highly significant. The arrangement suggests that within retinal ganglion cells there is specialization of function mediated by different neuronal connections from photoreceptors and that these different connections constitute parallel inputs. We will see that this dual theme of parallel processing and specialization of function carries through the entire visual system, including, in contradiction of some classical postulates about the nature of cerebral organization, cortical areas involved in vision.

RETINOFUGAL PROJECTIONS

In considering the projections from the retina to higher brain areas (termed **retinofugal,** from the Latin *fuga,* "to flee"), we first have to take another look at the structure of the retina itself. The retina can be divided into a **nasal hemiretina** and a **temporal**

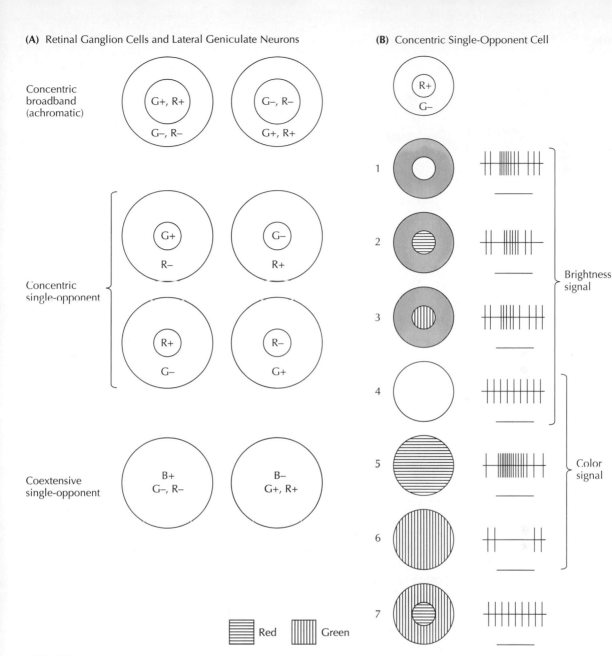

(A) Retinal Ganglion Cells and Lateral Geniculate Neurons

(B) Concentric Single-Opponent Cell

Concentric
broadband
(achromatic)

Concentric
single-opponent

Coextensive
single-opponent

Red Green

Brightness
signal

Color
signal

FIGURE 5.11 *(A)* P type retinal ganglion cells and neurons of the lateral geniculate nucleus, to which they project, have several types of receptive fields that can be defined in terms of how the three types of cones innervate their center and surround. *(B)* Concentric single-opponent cells code information about both color and achromatic brightness contrast because different cones feed the center and the surround. The figure shows the effect of shining light in the receptive field of a RED ON-center/ GREEN OFF-surround cell. Light in the center and darkness in the surround *(1–3)* will increase the firing of these cells. This is the case even for green light *(3)* because R cones are activated to some extent by green light. The effect of diffuse white light *(4)* will be canceled as it impinges on both the center and the surround. Diffuse red light *(5)* excites the cell, whereas diffuse green light *(6)* has an inhibitory effect. The effect of red in the center and green in the surround *(7)* tends to be minimal because the two cancel each other. *(Adapted from Kandel et al., 1995, p. 461)*

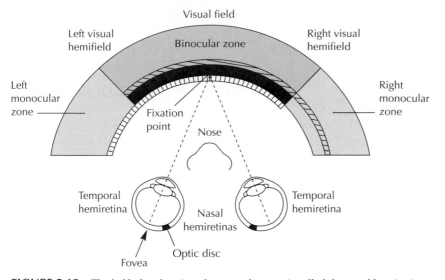

FIGURE 5.12   The half of each retina closest to the nose is called the nasal hemiretina, and the half closest to the temple, the temporal hemiretina. There is a binocular zone within the visual field, which projects to the retinas of both eyes, and two monocular zones, each of which, because of the position of the nose, projects to only one retina. *(Adapted from Kandel et al., 1995, p. 426)*

hemiretina (Figure 5.12). It can also be divided into a **ventral hemiretina** and a **dorsal hemiretina.** Because the lens of the eye left-right reverses and inverts the visual image, the right half of each retina receives light from the left side of space (i.e., the left **visual hemifield**), and the opposite is the case for the left half of each retina. In addition, the ventral half of each retina receives light from the upper visual field, while the dorsal half receives light from the lower half of the visual field. Within the entire visual field there is a **binocular zone,** which projects to both retinas, and two **monocular zones,** each of which, because of the position of the nose, projects only to one retina.

The **optic nerve** is composed of axons of ganglion cells. We have already mentioned that the more proximal layers of the retina (containing all of its cells except the photoreceptors) lie between the incoming light and the photoreceptors. There is, however, one area where this interference is minimized because the ganglion cell axons project away from the other cell layers at an acute angle, producing a kind of indentation in the retina called the **fovea** (from the Latin for "pit"). This allows more light to reach the

photoreceptors. The fovea is also the area of greatest density of cones and therefore the area that mediates the highest visual acuity. We are thus constantly moving our eyes in such a way as to fixate objects of interest on the fovea. The fovea has very few rods, their greatest concentration being in the part of the retina surrounding the fovea (see Figure 5.3). It is for this reason that one can more readily detect a dim point of light, such as a faint star, by looking just off to the side of its expected location.

The area where the ganglion cell axons leave the retina does not have any photoreceptors and is termed the **optic disc.** The absence of photoreceptors in the optic disc means that light falling in this area cannot be detected. The presence of this area within the visual field where stimuli cannot be detected (known as the **blind spot**) can be demonstrated in various ways. It is of great interest, however, that the blind spot requires special conditions for its demonstration, rather than being obvious. This shows that the visual system "fills in" areas of the visual field from which it is not actually receiving information. Apparently the visual system is constructing a coher-

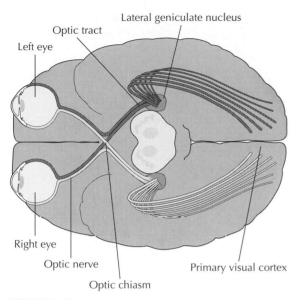

Lateral geniculate nucleus

Optic tract

Left eye

Right eye

Optic nerve

Optic chiasm

Primary visual cortex

FIGURE 5.13   A schematic depiction of the visual pathways as seen from below. At the optic chiasm, axons of ganglion cells from the nasal half of each retina cross over to the other side of the brain. Information is then projected to the lateral geniculate nucleus and the visual cortex. This is the basis for the contralateral relationship between visual field and the side of the brain to which information in that field is projected. *(From Hubel & Wiesel, 1979, p. 88)*

ent representation of the visual world based on information available to it, even when that information has major gaps.

The optic nerves leave each eye and course (project) toward the back of the brain. As they do so, they reach a point where they meet and the fibers from the nasal half of each retina cross over to the other side of the brain, while the fibers from the two temporal hemiretinas do not cross over. This point of crossing is called the optic chiasm (from the Greek letter χ, which it resembles). Posterior to the optic chiasm, the optic fibers are called the **optic tract.** Each optic tract carries information from the ipsilateral temporal hemiretina and the contralateral nasal hemiretina. This means that the optic tract on each side of the brain conveys information from the contralateral visual field (Figure 5.13).

The nature of the visual impairment seen after damage to different parts of the visual pathways re-

flects these anatomical relationships. Thus, damage to optic fibers anterior to the optic chiasm affects vision in one eye. In contrast, damage posterior to the optic chiasm results in a contralateral visual field deficit, termed an **homonymous hemianopia** (or, more often, simply **hemianopia**), when the one-sided postchiasmatic damage is complete. A hemianopia is a more serious impairment than blindness in one eye, because in hemianopia an entire visual field is lost, whereas in monocular blindness only one monocular zone (see Figure 5.12) is lost. Damage to the optic chiasm itself (as sometimes occurs, for example, in pituitary tumor), most often results in damage to its medial portions, causing a bitemporal hemianopia. Other patterns of visual field deficit are also possible, depending upon the location of the underlying lesion (Figure 5.14).

The Lateral Geniculate Nucleus of the Thalamus

The majority of the axons of the retinal ganglion cells (that make up each optic tract) synapse on the ipsilateral lateral geniculate nucleus of the thalamus, or LGN. Each LGN appears somewhat like a bent knee, hence the term *geniculate,* from the Latin for "knee" (Figure 5.15). Viewed in cross section, each LGN appears to have six layers of cells; these are traditionally numbered from one to six, with layer 1 being the most ventral layer and layer 6 being the most dorsal. Each layer represents the input from the hemiretina of one eye, with the eye-to-layer correspondence as indicated in Figure 5.15. The cells within each layer constitute a retinotopic (or topographic) representation of the hemiretina that innervates it. In other words, there is an orderly mapping of the hemiretinal surface onto the cells within each layer of the LGN. This mapping, however, like that of the body surface in the somatosensory cortex, is not a one-to-one mapping; the fovea receives a disproportionately large representation. The maps of the six layers are precisely in register, however, such that a line passing through the lateral geniculate perpendicular to its surface would pass through cells representing identical points in the visual field.

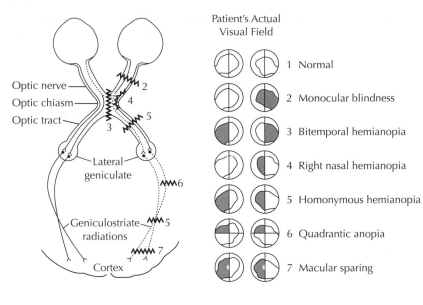

Patient's Actual
Visual Field

1 Normal

2 Monocular blindness

3 Bitemporal hemianopia

4 Right nasal hemianopia

5 Homonymous hemianopia

6 Quadrantic anopia

7 Macular sparing

FIGURE 5.14   Visual deficits associated with damage at different levels of the visual system. Dark areas indicate blind portion of the visual field. *(Adapted from Kolb & Whishaw, 1996, p. 252)*

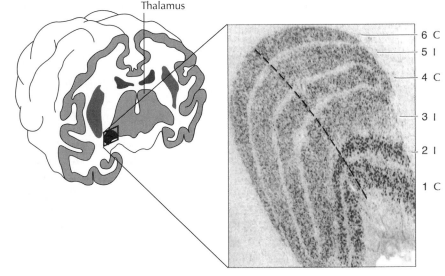

FIGURE 5.15   The lateral geniculate nucleus of the macaque monkey. The tissue has been stained to show cell bodies and reveals the LGN's six-layered organization, with the two ventral layers (magnocellular layers) composed of larger cells than the other four layers (parvocellular layers). Each layer receives input exclusively from either the contralateral *(C)* or ipsilateral *(I)* eye. *(Adapted from Bear, Connors, & Paradiso, 1996, p. 249)*

The layers within the LGN can be divided into two major categories. The ventral two layers (layers 1 and 2) consist of relatively large cells and are termed the **magnocellular layers;** the dorsal four layers (layers 3–6) contain small cells and are termed **parvocellular layers.** It turns out that the magnocellular layers receive their retinal input from M ganglion cells, whereas the parvocellular layers receive projections from P ganglion cells. Thus, the parallel processing that began in the retina is maintained in the LGN, and we will see

shortly that it is also maintained in areas of cortex devoted to vision. We will also find that specialization of function, first seen in the two major types of ganglion cell, is also maintained in higher visual areas.

The characteristics of the receptive fields of cells in the LGN were first identified by Kuffler in the 1950s and have been further delineated since that time. In general, LGN neurons have receptive fields with a center-antagonistic surround organization very much like that of retinal ganglion cells. There are, however, major differences between the cells in the magnocellular and parvocellular regions of the LGN. As we have noted, neurons of the magnocellular layers of the LGN receive their major input from the M type ganglion cells, whereas parvocellular LGN neurons are innervated by P type ganglion cells. The receptive field characteristics of cells in the LGN correspond to this anatomical organization. Thus, neurons in the magnocellular LGN are more sensitive to contrast than are those in the parvocellular layers. That is, the response of magnocellular neurons grows as a function of contrast more steeply than does the response of parvocellular neurons. In addition, magnocellular neurons respond strongly to movement but are insensitive to wavelength. In contrast, the majority of parvocellular neurons respond weakly to movement but are color opponent, most exhibiting one of the three types of color-opponent cells that we have already described as being typical of the P ganglion cells that feed them: concentric single-opponent, concentric broadband opponent, and coextensive single-opponent.

An Overview of Cortical Areas Mediating Vision

At this point we have laid the groundwork for some of the very important and generally unexpected findings that have emerged in the past 25 years about areas of cortex involved in visual processing. As we noted earlier, the classical view of the visual brain postulated a sequential hierarchical model of cortical processing whereby information first is projected to the primary visual cortex, where the processing of elementary components of vision takes place. We have seen that this conceptualization of the function of the primary visual cortex led the neurologist Henschen, at the turn of the century, to term this area the cortical retina. This idea seemed to be supported by the retinotopic organization of the primary visual cortex and the presumed absence of such organization in neighboring cortex. It is in these neighboring areas that the "higher" visual functions of perception and recognition were thought to be mediated, a notion embodied in the term *visual association cortex*, which was used to denote these areas. What has emerged

in recent years is a body of findings that requires an entirely different conceptualization of the organization of cortical visual areas.

This revised conceptualization includes, in most general terms, the following: (a) There are areas of cortex outside the primary visual cortex that are specialized for the processing of specific aspects of the visual world, such as form, motion, and color. (b) These specialized areas are retinotopically organized, although generally less precisely so than the primary visual cortex. (c) Within each area there is subspecialization of function and anatomical differentiation that is related to functional specialization. (d) Processing is parallel rather than sequential (as postulated by the classical model) in the sense that areas specialized for the processing of different aspects of the visual world, such as color or movement, receive direct input from primary visual areas. The sections that follow will further consider these unexpected changes in our view of the visual brain and the empirical basis for these changes.

Projections from the LGN to the Visual Cortex

There are four currently known parallel streams from the lateral geniculate nucleus to the visual cortex, two from the magnocellular layers of the LGN and two from the parvocellular layers. These streams and the specialized areas to which they project are schematically depicted in Figure 5.16. In the following paragraphs we will elaborate on this general schema, discussing in some detail the specialization of function and neuroanatomical connections that characterize these streams or subsystems. The findings that we will be discussing are summarized in Figure 5.16 and Table 5.1. Let's begin then with the areas of cortex receiving direct input from the LGN.

As we have already mentioned, the cerebral cortex is generally considered to be composed of six layers. In the visual cortex, however, there are actually nine layers. Therefore, to maintain the six-layered schema, it is necessary to subdivide one of the layers, layer IV, into four layers (Figure 5.17). The vast majority of fibers that project to the cortex from the LGN synapse in layer IVC of V1. (As you may recall from

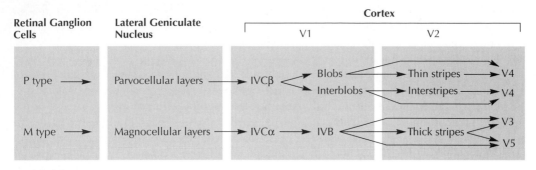

FIGURE 5.16   Schematic representation of the four known major parallel pathways involved in visual perception. *(Adapted from Kandel et al., 1995, p. 395)*

our earlier discussion, the primary visual cortex is usually now referred to as V1, and we will use this terminology from now on.) However, the anatomical segregation that we found in the LGN is maintained at this next level of synaptic connection: Magnocellular layers of the LGN synapse in layer IVCα, whereas parvocellular layers synapse in the neighboring but separate layer IVCβ.

If we consider the receptive fields of cells in these two cortical layers, we find that neurons in IVCβ have center-antagonistic surround receptive fields, many of which are color opponent. In other words, they have receptive fields very similar to those of the parvocellular LGN neurons that feed them. In contrast, the receptive fields of neurons in layer IVCα are elongated and are **orientation selective,** meaning that their firing rate is modified most by a bar-shaped stimulus presented at a particular orientation in a particular area of the visual field (Figure 5.18). In addition, like the magnocellular LGN neurons that innervate them, these neurons are insensitive to wavelength. David Hubel and Torsten Wiesel, students of Kuffler, who pioneered research in the neurophysiology of V1, discovered these cells and termed them **simple cells,** for reasons that will become apparent shortly.

SPECIALIZATION WITHIN CORTEX DEVOTED TO VISION

The development of a dye by Margaret Wong-Riley for the enzyme **cytochrome oxidase,** a marker of enhanced metabolic activity, revealed patches of darkly stained cells surrounded by lightly stained areas in layers II and III of V1. These stained areas have come to be known as **blobs,** and the surrounding unstained areas have been termed **interblobs.** It turns out that neurons in layer IVCβ in V1, those neurons receiving input from the parvocellular LGN, project to the blobs and to the interblobs. An examination of the receptive fields of the cells in these two regions and the projections from these regions to other areas of cortex reveals the presence of two different processing channels involving parvocellular input: the **parvocellular-blob channel** and the **parvocellular-interblob channel.**

The Parvocellular-Blob Channel

The blob regions of V1 have neurons with several different types of receptive fields. Many have center-surround and color-opponent receptive fields, like those already described for the P ganglion cells, the parvocellular layers of the LGN, and in layer IVCβ of V1. Others have **concentric double-opponent** receptive fields (Figure 5.19), making them highly sensitive to the presence of contrasting colors. To appreciate the potential importance of these cells for color perception, it is necessary to consider color vision in somewhat more detail.

As we have already discussed, the three cone types provide a basis for the coding of wavelength in that any particular waveband will produce a unique pattern of stimulation across the three receptors. For example, light in the 600 nm range will cause the R cones to fire at their highest frequency, the G cones

TABLE 5.1   Receptive field characteristics of neurons in retina, LGN, and cortical regions mediating visual processing.

RETINA

P ganglion cells	*M ganglion cells*
wavelength sensitive	not wavelength sensitive
most are color-opponent	sensitive to low contrast
sustained discharge	transient discharge
	large receptive fields

LGN

Parvocellular layers	*Magnocellular layers*
center-antagonistic surround receptive fields	not sensitive to wavelength
wavelength sensitive	response as a function of contrast grows more steeply than P neurons
most are color-opponent	respond strongly to movement
respond weakly to movement	

CORTEX

V1

Layer IVCβ
receptive fields like P LGN

Blobs
wavelength selective
single- and double-color opponent

Interblobs
not wavelength selective
simple cells
complex cells

V2

Thin stripes
wavelength sensitive
many are double-color-opponent
generally have larger receptive fields than color-opponent cells in V1

Interstripes
most are wavelength sensitive
similar to interblob neurons but larger receptive fields

V4

majority of cells are wavelength sensitive
many are orientation selective
some are truly color selective (i.e., their receptive field is a perceived color)
some are both color and orientation selective
projects mainly to inferotemporal cortex and neurons implicated in pattern recognition

V1

Layer IVCα
not wavelength sensitive
orientation selective (simple cells)

Layer IVB
orientation selective
direction selective
binocular receptive fields

V2

Thick stripes
similar to IVB, but larger receptive fields

V3

not color sensitive
majority are orientation selective
many are both orientation and movement selective

V5

all cells are movement sensitive
most are direction selective
not color sensitive
not form sensitive
large receptive fields
projects mainly to parietal cortex and neurons implicated in spatial location

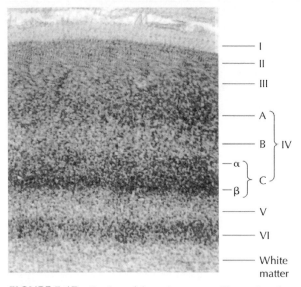

FIGURE 5.17   Section of the striate cortex illustrating the cytoarchitecture of this area. The section is Nissl stained to show cell bodies and reveals the presence of nine layers in this area. *(Adapted from Bear, Connors, & Paradiso, 1996, p. 253)*

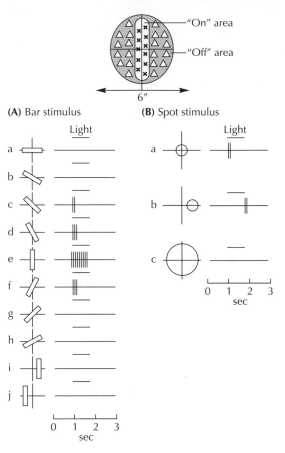

FIGURE 5.18   Simple cells, as defined by Hubel and Wiesel, in layer IVCα of the primary visual cortex (V1). These cells respond most strongly to a bar presented at a particular angle of orientation in a particular location within the visual field. Patterns of action potentials that occur in response to various stimuli are shown, and the bar above the response record indicates the duration of the stimulus. *(A)* This particular cell responds most strongly when a vertical bar is in a particular location within the visual field (e). Bars of all other orientations (a–h) or vertical bars in other locations within the visual field (i, j) are less effective or totally ineffective in driving the cell. Spots of light elicit only weak responses or no response at all. *(Adapted from Kandel et al., 1995, p. 435)*

to fire at a lower frequency, and the B cones to fire at a very low frequency (see Figure 5.4). The system is able to monitor the relative activation of the three types of cones and thus has a mechanism for coding the wavelength of light impinging on the retina. The coding of wavelength is, however, not sufficient for the perception of the color of an object because an object of a given color, say red, will be seen as red under different illumination conditions, even though the light reflected from its surface varies enormously across these conditions. This is something we commonly experience in everyday life: An apple looks red in sunlight and in candlelight, even though the wavelengths reflected from its surface differ radically in the two illumination conditions.

This can also be demonstrated experimentally. Suppose we have three lamps, one projecting long, one middle, and one short wavelength light, and a telephotometer, which measures the amount of light of any given wavelength reflected from a surface. Using these devices, we can manipulate the light reflected from a surface of a given color in various ways. For example, if we have a red surface, we can adjust the three lamps so that the surface reflects 70 units of short-wavelength light, 20 units of middle-wavelength light, and 10 units of long-wavelength light. If this surface is part of a larger array of colored surfaces, as, for example, part of a pattern of

(A) Concentric Double-Opponent Cells (cortex)

(B) Double-Opponent Red-Green Contrast Cell

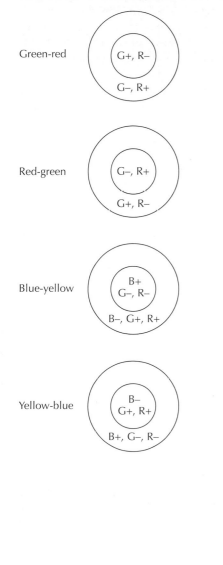

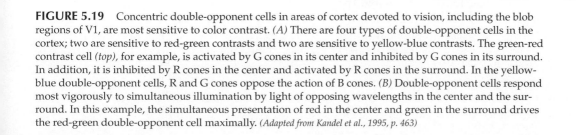

FIGURE 5.19   Concentric double-opponent cells in areas of cortex devoted to vision, including the blob regions of V1, are most sensitive to color contrast. *(A)* There are four types of double-opponent cells in the cortex; two are sensitive to red-green contrasts and two are sensitive to yellow-blue contrasts. The green-red contrast cell *(top)*, for example, is activated by G cones in its center and inhibited by G cones in its surround. In addition, it is inhibited by R cones in the center and activated by R cones in the surround. In the yellow-blue double-opponent cells, R and G cones oppose the action of B cones. *(B)* Double-opponent cells respond most vigorously to simultaneous illumination by light of opposing wavelengths in the center and the surround. In this example, the simultaneous presentation of red in the center and green in the surround drives the red-green double-opponent cell maximally. *(Adapted from Kandel et al., 1995, p. 463)*

different colored and different sized rectangular surfaces known as a Mondrian (after the Dutch painter Mondrian), then it will continue to be perceived as red, even though in this instance a relatively small percentage of the light reflected from it is long wavelength. This tendency of a surface to maintain its color across varying conditions of illumination is known as **color constancy.**

What is particularly interesting about color constancy is that it is maintained only when the surface in question is surrounded by surfaces of other colors. If the surface is viewed in isolation (termed the **void condition**), then changes in reflected wavelength do result in changes in perceived color. Evidently, then, the visual system engages in some comparative process that enables it to calculate the relative reflectance of a given object for a given waveband compared with other objects in the visual field. Precisely how this is accomplished is not known, but one hypothesis, put forward by Erwin Land, suggests that the system compares the relative reflectance of different objects for short-, middle-, and long-wavelength light. Such a comparison within each waveband is known as a **lightness record.** A comparison of the three lightness records would then enable the system to compute the relative reflectance for different wavelengths of the surfaces in view. This is the invariant information, independent of the particular conditions of ambient illumination, that the system requires for the construction of color. The word *construction* is used here deliberately, for, as we have just seen, assigning a color to a surface is a kind of abstracting process that specifies characteristics intrinsic to that surface, transcending the registration of the particular wavelengths reflected from the surface under any specific conditions of illumination.

With this as a framework, let's go back and consider what the color-opponent cells we have discussed so far may contribute to color perception. The simple color-opponent cells in the retina and the LGN are in fact really *wavelength*-opponent rather than *color*-opponent. In this sense, their conventional name is misleading. For example, suppose a blue surface is illuminated in such a way as to reflect, say, 70 units of long-, 20 units of middle-, and 10 units of short-wavelength light. An ON-blue center/OFF-

yellow surround simple color-opponent cell, the receptive field of which is activated by this light, will *reduce* its firing rate below baseline. In other words, it will respond on the basis of wavelength (in this case predominately in the long waveband) rather than in terms of the perceived color of the surface.

In contrast, the double-opponent cells of V1 (see Figure 5.19) seem to represent an advance toward color generation. They are still responding to particular wavelengths rather than color, so in that sense they cannot be the substrata of color generation. However, their receptive field characteristics require a minimum *difference* between the wavelengths impinging on their center and their surround. For example, the cell described in Figure 5.19B will fire maximally when long-wavelength light impinges on its center and middle-wavelength light impinges on its surround. Thus, these cells appear to be carrying out aspects of the comparative process that are necessary for an appreciation of the relative reflectance of surfaces within the field of view. The small size of the receptive fields of double-opponent cells in V1 suggests that they play only an initial role in that process.

To find cells with a receptive field that is a particular perceived color (rather than a particular wavelength), one must go to another area of cortex, called V4. We will discuss this critically important area for color perception shortly. First, however, let us consider some of the other projections from V1, starting with the projection of fibers from the blob regions. Their first synapse is in V2. Area V2 forms a ring around V1 (Figure 5.20), and within V2 there are areas that are defined by the same method for cytochrome oxidase staining described earlier for V1. In the case of V2 the subareas are called **thin stripes, thick stripes,** and **interstripes.** The destination of neurons originating in the blob areas of V1 is the thin stripes of V2. Neurons within the thin stripes are wavelength sensitive, and many are also double-opponent. They generally have larger receptive fields than the double-opponent cells of V1, a characteristic that would enhance the efficiency of the comparative process hypothesized to be carried out by the double-opponent cells. Neurons in the thin-stripe regions of V2 then project to V4. In addition, there are direct connections from the blob areas of V1 to V4 (see Figure 5.16).

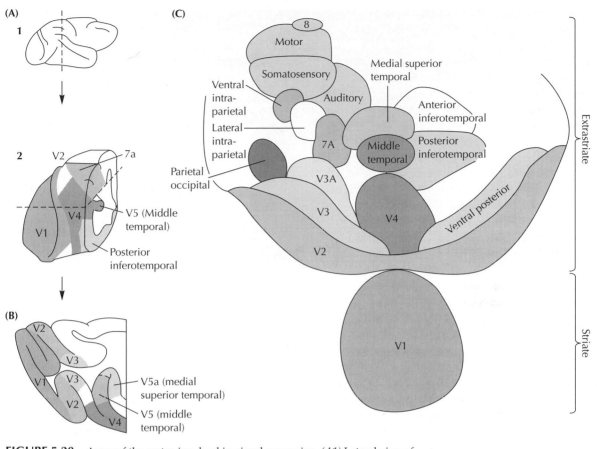

FIGURE 5.20   Areas of the cortex involved in visual processing. *(A1)* Lateral view of the right hemisphere of the monkey, from which parts of the striate cortex (V1) and extrastriate cortex (V2 and V4) are visible. *(A2)* Coronal section at the level of the vertical line in (A1); V1, V2, V4, and V5 can be seen. *(B)* Horizontal section at the level of the line in (A2) shows the known visual areas visible at this level. *(C)* The visual areas are unfolded and flattened to show their relative sizes. There are at least 14 known visual areas and probably many others. Areas V1, V2, V3, V4, and V5 (also called middle temporal, or MT) are currently the best understood of these cortical visual areas, but it is almost certain that others will be found to play critical roles in visual processing. *(Adapted from Kandel et al., 1995, p. 394)*

If we consider the receptive-field characteristics of cells in V4, we find many wavelength-selective cells. In addition, as already mentioned, we find cells whose receptive field is a particular perceived *color*. Thus, there are cells in V4 that respond to a blue surface positioned within a Mondrian field (i.e., an array of other colors) and will not respond to a surface of another color *even when the wavelengths reflected from the two surfaces are identical.* For example, light can be projected on a blue surface so that it reflects 50 units of long-, 30 units of middle-, and 20 units of short-wavelength light. When viewed in a Mondrian field, this surface will appear blue, even though it is reflecting more long-wavelength light, and it will cause our cell to fire. Next, if we project light on a red surface in such a way as to cause an identical composition of reflected light, the surface will nevertheless appear red, and our cell will not fire. Thus, unlike the

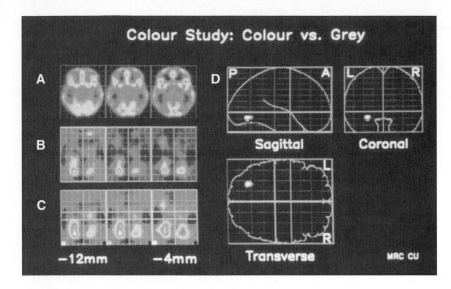

FIGURE 5.21 *(A)* PET images of blood flow obtained from subjects looking at a multicolored Mondrian. *(B)* The image resulting when the scan obtained from looking at a black-and-white array with the same formal aspects as the color array used in *A* is subtracted from *A*. *(C)* The statistical significance of the obtained differences. *(D)* The localization by this method of the area designated as Human V4 within the three principle anatomical planes. *(Adapted from Posner & Raichle, 1994, p. 75)*

color-opponent cells that we found in other areas of the visual system from the retina to V2, some of the cells in V4 are truly responsive to color and not wavelength.

The importance of V4 for color perception is also demonstrated by the occurrence of **achromatopsia,** or central color blindness. Patients with this impairment cannot generate color, or even form a mental image of color, even though their ability to differentiate between different wavelengths is unimpaired. This condition was poignantly described in an account by Oliver Sacks of an artist (Sacks, 1995; Sacks & Wasserman, 1987), who described a world of black, gray, and white that was intensely distressing to him, everything appearing dirty and disturbing. He described food as appearing particularly disgusting, and he had difficulty eating without closing his eyes. Particularly disturbing was the fact that this achromatic world was three-dimensional. Unlike a photograph or a black-and-white movie, one could not turn away from it but instead was trapped within it. Of particular interest, in the context of our discussion of color perception, is the preservation of wavelength discrimination in this patient. This was demonstrated by normal performance in tasks such as the sorting of yarn of different colors. The artist was able to discriminate between different wavelengths, even though he had no subjective experience of color. This dissociation emphasizes what has already become a recurring theme in our discussion: Color perception is more than wavelength discrimination.

Although the site of lesion in this patient was not determined, Semir Zeki and his colleagues (1991), using positron emission tomography, have compared cerebral blood flow in human subjects viewing a color Mondrian with blood flow while viewing an identical black-and-white pattern. They found that the highest increase in blood flow in the color condition was in the fusiform gyrus, although V1 and V2 also showed increased activity, and they designated this area **human V4** (Figure 5.21).

The Parvocellular-Interblob Channel

Let's consider a second channel, the **parvocellular-interblob channel.** Up to layer IVCβ this channel is not differentiated from the parvocellular-blob channel just discussed. However, as its name suggests, this channel's next synaptic connection is in the interblob regions of V1. Here the cells have receptive-field characteristics that are very different from those of cells in the blob regions. In contrast to blob neurons, interblob neurons are not wavelength selective. Instead, the majority of them are orientation selective. In some interblob neurons this orientation selectivity takes the form of a receptive field with an

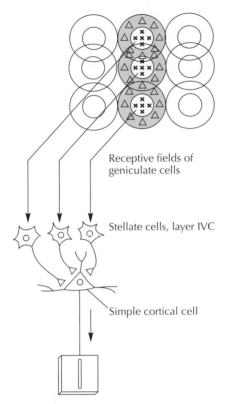

Receptive fields of geniculate cells

Stellate cells, layer IVC

Simple cortical cell

FIGURE 5.22   The mechanism by which the output of LGN cells with center-surround receptive fields is transformed into the elongated receptive fields of simple cortical cells is unknown. One hypothesis is that the simple cortical cell's receptive field is generated by the converging input of three or more ON-center LGN cells whose centers define its location and orientation. *(Adapted from Kandel et al., 1995, p. 435)*

(A) Response to Orientation of Stimulus

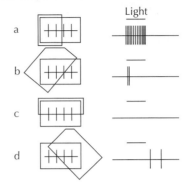

(B) Response to Position of Stimulus

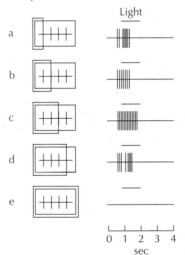

FIGURE 5.23   Complex cells, like simple cells, respond to stimuli of a particular orientation in the visual field. In contrast to a simple cell's response, however, the response of a complex cell is not dependent on the exact location of the stimulus within the cell's receptive field, and movement of the stimulus may actually enhance the responsiveness of the cell. In *(A)* the orientation selectivity of a complex cell is demonstrated. In *(B)* the responsiveness of this cell to vertical stimuli in different regions of its receptive field is seen. Note that the cell is actually responding to the edge between illumination and darkness, so that illumination of the entire receptive field *(A-c, B-e)* produces no response. *(Adapted from Kandel et al., 1995, p. 437)*

excitatory bar-shaped center of a particular orientation, flanked by inhibitory regions (see Figure 5.18), such as those found in layer IVCα. Hubel and Wiesel, who carried out the first systematic exploration of the physiology of the visual cortex and termed these neurons simple cells, hypothesized that their functional characteristics are defined by input from several concentric center-surround cells (Figure 5.22). Other cells within the interblob region, termed **complex cells,** are responsive to an edge of illumination in a particular orientation in any portion of the cell's receptive field (Figure 5.23). These cells have been hypothesized to have input from a number of simple cells. It is of interest that the blob and interblob regions have neurons with such different receptive-field characteristics even though they both derive their major input from cells in layer IVCβ. This emphasizes how the same input, processed differently, can be transformed in such a way as to extract information about very different aspects of the stimulus.

Neurons in the interblob regions of V1 project to the interstripe regions of V2. Cells in the latter area have similar receptive-field characteristics to those in the former, but again the receptive fields of neurons in V2 are larger. Neurons in the interstripe regions of V2 project to V4. There is also direct input from the interblob regions of V1 to V4. These inputs to V4 suggest that this area is not involved only with color, as our earlier discussion of blob inputs suggested. In fact, although the majority of cells in V4 are wavelength selective, and, as we have seen, some are truly color selective, many are orientation selective and some are both color and orientation selective. It appears, therefore, that V4 is involved in processing both color and form. Data demonstrating specific impairment in form perception following cerebral lesions analogous to the specific impairment in color perception we discussed earlier are lacking. This is probably due to the fact that the processes involved in form perception are more diffusely represented. As we will see in the next section, one of the magnocellular channels is also involved in the processing of form.

The Magnocellular-V5 Channel and the Magnocellular-V3 Channel

The two magnocellular layers of the LGN, deriving their input from M ganglion cells, project to layer IVCα of V1. Like the neurons in the magnocellular layers of the LGN, cells in layer IVCα are insensitive to wavelength. Instead, these neurons have elongated receptive fields that are sensitive to a bar of illumination in their center and that have inhibitory regions on their flanks. In other words, they have the characteristics of Hubel and Wiesel's simple cortical cells that we found in the interblob regions.

Neurons in layer IVCα project to neurons in layer IVB. The latter have receptive fields that are orienta-

tion selective. In addition, many neurons in this layer are **direction selective;** they fire when a stimulus moves in a particular direction. In addition, neurons in layer IVB have binocular receptive fields. This allows them to code depth by processing information about **binocular disparity,** the difference between the images of an object on the two retinas due to the slightly different locations of the two eyes relative to the viewed object.

Neurons in layer IVB of V1 project to the thick stripes of V2. Here again, as we saw with the projections of the two parvocellular channels from V1, the most striking elaboration is an increase in the size of the receptive fields. From V2 there are projections to two areas of cortex, V5 and V3. There are also direct projections from layer IVB of V1 to these areas (see Figure 5.16).

CORTICAL SPECIALIZATION FOR MOTION PERCEPTION: V5   The receptive-field characteristics of cells in V5 (also called **MT,** for middle temporal, the location of this area in the monkey) indicate that this area is specialized for processing involved in the perception of movement. All neurons in V5 are sensitive to movement, and most are selectively sensitive to movement in a specific direction. In contrast, no neurons sensitive to color or form have been found in V5. In addition, neurons in V5 have large receptive fields, which would appear to enhance their capacity to provide a basis for determining whether a number of points are moving together (i.e., are parts of a single moving object).

The existence of areas in cortex specialized for the processing of motion is also supported by the occurrence of specific impairment in the perception of motion after cerebral lesions, a condition called **akinetopsia.** Patients with this impairment cannot see objects in motion and describe experiencing objects suddenly appearing in front of them without moving toward them, much as one might suddenly see an approaching object illuminated only by a slowly flashing strobe light. In contrast, other aspects of objects are accurately perceived. Interestingly, these patients retain a sense that motion has occurred, even though their perception of it is severely impaired. This resid-

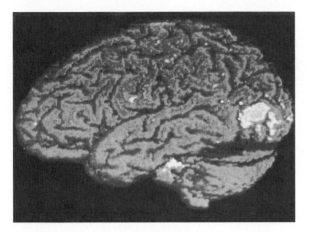

FIGURE 5.24   The area of cortex that shows increased activity when human subjects view moving stimuli (human V5), as determined by positron emission tomography. *(Adapted from Zeki, 1993, Plate 2)*

ual capacity for motion detection probably relies on intact mechanisms in V1 and V2, where cells sensitive to motion have also been identified.

PET studies of blood flow in normal subjects who are viewing moving black squares reveal increased activity in an area just lateral to V4; this area has been called **human V5** (Figure 5.24). As one might expect, V1 and V2 also show increased activity under these conditions, as we saw that they did under the stimulus conditions that revealed the presence of V4.

All of this evidence in support of a cortical area specialized for the processing of movement has recently been augmented by studies that demonstrate that perception of movement in the monkey can actually be manipulated by the stimulation of cells in V5. To describe these experiments it is necessary to consider another dimension of organization within the specialized areas of cortex that we have been discussing. All of these areas, including V1 and V2, have neurons organized in columns extending from the upper to the lower layers of the cortex. These columns are defined neurophysiologically: All of the cells within a column have very similar receptive fields. For example, in the orientation columns of V1, all of the neurons within a given column have the same orientation specificity, all firing to a bar-shaped

illumination oriented at the same angle, say 44°. We will have more to say about this elegant organization within the cortex, and we will also see that some remarkable investigations have been carried out that have made it possible to visualize these areas. In the present context, however, let us return to V5 and note that the neurons in this area also exhibit a columnar organization, each column containing cells that fire in response to movement in a particular direction.

With the columnar organization of V5 in mind, let's consider the experiments carried out by William Newsome and his colleagues, which we introduced in the previous paragraph. A monkey was first trained to report the direction of moving dots by moving his eyes in the direction of their movement. Then, using a microelectrode, neurons within a particular column of V5, and therefore sensitive to a particular direction of movement, were stimulated at an intensity that would increase their firing rate. The result of this stimulation was that the monkey moved his eyes in the direction encoded by the stimulated neurons within the direction-selective column being stimulated (Salzman, Britten, & Newsome, 1990; Salzman, Murasugi, et al., 1992). This is compelling additional evidence for the role of neurons in V5 in motion perception.

SPECIALIZATION FOR FORM-MOTION PERCEPTION: V3   The second magnocellular channel has circuitry very similar to that of the magnocellular channel projecting to V5 that we have just discussed (see Figure 5.16). In this channel, however, neurons from layer IVB of V1 project to V3. As in the magnocellular-V5 channel, IVB connects with V3 both directly and via the thick stripes of V2. The majority of neurons in V3 are orientation selective, and many are both orientation selective and movement selective. In contrast, none have been found that are sensitive to wavelength. Thus, V3 seems to be concerned with the shapes of objects in motion, an attribute that has been described as **dynamic form.**

We have seen that there are two areas specialized for the processing of form, V3 and V4. This probably accounts for why a specific impairment in form perception has not been observed after a cerebral lesion; the lesion would have to be very large and have a peculiar shape to include these two areas while leaving other extrastriate areas intact. There are reports that patients with V4 lesions, in addition to manifesting achromatopsia, also exhibit some form discrimination deficits when viewing stationary stimuli. Interestingly, when these patients are able to move their heads from side to side, their form discrimination is vastly improved, presumably because the resulting movement of the stimuli brings into play the dynamic form system mediated by V3.

In summary, there are four well-studied specialized channels projecting to three specialized extrastriate cortical areas mediating specific aspects of visual perception. The parvocellular-blob channel, projecting to V4, processes information contributing to color perception. The parvocellular-interblob channel, also projecting to V4, processes information related to form perception. Thus, V4 mediates processes involved in the perception of color and the perception of form and color. There are two magnocellular channels, one projecting to V5 and involved in motion perception and one projecting to V3 and involved in the perception of dynamic form.

THE MICROANATOMY OF THE VISUAL CORTEX AND THE CONCEPT OF MODULAR ORGANIZATION

In our discussion of the experimental manipulation of motion perception in the monkey through the stimulation of cells in V5, we alluded to the columnar organization of areas of the cortex involved in vision. Let's now consider this topic in somewhat greater detail. We will find that cortical areas involved in vision are indeed highly organized and that this organization has led to the notion that the visual cortex has a modular organization.

Hubel and Wiesel's discovery of orientation-selective neurons in the interblob regions of V1 was accompanied by the discovery that cells sensitive to a bar of illumination of a particular orientation are organized in columns, termed **orientation columns.** Thus, an electrode penetrating the cortex at an angle perpendicular to its surface will encounter cells that have receptive fields defined by bar-shaped visual

stimuli oriented at the same angle. Furthermore, when recordings were made from neighboring areas, the orientation specificity of adjacent columns was found to vary in a highly systematic manner (Figure 5.25).

Superimposed on this organization is another that has to do with the eye that drives a given cell. Recall that V1 in each hemisphere receives input from only one visual field, but from both eyes. Hubel and Wiesel found that each neuron in V1 shows a characteristic pattern of sensitivity to input to the two eyes. Thus, some cells fire only when the right eye is stimulated, some fire much more to right-eye stimulation and to a lesser extent to left-eye stimulation, some are driven equally by input to both eyes, and so on. When a perpendicular penetration is made, the cells encountered in a given column were found to have a characteristic pattern of responsiveness to input to the two eyes, although some variation among cells in a column was seen (Figure 5.26). These columns came to be known as **ocular dominance columns.**

Having identified orientation columns and ocular dominance columns on the basis of physiological methods, Hubel and Wiesel then attempted to discover anatomical correlates of these physiologically defined entities, using some sophisticated techniques. To visualize the ocular dominance columns, they injected a radioactive amino acid into one eye of an animal. They reasoned that cells in the visual system, like all neurons, would transport this amino acid along the chain of cells, in this case from the eye to V1. The resulting differences in the level of uptake by cells in V1 should therefore reveal a picture of the extent to which cells were receiving neural input from the injected eye. Using autoradiography, which allows quantitative measurement of uptake of radioactivity in tissue, a stunning visualization of the ocular dominance columns was achieved (Figure 5.27). The investigators also discovered that if one visualizes the cortical surface from above, these columns form an intricate pattern not unlike that of a zebra or in a fingerprint (Figure 5.28).

To visualize the anatomical substrate of the orientation columns, Hubel and Wiesel utilized a technique developed by Louis Sokoloff and his associates that involves the radioactive labeling of 2-deoxyglucose, a

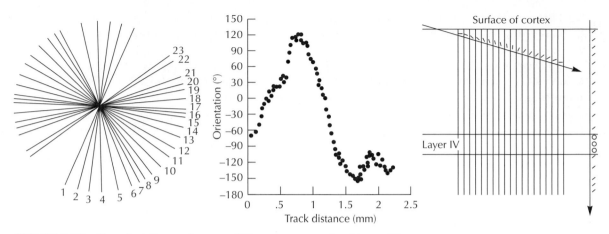

FIGURE 5.25   The orientation preferences of 23 neurons encountered in an oblique penetration of a microelectrode *(left, center)*. Note the highly systematic way in which the orientation specificity of neurons varies as the electrode moves to adjacent areas of cortex. Findings such as these, together with the finding that an electrode penetration made perpendicular to the cortical surface encounters neurons with the same orientation preference, have led to the idea that the cortex is divided into parallel orientation columns, each containing cells with the same orientation specificity. *(Adapted from Hubel & Wiesel, 1979, p. 91)*

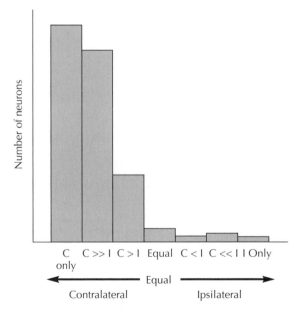

FIGURE 5.26   Neurons in V1 vary with respect to the eye to which a stimulus must be presented for each neuron to fire. Some will fire only to stimuli presented to one eye, others prefer one eye but will also respond to stimuli presented to the other eye, and still others fire equally in response to stimuli to either eye. This dimension of neuronal activity is referred to as ocular dominance. An electrode penetration made perpendicular to the cortical surface will encounter a population of cells with a characteristic response profile, as illustrated by the ocular dominance histogram shown here, in which the majority of cells are more responsive to stimuli presented to the eye contralateral (C) to the hemisphere being recorded and less to the eye ipsilateral (I). As one moves to adjacent areas of cortex, there is a systematic shift in the ocular dominance of cells. Findings such as these revealed the presence of ocular dominance columns.

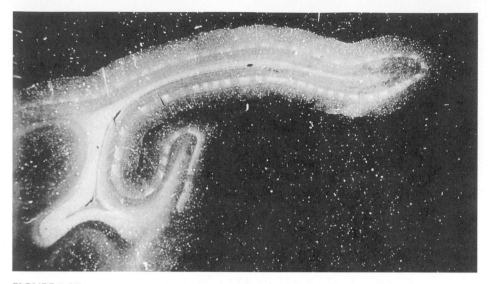

FIGURE 5.27 Cross section of cortex in V1 cut perpendicular to the surface, showing the ocular dominance columns revealed through an axon-transport autoradiograph. *(From Hubel & Wiesel, 1979, p. 85)*

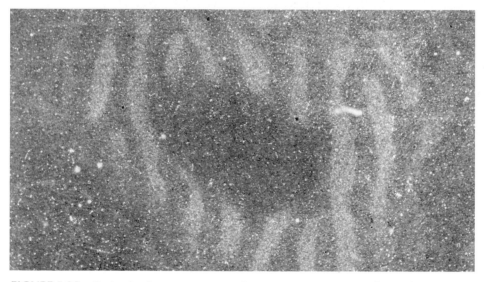

FIGURE 5.28 Ocular dominance pattern seen in an axon-transport autoradiograph of V1 cortex cut parallel to its surface. *(From Hubel & Wiesel, 1979, p. 85)*

metabolically active molecule that mimics the activity of glucose, the major source of energy for neural tissue. The basis of this technique is the demonstrated correlation between the rate of 2-deoxyglucose utilization and the level of metabolic activity in specific regions of the brain. This correlation reflects the fact that, although the initial steps in the metabolism of

2-deoxyglucose parallel those of glucose, the metabolism of 2-deoxyglucose stops with the production of a molecule that does not cross the cell wall and so accumulates in the cell. Thus, the examination of brain tissue immediately after metabolic activity, using autoradiological techniques similar to those utilized in the identification of ocular dominance columns,

FIGURE 5.29 A cross section of V1 cut perpendicular to the surface, showing the orientation columns revealed by the 2-deoxyglucose method. *(From Hubel & Wiesel, 1979, p. 91)*

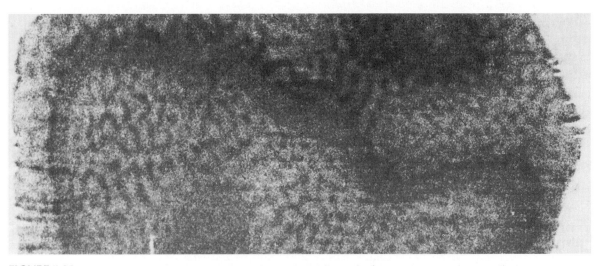

FIGURE 5.30 Orientation pattern seen in a 2-deoxyglucose autoradiograph of a section of monkey cortex in V1 cut tangential to its surface after the animal had been exposed to vertical stripes. *(From Hubel & Wiesel, 1979, p. 91)*

makes it possible to measure metabolic activity in different brain regions and under varying stimulus conditions.

The reasoning behind this investigation was that if the visual system of an animal is exposed to a stimulus of a particular orientation, those cells responsive to that orientation should be firing at the highest rate and should therefore be utilizing glucose at a high rate. In contrast, the opposite should be true for those cells that do not have that orientation as their receptive field. Using the 2-deoxyglucose method, Hubel and Wiesel were able to visualize the orientation columns that they had previously defined electrophysiologically (Figure 5.29). In addition, when they

viewed a slice of cortex cut parallel to its surface, they found that cells of a particular orientation were organized in a kind of honeycomb pattern (Figure 5.30). Finally, by modifying the deoxyglucose experiment so that a stimulus of a particular orientation was exposed to one eye only, it was possible to visualize neurons with both a particular orientation sensitivity and a particular ocular dominance. These neurons were also found to exhibit an orderly arrangement (Figure 5.31).

We have seen that in an electrode penetration that is oblique or parallel to the cortical surface, the orientation preferences of successive cells vary with great regularity (see Figure 5.25). If an electrode travels about 1 mm, it will encounter cells representing

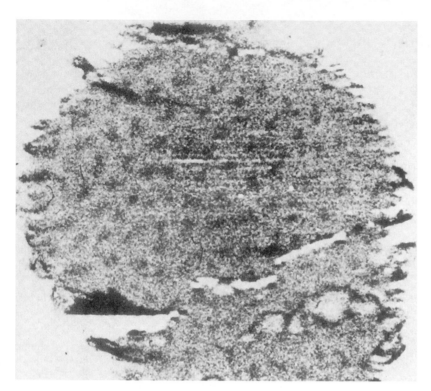

FIGURE 5.31   A 2-deoxyglucose autoradiograph of a tangential section of V1 showing the pattern of activity elicited by exposing one eye only to vertical stripes. *(From Hubel & Wiesel, 1979, p. 96)*

all orientations. This is referred to as an **orientation hypercolumn.** Analogously, an electrode must move about the same distance to cover the complete cycle of eye dominance, i.e., an **ocular dominance hypercolumn.** It has been established that the image of a point in space falls within the receptive fields of neurons across a 2 mm distance in V1. These findings, together with findings regarding the density of blobs in V1, indicate that a 2 × 2 mm block of cortex in V1 would contain 16 blobs, two ocular dominance hypercolumns, and two orientation hypercolumns. Hubel and Wiesel have suggested that such a block contains the machinery necessary to initiate the analysis of the contribution of a point in the visual field to the perception of color, form, and movement. This has led to the hypothesis that V1 possesses a modular architecture and that visual perception somehow involves the simultaneous processing of the visual scene by these **cortical modules.**

We have already mentioned that V5 also exhibits a columnar organization, such that neurons sensitive to a specific direction of movement are grouped together. V2 is also highly organized, as are, to a lesser extent, V3 and V5.

THE PROBLEM OF INTEGRATION AND THE CONSTRUCTION OF A REPRESENTATION OF THE VISUAL WORLD

We have seen that specialized areas within the visual cortex can be defined in terms of their function, as revealed by the physiological characteristics of single neurons, the effect of lesions, anatomical inputs and outputs, and anatomical and metabolic microarchitecture. On the basis of these lines of investigation, it has been established that there are a number of functionally specialized areas devoted to specific aspects of vision and that these areas process input largely in parallel. We have said that these findings were unexpected in that they did not fit into the traditional conceptualization of cortical processing. Taken together, these findings make cortex that processes vision the currently most completely understood area of the cortex.

This advanced level of understanding brings with it, of course, profound new problems that have yet to emerge in the study of other cortical areas. Knowing more about something as complicated as the visual cortex means having a clearer view of the deeper questions revealed by more complete understanding. Two of the major questions with which this depth of understanding confronts us is why these specialized areas exist and how the different aspects of the visual world processed in these separate areas of cortex are integrated into a unified representation of that world. We are a long way from being able to answer either of these questions satisfactorily.

With regard to the question of why this functional specialization is present, one may presume that it reflects the need for highly specialized neuronal organization for the processing of each aspect of the visual world. For example, consider the significance of the large receptive fields of cells in V5. These large receptive fields enhance the capacity of these neurons to make the comparisons necessary to evaluate which features of a field of view are moving in the same direction and at the same speed. Such an evaluation would seem to be a requirement for the differentiation of many points on a single moving object from points on different objects moving in different directions. In contrast, consider the small receptive fields of cells in V1. This suggests that V1 must be involved in the precise identification of the location of stimuli within the visual field. These two hypotheses sound reasonable enough, although they remain to be fully tested. But there is much about functional specialization within different visual areas that remains a mystery. Thus, the general proposition that the functional specialization that characterizes these areas reflects the processing requirements of the specific features of the visual world with which these areas are concerned is really a set of new and challenging questions about the relationship between neuronal organization and function.

Also awaiting an answer is the integration problem or, as it is generally called, the **binding problem.** How do the varied aspects of the visual input being processed in different cortical areas get put together to yield the integrated visual representation that we experience as the visual world? The most alluring and convenient answer to this question would seem to be that all of the specialized areas report to some master area, where integration takes place. There are serious problems with this solution, however, both on conceptual and empirical grounds. Conceptually, the master area hypothesis begs the question, for it immediately raises the question of who is looking at the master area. In addition, the master area would presumably contain cells with highly specific receptive fields that represent the culmination of the hierarchical integrative processes of the system. These are the hypothetical **grandmother cells** that have been proposed by some to mediate visual perception by firing to highly specific stimuli. Conceptually, it is difficult to imagine how there could be a sufficient number of neurons to represent all encountered visual images in all of their possible orientations and illuminations. Even the massive number of neurons in the human brain would seem to be insufficient for such a task.

The master area hypothesis also has serious problems on empirical grounds. The only evidence for such an area is the finding that about 10% of the neurons in the inferior temporal cortex of the monkey, receiving major input from V4, are selectively sensitive to specific images, such as hands or faces. Some neurons selective for faces respond best to a particular view of the face; others respond best to a particular facial expression. Considered alone, this detailed and specific selectivity of cells in the inferior temporal cortex seems to support the master area hypothesis; however, the representation of faces and other complex forms in the inferotemporal cortex appears to be a special case. The representation of a very limited class of stimuli in this way may have some specific adaptive value, but there is no evidence that this reflects a general mechanism for coding visual stimuli.

A second and related empirical problem with the master area hypothesis is the absence of anatomical evidence that the specialized visual areas all converge on one area. Instead, V4 projects mainly to the inferotemporal cortex, and V5 projects mainly to parietal cortex. Actually, the situation is somewhat more complicated because there are also projections from V4 to parietal cortex and projections from V5 to temporal cortex. Of particular interest in the present context, however, is the fact that each of these extrastriate areas projects to different areas within parietal and temporal cortex, again in contradiction to the master area hypothesis.

Far from converging on one master area, the four parallel channels are linked anatomically at every level, so that input from one can influence others. Thus, V3, V4, and V5 are richly interconnected and also project back to V1 and V2, which feed them. These latter returning projections have been termed **reentrant connections.** Zeki (1993) has proposed that reentrant connections from each specialized extrastriate area back to V1 and V2 provide a partial solution to the binding problem. This hypothesis is supported by anatomical evidence. For example, whereas projections from V1 and V2 to extrastriate areas are highly specific with regard to both their regions of origin within V1 and V2 and their destinations within extrastriate areas, reentrant connections from extrastriate areas back to V1 and V2 are diffuse and nonspecific. This diffuse reentrant input would appear to provide a basis for the integration of specialized processing carried out in one extrastriate area, such as motion in V5, with information on its way to other specialized areas, such as form-related information on its way to V3. Such an integration of information related to form and motion could manifest itself in the "dynamic form" receptive fields in V3. To take another example, reentrant connections from V4 to V2 project not only back to the thin stripes and interstripes, V4's major sources of input from V2, but also to the thick stripes of V2, which project to V3 and V5. This could represent a mechanism for integrating processing concerned with form and color (mediated by the two parvocellular channels) with the processing of form and motion mediated by the two magnocellular channels (Figure 5.32).

The notion that reentrant connections play a role in solving the binding problem is enticing and may well prove to be the case, although at the present time it remains hypothetical. Another perspective from which to try to understand the contributions of

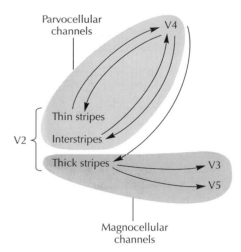

FIGURE 5.32 The reentrant connections from V4 to the thick stripes of V2 provide a possible mechanism whereby the processing of form and color mediated by the two parvocellular channels, including V4, could be integrated with the processing of form and movement mediated by the two magnocellular channels, including V3 and V5.

different visual areas is to examine what happens when components of the visual cortex are compromised through cerebral lesions. Damage to V1 results in blindness, so it would seem that V1 is needed to begin the cortical processing of visual input and/or to receive reentrant input from extrastriate areas. Interestingly, recent studies suggest that the latter process may be more critical than the former. These studies involve the phenomenon of blindsight and the demonstration of direct connections from the LGN to extrastriate areas. We have discussed blindsight briefly already and suggested that the preserved capacity to localize points of light in the presence of cortical blindness is mediated by the superior colliculus (see chapter 3). At that time we supported this contention with the argument that the superior colliculus is the homologue of the optic tectum, a structure that in lower species mediates visuomotor coordination. The neural basis of blindsight must, however, be more complicated than this because persons with blindsight are able to make discriminations that require the participation of cortical processing. These include simple pattern discrimination, the discrimination of motion in different directions, and wavelength discrimination.

What is the mechanism of this preserved function in the presence of damage to V1? As we have noted, there are direct connections from the LGN to extrastriate areas. For example, the existence of direct connections from the LGN to V4 and to V5 has been demonstrated. This would provide a mechanism whereby specific features of a stimulus could be processed, and even influence behavior, in the absence of an integrated conscious representation of the visual world. Apparently V1 is critical for such a conscious representation, although how it participates in its construction remains a mystery.

Another perspective from which to assess the function of V1 comes from the study of patients with a pattern of impairment complementary to that underlying blindsight: severe damage to extrastriate areas and relative preservation of V1. Such patients have an appreciation of local elements within the visual scene, as evidenced by their ability to sketch discrete features within a complex visual scene with considerable accuracy. They are, however, unable to place these elements within a larger perceptual context and thus have no comprehension of what they have drawn. The absence of extrastriate input renders these patients incapable of integrating the accurately perceived elements into a coherent picture of the whole scene.

SUMMARY

From the foregoing discussion it can be seen that a good deal is known about the parts of the brain directly involved in vision. From the physiological study of cells at all levels of the visual system, from the retina to the specialized visual areas of the cortex, receptive-field characteristics have been discovered that provide information about the features of the visual world being processed by particular cells and by particular brain areas, as well as the mechanisms whereby this processing is accomplished. Detailed anatomical studies have identified the sources of input and the destinations of output for many of the regions involved in vision. Studies of metabolic

microarchitecture have revealed subregions that are specialized both in terms of the receptive field characteristics of their neurons and their anatomical connections with other areas. Lesion studies have shown the presence of specific deficits, such as achromatopsia and akinetopsia, that are consistent with evidence of specialization derived from other methods. What is truly encouraging and exciting is the way in which these varied methods, these different perspectives and levels of investigation, have yielded findings that complement and inform each other. This has enabled us to have a more complete picture of the neural basis of vision than of any other domain of higher functioning.

In this sense, the extent to which different investigative approaches to the visual system have complemented each other and achieved an integrated view of the system might stand as a model to which the study of other domains of brain-behavior relationship might aspire. For a number of reasons our understanding of other domains is less complete. Sometimes this is because they have simply been less extensively studied. But more often, as in the case of the higher-order psychological functions that the rest of this book will consider, it is because the psychological processes that we are striving to understand on the neuropsychological level are even more complex than vision or at least pose less obvious questions. In such cases we must be content for now with the light we are able to shed, even when it is not powered by converging findings from a range of methodological perspectives, as it is in vision.

But if our current understanding of the visual system is a model of what can be known about brain-behavior relationships, it is also a harbinger of the kinds of baffling questions advances in the understanding of other areas will reveal. In the case of the visual system, we have seen how our relatively advanced knowledge has revealed the binding problem and the even larger problem of how neural activity in the system yields a conscious representation of the visual world. As our knowledge advances in other areas, we can be sure that it will bring us face to face with these problems and new ones that are equally baffling.

CHAPTER 6

Language

CHARACTERISTICS OF LANGUAGE

THE DEVELOPMENT OF LANGUAGE IN CHILDREN: NATURE VERSUS NURTURE

LANGUAGE DISORDERS: THE CONCEPT OF APHASIA
Broca's Aphasia
Wernicke's Aphasia
Global Aphasia
The Transcortical Aphasias
Other Central Language Disorders

THE DISCONNECTION SYNDROME HYPOTHESIS APPLIED TO LANGUAGE DISORDERS

MAJOR COMPONENTS OF LANGUAGE FUNCTION
Auditory Word Comprehension

Word Retrieval
Sentence Comprehension and Production
Speech Production
Acquired Reading Impairment
Spelling
Writing

FURTHER THEORETICAL CONSIDERATIONS

THE RIGHT HEMISPHERE AND LANGUAGE

HEMISPHERIC ANATOMICAL ASYMMETRIES

THE EVOLUTION OF HUMAN LANGUAGE

SUMMARY

Of all the psychological functions of which humans are capable, language is perhaps the most remarkable, important, and uniquely human. Other species, such as the honeybee, have evolved some elaborate systems for communicating information, and some primates have been taught to use components of human language. But as far as is currently known, no other species possesses a communication system comparable to human language.

There are several features that distinguish human language from these other communication systems. Human language is infinitely creative. Speakers don't simply repeat what they have heard; rather, they invent novel sentences, many of which must be unique. This

contrasts markedly with systems of other species, which, as far as is known, communicate a narrow range of rather specific and present-oriented information. To be sure, such information can be highly important, as when a honeybee conveys information about the location of a potential source of nectar to the rest of the hive or birds signal their readiness, perhaps even their yearning, for sexual union through intricate mating rituals. These are certainly kinds of communication that our species takes very seriously. Yet for all their importance, communications such as "Nectar 300 yards at 48 degrees left of the sun" and "I want to mate with you" are uncomplicated, and the communication systems that underlie them in other species appear to be limited with regard to the subtlety, nuance, and complexity of the messages that they can transmit. In contrast, human language is infinitely rich in possibilities of meaning, as exemplified by Prospero's speech in The Tempest:

Our revels now are ended: and our actors—
As I foretold you—were all spirits and
Are melted into air, into thin air;
And like the baseless fabric of this vision
The cloud capp'd towers, the gorgeous palaces,

The solemn temples, the great globe itself,
Yes, all which it inherit, shall dissolve
And like the insubstantial pageant faded
Leave not a trace behind: we are such stuff
As dreams are made on, and our little life
Is rounded with a sleep. . . .

But one need not quote Shakespeare to illustrate this point. We all use language to send and receive messages of infinite variety and subtlety of meaning.

CHARACTERISTICS OF LANGUAGE

Two of the aspects of language that make this infinite generativity possible are its form and its structure. Every language has a surprisingly limited number of individual sound elements, called **phonemes,** which are the smallest significant units of sound in a language. English, for example, has only about 40 phonemes, yet, when combined in various ways, these sound elements form all the words of our language.

Language may also be said to be highly structured. It is structured with regard to how phonemes may be combined into words (**morphology**) and how words may be combined into phrases and sentences (**syntax** or **grammar**). Syntax expands the possibilities for the specification of meaning by making word order and word form (e.g., word endings) vehicles for the expression of meaning, thereby rendering a sentence more than the sum of the meanings of its individual words. Thus, it is by virtue of the sentence's syntax that we understand *The lion kills the leopard* to mean that the leopard is dead and that the lion killed it; a sentence containing the same words in a different arrangement could denote the opposite outcome. Grammar, the explicit articulation of the principles governing syntax, need not be learned. Its principles are known implicitly by every competent speaker of a language, even without the laborious lessons in grammar that most of us suffered in our early school years.

The use of syntax has not thus far been conclusively demonstrated in the communication systems of other animals. They may produce a truly impressive array

of communications, yet, as far as we know, each is a discrete element of meaning and the order in which they are produced does not affect the meaning of the individual elements. In addition to the naturalistic study of animal communication, there have been some interesting attempts to train primates, mainly chimpanzees, to use sign language (Gardner & Gardner, 1969, 1975, 1978; Terrace, 1979) and artificial systems based on colored chips and symbols on a computer screen (Premack, 1976; Rumbaugh, 1977). These attempts at language training have shown that chimpanzees are able to learn to produce and understand signs or symbols corresponding to a vocabulary of several hundred words and are able to use these in meaningful interactions with humans and in certain problem-solving situations. However, do the communications of these animals exhibit syntax? Although there have been some reports that they do (Savage-Rumbaugh, 1987; Savage-Rumbaugh et al., 1986), a careful consideration of the data indicates that primates who have undergone language training have not learned syntax (L. R. Gleitman, 1995, p. 372; Kandel, Schwartz, & Jessell, 1995, p. 636). In fact, the inability of chimpanzees to use syntax appears to be one of the major limitations in their ability to truly learn human language, rendering their productions imitative and noncreative. (For a further discussion of the issue of language learning in other species, see Pinker, 1994; Seidenberg & Pettito, 1979; Van Cantfort & Rimpau, 1982).

Another key aspect of language (which is perhaps so intrinsic to it that it seems too obvious to state) is that language conveys meaning. The study of meaning is referred to as **semantics.** Language is also referential. That is, it refers to things and events in the world or to aspects of our subjective experience. As such, the use of language for expression and comprehension is intimately linked with our knowledge of the world and of ourselves and thus with the whole fabric of our cognitive and emotional being. The investigation of the relationship between linguistic meaning and knowledge of the world is known as **pragmatics.**

A final key aspect of language is its interpersonal nature. It is primarily a means of social communication, communication between people, although in the act of writing or engaging in an internal dialogue, individuals may use language as a vehicle for communicating with themselves.

In short, the study of human language users seems to be the most fruitful and most obvious avenue for investigating language. Within this domain, the study of what goes wrong with language when the brain is not working normally has proved to be a highly useful perspective. It will therefore be the focus of the bulk of this chapter.

Before moving to this perspective, let's briefly consider the problem of the origin of language. This question has at least two meanings: How does language develop in the individual, and how did language evolve? Aside from the intrinsic interest of these questions, tackling them illuminates our understanding of the biology of language, although the problem of individual language development is obviously far more amenable to empirical investigation than is the problem of the origin of language itself, shrouded as it is in the remote past. Let's then look at individual language development as a touchstone for understanding the biology of language. At the end of this chapter we will briefly consider the second question and suggest that what we know about the biology of language may provide some very tentative clues about the evolution of language.

THE DEVELOPMENT OF LANGUAGE IN CHILDREN: NATURE VERSUS NURTURE

In considering the development of language in the individual, one thing is clear: The strong forms of both the nativist and the empiricist positions must be wrong; that is, language is neither wholly innate nor wholly learned. Children isolated from the experience of language do not learn language. If the isolation is sufficiently prolonged, they fail to learn language competently, even after exposure to it. This has been shown from the few known cases of children who have grown up in the wild, isolated from other people (so-called wild children), and from children isolated during childhood due to extreme abuse. On the other hand, in contrast to the assertions of behaviorists such as John Watson and B. F. Skinner, language is not simply a learned habit. It is, as we have already asserted, creative and innovative. Children do not learn language by memorizing what they've heard and then emitting conditioned responses after being exposed to conditioned stimuli. Nor, except in some very specialized instances, do they learn language because their efforts are rewarded or punished (Chomsky, 1959). These assertions seem so obvious that it is difficult to appreciate now that a strong empiricist view of language acquisition was championed so vigorously and articulately in the past.

If the strong nativist and strong empiricist theories of language acquisition are both wrong, the reality must be somewhere in between. A position that is supported by a good deal of evidence is that, although language must be experienced to be learned, the capacity for language is an innate property of the human brain (Chomsky, 1975; Lenneberg, 1967). Thus, the brain has evolved in such a way that it is prepared to learn language, just as other organs have evolved in such a way that they are prepared to perform other functions.

There are several lines of evidence supporting this contention. Children seem to learn language effortlessly, as if they were programmed to do so. As long as there is language in the environment and the child is not significantly intellectually impaired, language acquisition proceeds without specific training. It is true that some parents seem to feel the need to provide their children with language instruction, carefully naming various objects in the environment for the child's edification. Yet such instruction is in fact not needed for the child to learn language. On the contrary, there are universal regularities in the process of language acquisition across individuals within a culture and across different cultures. Thus, although there is some individual variation, children pass through an orderly progression of stages, including babbling, one-word speech, two-word speech, and complex speech, and the average onset for each stage is the same for a wide range of cultures (L. R. Gleitman, 1995).

A second line of evidence for the biological preparedness of the human brain for language is the finding that there is a critical period for language acquisition. The study of rare cases of wild children and severely abused children who have been deprived of language experience in early life makes it clear that if a child is not exposed to language for an extended period between age 2 and puberty, that child will not learn language normally. This **critical period** for language acquisition is correlated with a large number of neurobiological variables that are considered indices of brain maturation (Lenneberg, 1967). This second line of evidence provides us with powerful, although circumstantial, evidence that genetically programmed processes of brain maturation provide the neurological substrata supporting language acquisition.

A third line of supporting evidence comes from the finding that infants at birth are sensitive to distinctions among an enormously broad range of phonemes. At birth, infants can discriminate between all of the phonemic distinctions in all languages. Then, as infants are exposed to the particular language in their environment, their capacity to make distinctions not present in the ambient language declines. This suggests that the genetic program constructs a brain that is prepared to make all phonemic distinctions necessary for the learning of any language and that language experience, in at least some metaphorical sense, prunes the neural connections underlying this capacity. Interestingly, this decline begins soon after birth and is perhaps the earliest index of language development identified to date.

A fourth line of evidence supporting the notion of the biological preparedness of the brain for language is the fact that, in the vast majority of right-handers, as well as a majority of left-handers, the left hemisphere is specialized for speech. This is true both for people who use spoken language and for individuals who are hearing impaired and use only sign language (Kimura, 1981). If neural structures within the left hemisphere were not somehow prepared for the acquisition of language, it is difficult to understand why there should be this propensity for language to develop on that side of the brain.

Additional support for the brain's biological preparedness has come from the discovery of anatomical asymmetries between the two hemispheres. We will return to a discussion of hemispheric anatomical asymmetries near the end of the chapter. However, for now we can briefly state that there is an area just posterior to the primary auditory area in the temporal lobe, called the **planum temporale,** that has been shown to be larger on the left than on the right side of the brain in a majority of individuals (Geschwind & Levitsky, 1968). It is implausible that this major structural asymmetry could have arisen as the result of experience. Therefore, if the larger planum temporale on the left is in fact a structural manifestation of the language specialization of the left hemisphere, as is widely believed, it would constitute further evidence for the biological preparedness of the brain for language. This conclusion is further supported by the finding that this asymmetry has been found to be present as early as the 31st week of fetal development (Wada, Clarke, & Hamm, 1975).

Given that the brain is biologically prepared to learn language, let's now move to the major focus of this chapter: the effects of cerebral lesions on language and the implications of these effects for an understanding of normal language.

LANGUAGE DISORDERS: THE CONCEPT OF APHASIA

Disorders of language following cerebral damage are generally termed aphasia. We have already encountered two types of aphasia (Broca's and Wernicke's), and we will find that there are other types as well. We may define aphasia, by exclusion, as a disorder of language not due to impairment in sensory or motor function or to deterioration of general intellectual functioning. Thus, an impairment in language due to deafness, paralysis, or dementia is not an aphasia. In the former two cases, the language disturbance is secondary to another disturbance; in general intellectual impairment, the language disorder is not specific but part of a general picture of cognitive impoverishment.

One of the first recorded cases of aphasia appears in a document known as the Ebers Papyrus, dating from about the middle of the third millennium B.C. This document describes a man with a head injury who "lost his ability for speech without paralysis of the tongue." Hippocrates, as was mentioned in chapter 1, had recorded observations that could have served as the basis for inferring that the left hemisphere is specialized for language, although he did not make this inductive leap. We also mentioned one of Gall's few empirical observations, a man whose speech was disrupted after a knife wound to the left eye. This observation caused Gall to add language functioning to his phrenological chart, locating it in the anterior left hemisphere not distant from Broca's area. We have also discussed the enormous importance of Broca's and Wernicke's findings. In what follows, we consider central disorders of language in somewhat more detail.

Broca's Aphasia

If we consider disorders of language production, we find that in addition to aphasia, there are two other general categories of dysfunction that may occur. The term **dysarthria** generally refers to the effects of dysfunction of peripheral structures involved in the mechanics of speech production, such as the face, jaw, tongue, and larynx. If one or more of these components of speech production are not working normally, speech production will be compromised. Speech may be distorted in various ways, and, depending upon the structures involved, particular sounds will be distorted. Unfortunately, the term *dysarthria* is used inconsistently in the literature. It is occasionally applied descriptively to distorted speech production without reference to the causal mechanism of the disorder and thus may be applied to the production problems of a person with Broca's aphasia.

In contrast to this impairment in the peripheral mechanisms of speech production, speech may be disrupted due to central processing deficits. The two major categories of central production deficits should be differentiated from the outset. In a **phonemic disorder of**

speech, the production of individual phonemes is unimpaired but the capacity to program rapid sequences of phonemes to produce fluent speech is disrupted. This impairment at the level of the combination and sequencing of phonemes is a central feature of Broca's aphasia. In contrast, in a **kinetic disorder of speech,** also often termed **apraxia of speech,**[1] the ability to organize movements of the speech musculature to produce previously learned phonemes is impaired, even though the speech musculature and the peripheral nerves activating it are intact. Thus, if you ask someone with a kinetic disorder of speech to produce a particular phoneme, the person may not be able to do so even though the ability to make the individual component peripheral movements that are necessary for the production of that phoneme is unimpaired. It is thus possible to conceptualize kinetic disorders of speech and phonemic disorders of speech as disruptions of two hierarchically related processes, the former disrupting the coordination of movement necessary to produce the most elementary components of speech (phonemes) and the latter disrupting the higher-order coordinated production of sequences of these elementary components of speech. It is important to note, however, that the two disorders are dissociable. Not only can a phonemic disorder coexist with the unimpaired production of individual phonemes, but a mild to moderate kinetic disorder of speech can coexist with retained capacity for the coordinated sequential articulation of those phonemes that can be produced.

Let's return now to a consideration of Broca's aphasia. Recall from chapter 1 that Broca's patient Tan exhibited a disturbance of language characterized by slow, effortful, and deliberate speech. As Broca described more patients in his series, it became clear that these symptoms are components of a characteristic disorder that, despite Broca's proposal of the term *aphemia*, has come to be known as *aphasia*, a term sug-

---

1. As we will discuss more fully in chapter 9, the term *apraxia* has a number of meanings, one of which would render it an appropriate descriptor for the *phonemic disorder of speech* that is a characteristic of Broca's aphasia. This ambiguity makes the term *apraxia of speech* somewhat confusing. It therefore seems appropriate to avoid its use when possible, even though it is frequently encountered in the literature.

gested by Armand Trousseau. The speech of patients suffering from Broca's aphasia is generally composed of very simple grammatical structures, creating a kind of "telegraphic" speech consisting mostly of nouns in singular form and verbs in their infinitive or participle forms. When asked what he is doing, a patient with Broca's aphasia might reply, "Make dinner" or "Eat dinner." These telegraphic productions do not reflect fatigue or a lack of the desire to communicate. The patient may make agonizing efforts to produce normal speech and yet remain unable to do so, even when assisted by the presentation of a model sentence to repeat or a printed passage to read.

In addition to impairment in the coordinated production of accurately produced phonemes, patients with Broca's aphasia may have difficulty finding the appropriate phoneme or word. This may result in complete inability to come up with the desired word (**anomia**), or it may result in distorted productions. These distorted productions are termed **paraphasias** and are of two types, phonemic and semantic. In **phonemic paraphasia,** the patient cannot come up with the desired phoneme but instead substitutes a phoneme that has some similarity to the desired sound (e.g., *ho* for *show*). In contrast, the patient who makes a **semantic paraphasia** makes an error that has a semantic similarity to the desired word (e.g., *look* for *show*).

Patients with Broca's aphasia often make grammatical errors in their speech (**agrammatism**). They may have difficulty repeating what they hear. As has already been emphasized, these patients show extreme slowness in their speech production and have difficulty producing words in uninterrupted strings, a symptom termed **reduced verbal fluency.**

Patients with Broca's aphasia have difficulties writing (**dysgraphia**), which parallel their impairments in spoken language. Thus, their written productions have many errors (**paragraphias**) that parallel the paraphasic errors we just described. These patients tend to produce the same utterance or the same written production again and again, even when it does not fit their intended meaning or may not even be a word. Such repetition, which does not serve an adaptive function, is termed **perseveration.**

Spoken language contains fluctuations in pitch and rhythm that produce the tonal pattern characteristic of a particular language as well as the individual differences in tonal pattern that are characteristic of a particular speaker of that language. In addition, the intonation of spoken language conveys emphasis and emotional tone. This aspect of language is termed **prosody.** Patients with Broca's aphasia exhibit significant disruptions in prosody. This may take the form of greatly diminished tonal fluctuation (**aprosodia**), abnormal or distorted prosody (**dysprosodia**), or exaggerated variations in the tonal and rhythmic features of spoken language (**hyperprosodia**).

It is often said that language comprehension is intact in Broca's aphasia, and this is largely true. Nevertheless, it can be shown that although these patients do have good comprehension for nouns and verbs, they have difficulty comprehending small function words (e.g., prepositions and pronouns) and inflected endings. Thus, patients with Broca's aphasia, who may be able to understand even infrequently occurring nouns, such as *dinosaur* and *glacier,* may be totally stumped when presented with problems like these: *That's my aunt's brother. Would that be a man or a woman?* or *The lion was killed by the tiger. Which animal died?* The inability of these patients to understand the significance of small function words and to appreciate nuances of meaning signified by grammatical context is particularly interesting because it cuts across the generalizations that are usually made in defining and contrasting Broca's and Wernicke's aphasia and suggests that Broca's area plays a role in language comprehension.

As has been mentioned, the critical area that, when injured, results in Broca's aphasia is the posterior part of the inferior frontal convolution in the left hemisphere (see Figure 1.8). This has come to be called Broca's area, and its lateralization on the left side of the brain has been confirmed using a number of different methods. Thus, electrical stimulation of exposed cortex during surgery and recent functional imaging techniques have made it possible to map out a specific area within the left hemisphere corresponding rather precisely to the intrahemispheric localization inferred from the study of cortical lesions. Broca's area lies just anterior to the portion of motor cortex that controls the muscles involved in speech production, including those in the throat, tongue, jaw, and lips (see Figure 1.8). As already emphasized, damage to Broca's area does not cause paralysis of the vocal musculature. Rather, Broca's area may be conceptualized as the motor association area for portions of motor cortex controlling the muscles necessary for speech.

Wernicke's Aphasia

During the decade following Broca's initial reports, a number of papers appeared describing patients with an aphasia like that of Broca, and it began to seem that all aphasias were of the Broca type. It was therefore an important landmark when the young German neurologist Carl Wernicke described an aphasia with an entirely different symptom pattern associated with damage to a different area of the cerebral cortex. The critical lesion associated with Wernicke's aphasia lies between Heschl's gyrus and the angular gyrus in the left hemisphere (see Figure 1.8). This cerebral localization has been corroborated using a variety of methods including cortical stimulation, rCBF, and PET.

In terms of symptom picture, the hallmark of Wernicke's aphasia is severely impaired comprehension together with hyperfluent (rapid and copious) spontaneous speech that retains the intonation pattern, rhythm, and pronunciation of normal speech but does not make sense. The comprehension problem seen in Broca's aphasia (which we discussed earlier) notwithstanding, patients with Broca's aphasia can understand much of what they hear. In contrast, patients with Wernicke's aphasia have severely impaired comprehension even for frequently occurring words presented in isolation. Furthermore, the comprehension problem of these patients is not confined to heard speech; reading is also severely impaired in these patients.

In Wernicke's aphasia the contrast between the normal intonation and pronunciation of the patient's spoken language and its confused or totally obscure content is striking. If not listened to carefully, the patient's speech may sound normal; yet, when one attends to meaning, the confused nature of the production is readily apparent. The patient might say, with normal intonation, pronunciation, and rhythm, "I

went deep to the a, er . . . the, a store and the shoots were in the cellar without zailfops so I went back and thought and then the man who sweeps and cleans up came out so the city was dark the rest of the lime."

Several factors make the content of this utterance incomprehensible. There are many paraphasias, both semantic (*deep* for *down*) and phonemic (*lime* for *time*). In addition, speech is **circumlocutory,** that is, the patient often talks around the topic or word at hand in a way that may make understanding very difficult (*man who sweeps and cleans up* for *janitor*). Anomia (difficulty finding the word *store*) is frequent, as is the distortion of two or more sounds within a word or the invention of novel words, referred to as **neologisms** (*zailfops*). An aphasia characterized by the pervasive use of neologisms is referred to as **jargon aphasia.** The writing of patients with Wernicke's aphasia parallels their speech and thus is severely impaired.

The well-articulated but extremely confused speech that is typical of Wernicke's aphasia has been metaphorically described as *word salad,* a term that has also been applied to the speech of patients with schizophrenia. In fact, an inexperienced clinician may mistakenly diagnose a patient with Wernicke's aphasia as suffering from schizophrenia. This is obviously a dangerous error because the abrupt onset of Wernicke's aphasia is usually a sign that the patient is experiencing an acute neurological emergency such as a stroke, which requires immediate medical attention. It is also an avoidable error because, for all its similarity to that of Wernicke's aphasia, the speech of patients with schizophrenia can often be identified as such, particularly when its content is frankly bizarre. More reliably differentiating is the frequent association of lateralized neurological signs, such as weakness or sensory loss, in Wernicke's aphasia and the infrequent occurrence of many categories of paraphasic errors in schizophrenia. This is one example, among many that could be adduced, of how important a basic understanding of neuropsychology is for the clinician working in a psychiatric setting.

In chapter 1 we introduced Wernicke's model of how language areas in the brain are connected and his conceptualization of various language disorders

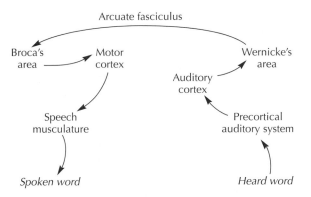

FIGURE 6.1   The structures involved in the repetition of a heard word, according to Wernicke's conceptualization of language function as comprising a sequence of processes carried out in different cerebral areas. Wernicke's disconnection syndrome model attributed language disorders to disconnections between these and other areas.

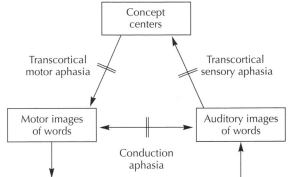

FIGURE 6.2   Schematic representation of Lichtheim's disconnection model for transcortical motor, transcortical sensory, and conduction aphasia. *(Adapted from McCarthy & Warrington, 1990, p. 13)*

as the consequence of disconnection between these areas. We noted, as an example, Wernicke's hypothesis that conduction aphasia, with its characteristic impairment in the ability to repeat spoken language, was the result of a lesion in the fiber bundle connecting Broca's area and Wernicke's area, the arcuate fasciculus. It could be argued that this model was Wernicke's most important contribution to neuropsychology, and we will see shortly that it does in fact provide a useful framework for understanding a variety of other language disorders.

Wernicke's model can be used to deduce the processes involved in normal language function. When a word is heard, the verbal stimulus is processed by peripheral components of the auditory system and projected to the primary auditory cortex, Heschl's gyrus, in the temporal lobes. From there, input is sent to the adjacent Wernicke's area. The nature of the processing carried out by Wernicke's area is something we approach later in the chapter. For now, let's assume that the heard word is simply to be repeated. In this case information is sent, via the arcuate fasciculus, to Broca's area, where the motor program organizing the required articulatory pattern is activated and transmitted to the motor cortex. This, in turn, activates the peripheral nerves, which set the vocal musculature in a dance of movement to produce the word (Figure 6.1).

Global Aphasia

Global aphasia is a syndrome characterized by the combined symptom picture of both Broca's aphasia and Wernicke's aphasia. As one would predict, the lesions associated with this disorder include both the anterior and posterior speech areas.

The Transcortical Aphasias

In the decade following Wernicke's discoveries, Lichtheim (1885) conceptualized yet another type of aphasia, **transcortical aphasia.** Lichtheim argued that there are cortical areas outside Broca's and Wernicke's areas that are centers for concepts (Figure 6.2). He was led to this position through his observation of patients who exhibited all the symptoms of Broca's aphasia, including severe impairment of spontaneous speech, except that, unlike the Broca's aphasic, they were able to repeat what they heard (**transcortical motor aphasia**). He described other patients who had all the symptoms of Wernicke's aphasia except that they also were able to repeat heard speech (**transcortical sensory aphasia**). In both cases the retained ability to repeat indicated that Broca's area, Wernicke's area, and the arcuate fasciculus connecting the two were all intact. In a third form, **mixed transcortical aphasia,** both spontaneous speech and comprehension were impaired, but, again, the transcortical syndrome differed from global aphasia in that the capacity to repeat was retained.

In transcortical motor aphasia the critical lesion involves cortex superior to Broca's area and/or fiber tracts connecting these areas with Broca's area. Analogously, transcortical sensory aphasia is associated with damage involving the cortex superior to Wernicke's area and/or the fiber connections between these areas and Wernicke's area. Mixed transcortical aphasia involves damage to (or disconnection from) both superior areas. Geschwind, Quadfasel, and Segarra (1968) reported a dramatic case illustrating an extreme form of mixed transcortical aphasia. Over the 9-year period their patient was studied, she was never observed to utter spontaneous speech and showed no indication of language comprehension. Nevertheless, she was able to repeat heard sentences perfectly. Postmortem examination revealed an extensive lesion that essentially isolated the speech areas from the rest of the cortex. This unusual syndrome, which can be conceptualized as an extreme form of mixed transcortical aphasia, is called **isolation of the speech area.**

These observations of Lichtheim and others support the idea that areas outside the classical language areas, connected to them by transcortical fibers (hence, the name of the disorders) make necessary contributions to normal speech production and language comprehension. Whether or not Lichtheim's designation of these areas as "concept centers" adequately describes their function, there can be no doubt of the critical role of areas outside the classical language areas in normal language processing. The transcortical aphasias thus corroborate the opinion of Hughlings-Jackson that widespread areas within the brain are involved in language. The transcortical aphasias also reveal that Wernicke's area is not sufficient for language comprehension, a point to which we will return later.

Other Central Language Disorders

There are several other language disorders that are associated with cerebral damage. We have already discussed conduction aphasia, the disorder predicted by Wernicke based on the disconnection syndrome hypothesis and then confirmed by him with the report of a patient whose ability to repeat what was heard was impaired even though expressive speech and language comprehension were intact. As Wernicke had predicted, this patient was found to have a lesion in the fiber bundle connecting Broca's area and Wernicke's area, the arcuate fasciculus. Some findings that have emerged in the past 20 years have cast doubt, however, on the validity of the notion of conduction aphasia. In particular, the discovery of a specific verbal-auditory short-term memory deficit (see chapter 10) associated with left parietal-lobe lesions (Shallice & Warrington, 1977) raises the possibility that in at least some cases this specific memory impairment underlies the symptoms that have been accounted for in terms of the disconnection posited in conduction aphasia.

A number of other highly specific deficits have been observed. **Pure word deafness** is the specific inability to understand heard speech in the absence of impaired comprehension for linguistic input presented in the visual or tactual modality. **Pure word dumbness** is the specific impairment in the production of spoken language in the absence of disturbance in other forms of language output, including writing. **Tactile aphasia** is a specific disturbance in the comprehension of language that is delivered through somatosensory input (i.e., touch), and **alexia** is specific impairment in the ability to understand language that arrives through vision (i.e., reading). We have also discussed (in chapter 1) the syndrome alexia without agraphia, impairment in the ability to read with preserved ability to write and preserved comprehension of language that is perceived through modalities other than vision. As we saw in the case of alexia without agraphia, the disconnection hypothesis can provide a conceptual framework for understanding the underlying mechanisms of seemingly puzzling dissociations. In the next section we will apply this framework to some of the language disorders we have just reviewed.

THE DISCONNECTION SYNDROME HYPOTHESIS APPLIED TO LANGUAGE DISORDERS

If we consider the cortical areas that are particularly important for language and the interconnections between those areas and other areas of the cortex, we

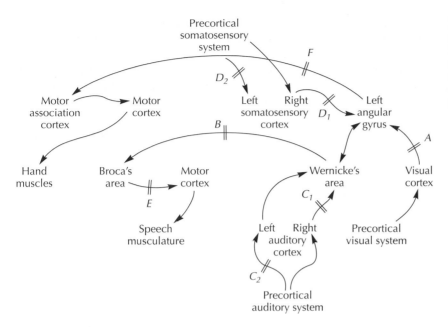

FIGURE 6.3 Schematic representation of the cortical areas important for language and some major interconnections relevant to disconnection syndrome explanations of language impairment.

can begin to consider mechanisms for some of the perplexing syndromes that we have just reviewed. These areas and interconnections are schematically represented in Figure 6.3.

Let's first consider the impairments that are associated with Wernicke's area and then see how the disconnection syndrome hypothesis helps us understand them. Lesions to Wernicke's area impair comprehension of language presented in any modality, whether auditory, visual, or tactual. In addition, a person with a Wernicke's area lesion cannot write, repeat what is heard, or spell to dictation. Further, lesions in this area interfere severely with the generation of meaningful verbal content, without disrupting the articulation of speech sounds. We will return later to consider what is actually processed by Wernicke's area, but let's first consider other syndromes.

Lesions to the angular gyrus disrupt reading, writing, and spelling to dictation. Apparently, processing by the angular gyrus is necessary both for the decoding of written information into a form that can be processed by Wernicke's area (i.e., reading) and the reverse process of coding verbal information into written form. If we consider the patient of Dejarine whom we discussed in chapter 1, we recall what happens when the angular gyrus is deprived of visual input. Reading of seen words was impaired, although

"reading" tactually, auditory comprehension, and writing were not. Such a disconnection may be represented by a lesion at point A in Figure 6.3. Note that the preserved areas and interconnections depicted in Figure 6.3 account for the preservation of tactual reading, writing, and auditory comprehension. It is of interest that angular gyrus lesions disrupt spelling to dictation. Apparently processing within this area is necessary for the transformation of the sounds of words into their component letters even when no explicit visual or motor processing is involved.

As we discussed earlier, the inability to repeat what is heard together with relatively intact comprehension and spontaneous expression can be understood in terms of the disruption of the direct connection between Wernicke's and Broca's area (lesion B in Figure 6.3).

From the perspective of the disconnection hypothesis, pure word deafness (the specific inability to understand heard speech without disruption in the comprehension of language presented in other modalities) can be understood as the result of depriving Wernicke's area of auditory input. This is diagrammatically represented by a lesion at points C_1 and C_2. It is important to emphasize that this and other disconnections depicted in Figure 6.3 are represented in highly schematic form. To take the last-discussed disconnection as an example, the lesion that would be required to effectively deprive Wernicke's area of auditory input is really rather complex because of the fact that this area receives input both from the ipsilateral auditory cortex and from auditory areas in the opposite hemisphere. Thus, pure word deafness would require a lesion that disrupted both these connections and would therefore have to involve both disruption of auditory radiations projecting to the left hemisphere from subcortical areas and disruption of callosal connections from the auditory cortex of the nonlanguage hemisphere (hence, the two lesion points shown in Figure 6.3). Lesions that affect both these connections but do not produce more widespread abnormality (e.g., Wernicke's aphasia) are extremely rare, making this syndrome rare as well. Nevertheless, there are reports of pure word deafness that contain pathological evidence consistent with the disconnection model (Albert & Bear, 1974; Klein & Harper, 1956).

Let's turn briefly to tactile aphasia, the specific impairment in the comprehension of language presented to the tactual modality (as in "reading" raised or textured letters while blindfolded). This disorder can be understood in terms of a disconnection analogous to that just described for pure word deafness. In this case the disconnection is again complicated, including disconnection of the right somatosensory cortex and the left angular gyrus and also disconnection of the somatosensory system and the somatosensory cortex in the left hemisphere (lesions D_1 and D_2 in Figure 6.3), although other mechanisms are possible.

Considering pure word dumbness, the inability to articulate spoken language without associated impairment in writing can be understood in terms of a disconnection of Broca's area from the motor mechanisms of speech (lesion E in Figure 6.3). Pure agraphia can be understood in terms of the disconnection of the motor association cortex from the angular gyrus (lesion F).

Although it may seem simplistic, the conceptualization of language disorders in terms of disconnection syndromes helps to provide some rational basis for the sometimes baffling dissociations that have been observed in these disorders. However, this explanatory framework is not only theoretically comforting; there is also a great deal of empirical support for this approach derived both from the study of human patients and from experimental work with other animals. We will return to this explanatory framework frequently as we consider other disorders.

Nevertheless, for all its usefulness, the disconnection syndrome approach has some major limitations. In particular, as the sections that follow will show, it is impossible to understand the symptom patterns of many disorders in terms of disconnections between processing centers. Therefore, the notion that language or other higher-order cognitive processing can be accounted for entirely in terms of a series of sequential processes, the central postulate of the disconnection syndrome model, cannot be the whole story. This view is further supported by some recent imaging studies suggesting that subtle differences in language functioning are associated with the activation of very different constellations of brain structures. In what follows we will review some of the more recent findings from lesion studies and from imaging studies, considering in turn each of the major components of language function. They suggest, among other things, that the processes underlying language are more parallel and more modular in their organization than those posited by the disconnection model.

MAJOR COMPONENTS OF LANGUAGE FUNCTION

Auditory Word Comprehension

Evidence from patients with cerebral lesions indicates that understanding a heard word requires at least three types of processing: detecting the elementary acoustic features of the word's sound (**auditory temporal acuity**), perceiving the phonemes composing the word (**auditory perceptual analysis**), and assigning a meaning to the word (**semantic processing**). The first and most basic of these processes appears to be an elementary aspect of audition that is not specific to language and that is mediated by the auditory cortex. Thus, bilateral lesions of the auditory cortices result in an impairment in the temporal resolution of stimuli such as is required for the discrimination of two rapidly pre-

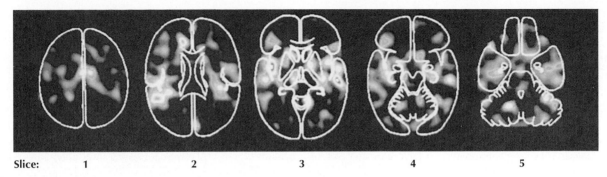

Slice: 1   2   3   4   5

FIGURE 6.4   PET images, seen in horizontal section, obtained when normal subjects passively listened to words. Activation is greatest in the temporal lobes of both hemispheres *(slice 3)* and in Wernicke's area in the left hemisphere *(slice 2). (Adapted from Posner & Raichle, 1994, p. 117)*

sented clicks from a single presentation. These patients require a greater delay between presentations to discriminate them. In contrast, such patients are able to accurately discriminate aspects of sounds, such as pitch and volume, that do not require a high level of temporal resolution for their perception.

Considering the next stage of processing, auditory perceptual analysis, one finds that lesions in many areas of the left hemisphere are associated with impairment in phoneme discrimination but that the most often associated area is Wernicke's area. In contrast, lesions in the right hemisphere in the area homologous to Wernicke's area are associated with impairment in the matching of linguistically meaningless sounds. This suggests that Lichtheim's designation of Wernicke's area as the center for auditory word images has captured an important aspect of the function of this area, despite the somewhat antiquated tone of Lichtheim's 19th-century terminology. Recent PET studies are consistent with inferences drawn from lesion studies. In particular, Posner and Raichle (1994) have reported increased activity in Wernicke's area as well as in the auditory cortices of both hemispheres during passive listening to words (Figure 6.4).

Semantic processing, the extraction of meaning from the stream of accurately perceived phonemes, is the next stage in the process. Impairment in the comprehension of heard words, as assessed, for example, by an auditory vocabulary test, is associated with le-

sions to various parts of the left hemisphere but most frequently with left temporal-lobe lesions. Of particular importance is the finding that patients with impaired auditory word comprehension do not necessarily have any impairment in the processing of word sounds, as measured, for example, by a phoneme discrimination task. This dissociation indicates that the process of perception and categorization of word sounds into psychologically distinct percepts (phonemes) and the process of assigning meaning to perceived combinations of phonemes (words) are separate processes, although the former is a prerequisite for the latter.

Also of great interest is the seemingly counterintuitive finding that a patient who is unable to comprehend a heard word may be able to retrieve and produce the same word in a confrontation naming task. This dissociation between auditory verbal comprehension and word retrieval is striking and suggests that the output processes of speech (Broca's area) can gain access to the semantic store of word meanings even though the products of phonemic analysis cannot. This is a picture consistent with the disconnection between areas mediating phonemic analysis (Wernicke's area) and areas mediating the representation of word meanings (other areas within the left hemisphere), a disconnection which Lichtheim postulated as the neural basis for transcortical sensory aphasia. Note that, according to Lichtheim's schema, in transcortical sensory aphasia semantic

TABLE 6.1   Example responses of two patients with a selective impairment in defining heard words denoting foods and living things, together with preserved comprehension of words denoting objects.

Target	Response	Target	Response
		J. B. R.	
Camel	Don't know	**Torch**	Device for showing way in dark
Wasp	Bird that flies	**Thermometer**	Device for registering temperature
Buttercup	Cup full of butter	**Helicopter**	Flying, for vertical take-off
Swan	Forgotten	**Binoculars**	A system for seeing things far away
		S. B. Y.	
Frog	Animal, not tamed	**Hammer**	Device used to hit things
Cheese	You eat one of your foods	**Taxi**	Machine that takes you around, a vehicle of transportation
Mutton	Some sort of rubbish	**Camera**	Device for taking photos
Butterfly	A thing that flies through the air, a bird that flies	**Pamphlet**	Written piece of work describing something

From McCarthy & Warrington, 1990, p. 132

information about word meaning can still reach areas mediating language output (see Figure 6.2).

In addition to providing evidence of a dissociation between phonemic processing and semantic processing, patients with impaired auditory word comprehension provide hints about the nature of the organization of the semantic store. These come from patterns of impairment that appear to represent disorders within the semantic system itself. It turns out that patients exhibit some curious dissociations with respect to the categories of words they are able to comprehend. For example, it has been known for some time that patients may exhibit a selective impairment in color naming (**color anomia**) or in the naming of parts of the body. In other patients one finds striking dissociations such as impairment specific to the comprehension of words denoting living things (but not objects), large (but not small) objects, or food and animals (but not objects). Table 6.1 illustrates the striking discrepancy in level of comprehension across different categories in two patients.

In addition to this **category specificity** of comprehension impairment, patients have been reported who can identify the category to which a word belongs but who are unable to differentiate it from other similar things. Thus, when required to choose from an array of pictures the one that matches a heard word, these patients do well when the choices are from distinct semantic categories but do poorly when the choices are all from the same semantic category as the target word. For example, if they hear the word *spoon,* they are able to match it to, say, a picture of a bowl of soup when the distractor pictures are not related to eating, but they perform poorly when all the distractors are food-related objects. It is as if they have access to information regarding the superordinate category to which the object belongs but are unable to access more specific knowledge about it. For this reason, this phenomenon has been termed **partial knowledge.** Category specificity and partial knowledge suggest the presence of a semantic processing deficit, a degradation of the word-knowledge base itself, and they provide hints as to the conceptual and hierarchical dimensions along which this knowledge base is organized.

It has often been assumed that there is a single semantic store that is shared between various sensory modalities. According to this hypothesis, the knowledge base that is accessed in comprehending the word *whale* and understanding a picture of a whale is the same. This reasonable assumption is challenged, however, by data indicating that there is a

TABLE 6.2 Example responses of a single patient demonstrating a dissociation between the abilities to comprehend pictures of animals and the heard names of the same animals.

Target	Word definitions Response	Picture descriptions Response
Kangaroo	Common name	Famous animal from Australia, jumps
Dolphin	Animal or bird	Some in Brighton, sea-animal trained to swim around
Rhino	Totally new word	Enormous animal, lives in Africa, weighs a ton
Swan	Another animal	Common for this country, on the Thames and canals

From McCarthy & Warrington, 1990, p. 150

TABLE 6.3 Category-specific impairment in confrontation naming and naming from auditory description in a single patient.

	Countries	Colors	Objects	Body parts	Animals
Naming to confrontation	13	0	2	10	1
Naming from auditory description	15	0	2	0	1

From McCarthy & Warrington, 1990, p. 160

double dissociation between defining a heard word and describing a corresponding picture. Patients with visual associative agnosia (see chapter 8) are impaired on the latter task but not the former, whereas the converse pattern is seen in some patients with an auditory verbal comprehension impairment (Table 6.2). We thus have evidence for a modality-specific impairment in semantic knowledge, an impairment that would seem to weaken the argument for a unitary semantic system. It remains possible, however, that these dissociations reflect modality-specific impairments in access to a unitary semantic store.

Word Retrieval

Word retrieval difficulties, variously termed **anomic aphasia** or **amnestic aphasia,** can occur as a relatively selective problem and are associated with lesions in a wide range of areas in the left hemisphere. Confrontation naming tasks frequently used to assess word retrieval require subjects to produce a name corresponding to a presented picture. In addition to being totally unable to produce the appropriate word, subjects may produce phonemic paraphasias, semantic errors, neologisms, and circumlocutions. It has long been established that the less frequently a word appears in a language, the higher the probability that problems will occur in the retrieval of that word.

Word frequency is not, however, the only factor determining the probability of retrieval problems. As with the comprehension of heard words, patients with word retrieval deficits frequently exhibit patterns of category-specific impairment and preservation. These include the inability to name colors (color anomia), letters (letter anomia), and parts of the body. Other examples include impairment in the naming of colors, objects, and animals together with preserved capacity to name countries and body parts (Table 6.3) and impairment in the naming of proper nouns (such as cities and countries) together with preservation of the capacity to name common nouns (such as vegetables and fruits) (Table 6.4). In addition, modality-specific impairments in naming have been reported. Patients have been found who are specifically impaired in naming visually presented material but who are unimpaired in the naming of objects presented by touch. The converse dissociation has also been reported. Finally, there are reports of patients who are

TABLE 6.4   Category-specific naming impairment in a single patient.

Common names	No. correct	Proper names	No. correct
Vegetables	15/15	Relatives	2/8
Fruits	15/15	Famous people	0/15
Body parts	18/18	Cities	0/15
Means of transportation	15/15	Mountains	0/5
Pasta types	6/6	Countries	0/10

From McCarthy & Warrington, 1990, p. 159

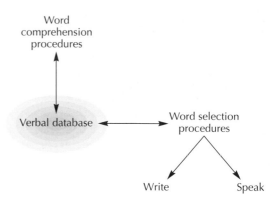

FIGURE 6.5   A model for the processes underlying word retrieval. *(From McCarthy & Warrington, 1990, p. 169)*

impaired in spoken word retrieval but who are unimpaired in written word retrieval. The presence of category-specific dissociations provides further evidence regarding the dimensions of organization of the semantic store. The modality-specific impairments may be accounted for in terms of disconnection between cortex dedicated to a particular sensory modality and the semantic store. Also, as we saw in an earlier section, modality-specific retrieval problems are often associated with damage to the corpus callosum and can often be usefully conceptualized in terms of disconnection syndromes. In addition, however, as we have already noted in the context of comprehension impairments, modality-specific errors may indicate that there are discrete modality-specific semantic systems that have been disconnected by these lesions. We will see in chapter 8 that visual associative agnosia provides evidence consistent with this hypothesis.

Perhaps the most striking dissociation is one that we have already noted in our discussion of auditory comprehension, namely, the double dissociation between auditory comprehension and naming. This double dissociation indicates that the retrieval processes underlying the comprehension of heard words and those mediating the production of words are separable. McCarthy and Warrington (1990) have proposed a model for word retrieval that reflects this observation (Figure 6.5). Note that their model depicts spoken and written word production as separate processes. This is supported by the dissociation

between spoken and written word retrieval that has been observed in some patients.

Sentence Comprehension and Production

In the previous paragraphs we have been considering the comprehension and production of single words. When we consider sentences, it is apparent that, to adapt the familiar dictum of Gestalt psychology, the sentence is more than the sum of its words. The combination and arrangement of words in a sentence produce a meaning beyond that of the individual words. As we noted earlier, the study of the meaning to which language refers is known as semantics (from the Greek *semantikos*, "to mean, to indicate"). Aspects of word order and form that specify the relationship between words in a sentence and thereby contribute to its meaning are referred to as syntax or grammar. (The word *syntax* comes from the Greek *syn*, "together," and *taxon*, "order"; thus, syntax is concerned with the relationship between word order and meaning. Variations in the form of a word that serve to specify its relationship to other words in the sentence, such as the addition of endings, are also the province of syntax.) To construct a meaningful sentence, we must transform its semantic content into a combination of specific words in an order that conforms to and uses the grammatical rules of our language. Analogously, understanding a sentence requires the reverse process; we must transform grammatical structures and specific word meanings into the semantic content that they represent.

Thus, the meaning of a sentence lies not only in the meaning of its individual words, but also in the relationship between the individual words inherent in the sentence's syntax. For this reason one would expect that the processing of sentences involves processes different from the processing of individual words, and the results of lesion studies support this notion. In particular, one finds patients whose sentence comprehension or production is disproportionately impaired relative to their processing of individual words. This dissociation is frequently seen in the comprehension ability of patients with Broca's aphasia. In this disorder, comprehension of heard individual words can be quite good, as can comprehension of sentences that do not require elaborate processing of syntax for their comprehension. Such sentences as, for example, *The man hoes the garden,* are termed **semantically constrained** because their meaning is constrained by the words that compose them (the garden couldn't be hoeing the man). In contrast, the meaning of some sentences, termed **semantically reversible** sentences, is not so constrained. An example of such a sentence is *The lion chases the tiger.* As we noted in our earlier discussion of Broca's aphasia, it is semantically reversible sentences that pose comprehension problems for these patients.

In the area of speech production, we have seen that patients with Broca's aphasia have difficulty on naming tasks and, at the sentence level, tend to produce speech that is markedly ungrammatical, an impairment termed **agrammatism.** There are two major categories of agrammatism. **Morphological agrammatism** is characterized by an impairment in the use of function words (conjunctions, articles, prepositions, etc.) and impairment in the appropriate use of word endings together with preservation of word order. The telegraphic speech so typical of Broca's aphasia illustrates this form of agrammatism (*Boy give ball referee*). In contrast, **syntactic agrammatism** is characterized by the converse pattern of impairment: intact use of function words and word endings together with disruption of word order and choice of words (*The boy ball the table on is giving the referee*).

Both of these types of agrammatism are common in Broca's aphasia, although they may also be seen in other types of aphasia, including Wernicke's aphasia.

The jargon aphasia so characteristic of fluent speech seen in Wernicke's aphasia has also been conceptualized as having two subtypes. **Semantic jargon** is characterized by the use of real words that are combined inappropriately. In **phonemic jargon** some real words are used, but speech also contains many nonwords (neologisms).

Speech Production

As described earlier, speech production requires at least three component processes: (a) selection and ordering of the specific phonemes required for a particular utterance, (b) coordination of the timing and positioning of the speech musculature to produce the selected phonemes, and (c) execution of the required movements. We have seen that these components of the speech production process can be selectively impaired. To review these disorders briefly: In a disorder of the first process, the selection and sequencing of phonemes is disrupted, but the production of individual phonemes is not impaired. This disruption of the sequencing of phonemes is a phonemic disorder of speech and is the most characteristic impairment in Broca's aphasia. In a disorder of the second process, the selection of individual phonemes is unimpaired but the coordination of the actions that are necessary for the production of individual phonemes is disrupted. This results in productions in which the intended phonemes appear in distorted but sometimes recognizable form and is a kinetic disorder of speech. In a disorder of the third process, the capacity to move the muscles involved in speech production may be impaired, producing a generalized motor disorder affecting speech but not specific to it. This disorder is dysarthria.

If we look more closely at phonemic disorders, we often find that the production of individual phonemes is entirely normal, with all phonemes produced belonging to the patient's language. In addition, when the sequence of phonemes produced is incorrect, the errors nevertheless are consistent with the sequencing rules of the speaker's language. In contrast, in kinetic disorders the sounds produced are often not characteristic of the speaker's native language, taking on a kind of abnormal or foreign sound. Whereas patients with a phonemic disorder of speech production usually also exhibit disrupted written language, a kinetic disorder may be seen together with unimpaired performance in other aspects of language, including writing.

If we consider the conditions that produce a phonemic disorder, we find that there are at least three: Broca's aphasia, conduction aphasia, and transcortical motor aphasia. It is thus clear that the presence of a phonemic disorder has very little localizing significance. In contrast, kinetic disorders are associated with damage to the anterior left hemisphere, including the **pars opercularis** of the inferior frontal gyrus and the inferior precentral gyrus.

In a study comparing conduction aphasia and transcortical motor aphasia McCarthy and Warrington (1984) revealed a double dissociation that has important implications for an understanding of speech production mechanisms. They required their patients either to passively process a heard sentence by simply repeating it or to actively process its meaning by supplying the missing last word of the sentence and judging whether or not the sentence was meaningful. Patients with conduction aphasia were impaired on the passive task but not the active task, whereas patients with transcortical motor aphasia exhibited the converse pattern of impairment and preserved function.

McCarthy and Warrington interpreted this dissociation as evidence that there are two distinct transcoding procedures for speech production: a passive transcoding process that transforms auditory input into a program for motor commands that results in the repetition of the input and an active transcoding process that transforms the semantic content of heard speech into semantically appropriate speech (Figure 6.6). Such a dissociation is also consistent with Lichtheim's conceptualization of transcortical motor aphasia (see Figure 6.2) as the result of a disconnection between areas mediating the representation of meaning (presumably throughout the left hemisphere and possibly also in the right hemisphere) and areas transforming these meanings into

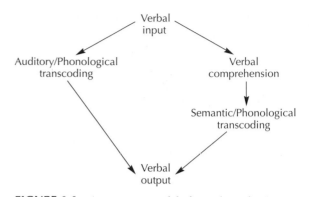

FIGURE 6.6 A two-route model of speech production. *(Adapted from McCarthy & Warrington, 1990, p. 209)*

the phonemic elements of the language and then organizing these phonemes for speech production (Broca's area and neighboring areas).

Recent functional imaging studies have addressed the question of which parts of the brain are activated during speech production and, in particular, whether different areas are activated during passive repetition versus active generation of words. Posner and Raichle (1994) reported a series of experiments addressing these issues, the results of which are consistent with the two-route model of speech production hypothesized by McCarthy and Warrington (1984). In addition, the imaging data revealed some unexpected findings.

To describe Posner and Raichle's findings we will have to consider their experiments in some detail. The investigators used a series of subtractions in an attempt to identify the structures specifically activated under different task conditions. First, as we already noted, they investigated the pattern of PET activation associated with passive listening to words (see Figure 6.4). Recall that in this condition activation was seen in the temporal cortex, bilaterally, and in Wernicke's area. Posner and Raichle then subtracted this pattern from that obtained when subjects passively repeated heard words; the result of this subtraction is seen in Figure 6.7. It reveals activation of four areas of the brain: (a) the motor cortex, bilaterally; (b) the insula; (c) the medial portion of the cerebellum; and (d) the supplementary motor area. These findings are particularly interesting because

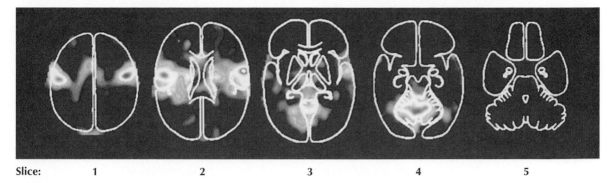

Slice: 1   2   3   4   5

FIGURE 6.7   To detect the pattern of activation specific to the speaking of words in normal sub-jects, the PET image obtained during passive listening to words (in Figure 6.4) was subtracted from the image obtained when subjects repeated words that they heard. The result of this subtraction showed activation in the motor cortex bilaterally *(slices 1, 2)*, the left insular cortex *(slice 2)*, the medial cerebellum *(slice 4)*, and the supplementary motor area *(slice 1)*. It should be noted that the areas showing activation during the passive listening condition were also activated during the speaking condition but are not seen in these images because of the subtraction procedure. *(From Posner & Raichle, 1994, p. 118)*

they implicate structures, such as the medial cerebel-lum, that are not generally considered to be specifi-cally involved in language function. Note that the subtraction method is presumed to reveal those areas of activation that are specific to the task being per-formed *relative to the task that is being subtracted from it*. Thus, in the word-production task there is also ac-tivation of the temporal cortex in both hemispheres and of Wernicke's area, but these activations are sub-tracted out and so do not appear in Figure 6.7.

Posner and Raichle then investigated the pattern of brain activation involved in more active and seman-tically based language-production processes by ask-ing subjects to generate verbs that described the ac-tion of heard nouns. Thus the subjects had to access their semantic knowledge related to the heard noun and generate a verb that meaningfully denoted a re-lated action. For example, if the subject heard the word *book*, he or she might say *read*. When the PET scans obtained from the previous passive repetition study were subtracted from this active generation task (Figure 6.8), activation was seen in four areas: (a) the left frontal cortex (including Broca's area), (b) the an-terior cingulate gyrus, (c) the left posterior temporal cortex (including Wernicke's area), and (d) the right cerebellum.

It can be seen how the difference in patterns of PET activation obtained during the active generation of words versus the passive repetition of words is con-sistent with McCarthy and Warrington's two-route model of speech production, which proposed that separate neural mechanisms underlie these two pro-cesses. Posner and Raichle (1994) also found evidence for two mechanisms of speech production within the domain of word generation, depending on whether or not the subject had practiced the task. They com-pared PET scans of subjects actively generating verbs from nouns in the way we just described with scans from the same subjects after they had had 15 minutes to study a different list of nouns and rehearse appro-priate verbs. When subjects were then presented with the list of nouns they had just used in rehearsal, they performed the generation task in a highly efficient manner, as one would expect. In addition, their scans were very different from those obtained in the unprac-ticed condition. The activations seen in the latter were not present (Figure 6.9). Moreover, it was discovered that the unpracticed condition was associated with a *decrease* in the activity of the insular cortex (which is active during the passive speaking of heard words) and that this decrease was not present in the practiced condition (Figure 6.10). After the practice task, the

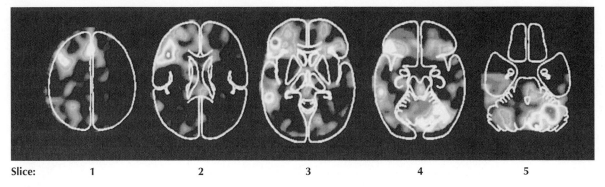

Slice: 1   2   3   4   5

FIGURE 6.8   The result of the subtraction of the PET image obtained when normal subjects passively repeated a heard word from the image obtained when subjects generated a related verb from heard nouns. Activation is seen in the left frontal cortex *(slices 1–4)*, the anterior cingulate gyrus *(slice 1)*, the left posterior temporal cortex *(slices 3, 4)*, and the right cerebellum *(slices 4, 5)*. As in Figure 6.7, the subtraction process has been utilized in an attempt to cancel out activations that are not specific to the task. *(From Posner & Raichle, 1994, p. 120)*

subjects were required to once again generate verbs from a novel list of nouns. In this control condition their scans returned to the pattern seen previously in the unpracticed condition.

These findings led Posner and Raichle (1994) to hypothesize that there are two pathways mediating the performance of generation tasks, one mediating automatic processing and involving insular cortex and a second mediating active, nonautomatic generation and involving activation of the left frontal cortex, anterior cingulate cortex, left posterior temporal cortex, and right cerebellum, together with decreased insular cortex activation.

Acquired Reading Impairment

In chapter 1 we saw how useful the disconnection hypothesis was in accounting for the symptom picture of Dejarine's classic case of alexia without agraphia. However, a more complete exploration of acquired reading impairment (alexia or, in its less severe form, **dyslexia**), emerges from the investigation of the patterns of impairment and retained functioning seen in different forms of acquired dyslexia. As we review the major types of reading disorders that occur after lesions to the brain, we find that not all of them are associated with lesions of the angular

gyrus. In fact, in some cases, the localization of the cerebral abnormality is not precisely known.

There are two major categories of dyslexia: the **visual word-form dyslexias** and the **central dyslexias.** The visual word-form dyslexias have been conceptualized as disrupting the initial processing of a word as a visual unit. In contrast, the central dyslexias have been understood as interfering with later stages of the reading process.

Within the word-form dyslexias, **spelling dyslexia** is characterized by loss of the ability to recognize words as coherent visual units. The normal ability to do this is reflected by the fact that whole words are read as rapidly as single letters. In contrast, the reading speed of patients with spelling dyslexia is slow and proportional to the length of the word; they are reading letter by letter. In **neglect dyslexia,** the initial or terminal part of a word is misread. These errors are not simple deletions but, rather, substitutions that produce a real, but erroneous, word. Examples are *floor* for *door* and *sight* for *sign.* **Attentional dyslexia,** a rare condition, is characterized by an inability to read words and letters when they appear with other written material, coexisting with preserved ability to read isolated words or letters.

Within the category of the central dyslexias, those disorders of processing that follow the initial visual

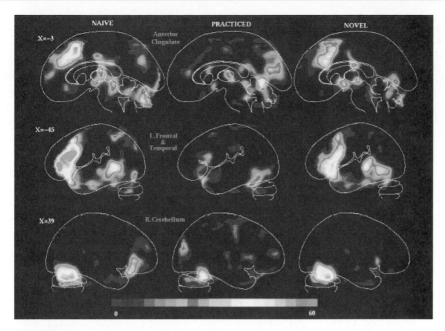

FIGURE 6.9 Midsagittal and lateral PET images showing activation in three conditions of the verb-generation task. In the naive condition, subjects who had not done the task before generated verbs from nouns. This is the same condition as the experiment in Figure 6.8 and resulted in activation of the same four areas. In the practiced condition, in which subjects were given the list of nouns 15 minutes before the test and were provided with an opportunity to practice generating verbs, the pattern of activation seen in the naive condition is not present. When, in the novel condition, subjects were given a new list of nouns without an opportunity to practice generating verbs, the original pattern of activation returned. *(From Posner & Raichle, 1994, p. 127)*

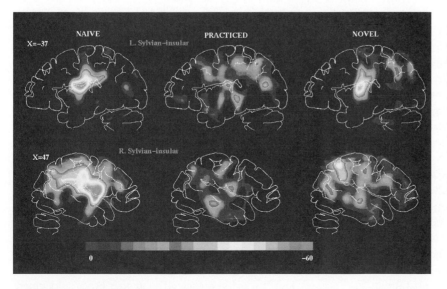

FIGURE 6.10 In these sagittal PET images the reverse of the ordinary scale is used so that markings indicate decreased activation. The three experimental conditions are the same as those depicted in Figure 6.9. These images reveal that during the "naive" condition, in addition to the four areas of activation seen in Figure 6.9, there is a decrease in activation of the insular cortex. This is not seen in the "practiced" condition. *(From Posner & Raichle, 1994, p. 128)*

TABLE 6.5   Reading performance for phonetically regular and phonetically irregular words in surface dyslexia and phonological dyslexia.

	Surface dyslexia (reading by sound)	Phonological dyslexia (reading by sight vocabulary)
Common phonetically regular words	normal	normal
Common phonetically irregular words	impaired	normal
Nonwords or uncommon phonetically regular words	normal	impaired

analysis of a printed word, there are two major types of disorder. In **surface dyslexia** (also termed **phonological reading** or **reading by sound**) reading appears to follow the standard print-to-sound rules of the language; the subject is reading by sound and cannot recognize words that do not follow these standard rules. In contrast, in **phonological dyslexia** (also termed **reading by sight vocabulary**) the patient's reading appears to utilize a learned sight vocabulary and reading by sound is impaired. The nature of the impairment in these two forms of dyslexia may be illustrated by comparing performance on the reading of common phonetically irregular words (which can be read via sight reading but not via phonological decoding) and the reading of nonsense words or uncommon phonetically regular words (which can be read via phonological analysis but not via sight reading). The two forms of dyslexia exhibit a double dissociation on these tasks (Table 6.5). Surface dyslexia is characterized by an inability to read phonetically irregular words with preserved ability to read nonsense words and uncommon phonetically regular words. Phonological dyslexia is characterized by the opposite pattern. Note that both groups are able to read common phonetically regular words because these words can be read either through phonological decoding or sight-reading.

There are patients in whom symptoms of both these dyslexias occur together. These patients are severely impaired in the phonetic decoding of words and have lost part of their sight vocabulary. Using their residual sight vocabulary, patients with this type of reading disorder may exhibit some surprisingly specific reading deficits. Some are impaired in the reading of specific grammatical forms, such as function words (e.g., *also* and *by*), inflected endings (e.g., *-ing* or *-ed*), adjectives, or nouns. In other instances the specificity of the impairment is along semantic dimensions. Thus, patients have been reported who are severely impaired in the reading of abstract words, whereas their ability to read concrete words is only slightly impaired. This type of impairment has been termed **deep dyslexia**. At least one case of a patient exhibiting the opposite pattern has been reported. In addition, investigators of patients with deep dyslexia have described three major types of errors made by patients with this disorder: semantic (*stroll* for *walk*), derivational (*sleep* for *slept*), and visual (*crack* for *crawl*). Patients with deep dyslexia generally make all three types of error, but the proportion of each type varies greatly from patient to patient.

The specificity of impairment observed in patients with surface dyslexia, phonological dyslexia, and the various forms of deep dyslexia provides important hints regarding the nature and organization of the cognitive systems underlying reading. In particular, on the basis of these data, a two-route model of the reading process has been proposed (Patterson, Marshall, & Coltheart, 1985). This model posits that after the analysis of the visual word form, disrupted in spelling dyslexia, there are parallel routes for the analysis of the sound of a word and the analysis of its meaning (Figure 6.11). This model has implications for remedial strategies for both persons with acquired dyslexia and children with developmental reading disabilities.

Spelling

It is not intuitively obvious that spelling and writing should be processes that are independent from other aspects of language, and, in fact, impairment in these areas is frequently associated with aphasia. Nevertheless, it was hypothesized soon after Broca's documen-

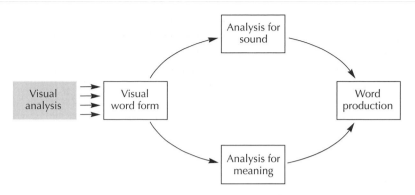

FIGURE 6.11   A generalized two-route model of reading. *(From McCarthy & Warrington, 1990, p. 229)*

tation of aphasia that specific disorders of spelling and writing exist. This was first proposed in 1865 by Benedikt (cited by Hecaen & Albert, 1978), who suggested that there were different neuroanatomical localizations for writing and spoken language, although he did not specify where the writing center might be located. In 1869 Ogle (cited by McCarthy & Warrington, 1990) coined the term **agraphia** to denote a specific impairment in writing ability. He also reported cases of aphasia without agraphia and cases of agraphia without aphasia. This double dissociation led him to also posit the existence of a separate center for writing. It remained for Exner (1881) to propose a specific area for the representation of writing at the foot (posterior portion) of the middle frontal gyrus in the left hemisphere. This is just superior to Broca's area, and so it is plausible that this area might have the same relationship to areas of the motor cortex mediating hand movement as Broca's area has to areas of the motor cortex mediating movement of the vocal musculature. It turns out, however, that there is very little evidence that the foot of the middle frontal convolution is in fact a writing center (but see Gordinier, 1899). Localization issues aside, however, the presence of specific impairments in spelling and writing is now well established.

As we have already mentioned, the term *agraphia* is used to denote a specific impairment in the movements required for writing. However, it is also used to indicate specific disorders of spelling. It is, in fact, this meaning of the term which Gerstman (1927) intended in his description of the syndrome that now

bears his name.[2] In what follows we consider three categories of spelling impairment: (a) linguistic or central disorders, (b) disorders of spelling assembly, and (c) disorders that are secondary to spatial processing impairment. We also discuss disorders confined to the act of writing.

There are two main types of **linguistic** or **central disorders of spelling:** spelling by sound and vocabulary-based spelling. In **spelling by sound** the patient spells according to the most common letter-to-phoneme correspondences in the language. These patients thus can spell words that follow these regular correspondences, such as *rod*, without difficulty. In contrast, words with irregular or unusual spellings, such as *high, although, knife,* and *language* are spelled very poorly, as are words that are ambiguous in the sense that they contain sounds that can be represented by more than one letter or letter combination, such as the final vowel sound in *stencil, camel,* and *moral.*

In **vocabulary-based spelling** (also called **phonological agraphia),** the second type of central spelling

2. Briefly, the Gerstman syndrome was hypothesized to consist of four co-occurring deficits resulting from left parietal-lobe abnormality: finger agnosia, acalculia (impairment in calculation), agraphia, and impairment in right-left discrimination. There is, however, compelling evidence that these four disorders do not truly constitute a syndrome because they are not more highly intercorrelated than are other disorders associated with left parietal abnormality (Benton, 1961).

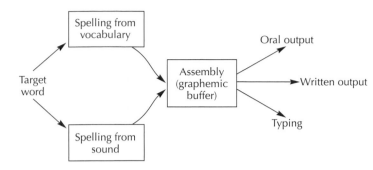

FIGURE 6.12   A generalized schema for two-route models of spelling. *(From McCarthy & Warrington, 1990, p. 255)*

disorder, the converse pattern is seen. Patients with this disorder are able to spell irregular words and regular words well; in fact, a spelling impairment may not be evident until they are asked to spell nonsense words phonetically. In this task their performance is extremely impaired, suggesting that their spelling relies on access to an established vocabulary of word-spelling correspondences rather than knowledge of letter-phoneme correspondences. It will be noted that spelling by sound is analogous to reading by sound and that vocabulary-based spelling is analogous to reading by sight vocabulary.

Disorders of spelling assembly take the form of specific impairment in the sequencing of letters. The tendency of patients with this disorder to retrieve the correct letters of a target word but not in the correct order has led to the hypothesis that information regarding order is lost between the time the letter sequence is accessed and the time the word is written or spelled aloud. This, in turn, has led to the hypothesis that there is a **graphemic buffer,** a short-term store for the retrieved letter sequences that spell words, that is analogous to verbal short-term memory (Caramazza et al., 1987).

A final area of unexpected dissociation in spelling is seen in the domain of output. There are reports of patients who are able to spell orally but not when writing, and the converse pattern has also been reported. There are even reports of dissociations between spelling when typing and spelling when writing. These dissociations have led to a two-route model of spelling (Figure 6.12) in which spelling is conceptualized as normally being achieved through two possible routes, vocabulary-based spelling and spelling from sound (McCarthy & Warrington, 1990).

The results of one or both of these processes are then briefly stored in the graphemic buffer until one of several output processes takes place.

Writing

As has been said, impairment in writing is frequently seen in association with aphasia. In contrast, selective impairment in the ability to write is relatively rare. Nevertheless, cases of such **pure agraphia** have been reported, and there is no doubt that the disorder does exist. Striking dissociations have been reported between impaired ability to produce written language and relative preservation of the ability to spell orally and to form words using block letters (Crary & Heilman, 1988; Zangwill, 1964). Pure agraphia is usually conceptualized as a specific type of the larger class of disorders of voluntary movement known as the **apraxias** (see chapter 9).

Spatial agraphia refers to impairments in spelling and writing that are secondary to impairments in spatial processing. These include errors in the orientation of written letters; neglect of the right or, more often, the left side of a word; and spacing errors. As such, they are not truly language errors. Spatial processing disorders will be discussed in more detail in chapter 7.

FURTHER THEORETICAL CONSIDERATIONS

At this point let's return to an issue to which we have already alluded several times: What is the nature of the processing that is being mediated by the great mass of neural tissue in the left posterior parietal lobe, which we traditionally designate as Wernicke's area? It is tempting to consider Wernicke's area the "storehouse of auditory associations," the great lexicon or dictionary of the brain within which words and their meanings are stored. There is, however, evidence that this is not the case. Perhaps the most powerful evidence comes from the transcortical aphasias. Recall that in transcortical sensory aphasia and mixed transcortical aphasia we observe patients in whom Wernicke's area is intact, but who nevertheless show significant impairment in language comprehension. As we concluded during our discussion of transcortical aphasia, this indicates that areas outside the classical language areas are critical for normal comprehension.

If Wernicke's area is not the great dictionary of the brain, then what is its function? Data from patients with aphasia, and, in particular, the impairments associated with transcortical aphasia, suggest that Wernicke's area functions as a kind of mediator or agent between structures supporting auditory processing, including internal auditory representations (i.e., the auditory cortex), and those supporting knowledge of language and language-meaning correspondences (the left posterior cortex and probably other areas of the left hemisphere and parts of the right hemisphere). Spontaneous speech production thus requires the transformation of meaning into auditory representations. Broca's area is then critically involved in the transformation of these auditory representations into programs for the coordinated movement of the vocal musculature. In language comprehension Wernicke's area again serves a transformational function, arousing meaning from those parts of the brain supporting language knowledge in response to ongoing auditory representations.

A metaphor may help clarify this view of the role of the language areas. The New York Public Library has a service, as part of its reference department, that allows people to phone in reference questions, such as What was the name of Caligula's fourth wife? The staff then searches for the answer and provides it to the caller. In this metaphor, Wernicke's area is the reference librarian who receives the call. The librarian understands the question and directs library staff to particular parts of the library where this information is stored. In this way the librarian is a liaison between the caller and the library shelves. The individual librarian does not possess the sought-after knowledge herself; yet she is able to elicit it from the areas of the library in which it is stored. If we wish to elaborate the metaphor to include Broca's area, we would imagine that an assistant brings the information back to the reference librarian, who then hands it to another librarian (Broca's area) who organizes and delivers a response to the caller.

The crux of this metaphor is that Wernicke's area is not a storehouse of language or meaning but an interface or mediator between linguistic sound representations (heard words) and meaning. As such, it operates in both directions, arousing meaning from auditory verbal representations (language comprehension) and transforming meaning into auditory verbal representations (a stage in language production).

It is possible that the neurons within the area of the angular gyrus play an analogous role with regard to visual-meaning transformations, serving as a mediator between seen language and meaning, although the fact that Wernicke's aphasia is associated with alexia indicates that Wernicke's area is a necessary component in this transformation process. As with Wernicke's area, the transformation process mediated by the angular gyrus can go in either direction, arousing meaning from visual-verbal representations (reading words) and transforming meaning into visual-written form (writing).

THE RIGHT HEMISPHERE AND LANGUAGE

Despite the early speculations of Hughlings-Jackson that the whole brain is involved in language, for a century after Broca's pioneering discovery the left hemisphere was considered dominant for language and the right hemisphere was considered to play no role. (Again we are talking about the vast majority of right-handed individuals. As we have already discussed, among left-handed persons there is more variability with regard to which hemisphere is specialized for speech.) Many of the methods that we have reviewed previously have provided evidence to support this notion. In particular, the right hemisphere can be shown to be extremely limited in its speech capabilities; it is capable of uttering only a few words. For example, words flashed to the right hemisphere of a commissurotomy patient cannot be read aloud, and in fact under these conditions the patient is unable to state verbally even that a word has been presented at all.

To access the comprehension capabilities of the essentially mute right hemisphere, it is necessary to test it without requiring the production of language, as in tests that require matching a word with a picture (picture vocabulary tests) or picking out or manipulating objects in such a way as to demonstrate comprehension (token tests). Using such methods with split-brain patients, Zaidel (1976) has demonstrated that the right hemisphere has a comprehension vocabulary equivalent to that of a 4-year-old child. This is obviously inferior to the vocabulary of the left hemisphere, yet it is a significant language capability when compared with the general linguistic incompetence that had been attributed to the right hemisphere.

There is another important domain of language in which the right hemisphere not only possesses competence but may be involved in routine language processing. The right hemisphere appears to play an important role in the production and comprehension of the emotional content inherent in the tonal qualities of speech, known as **prosody.** A disruption in the processing of prosody is termed **aprosodia** and may be either **expressive** or **receptive.** Oliver Sacks (1985) described a patient with a right-hemisphere lesion who, on hearing a speech by the president on television, was unable to perceive its emotional tone and so remained unaffected by its dramatic aspects, hearing only the logical argument (or lack thereof). In contrast, a group of patients with Wernicke's aphasia, when hearing the same speech, were observed to fall into uncontrolled laughter as they comprehended the emotional and dramatic tone of the speech (and apparently saw through it), even though they did not comprehend what was being said.

These anecdotal accounts are consistent with experimental studies that have demonstrated impairment after right-hemisphere lesions in the appreciation of the connotations of emotion and meaning implicit in the tonal aspects of language. There is also evidence that patients with right-hemisphere lesions are less able to utilize variations in the intonation of speech to express emotion or meaning (Ross, 1981). These and similar findings have led to the suggestion that there are a variety of aprosodias that are analogous to the varieties of aphasia (Gorelick & Ross, 1987). This remains to be fully investigated.

In addition to this important contribution of the right hemisphere to the processing of emotional components of language, there is evidence that the right hemisphere contributes to the comprehension of phonemically based semantic aspects of language in speakers of languages, such as Chinese, that extensively utilize subtle variations in tone as a marker for meaning. Thus, it has been shown that the incidence of receptive aphasia after right-hemisphere lesions is much higher in speakers of a highly tonal Chinese dialect than in speakers of European languages (Yu-Huan, Ying-Quan, & Gui-Qing, 1990).

The importance of the right hemisphere for processing tonal aspects of language is not, however, absolute. Disruption of production of the tonal aspects of language in a way that produces a distortion of articulation, termed **foreign language syndrome,** has been reported after anterior left-hemisphere damage that included the left basal ganglia (Graff-Radford et al., 1986; Gurd et al., 1988). Thus, despite the conceptual attractiveness of the association between right-hemisphere damage and prosodic difficulties, it remains unclear whether these difficulties are specific effects of right-hemisphere damage.

In an earlier section we argued that the transcortical aphasias support the proposition that areas outside the classical language areas are vitally important for language processes and that Wernicke's area, far from being *the* storehouse of language knowledge, serves to mediate and integrate language processes that are represented in widespread and diverse areas of cortex, presumably within the left hemisphere. This discussion of right-hemisphere language capabilities reinforces the idea that language is represented throughout the cerebral cortex. These considerations, taken together with the demonstrable fact that Wernicke's area, Broca's area, and the angular gyrus each play a particularly important role in language, have implications for the localizationist-holist controversy discussed earlier. It would seem that the extreme form of either position is untenable: Some areas of cortex are more important than others for lan-

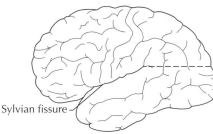

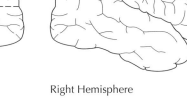

Sylvian fissure

Left Hemisphere   Right Hemisphere

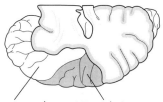

Planum temporale   Wernicke's area

FIGURE 6.13   Two instances of anatomical asymmetry in the human brain are detectable at the level of gross anatomy. In a majority of brains the Sylvian fissure rises more steeply on the right than on the left *(top)*. The second asymmetry is found in the planum temporale, which forms the upper surface of the temporal lobe and can be seen only when the Sylvian fissure is opened *(bottom)*. The posterior region of the planum temporale has been found to be larger on the left more often than on the right. *(From Geschwind, 1979, p. 115)*

guage processing, yet widespread areas outside these areas are critical for normal language competence.

HEMISPHERIC ANATOMICAL ASYMMETRIES

Ever since Broca's discovery of hemispheric functional asymmetry, attempts have been made to find corresponding anatomical asymmetries. For decades, however, no reliable anatomical asymmetry between the two cerebral hemispheres was detected, despite energetic searches and sometimes elaborate measurements (LeMay, 1984). It was not until the late 1960s that Geschwind and Levitsky (1968) reported two related findings of asymmetry that turned out to be detectable on the level of gross anatomy. They found that the angle of the Sylvian fissure was less steep on the left side (Figure 6.13) than on the right, an asymmetry that may reflect the relative enlargement of the parietal lobe in the language hemisphere. Their second and more important finding, to which we alluded in our earlier discussion of evidence for a biological predisposition for language, was that an area of the lower lip of the Sylvian fissure not visible when viewing the surface of the brain, called the **planum temporale,** is larger in the left hemisphere

than in the right (see Figure 6.13). This area includes part of Wernicke's area.

In addition to these asymmetries on the level of gross anatomy, Galaburda and his colleagues found that microscopic examination revealed a distinctive cytoarchitectonic region corresponding to the planum temporale and that this area was consistently larger on the left than the right (Galaburda et al., 1978; Galaburda & Sanides, 1980). Another asymmetry on the microscopic level, this one in the anterior speech area, has been reported by Scheibel (1984), who found increased dendritic branching in the left operculum (corresponding to Broca's area) compared with the homologous area in the right hemisphere and with adjacent precentral areas (Figure 6.14).

Although reliable anatomical asymmetries between the cerebral hemispheres have now been established, some qualifications are necessary. Geschwind and Levitsky (1968) reported that in 65 of the 100 brains they studied the planum temporale was larger on the left, whereas in 11 it was larger on the right and in 24 there was no detectable size difference. Although they did not know the handedness of the individuals whose brains they were studying, assuming that those studied were representative of the general population,

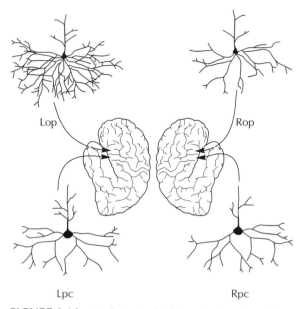

FIGURE 6.14   A schematic drawing showing the relative extent of dendritic arborization in neurons found in the left operculum *(Lop)*, right operculum *(Rop)*, left precentral *(Lpc)* area, and right precentral *(Rpc)* area. An increased number of higher-order segments was found in the left operculum (Broca's area) compared with all other areas. Areas outside the left operculum were also found to have relatively longer second- and third-order branches. *(From Scheibel, 1984, p. 50)*

the number of brains with the planum temporale larger on the left that Geschwind and Levitsky reported is less than the expected 93.[3] However, the proportion of cases with the larger planum temporale on the left is significantly greater than chance, almost six times as great as the number of brains with the right side larger, and comprises a region, part of the posterior speech area, where one would expect an asymmetry. Thus, it seems Geschwind and Levitsky discovered an anatomical asymmetry that corresponds to a functional asymmetry but that may not be a necessary condition for functional asymmetry.

The second qualification is a reminder of how very primitive our understanding of the neural substrate of language remains despite the identification of these anatomical asymmetries in areas that are important for language. We are still at the level of identifying an area that includes part of Wernicke's area

as being larger in the speaking hemisphere and an area corresponding to Broca's area as having more extensive dendritic arborization (branching) than the homologous area on the right. This is not to disparage what may prove to be the first steps toward an understanding of the processes on the neuronal level that underlie language; it is only to point out how far away we still remain from such an understanding.

THE EVOLUTION OF HUMAN LANGUAGE

We will end our consideration of language with a look at one of the most intriguing problems human language poses: How did it evolve? We have suggested that there is significant, though not conclusive, evidence that language is unique to humans. Whether or not this is the case, however, we may ask to what extent we are able to trace the evolution of the neural substrate for language back to our primate ancestors. This is clearly a very difficult issue to address, both because we do not have specimens of brains from our primate ancestors and because, even if we did, we do not possess a thorough understanding of the relationship between brain structure and language function.

Despite these serious obstacles, there are some hints that can be gleaned from the brains of other primates and from fossils of our early ancestors (LeMay, 1984). Fossilized skulls can yield data about the brain they once contained because the developing brain leaves impressions of its structural features on the inner surface of the skull. By making a cast of this inner surface of the skull—called an endocranial cast, or endocast—it is possible to get an idea of the structural features of the brain the skull contained.

Endocasts of the skull of the Neanderthal man of La Chapelle, who is believed to have lived approxi-

---

3. In the general population about 90% of people are right-handed and 10% left-handed. About 96% of right-handers have speech represented in the left hemisphere, with the remaining 4% having speech on the right side. In left-handers, 70% have speech on the left, whereas 15% have speech on the right and 15% have bilateral speech. Using these data, one can estimate the overall incidence of left-hemisphere speech to be about 93%, with 5% of people having speech represented in the right hemisphere and 2% having speech bilaterally represented.

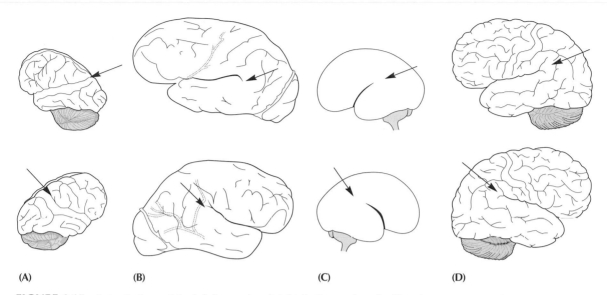

(A)   (B)   (C)   (D)

FIGURE 6.15   Lateral views of the left *(top row)* and right *(bottom row)* cerebral hemispheres of *(A)* an orangutan, *(B)* an endocranial cast of Peking man, *(C)* a human fetus, and *(D)* an adult male. Arrows mark the end of the Sylvian fissure, which is higher on the right than on the left. *(From LeMay, 1984, p. 32)*

mately 50,000 years ago, show the end of the Sylvian fissure to be higher on the right than on the left, a finding that we saw generally holds true for modern humans. This has also been found for endocasts of the skull of *Homo erectus*, who is believed to have lived 300,000–500,000 years ago, and of Peking man, who lived about 500,000 years ago. Similar asymmetries have also been observed in the brains of many species of great ape and are particularly prominent in the orangutan (Figure 6.15A). This asymmetry is also seen, to a lesser extent, in monkey brains.

The implications of these findings for an understanding of the evolution of language remain unclear, particularly because, as we emphasized earlier, we are not even certain that the asymmetry in the angle of the Sylvian fissure observed in humans is related to language. Nevertheless, it is tempting to speculate that the finding of this asymmetry in human ancestors who may have been without language and in contemporary primate species that, as far as we know, are also without language may indicate that the capacity for human language reflects the modification, through the process of evolution, of a basic primate neural apparatus rather than the evolution of a completely new neural apparatus for language. Reports that Japanese macaque monkeys show left-hemisphere specialization for the recognition of species-specific cries (Kandel et al., 1995) also would seem to be consistent with this view. Clearly, however, this will remain a speculative issue for some time to come and in any case must be a matter of degree because the structures mediating language must both be different from and derived from structures in ancestors who were without language.

SUMMARY

Language is the oldest and probably the most intensively studied area in neuropsychology. One reason for this intense interest is the importance of language for human beings. Language has enormous practical importance in our daily lives, and it has generated great theoretical interest, in part because there is reason to believe that it is a process that is unique to our species. In addition, language is a discrete phenomenon, in the sense that we know a good deal about what is and what is not language, and there is a long tradition of empirical and theoretical investigation of language that can be drawn upon to help us analyze and understand disorders in this domain. These factors also make the study of language disorders a fruitful avenue for the pursuit of a more general understanding of the relationship between brain and cognition.

In examining these disorders we have found that certain areas of the human brain are particularly important for language and that disorders of language can often be understood in terms of damage to these areas and the fiber tracts connecting them. This disconnection syndrome model has been useful in explaining some otherwise baffling patterns of impairment and preservation of function, such as the pattern of impaired repetition and preserved spontaneous speech that characterizes conduction aphasia and the syndrome of alexia without agraphia, to take just two examples.

Despite its usefulness, the disconnection syndrome model has some disadvantages. In particular, it cannot adequately account for certain dissociations that have emerged in the study of language disorders. This has led to a more cognitive approach, which attempts to infer the structure of the cognitive processes involved in language from the patterns of dissociation seen after cerebral damage. These inferences often take the form of models of information processing, and these, in turn, often conceptualize a particular aspect of linguistic processing as proceeding along parallel channels, as we saw, for example, in the two-route models of reading and spelling.

In most individuals, language representation is strongly lateralized to the left hemisphere and relatively focally localized within the anterior and posterior speech areas of that hemisphere. In fact, language is the most clearly localized of all higher-order cognitive functions. Nevertheless, there is compelling evidence that language processing, far from being confined to the classical language areas, is me-

diated by widespread cortical areas in both hemispheres. Examples of this evidence include the effect of left-hemisphere lesions outside the classical language areas on spontaneous speech in transcortical aphasia, the effect of lesions in either hemisphere on the production and comprehension of prosody, and the finding that the right hemisphere possesses a significant capacity for language comprehension. In addition, to paraphrase a conclusion drawn long ago by Hughlings-Jackson, primary impairment in a cognitive system that is not explicitly linguistic will nevertheless have a secondary effect that manifests itself in the domain of language, as when a patient with a spatial processing deficit cannot verbally describe how to get from one location to another.

Although functional asymmetry between the hemispheres was firmly established by Broca's work in the middle of the 19th century, it was not until 1968 that anatomical hemispheric asymmetries were definitively established. These anatomical asymmetries involve areas that are known to be involved in language function, and it is therefore presumed that they are related to the language specialization of the left hemisphere, although this remains to be fully established. One of these asymmetries, the finding that the posterior end of the Sylvian fissure is lower on the left than on the right, has been identified in the endocranial casts of several early ancestors of humans and in the brains of many contemporary primates. This provides a hint that the neural structures mediating language in modern humans evolved from structures already well developed in the more primitive primate brain rather than reflecting the evolution of a radically new neural substrate for language. At the present time, however, the data bearing on this problem are highly inconclusive. Therefore, attempted solutions based on our current understanding of the neurobiological basis of language remain highly speculative.

CHAPTER 7

Spatial Processing

GENERAL CONSIDERATIONS
  Problems in the Neuropsychology
    of Spatial Processing
  Types of Spatial Behavior
  Early Empirical Studies
BODY SPACE
  Body Surface
  Joint and Muscle Sense
EGOCENTRIC SPACE
  Visual Disorientation
  Visual Localization
  Neural Correlates of Visual Disorientation
    and Impairment in Visual Localization
ALLOCENTRIC SPACE
  Spatial Analysis
  Search for the Mechanisms Underlying
    Spatial Behavior
  Perception of Relative Spatial Location
  Orientation Discrimination
  Complex Spatial Tasks
  Topographical Orientation and Memory

The Two-Pathway Hypothesis for Object
    Recognition and Spatial Processing
**THE ROLE OF THE HIPPOCAMPUS
  IN SPATIAL PROCESSING**
  Unit Recording Studies
  Lesion Studies
  Neuroethological Studies
NEGLECT OF ONE SIDE OF SPACE
  Neglect as a Disorder of Attention
  Neglect as a Disruption of the Internal
    Representation of Space
SPATIAL THINKING AND MENTAL IMAGERY
  Electrophysiological Studies
  Imaging Studies
  Lesion Studies
  Hemispheric Specialization for Imagery
  Implications for Our Initial Questions
    About Imagery
**THE ROLE OF THE FRONTAL LOBES
  IN SPATIAL PROCESSING**
SUMMARY

If language is a uniquely human capacity, the ability to orient and direct movement in space is essential for the survival of all but the simplest of animals and must have emerged very early in the course of evolution. Consistent with these differences, the modes of cognition *mediating language and spatial processing are strikingly different. The mental representations underlying language are* **symbolic representations.** *For example, a word is a sound or a written pattern that does not usually bear any direct relationship to the thing that it*

denotes (although certain poetic uses of words such as buzz *or* hiss *strive toward such a relationship, a literary device called onomatopoeia). We all know the object to which the word* moon *refers, although there is nothing intrinsic to that word that has anything to do with the natural satellite that circles the earth each month.*

In contrast to this symbolic function, a mental representation may capture some of the actual characteristics of (and thus be analogous to) that which it represents. For example, the moon could be represented by a circle. Such representations are termed **analogical representations.** *Mental representations of space, such as an image of the layout of furniture in a familiar room or the relative locations of cities on a map, are analogical, although the content of these images could be represented symbolically in the form of a verbal description or coordinates of latitude and longitude.*

Actually this distinction is not quite as clear-cut as it appears. It is well known that mental images are not *veridical (true) representations of the external world. This is clear to most people who, having been asked to form an image of, say, the Parthenon, are then asked how many pillars line its facade. Although a small minority of people are able to form completely veridical images, termed* **eidetic images,** *most of us form images that contain far less information than a photograph. In fact, our mental representations of spatial relationships are strongly influenced by our symbolic or conceptual understanding of the world. A dramatic illustration of this is the finding that, when asked to imagine a map of the United States and then imagine the locations of Reno and San Diego, subjects tend to visualize Reno as lying east of San Diego because they believe this to be the case (Stevens & Coupe, 1978). In fact, Reno lies west of San Diego. As we will see, the fact that spatial information can be coded in multiple ways and is subject to multiple influences complicates attempts to understand its underlying neural basis.*

GENERAL CONSIDERATIONS

Problems in the Neuropsychology of Spatial Processing

As mentioned, spatial information can be encoded in a variety of ways. Thus, information that an experimenter has presented in spatial form may in fact be encoded verbally by an individual confronted with it. Although verbal information is also subject to multiple encoding, as when a subject forms a mental image of a concrete noun, there appears to be less encoding variability for verbal material. This means that in experimental situations designed to test spatial processing, it is often difficult to be confident that we have in fact induced a subject to engage in spatial processing rather than verbal processing.

The study of spatial processing and the brain is further complicated by the fact that spatial processing has not yielded to a systematic analysis like that which has been applied to language. Although we will find that spatial processing can be categorized in ways that provide a useful framework for attempting to understand underlying brain mechanisms, spatial

processing currently lacks (and may be intrinsically resistant to) the highly delineated conceptual analysis that has emerged from the study of language.

In chapter 6 we saw that such a conceptual framework was highly useful for understanding the brain mechanisms underlying language. In contrast, the absence of a differentiated grammar and syntax of spatial processing means that the subprocesses involved in complex spatial behavior are difficult to specify and dissociations of function are difficult to demonstrate. For example, if a subject performs poorly on a complex spatial test, such as replicating a pictured design by manipulating a number of cubes with different patterns on each face (Block Design Subtest of the Wechsler Adult Intelligence Scale–Revised [WAIS-R]), it may be unclear whether this is due to a spatial processing impairment, an impairment in motor function, or some other impairment.

In fact, the study of impairment in spatial processing in patients is plagued by the potential problem of confounds with other impairments. Language is such an overlearned function that its basic elements may persist in relatively undisturbed form even in the face of generalized interference such as is seen in delirium and confusion or even psychosis and dementia. In contrast, spatial processing, which requires a certain degree of comprehension of the immediate environment, is more vulnerable to the effects of nonspecific interfering factors.

There are other complicating factors as well. The right hemisphere appears to be less specialized for spatial processing than the left hemisphere is for language processing. This is suggested by findings that we will discuss in more detail later. At this point we can generally state that, whereas right-hemisphere lesions (again we are assuming a population of strong right-handers) generally have relatively slight impact on language, left parietal-lobe lesions may have a significant impact on spatial tasks (Gainotti & Tiacci, 1970; Mehta, Newcombe, & Damasio, 1987). Furthermore, it has been shown that, although the left hemisphere in split-brain patients is highly linguistically competent, the disconnected right hemisphere in these patients is less competent for spatial processing than the left hemisphere is for language processing (Milner & Taylor, 1972). An obvious interpretation of these and other studies is that the left hemisphere is more of a language specialist than the right hemisphere is a spatial specialist. It seems likely that this difference has at least in part to do with the heterogeneity of the many processes that we sometimes misleadingly lump into the unifying construct spatial processing. Many of these processes apparently require the participation of the left hemisphere for their successful execution.

There may be yet another sense in which the right hemisphere is less specialized for spatial processing than the left is for language. Whereas the left hemisphere exhibits significant intrahemispheric localization in its mediation of language, no areas analogous to Broca's area, Wernicke's area, or the angular gyrus have been demonstrated within the right hemisphere for the mediation of spatial processing. Thus, spatial processing appears to be more diffusely represented in the right hemisphere than language processing is in the left hemisphere (Semmes, 1968). The grounds for this difference constitute an interesting area for speculation. Once again, it is tempting to attribute the difference to intrinsic differences in the nature of language and spatial processing, but there may be other factors underlying these differences. For example, in the course of evolution, spatial processing obviously long preceded language processing. It may be that the more diffuse representation of spatial processing, both within the right hemisphere and within the brain as a whole, is related to its earlier evolutionary development.

Types of Spatial Behavior

There are several different aspects of spatial behavior and at least three basic frameworks from which to answer the question "Where?" We can conceptualize three major categories of spatial processing: (a) body space, (b) egocentric space, and (c) allocentric space. Within the domain of **body space** we can identify the sense of the body surface as a space on which stimuli can impinge and be localized (**localization on the body surface**). We also perceive the position of parts of our body relative to each other in space (**proprioception**) and changes in body position over time as we move our bodies through space (**kinesthesis**).

Egocentric space refers to the perception of spatial location outside the body but with reference to it. In other words, the coordinate system defining location within egocentric space has the body as its center, and all locations are defined as positions relative to that center. The familiar "clock" schema used by fighter pilots to identify the location of enemy planes is an example of an egocentric coordinate system, as are the less precise designations "left" and "right."

Allocentric space (from the Greek *allos*, "other") refers to representations of space in which place is defined by a coordinate system that is independent of the observer. The coordinate system may have distant points of reference, such as the global points used by the system of longitude and latitude or the positions of the stars used in celestial navigation. In fact, navigation may be considered a technology for defining one's position within an allocentric frame of reference. More often, place in allocentric space is defined in terms of a coordinate system that uses local features as points of reference, such as landmarks in a city, the floor plan of a room, or the relational properties of a number of objects. In sum, orientation within body space and egocentric space uses the body as a frame of reference, whereas orientation within allocentric space uses external objects to define a frame of reference. We will see that there is evidence that different neural mechanisms underlie orientation in these different frames of reference.

Early Empirical Studies

All of the factors just discussed may have contributed to the fact that the appreciation of disorders of spatial processing after cerebral damage came relatively late in the history of neuropsychology. It is true that John Hughlings-Jackson, whose ideas about the brain are so strikingly modern, speculated as early as 1864 that the right hemisphere might be the seat of visual perception (Hughlings-Jackson, 1864) and proposed in somewhat more detail 10 years later the notion that the right hemisphere also has functions for which it is specialized (Hughlings-Jackson, 1874). Among these he suggested visual imagery, visual object recognition, and getting around in space. Nevertheless, despite some well-executed early empirical work (for a review, see Benton, 1982), it was not until the 1940s and 1950s that the studies of Paterson, McFie, Zangwill, Hecaen, and others established unequivocally a specialized role for the right hemisphere in spatial processing, although, as we have already hinted, hemispheric specialization for spatial processing appears to be more complex than that seen in language. Let's turn now to an examination of spatial processing and its neural basis.

BODY SPACE

Body Surface

Evidence of cortical involvement in the mediation of elementary tactile function comes from studies of the effect of cortical lesions. Damage to the postcentral gyrus, the classical somatosensory cortex, is associated with impairment on the contralateral side of the body on tests of elementary somatosensory function such as pressure threshold and two-point discrimination. Physiological work with lower animals and cortical stimulation work carried out in humans dur-

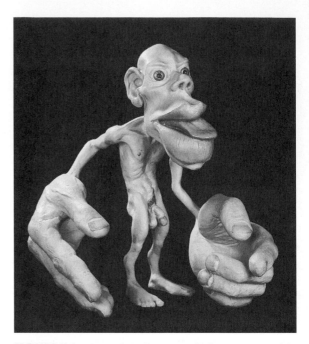

FIGURE 7.1   An artist's depiction of what a man would look like if the size of his various body parts was proportional to the area of somatosensory cortex devoted to them. *(From H. Gleitman, 1995, p. 41)*

ing neurosurgery have demonstrated that the body surface is topographically represented on the postcentral gyrus. For example, lesions to the most inferior part of the somatosensory area (adjacent to the Sylvian fissure) produce impairment in tactile sensitivity on the face, and lesions on the medial aspect of the postcentral gyrus are associated with tactile deficits on the feet. The relative area of the somatosensory cortex devoted to various parts of the body and the corresponding relative sensitivity of these parts are often depicted by the **sensory homunculus** (Figure 7.1).

Perhaps the most elementary identification of spatial location is detection of the location of a stimulus impinging on the body surface. **Point localization thresholds** are typically measured by stimulating neighboring points on the skin and determining the minimum distance between two successively touched points that can be reliably identified as different. Accuracy of localization on different parts of the body surface corresponds to the thresholds for two-point discrimination and pressure sensitivity represented by the sensory homunculus.[1]

Joint and Muscle Sense

Somatosensory input from the body not only registers passive stimuli impinging on the body surface, it also includes sensations that are the result of combined input from the joints and muscles that yield a perception of body position (proprioception) and body movement (kinesthesis). The proprioceptive and kinesthetic sensations resulting from active touch make possible the recognition of objects and spatial layouts, a process termed **tactual perception.** (The term *tactile* is often used in this context; however, limiting the use of the latter term to the perception of passively impinging stimuli and employing the term *tactual* for active touch has the advantage of emphasizing the very different nature of the two processes.) Lesions to the secondary somatosensory cortex (posterior to the primary sensory cortex) produce impairment in tactual functioning. It appears that these parietal areas are necessary for the complex integration of information about body movement (from joints and muscle) and skin sensation, an integration that results in the identification of the object being touched or the space that is being tactually explored.

EGOCENTRIC SPACE

Visual Disorientation

We first consider the simplest case of spatial localization, the location of a single point relative to the observer. This capability would seem to be a prerequisite for all more complicated spatial processing. We have seen that neural structures in the visual system

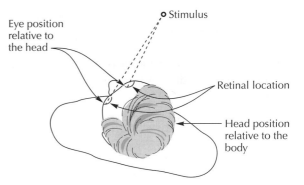

FIGURE 7.2   To determine the location of a visual stimulus relative to the body, information regarding retinal location, eye position relative to the head, and head position relative to the rest of the body must be integrated.

are retinotopically organized. This means that the specific location on the retina stimulated by a single point is coded in a number of structures, including the lateral geniculate nucleus and a number of cortical visual areas. But it is obvious that information about where a stimulus falls on the retina does not provide sufficient information to define its location relative to the observer because the eye, head, and body can move. Thus, the fact that a point stimulus falls on point X on the retina tells us nothing about where it is relative to the observer; such a determination requires the integration of information regarding retinal location, eye position relative to the head, and head position relative to the rest of the body (Figure 7.2).

One of the simplest breakdowns in this process is seen as an inability to move the eyes and head in such a way as to cause a stimulus to fall on the retinal fovea (i.e., to fixate an object), in the absence of primary visual impairment or impairment in eye and head musculature. The term **visual disorientation** has traditionally been used to specify this impairment (Holmes, 1918; McCarthy & Warrington, 1990), although when used in this way the term has a more restricted meaning than one might expect from colloquial usage. Visual disorientation can be measured in terms of the discrepancy, in degrees, between the location of a point stimulus and the direction of a subject's gaze. This is essentially a breakdown in the

---

1. Interestingly, about 40% of patients with cortical lesions who exhibit contralateral deficits in point localization on the hand have been reported to also have defects on the ipsilateral hand as well (Corkin, Milner, & Taylor, 1973). The reason for this variation in sensory findings in patients with quite similar lesions is unclear.

coordination of retinal information and eye and head movement. Visual disorientation may also manifest itself as impaired perception of depth. This can be detected by misreaching on the part of the subject or by errors in judgment regarding the relative distances of two or more objects.

Visual Localization

Deficits in **visual localization** have traditionally been defined as impairment in the ability to point to or touch a visual stimulus in the absence of primary visual, primary somatosensory, or primary motor impairment. Holmes (1918) reported patients who were unable to point to a visual stimulus but were unimpaired in fixating a visual stimulus and in pointing to the location of auditory and tactile stimuli. Since then, there have been many reports of impairment in pointing to a stimulus in the absence of primary visual disorientation or of proprioceptive, kinesthetic, or motor impairment. This impairment, which has been termed **optic ataxia,** constitutes a disruption in the coordination of visual and motor processes.

Neural Correlates of Visual Disorientation and Impairment in Visual Localization

The lesions associated with visual disorientation and impairment in visual localization are bilateral in the area of the occipitoparietal boundary (Ross-Russell & Bharucha, 1984; Warrington, 1986). In addition, it was recognized early (Riddoch, 1935) that both of these impairments can be confined to one visual field or even one visual quadrant and, in the case of visual localization, to one arm. Thus, the systems that underlie visual orientation and visual localization are bilaterally represented and have the same contralateral relationship between hemisphere and side of receptor surface as is seen in primary visual functioning. In addition, like primary sensory function, these systems are retinotopically organized.

Although our knowledge of the mechanisms on the neuronal level that underlie visual orientation and visual localization remains very incomplete, some hints have emerged from recent studies. As we have seen, to pinpoint a stimulus in space, it is necessary to integrate information about the areas of the retina on which the stimulus impinges with information about the location of the retina (eye) relative to the head and information about the location of the head relative to the rest of the body. The integration of this disparate information is necessary for localization within egocentric space.

We have seen that at levels of the visual system from the retina to the cortex one finds neurons with receptive fields that correspond to a particular area of retina. Of cortical neurons, those with the smallest receptive fields are found in V1 and V2, and these areas therefore code the most precise mapping of retinal location of stimulation. A major problem posed by attempts to understand the neural basis of egocentric localization is how information contained in these retinotopic maps is integrated with information about eye and head movement to yield information about the position of the stimulus relative to the body. Although this question remains to be answered, the receptive-field characteristics of certain cells in area V3 and in parietal cortex indicate that they are responding as if they were sensitive to the confluence of this information. To explain this more fully, we have to briefly discuss the size of the receptive fields of extrastriate neurons.

In general, as one moves downstream from V1 and V2 to extrastriate visual areas, the size of the receptive fields of neurons increases. For example, direction-specific neurons in V5 show a strong differential response to movement in their preferred direction, but they do so without regard to where in their relatively large receptive fields that movement occurs. Thus, in neurons in V5, the coding of movement takes priority over the coding of retinal location. Similarly, neurons in V3 and V4 have relatively large receptive fields, and in the parietal and inferior temporal cortex receptive-field sizes are even larger, resulting in a major loss of information regarding retinal location of stimulation that is exchanged for a more integrated coding of stimulus characteristics.

It is logical that a confluence of information from different parts of the retina should take place in extrastriate areas. This raises the problem, however, of how information about the retinal location of this now highly processed stimulus is coded. This is an

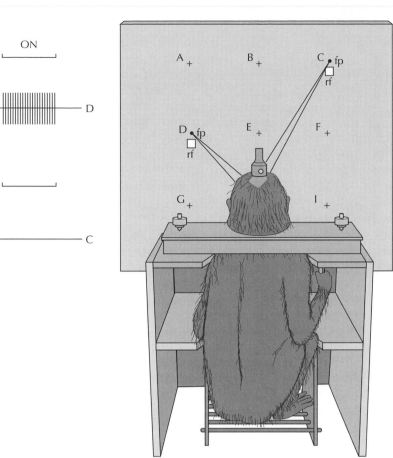

FIGURE 7.3   Response of a gaze-locked cell in area V3 of the alert, behaving monkey. When the animal fixates a point *(fp)* near D, the cell fires when a line of appropriate orientation appears in its receptive field *(rf)*, which in this neuron happens to be immediately below the fixation point. So far this is unremarkable. However, when the monkey shifts its gaze so that it now fixates a point *(fp)* near C, the neuron does not respond when the same stimulus appears in the same location relative to the fixation point. The horizontal lines to the left of the drawing indicate when the stimulus was in the cell's receptive field. *(From Zeki, 1993, p. 339)*

aspect of the larger binding problem that we have seen challenges attempts to achieve a comprehensive understanding of visual perception. Zeki (1993) has proposed that information about the locus of retinal stimulation may be reintegrated with other characteristics of a stimulus processed by extrastriate areas through reentrant connections from these areas back to the precisely topographically coded information in V1 and V2.

There is considerable support for this reentrant hypothesis (Zeki, 1993). However, at this point let's return to our original problem of how the system integrates information regarding location of retinal stimulation with eye, head, and body position to yield a representation of location within egocentric space. The hints from the receptive-field characteristics of neurons in area V3 and in parietal cortex (to

which we alluded earlier) are as follows. Unit cell recording in the alert, behaving monkey has revealed cells in these areas that respond only when a stimulus impinges on a particular area of the retina *and* the animal is gazing in a particular direction (Galletti & Battaglini, 1989). When the animal is fixating a different point, stimulation falling on the same area of retina that caused the cell to fire during its preferred direction of gaze will not produce a response (Figure 7.3). In other words, whether or not a particular locus of retinal stimulation will cause such a cell to fire is contingent on the point on which the animal is fixating, its direction of gaze. These cells have therefore been termed **gaze-locked cells.**

Here then are cells that are sensitive to position within egocentric space. However, some even more complex cells have been discovered in area V6 of

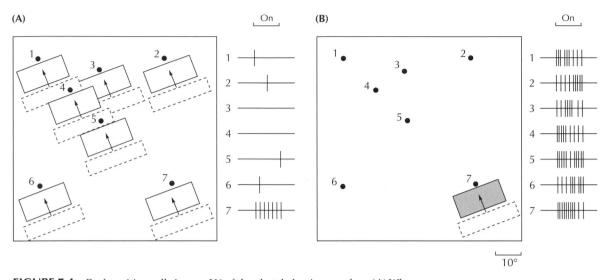

FIGURE 7.4   Real-position cells in area V6 of the alert, behaving monkey. *(A)* When the animal fixated on *point 7,* the cell gave a good response to a stimulus moving toward 11 o'clock. However, when the monkey fixated other positions *(1–6)* and identical locations relative to the fixation point were stimulated, the cell was unresponsive. So far the cell has the characteristics of a gaze-locked cell. *(B)* In addition, when the monkey fixated different positions *(1–6)* and the same moving stimulus was presented to *point 7,* the cell fired, regardless of the point of fixation. ON indicates that the stimulus was in the receptive field. *(From Zeki, 1993, p. 341)*

monkey parietal cortex. Some cells in V6 are sensitive to movement in a particular direction (like cells in V5), and many of these are gaze-locked. Thus, a given cell might fire, say, to a stimulus moving upward to 11 o'clock when the monkey is fixating a particular point, but not when it is fixating other points (Figure 7.4A). Of particular interest in the context of our discussion of egocentric space, however, is the discovery by Galletti and his colleagues (cited by Zeki, 1993, p. 341) of cells that have the same gaze-locked characteristics as those just described but which also fire to movement in a specific direction *in a specific position relative to the monkey regardless of the point being fixated* (Figure 7.4B). These have been termed **real-position cells.** Here we have cells that appear to be coding position in egocentric space. We are very far from understanding the neural mechanisms and connections that mediate the integration of proprioceptive and visual information underlying the response characteristics of these gaze-locked and real-position cells. Nevertheless, it is clear that the

response characteristics of these cells must be the product of such integration. We also do not understand how, or even whether, the response properties of these cells contribute to the construction of a representation of egocentric space, although their involvement in this process seems highly likely.

ALLOCENTRIC SPACE

We turn now to a consideration of allocentric space, spatial representations in which the environment serves as the frame of reference for a coordinate system that is independent of the observer. This may be an elaborate and highly abstract system of cartesian coordinates, such as the system of latitude and longitude, or it may be the coordinate system defined by landmarks in an extended space, the features of a room, or the relative positions of several objects. In everyday life egocentric and allocentric frames of reference interact to generate a sense of place for an individual organism. This happens, for example, when

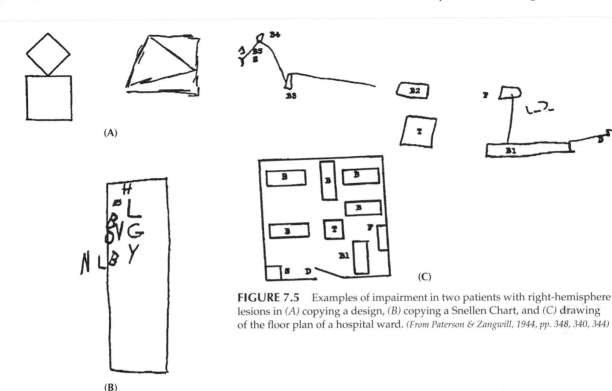

FIGURE 7.5   Examples of impairment in two patients with right-hemisphere lesions in *(A)* copying a design, *(B)* copying a Snellen Chart, and *(C)* drawing of the floor plan of a hospital ward. *(From Paterson & Zangwill, 1944, pp. 348, 340, 344)*

the representation of allocentric space defined by landmarks and the sense of the position of those landmarks relative to the individual's body together serve to guide the individual's movement through the spatial layout.

In the sections that follow we will examine several aspects of allocentric spatial processing and its neural basis. Again, it will be apparent that spatial processing is a highly complex and heterogeneous spectrum of activities that have not yet been fully integrated into a coherent conceptual model of cognitive functioning. The investigation of the neuropsychology of spatial processing will doubtless contribute to the development of this model.

Spatial Analysis

The early studies that emerged in the 1940s (Paterson & Zangwill, 1944, 1945) did not attempt to isolate aspects of spatial processing. Instead, they made the important contribution of documenting impairment in complex spatial processing after cerebral lesions in the absence of primary sensory, motor, or language impairment. In addition, these early studies demonstrated that performance on spatial tasks was dissociable from object recognition. This was an important finding because it indicated that the perception of objects and the perception of space are distinct processes. The investigators presented case studies of patients who were impaired in such tasks as the spontaneous drawing and copying of simple figures, making matchstick designs, counting the number of blocks in a solid cube with three blocks on a side, and marking places on a map (Figure 7.5). These findings were later corroborated by a large number of group studies (e.g., Newcombe, 1969; Warrington & James, 1988).

Perhaps the major contribution of these early studies was this demonstration that tasks with a spatial component, even though heterogeneous, could be selectively impaired after damage to the brain. The selectivity of deficits in behaviors that had to do with space led to the idea that perceptual impairment could be confined to spatial processing, a notion embodied in the term **visuospatial agnosia,** a term much used

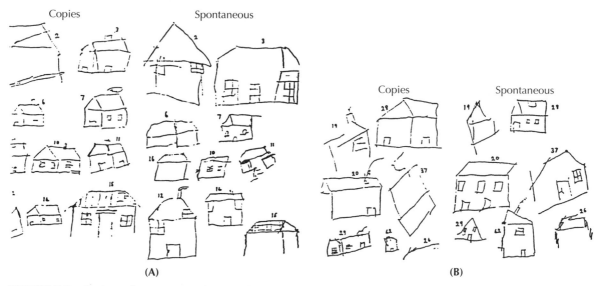

FIGURE 7.6   Copies and spontaneous drawings by patients with lesions in
(A) the left hemisphere and *(B)* the right hemisphere. *(From Piercy et al., 1960, p. 234)*

in the 1950s. This conceptualization was in line with other evidence, emerging from cognitive psychology (e.g., Cooper & Shepard, 1973; Jonides & Baum, 1978; Kosslyn, Ball, & Reisser, 1978), indicating that spatial thinking and behavior are mediated by cognitive processes that are distinctly different from those underlying other types of thinking and behavior. This was an important advance, but at the same time it posed new problems. In particular, it raised the question of whether a systematic taxonomy of spatial behavior that would explain the structure of underlying spatial processing is possible. This is a problem that remains to be adequately resolved, although we will see that neuropsychological investigations, particularly the patterns of dissociation observed after different cerebral lesions, have made contributions toward that goal.

Search for the Mechanisms Underlying Spatial Behavior

Although the deficits in spatial behavior observed by Paterson and Zangwill (1944, 1945) were associated with lesions in the posterior area of the right hemisphere, subsequent studies showed that certain complex spatial processing, such as that underlying drawing and other constructional behavior, is disrupted after damage to either the right or the left hemisphere (McFie & Zangwill, 1960; Piercy, Hecaen, & Ajuriaguerra, 1960). Thus, it appeared either that there was no strong hemispheric specialization for complex spatial processing or that some of the component processes underlying complex spatial behavior are mediated by the right hemisphere and others are mediated by the left hemisphere, so that damage to either hemisphere disrupts complex spatial behavior but in qualitatively different ways.

An example of a complex spatial behavior that could be so analyzed is drawing. Lesions in the parietal region of each hemisphere disrupt this behavior. However, although the issue is not absolutely settled, there is strong evidence that the two hemispheres are mediating different aspects of this behavior (Figure 7.6). In particular, it has been proposed that the right hemisphere is mediating perceptual aspects of the task, whereas the left hemisphere is mediating components of the task that are more explicitly executive in nature. This formulation is supported by a number of lines of evidence. First, as will be discussed in more detail in chapter 8, the right hemisphere is in general more specialized for perceptual processing than the left (McCarthy & Warrington, 1990). In addition, as we will discuss in more detail below, the right hemisphere is more specialized for the perception of space. Furthermore, as we will discuss in more detail in chapter 9, lesions of the left hemisphere are associated with disruptions of learned movement, termed **apraxia,** and it appears to be this breakdown in the capacity to execute learned action that underlies the impairment in drawing seen in association with left parietal-lobe damage. We will find that variations on this theme of complementary specialized contributions of the two hemispheres to complex spatial behavior will recur often in our discussion. In addition, we will identify areas mediating specialized aspects of spatial functioning within each hemisphere. In fact, much of the empirical work since the 1950s has been an attempt to further investigate these and other components of spatial processing through the study of the dissociations seen after cerebral lesions. We turn now to some of the evidence that has emerged from these studies.

Perception of Relative Spatial Location

A number of studies have investigated discrimination of relative spatial location. In its simplest form this has been tested by asking subjects to make same-different matching decisions about the location of a gap in a line (Warrington & Rabin, 1970) and the location of one or two dots within a square (Taylor & Warrington, 1973). In another variant, subjects were required to identify a number from a random array within a square corresponding to the location of a previously viewed dot (Hannay, Varney, & Benton, 1976; Warrington & James, 1988). These studies consistently found that impairment in the perception of relative spatial location was associated with lesions in the posterior right hemisphere.

Orientation Discrimination

Studies investigating discrimination of line orientation (Benton, Hannay, & Varney, 1975) have found impairment associated with right parietal-lobe damage (Figure 7.7). Impaired orientation discrimination

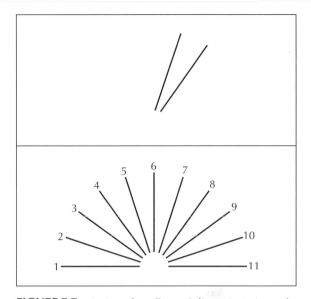

FIGURE 7.7   An item from Benton's line-orientation task. Subjects are presented with pairs of lines *(top)* and have to identify which of the numbered lines *(bottom)* have the same orientation. Patients with right parietal-lobe lesions are impaired on this task. *(Benton, Varney, & Hamsher, 1978, p. 365)*

has also been demonstrated after lesions of the right parietal lobe in a task that required patients to match the orientation of a movable rod to a sample in both visual and tactual conditions (De Renzi, Faglioni, & Scotti, 1971).

Complex Spatial Tasks

When we move from relatively simple tasks to more complex spatial tasks, we find that impairment follows lesions of either hemisphere and the clear specialization of the right hemisphere is no longer seen. We have already found this to be the case for impairments in copying and drawing tasks, impairments that are generally termed **constructional apraxia,** although this term confuses the issue of whether the underlying mechanism of the impairment is one of disturbed action *(praxis)* or disturbed perception. In fact, as mentioned earlier, there is evidence that different components of drawing are disrupted after lesions to the two hemispheres, based primarily on qualitative differences in the disruptions following left- and right-hemisphere lesions.

One of the ways this difference has been characterized is that a disturbance of spatial perception underlies the impairment in drawing associated with right-sided lesions and a disturbance of the organization of action underlies the effects of left-sided lesions. As mentioned, one of the first sources of evidence for this hypothesis came from some penetrating observations and inferences made by investigators in the 1950s. Drawings by patients with right-hemisphere lesions were described as having a kind of "piecemeal" character (Piercy et al., 1960), such that the individual elements might be adequately depicted but the depiction of the relationship between individual components was severely disrupted (see Figure 7.6). This disrupted performance was attributed to an underlying impairment in the perception of visual space (visuospatial agnosia) (Ettlinger, Warrington, & Zangwill, 1957).

Drawings made following left-hemisphere damage appeared to be disrupted in a different way, being described as more simplified and lacking in detail but as retaining the general spatial features of the depicted objects (Arrigoni & De Renzi, 1964; McFie & Zangwill, 1960; Warrington, James, & Kinsbourne, 1966). In addition, patients with left-hemisphere lesions were able to draw better when they had a model to copy, whereas patients with right-hemisphere lesions did not benefit from copying (see Figure 7.6). If we assume that an impairment in the organization of action would benefit from the presence of a model to copy, whereas perceptual deficits would not, then this observation is consistent with the praxic-perceptual division of labor between the left and the right hemispheres that we have been considering.

In the 1960s, as studies of commissurotomy patients began to be conducted, these early studies were complemented by reports that confirmed that each hemisphere was contributing to constructional tasks because neither hemisphere in isolation was able to draw normally (Geschwind, 1979). Furthermore, the characteristics of the impairments seen in the productions of each hemisphere could be reasonably interpreted as supporting the hypothesis that the two hemispheres are making different, specialized contributions to constructional behavior (Figure 7.8).

These observations and the inferences regarding qualitative differences between the two hemispheres proved to be highly heuristic conceptualizations for an understanding of both spatial behavior and hemispheric functional asymmetry. Nevertheless, the qualitative analysis of drawings runs the risk of being a subjective enterprise. Therefore, the search for a more objective basis for differentiating the role of each cerebral hemisphere in spatial behavior became important. These efforts yielded an important dissociation: Constructional impairment following right parietal-lobe lesions is associated with impairment in spatial tasks without an explicit motor component, such as the dot location and line orientation tasks discussed earlier (Benton et al., 1975; Taylor & Warrington, 1973), but not in tasks requiring the organization of action outside the spatial domain. In contrast, constructional impairment following left parietal-lobe lesions is associated with impairment in tasks requiring the organization of actions outside the spatial domain but not in tasks of spatial perception that do not require organized action (Costa & Vaughan, 1962; Dee, 1970). These findings support the notion that the right hemisphere is specialized for spatial perception and that the left hemisphere contributes a praxic (action) component to spatial tasks.

Whether this hypothesis adequately accounts for the effects of left- and right-hemisphere lesions on constructional behavior remains to be conclusively established. Let's, however, leave the question of the differential contribution of the two hemispheres to constructional behavior and turn to another complex spatial behavior: orientation in larger spatial layouts, such as a city or a geographic locale.

Topographical Orientation and Memory

Topographical disorientation refers to an inability to move about in spatial layouts due to a disruption in the ability to accurately perceive the spatial relationships and distances between landmarks. Individuals with this disorder are unable to use landmarks to guide movement through the spatial layout

Reproduced by left hand (right hemisphere)	Model pattern	Reproduced by right hand (left hemisphere)

FIGURE 7.8 The performance of a patient in whom the corpus callosum had been sectioned, isolating the two hemispheres. The subject had to reproduce the model in the center column by assembling colored blocks using either the left hand (right hemisphere) or right hand (left hemisphere). Errors were equally frequent for the two hands, but the kinds of errors were different, suggesting that each hemisphere is specialized for a different component of the task. The finding that neither hemisphere alone is competent in this task emphasizes the need for the cooperative activity of both hemispheres in the execution of complex spatial behaviors. *(From Geschwind, 1979, p. 109)*

because their ability to generate an internal representation of the environment has been compromised. In contrast, a **topographical memory disorder** (also called **topographical amnesia**) is an impairment in the ability to learn new spatial layouts (**anterograde topographical amnesia**) or a loss of the ability to move about in previously known spatial layouts (**retrograde topographical amnesia**) without, however, a primary disturbance of spatial processing. Thus, the patient with topographical amnesia is no more disoriented in a spatial environment than is a normal individual who had just been placed in a new environment. Anterograde and retrograde topographical amnesia are dissociable.

There is strong evidence that topographical disorientation is associated with right parietal-lobe damage (Hecaen, Tzortzis, & Romdot, 1980; Paterson & Zangwill, 1945). However, there is also evidence that the impaired representation of extended and distant extrapersonal space characteristic of topographical disorientation is dissociable from disruptions in allocentric space in the immediate environment of the individual (Hecaen et al., 1980), suggesting that different specialized areas within the right-parietal region may mediate the functions disrupted in these two types of disorder.

Anterograde topographical amnesia appears to be related to hippocampal abnormality, and, as discussed in more detail below, there is considerable evidence that the hippocampus is centrally involved in memory for spatial location and may serve as the site of representation of a spatial map of the environment (e.g., Wilson & McNaughton, 1993). In contrast, the neural structures involved in retrograde topographical amnesia, though unclear, appear not to include the hippocampus. This conclusion is based on the finding that this disorder has been reported in the absence of detectable hippocampal damage (Paterson & Zangwill, 1945). More compelling, however, is the finding that patients with extensive hippocampal damage and severe anterograde topographical amnesia may have preserved knowledge of spatial layouts learned before the onset of their lesion (Milner, Corkin, & Teuber, 1968).

Topographical orientation and topographical memory are intimately related. To form an internal representation of a spatial layout through which we are moving, such as a city, we must build up that representation from ongoing perceptual information accumulated over time (assuming we do not look at a map). Thus, topographical orientation is different from other types of visual spatial perception (and similar to tactual perception) in that it entails memory processing; it requires the retention and integration of spatial information over time to generate an internal representation of extended space.

The Two-Pathway Hypothesis for Object Recognition and Spatial Processing

A cornerstone of investigations into spatial processing has been the large body of evidence that disorders of object recognition (considered in some detail in chapter 8) and disorders of spatial location are doubly dissociable (Mishkin, Ungerleider, & Macko, 1983). For example, whereas bilateral lesions in area TE in the inferior temporal cortex of monkeys produces impairment in visual object discrimination, bilateral removal of posterior parietal cortex produces severe impairment on tasks requiring the discrimination of the relative spatial location of a "landmark" (Figure 7.9).

In addition to specifying specific cortical areas differentially involved in these two types of task, Mishkin and his colleagues, using the 2[14C]deoxyglucose method, were able to delineate the connections from the primary visual cortex (V1) to these two areas. The result was the detection of two pathways, a dorsal pathway projecting from V1 to area PG in the parietal cortex and a ventral pathway projecting from V1 to area TE in the temporal lobes (see Figure 7.9). Consistent with this hypothesis, these investigators found that the ventral pathway conveys information mainly from the fovea, the area most important for visual acuity and therefore most important for visual discrimination. In contrast, the dorsal pathway conveys information from both the central and peripheral retina, a finding consistent with the requirements of its role in the perception of location within an expanse of space.

This two-pathway model of visual functioning, positing a dorsal system for the perception of the "where" of a stimulus and a ventral system for the perception of the "what" of a stimulus, organizes a wealth of empirical data. In particular, it suggests a neural

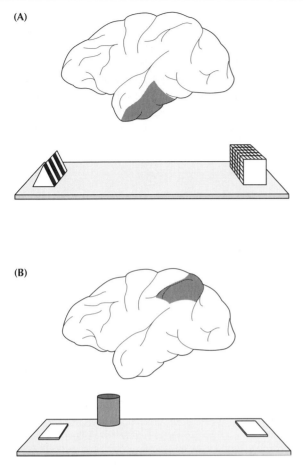

FIGURE 7.9   Behavioral tasks sensitive to lesions in the two cortical visual systems hypothesized by Mishkin and his colleagues. *(A)* Bilateral removal of area TE in the inferior temporal cortex in the monkey produces severe impairment in object discrimination tasks such as non-matching to sample. In this task, the animal is first shown an object in a central location and given time to become familiar with it. It is then presented with two objects, the one just shown and one that is novel. The animal is rewarded for choosing the unfamiliar object. *(B)* Bilateral removal of posterior parietal cortex produces severe impairment in landmark discrimination. In this task, the animal is rewarded for choosing the covered food well closest to the "landmark" (in this case, the tall cylinder), which is positioned randomly, from trial to trial, either closest to the left or the right food well. *(From Mishkin et al., 1983, p. 415)*

basis for the well-established double dissociation of impaired object discrimination and impaired land-mark discrimination. It also raises several interesting problems. How is the spatial and object information reintegrated into a unified representation of a particular object in a specific spatial location? As Mishkin and his colleagues acknowledge, this problem remains unsolved. They suggest, however, that since both pathways have connections to the limbic system and to the frontal lobes, one or both of these areas may be the site of these integrative processes. The finding that damage to the right hippocampus in humans disrupts memory for the spatial location of particular objects supports the hypothesis that the hippocampus might be involved in such integrative processes.

There are, however, some more fundamental problems with the two-pathway hypothesis. Zeki (1993) has criticized the model on the basis of emerging information about the extrastriate cortex and its connections to V1. In particular, he notes that there are direct projections from V1 to V3, V3A, V4, V5, and probably also to V6. Therefore, there are clearly not *only* two pathways emanating from V1. In addition, the properties of single cells within each system do not always correspond to their hypothesized functions. To cite one example, although area V3, considered part of the "what" system, contains orientation-selective neurons as we might expect, we have seen that it also contains gaze-locked cells, which presumably are involved in spatial processing. Perhaps even more problematic for a model that conceptualizes two largely isolated subsystems, one involved in the perception of form and one involved in the perception of location, is the fact that information from one of these domains can often provide critical information about the other. For example, the position of an object and its relationship to other objects can provide vital information regarding its identity. Conversely, the precise shape of an object can provide vital information about its position.

THE ROLE OF THE HIPPOCAMPUS IN SPATIAL PROCESSING

There is compelling evidence that the hippocampus plays a critical role in the coding of spatial location. This evidence comes from three domains: physiological recording from single cells in the hippocampus, the effect of hippocampal lesions on spatial behavior, and studies of the relative size of the hippocampus in animal species that utilize spatial memory extensively compared with those that do not. We consider each of these areas of evidence in turn.

Unit Recording Studies

One of the first indications that the hippocampus plays a role in spatial behavior was the report of O'Keefe and Dostrovsky (1971) that individual cells in the hippocampus fired selectively when the study animal was in a particular location and/or facing a particular direction. This finding led these investigators to propose that the hippocampus serves as a cognitive map of the environment, an idea that was subsequently elaborated in more detail (O'Keefe & Nadel, 1978).

These early reports of cells in the hippocampus sensitive to the spatial location of the animal were confirmed by later reports, and it is now clear that there are cells in the hippocampus whose receptive field is the presence of the animal in a particular place within the environment (Wilson & McNaughton, 1993). This place, for any given neuron, is referred to as that neuron's **place field,** and a cell with such sensitivity is referred to as a **place cell.** Recording from a place cell, it is possible to map its place field (Figure 7.10). Of particular interest is the finding that when an animal is introduced into a new environment, some hippocampal cells that did not have a place field in the old environment become, over time, sensitive to the location of the animal in the new environment.

Lesion Studies

The finding that hippocampal lesions disrupt spatial behavior is a second line of evidence for the role of the hippocampus in such processes. An example of such disruption involves the performance of rats in a radial-arm maze (Figure 7.11). When each arm of the maze is baited (has food at the end of it) the rat learns to go around and collect food from each arm, without unnecessarily returning to arms from which it has already collected food. In an alternative condition in which, over many trials, certain arms are never

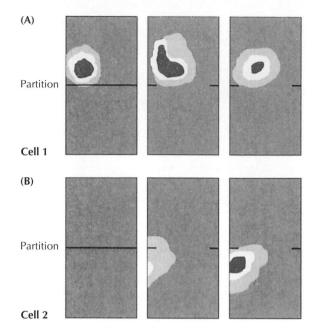

FIGURE 7.10   Place cells in the rat hippocampus. *(Left)* When the rat explored the area above the partition for 10 minutes, it was found that cell 1 fired maximally when the animal was in a particular location. This location is referred to as that cell's place field. The shading shows a gradient of firing frequency as the animal moves away from the center of the place field. Cell 2, another hippocampal cell, does not have a place field in the area above the partition. *(Middle)* When the partition is removed and the animal is allowed to explore the larger space, cell 1 continues to fire when the animal is in its place field, and cell 2 is found to have only a weak place field in the newly explored compartment. *(Right)* However, as the rat continues to explore the novel space beyond the partition, cell 2 develops a robust place field. *(From Bear, Connors, & Paradiso, 1995, p. 539)*

baited, the rat again does not make return trips to arms from which food has already been retrieved. In addition, it learns to avoid the always-unbaited arms altogether. After hippocampal lesions, the animal's behavior in the first condition is markedly disrupted: It frequently returns within the same trial to arms of the maze from which it has already collected food. Interestingly, in the partial-baited condition, the animal learns to avoid arms that are never baited but continues to inefficiently traverse arms from which food has already been retrieved. These findings suggest that the hippocampus is critical for the recognition of spa-

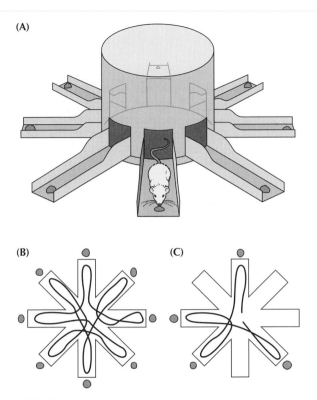

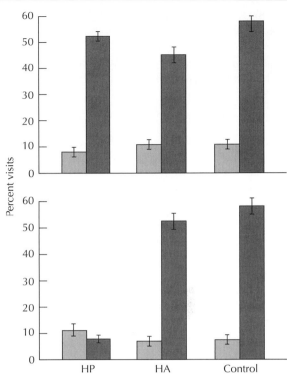

FIGURE 7.11 *(A)* An eight-arm radial maze used to investigate spatial behavior in rats. *(B)* When each of the arms is baited, the animal will go to one after another until the food is collected. *(C)* If certain arms are never baited, the animal will learn to ignore them and travel only to the baited arms. *(From Bear, Connors, & Paradiso, 1995, p. 537)*

FIGURE 7.12 The effect of bilateral hippocampal lesions on cache recovery accuracy in black-capped chickadees. Darker bars show visits to cache sites as a percentage of visits to all sites while searching for caches. Lighter bars show visits to these same sites before food was cached and indicate the random level of site visiting. *(Top)* The mean accuracy for birds in each of three groups prior to surgery. *(Bottom)* The mean accuracy after bilateral aspiration of the hippocampus *(HP)*, bilateral aspiration of the same volume of tissue from the hyperstriatum accessorium *(HA)*, or no surgical procedure *(Control)*. *(From Sherry, Jacobs, & Gaulin, 1992, p. 299)*

tial location over certain time intervals, although other structures appear to be involved in the long-term retention of such information.

In addition to laboratory studies, there have also been some lesion studies that have investigated the role of the hippocampus in spatial memory in the natural environment. In a study that combined ethological observation and the lesion method, Sherry and Vaccarino (1989) first documented the ability of black-capped chickadees to remember locations where food had been stored (cache sites). Birds were then subjected to either bilateral aspiration of the hippocampus or bilateral aspiration of the same volume of another brain region or received no surgery. When their visiting behavior was again observed in their natural environment, it was found that the post-

surgical behavior of birds with hippocampal lesions failed to demonstrate the normal preference for sites at which food had been stored (Figure 7.12).

Studies of patients with hippocampal lesions have demonstrated impairment in the performance of a number of spatial tasks, including maze learning in the visual (Milner, 1965) and tactual (Corkin, 1965) modalities, the recall of the position of a point on a line (Corsi, 1972), the recall of spatial location in the tactual modality (Rains & Milner, 1994a), and the recall of the location of seen objects (Smith & Milner, 1981).

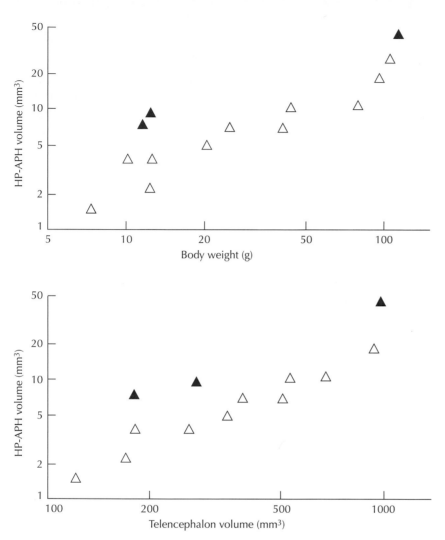

FIGURE 7.13   The volume of the hippocampal complex (HP-APH) in 3 food-storing *(filled triangles)* and 10 non-food-storing *(open triangles)* families and subfamilies of birds. *(Top)* Hippocampal volume is shown relative to body weight. *(Bottom)* Hippocampal volume is shown relative to telencephalon volume. Note that all axes are logarithmic. *(From Sherry, Jacobs, & Gaulin, 1992, p. 300)*

Although, as we will see in chapter 10, damage to the hippocampus in humans is also associated with impaired memory for nonspatial material, lesion studies in the macaque monkey indicate that the critical structures related to visual recognition in these animals are areas of cortex near the hippocampus known as the **perirhinal cortex** and the **parahippocampal cortex,** rather than the hippocampus itself (Zola-Morgan et al., 1989). This would indicate that the functional role of the hippocampus may be more specifically spatial than has previously been thought. Whether this is also the case for humans remains to be determined because the animal findings are based on the effects of very

specific and circumscribed experimental lesions that are not seen in human patients. (See chapter 10 for a more detailed discussion of this issue.)

Neuroethological Studies

Ethology is the study of the behavior of animals in their natural environment (Lorenz, 1966; Tinbergen, 1951). **Neuroethology** is the study of the relationship between such behavior and the brain. It typically takes the form of attempting to relate differences in the behavior of related species to differences in brain structure. Neuroethological investigations of the hip-

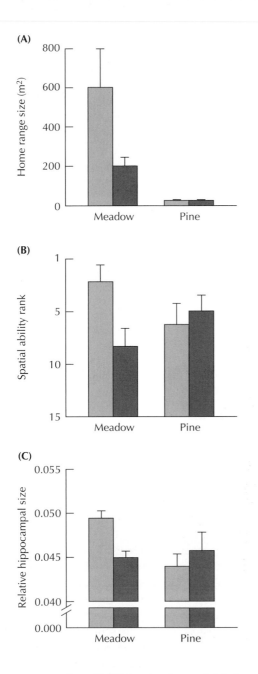

(A)

(B)

(C)

◀ **FIGURE 7.14** Sex differences in behavior and hippocampal size in two species of vole, the polygamous meadow vole and the monogamous pine vole. Lighter bars = males; darker bars = females. *(A)* Home range size as computed from telemetric observations of individual voles tracked under natural conditions during the mating season. *(B)* Spatial ability on the sunburst maze. Ranks were determined within each species separately because the species differed with regard to the number of trials required to reach criterion. The scale of the y-axis is reversed, a low score indicating good performance. *(C)* Relative hippocampal size (the volume of the hippocampus relative to the volume of the whole brain) in breeding adults. *(From Sherry, Jacobs, & Gaulin, 1992, p. 301)*

on spatial processing (Sherry, Jacobs, & Gaulin, 1992). This increase in hippocampal size represents an adaptive specialization that may be the result of natural selection, sexual selection, or, in species such as the homing pigeon, artificial selection. For example, the volume of the hippocampus relative to body weight and relative to the volume of the telencephalon has been shown to be larger in 3 food-storing than in 10 non-food-storing families and subfamilies of birds (Figure 7.13).

In a series of studies, the relationship between hippocampal size and behavior in the natural environment was investigated in two species of vole (a rat-like rodent): the polygamous meadow vole and the monogamous pine vole. It was found that the size of the home ranges of the two species, tracked by telemetry under natural conditions during the mating season, differed considerably (Figure 7.14A) and, in addition, that the male meadow vole had a larger home range than the female (Gaulin & FitzGerald, 1986, 1989). When spatial ability was assessed under laboratory conditions using a sunburst maze, it was found that males were superior to females in the polygamous meadow vole, whereas there was no sex difference in the monogamous pine vole (Figure 7.14B). The polygamous male meadow voles were found to have significantly larger hippocampal size relative to the size of the whole brain than did females of the same species (Figure 7.14C).There was no sexual dimorphism in hippocampal size in the monogamous pine vole (Jacobs et al., 1990).

We also should mention the remarkable navigational ability of certain species of birds. It is well

pocampus and spatial behavior have yielded some highly interesting findings.

In most general terms, in a diverse group of animals, an increase in hippocampal size has been observed in species that rely heavily on spatial abilities compared with related species that rely less heavily

known that migrating birds fly hundreds or even thousands of miles each migration season, often returning to precisely the same location each year. In addition, birds such as homing pigeons are able to return to a precise location even when elaborate means are undertaken to eliminate potential cues to guide their flight. For example, homing pigeons have been transported in trucks to distant locations, have had their eyes occluded, and have been fitted with devices intended to interfere with natural electromagnetic fields, without, remarkably, interfering with their return to their home location. Investigators even moved the home lofts of pigeons 100 yards after the birds had left the area, only to have the birds return to the precise location where the home loft *had been*, even though their relocated home lofts were still in view.

These migratory and homing behaviors are clearly examples of exquisitely precise spatial behavior. Although the mechanisms underlying these behaviors remain to be fully explained, hypotheses for the basis of migratory behavior include the use of the positions of stars for a kind of celestial navigation and a sensitivity to the earth's magnetic and electromagnetic fields. The mechanism of homing behavior is even more difficult to account for because it has been impervious to so many experimental manipulations. This remains a fascinating area for future investigation.

NEGLECT OF ONE SIDE OF SPACE

Neglect is one of the most curious and dramatic consequences of cerebral damage on behavior in humans. It turns out also to be an important touchstone for the understanding of spatial behavior. In **neglect** (or, as it is sometimes termed, the **neglect syndrome**) a patient ignores objects and people on one side of space. It is not that objects on one side of space are simply missed because they are not detected, as can occur after a hemianopia or sensory loss on one side of the body. Rather, the patient with neglect acts as if an entire side of space *does not exist.* This may occur in the absence or the presence of a primary sensory deficit. When there is sensory loss, patients with neglect are unable to learn to compensate for the lack of information in their blind field by directing the

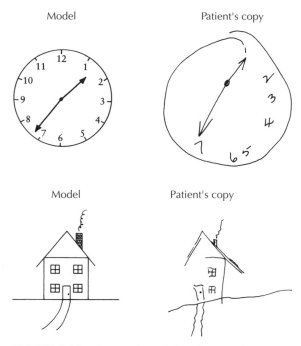

FIGURE 7.15   Copies of simple line drawings by a patient with left-sided neglect and a right parietal-lobe lesion. *(From Posner & Raichle, 1994, p. 158)*

movement of their head and eyes in that direction, as a patient with a simple hemianopia learns to do.

Neglect may lead to some bizarre behaviors, such as failing to draw the side of an object in the neglected hemispace (Figure 7.15), reading only the right half of lines of text, and leaving the food on one side of the plate uneaten, only to finish it enthusiastically when the plate is rotated so that the food appears on the nonneglected side. Patients may shave only one side of their face, dress only one side of their body, and react only to speech or other sounds coming from one side of space. An even more dramatic example of neglect is a distortion of body schema that makes patients totally unaware of one side of their body (usually the left). These patients may actually believe that an arm or a leg on the neglected side belongs to someone else and complain in alarm that a detached limb has been placed in their bed. In a possibly related phenomenon, patients may deny paralysis or other impairment on one side of the body, insisting that they have full use of a limb that they cannot move.

Neglect may be evident in only one or in more than one modality. In fact, all patterns of dissociation between neglect tasks presented in the auditory, visual, and tactile modalities have been reported (Barbieri & De Renzi, 1989). But it is neglect of visual space that has been most extensively studied. In its milder forms neglect is less dramatic, manifesting itself in spatial biases on tests such as line bisection and on tasks that require visual search, be they simple "cancellation" tasks (Figure 7.16) or tasks that require searching for a target within a complex visual array.

The majority of patients with neglect have neglect for the left side of space and have a lesion in the right parietal region, although it has also been reported after right prefrontal-cortex lesions (Posner & Raichle, 1994) and after unilateral lesions of the superior colliculus and the pulvinar (a nucleus of the thalamus). Right-sided neglect associated with left-sided lesions is also seen, although less often. It has been argued, however, that a mild form of this latter disorder is more common than is generally appreciated (Ogden, 1987).

There are two major theoretical frameworks within which attempts have been made to account for neglect. It has been conceptualized as (a) a disorder of attention and (b) a disorder of the internal representation of space. We examine each of these theories in turn.

Neglect as a Disorder of Attention

Perhaps the most developed attentional theory of neglect is that proposed by Posner and his colleagues (1994). Briefly, their theory states that neglect results from an impaired ability to disengage attention from the nonneglected side of space. Support for this theory comes from three areas: (a) unit cell recording in the parietal lobe of the awake monkey, (b) the study of parietal-lobe patients, and (c) imaging studies with normal subjects. To explain this theory and its empirical basis more fully, we need to go into some detail.

LOCATION-SPECIFIC ATTENTION-ENHANCED CELLS IN MONKEY PARIETAL CORTEX   It has been clear for some time that there are cells in the

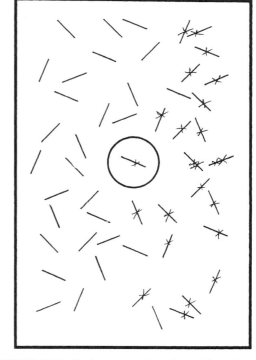

FIGURE 7.16   Performance of a patient with neglect for the left side of space on a line-cancellation task that required the subject to simply make an X on each line. *(From McCarthy & Warrington, 1990, p. 83)*

parietal lobe of the awake monkey that fire when the animal is attending to a stimulus (Wurtz, Goldberg, & Robinson, 1982). Monkeys were trained to fixate on a point on a computer screen and then, when a target appeared on the screen, to make a saccade (eye movement) to the target. Under these conditions it was found that some of these cells exhibited a burst of activity during the interval after the appearance of the target but before the onset of the saccade (Figure 7.17). This was not due simply to the appearance of the target in the cell's receptive field because such an appearance alone (without an anticipated saccade) produced a much less intense response. It can be seen that these two conditions are behaviorally identical, the only difference being that in the former condition the animal is attending to the location where a saccade is about to be made. This is why the burst of activity is believed to be the result of attention.

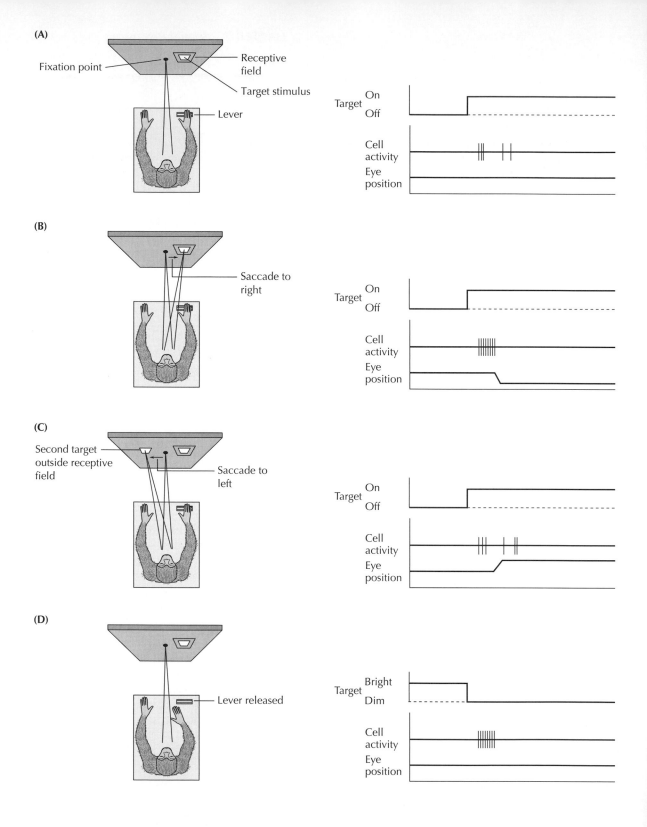

There were two other control conditions that supported this conclusion. The cell exhibited spatial specificity in that it would not fire intensely if the saccade was to be made outside its receptive field. In addition, it was shown that the anticipatory burst was not related to the mechanism of eye movement per se because the same activation was seen if the response to the target was an arm movement instead of eye movement. These studies appear to reveal an enhancement in cell activity that is a correlate of attention, and it is possible that this enhancement is involved in the behavioral effects of attention. Conversely, it seems plausible that a disruption of these mechanisms, due to a parietal-lobe lesion, would disrupt attention in the area of space represented in the receptive field of these cells. Cells in parietal cortex all have receptive fields that include part of the contralateral visual field.

STUDIES OF ATTENTION AND VISUAL ORIENTING IN PATIENTS WITH PARIETAL-LOBE LESIONS

These single unit studies in monkeys raised the question of whether parietal-lobe regions in humans mediate similar functions. One model for testing this hypothesis is a directed attention task that has been used extensively in the study of normal subjects. Subjects sit in front of a computer monitor and fixate a point, and a trial begins with a cue that indicates the side of the screen on which a target will appear. Subjects are instructed to press a button as soon as they detect the presence of the target. In addition to trials in which the appearance of the cue is informative about the future position of the target, on some trials there is no cue and on some trials the cue is misleading, indicating the wrong side (Figure 7.18). Eye position is monitored carefully to make sure that there is no movement because what is being measured here is the beneficial (or in the case of incorrect cues, the detrimental) effect of a cue on target-detection reaction time in the absence of any eye movement. Shifts of visual attention that occur independently of any eye movement are considered markers of **covert attention,** in contrast to **overt attention,** as exemplified by anticipatory eye movement in response to a cue. Covert attention is thus like a spotlight of visual attention that can move, although the eye is fixed.

As one might expect, under these conditions correctly cued trials result in shorter reaction times than trials without a cue, which in turn have shorter reaction times than incorrectly cued trials. This experimental procedure was then used to study directed attention in patients with parietal-lobe lesions. The patients in this study did not have a severe neglect syndrome; nevertheless, it was reasoned that because neglect is associated with parietal-lobe lesions, the study of these patients might provide clues to the nature of neglect. The results were that on trials without a cue, parietal-lobe patients had slower reaction times to targets appearing in the visual field contralateral to their lesion than in the ipsilateral field. However, on the correctly cued trials these patients' reaction times were not impaired; they were able to direct attention in response to the cue.

In contrast, incorrect cues increased reaction time. In particular, when incorrect cues were presented so as to direct attention to the same side of space as the lesion and the target then appeared in the contralateral

◄ **FIGURE 7.17**   The effect of attention on the response of a neuron in monkey posterior parietal cortex. *(A)* Response to a target stimulus appearing in the cell's receptive field. *(B)* When the animal is trained to make a saccade after the onset of the stimulus, there is enhanced activity in the neuron (beyond the level of simple response to the presence of the stimulus) during the time interval between the onset of the stimulus and the beginning of the saccade. This is the result of attention to a stimulus that is about to be the target of a saccade. *(C)* This enhancement is spatially selective because when the saccade is to be made to a point outside the cell's receptive field, there is no enhancement. *(D)* The enhancement effect is not specific to eye movement because when the animal responds to the stimulus target by releasing a lever rather than by a saccade, the enhancement effect is still seen. *(From Bear, Connors, & Paradiso, 1995, p. 610)*

FIGURE 7.18 In the visual orienting task, a cue (here, an arrow in the center of the screen) indicates the likely location of the target that is about to appear. The subject's attention (represented by the circle) shifts to the indicated location, which may or may not be correct. An alternative to this central cuing format is one in which the cue is presented at the target location (not shown). The results of the experiments with parietal-lobe patients were essentially the same for the two cuing conditions. *(From Posner & Raichle, 1994, p. 155)*

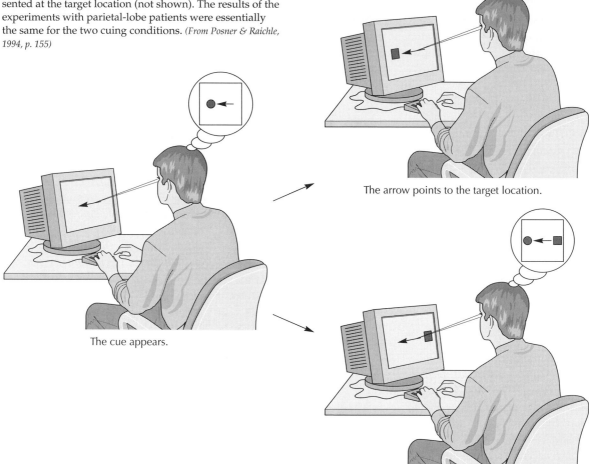

The cue appears.

The arrow points to the target location.

The arrow points away from the target location.

visual field, detection of the target was severely impaired, resulting in greatly increased reaction times or even missing of the target altogether. This impairment was greater for patients with right-parietal lesions. In the other incorrectly cued condition, presentation of the cue to the contralateral side prior to the appearance of the target on the ipsilateral side, the increase in reaction time was not as large (Figure 7.19).

Although, as was mentioned earlier, the parietal-lobe patients in these studies did not have a severe visual neglect, they did exhibit greatly increased reaction times (or even completely missed stimuli that were presented only briefly) when they were incorrectly cued to the side of space ipsilateral to their lesion before the appearance of the target on the contralateral side. Subsequent experiments showed that

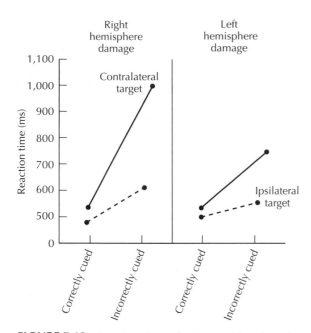

FIGURE 7.19   Reaction times of patients with right and left parietal-lobe lesions on a directed-attention task with peripheral cues were greatest when the target appeared in the field contralateral to their lesion after they had been cued to expect the target in the ipsilateral field. The effect was greatest for patients with right-sided lesions. *(From Posner & Raichle, 1994, p. 159)*

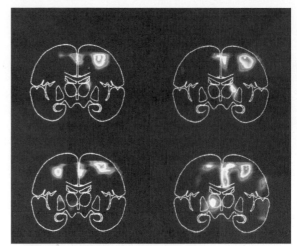

FIGURE 7.20   *(Top)* PET scan showing activation of right superior-parietal areas when attention is directed to (and shifted within) the left visual field and both right and left superior-parietal activation when attention is directed to (and shifted within) the right visual field *(Bottom)*. *(From Posner & Raichle, 1994, p. 161)*

this effect did not depend on the incorrect cue's actually appearing in the ipsilateral field; the effect was the same if an arrow appearing at the fixation point served as the incorrect cue. Posner and Raichle (1994) interpreted these findings as evidence that the major deficit in these patients was an inability to *disengage* attention from the side of space ipsilateral to the lesioned hemisphere and shift it to the side contralateral to the lesion, particularly in patients with right parietal-lobe damage. This is consistent with the idea that each parietal lobe mediates the movement of attention in the contralateral direction.

IMAGING STUDIES IN NORMAL SUBJECTS   Corbetta and his colleagues (1993) conducted a PET study with normal subjects to measure activation when attention is directed to and shifted within the left or right visual field. To do this they required subjects to maintain fixation at a central point but

covertly attend to shifting leftward/rightward movement within either the left or right visual field. Thus, subjects had not only to covertly attend to events within one or the other visual field, but they had to shift the direction of their attention within that field. This was compared with a central attention condition in which subjects attended to events at fixation while the same peripheral events were taking place but without attention being directed to them. No differences in activation were seen when subjects directed attention rightward versus leftward in the same half of the visual field. However, right-superior parietal-lobe activation occurred when attention was directed to (and shifted within) the left visual field, and both left- and right-superior parietal-lobe activation was seen when attention was directed to (and shifted within) the right visual field (Figure 7.20).

These findings bear on the observation that visual neglect is more often seen after right parietal-lobe lesions than after left. One attempt to account for this asymmetry has been to postulate that attention to the right side of space is mediated by both hemispheres (and hence preserved after unilateral lesions in either hemisphere), whereas attention to the left side of space is directed by the right hemisphere alone (and hence is vulnerable to right-sided lesions). Although this notion remains hypothetical, the imaging data from this experiment are consistent with it.

SUMMARY OF THE ATTENTIONAL HYPOTHESIS
We have seen that the hypothesis that an attentional deficit underlies neglect has considerable support. There is a contralateral relationship between side of parietal-lobe lesion and the side of the visual field that is neglected. Neurons in monkey parietal cortex have been discovered that show enhanced firing when the monkey is attending to a target that appears in that cell's receptive field (which also is in the contralateral visual field). Patients with parietal-lobe lesions show greatly increased reaction time in the detection of a target in the field contralateral to the lesion when they have been incorrectly cued to attend to the ipsilateral half of the visual field. In normal subjects attention to the left half of the visual field activates right parietal cortex, and attention to the right visual field activates both left and right parietal cortex. Taken together, these findings would seem to support the notion that neglect is the result of a disruption, resulting from unilateral parietal-lobe damage, of attentional processes directed to one side of space. Nevertheless, some important findings have made it necessary to consider an alternative theoretical approach to the understanding of neglect. We consider them next.

Neglect as a Disruption of the Internal Representation of Space

An alternative approach to understanding the phenomenon of neglect is in terms of a disruption of an internal representation of space. In a revealing experiment, Bisiach and Luzzatti (1978) asked patients with neglect to imagine that they were standing in the Piazza del Duomo in Milan facing the magnificent Gothic cathedral that dominates the square. They were then asked to describe what they "saw" in their mental image. These patients reported buildings and landmarks on their right in a lively manner, sometimes elaborating on their features at some length. In contrast, left-sided landmarks were often omitted altogether, and, if they were mentioned, it was in what

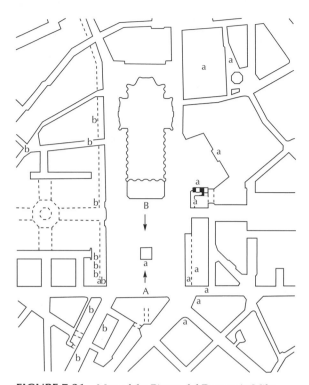

FIGURE 7.21   Map of the Piazza del Duomo in Milan. *A* and *B* indicate the two positions from which patients with neglect were asked to imagine viewing the piazza. The landmarks that they recalled from each position are labeled *a* and *b*, respectively. *(From Farah, 1995, p. 965)*

the investigators described as an "absent-minded, almost annoyed" tone. Following this, they asked their patients to report what they "saw" when they imagined themselves standing on the opposite side of the square with the cathedral behind them. In this condition patients reported landmarks that were on their right and neglected landmarks on their left from this *new* point of view. Thus they reported objects that had been neglected when they imagined viewing the square from the first perspective (Figure 7.21). These were striking findings because they suggested that neglect was not confined to a failure of registration or attention but involved a disruption of an internal representation of space that rendered conceptualization of the neglected side of space impossible.

This hypothesis received further support from the results of an ingenious experiment (Bisiach, Luzzatti, &

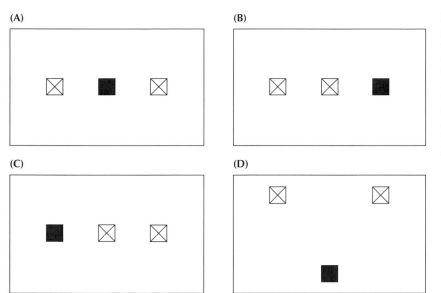

FIGURE 7.22 Stimulus display for *(A)* left visual field and right visual field, *(B)* two stimuli in the left visual field, *(C)* two stimuli in the right visual field, and *(D)* two stimuli that, when the head is tilted 90° to the left, fall into the right visual field. The blackened squares indicate fixation points. *(From Ladavas, 1987, p. 170)*

Peranni, 1979). On each trial, patients with neglect viewed two successively presented cloud-shaped forms, a thin portion of each being revealed as it was moved behind a slit. Subjects were then required to decide whether the two forms were the same or different. On trials in which the forms were different, they differed either on their left or their right side. Notice that to perceive the cloud under these conditions it was necessary for the subject to mentally construct a representation of the whole cloud from the varying information available over time at the slit. The question was, Would neglect be manifested under these conditions? The results showed that in fact patients with left-sided neglect made more errors when the forms differed on their left side. The fact that all of the stimuli were presented in central vision (through the slit) meant that no portion of any stimulus was ever presented in the neglected half of the visual field. These results were interpreted as supporting the notion that unilateral neglect results from a disruption of an internal representation of space.

An earlier experiment that investigated exploration of space in the visual and tactual modalities is open to a similar interpretation (De Renzi, Faglioni, & Scotti, 1970). In this study patients with neglect were required to search for a particular stimulus in a visual array and to search for a marble in a tactual array. The investigators reported that patients with

right posterior lesions found the target faster when it was on the right side of the visual or tactual array. The extension of these findings to the tactual modality is of considerable interest in the context of our present discussion. Whereas in vision one is able to perceive a space instantly, tactual exploration requires a complex series of active movements and resulting sensory input to build up a representation of a specific space. The fact that in the tactual task patients with right-parietal lesions were impaired in actively searching for the target when it was on the left side of the array suggests that this impairment reflects a disruption of an internal representation of space rather than inattention to sensory stimuli. The logic of this interpretation is similar to that of the "cloud form" experiment discussed earlier.

Further support for the internal representation hypothesis of neglect comes from a study by Ladavas (1987) indicating that the difficulty right parietal-lobe patients have attending to the left is tied to gravitational coordinates as well as retinal coordinates. Patients with neglect were asked to tilt their heads 90° to the left so that two stimuli that were to the left and right of each other were now above and below each other and both were in the right visual field (Figure 7.22D). It was found that reaction times to the stimulus that was on the left relative to gravitational coordinates were slower than were reaction times to the stimulus on the right even though, because of the patient's head tilt, both stimuli were in the right visual field. In another condition of this experiment, two stimuli both appeared on one side of fixation (Figure 7.22B and C). Thus, although the stimuli were to the right and left of each other, they were in the same visual field. Under these conditions, the left-most stimulus was responded to more slowly, whether both stimuli were in the right or the left visual field. These effects were found to coexist with the well-established visual field effects that characterize neglect. These findings are difficult to reconcile with a theory of neglect that emphasizes differences in the capacity to direct attention to one or the other visual field as the critical underlying mechanism. They support, rather, the notion that neglect is a disruption of an internal representation of space that is constructed at least in part in terms of gravitational coordinates and is not entirely dependent on retinal coordinates.

Theories that view neglect as a disturbance of an internal representation of space account well for these findings and for the disruption of spatial imagery that has been reported in patients with neglect. However, there are some data that are difficult to account for from this perspective. These include the finding that neglect may be present in only one or two modalities (Barbieri & De Renzi, 1989). Taking this into account would seem to require postulating modality-specific representations of space. In addition, the internal representation hypothesis is complicated by at least one report of a patient who exhibited neglect in his spatial behavior (e.g., he would turn to the right but not to the left) but who could describe familiar spatial layouts completely and accurately (Brain, 1941).

Whether neglect is most usefully viewed as a disorder of attention or a disruption of an internal representation of space remains to be resolved. The two theories are not mutually exclusive. It may be that the phenomenon of neglect is the result of an interaction between these two underlying disorders, in that an attentional disorder is likely to disrupt the construction of internal representations of space and

disrupted internal representations are likely to adversely affect attention. However this issue is finally resolved, it is clear that each of these hypotheses has generated a good deal of illuminating data.

SPATIAL THINKING AND MENTAL IMAGERY

Under the topic of spatial thinking one finds a variety of tasks that involve mental imagery. A consideration of the neural substrate of spatial thinking therefore inevitably leads us to mental imagery. We consider here three central questions: (a) Is imagery fundamentally different from verbal thought? (b) Is information in images represented in a spatial format? and (c) Does mental imagery share underlying mechanisms with visual perception? The first two questions have to do with the nature of imagery and therefore the nature of spatial thought. The third question ends up being a touchstone for attempts to answer the first two; therefore we consider the third question first.

We have already noted differences between imagery and perception, as when we form what we think is a vivid image of, say, a familiar building and then cannot answer a simple question about its appearance, such as how many windows it has on its facade. Experiments with imagery suggest, however, that for limited amounts of information, a visual image is very similar to a percept. For example, it has been shown that the time it takes a subject to decide if a string of letters contains a letter that ascends above the central line (e.g., *f* or *h*) is the same, for strings up to three letters, whether or not the letters are actually present. However, decisions about longer strings take longer when the letters are not available for viewing.

These and similar data suggest that under some circumstances an image and a percept may be much alike. This brings us then to the question of the extent to which images and percepts share the same neural mechanisms. To the extent that this is the case, one would predict that different components of imagery would be associated with different cortical areas in a manner analogous to the specialization of function seen in perception. We address this issue through the examination of three sources of evi-

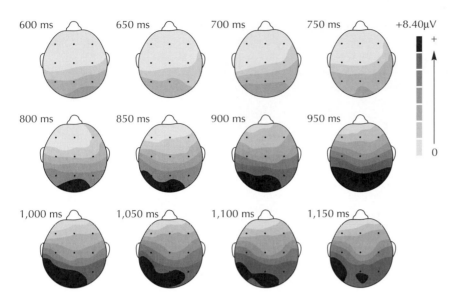

FIGURE 7.23 Scalp distribution of potentials synchronized with generation of a visual image from memory. These representations were obtained by subtracting the ERP when subjects passively listened to words from the ERP when they listened to the same words and generated images of their referents. The effect is shown at 50-ms intervals beginning 600 ms after word onset and continuing through 1,150 ms after word onset. *(From Farah, 1995, p. 970)*

dence: (a) electrophysiological studies with normal subjects, (b) imaging studies with normal subjects, and (c) the study of patients with cerebral lesions.

Electrophysiological Studies

Several electrophysiological studies have yielded results consistent with the notion that imagery and perception activate the same or similar areas of the brain. An event-related potential study (Farah, Levine, & Calvanio, 1988) compared the effect of seeing one letter while imaging another versus the effect of seeing a letter and forming an image of the same letter. The reasoning was that if imaging and perceiving the same letter had a systematic effect on the ERP, as compared with the different condition, then there must be some common brain locus at which perception and imagery interact. When the ERP in the condition in which the stimulus and image do not match was subtracted from the ERP in the condition when stimulus and image did match, the result was an effect localized at the occipital and posterior temporal sites. That this effect was specific to the visual modality was supported by the finding that the latency of its appearance after stimulus presentation coincided with the first negative peak of the visual ERP.

In a related study (Farah, Peronnet, et al., 1989), subjects were exposed to two conditions. They were instructed either to listen to a word or to listen to a word and form a visual image of its referent. The logic of the experiment was that the difference between the ERP in these two conditions should reflect the activity specific to the generation of images from memory. When the ERP in the former condition was subtracted from that in the latter, the maximal ERP was again seen over the occipital and posterior temporal regions (Figure 7.23), areas known to be activated in visual perception.

Imaging Studies

A rCBF study of spatial imagery in expanded extrapersonal space was carried out by Roland and Friberg (1985). Normal subjects were asked to imagine walking along a familiar street while observing landmarks along the route. Every second street they were to imagine that they were turning alternately to the right and to the left. The result was the finding of increased blood flow in the temporal and parietal regions of both hemispheres (Figure 7.24). The finding of bilateral activation in this route-finding task is of interest in the context of data suggesting that both hemi-

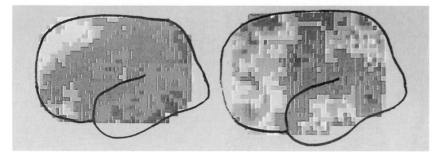

FIGURE 7.24   Roland's study of the effect of spatial imagery on regional cerebral blood flow. The image on the right shows blood flow when the subject imagined walking on a familiar street and periodically turning left and right. The image on the left is the same subject in the control condition of simply resting. The imagery task activated parietal-lobe regions in both hemispheres, whereas no such activation is seen in the control condition. Interestingly, frontal-lobe regions are also activated in the imagery condition. This may reflect the processes involved in planning and directing the imagined path of walking, when subjects were told that at every second street they should imagine turning alternately right and then left. *(From Posner & Raichle, 1994, p. 95)*

spheres may be involved in these tasks, although experimental findings are at odds with this study in that they suggest a dominant role for right-parietal areas.

In a PET study, Kosslyn (1988) presented subjects with a matrix of squares on a computer screen, in one of which was an X. There were three conditions. In one the subject was instructed to form an image of a particular letter and then to decide whether the X was within the letter (imagery condition). In a second condition the subject was presented with the probe (X) and the actual letter also appeared so that the judgment as to whether the probe fell within the boundary of the letter could be determined from visual inspection of the screen (perceptual condition). The third condition was a control task in which an X simply appeared on the screen but no decision was required (Figure 7.25). The control condition was subtracted from each of the experimental conditions, and then the two adjusted experimental conditions were compared. The result was that the perceptual and the imagery conditions were extremely similar, a finding again consistent with the hypothesis that similar or possibly the same brain areas are involved in constructing images and forming actual percepts. Some caution is required in the interpretation of these results, however, because limits in the resolution capacity of PET imagery may mask subtle differences in brain activation in the two conditions.

Lesion Studies

The data from lesion studies are also consistent with this conclusion. A particularly striking source of this evidence are reports that patients with achromatopsia (central color blindness) are also unable to form images of colors. This has been reported frequently and was described in Oliver Sacks's (1985) report of the colorblind painter whose distress at finding himself in a world drained of color was heightened by his inability to even imagine color. The report of Bisiach and Luzzatti (1978) that patients with left-sided neglect following right parietal-lobe lesions are impaired in the formation of an image of the visual field contralateral to their lesion is also consistent with this notion, as is the finding that patients with prosopagnosia (impaired face recognition) are unable to form images of faces (Shuttleworth, Syring, & Allen, 1982).

Particularly striking in this context is the report of two patients, one of whom was unable to form images of how objects appear and the other of whom was unable to form images of the location of objects (Levine, Warach, & Farah, 1985). The first of these, a patient with bilateral temporal-lobe lesions, was impaired in object recognition but not in the perception of spatial location, and his imagery capabilities paralleled this pattern. Thus, he could not describe the face of Abraham Lincoln even to the extent of specifying that he

Imagery task   Perceptual task   Passive control

"Is the X on the letter F?"   "Is the X on the letter F?"   No question

FIGURE 7.25   Kosslyn's PET study of visual imagery. *(From Posner & Raichle, 1994, p. 97)*

had a beard, but was able to accurately describe spatial relationships within familiar spatial layouts. In contrast, the second patient had bilateral parietal-lobe lesions and was impaired in the localization of objects, even to the degree that he got lost in his own house, but had unimpaired object recognition. In this case also, imagery and perception paralleled one another, with the patient's ability to create spatial imagery being severely impaired while his ability to generate images of objects was unimpaired. Taken together, these two patients manifest a dissociation in imaging ability corresponding to the dissociation in visual processing characteristic of the ventral and dorsal visual subsystems that we discussed earlier. This suggests that the normal visual imagery system includes subsystems for representing visual appearance and spatial location and that these subsystems share the same or similar neural mechanisms as the corresponding perceptual subsystems.

We close this section with one more example of a correlation between perceptual impairment and impairment in imagery. As we will discuss in more detail in chapter 8, there is evidence for category-specific impairment in object recognition. For example, some patients are able to recognize living things but not inanimate objects; others may manifest the reverse pattern. There are reports that in such cases a category-specific impairment in imagery generation parallels that seen

in perception, the same lesion evidently disrupting category-specific elements of both perception and imagery (Farah, Hammond, et al., 1989).

Hemispheric Specialization for Imagery

As mentioned earlier, Hughlings-Jackson suggested as early as 1874 that the right hemisphere is specialized for visual imagery. Although his assertion that the right hemisphere is not simply the "minor hemisphere" but is also functionally specialized was ahead of its time, the assignment of imagery as an exclusive function of the right hemisphere turns out to be wrong (Ehrlichman & Barnett, 1983). Instead, the evidence points to different components of mental imagery being mediated by the two hemispheres. More specifically, the left hemisphere appears to be specialized for the generation of images that are stored in long-term memory, such as evoking the image of a particular capital letter. In contrast, the right hemisphere appears to be specialized for processes that involve the spatial manipulation of images, such as those involved in mental rotation.

Evidence for left-hemisphere specialization for image generation comes from split-brain studies (Farah et al., 1985) in which uppercase letters were projected to either the left or the right hemisphere. Subjects had to classify the *lowercase* form of the same letter as ascending (*l, f*), descending (*g, p*), or neither. In a variant of this task, lowercase letters were presented to each hemisphere, and the subject had to decide if the uppercase form of the letter had a curve in it. These tasks thus required the subject to evoke or generate the image of the alternative form of the letter from long-term memory. The results were that the left hemisphere performed normally on these tasks but the right hemisphere was severely impaired. There are also reports of impairment after left-hemisphere lesions in answering questions that require the generation of a visual image from long-term memory (Farah, Levine, & Calvanio, 1988).

In addition to generating images from long-term memory, we mentally manipulate images to appreciate how a stimulus would look if it were moved in space. Mental rotation of an image is an example of such manipulation. There is considerable evidence that the right hemisphere is specialized for mental rotation. For example, studying a group of patients with penetrating head wounds, Ratcliff (1979) found that patients with right-posterior lesions showed the most impairment on mental rotation tasks. Similarly, in studies of split-brain patients, Corballis and Sergent (1988, 1989) found that the right hemisphere was far superior to the left in performing mental rotation tasks, although, interestingly, the left hemisphere was able to demonstrate some competence in this task. These findings, taken together with the data on image generation discussed previously, support the notion that the two hemispheres are functionally specialized for different components of mental imagery, the left hemisphere being specialized for the generation of images from long-term memory and the right hemisphere being specialized for the manipulation of images.

Implications for Our Initial Questions About Imagery

Of the three questions posed at the beginning of this section on imagery, we have focused on the third, whether or not imagery shares underlying mechanisms with visual perception. We have found that there are solid grounds for concluding that this is in fact the case, or at least neighboring and interrelated

structures mediate the two domains of function. These studies also provide some insight into the first two questions: Is imagery fundamentally different from verbal thought? and Is information from images represented in spatial form? With regard to the first of these questions, the finding that impairment in image generation and impairment in verbal thinking are dissociable after left-hemisphere lesions indicates that the two functions do not share the same neural substrate and strongly supports the notion that they are fundamentally different. With regard to the second question, we find ourselves in the opposite situation. Impairment in visual imagery and impairment in visual perceptual processes have not been shown to be dissociable. This suggests that they share the same or highly similar neural mechanisms and that the spatial format that characterizes visual percepts also holds for visual images.

THE ROLE OF THE FRONTAL LOBES IN SPATIAL PROCESSING

The frontal lobes have a highly complex function, which we explore in detail in chapter 12. We cannot do justice to this important topic here but will only suggest generally that frontal regions may be thought of as mediating executive function. Thus, these regions are critically involved in planning and motivating behavior, setting goals, monitoring progress toward those goals, and modifying behavior in response to ongoing feedback regarding its effectiveness. This means that damage to the frontal lobes will affect all complex behaviors, including spatial behavior.

An instructive example of the effects of frontal-lobe lesions on spatial behavior is the impairment in visual maze learning that has been found to be associated with such lesions (Milner, 1965). As one might expect, patients with right parietal-lobe lesions performed very poorly on this task due to impaired spatial processing. In addition, patients with right temporal-lobe lesions, particularly those with large removals of the hippocampus, performed poorly due to their impaired spatial memory. The performance of the frontal-lobe patients was particularly instructive, however. These patients not only had difficulty learning the maze, they often violated the simple instructions set by the examiner.

For example, in the bolt-head maze task in this study (Figure 7.26) the subject heard a loud click if she placed the stylus on an incorrect bolt and was told that in such a case she should return to the previous correct bolt and then choose a new path. Patients with frontal-lobe lesions would violate these rules in a number of ways. For example, when they heard the click, they might fail to return to the previous correct bolt or persist in backtracking toward the starting point. Sometimes they would omit part of the route or make diagonal moves (also against the rules). In addition, they would often repeat errors, immediately returning to the same wrong bolt.

This rule breaking and commission of repetitive errors by frontal-lobe patients was not due to poor recall of the instructions. These patients were able to articulate the rules even as they violated them, and all other patients, including three with severe amnesia, were able both to follow the rules and to avoid making repetitive errors (Figures 7.27 and 7.28). Thus, although the precise nature of the frontal-lobe impairment is elusive, it may be characterized as a limitation in the ability to control, modulate, and modify behavior in a manner that is adaptive in a particular context. More simply, it may be hypothesized that these frontal-lobe patients were less interested in obeying rules and avoiding errors.

Many other examples could be offered to illustrate this point, such as impairment in the efficiency of visual search (Luria, 1973, p. 218) and impairment in a spatial form of a task that has been termed **conditional associative learning** (Petrides, 1985). In this latter paired-associate learning task, subjects have to learn, through a process of trial and error, how each of six lights is paired with one of six cards placed in front of them (Figure 7.29). To eventually learn the correct light-card pairings, subjects have to use feedback about the correctness or incorrectness of their responses over a number of trials. Patients with unilateral frontal-lobe lesions in either hemisphere are impaired on this task, although they are not impaired in learning associations when they are explicitly informed of the correct pairings. This suggests that their poor performance stems

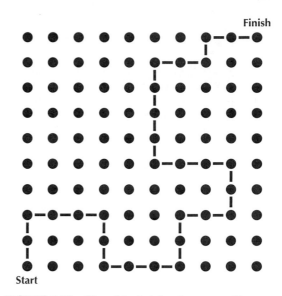

FIGURE 7.26   Plan of the bolt-head maze used by Milner. The black line, indicating the correct path, was of course not visible to the subject. *(From Milner, 1965, p. 325)*

from an inability to use feedback about their own behavior to learn the associations.

It should be emphasized that these effects of frontal-lobe lesions on spatial behavior are being understood as examples of the general effect of a superordinate disorder of executive function on behavior rather than as a specific disorder of spatial behavior. Thus, the kinds of errors made by frontal-lobe patients in maze learning and their impairment in the spatial conditional associative-learning task reflect an impairment that affects behavior generally, rather than being specific to spatial behavior. Petrides (1990) demonstrated this explicitly by showing that when a version of his conditional associative-learning task was used that required responses that were hand postures rather than spatial locations, frontal-lobe patients were equally impaired. Moreover, the generality of the frontal-lobe impairment is clear from the enormous range of tasks that are vulnerable to frontal-lobe lesion and the finding that the critical element in all of them has to do with motivational or executive aspects of the task that are not specific to its content.

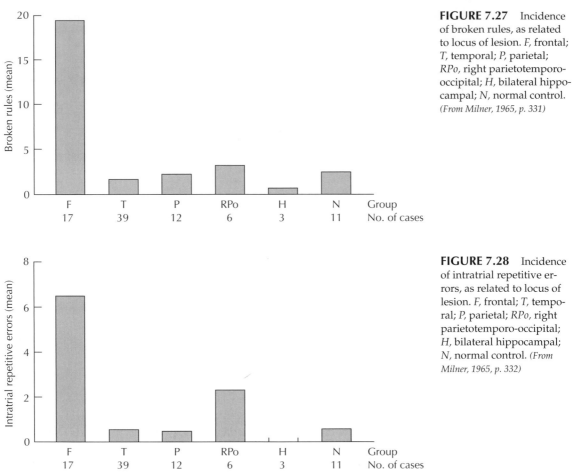

FIGURE 7.27   Incidence of broken rules, as related to locus of lesion. *F,* frontal; *T,* temporal; *P,* parietal; *RPo,* right parietotemporo-occipital; *H,* bilateral hippocampal; *N,* normal control. *(From Milner, 1965, p. 331)*

FIGURE 7.28   Incidence of intratrial repetitive errors, as related to locus of lesion. *F,* frontal; *T,* temporal; *P,* parietal; *RPo,* right parietotemporo-occipital; *H,* bilateral hippocampal; *N,* normal control. *(From Milner, 1965, p. 332)*

Given this generality, one might ask why the effects of frontal-lobe lesions were not discussed also in the context of language. The answer is that they clearly could have been (and we will discuss the effects of frontal-lobe lesions on language in chapter 12, which examines executive functioning). What is, however, different about language and spatial processing is that, because the former is highly overlearned, the impact of frontal-lobe lesions on it is not seen at the level of the elementary components of language (i.e., syntax) but in the relationship between the language user and the environment (i.e., pragmatics). In contrast, spatial processing, because it deals with the world of external space, constantly requires a relationship with that world. It is therefore particularly vulnerable to the disruptions in that relationship that are so characteristic of frontal-lobe lesions.

SUMMARY

Spatial processing is a highly complex group of heterogeneous subprocesses that together mediate a complex array of behaviors. These have yet to be integrated into a comprehensive and unified model of spatial cognition, and, therefore, attempts to organize the various aspects of spatial processing are not as systematic or differentiated as are the more theoretically grounded organizational schemas that have emerged from the study of language.

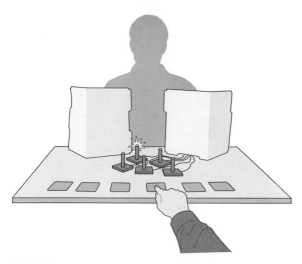

FIGURE 7.29 The conditional associative-learning procedure employed by Petrides. Each of six lights is associated with a specific card, but the pairings are unknown to the subject at the beginning of the experiment. At the beginning of each trial, a light goes on and the subject has to respond by touching one of the cards. At first, of course, she has no way of knowing which card goes with a particular light. As trials proceed, however, and the subject receives feedback regarding the correctness or incorrectness of her responses, she has the opportunity to learn the correct light-card pairings. Patients with frontal-lobe lesions are impaired on this task. *(From Petrides, 1985, p. 604)*

There are three types of spatial processes: those mediating perception in body space, in egocentric space, and in allocentric space. Within each of these spatial domains there are a number of subprocesses mediated by different underlying neural mechanisms. In some ways this is least true for body space because perception in this domain is relatively simple, involving perception of the location of a point on the sensory sheet innervating the skin and perception of body position and movement derived from the pattern of activity of receptors in the joints and muscles. Yet even within body space, dissociation between point localization on the body surface and body position sense is seen, although such dissociation is usually due to selective impairment at the level of the afferent pathways conveying information to the somatosensory cortex.

Perception of egocentric space, involving localization of stimuli relative to the body, adds a complicat-

ing dimension. The system has not only to calculate the position of a stimulus relative to the array of receptors registering it, but must also integrate this information with information about the position of the receptors relative to the rest of the body. This is exemplified by the eye and head movement necessary to bring a point of light into the fovea. Impairment in this ability, termed visual disorientation, is associated with lesions in occipital regions outside the primary visual cortex. Although the mechanisms underlying these processes remain to be fully explored, there are cells in area V3 of the monkey that fire only when a stimulus is in their receptive field *and* the monkey is fixating a particular point. In addition to these so-called gaze-locked cells, there are cells in area V6 of the monkey parietal cortex that fire when a stimulus is in a particular location regardless of where on the retina it falls. These have been called real-position cells, and it seems highly likely that they are involved in the mechanisms at the neuronal level underlying localization in egocentric space, although this has yet to be proved.

Perception and activity in allocentric space involve a wide range of processes, including perception of the location of objects relative to one another, drawing and other constructional tasks, spatial analysis and problem solving, and topographical orientation and memory. As spatial tasks become more complex, so does the participation of brain regions contributing to the task. In constructional tasks, for example, lesions to either the left or the right hemisphere disrupt performance, although they appear to affect different aspects of the task. The necessary contribution of each hemisphere to these tasks is also evident from studies of commissurotomy patients, which demonstrate that neither hemisphere in isolation is competent to execute constructional tasks. It has also been shown that neither hemisphere alone is competent to process the spatial components of a simple tactual form-recognition test. Thus, the contention that the right hemisphere is less specialized for spatial processing than the left hemisphere is for language processing has strong empirical support.

In addition to being less lateralized, spatial processing is less focally represented within each hemisphere when compared with the relatively circumscribed representation of language in Broca's and Wernicke's areas. Thus, we have seen that damage to occipital (extrastriate), temporal (hippocampal), frontal, and parietal regions in each hemisphere can disrupt spatial processing. However, representation in the spatial domain may be less diffuse than it seems. A case can be made that the parietal lobes are in fact highly specialized for spatial processing and that the effects of lesions in other regions affect spatial processing indirectly. From this point of view, the effect of extrastriate lesions is seen as specific to vision, rather than affecting spatial processing per se. This is supported by the retinotopic nature of disorders of visual orientation associated with occipital-lobe lesions and the resulting findings that the disorder can be confined to one half or even one quarter of the visual field. It is also supported by the finding of dissociations between impairment in visual orientation and orientation in other modalities.

There is strong evidence that the parietal lobes are the regions most specialized for spatial processing. This evidence comes from studies of patients with a range of impairments, from problems in orientation discrimination and perception of relative location to problems in constructional tasks and topographical orientation. The importance of the parietal lobes in spatial processing is also supported by lesion and unit recording studies in primates that have implicated these regions in the mediation of spatial processing. These findings have led to hypotheses such as the two-pathway hypothesis of Mishkin and his colleagues specifying a specialized role for the parietal lobes in spatial behaviors, in contrast to visual areas in the temporal lobes that are specialized for object recognition.

Considering the role of the hippocampus, there is evidence that this region is involved in *memory* for spatial location rather than spatial orientation itself. Thus, the cells in the hippocampus that fire when an animal is in a specific location do so only after the animal has had a certain amount of experience in the particular environment. Along the same lines, animals with hippocampal lesions and human patients with right or bilateral hippocampal lesions, although impaired in the recall of spatial location, are not spa-

tially disoriented when they are able to utilize cues already in long-term memory to guide their spatial behavior. The argument that the impairment in spatial behavior associated with hippocampal lesions is essentially the result of a memory impairment is particularly compelling in the case of topographical orientation. Here the construction of a mental representation of a spatial layout (cognitive map) requires the integration of perceived information regarding landmarks and their relationships that unfolds over time as the organism moves about its environment, a process that is clearly vulnerable to the effects of memory impairment.

Unilateral spatial neglect, a disorder in which a patient acts as if one side of space does not exist, is associated with parietal-lobe lesions contralateral to the neglected hemifield. Two major hypotheses have been proposed regarding the underlying mechanism of neglect. One attempts to account for neglect in terms of a disorder of attention, the inability to disengage attention from the nonneglected hemifield. The other hypothesis conceptualizes neglect as a disruption of the internal representation of space. This approach is supported by evidence that the visual images generated by patients with neglect show the same neglect for the side of space contralateral to their parietal-lobe lesion as is seen in their perception of space. This finding, together with evidence of a correspondence between the role of a structure in perception and its role in visual imagery, suggests that right parietal-lobe structures are critical for the maintenance of an internal representation of space. Nevertheless, a complete account of neglect will probably incorporate aspects of both theories and possibly others that have yet to be formulated.

Mental imagery and visual perception appear to share underlying mechanisms. Evidence for this comes from electrophysiological and imaging studies that implicate the same areas in occipitotemporal cortex in both imagery and visual perception. This idea is also supported by the finding that patients with specific central perceptual impairments report corresponding impairments in the formation of images. For example, patients with achromatopsia also report being unable to form *images* of color. This supports the idea that information inherent in images is represented in the same form as perceptual information.

The two hemispheres appear to be specialized for particular types of visual images, with the left hemisphere mediating the generation of images from long-term memory while the right hemisphere is specialized for the manipulation of images, as in mental rotation tasks. The finding that impairment in image generation and impairment in verbal thinking are dissociable after left-hemisphere lesions sug-gests that imagery is fundamentally different from verbal thought.

Frontal-lobe lesions are associated with severe impairments in behavior that has a spatial component. These impairments are not, however, essentially spatial in nature. Instead, they are secondary to an impairment in executive function that exerts a generalized effect on a wide range of complex behaviors, including spatial behavior.

CHAPTER 8

Visual Recognition

A CASE OF VISUAL AGNOSIA

DISORDERS OF VISUAL RECOGNITION

Early Attempts at Understanding

Partial Cortical Blindness

Apperceptive Agnosia

Associative Agnosia

Summary of the Classical View of Visual Agnosia

PROBLEMS WITH THE CLASSICAL MODEL

Perceptual Impairment in Associative Agnosia

Significance of the Apperceptive-Associative
Distinction

Perceptual Impairment in Prosopagnosia
and Pure Alexia

The Problem of Category-Specific Impairments
in Visual Recognition

THEORIES OF VISUAL AGNOSIA

Disconnection Model

Symbolic Search Model

Massively Parallel Constraint-Satisfaction Models
of Object Recognition

A Neurobiologically Based Conceptualization
of Visual Agnosia

**RESTORATION OF SIGHT IN ADULTHOOD
AFTER EARLY ONSET OF BLINDNESS**

SUMMARY

In this chapter we continue to pursue a question to which we have already devoted considerable time: How do we see the visual world as we do? We have seen that light impinging on the retina activates rods and cones and sets in motion a complex pattern of neuronal activity that, through the mediation of bipolar, amacrine, and horizontal cells, is highly complex even before it leaves the retina. The optic nerve conducts this pattern to a number of structures, the most important being the lateral geniculate nucleus of the thalamus, and from there information is projected to the cerebral cortex. We have also seen functional specialization within areas of cortex devoted to vision, such that certain areas are spe-

cialized for the processing of various subcomponents of vision, including color, form, and motion, and that these areas have distinct and specific microarchitectures. In addition, we have seen that we are beginning to understand the nature of the anatomical interconnections between these specialized areas. We are, however, still left with the question of how we see the world: How, within the darkness of the skull, does the activity of the brain generate a meaningful representation of the visual world?

It will come as no surprise that we are far from a complete answer to these questions. Nevertheless, the study of patients with impaired visual recognition due to brain lesions, together with the physiological and anatomical findings emerging from animal studies that we have already discussed, provides some insight into how we construct visual representations. Disorders of vision that are not due to disruption of elementary visual function (or the severity of which is incommensurate with relatively mild disorders of elementary function that may be present) and that are not due to generalized intellectual impairment are termed **visual agnosia.** We begin our discussion with an account of a case of visual agnosia described by Oliver Sacks. The striking nature of this patient's pattern of impaired and preserved functions dramatically depicts what can happen when higher visual functioning is disrupted in humans. We will then briefly review some of the early attempts to understand disorders of higher vision and their implication for an understanding of normal visual recognition. These disorders have traditionally been divided into three categories: partial cortical blindness, apperceptive agnosia, and associative agnosia, which together suggest a hierarchy of sequential processing stages mediating object recognition. According

to this hierarchical account, visual recognition can be divided into three general phases: (a) the processing of relatively elementary components of vision (such as acuity, simple shape, and color), (b) the integration and organization of these components to yield percepts, and (c) the assignment of meaning to these percepts. From this point of view, partial cortical blindness, apperceptive agnosia, and associative agnosia are seen as breakdowns in each of these three phases, respectively. We will see that this sequential-hierarchical model accounts for a good deal of data that has emerged from the study of patients with higher visual disorders.

Nevertheless, data also exist that are inconsistent with this model. They suggest that the division of object recognition into discrete sequential stages, particularly the separation of percept formation and meaning assignment, may be a serious oversimplification—that the seemingly obvious distinction between seeing and knowing may not be a useful framework for understanding how we represent the visual world. But we are getting ahead of our story; let's begin with a look at a patient with visual agnosia.

A CASE OF VISUAL AGNOSIA

In his essay *The Man Who Mistook His Wife for a Hat*, Oliver Sacks (1985) conveys a vivid description of a patient with visual agnosia. Dr. P was a music professor who began to have difficulty recognizing the faces of his students, although when they spoke, he readily recognized their voices. In addition, he exhibited some bizarre behaviors, such as patting parking meters and addressing them amiably, as if they were the heads of children. When Dr. P consulted an ophthalmologist, he was told that his eyes were normal but that he should consult a neurologist. This is how he came to be examined by Oliver Sacks.

Sacks noticed initially something strange about the way in which Dr. P looked at him. Instead of gazing at him and "taking him in" in the normal way, Dr. P made a series of rapid fixations on various parts of Sacks's face and head. He would fixate on Sacks's right ear, then his chin, and then his right eye, as if studying these individual features but not seeing the

whole of Sacks's face, not seeing Sacks as a whole. As Sacks (1985) writes, "He saw me, he scanned me and yet . . ." (p. 8).

As Sacks describes the routine neurological examination that followed, all was going uneventfully until Sacks invited Dr. P to put his shoe, which had been removed in the course of the examination, back on his foot. Dr. P then pointed to his *foot* and asked Sacks if it was his shoe. When Sacks replied that, no, he had pointed to his foot, Dr. P pointed to his *shoe* and announced that he thought *that* was his foot. Sacks then presented Dr. P with pictures of scenes from a magazine and discovered that Dr. P was completely unable to appreciate the scenes as a whole. As Sacks (1985) writes, "He never entered into relation with the picture as a whole—never faced, so to speak, its physiognomy" (p. 9). Dr. P's descriptions of these scenes were strikingly inaccurate, as exemplified by his description of a picture of the Sahara Desert as a river with a little guesthouse and people beside it. Dr. P presented this bizarre description without the slightest recognition of, much less concern about, his impairment. In general, the tendency to deny an impairment and act as if it were not present even when this entails behavior that is inconsistent with reality is termed **confabulation,** and this typified Dr. P's behavior. We will see that confabulation also accompanies many other impairments. For example, it is sometimes found in patients with severe amnesia. Thus, patients who have no memory of the person with whom they are talking may act as if they remember the individual vividly (see chapter 10).

In contrast to the severe visual recognition impairments that we have already described, Dr. P was able to recognize certain visual stimuli. He readily identified abstract geometric solids, for example. In fact, as if to emphasize how intact his general intellectual functioning remained, Dr. P was able to supply the technical names for these geometric forms, such as dodecahedron and eikosihedron. In addition, when shown cartoons of famous people, he was able to identify many of them from distinguishing characteristic details, such as Churchill's cigar. Photographs of people that contained distinguishing details were also well recognized, as was, for example, a photograph of Einstein that exhibited his characteristic hair. However, when confronted with photographs of people he knew well, including family members, Dr. P was unable to recognize them. Remarkably, this extended even to photographs of himself.

Dr. P was also unable to recognize objects with which he was confronted, even though he accurately perceived their individual elements. Thus, when presented with a rose, Dr. P was at a loss as to what it was, although he was able to provide an articulate description of it as "about six inches in length . . . A convoluted red form with a linear green attachment" (Sacks, 1985, p. 12). When invited by Sacks to smell it, Dr. P seemed puzzled; however, after inhaling its fragrance, he smiled with pleasure and immediately provided its correct name. Similarly, when presented with a glove, Dr. P seemed puzzled as to what it was, even as he provided an elegant description of it as "a continuous surface . . . infolded on itself . . . it appears to have five outpouchings, if this is the word" (p. 13). As Dr. P was handling the glove, he inadvertently put it on his hand. This resulted in immediate recogni-

tion. These two examples illustrate that Dr. P was able to recognize objects when information about them was available through modalities other than vision, a characteristic feature of visual agnosia.

According to Sacks, Dr. P no longer dreamed pictorially, suggesting a disruption in the ability to form images of objects. This is also suggested by the doctor's performance on a Bisiach-type imagery test in which he was asked to form an image of a scene and then describe it from opposite perspectives. Like the patients of Bisiach with neglect described in chapter 7, Dr. P described only the right side of the scene from each perspective. These findings led Sacks (1985) to conclude that Dr. P was "suffering from an internal agnosia as well" (p. 14). This was also suggested by a series of paintings by Dr. P that Sacks found on the wall of his apartment. Placed in chronological order, the last of the paintings was totally abstract and seemed to Sacks to depict "the pathology advancing—advancing toward a profound visual agnosia, in which all powers of representation and imagery, all sense of the concrete, all sense of reality, were being destroyed" (p. 16). It should be noted that Dr. P had a left homonymous hemianopia, an impairment not always present in visual agnosia, suggesting that his imaging impairment might be independent of the agnosia. This possibility is supported by the fact that Dr. P was apparently able to form images of objects on the right side of an imagined scene.

DISORDERS OF VISUAL RECOGNITION

Early Attempts at Understanding

In 1890 Herman Munk (1839–1912) produced brain lesions in dogs that resulted in an inability to recognize objects visually although the dogs were not blind and recovered visual recognition a few weeks after surgery. He termed this impairment **Seelenblindheit,** literally, "soul blindness." In the same year, the German neurologist Heinrich Lissauer (1861–1891) reported a patient with an analogous abnormality: intact elementary visual processing together with an inability to recognize objects visually in the absence of aphasia or general intellectual impairment. The term *agnosia* (from the Greek, "not knowing") was coined by Sigmund Freud in 1891 and carries the theoretical connotation that the problem is essentially one involving loss of knowledge about the visual world, either because that knowledge has been destroyed or has become unavailable.

But it is Lissauer's classification of agnosia into two categories, apperceptive agnosia and associative agnosia, that has had a profound influence on later attempts to understand impairments in object recognition. Lissauer used the term **apperception,** a word coined by the German mathematician and philosopher Gottfried Leibniz and popular among 19th-century psychologists, including Wundt, to indicate higher-order perception. Lissauer used the term *apperceptive agnosia* to designate impairment in visual recognition due to a disruption of perception. He designated as *associative agnosia* impairment in the assignment of meaning to an intact percept.

This distinction was based on both empirical and theoretical grounds. Empirically, it was found that although some patients with impaired object recognition were also impaired on tests of visual perception, such as a matching-to-sample task, other patients did not appear to have perceptual deficits. The apperceptive-associative distinction also fit well with psychological theories of the time that postulated a sequential chain of processes whereby objects were first perceived and then meaning was assigned to them. This framework had an enormous impact on ideas about how the brain is organized, an influence that is still very much with us today. This is embodied in the widely held notion that input for a given modality first arrives at the cortex at the primary sensory projection area for that modality, where perceptual (apperceptive) processes are mediated, and is then sent to association areas, where meaning is assigned.

We have already discussed the limitations of this schema at some length in previous chapters, where we learned that recent findings such as functional segregation and specialization within areas of cortex devoted to vision and parallel projections to these areas pose serious problems for the classical primary sensory cortex–association cortex view of cerebral organization. And we will see that these limitations, as well as empirical findings from the study of patients with visual recognition impairment, will compel us to expand our theoretical conceptualization of agnosia beyond Lissauer's framework.

Yet the plausibility of this sequential processing schema and the apperceptive-associative classification of agnosia that it generated had an enormous influence on attempts to understand visual recognition. Several factors contributed to this influence. It was a relatively simple schema, which was consistent with both common sense and with the dominant psychological theories of the day. In addition, findings from the study of patients with disorders of visual recognition seemed to fit neatly into either the apperceptive or the associative category. Furthermore, it seemed consistent with available neuroanatomical data, such as the finding by Paul Flechsig (1847–1929) that although the primary visual cortex was myelinated at birth, the so-called visual association cortex surrounding this area was myelinated during the course of postnatal development. Flechsig interpreted this as an indication that association areas remained open to modification after birth. This inference seemed to fit well with the idea that visual association areas are mediating processes involved in learning about the meaning of things experienced in the visual world, whereas the primary visual cortex mediates basic perceptual processes, hard-wired at birth.

For all of its plausibility, however, Lissauer's formulation did not have to wait for the recent developments alluded to earlier to evoke criticism. In fact, soon after Lissauer's and Freud's conceptualization of agnosia there were those who questioned the very existence of the disorder, and exponents of this skepticism continued to espouse their views as late as the 1950s. Typical of these views was Eberhard Bay's (1953) contention that impairment in object recognition was always the result of impairment in elementary visual processing, impaired general intelligence, or the interactive effect of the two. It turns out that Bay was wrong: Impairment in visual recognition *is* seen in patients who have no (or relatively mild) impairment in elementary visual functioning and who do not suffer from general intellectual impairment. Of course, the converse is not the case: Impairment in elementary visual function will disrupt visual recognition.

Let's then examine in more detail the symptomatology of visual agnosia, using, initially, Lissauer's categorization as our framework. Before doing this, however, it is necessary to examine disorders of relatively elementary visual processing—processing that is a prerequisite for the higher visual processing required for object recognition—that follow damage to the primary visual cortex.

Partial Cortical Blindness

Lesions to the primary visual cortex can result in blindness, a condition termed **cortical blindness.** Very often, however, damage to the occipital cortex does not result in complete blindness; certain functions are spared or reemerge during the course of recovery. This condition is termed **partial cortical blindness.** In chemistry, fractionation is a process whereby the components of a mixture are separated into different portions through a process such as distillation. Analogously, the patterns of sparing and impairment of function observed in partial cortical blindness after occipital-lobe lesions provide a basis for analyzing the elementary components of visual sensory processing.

ACUITY   In our earlier discussion of vision we saw that cortical lesions can produce a selective impairment in the perception of color (achromatopsia) and movement (akinetopsia). In addition, cortical lesions can, like lesions in peripheral structures in the visual system, such as the retina and the optic nerve, produce impairment in visual acuity. **Visual acuity** has been measured in a number of ways, including detecting the presence or absence of light, detecting the presence of a single target, determining whether one or more stimuli are present (two-point discrimination), detecting differences in spatial frequency, and detecting differences in brightness (contrast sensitivity). Clinically, it is often assessed through a letter discrimination task, such as the familiar eye chart known as the Snellen Chart.

SHAPE DISCRIMINATION   Impairment in shape discrimination, as measured by the ability to detect differences between two shapes, is also sometimes seen in partial cortical blindness. The Efron Squares Test (Efron, 1968) is a good example of a test of shape discrimination (Figure 8.1). In this test, a square is

FIGURE 8.1   Stimuli used in the Efron Squares Test. *(From McCarthy & Warrington, 1990, p. 25)*

paired with one of a series of rectangles, the ratios of whose sides progressively increase. The subject is required to judge whether the two figures are the same or different. The surface areas and luminous flux (the amount of reflected light) of the stimuli are equated so that relative brightness cannot serve as a cue to the subject. Discrimination of line lengths, sizes of figures, and curvature versus straightness of the lines of a figure (Figure 8.2) have also been used.

It would seem logical to presume that normal acuity would be necessary and sufficient for the discrimination of shape. In fact, however, impairment in acuity and impairment in shape discrimination are doubly dissociable. Thus, patients with impaired shape discrimination and normal acuity have been reported (Efron, 1968; Humphreys & Riddoch, 1984, 1987; Riddoch & Humphreys, 1987; Warrington, 1986), as has the converse pattern of impaired acuity and normal shape discrimination (Warrington, 1985). Furthermore, Warrington (1985) has demonstrated reciprocal dissociation of acuity, color discrimination, and shape discrimination (Figure 8.3) in patients with par-

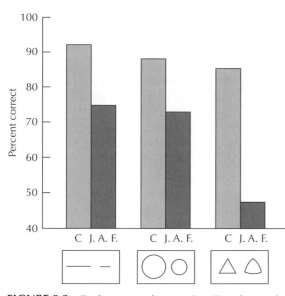

FIGURE 8.2   Performance of patient J. A. F. and control subjects on three tests of shape discrimination. *(From McCarthy & Warrington, 1990, p. 27)*

	Preserved		
Impaired	Acuity	Shape	Color
Acuity		C. O. T.	B. R. A. T. H. R.
Shape	J. A. F. R. B. C		B. R. A. T. H. R.
Color	J. A. F. R. B. C	C. O. T.	

FIGURE 8.3   Dissociation of preserved and impaired visual sensory processing in five patients (C. O. T., J. A. F., B. R. A., T. H. R., and R. B. C.) with partial cortical blindness. *(Adapted from McCarthy & Warrington, 1990, p. 45)*

tial cortical blindness. We could add movement discrimination to this list (Zihl, von Cramon, & Mai, 1983). Taken together, these findings corroborate our earlier conclusion, based on a confluence of findings from a number of methodologies (see chapter 5), that visual sensory abilities are not organized in any straightforward sequential-hierarchical manner.

In addition, as one might expect, there is no lateralization of visual sensory function, lesions in the left and right occipital lobes producing similar impairments. In the case of acuity, lesions anywhere from the eye to the brain can produce impairment. Cortical lesions producing impairments in acuity do so in a manner commensurate with the retinotopic organization of the visual cortex, so that the field affected is contralateral to the hemisphere involved. In contrast, impairment in shape discrimination is associated with bilateral posterior lesions. We have seen that achromatopsia is associated with bilateral lesions in the regions of the fusiform and lingual gyri, whereas akinetopsia is associated with bilateral lesions in an area of cortex just lateral to this area (see chapter 5).

Somehow these specialized visual sensory processes mediated by distinct areas of occipital cortex

undergo a process of synthesis and integration that yields percepts, organized representations of the visual world. We have already confessed our profound ignorance in the face of the great mystery as to what these integrative processes are. Nevertheless, we can derive some clues as to their nature from the ways in which they break down. This is one of the opportunities afforded by the study of visual agnosia. Let's now examine the impairment that Lissauer interpreted as occurring at the level of percept formation, apperceptive agnosia.

Apperceptive Agnosia

We have defined **apperceptive agnosia** as an impairment in the organization of visual sensations into percepts in the absence of (commensurately severe) impairment in visual sensory processing. To obtain a metaphorical appreciation of the experience of apperceptive agnosia, imagine that you are viewing a camouflaged object or a pattern of black and white areas that together depict a form by inducing perceptual closure (Figure 8.4). Viewing such patterns strains the perceptual organizational processing of normal subjects and creates an experience, in the moments before the form is recognized, that may be analogous to that of the patient with apperceptive agnosia when confronted with a normal visual scene.

Impairment in patients with apperceptive agnosia is readily apparent on measures such as the Efron

FIGURE 8.4   A figure from the Street Completion Test. Out of this array of black and white areas we are able to organize a coherent visual representation, although it may take a moment to do so. A patient with apperceptive agnosia may experience the visual world in a way analogous to our experience of this array in the moments before it coalesces into an organized percept. *(From Lezak, 1983, p. 356)*

Squares Test (see Figure 8.1) and tests requiring the matching of simple forms (Figure 8.5). These patients are also severely impaired in the copying of even very simple forms. More elaborate tests used to detect and study apperceptive agnosia typically consist of complex or degraded pictorial representations of common objects that place heavy demands on perceptual organization. For example, to exclude the effect of possible confounding naming problems, De Renzi, Scotti, and Spinnler (1969) used a modified version of Ghent's (1956) Overlapping Figures Test (Figure 8.6). Subjects had to identify objects in overlapping line drawings by pointing to identical objects drawn separately, using a multiple-choice format. These investigators found patients with normal elementary visual processing who were markedly impaired in the recognition of items in the overlapping figure, although when the same drawings were presented individually, the patients were unimpaired. This pattern is indicative of apperceptive agnosia.

Similarly, a dissociation between elementary visual processing and perceptual processing was demonstrated using the Gollin figures, a test that uses incomplete drawings to assess perceptual function (Gollin, 1960) (Figure 8.7). In this test, subjects are initially presented with a fragmented version of a drawing and asked to identify it. If they fail, increasingly complete drawings are presented until the

FIGURE 8.5   Performance of a patient with apperceptive agnosia on a simple form-matching test. Each row contains a target shape *(left)* and a set of four choices to be matched with the target. The patient's responses are marked. *(From Farah, 1990, p. 12)*

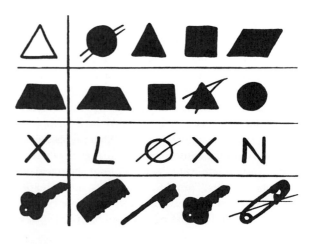

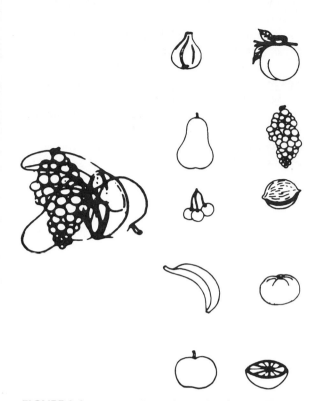

FIGURE 8.6 Example from Ghent's Overlapping Figures Test as modified into a multiple-choice version by De Renzi and his colleagues (1969). Subjects have to decide which of the 10 items shown on the right are part of the composite figure on the left. *(From De Renzi, Scotti, & Spinnler, 1969)*

FIGURE 8.7 An example from Gollin's incomplete drawings test. *(From McCarthy & Warrington, 1990, p. 31)*

subject succeeds in identifying the depicted object. Patients with cerebral lesions and normal or near-normal visual sensory processing have been shown to be impaired on this task, requiring more complete versions of the drawings for accurate identification than control subjects (Warrington & James, 1967a; Warrington & Taylor, 1973).

The overlapping figures and incomplete drawings in these two tests render the formation of a percept more difficult and thus make these tests sensitive to impaired perceptual processing. Warrington has used more naturalistic stimuli for the same purpose. By manipulating lighting conditions it is possible to unevenly illuminate objects so that they appear quite different than they do in typical lighting (Figure 8.8). Warrington (1982) has demonstrated that some pa-

tients show impairment in the identification of items in the unusual lighting conditions but not in the usual lighting condition.

In another test utilizing naturalistic stimuli, the Unusual Views Test, Warrington and Taylor (1973) presented patients with a photograph of an object taken from an unusual (nonprototypical) view (Figure 8.9). The patient was then presented with a pair of photographs, one of a different but visually similar object and the other of the target object seen from a prototypical view. The task was to choose the object that had been previously seen in the unusual view. Once again, some patients without visual sensory impairment were found to be impaired on this task, indicating a disruption of perceptual processing. Similarly, patients have been found to be impaired on

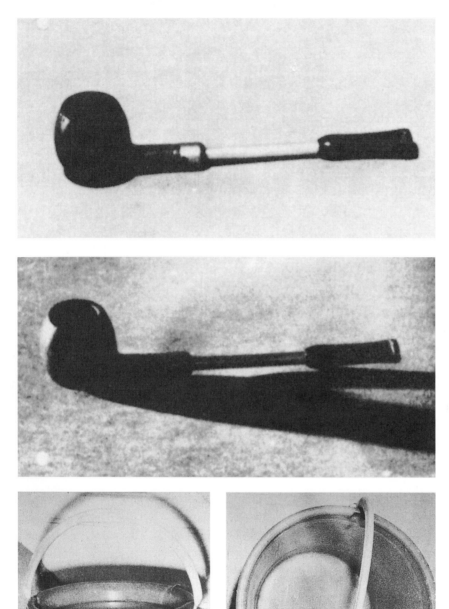

FIGURE 8.8 Example from an Uneven Lighting Test (Warrington, 1982). The pipe in the upper picture is seen in typical, even lighting, whereas that in the lower picture is seen in more unusual lighting. *(From Farah, 1990, p. 32)*

FIGURE 8.9 An example of an item from an Unusual Views Test. On the left is a pail seen from a typical view. On the right is a pail seen from above, an unusual view. *(From Warrington & Taylor, 1973)*

the identification of photographs of foreshortened objects (Humphreys & Riddoch, 1984; Riddoch & Humphreys, 1986) and foreshortened silhouettes of objects (Warrington & James, 1988). The particular perceptual mechanism impaired in these tests requiring identification of objects across different views would seem to involve **shape constancy,** that perceptual mechanism whereby we are able to extract the invariant (unchanging) shape of an object from the changing pattern of stimulation impinging on the retina.

There is considerable evidence that impairments characteristic of apperceptive agnosia are associated with posterior right-hemisphere lesions. De Renzi and his colleagues (De Renzi & Spinnler, 1966; De Renzi et al., 1969) report that impairment in tests using overlapping figures occurs more often after right-hemisphere than after left-hemisphere lesions and, within the right hemisphere, more often in association with posterior than with anterior lesions. The most severe impairments on the Gollin figures (Warrington & James, 1967a) and the Unusual Views Test (Layman & Greene, 1988; Warrington & Taylor, 1973) have been reported to be associated with right parietal-lobe lesions.

Associative Agnosia

According to the classical view, **associative agnosia** is an impairment in the assignment of meaning to a normally perceived object. To gain a phenomenological appreciation of this disorder, imagine that you are looking at a totally unfamiliar piece of machinery. Your visual sensory processing is normal, as is your perception of the object, yet you cannot identify it because you simply have not acquired knowledge of it. Or consider an abstract stabile by Alexander Calder. You see it, you perceive it, but if someone asks you what it is, you have no answer. It doesn't correspond to any information about the visual world that you have acquired, although you might make some association to such knowledge, saying it reminds you of some object, perhaps suggested by its title. In both cases we have accurate perception but a lack of any corresponding information about the visual world to enable us to identify, to *know,* the object.

If we extrapolate this lack of recognition to most of our visual experience, we may gain a flavor for the experience of the patient with associative agnosia. Much of the behavior of Oliver Sacks's patient Dr. P appears to fall into this domain. Although Sacks did not extensively test his patient's perceptual processing, a point to which we will return later, Dr. P's eloquent descriptions of the rose and the glove, which he nevertheless couldn't identify on the basis of vision, seem to point to a problem in assigning meaning to a normally perceived object. It is this sense of agnosia as a breakdown in the association of a percept with knowledge about the visual world (or a breakdown in that knowledge itself) that Freud had in mind when he coined the term *agnosia* and that Lissauer, in the same spirit, designated as associative agnosia.

Experimentally, one finds patients who have normal, or near-normal, visual perception, as measured by tests such as those described in the previous section, and who are yet unable to identify objects visually. For example, Taylor and Warrington (1971) report a patient who did quite well on the Unusual Views Test (16 out of 20 items correct) but who was able to recognize only four of the items. This is a rather striking dissociation, in that the patient was frequently able to match the usual and unusual views and yet not identify the object. As he correctly matched the two views, he complained, "There's the same object again. I didn't know what it was before and I still don't now."

In testing visual recognition, it is important to avoid the confounding effects of aphasia, particularly naming problems. This is generally not difficult. Qualitatively, patients with naming problems are often able to communicate the meaning of an object through verbal description, or even pantomime, even if its precise name is unavailable to them. In contrast, patients with a visual recognition impairment are likely to be at a complete loss as to the identity of the object, being unable to communicate its identity through any means. Experimentally, tests that require no verbal response, such as matching tests, go a long way toward obviating this problem.

We have noted the use of matching tests in measures of perceptual impairment, such as the Unusual Views Test. They are also useful in the assessment of

FIGURE 8.10   Stimuli from a visual-visual matching test used to detect associative agnosia. Subjects are required to match each object on the left with a semantically similar, but perceptually dissimilar, object on the right. *(From Warrington, 1992)*

associative agnosia. For example, De Renzi, Scotti, and Spinnler (1969) constructed a visual-visual matching test in which subjects were required to match semantically similar but perceptually dissimilar items. Similar tests (Figure 8.10) have also been devised by McCarthy and Warrington (1986). In addition, Warrington (1992) has devised tests that assess the ability of subjects to assign meaning to a pictured object by requiring them to decide which of three presented objects is the heaviest (Figure 8.11). Studies using such visual-visual matching tests have generated many reports of patients with normal or near-normal performance on perceptual tests and severely impaired performance on tests requiring the assignment of meaning to percepts. This is what one would expect if visual perceptual processing and visual semantic pro-

cessing were discrete functions, organized in a sequential and hierarchical manner. We will have occasion, however, to reconsider this issue later.

PARTIAL KNOWLEDGE   In analyzing the errors of patients with associative agnosia, some curious findings have emerged. It has been found that some patients who are unable to identify an object are nevertheless able to indicate the general class to which the object belongs, a phenomenon known as **partial knowledge.** This is exemplified by patients who correctly identify an object as, say, a household object but cannot identify it further. Or they may be able to correctly identify a pictured animal as a mammal but not be able to identify the animal more specifically (Warrington, 1975).

FIGURE 8.11   Stimuli from a "weight decision" test for associative agnosia. Subjects are required to indicate which of the three objects in each group is heaviest. *(From Warrington, 1992)*

CATEGORY SPECIFICITY   Another somewhat counterintuitive finding, known as **category specificity,** is that patients with visual associative agnosia are not necessarily equally impaired in recognizing all categories of objects. Most striking is the finding that some patients appear to be specifically impaired in the recognition of faces, a condition termed **prosopagnosia.** In addition, as discussed in chapter

6, impairment in reading without impairment in other linguistic skills (termed **pure alexia**) is a well-documented result of cerebral damage. Pure alexia may be thought of as a category-specific agnosia, an agnosia for written words.

In addition to these broad categories of agnosia, there are reports of patients who are impaired in the recognition of objects within somewhat less broad

FIGURE 8.12   Example of stimuli used to demonstrate a dissociation between impaired recognition of an isolated object and retained ability to recognize a visually presented action. In this case a patient with associative visual agnosia who is not able to recognize a cup *(left)* may be able to recognize the visually presented action of drinking from a cup. *(From McCarthy & Warrington, 1986, p. 1237)*

categories. For example, a patient may be impaired in the recognition of living things but unimpaired in the recognition of inanimate objects (Nielsen, 1937, 1946; Warrington & Shallice, 1984). The converse pattern of impaired recognition of inanimate objects with preserved recognition of living things has also been reported (Hecaen & Ajuriaguerra, 1956). There are also reports (McCarthy & Warrington, 1986) of selective preservation of knowledge of the abstract connotations of a scene and of visually presented action (Figure 8.12).

A number of reports indicate that the pattern of preserved perception and disrupted recognition that has traditionally been termed associative agnosia is seen following lesions of the posterior left hemisphere. The brain of the patient in Lissauer's (1890/1988) case study, who could see but could not recognize objects, was subsequently examined at autopsy and found to have a lesion in this area. Subsequent studies were consistent with this finding (De Renzi et al., 1969; Ferro & Santos, 1984; Hecaen & Ajuriaguerra, 1956; Hecaen et al., 1974; McCarthy & Warrington, 1986; Warrington & Taylor, 1973).

IMPLICATIONS OF MODALITY SPECIFICITY, PARTIAL KNOWLEDGE, AND CATEGORY SPECIFICITY

One of the most striking features of visual agnosia is its modality specificity, its confinement to the visual modality. We saw this in Sacks' patient, who, viewing a rose, was at a loss as to what it was until he inhaled its fragrance, whereupon he immediately recognized it. The literature contains innumerable other accounts of impaired recognition in one modality coexisting with normal recognition in other modalities. This is reflected in the terms used to describe these category-specific recognition impairments: *visual agnosia, auditory agnosia,* and *astereognosis* (tactual agnosia). What are the implications of this modality specificity for an understanding of the organization of semantic memory (knowledge about the world)? In particular, does the existence of a visual-specific agnosia mean that there is a visual semantic memory that is separate from other stored representations of knowledge about the world? Furthermore, do partial knowledge and category specificity reflect the results of a kind of fractionation process that reveals aspects of the organization of semantic memory? Some investigators believe that the answer to the last two questions is yes (McCarthy & Warrington, 1990). As we will see shortly, however, there are alternative ways of interpreting these data, and these questions remain far from settled.

Summary of the Classical View of Visual Agnosia

Let's summarize the classical conceptualization of visual recognition that we have discussed so far. According to this view, there are three major processes that result in object recognition: (a) visual sensory processes, including acuity, shape discrimination, color discrimination, and movement discrimination, mediated by the occipital lobes in each hemisphere; (b) perceptual processes that yield an organized percept, mediated by posterior structures in the right hemisphere; and (c) the assignment of meaning to percepts, mediated by the posterior left hemisphere. Further, according to this view, these processes are discrete, as demonstrated by their dissociability. They are

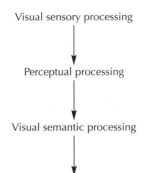

Visual sensory processing

↓

Perceptual processing

↓

Visual semantic processing

↓

FIGURE 8.13   Stages in visual recognition according to the classical model. *(Adapted from McCarthy & Warrington, 1990, p. 43)*

sequentially and hierarchically organized, each earlier stage being a prerequisite for later stages (Figure 8.13).

A factor, not yet mentioned, that complicates this sequential model is the finding that some patients with impairment on perceptual tests, such as Overlapping Figures or Unusual Views, are able to perform well on semantic matching tests when the stimuli are not perceptually difficult. This finding suggests that assignment of meaning is compatible with somewhat impaired perceptual processing, either through the assignment of meaning to percepts mediated by residual perceptual processing capacity or through the direct assignment of meaning to the results of visual sensory processing or both. From this perspective, the modality specificity of visual agnosia reflects the presence of an independent or partially independent visual semantic memory system. Partial knowledge and category specificity are seen as reflections of the organization of this semantic system.

PROBLEMS WITH THE CLASSICAL MODEL

The classical model has an alluring conceptual simplicity; however, it does not account for some important data from patients with visual agnosia. These data fall into two domains. The first has to do with the classical model's fundamental distinction between impairment in object recognition due to perceptual disorder (apperceptive agnosia) and impairment due to a disorder of the assignment of meaning in the ab-

sence of disrupted perception (associative agnosia). It turns out that there *are* perceptual deficits in patients with what is traditionally termed associative agnosia. Therefore, the simple presence or absence of perceptual impairment cannot serve as a basis for constructing a taxonomy of the visual agnosias. This finding has enormous implications for an understanding of visual recognition. In particular, as has been argued by Farah (1990) and by Zeki (1993), among others, it indicates that the distinction between seeing and understanding, between perception and knowing, which seems so logical and for which there seems to be empirical support, may in fact represent a serious misunderstanding of the processes involved in visual recognition.

The second critical domain of data bears on the classical model's interpretation of apparent category-specific impairments in visual recognition as markers of the organization of semantic memory. From the point of view of the classical model, prosopagnosia, pure alexia, and other apparently category-specific impairments in object recognition reflect the presence of specialized subsystems or modules within semantic memory. There is, however, growing evidence that what appear to be category-specific impairments are more parsimoniously conceptualized as the result of different types of perceptual impairment. What emerges from these findings is a model that, in contrast to the postulated separate systems of the classical model, views the different manifestations of visual agnosia as disruptions of different underlying perceptual processes. Figure 8.14 contrasts these two perspectives. In the sections that follow we consider some of the findings that do not fit the classical model and elaborate on the nature of the revisions in our conceptualization of the processes involved in visual recognition that they seem to require. We begin with evidence for perceptual impairments in associative agnosia.

Perceptual Impairment in Associative Agnosia

COPYING   The apparently intact copying ability of patients with associative agnosia (Figure 8.15) is often cited as evidence of their intact perceptual

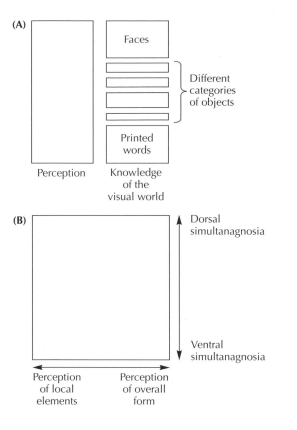

FIGURE 8.14 Schematic representation of two general models of visual recognition. *(A)* The classical model postulates that visual perception and visual semantic memory (knowledge of visual-meaning correspondences) are mediated by separate processes, the breakdown of which results in apperceptive agnosia and associative agnosia, respectively. Category-specific impairments such as prosopagnosia, pure alexia, and category-specific recognition impairments within object agnosia are seen as reflecting the disruption of specialized components or modules within semantic memory. *(B)* A model of visual recognition that conceptualizes the varying symptomatology of visual agnosia in terms of disruptions in different dimensions of perceptual processing. Apperceptive agnosia is seen as a severe impairment in organization that affects the perception of local elements, whereas associative agnosia is seen as a less severe impairment affecting the perception of overall form. From this point of view, apparently category-specific associative agnosias are understood as manifestations of varying degrees of two underlying perceptual-attentional impairments, dorsal simultanagnosia and ventral simultanagnosia. *(Based on Farah, 1990)*

processing (McCarthy & Warrington, 1990). The quality of their performance is particularly striking when compared with the severe impairment in copying even simple forms typical of patients with apperceptive agnosia (Figure 8.16).

In fact, however, reproductions of patients with associative agnosia are constructed very slowly and with what has been described as a "slavish" quality. They appear to be copying individual segments of lines without achieving an overall appreciation of the form of the figure. A particularly compelling example of this is a drawing of St. Paul's Cathedral in London by a patient with agnosia (Figure 8.17). Although the details of the picture are quite accurate, the overall layout and the relationships between buildings show a failure to grasp the broader forms of the scene. The copy was constructed in an extremely piecemeal fashion and, remarkably, took 6 hours to complete (Humphreys & Riddoch, 1987). This is consistent with

the verbal self-reports of these patients. For example, Zeki (1993) reported a patient who stated that when he copied a complex figure, "all he saw was a complex pattern of lines, which did not correspond to a particular object" (p. 315).

MATCHING TESTS A similarly slavish and piecemeal quality characterizes the performance of associative agnosic patients on perceptual matching tests. Although their performance can be quite accurate, it is extremely slow and appears to consist of a feature-by-feature matching of the two figures rather than a comparison of their overall forms.

SENSITIVITY OF THOSE WITH ASSOCIATIVE AGNOSIA TO THE QUALITY OF THE STIMULUS A number of studies indicate that the visual recognition of patients with associative agnosia is highly sensitive to the quality of the stimulus. Thus, they

(A)

(B)

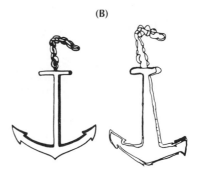

(C)

FIGURE 8.15 Copies of line drawings by patients with associative agnosia. None of these objects were recognized by the patients. *(A: Adapted from Rubens & Benson, 1971 [in McCarthy & Warrington, 1990, p. 35]; B: Copy of an anchor by patient M. S. from Ratcliff & Newcombe, 1982 [in Farah, 1990, p. 61]; C: Copy of a tea bag, ring, and pen by patient L. H. from Levine & Calvanio, 1989 [in Farah, 1990, p. 61])*

◀ **FIGURE 8.16** Severe impairment in the copying of simple letters and shapes by a patient with apperceptive agnosia resulting from carbon monoxide poisoning, which is believed to particularly damage V1. *(From Benson & Greenberg, 1969 [in Zeki, 1993, p. 314])*

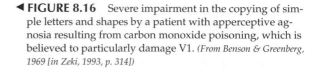

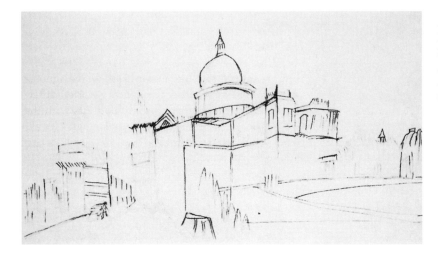

FIGURE 8.17   Drawing of St. Paul's Cathedral, London, by a patient with associative agnosia. In this patient V1 is intact, whereas extrastriate areas are damaged, a pattern commonly seen after strokes. *(From Humphries & Riddoch, 1987 [in Zeki, 1993, p. 315])*

are generally much better at identifying actual objects than photographs of objects, which in turn they identify more readily than line drawings of objects. Those with associative agnosia are also very sensitive to presentation conditions in which exposure to the object is limited in some way, such as partial occlusion of the object or brief tachistoscopic presentation. Of course, these conditions would compromise the performance of any subject. What is important in this context, however, is that the performance of associative agnosics is particularly disrupted, a finding that does not fit with the notion that their impairment is outside the perceptual domain. The same implication may be drawn from the finding that, in the majority of their errors, patients with associative agnosia misidentify the object as a similar-looking, rather than as a semantically related, object.

IMPAIRED PERFORMANCE ON PERCEPTUAL TESTS   In view of the findings just reviewed, it is not surprising that patients with associative agnosia have been found to perform poorly on a number of perceptual tests. As we have seen, those perceptual tests on which associative agnosics perform relatively well, such as copying lined figures and perceptual matching tests, are nevertheless performed slowly and in a piecemeal fashion, suggesting that the patient is not accurately appreciating overall form. This hypothesis is strengthened when one considers the perceptual

tasks that those with associative agnosia perform poorly. In general, these tasks tend to be precisely those that require an appreciation of overall form. For example, in a task in which subjects are required to decide whether there is an upside-down *T* amid a number of normally oriented *T*s, normal subjects are much faster in the "absent" condition when letters are arranged in a circle than when letters are in a random array. In addition, their response times are only weakly related to the number of letters in the circular arrangement, whereas response times are strongly related to the number of letters in the random arrangement. This suggests that normal subjects are using the overall configuration, or gestalt, of the circular arrangement to arrive at a rapid decision, whereas they are unable to do so in the random condition.

In contrast, a patient who met the classical criteria for associative agnosia failed to show an advantage in response time for the circular array compared with the random array (Humphreys & Riddoch, 1987). This case suggests an impairment in the perception of the overall configuration, or gestalt, in the circular condition.

In a study from which one might draw a similar interpretation, Ratcliff and Newcombe (1982) report a patient, M. S., who also met the classical criteria for associative agnosia. He was able to copy drawings of objects well (see Figure 8.15B), although he was unable to recognize the object he had copied. When

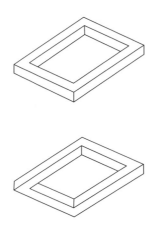

FIGURE 8.18   Example of a possible figure *(top)* and an impossible figure *(bottom)*. *(From Farah, 1990, p. 63)*

M. S. was confronted with "possible" and "impossible" figures, such as those shown in Figure 8.18, he was unable to distinguish between them. This discrimination requires an appreciation of the overall figure and cannot be made on the basis of a piecemeal inspection of separate details. In addition, Ratcliff (unpublished work cited by Farah, 1990, p. 63) found that unlike normal subjects, who copy possible figures much more rapidly than impossible ones, M. S. required the same extended amount of time to copy both figures, suggesting that he was unable to use the overall structure of the possible figure to guide his drawing.

Significance of the Apperceptive-Associative Distinction

Although the evidence just described indicates that visual perception may not be normal in associative agnosia, suggesting that the apperceptive-associative distinction may not be valid, this distinction nevertheless remains useful because it reflects empirically based differences in the capabilities of patients with visual agnosia. Thus, those with associative agnosia can match objects viewed under different conditions and copy drawings of objects (which, however, they cannot identify), whereas apperceptive agnosics show extreme impairment in both of these tasks. A

compelling example of this difference is seen when one compares the extreme impairment in copying typically shown by patients with apperceptive agnosia (see Figure 8.16) with the relatively preserved copying typical of patients with associative agnosia (see Figure 8.15). Another frequently reported difference between the performance of patients with the two classical agnosias is that associative agnosics are more likely to make identification errors based on the shape of the object in question (e.g., box for book). In contrast, the errors of apperceptive agnosics indicate that they are more likely to make identification errors based on elements other than form, such as color or texture (e.g., apple for tomato).

Even if we keep the apperceptive-associative distinction, however, these findings suggest that perceptual impairment underlies both apperceptive and associative agnosia and that it is the nature and severity of the perceptual impairment that distinguishes the two. In apperceptive agnosia the perceptual impairment is so severe that it impairs performance on a wide range of perceptual tasks. In contrast, in associative agnosia, perception is sufficiently intact to mediate the piecemeal inspection and copying of figures, while the perception of the overall structure or the whole configuration of a complex stimulus is disrupted. Moreover, the great variability among patients with visual agnosia suggests that, although we have been talking in dichotomous terms, there is a continuum of degrees of perceptual impairment underlying visual agnosia. Nevertheless, we will find it useful to retain the descriptive terms *apperceptive agnosia* and *associative agnosia* to designate the two halves of this continuum.

Perceptual Impairment in Prosopagnosia and Pure Alexia

An analogous case can be made that prosopagnosia and pure alexia are the result of impaired perceptual processing and that variations in the capacities of patients within each disorder represent degrees of perceptual impairment rather than selective impairment of discrete perceptual and semantic systems. In the case of prosopagnosia, there have been reports of impaired recognition of (previously) familiar faces coexisting with normal perception, as defined by preserved ability to discriminate unfamiliar faces (Bruyer et al., 1983). This has led to the notion, analogous to the apperceptive-associative distinction in object agnosia, that different systems or modules are involved in discriminating between unknown faces and in recognizing already well-known faces. However, despite some evidence to the contrary (Benton, 1980; Benton & Van Allen, 1972), the majority of studies of prosopagnosics that have looked carefully at perceptual ability report an association between the two impairments (Farah, 1990, p. 77; Newcombe, 1979; Shuttleworth, Syring, & Allen, 1982). Thus, there is reason to believe that impaired visual perception generally underlies prosopagnosia.

Similarly, although pure alexic patients are often without obvious perceptual impairment, there is evidence that their visual perception is impaired. For example, it has been shown that they are more likely to confuse visually similar than visually dissimilar letters (Patterson & Kay, 1982). We will elaborate further on the nature of the perceptual impairment in prosopagnosia and in pure alexia in the next section, as we return to the related problem of category specificity in visual agnosia.

The Problem of Category-Specific Impairments in Visual Recognition

One of the problems mentioned in an earlier section is that of category specificity in associative agnosia. We have seen that there is evidence for at least two material-specific impairments in visual recognition: impairment in face recognition (prosopagnosia) and impairment in the recognition of printed words in the absence of other language impairment (pure alexia). We have also seen that there is evidence for the existence, within object agnosia, of category-specific impairments in visual recognition (e.g., impaired recognition of living things with preserved recognition of inanimate objects). This evidence raises the possibility that these impairments are a reflection of the organization of semantic memory. From this point of view, observed dissociations provide relatively straightforward avenues for ana-

lyzing this organization. Thus, one would infer that there are separate independent (or quasi-independent) components or modules within semantic memory devoted to the recognition of printed words, faces, or objects. Furthermore, within the domain of objects, this perspective would posit several subcomponents of semantic memory, including, for example, inanimate objects and living things. This is the position taken by Warrington and her colleagues (see, for example, McCarthy & Warrington, 1990). On the other hand, observed dissociations that appear to be category-specific may be attributable to differences in the perceptual processes involved, a position argued by Farah (1990).

Following Farah's argument, let us consider prosopagnosia and pure alexia, disorders that have traditionally been considered to be category-specific impairments in the assignment of meaning in the absence of perceptual impairment. We have already seen that there is evidence contradicting the notion that perceptual impairment is absent in these patients. In this section we will review findings that place the category specificity of these disorders in doubt as well. Let's begin with prosopagnosia.

Since Bodamer (1947) introduced the term, prosopagnosia has been understood as a selective impairment in the recognition of faces. This fits with the intuitive sense that the human face is unlike anything else we encounter in our visual world. In addition, there seems to be a good deal of empirical support for the notion that face perception is somehow special. The argument that faces are simply particularly difficult stimuli and that prosopagnosia merely represents a more severe form of object agnosia is countered by the finding of a double dissociation between the two disorders, with some patients manifesting object agnosia without prosopagnosia and other patients showing the converse pattern (De Renzi, 1986). In addition, as discussed in chapter 5, it is well established that there are neurons in the temporal cortex of the monkey that respond selectively to faces (Desimone et al., 1984; Perrett, Rolls, & Caan, 1982). Moreover, face-sensitive cells have been found that reliably fire more to certain faces than to others (Baylis, Rolls, & Leonard, 1985), even across varying lighting conditions and facial expressions. Furthermore, these cells do not respond when features of their "preferred" face are changed, deleted, or rearranged (Desimone et al., 1984; Rolls, 1984). In sum, these cells are exactly what one would expect to find in a neural module specialized for the recognition of faces, just as selective impairment in the recognition of faces is the disorder one would expect as the result of damage to that module.

Despite the evidence just cited, there are grounds for doubting both that there is a specialized neural system or module for the recognition of faces and that there is a selective impairment in face recognition associated with cerebral damage. Perhaps most problematic for this notion is the frequently reported finding that patients with impaired face recognition often also have impaired visual recognition for material other than human faces. There are well-documented accounts of prosopagnosic patients who are also impaired in the recognition of buildings (Cole & Perez-Cruet, 1964), chairs (De Renzi & Spinnler, 1966), flowers (Newcombe, 1979), makes of automobile (Gomori & Hawryluk, 1984), photographs of animals (Damasio, Damasio, & Van Hoesen, 1982; Shuttleworth et al., 1982), different species of birds (Bornstein, 1963), plants (Whitely & Warrington, 1977), and articles of clothing and food (Damasio et al., 1982). There is even a report of a farmer who, previously able to recognize the individual faces of his cows, lost this ability when he became prosopagnosic (Bornstein, Stroka, & Munitz, 1969).

It is difficult to know how common these associated impairments are because their presence is not always adequately assessed in case studies. Nevertheless, it is clear that their association with prosopagnosia is not infrequent. This raises a major problem for material-specific accounts of prosopagnosia because it compels the adoption of an ad hoc approach that postulates that whatever prosopagnosics cannot recognize is processed by the hypothesized specialized module. Some of the associated recognition impairments, such as that for faces of cows, do not require radical revisions in conceptualizations of this hypothesized specialized subsystem. However, the full range of recognition impairments associated

with prosopagnosia, taken together, seem to defy explanation in terms of the disruption of any parsimoniously defined category-specific or material-specific module.

A similar argument can be made against the notion that pure alexia is a material-specific impairment in the recognition of printed words. For example, one influential theory of pure alexia as a material-specific disorder of visual recognition (Warrington & Shallice, 1980) postulates that the letter-by-letter reading characteristic of these patients is due to their inability to group individual letters into higher-order word units, which the investigators term **word forms.** This hypothesis is based on the assumption that pure alexics have good perception, an assumption that we have seen there is reason to question. In addition, there is evidence that, despite the inability of pure alexics to read, higher-order multiletter patterns are available to them.

To describe this evidence, a slight digression is required. Normal subjects are able to recognize a given letter more rapidly and more accurately when it is presented as part of a word than when it is presented as part of a nonword. For example, when required to indicate whether they saw the letter *r,* subjects respond more efficiently when the *r* is presented in the word *car* than when it is presented in the nonword *dar.* Furthermore, by using a forced-choice situation in which both choices would complete a real word (e.g., Did you see an *r* or a *t*?), it can be shown that this effect is not simply due to guessing the letter on the basis of the previous letters of the word. This phenomenon is termed the **word superiority effect** and demonstrates that processing a group of letters *as a word* enhances recognition of the individual letters.

The word superiority effect is not startling in itself, but it is startling that it is also seen in patients with pure alexia (Bub, Black, & Howell, 1989). This finding contradicts the contention that these patients are unable to group letters into higher-order word forms as proposed by the word form hypothesis (Warrington & Shallice, 1980). In other words, it is apparently not the material-specific, linguistic features of words that form the basis for their impaired recognition in pure alexia. This notion is further supported by evidence that patients with pure alexia are also impaired in the visual recognition of nonverbal material (Friedman & Alexander, 1984). Taken together, these findings suggest that there are no category-specific boundaries between prosopagnosia, object agnosia, and pure alexia and that what seem to be category-specific impairments in visual recognition can be accounted for in terms of different types of perceptual impairment.

An argument with this conclusion was put forward by Farah (1990), who suggested that varying degrees of impairment in two underlying perceptual abilities could account for the full range of visual recognition impairment, including prosopagnosia, object agnosia, and pure alexia. Reviewing the literature, she identified what she considered to be two related but distinct syndromes, dorsal simultanagnosia and ventral simultanagnosia. As the term implies, **simultanagnosia** is an impairment in the ability to perceive and attend to all of the features of an object or a scene at the same time. **Dorsal simultanagnosia,** which derives its name from its association with bilateral parietal-lobe lesions, is primarily an impairment in the ability to perceive the parts of objects, including complex parts, that cannot be easily decomposed into constituent parts or for which such decomposition does not aid perception. Faces are an example of such stimuli because they are typically perceived as gestalts rather than as a series of separate parts, but other stimuli, such as makes of cars and plants, share this attribute.

In contrast, **ventral simultanagnosia,** associated with left inferior temporal-lobe lesions, disrupts the ability to rapidly encode multiple parts, particularly stimuli whose perception requires their decomposition into discrete elements. Printed words are a prime example of such stimuli. Farah's hypothesis is that varying degrees and combinations of impairment in these two abilities underlie the range of manifestations of associative agnosia. From this point of view the apparently category-specific agnosias (prosopagnosia, object agnosia, and pure alexia) can be understood as resulting from dorsal simultanagnosia, ventral simultanagnosia, or some combination of the two. Farah reasoned further that this hypothesis would require that (a) there would never be a case of object

agnosia without either prosopagnosia or alexia and (b) there would never be a case of prosopagnosia or alexia that did not also have some degree of object agnosia. Her review of published case reports yielded results consistent with these requirements.

As Farah acknowledges, it is possible to account for differences in visual recognition along the prosopagnosia-alexia dimension in terms of underlying mechanisms different from those postulated above. It is possible, for example, that the right hemisphere is mediating processes involved in face recognition while the left hemisphere is mediating the recognition of printed words (Young, 1988). What is of particular importance in the present context is the idea that different patterns of visual recognition impairment can be accounted for in terms of varying degrees of impairment in different perceptual processes and need not be ascribed to category-specific disruptions in semantic memory.

Let's take a moment to consider the picture of visual agnosia that emerges from the data considered in the previous several sections. A central hypothesis generated by these data is that the distinction between apperceptive and associative agnosia and the distinction between prosopagnosia, object agnosia, and pure alexia are due to varying degrees of impairment in perceptual integration and varying degrees of impairment in two underlying perceptual processes, respectively. The hypothesis thus accounts for variations in agnosic phenomena in terms of performance on two continua of perceptual functioning (see Figure 8.14B) rather than in terms of the selective impairment of modules specialized for perceptual processing, for semantic processing, and for category-specific domains within semantic memory (see Figure 8.14A). Let's now consider how these data and hypotheses associated with them fit with some of the major general theories of visual agnosia.

THEORIES OF VISUAL AGNOSIA

We will consider here three theories of visual agnosia: (a) the disconnection model, (b) the symbolic search model, and (c) massively parallel constraint-satisfaction models.

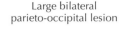

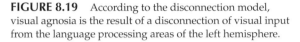

FIGURE 8.19   According to the disconnection model, visual agnosia is the result of a disconnection of visual input from the language processing areas of the left hemisphere.

Disconnection Model

We have already discussed the disconnection model in other contexts in some detail. As will be recalled, its central premise is that impairment following cerebral lesions can be understood in terms of the disconnection of centers in the brain that are specialized for particular functions. It was espoused by Wernicke (1874), Dejarine (1892), and Liepmann (1900) in the late 19th century and was energetically revived by Geschwind (1965). According to the disconnection model account put forward by Geschwind, visual agnosia is the result of a disconnection of visual input from the language processing areas of the left hemisphere (Figure 8.19) due to a large bilateral parieto-occipital-lobe lesion. In contrast to Dejarine's disconnection model of pure alexia (discussed in chapter 1), which posits a lesion in the left visual cortex and the splenium of the corpus callosum, the disconnection between visual and language areas hypothesized to underlie visual agnosia is anatomically more extensive, as one would expect if the language areas of the posterior left hemisphere were to be deprived of all visual input.

We have seen in earlier chapters that the disconnection model has certain strengths. Geschwind argued that we should abandon the concept of unitary cognitive processes, such as visual recognition, and instead focus on what a particular patient can and cannot do under particular conditions. From this perspective one can attempt to account for a patient's specific pattern of impaired and preserved function in terms of disconnection(s) between centers. In chapter 1 we saw how useful this approach could be in accounting for the seemingly baffling syndrome of alexia without agraphia. It also accounts neatly for the modality-specific nature of agnosia by positing a disconnection

between a particular primary sensory area and the posterior language area in the left hemisphere. Furthermore, in emphasizing the careful analysis of behavior as the starting point for inferring the mechanisms underlying cognitive impairment, this approach has much in common with and shares some of the strengths of strict behavioral methodologies (Skinner, 1965). Its attempt to then relate patterns of impairment and preserved function to disconnection between cerebral centers clearly goes beyond the black-box approach of the behaviorists. Nevertheless, in attempting to relate cognitive function to neuroanatomy, it does so with extreme parsimony, positing a relatively small number of centers mediating basic cognitive functions.

However, a closer examination of the account of impairment in visual recognition postulated by the disconnection hypothesis reveals some major problems, despite the theory's strengths. Most problematic is its basic contention that visual recognition impairment is due to a disconnection between visual areas and language areas. The underlying assumption of this account is that meaning for what is seen and words for what is seen are represented in the same cerebral center in the posterior left hemisphere. If this were the case, then impaired ability to name seen objects and impaired ability to demonstrate knowledge of their meaning through nonlinguistic means should always be found together. This is, however, clearly not the case, as is evidenced by the well-documented syndrome of **optic aphasia.** In this syndrome an inability to name seen objects is found in the presence of preserved ability to demonstrate knowledge of their meaning through nonlinguistic means, such as pantomime or the matching of pictures that are semantically similar but perceptually dissimilar. Thus, optic aphasia is clearly very different from visual agnosia in that the former may be conceptualized as an impairment in associating *words* to seen objects and the latter as an impairment in assigning *meaning* to seen objects. If associative agnosia were due simply to a visual-verbal disconnection, then patients with optic aphasia, like patients with associative agnosia, should be unable to demonstrate the meaning of an object through nonverbal behaviors. The ability of patients with optic aphasia to do this and to interact normally with objects in everyday life contrasts markedly with the profound impairment of associative agnosics in both these areas and argues against a visual-verbal disconnection as the mechanism of associative agnosia.

An additional limitation of the disconnection hypothesis in the context of visual recognition is its inability to account for apparent category-specific types of agnosia without positing specific pathways mediating processing critical for the recognition of faces, objects, and printed words. This necessitates, in turn, that the model postulate a number of distinct centers for the mediation of these apparently category-specific recognition processes, a schema which diminishes the parsimony of the disconnection approach by multiplying the number of required specialized centers.

Symbolic Search Model

The **symbolic search model** represents what we have termed the classical view of visual agnosia. According to this approach, the processes of normal perception generate an abstract representation of the stimulus, which is then compared with stored visual representations in semantic memory. A match between the abstract representation of the stimulus and a stored visual representation results in recognition. As an analogy for this process, imagine that you have been bird-watching for a number of hours and that during that time you have seen many birds that belong to a species you do not know. Suppose, further, that you are a talented illustrator of birds and that you return home and draw a picture of a bird that is a prototype of all the birds belonging to the unknown species that you saw. This drawing is analogous to the abstract representation of the stimulus. Now you open your field guide (semantic memory) and search for a picture of a bird corresponding to your drawing (stored visual representation). Finding a match constitutes recognition. The analogy of finding a book in a library (stored visual representation) using the title and call number written on the title slip (abstract representation of the stimulus) has also been used (Humphreys & Riddoch, 1987).

Like all analogies, these are imperfect, but hopefully they convey the flavor of the symbolic search model. From this perspective, apperceptive agnosia

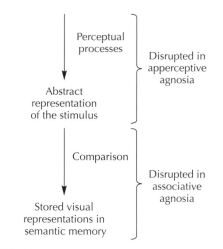

FIGURE 8.20   According to the symbolic search model, perceptual processes normally generate an abstract representation of the stimulus that is then compared with the stored visual representation in semantic memory. From this perspective, apperceptive agnosia results from impairment in perceptual processing that disrupts the formation of an abstract representation of the stimulus. Associative agnosia results from the inaccessability or destruction of stored visual representations in semantic memory.

is due to a disruption in the formation of the abstract representation of the stimulus (the drawing of the prototypical bird). Associative agnosia, on the other hand, is due to the inaccessibility or destruction of stored visual representations (Figure 8.20). Early writers expressed this in terms of loss of "stored visual memories" or "engrams for objects" (cited by Efron, 1968). More recently, the same mechanism has been described as an impairment in the "matching of signal to trace" (Brown, 1972) and the destruction of previously formed templates (Mesulam, 1985).

As already suggested, this model has considerable intuitive appeal and is consistent with a good deal of the findings from patients with visual agnosia, reviewed in earlier sections of this chapter. Those findings seem to indicate that the disruption of perceptual processes and the disruption of processes involved in the storage and/or accessing of percept-meaning correspondences are dissociable. Yet we have also seen that a closer look at patients with associative agnosia indicates that these patients are *not* free of perceptual impairment. We saw this in the slavish manner in which patients with associative agnosia copy drawings and perform matching tasks, the visual nature of their identification errors, the sensitivity of their recognition performance to the visual quality of the stimuli, and their own introspective report that they are not seeing normally. Furthermore, in a number of people with associative agnosia who have been subjected to experimental perceptual tasks, serious perceptual deficits have been reported (Humphreys & Riddoch, 1987; Levine & Calvanio, 1989; Mendez, 1988; Ratcliff & Newcombe, 1982). In fact, Farah (1990) has concluded that perceptual impairment has been found in every reported case of associative agnosia in which perception has been thoroughly studied.

These findings challenge the parsimony of a view that ascribes the mechanism of associative agnosia to damage to stored visual representations (or the mechanisms that make them accessible). Moreover, they raise serious doubts about the validity of the distinction, fundamental to the symbolic search model, between abstract visual representations derived from the stimulus and stored visual representations in semantic memory. This is the point of departure for the last general theory of visual recognition, which we will consider next.

Massively Parallel Constraint-Satisfaction Models of Object Recognition

The third viewpoint on visual recognition is represented by models known as **massively parallel constraint-satisfaction models,** variations of which are termed **parallel distributed processing, connectionism,** and **computation by constraint satisfaction.** These models have been generated within the framework of what is often referred to as **computational neurobiology.** In general, this framework attempts to provide both a rigorous definition of the problems facing the cognitive system in question and a mechanism by which the brain may solve these problems. A major strength of this approach lies in its rigorous analysis of the problems faced by the nervous system, a process that is enhanced by its formal attempts to generate models that can serve as possible solutions.

In describing this approach, let's begin with a general distinction between local representations and distributed representations. In a **local representation** there is a one-to-one correspondence between the entity being represented and the activity of a neuron (or group of neurons) encoding the representation. Each entity is thus represented by one neuron or one set of neurons. An extreme example of a local representation is the **grandmother cell,** a hypothetical neuron onto which cells with progressively more complex receptive fields ultimately converge so that the cell is able to encode a specific stimulus across variations in viewing conditions. In contrast, in a **distributed representation** the same set of neurons represents different entities, each entity being represented by a specific *pattern* of levels of activity over all the neurons of the system. We will see that distributed systems have several advantages, not the least of which is the mathematically derived fact that a set of neurons organized as a distributed system can encode a larger number of representations than the same number of neurons acting as individual, local representations. Note that, when looking at the brain as a whole, there is overwhelming evidence for local representation, as evidenced by findings that certain brain regions are specialized for certain functions. In other words, the brain as a whole is not one massive distributed system. The distributed-system hypothesis is more relevant as a possible account of mechanisms of representation *within* regions devoted to a functional system or subsystem. We consider now how the concept of distributed systems might contribute to an understanding of visual recognition.

In the case of visual recognition, the central problems are (a) How do we extract (or abstract) the invariant properties of an object from variations in shape, size, spectral composition, and so forth that characterize the image that it projects on the retina, thus enabling us to recognize the object as equivalent under these different conditions (a process often termed **perceptual categorization** or **perceptual constancy**), and (b) How do we relate this object to our knowledge of the visual world so that we recognize the object?

Massively parallel constraint-satisfaction models of visual recognition, and their variants, end up attempting to solve these two problems by proposing a single mechanism that explains them both, collapsing the apparently discrete processes of perception and understanding into a single process (Farah, 1990; Hinton, 1981). In general, this viewpoint postulates that a stimulus is represented as a specific pattern of activation across a highly interconnected set of neurons or neuronlike units. Activation of one unit will activate or inhibit neighboring units (and this unit will be activated or inhibited *by* neighboring units) in accordance with the connection strengths and weights (excitation versus inhibition) between them. At any given time, the network has specific properties, acquired presumably through accumulated visual experience (perceptual learning), such that all retinal images consistent with a particular object, regardless of its orientation, lighting, and so forth, will result in a particular pattern of activation of the network. Other objects will result in other patterns of activation. This is the case because units within the network representing consistent hypotheses regarding a particular object activate each other, whereas units representing inconsistent hypotheses inhibit each other. This is achieved through positive weights between units representing consistent hypotheses and negative weights between units representing inconsistent hypotheses.

Presenting a stimulus to the system, say, a wooden square, results in an initial pattern of varying activation levels across the units of the network. The activation level of each unit then begins to change, influenced by the activation levels of units to which it is connected and the weighting of these connections. As we first view the square from, say, an acute angle to its plane, the network pattern representing a square will be activated, but so will the pattern for a trapezoid. As the angle of orientation changes, however, the pattern representing a square will continue to be activated, whereas that representing a trapezoid will not. The network thus settles into a steady state representing a square, and we recognize the object as one. Note that this steady state is the result of the interaction between the stimulus and our knowledge of objects.

This theory provides a hypothetical mechanism whereby the unchanging features (e.g., shape) of an object can be abstracted from the constantly changing retinal image; at the same time this abstraction process constitutes recognition. In the example of the previous paragraph, the steady state achieved by the network represents a satisfaction of the constraints imposed by

(a) the knowledge of squares in various orientations, lighting, and so forth inherent in the connectivities and weightings of the network and (b) the changing image projected on the retina by the particular square being viewed.

Note that the *change* in the retinal image over different viewing angles is crucial here because from any single viewpoint the retinal image is often ambiguous, particularly if information from other sources, such as lighting and texture, are absent. For example, a trapezoidal retinal image may result from a true trapezoid or from a square seen in perspective. Let's suppose that the stimulus is actually a square. This information is inherent in the change in the retinal image over different viewing angles. According to the generalized distributed-network hypothesis that we have outlined here, the true shape of the stimulus is represented by the set of activations of the distributed system elicited by the changing retinal image, a set which, because of the constraints on the system, will correspond to the hypothesis "square."

Of course, if other information (such as lighting and texture) is available in the retinal image, as it usually is, this will contribute to the settling in of the network to the appropriate hypothesis. In addition, other objects visible at the same time will enter into these computations, providing a context that may, in turn, influence our perception of the first object. This may happen, for example, in the case of occlusion of an object by a second object. It may be seen that this model has the virtue of allowing many kinds of constraints to be applied simultaneously and of permitting development and change in constraints through experience. It also affords the possibility of modifying the entire network, either transiently or long term, through top-down processing.

ADVANTAGES OF MASSIVELY PARALLEL CONSTRAINT-SATISFACTION MODELS Massively parallel models of object recognition, such as that just outlined, make no distinction between stimulus representation and stored representation; they eliminate the traditional discontinuity between encoded percept and stored knowledge. To elaborate on this point a bit further, activation of the network by the changing retinal image produced by the object will eventually yield a stable state of network activation that represents recognition of the object. The stable state of the network is the result of the stimulus *and* stored knowledge inherent in the connection strengths and weightings between the elements of the network. The connection strengths and weightings manifest themselves only when stimulation occurs, the effect of stimulation depending on the connection strengths and weightings. Thus, there are no discrete stages of percept formation and matching of percept with stored knowledge, no separation between perception and recognition. The massively parallel recognition model fits well with the evidence from patients with visual agnosia reviewed earlier indicating that there is no sharp dividing line between perception and knowing, particularly the evidence that impaired visual recognition in associative agnosia always includes perceptual impairment.

The distributed-processing approach seems at first to be at variance with data from the macaque monkey, discussed earlier, indicating that there are cells in the inferior temporal cortex that have specific human faces as their receptive fields. These "face cells" seem to be the embodiment of the hypothetical grandmother cell, instances of local representation par excellence. Yet on closer examination one finds that, although each cell has a "preferred" face to which it fires most rapidly, each cell will also fire at a lower frequency to a number of other faces. Furthermore, a number of cells will fire, again at a frequency below their maximum, to the "preferred" face of other cells. In other words, the physiological data from face cells in the monkey inferior temporal cortex turn out to be entirely consistent with what one would predict within a distributed system.

Finally, distributed systems are consistent with the patterns of degradation of function that tend to result from brain lesions. In chapter 1, we argued that brain lesions are not analogous to removing a gear from a clock or a component from a computer; they seldom result in the complete obliteration of a particular function or even a subcomponent of a function. Instead, they typically disrupt or degrade a function that nevertheless retains some residual capacity. We have seen this to be the case in each of the domains we have examined thus far, and we will continue to see it as we explore action, memory, emotion, and executive function. Distributed-processing hypotheses are highly consistent with the pattern of degradation together with residual function so characteristic of the effects of brain lesions. As some of the units within a distributed network become inoperative, its overall function is compromised, but the remaining units mediate some residual capability.

LIMITATIONS OF MASSIVELY PARALLEL CONSTRAINT-SATISFACTION MODELS   One of the major motivations for postulating that a distributed network underlies visual recognition is its ability to accommodate data indicating that there is no sharp distinction between visual perception and visual knowledge. The most important of these data are consistent findings of perceptual impairment in all patients with associative agnosia in whom perception has been thoroughly studied. A note of caution is required here, however, because the absence of a demonstrated dissociation between perception and recognition is essentially negative evidence. This confronts us with some interpretive problems. Whereas the finding of a dissociation is grounds for inferring that the two processes underlying the dissociated impairments are at least partially independent, the absence of a dissociation (i.e., the consistent finding of association) does not conclusively exclude the possibility that two separate processes are involved. There are at least two reasons for this. Although a particular dissociation has not been demonstrated, there is always the possibility that a patient exhibiting that dissociation will be found at some future time. Thus, impairment in two independent processes may be consistently associated because the cerebral regions representing these processes are so near each other that a lesion confined to only one of them is extremely unlikely. In the context of our present discussion of visual recognition, there is the additional complication of the lack of universal agreement as to whether patients with associative agnosia who have already been studied always have impaired perception (McCarthy & Warrington, 1990), although we have seen that there is strong evidence that this is the case.

There is, however, an even more fundamental problem with parallel distributed models of visual recognition and, indeed, with most computational neurobiological models of psychological processes. Although they help us rigorously define the problems that the neural system in question must solve, they yield an account of how the system *could* work rather than an account of how it *does* work. This is largely because computational models are usually at a level of explanation that makes their details impossible to verify, given the present limits of our knowledge and experimental technology, however compatible their general schemas may be with available empirical evidence. This is not altogether useless. Knowing how a system could work tells us something about it, and attempts to verify such a model may lead to experimental investigations that yield illuminating data. But it is important to differentiate such an account from a model whose details currently have substantial empirical support.

One of the strongest critics of computational models is the neurobiologist Semir Zeki. He argues that attempts to understand the brain are likely to be more fruitful when they stay in close touch with the findings of experimental neurobiology than when they take the form of computational models that are not currently amenable to empirical testing. In addition, he contends that a focus on the findings of neurobiology can fruitfully serve as a touchstone for the formulation of theory. For example, the application of the concept of parallel processing to neural mechanisms, so prevalent in computational models, emerged, according to Zeki (1993, p. 118), from neuroanatomical studies that demonstrated its pervasiveness in cortical sensory systems, including the visual system. According to Zeki, before the demonstration of parallel *neuroanatomical* pathways, the concept of parallelism in neural mechanisms was not clearly articulated by computational theories. Zeki's own approach to visual agnosia, which we examine next, illustrates his position.

A Neurobiologically Based Conceptualization of Visual Agnosia

Zeki shares the conviction of Farah (1990) and others that what we have called the classical distinction between seeing and perception, on the one hand, and knowledge and understanding on the other (as embodied in the distinction between apperceptive agnosia and associative agnosia) represents a misunderstanding of visual recognition. His conclusion is grounded, in part, on data, such as those reviewed earlier indicating that patients with associative agnosia are not without perceptual impairment. In addition, Zeki also considers data from neurobiology (which we reviewed in some detail in chapter 5) demonstrating functional specialization, functional segregation, and parallel processing in cortical areas devoted to vision. Zeki argues that, as one goes from V1 to more central visual regions, there is a progressively higher-order level of integration of visual input. In the dimension of form, this is reflected in the larger visual fields of more central visual areas. Thus, V1 appears to mediate the recognition of very local form elements but cannot support integrative processes required for the recognition of more expansive forms. This is reflected in the severe perceptual impairment seen after damage to V1, in which patients are unable to copy even simple letters and forms (see Figure 8.16), and the preserved ability to recognize and construct local form elements (but not complex forms) seen in patients in whom V1 is intact, in the presence of extensive damage to prestriate areas (see Figure 8.17).

From this perspective, apperceptive agnosia is seen as an impairment in the integration of local form elements such as is seen in damage to V1, whereas associative agnosia is seen as an impairment in the integration of form in a more global context, so that individual form elements are perceived adequately but global forms are not, such as is seen after damage to prestriate visual areas (i.e., those outside V1). This account is consistent with the severe perceptual impairment characteristic of apperceptive agnosia and the specific types of perceptual impairment characteristic of associative agnosia. From this perspective, the latter would be characterized as impairment in the integration of global form elements to yield a whole percept.

This characterization is consistent with evidence that patients with lesions in V2 are impaired in the perception of **subjective contour** in a figure such as the Kanizsa triangle (Figure 8.21). Normal subjects

FIGURE 8.21   The Kanizsa triangle. Normal subjects see a central white triangle, although none of the sides of the triangle are actually present. This subjective contour effect is an example of the perceptual integration mediated by higher vision. One patient with visual agnosia reportedly described the figure as "a three cornered thing. . . . I see three edges and three circles." *(From Zeki, 1993, p. 263)*

"fill in" the gaps in this figure, perceiving a triangle, although none of its sides are actually present. In contrast, patients with lesions involving V2 are unable to make this completion (Wapner, Judd, & Gardner, 1978), presumably because their limited ability to integrate form leaves them "stuck" on the individual elements of the figure, unable to use the figure's overall form to influence their perception.

This account seems to fit well with descriptive accounts of associative agnosia, such as those of Sacks (1985). His patient described individual elements of objects accurately, even eloquently, whereas the overall form of the object eluded him. It also fits with experimental findings, such as the ability of associative agnosics to copy accurately when they adopt a piecemeal strategy, although they are unable to recognize what they have copied, and their ability to copy the local elements of "possible" and "impossible" figures fairly well, even though they cannot distinguish between the two types of figures.

Zeki (1993) was particularly interested in the severe impairment in form recognition accompanying damage to V1, damage that often results from carbon monoxide poisoning. For him, this impairment in elementary integration, the results of which would normally be subjected to higher-order perceptual processing by specialized areas of the prestriate cortex, was a paradigm for the inseparability of perception and understanding, an inseparability he believes permeates all agnosias. Zeki invoked Hughlings-Jackson's term **imperception,** as a substitute for the term *agnosia* ("not knowing"), to emphasize this point.

It can be argued, as Zeki does, that this notion of a continuum of increasing complexity of integrative processing can be extended to domains outside of form recognition. We have seen that patients with prestriate lesions that spare V1 have reasonably intact information about local form elements and can use this information to make reasonably accurate, albeit piecemeal, drawings of objects that they, however, cannot identify (see Figure 8.17). We may attribute this to intact orientation-selective cells in V1 that are able to detect lines and edges but are unable to integrate them into a whole. Analogously, achromatopsic patients (with lesions in V4 but sparing V1) can detect a boundary between two stimuli that reflect the same amount of light but are of different colors, even though they are unable to perceive (construct) color. This phenomenon can be understood as the result of the ability of intact interblob cells in V1 to detect differences in wavelength, although they are unable to generate color. Similarly, akinetopsic patients (with V5 lesions but sparing V1) are able to detect movement but not discriminate (perceive) its direction. Again, this is explicable in terms of the limited integrative capabilities of motion-sensitive neurons in V1.

These examples illustrate how fruitful an approach anchored in neurobiology can be. At this stage in our knowledge, it is obviously not a complete and definitive explanatory framework. Zeki would be the first to emphasize that all of the varied manifestations of visual agnosia cannot be accounted for in terms of the known specialized visual areas of the brain and their interconnections. In fact, the current incompleteness of our understanding of these specialized areas and their interconnections clearly limits the explanatory power of this approach. At the same time, what we do know about specialization and parallel processing within the striate and prestriate cortex constitutes a wellspring of potentially fruitful hypotheses bearing on the neural basis of visual recognition.

To take just one example, consider the binding problem, the perennial problem of how the various submodalities converge to form an integrated visual representation. As we saw in chapter 5, recent advances in the understanding of the neuroanatomy and neurophysiology of visually devoted cortex, although clearly not providing a definitive solution to this problem, provide some useful hints. In particular, the reentrant connections from specialized areas in prestriate cortex (including V3, V4, and V5) back to the areas that innervate them in V1 and V2 suggest that these latter areas may mediate the confluence and integration of different submodalities of visual information.

This possibility seems all the more plausible because, in contrast to specialized prestriate areas, whose cells have relatively large receptive fields, neurons in V1 and V2 have small receptive fields and constitute a precise retinotopic map. This characteristic provides for a precise localization of different aspects of stimuli. It also provides a mechanism whereby one aspect of a stimulus processed in a specialized area (say, motion in V5) can influence the processing of a different aspect of the stimulus (say, form in V3). For example, bars can obviously be generated by luminance difference, as shown in Figure 8.22A. However, if different regions of a texture (Figure 8.22B) are moved in different directions (e.g., right or left), an effect similar to the bars in Figure 8.22A can be produced. Thus, form is derived from motion.

Zeki (1993) attempted to investigate the reentry hypothesis by obtaining PET images in three viewing conditions: (a) vertically oriented bars created by luminance differences (form), (b) two sheets of textures moving in opposite directions (movement), and (c) a set of vertical bars identical to (a) except that they were generated by moving textures: textures within the bars moving in the opposite direction from the movement of textures between bars (form-from-motion). If movement processed by cells in V5 were influencing the processing of form in V3 via reentrant

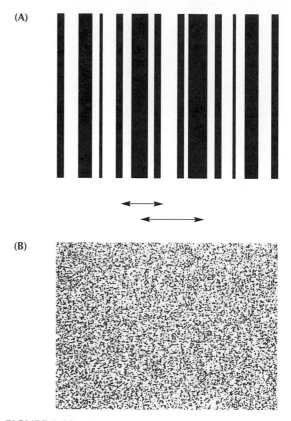

FIGURE 8.22 Form can be generated from motion. *(A)* A series of vertical lines generated from luminance differences. *(B)* Lines of the same size and orientation can be generated if sections of a texture corresponding to the white lines move in one direction and sections corresponding to the black background move in a different direction. *(From Zeki, 1993, p. 324)*

connections to V1 and V2 (Figure 8.23), then one would predict greater activation of V1 and V2 in the form-from-motion condition than in the other two conditions. Figure 8.24 shows that this was the result obtained by Zeki and his colleagues (1993).

Of course, this is not definitive evidence of the role of reentry connections in the integration of information in different submodalities and, clearly, as we have seen, one need not confine oneself to the neurobiological level in investigating visual recognition and the binding problem. Nevertheless, it has shown itself to be a highly fruitful approach and is certain to continue to do so in the future.

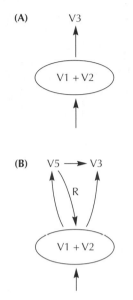

(A)

(B)

FIGURE 8.23   Schematic representation of two hypothesized pathways for the processing of form. *(A)* When form is generated from luminance differences, information is first processed by V1 and V2 and then conveyed to V3, an area specialized for the processing of form. *(B)* In contrast, when form is generated from motion, information first processed in V1 and V2 is then sent to V5, an area specialized for the processing of motion. From there it is sent back to V1 and V2, via reentrant connections *(R)*, before being sent to V3. There are also direct connections from V5 to V3.

RESTORATION OF SIGHT IN ADULTHOOD AFTER EARLY ONSET OF BLINDNESS

We conclude our discussion of visual recognition by turning briefly to a consideration of a disorder of visual recognition that results from a long period of visual deprivation. There are a number of reports of patients whose sight has been restored in adulthood after onset of blindness in early life (usually after removal of congenital cataracts). Contrary to what one might expect, after their surgery these patients experience a profound and distressing impairment of higher-order vision. In part, this appears to be a disruption of the convergence and integration of information from different visual submodalities. For example, von Senden (1932) quotes Grafe: "To begin with, the newly-operated patients do not localize their visual impressions. . . . they see colors much as we smell an odor of

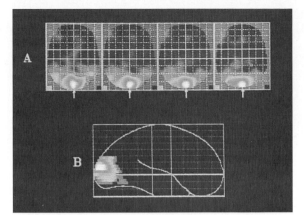

FIGURE 8.24   The result of a rCBF study in which the weighted mean activity when subjects viewed the motion stimulus alone and the form stimulus alone was subtracted from the form-from-motion condition. This revealed a significant increase in V1 and V2 activity as seen *(A)* in horizontal sections (with posterior of brain at bottom of the figures) and *(B)* in lateral view. *(From Zeki, 1993, plate 23, facing p. 309)*

peat or varnish . . . but without occupying any specific form of extension in a more exactly definable way." Sacks's patient Virgil, whose sight was restored at the age of 50 after 45 years of blindness, was similarly described: ". . . he saw colors but little else—and sometimes colors without objects: thus he might see a haze and a halo of pink around a Pepto-Bismol bottle without clearly seeing the bottle itself" (1995, p. 147).

In addition, patients with sight restored late in life exhibit other related impairments that have much in common with the visual recognition impairment seen in visual agnosia. Sacks's patient, after finally mastering the recognition of simple two-dimensional shapes (squares, triangles, etc.), a task which in the period following his restoration of sight had been difficult for him, nevertheless continued to experience visual recognition difficulties: "Solid objects, it was evident, presented much more difficulty because their appearance was so variable, and much of the past five weeks had been devoted to the exploration of objects, their unexpected vicissitudes and appearance as they were seen from near and far, or half-concealed, or from different places and angles" (1995, p. 127).

These impairments are not seen after restoration of sight following blindness that began in adulthood, suggesting a disruption in an underlying developmental process and emphasizing the importance of early visual experience for higher vision. The extent to which the mechanisms underlying these impairments involve atrophy or competitive elimination of genetically hard-wired connections through disuse, versus failure to establish or retain connections representing acquired knowledge of the visual world, is not known. It is almost certain, however, that both factors are at work here. Continued study of these patients is likely to increase our understanding of the mechanisms underlying visual recognition.

SUMMARY

Visual agnosias are specific impairments in visual recognition that are not due to disruption of elementary visual function or general intellectual impairment. The specificity of this disorder to the visual domain can be very striking, persons with visual agnosia being totally unable to identify a seen object, only to immediately recognize it as familiar when they have an opportunity to explore it through their other senses.

Agnosia is to be distinguished from partial cortical blindness, which involves the disruption of relatively elementary components of visual sensory processing, such as visual acuity and shape discrimination.

Traditionally, visual agnosia has been seen as taking two forms. Apperceptive agnosia was conceptualized as an impairment in the organization of visual sensations into percepts, whereas associative agnosia was viewed as an impairment in the assignment of meaning to normally perceived stimuli. Some patients with associative agnosia appear to have a specific impairment in recognizing faces (prosopagnosia); others appear to have a specific impairment in recognizing words (pure alexia). In addition, among patients with object agnosia, some puzzling dissociations have been seen. For example, some patients are able to recognize inanimate objects but not living things; others show the reverse pattern (category specificity). These phenomena have been interpreted by some as providing

evidence regarding the organization of visual semantic memory.

The distinction between apperceptive and associative agnosia has served as a basis for a sequential model of visual recognition. According to this model, there are three discrete stages in the processes that ultimately result in visual recognition: (a) relatively elementary visual processing, including those processes underlying acuity and shape discrimination, mediated by V1; (b) perceptual processes, mediated by the posterior right hemisphere; and (c) the assignment of meaning to the percept, a process mediated by the posterior left hemisphere.

There are, however, several problems with this classical view. Foremost among them is the finding that patients with associative agnosia also have perceptual impairments. In contrast to the perceptual impairment seen in apperceptive agnosia, which involves severe impairment in the perception of stimuli at both the local and the global levels, patients with associative agnosia exhibit an impairment in integrating local features of a stimulus into a unified global percept. This led Farah and others to propose that the apperceptive-associative distinction is more usefully conceived as reflecting different types of impairment within the domain of perceptual analysis, with apperceptive agnosia reflecting disruption of the analysis of local elements of a stimulus, whereas associative agnosia reflects impaired perception of overall form. Farah also attempts to account for category-specific impairments in associative agnosia (prosopagnosia, object agnosia, pure alexia) in terms of dorsal simultanagnosia (impaired ability to perceive parts of stimuli, such as faces, that cannot be easily decomposed into constituent parts), ventral simultanagnosia (impaired ability to perceive stimuli, such as words, when perception requires their decomposition into discrete elements), or some combination of the two.

Three general theories of visual agnosia were considered: the disconnection model, the symbolic search model, and the massively parallel constraint-satisfaction model. The disconnection model accounts for visual agnosia in terms of a disconnection between visual areas and language areas. This approach is, however, inconsistent with data demonstrating that patients with optic aphasia (inability to name seen objects) can nevertheless recognize and demonstrate the use of the object that they cannot name. The symbolic search model represents the classical sequential view of visual recognition, according to which the processes of normal perception generate an abstract representation of a stimulus that is then compared with stored visual representations in semantic memory. From this perspective, apperceptive agnosia results from a disruption of the formation of the abstract representation of the stimulus, and associative agnosia is due to the inaccessibility or destruction of stored visual representations. Although this model has considerable intuitive appeal, its assumption of a dichotomy between perceiving and knowing is inconsistent with the finding that patients with associative agnosia have significant perceptual impairments.

Massively parallel constraint-satisfaction models of object recognition propose a single mechanism to account for both perceptual categorization or perceptual constancy (perceiving an object under different conditions of presentation as a single object) and relating this object to our knowledge of the visual world. According to this perspective, a particular stimulus is represented as a specific pattern of activation across a highly interconnected network of neurons or neuronlike units. Activation of one unit will activate or inhibit (and be activated or inhibited by) neighboring units in accordance with connection strengths. At any given time, the network has specific properties, acquired presumably in the course of learning, such that all retinal images corresponding to a particular object will result in a particular pattern of activation of the network. This theory provides a single hypothetical mechanism whereby the unchanging features of an object can be abstracted from the constantly changing retinal image *and* the object can be recognized. It thus provides a mechanism that is consistent with evidence that there is no discrete

division between processes involved in perceiving an object and in relating it to prior knowledge. However, this model, and other computational models, have the limitation that they provide an account of how the system *could* work, rather than how it *does* work. This is because at our present state of knowledge we cannot verify the details of such models.

Zeki shares the belief that the distinction between perception and knowledge posited by classical theories of visual recognition represents a serious misunderstanding of the process. Rather than taking a computational approach, however, such as that seen in the massively parallel constraint-satisfaction model, Zeki anchors his hypothesizing in neurobiology. In particular, he notes that damage confined to V1 results in a very severe perceptual impairment in which patients are unable to copy even simple letter and forms. In contrast, damage to prestriate visual areas but sparing V1 results in preserved ability to recognize local form elements together with impairment in the recognition of global forms. This suggests that the apperceptive-associative distinction may be more usefully interpreted within the framework of different domains of visual perception, an idea embodied in his preference for Hughlings-Jackson's term *imperception* to the term *agnosia,* with its connotations of separation between perception and knowledge. Zeki also has speculated that reentrant connections from more central visual areas back to V1 play a critical role in normal visual recognition.

There have been several reports of people whose vision has been restored in adulthood after onset of blindness in early life. Sacks has described one such patient, Virgil, whose vision was restored at age 50 after 45 years of blindness. With the restoration of sight, Sacks's patient, and others like him, exhibited symptoms similar to the impairments seen in visual agnosia. These impairments are not seen after restoration of sight following blindness that began in adulthood, however, emphasizing the importance of early visual experience for normal visual recognition.

CHAPTER 9

Voluntary Action

VOLUNTARY MOVEMENT

THE COMPONENTS OF VOLUNTARY MOVEMENT
  Dimensions of Regulation of Movement
  Levels of Regulation of Movement

ELEMENTARY DISORDERS OF MOVEMENT

AN OVERVIEW OF HIGHER-ORDER CONTROL
  OF MOVEMENT

THE MOTOR CORTEX
  Defining the Motor Cortex
  Characteristics of Single Neurons in M1
  How M1 Neurons Code Movement
  Sensory Input to M1 Neurons

THE PREMOTOR AND SUPPLEMENTARY
  MOTOR AREAS
  Anatomical Considerations
  Stimulation and Lesion Studies
  Neuroimaging Evidence of Area 6's Role
    in Planning Movement Sequences
  Single Cell Recording

THE CEREBELLUM
  Anatomical Considerations
  Lesion Studies

THE BASAL GANGLIA
  Anatomical Considerations
  The Effects of Basal Ganglia Lesions
  The Contribution of the Basal Ganglia
    to Movement

APRAXIA AND THE LEFT PARIETAL CORTEX
  Early Conceptualizations of Apraxia
  Liepmann's Classification of the Apraxias
  A More Theoretically Neutral Approach to Apraxia
  The Role of the Left Hemisphere in the Control
    of Voluntary Movement

OTHER MOVEMENT-RELATED FUNCTIONS
  OF PARIETAL CORTEX

THE PREFRONTAL CORTEX

SUMMARY

Late in his life, the 20th-century French composer Maurice Ravel, the creator of marvelously original impressionistic music and one of the most brilliant orchestrators in the history of Western music, began to experience symptoms of a brain tumor that eventually killed him. He describes awakening one morning and finding to his distress that he had forgotten how to tie his necktie. It wasn't that he had lost the strength or dexterity necessary to perform the individual component movements; rather, it seemed that he had forgotten the sequence of movements, so often performed in the past, necessary to accomplish the task. He had, strangely, forgotten what to do. This symptom picture, which so frightened Ravel, is an example of a disorder termed

*apraxia. Although there are different types, **apraxia** can generally be defined as a disorder of learned movement not due to peripheral paralysis, weakness, loss of dexterity, sensory loss, or the effects of other impairments such as aphasia, dementia, or a psychiatric disorder. In other words, apraxia is a disorder of the execution of complex*

movements, which are generally termed voluntary, in the absence of primary motor or sensory impairment, general intellectual impairment, or a psychiatric disorder. We will have more to say about apraxia in subsequent sections of this chapter.

VOLUNTARY MOVEMENT

The use of the term *voluntary* is intended to differentiate these movements from reflexive or automatic movements that the person does not intend. For the present we will sidestep the fascinating and thorny question of how volitional behavior, free will, is possible in a biophysical system that we assume obeys all the laws of physics and chemistry in a deterministic way. Put differently, How, if our behavior is the result of brain activity and that brain activity obeys physical laws, can we decide anything freely? We will consider this issue, one of the most exciting and baffling in brain science, in the epilogue of this book. For the present, we will conceptualize voluntary behavior as those behaviors that, not automatic or reflexive, are relatively complex responses of the organism to external or internal variables and that, at least in humans, seem to be the result of decisions or plans.

On reflection, it will be seen that this is a vast topic. In fact, each of the systems that are discussed in the separate chapters of this book ultimately compels us to consider the functioning of the whole brain. It is as if each system is a gate through which we can enter into partially explored domains of the brain. Ultimately each gate leads us to the same territory but through different routes. This is one reason why investigators who seem at first sight to have chosen a narrow area of focus immediately find themselves facing some fundamental problems and find the fruits of their investigations to be highly related to those of investigators in seemingly distant areas. This is true for all systems, but it is particularly clear in the case of movement. Perceptual and cognitive systems would be of little use if their processing were not finally manifested in behavior. It might thus be argued that the organization and mediation

of movement, in the context of the organism's external and internal environment (as remembered, currently experienced, and anticipated), is the final product—one is tempted to be teleological and say goal—of all brain systems. Let's then, following our earlier metaphor, enter the domain of the brain through this gate.

THE COMPONENTS OF VOLUNTARY MOVEMENT

The complex planned movements shaped to the external or internal environment, which are our focus here, contrast markedly with spinal and brain-stem reflexes. The latter, remarkable in their own way, are, of course, highly useful for the organism. They are rapid and inflexible responses to environmental stimuli, and these attributes make them highly adaptive in situations where such responses are required, such as maintaining a standing posture on a slippery surface or extending one's arms to break a fall. Yet these characteristics, so adaptive in emergency situations, are obviously an enormous disadvantage when dealing with even minimally complex environments over time. Here, planning (the ability to anticipate future events) and flexibility (the ability to modify ongoing and planned behavior) are crucial. These requirements are particularly important for humans, with our enormously complex external environments and our at-least-equally-complex internal constellations of motivations, desires, and goals.

Dimensions of Regulation of Movement

Adaptive higher-order control of movement may be thought of as having two components: content and timing. One must have knowledge of the required movement and the ability to organize that knowledge into performance, and one must decide when to engage in a particular movement or movement sequence and when not to. In other words, knowledge of both how and when is required for the adaptive execution of complex movement (Heilman & Watson, 1991).

Levels of Regulation of Movement

Cutting across these two dimensions are three others: the execution, tactics, and strategy of movement. The final neural events leading to a movement are the stimulation of muscle by motor neurons whose cell bodies are in the spinal cord or brain stem. The pioneering physiologist Charles Sherrington called this the final common pathway, the direct and immediate cause of all muscle contraction. But a given movement, if it is at all complex, requires the highly organized activation of a specific set of muscles in a specific temporal sequence that takes account of the specific features of the environment. It also requires the simultaneous inhibition of opposing muscles. We can refer to this level of the organization of movement as the tactics of movement. The motor cortex, premotor area, supplementary motor area, and the cerebellum, all of which we discuss in the following sections, are major mediators of the tactics of movement.

The sequential and combined activation of specific movements over time to form meaningful, goal-directed actions constitutes the highest level in the hierarchical control of movement: the strategic control of movement. This involves the planning, timing, and monitoring of movement within the context of varying environmental and internal contexts. The time frame for this control varies considerably. In the short term it involves such actions as opening a can of tomatoes and then pouring its contents into a bowl. This, in turn, requires the evocation of stored patterns of movement (or, in computer terminology, the readout of a program) related to the activity of opening a can, pouring, and so forth. Areas in the left parietal lobe are critical for the storage of these motor programs, and disruptions in the execution of these programs manifest themselves in the form of apraxias such as that experienced by the composer Ravel. Of course, the successful execution of stored motor

programs also requires ongoing tactical adjustment to take account of the parameters of the specific situation: the size of the can, the type of can opener, the size of the bowl, and so on.

In contrast, long-term strategies of movement involve the control of movement within broader contexts. To use our current example, this would involve mediating the execution of the can opening and pouring sequence (together with other related actions) at a specific time in a particular recipe for creating a marinara sauce, taking into account the overall process of preparing the sauce and the entire meal. On reflection, it is apparent that the breadth of the context in which one considers movement strategies depends on one's perspective. A whole constellation of internal goals, desires, and plans, together with a multitude of external circumstances in the past, present, and anticipated future, may contribute to the act of creating this sauce at a particular time and place and within a particular social and interpersonal context.

In this chapter we are most concerned with (a) the tactics of movement, a level of control involving the motor cortex, the premotor and supplementary motor areas, and the cerebellum, and with (b) short-term strategies of movement, involving the basal ganglia, the posterior parietal cortex, and the prefrontal cortex. After a brief discussion of elementary disorders of movement and an overview of the higher-order control of movement, we will consider the contribution of each of these structures in more detail. In chapter 12 we consider further the role of prefrontal cortex in the organization of long-term action.

ELEMENTARY DISORDERS OF MOVEMENT

Abnormality of the motor system at any level will lead to impairment. The most severe and absolute impairments manifest themselves as paralysis and follow lesions of peripheral levels of the system. These include disorders directly affecting muscle (e.g., muscular dystrophy), the neurotransmitter link between motor neuron and muscle (e.g., myasthenia gravis), and the peripheral motor neuron or its cell body in the anterior horn of the spinal cord (e.g., poliomyelitis). In addition, it is well known that car crashes and other trauma often result in injury to the

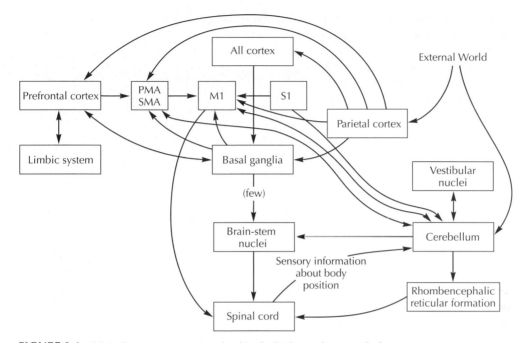

FIGURE 9.1 Major brain structures involved in the higher-order control of movement and their anatomical interconnections: *SMA,* supplementary motor area; *PMA,* premotor area; *M1,* primary motor cortex; *S1,* somatosensory cortex. (Efferents from basal ganglia to cortex and from cerebellum to cortex are via the thalamus.)

spinal cord and its motor pathways, resulting in a profound paralysis of parts of the body innervated by regions of the spinal cord distal to the injury. Depending on the level at which the spinal cord is damaged, paralysis may involve only the lower limbs (**paraplegia**) or all four limbs (**quadriplegia**).

AN OVERVIEW OF HIGHER-ORDER CONTROL OF MOVEMENT

In contrast to the profound impairments that result from lesions of the peripheral components of the motor system, the impairments that result from damage to higher levels of the motor system are complicated and multifaceted. Before going further, let's state what these higher levels are. As we have noted, it can be argued with justification that the entire brain is involved in movement, that movement is the final product of all the other perceptual, cognitive, and affective processes of the brain. Thus, every

brain structure is ultimately involved in the programming and control of movement (Nauta & Feirtag, 1986, p. 92), and it would be more correct to speak of a sensorimotor system or of some elaborately named and multiply hyphenated system whose label reflects the integration of movement with all other higher brain processes.

A physiological manifestation of this perspective is the fact that almost all areas of cortex, as well as many subcortical regions, will, when stimulated, elicit movement. Nevertheless, there are specific cerebral regions that are involved to a greater extent than others in higher-order voluntary movement. These regions include the **motor cortex (M1),** the **premotor area (PMA),** the **supplementary motor area (SMA),** the **somatosensory area (S1),** the **cerebellum,** the **basal ganglia,** the **parietal lobes** (particularly in the dominant hemisphere), and the **prefrontal cortex.** Let's consider the role of each of these areas in the higher control of movement.

Figure 9.1 shows the major structures involved in the higher-order control of movement; their major interconnections; and their connections with limbic structures, brain-stem nuclei, and the spinal cord. Parietal-lobe structures provide sensory information to frontal cortex, where long-term movement strategies are planned and where ongoing motor execution is monitored and, when necessary, maintained or revised in response to feedback regarding its effectiveness. Frontal cortex is also closely linked with limbic structures, thus enabling long-term strategies to be influenced by emotional processing. All cortical areas, including frontal cortex, project to the basal ganglia, which in turn project, via the thalamus, to prefrontal cortex, the premotor area, the supplementary motor area, and the motor cortex. This cortical-cortical loop mediated by the basal ganglia thus provides an anatomical route whereby the activity of wide areas of cortex can be funneled to areas of the cortex most directly involved with movement. These areas—PMA, SMA, and M1—prepare lower centers for the execution of specific movements by organizing the tactical aspects of movement.

The cerebellum is reciprocally linked with the PMA, SMA, and M1. In addition, it receives extensive sensory input (particularly vestibular, proprioceptive, and kinesthetic) that signals the position of the body in space. The cerebellum is thus in a position to serve as a comparator, comparing the motor commands mediated by M1 with the actual movement of the organism. It is also in a position, via its efferent links with cortical motor areas, to make adjustments to motor commands based on information about actual movement. The cerebellum also adjusts peripheral motor output by influencing brain-stem and spinal motor centers.

The posterior parietal cortex, in addition to its sensory function, has an area in the left hemisphere specialized for the representation of learned movement sequences. Damage to this area, or to connections from it to other areas involved in motor function, results in the disturbances in the reproduction of learned motor sequences known as the apraxias. Now that we've looked at this general schema of the neural control of motor function, let's consider each aspect in more detail.

THE MOTOR CORTEX

Defining the Motor Cortex

Many areas of the cortex contribute to movement. This is exemplified by the fact that the stimulation of widespread areas of cortex results in movement and that fibers in the corticospinal tract originate from diverse areas of cortex. The designation of the precentral gyrus as the primary motor cortex, or M1, is thus somewhat arbitrary. Nevertheless, the precentral gyrus has the lowest threshold for stimulation-elicited movement, indicating that its connections with motor neurons are more numerous and direct than are those of other areas of cortex. In addition, M1 contains a highly organized topographical representation of the body, as revealed by stimulation and lesion studies in animals. In humans, this was dramatically demonstrated by the stimulation studies of the neurosurgeon Wilder Penfield (Penfield & Rasmussen, 1950; Penfield & Roberts, 1959).

Characteristics of Single Neurons in M1

For a time it was thought that activity of an individual pyramidal cell in M1 caused movement of a specific muscle. Now it is clear that pyramidal cells drive groups of muscles so that a limb moves toward a desired goal. This means that pyramidal cells in M1 code movement, not individual-muscle contraction. Evidence for this comes from studies showing that stimulation of specific areas of M1 frequently leads to the coordinated movement of a limb toward a desired goal rather than to isolated muscle contractions. Studies of single-neuron activity in M1 in awake monkeys trained to perform simple tasks have revealed evidence consistent with this. In these studies it was found that different populations of neurons are active during flexion and extension of the same muscle.

Of particular importance for an understanding of the function of M1 is the finding that M1 neurons change their activity *before* as well as during the contraction of the muscles that they affect. This is illustrated in an experiment by Edward Evarts (1979) in which monkeys were trained to keep a handle in a

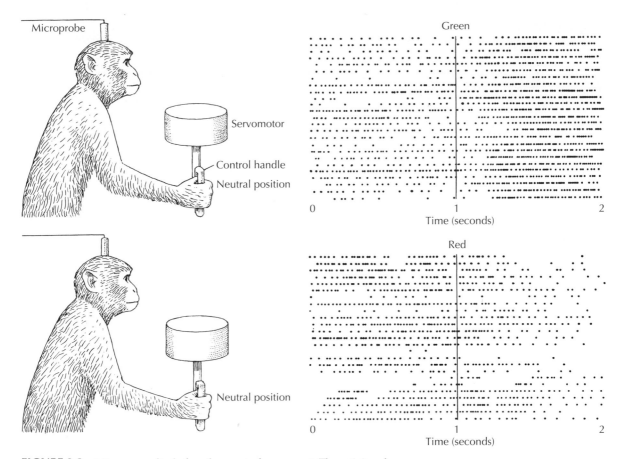

FIGURE 9.2   M1 neurons fire before the onset of movement. The activity of one neuron in M1 recorded for 1 second before and 1 second after the flashing of a signal light. The green signal light indicated that the monkey was to push the handle at some indefinite future time (signaled by a second stimulus), and the red light signaled that the monkey was to pull the handle. Each horizontal row of dots is a record of the activity of the neuron over one trial. The total record, termed a raster, indicates that the firing rate of the neuron increases before an anticipated push, relative to its frequency before the appearance of the signal light *(top)* and decreases prior to an anticipated pull *(bottom)*. *(From Evarts, 1979, p. 103)*

neutral position. If a green light was illuminated, this signaled that the animal should be prepared to push the handle when a second stimulus appeared. If a red light was illuminated, the monkey was to prepare to pull the handle. Figure 9.2 shows that preparing to pull and preparing to push produced different responses in an M1 neuron *before* any actual movement took place. In an extension of this experiment (Figure 9.3), Evarts showed that the activity of M1 neurons changed when actual movement took place. In addition, he found that this activity varied depending on whether the movement was reflex (performed as a response to a mechanical movement of the handle) or voluntary (performed in accordance with the anticipatory signal). Taken together, these findings suggest that neurons in M1 are involved both in preparation for voluntary movement and in its execution.

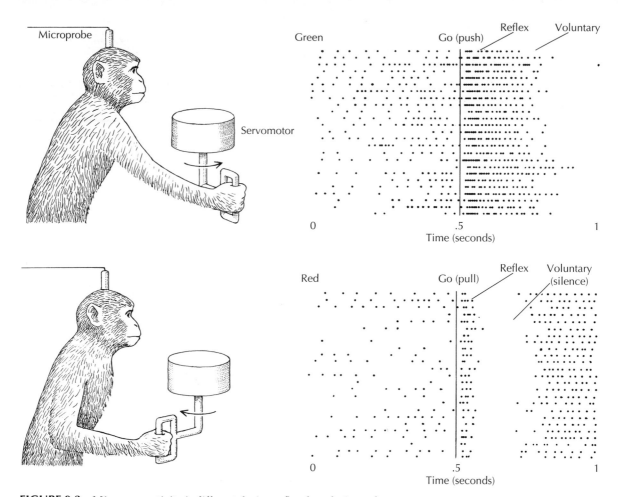

FIGURE 9.3   M1 neuron activity is different during reflex than during voluntary movement. In a variation of the previous experiment, the activity of a single M1 neuron is again recorded over many trials. From 1 to 5 seconds after the appearance of the signal light, a go signal, in the form of a motor displacement of the handle, occurred. The activity of the single neuron was recorded during the 0.5 second before and the 0.5 second after the handle displacement. When the signal light was green (push), the handle displacement was toward the monkey so that it elicited a reflex push *(top)*. This is reflected in the high firing rate of the neuron immediately after the go signal. When the monkey then recovered and initiated a voluntary push, the firing of the neuron decreased somewhat, but the neuron continued to be more active than during the anticipatory period. The far-right section of the raster shows that the activity of the neuron decreased when the monkey was pulling the handle back to the starting position. The difference in activity between a reflex and a voluntary pull *(bottom)*. To the far right is the activity during the voluntary push back to the starting position. These records show that the activity of the neuron is different during reflex than during voluntary movement and during voluntary pushing versus voluntary pulling. *(From Evarts, 1979, p. 104)*

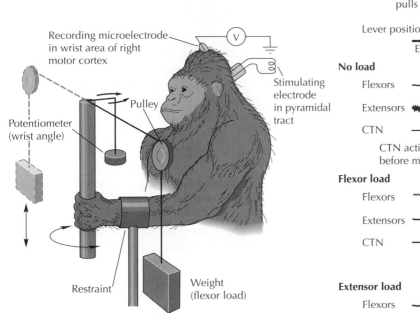
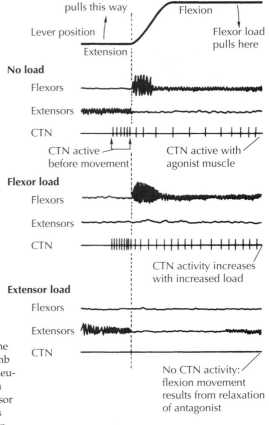

FIGURE 9.4 M1 neurons code force, not displacement. Using an apparatus that required a monkey to either flex or extend its wrist, the relationship between M1 neuron activity, muscle contraction, and limb displacement was studied. In this experiment the activity of an M1 neuron, which projects into the pyramidal tract *(CTN)* and is involved in the control of wrist flexion, and the activity of wrist flexor and extensor muscles are being recorded in the monkey. When the monkey moves from extension to flexion of the wrist with no load *(top)*, the neuron in the motor cortex begins firing before the flexor muscles contract. When a load opposing flexion (a flexor load) is applied, the M1 neuron fires more rapidly before the more intense excitation of the flexor muscles *(middle)*. When a load facilitating flexion (extensor load) is applied, so that relaxation of the extensors is sufficient for the required movement and no contraction of the flexors is needed, the same M1 neuron does not fire *(bottom)*. This shows that M1 neurons fire before the muscles that they innervate and that their rate of firing is related to the force exerted by the muscle rather than the displacement of the limb. *(From Kandel et al., 1995, p. 531)*

How M1 Neurons Code Movement

M1 neurons code both the force and the direction of movement. The firing rate of individual M1 neurons has been shown to code the force to be employed to move a limb rather than the actual displacement of the limb. Evidence for this comes from studies (e.g., Evarts, 1968) that have demonstrated that the activity of an M1 neuron involved in a given movement precedes the activation of the participating muscles. Furthermore, it was found that an M1 neuron's activity increases when a load that resists the movement is added and decreases when a load facilitating the movement is added (Figure 9.4).

A less obvious relationship exists between the activity of single neurons in M1 and direction of movement. It has been shown that cells in M1 fire at their maximum frequency prior to and during movement

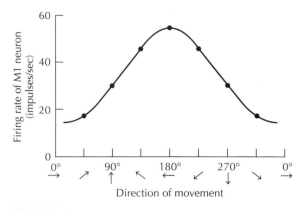

FIGURE 9.5   The tuning curve of an M1 neuron. A monkey is trained to move a handle in different directions in response to signal lights, and the activity of an M1 neuron is recorded. Each M1 neuron has a preferred direction, which is associated with its highest firing rate. Each cell also fires at a lower rate in association with a broad range of directions of movement. Plotting firing rate as a function of direction of movement yields a tuning curve such as that depicted in this figure. *(From Bear, Connors, & Paradiso, 1996, p. 393)*

in a particular direction. This is referred to as the cell's **preferred direction.** However, each cell also fires in association with movements over a wide range of directions. This range may be more than 90° (Figure 9.5). The range of movement over which an M1 neuron fires is referred to as that cell's **directional tuning.** Thus, while M1 neurons have a preferred direction, they also have a very broad directional tuning. This raises the question of how a single neuron in M1 could determine movement direction.

The answer appears to be that direction is not coded in M1 by single neurons but, rather, by ensembles of neurons (neuron populations). Evidence for this comes from the work of Apostolos Georgopoulos and his colleagues (1982) who, in one experiment, recorded simultaneously from approximately 200 M1 cells while a monkey made arm movements in different directions by moving a handle toward a small light. The investigators found that during an arm movement in a given direction a large number of M1 neurons were active, as one would expect given each neuron's broad directional tuning. They then represented the activity level of each neuron as a line of

varying length (depending on its level of activity) drawn in that cell's preferred direction (Figure 9.6). Each of these lines was termed the **direction vector** for that particular cell for movement in the given direction. If the sum of these individual direction vectors was then calculated, Georgopoulos and his colleagues found that the resulting **population vector** predicted the actual direction of movement made by the monkey. Thus, many neurons with many different preferred directions contribute to any given movement and that movement cannot be predicted by the activity of any single neuron. This mechanism of coding is a compelling example of distributed representation, representation embodied in the pattern of activity of a population of neurons, and is reminiscent of the massively parallel constraint-satisfaction models of visual object recognition discussed in chapter 8.

Although the significance of these patterns of neural activity for the control of movement is not completely understood, it is interesting to speculate about the adaptive advantage of this mechanism of encoding intended movement. Some precision of movement is probably sacrificed by a mechanism that codes movement in such a distributed representation rather than a mechanism in which there is a one-to-one mapping between individual specific neuron activity and direction of movement. Nevertheless, the "voting" process inherent in this distributed representation would seem to maximize the consistency or reliability of M1 output to the periphery because errors in the activation of one or even many neurons would have minimal impact on the population vector.

Sensory Input to M1 Neurons

We have repeatedly emphasized the close connection between motor and somatosensory processes. It makes sense that this should be the case because motor mechanisms must take information regarding current body position and movement into account to mediate effective future movement. There are a number of mechanisms whereby M1 receives such feedback, including input from the cerebellum. We will discuss this further in a later section. It is important to

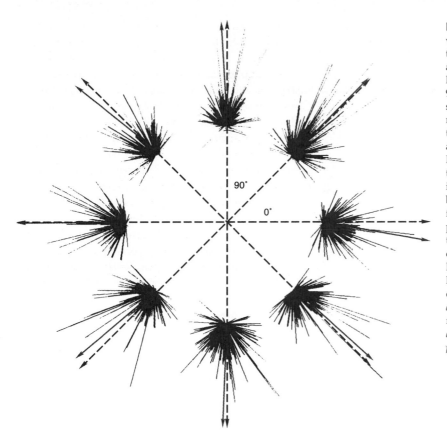

FIGURE 9.6 The population vector of M1 neurons predicts the direction of movement. In an experimental situation similar to that described in Figure 9.5, M1 neuron activity is measured in association with movements in different directions. In this experiment, however, the activity of approximately 200 M1 neurons is measured simultaneously. During a movement in a particular direction, a number of M1 neurons with different preferred directions (represented by the direction of the lines) are active to different degrees (represented by the length of the lines). The population vector of neurons active during a given movement *(solid arrows)* closely matches the direction of movement *(dashed arrows)*. *(From Kandel et al., 1995, p. 533)*

note, however, that M1 neurons also receive sensory input from the periphery via the somatosensory cortex. In fact, many M1 neurons actually have sensory receptive fields for tactile, proprioceptive, and kinesthetic information from specific parts of the body.

THE PREMOTOR AND SUPPLEMENTARY MOTOR AREAS

The premotor area (PMA) and the supplementary motor area (SMA) prepare the motor system for movement by playing a major role in the planning of goal-directed movement. Both are located in area 6 in the frontal lobes just anterior to M1, PMA on the lateral surface and SMA on the superior and medial surfaces (Figure 9.7). Penfield identified both in humans, again in the course of stimulation carried out

at the time of surgery. The two areas have been shown to be somatotopically organized.

Anatomical Considerations

The importance of area 6 for complex movement is suggested by an interspecies comparison of its size relative to body weight. Thus, whereas the ratio of the area of M1 to body weight is roughly constant across primate species, the ratio of the size of area 6 to body weight is six times larger in humans than in the macaque monkey. Area 6's anatomical connections also provide clues to its function (see Figure 9.7). It receives major input from posterior parietal cortex and from prefrontal cortex, and its major output is to M1. As we have already mentioned, posterior parietal cortex is extensively involved in sensory and perceptual

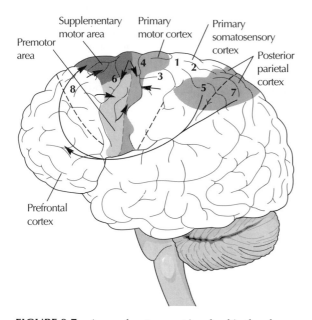

FIGURE 9.7   Areas of cortex most involved in the planning and organization of voluntary movement, and some of their major interconnections. The numbers refer to Brodmann's cytoarchitectonic areas. *(From Kandel et al., 1995, p. 534)*

processing. It is also important for storage and implementation of learned motor programs. Prefrontal cortex is involved in strategic planning of movement, processes that organize movement over time to bring it in line with the organism's goals. M1, as we have seen, is important in the preparation and execution of movement. Taken together, these anatomical considerations suggest that area 6 is at the interface between the areas of brain involved in organizing planned programs of movement to meet goals and the cortical area most directly involved in the execution of movement, M1.

Stimulation and Lesion Studies

The effect of stimulation of area 6 is the coordinated contraction of muscles at more than one joint. In addition, SMA stimulation often evokes movement on both sides of the body. These movements are different from those resulting from stimulation of M1 neurons, the latter often resulting in movement at only one joint and requiring smaller stimulus currents. This suggests that area 6 is involved in the organization of relatively complex movement sequences.

A comparison of the effect of lesions to area 6 and M1 supports this conclusion. Whereas lesions to M1 result in severe weakness and loss of fine-motor coordination, lesions to area 6 impair the ability to implement appropriate sequences of movement without impairment in the execution of simple individual movements. An example of this is the impairment in the production of sequences of phonemes (to form words) together with preserved ability to produce individual phonemes that is characteristic of Broca's aphasia. It will be noted that Broca's area is actually the region of PMA just anterior to the region of M1 mediating the movements necessary for vocalization.

Another example of the effect of PMA lesions on movement comes from experiments with monkeys. Consider a monkey with a lesion of PMA confronted with the situation depicted in Figure 9.8. Food is placed behind a transparent Plexiglas sheet; to obtain the food, the monkey cannot reach directly for it but must reach through an opening to the side. Normal monkeys have no difficulty organizing the sequence of movements necessary to reach through the opening and obtain the food. In contrast, monkeys with lesions of PMA tend to attempt to reach directly for the food, although the Plexiglas barrier prevents them from obtaining it. They are unable to organize the required sequence of movements.

A consideration of the effects of lesions to M1 provides some clues to the mechanism whereby area 6 influences movement. As we have noted, M1 lesions seriously disrupt movement of distal muscles, such as those of the fingers and hand. Thus a person with **hemiparesis** after an M1 lesion will have difficulty with fine-motor behavior such as grasping a cup or writing. In contrast, M1 lesions have minimal impact on axial and proximal musculature; the same patients who cannot grasp a cup handle are able to orient their body or direct their arm in a desired direction. This suggests that although area 6 influences distal muscles via M1, it organizes movements involving proximal muscles and axial muscles via direct projections to regions of the spinal cord controlling these muscles. Proximal and axial muscles

FIGURE 9.8   Experimental situation in which a monkey is unable to obtain food that is placed behind a Plexiglas shield by reaching directly for it but must, instead, reach around through an opening that is not adjacent to the food. Monkeys with PMA lesions are unable to organize the sequence of movements necessary for this task.

are particularly important in mediating the initial phases of action involving orienting the body and arm toward a target. It would seem that area 6 has a particularly important role in this phase of movement.

Neuroimaging Evidence of Area 6's Role in Planning Movement Sequences

A study by Per Roland and his colleagues (1980) compared rCBF while normal subjects were performing either a simple task that did not require sequential movements or a complex sequence of movements. The simple task, involving pressing a finger against a spring, revealed increased activity in M1 and in S1 (the primary somatosensory cortex). In contrast, during the complex task, which involved a complex sequence of finger movements, activation extended into SMA. Interestingly, in a third condition in which subjects mentally rehearsed the finger sequence but did not make any actual movement, SMA but not M1 showed activation (Figure 9.9). Taken together, these findings are consistent with other evidence that SMA is specifically involved in the planning and program-

(A)

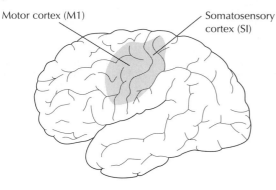

(B)

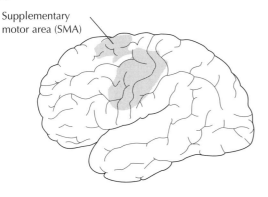

(C)

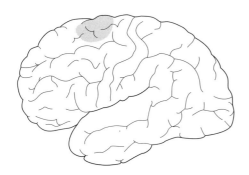

FIGURE 9.9 Regional increases in cerebral blood flow during *(A)* the performance of simple finger flexion, *(B)* the performance of a complex finger movement sequence, and *(C)* mental rehearsal of the same complex finger movement sequence. In condition A only M1 and S1 show increased activity. In condition B the increase also includes SMA. In condition C, only the SMA shows increased activity. *(From Kandel et al., 1995, p. 535)*

ming of movement sequences in distal musculature but is not directly involved in the immediate execution of such movements.

Single Cell Recording

Single unit recording studies add support to the notion that PMA plays a role in planning and preparing for specific movements. In one study (Weinrich & Weis, 1982) a monkey sat in front of four square panels, each of which could be illuminated. Below each panel was a smaller light (Figure 9.10). The monkey began each trial with his hand on one of the square panels. One of the other square panels was then illuminated, signaling to the monkey that this would be the location of his next movement (*instruction stimulus*). The monkey was not to actually make the movement, however, until the small light below the panel was illuminated (*trigger stimulus*). Thus, between the onset of the instruction stimulus and the appearance of the trigger stimulus, the animal does not move but has information regarding the direction of his next movement. Recording in PMA revealed neurons that increased their activity at the onset of the instruction stimulus but returned to baseline immediately after the onset of the trigger stimulus. Furthermore, specific PMA neurons were found to increase their activity only when the anticipated movement was to be made in one direction (say, left) but not in the opposite direction (see Figure 9.10).

We do not yet know the details of how preparation for movement is coded in PMA and SMA. However, the finding that cells in these areas are selectively active before movements are executed and that their activity is contingent on the direction of the anticipated movement lends support to the notion that these areas are involved in the preparation and planning of movement.

THE CEREBELLUM

The cerebellum does not directly initiate voluntary movement. Nevertheless, it does indirectly regulate movement by adjusting the output of the major cortical motor systems (M1, PMA, and SMA) and by

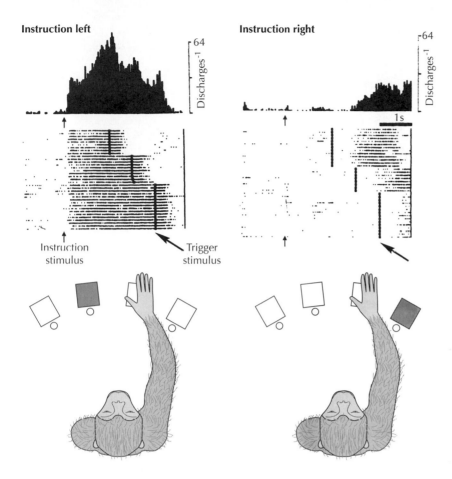

Instruction left

Instruction right

Discharges⁻¹ 64

Discharges⁻¹ 64

1 s

Instruction stimulus

Trigger stimulus

FIGURE 9.10   Neurons in PMA are active during preparation for specific movement but not during the actual movement. The raster on the left shows that the PMA neuron being monitored is active during the interval between the onset of the instruction stimulus (large illuminated square), which in this case informs the monkey that he is to move to the left, and the onset of the trigger stimulus (small illuminated circle), which indicates that the animal is to actually perform the movement. It is not, however, active during the movement itself. Each horizontal line is a single trial, and each dot indicates firing of the neuron. Because the interval between instruction stimulus and trigger stimulus varied, trials were grouped according to interval length. The raster on the right shows that this particular neuron is not active in preparation for movement to the right. *(From Kandel et al., 1995, p. 537)*

influencing brain-stem nuclei and the rhomben-cephalic reticular formation.

Anatomical Considerations

The anatomical interconnections between the cerebellum and the rest of the brain are consistent with a regulatory function for this very large and complicated structure. Afferent connections to the cerebellum include input from all sensory modalities, except, probably, taste and olfaction. This input is mainly through secondary sensory neurons, although the cerebellum receives some input from primary sensory neurons of the vestibular system. It also receives input from areas of cortex involved

in sensory-motor function, particularly M1 and S1. Cerebellar efferents project to the vestibular nuclei, to many brain-stem nuclei, and to the rhomb-encephalic reticular formation. The cerebellum also projects to the ventromedial nucleus of the thalamus, which, in turn, projects to M1, PMA, and SMA. The cerebellum thus receives information about intended movement (from cortical motor areas) and actual movement (from peripheral sensory receptors) and is therefore in a position to compare the two. Its output back to cortical motor areas provides a mechanism for readjusting cortical motor programs, and its connections with brain-stem nuclei and the rhomb-encephalic reticular formation provide an additional mechanism for refining output from higher motor centers (see Figure 9.1).

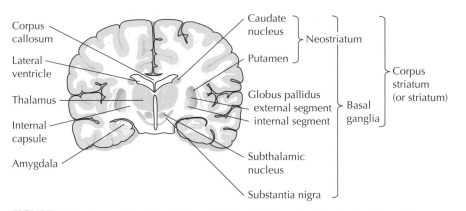

FIGURE 9.11   A coronal section of the cerebral hemispheres showing the basal ganglia.
(From Kandel et al., 1995, p. 545

Lesion Studies

The effect of cerebellar lesions provides evidence consistent with the comparator function suggested by the anatomical connections we have just considered. Thus, consistent with the absence of direct connections between cerebellum and motor neuron pools in the spinal cord, cerebellar lesions do not produce paralysis. Instead, cerebellar lesions produce disturbance of limb-eye coordination, impaired balance, and decreased muscle tone.

An example of impaired limb-eye coordination following cerebellar lesions is elicited by asking patients to extend their arm at full length in front of them and then move their arm so that they touch their nose with their forefinger. This task requires the coordinated and concurrent movement of the shoulder, elbow, wrist, and finger. Patients with cerebellar lesions have difficulty reaching the target, an impairment termed **dysmetria.** The required muscles are activated but not in a coordinated synergistic manner. The result is a decomposition of what normally would be a coordinated movement into individual components, a disorder termed **dyssynergia.** These impairments may be seen in many muscle groups, including those mediating posture and walking. Thus, cerebellar lesions frequently manifest themselves in a kind of general clumsiness, a disturbance termed **cerebellar ataxia** (*a*, "without" + *taxia*, "order"). The cerebellum is particularly sensitive to the effects of alcohol, and many of the tests used to assess alcohol in-

toxication, such as walking a straight line, are probes for the presence of cerebellar ataxia.

THE BASAL GANGLIA

The basal ganglia traditionally include the **caudate nucleus,** the **putamen,** and the **globus pallidus.** The caudate and the putamen have similar cell structures and may be considered one structure that is separated by the internal capsule. This separation is not complete; there are cell bridges connecting the two structures. They are therefore collectively termed the **neostriatum.** The globus pallidus has two parts, the **external segment** and the **internal segment.** The **substantia nigra** and the **subthalamic nucleus** are often also included as part of the basal ganglia (Figure 9.11).

Anatomical Considerations

DIFFERENCES BETWEEN THE CEREBELLUM-CORTEX LOOP AND THE BASAL GANGLIA–CORTEX LOOP

Like the cerebellum, the basal ganglia are part of a cortical-subcortical-cortical loop that influences motor functioning indirectly. However, there are some major differences in the connections formed by these two looping systems that parallel differences in their contribution to movement. First, as we have seen, the cerebellum receives most of its cortical input from M1, PMA, and SMA, areas intimately involved in movement. In contrast, the neostriatum, the destination of afferents to the basal ganglia from the cortex, receives input from all areas of the cortex. Second, whereas the cerebellum projects back to those areas of cortex specialized for movement from which it received input, basal ganglia efferents to the cortex, emerging from the globus pallidus, project more widely to include prefrontal cortex as well as the more specialized cortical motor areas. Finally, it will be recalled that the cerebellum receives input from secondary sensory neurons, including those in the spinal cord, and projects to brain-stem nuclei and the reticular formation, which in turn form efferent connections with spinal cord structures. In contrast, the basal ganglia receive no direct input from the spinal cord and have very few efferents to those brain-stem nuclei that eventually form efferent connections with motor areas of the spinal cord. In fact, the midbrain reticular formation is the lowest structure to which the basal ganglia send direct projections. These differences are summarized in Figure 9.12.

BASAL GANGLIA CIRCUITRY   Figure 9.13 shows a simplified account of the circuitry of the basal ganglia. Neurons from cortex form excitatory connections with neurons in the neostriatum (caudate and putamen). These neurons, in turn, form inhibitory connections with neurons in the internal segment of the globus pallidus, which then form inhibitory connections with neurons in the **ventrolateral nucleus of the thalamus (VL).** These then form excitatory connections with neurons in the SMA, PMA, and prefrontal cortex. In addition, neurons projecting from the subthalamic nucleus form excitatory connections with neurons in the internal segment of the globus pallidus. Further, neurons from the substantia nigra form excitatory connections with neurons in the neostriatum. This wiring diagram should aid understanding of the diverse range of disorders that follow lesions to the basal ganglia.

The Effects of Basal Ganglia Lesions

PARKINSON'S DISEASE   Parkinson's disease is characterized by **hypokinesia** (diminished movement), **bradykinesia** (slowed movement), or even **aki-**

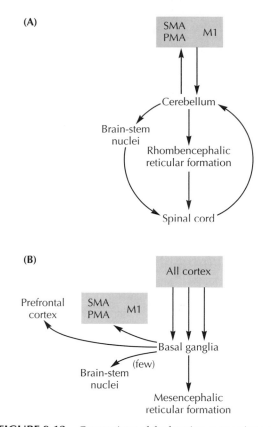

FIGURE 9.12   Comparison of the looping connections of *(A)* the cerebellum and *(B)* the basal ganglia: *SMA*, supplementary motor area; *PMA*, premotor area; *M1*, motor cortex. These connections suggest that the cerebellum is most intimately involved with areas of cortex, brain stem, and spinal cord directly involved with movement. In contrast, the basal ganglia have reciprocal connections with more diverse areas of cortex and less direct connections with lower motor and sensory areas, suggesting that their role in the control of movement is more directly related to processing at the cortical level. (Cerebellar efferents to cortex and basal ganglia efferents to cortex relay through the thalamus.)

nesia (absence of movement). **Cogwheel rigidity** (so-called because of the impression made when the patient's limbs are moved passively) and **resting tremor** are also seen. Parkinson's disease is associated with deterioration of dopamine-producing cells in the substantia nigra.

A consideration of our wiring diagram (see Figure 9.13) will provide a basis for understanding why this deterioration should produce a disorder charac-

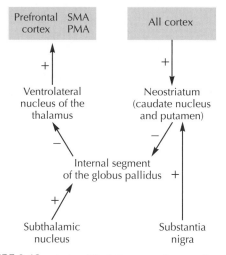

FIGURE 9.13   A simplified diagram of connections between different basal ganglia structures. The plus signs indicate excitatory connections, and the minus signs indicate inhibitory connections. *(From Banich, 1997, p. 140)*

terized by poverty of movement. Neurons in the substantia nigra project (via the **nigrostriatal bundle**) to the neostriatum, where they form excitatory connections. Diminished input from the substantia nigra in Parkinson's disease thus reduces the inhibitory effect of striatal neurons on neurons of the globus pallidus. This, in turn, increases the latter's inhibitory effect on neurons in the VL nucleus of the thalamus, which, in turn, reduces the firing rate of neurons in SMA and PMA, thereby producing hypokinesia.

HUNTINGTON'S DISEASE   In contrast to Parkinson's disease, some disorders following basal ganglia lesions are characterized not by hypokinesia but by the occurrence of **hyperkinesia,** unintended and unwanted movement. One such disorder is Huntington's disease. This disorder includes **chorea** (uncontrolled twitching) and **athetosis** (involuntary writhing and posturing of the body). Huntington's disease also involves dysfunction of the caudate and putamen, but in different regions than that affected in Parkinson's disease. One theory of the mechanism of Huntington's disease (Albin, Young, & Penney, 1989) is that the affected region of the caudate contains cells that,

through a series of synapses, normally exert an excitatory effect on neurons of the internal segment of the globus pallidus. The diminished activity of these striatal neurons thus reduces the inhibitory output of the globus pallidus on the VL nucleus of the thalamus, resulting in a dysfunctional hyperactivity of the VL nucleus and, in turn, of cortical motor regions.

BALLISM   Another hyperkinetic disorder, **ballism** is characterized by involuntary, violent flinging movements of the extremities. Often only one side of the body is involved, a condition known as **hemiballism.** This disorder is associated with lesions of the subthalamic nucleus. Because the subthalamic nucleus exerts an excitatory effect on the internal segment of the globus pallidus, its hypoactivity results in decreased inhibitory input by the globus pallidus on the VL nucleus. This, in turn, results in hyperactivity of cortical motor areas.

The Contribution of the Basal Ganglia to Movement

Although current understanding of the contribution of the basal ganglia to normal movement is incomplete, some intriguing hypotheses begin to emerge from a consideration of the effects of lesions to these structures. The hypokinesia (or, in extreme cases, even akinesia) of Parkinson's disease suggests that the loop involving the basal ganglia and the cortex is critically involved in the initiation of willed (intended) movements. Supporting the selective importance of this loop in specifically intentional movement is the striking finding that stimulus-triggered movement, such as catching a thrown ball, is generally preserved in parkinsonian disorders.

In this connection, it would appear that the basal ganglia serve to funnel widespread cortical activity into cortical areas more directly involved in the execution of movement (PMA, SMA, and M1). From this perspective one might speculate that one prerequisite for the execution of intentional movement is the activation of SMA and PMA beyond some threshold level by the cortical activity being funneled to these areas by the basal ganglia. But basal ganglia lesions do not result only in parkinsonian hypokinesia. We have also seen that in Huntington's disease and ballism they cause unwanted movements. This suggests that the basal ganglia loop also serves a kind of filtering function, selecting some movements and inhibiting others. Finally, as will be discussed at greater length in chapters 10 and 13, it is clear that the function of the basal ganglia is not confined to the motor sphere. These structures are involved in certain forms of memory, learning, and other aspects of cognition.

We have seen that a number of different neural structures participate in voluntary movement. We turn now to a group of disorders in which the problem is the execution of learned movements and movement sequences, disorders termed apraxia. In the example of Maurice Ravel, which began this chapter, we saw how debilitating and frightening these disorders can be. Let's now examine them in greater detail.

APRAXIA AND THE LEFT PARIETAL CORTEX

Early Conceptualizations of Apraxia

In 1870 John Hughlings-Jackson described a case of a patient who had difficulty making various oral and thoracic movements—such as coughing, protruding the tongue, and opening the mouth—to verbal command (Hughlings-Jackson, 1870/1932). It was clear that there was no paralysis of the muscles involved in these movements because the same actions could be carried out spontaneously in the course of normal daily activity. The following year, Steinthal (cited by Hecaen & Rondot, 1985) coined the term *apraxia* to describe a disorder of movement not due to primary motor or sensory impairment, although he did not explicitly distinguish apraxia as a disorder of action qualitatively different from a disorder of object recognition. It was Hugo Liepmann who made the first systematic investigation of apraxia and who first attempted to formulate a theoretical basis for it. In his seminal 1900 paper, Liepmann described a patient, known as M. T., who had no elementary motor dysfunction and yet was unable to make simple hand postures or to perform pantomimes with his right hand. He was, however, able to respond normally to

commands to make whole-body movements, such as assuming the pose of a boxer or walking to the other side of the room. Curiously, he was less impaired in the performance of actions produced by the left hand. It has been argued (Rothi & Heilman, 1996) that the most important contribution of this early case study was to more precisely characterize apraxia as a disorder of purposeful movement not explained by primary motor dysfunction or impairment in object recognition. In addition, Liepmann's demonstration that cerebral lesions can result in a specific disruption of planned, purposeful movement indicated that such movement has a localized cerebral representation, a notion that Liepmann conceptualized in terms of **movement formulas** contained in the left hemisphere.

Liepmann further developed his conceptualization of apraxia in his 1905 paper, the first large group study conducted in neuropsychology, in which he studied 83 patients with either left- or right-hemisphere lesions. He observed impairment in imitating gestures, pantomime of transitive actions (actions involving an object, e.g., opening a door), pantomime of intransitive gestures (actions without an object, e.g., saluting or waving good-bye), and actual object use. Three findings that are central to current understandings of apraxia emerged from this study. First, it clearly established apraxia as a distinct clinical entity, different from other higher-order impairments such as agnosia and aphasia. Second, whereas 20 of the 41 patients studied by Liepmann with left-hemisphere lesions were apraxic when tested with their nonparetic (left) hand, none of the 42 right-hemisphere patients was found to be apraxic. This finding, which has been confirmed by subsequent studies (e.g., Kimura & Archibald, 1974) indicates that the left hemisphere is specialized for the mediation of voluntary movement.

A third important finding of Liepmann was that a comparison of patients with apraxia revealed considerable variability of symptom picture. For example, some patients who were able to make simple movements, such as those involved in pouring water from a kettle into a cup, were impaired in performing a goal-directed series or sequence of movements, such

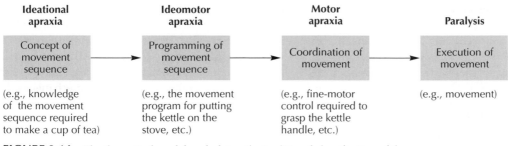

Ideational apraxia	Ideomotor apraxia	Motor apraxia	Paralysis
Concept of movement sequence	Programming of movement sequence	Coordination of movement	Execution of movement
(e.g., knowledge of the movement sequence required to make a cup of tea)	(e.g., the movement program for putting the kettle on the stove, etc.)	(e.g., fine-motor control required to grasp the kettle handle, etc.)	(e.g., movement)

FIGURE 9.14   The theoretical model underlying the traditional classification of the apraxias. The boxes represent the stages of processing involved in voluntary action according to this model. Shown above each stage is the disorder resulting from its disruption.

as those involved in making a cup of tea. These dissociations led to the idea that apraxia, far from being a unitary disorder, is actually a group of different disorders, each of which may be understood in terms of the disruption of a different stage in the sequence of processes involved in voluntary movement.

Liepmann's Classification of the Apraxias

HIERARCHICAL STAGES IN THE PROCESSING OF ACTIONS   Liepmann analyzed apraxia into three subtypes: motor apraxia, ideomotor apraxia, and ideational apraxia. According to Liepmann, clumsiness and impairment in fine-motor coordination characterize **motor apraxia,** but the basic movements and sequences of movement involved in learned behavior are intact. **Ideomotor apraxia,** in contrast, is characterized by an impairment in the ability to perform specific learned motor acts, such as saluting, waving good-bye, or showing how you would use a hammer or how you would brush your teeth. In **ideational apraxia,** the ability to perform specific movements is intact, but the ability to carry out acts that involve complex sequences of movement is impaired. For example, a patient with ideational apraxia would have difficulty executing the movements required for making a cup of tea or lighting a candle with a match, even though the ability to execute the component movements is intact.

Figure 9.14 shows the general theoretical model underlying Liepmann's classification of apraxia. The

model posits a series of stages of information processing whereby the concept of the sequence of movements involved in a complex act is superordinate to the movements involved in each component of the sequence, which, in turn, is superordinate to the smooth and coordinated execution of each movement. From this point of view, disruption of each of these processes would result in ideational, ideomotor, and motor apraxia, respectively.

PROBLEMS WITH THE CLASSICAL DISTINCTION BETWEEN IDEATIONAL AND IDEOMOTOR APRAXIA   The classical distinction between ideomotor and ideational apraxia rests on reports, beginning with Liepmann's early in the 20th century, of dissociation between impairment in the use of a single object and in the sequential utilization of a number of objects to perform a series of goal-directed actions. There is, however, reason to question the validity of inferring that qualitatively different mechanisms underlie these two types of task. In particular, there is evidence that the level of performance on these two tasks after cerebral lesions is highly correlated and that differences within subjects in level of performance reflects the greater level of difficulty of sequential tasks rather than qualitatively different underlying mechanisms (De Renzi & Lucchelli, 1988; Poeck & Lehmkuhl, 1980). This conclusion is also supported by the fact that there are few reported cases of patients with impairment in sequential tasks who do not also have impairment in simple tasks (Zangwill, 1960).

A More Theoretically Neutral Approach to Apraxia

There are many theoretical frameworks that can serve as a basis for classifying higher-order movement disorders. We have seen in the previous section how the framework that posits a distinction between ideational and ideomotor apraxia has some difficulty accounting for all the data. This is true of other theoretical frameworks that have been proposed to explain higher-order disturbances of movement, and there is as yet no single framework that has been generally accepted as a basis for understanding the apraxias. This lack of consensus makes the terminology of apraxia rather confusing. Sometimes the same terminology is utilized by different models to represent different conceptualizations of what is wrong, and sometimes different terms are used by different models to denote disruption of the same underlying mechanism. Rather than get lost in the somewhat arcane terminology in this area, it may be more useful to take an empirical approach, describing what kinds of impairments in voluntary movement are seen after cortical lesions and examining some of the associations and dissociations that have been reported.

UNFAMILIAR HAND POSTURES AND MOVEMENT SEQUENCES

Unfamiliar actions and action sequences are not overlearned and deeply stored. On the contrary, they must be learned by the individual as novel postures or movement sequences. In this respect they are different from familiar gestures and from the movements involved in the use of familiar objects, both of which are deeply learned in the course of an individual's experience.

Impairment in the learning of simple hand postures has been reported after left-hemisphere lesions (De Renzi et al., 1983; Kimura & Archibald, 1974). Kimura and Archibald (1974) reported that impairment in the learning of a simple sequence of novel movements was most commonly associated with lesions in the left parietal lobe, although impairment after left or right frontal-lobe lesions was also seen. Similar impairment after left parietal-lobe lesions was also reported (De Renzi et al., 1983; De Renzi, Motti, &

Nichelli, 1980; Kolb & Milner, 1981b). Impairment in the acquisition of single hand movements and impairment in the acquisition of sequences of unfamiliar movements are highly correlated and appear to lie on a continuum of task difficulty, rather than depending on qualitatively different neural mechanisms (De Renzi et al., 1980).

FAMILIAR GESTURES

Familiar gestures include actions like showing the thumbs-up sign, waving good-bye, and saluting. These are referred to as **symbolic gestures** and are differentiated from **expressive gestures,** such as shaking the fist, which communicate emotion more directly.

Lesions of the left parietal lobe have been consistently associated with disruption of familiar gestures (De Renzi et al., 1980; Hecaen & Rondot, 1985). Disruption of symbolic and of expressive gestures appears not to be dissociable (Hecaen & Rondot, 1985). In addition, impairment in the acquisition of unfamiliar movement sequences and the execution of meaningful gestures do not appear to be dissociable (De Renzi et al., 1983; Lehmkuhl, Poeck, & Williams, 1983).

OBJECT USE

Reports of impairment in object use after cerebral lesions are complicated by the fact that there are many different potential methods for assessing impairment. There are four major methods: (a) pantomiming the use of an object to verbal command when the object is absent, (b) pantomiming the use of an object that is in view but out of reach, (c) imitating, through pantomime, the use of an object, and (d) using an actual object that is placed in the subject's hand. It turns out that these different methods of assessment have yielded some informative dissociations. In particular, patients who are impaired in pantomiming the use of an object to verbal command when the object is absent may be able to demonstrate its use when the object is in view but out of reach (De Renzi, Faglioni, & Sorgato, 1982; Heilman, 1973). They may also be able to imitate the required action (Heilman, 1973) and be able to demonstrate the use of an object when actually holding it (Gazzaniga, Bogen, & Sperry, 1967; Geschwind & Kaplan, 1962; Heilman, 1973). We will have more to say about the mechanisms underlying these dissociations in a later section, when we discuss a patient with apraxia confined to the left side of the body. Impairment in object use is associated with left parietal-lobe lesions (De Renzi & Lucchelli, 1988; Heilman, 1973).

BODY-PART-SPECIFIC ACTIONS   Because different neural systems control different parts of the body, one might expect to see body-part-specific impairment in voluntary action. This is in fact the case.

Oral Apraxia and Limb Apraxia   As was mentioned earlier, the first clinical account of an impairment in voluntary action, recorded by Hughlings-Jackson, described a disorder that selectively affected the patient's mouth and tongue. This has come to be termed **oral apraxia,** and its occurrence as a highly selective impairment has been well documented (Goodglass & Kaplan, 1963; Kolb & Milner, 1981b; Mateer & Kimura, 1977). This stands in contrast to the more frequently encountered apraxic disorder that affects the limbs, particularly the hands, but does not affect the mouth and tongue. This is termed **limb apraxia.** No consistent dissociation has been found between apraxia affecting the upper and the lower limbs (Lehmkuhl et al., 1983). Whereas oral apraxia is associated with damage to left central operculum and insula (Tognola & Vignolo, 1980), limb apraxia is most often associated with damage to parietal cortex in the left hemisphere (De Renzi et al., 1980; Hecaen & Rondot, 1985).

Independence of Whole-Body Movements   Interestingly, limb apraxia typically does not affect movement involving the axial muscles. This results in some curious dissociations; a patient with severe limb apraxia may be easily able to make **whole-body movements,** such as standing in the pose of a boxer or walking across a room (Geschwind, 1975).

Unilateral Impairment   Impairment in voluntary movement may be confined to one side of the body. In such cases the nondominant hand is most often affected. One of the best-documented case studies of such a patient is that reported by Geschwind and Kaplan (1962). Their patient had a left glioblastoma that was partially removed at surgery. After surgery

he had a dense right hemiplegia and aphasia, both of which cleared postoperatively, leaving him with a mild weakness of the right shoulder and right leg and a grasp reflex of the right hand. The left hand had no trace of elementary motor impairment.

When this patient was tested, a peculiar pattern of performance emerged. Although the patient's ability to move his right hand was somewhat impaired due to that hand's grasp reflex and to some residual weakness, he was nevertheless able to use it to successfully carry out actions to verbal command. In startling contrast, he was apraxic when performing actions with the left hand, even though that hand had no motor weakness or other elementary motor impairment. For example, when asked to show with his left hand how he would brush his teeth, he pantomimed movements corresponding to lathering his face and combing his hair. When asked to draw a square, he drew a triangle.

This seemingly baffling discrepancy between the two hands can be accounted for in terms of a disconnection of the right motor area from language centers in the left hemisphere. Support for this comes from the presence of an analogous discrepancy between the performance of the two hands in the domain of language. Thus, the patient was able with his right hand (despite the presence of a grasp reflex) to write the alphabet, a simple sentence, and several words to dictation and was able to perform simple arithmetic calculations (Figure 9.15). In contrast, he was markedly impaired in the performance of the same or similar tasks when using the left hand (Figure 9.16). Furthermore, when holding an object in the left hand, he was unable to draw it with his right hand.

Figure 9.17 illustrates the disconnection that Geschwind and Kaplan hypothesized to underlie this pattern of impairment. Information from Wernicke's area is able to activate areas in the left hemisphere specialized for movement (the supramarginal gyrus), and from there output goes to the premotor area and then to the motor area of the left hemisphere. This input is, however, unable to get to the motor areas of the right hemisphere due to damage to the anterior corpus callosum. Examination of this patient's brain after death revealed massive infiltration of the left frontal lobe by tumor, but no involvement of the right hemisphere. In

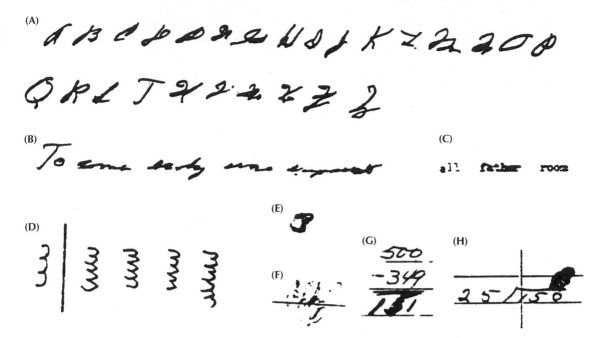

FIGURE 9.15   Sample of performance of the right hand of Geschwind and Kaplan's patient. *(A)* The alphabet. *(B)* The sentence *To come early was impossible* written to dictation. *(C)* The words *all, father,* and *room* typed with the right index finger. *(D)* Attempts to copy the model drawn to the left of the line. *(E)* The number 3 written to dictation. *(F)* The patient's writing of his first name. *(G)* and *(H)* The patient's correct solutions to problems written by the examiner. The additional loops in *(D)* and the overwriting in *(E), (G),* and *(H)* are due to the residual grasp reflex of the right hand. *(From Geschwind & Kaplan, 1962, p. 677)*

addition, however, there was a marked thinning of the anterior two thirds of the corpus callosum, indicating damage to this massive bundle of fibers connecting the two hemispheres. This was consistent with the disconnecting lesion hypothesized by Geschwind and Kaplan before the patient's death. Apraxia confined to the left hand was subsequently reported in patients with surgical section of the corpus callosum (De Renzi et al., 1982; Gazzaniga et al., 1967; Watson & Heilman, 1983).

There are several other aspects of this case that are instructive. First, the left-hand impairment means that information could not be transferred directly from the left parietal lobe to the right parietal lobe via the intact posterior part of the corpus callosum. Apparently the anterior connection between the left and right premotor cortices is critical for the transfer

of neural activity controlling verbally elicited movement from the left parietal lobe to right motor areas.

Second, some interesting dissociations were observed. Although the left arm and hand were impaired in the performance of actions to verbal command, the patient was able to demonstrate the use of an object with that hand when the object was in view and when the actual object was placed in his left hand. He was also able to imitate seen actions. We indicated in an earlier section that such patterns of dissociation are not uncommon in patients with apraxia. This has led some investigators to consider **dissociation apraxia** as a specific class of apraxic disorders (Heilman, Watson, & Rothi, 1996). These dissociations suggest that the cerebral representation for movement elicited by visual and tactile input may not be confined to the left hemisphere, as verbally activated

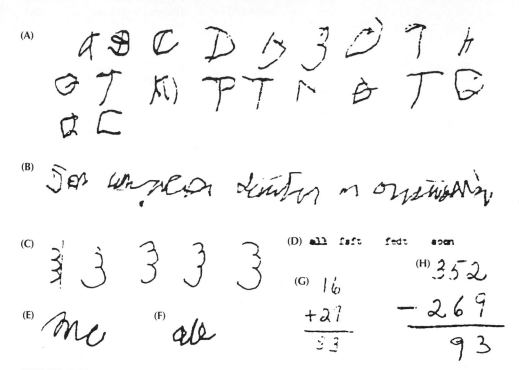

FIGURE 9.16 Sample of performance of the left hand of Geschwind and Kaplan's patient. *(A)* The alphabet. *(B)* The sentence *To come early was impossible* written to dictation. *(C)* Copies of the model to the left of the vertical line. *(D)* Attempts to type with the left index finger the words *all*, *father*, *father* (the second being a spontaneous attempt to correct the first error), and *room*. *(E)* Attempt to write *run* to dictation. *(F)* Attempt to write *go* to dictation. *(G)* and *(H)* The patient's incorrect solutions to problems written by the examiner. *(From Geschwind & Kaplan, 1962, p. 679)*

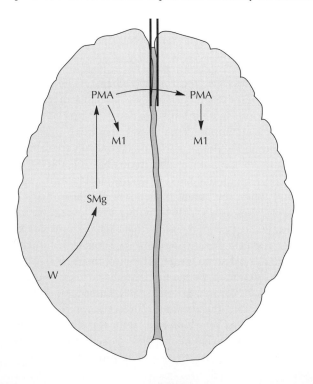

FIGURE 9.17 The disconnection of the left and right premotor cortices hypothesized by Geschwind and Kaplan in their patient with apraxia of the left hand: *W*, Wernicke's area; *SMg*, supramarginal gyrus; *PMA*, premotor area; *M1*, primary motor cortex. The presence of damage to the anterior portion of the corpus callosum was confirmed in subsequent postmortem examination. The double line indicates the site of the hypothesized (and later confirmed) callosal lesion. *(Based on Geschwind & Kaplan, 1962)*

motor programs seem to be. According to this view, Geschwind and Kaplan's patient was able to demonstrate the use of an object held in the left hand because activity in the right somatosensory cortex was able to activate stored tactually associated movement programs in the same hemisphere. An analogous mechanism involving the visual cortex could presumably underlie the ability of this patient to demonstrate the use of a seen object. The finding of similar dissociations in patients with complete section of the corpus callosum is consistent with this view (De Renzi et al., 1982; Gazzaniga et al., 1967; Heilman, 1973). It may also be the case, however, that in at least some apraxic patients without complete section of the corpus callosum—such as Geschwind and Kaplan's patient—preservation of the ability to imitate action or to use actual objects may be possible because motor areas in the right hemisphere can somehow gain access to stored motor programs in the left parietal lobe.

CONCEPTUAL APRAXIA   Heilman has made a distinction between impairment in the use of an object due to disruption of the programming of the necessary movements versus disruption of the conceptual knowledge underlying the movement. Thus, whereas in ideomotor apraxia the patient's actions are impaired because of an inability to program the sequences of movements involved in, say, using a hammer, in **conceptual apraxia** the patient may successfully carry out a sequence of movements but they do not correspond to the situation. Thus, the patient may pick up a hammer and make movements that would be appropriate for the use of a saw. In other words, the conceptual knowledge of object-movement correspondences rather than the programming of movement sequences, per se, is disrupted in conceptual apraxia. We saw this type of disorder in Geschwind and Kaplan's patient when he responded to a request to show how he would brush his teeth by making movements corresponding to lathering his face and combing his hair.

DISSOCIABILITY OF IMPAIRMENT IN THE COMPREHENSION OF MOVEMENT AND IN PERFORMANCE   Many patients who are not able to perform actions can comprehend them. In addition, specific

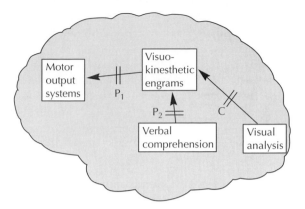

FIGURE 9.18   Heilman's model of the disconnections that would account for dissociations between impairment in performance and impairment in comprehension of learned movements. Lesions disconnecting areas representing visuokinesthetic engrams from motor output systems (P_1) or from areas mediating verbal comprehension (P_2) would result in a specific impairment in performance. Lesions disconnecting areas mediating visual analysis from areas representing visuokinesthetic engrams (C) would result in a specific impairment in the comprehension of movement. Damage in the area representing visuokinesthetic engrams would produce impairment in both the performance and the comprehension of learned actions.

impairment in the comprehension and discrimination of action (with performance intact) has been reported after left-hemisphere lesions (Heilman, Rothi, & Valenstein, 1982; Heilman, Watson, & Rothi, 1996). Heilman and Rothi (1985) have proposed that performance-specific impairments are attributable to a disconnection of areas in the left parietal lobe that represent what they term **visuokinesthetic engrams** or **praxicons** from areas involved in motor output. Evidence for this comes from the finding that performance-specific impairments are often seen in association with frontal-lobe lesions (Heilman et al., 1982). A second mechanism, proposed to underlie performance-specific impairments, involves a disconnection of visuokinesthetic engrams from areas involved in language comprehension (Heilman et al., 1996). In contrast, comprehension-specific impairments result from disconnection of movement-critical areas in the left parietal lobe and areas mediating visual analysis (Figure 9.18)

These two mechanisms proposed to underlie performance-specific impairment provide a basis for understanding some of the dissociations frequently seen when object-use is tested in different ways. A disconnection of visuokinesthetic engrams from areas mediating verbal comprehension would be expected to leave intact performance that is elicited by nonverbal means. On the other hand, disconnection of visuokinesthetic engrams from motor output systems would result in a more pervasive performance impairment.

The Role of the Left Hemisphere in the Control of Voluntary Movement

We have seen that disorders of action are associated with damage to the left hemisphere or to fibers connecting it with motor areas in the right hemisphere. This has led to the notion that the left hemisphere has a dominant role in the control of voluntary movement. This was Liepmann's (1905) conclusion, based on his extensive analysis of case material, and overwhelming supporting data from the study of patients with cerebral lesions has accumulated since his seminal findings (e.g., De Renzi & Lucchelli, 1988; Heilman et al., 1982; Kimura & Archibald, 1974; Shallice, 1988, p. 339). In addition, a special role for the left hemisphere in the control of movement was corroborated by studies of patients undergoing the sodium amobarbital test. It was found that only injection of the speaking hemisphere caused impairment in recently learned arm movements (Milner & Kolb, 1985), even though all testing was carried out with the hand ipsilateral to the injection.

The finding that the language hemisphere is also the hemisphere that controls voluntary action and that there is a frequent co-occurrence of language impairment and impairment in voluntary action has raised some interesting hypotheses. Using a disconnection syndrome framework, Geschwind (1975) has proposed that apraxia is the result of a disconnection of language areas and areas in the brain critical for the mediation of learned movement. Although Geschwind and Kaplan (1962) describe a case where such a mechanism is at work, there are clearly other cases of impairment in voluntary action that defy explanation in terms of disconnection syndromes. In particular, it is not unusual

to find patients who are impaired in the use of an object under conditions that do not require linguistic processing, such as imitating a seen action or using an object that is placed in their hand.

An interesting hypothesis put forward by Doreen Kimura (1982) proposes that the specialization of the left hemisphere for both language and voluntary action springs from a set of underlying processes that is common to both domains. In particular, both language and action require movement to be highly organized in time. From this perspective, then, language impairment is conceptualized as a special case of impairment in complex motor control. This approach also implies that, in the course of human cultural development, the evolution of language became possible by virtue of the evolving refinement and complexity of motor control systems within the left hemisphere.

In its conceptualization of language processing as a special case of voluntary movement, this hypothesis has an alluring parsimony. It is also supported by much of the empirical evidence, including the well-established finding that apraxia and aphasia often occur together after left-hemisphere lesions. Nevertheless, there are some complications. Although apraxia is often accompanied by receptive aphasia (De Renzi, 1985), it has also been shown to occur independently (De Renzi et al., 1980; Kertesz, Ferro, & Shewon, 1984). The comparison of lesion sites in cases in which apraxia and receptive aphasia occur together and cases in which only one disorder occurs provides clues regarding the cerebral localization of stored motor programs. This comparison has led to the hypothesis that the critical area is in the left parietal lobe, just posterior to but not including Wernicke's area, in the neighborhood of the supramarginal gyrus (Geschwind, 1975; Heilman & Rothi, 1993; Kimura, 1980).

Interestingly, dissociation between language ability and ability to carry out voluntary action has been reported even when the same body part is involved in both types of action. Thus, there are reports of deaf patients with impaired signing after a left-hemisphere lesion who are not apraxic (Poizner, Klima, & Bellugi, 1987) and reports of patients with oral apraxia who are unimpaired in the articulation of speech sounds (Kolb & Milner, 1981b). Although these data contradict the idea that cerebral specialization for speech and specialization for learned movements are mediated by the same cortical areas in the left hemisphere, they are not inconsistent with Kimura's hypothesis that the evolution of language is related to the evolution of skilled movement.

OTHER MOVEMENT-RELATED FUNCTIONS OF PARIETAL CORTEX

We have seen that left posterior parietal areas are critical for the control of learned movement. This area of the brain, and its homologue on the right, make two other important contributions to movement. As we noted earlier, the somatosensory cortex in each hemisphere receives input from receptors in muscles, tendons, joints, and skin that provide important information about ongoing movement utilized in the process of planning and programming future movement.

In addition, as we saw in chapter 7, damage to the parietal lobe in either hemisphere is associated with impairment in the execution of behaviors that require extensive spatial processing, such as drawing. We noted there that disruption of these actions is termed constructional apraxia and presented evidence that the impairment underlying this disruption varies depending upon the hemisphere involved, with right parietal-lobe lesions impairing spatial processing and left parietal-lobe lesions resulting in a primary disruption of movement. From this perspective, the term *constructional apraxia* is misleading if it is understood to imply that a disruption of a single mechanism underlies impairment in constructive behaviors, such as drawing, after left and right parietal-lobe lesions (Arrigoni & De Renzi, 1964; Warrington, James, & Kinsbourne, 1966).

THE PREFRONTAL CORTEX

We have already alluded to the role of prefrontal cortex in the control of voluntary movement and have suggested that the processes mediated by these structures represent the highest level of movement control. This includes the enormously complex processes involved in planning, implementing plans, monitoring the results of behavior in terms of these plans, and, when necessary, modifying behavior to bring it in line with plans. It also often requires modifying the plans themselves in the light of the results of the behaviors that they generate.

We will have much more to say about the executive function mediated by the frontal lobes in chapter 12. In the present context, however, we will confine ourselves to a look at some unit recording studies by Joaquin Fuster (1991) illustrating that neurons in dorsolateral frontal cortex play a role in the anticipation and planning of behavior. Fuster trained monkeys to choose either a left or a right response depending on the color of a cue light. A red or a blue cue light signaled a left choice, and a green or a yellow light signaled a right choice. In addition, within each choice direction, the color of the cue light signaled the probability that the indicated response direction would in fact be correct (red and green, 75%; blue and yellow, 100%). In the experiment, the monkey was first exposed to a preparatory flash, which was then followed by the cue light. There was then a delay interval of a few seconds, after which a pair of choice stimuli appeared. The monkey then was to make a choice corresponding to the direction indicated by the cue light.

Recording from individual neurons in dorsolateral frontal cortex, Fuster found neurons that were not active during the actual movement but that were active during the delay interval between cue onset and choice. Furthermore, he found that individual neurons were selectively active depending on the direction of the anticipated movement (Figure 9.19A) and, most strikingly, depending on the probability that the anticipated direction of movement was correct (Figure 9.19B). These findings demonstrate that there are cells in dorsolateral frontal cortex that are tuned not only to the direction of forthcoming movement but also to the probability that the anticipated movement is correct. They suggest that neurons in the prefrontal cortex play a role in planning and in evaluating the potential consequences of future behavior.

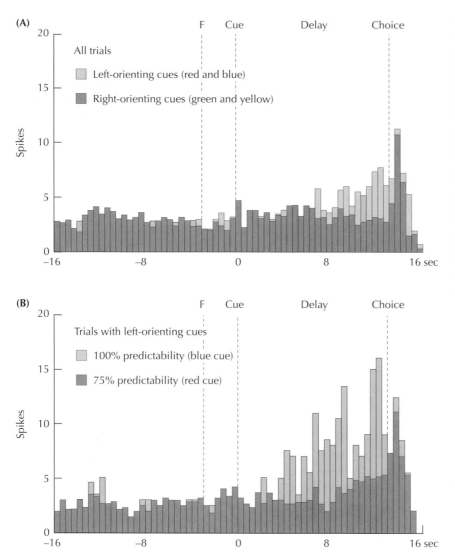

FIGURE 9.19   Activity of a prefrontal cell related to anticipated direction and probability of correctness of response. *(A)* The discharge of the cell during trials with left- or right-orienting cues. Discharge accelerates during the delay in trials with left-orienting cues. *(B)* The breakdown in cell activity according to whether the left-orienting cue is 100% predictive of a correct response or 75% predictive. Acceleration of firing during the delay is greater for the cue that is 100% predictive. *F* indicates the onset of a preparatory warning flash. *(From Fuster, 1991, p. 68)*

SUMMARY

Movement is the ultimate manifestation of all psychological processes within an individual. Without it there would be no behavior, and the myriad internal processes that inform and regulate action would have no consequences or meaning beyond the subjective experience of the individual.

Adaptive higher-order control of movement may be thought of as having two components: content

and timing. Content refers to knowledge of learned movement and the ability to organize that knowledge into movement required in a particular context. Timing refers to the ability to determine when a particular movement or movement sequence is to be executed. Cutting across these two dimensions are three others, the execution, tactics, and strategy of movement. Each of these levels of control regulates movement in progressively more global behavioral contexts, from the execution of a single movement, to the production of a sequence of coordinated movements, to the organization of long-term patterns of behavior.

Although it is true that all of the nervous system contributes to the control of movement, it is also true that certain regions are more directly involved than others. These are traditionally designated as components of motor systems. The peripheral motor system is perhaps the most obvious because dysfunction of the motor neurons innervating muscle, disruption of the neurochemical links between these neurons and muscle, and dysfunction of muscle itself all result in paralysis, the most profound and absolute impairment of movement.

Going upstream from the periphery, we come to the spinal cord and brain stem, extremely complex structures that, when separated from higher levels of the nervous system, are able to mediate some remarkable reflexes and patterns of movement. Rigid and stereotyped as these are, they may be highly adaptive in specific situations. Nevertheless, it is movement that takes into account a broad range of internal and external factors in the past, present, and future, movement, which—with some philosophical license—we label voluntary, that is the hallmark of intelligence and the capacity for adaptation. This movement is controlled by the forebrain.

The primary motor cortex (M1) is more directly involved in movement than any other cortical area. The importance of M1's role is suggested by the following: (a) of all cortical areas M1 has the lowest threshold for simulation-elicited movement, (b) M1's neurons fire both before and during movement, and (c) the firing rate of M1 neurons is related to the force of associated muscle contractions. Moreover, neurons in M1 code direction of movement, although they do so through the activity of populations of neurons rather than through the activity of single neurons. This is a striking instance of distributed processing and may serve to protect M1 movement-control mechanisms from the effect of "noise" in the system.

The premotor area (PMA) and the supplementary motor area (SMA), occupying area 6, stand at the interface between plans and strategies and specific actions. They prepare the motor system for organized movement and movement sequences. Precisely how PMA and SMA mediate this preparation is incompletely understood, but that they do so is indicated by a number of lines of evidence. These include (a) the selective disruption of movement sequences following lesions to these structures, (b) neuroimaging studies showing that neurons in SMA are more active during the rehearsal and execution of movement sequences than during the execution of simple movements, and (c) single unit studies showing that PMA neurons are selectively active in preparation for movement in a particular direction but not during the movement itself.

The cerebellum is a massive structure that compares the output of PMA, SMA, and M1 with the ongoing movement of the individual and, on the basis of this comparison, then adjusts both cortical motor output and peripheral motor mechanisms. It is thus an important regulator of tactical aspects of movement. Cerebellar lesions produce disruption in the accuracy and coordination of movement.

In contrast, the basal ganglia receive projections from all cortical areas and, after some elaborate connections between different basal ganglia structures and the thalamus, project to PMA, SMA, M1, and prefrontal cortex. They thus serve to funnel widespread cortical activity to prefrontal cortex and to areas of cortex more directly involved in movement. The fact that lesions to certain structures within the basal ganglia (most notably the substantia nigra in Parkinson's disease) result in a profound hypokinesia or even akinesia suggests that the basal ganglia are critical for the initiation and maintenance of voluntary movement. However, lesions of the basal ganglia may also result in unwanted movement, as seen in Huntington's disease and ballism. These disorders are poorly understood, although mechanisms have been proposed that attempt to account for them in terms of disruptions in basal ganglia circuitry. The hyperkinesias characteristic of these disorders suggest that, in addition to their funneling role, the basal ganglia normally serve to filter out unwanted movement.

Apraxia, the disruption of learned movement not due to elementary motor or sensory impairment, has many manifestations. This has been evident since Liepmann's early accounts of apraxia, which included its breakdown into ideational, ideomotor, and motor apraxia, depending on whether the concept of the movement, the organization of component movements, or the coordination of movement was impaired, respectively. Since Liepmann, no consensus has been reached with regard to a theoretical model that would account for the varying manifestations of apraxia. This has led to some confusion at both the descriptive and the theoretical levels, in that different models may categorize errors in strikingly different ways and then use similar or even identical terminology to denote very different conceptualizations of underlying impairment. One way of attempting to surmount this problem is to adopt an empirically based approach that makes a minimum of theoretical assumptions.

One of the most consistent notions to emerge from the study of apraxia is the idea that the left hemisphere is specialized for the control of learned movement sequences. This has led to the hypothesis that speech, a striking instance of learned movement, developed out of movement control mechanisms represented in the left hemisphere and that other language functions, including comprehension, came to be represented in neighboring regions. Evidence that representations of learned movement are localized in areas of the left parietal lobe bordering Wernicke's area, particularly the supramarginal gyrus, appears to support this hypothesis, although it seems clear that language and learned movement are represented in different areas of left-parietal cortex.

The parietal lobes play two other important roles in the control of movement. They process sensory information about both the outside world and the on-going movement of the individual. Both of these domains of information are critical for the control of movement. In addition, as we saw in chapter 7, the right parietal lobe plays a major role in spatial processing. Disturbances of spatial processing have a major secondary impact on movements that require spatial processing for their successful execution, such as drawing. Although the term constructional apraxia is traditionally used to denote disorders of construction after both left and right parietal-lobe lesions, the term is misleading when applied to construction problems following right parietal-lobe lesions because in these cases the underlying impairment is spatial rather than motoric. In contrast, as we also noted in chapter 7, there is compelling evidence that disruption of constructional tasks following left parietal-lobe lesions is due to an impairment in voluntary movement, although this has not been finally settled. If this turns out to be the case, it would seem more useful to reserve the term constructional apraxia for constructional problems following left parietal-lobe lesions, thereby denoting their kinship with other disorders of voluntary action.

Prefrontal cortex represents the highest level of control of voluntary movement. It is here that representations of the external world, generated by posterior cortex, and representations of internal state, generated by limbic structures, are integrated, a process that is perhaps the essence of intelligence. Out of this integration emerge long-term plans and strategies of action, as well as the capacity for their revision and modification in the light of feedback regarding the consequences of the behaviors that they generate.

CHAPTER 10

Memory Systems

AN OVERVIEW OF NORMAL MEMORY
Categorizing Memory in Terms of What
  Is Remembered
Categorizing Memory in Terms of Capacity
  and Duration
Component Processes of Memory
The Relationship Between Memory and Other
  Domains of Cognition
**MEDIAL TEMPORAL-LOBE AMNESIA AND
THE CONSOLIDATION HYPOTHESIS**
Patient H. M.
Some Implications of H. M.'s Memory Impairment
**MEMORY IMPAIRMENT AFTER UNILATERAL
TEMPORAL-LOBE LESIONS**
Complementary Specialization of Memory Function
  for the Left and Right Temporal Lobes
The Roles of Medial Temporal-Lobe Structures
  and Lateral Temporal Cortex in Memory
**THE CRITICAL STRUCTURES INVOLVED IN MEMORY
LOSS AFTER TEMPORAL-LOBE LESIONS**
H. M.'s Lesions
Discrepancy Between Findings in Animals and Humans
Apparent Resolution of the Discrepancy
Search for the Critical Structures Involved
  in Recognition Memory
Some Conflicting Findings
The Importance of Medial-Temporal Cortex
DIENCEPHALIC AMNESIA
Korsakoff's Disease
Other Causes of Diencephalic Amnesia

The Relationship Between Medial-Temporal
  and Diencephalic Amnesia
**WHERE IN THE MEMORY PROCESS
IS THE IMPAIRMENT?**
Registration/Encoding
Consolidation/Storage/Maintenance
Retrieval
PRESERVED ASPECTS OF MEMORY IN AMNESIA
Motor Learning
Perceptual Learning
Classical Conditioning
Cognitive Skill Learning
Priming
EPISODIC MEMORY AND SEMANTIC MEMORY
Global Amnesia
Selective Impairment of Episodic Memory
Selective Impairment of Semantic Memory
SHORT-TERM/WORKING MEMORY IMPAIRMENT
Short-Term Memory
Working Memory
The Frontal Lobes and Working Memory
**CONCEPTUALIZATION OF MULTIPLE
MEMORY SYSTEMS**
THE NEURAL SUBSTRATE OF LONG-TERM MEMORY
Lashley's Search for the Engram
Evidence That Long-Term Memory Is Stored
  in the Cortex
Hippocampal Binding of Different Memory
  Elements as an Integral Component
  in Explicit Memory

Storage of Implicit Memory
Protein Synthesis and the Structural Plasticity
   Underlying Long-Term Memory
So Where Is Memory Stored?

**FURTHER CONSIDERATION OF THE ROLE
   OF THE FRONTAL LOBES IN MEMORY**
The Frontal Lobes and Organization
Impairment in Metamemory
SUMMARY

❖ ❖ ❖

Memory is an extraordinary process, one of the most central aspects of being human. Through it, our nervous system codes past events in a way that sometimes allows us to consciously remember events in the distant past as vividly as if they had just occurred, and these memories often carry with them intense emotions ranging from the blissful to the tormenting. Other times, past events are represented in the nervous system in a way that does not yield conscious memories and yet affects subsequent behavior, as when we engage in a motor skill such as riding a bicycle. It seems as if everything except the slender sliver of the present moment is either memory of the past or imaginings of the future. Yet even our experience of the present moment is inextricably interwoven with our memory. The meaning and significance of the people and things in the present are dependent on our memory, so that the present loses its salience without the past, an idea that Gerald Edelman (1989) captured in the title of his book The Remembered Present.

What would it be like to have a devastating impairment of memory so that nothing new could be learned? The magnitude of such an impairment was brought home to me when, in the mid-1970s, I heard the eminent neurophysiologist John Eccles describe the famous patient known as H. M., who had undergone bilateral removal of medial temporal-lobe structures for the relief of epilepsy. This was a frankly experimental procedure that, although it achieved its aim of eliminating the patient's seizures, had horrible unintended consequences: H. M. was apparently unable to remember anything that happened to him, unable to learn anything new. Tragically, although he retained many of his memories from before the surgery, any memory of experiences after the surgery dissolved in a matter of seconds, lost forever in a blank void of amnesia.

When, a few years later, I had an opportunity to meet and work with H. M. myself, the poignancy of his impairment made an indelible impression. I found him to be an amiable and polite man who seemed to enjoy the casual conversation that we struck up on first meeting. But I had come too early to his room, a hospital-like room in a laboratory at MIT, where he was staying during one of his periodic visits to Boston. Because he was still in bed, I explained that we would chat a few minutes, and then I said I would leave so that he could get up and have breakfast before we began work. After a few more minutes of chatting, I began to excuse myself. As I did so, to my surprise, H. M. expressed concern. He asked why I was leaving, whether he had done something to make me leave, something perhaps inappropriate. I reassured him that he had not, but he continued to express his concern. It was clear that he had not only forgotten our earlier plan of only chatting briefly but also did not know what had just occurred in the immediate past. Later, in response to my questions, he described what his inability to remember felt like: "Well, it's a big question mark you have always. And you wonder, did I or didn't I? That's what I mean by a big question mark."

After a morning of work, during which I gave H. M. a variety of memory tests and talked to him at length about the nature of his experience, it was time for us to end our work. As we said good-bye, something happened that has stuck with me ever since. As we shook hands, H. M. grabbed my arm and, smiling, playfully held on to me for a long moment so that I could not leave. I have always wondered if this gesture perhaps came out of a desperate yearning to hold on to his past. Was it perhaps a manifestation of his awareness that when people leave him they are, for him, truly gone, leaving no trace in his memory?

AN OVERVIEW OF NORMAL MEMORY

We have learned much about memory from the study of H. M. In fact, he is probably the most studied single individual in the history of psychology. Patients with other memory impairments have also taught us a great deal about the nature of memory. In this chapter we examine some of the strange and often counterintuitive findings that have emerged from the study of patients with disrupted memory. We also explore the implications of these findings for an understanding of normal memory. To provide a context for later discussions, we begin with a brief survey of theories of normal memory. As we explore the relationship between brain and memory in later sections of this chapter, it will be seen that many aspects of our current understanding of normal memory have emerged from the study of patients with memory impairment.

Although we commonly talk about memory, it would be more accurate to talk about memory systems. These systems work with varying degrees of independence, but they are also intricately interdependent. They may be categorized along several dimensions: (a) What is remembered? There are different systems devoted to remembering different things. (b) How much is remembered and for how long? Some systems store only a limited amount of information for a brief time, whereas others store an apparently unlimited amount of information for as long as a lifetime. (c) What are the processes involved in remembering? It is possible to analyze memory into component processes, each of which makes a specific contribution to remembering. In later sections of this chapter, we will briefly examine systems of memory along these three dimensions. In this section, however, we will be didactic, confining ourselves to sketching out the territory to provide a context for later discussions.

Categorizing Memory in Terms of What Is Remembered

EPISODIC AND SEMANTIC MEMORY   Endel Tulving (1972) proposed a distinction between episodic and semantic memory. **Episodic memory** is memory for particular personal experiences, such as bobbing for apples at one's seventh birthday party, watching ravioli being made at a Venetian pasta factory, or a first kiss. **Semantic memory,** on the other hand, is memory for general information that is not consciously tied to a particular personal experience. The formula for table salt, the number of states in the U.S., and the capital of Italy are all pieces of information that we possess. Yet we would probably be hard-pressed to identify the personal experiences that occurred when we learned these things. Of course, in some instances there was something about the experience of learning that caused that experience to remain in our memory, such as a silly but endearing mnemonic device provided by a favorite teacher. But much of our knowledge of the world has an impersonal flavor. It's just something we know, without being tied to specific events in our lives.

EXPLICIT AND IMPLICIT MEMORY   **Explicit memory** refers to the conscious representation (recollection) of past events, in contrast to **implicit memory,** which refers to the nonconscious representation of past events (Graf & Schacter, 1985). In explicit memory, the effect of past experience takes the form of recollections of personal experiences (episodic memory) or conscious memory for impersonal knowledge of facts and concepts (semantic memory). In contrast, in implicit memory, the effect of past events is manifested in behavior, rather than consciousness. There are several types of implicit memory. It may take the form of performance of a **motor skill,** such as learning to ride a bike or throw a baseball accurately, or a **perceptual skill,** such as learning to quickly and accurately read the mirror images of words. Learning a **cognitive skill,** such as an efficient method for solving a particular kind of puzzle or problem, would also fall into the category of implicit memory. **Nonassociative learning** (e.g., habituation and sensitization) and **classical conditioning** also fall within the domain of implicit memory, as does **priming,** the nonconscious facilitating effect of prior experience on perception and other processes, in the absence of conscious recollection of the prior experience.

The terms **declarative memory** and **procedural (or nondeclarative) memory** (Cohen, 1981, 1984;

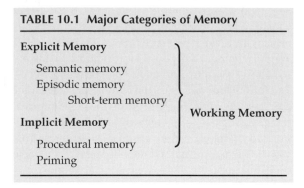

TABLE 10.1   Major Categories of Memory

Explicit Memory

   Semantic memory

   Episodic memory

      Short-term memory

Implicit Memory   **Working Memory**

   Procedural memory

   Priming

Cohen & Squire, 1980) have been used in a way roughly equivalent to *explicit* and *implicit,* respectively. Actually, some authors have articulated some important distinctions between these two sets of terms, but these are beyond the scope of this chapter.[1] Here we will mainly use the terms *explicit* and *implicit.* We will, however, use the term *procedural* to refer to the subset of implicit memory that comprises learning resulting from repetitive experiences, such as motor, perceptual, and cognitive skill learning, to distinguish that subset from implicit memory resulting from a single experience, such as priming. Working memory (discussed in the next section) has both explicit and implicit memory components. This terminology is summarized in Table 10.1.

FREDERICK: A GOLFER WITH ALZHEIMER'S DISEASE Daniel Schacter (1996) dramatically illustrates these distinctions in the course of his description of a golf game, played with a man he calls Frederick, who had Alzheimer's disease. Frederick

---

1. The relationship between the declarative-procedural (nondeclarative) distinction and the explicit-implicit distinction can be a source of confusion. This is particularly the case because the terms are used differently by different investigators, and even by the same investigator as his or her conceptualizations evolve. For example, the declarative-procedural distinction has undergone significant evolution, as may be seen by comparing Cohen and Squire (1980) and Cohen (1997). The reader should be aware of variation in the meaning assigned to these terms by different authors.

was an avid golfer who loved to talk about general aspects of the game and did so eloquently. He was able to play the game quite well, as well as he did before the onset of his disease. Yet all was not well. Schacter describes how, on a hole with a difficult water hazard, Frederick teed off and hit a drive that cleared the hazard and set him up nicely for a chip to the green. Frederick was pleased and began contemplating whether an eight iron or a seven iron would be better for his next shot. Meanwhile Schacter teed off and was about to proceed to his ball when he saw Frederick approach the tee again and prepare to drive another ball. When Schacter asked Frederick what he was doing, he received a bemused look and, to his surprise, heard Frederick say that he'd like to play the hole *too!*

From this description we see that Frederick's golf skill (implicit, procedural memory) was intact. So was his semantic memory, his accumulated knowledge about the world. In contrast, his ability to add to his semantic and episodic memory—that is, his ability to form new explicit memories—was devastated.

Categorizing Memory in Terms of Capacity and Duration

SENSORY REGISTERS: ICONIC AND ECHOIC MEMORY Although very few of us have photographic memory, all of us are able to retain precise representations of what we see and hear for a brief span of time, on the order of milliseconds. The highly accurate but short-lived representations in the visual modality are termed **iconic memory.** Those in the auditory modality are termed **echoic memory.** These systems contribute to our experience of our environment as continuous by providing us with a highly accurate representation of the immediate past. Impairment in sensory registers as the result of cerebral lesions has not been demonstrated.

SHORT-TERM MEMORY Everyone has had the experience of looking up a telephone number and then being distracted before having a chance to place the call, only to find that the number is forgotten. This is characteristic of **short-term memory,** an explicit memory system. Information in short-term memory is available for only a matter of seconds, unless continuous rehearsal takes place, and it is vulnerable to the effects of distraction. Short-term memory also has limited capacity (Miller, 1956). We are able to keep only about seven items in this store, as illustrated by the fact that most people have difficulty remembering many more than seven digits that are read to them. We are, however, able to inventively get around this capacity limitation by organizing information into parcels, a process called **chunking.** Much of the information that enters short-term memory is forgotten, but some enters intermediate-term or long-term memory, either because it is rehearsed or because it has particular salience.

WORKING MEMORY   The concept of short-term memory has been subsumed into a more inclusive concept, **working memory** (Baddeley, 1986, 1994). Working memory is important for the regulation and guidance of ongoing behavior and mental processes. Its content is temporary and constantly changing. Working memory includes short-term memory, but it is much more. It is generally considered to have two components: The first is a general temporary store, several types of specialized temporary storage systems, and particular processes applied to these contents at any given time. Together these have been termed the **workspace.** The second component is the **executive function,** which takes care of overall coordination of activities in working memory, including which contents and processes should be shuffled in and out of the workspace.

Thus, at any given time, working memory is the contents of the workspace, the processes in the workspace being brought to bear on those contents, and the executive function regulating both the contents of the workspace and the processes interacting with those contents. Within the workspace, the processes active at a given time influence the content, and vice versa. In addition, the result of processing and content in the workspace is influenced by the executive function, which in turn is influenced by the processing and content within the workspace. These reciprocal relationships are schematically illustrated in Figure 10.1.

An example may be useful at this point. Suppose I am given the following problem: Construct four equi-

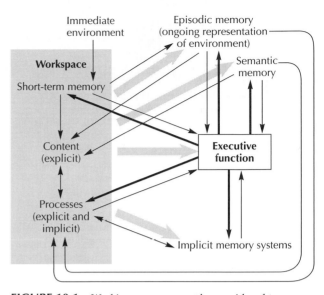

FIGURE 10.1   Working memory may be considered to be composed of two major elements: the workspace and the executive function. Within the workspace is conscious content and processes that are being applied to that content. The content of working memory is derived from the immediate environment (via short-term memory) and from already stored information (i.e., from episodic and semantic memory), which is moved into the workspace as needed. The processes within the workspace are derived from semantic and episodic memory and from implicit memory systems. The medium-weight lines indicate the regulation of the content and the processes within the workspace by the executive function. The regulation of content is via the regulation of attentional processes influencing short-term memory and the regulation of information coming into the workspace from episodic and semantic memory. The regulation of the processes within the workspace by the executive function takes place directly and via the activation of semantic, episodic, and implicit memory systems. The arrows feeding into the executive function represent the interactive nature of these processes. In particular, the executive function is itself modified by the ongoing processes within the workspace. Some of this modification will manifest itself in the formation of new semantic, episodic, and implicit memories. The thick arrows indicate the effect of processes within the workspace on other components of memory.

lateral triangles using only six matchsticks. When I am confronted with this problem, the content of the problem, the six matchsticks, enters the workspace. These have come from the environment, the stated problem, although I must bring my knowledge of the appear-

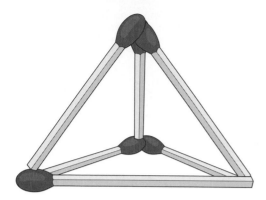

FIGURE 10.2   The application of working memory to the solution of the problem of constructing four equilateral triangles from six matches requires the regulation of content and process within the workspace by the executive function. The solution may be stored in episodic and semantic memory. It may also be represented in modified implicit memory and in alterations in the executive function of working memory.

ance of matchsticks from semantic memory into the workspace. I also bring into the workspace, from long-term memory, my knowledge of the characteristics of triangles and of equilateral triangles in particular. I then subject these contents to various mental processes. I try to imagine the six matches in various configurations, searching for the one that will result in four triangles. I lay them out on an imaginary table, move them about, but cannot come up with four triangles. Finally, after some effort, I manage to change my mental set and manipulate the matchsticks in three dimensions. This is a change of process regulated by the executive function of working memory. The result is manipulation of the content of working memory (matchsticks) into the form of a pyramid that contains four triangles (Figure 10.2).

Working memory is thus a confluence of explicit memory systems (semantic memory and episodic memory), implicit memory systems (processing in the workspace and executive function), and immediate environmental information in short-term memory. If we think back to Frederick, the golfer with Alzheimer's disease, we see that the semantic and implicit components of his working memory were relatively intact. He could bring knowledge of the world to bear on the problem at hand, such as which irons are best for which shots. The difficulty for Frederick was that his devastated episodic memory deprived him of a conscious representation of what the problem at hand was. He could not remember where he had hit the ball or even that he had hit it, and so, of course, he could not focus his attention on that task and use his intact implicit knowledge of golf skills.

RECENT, OR INTERMEDIATE-TERM, MEMORY   **Recent memory,** or **intermediate-term memory,** refers to a store that maintains information for a time period intermediate between short-term memory (seconds to minutes) and long-term memory (which may be maintained for a lifetime). An example of this is memory for what you had for breakfast this morning. This information is clearly not as transient as information in short-term memory, yet, unless today's breakfast was unusual in some way, it is unlikely that you will retain a specific memory of it for more than a few days.

LONG-TERM MEMORY   One of the great marvels of our cognitive endowment, **long-term memory** is a system that stores an enormous amount of information, an amount so large that its limits have not been defined. Furthermore, it maintains this information for years, or even a lifetime.

Component Processes of Memory

The process of memory is traditionally divided into three sequential subprocesses: registration/encoding, storage/maintenance, and retrieval. **Registration** refers to the obvious fact that a stimulus must make some impact on a nervous system for that system to form a representation of it. **Encoding** refers to the form in which the information is represented in the nervous system. Encoding may take many different forms, depending on the features of the stimulus that serve as a basis for it. This, in turn, will have a lot to do with the individual who is doing the encoding. For example, a person viewing the printed word *rosebud* might encode it on the basis of the visual aspects of the printed word, a visual image of a rosebud, the fragrance of a fresh rose, its significance in the movie *Citizen Kane,* or in any number of other ways.

After registration/encoding, the representation of the information in the nervous system must be stored or maintained in some way, if it is to be available at a later time. Precisely how this **storage** (and **maintenance**) occurs is one of the great mysteries of neurobiology, but that it must somehow happen is obvious. Not that the representation is necessarily a static one, like words etched in stone. On the contrary, as we will discuss in more detail in the next section, remembering is a dynamic process, influenced by a multitude of factors. Nevertheless, some representation, even if a dynamically changing one, must be stored in the brain for memory to work.

The last component process is **retrieval.** We have all had the experience of knowing that we know something, such as a person's name, but not being able to come up with it at a particular time. It is, as we say, on the tip of our tongue. Later, perhaps in an unrelated context, the name pops into our head. This is an example of a disruption of our ability to gain access to stored material, that is, a disruption of retrieval.

The Relationship Between Memory and Other Domains of Cognition

We will end this overview of memory with a brief word concerning the relationship between memory and other domains of cognition. Although it is commonplace to treat memory as if it were a discrete and separate function, it is clear from the foregoing discussion that it is in fact a collection of systems working together. This will be a recurring theme in the remainder of this chapter, as we examine the relationship between brain and memory. Moreover, memory is intimately related to other domains of cognition; what we remember is influenced by what we already know and what we infer about the past. This very important point was perhaps most eloquently articulated by Frederic Bartlett (1932) in his book *Remembering*. This title emphasizes Bartlett's view that memory is not a static record but, rather, a dynamic process, influenced by our general knowledge and conceptual frameworks (Bartlett termed these **schemas**) and the inferences we draw from them. For Bartlett, remembering is therefore not simply a matter of consulting a static record; it is a dynamic construction or reconstruction of the past.

More recently, Elizabeth Loftus has experimentally demonstrated the reconstructive nature of memory and the powerful role of schemas in this process by manipulating subjects' memory of an event through the introduction of information after the experience of the event. In one study, subjects saw a brief film showing a car accident. Immediately afterward, Loftus asked some subjects, "Did you see a broken headlight?" and others, "Did you see the broken headlight?" Although there was actually no broken headlight, subjects asked about *the* broken headlight were more likely to report seeing one than subjects asked about *a* broken headlight (Loftus & Zanni, 1975). In another study, Loftus showed subjects a brief film of an accident in which there was no school bus present. Shortly after the film, she asked some subjects whether they had seen the children coming out of the school bus. This manipulation caused a high percentage of subjects to report having seen a school bus when they were asked about the film a week later (Loftus, 1975). These are stunning examples of how influential our knowledge and concepts of the world, our schemas, are in forming the constructions that are the fabric of much of our memory.

Now that we have an overview of memory, we turn to a consideration of its neural basis.

MEDIAL TEMPORAL-LOBE AMNESIA AND THE CONSOLIDATION HYPOTHESIS

Patient H. M.

Although the first reported indication of a relationship between memory and the temporal lobes, by Bekhterev, appeared in 1900, the report by Scoville and Milner (1957) of patient H. M., the man described at the beginning of this chapter, was the first unequivocal demonstration of a localized cerebral lesion producing a specific memory impairment. In this case the lesion was well localized because it was the result of surgical removal. According to H. M.'s surgeon, William Scoville, the removal included medial temporal-lobe structures bilaterally, including the amygdala and the anterior 8 cm of the hippocampus, as well as the surrounding medial cortex, in an attempt to reduce H. M.'s seizures (Figure 10.3). The impairment was very specific. H. M.'s short-term memory, as measured by his ability to repeat back digits that were read to him (**digit span**), was above average. His general intellectual functioning, as measured by formal intelli-

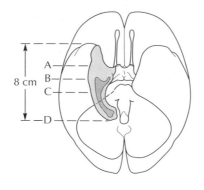

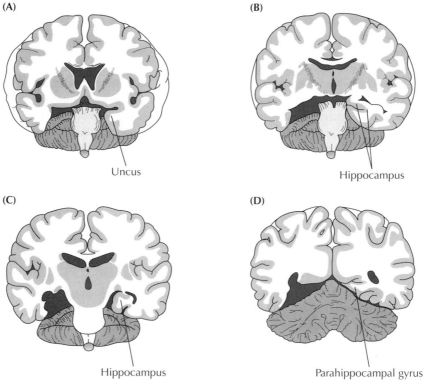

FIGURE 10.3   Ventral view of the extent of hippocampal removal in patient H. M. *(top)* and viewed in four coronal sections *(A–D, below)*. The removal was bilateral, but for illustrative purposes intact structures are shown on one side. *(From Milner, 1970, p. 35)* A more recent MRI study of H. M. has indicated that Scoville overestimated the extent of removal of the hippocampus and that only the anterior 5 cm of this structure were removed (Corkin et al., 1997). The remaining hippocampal tissue did, however, show some atrophy, and it may be that little functional hippocampal tissue remained.

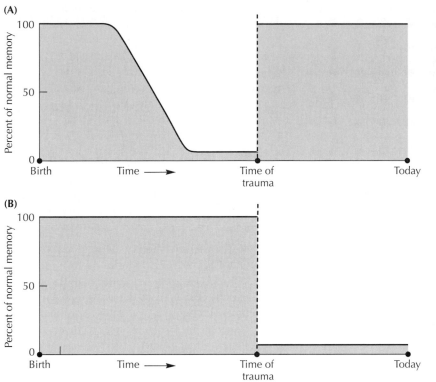

(A)

(B)

FIGURE 10.4   Retrograde and anterograde amnesia. *(A)* In retrograde amnesia, events for a period of time prior to the trauma are forgotten, but memories from the distant past and from the time period following the trauma are intact. *(B)* In anterograde amnesia, memory for events after the trauma is impaired, but events prior to the trauma are remembered. *(Adapted from Bear, Connors, & Paradiso, 1996, p. 519)*

gence testing, was also above average, and he had no intellectual impairment that was not secondary to his memory impairment. Yet nothing in short-term memory went on to be retained for a longer time, and so H. M. remembered almost nothing new since the time of surgery. He also had some impairment in memory for a period before the surgery.

Severely diminished ability to remember new material is termed **anterograde amnesia.** The memory impairment metaphorically extends forward in time from the onset of the amnesia. Major loss of previously remembered material is termed **retrograde amnesia.** In the case of H. M., this deficit went back about 10 years before the onset of the amnesia—i.e., before the surgery—disrupting old, already stored memories (Figure 10.4). Because H. M. does not have a global intellectual impairment, as many people with amnesia do, he provides a rare opportunity to study a pure amnesia, uncomplicated by other cog-

nitive impairments. The specificity of his impairment and the relatively precise localization of the lesion that caused it are the factors that have made him such an exhaustively studied patient over a period of more than 40 years and such an illuminating source of information about the brain and memory.

We have already seen some examples of the poignant nature of H. M.'s horrible loss of memory. Like some cursed mythological figure, he has been condemned since his surgery at age 27 to live eternally in a moving island of the present and the immediate past, although he also has many old memories from his life before the surgery. Understandably, this devastates his ability to deal with life. Thus, he does not recognize anyone he has met since his surgery. He cannot follow a conversation or understand ongoing events. For example, his amnesia makes it impossible for him to follow the plot of even a simple TV show, and he may watch the tape of the same program again

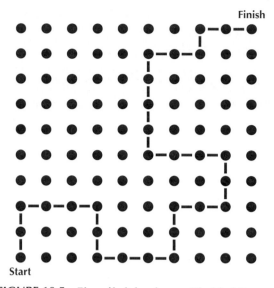

FIGURE 10.5   Plan of bolt-head maze. The black line (not shown on the actual maze) indicates the correct path. *(From Teuber & Milner, 1968, p. 354)*

and again, without any apparent recognition that he has seen it before. H. M. lacks knowledge of even the most salient events in his life since age 27. He wept when he heard that his favorite uncle had died, only to receive the news as if for the first time minutes later and again be consumed by tears. Years after his father's death, when I asked him about his father, H. M. said, tentatively, "I think my Daddy is dead." This response indicates that H. M. has retained some information about his past, although he is unsure about its accuracy. In fact, he often responded to questions about the past as if he were free-associating, without confidence in the accuracy of his responses, even when they happened to be correct.

Formal studies of H. M. provide a more quantitative picture of his impairment. This picture is exemplified by his performance on a maze learning task in which subjects had to discover and remember the correct path by moving a stylus from one bolt head to another (Figure 10.5). Every time a bolt head not on the correct path was touched, an error counter clicked loudly. Although normal control subjects learn this task quite quickly, H. M. failed to show any learning on it after 215 trials, spread over 3 days of training. In fact, despite the considerable amount of time he spent

doing the task, he did not remember doing it or seeing the apparatus before, even at the end of the extended training period (Milner & Teuber, 1968).

Some Implications of H. M.'s Memory Impairment

EVIDENCE THAT SHORT-TERM MEMORY AND LONG-TERM MEMORY ARE TWO SEPARATE SYSTEMS   We have noted that H. M. has normal short-term memory, as exemplified by his above-average digit span. Yet his long-term retention of new information is severely impaired. This dissociation is strong evidence supporting the notion that short-term memory and long-term memory are two separate systems, an idea proposed by William James (1890), using different terminology, in the 19th century.

MEDIAL TEMPORAL-LOBE STRUCTURES AS THE NEURAL SUBSTRATE OF MEMORY CONSOLIDATION   Since the initial report of H. M., other patients with damage to medial temporal-lobe structures have been reported to have a similar impairment. This damage may be due to a number of causes, including *Herpes simplex* encephalitis, vascular accident, hypoxia (oxygen deprivation), closed-head injury, electroconvulsive shock, and Alzheimer's disease. Amnesias involving medial temporal-lobe structures are collectively referred to as **medial temporal-lobe amnesia.** The anterograde amnesia of H. M. and other patients with medial temporal-lobe amnesia suggests that medial temporal-lobe structures are necessary for information to be stored in long-term memory, a process referred to as **consolidation.**

Limits to the Generality of the Consolidation Hypothesis   As intuitively appealing as this notion is, there is an important domain of findings showing that, although medial temporal-lobe structures play a critical role in the consolidation of explicit memory, they are not necessary for implicit memory, including procedural memory or priming. We will have much more to say about this in a later section.

Retrograde Amnesia and the Nature of the Consolidation Process   H. M.'s anterograde amnesia is the most salient feature of his memory impairment.

However, his impairment also has a retrograde component: He has impaired memory for specific events that occurred between age 16 and age 27, the decade *before* his surgery. In fact, the death of his favorite uncle, mentioned earlier, is one of these forgotten events that occurred before the surgery. H. M. exhibits no memory impairment for events before age 16. This pattern of retrograde amnesia represents a **temporal gradient,** whereby memory for more recently acquired information is more impaired than memory for more remote information. This pattern is seen in several different types of amnesia (Squire & Cohen, 1979, 1982), particularly in patients with Korsakoff's disease (discussed later). The presence of a temporal gradient in retrograde amnesia suggests that memory is a dynamic process that changes over time. It also suggests that medial temporal-lobe structures are involved in the retention of memories for a period of years. Apparently, these structures are involved in the storage of information, or in the maintenance of information stored elsewhere, for an extended time period, until memories are eventually stored in a system independent of medial temporal-lobe structures.

MEMORY IMPAIRMENT AFTER UNILATERAL TEMPORAL-LOBE LESIONS

Much of the work in the area of unilateral temporal-lobe lesions has been carried out by Brenda Milner and her colleagues at the Montreal Neurological Institute, who have studied patients who have undergone unilateral temporal lobectomy for the relief of focal seizures that cannot be successfully treated with anticonvulsant medication (Milner, 1975). These lesions differ from those seen in patients with medial temporal-lobe amnesia in that they are confined to one side of the brain, include less extensive damage to medial temporal-lobe structures, and include removals of larger portions of temporal neocortex. These unilateral temporal-lobe lesions do not cause the devastating amnesia seen after bilateral temporal-lobe damage. Instead, lesions confined to one temporal lobe result in relatively mild memory impairments, which can nevertheless still be quite troublesome to individuals affected by them.

Complementary Specialization of Memory Function for the Left and Right Temporal Lobes

The nature of the memory impairment seen after a unilateral temporal-lobe lesion varies depending on the hemisphere involved. Lesions of the left temporal lobe are associated with impairment in the retention of verbal material (or material that is coded verbally) but with normal performance on tests assessing memory for material that is difficult to verbalize. For example, patients with left temporal lobectomy are impaired in the delayed recall of words, stories, and verbal paired associates (Milner, 1975), but they are unimpaired in the recall of geometric figures and the recognition of pictures of faces. In contrast, patients with right temporal-lobe lesions exhibit the complementary pattern of impaired and preserved memory function. For example, these patients show impaired recall of geometric figures (Taylor, 1969) and face recognition (Milner, 1968; Warrington & James, 1967b), but are not impaired in the retention of verbal material.

The Roles of Medial Temporal-Lobe Structures and Lateral Temporal Cortex in Memory

H. M. and patients with similar lesions exhibit a severe amnesia after extensive damage to medial temporal-lobe structures and relative sparing of lateral temporal neocortex. This raises the question of whether the severity of the memory impairment seen after unilateral temporal-lobe lesions is related to the extent of damage to the hippocampus and other medial temporal-lobe structures. The answer that has emerged is that it depends on the task. The magnitude of impairment on some tasks, such as delayed recall of verbal paired associates and face recognition, is related to the extent of removal of temporal neocortex, but not the extent of medial temporal-lobe removal. This shows that the temporal neocortex plays a role in the retention of at least certain types of information.

On some tasks, however, the degree of memory impairment after unilateral temporal lobectomy is related to the extent of medial temporal-lobe removal. Studies by Philip Corsi (1972) first demonstrated this

Group 1

Hippocampus spared

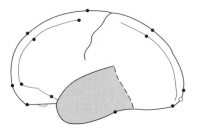

Group 2

Pes hippocampi excised

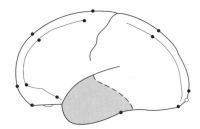

Case T. H.

Case R. S.

Group 3

Pes hippocampi and
approximately 1 cm
of body excised

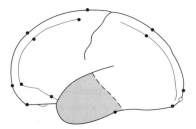

Group 4

Radical excision
of hippocampus

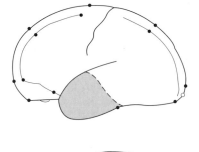

Case J. W.

Case M. O.

FIGURE 10.6 Brain maps, based on drawings made at surgery, showing representative left temporal lobectomies in four groups of patients classified by extent of medial temporal-lobe removal. The pes hippocampi is the anterior tip of the hippocampus. Shading indicates the extent of surgical excision. *(From Milner, 1970, p. 31)*

relationship. In one study, he gave patients with unilateral temporal lobectomy the Hebb Recurring Digits Test, a task in which strings of digits that are longer than the subjects' digit spans are presented to them. As expected, all subjects learned these novel strings

poorly. However, every third string was repeated, and, over many presentations, normal control subjects learned the repeated sequence. Corsi divided patients who had undergone left temporal lobectomy into four groups, according to the extent of medial temporal-

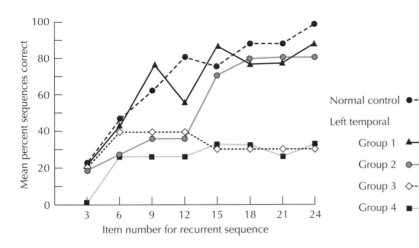

FIGURE 10.7   Learning curves for the normal control and for left temporal-lobe subgroups (see Figure 10.6) for each presentation of the recurring sequence on the Hebb Recurring Digits Test. The ordinate indicates the proportion of subjects correctly recalling the recurring sequence. The abscissa indicates the ordinal position of the recurring sequence. *(From Corsi, 1972)*

lobe removal (Figure 10.6). On this task, patients with extensive removal of left medial-temporal structures were severely impaired, whereas patients with small left medial-temporal removals and patients with either slight or extensive right medial-temporal lesions showed no impairment (Figure 10.7). Degree of impairment was also found to be unrelated to the extent of neocortical removal.

In a spatial analogue of this task, the Block-Tapping Test, Corsi required subjects to repeat a sequence tapped out by the examiner on an array of blocks (Figure 10.8). As in the Recurring Digits Test, the length of the sequence was longer than the subjects' immediate spans, but every third sequence was repeated. On this task, patients with extensive right medial temporal-lobe removals were impaired in learning the repeating sequence, whereas patients with only small right medial temporal-lobe removals and patients with left temporal-lobe removals were unimpaired. As in the Recurring Digits Test, no relationship was found between the extent of temporal neocortex removal and magnitude of impairment.

These studies of Corsi were followed by a number of studies showing a relationship between extent of unilateral medial temporal-lobe removal and memory impairment. However, for some tasks no such relationship was apparent, the extent of lateral neocortex being the critical factor. Although the different contributions of each of these areas to memory processes re-

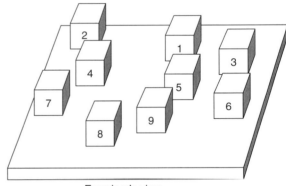

Examiner's view

FIGURE 10.8   Corsi's Block-Tapping Task. The nine black blocks (1.25-in. cubes), mounted on a black board (8 × 10 in.), are numbered on the examiner's side for ease in recording performance. The numbers are not visible to the subjects. *(From Milner, 1971, p. 275)*

main to be fully elucidated, there is compelling evidence that right medial temporal-lobe structures are particularly important for the retention of spatial information (Corsi, 1972; Rains & Milner, 1994a; Smith & Milner, 1981) but not for the retention of visual patterns (Taylor, 1969) or for the recognition of faces (Milner, 1968). The difference in the functional role of left medial temporal-lobe structures as opposed to left temporal neocortex is less easily characterized and is an active area of current investigation.

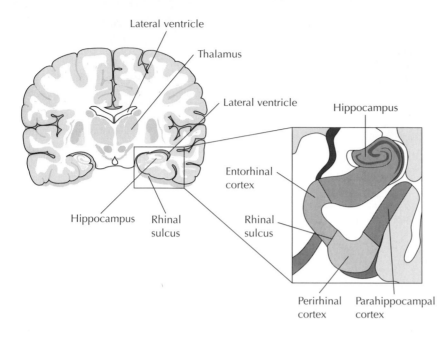

FIGURE 10.9   A coronal section of the brain, showing the hippocampus and the cortex of the medial temporal lobe, including the entorhinal cortex, the perirhinal cortex, and the parahippocampal cortex. *(From Bear, Connors, & Paradiso, 1996, p. 531)*

THE CRITICAL STRUCTURES INVOLVED IN MEMORY LOSS AFTER TEMPORAL-LOBE LESIONS

Whatever the differential role of medial temporal-lobe structures and temporal neocortex, the severe amnesia manifested by H. M. and other patients with medial temporal-lobe lesions shows that these structures are critical for memory. Up to now we have used the umbrella term *medial temporal-lobe structures.* In this section we examine more closely what structures within this area are crucial for memory.

H. M.'s Lesions

H. M.'s surgery included bilateral removal of the following structures: the anterior 8 cm of the hippocampus, the amygdala, and the rhinal cortex. The rhinal cortex comprises the entorhinal cortex, the perirhinal cortex, and the parahippocampal cortex (Figure 10.9). The findings in H. M. and patients with similar lesions were initially interpreted as evidence for the crucial role of the hippocampus in memory. This idea has undergone an interesting process of evolution in the course of the 40 years since its inception, a process that serves as an instructive model of fruitful

reciprocal interaction between hypothesis and experiment. For this reason we will trace this evolution in some detail in the following sections.

Discrepancy Between Findings in Animals and Humans

After the report of H. M., intensive efforts were made to produce an animal model of his impairment, that is, to produce a lesion in an animal that would cause a similar amnesia. The intent was to enable investigators to study anterograde amnesia in the animal laboratory and to learn more precisely which medial temporal-lobe structures were critical for memory. Based on patient H. M., an obvious candidate was the hippocampus. Investigators proceeded to study the effects on memory of experimental lesions in this structure in monkeys.

To the surprise of investigators who followed this line of reasoning, animal studies involving lesions to the hippocampus failed to produce impairment in memory. This was interpreted by many as evidence that the neural substrate of memory is fundamentally different in animals and humans. This would preclude the creation of an animal model for medial temporal-lobe amnesia and present animal researchers with the

Sample
presentation

Delay

Test

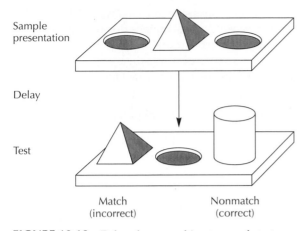

| Match | Nonmatch |
| (incorrect) | (correct) |

FIGURE 10.10 Delayed nonmatching to sample test.
(From LeDoux, 1996, p. 188)

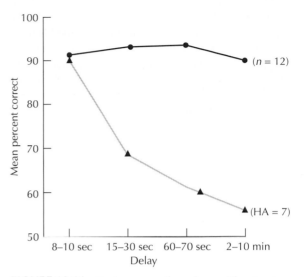

FIGURE 10.11 Performance of monkeys with extensive medial temporal-lobe lesions *(HA)* and normal controls *(N)* on delayed nonmatching to sample at different delay intervals. *(From Squire, 1987, p. 191)*

problem of finding a structure whose function is analogous to that of the hippocampus in humans.

Apparent Resolution of the Discrepancy

For a time, this discrepancy seemed to be resolved by the discovery of a task that was sensitive to hippocampal lesions in monkeys. Gaffan (1974) showed that macaque monkeys with hippocampal lesions performed poorly on a task called **delayed nonmatching to sample (DNMS).** In this task a monkey is first presented with an object that covers one of several food wells on a table in front of him. Then, a screen comes down for a period of time: the delay interval. When the screen is lifted, the monkey now sees two objects, one of which was recently seen and one of which is new. If the monkey then moves the new object aside, he finds food in the well, but there is no food under the previously seen object. In this way, the monkey can be trained to choose the novel object, a process that is facilitated by the macaque's natural curiosity (Figure 10.10). Because this task requires identifying a previously seen object, it is a form of **recognition memory.**

Normal monkeys are able to perform this task with a high level of accuracy for intervals as long as 10 minutes. Animals with medial temporal-lobe lesions, however, are markedly impaired on this task for delay intervals longer than a few seconds (Figure 10.11). The

finding that they are able to perform well at short delay intervals shows that the impairment is not due to a perceptual deficit or to failure to remember the task procedure. It also supports the notion that the impairment parallels the anterograde amnesia seen in H. M. and other patients with medial temporal-lobe amnesia, because in these patients short-term retention is also unimpaired.

Search for the Critical Structures Involved in Recognition Memory

With the achievement of this animal model, the search for the critical structures involved in recognition memory was intensified. At first it was thought that the hippocampus was the critical structure. But the initial experiments demonstrating impairment in DNMS were with monkeys with large medial temporal-lobe lesions which, like H. M.'s, included the hippocampus, amygdala, and the rhinal cortex (entorhinal cortex, perirhinal cortex, and parahippocampal cortex). Experiments with more circumscribed lesions that selectively damaged only the hippocampus produced only a mild deficit. Mishkin (1978) then studied the effect of damage to both the amygdala and the hippocampus and found that the combined lesions produced a severe impairment. These findings fit with H. M.'s damage because he also had damage to both the amygdala and the hippocampus. As if the two structures had redundant functions, it seemed that damage to both the amygdala and the hippocampus was necessary to disrupt recognition memory.

Some Conflicting Findings

It is a truism that the promising theories of today are overturned by new findings tomorrow. So it was with the conclusion that combined damage to the amygdala and the hippocampus is the critical lesion in medial temporal-lobe amnesia.

PATIENT R. B.   One source of conflicting data was the report of a patient, known as R. B., who had a severe anterograde amnesia (though milder than H. M.'s) and had a lesion confined to the hippocampus (Zola-Morgan, Squire, & Amaral, 1986). This finding had two important implications: (a) Amnesia can occur after damage confined to the hippocampus, and (b) such amnesia is less severe than that resulting from more extensive medial-temporal lesions. Taken together, these findings suggested that the hippocampus is important for recognition memory but that it is not the only important structure.

EXCLUDING THE AMYGDALA   Based on Mishkin's (1978) findings, an obvious candidate for another contributing region was the amygdala. However, the interpretation of Mishkin's finding that combined lesions of the amygdala and the hippocampus resulted in memory impairment was complicated by the fact that his amygdala lesions also included damage to neighboring regions of cortex. To explore this further, Zola-Morgan and his colleagues (1989) carried out a study with monkeys in which they made selective removals of only the amygdala, without disturbing adjacent cortical areas. When these monkeys were then subjected to memory testing, it was shown that amygdala lesions alone do not cause impairment in DNMS. More im-

portant, it was also shown that amygdala lesions that spare adjacent cortical regions do not exacerbate the memory impairment that follows hippocampal lesions. The structure outside the hippocampus critical for recognition memory was not the amygdala.

The Importance of Medial-Temporal Cortex

The critical structures turned out to be the entorhinal cortex, the perirhinal cortex, and the parahippocampal cortex, all parts of the cortex adjacent to the hippocampus (see Figure 10.9). Collectively these regions are referred to as rhinal cortex. That these structures are critical became clear from a number of studies, including those showing that selective lesions of perirhinal, entorhinal, and parahippocampal cortex that spared both the amygdala and the hippocampus produced severe memory impairment in monkeys (Meunier et al., 1993; Murray, 1992; Murray, Gaffan, & Mishkin, 1993; Squire & Zola-Morgan, 1991; Zola-Morgan, Squire, Amaral, & Suzuki, 1989).

The conclusion that the hippocampus and surrounding rhinal cortex are both critical for recognition memory, drawn from these animal studies, fits with findings from studies of medial temporal-lobe amnesia in humans. H. M. had damage to rhinal cortex, in addition to his hippocampal lesion. R. B., with damage confined to the hippocampus, was amnesic but did not manifest a memory impairment as severe as H. M.'s. This conclusion is also consistent with the anatomical relationship between the hippocampus and its neighboring cortex. The perirhinal and parahippocampal cortices receive highly processed sensory input converging on them from each of the major cortical sensory areas. These cortices in turn project to the entorhinal cortex, which is the major source of input to the hippocampus. It is plausible, therefore, that damage to rhinal cortex produces a severe memory impairment because it deprives the hippocampus of highly processed sensory input necessary for the laying down of memories (Figure 10.12). In addition, rhinal cortex may be the site of temporary storage of information. This is suggested by the fact that R. B., who has hippocampal but not rhinal cortex damage, has a much milder retrograde amnesia than patients such as H. M., whose lesions include the rhinal cortex.

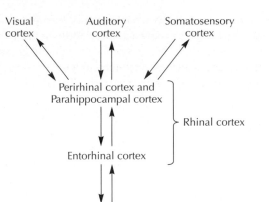

FIGURE 10.12 Cortical input to the hippocampus. Highly processed input from all of the major sensory modalities projects to the perirhinal and parahippocampal cortices. These, in turn, project to the entorhinal cortex. The entorhinal cortex is the major source of input to the hippocampus. The hippocampus projects back to the neocortex by way of the same pathways. *(After LeDoux, 1996, p. 194)*

DIENCEPHALIC AMNESIA

We turn now to another type of severe amnesia, diencephalic amnesia. Diencephalic amnesia differs from medial temporal-lobe amnesia both in its symptomatology and in the location of the lesions producing it. The most common form of diencephalic amnesia is seen in **Korsakoff's disease,** a thiamine (vitamin B$_1$) deficiency disease usually caused by malnutrition secondary to severe alcoholism. Most investigations of diencephalic amnesia have studied patients with Korsakoff's disease, and this will be our focus here. There are, however, other less frequent causes of damage to diencephalic structures, such as trauma and stroke.

Korsakoff's Disease

Like patients with medial temporal-lobe amnesia, patients with Korsakoff's disease have severe anterograde amnesia. However, they generally have a number of other components to their disorder that make it different from that seen in medial temporal-lobe amnesia.

MEMORY IMPAIRMENT IN KORSAKOFF'S DISEASE In addition to having a severe anterograde amnesia that is as profound as that seen in medial

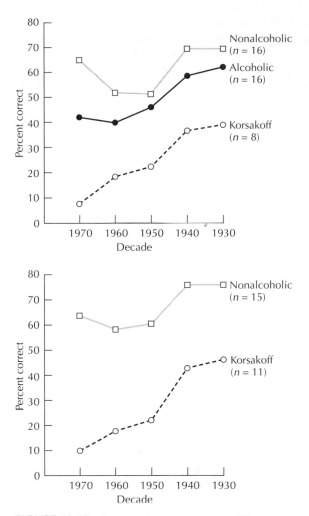

FIGURE 10.13 Retrograde amnesia in two different populations of patients with Korsakoff's disease as measured by a test that involves the identification of pictures of famous faces from different decades. *(Top)* Results from Cohen and Squire (1981). *(Bottom)* Results from Albert, Butters, and Levin (1980). The impairment is more severe for faces that came into the news during the most recent two decades before administration of the test. This is presumably because the anterograde amnesia was present or developing during that period. *(From Squire, 1987, p. 216)*

temporal-lobe amnesia, Korsakoff's disease is accompanied by a retrograde amnesia. This typically stretches further back in time than the retrograde amnesia in medial temporal-lobe amnesia, often extending back for decades (Figure 10.13).

Disturbance of Metamemory   Diencephalic amnesia also differs from medial temporal-lobe amnesia in that patients with diencephalic amnesia often exhibit an impairment in the ability to accurately appraise their memory capability, a process called **metamemory.** When presented with a memory task and asked to estimate how well they will perform on it, patients with diencephalic amnesia tend to overestimate their memory abilities (Gardner, 1975, pp. 181–182).

Confabulation   Patients with diencephalic amnesia may go further and exhibit an apparent total unawareness of their impairment. This may be accompanied by **confabulation,** acting as if one remembers people and situations that one in fact does not recognize. For example, a former delicatessen owner with Korsakoff's disease greeted his physician on the hospital ward as if the two were in his delicatessen in a distant city and his physician was an old, familiar customer for whom he was about to prepare his favorite sandwich (Sacks, 1985). Confabulatory behavior in patients with severe amnesia can reach tragic-comic proportions, as they seem to blatantly disregard their lack of knowledge of situations and people and plunge ahead as if they were on the most familiar terrain.

Source Amnesia   **Source amnesia** is impairment in the ability to remember the source of information together with preservation of the information itself. For example, a patient might be told some made-up bit of trivia, such as "Yogi Berra's favorite food is pizza." When asked a few minutes later about Yogi Berra's favorite food, they might respond "pizza" but then be unable to accurately respond to questions about where they learned that information. In response to such questions they might produce a confabulatory response, such as claiming that they had picked up the information while watching television or reading magazines.

Memory for Temporal Order: Recency Discrimination
Being able to recall and recognize past experience is obviously a major function of memory, and it is clearly highly useful. But it is important to be able to go further and identify when events in the past happened relative to other past events—in other words, to remember the order of their occurrence. It may simply

be important to know what happened before such and such and what happened after. In addition, the elaborative process of reconstruction, which Bartlett and others have argued is a hallmark of long-term remembering, achieves greater accuracy when it is possible to "tag" specific events to particular times and contexts. This all-important memory for temporal order is often impaired in patients with Korsakoff's disease.

Failure to Release From Proactive Interference   **Proactive interference (PI)** is the tendency of previously presented information to interfere with memory for material that is presented later. For example, suppose a subject is presented a list of names of fruit (list F_1) and asked to remember it. Following this, she is given a second list of different fruit names (list F_2) to remember. Suppose list F_3 and list F_4, both also composed of fruit names, are then given. In recall of the fourth list of names of fruit, there will be a tendency for the subject to insert words from previous lists. This is proactive interference. If a list of names from an entirely different category, say animals, is then given, the tendency for intrusions from the prior lists is reduced. We say the shift of category has caused a **release from proactive interference.** Release from PI is thought to reflect aspects of memory organization. Korsakoff's patients frequently fail to show release from PI; intrusions from prior lists occur even after a category shift.

OTHER IMPAIRMENT IN KORSAKOFF'S DISEASE   In addition to aspects of disrupted memory in Korsakoff's disease, certain pervasive impairment in cognitive and emotional functioning is often seen. Patients with this disease have been described as cognitively apathetic and unmotivated, frequently not mustering the attention and concentration required to solve a problem that otherwise would be in the compass of their intellectual ability. In addition, a reduction in the range and intensity of emotional expression is often seen. This may be reflected in a tendency to minimize, or even completely deny, the devastating severity of their memory impairment.

THE NEUROPATHOLOGY OF KORSAKOFF'S DISEASE   What is wrong with the brains of people with Korsakoff's disease? Neuropathological studies of these patients suggest that there are lesions in the diencephalon and in the frontal lobes.

Diencephalic Lesions   The two most frequently reported lesions in postmortem studies of patients with Korsakoff's disease are in two diencephalic structures: the mamillary bodies and the dorsomedial nucleus of the thalamus (Mair, Warrington, & Weiskrantz, 1979; Parkin & Leng, 1993; Victor, Adams, & Collins, 1989). MRI studies of living patients are also consistent with these postmortem findings (Jernigan et al., 1991). In addition, there have been some reports of lesions to the anterior nucleus of the thalamus in patients with Korsakoff's disease, although these lesions are seen less consistently.

Lesions Outside the Diencephalon   Many patients with Korsakoff's disease, in addition to their diencephalic lesions, have lesions that include areas of the frontal lobes. It is likely that these frontal-lobe lesions account for many of the features that differentiate Korsakoff's disease from medial temporal-lobe amnesia. Support for this comes from the fact that all of the features differentiating Korsakoff's disease from medial temporal-lobe amnesia, except the extended retrograde amnesia in Korsakoff's disease, are also seen in lesions confined to the frontal lobes. These include disturbance of metamemory, confabulation, source amnesia, disturbance of memory for temporal order, failure to release from PI, cognitive apathy, motivational disturbance, and reduced emotional expression. Furthermore, it has been shown that at least some of these impairments, such as confabulation, are seen only in Korsakoff patients who have frontal-lobe pathology (Shimamura, Jernigan, & Squire, 1988).

Other Causes of Diencephalic Amnesia

As mentioned earlier, Korsakoff's disease is not the only cause of diencephalic amnesia. Any disease or trauma that damages critical diencephalic structures will cause severe memory impairment. Although trauma confined to these critical diencephalic structures is rare because of their position deep within the forebrain, such cases have been reported.

PATIENT N. A.   In 1959, the patient known as N. A. was accidentally stabbed by his roommate with a miniature fencing foil. The foil entered N. A.'s right nostril and penetrated leftward into his brain. As a result, he sustained a severe anterograde amnesia. Although not as severe as H. M.'s (he was able to form sketchy memories of some events and faces), it was nevertheless extreme. He also had a retrograde amnesia for a period of about 2 years prior to his accident. In several other respects his memory impairment was similar to that of H. M.: His short-term retention was normal, his recall of old memories was intact, and there was no impairment in general intellectual functioning. CT scan revealed a lesion of the left dorsomedial nucleus of the thalamus.

OTHER EVIDENCE OF THALAMIC AMNESIA
There have been a number of other reports of amnesia following thalamic lesions (e.g., Von Cramon, Hebel, & Schuri, 1985), including lesions involving the anterior nucleus of the thalamus (Aggleton and Brown, 1999). In addition, impairment in memory during thalamic stimulation carried out in the course of surgery has been reported (Ojemann, Blick, & Ward, 1971).

The Relationship Between Medial-Temporal and Diencephalic Amnesia

If we discount the impairments in Korsakoff's disease due to frontal-lobe lesions, the patterns of impaired and preserved memory function associated with medial temporal-lobe amnesia and with diencephalic amnesia are strikingly similar. Both are characterized by severe anterograde amnesia. They also exhibit retrograde amnesia stretching back a few years. (Korsakoff's disease may be associated with a longer retrograde amnesia, but this is not seen in amnesia in which the lesion is known to be confined to the diencephalon.) In addition, both medial temporal-lobe amnesia and diencephalic amnesia show preservation of short-term memory, old memories, and general intellectual functioning. The fact that damage to either medial temporal-lobe structures or diencephalic structures produces a very similar amnesia suggests that these two regions are part of a common system that mediates the formation of new declarative long-term memories.

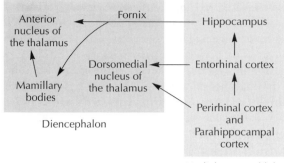

FIGURE 10.14   Two different circuits connect medial temporal-lobe cortex and the diencephalon. One circuit connects the hippocampus to the anterior nucleus of the thalamus, both directly and via the mamillary bodies. The other connects perirhinal and entorhinal cortex to the dorsomedial nucleus of the thalamus. *(Adapted from Aggleton and Brown, 1999, pp. 426, 427)*

For a time, there were findings that did not seem to fit with this notion of a common, unitary system including both medial-temporal and diencephalic structures. These findings had to do with the effect of lesions to the fornix, the fiber tract that conveys impulses from the hippocampus to the mamillary bodies. The problem was that early clinical reports indicated that lesions to this obvious link between medial-temporal regions and the diencephalon did not produce memory impairment. Although more recently it has been shown that patients with fornix lesions do experience some memory impairment, the magnitude of their impairment is not comparable to that seen in amnesia (Gaffan, Gaffan, & Hodges, 1991). These findings do not fit with the notion that the two regions are part of a common system.

There are, however, anatomical findings consistent with the unitary system hypothesis. The fornix is not the only major connection between medial temporal-lobe structures and diencephalon; as illustrated schematically in Figure 10.14, there is also a route from the perirhinal and entorhinal cortex to the dorsomedial nucleus of the thalamus that does not involve the fornix (Aggleton and Brown, 1999). Moreover, Aggleton and Brown have hypothesized that episodic memory is dependent on the hippocampal-anterior thalamic axis, while semantic memory depends on the perirhinal cortex-dorsomedial thalamic pathway, although in the large majority of amnesic cases structures integral to both pathways are compromised.

WHERE IN THE MEMORY PROCESS IS THE IMPAIRMENT?

In an earlier section, we outlined the processes into which memory can be analyzed. Which of these components of memory are disrupted in amnesia? And which are disrupted in the less severe memory impairment seen after unilateral temporal-lobe lesions?

Registration/Encoding

If we look at the initial stage of the memory process, we find that there is no evidence of disruption in the registration or encoding of information in H. M. (Milner, Corkin, & Teuber, 1968) or in patients with unilateral temporal lobectomy (Rains & Milner, 1994b). Furthermore, at least the retrograde component of memory loss in patients with amnesia cannot be due to disruption of registration or encoding because the lost information was accurately retained during the time period before the onset of the amnesia.

Consolidation/Storage/Maintenance

The next stage in memory processing that might be disrupted in amnesia may be variously conceptualized as consolidation, storage, or maintenance of information. Disruption at this level seems consonant with the anterograde component of amnesia; H. M. and other amnesic patients do not seem to consolidate information that is nevertheless accurately encoded and accurately retained over the short intervals mediated by short-term memory.

However, several aspects of the retrograde component of amnesia complicate this interpretation. First, the period of retrograde amnesia can be quite long, up to 10 years in H. M. and several years in other patients. If this retrograde component is due to a consolidation problem, then consolidation is a very long process, on the order of years. A disruption of maintenance has also been proposed to explain this effect. According to this hypothesis, the retrograde amnesia results because the lesioned structures are unable to mediate processes that normally would maintain the memory trace until it is fully consolidated in long-term memory. That information should be kept in some intermediate state between short-term memory and long-term memory for a long time period seems unlikely, although it remains a possibility.

A second problem with the consolidation hypothesis also has to do with retrograde amnesia, in particular, the fact that its extent is highly variable across amnesic patients. Some amnesic patients have a retrograde amnesia stretching back 1 or 2 years. For others it stretches back for a decade or even several decades. If the retrograde amnesia is due to an impairment in consolidation, it is unclear why the duration of this process should be so variable across patients.

A third problem for the hypothesis that a consolidation impairment underlies retrograde amnesia is the finding of retrograde amnesia in a patient who, before the onset of his Korsakoff's syndrome, had written an autobiography that documented that he had had excellent recall for events that were subsequently lost within the period of retrograde amnesia (Butters & Cermak, 1986). Findings such as this do not seem to fit well with the idea that the amnesia is due to a disruption of the consolidation process.

It should be noted that it remains possible that the disruption of different components of the memory process underlie the anterograde and the retrograde components of amnesia. Thus, the anterograde component may be due to a disruption of consolidation, while the retrograde component is due to the disruption of already stored information.

Retrieval

A **retrieval cue** is a stimulus that is perceptually, semantically, or in some other way similar to or related to information that one is trying to recall. We have all had the experience of being unable to remember something and then, after being exposed to a cue, having the elusive information suddenly come to mind. When this happens, it indicates that the information was "in there somewhere" but that we couldn't get to it. This is a disorder of retrieval.

In amnesic patients, the recall of past events within the period of time encompassed by their retrograde amnesia is often improved when cuing is employed. This has been interpreted as evidence that a disorder of retrieval underlies at least the retrograde component of their amnesia (Warrington & Weiskrantz, 1970). However, improved recall after cuing means only that there was more information stored than was available in the uncued condition. The mechanism whereby this information was unavailable in uncued recall is not necessarily a disorder of retrieval. The basic problem could be one of encoding or storage; poorly or inefficiently encoded or stored material could also be recalled better with the aid of a retrieval cue.

It is clear from the foregoing discussion that evidence regarding the stage (or stages) of memory processing that is (are) disrupted in amnesia remains inconclusive and that this is an active area of ongoing investigation.

PRESERVED ASPECTS OF MEMORY IN AMNESIA

We have seen that, despite severe impairment in the ability to retain information for any appreciable length of time, patients with medial temporal-lobe amnesia and diencephalic amnesia retain certain memory capacity. In particular, short-term memory is unimpaired. Under certain conditions working memory can be quite efficient, although it is secondarily disrupted whenever there is a need to draw on information from the past that normally, in a person without amnesia, would be available in long-term memory.

But short-term and working memory are not the only memory domains that are preserved in amnesia. We turn now to a discussion of preserved memory in amnesia, beginning with a famous report by the French physician Claparède (1911/1951). He had been caring for a severely amnesic patient, a patient so amnesic that she did not recognize Claparède despite having daily contact with him over a considerable period of time. In an effort to further assess his patient's

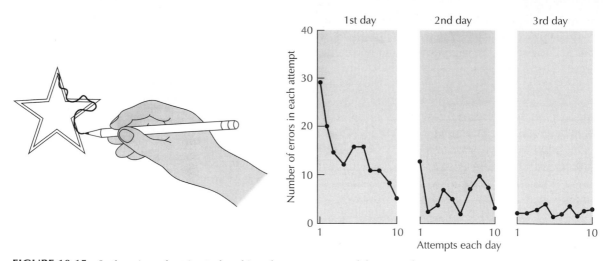

FIGURE 10.15   In the mirror drawing task, subjects have to trace a path between the outlines of two stars while viewing their hand and the star in a mirror. Over a 3-day period, H. M. showed learning, as measured by the number of lines straying outside the path per trial. *(From Milner, 1970, p. 44)*

memory impairment, Claparède performed an informal experiment. He placed a pin in his hand and approached his patient on the hospital ward with his hand extended, offering to shake hands. When his patient reciprocated, she felt a painful prick. Later that day, Claparède again approached his patient on the hospital ward, once again offering a handshake. This time the patient refused to shake his hand. When asked to explain her socially unconventional behavior, the patient, momentarily flustered, finally said, "Maybe you have a pin in your hand." Claparède's patient didn't explicitly remember the unpleasant experience that had occurred only hours before. She didn't say, as we might, "Hey, I'm not going to do that *again*." Instead, the prior experience had caused a change in the patient's behavior without leaving a memory of the event itself. The patient only had a sense, or perhaps made an inference from her own behavior, that to shake hands would be painful.

The behavior of Claparède's patient is an example of implicit memory, which we have defined as a change in behavior as a result of past experience without conscious awareness, without conscious recollection, of the past experience. It will be recalled from our earlier discussion that explicit memory, in

contrast, is conscious memory of the past. It is implicit memory that is intact in amnesic patients. In the following sections we will explore further this preserved domain of memory in amnesia.

Motor Learning

Early studies of H. M. revealed that his severe impairment in explicit memory was accompanied by an ability to show improvement on tasks involving the learning of skilled movement. For example, he was able to improve on a mirror drawing task (Figure 10.15) that required him to learn to trace a path between two outlines of stars while seeing only the reflection of his hand and the lines in a mirror (Milner, 1965a). This task is quite difficult for normal subjects at first, but they readily learn it after repeated trials. H. M. also showed continued learning on this task over a 3-day period, showing retention of learned skill from one day to the next, even though he could not remember doing the task previously if he was away from it for more than a few minutes. Similarly, H. M. showed learning in a pursuit rotor task that required him to move a stylus in such a way as to keep it in contact with a dot mounted on a moving turntable (Corkin, 1968). Again, this learning took place without conscious memory of having performed the task. Preserved motor learning is also seen in patients with diencephalic amnesia.

Evidence regarding the areas of the brain critical for motor learning points to the basal ganglia and the cerebellum. Patients with Huntington's disease, which affects the basal ganglia, are impaired in motor learning, but not in tests of explicit memory or priming (discussed later) (Heindel, Butters, & Salmon, 1988). In addition, PET studies of normal subjects engaged in motor learning tasks show activation of the basal ganglia. Impaired motor learning has also been reported in association with cerebellar lesions (Pascual-Leone et al., 1993).

Perceptual Learning

H. M. and other amnesic patients are able to show improvement on a number of perceptual tasks. For example, consider Gollin's incomplete drawings test. On this task the subject is first presented with a series of degraded line drawings of familiar objects, shown one at a time. Following this, a second set of somewhat less degraded drawings of the same objects is shown. This is followed by several additional series of progressively less degraded drawings, until the subject is able to identify all the objects (Figure 10.16). After a delay, the subject is again shown the drawings, from most degraded to progressively less degraded. Both normal control subjects and amnesic patients are able to benefit from prior viewing; they are able to identify more-degraded versions of the pictures after the delay than on initial presentation (Milner, Corkin, & Teuber, 1968; Warrington & Weiskrantz, 1968, 1970).

Another example of perceptual learning in amnesic patients is improvement, after repeated trials, in reading the mirror images of words (Figure 10.17). At first, this is a difficult task, but, after practice, normal control subjects learn mirror reading quite well. Amnesic subjects have been shown to learn this skill as rapidly as normal control subjects, even though they fail to recall or recognize the specific words that they read or other aspects of the training sessions (Cohen, 1981; Cohen & Corkin, 1981; Cohen & Eichenbaum, 1993; Cohen & Squire, 1980).

FIGURE 10.16   Examples of visually degraded line drawings for which amnesic subjects are able to show perceptual learning. *(From Cohen, 1997, p. 332)*

Classical Conditioning

Classical conditioning is preserved in amnesic patients. Weiskrantz and Warrington (1979) have demonstrated conditioning of eye blink response in amnesic patients. This finding is consistent with studies in animals that have shown preservation of condi-

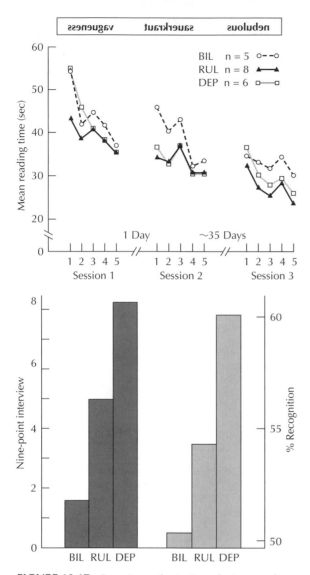

FIGURE 10.17   Learning and retention of mirror-reading skill despite amnesia for the learning experience. *(Top)* Patients given bilateral *(BIL)* or right unilateral *(RUL)* electroconvulsive therapy *(ECT)* and depressed patients *(DEP)* not receiving ECT practiced mirror reading for three sessions (50 trials/session). For the patients receiving ECT, one ECT treatment intervened between the first and second sessions, and an average of seven treatments intervened between the second and third sessions. *(Bottom)* At the beginning of the third session, subjects were tested for their recollection of the previous testing sessions (nine-point interview) and for the words they had practiced (recognition test, chance = 50%). *(From Squire, 1987, p. 154)*

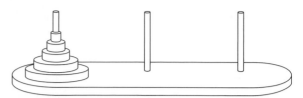

FIGURE 10.18   The Tower of Hanoi puzzle. To solve this puzzle the subject must move five disks from their starting position on the left-most peg to the right-most peg. The rules are that only one disk can be moved at a time and a larger disk cannot be placed on top of a smaller disk. The optimal solution requires 31 moves. *(From Cohen, Eichenbaum, et al., 1985, p. 57)*

tioned eye blink response after removal of the brain above the midbrain and abolition of classical conditioning after lesions to the interpositus nuclei of the cerebellum (Thompson, 1990).

Cognitive Skill Learning

Many studies have shown that amnesic patients are able to develop cognitive skills. In particular, they are able to learn procedures and strategies that lead to the successful solution of certain problems, even though, as in other situations in which learning takes place in amnesic patients, they have no explicit recollection of doing the task.

A striking example of this is the Tower of Hanoi puzzle. In this task the subject has to move five disks with holes in their centers from one peg to another, with the constraints that only one disk can be moved at a time and a larger disk cannot be placed on top of a smaller disk (Figure 10.18). Learning on this task can be measured in terms of the number of steps a subject takes to solve it, the optimal solution requiring 31 steps. It has been shown that amnesic patients learn the cognitive skills required for this solution as rapidly as normal controls (Cohen, Eichenbaum, et al., 1985). The learning curves for both groups are shown in Figure 10.19.

If you try this puzze yourself, you will find that you improve over trials, even though you may not explicitly remember the steps that you took on the previous trials; you get the knack of the problem, without remembering exactly what you did. Am-

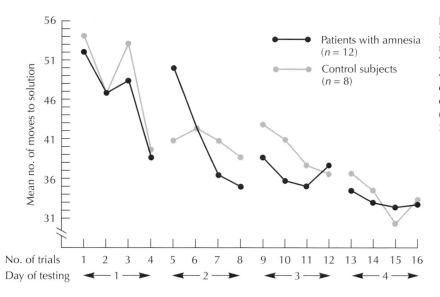

FIGURE 10.19   The performance of amnesic patients and normal control subjects on the Tower of Hanoi puzzle. Over a 4-day period the performance of both groups approaches the optimal solution in 31 steps. *(From Cohen, Eichenbaum, et al., 1985, p. 63)*

nesic patients are able to do this also. Interestingly, amnesic patients are able to remember the rules (one disk at a time and no larger disk on top of a smaller one) and the goal of the task. This is also seen in the performance of amnesic subjects on other tasks, such as their very infrequent rule breaking on a visual maze-learning task, although in that instance they were unable to learn the maze (Milner, 1965b). The neural structures mediating the learning of cognitive skills are not known, although it seems likely that the frontal lobes are important in these processes.

Priming

Perceptual priming is yet another instance of the effect of prior exposure to information on subsequent behavior, in the absence of conscious recollection of the previously experienced information. However, in contrast to the instances of implicit memory discussed earlier, which require repeated exposure to a stimulus or repeated action in a situation, in perceptual priming a single, brief exposure to a stimulus facilitates and enhances the perception of the stimulus on a later occasion. This facilitation may take the form of more rapid perception or accurate perception of a degraded stimulus that would not otherwise be recognized. For example, in **repetition priming** a

subject is first exposed to a list of words. A test of recall follows. Then, words are tachistoscopically flashed to the subject so briefly that under normal circumstances very few are read accurately. However, under these conditions, subjects are more likely to accurately read words that appeared on the prior list, including words that they did not recall on the intervening memory test. Thus, prior exposure to the stimulus facilitates perception, even in the absence of conscious memory of the stimulus.

Another example is the stem completion task. In this task the subject's prior exposure to a list of words facilitates the completion of word stems with the previously seen words. For example, suppose the word *elephant* appears on the list. The subject is then presented with three letters that could be the beginning of a word (the stem), followed by blanks for the missing letters (e.g., ELE _ _ _ _ _), and asked to fill in the blanks to form any word that comes to mind. In other words, the subject is not explicitly asked to complete the stem with a word from the prior list. Despite these instructions, subjects more often complete the stem with words that occurred on the prior list than with other words that meet the constraints of the stem and occur equally frequently in English. This is the case even when they are unable to recall the word as one that appeared on the prior list. Here again we see the effect on behavior of past exposure to a stimulus, in the absence of conscious awareness of having seen the stimulus.

These and other priming effects have been reported in normal subjects (e.g., Tulving, Schacter, & Stark, 1982) and have contributed to the formulation of the distinction between implicit and explicit memory put forth by Graf and Schacter (1985). (For reviews of implicit memory in normal subjects see Roediger & McDermott, 1993; Schacter, 1987; Schacter, Chin, & Ochsner, 1993.)

INTACT PRIMING IN AMNESIC PATIENTS Priming effects are seen in amnesic patients. Thus, although amnesic patients are impaired in the free recall and cued recall of recently seen words, they do not differ from normal controls in their ability to complete stems with words that were seen on a prior list when they are simply asked to complete the stem with any word that comes to mind (Graf, Squire, & Mandler, 1984; Squire, 1987; Warrington & Weiskrantz, 1970). This is shown in Figure 10.20. Interestingly, in contrast to the data shown in Figure 10.20, the performance of amnesic patients on the stem completion task may *decline* if, instead of being asked to complete the stem with any word that comes to mind, they are asked instead to complete the stem with a word from the recently seen list (Graf et al., 1984).

DIFFERENT RULES FOR PRIMING THAN FOR EXPLICIT MEMORY IN NORMAL SUBJECTS Further evidence that priming and explicit memory are mediated by different systems comes from differences in the rules governing the two forms of memory. Priming does not show the depth of processing effects seen in explicit memory. An example of depth of processing effects is the finding that when subjects are induced to encode words semantically (e.g., by answering questions about their meaning) they subsequently recall and recognize these words better than words that have been encoded phonemically (e.g., by answering questions about their sound). Phonemically encoded words, in turn, are remembered better than words encoded according to their physical features (e.g., by answering questions about whether the word is printed in capital letters).

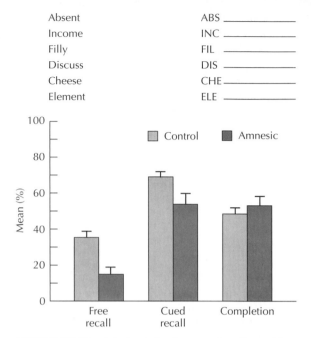

FIGURE 10.20 Intact priming in amnesic patients. After exposure to a word list, amnesic patients were impaired in the free recall of words from the list. If, however, subjects were given the first three letters of words and instructed to simply say the first word that came to mind (completion), amnesic patients performed as well as normal control subjects. (The baseline guessing for the word completion condition was 9%.) The performance of control subjects, but not amnesic subjects, improved relative to the completion condition when subjects were given the first three letters and asked explicitly to recall the words seen on the prior list (cued recall). *(From Squire, 1987, p. 155)*

These depth-of-processing effects presumably depend on the interaction of systems mediating memory with systems mediating semantic and phonemic processing. Apparently, the system mediating priming does not interact with these systems. Instead, priming seems to be closely linked with perceptually based processing. This is indicated by the finding that priming does not occur if the initial presentation of the to-be-remembered words is in a different modality than the later test of priming (termed **study-test modality shift**). For example, subjects first exposed to heard words will not show priming effects for visually presented words.

THE NEURAL SUBSTRATE OF PRIMING   The hypothesis that priming is closely linked to perceptual processing is supported by findings in imaging studies and lesion studies. Although PET studies show that temporal and frontal regions are activated when a subject thinks of a word, seeing a word activates occipital areas. This is to be expected because occipital cortex is involved in the initial stages of cortical visual processing. There is evidence that in normal subjects changes in occipital activity occur in conditions that promote visual priming (Buckner et al., 1995), whereas activation of the hippocampus is seen in recall and recognition (Squire, Ojemann, et al., 1992). In addition, there are reports of impairment in priming after occipital-lobe lesions (Gabrieli et al., 1995; Keane, Clarke, & Corkin, 1992). Taken together, these findings support the idea that priming is mediated by a system closely linked to systems mediating perceptual processing. This is embodied in Daniel Schacter's hypothesis of a **perceptual representation system,** or **PRS** (Schacter, 1996).

The link between perceptual processing and perceptual priming is further supported by the finding that patients with impairment in perceptual priming are not impaired in conceptual priming. An example of conceptual priming would be first hearing the sentence *The haystack was important because the cloth ripped* and then hearing the word *parachute.* When the sentence is then heard again after a delay, normal subjects can make sense of it because they had heard the key word. Interestingly, amnesic subjects also retain this capacity. In the present context what is particularly important, however, is the finding that patients with impaired perceptual priming may have unimpaired conceptual priming (Keane et al., 1992). This dissociation provides further evidence that perceptual priming is linked to systems mediating perceptual processing rather than to more general cognitive systems.

A ROLE FOR PRIMING IN COGNITIVE REHABILITATION   For many years efforts to help people with impaired memory have focused on the use of memory aids similar to those employed by normal people who want to improve their memory. These include approaches such as the **method of loci,** in which a subject forms interactive visual images with an overlearned sequence of imaged locations. These methods have been shown to help some patients with relatively mild memory impairment (e.g., Jones, 1974).

More recently, however, cognitive rehabilitation has begun to focus on the use of implicit memory capabilities in patients with severe explicit memory impairment. A dramatic example of this is the training of a woman who suffered from a severe anterograde amnesia caused by an encephalitis. Because priming is intact in amnesic patients, Schacter and his colleagues attempted to train their patient, whom they called Barbara, to enter data from invoices and other business documents into a computer, using a method that they called the **method of vanishing cues.** To gain a sense of whether implicit memory could be used to train an amnesic patient on such a task, Schacter and his colleagues began by attempting to train her in computer terminology. To do this they flashed a definition on a computer screen, such as "a repeated portion of a program." If she failed to provide the correct term, letter cues started appearing until she came up with the correct term, in this instance *loop.* Later the definition was presented repeatedly, each time with one fewer letter in the cue than had been required on the previous trial, until Barbara was able to come up with the correct term on her own. Using this method over a period of about 6 months, Barbara was able to learn to enter data into the computer from 11 different business documents, a process requiring the correct use of more than 250 rules, symbols, and codes. She was able to do this even though she had a profound anterograde amnesia that made it impossible for her to consciously remember new information (Glisky, Schacter, & Tulving, 1986; also see Glisky & Schacter, 1987, 1988, 1989). Her performance was so accurate and efficient that she was able to hold a full-time paid position.

EPISODIC MEMORY AND SEMANTIC MEMORY

As will be recalled from an earlier section, Endel Tulving (1972) made a distinction between episodic memory and semantic memory: Episodic memory is memory for the specific events and incidents that are part of our personal history. Semantic memory is composed of conceptual and factual knowledge that is not consciously linked to events in our personal lives. There is thus a strong phenomenological difference between these two types of memory, a difference described poignantly by William James more than a century ago. Speaking of what is now called episodic memory, James (1890) wrote, "Memory requires more than mere dating of a fact in the past. It must be dated in *my* past. In other words, I must think that I directly experienced its occurrence" (p. 650). In contrast, no such intimacy accompanies facts in semantic memory; they are simply things we know, without any connection to personal experience.

Global Amnesia

There are reports of patients with severe **global amnesia,** a total devastation of memory that includes the loss of both semantic and episodic memory. This leaves the patient without facts and concepts that had been accumulated in semantic memory and without the memories of a personal past previously mediated by episodic memory. One such patient, described by Schacter (1996, pp. 140–143), could remember nothing from his personal past and was unable to speak, comprehend heard language, or read. He was reported to have an encephalitis that included the left temporal lobe. It is, however, doubtful that damage to this area alone could have been the cause of his deficit because global amnesia is not typically seen after damage confined to left temporal-lobe structures.

More informative from the point of view of understanding the organization of memory, however, are patients with selective impairment of episodic or semantic memory. These dissociations, which provide further evidence for the validity of the distinction between the two systems, are considered next.

Selective Impairment of Episodic Memory

A patient known as Gene suffered a selective impairment of episodic memory as the result of head trauma sustained in a motorcycle accident (Schacter, 1996; Tulving, Schacter, et al., 1988). He was able to remember virtually no personal events or experiences from his life. In contrast, his semantic memory was only very mildly impaired. Interestingly, he retained knowledge of his own past, knowledge that is like the impersonal knowledge we have of another person's life. This impersonal autobiographical memory is mediated by the semantic memory system. For Gene and other patients like him (see Cermak & O'Connor, 1983; Damasio, Tranel, & Damasio, 1989), all knowledge of the self is in this impersonal form. These patients alert us to the fact that, in normal subjects, semantic memory serves as the basis for a good deal of autobiographical knowledge, such as knowledge of when and where we were born.

Selective Impairment of Semantic Memory

MULTIPLE SEMANTIC KNOWLEDGE SYSTEMS In previous chapters we have discussed aphasia, agnosia, and apraxia in some detail. Each of these disorders can be understood as an impairment in a specific semantic knowledge system. The selectivity of these impairments indicates that each of these systems can operate separately from the others, although under normal circumstances they constantly interact with one another.

GENERAL SEMANTIC MEMORY IMPAIRMENT AND PRESERVED EPISODIC MEMORY Patients with general impairment in semantic memory together with preserved episodic memory have been reported. In one case (De Renzi, Liotti, & Nichelli, 1987), the patient was impaired in memory for word meanings, historical events, familiar people, and the attributes of objects, such as the color of a mouse or where one would find soap. These impairments were seen in the absence of impairment in episodic memory.

SEMANTIC DEMENTIA **Semantic dementia** is a selective impairment in semantic memory seen in association with dementia. Episodic memory is not always normal in patients with semantic dementia, but any impairment in episodic memory is mild relative to the severity of the semantic memory deficit. This condition differs from that typically seen in Alzheimer's disease, where both episodic and semantic memory are impaired (Hodges et al., 1992).

SOME BIZARRE BREAKDOWNS IN SEMANTIC MEMORY   Some rather unexpected patterns of breakdown in semantic memory have been reported. For example, some patients have been reported to be impaired in identifying living things when given their name (e.g., What is a horse?), but not in identifying manufactured objects (e.g., What is a car?) (Hillis & Caramazza, 1991; Warrington & Shallice, 1984). The converse pattern has also been reported (memory for living things unimpaired and memory for manufactured objects impaired). In addition, some even more fine-grained dissociations have been reported, including a patient who can explain the function of tools but not articles of clothing and another patient who can describe manufactured objects, except for musical instruments (Damasio, 1990).

One interpretation of these dissociations is that they provide clues to the structural organization of semantic memory, suggesting an organization along the lines of the observed dissociations. Thus, it has been suggested that some information, such as that having to do with animals, is stored in a system organized along dimensions of appearance (the most salient feature in differentiating animals), whereas other information, such as that having to do with tools, is stored in systems organized along dimensions of function (Damasio, 1990; McCarthy & Warrington, 1990, pp. 146–150).

Support for this notion comes from PET studies of cerebral activation during the identification of pictures of objects. When subjects identify pictures of either animals or tools, there is an increase in the activity of lower temporal cortex, an area important for the perception of complex objects. However, when subjects identify pictures of tools (but not animals) there is also an increase in activity of the precentral cortex (Martin et al., 1996), an area that is also active when people imagine movements (Decety et al., 1994). These findings are consistent with the view that at least some category-specific impairments in semantic memory reflect the breakdown of distinct brain networks responsible for knowledge of different properties of objects.

Although the interpretation of category-specific impairments in semantic memory remains a matter of active investigation and debate, the double dissocia-

tion of impairment in episodic and semantic memory has a clearer interpretation. It provides strong support for the idea that episodic and semantic memory are distinct memory systems.

SHORT-TERM/WORKING MEMORY IMPAIRMENT

Short-Term Memory

SHORT-TERM MEMORY FROM THE PERSPECTIVE OF GATEWAY THEORY   As we saw in an earlier section, the serial model of consolidation viewed short-term memory (STM) as the gateway through which information must pass in order for it to be consolidated in long-term memory (McGaugh & Herz, 1972; Scoville & Milner, 1957). According to this view, retention of information in short-term memory is also an obligatory step in the sequence of processes underlying complex cognitive operations such as language comprehension, language production, and problem solving. As intuitively obvious as these notions may appear, there is now compelling evidence that they are wrong; short-term memory is not an obligatory component in any of these processes. Evidence for this comes from patients with selective short-term memory impairment.

PROBLEMS WITH THE GATEWAY THEORY: SPECIFIC IMPAIRMENT IN SHORT-TERM MEMORY Patients have been identified who have selective impairment in short-term memory (Shallice & Warrington, 1979; Vallar & Baddeley, 1984). What is particularly striking about these patients is that they have no impairment in long-term memory. For example, patient K. F., studied by Shallice and Warrington, was severely impaired in the immediate repetition of auditory-verbal material. Thus, although he was able to repeat single numbers or letters correctly, he was impaired in the immediate repetition of strings of two or more of these stimuli (Figure 10.21). In contrast, his long-term memory was unimpaired. For example, he was able to learn word lists and verbal paired-associates normally. Similar findings have been observed in a number of patients (Caplan & Waters, 1990). Interestingly, as can be seen in Figure 10.21,

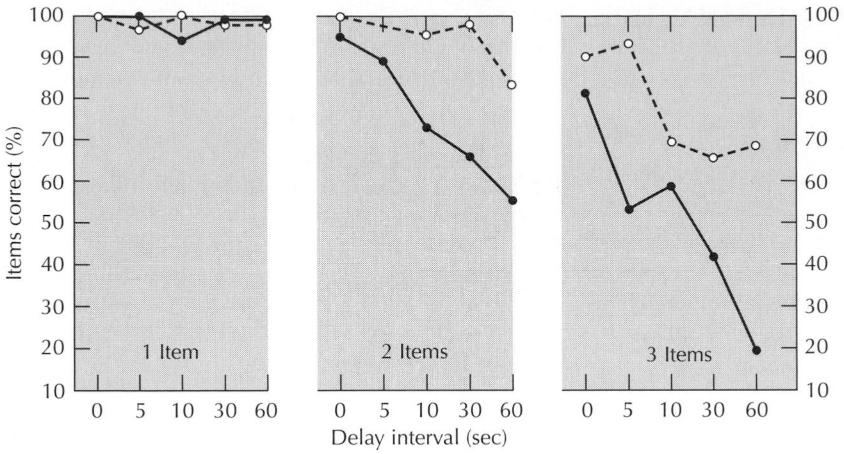

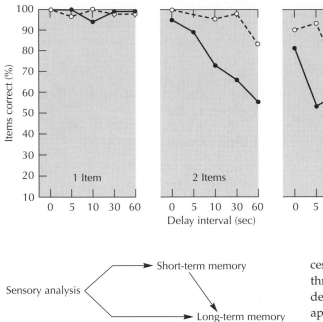

FIGURE 10.21   Forgetting of one-, two-, and three-item lists with auditory and visual presentation in patient K. F. (dotted line = visual; solid line = auditory). *(From McCarthy & Warrington, 1990, p. 279)*

FIGURE 10.22   Model suggested by patients with impairment in short-term memory but preserved ability to acquire new long-term memories. This dissociation suggests that short-term memory is not an obligatory stage in the formation of long-term memories. *(Adapted from McCarthy & Warrington, 1990, p. 288)*

K. F.'s impairment was most severe for auditory-verbal material, although his short-term retention of visually presented verbal material was also impaired. This suggests that there are several different short-term memory stores, a point to which we will return shortly.

This pattern of preservation and impairment, complementary to that seen in anterograde amnesia, presents an obvious problem for a serial model positing that information must first be held in short-term memory before being consolidated into long-term memory. It suggests, rather, that there are parallel routes of input to short-term memory and long-term memory (Figure 10.22). Also, patients with selective impairment of short-term memory are unimpaired in language comprehension, language production, and many problem-solving tasks, indicating that short-term memory is not required for these pro-

cesses. Apparently, STM is not an obligatory gateway through which information must pass in order to undergo deeper processing and long-term retention. It appears, rather, to be part of a system that, when necessary, holds information in consciousness so that it can be further processed.

Working Memory

THE WORKSPACE AND THE EXECUTIVE FUNCTIONS   The considerations just discussed and others like them have led to the idea that STM is part of the more elaborate system called working memory (WM), which we introduced in an earlier section. Within the framework of working memory, short-term memory may be conceptualized as being composed of several specialized temporary storage systems, each specialized for the retention of certain aspects of incoming stimuli. These are sometimes referred to as **buffers.** As used in computer technology, a buffer is a temporary storage unit that usually accepts information at one rate and delivers it at another. We will see that there are several types of buffers.

THE BUFFERS   Evidence for several types of temporary stores, or buffers, comes from the study of patients with selective short-term memory impairments. For example, we noted that K. F.'s impairment was more severe for auditory-verbal than for visual-verbal mate-

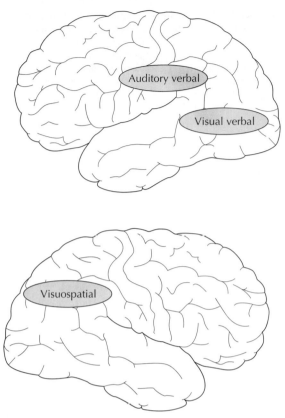

FIGURE 10.23 The approximate location of cortical lesions associated with specific impairments in short-term memory. *(From McCarthy & Warrington, 1990, p. 283)*

rial. This suggests that there is a specific short-term store for auditory-verbal information, a store that has been referred to as the **phonological store** or the **phonological buffer** (Caramazza et al., 1985). Other patients have been reported with selective impairment in visual-verbal short-term memory, and yet others with selective impairment in visuospatial short-term memory. The latter system has been referred to as the **visuospatial scratchpad** (Baddeley, 1986).

Each of these selective impairments is associated with specific lesion sites. Auditory-verbal STM deficits are seen after left parietal lesions, whereas visual-verbal STM deficits are seen after damage to a neighboring area within the left occipital lobe (Figure 10.23). Impairment in visuospatial STM has been reported after right occipitoparietal lesions and after

hippocampal lesions (Olton, Becker, & Handleman, 1979). These findings indicate that there are multiple short-term memory systems, each linked to specific information-processing modules in the brain.

The Frontal Lobes and Working Memory

We have seen that there are a number of different buffer systems that supply input to the workspace of working memory. There is also evidence that the frontal lobes are involved in working memory. To consider this evidence, it is necessary to look briefly at the now-classic experimental investigations of the frontal lobes carried out in the 1930s.

DELAYED RESPONSE In animal studies of frontal-lobe function, monkeys have been the subjects of choice because of their extensively developed frontal lobes and their evolutionary relationship to humans. Although there had been some earlier astute observations of motivational changes after lesions of the frontal lobes in monkeys, Jacobsen (1936) was the first to experimentally investigate the cognitive effects of frontal-lobe lesions in monkeys. He demonstrated impairment in **delayed-response tasks.** In the classic version of a delayed-response task, the monkey first watches the experimenter bait one of two food wells. Covers are then placed over the wells, and then there is a delay during which an opaque screen is lowered, blocking the monkey's view of the food wells. After the delay, the screen is raised, and the monkey must uncover the well containing the food in order to be rewarded (Figure 10.24). In a variation of this task, termed a **delayed-alternation task,** the location of the bait is alternated between trials, but the monkey does not see the baiting. In this condition the monkey must remember the response that he made on the previous trial in order to find the food.

Successful performance on delayed-response tasks has a number of components, including registering the relevant information and initiating the necessary motor responses. There is clearly also a memory component: the ability to hold information about the location of the food (in delayed response) or the location of the last response (in delayed alternation) over the delay interval. At the end of the delay interval, the

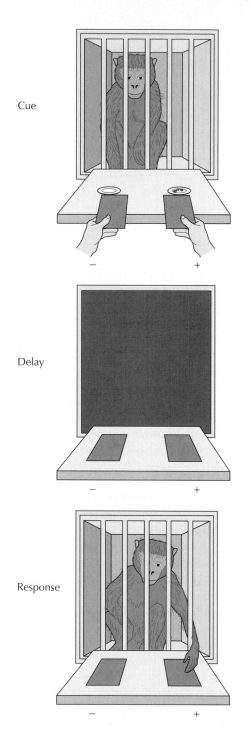

Cue

Delay

Response

–   +

◀ **FIGURE 10.24**   The three components of the delayed-response task. *(Top)* The monkey sees the experimenter bait one food well (cue) before both wells are covered. *(Middle)* An opaque screen is lowered and remains lowered (delay). *(Bottom)* The screen in raised, and the monkey chooses one well by removing its cover (response). *(From Goldman-Rakic, 1987, p. 377)*

monkey sees only two covered food wells and must decide which has the food. Therefore, the monkey's decision regarding which food well to choose must be guided by an internal representation of past events, not by the recognition of a present stimulus, as in, for example, delayed nonmatching to sample. It is in this sense that delayed response requires short-term representational memory or working memory (Goldman-Rakic, 1987).

Lesion studies such as Jacobsen's are not the only source of data supporting a role for prefrontal cortex in delayed-response tasks. As we saw in chapter 9 (see Figure 9.19), cells in the lateral prefrontal cortex have been shown to be active during the delay period in delayed-response tasks. Interestingly, these same cells do not fire when the animal makes a mistake on a delayed-response task (Funahashi, Bruce, & Goldman-Rakic, 1989, 1991; Fuster, 1989; Niki & Watanabe, 1976).

AN OCULOMOTOR ANALOGUE OF THE DELAYED-RESPONSE TASK   In an attempt to further investigate the role of prefrontal cortex in delayed-response tasks, Goldman-Rakic (1987, 1988) recorded from cells in the principal sulcus of the monkey during an oculomotor analogue of the classical delayed-response task. In this task, monkeys were trained to fixate on a central point on a screen and to continue to fixate on that point while a target was flashed at some peripheral location. After a delay, the central (fixation) point is turned off, at which time the monkey is to move its eyes to the target. If the target is turned off before the central point, the task becomes a delayed-response task (Figure 10.25).

Goldman-Rakic found that unilateral frontal-lobe lesions produced impairment in the delayed-response condition. The impairment was severe even after a

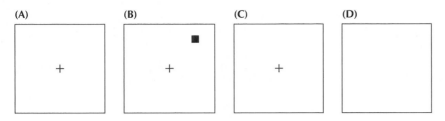

(A)   **(B)**   **(C)**   **(D)**

FIGURE 10.25   The oculomotor analogue of the delayed-response task. *(A)* The monkey fixates on the central cross and continues to do so as *(B)* the target appears in the upper right and then *(C)* disappears. *(D)* When the central point is turned off, the monkey is then to move his gaze to the point where the target had appeared. *(Adapted from Goldman-Rakic, 1987)*

delay of only a few seconds but was not seen on the nonmemory task (i.e., when the fixation point went off while the target stayed illuminated). It should also be noted that these animals had no difficulty moving their eyes. In addition, right frontal-lobe lesions disrupted memory for the position of the target only when it was in the left visual field, whereas left frontal-lobe lesions followed the opposite pattern. What is more, Goldman-Rakic and her colleagues found a topographical relationship between the area within the principal sulcus that was damaged and the region of the visual field in which delayed response was disrupted (Figure 10.26). They also found cells near the principal sulcus that began firing when the target was presented at a certain location (but not others) and that continued firing over the delay interval until the fixation point had been turned off and the eye movement had begun (Figure 10.27). These findings provide evidence that cells in the principal sulcus play a role in the mediation of representational memory, in this case the guiding of response on the basis of stored information, in the absence of the stimulus that was present initially.

There are extensive reciprocal connections between the principal sulcus and posterior parietal areas known to process information regarding the spatial location of objects and the locations of the body in space. It is probable that the prefrontal areas mediating the short-term representation of spatial location do so by interacting with systems within the parietal lobes that process spatial information (Gnadt & Andersen, 1988; Goldman-Rakic, 1992).

EVIDENCE FOR SPECIALIZATION OF WORKING MEMORY WITHIN PREFRONTAL CORTEX There is evidence that the prefrontal areas mediating WM for spatial location are different from those mediating WM for objects (Wilson, Scalaidhe, & Goldman-Rakic, 1993). Thus, there are prefrontal cells that fire during the delay interval after the presentation of an object. These prefrontal cells are in areas different from those involved in WM for spatial location. They are also reciprocally connected with areas of inferotemporal cortex that mediate object perception. This suggests that prefrontal cortex is not a generalized working memory processor. Rather, there appear to be at least two visual working memory systems, each dependent on interactions between specific lateral prefrontal regions and specialized areas of visual cortex. This conclusion is supported by a PET study of human subjects showing activation of frontal and parietal regions during tasks requiring WM for spatial location, but frontal and temporal activation for tasks requiring WM for objects (Jonides et al., 1993).

WORKING MEMORY AND ATTENTION: THE IMPORTANCE OF RECIPROCAL FRONTAL-CORTICAL INTERCONNECTIONS Attention gates access to memory: We are more likely to remember stimuli to which we attend. But the converse is also the case: Memory guides attention. What we already know partially determines those aspects of the sensory array to which we attend. In a sense, working memory lies at the interface between what is already known (LTM) and what is currently perceived

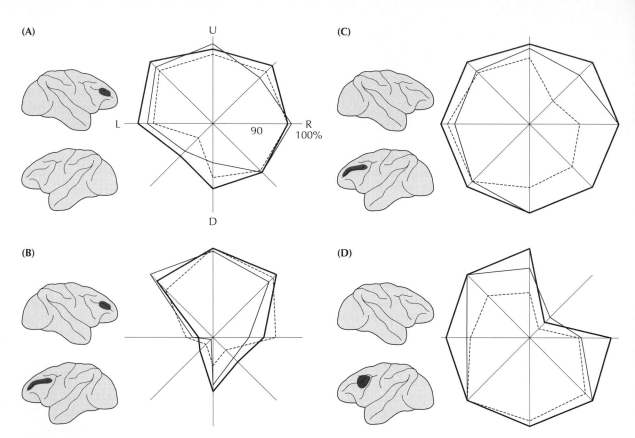

FIGURE 10.26   Results of three monkeys tested on a delayed eye-movement task: *Thick line:* performance at shortest delay (usually about 1 sec); *thin line:* performance at 3-sec delay; *dashed line:* performance at 6-sec delay. Correct performance percentage is indicated along axes drawn through central fixation point. Eight positions of target stimulus are located at a constant distance from the fixation point. *(A)* and *(B)* Monkey with sequential lesions of the middle third of the principal sulcus. *(A)* Monkey showed deficit in the lower left visual field and milder deficit in the lower right visual field after lesion on the right side. *(B)* The lower right visual field deficit was more severe after prefrontal lesion in the middle principal sulcus in the left hemisphere. *(C)* Monkey with unilateral lesion of entire principal sulcus showed loss of ability to remember targets in both upper and lower contralateral visual fields at 6-sec delay. *(D)* Monkey with lesion confined to the posterior portion of the principal sulcus and the anterior bank of the arcuate sulcus showed severe deficit in contralateral upper visual field at all delays. All three monkeys performed without difficulty in all locations as long as the visual target was present at the time of response. *(From Goldman-Rakic, 1987, p. 383)*

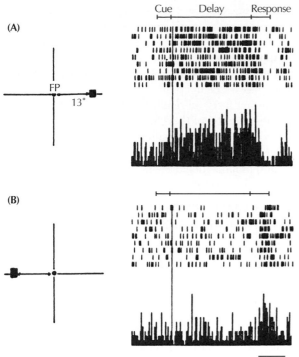

(A)

Cue   Delay   Response

FP

13°

(B)

1 sec

FIGURE 10.27 Neuronal activity of cell recorded near the principal sulcus during multiple trials of delayed-response eye-movement task. *(A)* When target was presented 13° right of fixation, the cell was activated during the delay. *(B)* When the target was presented 13° left of fixation, the cell did not increase its baseline firing rate during the delay. *(From Goldman-Rakic, 1987, p. 384)*

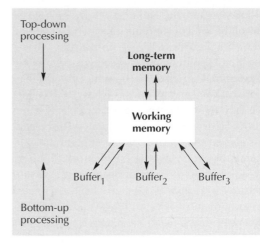

FIGURE 10.28 Working memory serves as the interface between short-term buffers and long-term memory. The content and processes constituting WM at any given time are derived from information from the environment (represented initially in sensory buffers) and already stored information and processes (moved into the workspace from LTM) applied to this incoming information. Thus, WM is a confluence of bottom-up and top-down processing. Depending on the particular instance, the major net effect of these processes may be to interpret new information in terms of what is already known (top-down processing) or to modify what is known in the light of new information (bottom-up processing). *(From LeDoux, 1996, p. 273)*

(sensory systems). As such, it mediates both bottom-up and top-down processing (Figure 10.28). By maintaining information from sensory systems and from LTM, working memory provides an opportunity for sensory information to influence and modify LTM (bottom-up processing) and for information in LTM to direct attentional processes, thereby leading to particular sensory input (top-down processing). Both of these modes of processing are always active, although one of them will be more dominant at any given time.

The reciprocal connections between visual sensory cortex and prefrontal cortex provide pathways that may mediate these processes. What information

is maintained in working memory will depend partly on the input to prefrontal areas from sensory areas. However, the reentrant connections from specific areas of prefrontal cortex back to the sensory areas that feed them provide a pathway through which working memory processes, interacting with LTM, could influence attentional processes (Desimone et al., 1995).

EVIDENCE FOR A GENERAL PROCESSOR MEDIATING THE EXECUTIVE COMPONENT OF WORKING MEMORY   Although we have seen that there is evidence for specialized working memory subsystems within prefrontal cortex, this does not preclude the possibility that there is also a general processor within the frontal lobes that coordinates the activities of the specialized subsystems. Evidence for this comes from studies of human subjects indicating that frontal-lobe lesions cause an impairment in WM, regardless of the kind of stimulus information involved (Fuster, 1989; Petrides, 1994a). In addition, brain imaging studies in humans have shown activation of lateral prefrontal cortex during a number of different kinds of working memory tasks (D'Esposito et al., 1995; Grasby et al., 1993; Jonides et al., 1993; Petrides et al., 1993; Schwartz et al., 1995). Anatomical considerations also support a role for lateral prefrontal cortex in general-purpose working memory function. This area is intimately interconnected with sensory systems, motor areas, and systems of the brain related to long-term memory (Fuster, 1989; Goldman-Rakic, 1987; Reep, 1984; Uylings & van Eden, 1990).

Areas other than lateral prefrontal cortex have been implicated in the mediation of working memory. These include cingulate cortex, which receives input from sensory buffers (Corbetta et al., 1991; D'Esposito et al., 1995; Posner & Peterson, 1990) and projects to lateral prefrontal cortex (Goldman-Rakic, 1988). In addition, lesions of orbital frontal cortex have been associated with disruption of short-term retention of information about the reward aspects of stimuli (Gaffan, Murray, & Fabre-Thorpe, 1993), and cells in orbital frontal cortex have been shown to be sensitive to whether a stimulus has led to punishment (Thorpe, Rolls, & Maddison, 1983). Further, humans with orbital frontal lesions become oblivious to social and emotional cues (Damasio, 1994). Orbital frontal cortex receives input from sensory buffers and also from the amygdala and cingulate cortex. We examine the neural basis of emotion in more detail in chapter 11; for the present we simply state that the amygdala is important for emotional processing. In the context of working memory, it is possible that orbital frontal cortex is a link by which emotional processing by the amygdala might be related in WM to sensory information and to information in LTM.

If there is a general-purpose working memory processor, it may nevertheless not be localized within one area of the frontal lobes. It may, instead, be distributed over the multiple WM systems. Evidence for this comes from the finding that some cells in specialized areas of prefrontal cortex participate in many different working memory tasks (Petrides, 1994a). There are many other questions that remain to be resolved concerning working memory and the frontal lobes. For example, it is not yet known whether anything is actually stored in the frontal lobes or whether frontal areas mediate WM by controlling the activity of other areas.

In addition to their role in WM, the frontal lobes also play a role in memory when organization is an important factor in retention. We explore this role in the last section of this chapter. First, let's step back and consider the implications of the findings that we have reviewed so far for an understanding of the neural organization of memory.

CONCEPTUALIZATION OF MULTIPLE MEMORY SYSTEMS

We have seen that medial-temporal structures (particularly the hippocampus and the entorhinal, perirhinal, and parahippocampal cortices) and diencephalic structures (particularly the mamillary bodies and the anterior and dorsomedial nuclei of the thalamus) are critical for the creation of new explicit memories. Patients with lesions in these structures have severe anterograde amnesia and varying degrees of retrograde amnesia. In contrast, patients with temporal-lobe or diencephalic amnesia are able to demonstrate a number of forms of learning, many related to repetitive exposure to past situations and conceptualized under the category of implicit memory. These include motor learning, perceptual learning, classical conditioning, problem solving, and priming. Furthermore, there are dissociations within the domain of implicit memory. Patients with lesions of the basal ganglia are impaired in motor learning but not in other forms of learning. Patients with lesions of the occipital lobes are impaired in visual perceptual priming but not in other forms of learning. Cerebellar lesions selectively impair simple classical conditioning. We have also seen that lesions of the parietal lobes result in specific impairment in short-term memory, whereas lesions of the frontal lobes result in disturbances of working memory.

Taken together, these findings constitute a pattern of dissociations that suggests that there are five major memory systems: procedural memory, the perceptual representation system, working memory, semantic memory, and episodic memory. In addition, at least three of these systems include a number of subsystems (Table 10.2). The procedural memory subsystems

TABLE 10.2   Major Systems of Human Memory and Learning

System	Other Terms	Subsystems
Procedural	Nondeclarative	Motor skills Perceptual skills Cognitive skills Nonassociative learning Simple conditioning
Perceptual representation system (PRS)	Priming	Visual word form Auditory word form Structural description
Semantic	Generic Knowledge	Spatial Relational

Working		Workspace
		  Short-term (buffers)
		    Visual
		    Auditory
		    Spatial
		  Content from LTM
		  Processes
		Executive function

Episodic	Autobiographical Personal	

are behavioral or cognitive *action* systems that are expressed in the form of learned and often skilled behavioral or cognitive procedures, performed in the absence of conscious recollection of the past experiences that generated them (i.e., implicit memories). There are several subsystems within the domain of procedural memory. In perceptual priming, prior exposure to a stimulus facilitates the perception of the stimulus on a later occasion. Because the subject does not necessarily retain a conscious representation of the past experience, priming also falls within implicit memory. Semantic and episodic memory fall within the domain of explicit memory. Working memory cuts across the explicit-implicit distinction, with the content of the workspace being explicit, while the processes active in the workspace and the executive function may be either explicit or implicit.

Tulving (1995) has suggested that the order of arrangement of the five major memory systems reflects their order of emergence, both in terms of evolution and individual development. According to this view, procedural systems and perceptual representation systems, essential for even simple and immediate interactions with the environment, evolved first and develop earliest in the human infant. Semantic memory, working memory systems, and episodic memory evolved and develop later, as explicit representations of past events become essential for the regulation and execution of complex adaptive behavior.

THE NEURAL SUBSTRATE OF LONG-TERM MEMORY

Long-term memory has a vast capacity, so vast that it has not been possible to specify its limits. Its duration is equally vast, at least on the time scale of an individual person: Many memories last a lifetime. Yet where and how long-term memories are stored remain alluring mysteries.

Lashley's Search for the Engram

The term **engram** is used to refer to the hypothetical, currently unknown, neural representation of memory.

The neuropsychologist Karl Lashley set out to localize the engram by first training rats to learn a maze and then damaging different parts of their cerebral cortex. His reasoning was simple: The location of lesions disrupting the running of the maze would also be the location of the engrams storing knowledge of the maze. Lashley found that lesions in different cerebral areas (outside the primary sensory and motor areas) disrupted memory of the maze equally; he was unable to find the engram in any single restricted location. This led him to conclude that the engram must be distributed throughout the cortex. Although his more general holistic conclusion that there is no specialization of function within the cortex (outside the primary sensory and motor areas) is clearly wrong, his conclusion that long-term memory is stored throughout the cortex has turned out to have a firmer foundation.

Evidence That Long-Term Memory Is Stored in the Cortex

In the 1950s the neurosurgeon Wilder Penfield reported that when he stimulated the temporal lobes of patients in the course of surgery for the relief of seizures, patients, awake under local anesthesia, often said that they were experiencing vivid memories from their distant past. These patients were sometimes very emotional as they poignantly described the content of these experiences. This led Penfield to conclude that the temporal lobes are the area of the brain in which long-term memories are stored. He went further and postulated that *all* past memories are represented there, forming a permanent and accurate record of past experience (Penfield & Perot, 1963). Unfortunately, Penfield failed to verify that his patients' verbalizations were reports of actual memories by comparing them with documented information from these individuals' pasts. This left open the possibility that patients were reporting dreamlike experiences or hallucinations. Despite problems with this dramatic source of evidence, there are grounds for believing that the cerebral cortex is the site of storage of long-term memories. We examine a number of these grounds in the following sections.

THE PLASTICITY OF THE CORTEX   Although we do not know what changes in the nervous system underlie long-term memory, it is obvious that some changes must occur. The cerebral cortex is the leading candidate for the site of these changes because, of all regions of the mammalian brain, it is the one where changes resulting from experience have been most clearly demonstrated. Evidence for this comes from the now-classic work of Mark Rosenzweig (1977; Rosenzweig, Bennett, & Diamond, 1972), that compared the brains of rats raised in an enriched environment with those of rats raised in an impoverished environment. Rats in enriched environments were housed in large cages containing stimulating objects like exercise wheels and, most important, other rats with which to interact. Rats in impoverished environments were housed alone, in small cages without stimulating objects.

Gross Cortical Changes   When the brains of the rats in these two groups were compared, a number of differences between the two groups were found. The brains of rats in the enriched environment had a greater cortical thickness. In addition, the occipital cortex had greater weight in the enriched group. No such changes were seen in areas outside the cortex.

Dendritic Changes   When fine structural features at the level of the single neuron were measured on electron micrographs, several differences were found in cortical tissue. The enriched group had a greater number of dendritic spines per unit length of dendrite. (**Dendritic spines** are little knobs, protruding from dendrites, that increase the area of the dendritic surface. The number of spines on a dendrite is correlated with the number of axonal inputs to the dendrite.) The basal dendrites of cortical neurons in the enriched group also showed more dendritic branching, another correlate of the number of incoming axons (Figure 10.29). More recently, when the number of synaptic contacts was measured directly, the brains of animals in the enriched group were found to have more of them.

Neurochemical Changes   Cortical tissue of rats in the enriched group contained more acetylcholine per unit weight than did cortex of rats in the impoverished condition. It is important to note that all of the changes just discussed were seen in cortex, but not in other

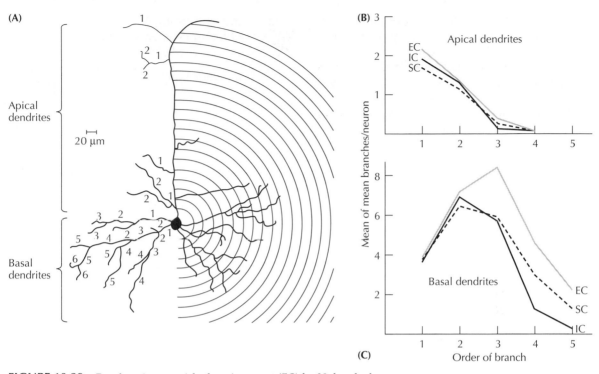

FIGURE 10.29   Rats kept in an enriched environment *(EC)* for 30 days had more elaborate branching of basal dendrites of cortical neurons than did rats kept in standard *(SC)* or impoverished *(IC)* conditions. *(A)* Dendritic branching can be quantified either by counting the number of branches of different orders *(left)* or by counting the number of intersections with concentric rings *(right)*. *(B)* and *(C)* The results of the number-of-branches measure are shown in these graphs. Basal dendrites, but not apical dendrites, from rats kept in the enriched environment show increased higher-order branching relative to the other two groups. *(From Rosenzweig & Leiman, 1989, p. 666)*

areas of the brain. Although the effect on the brain of an enriched environment over a period of time must be more general and greater in magnitude than the effect of a single event, these findings nevertheless demonstrate changes in cortical tissue as the result of experience. In doing so, they provide evidence consistent with the idea that the cortex is the site of the neural changes underlying long-term memory. We discuss the neuronal mechanisms of long-term memory in more detail in a later section.

SPLIT-BRAIN STUDIES   Another source of evidence that the cortex is the site of storage of long-term memories comes from studies of split-brain animals. In monkeys and cats the optic chiasm (not sectioned in

humans with split-brain surgery) can be sectioned, in addition to the forebrain commissures (anterior commissure and corpus callosum). If one eye of such an animal is covered and the animal is then trained on a visual discrimination task, the learning will not later transfer to the previously occluded eye (Myers, 1955; Sperry, 1961). The previously occluded eye can even be trained to learn the opposite discrimination from that learned by the first eye. Thus, in this experimental situation, the neural substrate of the discrimination learning mediated by the trained eye is confined to the ipsilateral hemisphere, so that input from the other eye cannot gain access to it. The failure of visual discrimination learning to show interocular transfer in such split-brain animals is evidence that the neural substrate of this learning is stored in the cortex. If the engram were represented subcortically, one would expect that the visual discrimination would be transferred between the hemispheres by intact subcortical pathways.

THE EFFECT OF LESIONS TO INFEROTEMPORAL CORTEX   Further evidence for the role of the cerebral cortex in the storage of long-term memories comes from lesion studies in monkeys showing that lesions to the inferotemporal cortex (area TE), in addition to impairing the ability to acquire new information, also impairs previously learned visual discriminations (Mishkin, 1966). Area TE is thus involved both in perception and in memory. Information from prestriate areas is funneled into area TE, making this area well suited to serve both as an area mediating higher-order visual perception and as the site of storage for visual representations (Mishkin, 1982).

A study of the physiological properties of individual neurons in TE provides further support for the role of this area in both visual perception and memory. Sakai and Miyashita (1991) exposed monkeys to a paired-associate learning procedure. After training, they found cells that fired when the monkey saw a certain stimulus and then continued to fire in anticipation of the associate to that stimulus. If the associate was presented next, the cell continued to fire. If, however, a stimulus other than the associate followed, the cell stopped firing. In other words, the cell was coding the presence or absence of the associate.

There have also been a number of imaging studies showing that inferotemporal cortex is active during tasks requiring visual recognition (e.g., Haxley et al., 1994). Taken together, these findings suggest that some visual representations of past experience are stored in the temporal cortex. There is evidence that parietal areas may be the site of storage of spatial information and somatosensory cortex may be the site of storage of tactile information (Squire, 1987, p. 123). These findings support the notion that at least some types of information are stored in the cortex. More specifically, they suggest that the engram may be stored in the same regions as those mediating late stages in perceptual processing and recognition.

Hippocampal Binding of Different Memory Elements as an Integral Component in Explicit Memory

Explicit memory is relational or associative: One memory brings others to mind. When we smell bacon, it may remind us of breakfast on a camping trip years ago, of the crisp, clear air and the sights and companions we experienced. This may lead us to remember a particular person's face, which, in turn, leads us to remember aspects of his or her work. We also experience the relatedness of memories within semantic memory in tasks such as problem solving, when one element of knowledge leads to another in a way that helps us reach our goal. How do the different contents in memory become related to each other?

It has been suggested that this relatedness is the hallmark of explicit memory, as distinct from implicit memory, which represents experience in a way that is tied to the processing operations that were engaged at the time of learning (Cohen, 1997; Cohen & Eichenbaum, 1993).[2] It has been proposed, further, that the hippocampus mediates the binding process characteristic of explicit memory, whereas structures outside the hippocampus mediate implicit memory. Evidence for the role of the hippocampus in binding different elements comes from studies, such as those discussed in earlier sections, indicating that it is the relatedness characteristic of explicit memory that is disrupted by medial-temporal and diencephalic lesions, whereas implicit memory is disrupted by lesions outside this system. In addition, the fact that the hippocampus receives highly processed sensory and limbic input and that it has extensive projections back to cortex argues for its role in the association and integration of different memory contents. Further evidence for this notion comes from a functional magnetic resonance imaging (fMRI) study in which subjects were required to associate faces with icons and names. Subjects were then required to distinguish previously studied face-icon-

---

2. These authors use the terms *declarative* and *procedural* where I have used *explicit* and *implicit,* respectively. I have substituted the latter, basically equivalent, distinction to maintain consistency within the current discussion.

name combinations from novel combinations. This task elicited activation of the hippocampus (Cohen, Ramzy, et al., 1994).

Storage of Implicit Memory

We have seen that the effects of procedural memory and priming are manifested only when the subject is engaged in actions or operations similar to those engaged in at the time of learning. This suggests that the neural mechanisms underlying implicit memory may be closely linked to the mechanisms mediating the initial actions and operations. Evidence for this comes from a number of different findings. As we noted in an earlier section, visual priming results in a lowering of occipital cortex activation as measured by PET (Buckner et al., 1995; Squire, Ojemann, et al., 1992). Impairment in visual priming has also been reported after lesions of right occipital cortex (Gabrieli et al., 1995; Keane et al., 1992). In the somatosensory modality, tactile discrimination learning has been reported to cause enlargement of receptive fields of neurons in the area representing the body area trained (Merzenich et al., 1990). Analogously, changes in the receptive-field properties of neurons in the auditory cortex have been seen after tone discrimination learning in classical conditioning (Diamond & Weinberger, 1986). Other studies have shown changes in the activation of motor cortex (Karni et al., 1995) and cerebellum (Kim, Ugurbil, & Strick, 1994) after the learning of motor sequences. We may speculate, therefore, that neural changes underlying diverse types of implicit memory in higher animals and humans may be broadly analogous to the modification of existing circuits that underlie habituation, sensitization, and classical conditioning in *Aplysia* (see chapter 2), although obviously at a far greater level of complexity.

Protein Synthesis and the Structural Plasticity Underlying Long-Term Memory

As we have pointed out, precisely how long-term memories are formed and maintained remains a great mystery. There is evidence, however, that protein synthesis and the formation of new synapses are critical components in the formation of long-term memory.

Although not a focus of our discussion in chapter 2, alterations in existing proteins have been shown to be a critical component in short-term sensitization and habituation in *Aplysia*. While this mechanism helps to explain relatively short-term memory processes, the fact that proteins are constantly being degraded and synthesized (with a turnover rate of about 2 weeks) makes it highly unlikely that alterations in existing proteins alone could be the basis of long-term memory.

It is now clear that the synthesis of *new* proteins (rather than alterations in existing proteins) is an integral component in the retention, but not the learning, of new tasks in mammals. This is clear from studies (e.g., Davis & Squire, 1984) demonstrating that when drugs that selectively inhibit the synthesis of protein are injected into an animal as it is trained to perform a task, the animal fails to remember the task when tested after a delay, although the process of learning takes place normally (Figure 10.30). Impairment in retention is also seen if the protein inhibitor is administered shortly after training, but its disruptive effect decreases as the interval between training and injection increases. A similar disruptive effect of inhibition of protein synthesis is seen in long-term sensitization, but not in short-term sensitization, in *Aplysia.*

Taken together, these findings suggest that the early stages of memory formation involve the rapid modification of *existing* synaptic proteins, whereas the synthesis of *new* proteins is a necessary component for the formation of long-term memory. A major consequence of the synthesis of new proteins, with obvious implications for long-term memory, is the construction of new synapses. This has been demonstrated in long-term (but not short-term) sensitization in *Aplysia*. It is also seen in long-term potentiation in the hippocampus. Further, as we saw earlier, an increase in the number of synapses is seen in rats exposed to enriched environments.

Each protein molecule is the product of a sequence of DNA that codes that protein's particular sequence of amino acids. A DNA sequence generating a specific protein is called a gene. It therefore should in principle be possible to identify the genes coding the synthesis of proteins that are involved in the formation of new synapses underlying long-term

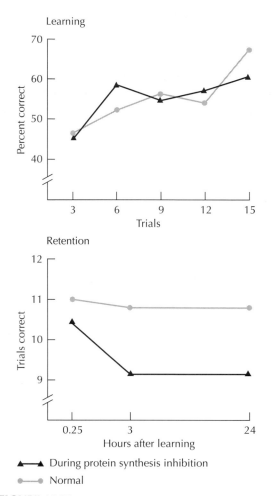

FIGURE 10.30 *(Top)* Protein synthesis inhibitors typically have no effect on the rate of learning of a new task. *(Bottom)* Long-term retention will fail to take place, however, if new protein synthesis is prevented during training. *(From Bear, Connors, & Paradiso, 1996, p. 573)*

II, an enzyme important for the induction of long-term potentiation. The result was a deficit in long-term potentiation in the hippocampus of these animals (Silva, Stevens, et al., 1992). In addition, when tested in the Morris Water Maze, these animals were found to have severely impaired spatial memory (Silva, Paylor, et al., 1992). Although these findings provide an enticing glimpse into the processes at the neural level underlying long-term memory, there is much in this area that remains obscure. In particular, it is unclear how the formation of new synapses contributes to the formation of complex memories, particularly explicit memories.

So Where Is Memory Stored?

Lashley (1950) was correct in his conclusion that long-term memory is not stored in one place, yet he was wrong in his further inference that it must therefore be stored equally everywhere. In fact, memory is both distributed and localized; many different areas of the brain store memory, *and* at least some specific types of memory are stored in specific brain regions. As we have seen, the most probable site of storage of explicit memory is the cortex, and explicit memory appears to be widely distributed in different cortical areas. In contrast, priming appears to be subserved by a number of specific systems, each closely related to cortical areas specialized for early stages of processing within a specific sensory modality. There is most evidence for this in visual priming, where there is accumulating evidence for a relationship between the occipital cortex and perceptual priming. Within other domains of implicit memory, there is evidence that procedural memory also involves the modification of processing systems involved in initial motor and cognitive operations. This is most clear in motor learning, where areas within motor systems, including the basal ganglia and cerebellum, appear critical.

FURTHER CONSIDERATION OF THE ROLE OF THE FRONTAL LOBES IN MEMORY

We have already considered the role of the frontal lobes in working memory. This is not, however, the only domain of memory in which the frontal lobes are involved; they are also important whenever organiza-

memory. One way of tackling this problem has been to produce mutant strains of the fruit fly *Drosophila* (by subjecting the insects to X rays or drugs) and then to search for strains with specific learning problems. This has resulted in the identification of at least three such mutants, each of which has a defective gene coding the synthesis of a particular enzyme in a cAMP-associated pathway (Dudai, 1989). More recently, using genetic engineering in mice, investigators have been able to specifically delete the gene coding the synthesis of the protein α-calcium kinase

tion is a critical component of memory and whenever information must be extracted from a series of events. The frontal lobes also are critical for an individual's accurate assessment of his or her own memory capability. We reviewed these roles of the frontal lobes in Korsakoff's disease, presenting evidence supporting the hypothesis that organization-related memory impairments and impairment in metamemory are found only in cases of Korsakoff's disease that also involve frontal-lobe abnormality (Shimamura, Jernigan, & Squire, 1988). In this section we examine further the role of the frontal lobes in memory, focusing on their role in the organizational processes underlying memory and metamemory.

The Frontal Lobes and Organization

Organization and memory are intimately related. Not only do we remember organized material better than unorganized material, the reconstructive nature of remembering means that the way in which we perceive and organize events determines to a large extent how we reconstruct our memory of our past. Organization affects memory through its impact on encoding, on retrieval, and on processes intermediate between these two points. When we attend to material that we want to remember, we may actively organize it for later recall. This organization may take place during or after initial exposure (**elaborative encoding**) or it may consist in the manipulation and processing of information that has already been encoded (**elaborative rehearsal**). Finally, at the time of recall, we may search for the information in an organized way, a process termed **strategic retrieval.** Evidence for frontal-lobe involvement in these processes and the possibility of hemispheric specialization within the frontal lobes for specific processes comes from a PET study showing activation of left frontal-lobe areas during the encoding of information and activation of right frontal-lobe areas during retrieval (Tulving, Kapur, et al., 1994).

IMPAIRMENT IN THE USE OF INHERENT ORGANIZATION The most compelling evidence for the involvement of frontal cortex in organizational processes related to memory comes, however, from lesion studies. Although under many conditions frontal-

lobe lesions do not disrupt memory, patients with frontal-lobe lesions are impaired on memory tasks that normally require organizational processes.

We have already discussed some examples of the impact of frontal-lobe lesions on memory in the context of our discussion of Korsakoff's disease. There we saw that patients with Korsakoff's disease who also had damage to the frontal lobes showed impaired release from proactive interference, memory for temporal order, and memory for the source or context in which information was obtained. Furthermore, some of these patients showed impairment in metamemory and also showed confabulation. These impairments, not seen in Korsakoff's patients who do not have damage to the frontal lobes, are seen in patients with damage confined to the frontal lobes. Each of these impairments results in a breakdown in the ability to utilize features inherent in the context of an event (conceptual, temporal, or temporal-spatial) for its subsequent recall, an ability that is a critical component of effortful, strategic memory processes (Jetter et al., 1986).

IMPAIRMENT IN SUBJECTIVE ORGANIZATION Because human cognition is flexible and creative, we do not have to rely on organization inherent in stimuli; we can impose subjective organization. Not unexpectedly, patients with frontal-lobe lesions are impaired on memory tasks that tap this capacity. A study by Petrides and Milner (1982) illustrates this. They presented patients with a series of cards with a 3 × 4 array of words (or, in another condition, pictures). Each card had the same 12 stimuli, but in different positions within the array. As the cards were presented, one at a time, the subject had to point to one of the stimuli that had not been touched on a previous trial. Performance on this task is greatly facilitated if subjects adopt a plan or strategy that organizes their responses. Frontal-lobe patients were severely impaired on this task. Significantly, when Petrides and Milner debriefed their subjects after the experiment, patients with frontal-lobe lesions were less likely to report initiating organizing strategies to aid their performance than were patients with temporal-lobe lesions or normal control subjects. An analogous impairment in a self-ordering task in monkeys after frontal-lobe lesions has been reported (Passingham, 1993). These impairments are striking because frontal-lobe patients are unimpaired on tasks with an equally heavy memory load when subjective organization is not required for a high level of performance.

IMPAIRMENT IN THE EXTRACTION OF INFORMATION FROM THE CONSEQUENCES OF ONGOING BEHAVIOR   In everyday life it is often the case that what must be remembered is not simply presented, but must be actively extracted from a series of events resulting from our own behavior. An experimental analogue of this situation is a conditioned paired-associate learning task in which the subject is not told which stimulus goes with which, but must learn the associated pairs by trial and error. As we saw in chapter 7, Petrides (1985) has shown that patients with frontal-lobe lesions were impaired in learning to associate a specific colored light with a specific spatial location when that information had to be extracted from trial-and-error attempts (see Figure 7.29). This contrasts markedly with the normal performance of frontal-lobe patients on memory tasks that do not require the extraction of information from an ongoing series of events, such as paired-associate learning tasks in which the associates are directly presented in pairs.

Impairment in Metamemory

In our discussion of Korsakoff's disease, we found that those patients with the disease who were unaware of their memory impairment and those who confabulated had frontal-lobe pathology in addition to their diencephalic lesions (McGlynn & Schacter, 1989; Schacter, 1991). The involvement of frontal cortex in the self-appraisal of memory capability is also supported by a number of studies showing that frontal-lobe patients are impaired in the accurate estimation of their own memory (e.g., Schacter, 1991; Shallice & Evans, 1978; Smith & Milner, 1984).

One might think that a severe amnesia would produce impairment in the appraisal of memory capacity because affected persons would not be able to remember how often their memory had failed them. There are, however, patients with severe amnesia who are nevertheless acutely aware of their memory impairment. In the face of their profound inability to learn anything new, some of these patients are in a constant state of anxiety and torment. Yet there are other amnesic patients who seem oblivious to their impairment, engaging in confabulatory pretending to remember. What differentiates these two groups seems to be that the group with impaired awareness has frontal-lobe damage in addition to the lesion causing primary memory loss. This is consistent with the finding of impaired metamemory in patients with lesions confined to the frontal lobes, despite these patients' unimpaired performance on many memory tasks. Taken together, these findings suggest that the contribution of frontal-lobe pathology to impairment in self-appraisal of memory capacity is part of a more general impairment in self-monitoring. This is not altogether a surprising conclusion, given the importance of the frontal lobes in executive function, a topic that we will address in more detail in chapter 12. Before turning to that topic, however, we first consider the neuropsychology of emotion in chapter 11.

SUMMARY

What we call memory is the result of the interaction and integration of many different memory systems. These may be conceptualized along a number of dimensions, including what is remembered, memory capacity and duration, and the component processes of memory. Within the dimension of what is remembered, a distinction has been made between episodic memory, memory for particular personal experiences, and semantic memory, memory for general information that is not consciously tied to a particular personal experience. Another dimension of memory content is conceptualized in the distinction between explicit memory and implicit memory. Explicit memory refers to the conscious representation of past events, in contrast to implicit memory, which refers to the nonconscious representation of past events. Explicit memory includes both episodic and semantic memory. Implicit memory has several subtypes, including motor skill, perceptual skill, cognitive skill, nonassociative learning, classical conditioning, and priming. The terms *declarative memory* and *procedural memory* have been used in a way roughly equivalent to *explicit* and *implicit,* respectively, although some important distinctions between these dimensions have been proposed by some authors.

Along the dimension of capacity and duration, short-term memory is a limited-capacity memory store that, in the presence of interference, retains information for only a matter of seconds. The concept of short-term memory has been subsumed into the concept of working memory. Working memory is conceptualized as having two main components, a workspace, consisting of temporary memory stores and processes applied to their contents, and executive function, which regulates the overall coordination of activities in working memory. Recent, or intermediate-term, memory refers to a memory store that maintains information for a time period intermediate between short-term memory (seconds to minutes) and long-term memory. Long-term memory is a store that can retain an enormous amount of information for as long as a lifetime.

Memory processes may be divided into three sequential stages: registration/encoding, consolidation/storage/maintenance, and retrieval. Attempts have been made to analyze various impairments in memory following cerebral damage in terms of the components of memory that are disrupted.

Not only is memory a collection of interacting systems, it is intimately related to other domains of cognition, including prior knowledge, inferences drawn from that knowledge, and aspects of cognitive organization.

Although there were indications of the multifaceted nature of memory from the study of normal subjects, the notion of multiple memory systems was deepened and extended by the finding of specific memory impairments in patients with cerebral lesions. The first of these was the severe impairment in the acquisition of new information after medial temporal-lobe damage in H. M., although he also lost some information acquired prior to his surgery.

Unilateral temporal-lobe lesions produce impairments in memory, although the magnitude of these impairments is much less severe than that following bilateral damage to medial temporal-lobe structures. The temporal lobes in each hemisphere show a complementary specialization of memory function that generally parallels the specialization of the two cerebral hemispheres.

The search for the anatomical basis of medial temporal-lobe amnesia serves as an instructive model of how theories evolve as new data are obtained. The conclusion that damage to either the hippocampus or rhinal cortex (entorhinal cortex, perirhinal cortex, and parahippocampal cortex) underlies medial temporal-lobe amnesia was reached only after years of investigation of both human patients and animal models of the disorder. During this period, there were many false resolutions of this issue, each of which eventually cracked under the weight of new empirical findings.

A second type of amnesia, diencephalic amnesia, is associated with lesions of the mamillary bodies and the anterior and dorsomedial nuclei of the thalamus. The most common form of diencephalic amnesia is Korsakoff's disease. In contrast to medial temporal-lobe amnesia, which is a relatively pure memory disorder, the severe anterograde amnesia and several years of retrograde amnesia characteristic of Korsakoff's disease are often associated with other cognitive impairments, including impairment of metamemory, confabulation, source amnesia, impaired memory for temporal order, and failure to show release from proactive interference. In addition, these patients are often cognitively apathetic, unmotivated, and emotionally unexpressive. These cognitive impairments suggest that, in addition to lesions in the diencephalon, these patients have also sustained damage to prefrontal cortex.

If we exclude the symptoms of Korsakoff's disease that appear to be associated with prefrontal dysfunction, the memory impairment seen in Korsakoff's disease and other forms of diencephalic amnesia share common features with that seen in medial temporal-lobe amnesia. This suggests that diencephalic and medial temporal-lobe regions are part of a common system that mediates the formation of new declarative long-term memories.

Evidence regarding the stage (or stages) of memory processing that is (are) disrupted in amnesia remains inconclusive. While there is little evidence that disruption at the registration/encoding stage underlies these memory impairments, disruption at the consolidation/storage/maintenance stage has been hypothesized by some investigators. Although disruption of consolidation may underlie the anterograde component of amnesic syndromes, this mechanism appears to be inconsistent with their retrograde component, in which information that had been retained for years is lost. Retrieval cues often enhance memory in amnesic patients. This does not necessarily mean, however, that the mechanism underlying amnesia is a disorder of retrieval, because the beneficial effect of cuing could occur regardless of the components of the memory process that are disrupted.

Since the first report of H. M., there has been accumulating evidence that, although amnesic patients are able to consciously remember very little new information for more than a few seconds, they do exhibit some preserved memory function. In particular, their behavior can be shown to be affected by past experience, even though they retain no conscious awareness of those events, a phenomenon that has given rise to the concept of implicit memory. Preserved implicit memory in amnesic patients takes several forms, including motor learning, perceptual learning, classical conditioning, the learning of cognitive skills (e.g., procedures and strategies that lead to successful solutions of problems), and perceptual priming. This suggests that each of these domains of memory depends on neural structures different from those necessary for normal explicit memory, and some progress has been made in further identifying their neural substrates. In addition to deepening our understanding of the functional organization of memory, preserved implicit memory in amnesic patients is being used in rehabilitation to help these individuals expand their functional capabilities.

The notion that there are two long-term memory systems, episodic memory (memory for specific events of an individual's life) and semantic memory (knowledge of the world not consciously related to one's own past) emerged out of the study of normal subjects. The study of neurological patients has revealed the existence of specific impairments in episodic memory and in semantic memory, suggesting that these two types of memory have specific neural substrates. In addition, within the domain of semantic memory impairment, some curious dissociations have been reported, including patients who are impaired in knowledge of living things but not manufactured objects. The converse pattern has also been

reported. These dissociations may provide clues about the structural organization of semantic memory. In particular, information about animals may be stored on the basis of appearance, whereas information about manufactured objects may be stored on the basis of function.

Specific impairments in short-term memory in the absence of impairment in long-term memory have been reported. This presents problems for the gateway theory, which posits that information must pass through short-term memory before it can enter long-term storage. Several specific types of short-term memory impairment are seen, including selective impairment for auditory-verbal, for visual-verbal, and for visuospatial material. The first two of these impairments are associated with lesions in left parietal cortex; the last is associated with lesions in right parietal cortex.

Because delayed-response tasks require the maintenance of an internal representation of past events, they are useful measures of working memory. Using an oculomotor analogue of the delayed response task, Goldman-Rakic has demonstrated that lesions of the principal sulcus in the monkey cause selective impairment in the ability of these animals to move their eyes to the location of a previously presented target. These findings implicate prefrontal cortex in the mediation of spatial working memory. In addition, there is evidence that other prefrontal regions are involved in other domains of working memory, such as object representation. Moreover, there is evidence that prefrontal cortex mediates the general executive component of working memory. Support for this notion comes from evidence that prefrontal lesions disrupt working memory, regardless of the kind of information involved. Imaging studies reporting prefrontal activation during a wide range of working memory tasks also support this view.

The patterns of dissociation that we have encountered suggest that there are five major memory systems: procedural memory, the perceptual representation system, working memory, semantic memory, and episodic memory. At least three of these contain a number of subsystems. Tulving has suggested that these systems emerged in the order just stated, both in the course of evolution and of individual development. From this perspective, procedural memory and the perceptual representation system are seen as essential for even the simplest interaction with the environment, whereas working memory, semantic memory, and episodic memory evolved (and develop) later, as the conscious representation of past events becomes essential for the execution and regulation of complex behavior.

The neural substrate of long-term memory is not known with certainty. However, there is strong evidence that explicit long-term memory is represented in the cerebral cortex. Furthermore, there is some evidence that explicit memory may be stored in cortical regions that mediate late stages in perceptual processing and recognition.

Implicit memory appears to involve the modification of structures that take part in the initial processing of information. There is evidence that perceptual priming is mediated by a number of specific systems, each closely linked to the cortical areas specialized for early stages of processing within a specific sensory modality. In addition, there is evidence that the neural substrate of procedural memory involves the modification of structures mediating the initial execution of perceptual, motor, and cognitive operations. This is most clear in the domain of motor learning, where areas within the motor system, including the basal ganglia and cerebellum, are known to be important.

Although under many conditions frontal-lobe lesions do not disrupt memory, damage to these brain regions causes impairment in working memory and in metamemory. Frontal dysfunction also disrupts memory whenever organization is critical for remembering. This includes the use of elaborative encoding, elaborative rehearsal, and strategic retrieval. It also includes the use of inherent organization within the to-be-remembered material, as well as the imposition of subjective organization. Frontal-lobe lesions also impair memory when the extraction of information from the consequences of one's own behavior is an essential component of the memory task.

What we know about the neural basis of memory suggests that it is both distributed and localized. It is distributed on at least two levels. First, structures throughout the brain are involved in memory. Indeed, it is becoming increasingly difficult to identify an area of the brain *not* involved in some aspect of memory. Second, within each structure the neural mechanisms underlying the representation of the past appear to involve vast arrays of neurons, rather than one or a few. The distributed nature of memory storage on this level is most clear for storage of long-term episodic memory in the cerebral cortex; localized cortical lesions do not selectively disrupt specific portions of long-term episodic memory. Yet if memory can be conceptualized as distributed, it can also be considered localized. Different neural structures are highly specialized for the mediation of specific aspects of memory.

CHAPTER *11*

Emotion

THEORIES OF THE RELATIONSHIP BETWEEN BRAIN AND EMOTION
The James-Lange Theory of Emotion
The Cannon-Bard Theory
Importance of the Hypothalamus for Emotion
The Papez Circuit
The Kluver-Bucy Syndrome
The Concept of the Limbic System
THE NEURAL BASIS OF LEARNED FEAR AS A MODEL SYSTEM
Advantages of Studying Fear
Fear Conditioning
Critical Structures for Conditioned Fear
The Amygdala: Interface Between Information About the World and Emotional Response
The Interspecies Generality of the Amygdala's Role in Fear Conditioning
EMOTIONAL MEMORY
Emotional Memory and Memory of Emotion

Brain Systems Mediating Emotional Memory and Memory of Emotion
THE CORTEX AND EMOTION
The Cortex and Mood
The Cortex and the Perception and Interpretation of Emotion
The Cortex and Emotional Expression
The Temporal Lobes and Emotion
THE INTERACTION OF CORTEX AND AMYGDALA IN THE HIGHER-ORDER MEDIATION OF EMOTION
Amygdala Influences on Cortex
Integration of Cortex and Amygdala
EMOTION AND CONSCIOUS EXPERIENCE
Requirements for the Conscious Experience of Emotion
Thoughts and Feelings
SUMMARY

❖ ❖ ❖

The importance of emotion for human functioning is obvious. On an immediate level, love or fear may absorb our attention and dominate our conscious experience, leaving us unable to deal with other matters. This may have enormous survival value; faced with an angry bear, it is not very adaptive to contemplate one's stock portfolio. From a longer-term perspective, emo-

tions are behavioral and physiological specializations that have evolved because they increase the chances that a particular species will survive. The process of natural selection that drives evolution means that organisms with certain characteristics will survive and transmit these characteristics to their offspring, whereas organisms with less-adaptive characteristics will fail to do so. The net result of evolution's tinkering with the gene pool is a combination of change and conservation of characteristics, depending on the demands of the environment. Although emotional systems have evolved, their evolution has been strikingly conservative. This means that emotional processes are more similar across different species than are most other psychological processes. This conservatism is understandable when one considers that maladaptive characteristics in a system so closely keyed to survival and procreation may rapidly lead to the death of the individual with those characteristics. When it comes to survival mechanisms, maladaptive characteristics are ruthlessly expunged from the gene pool.

For all of its importance, emotion and its neural mechanisms have been less studied than most other areas of psychological functioning. This is partly due to the difficulties inherent in studying emotion. In particular, the subjective nature of conscious emotional experience has alienated many researchers. This is partly a by-product of behaviorism and its repudiation of subjective experience as a fruitful domain of study. But the study of emotion in its own right has also been largely excluded from the cognitive psychology that has dominated psychology for the past three decades. Instead, emotion has been approached as if it were a province of cognition.

An example of cognitive approaches to emotion is Schachter and Singer's (1962) **cognitive arousal theory of emotion.** *In their classic study, Schacter and Singer injected subjects with epinephrine and then exposed them to a social situation that was likely to evoke either positive or negative emotions. In this case, the social situation was the presence of a confederate of the experimenter who was either in a buoyant, happy mood or an angry, hostile mood. The critical manipulation of the experiment was that some of the subjects were told that they had received epinephrine and that they should expect to experience autonomic arousal (e.g., increased heart rate), whereas others were not told that they were receiving epinephrine and that they were about to experience sympathetic arousal. Most subjects experienced the same quality of emotion (positive or negative) as that displayed by the confederate. The most important finding, however, was that subjects who were not told that they were receiving epinephrine experienced*

FIGURE 11.1   The Schacter-Singer cognitive arousal theory of emotion. According to this theory, bodily arousal sets in motion cognitive processes that interpret the cause of the arousal. It is this interpretation that determines the quality and intensity of experienced emotion. *(Adapted from LeDoux, 1996, p. 48)*

stronger emotions than those who were told to expect sympathetic arousal. Uninformed subjects apparently attributed their arousal to their emotional state, and this attribution enhanced the intensity of their emotional experience. Informed subjects, in contrast, attributing their arousal to the epinephrine and not to their emotional state, experienced less-intense feelings. The key factor, the investigators concluded, was the subjects' cognitions about their arousal, rather than the arousal per se. In fact, it was subsequently shown that a subject's belief that he or she is being aroused influences emotional experience, even when that belief is based on false information (Valins, 1966).

These were seminal studies and are representative of a large number of studies emphasizing the importance of cognitive interpretation as a factor contributing to emotional experience (Figure 11.1). The cognitive approach to emotion has been useful in that cognitive attributions and interpretations clearly do influence what we feel (Arnold, 1960; Lazarus, 1966). In addition, applications of this approach in the form of cognitive therapy have been effective in the treatment of mood disorders (Beck, 1967; Kelly, 1955). Nevertheless, cognitive approaches to emotion leave out aspects of emotion that lie outside the cognitive domain, aspects that made their appearance in the course of evolution long before cognition. These essentially emotional systems are conserved in the biologically based survival mechanisms of present-day animals, and a biological approach to emotion therefore offers the possibility of attaining a more complete and balanced understanding than is attainable through the exclusive use of the cognitive perspective.

A biologically based approach also affords the possibility of integrating cognitive and emotional factors into a more unified view of human decision making. Emotion and cognition ultimately work together to mediate higher-order human behavior. This idea, espoused by poets and philosophers for centuries, has recently gained empirical support from investigations in the neurobiology of emotion. There is evidence, for example, that the impairment in reasoning seen in patients with orbital frontal lesions is not due to a primary deficit in thinking but, rather, to the unavailability of emotional input to the reasoning process. Such patients have been shown to reason well in laboratory tests that do not require an emotional contribution, only to be very impaired in real-life decision-making situations that depend on being in touch with one's emotions for their adaptive solution (Damasio, 1994). This interdependence of emotion and cognition has led some to suggest that, in studying the neural basis of psychological functioning, the much-used term cognitive neuroscience *is too restrictive and biased, implying some kind of priority to cognition over other processes, including emotion. The term* mental neuroscience *has been proposed as an alternative (LeDoux, 1996). The term* psychic neuroscience *might be preferable because it would seem to be burdened with even fewer assumptions about the basic elements of psychological processes.*

Whatever we call it, making the brain the focus of the investigation of psychological processes has the advantage of providing a perspective that may help free us from some of the biases inherent in cognitively based perspectives. In this chapter, we will address the question of what the brain tells us about emotion. This approach will allow us to avoid some of the assumptions inherent in cognitive approaches to emotion. Framing the question in this way also provides an opportunity to apply what is sometimes called reverse engineering (Pinker, 1995). This is the idea that, because evolution has "engineered" (through the process of natural selection) a highly adaptive biological mechanism for a certain psychological process, a strategy making that mechanism the focus of investigation is likely to reveal much about the nature of both the brain mechanism and the psychological process it mediates.

Emotion can be divided into three components: body changes mediated by the autonomic nervous system and the endocrine system (such as increased heart rate),

behavior, and subjective experience. The last of these domains presents a problem. Whereas body changes and behavior can be objectively measured, feelings, being subjective, cannot. As mentioned earlier, this has had a dampening effect on the experimental study of emotion. The position taken here (and advocated by a number of neuroscientists studying emotion, e.g., LeDoux, 1996) is that, as important and interesting as feelings are, it is not necessary that they be tackled directly in order to study emotion. Analogously, cognitive psychology has found ways to study a wide variety of processes, from mental rotation to priming, through the analysis of observable data. According to this approach, the study of emotion can focus on understanding how various specialized brain systems process information and produce responses that are characteristic of various classes of emotion. This can be done without reference to conscious emotional experience.

In the sections that follow, we will first discuss some of the early attempts to understand the relationship between brain and emotion. Some of these are enticingly inventive and have stimulated some illuminating experimentation. In the end, however, they leave us disappointed. One reason for this is that they attempt to deal with emotion as if it were a global phenomenon. We have seen that when Karl Lashley treated memory as a global phenomenon, he was unable to devise experiments that shed light on its neural basis. It was only as it was realized that memory comprises a number of different systems that it became possible to gain some meaningful understanding of the neural basis of each of these systems (see chapter 10). There is every reason to believe that the search for the neural mechanisms of emotion will follow a similar course, and, in the second section of this chapter, we examine the neural basis of conditioned fear as a model system. In the third section, we examine emotional memory and compare it with explicit memory for emotion. We will find that different systems underlie these two domains of memory. In the fourth section, we examine the role of the cerebral cortex in emotion, and, in the fifth section, we discuss the interactive relationship between cortex and amygdala in the higher-order mediation of emotion-based action. Finally, in the last section we will briefly tackle the problem of emotion and consciousness.

FIGURE 11.2   The most intuitive idea about the relationship between subjective emotional experience, bodily arousal, and emotional behavior is that subjective emotional experience is primary and causes the other two components. *(Adapted from LeDoux, 1996, p. 44)*

THEORIES OF THE RELATIONSHIP BETWEEN BRAIN AND EMOTION

As we have said, emotion can be conceptualized as having three components: bodily arousal, behavior, and subjective experience. Early theories attempted to relate these basic components to each other and to the stimulus that sets them in motion. They also attempted to relate each of these components to particular regions of the brain and body. Some aspects of these theories remain viable and continue to stimulate research investigations. Others have contributed to scientific progress by stimulating research that has led to their disproof. We will review some of the more important of these theories in this section.

The James-Lange Theory of Emotion

The first modern theory of the relationship between brain and emotion was proposed independently by William James (1884) and the Danish psychologist Carl Lange (1887). Although the most intuitive relationship would seem to be that a stimulus elicits feelings (subjective emotional experience), which in turn cause peripheral arousal and behavior (Figure 11.2), the James-Lange theory proposed a different relationship between these components. It proposed that emotional experience is the result of feedback from the body regarding its internal state (i.e., peripheral arousal) and the behavior in which it is engaged (Figure 11.3). This counterintuitive view is often illustrated by the example of a man meeting a bear in the woods. According to the James-Lange theory, we feel fear because of feedback from our body regarding its internal state (trembling and sweating) and the behavior in which we are engaging (running). James proposed that the cortex processes the stimulus and then organizes behavior and an internal body response, which are then fed back

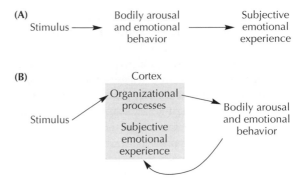

FIGURE 11.3   *(A)* According to the James-Lange theory of emotion, bodily arousal and emotional behavior cause subjective emotional experience. *(B)* James believed that the cortex organizes an emotional response (bodily arousal and emotional behavior) to a stimulus. The emotional response is then fed back to the cortex, where subjective emotional experience is generated. *(Adapted from LeDoux, 1996, p. 45)*

to the cortex. It is this feedback to cortex that generates the experience of an emotion. James suggested that peripheral body activity and behavior are analogous to the sounding board of a piano. After the hammer strikes the string, the sounding board resonates with the vibrating string, amplifying and enriching the sound. Analogously, peripheral arousal and behavior amplify the initial cortical activity, yielding emotional experience (James, 1884).

Although this theory may appear counterintuitive, it may not be as foreign to everyday experience as it initially sounds. Is it not the case that we often feel an emotion more strongly when we realize that our heart is pounding and our legs are shaking? Could this peripheral arousal not also be the cause of the quality of our feelings? Indeed, this is the basis of certain forms of yoga and meditation and certain drugs, such as beta blockers, that attempt to control anxiety by controlling peripheral arousal.

Although this theory was proposed more than a century ago, the degree to which it accurately accounts for emotion remains inconclusive. There is evidence that persons with spinal cord transection experience emotions normally (Cannon, 1927), although there are some reports that people with these lesions experience emotions less intensely (LeDoux, 1987). However, even if emotional experience is intact after spinal transection, this does not finally settle the issue, because there are a wealth of autonomic connections from the body to the brain, such as those made by the vagus nerve, that bypass the spinal cord. Another source of data consistent with the James-Lange hypothesis are reports that inducing subjects to adopt a particular facial expression (such as smiling), by giving them emotionally neutral instructions as to how to contract certain facial muscles, results in feelings corresponding to the facial expression (Izard, 1971, 1992; Tomkins, 1962). Findings such as these have been interpreted as evidence for the **facial feedback hypothesis,** the view that the configuration of facial muscles determines emotional experience.

One of the most modern aspects of the James-Lange theory is the notion that emotional experience is not a primary causal factor in overall emotional response; bodily arousal and behavior do not require subjective experience for their organization. We have already alluded to the heuristic usefulness of this idea and will return to it later.

The Cannon-Bard Theory

Walter Cannon (1927) and his student Philip Bard (1929) criticized the James-Lange theory. Cannon argued that feelings occur too rapidly to be the result of feedback from the body and that, in any case, patterns of autonomic arousal are basically the same for different emotions. His belief that there are not specific autonomic signatures corresponding to particular emotions led him to an alternative theory. He proposed that an emotional stimulus first activates the thalamus, from which it then simultaneously activates the cortex and the hypothalamus (Figure 11.4). The cortical activation results in emotional experience, while the hypothalamic stimulation organizes behavioral and autonomic response. Because Cannon believed that autonomic response is essentially standard for all emotions, he argued that it contributes to emotional experience by feeding back to the cortex and amplifying the intensity of the specific emotional experience that had already been organized there by direct thalamic input.

Whereas James's theory did not propose that there were brain areas devoted specifically to emotion, the

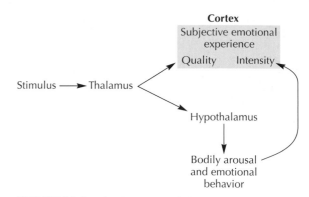

FIGURE 11.4   The Cannon-Bard theory of emotion proposed that the processing of emotional stimuli begins with its parallel projection, via the thalamus, to the cortex and to the hypothalamus. The cortex then organizes the quality of subjective emotional experience, while the hypothalamus simultaneously organizes peripheral arousal. Information about peripheral arousal, fed back to the cortex, influences the intensity, but not the quality, of emotional experience. *(Adapted from LeDoux, 1996, p. 84)*

Cannon-Bard theory of emotion emphasized the importance of subcortical structures, particularly the hypothalamus, for the mediation of emotional response. In the next section, we will explore further the role of the hypothalamus in emotion.

Importance of the Hypothalamus for Emotion

Many subcortical structures have been implicated in the mediation of emotion. However, the hypothalamus, a structure long known to be important in the regulation of autonomic and endocrine function, was the first subcortical structure for which a role in emotional behavior was clearly established. As early as the 1920s, it was shown that animals that had had their cerebral hemispheres removed were nevertheless able to engage in certain kinds of emotional behavior patterns. For example, a dog or cat that has undergone removal of all neural tissue anterior to the posterior portion of the hypothalamus is able to exhibit a pattern of aggressive behavior that is very similar to that of the intact animal. There were, however, some important differences between these animals and intact ones. Although before surgery the animals were not easily provoked, after surgery they

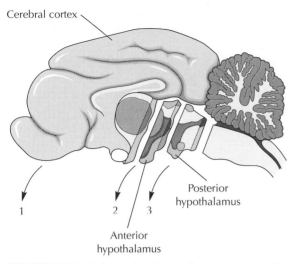

Cerebral cortex

Posterior
hypothalamus

Anterior
hypothalamus

1   2   3

FIGURE 11.5   If the cerebral hemispheres are removed
and the hypothalamus is left intact (*1*), sham rage occurs.
A similar result is obtained if the anterior hypothalamus is
also removed (*1 + 2*). If the posterior hypothalamus is also
removed (*1 + 2 + 3*), sham rage does not occur. *(From Bear,
Connors, & Paradiso, 1996, p. 447)*

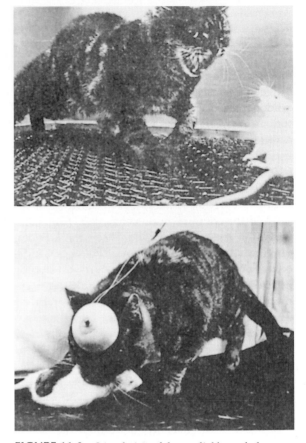

FIGURE 11.6   Stimulation of the medial hypothalamus
produces affective aggression *(top)*, whereas stimulation of
the lateral hypothalamus produces predatory aggression
(bottom). *(From Bear, Connors, and Paradiso, 1996, p. 448)*

went into a rage after mild stimulation. In addition,
animals that had had the operation did not direct
their rage toward a specific target but instead exhibited a kind of generalized and undirected rage. The
term **sham rage** was used to describe behaviors with
these characteristics. The critical structure organizing sham rage is the posterior hypothalamus. This is
shown by the finding that, although removal of all
tissue anterior to the posterior hypothalamus results
in sham rage, removal including the posterior hypothalamus abolishes it (Figure 11.5).

In the 1920s, Hess (1954) conducted a series of experiments investigating the effect of stimulating different regions of the hypothalamus, using **stereotaxic
technique,** a method that makes possible the implan-
tation of electrodes in precise locations within the
hypothalamus. Electrodes in different regions of the hypothalamus were found to elicit different components
of behavior. Some evoked sniffing and components of
eating. Other sites evoked components of anger and
rage responses, such as hissing, growling, and the
standing of hair on end in the cat.

More recently, Flynn (1967) has shown that the
stimulation of different regions of the hypothalamus
results in different forms of aggressive response. Cats
exhibit two different forms of aggressive response,
predatory aggression and **affective aggression.** Predatory aggression occurs when an animal is killing an
animal of another species for food. It is typically unaccompanied by vocalization or by elaborate display behaviors and is aimed at vulnerable parts of the prey's
body. In contrast, affective aggression is for show. It is
often accompanied by intense vocalization and other
aggressive displays, such as a threatening posture
(Figure 11.6). Flynn showed that stimulation of the
medial hypothalamus evoked affective aggression,

whereas stimulation of the lateral hypothalamus evoked predatory aggression.

These findings, together with clear evidence of the central role of the hypothalamus in the control of autonomic and endocrine function, established that the hypothalamus plays an important role in the mediation of emotion. This role is so important that some theories of emotion have gone so far as to define the emotional brain as those structures in close synaptic proximity to the hypothalamus (Nauta & Feirtag, 1986). Although this view enjoys much support, it has also been criticized on the grounds that the staggering number of interconnections between structures in the complex brains of mammals makes a definition of "close synaptic proximity" difficult (LeDoux, 1996). In any case, as we will see shortly, it is clear that other structures are centrally involved in emotion. These include other subcortical structures, particularly the amygdala, and certain cortical regions, particularly prefrontal cortex.

The Papez Circuit

The notion of the emotional brain that began to emerge from these and other investigations was that subcortical structures, particularly the hypothalamus, mediate bodily arousal (through autonomic and endocrine activation) and organize basic emotional responses such as aggression. The cerebral cortex, in contrast, was thought to mediate emotional experience and the organization of more complex and longer-term emotional behavior. It also seemed apparent that, whatever theory of emotion one embraced, peripheral arousal and emotional experience influence each other. The question arose then as to the neural mechanisms by which subcortical processes mediating bodily arousal and cortical processes mediating emotional experience influence each other.

TWO PATHWAYS MEDIATING EMOTIONAL EXPERIENCE   The neuroanatomist James Papez (1937), made a bold attempt to address the problem of the neural mechanisms underlying the reciprocal influence of bodily arousal and emotional experience. Like Cannon and Bard, Papez believed that after sensory input reaches the thalamus, it is then directed to

the cortex and to the hypothalamus. Papez considered the cingulate gyrus to be the cortical area mediating emotional experience, serving as a kind of cortical projection area for emotion analogous to the primary cortical sensory areas. According to his theory, there are two mechanisms by means of which conscious feelings may arise. In one, which Papez termed the **stream of thought,** sensory input reaches the cingulate gyrus via the thalamus and cortex. Also within this stream would be input to the cingulate gyrus from cortical areas storing long-term memory, a pathway through which memory could evoke feelings. In the other mechanism, which Papez called the **stream of feeling,** input from the thalamus goes first to the hypothalamus and then projects to the cingulate gyrus via the anterior thalamus (Figure 11.7).

THE CIRCUIT   To account for the reciprocal influence of cortical and subcortical mechanisms of emotion, Papez proposed the following circuit: The cingulate cortex projects to the hippocampus via the massive fiber bundle known as the cingulum. The hippocampus projects to the mamillary bodies (part of the hypothalamus) via the fornix. The mamillary bodies then project to the anterior thalamus via the mamillothalamic tract. Finally, to complete the circuit, the anterior thalamus projects to cingulate cortex, via the thalamocortical radiations (see Figure 11.7).

Here then is a hypothetical neural circuit that was proposed to account for the reciprocal interaction of emotional experience and emotional response. It also attempted to account for the difference between feelings resulting from cortical processes (cortical activation of emotion) and feelings springing from hypothalamic activity (subcortical activation of emotion). Papez further speculated that the tendency of emotions to cause extended periods of autonomic activation and mental preoccupation was due to prolonged reverberation of input around this circuit.

PROBLEMS WITH PAPEZ'S THEORY   In support of his proposal, Papez drew heavily on evidence derived from the clinical literature. For example, he included the hippocampus because damage to that structure is seen in rabies, a disease causing emotional dysfunction. Papez included the cingulate gyrus and

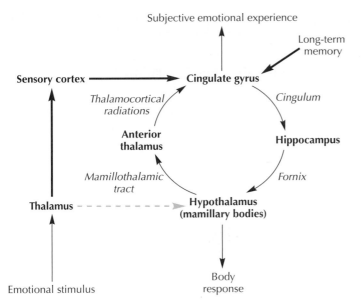

Subjective emotional experience

Long-term memory

Sensory cortex ⟶ **Cingulate gyrus**

Thalamocortical radiations

Cingulum

Anterior thalamus

Hippocampus

Mamillothalamic tract

Fornix

Thalamus ⤑ **Hypothalamus (mamillary bodies)**

Body response

Emotional stimulus

FIGURE 11.7   Schematic depiction of the Papez circuit. The stream of thought *(thick lines)* was proposed as a pathway mediating the cortical activation of emotion. This could be achieved either through the processing of sensory input to the cortex or through input from cortical areas storing long-term memory. The stream of feeling *(broken line)* was proposed as a pathway mediating the subcortical activation of emotion. The postulation of these two streams assumes that some emotional experiences are primarily the result of cortical activity, whereas others are primarily the result of hypothalamic activity. Because the Papez circuit was an attempt to account for how cortical emotional processes (mediating conscious emotional experience and complex emotion-based action) and hypothalamic emotional processes (mediating emotional autonomic arousal and simple behavioral response) can influence each other, each stream is likely to activate components of the other. *(Adapted from LeDoux, 1996, p. 89)*

assigned it a central role in emotional experience because damage to it results in apathy, depression, and emotional blunting. Unfortunately, he was not able to subject his speculations about the connections within his circuit to definitive empirical testing because, at the time, techniques for determining neuronal connections were relatively crude. Interestingly, however, Papez's anatomical speculations were prescient; subsequent research has verified the existence of the connections that he proposed. There have been some refinements, of course. For example, only 50% of fibers in the fornix reach the mamillary bodies, the other 50% projecting to the septum. In addition, there are many connections between the hypothalamus and other structures, including the amygdala, not predicted by Papez, that have turned out to be important (Figure 11.8).

The most important problem with the Papez circuit, however, is that subsequent research has failed to establish a role for the circuit in the mediation of emotion. As we have seen, the hypothalamus has obvious relevance to emotion. We will see that the cingulate gyrus also plays a role in the higher-order regulation of emotion. However, the anterior thalamus and the hippocampus have not been shown to have direct involvement in emotion, and there is no evidence that the connections between the four structures in the Papez circuit serve the role that Papez proposed for them. The Papez circuit is thus an example of how the beauty and aesthetic simplicity of a scientific theory have nothing to do with its validity. We might have said "yet another" example, for the history of science is strewn with plausible synthesizing theories that

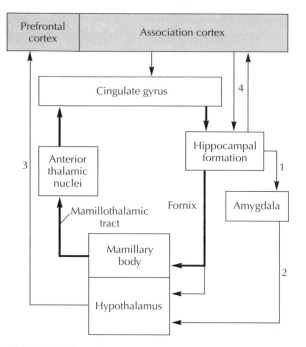

FIGURE 11.8   The circuit originally proposed by Papez *(thick lines),* together with some more recently discovered connections *(thin lines).* Of particular interest are *(1)* hippocampal connections to the amygdala; *(2)* amygdala connections with hypothalamus; *(3)* hypothalamic connections with prefrontal cortex, particularly orbital (ventromedial) frontal cortex; and *(4)* reciprocal connections between hippocampus and association cortex. Some of these pathways, particularly those involving the amygdala and orbital frontal cortex, have turned out to be more involved in emotion than the circuit originally proposed by Papez. *(From Kandel et al., 1995, p. 607)*

have not survived attempts at empirical validation. Nevertheless, Papez's bold attempt to achieve a general theory of the neural mechanisms of emotion is of historical interest because it encouraged theorizing about the neural mechanisms of emotion and it influenced the development of the concept of the limbic system, which we will consider shortly. In addition, although his attempt to account for the interaction of cortical and subcortical mechanisms of emotion failed, Papez's focus on the problem helped to define a central problem in the neurobiology of emotion. The failure of his attempt also ultimately contributed to movement away from general theories of brain and emotion

toward investigations of more specialized biological systems mediating specific emotions.

The Klüver-Bucy Syndrome

Shortly after the appearance of Papez's proposal, some very important empirical findings bearing on brain mechanisms of emotion were reported. Heinrich Klüver and Paul Bucy observed major behavioral changes in monkeys that had undergone bilateral temporal lobectomy (Klüver & Bucy, 1937, 1939). This constellation of changes, which has come to be known as the **Klüver-Bucy syndrome,** includes five categories of change: decreased fear, psychic blindness, oral tendencies, hypermetamorphosis, and changes in sexual behavior.

DECREASED FEAR   Wild monkeys normally are quite fearful of humans. They will often cower in the corner of their cage when approached and will avoid being handled. After bilateral temporal lobectomy, wild monkeys showed no fear of humans, allowing experimenters to touch them and pick them up without objection. In addition, these monkeys were observed to repeatedly approach a natural enemy, even after being attacked. These findings represent a severe impairment in response to what would normally be fear-evoking stimuli.

PSYCHIC BLINDNESS   Monkeys with bilateral temporal lobectomy were unable to recognize seen objects, although they were not blind. In other words, they had a visual agnosia. Borrowing a term from 19th-century neurology, Klüver and Bucy termed this **psychic blindness.**

ORAL TENDENCIES   These monkeys tended to explore objects by putting them in their mouth. They seemed to be using the tactile stimulation this behavior afforded to identify objects.

HYPERMETAMORPHOSIS   The oral tendencies of these monkeys can be explained in part as an attempt to compensate for their visual agnosia. However, these animals also seemed to be driven to run about and explore everything in their environment.

Klüver and Bucy called this restless urge to explore **hypermetamorphosis.**

CHANGES IN SEXUAL BEHAVIOR   Many of these monkeys exhibited a profound change in sexual behavior. They showed greatly increased interest in sex and engaged in an abnormally wide range of sexual behaviors. In addition to heterosexual acts, they masturbated and engaged in homosexual behavior. All of the components of the Klüver-Bucy syndrome have been observed in human patients with extensive bilateral temporal-lobe damage (Poeck, 1969).

INTERPRETATION OF THE KLÜVER-BUCY SYNDROME: THE CENTRAL ROLE OF THE AMYGDALA IN EMOTION   A large amount of tissue was removed in these monkeys, including bilateral removal of extensive areas of temporal cortex, the hippocampus, and the amygdala. Based on our current understanding of the brain, it is possible to associate components of the syndrome with particular regions within the removal area. Thus, it seems probable that the psychic blindness is the result of damage to visual areas in posterior temporal cortex. The oral tendencies are most likely attempts to compensate for the visual agnosia through tactile exploration. The hypermetamorphosis may also be a secondary effect of the visual agnosia, although that is less certain.

Of particular relevance to our current discussion are the emotional changes in these monkeys, particularly their decrease in fear. Subsequent research has indicated that this is the result of damage to the amygdala. Thus, bilateral damage confined to the amygdala results in flattened emotional expression. In particular, animals with bilateral amygdala lesions exhibit reduced fear. Rats with these lesions will fearlessly approach a sedated cat, and wild animals will become docile and tame (LeDoux, 1993b).

Not surprisingly, it has been shown that amygdala lesions have a profound effect on the social behavior of animals. Thus, if the dominant monkey of a troop is subjected to a bilateral amygdalectomy, after recovery from surgery and return to the troop, he fails to exhibit the aggressive displays that normally serve to maintain his dominant position and rapidly falls to the bottom of the dominance hierarchy (Pribram, 1954). Monkeys lower in the hierarchy subjected to bilateral amygdala lesions tend to get beaten up by the dominant monkey when they return to the troop. This appears to happen because they fail to emit the appropriate submissive displays that normally prevent such treatment. Their behavior does not appear to be regulated by an emotional appreciation of their social context. An even more dramatic effect is seen in monkeys living in a troop in a free-ranging natural environment. After bilateral amygdalectomy, these monkeys ostracize themselves from the troop, sometimes literally walking straight into the wild (Dicks, Myers, & Kling, 1969; Franzen & Myers, 1973; Myers, 1972). This inability to engage in social behavior results in extreme isolation and even death.

Although selective bilateral amygdala damage in humans is extremely rare, one such patient, known as S. M., has been reported to have a specific impairment in the ability to recognize facial expressions of anger, fear, and aggression. In contrast, she was able to recognize photographs of emotionally neutral facial expressions and facial expressions of sadness, happiness, and disgust (Adolphs et al., 1995).

Stimulation of the amygdala in animals produces aggressive behavior and other behavior that suggests the animal is fearful and anxious (LeDoux, 1993b). Amygdala stimulation has also been carried out in humans. As part of the EEG assessment of seizures in certain patients, depth electrodes are inserted through burr holes in the skull to positions deep in the temporal lobes (Figure 11.9). They can then be stimulated at specific locations along the electrode tracts. This may elicit seizures like those from which the patient is suffering, which can then be accurately recorded from the same electrodes. Using this technique, it has been reported that stimulation of the amygdala is associated with feelings of anxiety, apprehension, and fear (Gloor, Olivier, & Quesney, 1981).

The association of the amygdala with aggressive behavior has led some to advocate bilateral amygdalectomy as a treatment for otherwise intractable violence, and there have been reports that this procedure is effective in reducing aggression in some of these patients (Mark & Ervin, 1970; Mark, Sweet, & Ervin, 1972). Although this procedure is being advocated only for persons manifesting extreme and

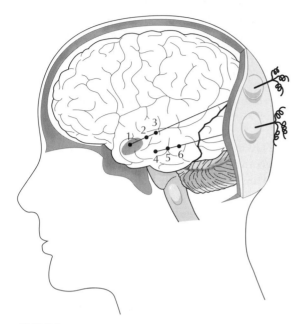

FIGURE 11.9   Insertion of depth electrodes in the temporal lobes. The numbers indicate points along the electrode tracts that are stimulated to elicit a seizure that can then be recorded from the same electrodes. This also provides an opportunity for patients to report emotional experiences that result from the stimulation. The amygdala is the oval body penetrated by the tip of the upper electrode at point 1. *(From Rosenzweig & Leiman, 1989, p. 599)*

chronic violence that is untreatable by other means, the ethical implications of a procedure that irreversibly destroys these important brain centers are worrisome.

Now that we have presented evidence for the importance of the amygdala in emotion, we are ready to examine its role in a specific emotion system. Before doing so, however, we will consider one more global theory of emotion, the limbic system. This will also provide an opportunity for us to touch on some of the other structures involved in emotion.

The Concept of the Limbic System

The term **limbic system** is widely used to denote the part of the brain most directly involved in mediating emotions. The term originated from a hypothesis proposed by Paul MacLean (1952), who argued that there is a set of neural structures, functioning as

a system, that is centrally important for emotion. These are located around the border between the telencephalon and the diencephalon; hence, the term *limbic,* meaning "border."

MacLean formulated the limbic system hypothesis in an attempt to address the same problem addressed by Papez: How do cortical and subcortical emotional processes interact to produce coordinated emotional response and experience? MacLean hypothesized that the structures of the limbic system mediate this interaction.

LIMBIC SYSTEM STRUCTURES

The Hippocampus, Parahippocampal Gyrus, and Cingulate Gyrus   Central among the structures of the limbic system for MacLean was the hippocampus, which he believed received information from the external world and from the internal visceral environment. In his view, the limbic system also included the cingulate gyrus, that rim of cortex along the medial surface of the hemispheres adjacent to the diencephalon, and the parahippocampal gyrus. This was cortex that Paul Broca (1878) had designated *le grand lobe limbique* in the 19th century. MacLean argued that limbic cortex is a common denominator in the brains of mammals, maintaining its size across species, in contrast to lateral neocortex, which enlarged greatly late in the course of evolution (Figure 11.10).

The Septum   Other structures considered by MacLean to be part of the limbic system were the hypothalamus, amygdala, septum, and prefrontal cortex. We have already presented evidence for the role of the amygdala and hypothalamus in emotion. Evidence for the role of the septum, neural tissue separating the anterior portion of the two lateral ventricles, came initially from the work of Olds and Milner (1954). They implanted electrodes in a number of subcortical areas and then provided the animal with an opportunity to deliver **electrical self-stimulation** to these areas by pressing a bar. Olds and Milner reported that the animals would energetically press the bar that delivered stimulation to the septum. The animals seemed to be deriving pleasure from this stimulation, although this is obviously an inference. It is perhaps more parsimonious to say that septal electrical self-stimulation is highly reward-

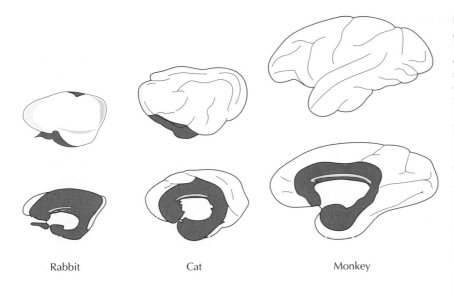

Rabbit   Cat   Monkey

FIGURE 11.10 Lateral *(top)* and medial *(bottom)* views of the rabbit, cat, and monkey cerebrum, drawn roughly to scale. The limbic lobe (limbic cortex) is found throughout the mammalian series. According to MacLean, as one ascends the phylogenetic scale, the limbic lobe enlarges very little, in contrast to the neocortex, which expands enormously. Thus, the phylogenetically older limbic cortex constitutes a smaller proportion of total cortex in more advanced mammals. These anatomical considerations have been seen as evidence that, over the course of evolution, limbic cortex has remained static and primitive, in contrast to the vastly expanding neocortex. *(From MacLean, 1970, p. 340)*

ing. It turns out that the septum is not the only brain region where electrical stimulation is rewarding. Other areas include the lateral hypothalamus, the medial forebrain bundle, the ventral tegmental area, and the dorsal pons (Figure 11.11).

Although self-stimulation studies in humans are rare, there is a report of a patient with narcolepsy who had 14 electrodes implanted in different brain regions in an effort to find a region that, when stimulated, would keep him awake and alert. The site that this patient chose to stimulate most frequently was the septum. He reported that stimulation to this region produced extremely pleasurable sexual feelings that felt like a building up to orgasm (Heath, 1963).

Prefrontal Cortex MacLean included prefrontal cortex, particularly orbital frontal cortex, in the limbic system because of its direct connections with the hypothalamus. Indeed, direct synaptic connection with the hypothalamus has been proposed as a criterion for inclusion of a structure within the limbic system (Nauta, 1971; Nauta & Feirtag, 1986). In addition, prefrontal cortex has been shown to play an important role in the modulation of emotion. We will have more to say about the role of frontal cortex in emotion later.

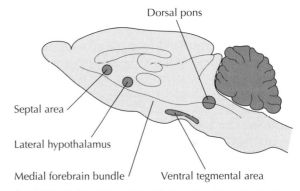

FIGURE 11.11 Rats will self-stimulate when electrodes are placed in these sites. *(From Bear, Connors, & Paradiso, 1996, p. 452)*

MacLean proposed that the structures of the limbic system, which he viewed as phylogenetically earlier than neocortex, work together as a coordinated system to ensure the survival of the individual and, ultimately, the species. He saw the system as coordinating basic drives, including fighting, defense, feeding, and reproduction, with input from the environment.

THE TRIUNE BRAIN HYPOTHESIS In 1970, MacLean further developed his conception of the limbic system by placing it within a broader theory that attempted to account for emotional processes at all levels of complexity. This was the **triune brain hypothesis** (MacLean, 1970). According to this view, the brain has undergone three major stages of evolution so that in higher mammals there exists a hierarchy of three brains in one—hence, the term *triune brain*. The **reptilian brain,** comprising the brain stem, mediates the most basic elements of survival, such as homeostasis. It is compulsive and stereotyped. MacLean illustrates its function by suggesting that it organizes the processes involved in the return of sea turtles to the same breeding ground year after year. The **paleomammalian brain,** comprising the limbic system, adds current and recent experience to the basic drives mediated by the reptilian brain. The limbic system allows the basic survival processes of the reptilian brain to interact with elements of the outside world, resulting in the expression of general emotion. For example, the drive for reproduction would interact with the presence of an attractive member of the opposite sex, generating feelings of sexual desire.

The **neomammalian brain,** the neocortex, mediates specific emotions based on the perceptions and interpretations of the immediate world. Feelings of love toward a particular individual would be an example of this kind of emotion. According to MacLean, in humans and other advanced mammals all three brains exist. Lower mammals have only the paleomammalian and the reptilian brains. All other vertebrates have only the reptilian brain. The evolution of the paleomammalian brain (limbic system) was thus seen as liberating animals from the stereotyped expression of drives dictated by the reptilian brain. The neomammalian brain added further flexibility to emotional behavior by enabling higher mammals to base emotional behavior on complex interpretive processes and to utilize problem solving and long-term planning in the expression of emotion (Figure 11.12).

PROBLEMS WITH THE LIMBIC SYSTEM CONCEPT   As we have seen, there is compelling evidence for a role in emotion for many structures assigned to the limbic system. What is more, the limbic

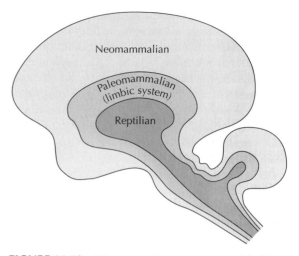

FIGURE 11.12   Diagrammatic representation of the hierarchical organization of the three basic brain types proposed in MacLean's triune brain hypothesis. *(From MacLean, 1970, p. 338)*

system constitutes an appealing organizing schema for the understanding of brain and emotion. It unifies a number of diverse structures into a coherent conceptualization based on anatomical considerations that seem to make sense within an evolutionary perspective. The power of this conceptualization is evidenced by the current wide use of the term *limbic system* to mean "emotional brain." However, despite its theoretical plausibility and its wide use, there is a serious problem with the limbic system concept. The theory posits more than that there are a number of brain structures involved in emotion; it argues that there are a number of structures that *work together in a system* to mediate emotion. The problem is that it is unclear by what criteria a structure should be included in the system (LeDoux, 1991).

One of the most conceptually attractive criteria is directness of connection to the hypothalamus (Nauta & Feirtag, 1986). The hypothalamus is clearly an important component in brain mechanisms of emotion. It is critical for the control of autonomic and endocrine functions (which activate peripheral arousal), it is involved in the organization of basic emotional behavior, and it is the recipient of highly processed cortical input. Directness of connection to the hypothalamus would seem, therefore, to be a compelling criterion for inclusion of a structure in the limbic system. However, as neuroanatomical techniques become more refined, more and more structures have been shown to have direct connections to the hypothalamus (Brodal, 1982; Kotter & Meyer, 1992).

Another major criterion formulated by MacLean for inclusion of a structure in the limbic system was that the limbic system is made up of phylogenetically older cortex and related subcortical structures. Phylogenetically older cortex is cortex that was present in species early in the course of evolution. The most prominent recently evolved structure is the neocortex, which is presumed to have evolved late in the course of evolution (hence, the prefix *neo*). According to this view, it is the phylogenetically old cortex that is mediating emotional processing, processing that is necessary for survival and therefore present at all stages of evolution.

We have seen that MacLean drew some of his evidence for this view from his understanding of comparative mammalian neuroanatomy (see Figure 11.10). However, more recent neuroanatomical investigations, surveying the brains of a broad range of animals (including fish, amphibians, birds, and reptiles), have shown that so-called primitive creatures have areas of cortex that meet the criteria for neocortex (Karten & Shimizu, 1991; Nauta & Karten, 1970; Northcutt & Kaas, 1995). These findings bring into question inferences about the relative evolutionary development of neocortex as compared with limbic cortex because they suggest that limbic cortex may have evolved from regions that are analogous to neocortex (LeDoux, 1991; Swanson, 1983).

A related assumption of the phylogenetic perspective is also open to question. It had been assumed that the apparent simplicity of a neural structure is an index of its early appearance in the course of evolution, and therefore a criterion for inclusion in the limbic system. For example, the hippocampus has often been considered to be more primitive than other areas of cortex because it has only three cell layers, rather than the six layers seen in most other cortical regions. This conclusion, apparently compelling on neuroanatomical grounds, does not fit well with the estab-

lished role of the hippocampus in highly complex aspects of declarative and explicit memory. The same argument applies to the mamillary bodies, structures with an apparently simple structure that nevertheless are involved in complex memory function.

Yet another criterion for the inclusion of a structure in the limbic system has been whether the structure plays a direct role in the regulation of visceral function. However, this also does not appear to be a useful criterion because some structures traditionally included in the limbic system, such as the hippocampus, do not have a direct role in the regulation of the viscera. Conversely, some structures not included in the limbic system, such as the lower brain stem, are directly involved in regulation of the viscera.

Finally, the requirement that a structure be involved in emotion is not a satisfactory criterion for inclusion in the limbic system because the whole purpose of the theory was to define the neuroanatomical substrate of emotion on a basis other than function. Identifying structures that play a role in emotion should lead eventually to an understanding of the emotion system(s) of the brain. However, this process cannot define which structures are part of the limbic system, a concept derived from assumptions outside the domain of functional analysis, such as the relative phylogenetic age of different brain regions.

These considerations lead to the inescapable conclusion that the limbic system concept, for all its intuitive appeal, does not provide a basis for defining which structures should be included in the system. If the limbic system cannot be defined, then it cannot be a useful explanatory construct and should be abandoned (LeDoux, 1996, p. 101; see also Brodal, 1982; Kotter & Meyer, 1992). Where does this leave us? We have already alluded to the fact that brain mechanisms of memory began to be elucidated when attempts to understand the neural basis of memory in general were supplanted by investigations of specific memory subsystems and their neurological bases. There is every reason to expect that progress will take the same form in the area of brain and emotion. In fact, there are already findings verifying this expectation. We therefore leave general theories of brain and emotion and turn to investigations of the neural mechanisms of a specific domain of emotion and its neurological basis, conditioned fear.

THE NEURAL BASIS OF LEARNED FEAR AS A MODEL SYSTEM

Advantages of Studying Fear

If there are many emotion systems in the brain, just as there are many memory systems, which should be studied? One candidate is the neural substrate of learned fear. Studying this system has certain advantages that have made it the focus of intense investigation by a number of brain researchers.

First, fear is universally recognized as an emotion. In studying its neural basis, therefore, we can be reasonably confident that we are investigating at least one aspect of emotional processing. Second, fear reactions are basic to the survival of the individual and, ultimately, the species. The selection pressures for the evolution of these reactions or, so long as they remain adaptive, for their perpetuation across generations, have therefore been very intense. These factors account for why fear responses are easily and reliably elicited. A third advantage of studying fear is that its behavioral and autonomic manifestations can be readily observed. These include behaviors such as startle, orienting, freezing, fleeing, and attacking, as well as autonomic responses, such as changes in blood pressure, heart rate, and defecation. Finally, fear responses can be readily elicited in the laboratory, using aversive classical conditioning.

Fear Conditioning

In natural conditions, some stimuli produce a response; others do not. A stimulus naturally producing a response is termed an **unconditioned stimulus** and the response produced is termed an **unconditioned response.** When a **neutral stimulus** (one that does not naturally produce an unconditioned response) just precedes an unconditioned stimulus on a number of occasions, the neutral stimulus, when presented alone, will come to produce a response that is usually (but not always) similar to the uncon-

ditioned response. This learned response is termed a **conditioned response** and the previously neutral stimulus that now elicits it is termed a **conditioned stimulus.** The entire process, termed **classical conditioning,** was discovered by Ivan Pavlov (1927). When the conditioned response is fear, the process is termed **fear conditioning.** For example, a shock is an unconditioned stimulus, naturally producing freezing and autonomic arousal (unconditioned response). If a tone that would not normally produce these responses (neutral stimulus) precedes a shock on a number of trials, the tone alone will become a conditioned stimulus, evoking freezing and autonomic arousal (conditioned response).

In fear conditioning, as in all forms of classical conditioning, the response is hardwired, genetically programmed in the individual. A rat that is bred in the laboratory will freeze and exhibit autonomic arousal the first time it sees a cat. Fear conditioning is thus stimulus learning, not response learning, and may be thought of as expanding the range of stimuli that will elicit the evolutionarily based fear response pattern that is hardwired in the animal's nervous system.

Critical Structures for Conditioned Fear

One of the most studied forms of fear conditioning utilizes a tone as the conditioned stimulus. Using this paradigm, one can then damage various structures and see which lesions interfere with the conditioning process.

THE AUDITORY PATHWAY   Figure 11.13 shows a simplified diagram of the auditory pathway. The first step in searching for the structures critical for fear conditioning is to damage different regions within the auditory pathways and then observe which lesions interfere with fear conditioning. It turns out that lesions of the medial geniculate nucleus of the thalamus, the destination of the auditory pathway at the thalamic level, interfere with auditory fear conditioning. Lesions of the inferior colliculus, a midbrain auditory center upstream in the pathway, also disrupt auditory fear conditioning. In contrast, lesions of the auditory cortex do not disrupt fear conditioning to a simple tone.

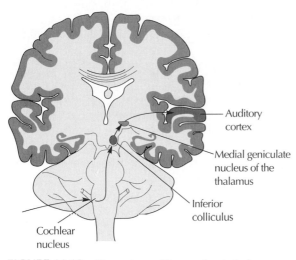

Auditory
cortex

Medial geniculate
nucleus of the
thalamus

Inferior
colliculus

Cochlear
nucleus

FIGURE 11.13   The major auditory pathway in humans. (A similar pathway exists in other vertebrates.) Input from the ear is transmitted along the auditory nerve *(bottom arrow)* to the cochlear nucleus in the brain stem. From there, input mainly crosses over and ascends to the inferior colliculus in the midbrain. Neurons in the inferior colliculus project to the medial geniculate nucleus, the auditory processing center of the thalamus. Neurons in the medial geniculate nucleus project to the auditory cortex. Although the contralateral connections from ear to auditory cortex are stronger than the ipsilateral connections, there are cross-connections at the lower brain stem and midbrain levels of the system, so that there is significant ipsilateral input from ear to auditory cortex. *(From LeDoux, 1996, p. 153)*

These findings indicate that the medial geniculate nucleus is the highest level of the auditory system required for fear conditioning. The finding that the auditory cortex is not required for fear conditioning was somewhat surprising because the auditory cortex was considered to be the major target of projections from the medial geniculate nucleus. If the auditory cortex is not required for fear conditioning, the next question is What targets of the medial geniculate nucleus are crucial? Staining techniques utilizing anterograde transport revealed that there are four subcortical structures to which the medial geniculate projects (LeDoux, Sakaguchi, & Reis, 1984). Studies that damaged the connection between the medial geniculate nucleus and each of these struc-

tures revealed that only damage to the connection to the lateral nucleus of the amygdala disrupted fear conditioning (LeDoux et al., 1986). In addition, retrograde labeling studies that injected stain into the lateral amygdala confirmed that the cell bodies of origin were located in the medial geniculate nucleus. These findings indicated that the amygdala plays a crucial role in fear conditioning and that the lateral amygdala is the target of neurons conveying auditory information from the medial geniculate nucleus.

THE CENTRAL ROLE OF THE AMYGDALA

These findings fit with a growing body of evidence that the amygdala plays a central role in emotion. We have previously reviewed some of the evidence for such a role for the amygdala. In addition, there is evidence that particular regions within the amygdala are specialized for particular components of emotion. The amygdala is composed of a number of nuclei, which traditionally have been divided into three major groups: the **corticomedial nuclei** (or **corticomedial nuclear group**), the **basolateral nuclei** (or **basolateral nuclear group**) and the **central nucleus** (Figure 11.14). The central nucleus of the amygdala (ACe) and the lateral nucleus (a component of the basolateral nuclear group) have been shown to be involved in specific aspects of conditioned fear.

The Central Nucleus of the Amygdala and Conditioned-Fear-Response Mediation   For some time it has been known that damage to ACe disrupts fear conditioning in the rabbit (Kapp, Frysinger, et al., 1979). More recently, however, it has been shown that ACe is specifically involved in the expression of conditioned fear. In fact, damage to ACe results in disruption of every measure of conditioned fear (Davis, 1992a, 1992b; Kapp et al., 1990; LeDoux, 1990, 1993a, 1995a). A particularly interesting result of these studies is the finding that specific elements of the fear response are disrupted by damage to specific outputs of ACe. For example, damage to connections between ACe and the dorsal motor nucleus of the vagus results in a specific disruption of conditioned parasympathetic responses, such as bradycardia (reduced heart rate) (Kapp, Wilson, et al., 1990). In contrast, damage to

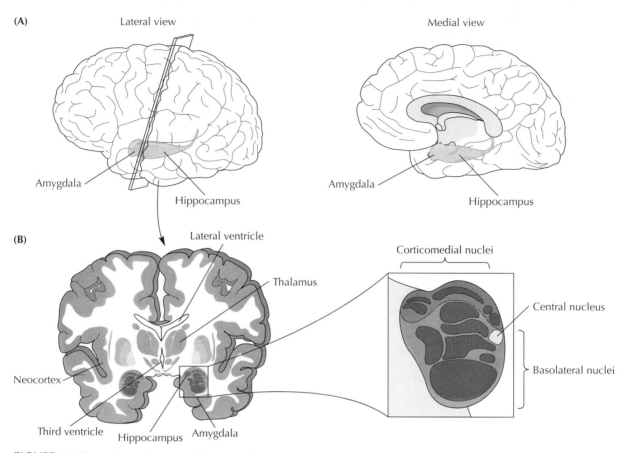

FIGURE 11.14   *(A)* Lateral and medial views of the temporal lobes, showing the location of the amygdala in relation to the hippocampus. *(B)* Coronal section showing the amygdala. The amygdala has many nuclei. These have been divided into three groups: the basolateral nuclei receive input from visual, auditory, gustatory, and tactile afferents. The corticomedial nuclei receive olfactory afferents. The central nucleus is the main source of amygdala efferents. The nomenclature of the amygdala can get somewhat confusing. For example, within the basolateral nuclei (or basolateral nuclear group, as it is also called) one finds a number of nuclei, including the lateral nucleus, the basolateral nucleus, and the basomedial nucleus. The lateral nucleus is the major amygdala target of neurons from the medial geniculate nucleus; the basolateral and basomedial nuclei are part of the pathway from the lateral amygdala nucleus to the central nucleus. *(From Bear, Connors, & Paradiso, 1996, p. 444)*

connections between ACe and periaquiductal gray results in a specific disruption of conditioned emotional behavior, such as freezing (LeDoux, Farb, & Ruggiero, 1990). Damage to connections between ACe and lateral hypothalamus (which projects to the rostral ventral lateral medulla) disrupts conditioned sympathetic responses, such as increase in blood pressure (LeDoux, Farb, & Ruggiero, 1990). Finally, damage to connections between ACe and the paraventricular nucleus of the hypothalamus disrupts conditioned endocrine responses. The four categories of conditioned fear responses controlled by different outputs of ACe are summarized in Figure 11.15. Taken together, these findings demonstrate

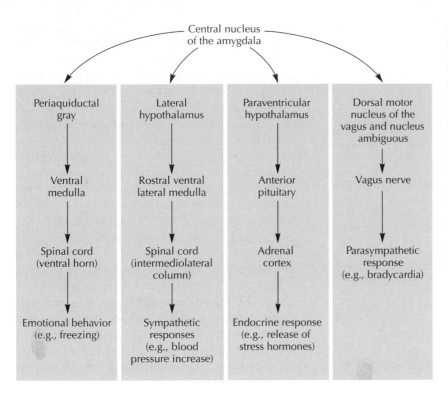

FIGURE 11.15 There are four categories of conditioned fear response: emotional behavior, sympathetic response, endocrine response, and parasympathetic response. Damage to efferents from the central nucleus of the amygdala (ACe) to the periaquiductal gray, lateral hypothalamus, paraventricular hypothalamus, or motor nucleus of the vagus selectively disrupts a specific type of conditioned fear response. These are shown at the end of each stream. Some of the intermediate neural connections involved in each response type are also shown. *(Adapted from LeDoux, 1995b, p. 1052)*

that ACe has a central role in the expression of conditioned fear.

The Lateral Nucleus of the Amygdala: Interface Between Sensory Stimuli and Conditioned Fear Responses We have seen that the central nucleus of the amygdala activates emotional response via its connections with other subcortical structures. We also saw that the lateral nucleus of the amygdala is the major target of auditory input projected to the amygdala from the medial geniculate nucleus. Thus, in fear conditioning, the lateral amygdala receives input activated by the conditioned stimulus, and the central nucleus mediates the autonomic activity, endocrine activity, and behavior that constitute the conditioned response. Connections between the lateral nucleus of the amygdala and the central nucleus of the amygdala would therefore be expected. It turns out that there are only sparse direct connections between these structures but that there are strong connections via the basolateral and basomedial nuclei of the amygdala (Amaral et al., 1992; Pitkämen et al., 1995; Price, Russ-chen, & Amaral, 1987). We thus have a pathway mediating conditioned fear. The pathway starts from auditory sensory neurons and ends with neurons activating autonomic, endocrine, and behavioral responses. Notice that this pathway bypasses the auditory cortex. This raises the question of the role played by the auditory cortex in fear conditioning.

THE ROLE OF THE AUDITORY CORTEX IN CONDITIONED FEAR We have seen that when shock is paired with a simple tone, destruction of the auditory cortex has no effect on fear conditioning. However, there are conditions under which the auditory cortex is required for fear conditioning. Suppose an animal is presented with two tones of slightly different frequencies, one of which is paired with shock and the other of which is not. The auditory cortex is required for this discrimination learning. If the auditory cortex is damaged, the animal will fail to make the discrimination and will respond to *both* tones (Jarrell et al., 1987). This indicates that the auditory discriminations mediated by the auditory cortex

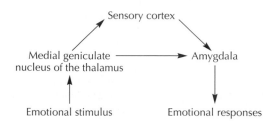

FIGURE 11.16 Auditory information from the outside world can reach the amygdala by two pathways: directly, via the medial geniculate nucleus of the thalamus, and indirectly, via a thalamus-cortex-amygdala pathway. The direct thalamus-amygdala connection conveys less information, but it is faster and biased toward response. The thalamus-cortex-amygdala pathway conveys more information, but it is slower. Each pathway has certain advantages. When speed of response is the critical factor, as in dodging a bullet, the direct thalamus-amygdala connection has an advantage. In complex social environments, the discriminating and interpretive function of the cortex is an important moderator of amygdala activity. *(Adapted from LeDoux, 1996, p. 164)*

influence fear conditioning by inhibiting amygdala-activated responses to the stimulus that had not been paired with the unconditioned stimulus. This discriminative role for the auditory cortex also fits with the finding that medial geniculate neurons projecting to the auditory cortex are tuned to (i.e., will fire only in response to) a narrow band of frequencies, whereas medial geniculate neurons projecting to the lateral amygdala are broadly tuned. This inhibitory process is made possible by a pathway from the medial geniculate nucleus to the auditory cortex and then to the lateral amygdala.

THE FUNCTION OF THE TWO PATHWAYS   There are thus, as illustrated in Figure 11.16, two pathways by which auditory information from the external world can reach the lateral amygdala (Davis, 1992a; Fanselow, 1994; Kapp et al., 1992; Weinberger, 1995). The cortical pathway allows for finer discrimination learning than the direct thalamus-amygdala connection. This raises the question of the adaptive significance of these two pathways for the functioning of animals in their natural setting.

Inferences about the neuroanatomy of evolutionarily early animals, based on the study of their living ancestors, suggest that the direct thalamus-amygdala pathway was strong in these animals, whereas the thalamus-cortex-amygdala pathway was relatively weak (Nauta & Karten, 1970; Northcutt & Kaas, 1995). In contrast, in modern mammals, the cortical channel is more elaborate and important. This suggests that in more recently evolved animals the direct thalamic-amygdala connection may be an evolutionary relic, serving no function, whereas the cortical channel, with its discriminatory capability, supplies detailed information to the amygdala about specific emotional stimuli in the world.

There is, however, reason to doubt that this is the case. As we have seen, the direct connection has a distinct advantage: speed. It is about twice as fast as the cortical channel. In addition, in contrast to information conveyed via the cortical channel, information conveyed via the direct connection is unfiltered and biased toward activating a response. This means that this connection will sometimes activate an emotional response when none is required; however, when dealing with stimuli that potentially threaten the survival of the individual, false negatives are generally more costly than false positives. That sound in the grass may not be a prowling lion, but for the gazelle it is likely to be less costly if it rapidly activates a fear response to a wide range of unexpected sounds, rather than waiting for slower, albeit more discriminating, cortical processing of stimuli. However, the cortex has a potentially important role in fear conditioning.

CONTEXTUAL CONDITIONING AND THE HIPPOCAMPUS   When a rat in a box repeatedly hears a tone followed by a shock, it starts to respond to the tone presented alone in the same way that it responds to the shock. This is the classical conditioning of a fear response. However, something else interesting happens; the rat also becomes conditioned to the box. If it is taken from some neutral place and simply put into the box, the rat will exhibit a fear response even though no tone or shock is delivered. This is called **contextual conditioning;** the animal has become conditioned to the context in which it received the unconditioned stimulus. Contextual fear conditioning is adaptive for an organism. It is likely to be adaptive for an animal to exhibit a conditioned fear response to a place where it had previously encountered an unconditioned stimulus that evoked fear. An impala that, walking under an acacia tree, is suddenly set on by a hungry leopard that was hidden in its branches would do well to react with fear next time it encounters an acacia tree, assuming that the leopard hasn't eliminated the possibility of a "next time."

A context is not just one particular stimulus. It is composed of many integrated stimuli. In our discussion of memory we found that the hippocampus receives highly processed input from polymodal association cortex (Amaral, 1987; Van Hoesen, 1982). We also saw that there is evidence that the hippocampus plays a central role in memory for the relationship between items in a conceptual or spatial context (Eichenbaum & Otto, 1992; Nadel & Willner, 1980; O'Keefe & Nadel, 1978; Sutherland & Rudy, 1989).

There is also direct evidence that the hippocampus plays a role in contextual conditioning. Lesions to the hippocampus disrupt contextual conditioning (e.g., fear response in the presence of the conditioning box), but not fear conditioning (e.g., fear response to a tone) (Kim & Fanselow, 1992; Phillips & LeDoux, 1992). The selective elimination of fear response to contextual stimuli after hippocampal lesions is consistent with the idea that conditioning to simple stimuli, such as a tone, can be mediated by the direct thalamus-amygdala pathway, whereas contextual conditioning requires that the hippocampus integrate stimuli into a context and feed the product of this integration to the amygdala. The involvement of the amygdala in both fear conditioning to simple stimuli and contextual conditioning is supported by findings that lesions of the amygdala disrupt both (Blanchard, Blanchard, & Fial, 1970; Selden et al., 1991).

The Amygdala: Interface Between Information About the World and Emotional Response

The picture emerging from these findings is that the amygdala is an emotional processing center that receives inputs from a range of levels of cognitive processes and then organizes emotional responses to this input through the activation of a number of different subcortical centers. In particular, the lateral amygdala appears to serve as the sensory interface for the amygdala, receiving a range of information from thalamic and cortical regions (Figure 11.17). The amygdala receives relatively crude sensory information about stimulus features from the thalamus. Thus, thalamic connections to the amygdala are sufficient to mediate simple fear conditioning (e.g., one tone paired with a shock). Cortical connections are also sufficient for this.

Higher-order sensory and perceptual information is projected to the amygdala from cortical sensory areas. For example, we have seen that input from auditory cortex to the amygdala is necessary for discrimination learning, that is, when one tone is paired with shock and another tone is not. Information about past events is projected to the amygdala from entorhinal cortex, and information about past events and higher-order contextual information reaches the amygdala via connections from the hippocampus. It also appears that input from medial frontal cortex is important for extinction of conditioned fear (Morgan, Romanski, & LeDoux, 1993). We will have more to say about the role of the frontal lobes in emotion later.

As we have seen, the central nucleus of the amygdala, receiving input from the lateral nucleus of the amygdala via the basomedial and basolateral nuclei, organizes the behavioral, autonomic, and endocrine components of emotional response. It then activates these responses via its connections to emotional response mechanisms represented in a number of subcortical areas (see Figure 11.15).

The Interspecies Generality of the Amygdala's Role in Fear Conditioning

Much of the research indicating a central role for the amygdala in fear conditioning has been carried out on the rat. To what extent are these findings applicable to other vertebrate species, including humans? The answer seems to be that, although different vertebrate species vary marvelously with regard to the specific sensory mechanisms each depends on to detect danger and the specific responses they employ to deal with it, the role of the amygdala in fear

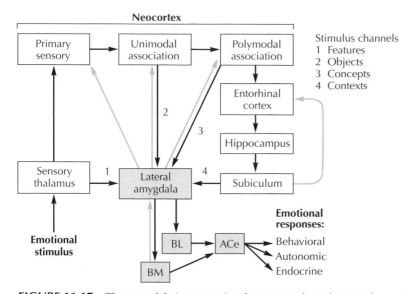

FIGURE 11.17   The amygdala is an emotional processor that takes in information about the world through a number of afferent channels projecting to the lateral nucleus and organizes components of response through a number of efferent channels projecting from the central nucleus (see Figure 11.15). The lateral amygdala, the gateway for stimuli influencing fear conditioning, may process information in parallel from various channels. It receives input from sensory processing areas in the thalamus *(1)* and neocortex *(2)*, and input from higher-order association regions in the neocortex *(3)* and the hippocampus *(4)*. Fear conditioning may be mediated by pathway 1 or 2 when no discrimination is required to identify the conditioned stimulus. Pathway 2 must be involved when discrimination between stimuli is required. Pathway 4 is involved in contextual conditioning. Medial prefrontal cortex, one of the origins of pathway 3, plays a role in extinction. Information is relayed within the amygdala from the lateral amygdala to the central nucleus of the amygdala (ACe) via the basolateral (BL) and basomedial (BM) nuclei. *(From LeDoux, 1995b, p. 1053)*

conditioning, at the interface between emotion-evoking stimulus and emotional response, appears to be universal in all animals with an amygdala.

This conclusion is based on evidence that lesions to the amygdala disrupt fear conditioning in a number of species, from mammals to pigeons. In addition, stimulation of the amygdala in anesthetized animals has been shown to produce autonomic components of fear response in rats, rabbits, dogs, cats, and monkeys, while stimulation of the awake animal produces freezing, escape, and defensive attack, in addition to autonomic changes, in these species (LeDoux, 1987). Stimulation of the medial nucleus of the amygdala produces defensive responses in a number of lizards (Greenberg, Scott, & Crews, 1984; Tarr, 1977).

In humans, stimulation of the amygdala produces a sense of foreboding, danger, and fear; these subjective experiences are also reported by patients with seizures involving the amygdala (Gloor, Olivier, & Quesney, 1981; Halgren, 1992). In addition, disruption of autonomic conditioned responses has been reported in human patients with temporal-lobe lesions that include the amygdala (LaBar et al., 1995) and in a patient with damage confined to the amygdala (Adolphs et al., 1995; Bechara et al., 1995). These findings suggest that conclusions about the role of the amygdala in fear conditioning drawn from animal studies are likely to be generally applicable to a wide range of vertebrate species, including humans. Let's turn now to the role of the amygdala in memory.

EMOTIONAL MEMORY

As we saw in chapter 10, memory is not a unitary process; there are many memory systems. Some of these systems are explicit (or declarative) and some are implicit (or procedural). This distinction is also highly relevant to the domain of memory and emotion.

Emotional Memory and Memory of Emotion

Consider a past event that was accompanied by a strong emotional response. Perhaps it was a terrifying accident or a devastating sudden emotional loss. As we think back, our memory of the episode may include both remembered details of the event and emotional arousal in the present. These two aspects of memory often seem inseparable, seamlessly fused into a remembered experience that fills us with emotion. However, sometimes this fusing of content and emotional arousal does not take place and we experience one without the other. We may have a memory of an event that we also remember as being highly emotional, but not experience emotional arousal as we remember it. This may happen, for example, in the case of a remembered emotional event that occurred a long time ago; we remember, without feeling emotion now, that, oh yes, that was very upsetting at the time. We remember the emotion, but it has been drained of the capacity to arouse us viscerally. This may be termed **memory of emotion.** Extreme forms of this type of memory are seen in certain **dissociative disorders,** disorders in which individuals may remember facts about past traumatic events without experiencing any associated emotion or even the sense that the events happened to them.

Conversely, we may experience emotional arousal without conscious memory for the past event to which that arousal is related. This is not an infrequent experience for most of us; we experience emotional arousal that seems to come out of the blue or to result from an immediate event, only to perhaps realize later that our intense feelings were related to our past. We saw this in Claparède's famous amnesic patient, who had feelings of apprehension when the physician offered his hand in greeting, without ex-

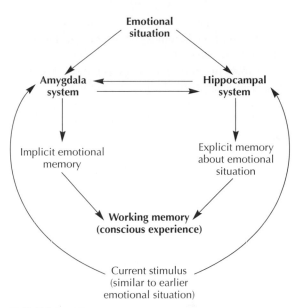

FIGURE 11.18 The hippocampal system mediates explicit memory of emotion, the facts of the past emotional situation. The amygdala system mediates implicit emotional memory, the bodily arousal associated with the past emotional situation. Usually the experiences generated by these two systems are seamlessly fused in a unified experience in working memory. However, under certain conditions, memory of emotion and emotional memory may be dissociated. *(Adapted from LeDoux, 1996, p. 202)*

plicitly recalling the pin that Claparède had concealed in his palm earlier in the day (see chapter 10). This may be termed **emotional memory.**

Brain Systems Mediating Emotional Memory and Memory of Emotion

Memory of emotion will be recognized as a form of conscious, declarative, or explicit memory. We saw that explicit memory is mediated by hippocampal and diencephalic memory systems. In contrast, emotional memory is implicit and may occur without conscious content. This is mediated by the amygdala (Figure 11.18). Thus, the hippocampal system will activate explicit memory for the details of an event and the dispassionate recollection that the situation was highly emotional (memory of emotion). The amygdala system will activate previous autonomic arousal (emotional memory). Support for the amygdala's role in a specialized emotional memory system comes from the finding that, although lesions of the hippocampal system disrupt explicit memory but not conditioning, lesions of the amygdala disrupt conditioning but not explicit memory (Bechara et al., 1995).

As we have said, explicit memory of an event and the implicit activation of associated emotional arousal are often fused, the hippocampal and amygdala systems processing in parallel. The results of this dual processing enter working memory, where they are integrated into a unified experience (see Figure 11.18). This parallel activation often involves some complex interactions between the hippocampal-diencephalic system and the amygdala system. Thus, the explicit memory system may activate the amygdala, producing current emotional arousal. This happens when an explicit memory unleashes a flood of emotion. Alternatively, amygdala-mediated emotional arousal may activate the hippocampal explicit memory system. This seems to be the basis for such phenomena as **mood congruity of memory,** the tendency of a person to remember information better when in the same or a similar emotional state as when the information was initially encountered. This also may account for how an intense emotional state may activate explicit memories associated with prior similar emotional states, a phenomenon not infrequently encountered in the course of our interactions with significant people in our lives.

THE CORTEX AND EMOTION

So far we have focused on the importance of subcortical structures in emotion. There has, however, been a growing recognition of the importance of cortical processes in emotion. The cortex plays an important role in the interpretation, expression, and regulation of emotion. It is also presumed to play a role in emotional experience. In this section, we will examine the contribution of the cortex to mood, to the perception and interpretation of emotion, and to emotional expression. We will also examine the role of the temporal lobes in emotion.

The Cortex and Mood

Some of the earliest investigations of the role of the cortex in emotion focused on the effects of cortical lesions on the long-term quality of emotional experience. In the past, this was termed **affect,** but it is now generally termed **mood.** Alford (1933) and Goldstein (1939) observed that patients with left-hemisphere lesions were often extremely depressed, a condition that Goldstein termed **catastrophic reaction.** In contrast, patients with right-hemisphere lesions were reported to be more likely to exhibit what was termed an **indifference reaction,** an apparent lack of negative emotional response to undesirable aspects of their lives, including the symptoms caused by their right-hemisphere lesion. They might also exhibit anosagnosia, outright denial of obvious symptoms, or even euphoria (Gainotti, 1972). There are now a significant number of studies reporting findings consistent with these observations (Gainotti, 1972; Gainotti & Caltagirone, 1989; Gasparrini et al., 1978; Robinson & Benson, 1981; Robinson et al., 1984; Sackheim et al., 1982; Silberman & Weingartner, 1986). These findings have been interpreted as evidence that the left hemisphere is dominant for positive emotion and the right hemisphere is dominant for negative emotion, a theory that has been termed the **valence hypothesis** (Davidson, 1992; Silberman & Weingartner, 1986). A corollary to this hypothesis is that some forms of clinical depression may be due to an imbalance between the activation level of the two hemispheres, with the left hemisphere being less active than the right (Henriques & Davidson, 1991). Although there is some evidence supporting this idea, findings are inconsistent, and the extent to which imbalance in the activation of the two hemispheres may be a factor in depression remains to be determined.

Mood is a rather global and subjective state, inferred from behavior and self-report. An alternative approach to the investigation of the role of the cortex in emotion is to attempt to analyze the role of each hemisphere in more specific components of emotion, particularly the interpretation and expression of emotion. These studies have provided evidence that the right hemisphere is specialized for the interpretation and expression of emotion, regardless of whether the emotion is positive or negative (Borod, Koff, & Caron, 1983). This view, which may be called the **right-hemisphere hypothesis,** is consistent with much of the data, although we will see that there is evidence that the left hemisphere also plays a role in these processes. We now turn, then, to an examination of hemispheric specialization for components of emotion.

The Cortex and the Perception and Interpretation of Emotion

PROSODY   As we mentioned in chapter 6, spoken language conveys two types of information: that derived from its content and that derived from its tone, or prosody (Monrad-Krohn, 1947). More recently, a distinction has been made between two types of prosody: Intonation supplying meaning to a sentence is termed **propositional prosody,** whereas intonation communicating emotion is termed **affective prosody.** Considerable evidence has accumulated indicating that the right hemisphere is specialized for the interpretation of affective prosody. Patients with right-hemisphere lesions are impaired in the perception of the emotional tone of heard sentences (Heilman, Bowers, & Valenstein, 1993; Heilman, Scholes, & Watson, 1975; Ross, 1981; Schmitt, Hartje, & Willmes, 1997; Tucker, Watson, & Heilman, 1977). Studies with normal subjects have yielded results consistent with these findings. Thus, dichotic listening studies have revealed a left-ear advantage for the perception of the emotional tone of a sentence (Ley & Bryden, 1982) and for discriminating emotional nonspeech sounds (King & Kimura, 1972).

PERCEPTION OF EMOTIONAL FACIAL EXPRESSIONS   A number of studies have shown that patients with right-hemisphere lesions are specifically impaired in the perception of emotional facial expressions but not simple identification of faces (Borod, Koff, & Buck, 1986; Borod, Koff, Lorch, & Nicholas, 1986; DeKosky et al., 1980; Etkoff, 1984; Schmitt, Hartje, & Willmes, 1997; Strauss & Moscovitch, 1981). It is important to emphasize that although right-hemisphere lesions can disrupt simple facial recognition, these reports demonstrate that impairment in

recognition of emotional facial expressions after right-hemisphere lesions is dissociable from impairment in simple face recognition (see also Pizzamiglio et al., 1983).

Laterality studies with normal subjects have also yielded data consistent with right-hemisphere superiority for the perception of emotional facial expression. In tachistoscopic studies, subjects have been shown to identify emotional facial expressions better when the face is presented to the left visual field (Bryden & Ley, 1983; Buchtel et al., 1978; Ladavas, Umilta, & Ricci-Bitti, 1980; Pizzamiglio et al., 1983; Strauss & Moscovitch, 1981). A left visual-field advantage has also been shown in matching a facial expression to a verbal description (Hansch & Pirozolo, 1980) or to a drawing of a face (Landis, Assal, & Perret, 1979). In addition, a stronger left visual-field effect has been reported for the recognition of emotional faces than of nonemotional faces (Suberi & McKeever, 1977). Consistent with these reports is a sodium amobarbital study in which patients were asked to rate the intensity of emotional expression of photographed faces. Patients rated photographs of faces as exhibiting less emotional expression after nondominant hemisphere injection than after dominant hemisphere injection (Abern et al., 1991).

Although the majority of studies point to the role of the right hemisphere in the perception of facial expression, there are some inconsistent findings. Kolb and Taylor (1981) have reported that, while patients with right-temporal and right-frontal lesions are impaired in the matching of faces according to facial expression (and patients with left-temporal and left-parietal lesions are not), patients with left-frontal lesions are also impaired on this task. This finding is at odds with the bulk of the literature, and its interpretation remains unclear. It may indicate that left-frontal cortex plays a role in the perception of facial expression.

HUMOR COMPREHENSION   The ability to experience humor is an emotional response that may be uniquely human. In general, right-hemisphere lesions disrupt the comprehension of humor more than left-hemisphere lesions. For example, patients with right-hemisphere lesions are impaired in choosing the punch line to a joke from four alternatives (Brownell, 1983; Wapner, Hamby, & Gardner, 1981), and they judged unfunny stories to be funny more often than did left-hemisphere patients (Wapner et al., 1981). Patients with right-hemisphere lesions have also been reported to be impaired in the appreciation of humorous cartoons, films, and stories (Gardner et al., 1975; Wapner et al., 1981; Winner & Gardner, 1977).

Patients with right-hemisphere lesions have been reported to more frequently exhibit spontaneous outbursts of laughter that are not appropriate to the situation (Sackheim et al., 1982), and right-sided injection in sodium amobarbital tests has been reported to be more frequently associated with laughter than left-sided injection (Perria, Rossalini, & Rossi, 1961). In addition, as a group, patients with right-hemisphere lesions have been reported to show extreme variability in their appreciation of humor— some laughing at every item, even those that were not humorous, and others failing to laugh, even at humorous items that they apparently understood (Gardner et al., 1975).

Some studies have suggested a role for the left hemisphere in the appreciation of verbally expressed humor. When patients with cerebral lesions were asked to judge which of four cartoons was the funniest, patients with left-hemisphere lesions were impaired when the cartoons had captions, whereas patients with right-hemisphere lesions were impaired when the cartoons had no captions (Gardner et al., 1975). Patients in this study were not aphasic or alexic, so the impaired performance of the left-hemisphere patients in the verbal condition cannot be attributed to failure to understand the verbal content of the captions. Taken together, these results suggest that although the right hemisphere is more involved in the appreciation of humor, the left hemisphere may also play a role, at least under certain conditions.

COMPREHENSION OF EMOTIONAL SITUATIONS

The appreciation of emotional situations is another aspect of emotion that is profoundly important for adaptive social behavior. Studies of the effect of cortical lesions on this capacity have taken a number of forms. In one study, patients were shown a scene depicting an emotional situation. They were then shown four other scenes, one of which depicted the same emotion but in a different situation. Patients with right-hemisphere lesions were impaired on a purely visual version of this test (Cicone et al., 1980). Dimond utilized an ingenious technique to study the processing of emotional stimuli by the two hemispheres in split-brain patients. He mounted a miniature film projector on a contact lens in such a way that the film was projected to only one visual field. In this way he was able to show an emotionally disturbing film to each hemisphere separately. He found that when a disturbing film was projected to the right hemisphere in split-brain patients, it was rated as being more unpleasant and was associated with greater autonomic activation than when it was projected to the left hemisphere (Dimond & Farrington, 1977; Dimond, Farrington, & Johnson, 1976).

Parenthetically, it is interesting that in split-brain patients the left hemisphere also experiences an appropriate emotional response to a stimulus projected to the right hemisphere, even though the left hemisphere does not experience the actual stimulus evoking the response. Thus, split-brain patients who have had a frightening film projected to their right hemisphere will verbally report feelings of fear, even though they cannot describe the stimulus that has triggered it (Gazzaniga & LeDoux, 1978). Apparently the subcortical pathways connecting the two hemispheres, which remain intact in split-brain patients, are sufficient for the transfer of the quality of an emotion, although these pathways are not sufficient for the interhemispheric transfer of structural features of the stimulus.

As in other domains of emotion, although the majority of studies point to the dominant role of the right hemisphere in the comprehension of emotional situations, there is also evidence for a left-hemisphere contribution to these processes. In one study, for example, subjects were shown a drawing depicting an emotional situation in which the face of the protagonist was blank. They were then shown six photographs and asked to choose the one that matched the situation. Patients with left and right temporal-lobe lesions and left and right frontal-lobe lesions were impaired (Kolb & Taylor, 1988).

These findings, taken together, indicate that the right hemisphere is more involved in the interpretation of emotion than is the left hemisphere. Nevertheless, there is evidence that the left hemisphere is involved in the comprehension of emotion, at least under certain conditions. Bowers, Bauer, and Heilman (1993) have drawn a distinction between the comprehension of the emotional significance of a nonverbal stimulus (such as a facial expression, gesture, or tone of voice), which is mediated by what they term the **nonverbal affect lexicon,** and cognitive knowledge of the relationship between an event and emotion (such as knowing that sadness is a response to loss), which they term **emotional semantics.** They suggest that the nonverbal affect lexicon may be disrupted by right-hemisphere lesions, whereas emotional semantics may be impaired by more widely distributed lesions, including lesions in the left hemisphere. Consistent with this hypothesis are the results of a study in which normal subjects had to rate the emotionality of monaurally presented passages in which the emotion conveyed by the tone of voice and by the passage's content were in conflict. It was found that when subjects attended to the passages presented to the left ear, they rated the emotionality of the passage according to the tone of voice. When, however, they attended to the passage presented to the right ear, they rated it according to its content (Safer & Leventhal, 1977). These findings suggest that the two hemispheres make different contributions to the interpretation of emotion because they process different domains of information.

Alternatively, it may be possible that the contribution of the left hemisphere to emotional comprehension is rather minor after all, and that the right hemisphere has a dominant role in the comprehension of emotion. The large number of studies showing disruption of emotional comprehension after right-, but not after left-hemisphere lesions are consistent with this view. Perhaps even more compelling is the well-established relationship between anosognosia (denial of illness) and right posterior lesions. Denial of and emotional indifference to a major neurological impairment would seem to be an extreme form of impairment in emotional comprehension.

The Cortex and Emotional Expression

PROSODY There are a number of studies indicating that right-hemisphere lesions are associated with impairment in the expression of affective prosody. Typically, patients were presented with a sentence and then asked to repeat it with a specified emotion. Patients with right-hemisphere lesions spoke in more of a monotone than did patients with left-hemisphere lesions (Kent & Rosenbek, 1982; Tucker, 1981; Tucker et al., 1977). The report of at least one right-hemisphere patient whose speech was devoid of emotional expression but who nevertheless showed intact capacity to comprehend emotions suggests that impaired expressive aprosodia may be a specific impairment and not simply the result of generalized impairment in emotional processing (Ross & Mesulam, 1979).

EXECUTION OF FACIAL EXPRESSIONS There are a number of studies indicating a specialized role for the right hemisphere in the execution of emotional expression. Patients with right-hemisphere lesions have been reported to exhibit less emotionally expressive facial expressions (Blonder, Bowers, & Heilman, 1991) and to be poorer at posing specific emotional facial expressions (Borod, Koff, Lorch, & Nicholas, 1986).

Studies of normal subjects have focused on which side of the face is more emotionally expressive. Because each side of the face is controlled by the contralateral hemisphere, the finding that one side of the face is more emotionally expressive could be interpreted to mean that the contralateral hemisphere is more involved in emotional facial expression. Most studies report that the left side of the face is more emotionally expressive, whether rated by judges or assessed by coding the contraction of relevant muscles of the face (Moscovitch & Olds, 1982; Sackheim et al., 1982), suggesting more involvement of the right hemisphere in the execution of facial expressions.

This conclusion was also drawn from the results of studies of chimeric faces. A **chimeric face** is composed by splitting a photograph of a face down the middle and then splicing together each side with its mirror image. This results in composites consisting

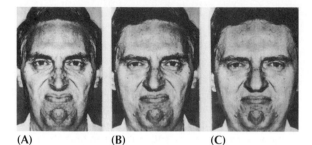

(A)   (B)   (C)

FIGURE 11.19   A chimeric faces test of the role of the two cerebral hemispheres in the execution of emotional facial expression. Normal subjects more often judge a chimeric face composed of two left-half faces *(A)* to be more emotionally expressive than one composed of two right-half faces *(C)*. *(B)* is the original photograph. *(From Sackheim, Gur, & Saucy, 1978, p. 434)*

of two left-half faces or two right-half faces (Figure 11.19). Studies using this method have shown that subjects judge chimeric faces composed entirely from the left side of the face to have a more intense emotional expression than those composed entirely from the right side (Sackheim, Gur, & Saucy, 1978).

There are, however, some findings inconsistent with this conclusion. In a review of the literature, Borod (1993) concluded that although there is strong evidence that the left side of the face is generally judged to be more emotionally expressive for negative emotions, the right side of the face is more expressive for positive emotions. This is consistent with the hypothesis that the two hemispheres may be specialized for the expression of different emotions. There are some reports that anterior lesions in either the left or the right hemisphere are associated with impairment in the ability to pose specific emotional facial expressions (Weddell, Milner, & Trevarthen, 1990) and a decrease in spontaneous facial expressions (Kolb & Milner, 1981a).

In summary, there is evidence suggesting that the right hemisphere is more involved than the left hemisphere in emotional expression, whether through emotional tone or through facial expression. However, there is evidence that the left hemisphere may play a role in the expression of emotion. There is also evidence that the frontal cortex in both hemispheres may play an important role in emotional expression.

We will turn to the important role of frontal cortex in emotion in the next section. First, we'll consider the role of the temporal lobes.

The Temporal Lobes and Emotion

Complex partial (focal) seizures of the temporal lobes have complicated behavioral and experiential manifestations (as opposed to seizures with relatively simple sensory or motor manifestations). Complex partial seizures of the temporal lobes have long been associated with emotional changes. This is a difficult area of investigation to evaluate because many of the studies are clinical case studies. Although this is a potentially rich source of information, it is also open to all of the biases to which uncontrolled studies are prone.

Fear is the most common symptom seen in patients with temporal-lobe seizures. Aggression is also seen in some patients. These symptoms are consistent with the role we have seen the amygdala plays in fear and response to fear. Some clinicians, however, have gone farther and described an overall pattern of behavior that they believe to be characteristic of these patients (Blumer & Benson, 1975; Geschwind, 1977). This has been called the **temporal-lobe personality.** Symptoms attributed to this disorder include deepening of emotions, taking a "cosmic" view of events in which even small events may be construed as having a bearing on personal destiny, and hyperreligiosity (or intense atheism). These patients are also often reported to be excessively concerned with details. This may lead them to write about their lives in great detail, a condition termed **hypergraphia** (Waxman & Geschwind, 1974). These patients have also been reported to be highly circumstantial.

There have been attempts to study these emotional changes quantitatively. Bear and Fedio (1977) asked patients with temporal-lobe epilepsy and their families and friends to fill out questionnaires that rated the patient's personality characteristics, and Bear and his colleagues (1982) conducted quantitative interviews with blind raters. They reported that patients with right temporal-lobe seizures were more likely to have emotional symptoms such as elation, sadness, or denial, whereas patients with left temporal-lobe seizures were more likely to have ideational symptoms, such as a highly reflective thinking style, hyperreligiosity, and a sense of personal destiny. Interestingly, Fedio and Martin (1983) reported a decrease in symptomatology in patients with temporal-lobe seizures who subsequently underwent surgical excision of temporal-lobe tissue for the relief of their seizures.

These studies and the inferences that have been drawn from them have generated a good deal of discussion and controversy. They have been found to have a number of methodological problems (Bear, 1983; Mungas, 1983; Silberman, 1983), and attempts to replicate their results have not always been successful (e.g., Brumbach, 1983; Mungas, 1982). In particular, the designation "temporal-lobe epilepsy" does not mean that seizure activity is confined to one or both temporal lobes, as abnormality and seizure activity may spread well beyond the focus of the seizures. Perhaps even more important are the problems inherent in making inferences about personality traits, even (or perhaps especially) when the patient is making the assessments. Personality, the complex pattern of behavior that characterizes our individuality, is likely to be the last domain of brain-behavior relationship that will be adequately understood because it is the most complex, both in terms of behavior and, presumably, in terms of underlying neural mechanisms.

We have seen that the cortex is critically involved in the interpretation of emotion in complex perceptual and social contexts. Tone of voice, nuance of facial expression, and details of a social context serve as bases for making fine discriminations and interpretations of the interpersonal and social world. The cortical processes mediating these complex perceptions and interpretations stand at the high-order end of the continuum of discriminative and interpretative capacity that has the discrimination between two stimuli in a fear conditioning paradigm at its lower end. We have also seen that the cortex is involved in subtle expressions of emotion, such as tone of voice and facial expression, expressions that can be so crucial for adaptive behavior in complex social contexts. It remains now for us to attempt to link cortical and subcortical contributions to emotion into an integrated system. This is the elusive goal that has been pursued ever since James's theory. Although we have not fully achieved this goal, we do have the beginnings of a coherent picture. We turn to this next.

THE INTERACTION OF CORTEX AND AMYGDALA IN THE HIGHER-ORDER MEDIATION OF EMOTION

We have seen that a direct thalamus-amygdala pathway mediates conditioned fear in lower animals. This is a kind of autonomic pilot. On the basis of innate programming, a rat that has never before seen a cat will respond to the sight with a fear response. On the basis of learning, a rat will respond with fear to a tone that had previously been paired with a shock. In either case, the response is automatic and rapid. These are enormous advantages when failure to make an immediate appropriate response is likely to lead to death. The genes of animals unable to make such responses are mercilessly culled from the gene pool by the process of natural selection.

Many animals are able to get along rather well on the basis of these automatic mechanisms. However, the more complex the animal's environment, the more flexibility of response is required. The gazelle that detects a stalking lion might have a better chance of escape if it waits for an opportune moment to flee, rather than automatically activating a flight response. This need for flexibility of response reaches its epitome in humans. The corporate junior executive whose competence has been publicly challenged by a competing peer may experience automatic signs of emotional arousal and a desire to deal with the situation with physical force. Yet it will be far more adaptive for him to channel his emotional response in a way that enables him to confront the challenge more deliberately, addressing the specific issues raised in an organized and rational manner. In such a context, automatic responses are likely to have disastrous consequences. And this is true not only in our complex social environment. A lone hiker in the backcountry who stumbles on a hungry grizzly bear may first automatically freeze. But if he is to survive, he must shift to deliberate, cortically mediated behavior, even if that behavior is the deliberate action of continuing to remain still.

FIGURE 11.20   Diagrammatic depiction of the connections between the amygdala and areas of cortex devoted to sensory processing, in this case, vision. The amygdala receives highly processed input from cortical areas mediating the advanced stages of sensory processing. In contrast, it projects back to a number of cortical areas involved in all stages of sensory processing. This suggests that, at the same time the amygdala is receiving refined input about the world, it is also influencing ongoing processing of information about the world by affecting multiple aspects of sensory-related processing, including perception, short-term memory, and, probably, attention. *(Adapted from LeDoux, 1996, p. 286)*

The ability to shift from automatic emotional *reaction* to deliberate, willed, emotion-based *action* has enormous adaptive advantages in complex situations. Crucial for this shift is the integration of amygdala and cortical processing. In the remainder of this section, first, we examine mechanisms by which the amygdala influences the cortex. Then, we look at how the results of this influence on the cortex moderate emotional reaction and organize emotion-based action.

Amygdala Influences on Cortex

The amygdala influences the cortex in three major ways: through direct connections, through amygdala-triggered cortical arousal, and through amygdala-triggered bodily feedback to cortex.

DIRECT AMYGDALA INFLUENCE ON CORTEX
The amygdala receives input from the most advanced stages of sensory processing. This highly processed input provides the amygdala with refined information about the external world. The amygdala sends projections back to the sensory cortical areas. What is particularly important about these connections is that the amygdala projects to *all* levels of cortical sensory processing (Figure 11.20). This provides a mechanism for the amygdala to influence processing at all of these levels, including perception, short-term memory, and (probably) attention.

The amygdala also has strong projections to the hippocampus. These provide a mechanism for the amygdala to influence whether or not an experience is consolidated into long-term memory. These projections may also be involved in some emotion-activated retrieval from long-term memory.

Although amygdala projections to lateral prefrontal cortex are relatively sparse, there are strong connections from the amygdala to the anterior cingulate and orbital frontal cortex (via the hypothalamus). Anterior cingulate cortex (together with dorsolateral prefrontal cortex) is involved in working memory, and the orbital frontal region may be particularly important for emotional aspects of working memory. Amygdala projections to anterior cingulate and orbital frontal regions provide a mechanism whereby the amygdala can directly influence the content of working memory. In addition, there are strong reciprocal connections between the amygdala and medial frontal cortex. This region is involved both in the regulation of the amygdala and the organization of emotion-based action. (We will discuss the significance of these amygdala-frontal connections in more detail shortly.) Finally, connections from amygdala to sensory cortex and from amygdala to hippocampus influence working memory indirectly, by influencing the stream of information flowing to working memory from attentional and perceptual systems, short-term memory buffers, and long-term memory (Figure 11.21).

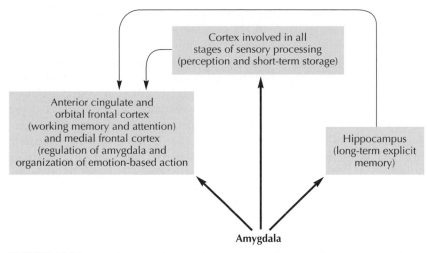

FIGURE 11.21   In addition to having direct input to all stages of sensory processing, the amygdala has strong connections with the hippocampus. This allows the amygdala to influence memory consolidation and retrieval. The amygdala also has strong connections with areas of frontal cortex known to be involved in working memory, including anterior cingulate cortex and orbital frontal cortex. The amygdala is also in a position to influence working memory indirectly *(thin lines)*, through its influence on attention, perception, short-term memory, and long-term memory. The amygdala also has strong connections with medial frontal cortex, a region involved in the regulation of amygdala activity and the organization of emotion-based action. *(Adapted from LeDoux, 1996, p. 287)*

AMYGDALA-TRIGGERED AROUSAL   Arousal is obviously a very important component in emotional response. Without it, we would not direct sustained attention toward dangerous stimuli and would not react adaptively. Novel stimuli, which may be potentially dangerous, result in arousal. Arousal to novel stimuli, however, is mediated by direct input from sensory systems to arousal systems. If the stimulus is not associated with danger, the animal rapidly habituates to it. In contrast, the amygdala triggers arousal that is evoked by stimuli that are deemed dangerous, either through genetic programming or through learning.

There are at least four brain-stem systems that arouse the cortex, each with its specific neurotransmitter. Although all of these systems probably contribute to the activation of the cortex in the presence of danger, one of them, known as the **nucleus basalis,** is closely linked to the amygdala and appears particularly important in danger-induced arousal. This has been shown by experiments in which the amygdala

or the nucleus basalis has been lesioned. The result is impairment in arousal by dangerous stimuli, such as a tone that had become a conditioned stimulus for a shock. Stimulation of the amygdala or the nucleus basalis, on the other hand, produces cortical arousal (LeDoux, 1995a; Gallagher & Holland, 1994).

The nucleus basalis utilizes acetylcholine as its neurotransmitter. Apparently, when the amygdala detects danger, it activates the nucleus basalis, which in turn releases acetylcholine into widespread areas of the cortex. One of the effects of this arousal (as well as arousal from other systems) is perpetuation of amygdala activation. This is due to connections from arousal systems back to the amygdala. The amygdala's being a target of its own activated arousal creates a self-perpetuating positive feedback loop and helps ensure that the activation is maintained during periods of danger.

The effect of cortical arousal is not necessarily global and diffuse cortical activation. This is because the major mechanism of arousal is a lowering of the threshold for firing of neurons. Thus, depending on other aspects of brain activity during arousal, the effects of cortical arousal can be quite specific. Nevertheless, the arousal systems themselves do not carry a lot of information. Their major purpose is to alert the cortex that something important is happening. A determination of what exactly it is that is happening, and what response or action is needed, requires the convergence of information in working memory (discussed later).

BODILY FEEDBACK   A third way in which the amygdala can influence the cortex is via feedback from amygdala-induced body changes. We have seen that the amygdala activates species-specific behaviors, autonomic activation, and endocrine response. At the very least, behavioral and autonomic activation contribute to the *intensity* of the emotion, as Cannon postulated. However, there is also evidence supporting James's idea that specific patterns of body activation correspond to specific emotions. Thus, there is evidence that autonomic activation in different emotions is not uniform (Ekman, Levenson, & Friesen, 1983; Levenson, 1992). There is also evidence that feedback from somatic muscles, particularly facial muscles, contributes to emotion (Izard, 1971, 1992; Tomkins, 1962). More generally, there is growing appreciation that feedback regarding body activation is a crucial component of emotion and reasoning. This is captured, for example, in Damasio's somatic marker hypothesis (Damasio, 1994).

As we have seen, the idea that feedback from the body is important for emotion fits with experience. Who has not suddenly experienced an emotion and at the same time become aware of their heart pounding or their knees shaking? Experimental studies of persons with spinal cord transections have been inconclusive with regard to the importance of feedback. This is partly because results of these studies have been inconsistent. More important, even the finding of intact emotional experience after spinal transection leaves open the possibility that connections via nonspinal autonomic afferents are supplying the brain with the required feedback. Finally, there is experimental evidence that feedback from the body con-

tributes to the quality of emotional response (Adelman & Zajonc, 1989; Ekman, 1992, 1993).

More than a century after William James proposed his theory, we still lack a definitive account of the role of body states in emotion. In particular, it is unclear whether there is a specific body-state signature corresponding to specific emotions and, to the extent there is, whether body states play a causal role in emotion. Having said this, there is probably wide agreement that body states, triggered by the amygdala and monitored by the cortex, play an important role in the experience of intensity of emotion, although whether this role extends to qualitative aspects of emotional experience remains an area of controversy.

Integration of Cortex and Amygdala

We have seen that innate and conditioned fear reactions can be mediated by a pathway involving the sensory thalamus and amygdala. In more complex environments, such reactions are unlikely to be adaptive and, in fact, are often disastrously counterproductive. Thus, although the automatic response may buy time, what is frequently needed is more deliberate action that takes into account a number of factors besides the immediate emotional state of the organism. These factors include the external situation; the acquired knowledge of the organism; the organism's repertoire of potential behaviors; and the organism's ability to anticipate, plan, and monitor future behavior. There is strong evidence that the frontal lobes are critically involved in the organization of behavior that takes these factors into account (Damasio, 1994; Fuster, 1989; Goldman-Rakic, 1992; Luria, 1966; Milner, 1964; Nauta, 1971; Stuss, 1991). We'll explore this important area in more detail in chapter 12. In the following section, we explore the role of the frontal lobes in the mediation of higher-order emotion-based action.

MEDIAL FRONTAL CORTEX AS THE INTERFACE BETWEEN SENSORY CORTEX AND AMYGDALA
As we have seen, medial frontal-lobe regions receive highly processed input from all cortical sensory areas. They also have extensive reciprocal connections with the amygdala. The amygdala also receives highly processed sensory input. In addition, medial frontal

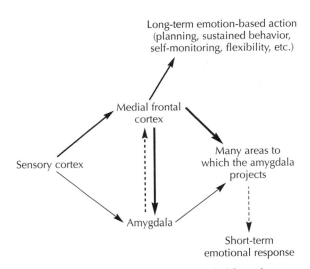

Long-term emotion-based action
(planning, sustained behavior,
self-monitoring, flexibility, etc.)

Medial frontal
cortex

Sensory cortex

Many areas to
which the amygdala
projects

Amygdala

Short-term
emotional response

FIGURE 11.22   The amygdala and medial frontal cortex modulate and regulate each other's functions and effects. The pathway of amygdala-triggered short-term emotional response *(thin lines)* is modulated by input from medial frontal cortex *(thick lines)* both to the amygdala and to many of the amygdala's targets. This input is the result of high-level processing of sensory information by the frontal cortex. Conversely, the pathway of frontal cortex organization of long-term action *(mid-weight lines)* is modulated by input from the amygdala *(dashed line)* based on the amygdala's emotional coloring of sensory information. This reciprocal regulation means that amygdala-triggered short-term emotional response may be inhibited by medial frontal cortex. However, because the amygdala projects to medial frontal cortex, it may override this inhibition. The amygdala may also regulate medial frontal cortex by stimulating the organization of long-term emotion-based action by medial frontal cortex. (The different line thicknesses in the figure are for identification purposes and do not represent the relative strength of the connections.)

cortex projects to many areas that are targets of the amygdala (Figure 11.22). These connections suggest that medial frontal cortex is in a position to regulate the effects of amygdala activation, both through direct connections to the amygdala and through connections to targets of the amygdala. At the same time, connections from the amygdala to medial frontal cortex suggest that the amygdala influences medial frontal cortex and its outputs to the amygdala's targets. The amygdala also influences frontal-lobe organization of emotion-based action. Taken together, these anatomi-

cal connections suggest that medial frontal cortex serves as an interface between the representation of the outside world, mediated by sensory cortex, and the emotional coloring of that representation, mediated by the amygdala. In other words, medial frontal cortex would seem to be an area where world representation and emotional coloring of the world are integrated, coming together to influence each other and to organize an action, or planned sequence of actions, that is the product of that integration. The result of this integration may be highly varied, ranging from inhibition to enhancement of amygdala-triggered short-term emotional response and from activation to disruption of cortically mediated long-term action.

A brief example might help illustrate these interactions. Consider our junior executive who has been rudely challenged by a competitive peer at an important meeting. This is dangerous: His chances for promotion may be threatened—or even his job—and his amygdala is activated. This activation could propel him into physically assaulting his rival. Medial frontal cortex, taking into account the social context, comes to the rescue and inhibits the physically aggressive response. However, that does not have to be the end of the story. The amygdala activation can stimulate medial frontal cortex to organize a long-term plan of action that will enable him to surpass his rival by succeeding brilliantly in the complex corporate environment. The old adage, Don't get mad, get even! could be neurologized into Inhibit amygdala-triggered short-term emotional response (via input from medial frontal cortex) and then direct amygdala output to medial frontal cortex and the organization of long-term action plans.

What is the empirical support for this rather elaborate hypothesis? Support comes from evidence that lesions of medial frontal cortex interfere with extinction of conditioned fear (Morgan et al., 1993). Thus, if a tone that was paired with shock until it became a conditioned stimulus is then repeatedly presented without ever being followed by a shock, a normal rat will eventually stop responding to the tone with a conditioned response. However, rats with medial frontal lesions continue to respond to the tone with a conditioned fear response, even though it has been repeatedly presented without being followed by a shock.

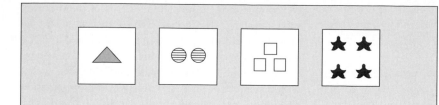

FIGURE 11.23   The Wisconsin Card Sorting stimuli. *(From McCarthy & Warrington, 1990, p. 352)*

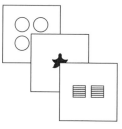

Extinction may not sound like a higher-order behavior, but it is an instance of cortex-amygdala integration. During the learning phase, the tone is followed by a shock over a number of trials, and as a result the amygdala mediates a conditioned fear response. During the extinction phase, the animal is receiving sensory information about the world, including the relationship between tone and shock. In this case, the information is that there is no longer an association between tone and shock because the tone is now never followed by shock. Normally, medial-frontal processing of these environmental events regulates amygdala activity, and the conditioned fear response disappears. After damage to medial frontal cortex, however, this integration of amygdala and medial-frontal activity does not take place, and the conditioned response does not undergo extinction.

An alternative way of conceptualizing this impairment is in terms of **perseveration,** the maintenance of a behavior despite continuing feedback that it is not adaptive. It has been well established that lesions to dorsolateral frontal cortex produce perseveration in cognitive tasks (Damasio, 1994; Luria, 1966; Milner, 1964; Petrides, 1994a). An example is performance on the Wisconsin Card Sorting Test (Milner, 1964). In this task, a subject is given a deck of cards that differ along three dimensions: color, form, and number. The task is to sort these cards into one of four piles, using only feedback from the examiner as a guide to behavior

(Figure 11.23). The first criterion is *color,* and normal controls and patients with dorsolateral frontal lesions figure this out quite easily on the basis of feedback. After the subject has made 10 consecutive sorts by color, the examiner shifts the criterion to *form.* The subject is not told explicitly about the shift, but must infer it from the feedback the examiner gives. The solution is for the subject to use alternative sorting criteria (that is, to shift set) until feedback indicates that the correct criterion is being used. This shift, easy for normal subjects, is difficult for patients with dorsolateral frontal-lobe lesions. They tend to continue to sort to color, despite consistent, ongoing feedback that this is now incorrect.

The disruption of extinction after medial frontal-lobe lesions may be thought of as **emotional perseveration,** analogous to the cognitive perseveration seen after damage to dorsolateral frontal cortex. After lesions in either region, there is a breakdown in the regulation of behavior on the basis of information about the world; however, the driving forces underlying the behaviors regulated by the two regions differ. Medial frontal lesions disrupt shifts of emotion-based behavior, whereas dorsolateral frontal lesions disrupt shifts of cognitively based behavior.

ORBITAL FRONTAL CORTEX AND EMOTIONAL WORKING MEMORY   In chapter 10, we saw that dorsolateral frontal cortex and anterior cingulate cortex are involved in working memory. Further, there is evidence that orbital frontal cortex is specifically involved in the short-term retention of reward information. This evidence includes the results of lesion studies that have shown that damage to orbital frontal cortex disrupts short-term retention of reward information (Gaffan, Murray, & Fabre-Thorpe, 1993). In addition, neurophysiological studies have shown that neurons in orbital frontal cortex are sensitive to whether a stimulus is followed by a reward (Ono & Nishijo, 1992; Rolls, 1992; Thorpe, Rolls, & Maddison, 1983).

Human patients with orbital frontal lesions show a pattern of impairment consistent with the results of these animal studies. These patients tend to be oblivious to social and emotional cues, and their behavior does not seem to be influenced by emotional factors. In addition, these patients' reasoning and decision-making processes are extremely impaired. This is not because of a breakdown in logical thinking per se, because patients with orbital frontal lesions perform well on a wide variety of tests in this domain. Rather, their decision making seems not to be informed by emotional factors. They do not seem to be able to integrate their emotions into their decision-making processes (Damasio, 1994). For example, Damasio (1994) describes a patient with an orbital frontal lesion who, when offered two potential future appointment dates to choose from, spent half an hour in vacillating indecisiveness, unable to choose one of the dates. Without an emotional component to his working memory, he had no basis for making a choice.

These findings suggest that orbital frontal cortex provides an interface or gateway through which emotional processing by the amygdala can be funneled into working memory in dorsolateral frontal and anterior cingulate cortex. This hypothesis fits with current understanding of the neuroanatomical connections involved (Figure 11.24). Like medial frontal cortex, orbital frontal cortex has reciprocal connections with the amygdala and receives input from all sensory systems. This suggests that, like medial frontal cortex, orbital frontal cortex is a site of integration of world representation and emotional processing. In addition, there are strong connections from orbital frontal cortex to dorsolateral frontal cortex and anterior cingulate cortex, areas known to be important for working memory. Taken together, these findings support the idea that orbital

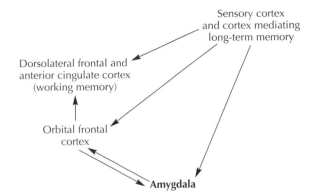

FIGURE 11.24   For reasoning and decision making to be effective, current sensory information, stored information about the past, and emotional input must all be integrated in working memory. Like medial frontal cortex, orbital frontal cortex provides an arena in which emotional processing (mediated by the amygdala) can be integrated with current and past information about the outside world (represented in cortex). Orbital frontal cortex also serves as a gateway through which the result of this emotionally infused integration may gain access to working memory processes mediated by dorsolateral frontal cortex and anterior cingulate cortex.

frontal cortex is the gateway through which the amygdala infuses an emotional component into working memory, albeit a component that has already been tempered by integration with information about the world. This emotional infusion is critically important for reasoning, decision making, and adaptive social behavior.

EMOTION AND CONSCIOUS EXPERIENCE

In this chapter we have avoided getting bogged down in the problem of the neural basis of conscious emotional experience. It's not that the problem isn't important or interesting. On the contrary, the neural basis of consciousness is one of the most fascinating questions confronting neuroscience. We have avoided the problem because its difficulty has plagued the investigation of the neural basis of emotion in a way that has retarded its development. The approach taken here, and one shared by many leading investigators in the area of emotion (e.g., LeDoux, 1996), is that the problem of the neural basis of consciousness is not a problem specific to the domain of emotion. We are as unable to explain the neural basis of conscious memories or perceptions as we are conscious emotions. The problem of the neural basis of consciousness is therefore a general problem shared by all of neuroscience.

A consequence of this idea is that progress in understanding the neural basis of emotion is most likely to be forthcoming if investigations in this area follow the strategy taken by those into the neural basis of cognitive processes. These investigations have focused on the behavioral and physiological manifestations of cognition (and its breakdown) and have used these manifestations to infer the nature of underlying cognitive processes, without being concerned about the conscious aspects of cognition. This strategy has been enormously successful for understanding cognition. There is no reason why it should not also be applied to emotion, and this has been the emphasis in this chapter. Before leaving this area, however, it might be useful to examine what we do know about emotion and consciousness.

Requirements for the Conscious Experience of Emotion

Although we do not understand the basis of conscious emotional experience, there are certain processes that we can identify as requirements for it. These include working memory, amygdala input to working memory, amygdala-triggered cortical arousal, and feedback from the body.

WORKING MEMORY   Working memory is the arena of consciousness, and a specific conscious content may be defined as the representation of specific psychological processes in working memory. We saw in chapter 10 that working memory includes several components: short-term buffers, which briefly hold information about present stimuli, and a working memory executive. The executive keeps track of information in short-term buffers; retrieves information from long-term memory; interprets the contents of the short-term buffers in terms of long-term memory; and directs attentional, perceptual, and cognitive processes. Working memory is essential for consciousness, including conscious emotional experience.

AMYGDALA INPUT TO WORKING MEMORY   We have seen that the amygdala provides input to work-

ing memory, probably via orbital frontal cortex. We have also seen that emotional response in the absence of this input is possible, as in the case of conditioned fear. However, to take advantage of the enhanced flexibility of choice of action afforded by consciousness, input from the amygdala must influence working memory. Without that influence, the contents of working memory would be bleached of emotional color. We would be left with dry intellectual ideas, without feelings to guide our decision making and behavior. In fact, we can define a feeling as a representation of emotional processes in working memory.

AMYGDALA-TRIGGERED CORTICAL AROUSAL   We have seen that the amygdala can initiate cortical arousal. This arousal serves to focus attention on emotional state and, in some instances, on the stimulus initiating it. Without this arousal, emotional experience would be fleeting, flickering through consciousness like a random thought. Part of this arousal process involves amygdala-triggered arousal of the amygdala itself. This helps to ensure that attention remains focused on emotion-arousing experience and associated events.

FEEDBACK FROM THE BODY   Bodily feedback provides a component that is essential to emotional experience. As James pointed out (1884), without that feedback a feeling would be a dry intellectual idea, without the force of an emotional experience. Long-term memory of past bodily feedback may also evoke an emotional experience.

Thoughts and Feelings

The considerations just presented suggest some differences between the neural basis of conscious thoughts and conscious emotional experience. Although we clearly have an enormous amount to learn about the neural basis of both of these elements of consciousness, we are in a position to speculate about some of their differences.

Thoughts and feelings appear to be due to different neural systems. Although these systems may converge in working memory, the neural bases of the two elements appear to be very different. Interestingly, what we know about the subcortical components of feelings, particularly the contribution of the amygdala, is one of the strongest sources of support for this statement. Despite the apparent mysteriousness of emotion, we know more about its neural basis than about the neural basis of thought.

A related speculation is that emotions involve more brain systems than are involved in thoughts and that emotions are associated with an intense mobilization of brain activity that is not a hallmark of thoughts. We have all had the experience of having our thoughts wander while reading, so that we have no notion of what the last three pages were about. We have also had the experience of being overwhelmed by a feeling, so that we can't get away from it for more than a moment without being involuntarily reemerged in its intensity. This is further evidence that different brain processes underlie the two phenomena.

Finally, amygdala influence on the cortex is stronger than cortical influence on the amygdala. We know from experimental cognitive psychology that cognition can have an important effect on emotion (Schacter & Singer, 1962; Valins, 1966). But we also know that when we are in the throes of a strong emotion, it grips us with a pervasive intensity that is unaffected by whatever countervailing cognitions we may muster. There is evidence that more recently evolved species exhibit a higher degree of connectivity from cortex to amygdala than less-advanced species. This raises the possibility that if this trend continues, evolution may yield a more harmonious balance between cognition and emotion, a balance that might significantly enhance our ability to live with each other, with our natural environment, and even with ourselves.

SUMMARY

Emotion has been a relatively neglected area of investigation in both experimental psychology and neuropsychology. This is due, in part, to the belief that it is necessary to understand the basis of conscious experience in order to understand emotion. The power of this belief is understandable when one considers how intense and consuming emotional experience can be. Nevertheless, it has retarded the understanding of the neural basis of emotion by burdening this area with neuroscience's most enigmatic problem. It is now

recognized that the problem of consciousness is not specific to emotion and that, as is the case with cognition, progress toward understanding emotion can be made by studying its behavioral and physiological manifestations. This places the investigation of emotion and its neural basis on the same empirical footing as the study of cognition.

Emotion may be thought of as comprising three components: physiological arousal, behavior, and conscious experience. Early theories of emotion and the brain attempted to relate these components to specific areas of the nervous system. The James-Lange theory proposed that conscious experience is the result of feedback to the cortex about bodily arousal and behavior. The Cannon-Bard theory argued that the thalamus responds to an emotional stimulus by simultaneously activating the cortex and the hypothalamus. The hypothalamus is critically important for the activation and organization of autonomic and endocrine components of emotional response. It also organizes certain emotional behaviors, such as uncomplicated aggression and rage. The Cannon-Bard theory proposed that cortical activation results in emotional experience, although the intensity of this experience may be enhanced via physiological arousal fed back to the cortex.

An important feature of the Cannon-Bard theory is the idea that parts of the brain are specialized for emotion. The search for these regions, for the emotional brain, has yielded a number of different theoretical formulations. The Papez circuit attempted to account for the interaction of cortical and subcortical components of emotion, through a connecting neural circuit. The limbic system hypothesis held that the emotional brain could be defined on the basis of neuroanatomical criteria. Each of these approaches has been heuristic, but each has definite limitations.

The Klüver-Bucy syndrome, resulting from bilateral removal of the temporal lobes in monkeys, comprises a number of different symptoms. One of them, extreme tameness, has subsequently been linked to damage to the amygdala. More recent research has shown that the amygdala is central to conditioned fear. This structure serves as an emotional processor in the sense that it organizes sensory input, arriving at the lateral nucleus of the amygdala, into fear responses, executed by the central nucleus of the amygdala. The amygdala also receives input from sensory cortex, sensory association cortex, polymodal cortex (including medial frontal cortex), and the hippocampus. These inputs serve to refine and modulate amygdala activity. This means that, at least in more recently evolved species, the individual is not always at the mercy of the most direct and automatic pathway involving the amygdala. Instead, cortical processes can modulate the effect of amygdala activity in the light of other internal and external factors.

A distinction may be made between memory of emotion and emotional memory. Memory of emotion is explicit memory of past events and feelings, memories that involve the hippocampus and diencephalic structures. Emotional memory is implicit memory that manifests itself as current autonomic arousal. Often these two types of memory are seamlessly merged, producing a unified experience in working memory of a memory of an event together with a current experience of physiological arousal. These two domains of memory may, however, be dissociated. We may remember an event, but the memory may be unaccompanied by physiological arousal. Alternatively, we may experience physiological arousal without accompanying explicit memory regarding its source.

Early investigation of the relationship between the cortex and emotion indicated that lesions of the left hemisphere were associated with depression, whereas lesions of the right hemisphere were associated with indifference, denial, or even euphoria. This led to the notion that the left hemisphere is specialized for positive emotions, and the right hemisphere is specialized for negative emotions.

This so-called valance theory has more recently given way to a focus on the contribution of each hemisphere to specific components of emotion. There is now strong evidence that the right hemisphere is specialized for the interpretation and expression of emotion, although the left hemisphere also appears to play a role in these processes, at least under certain conditions.

The amygdala exerts an influence on the cortex via strong and multiple projections to sensory-related cortex, amygdala-triggered arousal of cortex (via brain-stem arousal systems), and feedback to cortex of information about amygdala-triggered bodily arousal. Cortical influences on the amygdala are less extensive, but very important. Medial frontal cortex, a region receiving extensive sensory input and projecting both to the amygdala and to many targets of the amygdala, appears to exert a regulatory influence over the effect of amygdala activation in the light of environmental events. Evidence for this comes from the failure of animals with medial frontal lesions to undergo extinction. Orbital frontal cortex appears to be an interface between the amygdala and working memory, providing a link whereby emotional input can gain access to working memory. The breakdown of emotional input to working memory, a result of orbital frontal damage, has severe consequences for reasoning and decision making.

Although the neural mechanism of conscious emotional experience remains one of the great unsolved mysteries of neuroscience, one that we have deliberately avoided in this chapter, our discussion has nevertheless placed us in a position to appreciate some of the processes required for it. These include working memory, amygdala input to working memory, amygdala-triggered cortical arousal, and feedback from the body to the brain.

Thoughts and feelings appear to have different neural bases, with feelings apparently involving more of the brain than thoughts. The amygdala has more projections to cortex than the cortex has to the amygdala. This may be part of the neural basis for the dominance strong emotions have over thoughts. It appears that recently evolved animals have relatively more connections from cortex to amygdala than less-advanced animals. This may mean that evolution is moving toward a more harmonious balance between cognition and emotion.

The Prefrontal Cortex and the Higher-Order Regulation of Behavior

TOWARD A WORKING MODEL OF PREFRONTAL CORTEX FUNCTION
The Essence of Intelligence
Phineas Gage: A Case of the Disruption of Goal-Directed Behavior
Anatomical Considerations
Problems in the Interpretation of Deficits Following Prefrontal Lesions
A Working Model of Prefrontal Function
IMPAIRMENT IN FUNCTION AFTER PREFRONTAL LESIONS IN HUMANS
Emotion and Motivation
Social Behavior
Memory
General Intelligence
Language
Inventiveness, Ideational Fluency, and Divergent Thinking
Abstract and Conceptual Thinking

Executive Function: Planning and the Goal-Directed Organization of Behavior
The Channeling of Drive Into Goal-Directed Behavior: Inhibiting the Disruptive Effect of Impulsive Behavior
Goal-Directed Behavior and Environmental Stimuli
Integrating Goal-Directed Behavior With Its Consequences
Prefrontal Syndromes
THEORIES OF PREFRONTAL FUNCTION
An Animal Model of Prefrontal Function
Breakdown in the Guidance of Behavior by Representational Knowledge as the Essence of Impairment in Delayed Response
Specialization of the Principal Sulcus for Visuospatial Delayed Response in the Monkey
Other Prefrontal Subsystems
The Problem of Integration in Prefrontal Cortex
SUMMARY

We turn now to a discussion of the higher-order regulation of behavior mediated by the prefrontal cortex, cortex lying anterior to motor cortex and premotor cortex. This is not our first encounter with the functioning of this region of the brain; our discussion of every domain of functioning eventually led us to a consideration of the role of prefrontal cortex. To paraphrase the Roman proverb: All roads—all quests to understand the neural basis of specific domains of behavior—lead to prefrontal cortex.

TOWARD A WORKING MODEL OF PREFRONTAL CORTEX FUNCTION

The Essence of Intelligence

Prefrontal cortex is critical for the formulation, implementation, and regulation of goal-directed behavior. The ability to pursue goals in the face of obstacles is at the core of intelligence. This view of intelligence is expressed beautifully by William James (1890) in the first chapter of his famous textbook. After pointing out that attraction between inanimate objects, exemplified by a magnet and metal filings, can be easily impeded by, for example, the insertion of a card between them, James continues:

> If we now pass from such actions as these to those of living things, we notice a striking difference. Romeo wants Juliet as the filings want the magnet; and if no obstacles intervene he moves toward her by as straight a line as they. But Romeo and Juliet, if a wall be built between them, do not remain idiotically pressing their faces against its opposite sides like the magnet and the filings with the card. Romeo soon finds a circuitous way, by scaling the wall or otherwise, of touching Juliet's lips directly. With the filings the path is fixed; whether it reaches the end depends on accidents. With the lover it is the end which is fixed, the path may be modified indefinitely. (Vol. 1, p. 7)

A little further James writes, "*The pursuance of future ends and the choice of means for their attainment are thus the mark and criterion for the presence of mentality* in a phenomenon" (Vol. 1, p. 8, James's italics).

The very concept of intelligence is meaningless without goals (Pinker, 1997, p. 61). People differ, of course, with regard both to the nature of the goals they pursue and the way in which goals are hierarchically organized into superordinate and subordinate goals. Each goal is reached by a chain of subgoals, which, however, requires constant monitoring and modification in light of the results of attempts to reach earlier subgoals or on the basis of unforeseen events. This monitoring may even result in revision of the superordinate goal itself. An example may illustrate these processes. Suppose I want to make dinner (superordinate goal) and there is no food in the house. Achieving the goal of making dinner requires accomplishing the subgoal of going to the store and buying food. As I get into my car to go to the grocery store (subgoal dictated by environmental contingencies), I find that I have a flat tire and begin changing it. At this point I realize that the jack is in the cellar and walk toward the cellar stairs, only to find that the cellar lightbulb has blown out. Eventually, I may accomplish this mushrooming series of subgoals and produce an eatable dinner. On the other hand, midway through the series I may decide that the effort required to accomplish these subgoals is not commensurate with the benefits of cooking dinner, at which point I revise my subgoal series and head for the telephone to order a pizza. But suppose that when I reach the cellar I see that there is a seriously leaking pipe. At this point I postpone my superordinate goal of having dinner and replace it with a new superordinate goal: stopping the leak. I will then formulate new subgoals directed toward this superordinate goal, monitor their effectiveness, and revise them as needed.

As mentioned, each individual has a complex hierarchy of goals. Having dinner is superordinate to the subgoals devised to reach it, but subordinate to other goals, such as maintaining a healthy nutritional status and general good health. One might ask where the topmost goal in the hierarchy comes from. There are many possible answers to this daunting question, but one of the most plausible comes from evolutionary psychology: Natural selection has evolved a brain that strives to put the individual in circumstances like those that caused its ancestors to reproduce. For humans this means not only equipping individuals with the motivation and behavioral repertoire required for sexual reproduction. It also requires understanding the environment and securing the cooperation of others (Pinker, 1997).

Phineas Gage: A Case of the Disruption of Goal-Directed Behavior

What evidence is there that prefrontal cortex plays a critical role in the higher-order regulation of behavior? Some of the earliest evidence comes from the well-known case of Phineas Gage (Harlow, 1848, 1868). In 1848 Gage was working in Vermont for the Rutland and Burlington Railroad as the foreman of a construction gang laying down new track. Gage was considered to be a highly responsible worker and was held in high esteem by his employers. Part of his job involved setting explosive charges in rock that was blocking the path of the rail line. Setting the charge involved drilling a hole in the rock, filling it about halfway with powder, inserting a fuse, and then inserting sand. The sand served the purpose of directing the explosion toward the interior of the rock, rather than allowing its force to escape through the borehole. The final stage of the preparation before lighting the fuse involved gently compressing (tamping) the sand with a long iron rod. During one of these preparations, Gage started tamping before sand had been inserted into the hole. In the process he created sparks, igniting the powder and creating an explosion that propelled the rod out of the borehole and into his head. It entered his left cheek and penetrated the base of the skull. The rod then traveled through the front of the brain and exited from the top of his head (Figure 12.1).

The effects of this horrible accident were acute, and it originally appeared that Gage might die from his massive wound. However, to the surprise of everyone, he survived. As surprising as his survival was the fact that he had no obvious neurological deficits. He exhibited no sensory or motor loss and was able to talk coherently, even in the time period immediately following the accident. However, as the acute effects of the injury subsided, it became clear that something about Phineas Gage had changed utterly. Whereas before the accident he had been a highly responsible and skilled foreman, he was now unable to take responsibility for even routine menial work. In Harlow's (1868) words, "The equilibrium or balance, so to speak, between the intellectual faculty and animal properties" had been destroyed. Harlow goes on to describe Gage as

> fitful, irreverent, indulging at times in the greatest profanity which was not previously his custom, manifesting but little deference for his fellows, impatient of restraint and advise when it conflicts with his desires, at times pertinaciously obstinate,

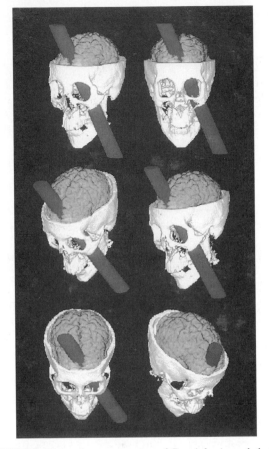

FIGURE 12.1   A reconstruction of Gage's brain and skull with the probable trajectory of the iron bar marked in dark gray. Gage's skull and tamping iron are at the Warren Anatomical Medical Museum at Harvard University. *(From Damasio, 1994, p. 32; based on H. Damasio, Grabowski, et al., 1994)*

yet capricious and vacillating, devising many plans of future operation, which are no sooner arranged than they are abandoned . . . a child in his intellectual capacity and manifestations, he has the animal passions of a strong man.

As far as we know, Gage's life after his accident was an unhappy one. In the 1850s, he joined Barnum's Museum in New York City, exhibiting his wound and his long tamping iron to curious visitors.

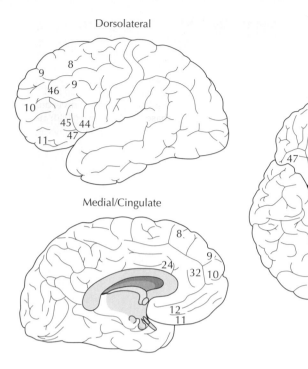

Dorsolateral

Medial/Cingulate

Orbital

FIGURE 12.2   Lateral, ventral (orbital), and medial views of the human cerebral cortex, illustrating the three major regions of prefrontal cortex. The numbers indicate the cytoarchitectonic areas defined by Brodmann. *(From Fuster, 1997, p. 173)*

According to Harlow, Gage carried his tamping iron with him everywhere he went. Later in the decade, he traveled to South America, returning to the United States in 1860, when he went to live with his mother and sister in San Francisco. There he found laboring jobs but, by all accounts, never stayed long at any one of them and never became financially independent. He died in 1861, at the age of 38.

It is not easy to characterize precisely what was wrong with Phineas Gage. His impairment is complex, not obviously confined to a specific domain of functioning. What is clear, however, is that something having to do with the higher-order control and regulation of behavior was tragically disrupted by his accident. A great deal has been learned about the function of the prefrontal cortex in the century and a half that has followed Phineas Gage's injury. This developing knowledge has not, however, yielded a definitive theoretical account of prefrontal function. In this chapter, we will examine the behavioral effects of lesions to prefrontal cortex and explore some of the attempts to provide a theoretical basis for understanding frontal-lobe function and its disruption. We

begin with a consideration of the anatomy of the frontal lobes.

Anatomical Considerations

SURFACE FEATURES OF PREFRONTAL CORTEX
The frontal lobes are the most anterior portion of the cortex, lying in front of the central sulcus. As already mentioned, prefrontal cortex refers to cortex anterior to motor cortex and premotor cortex. This is a massive area, comprising nearly 30% of the total cortex in humans (Brodmann, 1912). In humans, prefrontal cortex is traditionally divided into three regions: **dorsolateral prefrontal cortex, medial prefrontal cortex,** and **orbital (**also termed **ventral) prefrontal cortex** (Figure 12.2). We will discuss the surface features of monkey prefrontal cortex in a later section.

BASIC PHYSIOLOGICAL CHARACTERISTICS
Like other regions of cortex traditionally termed association cortex, prefrontal cortex has long been known to be relatively unresponsive to electrical

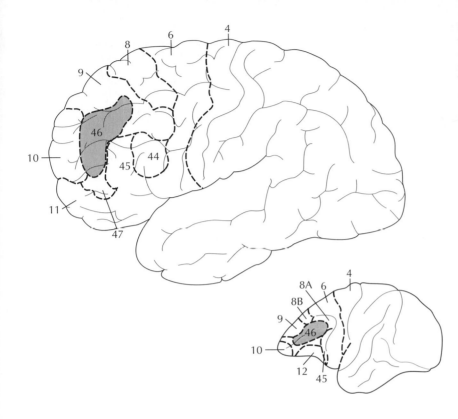

FIGURE 12.3   Lateral view of the human *(top)* and monkey *(bottom)* cerebral cortex, showing human prefrontal divisions based on Brodmann's (1925) cytoarchitectonic map and monkey prefrontal divisions based on Walker's (1940) attempt to designate homologous cytoarchitectonic areas in the two species using the same numbers. The shading indicates area 46, the area of the principal sulcus in the monkey. *(From Goldman-Rakic, 1987, p. 375)*

stimulation (Ferrier, 1886; Fritsch & Hitzig, 1870). In contrast to premotor and motor cortex, prefrontal cortex is not somatotopically organized and does not make direct connections to motor nuclei in the brain stem and spinal cord. It thus does not participate directly in the execution or fine-tuning of motor output. Nevertheless, prefrontal cortex has an enormous influence on voluntary behavior. As we will see, this influence is exerted via multisynaptic pathways that connect prefrontal cortex with a number of motor control centers, including those in premotor and motor cortex, the neostriatum (caudate and putamen), the thalamus, and the superior colliculus.

CYTOARCHITECTURE OF PREFRONTAL CORTEX   Brodmann described six different prefrontal areas in the macaque monkey and more than ten different prefrontal areas in humans. Because Brodmann's numbering in his cytoarchitectonic map of the macaque and his map of the human cortex do not correspond, Walker (1940) remapped macaque cor-

tex, describing and renaming areas that he considered to be homologous in the two species (Figure 12.3). One of the most distinctive features of primate prefrontal cortex, distinguishing it from posterior frontal cortex, is a profusion of granule cells in cortical layer IV (Bonin & Bailey, 1947; Carpenter, 1976; Walker, 1940). For this reason, prefrontal cortex is sometimes referred to as frontal granular cortex.

CONNECTIONS BETWEEN PREFRONTAL CORTEX AND OTHER BRAIN REGIONS   The connections between prefrontal cortex and the rest of the brain provide important clues regarding its function. In this section, we will discuss these connections in general terms and briefly consider their functional implications. In later sections, we will consider some of these connections in greater detail.

Afferents   There are four major sources of input to prefrontal cortex. (Figure 12.4). First, prefrontal cortex receives highly processed information about the

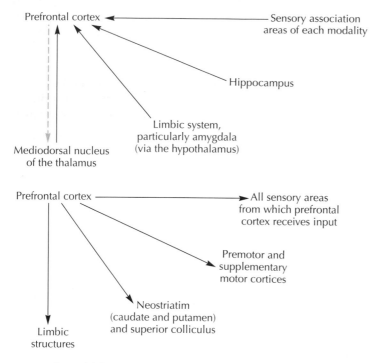

FIGURE 12.4   The four major sources of prefrontal afferents in primates. The dashed line indicates that the mediodorsal nucleus of the thalamus receives much of its input from prefrontal cortex.

FIGURE 12.5   The four major destinations of prefrontal efferents in primates.

external world from cortical areas involved in the processing of information from each of the five major sensory modalities. This information is not received directly from primary sensory cortex. It is received, rather, from sensory association areas, cortical regions mediating higher-order perceptual processing. Second, prefrontal cortex receives afferents from the hippocampus, via the uncinate fasciculus. This provides it with information from long-term memory. Third, prefrontal cortex receives information about the internal physiological and motivational state of the organism via input from the limbic system, particularly (via the hypothalamus) the amygdala. Fourth, prefrontal cortex receives extensive input from several thalamic nuclei. The most important thalamic input is from the mediodorsal nucleus, which in turn receives much of its input from prefrontal cortex (as well as from limbic structures). These return pathways to prefrontal cortex may provide routes for the communication of information between different prefrontal regions.

Efferents   There are four major destinations of efferents from prefrontal cortex (Figure 12.5). Prefrontal

cortex projects back to all sensory areas from which it receives input. These reentrant projections are believed to play a role in prefrontal control of attentional processes. Prefrontal cortex also projects to premotor cortex and to supplementary motor cortex, which in turn project to motor cortex. In addition, prefrontal cortex projects to the neostriatum (caudate and putamen), which in turn projects, via the thalamus, back to prefrontal cortex and to the premotor and motor cortex. Prefrontal cortex also projects to the superior colliculus. These prefrontal efferents to motor structures provide pathways through which prefrontal cortex can influence the initiation and regulation (continuation or inhibition) of movement. Finally, prefrontal cortex has direct connections with limbic structures, particularly the hypothalamus, providing a mechanism for influencing autonomic and endocrine function and for the regulation of emotional behavior.

Taken together, this pattern of prefrontal afferents and efferents suggests that prefrontal cortex mediates the higher-order regulation of behavior. Prefrontal cortex receives highly processed information about the external world; past experience; and the internal physiological, emotional, and motivational state of the organism. It is therefore in a position to integrate information from all of these sources in a manner that yields a schema for the overall regulation of behavior. This regulation can then be implemented via prefrontal efferents influencing attentional processes; internal physiological, emotional, and motivational state; and voluntary movement. This general conceptualization of prefrontal function will be further developed in the sections that follow.

Problems in the Interpretation of Deficits Following Prefrontal Lesions

Since Phineas Gage, many patients with prefrontal lesions have been studied, both clinically and in more systematic neuropsychological investigations. These have revealed a very broad array of deficits associated with prefrontal damage, including impairment in the control of voluntary action, problem solving, cognitive estimation, cognitive flexibility, planning, memory, and emotional behavior. In addition, different patients, or even the same patient over time, may exhibit contradictory symptoms. For example, individuals with prefrontal lesions engaged in a problem-solving task may stop working on the task before it is completed, even though they are using what would have been a successful strategy if it had been continued. Or, they may continue using an unsuccessful strategy, even though they are receiving consistent feedback that the strategy is not achieving its intended aim.

The problem in evaluating findings on the behavioral effects of prefrontal lesions is partly the proverbial one of the many blindfolded persons exploring different parts of an elephant and reporting the characteristics of the parts of the animal that they are touching. However, there is an even more serious problem: Inferences regarding the mechanisms underlying an observed deficit tend to intrude into the description of the deficit itself. A certain degree of conceptualization regarding the underlying nature of observed deficits is inevitable, and even desirable, lest we be confronted with a bewildering laundry list of all the things that can go wrong after prefrontal lesions. However, implicit conceptualization embed-

ded in descriptions of deficits runs the risk of misleading attempts to formulate a comprehensive theory of prefrontal function by contaminating conceptualizations regarding the underlying basis of observed deficits. In particular, we are faced with the problem of whether a particular deficit is a direct consequence of a primary impairment in a specific underlying function, x, or a compensatory response of the system to disruption of some superordinate function, y, that impacts on x. For example, consider the tendency of some prefrontal patients to respond to environmental stimuli that are unrelated to the task at hand (environmental dependency syndrome). This could be conceptualized as a primary disruption of selective and/or exclusionary attention. On the other hand, the guidance of behavior by irrelevant environmental stimuli may be the individual's compensatory attempt to adaptively direct behavior when planned strategies are disrupted or become unavailable. It is also possible, of course, that both of these mechanisms are operative or that yet another underlying mechanism accounts for the environmental dependency syndrome.

The account of the consequences of prefrontal lesions that follows will not entirely escape this problem. In fact, in an effort to impose some kind of order on the array of deficits reported after prefrontal lesions, deficits will be classified in terms of impairment in underlying functions. Nevertheless, it is hoped that the preceding discussion will make it clear that conceptualizations in this account are provisional, thereby protecting us from the potentially misleading theoretical connotations of our descriptions. In a later section of the chapter we will explore more explicit and deliberate theoretical formulations of prefrontal function.

A Working Model of Prefrontal Function

The working model of prefrontal function presented in this section is proposed as a framework for a discussion of the impairments resulting from prefrontal lesions. We will find that damage to prefrontal regions disrupts every component of this model.

Goal-directed behavior requires the activity of a number of underlying component functions

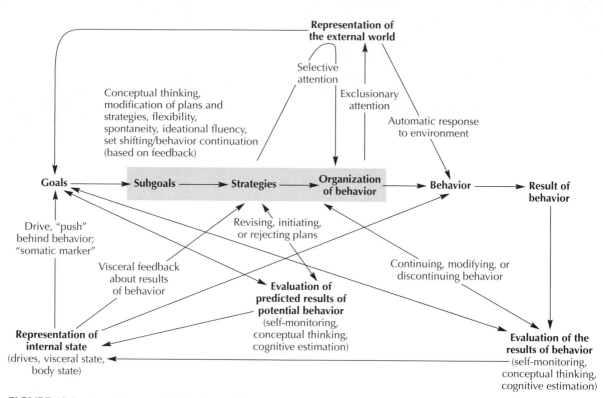

FIGURE 12.6 A working model of prefrontal function.

(Figure 12.6). Information about the environment must be integrated with information about internal state, including drives, resulting in goals. Goals must be translated into subgoals, which in turn must lead to the formulation of behavior strategies. These strategies must then be translated into the organization of specific behaviors, which are then initiated. Among the subfunctions supporting these functions are conceptual thinking, flexibility, spontaneity, ideational fluency, and the ability to initiate and maintain behavior.

Except in the case of very simple subgoals, a particular course of behavior rarely leads directly to the realization of our goals. Difficult, long-term goals require sustained and varied action over a considerable period of time. In addition, even the attainment of relatively simple subgoals requires the ongoing monitoring of behavior and an evaluation of the extent to which the results of our behavior are consistent with reaching our

goal. When there is a discrepancy between the results of our behavior and our goals, this requires a modification of subgoals, strategies, and organization of ongoing behavior. But, if our behavior is deemed to be commensurate with our goals, this evaluation will lead to a continuation of the behavior. Flexibility of response to the results of behavior monitoring is critical to the execution of goal-directed behavior.

Subgoals, strategies, and the organization of ongoing behavior will lead to the direction of selective attention to specific aspects of the environment that are salient to the task at hand. They will also lead to the exclusion of attention (exclusionary attention) to irrelevant aspects of the environment that, outside the context of the goal-directed behavior in question, might ordinarily evoke or facilitate a response. Drives and internal state can directly influence behavior. This is not, however, likely to be useful for the implementation of complex goal-directed behavior, and therefore goal-directed behavior will entail inhibition of impulse-triggered behavior. However, internal states *do* provide essential contributions to goal-directed behavior, both in the formulation of the goal itself and in providing a visceral response to discrepancies between the results of behavior and goals. This visceral response can be a strong motivation for behavior change.

As stated earlier, this model is intended as a framework for discussing prefrontal impairments. Until we possess a comprehensive theory of prefrontal function that accounts for the range of observed impairments in terms of the disruption of one (or a few) underlying function(s), we do not have a definitive way of conceptualizing and categorizing prefrontal impairments. Nevertheless, let's turn now to a discussion of these impairments. First, we will examine the effects of prefrontal lesions in humans. Then, later in the chapter we will explore theories of prefrontal function, focusing on Patricia Goldman-Rakic's hypothesis that the essence of prefrontal function is the regulation of behavior by representational knowledge.

IMPAIRMENT IN FUNCTION AFTER PREFRONTAL LESIONS IN HUMANS

Emotion and Motivation

Since the report of Phineas Gage, it has been clear that prefrontal lesions impair emotional functioning. In chapter 11, we examined the modulatory role exerted by prefrontal regions on subcortical regions important for emotion, particularly the hypothalamus and the amygdala. In this section we examine further some of the effects of prefrontal lesions on emotional functioning.

The investigation of the effects of prefrontal lesions on emotion has received much less attention than prefrontal-related cognitive impairments. This is partly due to the difficulty of defining emotion, an issue that we addressed in chapter 11. It is also partly due to the difficulty of determining to what extent emotional problems associated with prefrontal le-

sions are primary, as opposed to being secondary to the cognitive impairments seen in these patients. (It should also be emphasized that a similarly troublesome problem confronts us as we attempt to understand the nature of the cognitive impairments in these patients. It is often difficult to determine to what extent cognitive deficits associated with prefrontal lesions are primary cognitive impairments versus cognitive impairments secondary to emotional impairment.)

These problems of interpretation aside, advancement in this area has been clouded by the fact that case studies, rather than experimental studies, are a major source of information about the emotional consequences of prefrontal lesions in humans. These reports are sometimes prone to vagueness, imprecision, and the contamination of observation with unwarranted inferences about underlying mechanisms. Finally, all of these problems are compounded by the extremely complicated and highly variable (even contradictory) nature of the emotional changes resulting from prefrontal lesions.

These problems notwithstanding, let's examine the emotional changes associated with prefrontal lesions. These can be divided into negative or deficit symptoms (the absence of certain adaptive behaviors, or things individuals with lesions cannot do) and positive symptoms (behaviors that are present but not adaptive).

NEGATIVE SYMPTOMS

Disturbed Arousal   Individuals with lesions of the prefrontal cortex often exhibit low levels of arousal and alertness, particularly after large dorsolateral prefrontal lesions (Luria, 1966). This often leads to a dramatic reduction in the scope of their behavior. They tend to lack spontaneity and to be minimally responsive to their environment (Klages, 1954; Kleist, 1934).

Apathy   Individuals with prefrontal lesions are often apathetic. They may act as if they have no goals and do not care about their fate. This apathy may pervade their functioning, profoundly affecting many other aspects of cognitive and emotional processing. Prefrontal-related apathy may take the form of diminished awareness of the environment, diminished initiative, decreased movement (hypokinesia), blunted emotional expression, and diminished emotional experience and responsiveness (Cummings, 1993; Greenblatt, Arnot, & Solomon, 1950; Holmes, 1931; Stuss & Benson, 1986). Decreased movement is seen in all spheres, including talking (Kolb & Milner, 1981a), change of facial expression (Kolb & Taylor, 1981), and general motility (Fuster, 1997). Luria (1966) conceptualized individuals with prefrontal lesions as suffering from **psychic inertia,** the inability to initiate movement or to discontinue movement in progress.

Depression   Closely related to apathy is the tendency of patients with dorsolateral prefrontal lesions to experience depressed mood (Starkstein & Robinson, 1991; Stuss & Benson, 1986). There is some evidence that depression more often results from left prefrontal lesions than from prefrontal lesions in the right hemisphere (Gainotti, 1972; Robinson et al., 1984). As we have mentioned, in attempting to understand the emotional disorders associated with prefrontal lesions it is often difficult to determine whether an emotional impairment is a primary effect of prefrontal dysfunction, a secondary effect of the cognitive impairments known to follow these lesions, or some combination of both. This problem is particularly challenging to attempts to understand prefrontal-related depression.

Because this constellation of symptoms overlaps with many of the symptoms of major depressive disorder, it has been termed **pseudodepression** (Blumer & Benson, 1975). Apathy has been more often reported in association with lesions to the prefrontal convexity (dorsolateral prefrontal region) than orbital prefrontal cortex. It has also been reported after medial prefrontal lesions (Fuster, 1997, p. 169).

POSITIVE SYMPTOMS: EUPHORIA AND DISINHIBITION   Individuals with prefrontal lesions may exhibit a number of symptoms that are traditionally termed euphoria (Grafman et al., 1986; Greenblatt et al., 1950; Holmes, 1931; Kleist, 1934; Lishman, 1968; Rylander, 1939). These individuals tend to be nervous, distractible, and hyperactive. They are fre-

quently irritable and irascible. Particularly striking is their apparent disregard for the consequences of their behavior on others, a characteristic that has been termed **pseudopsychopathy** (Blumer & Benson, 1975). For example, these patients often engage in a shallow, childlike humor that is replete with sexual connotations or that may be overtly erotic in its content. These patients may be overtly hypersexual, exhibiting what seems to be a disinhibition of instinctual drives.

These behaviors are seen more often with prefrontal lesions involving orbital (ventral) prefrontal cortex. However, as with all prefrontal lesions, a range of symptoms is reported after orbital prefrontal lesions, and euphoria is not seen after all lesions of orbital prefrontal cortex. In addition, although some individuals with prefrontal lesions who exhibit euphoria also exhibit disinhibition, disinhibition is not always seen in prefrontal patients with elevated mood.

Social Behavior

In view of the emotional and motivational impairments just described, it is not surprising that prefrontal lesions have a major impact on social behavior, an impact that is probably always negative. In addition, the broad range of cognitive impairments that we will discuss shortly also contributes to the profoundly debilitating effect of prefrontal lesions on social behavior. This is particularly true for those who were functioning at a high social and occupational level before the onset of their lesion, although the nuances of even relatively uncomplicated social relations are sufficiently complex to be affected by the behavioral changes following prefrontal lesions.

It is not difficult to envisage how the apathy and depression associated with dorsolateral prefrontal lesions would result in behavior that negatively affects a person's social relations. Perhaps even more problematic for satisfying social interaction, however, are the euphoric symptoms associated with orbital prefrontal lesions. In particular, the disinhibition of instinctual drives associated with these lesions can be problematic. For example, individuals with orbital prefrontal lesions may eat excessively (Erb et al., 1989;

Hofstatter, Smolik, & Busch, 1945). More disruptive for social interaction is the pronounced hypersexuality frequently observed in individuals with orbital prefrontal lesions (Hecaen, 1964; Jarvie, 1954). These disinhibitions of drive seem to be accompanied by a loosening of conventional moral restraints. The extent to which this disinhibition results from a failure of these individuals to assess the effects of their behavior on social interactions, rather than from an inability to regulate behavior in the context of a reasonably accurate assessment of its impact, remains unclear. What is clear is how socially inappropriate their behavior can be, as if it were barely influenced by knowledge of the boundaries of normative behavior in the immediate social and interpersonal context. These changes are so fundamental as to radically change an individual's patterns of behavior, his or her very personality, as we saw in the case of Phineas Gage (Harlow, 1868) and as has been described many times since (e.g., Damasio, 1994).

Memory

As we saw in our discussion of memory in chapter 10, patients with prefrontal lesions do not show the severe impairment in the ability to learn new material seen in patients with medial temporal-lobe or diencephalic lesions. Nevertheless, individuals with frontal-lobe lesions do show impairment in certain types of memory. This section briefly summarizes these impairments. (A more lengthy discussion can be found in chapter 10.)

IMPAIRMENT IN MEMORY SECONDARY TO MORE GENERAL ATTENTIONAL IMPAIRMENT OR APATHY   Insofar as individuals with prefrontal lesions have impaired attention, this will obviously result in secondary impairment in memory. In addition, prefrontal patients may fail to remember because of a more general apathy and lack of interest in the material to be remembered or in the very process of remembering (Hecaen & Albert, 1978).

PREFRONTAL CONTRIBUTION TO ORGANIZATIONAL PROCESSES INVOLVED IN MEMORY Although individuals with prefrontal lesions show

normal memory on a variety of recall and recognition memory tasks, they show impairment when organization is a critical component of the task. This organization may take place during any stage of memory processing, including encoding, storage, and retrieval. The organizational process at each of these stages is referred to as elaborative encoding, elaborative rehearsal, and strategic retrieval, respectively, and there is evidence that prefrontal cortex is critically involved in each of these processes. Individuals with prefrontal lesions are impaired in the utilization, for later recall, of organization inherent in stimuli. This is seen, for example, in the failure of these patients to show the release from proactive inhibition seen in normal subjects.

Another manifestation of the contribution of prefrontal cortex to organizational processes involved in memory is seen in the impairment of individuals with prefrontal lesions on memory tasks that require the extraction of information from an ongoing series of events. An example of this is impairment in conditional paired-associate learning tasks that require subjects to learn the associated pairs by trial and error (Petrides, 1985, 1990). Prefrontal lesions also impair memory when performance depends on the ability of the subject to impose subjective organization on the to-be-remembered stimuli (Petrides & Milner, 1982).

IMPAIRMENT IN TEMPORAL MEMORY   Individuals with prefrontal lesions are impaired in temporal memory, memory for the chronological order of a sequence of stimuli. Thus, they are impaired in identifying which of two previously presented stimuli they saw most recently (Milner, Corsi, & Leonard, 1991). As we have mentioned, individuals with prefrontal lesions are unimpaired on simple recognition tests; this deficit thus has to do with remembering the temporal order of stimuli, not the stimuli per se.

SOURCE AMNESIA   Prefrontal lesions are associated with source amnesia, impairment in the recall of the source of information (Janowsky, Shimamura, & Squire, 1989).

IMPAIRMENT IN METAMEMORY Metamemory, the appraisal of one's own memory capability, is impaired in individuals with prefrontal lesions (Shallice & Evans, 1978; Smith & Milner, 1984). We will find that prefrontal lesions disrupt the capacity for self-evaluation in a number of contexts.

IMPAIRMENT IN WORKING MEMORY From our discussion in chapter 10, we have seen that prefrontal cortex plays a crucial role in the mediation of working memory (see the section The Frontal Lobes and Working Memory in chapter 10). We will discuss this important topic further in later sections of this chapter, particularly when we examine the hypothesis that the wide range of impairments associated with prefrontal lesions may be accounted for in terms of an impairment in working memory.

General Intelligence

Because the prefrontal cortex is far more developed in humans than in any other species, it would seem plausible that it plays a major role in aspects of intelligent behavior, such as those assessed by standard intelligence tests. This has not, however, been shown to be the case. Many studies have reported that patients with prefrontal lesions have normal IQs, as assessed by standard tests of intelligence (Hebb, 1939; Stuss & Benson, 1986). However, poor performance is often seen on components of these tests that tap working memory, such as the Arithmetic (solving math problems) and Digit Span (repeating recently heard strings of digits) subtests of the Wechsler Adult Intelligence Scale. In addition, some impairment may be apparent in subtests that tap abstract thinking, particularly Similarities, a point to which we will return shortly.

The finding that individuals with prefrontal lesions perform at a normal level on many portions of standard IQ tests testifies to the many aspects of cognitive functioning that remain unaffected by these lesions. However, it also alerts us to the restricted nature of the cognitive functions tapped by these tests. When more broad and ecologically valid measures of intelligence are utilized, such as those assessing the fluid intelligence required to creatively solve problems and plan extended goal-directed behavior, individuals with prefrontal lesions are found to be impaired (Duncan, Burgess, & Emslie, 1995; Duncan

et al., 1996). We will discuss these impairments in more detail in later sections.

Language

In chapter 6 we saw that lesions in specific regions of the left hemisphere are associated with central language disorders, the most common of which are Broca's aphasia (expressive aphasia) and Wernicke's aphasia (receptive aphasia). Broca's aphasia, resulting from damage to the posterior portion of the inferior frontal gyrus (Brodmann's areas 44 and 45), is characterized by slow, effortful speech that is poorly articulated, nonfluent, and agrammatic. Lesions of the premotor area (lateral portion of area 6) and the supplementary motor area (medial portion of area 6) in the left hemisphere result in a disruption of the spontaneity and natural smoothness of speech (Damasio, 1992; Luria, 1970; Masdeu, 1980). In severe lesions of the supplementary motor area, the patient may become completely mute.

Prefrontal lesions do not produce the gross symptoms of expressive aphasia seen after lesions to Broca's area. However, although individuals with prefrontal lesions have no difficulty pronouncing words and combining them into intelligible sentences, these lesions do result in definite, if subtle, alterations of speech. These changes have been termed **central motor aphasia** (Goldstein, 1948), **frontal dynamic aphasia** (Luria, 1970), or simply **prefrontal aphasia** (Fuster, 1997, p. 167). Despite this terminology, these alterations do not represent aphasia in the narrow sense of the term. They take the form, rather, of a reduction in spontaneous speech, diminished verbal fluency, and reduction in the volume and scope of narrative expression (Benton, 1968; Hughlings-Jackson, 1915). Thus, the sentences spoken by individuals with prefrontal lesions tend to be short and grammatically simple (Albert et al., 1981), having, for example, few dependent clauses. These impairments have been reported after lesions to either left or right prefrontal cortex, although they are more severe after left prefrontal lesions (Benton, 1968; Kaczmarek, 1984).

In considering the relationship between these prefrontal-related language impairments and the impairment in executive function seen after prefrontal

(A)   (B)   (C)

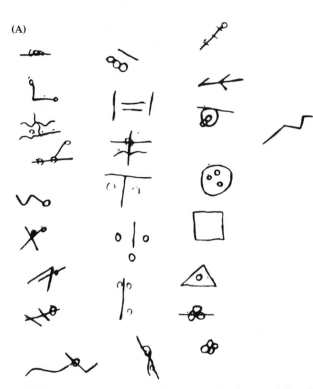

FIGURE 12.7   Performance of *(A)* a normal subject and *(B and C)* two individuals with right prefrontal lesions on the Design Fluency Test (Jones-Gotman & Milner, 1977). In the part of the test shown here, subjects are required to draw as many different drawings as they can in 4 minutes, using only four lines. Although the normal subject's drawings show variation among the designs, the drawings of the individuals with right prefrontal lesions show perseveration *(B)* and diminished capacity to generate responses *(C)*. *(From Jones-Gotman & Milner, 1977, pp. 661, 665, 669)*

lesions, two positions have been taken. Luria and his colleagues (Luria, 1966, 1970; Luria & Homskaya, 1964) have argued that impairment in executive function following prefrontal lesions is a consequence of impairment in the normal regulatory role of language on behavior. This position obviously postulates a central role for language or linguistic schemas in the regulation of higher-order behavior. Although impaired language capability may disrupt a subset of specialized behaviors that rely heavily on verbal guidance, it seems more plausible that the causality is in the reverse direction. From this perspective, the language impairment associated with prefrontal lesions is a specific instance of a more general disorder in the regulation of behavior (Drewe, 1975; Zangwill, 1966).

Inventiveness, Ideational Fluency, and Divergent Thinking

Individuals with prefrontal lesions tend to show limited inventiveness and flexibility in their thinking. For example, when given four minutes to produce as many different drawings, composed of only four lines, as they can, individuals with right prefrontal lesions produce fewer and less varied drawings than do those without such lesions (Jones-Gotman & Milner, 1977). An example is shown in Figure 12.7.

Closely related to the notion of inventiveness are the concepts of **ideational fluency** and **divergent thinking.** These refer to thinking that expands outward from a starting point, generating novel possibilities and ideas, as opposed to **convergent thinking,** which hones in on the unique solution of a problem. The two modes of thinking are thus useful for the solution of different kinds of problems. Divergent thinking is essential for the solving of problems that are unstructured and have many possible solutions, such as what kind of advertising campaign to mount to sell a new perfume or the invention of the plot of a novel. Standard intelligence tests and achievement tests typically assess convergent thinking (e.g., What is the capital of France? How much is four plus five?), tasks that are generally unaffected by prefrontal lesions. Tests of divergent thinking are exemplified by the Uses of Objects Test (Getzels & Jackson, 1962), which requires the subject to name as many different uses for objects as possible (e.g., Name different uses for a shoe). Many control subjects are able to generate novel and inventive uses for common objects (a shoe can be used as a doorstop, a paperweight, to bail out a boat, as a glove, etc.). In contrast, individuals with prefrontal lesions tend to focus on the main and conventional use of an object, failing to think of less probable uses (Zangwill, 1966). This diminished flexibility in unstructured settings is reminiscent of the impairment seen after prefrontal lesions on tasks such as the Wisconsin Card Sorting Test, which require flexibility of thinking within the specific constraints of a particular context (Eslinger & Grattan, 1993).

Abstract and Conceptual Thinking

DIRECT MEASURES OF ABSTRACT THINKING As mentioned in our discussion of general intelligence, patients with prefrontal lesions may exhibit impairment in abstract and conceptual thinking. This may be seen in their interpretation of proverbs such as One swallow does not make a summer. Individuals with prefrontal lesions may interpret this saying concretely, as a specific proposition about the relationship between a particular bird and a particular season of the year, rather than in its more general metaphorical sense. As mentioned earlier, another example of impairment in abstract thinking is the tendency of individuals with prefrontal lesions to provide concrete responses on the Similarities subtest of the Wechsler

Adult Intelligence Scale, a subtest that requires the subject to specify in what way two objects are the same or alike. For example, when asked how an apple and a pear are alike, patients with prefrontal lesions may respond that they "both have skins," rather than responding with the conceptualization of both objects as "fruit."

CONCEPTUAL CATEGORIZATION Not all patients with prefrontal lesions exhibit the severe impairments in abstract thinking described in the previous section. More common, however, are impairments in more demanding conceptual tasks. For example, Delis and colleagues (1992) presented individuals with prefrontal lesions with six cards that differed along eight dimensions, so that there were potentially eight different conceptual bases that could be used to sort them into two groups. The individuals had difficulty sorting the cards into meaningful groups, even when they were given cues to aid their sorting. In addition, individuals with prefrontal lesions were unable to verbally describe the basis for their own sorting or for sorting carried out by the examiner that they observed. These findings, particularly the inability to describe the rules of observed sorting, indicate impairment in conceptual thinking in individuals with prefrontal lesions.

INFERRING SHIFTS IN THE CONCEPTUAL BASIS FOR BEHAVIOR Individuals with prefrontal lesions are particularly impaired when they are required to successfully guide their behavior using feedback about the success of that behavior. This is seen, for example, in the most widely used test of prefrontal functioning, the Wisconsin Card Sorting Test. As discussed in chapter 11, this test requires subjects to determine the correct criterion for sorting cards on the basis of feedback about their behavior. Although most prefrontal patients learn to sort to the first criterion, *color,* they have difficulty shifting the conceptual basis of their sorting from *color* to *form* (and then to *number*), even though on every trial they receive information regarding the currently correct conceptual basis for sorting. It is important to note that many patients with prefrontal lesions who are unable to shift the conceptual basis for their sorting are nevertheless able to verbally state the alternative categories that could serve as the basis for sorting. For example, after sorting only to color throughout the test, they often say something like, "Oh yes, it was color, form, and number." This suggests that, in at least some prefrontal patients, it is not conceptual categorization per se that is impaired, but the ability to use conceptual thinking to guide behavior and/or the ability to use information implicit in feedback about one's own behavior to infer the conceptual basis for behavior.

INFERENTIAL THINKING   Individuals with prefrontal lesions have been shown to be impaired on tasks that require them to make inferences from already acquired knowledge. For example, Shallice and Evans (1978) asked subjects to estimate the length of the spinal cord of the average woman. To infer the answer, subjects must use information in their possession about the average height of women and the length of the spinal cord relative to overall height. Individuals with prefrontal lesions have difficulty making these inferences, even though they possess the required basic knowledge.

Executive Function: Planning and the Goal-Directed Organization of Behavior

Impaired ability to formulate and carry out plans is one of the most salient and most profoundly debilitating consequences of prefrontal lesions. This is poignantly evident in what we can glean from reports of Phineas Gage's life after his accident (Harlow, 1868). Since this first report, impaired planning has perhaps been the most consistently reported and extensively investigated impairment associated with prefrontal dysfunction (e.g., Ackerly & Benton, 1947; Brickner, 1936; Eslinger & Damasio, 1985; Freeman & Watts, 1942; Penfield & Evans, 1935).

Formulating and carrying out a plan requires a number of different component processes. These include (a) identification of goals and subgoals and the motivation to reach them; (b) formulation of plans and subplans for achieving these goals; (c) the holding of these plans and subplans in memory so that they are

available for reevaluation and, ultimately, execution or, in some instances, rejection; and (d) the implementation of the plans in the form of motor activity. The breakdown of any one of these components will disrupt planned behavior. However, it is not always clear in any given instance of impaired planning which component or combination of components is disrupted. This analysis is further complicated by the fact that these components are overlapping and interdependent. For example, it is necessary to hold provisional subplans in memory to determine if they will interface with other prospective subplans in a way that will lead to achieving the desired goal.

THE TOWER OF LONDON   An example may help illustrate these processes. Performance on the Tower of London Test, a task requiring planning, is extremely sensitive to prefrontal lesions (Shallice, 1982). In this task, the subject is presented with three vertical wooden sticks attached to a board and three balls of different colors that can slide on and off the sticks. The vertical sticks are of different lengths, so that the left-most stick can accommodate all three balls, the middle stick two balls, and the right-most stick only one. The task is to move the balls from a starting position to a goal position by moving the rings one at a time in a specified number of moves (Figure 12.8).

If we consider the processing required for successful completion of this task, we see first of all that, unlike the case in more naturalistic situations, the goal is clearly identified. Nevertheless, subjects must be motivated to reach this goal. In addition, they must be able to plan a series of subgoals in order to reach the final goal. This planning of subgoals entails the monitoring of the effectiveness of each prospective subgoal relative to other prospective subgoals (e.g., If I move a ring *here,* will I be able to get to my final goal in the required number of steps?). Anticipating the effects of a given move relative to the ultimate goal, rejecting or accepting a given move as one of the correct series, and holding the resulting sequence of correct moves for final execution all place demands on working memory. In other words, working memory is a critical component both in the

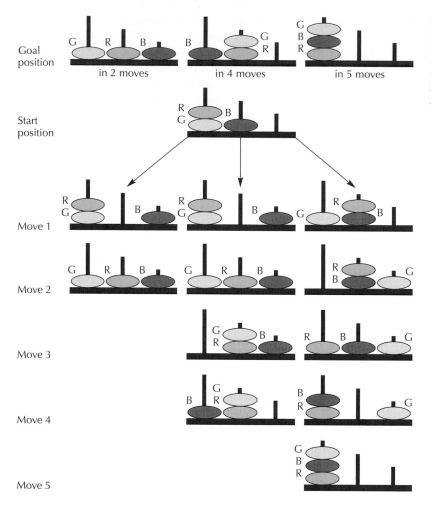

FIGURE 12.8 An example of three problems and their solutions in the Tower of London Test: *R*, red; *G*, green; *B*, blue. The same initial position is used in each problem, and the balls must be moved one at a time. *(From Fuster, 1997, p. 162)*

solution of the problem (the planning of the correct sequence of moves) and the execution of the ultimately determined sequence of moves. The particular aspect of working memory heavily involved in anticipating future events both for the formulation of plans and for the execution of plans is termed **prospective memory** (Dobbs & Rule, 1987; Meacham & Leiman, 1982). Prospective memory may be thought of as foresight, the capacity to internally represent future events and to utilize these representations to guide problem solving and future behavior. Prefrontal patients seem to lack this "memory for the future" (Ingvar, 1985).

VISUAL SEARCH   Another illustration of impaired planning after prefrontal lesions is seen in visual search tasks. For example, Teuber (1964) required subjects to find the location of a specific shape within an array of other shapes (Figure 12.9). Individuals with prefrontal lesions were impaired in locating the target shape.

Perhaps a clearer demonstration of the inability of individuals with prefrontal lesions to organize their behavior in accordance with a goal-directed plan is a study that tracked the eye movements of subjects who were required to answer specific questions about people in a photograph (Karpov, Luria, & Yarbuss,

FIGURE 12.9 The visual search task used by Teuber. Subjects had to locate a duplicate of the shape shown inside the central box. *(From Teuber, 1964, p. 425)*

1968). The eye movements of normal subjects varied in a systematic way, depending on the aspects of the photograph that required exploration in order to answer the question. In contrast, the eye movements of individuals with prefrontal lesions were grossly disorganized, providing a powerful graphic representation of the degree to which their behavior is unguided by a goal-directed plan (Figure 12.10). It is important to emphasize that the disorganized eye movements observed in these search studies were not the result of a primary paresis or ataxia of gaze. Prefrontal lesions do not affect the elementary components of eye movement, just as they do not affect the elementary components of other movement.

IMPAIRMENT IN TASKS SECONDARY TO PLANNING IMPAIRMENT Impairment after prefrontal lesions has been reported on a variety of other tasks that require the planning of self-initiated and self-ordered behavior (Grafman, 1995; Karmath & Wallesch, 1992; Karmath, Wallesch, & Zimmerman, 1991; Luria, 1966; Milner, 1982; Petrides & Milner, 1982). In addition, impaired planning may also con-

tribute to poor performance on tasks that, although not explicitly planning tasks, nevertheless have a critical planning component. This may account, at least in part, for impairment after prefrontal lesions in tests of verbal fluency (Milner, 1964) and design fluency (Jones-Gotman & Milner, 1977). In the verbal fluency task, impaired planning and organization would render the search of the lexicon inefficient, whereas in the design fluency task, impaired organization could interfere with the systematic generation of novel figures. These impairments in planned behavior underlie the frequently expressed notion that prefrontal cortex mediates the highest level of control of behavior, a level often characterized as **executive function** (Baddeley, 1986; Glosser & Goodglass, 1990; Pribram, 1973; Shallice, 1982; Stuss & Benson, 1986; Stuss & Gow, 1992).

THE TEMPORAL INTEGRATION OF BEHAVIOR
Another way of conceptualizing the prefrontal functions subsumed under the concept of executive function is in terms of the **temporal integration of behavior** (Fuster, 1997). This refers to the ability to initiate and carry out novel patterns of goal-directed behavior over extended time periods. Patients with prefrontal lesions generally have no difficulty executing familiar, well-rehearsed behavioral sequences, even when these must transpire over relatively long time periods. Thus, they may be able to carry out many of the routine activities of everyday life quite well. In contrast, they have great difficulty when confronted with novel and challenging situations that require them to develop new strategies and patterns of behavior and to organize these in a sequence of actions over an extended time period. This impairment may be at the root of the prefrontal patient's tendency to behave as if oriented almost entirely in the present, seemingly dominated by momentary impulse, immediately available strategies, and current environmental stimuli (Ackerly, 1964). Without the capacity to engage in planned, temporally integrated behavior, these patients appear to be struggling to organize their behavior in terms of direct reactions to immediately available internal and external information.

Whether one conceptualizes the basic function of prefrontal cortex in terms of executive function, the

(A)

1

2

3

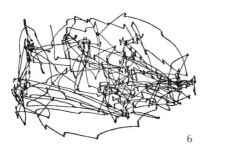

4

5

6

7

FIGURE 12.10   Eye movements during visual search tasks with different instructions. *(A)* normal subject; *(B)* individual with prefrontal lesion. The instructions were *(1)* Free observation, no instructions. *(2)* "Is the family poor or wealthy?" *(3)* "How old are the people in the picture?" *(4)* "What were they doing before the man entered the room?" *(5)* "Try to memorize the clothing that the people are wearing." *(6)* "Try to memorize the placement of the furniture." *(7)* "How long had the man been away from his family?" *(From Luria, 1966, pp. 274–275)*

(B)

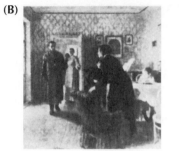

1

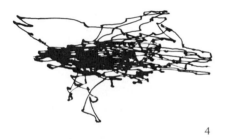

2

3

4

5

6

7

temporal integration of behavior, or some other construct, it seems clear that this basic function depends on a number of component functions. These include attention, inhibition of external and internal interference, working memory, and long-term memory. It also seems clear that interactions between prefrontal cortex and other cerebral areas are required for the mediation of these component functions, a topic to which we will return later.

The Channeling of Drive Into Goal-Directed Behavior: Inhibiting the Disruptive Effect of Impulsive Behavior

We have seen that the uncoupling of drive from behavior, a symptom of some individuals with prefrontal lesions, leads to apathy and depression, severely disrupting goal-directed behavior. On the other hand, the disinhibited expression of impulse, an impairment seen in other individuals with prefrontal lesions, is also rarely adaptive. Most often, the direct expression of impulses is likely to lead to behavior that evokes a negative response from others, thwarts attempts to meet short-term needs, and disrupts ongoing goal-directed behavior. This is true across the enormous range of our complex interactions with our environment, particularly our social environment. From flirtation with a prospective sexual partner to negotiations with our boss, what is needed for adaptive behavior is not the suppression of drive seen in the pseudodepression following some prefrontal lesions. Nor is the disinhibited eruption of impulse, seen after other prefrontal lesions, likely to be adaptive. Rather, we are most likely to achieve the ends we seek through the channeling of drive into motivated, organized, goal-directed behavior. Prefrontal cortex appears to be critical for this process.

Goal-Directed Behavior and Environmental Stimuli

Adaptive behavior requires that we both attend to features of the environment that are relevant to goal-directed behavior (**selective attention**) and inhibit response to features that are not relevant to our goals (**exclusionary attention**). Both of these processes are disrupted after prefrontal lesions.

SELECTIVE ATTENTION: FOCUSING ON TASK-RELEVANT STIMULI Individuals with prefrontal lesions are impaired in the ability to attend to features of the environment that are important for the execution of goal-directed behavior. In Karpov, Luria, and Yarbuss's (1968) study, reviewed previously, we saw this disruption powerfully represented in the disorganized eye movements of individuals with prefrontal lesions who were asked to answer specific questions about a visual scene.

Another example of impairment in the ability to attend to salient features of the environment is seen in a study by Alivisatos (1992). Subjects were given a standard mental rotation task in which they had to specify whether a briefly flashed, rotated letter was presented in a normal or mirror-image orientation. Shepard and Cooper (1982) had shown that the reaction time required to make an accurate determination regarding the orientation of the target letter was a function of the number of degrees that it was rotated from the vertical. From this they inferred that subjects were mentally rotating the target letter to determine its orientation. Alivisatos (1992) added a component to this standard task. On some trials, just before the target letter was presented, a cue letter appeared that was always in the normal orientation (not mirror-image) and rotated to the same position as the subsequent target letter. Subjects could thus determine the orientation of the target letter simply by comparing it with the cue, rather than subjecting it to mental rotation. If the orientations were the same, then the target letter was in the normal orientation. If they were different, then the target was in the mirror-image orientation. Not surprisingly, in the cue condition, the reaction times in normal subjects were unrelated to the angle of rotation of the target letter, the cue making the mental rotation unnecessary. In contrast, even in the cue condition, the reaction time of individuals with prefrontal lesions continued to be a function of the degree of rotation of the stimulus letter, indicating that they were continuing to mentally rotate the stimulus letter rather than using the information inherent in the cue.

Although unilateral sensory neglect is most often associated with right parietal-lobe lesions, it is also seen in some individuals with prefrontal lesions (Damasio, Damasio, & Chui, 1980; Guariglia et al.,

1993). Typically it is confined to the side of space (or the body, in the case of somatosensory neglect) contralateral to the lesion. Although the mechanism for this neglect remains to be fully clarified, it may be conceptualized as an extreme instance of the focusing of attention on a particular aspect of the sensory world, in this case a highly maladaptive focusing.

EXCLUSIONARY ATTENTION: IGNORING TASK-IRRELEVANT STIMULI   Just as goal-directed behavior requires the focusing of attention on task-related features of the environment, it also requires withholding attention from stimuli that are unrelated to the task at hand. Individuals with prefrontal lesions have difficulty doing this. For example, consider an associative learning task in which the subject is given the following instructions: *When the blue light goes on, press the red button; when the red light goes on, press the blue button.* To make the correct responses, a subject must override the most obvious stimulus-response associations (see blue light, press blue button, etc.). Individuals with prefrontal lesions are impaired on associative learning tasks such as this that require the inhibition or overriding of overlearned or automatic responses to the stimulus. In this sense their behavior may be said to be **stimulus bound.** Another example of this phenomenon is seen in a study of the effect of prefrontal lesions on the Stroop Test, a task that confronts subjects with words that are color names printed in incongruously colored ink (e.g., the word *red*, printed in yellow ink). Subjects are told to say the color in which the word is printed (rather than reading the word). Individuals with prefrontal lesions have difficulty suppressing the overlearned tendency to react to seen words by reading them and so do poorly on this task (Perret, 1974; Vendrell et al., 1995).

An experiment by Guitton, Buchtel, and Douglas (1982, 1985) provides another example of this phenomenon. Subjects had to first focus their gaze on a fixation point. A target then appeared somewhere in the visual field to the left or right of the fixation point. On some trials, subjects had to make a saccade (a rapid eye movement) to the target. Prefrontal lesions had no effect on this response. However, on other trials, subjects had to make a saccade to the point in the visual field directly *opposite* the one in which the target appeared. In this condition, individuals with prefrontal lesions were impaired in their ability to inhibit saccades to the target. In addition, after incorrectly beginning a saccade toward the target, individuals with prefrontal lesions were impaired in their ability to make corrective saccades to the opposite visual field when that field was contralateral to the side of their lesion.

These experimental findings indicating the stimulus-bound nature of the behavior of individuals with prefrontal lesions have striking parallels in more naturalistic observations of these patients. They tend to use objects that they confront in their environment, even though they have no obvious prior intention of doing so. For example, entering the house of someone they know only slightly and seeing pictures that need to be hung, together with a hammer and nails, individuals with a prefrontal lesion may begin hanging the pictures, although such behavior in this context is extremely socially inappropriate (Lhermitte, 1986; Lhermitte, Pillon, & Serdaru, 1986). This tendency to use objects in the environment without obvious prior intention to do so is termed **utilization behavior,** and the more general tendency of individuals with prefrontal lesions to rely on the environment for cues to regulate their behavior has been termed **environmental dependency syndrome.** It is possible to conceptualize this tendency as an impairment in the ability to inhibit environmentally evoked behavior. Alternatively, the basis of this tendency may be the unavailability of internally generated, goal-directed behavior, in the absence of which individuals with prefrontal lesions turn to the environment for guidance. It also remains possible that environmental dependency syndrome may result from the interactive effect of both of these factors.

Integrating Goal-Directed Behavior With Its Consequences

Plans are obviously critically important for goal-directed behavior. However, our plans do not always work, a truism that embodies much of the comedy and tragedy of life. Our plans do not always yield the results expected; and, when they do, we may find that those results do not, after all, help us reach our goal. Sustained adaptive behavior over time thus requires the comparison of the results of ongoing behavior with intended goals and subgoals and, when necessary, the modification of behavior on the basis of that comparison. This monitoring and comparative evaluation may be self-initiated, as we spontaneously evaluate our own prospective or actual behavior, or it may be initiated directly by the environment, in the form of explicit feedback.

SELF-GENERATED EVALUATION OF BEHAVIOR

Evaluation of Prospective Behavior   Individuals with prefrontal lesions are impaired in the ability to use knowledge of themselves and their world to spontaneously evaluate the future effects of their own prospective behavior. This is exemplified by the inappropriate tone of many of their social interactions. They seem to be unable to assess the likely impact of their behavior on those with whom they interact and so may be rude or even emotionally hurtful, apparently without intending or expecting to be so. In the domain of goal-directed behavior, prefrontal lesions often disrupt the ability to accurately assess whether a prospective behavior pattern will lead to the achievement of a particular goal. This may account in part for the tendency of individuals with prefrontal lesions to wander off-task, failing to sustain a consistent strategy of behavior over time.

Cognitive Estimation   Studies of cognitive estimation provide experimental evidence supporting these observations. For example, when individuals with prefrontal lesions were shown toy models of objects such as cars and refrigerators and asked to estimate the cost of the real item, a significant proportion of their estimates were totally off (Smith & Milner, 1984). This indicates a severe impairment in the self-generated evaluation of their estimates. We have seen that prefrontal lesions impair metamemory, the ability to estimate one's own capacity to remember. Not unexpectedly, impairment in the self-generated evaluation of prospective behavior extends to these individuals' assessments of their own ability to successfully engage in a wide range of everyday cognitive and emotional tasks. They tend to overestimate their abilities in these areas (Prigatano, Altman, & O'Brian, 1990).

Corollary Discharge   What may be an analogous impairment in the ability to monitor the effect of one's own behavior in the sensory-perceptual-motor domain has been reported after prefrontal lesions. Consider the following: If you place your finger on the corner of your eye and gently apply pressure, the world seems to move. In contrast, if you move your eyes slightly, this phenomenon is absent; you simply experience movement of the eyes. This suggests that our sensory-perceptual system somehow takes account of our voluntary eye movement, so that changes in the scene within the visual field can be interpreted as the result of that movement rather than the result of movement of the world. This hypothetical mechanism by which input to the sensory-perceptual system is integrated with activity of the motor system (and resulting body position) has been termed **corollary discharge** (Teuber, 1972), and there is evidence that prefrontal cortex is important for this process. This comes from an experiment in which subjects in a dark room had to adjust a luminous rod to a vertical position while their bodies were tilted in various orientations. Individuals with prefrontal lesions had no difficulty with this task when their bodies were in the upright position but were impaired in adjusting the rod to the vertical when their bodies were in the tilted position (Teuber, 1964, 1966; Teuber & Mishkin, 1954). This impairment appears to reflect a breakdown in the normal integration of information about body position, derived from proprioception and vestibular input, with information about the external world derived from vision (the darkness of the room excludes vision as a source of information about body position). More generally, this impairment may be a particular instance of the disruption, after prefrontal lesions, of the normal integration of information about the state of the individual (body position) and the external world (position of the rod).

Discrepancy Between Knowledge and Behavior   One of the hallmarks of the effects of prefrontal lesions is a discrepancy between knowledge and behavior. For all of us there is a discrepancy between what we know and what we do or don't do. But for individuals with prefrontal lesions this discrepancy is a pervasive aspect of their behavior. This is exemplified by a study that showed a discrepancy between accurate assessment of required prospective behavior and actual subsequent behavior. Individuals with prefrontal lesions were first shown to be accurate in estimating the number of clues they would need to solve a problem. So, in this case, their self-generated evaluation of required prospective behavior was unimpaired. However, when they actually engaged in the problem, this evaluation process failed to regulate their behavior; they tried to solve the problem before receiving the number of clues that they had already accurately determined to be necessary for its solution (Miller, 1992).

MODULATION OF BEHAVIOR IN RESPONSE TO DIRECT FEEDBACK REGARDING ITS RESULTS

Sooner or later the results of our behavior generate direct feedback from the environment regarding the extent to which that particular behavior is adaptive. Once feedback indicates that our behavior is not working (i.e., not having the effect that we intended), we are then faced with two problems: whether to change our behavior and, if so, in what way. Individuals with prefrontal lesions have difficulty solving both of these problems.

Adaptive Continuation of Behavior Strategies Sometimes it is the case that, although our behavior has not yet achieved its intended goal, we have sufficient feedback (or memory of feedback from previous similar efforts) to indicate that a continuation of that behavior is what is needed. This is particularly true of long and highly complex tasks, in which the intermediary stages provide little or no direct reward or feedback about the success of our strategies. Prefrontal lesions disrupt the sustained execution of strategies of behavior grounded in prior knowledge and experience, in the absence of direct feedback and immediate reward. Individuals with these lesions easily wander off-task (or become distracted by environmental stimuli), abandoning what would ultimately have been a successful strategy if it had been maintained (Rylander, 1939). This is illustrated by a study in which subjects were required to play the familiar game "20

Questions." As participants in long family car rides know, the best strategy for this game is to pose questions that allow the questioner to systematically narrow the category to which the mystery item belongs. Individuals with prefrontal lesions have difficulty executing this systematic question sequence. In addition, if they are able to determine that the mystery item is, say, an animal, they may abruptly abandon this narrowing strategy and guess that it is an automobile (Grafman, Sirigu, et al., 1993).

Adaptive Revision of Behavior Strategies If reaching our goal sometimes means doing more of the same, more often it means flexibly changing our behavior strategies to adapt to changing aspects of the environment. Impairment in this ability is one of the most maladaptive and most intensively studied effects of prefrontal lesions. This impairment is exemplified by performance on the Wisconsin Card Sorting Test. As we have seen, individuals with prefrontal lesions have great difficulty shifting their basis for sorting, in spite of consistent feedback that the examiner has changed the sorting criterion and that the previously correct criterion is now incorrect (Milner, 1963, 1964). We have also seen that this tendency to continue to maintain behavior strategies, in the face of feedback indicating that they are no longer adaptive, is termed perseveration.

There are many experimental findings exemplifying perseveration. In chapter 7 we saw that individuals with prefrontal lesions make more repetitive errors on a visual maze-learning task than patients with parietal-lobe or temporal-lobe lesions (Milner, 1965). That is, they more often go back to the same incorrect location after just receiving information that that move is incorrect (see Figure 7.28). In addition, prefrontal lesions are associated with more instances of broken rules, such as making a diagonal path from one location to another or failing to return to the immediately previous location after making an error (see Figure 7.27).

Repetitive errors and broken rules on visual maze learning are instances of perseveration in situations when avoiding such behavior would seem to be very simple. Individuals with prefrontal lesions remember the rules and can recount them when asked; yet they continue to violate them, despite consistent feedback that they are responding incorrectly. In view of these impairments, it is not surprising that prefrontal lesions disrupt more complex instances of interaction between feedback and resulting behavior. For example, individuals with prefrontal lesions are impaired in the learning of conditional associative learning tasks that require them to utilize feedback from their behavior to learn the correct associations between stimulus and response (Petrides, 1985, 1990). A similar impairment in the ability to extract behavior-directing information from feedback about prior behavior probably contributes to the impaired performance of individuals with prefrontal lesions on visual (Milner, 1965) and tactual (Corkin, 1965) maze-learning tasks.

In conditional associative tasks and maze-learning tasks, the modification of behavior in response to feedback entails a choice between a relatively limited set of alternatives. Even more sensitive to prefrontal lesions are tasks that require shifting from one behavioral strategy to another on the basis of feedback. The Wisconsin Card Sorting Test is one example of such a task. Another task requiring subjects to shift set that is sensitive to prefrontal lesions was devised by Owen and colleagues (1991). Subjects first learn a simple visual discrimination (e.g., between two black shapes). On subsequent trials they must continue to perform this discrimination and then learn new ones involving other black shapes (intradimensional condition). As the test goes on, superimposed white shapes appear over the black shapes. At first the black shapes remain the basis for the discrimination learning and the white shapes are irrelevant, so subjects learn to ignore the superimposed white shapes. Up to this point, individuals with prefrontal lesions show no impairment in learning the discriminations. Then, without subjects' being explicitly informed of the change, the criterion for the discrimination shifts to the superimposed white shapes, and subjects must shift the basis of their discrimination learning accordingly. It is the ability to make this shift in the basis of discrimination learning (extradimensional condition) that is particularly impaired by prefrontal lesions.

Prefrontal Syndromes

The findings reported in the preceding sections make it clear that the effects of prefrontal lesions are highly variable; there is no one pattern of impairment that is reliably associated with prefrontal damage. In fact, we have seen that prefrontal lesions may cause highly contrasting and even contradictory symptoms. Part of this variability appears to result from the fact that lesions to different regions of prefrontal cortex are associated with certain symptom clusters, although this association is by no means absolute. These associations have led to the conceptualization of three prefrontal syndromes, associated with dorsolateral, orbital, and medial prefrontal lesions (Fuster, 1997). Because we have already discussed many of the symptoms that make up these syndromes in some detail, we will not discuss them at length in describing these syndromes.

DORSOLATERAL PREFRONTAL SYNDROME   Dorsolateral prefrontal lesions are often associated with a lowering of general arousal. They are also associated with impaired attention, both selective and exclusionary, and behavior that is consequently highly vulnerable to interference. These lesions are also associated with apathy, diminished drive, reduced awareness, and depressed mood. Working memory and the temporal integration of behavior are also impaired after dorsolateral prefrontal damage. Patients with these lesions often engage in perseverative behavior. Planning ability is severely disrupted, as is the ability to initiate spontaneous and deliberate behavior and to maintain such behavior in a manner necessary for attaining goals. Because this syndrome has such a devastating effect on executive function, it has been called the **dysexecutive syndrome.** Patients with these lesions may also exhibit spatial neglect and disorders of gaze.

ORBITAL PREFRONTAL SYNDROME   Patients with orbital (ventral) prefrontal lesions exhibit a syndrome characterized by disinhibition of drives and release of behavior from normal regulatory mechanisms. Thus, in contrast to patients with dorsolateral lesions (who show diminished drive, apathy, and depression), patients with orbital prefrontal lesions exhibit disinhibited expressions of drive, impulsive responses to environmental stimuli, and elevated mood. These patients may be hyperactive and appear to have limitless energy, which they direct in an unorganized way. They are prone to imitation behavior and utilization behavior. As is the case with dorsolateral lesions, orbital lesions are associated with impaired attention. However, orbital-associated attention problems appear to result from interference from internal drives and external stimuli, rather than from a primary impairment of attentional control processes, as may be the case with dorsolateral lesions.

Patients with orbital prefrontal lesions are also more likely than patients with dorsolateral lesions to exhibit a disregard for social and ethical conventions and a lack of concern about the impact of their behavior on others. These behaviors have caused them to be compared with persons with sociopathy (Blumer & Benson, 1975).

MEDIAL PREFRONTAL SYNDROME Of the three major prefrontal syndromes, medial prefrontal syndrome is the least consistently observed and the least well defined. However, lesions of medial prefrontal cortex, including the cingulate gyrus, are associated with impairment of attention and disruption of motility. In particular, lesions of the supplementary motor area (SMA) are associated with impairment in the initiation and performance of limb and speech movement, whereas lesions of the frontal eye fields (area 8) are associated with disorders of voluntary gaze. Apathy is also a frequently observed impairment after medial prefrontal lesions. Lesions of the anterior cingulate gyrus may result in hypokinesia or, with large lesions, total akinesia (Meador et al., 1986; Verfaellie & Heilman, 1987).

COMMENT Although the idea that the effects of prefrontal lesions in humans can be categorized into the three syndromes just discussed is widely accepted in the clinical literature, two caveats are in order. First, across individuals there is considerable variation in the effect of lesions in what appears

to be the same region. It is always possible to attribute this variation to inaccuracies in the precise localization of lesions in different prefrontal regions in human patients. Nevertheless, this variation raises concern as to the validity of these syndromes.

A second problem with traditional characterizations of these syndromes, such as those just presented, is that they conceptualize differences in the effect of lesions to different prefrontal subareas in terms of the disruption of different essential functions. Thus, dorsolateral prefrontal regions are traditionally seen as disrupting aspects of cognition, including attention, working memory, planning, executive function, and the initiation of movement. In contrast, orbital prefrontal lesions are conceptualized as disrupting regulatory processes that normally inhibit maladaptive expressions of drive. Although these conceptualizations may convey a kind of metaphorical sense of the qualitative differences between the effects of lesions to these two regions, it is not clear that they accurately capture the essence of the mechanisms that each of these areas supports. To explore the question of underlying mechanism(s) of prefrontal function further, we next consider theories of prefrontal function, particularly concentrating on Patricia Goldman-Rakic's (1987, 1992) hypothesis that the essence of prefrontal function is the regulation of behavior by representational knowledge. We will find that experimental studies of nonhuman primates, in whom it is possible to make precisely localized lesions in discrete prefrontal subareas, have made invaluable contributions to these theoretical formulations.

THEORIES OF PREFRONTAL FUNCTION

How is one to make sense of the bewildering array of impairments associated with prefrontal lesions in humans? This question has generated an equally bewildering array of theories of prefrontal function. Thus, deficits associated with prefrontal lesions in humans have been conceptualized as the effect of a disorder of attention (Knight, 1984; Luria, 1966, 1973; Luria, Karpov, & Yarbuss, 1966; Mesulam, 1981), of reasoning and planning (Brickner, 1936; Goldstein, 1949; Milner, 1964; Shallice, 1982), of corollary discharge (Teuber,

1972; Teuber & Mishkin, 1954), of a supervisory-attentional system that regulates the activation of behavior-controlling schemas (Norman & Shallice, 1986; Shallice, 1982, 1988), and of the ability to grasp the essence of a situation and utilize past experience to regulate behavior through one's own or through another's verbal instruction (Denny-Brown, 1951; Luria, 1966, 1973; Luria et al., 1966; Milner, 1964). The effects of prefrontal lesions have also been characterized as resulting from impairment in the initiation and spontaneous activation of behavior (Jones-Gotman & Milner, 1977; Kleist, 1934; Milner, 1964). Some of the effects of prefrontal lesions have been characterized as impairment in behavioral restraint, social emotionality, and global features of personality (Brickner, 1936; Luria et al., 1966; Rylander, 1939).

Some theories conceptualize prefrontal function entirely in terms of cognitive or information processing. For example, Duncan (1986) has conceptualized prefrontal function in terms of the mediation of a goal list, the goals that an individual wants to achieve. Many of the impairments seen after prefrontal lesions are consistent with the notion that behavior is no longer guided by goals. A somewhat related theory (Grafman, 1989) posits that prefrontal cortex is critical for the execution of action that is based on knowledge of the behavior that is adaptive in particular situations, knowledge that has been termed **scripts** (Schank, 1982). Disruption of execution of scripts is a construct that is consistent with many of the effects of prefrontal lesions, including the disruption of goal-directed behavior.

Other theories are more anchored in neurobiology. For example, Damasio and his colleagues (Bechara, Damasio, & Damasio, 1994; Damasio, 1994, 1995) have conceptualized the disruptive effects of prefrontal lesions on the capacity to modify behavior (on the basis of feedback) as a breakdown in the processing of visceral and skeletal input by orbital prefrontal cortex and a resulting absence of an emotional response of the individual to the consequences of personal behavior. These investigators found that individuals with orbital prefrontal lesions failed to show the increase in skin conductance response (an index of autonomic arousal) exhibited by normal subjects, while in the process of choosing behavior that they knew would lead to negative consequences. Rolls (1995) has suggested that orbital prefrontal cortex is involved in correcting responses made to stimuli that were previously associated with reinforcement. This hypothesis is based on animal studies showing that during reversal learning, some orbital prefrontal neurons fire during the extinction phase, whereas others fire during trials reinforcing the reversal.

What is one to make of these diverse hypotheses regarding the underlying mechanism(s) disrupted after prefrontal damage in humans? There is no definitive theory of prefrontal functioning that explains all of the known effects of prefrontal lesions. In a sense, each theory gives us a grasp of part of the picture. There is one theory, however, that is particularly explanatory: Goldman-Rakic's conceptualization that the essence of prefrontal functioning is the regulation of behavior by representational knowledge. This approach has not only provided an explanatory framework for understanding the myriad effects of prefrontal lesions, it has also generated a number of specific and empirically testable hypotheses, the testing of which is likely to significantly advance our understanding of prefrontal functioning. Much of Goldman-Rakic's theory is based on findings from experiments with nonhuman primates. We turn to a discussion of some of that work next.

An Animal Model of Prefrontal Function

Nonhuman primates provide the most suitable animal model for prefrontal functioning. Their close evolutionary relationship to humans is paralleled by a relatively well-developed prefrontal cortex. The surface features and the major cytoarchitectonic areas of the lateral and orbital prefrontal cortex in the monkey are shown in Figure 12.11. There are two important landmarks on the lateral prefrontal surface: the **principal sulcus** and the **arcuate sulcus.** Other important prefrontal areas include the **arcuate convexity** (the anterior portion of which is also called the **frontal eye fields,** or **FEF**), the **superior prefrontal convexity,** the **inferior prefrontal convexity, orbital prefrontal cortex,** and **medial prefrontal cortex.**

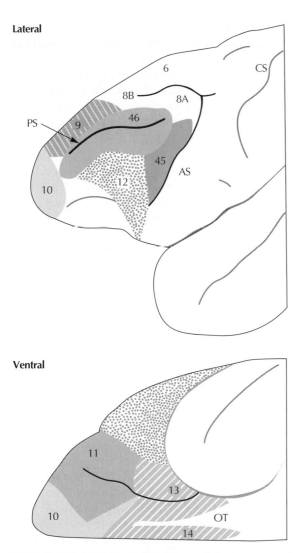

Lateral

Ventral

FIGURE 12.11 Walker's (1940) cytoarchitectonic map of monkey prefrontal cortex. The lateral view shows the principal sulcus *(PS)*, the arcuate sulcus *(AS)*, and the central sulcus *(CS)*. It also shows the approximate location of the frontal eye fields (areas 8A and 45), the inferior prefrontal convexity (area 12), and the superior prefrontal convexity (area 9). The ventral view shows the olfactory tract *(OT)* and orbital prefrontal cortex (areas 13 and 14). Many investigators include the medial portion of area 11 and the ventral portion of area 10 as part of orbital prefrontal cortex. *(From Goldman-Rakic, 1987, p. 400)*

Lesions of prefrontal cortex in monkeys have long been known to result in impairments in the cognitive (Harlow et al., 1952; Jacobsen, 1936), motivational (Bianchi, 1922; Ferrier, 1886), and social (Franzen & Myers, 1973; Myers, Swett, & Miller, 1973) domains that appear comparable in their complexity to those seen in humans.

EARLY STUDIES   The earliest descriptions of the effects of prefrontal lesions in monkeys (Ferrier, 1886; Hitzig, 1874) reported a significant loss of interest in the environment and deterioration of cognitive and emotional behavior, together with sparing of sensory and motor skills. Although there were some early experimental studies of prefrontal function in monkeys (Bianchi, 1895, 1922; Franz, 1907), Jacobsen (1936) conducted the first animal studies that captured an essential aspect of this function.

IMPAIRMENT IN DELAYED-RESPONSE TASKS
Jacobsen (1936) found that monkeys with prefrontal lesions were severely impaired on spatial delayed-response tasks. As may be recalled from our discussion in chapter 10, the classical delayed-response task involves presenting the monkey with two food wells, side by side. The monkey watches as one of them is baited (food placed in the well) and then covered. An opaque screen is then lowered, blocking the food wells from the monkey's view during the retention interval. At the end of the retention interval, the screen is raised and the monkey has an opportunity to respond by uncovering one of the food wells (see Figure 10.24). Monkeys with prefrontal lesions are extremely impaired on this task. They are also impaired on variations of the classical spatial delayed-response task, such as spatial delayed alternation, in which the food well that is baited alternates between trials, so that the monkey has to remember which of the wells was baited on the previous trial.

The ability to perform these delay tasks has been shown to depend on the integrity of dorsolateral prefrontal cortex in both hemispheres, and it has therefore been seen as a potential touchstone for an understanding of prefrontal functioning. There has, however, been considerable disagreement as to the nature of the processes tapped by these tasks. Jacobsen (1936) focused on the memory processes required for the task, and many later investigators have concurred with this notion (Fuster, 1985; Milner, 1982; Passingham, 1985b; Petrides & Milner, 1982; Pribram & Tubbs, 1967). Others, however, have suggested that delay tasks tap other processes, including spatial perception and orientation (Pohl, 1973; Pribram & Mishkin, 1956), attention (Kimble, Bagshaw, & Pribram, 1965), motor control (Teuber, 1972), kinesthesis (Konorski, 1967), and proprioception (Gentile & Stamm, 1972).

Breakdown in the Guidance of Behavior by Representational Knowledge as the Essence of Impairment in Delayed Response

It seems clear that delayed-response tasks tap at least three functions: (a) the ability to access relevant information at the time of presentation, (b) the ability to hold that information "on-line" over the retention interval, and (c) the ability to initiate the motor commands necessary for an accurate response. Goldman-Rakic has hypothesized that the essence of prefrontal function, including its contribution to the delayed-response tasks, is the regulation of behavior by representational knowledge. Thus, at the end of the delay interval in the delayed-response task, when the animal is confronted with two covered food wells, there is no information available in the external environment that the animal can use to guide its behavior. For the animal to consistently choose the correct food well, therefore, its choice must be based on an internal representation of prior events. According to Goldman-Rakic's hypothesis, it is under such circumstances, when behavior must be regulated by representational knowledge in working memory, that the essence of prefrontal functioning is tapped.

We have seen that in humans the prefrontal cortex is involved in certain domains of memory, but not others. This is also the case in nonhuman primates. For a time this seemed confusing and paradoxical, but now we are very much at home with the idea that there are different domains of memory that are mediated by different neural systems (see chapter 10). In monkeys, prefrontal lesions do not disrupt associative memory tasks in which the to-be-remembered

stimulus is present at the time of response. An example of such a task is visual discrimination learning. The animal comes to learn that, say, the vertically striped stimulus has food under it, whereas the horizontally striped stimulus does not. The essential difference here is that visual discrimination learning does not require an internal representation of the to-be-remembered stimulus; it merely requires the association of the seen stimulus with reward. Although the distinction between associative learning and memory involving an internal representation may appear somewhat technical, it has enormous implications for the adaptive functioning of an organism. Associative learning is sufficient to enable an organism to respond adaptively when in the presence of salient environmental stimuli. In contrast, the evolution of the ability to guide behavior by internal representations of stimuli, rather than by the actual stimuli themselves, is fundamental to the ability to guide behavior by plans.

Many effects of prefrontal lesions in both humans and animals fit with the hypothesis that the essence of the disorder is a disruption of the regulation of behavior by representational memory. For example, consider the distractibility so common after prefrontal lesions. The tendency of the behavior to be captured by environmental stimuli that are unrelated to the task at hand is consistent with the loss of the ability to guide behavior by internal representations. With the loss of this internal guidance, the organism is forced to rely on external stimuli present at the time of response. Perseveration can also be understood within this theoretical context. From this perspective, it reflects the organism's attempt to compensate for the absence of an adaptive guiding internal representation by basing responses on whatever internal program may be currently available, however maladaptive the behavior generated by that program may be in the current situation.

Other effects of prefrontal lesions in humans can also be accounted for in terms of impairment in the mechanism or mechanisms by which internal representations are held "on-line" to guide behavior in the absence of (or in spite of) stimuli in the environment. Thus, spatial delayed-response impairments analogous to those seen in monkeys have been reported in humans with prefrontal lesions (Chorover & Cole, 1966; Freedman & Oscar-Berman, 1986). Goldman-Rakic (1987) has suggested that impairment on the Wisconsin Card Sorting Test after prefrontal lesions can also be understood within this framework. In particular, although at the time of category shift there are many stimuli present, these provide no information as to the correct response. Instead, the subject must use an internal representation constructed from past events to guide response. Continued sorting within a category, on the other hand, can be done on the basis of stimulus-response associations because information regarding the ongoing sorting criterion is immediately available to the subject. It is this associative mode of memory that individuals with prefrontal lesions continue to utilize at the point when representational knowledge should be guiding them to shift category. Perseverative responses are the result.

Within the same conceptual framework, impairment on the Stroop Test (Perret, 1974) can be interpreted as a failure to keep the task instructions "on-line," allowing more automatic mechanisms to predominate. Impairment in remembering the temporal order of past events, including the sequence of one's own past responses, can also be understood within this framework (Milner & Petrides, 1984; Petrides & Milner, 1982). Tasks such as the Tower of London (Shallice, 1982), which require the analysis of a goal into subgoals that must be pursued in a particular order, clearly rely on this capacity. Furthermore, impairment after prefrontal lesions on tasks requiring the generation of novel responses, such as verbal fluency (Milner, 1964) and design fluency (Jones-Gotman & Milner, 1977), may be understood as a breakdown in the capacity to keep information, including task instructions and facilitating strategies, "on-line" for the guidance of behavior.

Specialization of the Principal Sulcus for Visuospatial Delayed Response in the Monkey

Because prefrontal lesions in humans cannot be precisely localized and usually involve large areas of frontal tissue, it is difficult to identify particular prefrontal regions as being critical for particular functions. One of the major advantages of studying animals is the ability to make small, well-localized lesions and then study their effects. This has revealed some stunning specializations of function within prefrontal cortex, one of the most important of which is the finding that lesions confined to the principal sulcus produce deficits in visuospatial delayed-response tasks that are as severe as those seen after larger lesions of dorsolateral prefrontal cortex (Blum, 1952; Goldman et al., 1971; Gross & Weiskrantz, 1964). In contrast, no such impairment is seen after lesions to other areas of cortex, including posterior parietal cortex (Harlow et al., 1952; Jacobsen, 1936; Pohl, 1973), or superior and inferior temporal, periarcuate, or premotor areas (Goldman et al., 1971; Jacobsen, 1936).

It should be emphasized that lesions of the principal sulcus were found to impair only delayed response in the visuospatial domain. Thus, after lesions of the principal sulcus, these animals perform normally on a wide range of memory tasks that do not require memory for objects in visual space, including visual pattern discrimination (Passingham, 1972), object learning set (Shallice, 1982), object discrimination reversal (Goldman, 1971), delayed object alternation (Mishkin et al., 1969), delayed matching to sample (Mishkin & Manning, 1978), "go–no go" (Goldman et al., 1971), conditional discriminative tasks (Passingham, 1985a), and cross-modality matching (Petrides & Iversen, 1976). Although many of these tasks require representational memory (because there are no cues available at time of response), they do not require the representation of *visuospatial* information. In addition to demonstrating the specialized function of the principal sulcus for working memory in the visuospatial domain, these findings show that the delayed-response deficit associated with these lesions is not due to sensory or motor problems, motivational disturbance, global memory loss, or the general difficulty or complexity of delayed-response tasks.

Single unit recording of neurons in the principal sulcus has yielded findings consistent with this picture. Some of these data were presented in chapter 10, where we discussed the visuospatial delayed-response task involving eye movements devised by Goldman-Rakic (1987, 1992) and her colleagues. From these and other studies (reviewed by Fuster, 1997, pp. 102–149) it is clear that some neurons in the area of the principal sulcus fire during the retention interval, indicating their involvement in the processes underlying the holding of information during that interval. In addition, these neurons code the location of the to-be-remembered stimulus, such that particular neurons are responsive to the prior appearance of a stimulus in a specific location (see Figure 10.27). Moreover, the activity of some neurons in the area of the principal sulcus reflects the position of the stimulus relative to the arbitrary axes defined by the body, rather than the absolute position of the stimulus. These firing characteristics suggest that prefrontal neurons are coding highly processed information that is the product of the integration of information about body position and information about spatial aspects of the environment.

ACCESSING SPATIAL INFORMATION: PREFRONTAL-PARIETAL CONNECTIONS   Where does this spatial information come from? The answer is the posterior parietal cortex. Evidence for this comes from the clear importance of posterior parietal cortex for spatial processing (see chapter 7) and the similarity of the firing characteristics of neurons in the principal sulcus and neurons in the posterior parietal cortex (Andersen, Essick, & Siegel, 1985; Mountcastle et al., 1984). It is true, as we have seen, that prefrontal lesions are associated with impairment on a number of tasks that have a spatial component, including maze learning (Corkin, 1965; Milner, 1965), the ability to adjust a luminous rod to the vertical in a dark room when the head and body are tilted (Teuber & Mishkin, 1954), and a number of delayed-response tasks. Visuospatial neglect is also seen after some prefrontal lesions (Damasio, Damasio, & Chui, 1980; Heilman & Valenstein, 1979). However, individuals and animals with prefrontal lesions exhibit no impairment on tasks assessing basic sensory-perceptual functioning in the spatial domain, such as the discrimination of spatial location or eye movement from the fixation point to a peripheral target when no delay is involved (Goldman-Rakic, 1987). In addition, neurons in the principal sulcus that code spatial information increase their firing rate only when the information must be remembered, not when the information is available during the delay interval (Fuster, 1973; Kojima & Goldman-Rakic, 1984). Furthermore, even in delay conditions, the firing rate of these cells is unrelated to the actual execution of the response. It appears, therefore, that the impairments in spatial tasks associated with prefrontal lesions have to do with the representation and manipulation in working memory of information about spatial location, rather than with spatial or motor processing per se.

Anatomical investigations have established the existence of major connections between parietal and prefrontal cortex (Bailey et al., 1944). In addition, more recently developed methods have revealed a precise topographically organized network of connections between particular regions of parietal cortex and specific areas of the principal sulcus (Barbas & Mesulam, 1985; Pandya & Seltzer, 1982; Petrides & Pandya, 1984). In particular, area 7a is interconnected with the fundus (bottom) and lower portion of each bank of the principal sulcus; area 7m is interconnected with the dorsal bank of the principal sulcus; area 7b is interconnected with the ventral bank of the principal sulcus; and area 7ip, in the caudal bank of the intraparietal sulcus, is interconnected with the caudal tip of the principal sulcus (Figure 12.12).

These parietal-prefrontal connections are organized as a set of parallel pathways, raising the question of whether each pathway transmits specific types of information. An examination of the respective parietal areas suggests that this is the case. Thus, areas 7a and 7m receive direct projections from visual association areas, including area 19 and area PO. Cells in area 7a are visually responsive, and some are activated when the animal moves its eyes and hands toward an object. This suggests that these cells are coding the spatial location of stimuli relative to body position. Areas 7a and 7m also receive input from areas of the superior temporal sulcus, and area 7a receives input from the superior temporal polysensory area. Neurons in this area, true to its name, respond to more than one modality. Those that respond to visual input generally have large receptive fields and are sensitive to the direction of movement of stimuli. These characteristics suggest that these temporal-lobe inputs to areas 7a and 7m are more involved in

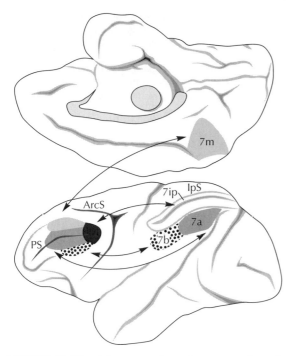

FIGURE 12.12   Subarea-to-subarea interconnections of parietal and prefrontal cortex in the monkey that may be essential for spatial working memory. *PS*, principal sulcus; *ArcS*, arcuate sulcus; *IpS*, intraparietal sulcus. *(From Goldman-Rakic, 1987, p. 385)*

orientation and spatial function than in pattern recognition, although some neurons in the superior temporal polysensory area do respond to visual patterns, including faces. Area 7ip receives projections from area PO and from visual areas corresponding to V2, V3, and V4. It also receives projections from temporal-lobe areas believed to be involved in visuospatial processing.

The firing characteristics of neurons in 7a, 7m, and 7ip, as well as the nature of the input they receive, suggest that these parietal areas are involved in the transformation of visual input into spatial coordinates. In contrast, neurons in area 7b receive only sparse input from visual association areas, receiving input instead from primary somatosensory cortex, supplementary somatosensory cortex, and area 5 of the parietal lobes. As would be expected from the nature of this input, neurons in 7b respond mainly to

cutaneous stimulation. Thus, we find at least some modality specificity among the parallel pathways from parietal to prefrontal cortex. It also remains possible that future investigations will reveal differences among the visuospatial information conveyed by areas 7a, 7m, and 7ip to their respective prefrontal targets.

The parietal-prefrontal interconnections that we have been discussing include strong prefrontal-parietal reentrant projections (Cavada & Goldman-Rakic, 1985; Schwartz & Goldman-Rakic, 1984). Although the function of these reentrant connections is not completely understood, at least two possibilities present themselves. First, this reciprocal parietal-prefrontal circuitry may be part of a reverberating circuit that mediates the short-term maintenance of visuospatial representations. It is tempting to further speculate that similar reverberating circuits between specific areas of prefrontal cortex and specific regions of posterior cortex underlie other types of short-term memory. Such a notion is consistent with evidence that specific prefrontal areas play a critical role in specific domains of working memory (see the following section) and that specific regions of posterior cortex are critically involved in specific types of short-term memory (see chapter 10). Furthermore, the mediation of working memory by a mechanism involving reverberating circuits between posterior areas (that mediate the perceptual processing of stimulus information) and prefrontal areas (involved in the organization of action based on that processing) would seem to be more economical and less prone to error than a mechanism that required the recoding of to-be-remembered information.

Second, prefrontal-parietal reentrant connections may also play a role in attentional processes, providing a regulatory mechanism for selecting, adjusting, and maintaining the flow of relevant information from parietal cortex to prefrontal cortex. Such a mechanism could thus participate in directing attention to stimulus features that are relevant to the task at hand, in addition to maintaining access to representations of these features during the delay period. This hypothesis fits with evidence that prefrontal cortex is involved in the mediation of selective attention (Knight, 1984; Knight et al., 1981).

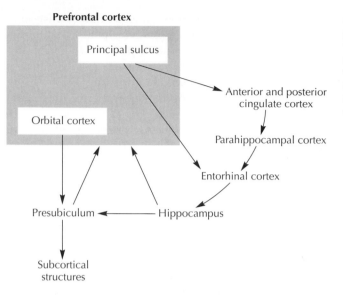

Prefrontal cortex

Principal sulcus

Orbital cortex

Anterior and posterior
cingulate cortex

Parahippocampal cortex

Entorhinal cortex

Presubiculum ◄──────── Hippocampus

Subcortical
structures

FIGURE 12.13   Some major connections between prefrontal cortex and the hippocampus. Connections shown include direct and multisynaptic input from the principal sulcus to entorhinal cortex, return connections from hippocampus to prefrontal cortex, and orbital prefrontal input to the presubiculum. (Connections between these structures and posterior cortex are not shown.)

ACCESSING LONG-TERM MEMORY: PREFRONTAL-LIMBIC CONNECTIONS   The regulation of behavior by prefrontal cortex is a joint function of at least two sources of information: (a) information about the immediate environment arriving at prefrontal cortex via transcortical pathways, an example of which we have just discussed, and (b) information in long-term memory requiring hippocampal mechanisms. For a long time the effects of hippocampal lesions on spatial memory appeared to be species-specific; hippocampal lesions were reported to disrupt spatial memory in rodents (Gaffan et al., 1984; O'Keefe & Nadel, 1978) but not in primates (Waxler & Rosvold, 1970). However, it is now clear that combined lesions of the hippocampus and the amygdala in primates cause impairment in delayed-response tasks at delays of 15 seconds or greater (Zola-Morgan & Squire, 1985). Thus, the integrity of the principal sulcus is required for both short (less than 15 seconds) and long delays, whereas the integrity of medial temporal structures is required for long delays. It is therefore reasonable to conclude that principal sulcal neurons convey information to the hippocampus for storage during more extended delay conditions.

This notion is supported by the finding that unit recording of hippocampal neurons in monkeys per-

forming delayed-response tasks reveals a profile of neural activity resembling that seen in principal sulcus neurons. Thus, like principal sulcus neurons, some hippocampal neurons show a higher level of activity during the delay period of delayed-response trials than during other components of the task. In addition, in spatial delay tasks, neurons in the hippocampus resemble neurons in the principal sulcus in showing spatial selectivity, some hippocampal neurons being more active when the cue is placed to one side or the other of the animal (Watanabe & Niki, 1985) and other neurons being more active when the animal makes a response in a particular direction (Wilson, Brown, & Riches, 1986). The mirroring of prefrontal activity by hippocampal neurons is also consistent with the finding that prefrontal lesions and hippocampal lesions in humans produce similar impairments in the performance of a self-ordering task that taps working memory for events occurring over a relatively long time period (Petrides & Milner, 1982).

The concept of a close functional relationship between prefrontal cortex and limbic cortex is also consistent with anatomical evidence of extensive connections between these two regions (Figure 12.13). The principal sulcus sends direct projections to entorhinal cortex (the gateway to the hippocampus), via the fronto-occipital fasciculus, and multisynaptic relays to entorhinal cortex, via anterior and posterior cingulate cortex and parahippocampal cortex. Virtually all hippocampal targets of prefrontal cortex send return connections back to prefrontal cortex. These return connections may provide routes for the transmission of information in long-term memory, accessed by the hippocampus, to prefrontal areas and may thus be components of a mechanism by which this information could influence the final motor output regulated by prefrontal cortex. Also of particular interest are projections from orbital prefrontal cortex to the presubiculum, a major output of the hippocampus to cortical and subcortical structures. Prefrontal terminals in this area are in a position to regulate, or gate, the output of the hippocampus, providing anatomical connections that may contribute to the prefrontal regulation of the influence of long-term memory on behavior.

MOTOR-CONTROL FUNCTIONS OF PREFRONTAL CORTEX: THE INITIATION AND INHIBITION OF ACTION

We have seen that a salient feature of damage to prefrontal cortex is the absence of primary motor impairment, together with a disruption of higher-order organizational aspects of behavior, disruption which we have characterized as the breakdown of the guidance of behavior by representational knowledge. In particular instances, this breakdown manifests itself as impairment in the ability to inhibit or to initiate action. In the absence of guiding representations, individuals with prefrontal lesions may fail to inhibit the use of a strategy that had been previously reinforced but, because of changing conditions, is now no longer adaptive. An example of this is perseverative sorting to a previously correct category on the Wisconsin Card Sorting Test. Disruption of guiding representations may also result in heightened vulnerability to compelling environmental stimulation, as exemplified by the difficulty individuals with prefrontal lesions have inhibiting a saccade to the cue in the antisaccade task of Guitton and his colleagues (1985), discussed previously. In both instances, the result is a failure to inhibit incorrect responses. However, prefrontal lesions also impair the initiation and generation of correct responses, partic-

ularly in unstructured tasks such as the generation of verbal lists (Milner, 1964); the invention of abstract designs (Jones-Gotman & Milner, 1977); and the solving of problems, like the Tower of London, that require the analysis of goals into subgoals and the sequential organization of behavior to achieve those subgoals (Shallice, 1982).

In line with its regulatory role on higher-order aspects of behavior, prefrontal cortex does not generate action directly. Rather, it regulates motor output by inhibiting and facilitating structures directly involved in the programming and performance of specific motor acts. These structures include the basal ganglia, the superior colliculus, and the premotor and supplementary motor cortices. In addition, prefrontal cortex receives extensive afferents from thalamic nuclei that, in turn, receive input from the basal ganglia and superior colliculus. This thalamic input appears to provide prefrontal cortex with feedback regarding the effect of its regulatory input on structures more directly involved in the execution of action. In the following sections we will briefly consider each of these mechanisms of prefrontal influence on motor function.

Cortical-Striatal Pathways   Much of the cerebral cortex projects to the caudate and the putamen (collectively termed the neostriatum). This is termed the cortical-striatal system. Prefrontal cortex, particularly the principal sulcus, projects to all regions of the caudate nucleus and the rostral putamen (Goldman & Nauta, 1977; Passingham, 1985a). Cortical projections to the neostriatum are very orderly, each cytoarchitectonic subdivision of the cortex projecting to a specific region of the neostriatum. These then project, via the substantia nigra and then the thalamus, to premotor cortex and back to prefrontal cortex (Figure 12.14). The striatal-nigral and the nigral-thalamic synapses in this circuit are GABAergic and therefore inhibitory (Penney & Young, 1981), thus producing back-to-back inhibitory synapses within the circuit. This arrangement suggests one mechanism whereby prefrontal cortex may regulate motor behavior. A prefrontal-activated decrease in striatal activity would have the net effect of inhibiting motor behavior, whereas an increase in prefrontal-activated striatal activity would have the opposite effect of generating motor behavior

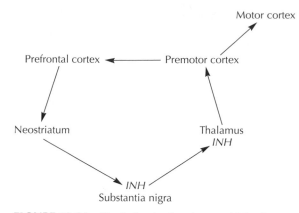

FIGURE 12.14   Cortical-striatal pathway with back-to-back inhibitory synapses, indicated by *INH*, whereby the activity level of prefrontal cortex can inhibit or increase premotor cortex activity.

(see Figure 12.14). The back-to-back inhibitory synapses in this circuit are an important component in the inhibition of behavior because they provide a mechanism whereby a decrease in prefrontal activity can *actively* inhibit premotor cortex activity.

Cortical-Tectal Pathways   Pathways from prefrontal cortex to the superior colliculus constitute another connection between prefrontal cortex and structures directly involved in the execution of movement. Intermediate and deep layers of the superior colliculus, containing cells that discharge in association with head and eye movements, receive connections from prefrontal cortex, including the principal sulcus and the frontal eye fields. It is possible that the intermediate and deep layers of the superior colliculus are points at which neurons in the principal sulcus influence head and eye movement, particularly in relation to stored information. This would provide a mechanism that could explain the tendency of individuals with prefrontal lesions to direct their gaze toward the cue (instead of to the same point in the opposite field, as instructed) in Guitton and colleagues' antisaccade task. From this perspective, this impairment would reflect a disruption of the normal inhibition of tectal-mediated head and eye movement by prefrontal neurons involved in

the regulation of behavior through representational memory of the task instructions.

Thalamic-Cortical Pathways   The mediodorsal nucleus of the thalamus was long thought to be the exclusive thalamic projection to prefrontal cortex (Akert, 1964; Freeman & Watts, 1948; Pribram, Chow, & Semmes, 1953; Rose & Woolsey, 1948), and prefrontal cortex was traditionally defined as that portion of cortex receiving projections from the mediodorsal nucleus. More recently, however, it has become clear that prefrontal cortex receives afferents from a number of other thalamic nuclei, including the anterior nucleus, the ventral anterior nucleus, and the medial pulvinar (Kievit & Kuypers, 1977). Further, each cytoarchitectonic subdivision of prefrontal cortex has a distinct and topographically specific input from each of these nuclei (Goldman-Rakic & Porrino, 1985).

Although the nature of the input conveyed by thalamic-prefrontal pathways remains obscure, there are some hints as to the nature of the information conveyed. Thus, although projections from prefrontal cortex to the neostriatum and to the superior colliculus, discussed earlier, are not reciprocal, the neostriatum projects to the ventral anterior nucleus and parts of the mediodorsal nucleus, which, in turn, project to prefrontal cortex. In addition, input from the superior colliculus reaches prefrontal cortex via the medial pulvinar and the mediodorsal nucleus (Figure 12.15). These pathways provide mechanisms whereby prefrontal cortex may receive feedback regarding the activity of motor structures that it influences. Information about the activity of structures directly involved in the execution of movement is an important component in the regulation of behavior by prefrontal cortex. In addition, the integration, in prefrontal cortex, of this feedback with information from sensory systems may be a component of the hypothetical corollary discharge mechanism proposed by Teuber (1972; Teuber & Mishkin, 1954).

Prefrontal-Premotor Cortex and Prefrontal-Supplementary Motor Cortex Connections   Connections between prefrontal cortex, premotor cortex,

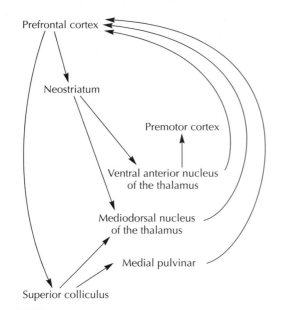

FIGURE 12.15   Prefrontal-striatal-thalamic-prefrontal and prefrontal-tectal-thalamic-prefrontal loops whereby prefrontal cortex may receive feedback regarding the activity of the motor structures that it influences.

and primary motor cortex (M1) are highly organized. Thus, somatotopically organized areas of the premotor cortex are connected to areas of M1 representing the same body areas. In addition, neurons in specific areas of the principal sulcus project to specific areas of premotor cortex. Prefrontal neurons are thus only one synapse removed from M1. A similar relationship obtains for connections between prefrontal cortex, the supplementary motor area (SMA), and M1. Both premotor cortex and SMA have been implicated in motor programming. Prefrontal cortex, therefore, is in a position to activate or to cancel the release of motor programs organized by these regions. Unlike SMA, premotor cortex, and M1, specific areas of prefrontal cortex are not specialized for the activation of any single muscle group or any specific movement. For example, in the monkey, the principal sulcus is able to regulate (initiate or cancel) responses of any part of the upper body (including the head, mouth, and eyes) to environmental stimuli.

Other Prefrontal Subsystems

In our earlier discussion of the effects of prefrontal lesions on humans, we saw how bewilderingly diverse these effects can be. We have also seen that the interpretations of the fundamental impairment(s) underlying these effects are highly diverse. From our discussion of animal models of prefrontal function, we have seen that lesions confined to the principal sulcus in the monkey result in specific impairment in visuospatial tasks that require a deferred response made in the absence of immediately available cues. Goldman-Rakic (1987) has conceptualized this process as the guidance of behavior by a visuospatial representation accessed and held "on-line" by neurons in the principal sulcus.

As we have mentioned, the demonstration of such a relationship between a specific region of prefrontal cortex and a particular function has not been possible in humans with prefrontal lesions because lesions in humans are seldom restricted to small and cytoarchitectonically homogeneous regions of prefrontal cortex. We therefore must again turn to animal studies to address the problem of specialization of function within prefrontal cortex. A particular question of interest is whether neurons in other prefrontal regions mediate the same basic function as neurons in the principal sulcus (but in different domains of information) or whether different prefrontal areas mediate basically different processes. Although there is no definitive answer to this question, there is considerable evidence supporting the hypothesis that different prefrontal subdivisions perform the same basic operation of accessing and holding information "on-line" for the guidance of subsequent behavior, but that each subdivision is specialized with regard to the domain of information processed. In the sections that follow we will review some of this evidence, derived from the study of three other prefrontal subareas: the frontal eye fields, the inferior prefrontal convexity, and orbital prefrontal cortex.

THE FRONTAL EYE FIELDS   The frontal eye fields (FEF) in each hemisphere constitute an area corresponding to Walker's areas 8A and 45 in the anterior bank of the arcuate sulcus (see Figure 12.11). The FEF is involved in the cortical control of purposive eye movement (Bruce & Goldberg, 1984). Fifty percent of neurons in FEF discharge in advance of visually guided saccades, and almost half of these are selectively activated by visual targets in specific locations (Bruce & Goldberg, 1984, 1985; Bruce et al., 1985). Moreover, this coding by FEF neurons is seen during the delay interval of delayed-response trials. Thus, as is the case with neurons in the principal sulcus, the activity of neurons in FEF appears to code the coordinates of a purposive saccade over a delay interval. In addition, FEF is also similar to the principal sulcus in that lesions to both areas impair delayed eye movement to visual targets that are no longer present. Furthermore, the two areas have some similar connections to other cerebral structures, both receiving afferents from the parvocellular portion of the mediodorsal nucleus of the thalamus and both sending efferents to the neostriatum and the superior colliculus. The major difference between the function of the two areas is that FEF appears to be concerned with keeping track of visuospatial information over time as it pertains specifically to eye movements, whereas the principal sulcus is concerned with keeping track of such information as it pertains to eye *and* hand movement. This is reflected in the effects of lesions to the two areas, with FEF lesions disrupting saccades to a target after the target is no longer present and principal sulcus lesions disrupting a broader range of movement to a target after a delay, including both eye and hand movement. This is also reflected in the pattern of efferents from the two areas. The motor output of FEF is restricted to regions involved in the production of eye movement, whereas the principal sulcus, in addition to sending efferents to FEF (Barbas & Mesulam, 1981; Pandya & Kuypers, 1969), sends output to a number of regions involved in organizing movement of parts of the body other than the eyes, including SMA, the region of frontal operculum representing the perioral and laryngeal musculature, and the region of premotor cortex representing the mouth (Matelli et al., 1984). These findings suggest that principal sulcal cortex may be superordinate to FEF, sending output to several motor-organization centers, including FEF, and commanding them to action or inaction, depending on environmental and internal factors. Further research is required to adequately explore this possibility.

THE INFERIOR PREFRONTAL CONVEXITY A comparison of the principal sulcus and the inferior prefrontal convexity (see Figure 12.11) provides an even more compelling instance of specialization of function within prefrontal cortex. The inferior prefrontal convexity and parts of the adjacent lateral orbital cortex (area 11) receive major afferents from inferior temporal cortex, an area specialized for the processing of visual features such as form, color, and other nonspatial aspects of stimuli. In line with these connections, there is evidence that the inferior prefrontal convexity is concerned with memory for nonspatial visual features of stimuli. Thus, lesions of the inferior prefrontal convexity impair performance on a number of tasks requiring memory for visual features of objects, such as delayed object alternation (Mishkin & Manning, 1978), delayed object matching, and delayed color matching (Jones & Mishkin, 1972; Mishkin & Manning, 1978; Passingham, 1972, 1975). These lesions do not, however, impair performance on spatial delayed-response tasks. These findings, taken together with the effects of principal sulcus lesions, reveal a double dissociation between the effects of principal sulcus and inferior prefrontal convexity lesions, the former disrupting performance of delay tasks with visuospatial components but not visual features, such as form and color, and the latter showing the opposite pattern. This dissociation is also supported by physiological studies that have revealed neurons in the inferior prefrontal convexity that respond to complex visual stimuli and respond best to stimuli presented foveally (Pigarev, Rizzolatti, & Scandolara, 1979). This contrasts markedly with the response profile of neurons in the principal sulcus. As we have seen, the majority of these cells respond best to spatial aspects of peripherally presented stimuli.

A reciprocal interaction between inferior temporal cortex and cortex of the inferior prefrontal convexity, paralleling the interaction between parietal cortex and principal sulcal cortex, has been demonstrated by cooling experiments (Fuster, Bauer, & Jervey, 1985). These have shown that cooling inferior temporal cortex influences the activity of neurons in the inferior prefrontal convexity that are normally active during the retention of nonspatial stimulus features, such as color, over the delay period of a delayed-matching task. Conversely, cooling the inferior prefrontal convexity influences the activity of inferior-temporal neurons normally active during nonspatial delayed-matching tasks.

Taken together, these findings indicate the existence of distinct prefrontal processing centers, one in the principal sulcus specialized for the retention of visuospatial aspects of stimuli and one in the inferior prefrontal convexity specialized for the retention of visual features of stimuli, such as form and color. This dissociation is consistent with the concept of dual visual processing in the cortex (Mishkin, Ungerleider, & Macko, 1983). From this perspective, the dorsal and ventral streams would achieve their ultimate level in the principal sulcus and the inferior prefrontal convexity, respectively.

ORBITAL PREFRONTAL CORTEX   Orbital prefrontal cortex (see Figure 12.11) has been less thoroughly explored by modern neurobiological techniques than other areas of prefrontal cortex, and its function therefore remains somewhat obscure. It has, however, long been associated with social, emotional, and motivational aspects of behavior (Denny-Brown, 1951; Fulton, 1950). In analyzing the functions mediated by this structure, it is useful to return to a consideration of the effect of prefrontal lesions in humans.

The importance of orbital prefrontal cortex for motivation has been highlighted by observations of the patient known as E. V. R., who sustained bilateral removal of ventromedial prefrontal cortex after surgery for an orbitofrontal meningioma (Damasio, 1994; Eslinger & Damasio, 1985). Following surgery, E. V. R. was found to have an IQ in the superior range. As we have seen, the absence of impairment on standard tests of intelligence is not unusual for individuals with prefrontal lesions. More striking, however, was E. V. R.'s unimpaired performance on tasks that are sensitive to dorsolateral prefrontal lesions, including the Wisconsin Card Sorting Test. Instead, E. V. R. showed severe impairment in motivation. He appeared to have no spontaneous motivation to act, no internal program to propel him into action. If goals were presented to him

externally and repeatedly, they triggered related actions, even if these goals were unrealistic and the strategies proposed for achieving them were not practical. As a consequence, E. V. R. was led into several obviously flawed business ventures. However, in the absence of externally presented goals, he maintained a goal-less, undirected existence. Finally, although information about E. V. R.'s emotional state was not reported, individuals with orbital prefrontal lesions typically exhibit shallow and socially inappropriate affect, and it is probable that E. V. R. did also.

This picture of the effects of orbital prefrontal lesions, in terms of impairment in motivation together with preservation of function in the cognitive domain, differs markedly from that seen after dorsolateral prefrontal lesions. However, lesions to these two regions are similar in that they both result in disruption of the regulation of behavior when external cues are not present, together with relative preservation of behavioral regulation by external stimuli. This suggests that an impairment in representational memory may also underlie the deficits seen after orbital prefrontal lesions, a point to which we will return in a moment.

At present there is no test of orbital prefrontal function that is as specifically sensitive to lesions in that region as delayed visuospatial tasks are to lesions of the principal sulcus. Thus, orbital prefrontal lesions in nonhuman primates are associated with impairment in a number of tasks, including object reversal, learning set, and recognition memory (Bachevalier & Mishkin, 1986; Goldman, 1971; Mishkin, 1964). Orbital prefrontal lesions also impair olfactory discrimination (Tanabe et al., 1975). These tasks do not have the obvious common element shared by delayed visuospatial response tasks, although like those tasks they include a complex combination of sensory, mnemonic, and motor control functions.

The anatomical connectivity of orbital prefrontal cortex is also less well understood than that of the principal sulcus. However, it is clear that afferents to orbital prefrontal cortex include input from the magnocellular portion of the mediodorsal nucleus of the thalamus (Fuster, 1997), the amygdala (Porrino, Crane, & Goldman-Rakic, 1981; Russchen, Amaral, & Price, 1985), the temporal pole (Markowitsch et al., 1985), olfactory regions (Yarita et al., 1980), and

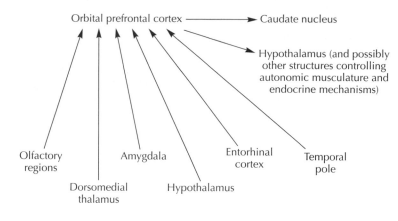

FIGURE 12.16   Major orbital prefrontal afferents from subcortical and limbic cortical regions, together with major orbital prefrontal efferents to the hypothalamus and caudate nucleus. These connections are consistent with the idea that orbital prefrontal cortex guides autonomic and endocrine responses (and ultimately behavior) on the basis of representational knowledge in the interoceptive domain, in a manner analogous to the way in which dorsolateral prefrontal cortex guides somatic motor output on the basis of representational knowledge of the environment.

entorhinal cortex (Van Hoesen & Pandya, 1975; Van Hoesen, Pandya, & Butters, 1975). Orbital prefrontal cortex also receives input from the hypothalamus (Figure 12.16). These afferents from limbic cortex and from subcortical areas supply orbital prefrontal cortex with olfactory and interoceptive information.

Major orbital prefrontal efferents include input to the caudate nucleus, although to different sectors than those receiving input from dorsolateral prefrontal cortex. In addition, orbital prefrontal cortex is known to send direct projections to the hypothalamus. In fact, as we noted previously, orbital prefrontal cortex is the only cortical area to send direct input to the hypothalamus. This connection is probably the route by which prefrontal cortex influences the regulation of autonomic musculature and endocrine mechanisms. Whatever the connections involved, however, there is ample evidence that prefrontal cortex exercises such influence. For example, stimulation of orbital prefrontal cortex results in autonomic changes, including slowing of respiration, increase in blood pressure, and irregularities of heart rate (Hall, Livingston, & Bloor, 1977; Hoff, Kell, & Carroll, 1963).

Evidence that orbital prefrontal cortex has access to information regarding interoceptive and olfactory stimuli and that it projects to areas mediating autonomic and endocrine functioning suggests that it may regulate autonomic and endocrine function on the basis of representational knowledge of interceptive status in a manner analogous to the way in which dorsolateral prefrontal cortex (principal sulcus cortex,

FEF, and the cortex of the inferior prefrontal convexity) regulates somatic motor output. Thus, according to this hypothesis, orbital prefrontal cortex would participate in the guidance of visceral and hormonal responses by holding "on-line" representational knowledge in the interoceptive-olfactory domain, just as dorsolateral prefrontal cortex guides somatic motor output by holding representational knowledge about past events "on-line." This hypothesis is consistent with the severe blunting of emotional suffering in response to pain seen after orbital prefrontal lesions. From this perspective, emotional blunting after these lesions results from failure to access the central representation of pain and current visceral (autonomic) status, so that these representations cannot be brought "on-line" to influence emotional state, motivation, and behavior. This constitutes an impairment in working memory for the central representation of reward and punishment and for motivational and emotional state. If this is the primary deficit in orbital prefrontal lesions, it could account for the blunting of response to reinforcement and the nonspecific pattern of cognitive impairment seen in individuals with these lesions.

The idea that an impairment in visceral or emotional working memory underlies the deficits seen after orbital prefrontal lesions is also consistent with E. V. R.'s inability, after bilateral orbital prefrontal lesions, to regulate his behavior on the basis of an emotional or visceral response to its consequences (Bechara, Damasio, & Damasio, 1994). Bechara and colleagues interpret E. V. R.'s impairment as a breakdown in the processing of autonomic feedback by neural centers contributing to the control of behavior (disruption of somatic marker). This interpretation may not be inconsistent with the notion argued here, that orbital prefrontal lesions disrupt working memory for interoceptive state, so that "on-line" representations of emotional and motivational state are not available to contribute to the guidance and organization of behavior.

The Problem of Integration in Prefrontal Cortex

Over the past hundred years, conceptualizations of prefrontal functioning have undergone an evolution. Early views of prefrontal cortex as basically homogeneous in structure and as mediating global functions such as intelligence, personality, and moral behavior gave way to the view that the region had two specialized subdivisions, dorsolateral prefrontal and orbital prefrontal, mediating cognitive and emotional processing, respectively. More recently, as we have seen, it has been appreciated that prefrontal cortex is highly differentiated into multiple subdivisions, based on anatomical, physiological, and behavioral criteria. In the foregoing sections we have examined four of these subdivisions: the principal sulcus, the frontal eye fields, the inferior frontal convexity, and orbital prefrontal cortex.

The problem of synthesizing recent findings into a general theory of prefrontal function remains to be solved. In our discussion we have followed Goldman-Rakic's hypothesis that all prefrontal subdivisions mediate the same essential attentional, working memory, and motor control processes, but that each does so in relation to different domains of information. From this perspective, the capacity to access and hold "on-line" information that is relevant to the task at hand is the essential mechanism underlying many higher-order functions, including language, concept formation, and planning. As we have seen, this is a compelling conceptualization that is well supported by anatomical, physiological, and behavioral data. Alternative interpretations of the available data remain possible, however. For example, Fuster (1997, pp. 230–238) has

proposed that different prefrontal processes are distributed across prefrontal cortex in distinctly different memory and motor control centers, with dorsolateral prefrontal cortex mediating working memory processes and orbital prefrontal cortex mediating inhibitory processes. Much of the data we have reviewed, including the fact that dorsolateral prefrontal cortex has more direct efferent connections to major somatic motor centers than does orbital prefrontal cortex, seem to favor Goldman-Rakic's hypothesis. However, the issue has not been definitively resolved.

Whether prefrontal cortex is composed of multiple subdivisions carrying out common processes on different domains of information or whether each subdivision has a distinctly different function, the processing of all prefrontal subdivisions must somehow be integrated in a way that makes possible a smoothly functioning individual with a coherent personality. This problem may be thought of as a variation of the binding problem that challenges our understanding of the neural mechanisms of object recognition, the problem of how the processing of specific features of an object in different subdivisions of posterior cortex is integrated into a single percept. Here the problem is how the processing of different aspects of the environment and aspects of an individual's emotional and motivational state, all processed in specialized subdivisions of prefrontal cortex, are integrated in a way that makes possible the formulation of coherent, adaptive, goal-directed plans that consistently regulate action and sequences of actions.

SUMMARY

In previous chapters of this book we have explored aspects of the brain's capacity to process information and to execute action. Thus, we have seen that posterior regions of the brain (the occipital, parietal, and temporal lobes), interacting with subcortical regions (including limbic structures), mediate a truly marvelous range of processes that enable us to construct internal representations of the external world and of our internal emotional and motivational state. We have also seen that premotor cortex and motor cortex, in posterior frontal regions, execute and coordinate the movements of our body necessary for action in the world. Between these two domains lies prefrontal cortex, the interface between our *internal representations* (of ourselves and of the world) and our *action* in the world. As such, prefrontal cortex represents the highest development, the apotheosis, of the forces of evolution that have formed our brain into such an astonishingly versatile and flexible mediator of adaptive behavior.

This picture of prefrontal functioning has emerged from a number of converging lines of evidence. The study of humans with prefrontal lesions has revealed a rich, if sometimes bewildering, array of data. This includes evidence of impairment in the areas of emotion, social behavior, memory, conceptual thinking, language, inventiveness, divergent thinking, planning, the goal-directed organization of behavior, and the revision and modulation of behavior on the basis of self-initiated evaluation and external feedback regarding its results.

Animal studies have greatly expanded our understanding of prefrontal function by making possible the study of the physiological activity of prefrontal neurons and the relation between that activity and behavior. They have also made possible more detailed and revealing studies of neuroanatomical connections between prefrontal cortex and other areas of the brain than is possible in humans. In addition, animal studies have made it possible, through the study of the effects of small, well-localized lesions in different prefrontal subareas, to discover and delineate specialization of function within monkey prefrontal cortex. These converging lines of evidence have led to the hypothesis that prefrontal cortex supports working memory processes that hold "on-line" internal representations of the immediate environment (from posterior perceptual centers) and the past environment (from a number of structures contributing to the mediation of short-term and long-term memory), together with representations of the organism's internal motivational and emotional state (from limbic processing centers). The integration of these elements, via prefrontally mediated working memory, generates plans that are ultimately expressed in the form of commands to motor centers. These commands initiate, organize, and regulate behavior on the basis of representational knowledge.

We are just beginning to understand the functional role of prefrontal cortex, the region of the brain that is most essentially related to who we are, both as human beings and as individuals. No current theory explains all of the known complexities of its functioning. Nevertheless, the hypothesis that the essence of prefrontal function is the regulation of behavior by representational knowledge held "on-line" in working memory provides a coherent framework for our attempts to understand its function. It also has generated many detailed and testable subhypotheses that have deepened our understanding of the relationship between prefrontal cortex and the higher-order regulation of behavior, and it holds the promise of continuing to do so in the future.

CHAPTER 13

Psychopathology

WHAT IS PSYCHOPATHOLOGY?

THE SCHIZOPHRENIC DISORDERS
Description
The Hypothesis of Multiple Etiologies
  of Schizophrenia
Genetic Factors
The Dopamine Hypothesis of Schizophrenia
Gross Structural Abnormalities
Microstructural Abnormalities
Abnormalities Revealed by Functional Imaging
Neurological Abnormalities in Schizophrenia
Neuropsychological Functioning in Schizophrenia
The Hypothesis That Prefrontal Dysfunction
  Underlies Schizophrenia

MOOD DISORDERS
Major Depressive Disorder
Seasonal Affective Disorder
Bipolar Disorder

ANXIETY DISORDERS
General Neurochemical Factors
Simple Phobias
Generalized Anxiety Disorder
Panic Disorder
Obsessive-Compulsive Disorder

SOCIOPATHY

DEMENTING DISEASES
Alzheimer's Disease: A Cortical Dementia
Subcortical Dementias

UNSOLVED PROBLEMS
The Heterogeneity of Diagnostic Categories
Invalid Findings
Inferring Cause Based on the Effective Treatment
  of Symptoms
Disentangling Cause and Effect
Levels of Explanation

SUMMARY

Major psychiatric disorders can severely disrupt behavior and cause enormous suffering. They are also quite common; we all know someone afflicted with a serious psychiatric disorder, perhaps someone very close to us. In this chapter we examine some of the evidence indicating that neurobiological factors play a major role in at least some forms of psychopathology. We begin with a brief discussion concerning problems confronted in attempts to formulate a satisfactory definition of psychopathology. One of these problems is the tension between biological and psychological approaches to its understanding. We will see that how we define psychopathology has important implications for our attitude toward these disorders and their treatment. In subsequent sections we examine biological factors in schizophrenia, mood disorders, anxiety disorders, sociopathy, and degenerative dementing

disorders, including Alzheimer's disease. We will pay particular attention to schizophrenia, both because of the importance of the disorder and because a wide range of evidence regarding biological factors in schizophrenia has

emerged in recent years. We end with a consideration of problems in the interpretation of biological factors in psychopathology.

WHAT IS PSYCHOPATHOLOGY?

In attempting to reach a definition of psychopathology, it is important to note that the very word we use to designate the problems people face has theoretical connotations. Thus, *psychopathology* means "soul (*psycho*) sickness (*pathos*)," indicating an *illness.* This is a construct that replaced the earlier idea, common well into the 19th century, that people with psychiatric problems were possessed by evil spirits or somehow bad or morally deficient. The illness, or medical, model took the onus off the individual. If someone's problems were the result of an illness, then punishment and condemnation would not be effective forms of treatment. This view changed the manner in which people with psychiatric disorders were treated, making such treatment much more humane (Figure 13.1).

The concept of mental illness turns out, however, to be somewhat complicated. What exactly do we mean when we designate people with certain problems as ill? Do we mean that in each case there is an at least potentially demonstrable lesion that is responsible for the disorder? This conception is problematic because many psychiatric disorders are not accompanied by known physical abnormalities. This has led some to criticize the medical model and to speak instead in terms of constructs that do not connote health or illness, such as *problems in living* (Szasz, 1961). In addition, as we will see in this chapter, those disorders that do have specific neurobiological correlates do not have unequivocally established biological causes. Moreover, suppose we accept the assumption that all behavior patterns are determined by specific brain states, and assume further that at some point in the future we will be in a position to understand the neurobiological basis of psychiatric disorders. It nevertheless remains unclear, given the present state of our knowledge, to what extent the neurobiological level

FIGURE 13.1   William Norris in chains in Bethlehem Hospital. *(Anonymous etching, 19th century, Clements C. Fry Collection, Yale Medical Library [in Andreasen, 1984, p. ii])*

of analysis is currently useful for the understanding and treatment of specific psychiatric disorders. To illustrate this point, consider Gleitman's (1995) example of an individual who has no cognitive disability but has simply not been taught to read. Although it may someday be possible to understand this lack of skill in terms of neurobiological mechanisms (or the absence of mechanisms), it is likely to be more useful to understand the person's inability to read simply in terms of the absence of instruction in this skill. A similar argument may apply to at least certain forms of psychopathology, regardless of our level of understanding of the brain mechanisms underlying them.

Although these distinctions may appear somewhat abstract and esoteric, they are actually of critical importance because how we conceptualize the causal basis of psychopathology profoundly influences what we conceive an adequate understanding of these disorders to be and how we go about trying to achieve that understanding. It also influences how we attempt to help individuals with these disorders. A glance at the history of psychiatry reveals how diverse conceptions of psychopathology have been. Consider, for example, the second decade of the 20th century. At that time Sigmund Freud was attempting to understand psychopathology as the result of dynamic conflict between conscious mental processes, known to the individual, and unconscious mental processes that he believed could be inferred from studying and treating his patients (Freud, 1940/1949). Freud adopted this approach after abandoning earlier attempts to formulate a biologically based theory of psychopathology. This attempt is exemplified by his unfinished *Project for a Scientific Psychology* (Freud, 1895/1966). Thus, despite his enthusiastic dedication to neurobiology in the early period of his career and his subsequent attempt in the *Project* to formulate a neurobiological theory of psychopathology, Freud nevertheless came to believe that such attempts were hopelessly premature. He therefore focused on psychological factors contributing to psychopathology, although he continued to emphasize the importance of biological factors, particularly drives.

A bold example of Freud's eventual emphasis on psychological factors is his *Schreber* case study, in which he attempts to understand a case of psychosis in terms of dynamic conflict (Freud, 1913/1958). Treatment, for Freud, consisted in making unconscious content and motivation conscious, so that individuals could come to know themselves more completely and thereby exercise greater conscious control over their experience and behavior. In contrast, this is also the decade in which John Watson (1913) made his emphatic argument that the only legitimate study of psychology is behavior. From the behaviorist perspective, psychopathology results from prior learning, and its treatment must therefore involve the application of the principles of learning theory, including classical and operant conditioning.

At the same time that these two very different conceptions of the cause of psychopathology were being espoused, biologically oriented approaches were also being pursued. These are epitomized by Emil Kraepelin's attempts to discover the neurobiological causes of psychopathology, particularly schizophrenia (or *dementia praecox*, as it was then called). Kraepelin (1921) is deservedly enshrined in the history of psychopathology for his magnificently accurate and detailed descriptions of psychiatric symptoms and his attempts to classify these into valid and useful diagnostic categories. He is less well known for his intense research into the biological basis of psychopathology, particularly schizophrenia. To conduct this research, Kraepelin brought together in his Munich laboratory some of the most prominent neuroscientists of his day. These included Alois Alzheimer, who had recently identified some of the neuropathological correlates of the disease that now bears his name, and Korbinian Brodmann, whose cytoarchitectonic map of the cerebral cortex has since proved to be so useful to neuroscience. Also in Kraepelin's laboratory was Franz Nissl, a psychiatrist who also developed the histological stain (that now bears his name), which selectively reveals neuron cell bodies and which was used by Brodmann in his cytoarchitectonic analysis of the cortex.

At the time, there was reason to hope that this stellar group would discover something important about the biological causes of schizophrenia and other psychiatric disorders. As mentioned, Alzheimer had recently identified neuropathological abnormalities in the brains of persons who had suffered from dementia. In addition, a few years earlier, in 1897, Richard von Krafft-Ebbing had made an important discovery that provided encouragement to biologically oriented approaches to psychopathology. His discovery had to do with the condition then known as general paresis and now known to be a form of syphilis. **General paresis** was characterized by a progressive general decline of physical and psychological functioning, culminating in personality changes, disturbed gait, delusions, and, ultimately, dementia and death. **Syphilis** is caused by a bacterial infection, the overt symptoms of which are usually evident from the beginning. In a small percentage of cases, however, the acute signs of infection clear and may not reappear until years after the infection is contracted. Krafft-Ebbing demonstrated that patients with general paresis in fact had a form of syphilis with delayed onset of symptoms. He established this by injecting material from the sores of syphilitic patients into patients with general paresis and showing that they did not develop any of the early symptoms of syphilis, thus demonstrating that they already had contracted the infection. Krafft-Ebbing had thus shown that general paresis, considered in the 19th century to be a major psychiatric disorder, was caused by a bacterial infection. By 1911, Hideyo Noguchi had identified the specific bacterium responsible for syphilis, *Treponema pallidum,* and the later discovery of penicillin provided a highly effective treatment for this disease.

That a bacterium could cause the disordered thinking that characterizes the psychotic symptoms and ultimate dementia of general paresis dramatically illustrated the potential influence of biological factors in psychopathology and encouraged the hope that biological factors underlying other psychiatric disorders could be discovered. Nevertheless, in spite of this promising and exciting atmosphere, and a great deal of work by some highly talented neuroscientists and clinicians, the results of the efforts of Kraepelin's team were disappointing. No reliable biological correlates of psychopathology emerged from Kraepelin's laboratory. An example of a seemingly promising but ultimately invalid finding that came out of this work was Alzheimer's (1913) report of cell abnormality in layer III of prefrontal cortex in a patient with schizophrenia. We will see that this is not the last false lead generated by neurobiological investigations of psychopathology.

We have gone into these diverse approaches to psychopathology to place the following discussion of biological factors in context. This is very important because the current intellectual climate is factionalized in a way that tends to generate extreme positions regarding biological factors in psychopathology. Some proclaim that psychopathology is biologically determined in a manner precisely analogous to physical illness and that, therefore, all investigative strategies should be directed toward the discovery of biological factors and all treatments should be directed to the manipulation of such factors. In contrast, others emphasize the critical importance of psychological and social factors, paying little attention to biological determinants or treatments. What are desperately needed are investigators and clinicians who are able to take a middle ground, sailing, like Odysseus, safely between the Sylla of ignoring biological factors and the Charybdis of ignoring psychosocial factors. In the remainder of this chapter, true to the emphasis of this book, we will be focusing on biological factors in psychopathology. However, we should not lose sight of the ultimate need for a balanced approach to the understanding and treatment of psychopathology. Indeed, many of the recent findings of neurobiological correlates of psychiatric disorders discussed in this chapter, exciting as they are, raise more questions than they answer and reinforce the need to approach the riddle of these disorders from every potentially fruitful level of analysis. With this caveat in clear focus, let's proceed to an examination of neurobiological factors in psychopathology.

THE SCHIZOPHRENIC DISORDERS

Schizophrenia, a diagnostic term coined by Eugen Bleuler (1911/1950), is a severely debilitating disorder, or, more probably, a group of disorders, that has a lifetime prevalence of 1–1.5% (Zigmond et al., 1999, p. 1553). At any given time, about 400,000 people are hospitalized for this condition in the United States (Black & Andreasen, 1994). Schizophrenia is thus a major health problem, and it is estimated that as many as 30% of *all* (i.e., not just psychiatric) hospital beds in the United States are occupied by people with this disorder (Andreasen, 1984). Schizophrenia is typically chronic. Thus, although people with the disorder have times when their symptoms are more or less intense, they rarely recover permanently. The high prevalence of the disorder and the long-term and extremely debilitating nature of its symptoms make its understanding and treatment perhaps the most important research goal in psychiatry today.

Description

Schizophrenia is an extremely complicated condition, with a broad range of symptoms. Different patients may exhibit very different symptom pictures, a finding that has led to the notion, alluded to previously, that what we refer to as schizophrenia is actually a group of disorders. What is more, individual patients may exhibit extreme variability of symptoms over time. Emil Kraepelin's (1919, 1921) classic descriptions of the disease that he called *dementia praecox* were so brilliant that they could still serve as textbook accounts of the disorder. Since Kraepelin's descriptions, however, the notion has emerged that there are two basic domains of symptoms in schizophrenia: positive and negative. We have already confronted this distinction, first articulated by John Hughlings-Jackson, in our discussion of the effects of cerebral lesions, particularly lesions to prefrontal cortex. It will be recalled that positive symptoms are symptoms and behaviors that are present but should not be (e.g., delusions and hallucinations) and negative symptoms are behaviors that are not present but should be (e.g., taking care of one's personal hygiene and engaging in social interaction). Patients with schizophrenia may exhibit one or both types of symptoms.

POSITIVE SYMPTOMS   Positive symptoms in schizophrenia include delusions, hallucinations, bizarre behavior, and formal thought disorder. **Delusions** are beliefs that are not based on reality. Of course, this is a potentially slippery definition because reasonable people can disagree about aspects of reality. To avoid this problem, the most utilized diagnostic criteria for schizophrenia, contained in the American Psychiatric Association's *Diagnostic and Statistical Manual of Mental Disorders*, Fourth Edition (*DSM-IV*) (1994), require that delusional beliefs be patently unrealistic. Believing that people are inserting thoughts into one's thinking (thought insertion) and that they are controlling one's thinking (thought control) are examples of patently unrealistic delusional beliefs. Such beliefs are often extremely frightening for individuals who have them.

Hallucinations are perceptual experiences that are not based on sensory stimuli. They are most often auditory, but may also be visual, somatosensory, olfactory, or gustatory. These are to be distinguished from **illusions,** distortions in perception that most people would make under particular stimulus conditions.

Bizarre behavior is behavior outside the conventional range of behavior for a given context that does not serve any apparent adaptive function. **Formal thought disorder** is disorganization of the form of thinking. This typically manifests itself through the verbal productions of the individual. Speech moves haphazardly and rapidly from one fragmentary referent to another, so that ideas are touched on fleetingly, rather than being logically developed (**loose associations**). The disconnected and disorganized character of this speech has led some to describe it as **word salad.** Patients who exhibit one of these types of positive symptoms may or may not exhibit others.

NEGATIVE SYMPTOMS   Negative symptoms of schizophrenia include the apparent absence of motivation (**avolition**), **social withdrawal,** diminished emotional expression (**blunted affect**), diminished verbal expression (**alogia**), poor judgment, and poor personal hygiene. Individuals with these symptoms often exhibit a general decrease in level of attention, activity level, and self-direction that has led some to characterize them as burned out. As with positive symptoms, there is considerable variability with regard to the nature and the severity of negative symptoms exhibited by different patients. It should also be added that a given individual with schizophrenia might exhibit both positive and negative symptoms.

The Hypothesis of Multiple Etiologies of Schizophrenia

The extreme variability of symptom picture in patients with schizophrenia presents a problem for the idea that schizophrenia is a single disorder. In fact, according to the *DSM-IV*, it is possible for two persons to each receive the diagnosis of schizophrenia without any overlap of symptoms (American Psychiatric Association, 1994, pp. 285–286). In addition, as we will see shortly, there is no single biological abnormality that has been found in all people with the diagnosis of schizophrenia. This suggests that what we refer to in the singular as schizophrenia is in fact a group of disorders with different **etiologies** (from the Greek *aitia,* "cause") and, consequently, different underlying neurobiological abnormalities. We will develop this notion further in later sections. Let's turn now, however, to an examination of neurobiological factors in schizophrenia, beginning with evidence of genetic factors.

Genetic Factors

There is overwhelming evidence that genetic factors contribute to schizophrenia. One of the most informative methods of exploring these factors is **twin studies,** in which the concordance rate for schizophrenia for monozygotic (identical) twins is compared with that for dizygotic (fraternal) twins. **Concordance rate** is the technical term for the probability that if one member of a set of twins has a particular condition, the other member of the set will also. The rationale for this method is that if monozygotic twins, who share all their genes, have a higher concordance rate than dizygotic twins, who share, on average, half their genes, then that constitutes evidence for the presence of a genetic factor. Monozygotic twins have a concordance rate for schizophrenia of about 55%, whereas dizygotic twins have a concordance rate of about 10% (Gottesman & Shields, 1972, 1982; Gottesman, McGuffin, & Farmer, 1987; Tsuang, Gilbertson, & Faraone, 1991).

Further evidence for genetic factors in schizophrenia comes from **adoption studies,** in which children at risk for a condition who have been adopted shortly after birth are studied. The rationale for adoption studies is that if the removal of an infant from a family environment that is correlated with a condition nevertheless results in an incidence of the condition that is higher than baseline, then that environment alone cannot account for the condition. In the case of schizophrenia, about 15% of children of schizophrenic mothers who grow up with those mothers become schizophrenic. One might reasonably speculate that this high incidence of the disorder is due to growing up with a schizophrenic mother. However, the results of adoption studies show that this percentage is unchanged for children of schizophrenic moth-

ers who are adopted immediately after birth (Kendler & Greenberg, 1984; Kety, 1983; Tsuang et al., 1991).

It is important to emphasize that, although twin studies demonstrate the presence of a genetic factor in the etiology of schizophrenia, they also show that the disorder is not entirely genetically determined. If it were, then the concordance rate for monozygotic twins would be 100%, just as it is for such genetically transmitted traits as eye color. In addition, patterns of transmission do not follow any simple pattern, indicating that many genes are involved. None of these genes have been conclusively identified as yet.

The Dopamine Hypothesis of Schizophrenia

EVIDENCE FOR THE DOPAMINE HYPOTHESIS According to the **dopamine hypothesis of schizophrenia,** abnormally increased dopamine activity in the brain is an important factor in schizophrenia. The development of medications formerly known as **antipsychotics,** and now termed **neuroleptics,** such as chlorpromazine (Thorazine) and haloperidol (Haldol); has led to significant control of schizophrenic symptoms in many patients, although the disorder is by no means cured by these drugs. Neuroleptics block dopamine receptors. Evidence for this comes from the parkinsonian symptoms these drugs typically induce and from more direct biochemical and imaging evidence (Bannon & Roth, 1983; Crow, 1982a; Sedvall, 1990). Different neuroleptic medications block dopamine receptors to different degrees, and the magnitude of the therapeutic effect of different neuroleptics is proportional to the magnitude of their dopamine blocking effect (Snyder, 1976). Also consistent with the dopamine hypothesis is the finding that dopamine-enhancing drugs, such as amphetamines, may produce transient psychotic states, as may L-dopa, a dopamine precursor administered for the relief of the symptoms of Parkinson's disease.

In considering the mechanism of dopamine hyperactivity posited by this theory, evidence points to an overabundance of dopamine receptors rather than to the presence of too much dopamine per se. Thus, dopamine levels have not been found to be elevated in patients with schizophrenia, nor have levels of dopamine metabolites such as homovanillic acid (Zigmond et al., 1999, p. 1560). Instead, autopsy studies and PET studies that have labeled dopamine receptors have demonstrated an abnormally high number of dopamine receptors in the brains of people with schizophrenia, including individuals who have never received antipsychotic medication (Andreasen, 1988).

PROBLEMS WITH THE DOPAMINE HYPOTHESIS   There are a number of problems with the dopamine hypothesis. Although the blockade effect of antipsychotic drugs on dopamine receptors is rapid, on the order of hours, the effect of these drugs on the symptoms of schizophrenia is relatively slow, taking weeks (Davis, 1978). This time lag does not seem to fit with the hypothesis that dopamine hyperactivity is the cause of the symptoms. Another problem for the dopamine hypothesis is the diverse response of patients to antipsychotic drugs, ranging from marked reduction in symptoms to no reduction. In addition, as already mentioned, highly variable symptom pictures are seen across different individuals with schizophrenia. It is unclear why dopamine hyperactivity should cause such variable symptom patterns. Moreover, there is significant variability in symptom pattern within individuals, particularly over the course of the disorder. Typically, positive symptoms are pronounced in the early or acute stage of the disorder. This is often followed by a longer period characterized by negative symptoms. Again, it is not obvious how dopamine hyperactivity could account for this changing clinical course.

These problems suggest that in some instances schizophrenia may not be related to dopamine hyperactivity. Alternatively, it has been proposed (Crow, 1982b, 1985) that positive symptoms, often seen in the acute stage of the disorder, are related to an abnormality of dopamine activity, whereas negative symptoms, typically seen later in the course of the disorder, are due to structural abnormalities. We will return to this hypothesis shortly. Finally, it remains possible, indeed it seems likely, that even for those schizophrenic patients with a dopamine abnormality, this may not be the only underlying neurobiological abnormality contributing to their disorder.

REFINEMENT OF THE DOPAMINE HYPOTHESIS   The recent development of so-called **atypical antipsychotics,** such as clozapine (Clozaril), risperidone (Risperdal), and olanzapine (Zyprexa), has led to a refinement of the dopamine hypothesis. These atypical antipsychotics, which appear to act by blocking both dopamine and serotonin receptors, are more effective than the classical neuroleptics in treating many patients with schizophrenia, particularly those with predominantly negative symptoms. This has led to the **dopamine-serotonin interaction hypothesis,** which posits that the neurochemical abnormality in schizophrenia involves both dopaminergic and serotonergic systems (Kapur & Remington, 1996; Megens & Kennis, 1996). It is also possible that the atypical antipsychotics exert their effect by blocking specific types of dopamine receptors that are only minimally blocked by the classical neuroleptics. The latter block primarily D_2 receptors, whereas clozapine, for example, blocks primarily D_4 receptors (Van Tol et al., 1991).

Gross Structural Abnormalities

ENLARGED VENTRICLES   Since early pneumoencephalographic studies, beginning in the 1920s, there has been accumulating evidence that the lateral ventricles of patients with schizophrenia are enlarged. The advent of the CT scan, which yields a much more accurate estimate of ventricular size, provided the opportunity to further assess this variable, and the first reports of ventricular enlargement in schizophrenic patients using CT appeared soon after the development of that technique (Johnstone et al., 1976; Johnstone et al., 1978; Weinberger, D. R., et al., 1979). Figure 13.2 shows enlarged ventricles in a patient with schizophrenia. Since these initial reports, this finding has been reported in a number of other studies (e.g., Crow & Johnstone, 1987; Weinberger, 1995). The precise nature and location of the structural damage causing ventricular enlargement is unclear, although it presumably reflects cell loss in wide areas of the telencephalon.

In some quarters, these reports were interpreted, and continue to be interpreted, as proof that schizophrenia is a brain disorder and that psychological

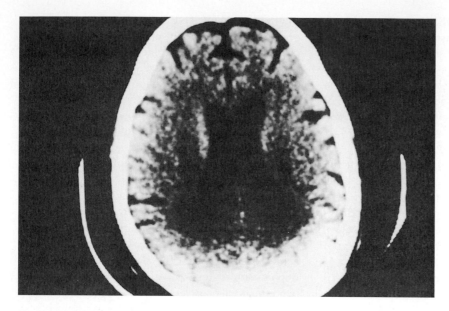

FIGURE 13.2 Ventricular enlargement in a patient with schizophrenia. *(From Andreasen, 1984, p. 169)*

variables therefore do not play a role in its etiology. There are two problems with this conclusion, however. The first is a general problem that applies to the interpretation of many of the findings presented in this chapter: The correlation of a psychiatric disorder with a neurobiological abnormality does not necessarily mean that the neurobiological abnormality is the cause of the disorder. It remains possible that psychological factors may be affecting biological variables. This is perhaps more obvious when considering neurochemical abnormalities, because we have become accustomed to psychological factors, such as stress, influencing neurochemical variables, such as hormone secretion. However, there is no a priori reason for excluding the possibility that psychological factors may cause other neurobiological abnormalities, including structural change.

The second problem with the finding of enlarged ventricles in schizophrenia is more specific to this particular issue. Like every other variable investigated in the history of schizophrenia research, ventricular enlargement is not found reliably in all patients with schizophrenia. This may be seen in Figure 13.3, which shows significant overlap between patients with schizophrenia and normal control subjects in the ratio of ventricular volume to overall brain volume (**ventricular-brain ratio,** or **VBR**).

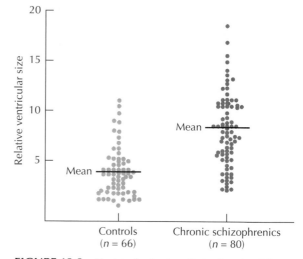

FIGURE 13.3 Ventricular-brain ratio in chronic schizophrenics and normal controls. *(From N. R. Carlson, 1999, p. 444)*

CORTICAL ATROPHY CT scans of the brains of some patients with schizophrenia show evidence of cortical atrophy (Weinberger, D. R., et al., 1979). An

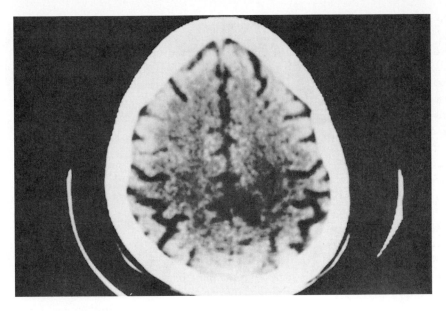

FIGURE 13.4 Cortical atrophy in the brain of a schizophrenic patient. The dark lines are widened sulci. *(From Andreasen, 1984, p. 169)*

example of this appears in Figure 13.4. As with abnormally high VBR, cortical atrophy is not seen in all patients with schizophrenia. Those patients with evidence of ventricular enlargement and/or cortical atrophy presumably have suffered loss of neural tissue. This loss appears, however, to be diffuse in nature, there being no evidence that the abnormality is confined to particular regions of the brain.

THE TWO-SYNDROME HYPOTHESIS OF SCHIZO-PHRENIA   How are we to interpret the finding that some patients with schizophrenia show enlarged ventricles and cortical atrophy, while others do not? Timothy Crow (1982a, 1982b, 1985; Crow & Johnstone, 1987) proposed that these findings may mean that there are two underlying pathological processes in schizophrenia, which he termed Type I and Type II. **Type I** is associated with normal ventricle size, the absence of cortical atrophy, and predominantly positive symptoms; **Type II** is associated with enlarged ventricles, cortical atrophy, and predominantly negative symptoms. This two-syndrome hypothesis was supported by previous findings that VBR was not correlated with race, age, length of illness, length of hospitalization, or type of antipsychotic medication

(Weinberger, D. R., et al., 1979). It was also supported by the well-established finding that antipsychotic medications are far more effective in alleviating positive symptoms of schizophrenia than negative symptoms.

The two-syndrome hypothesis has, however, been beset by a number of problems. One problem is whether the two types represent discrete diseases or different developmental phases of a single syndrome. According to the latter view, Type I, with its positive symptoms and absence of structural abnormality, would represent the early phase of the disorder, which then progresses into the negative symptoms and structural abnormalities characteristic of Type II. The evolution of many cases of schizophrenia from an acute phase, characterized by positive symptoms and improvement with antipsychotic medication, to a longer chronic phase, characterized by negative symptoms and the absence of positive response to neuroleptic medication, would seem to fit with the notion that the two types represent different phases of a single disease entity. On the other hand, some cases have been reported in which enlarged ventricles were seen at the time of acute onset of symptoms. This suggests that structural damage precedes onset of the disease or occurs during the first episode, which is consistent with the notion that the presence or absence of structural abnormality is a marker of two different diseases. The evaluation of these interpretations is further complicated by evidence that the relationship between structural abnormality and negative symptoms may not be as strong as was originally thought. It is clear that a number of issues in this area, both empirical and interpretative, remain unresolved (Andreasen, 1985; Andreasen et al., 1989; Cannon, Mednick, & Parnas, 1990; Zorilla & Cannon, 1995).

CEREBELLAR ATROPHY   There have been reports of cerebellar atrophy in patients with schizophrenia (Jacobsen et al., 1997; Martin & Albers, 1995). It remains unclear at this time what proportion of patients have this abnormality and what its functional significance may be.

FALSE LEADS   There have been a number of reports of structural abnormality in schizophrenia that have later been shown to be invalid. Although such findings are usually omitted from reviews of current knowledge, a brief look at two examples may prove useful as reminders of the caution required in interpreting new findings.

Abnormally Small Prefrontal Lobes   The hypothesis that prefrontal dysfunction is a critical component of schizophrenia was proposed early on by Emil Kraepelin (1919), and, as we will soon see, there is considerable support for this idea. Thus, when Andreasen and her colleagues (1986) reported the results of an MRI study in which patients with schizophrenia had abnormally small frontal lobes, this finding fit nicely into a compelling theoretical framework. Unfortunately, subsequent attempts by Andreasen to replicate her findings were unsuccessful.

Reversed Cerebral Asymmetry   In contrast to the report of smaller frontal lobes in schizophrenia, which was consistent with a theory of dysfunction in the disease, reports of reversed cerebral asymmetry emerged out of an atheoretic empiricism that cast as wide a net

as possible in its search for structural abnormalities. In this case the reported asymmetry was rather esoteric. In a majority of normal brains the left frontal pole curves slightly across the midline, as does the right occipital pole. This lends a slight clockwise torque to the brain. Patients with schizophrenia were reported to more often exhibit the opposite torque (Tsai, Nasralla, & Jacoby, 1983). The functional implications of such a reversal are far from obvious. However, as we mentioned, this report has not been corroborated by the results of subsequent studies.

Microstructural Abnormalities

Turning now to structural changes in schizophrenia revealed by microscopic examination of the brains of schizophrenic patients at autopsy, the most reliable finding is that of structural abnormalities in medial temporal-lobe structures, including the parahippocampal gyrus and the hippocampus (Roberts, 1990). In particular, alterations in pyramidal cell orientation in the anterior and middle hippocampus (Figure 13.5) have been reported (Kovelman & Scheibel, 1984; Scheibel & Kovelman, 1980). This abnormality is not seen in chronic alcoholism, temporal-lobe epilepsy, Huntington's disease, or Alzheimer's disease and may be specific to schizophrenia. It has been suggested that these abnormalities may be a milder form of the disruption in cell migration during embryogenesis seen in certain genetic strains of mice (Kovelman & Scheibel, 1984).

There are also reports of pathological changes associated with decreased volume in the hippocampus and entorhinal cortex (Bogerts, Meetz, & Schonfeldt-Bausch, 1985). These findings suggest that schizophrenia is a developmental abnormality that preferentially affects medial temporal-lobe structures, particularly the hippocampus. Given the importance of the hippocampus for integrating and remembering aspects of the environment, disrupted synaptic connections in this area might contribute importantly to the disorganizing effects of schizophrenic symptoms.

Other areas implicated by postmortem studies include limbic, neostriatal, and brain-stem structures, including the septal nuclei, the nucleus accumbens,

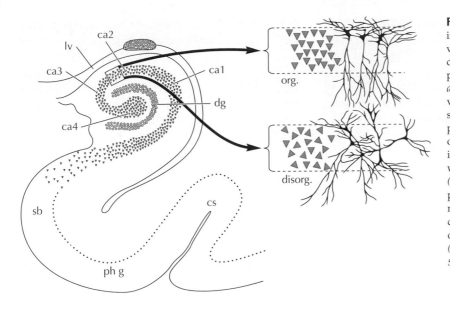

FIGURE 13.5 A conceptualized coronal section through the ventromedial temporal lobe: *cs,* collateral sulcus; *ph g,* parahippocampal gyrus; *sb,* subiculum; *dg,* dentate gyrus; *lv,* lateral ventricle; *ca1, ca2, ca3,* and *ca4,* standard divisions of the hippocampus. The area of *ca1/ca2* outlined in the square is shown in enlarged form to the right, where disorganized tissue (*disorg.*), seen in schizophrenic patients, is contrasted with organized tissue (*org.*), seen in normal controls. The histology is based on cresyl violet (*left*) and Golgi (*right*) stains. (*From Kovelman & Sheibel, 1984, p. 1613*)

the substantia innominata, the globus pallidus, and the bed nucleus of the stria terminalis (Fishman, 1975; Nieto & Escobar, 1972; Stevens, 1982). Abnormalities have also been reported in the cortex and thalamus (Heckers, 1997). There have been some reports of neuropathological abnormalities in prefrontal cortex (Miyakawa et al., 1972; Tatetsu, 1964), including abnormalities in the density and processes of neurons in anterior cingulate cortex (Benes & Bird, 1987; Benes, Davidson, & Bird, 1986), although it is unclear whether these abnormalities are specific to prefrontal structures.

Abnormalities Revealed by Functional Imaging

Ingvar and Franzen (1974a, 1974b) were the first to report an abnormality in cerebral blood flow (rCBF) in patients with schizophrenia. They found that, although cerebral blood flow is higher in frontal cortex than in other cortical regions in normal subjects at rest (see also Ingvar, 1979), patients with schizophrenia fail to exhibit this effect. They termed this abnormality **hypofrontality.** These patients also failed to exhibit the normal increase in frontal blood flow that follows visual, haptic, or noxious stimuli (Franzen &

Ingvar, 1975a, 1975b; Ingvar, 1980). They also reported that the degree of hypofrontality was correlated with the severity of negative symptoms, whereas patients with positive symptoms had abnormally high posterior rCBF.

Since these initial reports, there have been many other reports of decreased frontal activity in schizophrenia. These include decreased blood flow (Ariel et al., 1983; Berman & Weinberger, 1986; Weinberger, Berman, & Zec, 1986) and decreased glucose metabolism (Figure 13.6), as assessed by PET (Buchsbaum et al., 1984; Buchsbaum et al., 1982; DeLisi et al., 1985; Farkas et al., 1984; Wolkin et al., 1985). However, decreased frontal activation has not been reported in all studies of schizophrenic patients in the resting state (Gur et al., 1987; Mathew et al., 1982; Rubin, Holm, et al., 1991; Sheppard et al., 1983). Fuster (1997, p. 202) has suggested that this discrepancy may be due to a number of factors, including differences in the definition of resting state, the multifaceted character of schizophrenia, unreliability of diagnostic criteria (including those stipulated by the *DSM-IV*), technical and methodological differences between studies, and the confounding effects of antipsychotic medication.

Functional imaging studies that have required subjects to perform specific tasks have yielded more

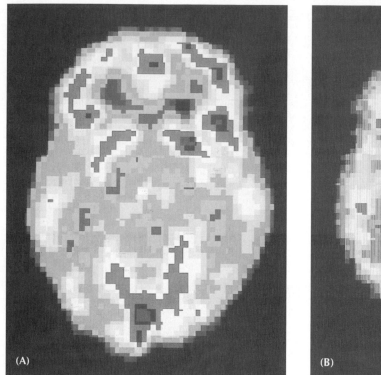
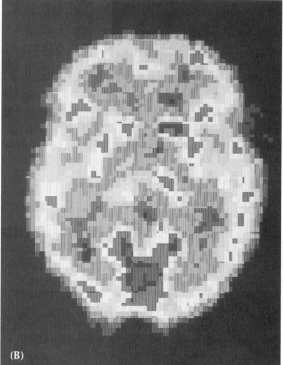

FIGURE 13.6   PET scan showing brain metabolic activity of *(A)* a normal control subject and *(B)* a patient with schizophrenia who was not receiving antipsychotic medication. The schizophrenic patient shows lower frontal metabolic activity than the control subject. *(From Sarason & Sarason, 1999, p. 337)*

consistent results. This is because these studies control for variation of activity during the resting state. In addition, by requiring subjects to perform a task that is known to involve a particular brain region, it is possible to assess whether individuals with a particular disorder show the expected increase in activity in that region. For example, Weinberger and his colleagues (Berman, Zec, & Weinberger, 1986; Weinberger, Berman, & Illowsky, 1988; Weinberger, D. R., et al., 1986) studied rCBF in patients with schizophrenia who were performing an automated version of the Wisconsin Card Sorting Test in which they indicated their sorting choice by pressing one of four buttons. The control task was a simple number-matching task that involved similar sensory stimuli and motor responses. Regional cerebral blood flow was also tested during the resting state. No differences were found between the patients with schizophrenia and normal subjects in the resting state and in the number-matching task. However, during performance of the Wisconsin Card Sorting Test, patients with schizophrenia failed to exhibit the increases in blood flow in dorsolateral prefrontal and in precentral cortex that were seen in normal control subjects (Figure 13.7). In subsequent studies of monozygotic twins discordant for schizophrenia, each twin with schizophrenia was found to be hypofrontal relative to the well twin in the card sorting but not the control or resting condition (Berman & Weinberger, 1992; Weinberger, D. R., et al., 1992). Patients with schizophrenia fail to exhibit prefrontal activation during the performance of other tasks normally associated with such activation (and normally depending on prefrontal pro-

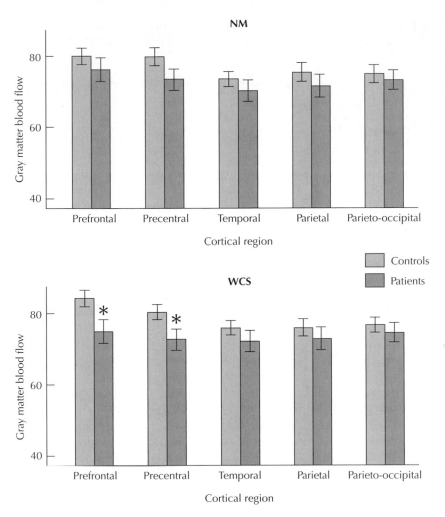

FIGURE 13.7 Regional analysis of cerebral blood flow for control subjects and patients with chronic schizophrenia during number matching (NM) and during performance of the Wisconsin Card Sorting Test (WCS). Asterisks indicate that, during the WCS Test, values for patients were lower than for controls in prefrontal and precentral regions. *(From Berman, Zec, & Weinberger, 1986, p. 129)*

cessing). These tasks include the Tower of London task (Andreasen et al., 1992), the Stroop Test (Carter et al., 1997), and others (Andreasen et al., 1994).

Positron emission tomography has been used to assess the number of dopamine receptors in the brains of schizophrenics (Andreasen, 1988). These studies have revealed an overproduction, or hypertrophy, of D_2 receptors in the basal ganglia (Wong et al., 1986), although there is some question as to whether this is a secondary effect of prolonged use of neuroleptic medication (Farde et al., 1990; Jaskiw & Kleinman, 1988). Imaging studies of receptor characteristics in schizophrenia, particularly those investigating never-medicated patients, show great promise in further revealing the mechanisms of the biochemical abnormality in this disorder.

Neurological Abnormalities in Schizophrenia

No reliable neurological abnormalities have been reported in schizophrenia. Neurological "soft signs," such as slightly hyperreactive or hyporeactive reflexes, have been reported to be present in 35–75% of schizophrenic patients. However, the significance of these findings is unclear because soft signs comprise a heterogeneous group of abnormalities, no one of

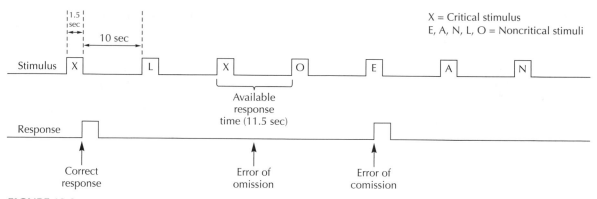

FIGURE 13.8   An example of the simple form of the Continuous Performance Test. The subject must respond whenever an X appears, but not when other stimuli appear. In the example, the stimulus appears for 1.5 seconds and then there is a 10-second inter-stimulus interval. In more complicated versions of the test, the subject must respond to a given stimulus (e.g., X) only when it is preceded by another specific stimulus (e.g., L).

which is exhibited by a significant proportion of patients with schizophrenia. EEG evidence of seizure abnormality is not consistently seen in patients with schizophrenia.

Impairment in smooth pursuit eye movement is seen in some patients with schizophrenia. This is the type of eye movement employed when one is following the movement of an oscillating object, such as a pendulum, without moving one's head. In schizophrenic patients with this impairment, smooth pursuit eye movements are jerky and disorganized. This impairment is not seen in all schizophrenic patients. In those who do show it, however, it is seen in a high proportion of first-degree relatives (parents and siblings), suggesting that its determinants are at least partly genetic. It has been hypothesized that a disruption of brain-stem mechanisms and/or prefrontal dysfunction may underlie this impairment.

Neuropsychological Functioning in Schizophrenia

ATTENTIONAL IMPAIRMENT   As one might expect, patients with schizophrenia do poorly on a wide range of tests of cognitive function (Heaton &

Crowley, 1981). This is hardly surprising, given the vulnerability of most cognitive processes to the disruptive effects of both the positive and negative symptoms of the disorder. In particular, symptoms of schizophrenia severely disrupt attentional processes. Evidence for this comes from the responses of patients with schizophrenia on the Continuous Performance Test (Heaton, Budde, & Johnson, 1978). On this test, subjects are presented with a series of stimuli. They must respond either to a particular stimulus or, in more difficult versions of the test, to a particular stimulus when it is preceded by another specific stimulus (Figure 13.8).

TEMPORAL-LOBE AND PREFRONTAL DYSFUNCTION   Attentional impairments are likely to result in impairment on a number of measures of cognitive functioning. Nevertheless, there is evidence that schizophrenia may cause specific impairment in measures of temporal-lobe and prefrontal function (Kolb & Whishaw, 1983). Thus, patients with schizophrenia have been reported to be impaired on tests of verbal and nonverbal memory and on measures of prefrontal functioning, including tests of working memory, cognitive flexibility, and planning (Goldman-Rakic, 1987; Weinberger, D. R., et al., 1988). They are less impaired on tasks tapping parietal-lobe function, including tests of spatial orientation or visual discrimination. Efforts to relate particular subtypes of schizophrenia to different patterns of neuropsychological functioning have not been highly successful (Bernstein, Riedel, & Graae, 1988). There are, however, reports that neuropsychological impairment is more severe in patients with negative symptoms than in patients with positive symptoms (Crow & Johnstone, 1987). In a later section, we will examine further the hypothesis that prefrontal dysfunction is an important component in schizophrenia.

THE LEFT-HEMISPHERE HYPOTHESIS Flor-Henry (1969) has proposed that schizophrenia is caused by an abnormality of the left hemisphere, whereas mood disorders are associated with right-hemisphere abnormality. This hypothesis has a certain conceptual appeal, because the impairments of speech and logic and the verbal auditory hallucinations seen in many patients with schizophrenia appear, on the face of things, to be more related to abnormality of the hemisphere specialized for speech. There has also been some empirical support for the idea that schizophrenia is related to overactivation of the left hemisphere (Bruder, 1995; Gur, 1978). There is also some evidence that the positive symptoms of schizophrenia are related to left-hemisphere overactivation, whereas the negative symptoms are associated with right-hemisphere activation (Gruzelier, 1981, 1984; Gruzelier & Hammond, 1980).

Inconsistent with the left-hemisphere hypothesis is evidence that patients with a known left temporal-lobe seizure focus are no more likely to have schizophrenia than patients who have a right temporal-lobe focus (T. Rasmussen, personal communication, 1981). In addition, in spite of the word salad character of the speech of patients with Wernicke's aphasia, discussed in chapter 6, true schizophrenic symptoms very rarely occur after lateralized lesions to either hemisphere. Finally, the structural abnormalities in the brains of patients with schizophrenia that have been revealed by CT and MRI studies have been bilateral, as have functional abnormalities reported in rCBF, PET, and fMRI studies. Taken together, evidence for a lateralized brain abnormality in schizophrenia is not compelling at this time.

The Hypothesis That Prefrontal Dysfunction Underlies Schizophrenia

Since Kraepelin's initial hypothesis that schizophrenia is caused by prefrontal abnormality, schizophrenia has often been related to abnormality of this part of the brain (Alzheimer, 1913; Franzen & Ingvar, 1975b; Ingvar, 1980; Luria, 1966; Weinberger, D. R., et al., 1986; Winn, 1994). This hypothesis fits with similarities in the symptom picture of schizophrenia and prefrontal lesions. Thus, in both conditions, elementary sensory-motor function is unimpaired, whereas the capacity for the higher-order regulation of behavior is severely disrupted. Furthermore, both conditions are characterized by the disorganization and fragmentation of behavior, with the result that behavior tends to be bizarre, idiosyncratic, and unrelated to long-range goals and plans. Rather than being regulated by the integration of current, past, and internal information, behavior is often dominated by immediate stimuli, irrelevant to long-term goals, or by internal drive states, the expression of which is also not in the individual's long-term interest. Fuster (1997, p. 203) has characterized this similarity of abnormality in schizophrenia and prefrontal lesions as disruption of the ability to construct logically coherent temporal gestalts and to use these to guide behavior.

Consistent with these similarities in symptom picture is evidence that patients with schizophrenia are impaired on formal measures of cognitive functioning that are sensitive to the effects of prefrontal lesions (Goldberg et al., 1987; Levin, 1984a, 1984b; Taylor & Abrams, 1984). These include tests of attention (Nuechterlein & Dawson, 1984), working memory (Goldman-Rakic, 1987, 1991; Park, 1995; Park & Holzman, 1992), oculomotor function (Levin, 1984a, 1984b; Levin et al., 1981; Mialet & Pichot, 1981), and the capacity to flexibly shift the conceptual basis of behavior (Kolb & Whishaw, 1983; Malmo, 1974). Of particular interest is the hypothesis that impairment in working memory is a major component of schizophrenia. From this perspective, many of the behavioral abnormalities in schizophrenia result from a breakdown in the process by which representational knowledge regulates behavior, a process mediated by prefrontal cortex (see chapter 12).

This notion is consistent with evidence from functional imaging studies, reviewed earlier, that patients with schizophrenia fail to show activation of prefrontal cortex during the performance of tasks that normally are associated with such activation. It is also consistent with reports of prefrontal EEG abnormality (Knight, 1984; Knight et al., 1980; Morihisa, Duffy, & Wyatt, 1983) and prefrontal morphological abnormality (Benes et al., 1986; Benes & Bird, 1987; Miyakawa et al., 1972) in schizophrenia. Moreover, the hypothesis of prefrontal abnormality in schizophrenia is consistent with evidence of an abnormality of dopamine activity in the disorder. Prefrontal cortex has among the highest dopamine concentrations of any brain region (Brown, Crane, & Goldman, 1979). This dopaminergic input to prefrontal cortex arises from the substantia nigra and neighboring groups of cells in the midbrain, which make diffuse and widely spread connections to the basal ganglia, via nigrostriatal pathways, as well as to prefrontal cortex, via mesocortical connections. In contrast to the vast majority of neurons, which are engaged in the rapid point-to-point excitatory or inhibitory transmission of signals, these nigral-prefrontal dopaminergic connections exert a relatively slow, long-term, and widespread neuromodulatory effect on prefrontal cortex, via the activation of second messenger systems (see chapter 2). It seems probable that disruption of this neuromodulatory dopaminergic input to prefrontal cortex is an important factor in the compromised prefrontal function and activation seen in schizophrenia.

In our previous discussion of the dopamine hypothesis, it was proposed that the positive symptoms of schizophrenia may be due to dopamine hyperactivity, whereas the negative symptoms may be due to some other factor or factors. One candidate for a factor contributing to negative symptoms is a *decrease* in dopamine activity in prefrontal cortex (A. Carlson, 1988; Crow, 1980; K. L. Davis et al., 1991; Grace, 1991; Heritch, 1990; MacLay, 1980; Weinberger, D. R., et al., 1988). This could account for the prefrontal-related impairments seen in schizophrenia, including impair-

ment in working memory (Luciana et al., 1992). From this perspective, positive symptoms are associated with dopamine hyperactivity in limbic structures, whereas negative symptoms are associated with dopamine underactivity in prefrontal cortex. The pattern of positive and negative symptoms seen in any one patient would thus result from the relative prominence of these two factors. As mentioned earlier, schizophrenia often begins with prominent positive symptoms and then evolves into a negative symptom picture. It may be that the initial positive symptom picture results from dopamine hyperactivity in limbic structures and that the mechanism of the disorder then somehow shifts to prefrontal hypoactivity, leading to a predominance of negative symptoms. Consistent with the hypothesis that prefrontal dopamine hypoactivity underlies the negative symptoms of schizophrenia are reports that depletion of prefrontal dopamine in monkeys produced by lesions of the ventral tegmental area (Simon, Scatton, & Le Moal, 1980) or by destruction of prefrontal cortical terminals (Brozoski et al., 1979) is followed by cognitive and motivational impairments like those characteristic of prefrontal dysfunction. This hypothesis also would account for the well-established finding that negative symptoms are generally not improved by dopamine-blocking medication.

MOOD DISORDERS

Mood disorders, formerly termed **affective disorders,** include disorders that have a long-term disturbance of mood as their predominant feature. In this section, we will consider biological aspects of three mood disorders: major depressive disorder, seasonal affective disorder, and bipolar disorder.

Major Depressive Disorder

DESCRIPTION   Major depressive disorder (also called **unipolar depression**) is characterized by dysphoric (sad, depressed) mood and/or loss of interest and pleasure in nearly all activities. Associated symptoms include changes in appetite and weight (increase or decrease), sleep disturbance, decreased psychomotor activity, decreased energy, feelings of worthlessness or guilt, difficulty concentrating and making decisions, and thoughts of death. The disorder may be life threatening; as many as 15% of persons with the disorder die by suicide. The lifetime risk of major depression is estimated to be about 12%, while the prevalence at any given time is estimated to be about 5%. The writer William Styron (1990) has provided a vivid personal account of his struggle with severe depression.

In the past, major depression was categorized as endogenous or reactive. **Endogenous depression** referred to depression caused by internal factors, presumably biological, whereas **reactive depression** referred to depression caused by external (i.e., interpersonal and social) factors. Depression is no longer conceptualized as falling into these two discrete categories because it is now realized that, like most psychiatric disorders, it almost always is caused by the interaction of environmental factors and internal, predisposing factors. In a minority of cases, major depression is accompanied by delusional thoughts that are usually congruent with the individual's depressed mood. These may include unrealistic beliefs about supposed personal transgressions, unrealistic feelings of guilt, and the belief that one deserves to be punished.

Vegetative symptoms refer to symptoms of depression that are presumed to be more directly related to brain dysfunction. These include disturbances of sleep (trouble falling asleep, early awakening, or excessive sleeping), loss of appetite, diurnal mood variation, and decreased sex drive. Sleep disturbance may also include more rapid onset of rapid eye movement (REM) sleep.

THE MONOAMINE HYPOTHESIS OF DEPRESSION   The three major monoamine neurotransmitters in the brain are the catecholamines dopamine and norepinephrine and the indoleamine serotonin. Drugs that increase brain monoamine levels, such as the **tricyclic antidepressants** and the **monoamine oxidase inhibitors,** alleviate depression. In addition, drugs that decrease monoamine levels, such as **reserpine,** may induce depression in individuals who were not previously depressed. These findings have led to the **monoamine hypothesis of depression,** which posits

that abnormally low levels of monoamines play a role in depression. Although dopamine agonists, such as amphetamine or cocaine, may transiently elevate mood in normal individuals, they do not alleviate the symptoms of major depression. For this reason, research on the biochemistry of depression has focused on norepinephrine and serotonin, and there is some evidence that there may be two subtypes of depression related to decreased levels of each of these two neurotransmitters. Evidence for this comes from the finding that increasing activity of either one has been shown to alleviate the symptoms of depression (Andreasen, 1984, p. 234; Duman, Heninger, & Nestler, 1997; Miller et al., 1996). This has led to more specific refinements of the monoamine hypothesis: the **catecholamine hypothesis of depression** and the **serotonin hypothesis of depression.**

Other evidence for a specific role of serotonin in depression includes the finding that as many as 45% of persons with major depressive disorder have an abnormally low level of **5-hydroxyindoleacetic acid,** a metabolite of serotonin. Also consistent with the serotonin hypothesis is the effectiveness of the antidepressants known as **selective serotonin reuptake inhibitors (SSRIs),** which, as their name implies, elevate the activity level of brain serotonin by selectively inhibiting its reuptake by presynaptic axon terminals (see chapter 2). The first drug in this class, fluoxetine (Prozac), has been effective in treating the symptoms of major depression (Kramer, 1993). Other SSRIs include paroxetine (Paxil) and sertaline (Zoloft).

POSSIBLE ENDOCRINE DYSFUNCTION IN DEPRESSION   Stress induces a number of endocrine responses, including the release of cortisol from the adrenal cortex. This involves a cascade of processes that eventually activates the hypothalamus, triggering its release of **corticotropin releasing hormone (CRH).** This, in turn, triggers the release of **adrenocorticotrophic hormone (ACTH)** by the pituitary, which causes the adrenal cortex to release **cortisol.** In normal individuals, when the blood level of cortisol reaches an optimum level for the activation of a stress response, negative feedback loops to the pituitary and hypothalamus shut down the release of ACTH and CRH, respectively. However, some patients with depression continue to release cortisol beyond optimum levels, presumably due to a disruption of the regulatory mechanisms mediated by the hypothalamic-pituitary-adrenal axis, the hypothalamic component of which is probably regulated by norepinephrine neurons in the locus ceruleus. The net result is an abnormal increase in cortisol levels that exerts a widespread influence on cerebral functioning (Andreasen, 1984).

ABNORMALITIES REVEALED BY FUNCTIONAL IMAGING   There have been reports that major depression is associated with decreased blood flow and reduced metabolic activity in frontal regions (Baxter et al., 1989; Buchsbaum et al., 1984; Buchsbaum et al., 1986; Cohen et al., 1989; Lingjaerde, 1993; Martinot et al., 1990) and in the whole brain (Baxter et al., 1985). An example of these findings is shown in Figure 13.9. It has also been reported that depressed patients who respond well to ECT show a specific increase in blood flow in prefrontal cortex that is correlated with the amount of reduced prefrontal blood flow that they had shown prior to treatment (Nobler et al., 1994). This hypofrontality in depression resembles that seen in schizophrenia (Cohen et al., 1989). However, it has been reported that patients with depression differ from patients with schizophrenia in that the former do not show an absence of prefrontal activation when challenged with tasks, such as the Wisconsin Card Sorting Test, that normally are associated with such activation (Berman et al., 1993). In addition, unlike schizophrenic patients, patients with major depression do not exhibit a pattern of cognitive impairment that is characteristic of abnormality in any specific brain region. Because major depression severely disrupts attention, concentration, and motivation, it is associated with impairment on all cognitive tasks that significantly draw on these processes.

In contrast to these reports of decreased prefrontal activity in patients with depression, Drevets and colleagues (1992) have reported increased metabolic activity in depression in an area extending from the ventromedial area of the left prefrontal cortex, through its anterior convexity, and into its medial surface; this study also reported increased activity in the left

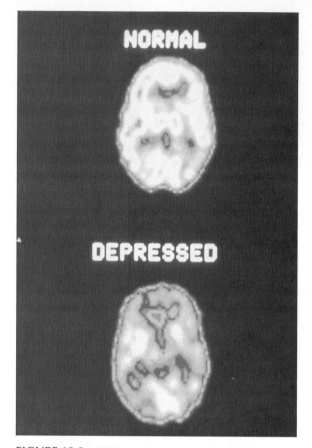

FIGURE 13.9   PET scan showing reduction in brain metabolic activity, particularly in the frontal areas, in a patient with major depression. The scan of a normal control subject is included for comparison. *(From H. Gleitman, Fridlund, & Reisberg, 1999, p. 20)*

amygdala. Increased blood flow in the cingulate gyrus in depressed patients has also been reported (Wu et al., 1992). In addition, studies of normal subjects experiencing depressed mood have reported increased mediofrontal and orbitofrontal activity, together with anterior temporal activation (George et al., 1995; Pardo, Pardo, & Raichle, 1993).

The interpretation of coexisting hypoactivation and hyperactivation in depression is not entirely clear. Fuster (1997, p. 206) has speculated that hypofrontal activity reported in major depression is consistent with the psychomotor retardation, aspontaneity, and avolition so characteristic of the disorder, whereas hyperactivity in the amygdala, orbitofrontal cortex, and medial frontal cortex may be related to the anxiety and psychological pain associated with the experience of depression.

GENETIC FACTORS Relatives of people with major depression are more likely to also have the disorder. Evidence for this comes from reports that the concordance rate for major depression for monozygotic twins is four times higher than for dizygotic twins (Andreasen & Black, 1996; Siever, Davis, & Gorman, 1991). As with schizophrenia, the fact that the concordance rate for monozygotic twins is not 100% indicates that genetic factors cannot entirely account for major depression.

Seasonal Affective Disorder

Some people become depressed during the winter months, when the days are short and the nights are long (Rosenthal et al., 1984). This form of depression, known as **seasonal affective disorder (SAD),** has been successfully treated by exposing patients to bright light for several hours a day (Rosenthal et al., 1985; Stinson & Thompson, 1990). As mentioned in chapter 3, the hypothalamus is involved in the entrainment of normal daily activity rhythm by changes in dark-light onset times. It is possible, therefore, that seasonal affective disorder is caused by a disruption of this mechanism of entrainment. Inconsistent with this hypothesis, however, is evidence that light therapy is effective in relieving depression in these patients regardless of the time during the 24-hour day that it is employed (Meesters et al., 1995; Wirz-Justice et al., 1993).

Bipolar Disorder

Bipolar disorder (formerly called manic-depressive disorder) is characterized by fluctuations between periods of depression and periods of **mania,** with normal periods interspersed between these episodes. The manic and depressed phases may be as short as a

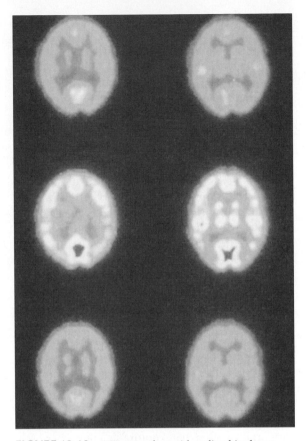

FIGURE 13.10 PET scan of a rapid-cycling bipolar patient. The top and bottom rows were taken on a day in which the patient was depressed. The middle row was taken on a day in which he was hypomanic. *(From H. Gleitman et al., 1999, p. 780)*

few hours, or they may last as long as several months (Figure 13.10). Bipolar disorder occurs in about 0.5–1% of the population (Andreasen & Black, 1996). Manic episodes are characterized by a persistently elevated, expansive, or irritable mood, which may include inflated self-esteem, a decreased need for sleep, and an increased tendency to talk. Mania may also include flight of ideas, distractibility, increased goal-directed behavior, hypersexuality, and an excessive tendency to engage in pleasurable activities that have a high potential for painful or dangerous consequences (American Psychiatric Association, 1994).

This behavior may continue for many days and sleepless nights, until the individual becomes exhausted. Kay Redfield Jamison (1995) has provided a powerful personal account of her own experience with bipolar disorder.

NEUROCHEMICAL FACTORS   The first medication used for the treatment of bipolar disorder was lithium carbonate (Eskalith). This medication usually dramatically reduces manic symptoms within a matter of days. The mechanism of its action is unknown, although it has been hypothesized that it may regulate neural transmission by stabilizing the influence of calcium on the presynaptic membrane (Meltzer, 1986; Wood & Goodwin, 1987). More recently, the anticonvulsants carbamazepine (Tegretol) and sodium valproate (Depakote) have been shown to be effective in treating the symptoms of bipolar disorder. Bipolar disorder is more effectively treated by psychoactive medications than any other major psychiatric disorder. Ironically, the therapeutic effectiveness of these medications has yet to reveal very much about the neurochemical basis of the disorder.

GENETIC FACTORS   Genetic studies appear to support the notion that there are separate inheritance pathways for major depression and bipolar disorder. Evidence for this comes from the finding that people with one of the disorders tend to have relatives with the same disorder (Gershon et al., 1985; Torgersen, 1986; Wender et al., 1986). Some genetic linkage studies of extended families with many members who have bipolar disorder indicate that individuals with bipolar disorder tend to have a particular type of enzyme deficiency as well as a particular type of color blindness. Because both of these anomalies are known to be due to genes on the X chromosome, the gene or genes causing bipolar disorder in these individuals may also be on that chromosome (Hodgkinson, Mullan, & Gurling, 1990). Although these and other studies bearing on specific mechanisms of the genetic transmission of bipolar disorder initially generated a great deal of excitement, it soon became apparent that no single mechanism of genetic trans-

mission can account for all cases of bipolar disorder and that a precise analysis of the genetic components of the disorder will be more elusive than initially hoped (Owen & Mullen, 1990).

ANXIETY DISORDERS

Anxiety disorders are characterized by feelings of anxiety and behavioral efforts to cope with these feelings. Four of the most serious categories of anxiety disorder are phobic disorders, generalized anxiety disorder, panic disorder, and obsessive-compulsive disorder. **Phobic disorders** involve anxiety related to a particular type of object or situation. This may be quite focal, as in snake phobia, or it may be general, as in **social phobia** (fear of social situations) or **agoraphobia** (fear of public, unprotected places). In contrast, in **generalized anxiety disorder (GAD)** no particular type of stimulus triggers anxiety. Instead, the person is plagued by a chronic feeling of anxiety that is not related to anything in particular, a "free-floating" anxiety. **Panic disorder** is characterized by intermittent but highly intense episodes of anxiety. People with this disorder describe the intensity of their anxiety as overwhelming. In **obsessive-compulsive disorder (OCD),** preoccupying thoughts involuntarily dominate the patient's thinking. These **obsessions** are often related to a particular theme, such as dirt and contamination, aggression, religion, or balance and symmetry. In an effort to deal with the anxiety generated by these thoughts, the individual engages in **compulsions,** behaviors that they cannot keep from performing. In this section, we will examine the neurobiological components of these disorders.

General Neurochemical Factors

As with the other forms of psychopathology we have considered so far, attempts have been made to infer the mechanism of anxiety disorders from what is known of the mechanisms of therapeutically effective medications. Most **anxiolytics** (antianxiety medications) bind to benzodiazepine receptors in the brain, and the magnitude of the therapeutic effect of different anxiolytics is correlated with the degree of binding to these sites. Benzodiazepine receptors are widely distributed throughout the cortex and are closely linked to gamma-aminobutyric acid (GABA) binding sites, forming a benzodiazepine-GABA complex. As we have seen, GABA is a major inhibitory neurotransmitter in the brain, and it appears that the binding of benzodiazepines to its receptors enhances the sensitivity of GABA receptors. This enhanced efficiency of GABA binding serves to enhance its inhibitory effect (Shader & Greenblatt, 1995). These mechanisms of benzodiazepine anxiolytics suggest that at least some anxiety disorders are associated with a disruption of the benzodiazepine-GABA complex. This could take various forms, including a diminished number of benzodiazepine receptors and/or the blocking of these receptor sites.

It has also been found that serotonin agonists, such as fluoxetine (Prozac), are effective in treating anxiety in disorders as different as panic disorder and OCD (Coplan, Gorman, & Klein, 1992), whereas antidepressants such as desipramine, which do not enhance serotonin activity, have no beneficial effect on the symptoms of anxiety disorders (Leonard et al., 1989). The mechanism of the effect of serotonin agonists on anxiety remains unclear.

The notion that anxiety is related to some abnormality of receptors distributed widely throughout the cortex (the benzodiazepine-GABA complex) is consistent with the finding that anxiety is not associated with a pattern of cognitive impairment that points to abnormality in any specific cortical region. Instead, anxiety disrupts the performance of any task that requires significant attention, concentration, and sustained effort.

Simple Phobias

Although conditioning is often invoked as an explanation for simple phobias, most phobias are fears related to a limited number of objects or situations, such as snakes, spiders, and heights, but not objects that are in reality more likely to cause harm, such as light sockets and automobiles. This has led to the **preparedness theory of phobias,** the notion that phobias for certain

stimuli were adaptive in the more naturalistic settings in which our early ancestors found themselves and that natural selection thus favored the survival of animals that were genetically programmed to rapidly learn to fear these stimuli. This notion that phobias may have a genetic basis is consistent with the fact that most people with a snake or insect phobia have never been harmed by these animals.

Generalized Anxiety Disorder

Although generalized anxiety disorder is the most common anxiety disorder, occurring in as much as 6% of the population in any given year (Weissman, 1985), neurobiological factors underlying it remain poorly understood. One hypothesis, based mainly on the finding that GABA agonists reduce the pervasive anxiety associated with GAD, is that this disorder may involve abnormalities of GABAergic transmission that reduce GABA's normal inhibitory effect. From this perspective, the prolonged overactivation of the sympathetic nervous system, so characteristic of GAD, is a consequence of this reduced inhibition (Costa, 1985). Whether genetic factors play a role in the etiology of GAD remains unclear.

Panic Disorder

Current theories of the etiology of panic disorder emphasize the interactive effects of neurobiological and cognitive factors. They posit an underlying overexcitability of the sympathetic nervous system (Andreasen & Black, 1996), which is then misinterpreted by the individual as an indicator that something is seriously physically wrong (e.g., heart attack). This makes the person more fearful, further activating sympathetic arousal, and so on. The result is the creation of a vicious positive feedback loop that generates the extremely high levels of anxiety that make panic attacks so terrifying and debilitating.

Panic attacks can be induced in people with a history of the disorder by conditions that activate the sympathetic nervous system. This includes the injection of lactic acid (lactate), a by-product of muscular activity (Stein & Uhde, 1995). There is evidence of a hereditary component to susceptibility to lactate-induced panic attacks (Balon et al., 1989). Evidence that panic disorder has a genetic component also comes from reports of higher concordance rates for the disorder for monozygotic twins than for dizygotic twins (Slater & Shields, 1969).

Obsessive-Compulsive Disorder

There is evidence that obsessive-compulsive disorder may involve prefrontal abnormality. OCD has been associated with increased glucose metabolism rates as measured by PET in orbital prefrontal cortex (Baxter et al., 1987; Baxter et al., 1988; Lucey et al., 1997; Nordahl et al., 1989; Rubin et al., 1992; Swedo et al., 1989). Increased metabolic rate in anterior cingulate gyrus has also been reported (Swedo et al., 1989). There is also evidence from a fMRI study of additional increases in metabolic activity in the basal ganglia, cingulate gyrus, amygdala, and prefrontal cortex when patients with OCD believed they were holding contaminated objects (Breiter et al., 1996). Imaging studies comparing cerebral blood flow before and after successful pharmacological or behavioral treatment of OCD have indicated that improvement of the patient's symptoms is correlated with reduction in the activity of prefrontal cortex (Rubin et al., 1995; Swedo et al., 1992).

Also implicating prefrontal cortex in OCD is evidence that serotonin agonists that beneficially affect the symptoms of OCD increase serotonin activity most in the basal ganglia and prefrontal cortex (Insel, 1990, 1992; Piccinelli et al., 1995; Swedo et al., 1992; Winslow & Insel, 1990; Zohar et al., 1988). In addition, symptoms of OCD are more likely to occur after damage to the basal ganglia, cingulate gyrus, and prefrontal cortex than to other brain regions (Giedd et al., 1995; Robinson et al., 1995). Furthermore, orbital prefrontal and anterior cingulate psychosurgery (the latter partially disconnecting prefrontal cortex from limbic and temporal-lobe structures) have been reported to have beneficial effects in some cases of the disorder (Bridges, Goktepe, & Maratos, 1973; Rees, 1973). Given the critical role of prefrontal cortex in the regulation of behavior, it is not surprising that abnormal prefrontal activation appears to be a component of OCD, although its precise role remains elusive. Fuster (1997, p. 204) has speculated that hyperfrontality in OCD is related to the excessively focused attention that has captured the OCD patient's thoughts and behavior.

As with panic disorder, genetic factors also play a role in OCD. Twin studies have revealed a higher concordance for monozygotic twins than for dizygotic twins in OCD (Black & Noyes, 1990; Rasmussen, 1993).

SOCIOPATHY

The terms **psychopathy, sociopathy,** and **antisocial personality disorder** have all been used to refer to individuals who behave in a manner that indicates an extreme lack of concern for the immediate or future consequences of their behavior. Individuals with this disorder are callous, selfish, and irresponsible. They frequently manipulate and exploit others, exhibiting little or no empathy, and they often engage in illegal behavior, without feeling guilt or remorse. Focused on their present needs and their gratification, these individuals feel little or no sense of emotional connection or loyalty to others and seem to view interpersonal relationships as merely vehicles for meeting their needs.

Lack of subjective anxiety and fear, together with the absence of autonomic arousal, in situations that would evoke these responses in most people is a striking characteristic of sociopathy. For example, in one study, normal control subjects and sociopaths were told that they would receive a shock in 10 minutes. As the time drew near, normal subjects experienced anxiety and exhibited high levels of autonomic arousal, as measured by galvanic skin response (GSR), whereas sociopaths showed only a slight increase (Lippert & Senter, 1966). Consistent with the absence of anxiety and disinhibition of impulse seen in sociopathy is evidence of decreased orbitomedial prefrontal activity in at least some criminals (Raine et al., 1994). It has also been hypothesized that sociopathy is associated with a more general underarousal of cortex (Hare, 1978; Quay, 1965). This could account for why individuals with this disorder often tirelessly seek stimulation.

DEMENTING DISEASES

Alzheimer's Disease: A Cortical Dementia

There are several different dementing diseases that primarily affect the cerebral cortex. These include Pick's disease, Creutzfeldt-Jacob disease, and Alzheimer's disease. Because it is the most common and the best-understood form of the cortical dementias, we will focus on Alzheimer's disease.

Alzheimer's disease is characterized by a horrible progressive deterioration of function that often begins with symptoms of mild memory loss, such as forgetting an appointment or people's names, and progresses through increasing memory loss and increasingly serious impairment in all other domains of cognitive and emotional functioning. Individuals with this disorder reach a point where they do not recognize family members and even lose a sense of their own identity. In the final stages of the disease, the patient becomes bedridden, completely helpless, and ultimately dies of the disease (Terry & Davis, 1980). Alzheimer's disease affects 5–10% of persons over age 65, and, because it is projected that the proportion of the population of the United States over 65 will continue to increase over the coming decades, the number of people with the disease will also increase. It is currently the fourth leading cause of death in the United States.

In 1906, after postmortem examination of the brain of a 51-year-old woman who had exhibited symptoms of severe cognitive deterioration, Alois Alzheimer reported the first specific neuropathological findings associated with these symptoms. Since that time, a great deal has been learned about the neurobiological basis of Alzheimer's disease. In fact, we know more about the neuropathology of Alzheimer's disease than of any other psychologically devastating disease, although, as in so many other domains, here too a full understanding continues to elude us. One thing that is clear is that, as with schizophrenia and the other psychiatric disorders we have considered, Alzheimer's is not a single disease entity. Rather, it is a group of closely associated diseases. For example, some forms of the disorder are genetically transmitted; others are not. Although we will continue to refer to Alzheimer's *disease*, in the singular, the fact that we are dealing with a group of disorders should be kept in mind.

NEUROCHEMICAL ABNORMALITIES Acetylcholine-containing neurons are particularly prone to destruction in Alzheimer's disease. In particular, degeneration of cholinergic neurons in the basal forebrain appears to be a major feature of the disorder (Coyle, Price, & Delong, 1983). Because cholinergic neurons originating in the basal forebrain project to the hippocampus and to widespread areas of neocortex, their degeneration would be expected to affect the broad range of cognitive and emotional functioning disrupted in Alzheimer's disease.

These findings have led to the study of cholinergic agonists as possible medications for the symptoms of Alzheimer's disease. Unfortunately, to date, the therapeutic efficacy of these agents has been disappointing. Potentially more promising are the results of transplant studies in aged rats or rats that have received lesions of cholinergic-releasing pathways that are analogous to those believed to be present in Alzheimer's disease. These animals were initially quite impaired on a number of learning tasks. However, after receiving implants of tissue containing cholinergic neurons, they showed improvement in cognitive functioning (Bjorklund & Stenevi, 1984; Gage & Bjorklund, 1986). Whether these promising results will lead to an effective treatment for Alzheimer's disease remains to be seen.

STRUCTURAL ABNORMALITIES The examination of brains of patients with Alzheimer's disease reveals degenerative changes throughout the brain. This would be expected, given the global nature of the cognitive and emotional impairments seen in the disease. Widespread neuropathology is also consistent with functional imaging studies showing decrease in metabolic functioning throughout the forebrain (Figure 13.11).

Two of the most prominent degenerative changes in Alzheimer's disease are cortical atrophy (Figures 13.12 and 13.13) and ventricular enlargement (Figure 13.13). Both of these are caused by the death of neurons and resulting decrease in brain volume.

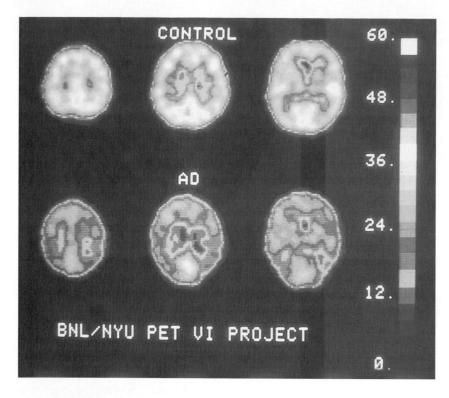

FIGURE 13.11 PET scan showing the characteristic global decrease in brain metabolic activity in a patient with Alzheimer's disease *(bottom)* compared with brain metabolic activity of an age- and sex-matched control subject *(top)*. *(From Sarason & Sarason, 1999, p. 377)*

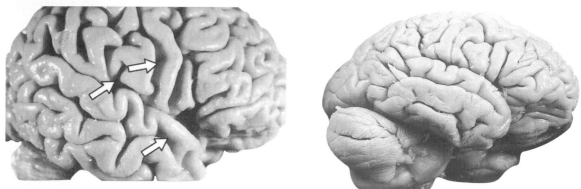

FIGURE 13.12 Cortical atrophy in Alzheimer's disease. *(Left)* Lateral view of the right side of the brain of a person with Alzheimer's disease. The widened sulci *(arrows)* are the result of degeneration of the neocortex. *(Right)* The lateral view of the right side of a normal brain. *(From N. R. Carlson, 1999, p. 430)*

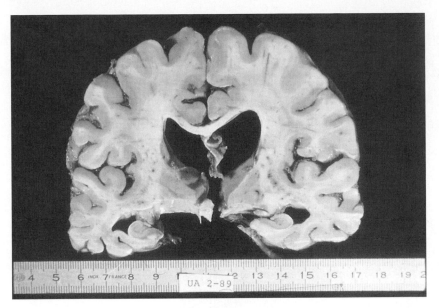

FIGURE 13.13   Cortical atrophy and ventricular enlargement in the brain of a patient with Alzheimer's disease. *(From Beatty, 1995, p. 488)*

Cell death is also seen on the microscopic level, directly in the form of dead and dying neurons, and in the form of diminished neuron density in certain brain regions. In addition, many other changes on the microscopic level have been observed. The dendritic branches of many neurons have thinned, so that the dendritic trees of neurons are much reduced in size (Figure 13.14). This diminishes the number of incoming synapses that can be formed. Another microscopic change is the filling of neuron cytoplasm with **neurofibrillary tangles.** These microscopic tubelike structures are seen in normal neurons and are thought to provide a kind of internal structural support. However, in Alzheimer's disease their numbers are greatly increased. It is believed that neurofibrillary tangles are associated with the dying of the neuron. Also seen in Alzheimer's disease is **granulovacular degeneration.** The significance of this abnormality for cell functioning is not known. A particularly important cellular abnormality is the presence of **neuritic plaques,** areas of incompletely destroyed neurons in the cortex. These plaques consist of a dense core of a protein known as **β amyloid,** surrounded by degenerating axons and dendrites, together with reactive astrocytes and activated microglia. Eventually the glial cells completely destroy the degenerating neurons and leave a core of β amyloid protein (Figure 13.15). All of the changes just discussed are seen to some degree in normal aging; however, they are much more extensive and pervasive in the brains of patients with Alzheimer's disease.

There is evidence that the formation of neuritic plaques is caused by a defective form of β amyloid protein. The normal *short form* of β amyloid protein consists of a string of 40 amino acids. However, a defective *long form* of the protein, consisting of 42 or 43 amino acids, has been found in patients with Alzheimer's disease. In some cases, this defective form has been shown to be the product of mutated genes. We turn to a discussion of genetic factors in Alzheimer's disease next.

GENETIC FACTORS   At least some forms of Alzheimer's disease run in families, indicating that genetic factors are involved in their cause. It has been demonstrated (St. George-Hislop et al., 1987) that chromosome 21 contains a gene that programs the synthesis of **β amyloid precursor protein (APP),** a long chain of amino acids that is cut apart by enzymes to produce β amyloid protein. Since the discovery of the APP gene, several specific mutations of that gene

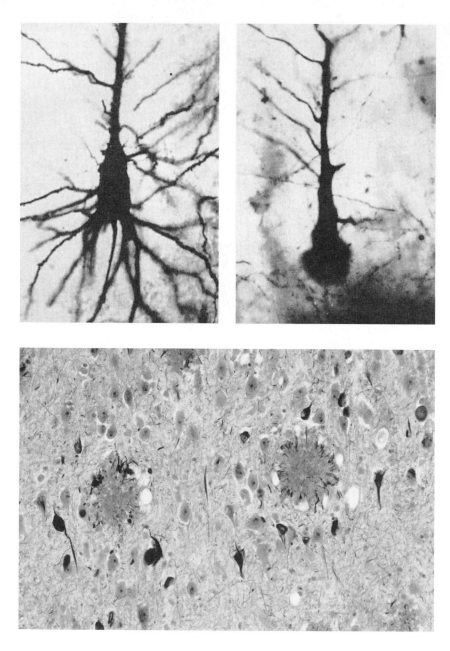

FIGURE 13.14 Golgi-stained dendritic trees of cortical neurons in *(A)* the normal brain and *(B)* the brain of an Alzheimer's patient. *(From Beatty, 1995, p. 488)*

FIGURE 13.15 A photomicrograph of cortical tissue from the brain of a patient who died from Alzheimer's disease. The two dark masses in the center are neuritic plaques, consisting of β amyloid protein surrounded by degenerating axons, dendrites, and cell bodies. *(From N. R. Carlson, 1999, p. 430)*

have been discovered in cases of familial Alzheimer's disease (Farlow et al., 1994; Martinez et al., 1993). Other studies have found mutations of additional genes involved in the synthesis of β amyloid, the **presinilin** genes on chromosomes 1 and 14. Thus, mutations of the APP gene or the presinilin genes cause defective forms of β amyloid protein to be produced in at least some cases of familial Alzheimer's disease (Hardy, 1997). It has also been found that a high percentage of patients with familial forms of Alzheimer's disease have at least one gene that programs the synthesis of **apolipoprotein E4,** and it may be that this gene represents a risk factor for familial forms of the disorder (Corton, 1994).

OTHER FACTORS IN ALZHEIMER'S DISEASE

The findings discussed in the previous section represent significant progress toward understanding the genetic and biochemical bases of familial Alzheimer's disease. However, most forms of Alzheimer's disease are not hereditary, raising the problem of what factors are responsible for these forms of the disorder and for the neuropathological changes, particularly the accumulation of β amyloid protein, that accompany them. This problem has yet to be solved; however, a number of possible causal factors contributing to some forms of the disorder have been proposed. These include extended alcohol or drug abuse, various toxins, and slow viruses, the effects of which appear long after the time of infection. Injury to the brain has also been proposed as a factor and postmortem examinations of the brains of prizefighters have revealed abnormally large numbers of amyloid plaques. The possibility of endocrine-related mechanisms in Alzheimer's disease has been raised by the finding that estrogen replacement therapy in postmenopausal women reduces the risk of the disease (Henderson, 1997).

Finally, there is some evidence that abnormal activity of the immune system may contribute to the brain abnormalities associated with Alzheimer's disease. This comes from the finding that the amyloid plaques seen in the disease contain substances characteristic of an immune reaction. These substances include activated microglia and reactive astrocytes, phagocytic glial cells that remove fragments of necrotic (dead) neurons in a manner analogous to the way in which white blood cells remove necrotic tissue in other parts of the body (McGeer & Rogers, 1992). The notion that an immune response contributes to the destruction of neurons in Alzheimer's disease is further supported by reports that people treated with anti-inflammatory drugs have a lower rate of Alzheimer's disease. In addition, some improvement in cognitive impairment was seen in patients with moderately severe Alzheimer's disease who received the anti-inflammatory drug indomethacin (Rogers et al., 1993).

Subcortical Dementias

Subcortical dementia refers to dementing diseases that primarily affect subcortical structures. It should be emphasized that this does not mean that cortical structures are not also involved, but only that the most prominent symptoms are believed to be caused by abnormality of subcortical structures. In fact, in the two subcortical dementias that we will consider, Huntington's chorea and Parkinson's disease, we will find that there is evidence of abnormal prefrontal function. It should also be noted that because of the prominence of motor symptoms in Huntington's chorea and Parkinson's disease, the two are sometimes conceptualized as movement disorders.

HUNTINGTON'S CHOREA The last two disorders that we will examine in this chapter, Huntington's chorea and Parkinson's disease, are not typically considered to be forms of psychopathology. Both, however, are associated with psychiatric symptoms and with cognitive impairment. In addition, our understanding of the neurological factors underlying these disorders may serve as a model for the kind of understanding of major types of psychopathology that may be possible in the future.

Huntington's chorea (from the Greek word for "dance") was first described in detail by George Huntington (1872). We discussed the disease briefly in chapter 9, in the context of movement disorders. Here, we elaborate further on aspects of the disease, with special attention to its cognitive aspects.

Huntington's disease often begins with cognitive loss and psychiatric symptoms, including anxiety, depression, mania, and psychosis. These symptoms may precede the movement disorder by as much as a year. Problems with movement may begin with restlessness and small involuntary movements. These movements increase in frequency and amplitude until parts of limbs, or whole limbs, are involved. As the disease progresses, involuntary movements and cognitive deterioration become more pronounced. Eventually the patient dies; the average time between the onset of symptoms and death is 12 years.

We know a good deal about the genetics of Huntington's chorea. Some of the biochemical and structural abnormalities associated with the disorder have also been identified. After reviewing these aspects of the disease, we briefly present the hypothesis that prefrontal dysfunction is a significant component of the disorder.

Genetic Factors   The genetics of Huntington's chorea has been worked out in some detail. It has long been known (Vessie, 1932) that the disease is caused by an autosomal dominant gene (an autosome is a chromosome other than a sex chromosome). This means that, on average, half of the offspring of an affected individual, regardless of the sex of the offspring, will receive the gene and develop the disease. The gene responsible for the disorder has been identified and found to be located on the short arm of chromosome 4. In addition, a genetic marker linked with the gene has been identified that makes possible a test that will reveal whether a particular individual carries the gene (Gusella et al., 1983). This test is particularly important because the onset of symptoms usually occurs between the ages of 30 and 50, after the person may have had children.

Biochemical and Structural Abnormalities   Postmortem studies of the brains of patients with Huntington's chorea show neuronal degeneration and cell loss in the caudate and putamen. The disease is also associated with a neurotransmitter abnormality in these structures, probably caused by cell death. The precise nature of this abnormality has not been established, but it appears to involve destruction of cholinergic and GABAergic neurons, with resulting disinhibition of dopaminergic activity. This disinhibition is thought to cause the disease's involuntary movements by activating movement-related regions of the thalamus and/or cortex. The hypothesis that an abnormal increase in dopamine activity plays a role in Huntington's disease is supported by the finding that dopamine antagonists, such as neuroleptics, decrease the involuntary movements of the disease, whereas dopamine agonists, such as amphetamine, increase these movements.

Cognitive Impairment and the Hypothesis of Prefrontal Dysfunction in Huntington's Chorea   Patients with Huntington's chorea exhibit a pattern of cognitive functioning that has some similarity to that seen in patients with prefrontal lesions (Goldman-Rakic, 1987). Thus, both conditions are associated with impairment on the Stroop Test, tests of sequencing and organizing, tests of working memory, and other measures of prefrontal functioning (Butters & Grady, 1977; Fedio et al., 1979; Fisher et al., 1983; Wexler, 1979). In addition, language and general information are relatively spared in both conditions (Fisher et al., 1983).

From animal studies it is known that the principal sulcus and surrounding dorsolateral prefrontal cortex send highly organized projections to the central part of the caudate nucleus, an area that shows degeneration in Huntington's disease. The magnitude of this degeneration is such that it is highly unlikely that it could occur without retrograde changes in prefrontal cortex. It seems possible, therefore, that the cognitive impairment seen in Huntington's disease may be the result of disconnection of the caudate from its prefrontal source of afferent input and/or degeneration of prefrontal cortex itself, thereby depriving motor centers of representational knowledge mediated by prefrontal cortex (Goldman-Rakic, 1987).

PARKINSON'S DISEASE   As discussed briefly in chapter 9, Parkinson's disease is characterized by profoundly diminished ability to perform voluntary movements (hypokinesia). There is also evidence of cognitive impairment in the disorder, although this is more controversial than in Huntington's chorea. It is well established that Parkinson's disease is associated with the degeneration of dopamine-producing cells in the substantia nigra. The hypokinesia of Parkinson's disease appears to be due to low levels of dopamine in the basal ganglia caused by the degeneration of the cells in the substantia nigra that normally convey dopamine to these structures via the nigrostriatal pathway.

Patients with Parkinson's disease have been reported to be severely impaired on the Wisconsin Card Sorting Test and on other measures of prefrontal function (Dalrymple et al., 1994; Henik et al., 1993; Lees & Smith, 1983; Taylor, Saint-Cry, & Lang, 1986), but not on measures of spatial processing. The substantia nigra can influence prefrontal cortex in a number of ways. Depletion of dopamine in the nigrostriatal pathways, mentioned earlier, in the context of the hypokinesia of Parkinson's disease, includes the reduction of dopaminergic activity in the portions of the caudate nucleus receiving input from prefrontal cortex. In addition, the substantia nigra influences prefrontal cortex via direct connections (Porrino & Goldman-Rakic, 1982) and via indirect connections through the thalamus (Ilinsky, Jouandet, & Goldman-Rakic, 1985). These pathways provide mechanisms whereby the degeneration of dopaminergic neurons in the substantia nigra could cause the impairments in prefrontal function reported in Parkinson's disease.

This picture of the lowering of prefrontal dopaminergic activity as the cause of the cognitive impairment in Parkinson's is complicated by evidence that the magnitude of cognitive impairment in the disorder may be unrelated to level of dopaminergic activity. For example, L-dopa treatment, which significantly decreases motor symptoms, has only a moderate and short-term effect on the cognitive symptoms of the disorder. In addition, little relationship has been shown between the degree of intellectual impairment and the magnitude of cell loss in the substantia nigra (Dubois et al., 1991). These findings raise the possibility that the degeneration of regions other than the substantia nigra may be the cause of the cognitive impairments seen in Parkinson's disease.

UNSOLVED PROBLEMS

As may be seen from the findings reviewed in this chapter, a good deal has been learned about the biological basis of psychopathology. However, like the head of the Hydra in Greek mythology, for every question that is answered, two unsolved problems spring to life. In this section we examine some of these problems.

The Heterogeneity of Diagnostic Categories

There are two problems having to do with the heterogeneity of diagnostic categories. First, there is the problem of reliability. The *DSM-IV* attempts to provide the basis for reliable diagnosis, and its requirement that specific criteria be met for a particular diagnosis to be made is clearly an improvement over earlier diagnostic schemas. Nevertheless, not all of the criteria can be objectively evaluated, and the interrater reliability for some criteria remains quite low.

The second problem of heterogeneity is that many diagnostic categories, including some for which there are reliable criteria, nevertheless include more than one disorder. This may be because several different disease entities produce similar symptom pictures, as is almost certainly the case in bipolar disorder. Or it may be because patients with quite different symptoms meet the criteria for a particular disorder, as is the case, for example, with schizophrenia. The net result of this heterogeneity is to blur the results of investigations into the neurobiological correlates of a patient group. One attempt to remedy this problem is to search for biologically based criteria that could serve as valid bases for identifying specific disease entities within a broader diagnostic category. Examples of such attempts are Crow's two-syndrome hypothesis of schizophrenia and the differentiation of genetically and nongenetically based forms of Alzheimer's disease.

Invalid Findings

Inevitably, well-designed and carefully conducted studies nevertheless yield findings that are later shown to be invalid. An example of this is Andreasen and colleagues' (1986) report, discussed earlier, that patients with schizophrenia have smaller frontal lobes and smaller cranial volume than those without the disease. Andreasen later reported failure to replicate these findings. Time tends to weed out studies with invalid results. However, their occurrence emphasizes the importance of replication studies and the need to very cautiously interpret data when such studies are lacking.

Inferring Cause Based on the Effective Treatment of Symptoms

It may be very misleading to infer biological mechanisms underlying psychopathology from the effectiveness of a somatic treatment agent. This is because the fact that an agent improves symptoms does not mean that its mechanism of action is related to the neurobiological mechanisms actually causing the symptoms. For example, serotonin agonists are effective in relieving symptoms of depression. This does not necessarily mean that depression is due to below-normal serotonin activity. Serotonin activation may have an antidepressant effect that is independent of the neurobiological abnormality underlying depression. The same argument can be made regarding dopamine antagonists and the symptoms of schizophrenia. Despite considerable circumstantial evidence, we do not know whether schizophrenia involves an abnormality of dopamine activity.

Disentangling Cause and Effect

The problem of distinguishing cause and effect is particularly pertinent to functional imaging studies of patients with psychopathology. In essence, the problem is that the presence of functional abnormality in a particular brain region does not necessarily mean that the abnormality is the *cause* of the condition under study. For example, consider hypofrontality in schizophrenia. Can we conclude from this phenomenon that prefrontal abnormality is the cause of schizophrenia? Certainly not, because it is clearly possible that the observed deviation from normal function seen in prefrontal cortex is not the cause of the disorder but an effect, a consequence, of it. This is not to say that hypofrontality in schizophrenia does not have an impact on cognitive and emotional functioning. It well may have such an impact, but it may do so without being the cause of the disorder.

Levels of Explanation

The considerations just discussed lead to the idea that there are multiple levels of explanation of the cause of a disorder, an idea embodied in the concepts of proximate cause and ultimate cause. **Proximate causes** are the immediate causes of the syndrome or disorder. For example, in diabetes, the proximate cause is insufficient insulin. A more complete understanding of a disorder, however, requires an understanding of more remote or **ultimate causes.** These may be divided into two categories: a **predisposition** for the disorder (technically termed a **diathesis**) and an environmental component (termed **stress**). In diabetes, the diathesis is a genetic factor that predisposes an individual to the disease. It is then triggered by environmental stressors, such as obesity (H. Gleitman et al., 1999). To take another example, a proximate cause of pneumonia is the breakdown of the normal function of cells in the lungs. The ultimate cause is bacterial infection.

Psychiatric disorders also have proximate and ultimate causes, although these are obviously less well defined than in the case of diabetes or pneumonia. For example, in schizophrenia, the high but less than 100% concordance rate for monozygotic twins indicates that, in at least some forms of this disorder, a hereditary predisposition and some other nongenetic factor, probably environmental stress, are ultimate causes. Proximate causes appear to include some form of biochemical abnormality. It will be appreciated that the many neurobiological aspects of psychopathology reviewed in this chapter fall on different points of the ultimate cause–proximate cause continuum. Furthermore, as we have already emphasized, some of them, like hypofrontality in schizophrenia, may not be causes at all, but effects.

The findings reviewed in this chapter convey a double-edged message. On the one hand, they represent new and potentially illuminating glimpses into these disorders and hold out the promise that additional findings will continue to be forthcoming. On the other hand, they alert us to how much more research is needed before we can truly understand the nature and causes of these debilitating disorders.

SUMMARY

The problem of achieving a satisfactory definition of psychopathology has not been thoroughly resolved. Nevertheless, a certain level of consensus about how to operationally define various psychiatric disorders has enabled us to make some progress toward an understanding of the biological factors contributing to disorders of experience and behavior, and in recent years the pace of this progress has been accelerating.

What we refer to as schizophrenia is almost certainly a group of disorders with varying symptomatology and underlying causation. This greatly complicates attempts to understand the biological basis of these disorders. Nevertheless, there is strong evidence that genetic factors contribute to schizophrenia, although these must not be absolutely decisive, because the concordance rate for schizophrenia for monozygotic twins is well below 100%. The dopamine hypothesis, in its simplest form, states that schizophrenia is associated with abnormally high dopamine activity. Although there are some problems with the simplest form of this hypothesis, abnormal dopamine activity does appear to be a correlate of schizophrenia. This may result from a hypertrophy of dopamine receptors.

Structural abnormalities, including ventricular enlargement and cortical atrophy, are seen in some patients with schizophrenia. These appear to reflect generalized tissue loss, rather than damage to a particular brain region. These structural abnormalities are not seen in all patients, and attempts have been made to correlate the presence or absence of structural abnormalities with particular symptom patterns. There is some evidence that ventricular enlargement and cortical atrophy are correlated with negative symptoms, whereas the absence of these abnormalities is associated with positive symptoms. The validity of these putative relationships is unclear, however.

Various microstructural abnormalities have been reported in schizophrenia. The most reliable of these are found in limbic structures, although there are some reports of abnormality in prefrontal cortex.

Functional imaging studies have revealed decreased blood flow and metabolic activity in pre-frontal cortex. This is most reliably seen when subjects are engaged in tasks that tap prefrontal function, where it manifests as an absence of the increase in prefrontal activity normally seen during such tasks.

Patients with schizophrenia perform poorly on a wide range of cognitive measures. However, they are particularly impaired on tasks that require processing mediated by prefrontal cortex, including those involving attention, voluntary eye movement, working memory, planning, and the modification of behavior in response to feedback. Taken together, these findings suggest that at least some symptoms of schizophrenia may represent a breakdown in the processes, mediated by prefrontal cortex, by which representational knowledge governs behavior.

Drugs that increase brain monoamine activity are effective in treating symptoms of major depression. This has led to the hypothesis that an abnormality of monoamine biochemistry underlies major depression (the monoamine hypothesis of depression). More recently, drugs that selectively enhance serotonin activity have been shown to be effective in treating depression, leading to the more specific serotonin hypothesis of depression. Genetic factors also play a role in some forms of depression.

Imaging studies of patients with major depression have reported prefrontal hypoactivity, a finding that may be related to the psychomotor retardation, aspontaneity, and apathy seen in these patients. Some imaging studies have reported hyperactivity in the amygdala, cingulate gyrus, and orbitomedial prefrontal cortex in depressed patients. The significance of these findings is not entirely clear, but they may be related to the experiences of anxiety and psychological pain that are such poignant aspects of severe depression.

Seasonal affective disorder is a form of depression that occurs during the winter months, when there are fewer hours of daylight in each day. Exposure to artificial light has been shown to be an effective treatment for this disorder, although the underlying cause of the disorder and the mechanism of light therapy's effectiveness are not known.

Bipolar disorder is effectively treated by lithium carbonate and certain anticonvulsant medications, although the underlying biochemistry of the disorder remains obscure. Genetic factors have been established as contributing to the cause of some forms of the disorder.

There are several different types of anxiety disorders. Many of them are effectively treated by benzodiazepines, which enhance the activity of the inhibitory neurotransmitter GABA. Serotonin agonists also effectively treat anxiety, particularly generalized anxiety disorder, although the extent to which abnormalities of serotonin biochemistry play a role in anxiety is unknown.

Phobias were long believed simply to be learned. However, the observation that phobias for certain animals and situations (such as snakes and heights) may be present even when the individual has not had unpleasant experiences with them in the past, suggests that humans may be biologically prepared to experience certain phobias. Panic disorder appears to involve a combination of sympathetic nervous system overactivation together with cognitive misinterpretation of that arousal as a signal of a physical crisis. This leads to a vicious positive feedback loop that creates extremely intense levels of anxiety. Functional imaging studies have reported that obsessive-compulsive disorder is associated with increased prefrontal activity. This may be related to the extremely narrow and intense focus of attentional processes characteristic of these patients.

Sociopathy has long been associated with diminished or absent autonomic arousal in situations that would cause such arousal in normal individuals.

Alzheimer's disease is a cortical dementia characterized by progressive deterioration of cognitive and emotional functioning. As with other psychiatric disorders, there is evidence that Alzheimer's disease is actually a group of associated disorders. Many neurobiological abnormalities have been identified in Alzheimer's disease. Cholinergic activity is disrupted.

Neuron death, as inferred from ventricular enlargement and cortical atrophy and as assessed directly by histological methods, is a prominent correlate of the disease. Dendritic atrophy, neurofibrillary tangles, granulovacular degeneration, and amyloid plaques, all present in the normal aging brain, are seen in far greater numbers in the brains of Alzheimer's patients. Amyloid plaques are areas of incompletely destroyed cortical neurons. Their core contains a defective form of β amyloid. In familial forms of Alzheimer's disease, the defective protein has been related to mutations of specific genes. In nonfamilial forms of the disease, the cause of the defective β amyloid protein has not been established, although several hypotheses have been proposed.

Huntington's chorea is associated with cognitive changes similar to those seen in patients with prefrontal lesions. It is possible that the caudate lesions seen in this disease disconnect the caudate from its prefrontal sources of afferent input, disrupting this important pathway that normally serves as a mechanism by which prefrontal cortex influences motor centers. Parkinson's disease is also associated with cognitive impairments similar to those seen after prefrontal lesions. The degeneration of dopamine-producing neurons in the substantia nigra in Parkinson's disease deprives prefrontal cortex of dopaminergic activation that would normally reach it via direct mesocortical connections and via the basal ganglia. Diminished prefrontal dopamine activity may underlie the cognitive impairments seen in this disorder.

There are many unsolved problems in the neurobiology of psychopathology. These include the heterogeneity of diagnostic categories, problems in inferring causal factors from the mechanisms of action of effective treatment agents, disentangling cause from effect, and different levels of explanation that may be used to address the problem of the causes of psychiatric disorders.

CHAPTER 14

Developmental Neuropsychology

DEVELOPMENT OF THE BRAIN
Induction
Neuroblast Proliferation
Cell Migration
Axonal Growth
Dendritic Growth
The Formation of Connections and
  the Contribution of the Environment
Myelination
**BRAIN DEVELOPMENT AND THE DEVELOPMENT
OF HIGHER-ORDER FUNCTION**
Development of Visual Acuity
Development of Control of Visual
  Orienting
Development of Executive Function
Language Development

**KNOWN CAUSES OF
DEVELOPMENTAL ABNORMALITY**
Inherited Disorders
Chromosomal Disorders
Structural Abnormalities
Prematurity and Low Birth Weight
Infection
Toxin-Related Damage
Nutritional Disorders
Anoxic Episodes
Traumatic Brain Injury and Focal
  Cerebral Abnormality
DEVELOPMENTAL DISORDERS OF UNKNOWN CAUSE
Learning Disorders
Attention Deficit Disorder
Autism
SUMMARY

❖ ❖ ❖

The physical development of an individual from zygote (fertilized egg) to mature adult is one of the most awe-inspiring and wondrous processes in all of nature. This is especially true for the development of the human brain, with its enormously complex organization, and for the development of the complex behaviors that are the fruit of its biological development. Understanding the fascinating process of brain development illumi-nates our understanding of the mature brain because knowing how something has come into being illumi-nates our understanding of its current state. We will see that this is true from a number of perspectives, from neuroanatomy (Why do the lateral ventricles have such peculiar shapes?) to functional neuroanatomy (What are the neurobiological correlates of developing visual acuity in the infant?).

The process of development does not always run smoothly. An understanding of disorders of development, important for the understanding and treatment of people *with developmental disorders, can also shed light on the process of normal development. We turn now to a discussion of these domains.*

DEVELOPMENT OF THE BRAIN

The cellular processes underlying the development of the human brain, with its array of structures and its bewilderingly complex and highly organized patterns of connections between neurons, are immensely complicated and incompletely understood. Nevertheless, certain aspects of the processes contributing to brain development have come to light. These processes include (a) induction of the neural plate, (b) cell proliferation, (c) cell migration, (d) cell aggregation, (e) differentiation of neuroblasts (undifferentiated nerve cells) into specialized neurons, (f) the formation of connections with other neurons, (g) selective cell death, and (h) the elimination of some connections

and the stabilization of others. In the following sections we consider these processes in detail.

Induction

During the third week of gestation, the flat sheet of cells in the ectoderm, or outer layer, on the dorsal surface of the developing embryo becomes transformed into specialized tissue that will become the brain and spinal cord (Figure 14.1). The resulting pear-shaped sheet of specialized cells is called the **neural plate,** and the transforming process that generates it is called **induction** (Saxon, 1980). The mechanism underlying induction of the neural plate is not completely under-

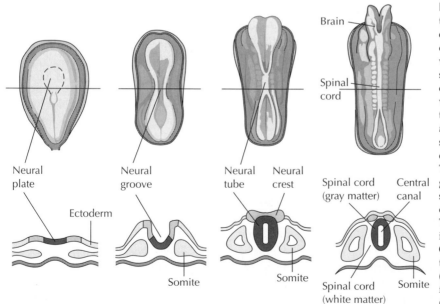

FIGURE 14.1   The genesis of the nervous system from the ectoderm of a human embryo during the third and fourth weeks after conception is represented in these four pairs of drawings. *(Top)* An external view of the dorsal surface of the developing embryo. *(Bottom)* The corresponding cross-sectional view at about the middle of the future spinal cord. The central nervous system begins as the neural plate, a flat sheet of ectodermal cells on the dorsal surface of the embryo. The plate subsequently folds into the hollow neural tube. Over the course of development, the head end of the central canal (former neural tube) widens to form the ventricles of the brain. *(From Cowan, 1979, p. 58)*

stood; however, it is known to involve some form of interaction between the ectoderm cells that will eventually form the neural plate and underlying mesoderm cells. This probably includes the transfer of substances from the mesoderm to the ectoderm.

Following induction, the neural plate folds into an elongated **neural groove,** which eventually deepens and folds over onto itself and begins to close, forming the **neural tube.** Closure begins in the middle of the neural groove and progresses both rostrally and caudally, until it is complete at about day 25 of gestation.

Neuroblast Proliferation

Immature neurons, which have not formed their axonal and dendritic processes, are called **neuroblasts**. The proliferation of neuroblasts occurs through the process of mitotic cell division and is believed to take place only during gestation. Thus, the newborn infant has all of the neurons it will ever have, although other important developmental changes, such as cell differentiation and the formation of connections between neurons, continue into the postnatal period. Neurons proliferate at an astounding rate. The neural plate has only about 125,000 neuroblasts, yet the entire final complement of the central nervous system's 100 billion or so neurons is present at birth. This means that during gestation the number of neuroblasts increases at the rate of about 250,000 per minute.

Proliferation occurs at different times and rates in different regions of the developing nervous system and, although the factors regulating the onset and cessation of proliferation are poorly understood, it is clear that these processes are rigidly determined. One of the consequences of this differential cell proliferation is the development of gross structural features in the embryonic nervous system. Just as adding clay to specific areas of a sculpture changes its shape, adding cells at a faster rate to specific regions of the developing nervous system determines its form. The results of differential proliferation are seen in all stages of neurogenesis. For example, at approximately day 35 of gestation three bulges appear at the rostral end of the embryonic nervous system. During the following weeks, differential cell proliferation fashions them

into the three major subdivisions of the brain: the forebrain, midbrain, and hindbrain (Figure 14.2).

Cell Migration

At some stage in the life of an embryonic neuron it permanently stops dividing. This triggers its movement, or **migration,** from the ventricular layer on the inner surface of the developing nervous system, where most cell division takes place, to new destinations. Neurons in different regions withdraw from the mitotic cycle at different times. The ultimate destination of the migrating neuron is tied to the time when it loses the capacity for DNA replication, a time in the life of the cell that is sometimes referred to as its **birth date.** For example, among those cells that will eventually form the cerebral cortex, the first to stop dividing will ultimately come to occupy the deepest cortical layer, and the next group to stop dividing will migrate to the next deepest layer, and so on. Thus, the cerebral cortex is formed inside out by successive waves of cell migrations, each wave passing though the previously established deeper layer (Rakic, 1995). There are, however, some exceptions to the general rule that proliferation ceases before migration begins. For example, deep gray-matter structures of the cerebral hemispheres, such as the basal ganglia, develop from cells that have undergone continued proliferation after migrating to a position between the ventricular and cortical layers.

The mechanism of neuronal migration involves specialized glial cells that radiate out from the ventricular layer and serve as scaffolding that guides the movement of migrating neurons to their final destinations (Figure 14.3). The actual movement with which migrating neurons progress along radial glial cells is amoeboid in nature, with the leading process of the developing neuron extending along its guiding glial cell and the trailing end progressively detaching itself. This is depicted diagrammatically in Figure 14.3 and is shown in an electron micrograph in Figure 14.4. That these glial processes perform this critical guiding role has been demonstrated in strains of mice with genetic mutations that led to early degeneration of these processes. Examination of the cerebral cortex in these

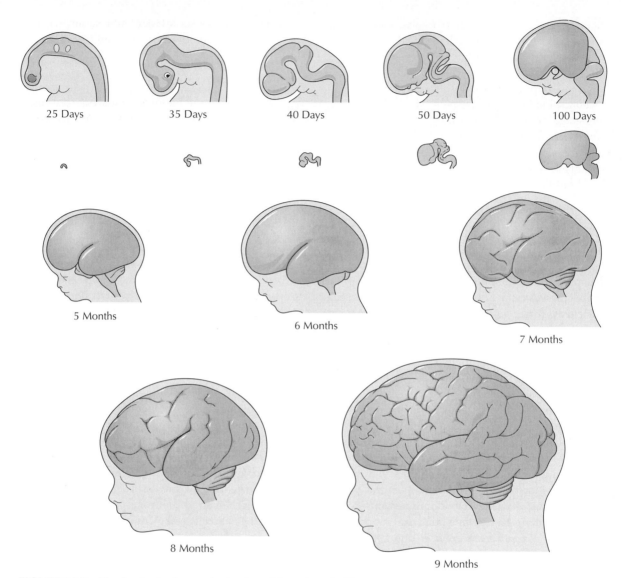

FIGURE 14.2   The developing human brain viewed from the side. The top row shows the developing brain enlarged to an arbitrary common size to emphasize the details of the developmental process. The drawings in the bottom three rows are approximately four-fifths life-size. The three major parts of the brain (the forebrain, the midbrain, and the hindbrain) originate as prominent swellings at the rostral end of the early neural tube. The enlargement and bending of these structures lead to changes in the shape of the neural tube that eventually define the shape of the cerebral ventricles. *(From Cowan, 1979, p. 59)*

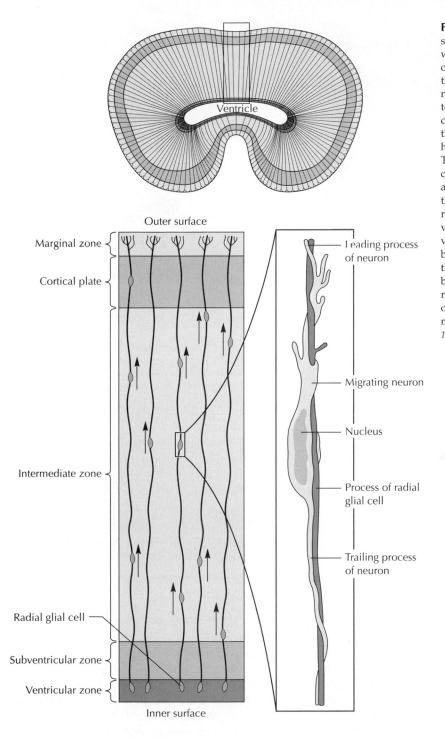

Ventricle

Outer surface

Marginal zone

Cortical plate

Intermediate zone

Radial glial cell

Subventricular zone

Ventricular zone

Inner surface

Leading process of neuron

Migrating neuron

Nucleus

Process of radial glial cell

Trailing process of neuron

FIGURE 14.3 Specialized supporting radial glial cells, which guide the movement of migrating neuroblasts, span the thickness of the wall of the neural tube. The drawing at the top shows how the radial glial cells look in a transverse section through the wall of the cerebral hemisphere of the fetal monkey. The cell bodies of the radial glial cells lie in the ventricular zone, and their processes extend to the outer surface of the surrounding layers. An enlarged view of a segment of this transverse section is shown at the bottom left. The magnified three-dimensional view on the bottom right shows the close relation between the processes of the radial glial cell and the migrating neuron. *(From Cowan, 1979, p. 62)*

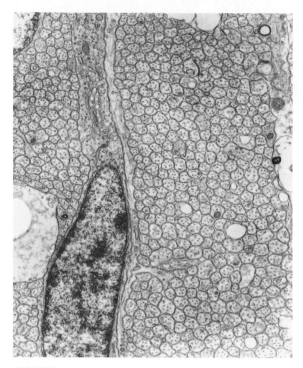

FIGURE 14.4 An electron micrograph of a migrating neuron (broader of the two vertical bands running all the way across the micrograph) and its supporting and guiding elongated radial glial cell (lighter, narrower band to the right of the neuron). The dark oblong object inside the lower part of the neuron is its nucleus. The migrating neuron travels through a dense neuropile of nerve fibers that runs in various directions. Some of these are cut in cross section in this micrograph and are seen as circular structures. The migrating neuron thus has contact with many fibers during the course of its migration. Nevertheless, it remains in intimate contact with its radial glial cell. *(Courtesy of Pasko Rakic)*

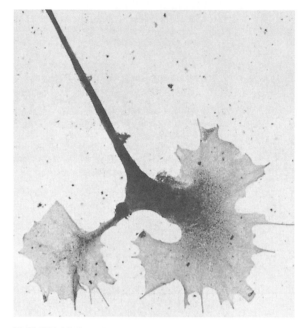

FIGURE 14.5 This transmission electron micrograph shows a pair of growth cones at the end of a developing axon. The fine fingerlike extensions are filopodia, and the flattened sheets between them are lamellipodia. *(From Cowan, 1979, p. 63)*

gregate with similar neurons to form layers or nuclei. They also assume a particular orientation, a process that we saw is disrupted in the hippocampal cells of some patients with schizophrenia (see chapter 13). Cell ligands on the membrane of neurons are presumed to be involved in this aggregation of neurons of similar type into discrete anatomical units and in their orientation within these units.

Axonal Growth

Most migrating neurons do not have the characteristic form of mature neurons; with a few exceptions, they begin to develop their processes (axons and dendrites) only after they have migrated to their final destination. At the distal end of the developing axon is a structure called a **growth cone,** which is involved in guiding the growing axon to its target (Figure 14.5). On the edge of the growth cone are threadlike exten-

mice showed extensive disruption of neuronal migration, and these animals also evidenced severe behavioral impairment (Rakic, 1988a).

The molecular events underlying neuronal migration are complex and incompletely understood. They are known to involve strong bonds between migrating neurons and radial glial cells, which are presumably mediated by cell adhesion molecules (Rakic, 1995). Once neurons reach their destination, they ag-

sions, known as **filopodia,** with flattened sheets between them, known as **lamellipodia.** Precisely how the growth cone guides the growing axon to its target is one of the most important and baffling problems in developmental neurobiology. Clues that the process is at least partially under genetic control come from studies showing that neuroblasts grown in cell culture grow processes that look normal (Cowan, 1979), although neuroblasts in cell culture do not of course make connection with their intended targets. Growth along the correct pathway and termination on the axon's ultimate target appear to involve specific molecules on the growth cone that enable it to respond to structural or chemical cues along its route and at its final destination.

Dendritic Growth

The major factor determining dendritic growth and branching appears to be the presence and pattern of afferent axonal fibers approaching the dendritic end of the developing neuron. Thus, the dendrites of many neurons remain in a relatively undeveloped state until the arrival of their afferent axons, at which point dendritic processes sprout to meet them (Figure 14.6), eventually forming the neuron's full dendritic tree (Courchesne, 1991a).

The Formation of Connections and the Contribution of the Environment

As we have said, the problem of how developing neurons make specific connections with other neurons remains unresolved. It is clear, however, that this critical process, the results of which serve as the basis for the enormously complex functional capacity of advanced nervous systems, involves an elaborate interaction of genetic and environmental determinants. In this section, we will discuss these determinants and their interaction.

In principle, one solution to the problem of forming the right connections could be to first form a random set of connections and then to retain those that are functionally active and eliminate those that are not. This connectivity through functional selection

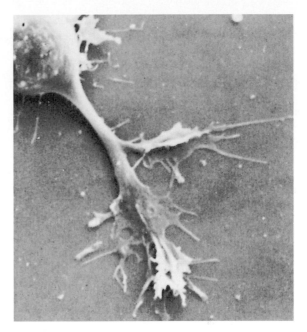

FIGURE 14.6 A scanning electron micrograph of a growing dendrite, showing growth cones on its surface. *(From Cowan, 1979, p. 63)*

would be analogous to building a complex network of interstate highways connecting all towns and then closing or reducing the size of those that do not have a certain level of traffic. There is evidence that most developing neurons generate more processes than they need or than they ultimately maintain and that they make more connections than are maintained in the mature state (Rakic, 1995). This suggests that some kind of functional selection contributes to the development of the neuronal connections that culminate in the mature nervous system. However, functional selection cannot be the only determinant of neuronal connectivity because of the sheer complexity of the enormous number of connections that are formed prenatally, before any significant environmental input is available. Thus, both genetically determined intrinsic factors and environmentally generated extrinsic factors contribute to the connectivity of the mature nervous system. We will examine each of these factors in turn.

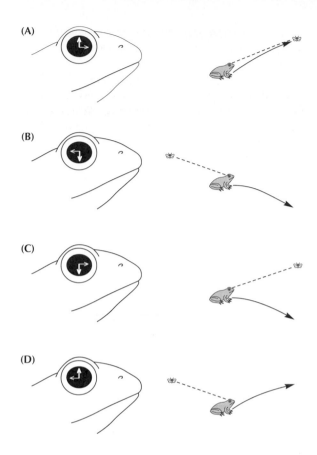

(A)

(B)

(C)

(D)

FIGURE 14.7   Sperry's experiments involving rotation or transplantation of the eye of a frog to determine how the regenerating optic nerve forms new connections with the optic tectum. When connections are reformed, their functionality can be assessed by observing the frog's visual behavior. (*A*) The behavior of the control frog with its eyes in the normal condition. (*B*) When the right eye is rotated 180° and the animal is then presented with a lure in the upper field, it strikes exactly 180° in the wrong direction. (*C*) In this experiment, the left eye is substituted for the right eye and rotated 180°, resulting in an inversion only in the dorsoventral axis: The frog directs its strike forward toward the lure, but in the direction of the lower, instead of the upper visual field. (*D*) When a similar transplantation is done, but the eye is not rotated, so that only the anteroposterior axis is inverted, the frog correctly senses that the lure is in the upper visual field, but strikes forward rather than backward. These results indicate that during regeneration, the fibers of the optic nerve always grow back to the part of the optic tectum they originally innervated. The results are thus consistent with the hypothesis that the fibers of the optic nerve and neurons in the optic tectum have chemical characteristics that enable them to identify each other. *(From Cowan, 1979, p. 64)*

INTRINSIC FACTORS   Impressive instances of genetically determined neuronal connections abound in the developing nervous system. For example, mice that are congenitally anophthalmic (born without eyes) and animals whose eyes have been surgically removed in early stages of embryonic development nevertheless develop correct topographical connections in the visual cortex in the absence of any information from the photoreceptors (Kaiserman-Abramoff, Graybiel, & Nauta, 1980; Olavarria & Van Sluyters, 1984; Rakic, 1988b). In addition, V1 in monkeys acquires area-specific cytochrome oxidase patches (see chapter 5) in the absence of any input from receptors in the retina (Kuljis & Rakic, 1990).

One theory of how these connections are made is the **chemospecificity hypothesis** of Roger Sperry (1968, 1971). According to this theory, neurons be-

come chemically differentiated at an early stage in their development in such a way that their membranes come to have distinguishing chemical labels that enable the neurons to recognize their target. Evidence for this position comes from classic experiments by Sperry in which he cut the optic nerve in embryonic and adult amphibians, such as the frog. These species are able to extensively regenerate neural tissue, so that even when the optic nerve is cut in the adult, fibers from the eye grow back to the optic tectum and form connections.

After cutting the optic nerve, Sperry either rotated the eye within its socket or removed the eye and replaced it with the eye transplanted from the other socket. His reasoning was that if each neuron in the optic nerve has a specific chemical label that determines its target in the optic tectum, then the experimental manipulations he performed should result in the reestablishment of the original connections. However, if function is a significant factor in the formation of connections between the optic nerve and the optic tectum, then manipulation of the position of the eye should lead to different, presumably more functionally adaptive, connections. Sperry's experiments showed that the original connections are in fact reestablished (Figure 14.7), supporting the notion that some kind of chemical labeling, rather than functionally related factors, determines the connections. This is the essence of Sperry's chemospecificity hypothesis.

EXTRINSIC FACTORS   The results of Sperry's experiments and similar findings by other investigators verify that internal factors, primarily genetic in nature, are important determinants of neural connections. This is not altogether surprising. It makes sense that the genetic code should contain information about how neurons in the brain are hooked up, particularly because much of the development of connections takes place prenatally, before significant environmental input is available. However, environmental input turns out to also be an important factor contributing to the ultimate pattern of neuronal connections. This too is not entirely unexpected when one considers that the information storage required for the genetic programming of all connections in the mature mammalian brain would far exceed the information storage capacity of the genome. In addition, such a hard-wiring of all connections, even if possible, would have the disadvantage of diminishing the developing nervous system's capacity to undergo adaptive modification in response to environmental or genetically based disruptions of normal development, a capacity termed **plasticity.**

The influence of the environment is evident most in later stages of development. In many instances, genetic instructions have programmed an overabundance of connections, which eventually diminish through the elimination of axons and synapses, as well as through the death of neurons. It is in these processes of pruning and attrition that functional activity (and the environmental stimuli that spark it) becomes important, for, in many instances, which connections survive depends on which connections receive the most environmental stimulation.

An example of this competitive process is the development of ocular dominance columns in V1. As will be recalled from chapter 5, although the vast majority of neurons in V1 respond to stimuli presented

to either eye, some respond more vigorously to stimuli presented to the ipsilateral eye, and others respond more vigorously to stimuli presented to the contralateral eye. This preference for firing in response to stimuli presented to a given eye is referred to as the neuron's ocular dominance. We also saw in chapter 5 that neurons in V1 are arranged in orderly ocular dominance columns, about 400 μm in width, that receive input predominantly from the right eye or the left eye (see Figure 5.27).

Experiments conducted by Hubel and colleagues (Hubel, Wiesel, & LeVay, 1977; Hubel, Wiesel, & Stryker, 1978) have shown that if one eye of a kitten is sutured shut shortly after birth so that its retina is never exposed to patterned illumination, the ocular dominance bands connected to that eye shrink, while those connected to the other eye enlarge, the combined width of the two bands remaining constant. Normally, ocular dominance bands do not develop until after the first month of life. This suggests that initially there is widespread input from both eyes to all neurons in V1, but that during the first postnatal month connections from one eye to neurons in a given ocular dominance band drop out. Apparently, in Hubel and Wiesel's experiments the absence of competing input from the deprived eye leaves the widespread input from the nondeprived eye intact, while the corresponding widespread input from the deprived eye drops out. These findings indicate that the neural hardware required for ocular dominance is prewired by genetic factors, but that manifesting or activating ocular dominance requires function.

The same conclusion may be drawn from experiments investigating the effect of sensory deprivation on the organization of the somatosensory cortex of the mouse. Mouse sensory cortex has specialized aggregates of cells, known as **barrels,** each of which receives input from a single whisker on the contralateral side of the animal. If a row of whiskers is removed in a young animal, the barrels that had represented those whiskers will disappear and those representing adjacent whiskers will expand (Woolsey et al., 1981). This is illustrated in Figure 14.8. These findings provide another example of the dependence of the developing nervous system on environmental inputs, as well as

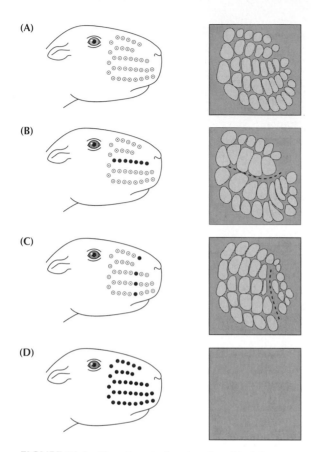

FIGURE 14.8 Experiments showing the critical dependence of the developing nervous system on its input. In the mouse, (*A*) specialized aggregates of cells in the somatosensory cortex, termed barrels, receive input from a single whisker on the opposite side of the animal's snout. (*B*) and (*C*) If one row of whiskers is destroyed shortly after birth, the corresponding row of barrels in the cerebral cortex will later be found to be missing and the adjacent barrels will have enlarged. (*D*) If all of the whiskers are destroyed, all of the barrels will disappear. *(From Cowan, 1979, p. 66)*

on genetic prewiring. As Rakic (1995) has noted, environmental input sculpts the final pattern of neuronal organization from an initial genetically determined state of excess cells, axons, and synapses. These examples also illustrate the capacity of the developing brain to reorganize itself in response to external influences or local injury, a theme to which we will return in chapter 15.

Myelination

Before ending our discussion of development on the neuronal level, let's briefly consider a process that occurs after the formation of connections between neurons. **Myelination** is the process whereby the developing axon becomes wrapped in a glial sheath. It is known to enhance the speed of neuronal transmission and therefore, presumably, its general efficiency (see chapter 2). Since the pioneering work of Flechsig (1901), it has been known that myelination does not take place all at once in the developing nervous system; different structures myelinate at different times, a phenomenon that has led to the concept of **myelogenetic cycles.** These are summarized in Figure 14.9. Attempts have been made to correlate myelogenetic cycles with the development of specific functions (Lecours, 1975; Lenneberg, 1967), particularly the function of the late-myelinating posterior parietal and prefrontal cortices. The finding that regions mediating higher-order functioning myelinate late, whereas structures such as sensory and motor pathways myelinate early, seems to fit with the notion that the time during development when myelination is complete is a marker of the maturation of a particular pathway or structure. Although this is a plausible hypothesis, it is by no means unequivocally established. Because unmyelinated axons are perfectly capable of neuronal transmission, albeit more slowly than myelinated axons, myelination is not a marker of neuronal activity per se. It is thus possible that regional differences in the completion time of myelination may prove to be rather crude markers of functional maturation.

BRAIN DEVELOPMENT AND THE DEVELOPMENT OF HIGHER-ORDER FUNCTION

Attempts to relate the development of higher-order function to brain development are complicated by the limits of our understanding of the neural mechanisms mediating complex functions. We simply do not know precisely which aspects of nervous system development are the most valid markers for the development of the neural mechanisms mediating complex

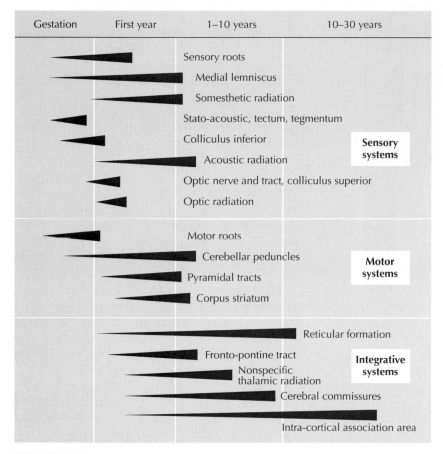

Gestation	First year	1–10 years	10–30 years

Sensory roots
Medial lemniscus
Somesthetic radiation
Stato-acoustic, tectum, tegmentum
Colliculus inferior
Acoustic radiation
Optic nerve and tract, colliculus superior
Optic radiation

Sensory systems

Motor roots
Cerebellar peduncles
Pyramidal tracts
Corpus striatum

Motor systems

Reticular formation
Fronto-pontine tract
Nonspecific thalamic radiation
Cerebral commissures
Intra-cortical association area

Integrative systems

FIGURE 14.9   Myelogenetic cycles of regional myelination in the human brain as summarized by Yakovlev and Lecours (1967). *(From Spreen et al., 1995, p. 20)*

behavior. Despite this daunting problem, some illuminating correlations between the development of function and aspects of neural development have been found. In addition, lags in the course of development between the attainment of knowledge and the ability to perform actions based on that knowledge may be markers of prefrontal development. In this section, we examine some of these findings.

Development of Visual Acuity

Infants have been shown to prefer looking at a grating as opposed to a plain, homogeneous stimulus. This tendency can be used to test visual acuity by exposing an infant to progressively finer gratings, each paired with a plain stimulus, until the infant fails to show a preference (Figure 14.10). Using this method, Gwiazda, Bauer, and Held (1989) have shown that an infant's visual acuity improves markedly over the first 12 months of life, reaching the adult level of acuity at approximately the end of that period (see Figure 14.10). This increase in visual acuity during the first 12 postnatal months is correlated with striking changes in the visual cortex (Conel, 1939–1967). At birth, migrating cells have populated only the deepest, sixth layer of V1; however, during the next 12 months all six layers of V1 are filled with neurons, and V1 appears very much as it does in the adult.

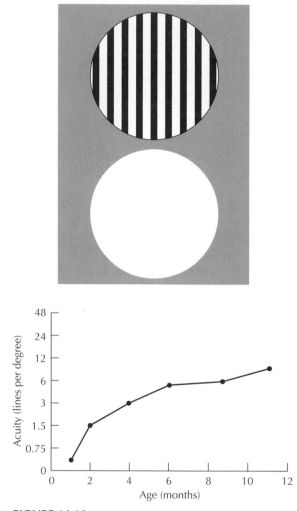

FIGURE 14.10   *(Top)* An example of the type of display used to study visual acuity in infants. *(Bottom)* Graph showing the results of one study in which the acuity of the infant is measured in terms of the largest number of lines per degree of visual angle that the infant prefers over a homogeneous field. *(From Posner & Raichle, 1994, p. 182)*

Development of Control of Visual Orienting

DEVELOPMENT OF INHIBITION OF RETURN Before age 1 month infants cannot consistently fixate on a visual stimulus. After the first month, V1 has developed sufficiently to allow for fixation. However, from about age 1 month to 4 months infants have the new problem of being unable to disengage from stimuli on which they are fixating, particularly when these include highly contrasting contours. This **obligatory looking** begins to decrease at about age 4 months, and by age 6 months infants are able to control orientation to the extent that they will consistently show a preference for looking at a novel object or novel visual location, a tendency termed **inhibition of return** (Posner & Raichle, 1994). This is illustrated in Figure 14.11.

DISENGAGING ATTENTION FROM A VISUAL LOCATION At about the same time that inhibition of return is developing, infants are developing the ability to disengage attention from a visual location and look at a newly appearing stimulus. This is illustrated by an experiment in which an infant is fixating on a central attractor; then a new stimulus, blinking on and off to attract the infant's attention, appears while the central attractor remains on. The probability that the infant will orient to the blinking stimulus has been shown to increase significantly between 2 and 4 months of age (M. H. Johnson, Posner, & Rothbart, 1991; Posner & Raichle, 1994).

In adults, it has been shown that disengaging attention from a visual location involves the superior parietal lobe. PET studies of infants have shown that the metabolic activity of this region reaches adult levels at about age 4 months. This finding fits nicely with the finding of a marked improvement in this function during the period just before age 4 months.

Development of Executive Function

As children mature, they develop increasing capacity to regulate their behavior on the basis of plans, goals, and other internal representations, processes that are mediated by prefrontal cortex. Although it is known that the process of myelination is not completed in prefrontal cortex until the second decade of life, little more is known about the developmental changes on the neuronal level that are correlated with the maturation of prefrontal cortex. On the behavioral level, however, there are clear indications of development of executive function throughout the course of the first two decades of life and beyond. In-

1 Central attractor on

3 Central attractor on

2 Stimulus at 30 degrees left

4 Stimulus at 30 degrees left and right

FIGURE 14.11 Stimuli used to study inhibition of return in infants. The infant faces a display of three monitors. *(1)* A central attractor on the center monitor first attracts the infant's attention. *(2)* The central attractor then goes off and a stimulus appears on the left monitor, which attracts the infant's attention. *(3)* The left stimulus then goes off, and the central attractor goes on. *(4)* Finally, the central attractor goes off, and stimuli appear on both the left and right monitors. Only after 6 months do infants show a consistent tendency to avoid the previously seen (left-hand) stimulus when presented with stimuli on the right and the left (inhibition of return). *(From Posner & Raichle, 1994, p. 186)*

deed, we might be tempted to ascribe the development of personality and character to the maturation of prefrontal cortex.

It will be recalled from our discussion of prefrontal function in chapter 12 that patients with prefrontal lesions often *understand* what is required in a particular situation but are not able to *organize behavior* based on that knowledge. This is dramatically exemplified by the not-uncommon occurrence of a patient with a prefrontal lesion who, after perseveratively sorting only to color on the Wisconsin Card Sorting Test, cheerfully announces at the end of the test that form and number could also have been used as bases for sorting. Recently, there have been some illuminating investigations of infant behavior that show the development of knowledge in a particular domain before the development of the capacity to act on that knowledge. These discrepancies in time of onset of *knowledge* versus *knowledge-based action* appear to be manifestations of the development of prefrontal executive function. Two examples are discussed below.

OBJECT PERMANENCE Knowledge that an object continues to exist even though it is no longer present

in the immediate environment is termed **object permanence.** The pioneering observations of Piaget (1952) indicated that before the age of about 9 months an infant will not search for an object that is removed from view, even when this is done right in front of the infant. Piaget concluded from these observations that before age 9 months infants do not have knowledge that the object continues to exist after it is removed from sight.

In some ways, experiments are like the evil genie in fairy tales who grants the wishes that the protagonists ask for rather than the ones they *think* they are asking for. In this case, Piaget's experiment was not actually asking, At what age does the infant know that the object continues to exist when it is out of sight? but, At what age will the infant actively search for the object? These are, of course, different questions. Experiments using the **dishabituation method** have shown that infants have knowledge that the object exists as early as age 4 months. This method takes advantage of the fact that infants show intense interest in novel objects, looking intently at them and sucking when that is rewarded by keeping the novel object in view. However, they also become bored after an object has been around for a while, a phenomenon termed **habituation.** If, after an infant has habituated to a particular stimulus, a new stimulus is introduced, the infant will **dishabituate,** looking and showing apparent surprise at the new stimulus, and, if the conditions of the experiment allow, working (e.g., sucking) to keep the novel object in view.

Baillargeon and her colleagues (1985; see also Baillargeon, 1987, 1991, 1995) used the dishabituation method to investigate object permanence in infants. In one experiment, 4-month-olds were shown a miniature stage with a screen attached to a rod in the middle of the stage so that the screen could be rotated upward, like a drawbridge, away from the infant (Figure 14.12A). The infant rapidly habituated to this event. Following this, a block was placed at the end of the stage so that it was clearly visible initially, but then became hidden by the screen as the screen rotated away from the infant and eventually was stopped by the block (Figure 14.12B). After the infant habituated to this condition, she was exposed to the critical condition. With the block in place, the screen was rotated back, but instead of hitting the block, the screen continued to move backward a full 180°. This should be an impossible event, but it was possible because the experimenter, out of sight of the infant, removed the block (Figure 14.12C). Just as adults would be surprised by this event, 4-month-old infants evidently found the event surprising because they spent more time looking at it than at the other two conditions, to which they had habituated. These results demonstrate that infants have knowledge of object permanence months before they are able to utilize that knowledge to guide goal-directed search behavior. Presumably the maturation of executive and representational systems in prefrontal cortex between 4 and 9 months of age is necessary for the development of this behavior.

NOVEL OBJECT PREFERENCE   An analogous discrepancy is seen in infants' response to novel objects. At age 6 months, infants will look more at a novel object than at one they have seen previously. However, it is not until age 18 months that they will preferentially reach for the novel object (Posner & Raichle, 1994). Again, this lag between knowledge (as demonstrated by preferential looking) and the regulation of organized behavior based on that knowledge (as demon-

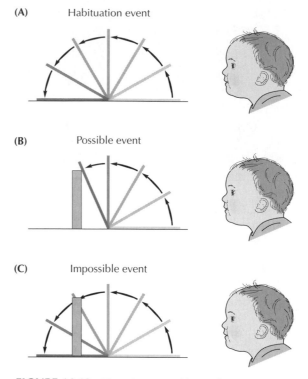

FIGURE 14.12   Experiment used by Baillargeon to test object permanence in 4-month-old infants. *(Modified from Posner & Raichle, 1994, p. 194)*

strated by reaching) may be ascribed to the maturation of prefrontal executive function during the interval.

RESOLUTION OF CONFLICT   Prefrontal cortex has been shown to be critical for the mediation of processes involved in the resolution of conflict, such as that created in the Stroop Test. It will be recalled from chapter 12 that the Stroop Test presents subjects with words that are color names but that are printed in colors different from the names, so that a conflict is created between the automatic tendency to read the word and the task requirements of saying the color in which the word is printed. As we have seen, patients with prefrontal lesions have extreme difficulty with this task (Vendrell et al., 1995).

Diamond (1990) created a somewhat analogous conflict for infants. She showed them an attractive toy inside a transparent box. The box had an opening on the front, but the infants viewed the toy through the

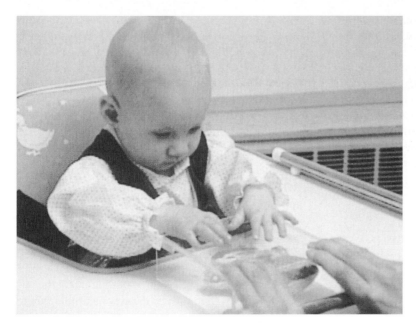

FIGURE 14.13   Experimental set-up used by Diamond to assess an infant's ability to resolve a conflict between line of sight and trajectory for reaching. Here the infant is unable to retrieve the toy from a transparent box that is closed on all sides except for the front. *(From Posner & Raichle, 1994, p. 196)*

top of the box (Figure 14.13). Infants 6½ to 8 months of age are unable to retrieve the toy unless the box is positioned in such a way that they can look through the opening and see the toy. When infants can see the toy only through the top, they try vainly to retrieve the toy through the closed top. Thus, infants at this age are unable to adaptively resolve the conflict between line of sight and trajectory for reaching.

By age 9 months, infants are able to look through the top of the box and retrieve the toy when the opening is in the front of the box, but not when the box is positioned so that the opening is on the side. Only at age 12 months are they able to reach through the side of the box to retrieve the toy. The mastering of this conflict between line of sight and trajectory for reaching requires both the inhibition of direct reaching along the line of sight and the development and execution of a plan to reach the object by a circuitous route. This achievement is yet another manifestation of the maturation of prefrontal executive function.

In this brief account of the development of executive function we have focused on disparities between the *achievement of knowledge representations*, at one point in development, and the later development of the *capacity to guide and regulate behavior on the basis of those*

representations. Infants are particularly well suited for an investigation of this development because of the rapid and extensive neurobiological changes that are taking place during this period and because confounding variables such as personality and experience have had less of an opportunity to complicate the picture. Nevertheless, it should, in principle, be possible to trace the resolution of analogous disparities throughout development. Although this would be extremely interesting, it is beyond the scope of our present account. We turn instead to the consideration of another critically important function: language.

Language Development

Although it is indisputable that the presence of language in the infant's environment is necessary for language acquisition, there is also evidence that language acquisition depends on the maturation of neural systems that have evolved to specifically support the development of language. From this perspective, the development of language is like the development of the physical structure of the body in that it unfolds under the direction of genetic factors (Lenneberg, 1967). More recently, this notion has been represented by the idea that language is an "organ" (Chomsky, 1988, 1991, 1993) or an "instinct" (Pinker, 1994).

Support for the hypothesis that language acquisition unfolds as the result of a biologically determined maturational process comes from a number of sources. Some of the evidence was discussed in chapter 6, including the ability of infants at age 1 month to discriminate between different phonemes (Eimas et al., 1971) and the finding of structural hemispheric asymmetries that are correlated with hemispheric specialization for language in both human adult and fetal brains (Wada, Clark, & Hamm, 1975). In this section, we review further evidence supporting this notion.

THE REGULARITY OF ONSET OF LANGUAGE MILESTONES Language milestones occur with marked regularity across different children and across different cultures. For example, in the absence of extreme environmental deprivation or neurological impairment, most children start forming two-word sentences at about 18–20 months of age. And they do so effortlessly, without explicit instruction. This is analogous to the way in which children develop such maturationally determined behaviors as crawling and walking.

THE RELATIVE INDEPENDENCE OF LANGUAGE CAPACITY FROM ENVIRONMENTAL FACTORS It is obvious that language must be available in the environment of children for them to learn it, and, of course, the particular language and dialect they learn will depend on what language they hear. Nevertheless, as long as a critical minimum of language is present in the child's environment, the capacity to develop language is not dependent on the nature or amount of that language. The idea of *capacity* for language development is emphasized because it is the case that children living in orphanages, in which there is little linguistic stimulation, or children of deaf parents exhibit a lag in language development. However, once they are exposed to a normal linguistic environment, their language abilities catch up, suggesting that the capacity for language was unaffected by the temporary reduction in language experience.

UTILITY NOT A MAJOR FACTOR IN THE DEVELOPMENT OF LANGUAGE Deaf infants vocalize in ways that are similar to hearing children, although they do not develop words (Lenneberg, 1967).

For example, cooing and babbling develop at about the same time in hearing-impaired children as they do in hearing children. In addition, deaf children at about age 2 are able to express their needs quite well through intuitively developed signs. This suggests that the development of language in hearing 2-year-olds is not occurring out of a response to an experienced need, but, rather, represents the result of a natural maturational process (Lenneberg, 1967).

CRITICAL PERIOD FOR LANGUAGE DEVELOPMENT Another source of evidence supporting the notion that language emerges as the result of a genetically programmed maturational process is the presence of a critical period for language acquisition. Studies of children who have experienced extreme environmental deprivation demonstrate that if a child is not exposed to language by approximately the onset of puberty, then the child cannot learn language normally. This finding is consistent with the idea that the brain of the young child is particularly prepared for language learning and that this preparedness disappears as the brain matures further.

As is the case with the development of other complex behaviors, we do not yet understand the neuronal mechanisms underlying language acquisition. It is therefore not yet possible to study the development, during the critical period, of the neurobiological mechanisms that support language development. We are therefore left with seeking markers of maturation during the critical period that we have reason to believe may have something to do with language acquisition and language function. Not surprisingly, there are many changes on the neuronal level that occur during the critical period for language acquisition. These include increase in neuronal volume, increase in neuronal weight, increase in the number of interconnections between neurons, and the development of higher-order (fuller) dendritic branching (Lenneberg, 1967). Although it remains to be seen which of these and which other maturational changes are directly related to language development, it is clear that the critical period for language is a period of intense maturational change.

CRITICAL PERIOD FOR THE RECOVERY OF LANGUAGE AFTER CEREBRAL DAMAGE A related phenomenon that supports the notion that the young brain is particularly prepared to develop language is the presence of a critical period for the recovery of language function after cerebral damage. Adults who become aphasic may experience some improvement over the first year following the lesion. The degree of recovery varies greatly and may be very incomplete. In contrast, of children who lose language after a cerebral lesion that occurs before puberty almost all experience full recovery. We will discuss this phenomenon further in our examination of recovery of function (see chapter 15).

THE DEVELOPMENT OF LEFT-HEMISPHERE SPECIALIZATION FOR LANGUAGE Looking at the probability that a left- or right-hemisphere lesion will produce language disturbance in children of different ages can give us clues about the development of lateralization of language. Studies exploring this relationship report that with increasing age, up to puberty, there is an increasing probability of language disturbance after left-hemisphere damage and a decreasing probability of language disturbance after right-hemisphere damage (Basser, 1962; Hecaen, 1976). Thus, as can be seen from Tables 14.1 and 14.2, before the onset of speech, lesions of the left and the right hemispheres are equally likely to disrupt the onset of speech. However, during the period from onset of speech to age 10, right-hemisphere lesions are far more likely to result in language disturbance than they are in adulthood, but less likely to do so than left-hemisphere lesions. These data suggest that there is a period in infancy during which the two hemispheres are equipotential for the development of language. After this period, and extending up to puberty, there is a gradual lateralization of language to the left hemisphere, culminating around puberty in the adult pattern of functional asymmetry. This process of lateralization, including its openness to modification as a result of early left-hemisphere lesions, is consistent with the notion that the capacity for language development is biologically determined. It is difficult to understand how environmental events could cause the lateralization of language to a specific hemisphere.

KNOWN CAUSES OF DEVELOPMENTAL ABNORMALITY

A number of factors are known to interfere with neural development during the prenatal period and during early life. Some, like gross malnutrition, serious maternal illness during pregnancy, and brain trauma during birth, are obvious causes of developmental abnormality. Others, like mild infection during pregnancy and premature birth, are more subtle causes of disturbed development. There is considerable variation with regard to the effect of any given factor on development, so that the behavioral and neurological consequences of a particular factor are not always predictable. This is the case even for factors that are relatively homogeneous in their causal mechanism, such as Turner's syndrome, a chromosomal abnormality, and phenylketonuria, a genetic abnormality. Variability is even more of a problem in less homogeneous conditions, such as seizure disorders or hydrocephalus. In addition, other influences complicate the relationship between a particular factor and its behavioral consequences. These include age of onset, environmental factors, predisposing factors, and the location in the brain of disease processes and trauma. In this section, we briefly review some of the major factors affecting neural development. A more detailed discussion of these factors can be found in Spreen, Risser, and Edgell (1995).

TABLE 14.1 Lesions Before Onset of Speech

	Onset of Speech		
	Normal	Delayed	Never
Left hemisphere	18	15	1
Right hemisphere	19	15	4

Based on Basser, 1962 (from Lenneberg, 1967, p. 151)

TABLE 14.2 Lesions After Onset of Speech and Before Age 10

	After Catastrophe, Speech Was:	
	Normal	Disturbed
Left hemisphere	2	13
Right hemisphere	8	7

Based on Basser, 1962 (from Lenneberg, 1967, p. 151)

Inherited Disorders

Genetically based disorders cover a spectrum from subtle cognitive deficits and learning disorders to severe impairment, including retardation (Baron, Fennell, & Voeller, 1995; Bellugi, Klima, & Wang, 1996). Genetic abnormalities can be transmitted in several ways. **Autosomal dominant transmission** refers to transmission via chromosomes other than the sex chromosomes and requires the gene from only one parent for the trait or disorder to occur. **Autosomal recessive transmission** requires two genes, one from each parent, for the trait or disorder to occur. **Sex-linked transmission** refers to any genetic disorder affecting one sex selectively, which is thus presumably due to a gene on the sex chromosome. In addition, the genetic predisposition for a particular disorder may be transmitted via the interaction of several genes. This is referred to as **polygenic inheritance** and may require the interaction of environmental factors for the trait or disorder to occur.

An example of an autosomal recessive disorder is **phenylketonuria (PKU),** a disorder that causes an alteration of the enzyme **phenylalanine hydroxylase,** which normally converts the amino acid phenylalanine to tyrosine. This alteration causes phenylalanine to build up, exerting a toxic effect on developing neural tissue and causing mental retardation. The disorder can be detected by an overflow of unmetabolized phenylalanine through the kidneys and the excretion of phenylpyruvic acid in the urine. This has led to a simple screening procedure for the disorder, performed at birth, and to the virtual elimination of undiagnosed infants. Treatment, which consists of restricting the amount of phenylalanine in the diet, is highly effective. Phenylketonuria serves as an example of a genetic disorder that is being successfully treated (controlled), reminding us that the negative consequences of genetic transmission are not necessarily incontrovertible.

Chromosomal Disorders

Chromosomal disorders include a group of defects of the chromosomes as identified by abnormalities of their configuration **(karyotype).** Chromosomal disorders may be due to either environmental or genetic factors. They may take the form of extra chromosomes, as in **trisomy,** in which three chromosomes of a particular type are present instead of two; **translocation,** the mismatching of chromosome pairs or portions of a chromosome; or structural abnormalities involving partial or complete **deletion** of a chromosome.

Down syndrome (trisomy 21) is a relatively common chromosomal abnormality, the incidence of which is a function of the age of the mother, although there is also an inherited form. The major symptom is mild to severe retardation.

An example of a chromosomal deletion is **Turner's syndrome,** which results from a missing X chromosome. Patients with Turner's syndrome appear to exhibit a specific pattern of neuropsychological dysfunction characterized by impairment in the perception of form and space. There is some disagreement as to whether these deficits represent a specific impairment of right-hemisphere functioning (Kolb & Heaton, 1975; Waber, 1979).

Structural Abnormalities

Disruptions of development can result in a wide range of structural abnormalities, depending on the period of development during which the disruption takes place. Many of these abnormalities result in the death of the embryo or fetus; others cause severe impairment. The latter disorders include **anencephaly,** the lack of brain development, and **microcephaly,** very reduced brain development.

Prematurity and Low Birth Weight

Prematurity has been defined as either a birth weight of less than 2,500 g (5.5 lbs) or birth before 37 weeks of gestation (World Health Organization, 1961). Risks of prematurity include respiratory problems due to immaturity of the lungs, and related **hypoxic-ischemic encephalopathy** (abnormality of the brain due to oxygen and blood deprivation). Although these and other abnormalities are more likely after premature birth, prematurity does not necessarily place the newborn at risk; many premature infants develop normally.

Infection

Infections, particularly prenatal infections, can have major consequences for development. Perhaps the best-known complication of pregnancy is **rubella,** which is associated with microcephaly, meningoencephalitis, and mental retardation. More recently, much attention has been directed to infants infected with **human immunodeficiency virus (HIV)** (Armstrong, Seidel, & Swales, 1993). Cognitive impairments have been reported in children infected with HIV who have not yet developed AIDS (Condini et al., 1991).

Possible links between subclinical perinatal infection and the development of intelligence, learning disabilities, and serious psychopathology (including schizophrenia) have been hypothesized. To date, support for these hypotheses is weak, although future research may yield more compelling evidence.

Toxin-Related Damage

Various toxins introduced during the perinatal period result in disorders of development and behavior. One of the more extensively studied disorders is **fetal alcohol syndrome,** seen in children of alcoholic mothers (Don & Rourke, 1995). It is characterized by facial malformations, intrauterine growth retardation, and neurobehavioral dysfunction. In the neonatal period, these behavioral dysfunctions include increased periods with eyes open, body tremors, and decreased vigorous body activity (K. L. Jones, 1977).

Another important toxic disorder is lead poisoning. High blood levels of lead in children have been associated with hyperactivity (David, Clark, & Voeller, 1972) and poor performance on intelligence tests (Beattie et al., 1975; Klein, Sayre, & Kotok, 1974; Marlowe et al., 1984).

Nutritional Disorders

Nutritional disorders take several forms. A predominantly protein-deficient diet is associated clinically with a syndrome known as **kwashiorkor,** whereas a predominantly energy-deficient diet may result in a syndrome known as **marasmus.** Nutritional deficiency is seldom seen in isolation, usually being accompanied by other environmental and health-related problems. This has led to the concept of the **malnutritional milieu.**

At birth, the most obvious consequence of prenatal malnutrition is low birth weight, including a reduction in gross brain weight. The reduction in brain weight appears to be due to reduction in neuron proliferation during gestation. As one would expect, these consequences of the malnutritional milieu during early life profoundly influence cognitive abilities later in life.

Permanent cognitive impairments usually do not occur during a temporary period of nutritional deficiency in adulthood. However, specific nutritional deficiencies in adulthood may result in specific cognitive impairments. An example of this is the amnesic disorder that is part of the Wernicke-Korsakoff syndrome, caused by thiamine (vitamin B_1) deficiency associated with alcoholism (Adams & Victor, 1993).

Anoxic Episodes

Of all the organs of the body, the brain has the highest demand for oxygen. This fact, together with the inability of neurons to regenerate, makes the brain highly vulnerable to damage as the result of an **anoxic episode,** a period of oxygen deprivation, which can result in hypoxic-ischemic encephalopathy. Nevertheless, a perinatal anoxic episode alone is a weak predictor of later childhood disability (Spreen et al., 1995). Some investigators have hypothesized that undiagnosed anoxia in early life may cause subclinical anoxic pathology that results in neuropsychological impairment, including learning disabilities, later in life. Although these hypotheses have a certain plausibility, they have actually received little empirical support.

Traumatic Brain Injury and Focal Cerebral Abnormality

Like the adult brain, the fetal brain and the brains of infants and children are vulnerable to the effects of traumatic brain injury and neurological diseases such as neoplasms and stroke (Lord-Maes & Obrzut, 1996; Reynolds, 1996). In our earlier discussion of language development, we saw that early lesions differ both with regard to their short-term effects on

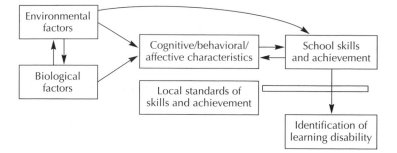

FIGURE 14.14 Taylor's (1987) model of the factors contributing to the diagnosis of a learning disability. The model assumes that a child's cognitive, behavioral, and affective characteristics emerge out of an interaction between biological and environmental factors. These characteristics then interact with current school skills to influence the development of further school achievement. Local standards enter the picture because whether or not an individual will be diagnosed as having a learning disability depends, in part, on performance relative to local standards. The model has the advantages of placing no restriction on the type and origin of learning problems and of emphasizing that multiple factors contribute to the disorder. It also does not assume any simple one-to-one correspondence between biological state and learning problems.

language function and the long-term prognosis for recovery. We will have more to say about the effects of early lesions in chapter 15, which deals with recovery of function.

DEVELOPMENTAL DISORDERS OF UNKNOWN CAUSE

In the preceding sections we have reviewed some of the abnormalities that can affect the developing brain and provided examples of some of the resulting impairments. We now change perspectives and focus on the symptom picture of three categories of developmental disorders for which the underlying neuropathology and remote causes are unknown: learning disorders, attention deficit disorder, and autism.

Learning Disorders

A **learning disorder,** sometimes called a **learning disability,** is an impairment in a specific domain of cognition, such as reading, mathematics, or spatial processing, that is not attributable to inadequate general intelligence, lack of opportunity to learn, inadequate home environment, inadequate motivation, or the presence of a handicapping condition, such as a sensory deficit. A critical criterion for the diagnosis is the

specificity of the impairment; poor functioning across a broad range of areas is usually due to some factor with generalized effects, such as one of those just discussed. These specific cognitive impairments are presumed to be due to central nervous system dysfunction, although the nature of this dysfunction is often unknown.

Although this definition seems straightforward enough, in practice, the diagnosis of a learning disorder is fraught with problems. In particular, when evaluating an individual child, it is not always clear to what extent socio-cultural-economic factors contribute to impairment in a specific skill. Taylor (1987) has formulated a model for the identification of learning disorders that attempts to acknowledge the complexity of factors involved in the process (Figure 14.14). The importance of sociocultural factors in the definition of learning disorders is also evident from the fact that these disorders were first identified in areas that are most salient for school performance, such as reading, math, and writing—rather than in skills that receive less emphasis in the school setting, such as spatial orientation and other nonverbal processing (Semrud-Clickeman & Hynd, 1991)—although the importance of nonverbal learning disorders is now recognized. In the sections that follow, we examine three categories of learning disorder: dyslexia, dyscalculia, and nonverbal learning disabilities. Because dyslexia is the most common learning disorder and the one about which we know the most, we consider it in more detail than the other two disorders.

DEVELOPMENTAL DYSLEXIA   Consistent with the general definition of learning disorders, **developmental dyslexia** is a specific disorder of reading not due to a known cerebral lesion (i.e., not acquired dyslexia) and not due to inadequate intelligence, environmental factors, or sensory handicap (Critchley & Critchley, 1978).

Acquired Dyslexia as a Model for Developmental Dyslexia   Developmental dyslexia was the first learning disorder to be identified. The concept emerged in the context of the rapidly accelerating knowledge of acquired language disorders that was taking place at the end of the 19th century. In the area of reading, these discoveries included Kussmall's identification in 1877 of a patient with what he called *word blindness* following a cerebral lesion. Ten years later Berlin coined the term *dyslexia,* and not long afterward Hinshelwood (1895) presented evidence for an association between acquired dyslexia and lesions of the left angular gyrus. In the context of these advances in the understanding of acquired dyslexia as a specific consequence of cerebral lesions, Morgan (1896) reported the case of a child whose inability to read was not associated with a known lesion or with other cognitive deficits, a condition which he termed *congenital word blindness.*

Features of Developmental Dyslexia   In chapter 6, we reviewed the types of dyslexia seen after cerebral damage. It may be recalled from that discussion that acquired dyslexia can be divided into two broad categories: the visual word-form dyslexias, involving the initial processing of a word, and the central dyslexias, involving later stages in the reading process. Developmental dyslexia resembles the acquired central dyslexias in having three basic forms, although there is often considerable overlap in individual cases. These are surface dyslexia, phonological dyslexia, and deep dyslexia. **Surface dyslexia,** also called **phonological reading,** is the inability to form word-sound correspondences without subject-

ing the word to phonological analysis, which is unimpaired. Individuals with this form of dyslexia can read phonetically regular words and nonsense words, but not phonetically irregular words. **Phonological dyslexia,** also called **reading by sight vocabulary,** is the converse: These individuals can read words by sight, but not on the basis of phonological analysis. They are thus unable to read uncommon phonetically regular words or nonsense words, but they can read common regular or irregular words that have entered their sight vocabulary. Some children with developmental dyslexia have an impairment that takes the form of confusions of meaning. This disruption of reading on the semantic level, termed **deep dyslexia,** is exemplified by reading *jog* for *run* or *bread* for *cake*.

Theories of Developmental Dyslexia   The causes and mechanisms of developmental dyslexia are not well understood. However, there are several theories that attempt to account for the disorder.

One of the first theories, put forward by Orton (1925, 1927), was that dyslexia is due to incomplete or mixed cerebral dominance. Noting that dyslexic children sometimes write letters and words in their mirror-image forms, Orton hypothesized that the right hemisphere stored these forms and that a lag in the development of the left hemisphere released these images from their normal suppression, disrupting writing and reading.

Although there is little empirical evidence for Orton's imaginative notion that the right hemisphere stores letters and words in their mirror-image form, less specific hypotheses invoking delayed, incomplete, or abnormal language lateralization as a cause of developmental dyslexia appear, at least on the face of things, somewhat more plausible (Geschwind, 1982; Geschwind & Galaburda, 1987; Witelson, 1976, 1977). Although these theories differ in certain ways, they share the premise that incomplete lateralization of language would render language processing somehow less efficient in a way that would adversely affect reading. Incomplete lateralization hypotheses of dyslexia rest on the fundamental fact that language is usually strongly lateralized to one hemisphere. However, it turns out there is little support for the idea that developmental dyslexia is associated with incomplete lateralization of language.

As pointed out by Zangwill (1962), if poorly developed cerebral lateralization were a cause of cognitive impairment, one would expect a more general learning or linguistic impairment rather than impairment specific to the domain of reading. In addition, left-handed individuals with bilateral speech, as assessed by sodium amobarbital testing, do not evidence specific reading problems or any other language problems. Also, attempts to assess hemispheric specialization for language in children with dyslexia, using laterality measures such as dichotic listening, have failed to establish consistent abnormalities of lateralization (Bryden, 1988; Porac & Cohen, 1981; Satz & Soper, 1986).

Although we are arguing here that abnormal laterality is not the cause of developmental dyslexia, it is important to recognize that the contribution of each hemisphere to abilities involved in *learning* an academic skill may be very different from those involved in the *execution* of that skill in older children and adults who have already mastered it (Witelson, 1985). For example, there is evidence that the right hemisphere is involved in the initial stages of reading because of the high visuospatial demands of that stage (Fletcher & Satz, 1980; Hinshaw, Carte, & Morrison, 1986; Licht et al., 1986) or because the right hemisphere is better at handling novel tasks (Goldberg & Costa, 1981). This would mean that the relative contribution of the two hemispheres to reading would change as the skill develops and that problems in learning to read may be the result of dysfunction of either the left or the right hemisphere, depending on the stage in the learning process at which the problem develops.

An alternative hypothesis is that some abnormality of left-hemisphere functioning, other than abnormal lateralization, is a major causal factor in developmental dyslexia. The simplest form of this hypothesis is that the left hemisphere has sustained some form of subtle damage. Evidence for this appears to come from the finding that a higher proportion of dyslexic than nondyslexic children are left-handed (Vernon, 1971), suggesting that some of them may have sustained early left-hemisphere damage that caused the control of handedness to move to the right hemisphere. There are, however, a number of problems with this hypothesis. Many dyslexic children are not left-handed. In addition, one would not expect an early left-hemisphere lesion that was sufficiently disruptive to cause the control of handedness to move from the left to the right hemisphere to result in a specific reading disorder, leaving all other left-hemisphere function intact.

It is well established that boys are more likely to be dyslexic than girls, the ratio being about 4:1 (Ansara et al., 1981; Buffery, 1976; Critchley & Critchley, 1978; Lansdell, 1964; Rourke, 1978; Singer, Westphal, & Niswander, 1968). Geschwind and Galaburda (1987) have proposed a hypothesis that uses this finding as a point of departure. According to their hypothesis, the fetal surge in testosterone, seen only in males, delays left-hemisphere development, which, in turn, allows the right hemisphere to develop more completely. This results in the general inferiority of boys on verbal tasks and their higher prevalence of dyslexia. It also provides an explanation for the superiority of males on spatial tasks. Geschwind and Galaburda also attempted to account for another set of findings with their hypothesis. There have been reports that children with dyslexia have a higher incidence of immune disorders, such as myasthenia gravis. The investigators therefore proposed that the fetal surge in testosterone also adversely affects the immune system, as well as delaying the development of the left hemisphere, thus accounting for this correlation. Assuming that delayed left-hemisphere development also causes a higher proportion of left-handedness, this hypothesis could also be invoked to account for the higher proportion of left-handers among children with dyslexia.

There are, however, a number of problems with the Geschwind-Galaburda hypothesis. Most important, the prediction that the left hemisphere of persons with dyslexia should show selective abnormality has not been confirmed. As we will see in the next section, autopsy studies of the brains of people who had dyslexia do not reveal a consistent pattern of lesions confined to the left hemisphere. In addition, the theory makes assumptions about the effect of fetal testosterone on the development of the left hemisphere that have not been confirmed.

Structural Lesions   Although the concept of developmental dyslexia grew out of the concept of acquired

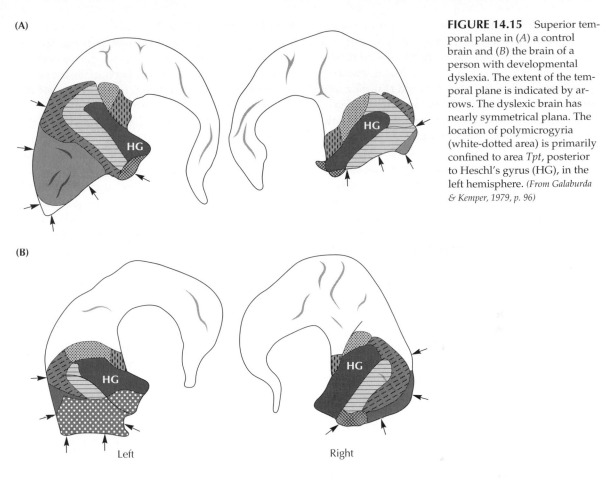

(A)

(B)

Left

Right

FIGURE 14.15 Superior temporal plane in (*A*) a control brain and (*B*) the brain of a person with developmental dyslexia. The extent of the temporal plane is indicated by arrows. The dyslexic brain has nearly symmetrical plana. The location of polymicrogyria (white-dotted area) is primarily confined to area *Tpt*, posterior to Heschl's gyrus (HG), in the left hemisphere. (*From Galaburda & Kemper, 1979, p. 96*)

dyslexia, the search for a lesion in developmental dyslexia that is analogous to that seen in persons with acquired dyslexia has not been successful. Thus, people with developmental dyslexia do not exhibit the symptoms of posterior left-hemisphere damage, such as right hemianopia, often seen in acquired dyslexia. In addition, modern radiological techniques, including CT and MRI, have failed to consistently identify lesions in the brains of people with developmental dyslexia.

However, autopsy studies do provide some hints concerning the neural basis of dyslexia. The first such study, investigating the brain of a 12-year-old dyslexic boy who had died of a cerebral hemorrhage (Drake, 1968), revealed atypical gyral patterns in the parietal lobes and an atrophied corpus callosum. Galaburda

and Kemper (1979) studied the brain of a man with a well-documented history of developmental dyslexia who died at age 20. They found a consistently wider left cerebral hemisphere; an area of polymicrogyria (small abnormal gyri) in the left-temporal speech region; and mild cortical dysplasias in the limbic, primary sensory, and association cortices. They also found many **ectopic cells,** neurons in white-matter regions where they are normally not seen. These changes were more frequent in the left hemisphere, but they have also been reported in the right hemisphere (Bigler, 1992).

Galaburda and Kemper also reported the absence of the normal asymmetry in the extent of the temporal plane in the left and right hemispheres (Figure 14.15). It may be recalled from chapter 6 that the temporal plane is larger in the left hemisphere than the right in a majority of individuals, and this is believed to be a structural correlate of the left hemisphere's specialization for language. The absence of such an asymmetry in the brains of persons with dyslexia was therefore striking. Findings of left parietal abnormality have been replicated in several other studies (Galaburda, 1989; Galaburda et al., 1985; Humphreys, Kaufmann, & Galaburda, 1990; Rosen, Sherman, & Galaburda, 1986). Interestingly, the deviation from the normal asymmetry typically takes the form of *large* temporal planes in both hemispheres, rather than small ones in both, as might be expected. However, the absence of the normal asymmetry is not seen consistently and is not a necessary or sufficient condition for the presence of dyslexia (Rourke, 1978). In addition, some studies showing an absence of asymmetry have been criticized on methodological grounds, which included some subjects identified as dyslexic not meeting the rigorous definition of the disorder, particularly the requirement that the disorder be specific to the domain of reading (Hynd & Semrud-Clickeman, 1989). At any rate, it is clear that many different neuroanatomical abnormalities have been associated with developmental dyslexia. This probably reflects the diversity of the causal factors contributing to the many forms of the disorder.

Metabolic Abnormalities   There have been some reports of metabolic abnormality in dyslexia. Less cerebral blood flow, as measured by PET, was seen in the left-temporal perisylvian region during a reading task in adults who had been childhood dyslexics (Flowers, Wood, & Naylor, 1991; Gross-Glenn et al., 1991). In addition, less asymmetry in activity in the prefrontal and inferior occipital regions has been reported (Gross-Glenn et al., 1991). However, less activation in the right hemisphere and bilaterally in a subject with deep dyslexia has also been reported (Hynd & Willis, 1987). It is possible that this finding reflects the normal involvement of the right hemisphere in semantic processing. Or, the inconsistencies of these findings may reflect the limits of metabolic imaging studies in identifying abnormalities in developmental dyslexia.

The Maturational Lag Hypothesis   According to the most general form of the maturational lag hypothesis, developmental dyslexia is due to delayed maturation of the brain in certain specific areas. On the neuronal level, this delay might consist of delayed myelination or the delayed formation of critical connections. There is very little evidence for this hypothesis, either from studies on the neuronal level or from studies attempting to identify delays in other areas of cognition in children with dyslexia. In addition, studies of the long-term outcome of children with dyslexia indicate that moderate to severe forms of the disorder persist into adulthood (Frauenheim, 1978; Spreen, 1988a, 1988b). Even children with milder forms of the disorder, who eventually acquire the fundamental skills of reading, often do not read for pleasure. The persistence of the disorder into adulthood argues against the notion that it is due to a maturational lag.

Genetic Determinants of Dyslexia   There is evidence that genetic factors contribute to at least some forms of dyslexia. This comes from the finding that dyslexia is seen in a high percentage of relatives of dyslexic individuals (Byring & Michelson, 1984) and that monozygotic twins have a higher concordance rate for the disorder than dizygotic twins. No genetic model for the inheritance of dyslexia has, however, been worked out.

Conclusion   The findings reviewed in this section, taken together, suggest that there are a number of different forms of dyslexia, each with its own characteristics and, presumably, it own causal factors (Benton, 1975; Yule & Rutter, 1976). This suggests that a multisyndrome approach to dyslexia, which recognizes that there are several neurologically based forms of the disorder, as well as many non-biologically based causal factors contributing to reading problems, will prove to be the most useful guiding framework for understanding the reading problems confronted by children.

DEVELOPMENTAL DYSCALCULIA   Dyscalculia, impairment in the ability to perform arithmetic operations, may occur after lesions to the posterior regions of either the left or the right hemisphere (Grafman et al., 1982). Acquired dyscalculia after posterior left-hemisphere lesions is often accompanied by other impairments, including finger agnosia, agraphia, and impaired right-left discrimination. These four impairments have been conceptualized as forming the **Gerstmann syndrome,** although, more recently, it has been shown that these symptoms should not be considered a syndrome because they are not in fact highly correlated (Benton, 1985). The dyscalculia seen after left parietal-lobe lesions seems to be an impairment of the essential operations of arithmetic in that patients with these lesions make fundamental errors in even simple addition problems. In contrast, acquired dyscalculia after right-hemisphere damage disrupts spatial aspects of calculating, such as lining up numbers, attending to the place value of a digit, and placing numbers in correct locations after performing operations (Levin & Eisenberg, 1979).

Developmental dyscalculia appears to have two forms, analogous to those seen after cerebral lesions. Thus, there is evidence that some children with calculation problems also have difficulty with spelling and reading, but not with visual or tactual perception. This pattern, sometimes termed **language-based dyscalculia,** is similar to the dyscalculia seen after left-hemisphere lesions. Other children with calculation difficulty show a pattern, sometimes termed **spatial dyscalculia,** that is similar to that seen after right-hemisphere lesions (Rourke, 1978, 1993; Rourke & Finlayson, 1978; Rourke & Strang, 1981). Despite these similarities between the developmental and acquired dyscalculias, no definitive neuroanatomical correlates of the developmental dyscalculias have been established.

NONVERBAL LEARNING DISABILITIES Non-**verbal learning disabilities,** a term first used by Myklebust (1975), are characterized by difficulty in areas that are not explicitly verbal and that are, therefore, less emphasized in the academic environment. These difficulties are heterogeneous and include impairment in the domains of perception, spatial processing, and social-emotional processing. Children may have difficulty with visual organization, face recognition, and tactual perception. They may have difficulty with spatial tasks, such as those involved in geometry or in map reading. People with nonverbal learning disabilities may have difficulty comprehending and interpreting aspects of their social-emotional environment, including the emotional communication inherent in the facial expressions and gestures of others. They may act socially and emotionally immature, have great difficulty making social judgments, and find it hard to develop social relationships. Although, in some individuals, these features may coexist with features of verbal learning disorders (Hooper & Willis, 1989; Rourke, 1989), there is strong evidence that features of nonverbal learning disabilities can occur without associated verbal features (Casey, Rourke, & Picard, 1991; Fuerst, Fisk, & Rourke, 1990; Rourke, 1989, 1995; Rourke et al., 1990; Rourke & Fuerst, 1992). Right-hemisphere dysfunction, possibly involving white-matter connections, has been hypothesized to underlie nonverbal learning disabilities.

Before ending our discussion of learning disorders, it should be pointed out that neuropsychological evaluation can be highly useful in their identification and treatment. The broad range of specific cognitive measures employed in such testing allows detection of the specific patterns of strength and weakness that characterize specific learning disorders. In addition, knowing in which cognitive domain or domains an individual is having selective difficulty makes it possible to focus educational interventions toward improvement in those areas. Perhaps equally important, from a treatment perspective, detection of an individual's relative strengths can contribute to the formulation of alternative cognitive strategies that utilize those strengths to achieve goals.

Attention Deficit Disorder

BEHAVIORAL FEATURES Attention deficit disor-**der (ADD)** is characterized by distractibility, impulsivity, and restlessness. Although it is now recognized that the symptoms of ADD can extend into adulthood

(Hallowell & Ratey, 1994), ADD is most often diagnosed in children. People with ADD have great difficulty attending to relevant cues and information in their environment. They may often act as if they are not listening or do not hear what is being said to them. Individuals with ADD have difficulty keeping their attention focused long enough to complete even relatively simple tasks, often moving on to a second or even a third task without completing any of them. Work is often highly disorganized, with material required to do a task scattered or lost. Individuals with ADD often have difficulty delaying gratification and taking the potential consequences of their actions into account when making decisions, even when they recognize on a cognitive level that it is in their long-term interest to do so. They are often restless, engaging in a great deal of nervous fidgeting and other hyperactive motor behavior, although hyperactivity is not always seen. Emotional immaturity, shallow social relationships, and poor academic and work performance are often part of the picture. Oppositionality may be seen, but this is usually secondary to the frustration experienced in the course of not being able to successfully complete tasks that require sustained attention and organization. For a further description of the behavioral features of ADD see American Psychiatric Association (1994, pp. 78–85) and Hallowell and Ratey (1994).

As is the case with so many of the disorders we have discussed in this and the previous chapter, ADD is almost certainly not a unitary disorder, but a spectrum of disorders with overlapping symptoms. It is therefore to be expected that attempts to identify biological factors in ADD will yield a number of factors, all of which may not be operative in all of the hypothetical subtypes of ADD. With this caveat in mind, let's review some of what has been learned about the biological factors contributing to ADD.

BIOLOGICAL FACTORS IN ADD   The strongest evidence for biological factors in ADD focuses on neurotransmitter abnormality and genetic determinants. There have also been a number of theories regarding the brain system that is dysfunctional in ADD. We review some of this evidence and a number of these theories in this section.

Neurotransmitters   Bradley (1937) reported that benzedrine, a stimulant, alleviated symptoms that are now characterized as indicative of ADD. More recently, other stimulants, including methylphenidate (Ritalin), pemoline (Cylert), and a combination of amphetamine and dextroamphetamine (Adderall) have also been reported to be effective. Some tricyclic antidepressants have also been shown to be effective in treating ADD, the most commonly used of these being desipramine (Norpramin). All of these medications increase neurotransmitter activity, particularly dopamine, norepinephrine, and serotonin. This has led to the **catecholamine hypothesis of ADD,** proposed by Kornetsky (cited in Hallowell & Ratey, 1994, p. 274), which posits that because the stimulants and tricyclic antidepressants that are effective in treating ADD raise catecholamine and indoleamine activity, ADD must be due to a decrease in these transmitters and/or a decrease in their activity level. Although this would appear to be a plausible inference, studies directly measuring neurotransmitter level in ADD have not shown a decrease. It remains possible that, in the future, direct measures may reveal neurotransmitter abnormality in ADD; this, of course, may also not happen. We know from our discussion of the neurobiology of psychopathology (see chapter 13) that the mechanisms of agents that alleviate the symptoms of a condition are not infallible clues to the mechanism of the condition itself.

Genetic Factors   ADD clusters in families. Thirty percent of parents of ADD children have ADD themselves, and, overall, relatives of children with ADD have a greater risk of ADD than do relatives of controls (McMahon, 1980). In addition, monozygotic twins have a higher concordance for ADD than dizygotic twins (Goodman & Stevenson, 1989; Safer, 1973; Willerman, 1973). Support for genetic factors in ADD also comes from adoption studies (Cadoret et al., 1975; Morrison & Stewart, 1971). There is also evidence that ADD may have a common genetic element with autism, Tourette's syndrome, and alcoholism. A gene for dopamine D_2 receptors has been found in all four conditions (Comings & Comings, 1984). Despite this evidence for genetic factors in ADD, no specific gene has been identified as the cause of ADD. Thus, genetic factors appear to be one of many factors contributing to at least some forms of the disorder.

Arousal Theories   Arousal theories of ADD take two basic forms: overarousal theories and underarousal theories. Overarousal theories posit that filter systems in lower brain centers, such as the reticular activating system, fail to filter stimuli normally, so that irrelevant information is not screened out. The resulting overload leads to a kind of cognitive shutdown. This theory accounts for the extreme difficulty some children with ADD have in selectively attending to one auditory stimulus in the presence of other competing stimuli. They may simply not be able to listen to what someone else is saying when it is said in the presence of competing environmental stimuli.

In contrast, underarousal theories posit that higher brain centers do not receive enough input from lower centers. From this perspective, the distractibility, hyperactivity, and risk-taking behaviors often seen in children with ADD are attempts to heighten the level of arousal in these higher centers. This is sometimes referred to as the **optimum arousal theory.**

The contradictory nature of these two theories is indicative of how far we have to go before we possess a coherent arousal-based theory of ADD. Although each type of arousal theory explains some of the characteristics of ADD, there is no solid neurobiological evidence for either.

Reward Theories   Reward theories hypothesize that ADD is due to a disruption of brain reward centers and/or their connections with other parts of the brain (e.g., Wender, 1971). As a result, the individual's behavior is not conditioned by its consequences. These theories fit well with the frustrating inability of many children with ADD to modify their behavior, even when the consequences of their behavior are explicitly and emphatically designed to foster such change.

Motivation Theories   Motivation theories propose that the motivational systems normally guiding and regulating behavior are dysfunctional in individuals with ADD (e.g., Barkley, 1990). The absence of such regulation would account for the inability of those with ADD to stay on-task and to complete tasks that

require sustained attention and effort in the absence of ongoing feedback or reward. Children who have difficulty with such tasks may perform quite well when reinforcement is frequent and constant. As R. A. Barkley says "There's no ADD while playing Nintendo" (quoted in Hallowell & Ratey, 1994). The fact that immediate reinforcement can guide and sustain attention on a specific task shows that the most extreme of the disrupted reward system hypotheses must be incorrect.

Theories of Prefrontal Dysfunction in ADD   Prefrontal cortex is known to play a critical role in the planning, initiation, and regulation of behavior (see chapter 12). It is thus a prime candidate for the site of disturbance in ADD. Some support for this hypothesis comes from similarities in the effects of ADD and prefrontal lesions on attention (Johnson & Roetig-Johnson, 1989). Not that the two groups have identical characteristics. However, both have similar profiles when it comes to attention: extreme difficulty inhibiting the distracting effect of immediate stimuli and maintaining goal-directed behavior.

Additional support for this hypothesis comes from the results of functional imaging studies. In a PET study assessing adults with ADD while they engaged in the Continuous Performance Test (a test tapping attentional processes), the ADD group had an 8% lower rate of glucose metabolism in widespread areas of the cerebral cortex. In addition, the largest decrease was seen in the prefrontal and premotor cortex (Zametkin et al., 1990). Regional cerebral blood flow studies have also reported reduced profusion in prefrontal cortex and in the closely related caudate-striatal region in ADD (Lou, Henrikson, & Bruhn, 1984; Lou et al., 1989). In the behavioral domain, individuals with ADD have been shown to perform poorly on measures of prefrontal function, including the Continuous Performance Test, the Wisconsin Card Sorting Test, and tests of planning (Boucugnani & Jones, 1989; Chelune et al., 1986).

Finally, as we discussed in some detail in chapter 10, prefrontal cortex is critical for the mediation of working memory, that collection of processes that enables behavior to be guided and regulated by internal representations. Among other things, working memory enhances the capacity to profit from experience, to anticipate the consequences of one's actions, and to use these anticipations to guide future action. These are among the processes disrupted in ADD, and it is possible, therefore, to conceptualize ADD as an impairment in working memory or, more generally, in executive function. Taken together, the similarities between ADD and the effects of lesions of the prefrontal cortex, the evidence from functional imaging studies of prefrontal hypoactivity in ADD, the poor performance of individuals with ADD on tests sensitive to prefrontal lesions, and the conceptualization of the fundamental impairment in ADD as one of working memory and executive function all point to prefrontal cortex as the site of abnormality in ADD. Clearly, more investigation is needed to further evaluate the prefrontal theory of ADD; however, it already has significant support and holds promise as a touchstone for future understanding of this serious disorder.

Autism

Autism, named and first described independently by Kanner (1943) and by Asperger (1944), is an extremely disabling disorder that almost always begins before age 30 months and lasts a lifetime, though sometimes with some improvement. It has three basic characteristics: severe impairment in verbal and nonverbal communication; failure to develop social relationships; and stereotyped and repetitive patterns of behavior, interests, and activities (American Psychiatric Association, 1994; Rutter, 1978). In addition, infants with autism seem not to care if they are held and may arch their backs in anxiety if they are picked up. They tend not to seek comfort or even look at their caregivers. At developmental levels at which imaginative play is appropriate, such play is absent in these children. Many children with autism are retarded, and 75% have an IQ below 50. Some, however, have normal intelligence. Some people with autism, including some who are retarded, have a special skill or talent in a specific area, such as music, the ability to memorize, art, or the ability to perform calculations. These individuals have been termed **autistic savants.** Some remarkable examples of autistic savants with unusual talents, including

one individual with a wonderful gift for drawing, are described by Sacks (1995, ch. 6).

Cognitive theories of autism have suggested that individuals with autism lack a **theory of mind,** a concept or sense that others have mind or consciousness (Baron-Cohen, Leslie, & Frith, 1985; Frith, 1989; Hermelin & O'Connor, 1990; Wing, 1991). This inability to attribute mind to other people (or even to themselves) is exemplified by their performance on tests of knowledge of other minds, such as tests that require the attribution of false beliefs to others. In one such test, a child first opens a box that normally contains a familiar brand of candy, only to be surprised to find pencils inside instead of the expected candy. The child is then asked what another child coming into the room would expect to find in the box. By age 4 normal children are able to put their knowledge of the real contents of the box aside and, assuming the mental perspective of the new child, answer that she will expect candy. Autistic children are unable to do this; they are unable to assume the perspective of a new child by excluding their acquired knowledge of the situation (see also Frith, Morton, & Leslie, 1991; Pinker, 1997, pp. 330–332).

Many autistic children grow into severely impaired adults. However, some develop language, learn minimal social skills, and even attain significant intellectual achievement, although they retain many of the other characteristics of autistic individuals, including the absence of a theory of mind. Individuals with this relatively high-functioning symptom picture are diagnosed as having Asperger's syndrome, named after the early investigator who was more aware than Kanner of these relatively high-functioning people with autism (Asperger, 1944). It has been suggested that the most salient difference between people with classical autism and people with Asperger's syndrome is that people with the latter are able to introspect about their condition and to tell others about it (Sacks, 1995). An example of this is Temple Grandin, a woman with Asperger's syndrome who holds a Ph.D. in animal science and is a recognized authority on the design of humane and efficient animal slaughtering facilities. She has also written an autobiography describing her disorder (Grandin & Scariano, 1986). Despite her many achievements, Grandin is unable to understand the minds of other people, a lack of understanding that she poignantly describes as feeling as if she were "an anthropologist on Mars" (Sacks, 1995, ch. 7). Whether classical autism and Asperger's syndrome are distinctly different disorders or different levels of severity of the same disorder is unresolved (Frith, 1991; Wing, 1991).

PSYCHOGENIC THEORIES OF AUTISM   Early theories of autism stressed the personality of the child's parents as causal factors (Bettelheim, 1959, 1967; Kanner, 1943). Parents, particularly mothers, of autistic children were described as cold, anxious, solitary, and obsessive, and parent-child dynamics were construed as the cause of the disorder. However, this line of thinking is not consistent with evidence that even extreme physical and emotional deprivation during early development does not cause autism. Thus, although extreme environmental stress early in development may cause symptoms that share some features with autism, including delayed development, passivity, lack of responsiveness to human contact, and repetitive behavior (Spitz & Wolf, 1946), these symptoms are usually entirely reversible when the environmental stressors are removed (McBride, 1975). In contrast, autism is not generally associated with extreme environmental stress, and its symptoms are not decreased by environmental change. These findings, together with the absence of evidence supporting the hypothesis that parents of autistic children have characteristic personality features (Cox et al., 1975; DeMyer et al., 1972; McAdoo & DeMyer, 1978), led to the abandonment of the notion that autism is caused by parental or other environmental factors. Autism is now generally considered to have biologically based causes. We discuss some of the evidence for biological factors in autism in the next sections.

GENETIC FACTORS   There is compelling evidence that at least some forms of autism are inherited. Between 2% and 3% of siblings of people with autism are themselves autistic (Bailey, 1993), about 50 times the expected frequency of the disorder in the normal population. The concordance rate for monozygotic twins has been reported to be as high as 96%, whereas the concordance rate of dizygotic twins is no higher than

that for non-twin siblings (Bailey et al., 1995; Folstein & Piven, 1991). The extremely high concordance for monozygotic twins clearly indicates that autism is highly heritable. In addition, the large difference between monozygotic and dizygotic concordance rates suggests that autism is caused by a combination of several genes, all of which are rarely present in both members of a dizygotic twin pair. Not all studies report such a high concordance in monozygotic twins. For example, Folstein and Rutter (1977) report concordance rates of approximately 36% for monozygotic twins and 0% for dizygotic twins. This suggests that the hereditary component is not the sole determinant of all forms of autism; what is inherited may be increased vulnerability to other influences. Even in the Folstein and Piven study, the autistic twin in the 4% of monozygotic twins who were discordant was reported to have had birth complications, indicating that factors other than hereditary factors are associated with autism. In the next section we examine some of these.

OTHER FACTORS ASSOCIATED WITH AUTISM
Autism has been associated with a number of pathological processes that adversely influence development. For example, women with rubella during pregnancy are more likely to give birth to an autistic child (Chess, Fernandez, & Corn, 1971). In addition, more than 20% of children with infantile hydrocephalus have autistic symptoms (Fernell, Gillberg, & Von Wendt, 1991). Autistic children have a higher rate of perinatal complications than normal children (Ornitz, 1973), and more than 20% of autistic children have indications of major organic disorders, such as cerebral palsy and congenital rubella (Ornitz, 1978). Minor neurological signs are also seen more frequently in autistic children, as are minor physical abnormalities (Konstantareas, Homatidis, & Busch, 1989). There is also some evidence of monoamine imbalance in children with autism (Martineau et al., 1991).

A diverse number of structural abnormalities have also been reported in autism, but, again, not consistently in all autistic individuals. These include abnormalities in the medial temporal lobe, the brain stem, and the cerebellum (DeLong, 1992; Happe & Frith, 1996); polymicrogyria and other general brain abnormalities (Piven et al., 1990); and enlargement of the third ventricle (Jacobson et al., 1988). The vermis (medial portion) of the cerebellum has been reported to be undeveloped in some children with autism (Courchesne, 1991b). In addition, children with **Joubert syndrome,** a genetic disorder with symptoms similar to autism, show profound or even complete agenesis of the cerebellar vermis (Holroyd, Reiss, & Bryan, 1991). A number of other studies have reported abnormalities of cerebellar development in autism (Haas et al., 1996; Hashimoto et al., 1995). However, no focal brain lesions occurring later in life, including cerebellar lesions, have been associated with symptoms of autism (Happe & Frith, 1996), and some studies have reported no structural abnormalities in children with autism (Garber et al., 1989).

Taken together, evidence of biological abnormality in autism leads to the conclusion that has become a recurring theme in our discussions of brain-psychopathology relationships: There is no specific brain abnormality or dysfunction that is seen in all cases of autism. And yet, there is evidence of genetic factors in at least some forms of autism. There is also a higher rate of perinatal neurological disorders and other physical abnormalities associated with autism, as well as developmentally related structural abnormalities in some children with the disorder. These findings suggest that autism is not a homogeneous entity (Hooper et al., 1993) but a group of disorders, each of which may be caused by different combinations of genetic factors and brain abnormality occurring early in development (Gillberg, 1992). The elucidation of the genetic and biological factors necessary and sufficient for the occurrence of autistic disorders clearly requires further investigation.

SUMMARY

The development of the human brain is one of the most wondrous processes in all of nature. The early phases of this process are entirely under genetic control; however, the determination of the final pattern of interconnections in many regions of the brain requires environmental input. This interaction between genetic programming and experience is most fully understood in the development of ocular dominance columns in the visual cortex during the first weeks of life, but the modification of neural structures by experience continues throughout the life span in the form of learning and memory.

The development of enhanced visual acuity during the first year of life is correlated with the development of the primary visual cortex. In investigating more complex behavior, such as executive function, the search for specific correlates on the neuronal level is more elusive. However, disparities between the development of knowledge representations and the development of the capacity to regulate goal-directed behavior based on those representations can be identified and can serve as markers for the development of executive function.

Although language development obviously requires exposure to a language, there is evidence that the *capacity* to develop language is the result of a maturational process that is a genetically programmed product of human evolution. This evidence includes the ability of infants as young as age 1 month to discriminate phonemes, the regularity of language milestones across individuals and in different cultures, and the relative independence of the development of language capacity from the amount of language in the environment (assuming that the minimum amount of environmental language is present). In addition, indications that language is not need-driven but occurs even though infants are able to get their needs met through other means, and the presence of critical periods for language acquisition and for full language recovery after left-hemisphere lesions that disrupt language, all support the notion that a genetically determined maturational process is central to the development of language.

Disease or injury can have particularly devastating effects on the developing brain, especially in its earliest stages of development, because they disrupt the programmed sequence of events that normally results in the marvelously ordered complexity of the mature brain. Unfortunately, there is no shortage of such disruptive processes, ranging from chromosomal disorders, genetic disorders, structural abnormalities, and prematurity to infection, toxins, malnutrition, anoxic episodes, focal cerebral disease processes, and injury. Not surprisingly, there is considerable variation in the effects of each of these processes, depending on a number of variables, including the age of the fetus or child, the severity of the insult, and the region or regions within the brain that are affected.

A number of developmental disorders have so far defied attempts to identify the specific neurobiological abnormalities underlying them. These include learning disorders, attention deficit disorder, and autism. There is strong evidence that biological factors contribute to the cause of each of these disorders, yet the specific nature of these factors has remained elusive. This is partly because each of these labels actually comprises a heterogeneous group of disorders. Further understanding of the nature of this heterogeneity is necessary before consistent biological factors contributing to the causes of these disorders can be identified.

CHAPTER 15

Recovery of Function

THE EFFECTS OF BRAIN DAMAGE
Cellular Effects
Physiological Effects
FUNCTIONAL RECOVERY AFTER BRAIN DAMAGE
Factors Affecting Recovery of Function
Age at the Time of Lesion as a Factor in Recovery
**NEURAL MECHANISMS OF RECOVERY
OF FUNCTION**
Rerouting
Sprouting

Denervation Supersensitivity
The Neural Basis of Cerebral Reorganization
**THERAPEUTIC APPROACHES TO THE
CONSEQUENCES OF BRAIN LESIONS**
Rehabilitation
Pharmacological Treatments
Brain Tissue Transplantation
SUMMARY

Like all things mortal, the fragile contents of the cranium are subject to the slings and arrows of outrageous fortune; disease and trauma can ravage the marvelous organ that regulates our behavior and generates our consciousness. Yet loss of function is not always permanent. Galen gave testimony to this almost two millennia ago when he pronounced with simple elegance, "I have seen a wounded brain heal." In this final chapter, we briefly examine some of the ways in which dam-
age affects the brain. We then turn to a consideration of the factors affecting recovery of function and the neural mechanisms underlying that recovery. Finally, we look at perhaps the most exciting and fruitful application of our developing knowledge of brain-behavior relationships: therapeutic approaches to the consequences of brain lesions. Great progress is being made in this area, and no one could wish for a more bountiful yield of our knowledge than that it help suffering individuals.

THE EFFECTS OF BRAIN DAMAGE

Many factors can cause the death or dysfunction of neurons. These include trauma, hemorrhagic strokes (bleeding), ischemic strokes (loss of blood to part of the brain), tumors, infection, metabolic disorders, and developmental disorders. In this section, we will review the effects of these processes on the cellular and physiological levels.

Cellular Effects

CHANGES AT THE SITE OF DAMAGE   Cell death, or **necrosis,** is obviously an event of major importance at the site of damage. Within 24 hours, phagocytes (astrocytes and microglia) engulf dead neurons and break them down. Within a matter of days, new capillaries infiltrate the area, as the phagocytes continue to remove the debris of dead neurons. As removal becomes complete, only glial cells remain in the area. These cells are supplemented by a reactive proliferation of additional glial cells, forming a scar in the area. This process, termed **gliosis,** may interfere with the function of any surviving neurons in the area.

CHANGES DISTANT FROM THE SITE OF DAMAGE   The death of a neuron means that neurons to which it projects will be deprived of input and neurons that project to it will be deprived of their target. The result is that a brain lesion is never truly localized in one area. An obvious example of this phenomenon is hemiparesis following lesions to the motor cortex, an effect that results when motor neurons in the anterior horn of the spinal cord are deprived of input from neurons in the precentral gyrus.

Neuronal connections can also be disrupted by damage that severs axons, without necessarily killing the cell. The severing of an axon leads to degeneration of the remaining axon distal to the point of damage, which is termed **anterograde** or **Wallerian degeneration.** In some instances, degeneration occurs in the opposite direction as well, spreading from the point of transection back to the cell body. This is termed **retrograde degeneration.** Degeneration can also extend to neurons with which the damaged neuron synapses, a phenomenon termed **transneuronal degeneration.** The effect of all of these degenerative processes is to cause damage and dysfunction at sites distant from the site of the initial lesion.

Physiological Effects

There are a number of physiological effects of brain lesions. Before discussing some of these effects, it should be pointed out that, like neuronal degenera-

tion, some produce disruption of function in tissue at sites distant from the lesion. However, unlike neuronal degeneration, which is permanent because neurons in the central nervous system cannot regenerate, some conditions causing distant effects, such as edema (swelling), are reversible, subsiding after a certain period of time. This is because they damage neurons, rather than cause their death. These time-limited disruptive effects on neural tissue outside the immediate area of the lesion are termed **diaschisis** (von Monakow, 1911). They are frequently seen after brain lesions, making the immediate consequences of a brain lesion more severe than the later persistent effects.

SHOCK   **Shock** is exemplified by **spinal shock,** the temporary loss of spinal reflexes after spinal transection. It will be recalled that spinal reflexes are mediated by neurons entirely within the spinal cord, a fact that is confirmed by their reappearance approximately three weeks after spinal transection. Apparently, the spinal neurons mediating these reflexes are temporarily depressed after their input from higher brain centers is removed.

EDEMA   **Edema,** from the Greek word for "swelling," is the presence of abnormally large amounts of fluid in the intercellular spaces of the body. Edema in brain tissue can cause a rise in intracranial pressure, resulting in widespread tissue damage and, if the damage is sufficiently severe, death. As already mentioned, many of the dysfunctional effects of edema are reversible once the swelling subsides. Therefore, the behavioral consequences of a brain lesion may not be apparent until this period passes. Cortisone reduces edema and is often used to help attenuate its acute effects.

BLOOD FLOW   Brain metabolic activity releases carbon dioxide, which, in turn, triggers an increase in cerebral blood flow. Cerebral blood flow is thus an index of brain metabolic activity. As we have seen, this relationship is the foundation for regional cerebral blood flow (rCBF) studies. Damage to brain tissue disrupts that tissue's metabolic activity, reducing its production of carbon dioxide and the resulting amount of blood perfusing the area.

GLUCOSE UTILIZATION   Cerebral lesions may temporarily decrease the rate of glucose utilization in brain tissue not directly affected by the lesion. This has been shown not to be due entirely to edema and may represent another mechanism whereby lesions result in a generalized reduction in cerebral function.

AUTONEUROTOXICITY   Oxygen deprivation causes neuronal death in all regions of the nervous system. However, certain regions, such as the CA region of the hippocampus, are particularly vulnerable to the effects of oxygen deprivation and are therefore selectively damaged during short-term hypoxic episodes that do not result in death. One mechanism for this selective vulnerability is the excessive release of glutamate in response to oxygen deprivation. Glutamate, an excitatory neurotransmitter, then overexcites neurons with which it binds, causing cell death. Thus, substances that excite glutamate receptors are potent neurotoxins. It is also possible that agents that block these receptors, or that block the release of glutamate, may potentially be effective in ameliorating the effects of hypoxic episodes and other neurotoxic events that utilize this mechanism.

CHANGES IN THE BLOOD-BRAIN BARRIER   Lesions can result in changes in the properties of the blood-brain barrier, allowing blood-borne substances that normally would not affect brain function to exert inhibitory or other disruptive effects (Seil, Leiman, & Kelly, 1976). Now that we have examined some of the cellular and physiological changes underlying the effects of brain lesions, we will examine recovery of function on the behavioral level.

FUNCTIONAL RECOVERY AFTER BRAIN DAMAGE

After the short-term effects of a brain lesion subside, individuals with brain lesions may continue to show some recovery. In adults, any significant recovery that takes place happens in the first year or so; after this period the chances for improvement are small. In children, recovery typically continues for a longer period and is more complete. In both adults and children, the pattern and degree of recovery is highly variable. In this section, we examine some of the factors affecting recovery of function. These include sex, familial left-handedness, intelligence, personality, lesion momentum, and the age of the individual at the time the lesion occurs.

Factors Affecting Recovery of Function

SEX   There is evidence that recovery from aphasia is better for females than for males. This finding, together with the results of some laterality studies, has led to the hypothesis that language functioning is less lateralized in females than in males. According to this hypothesis, then, the effect of a particular lesion in females is attenuated to some extent by the remaining functional representations in the nonlesioned hemisphere. The status of this hypothesis is unclear, as there is evidence that any sex effect that emerges from laterality studies is very small (Hiscock, Inch, et al., 1994; Hiscock, Israelian, et al., 1995). In addition, although there is some evidence of sex differences in brain anatomy in animals (Juraska, 1991), it is not yet possible to validly relate these to differences in functional organization. This is also the case for reported sex differences in the pattern of activation in functional imaging studies that require human subjects to process language (e.g., Shaywitz et al., 1995). It remains possible that the differences seen in these studies are due to the use of different cognitive strategies, determined by cultural factors, rather than different cerebral functional organization. In short, attempts to account for the seemingly straightforward finding that, on average, women recover more fully from aphasia than men raise a host of tantalizing, but as yet unconfirmed, hypotheses.

HANDEDNESS   Persons with familial left-handedness recover more fully from aphasia. In this case there is compelling evidence from sodium amobarbital studies that about 15% of individuals with familial left-handedness have bilateral speech representation (Rasmussen & Milner, 1977). Seventy percent have speech represented in the left hemisphere, and the remaining 15% have speech represented in the right hemisphere. Thus, 85% of familial left-handers do not show less lateralization of speech, as assessed by the sodium amobarbital test. Whether this group also has some diminished degree of lateralization of speech that has not yet been detected remains to be investigated.

INTELLIGENCE   Pre-lesion intelligence has been reported to be a factor in recovery of function, with individuals with high intelligence recovering more fully. It is unclear, however, whether pre-lesion intelligence actually facilitates recovery or whether the degree to which persons with high premorbid intelligence are working below their potential is masked by the fact that they continue to perform at a higher level than the majority of people who have suffered a comparable lesion.

PERSONALITY   People who are optimistic, both about life in general and about their prospects for recovery, appear to recover more fully from a brain lesion. Because left-hemisphere lesions are more often associated with depressed mood, this raises the possibility that depressed mood and the presence of a left-hemisphere lesion may be confounded in these studies. In any case, personality factors can be highly important determinants of extent of recovery. This underinvestigated area clearly deserves further study.

LESION MOMENTUM   Different kinds of lesions develop at different rates. For example, some brain tumors grow extremely rapidly; others grow very slowly. The rate of lesion development is referred to as **lesion momentum** (Finger, 1978). Lesion momentum is an important factor in recovery because the same amount of tissue destruction may have much less effect on behavior if it occurs gradually than if it occurs rapidly.

The effect of lesion momentum is most clearly seen in animal experiments in which lesions are made in stages. The effect of staged lesions is much less than the effect of a single lesion of the same size and in the same location, a phenomenon known as the **staged-lesion effect.** It is as if in the staged-lesion condition, the earlier lesion primes the system to re-

spond to the subsequent lesion (Scheff, Bernardo, & Cotman, 1978).

An example of lesion momentum in humans is seen in an adult patient who, in the course of attempts to remove a cerebral tumor, had a series of operations, spread over many months, in which progressively more of the speech area was removed. This resulted in much less impairment in language than is typically seen after a single lesion of the same size (Geschwind, 1976). The phenomenon of lesion momentum emphasizes the dynamic nature of neural processing: Unlike a fixed piece of machinery, the brain is a plastic system that adapts to changes within its structure.

Age at Time of Lesion as a Factor in Recovery

The most important factor affecting recovery of function following a brain lesion is the age of the individual at the time of the lesion.

THE KENNARD PRINCIPLE   One view of the relationship between the age of the individual at the time the lesion occurs and the lesion's behavioral effect is embodied in the **Kennard principle.** It states that the earlier in life a lesion is sustained, the better the recovery (Kennard, 1936, 1942).

Kennard's original work involved the investigation of motor function after lesions of motor cortex in animals. However, there are data from humans consistent with this principle. Perhaps the most dramatic example is the recovery from language disturbance after cerebral lesions in childhood. As we noted in an earlier section, children who become aphasic before puberty usually recover language fully. In contrast, adults who become aphasic often experience only limited recovery, although recovery can sometimes be nearly complete in adults as well.

More specifically, after a left-hemisphere lesion, children ages 2 to 3 may be verbally unresponsive for weeks; after that, they start to learn language seemingly from the beginning, going through the stages they had previously passed through. Within a year or two, their language is equivalent to that of normal children of the same age (Lenneberg, 1967). Children between the ages of 3 and puberty who sustain a left-hemisphere lesion go through a period of aphasia similar to that seen in adults, although fluent (Wernicke's) aphasia is not seen. They also recover language, the majority of them catching up to their age mates within as little as 2 years' time (Lenneberg, 1967; Woods & Teuber, 1978). Even children in whom the entire left hemisphere has been removed, because early massive damage was causing uncontrolled seizures, may show recovery of language function, presumably mediated entirely by the remaining right hemisphere (Smith & Sugar, 1975).

As we noted in a previous section, the remarkable capacity of the young brain to learn language, even in the face of left-hemisphere lesions that would often leave an adult with a permanent aphasia, is one of the strongest sources of evidence that the brain is specifically programmed for language development. In addition, what we know about the mechanism of this recovery provides insight into the nature of the plasticity of the developing brain.

REORGANIZATION OF HEMISPHERIC SPECIAL-IZATION   One of the most striking aspects of recovery of language after early left-hemisphere damage is the finding that in some cases the right hemisphere *takes over* language function. Whether or not the right hemisphere assumes language function after left-hemisphere damage can be determined in a given individual by sodium amobarbital testing. Studies using this technique have revealed that one factor influencing whether the right hemisphere takes over language representation is age at the time of lesion: Reorganization after age 6 is unusual, and puberty appears to be the upper age limit for such reorganization. This suggests that recovery between approximately age 5 and puberty generally results from reorganization *within* the left hemisphere, probably involving intact regions close to the speech areas. However, not all left-hemisphere lesions sustained before age 5 result in right-hemisphere speech representation. Sodium amobarbital studies indicate that even among individuals who have become left-handed or ambidextrous after an early left-hemisphere lesion only approximately 30% have right-hemisphere speech representation, while 20% have bilateral representation, and in 50% language remains in the left hemisphere (Rasmussen & Milner, 1977).

The critical additional factor determining functional reorganization, perhaps not surprisingly, is the location of the early lesion within the left hemisphere. Thus, even extensive left-hemisphere lesions that do not encroach on the language areas do not result in the movement of language representation to the right hemisphere, whereas even relatively small lesions that involve the language areas do. In addition, lesions involving only one language area result in the movement of the functions mediated by that area to the right hemisphere, while the undamaged area remains functional (Figure 15.1).

The effect of age at the time of lesion and location of lesion on cerebral reorganization is illustrated by the case of Sho, a girl who sustained severe damage to her left parietal lobe at age 2½ years in an accident aboard ship. Prior to the accident, she had been right-handed and had been exhibiting normal language development. Following the accident she remained unconscious for 2 days and had right-sided seizures the day following her injury. When she regained consciousness, she was hemiparetic and remained speechless for 5 weeks. At age 4, 1½ years after the lesion, she had a right hemianopia, right hemiparesis, and right hemisensory loss. However, her language was normal. When seen at age 16, she was found to be left-handed, and a sodium amobarbital test revealed that she had bilateral speech representation. Subsequent surgery for the relief of seizures revealed massive damage to the posterior portion of the left hemisphere, including the area that would normally have been Wernicke's area (see Figure 15.1E). This area of damage was removed without affecting her language functioning, confirming that the functions normally mediated by the posterior speech area were now represented elsewhere in the brain, presumably in the right hemisphere. The finding of bilateral speech on the sodium amobarbital test indicated that the anterior speech area, outside the area of damage, remained in the left hemisphere.

It is interesting to note that cerebral reorganization is seen not only in response to lesions; it also appears to be a component of normal development. This is illustrated by a study of the effect of lesions to prefrontal cortex on delayed-response performance in 3-year-old (adult) and 18-month-old (juvenile) monkeys. Pre-

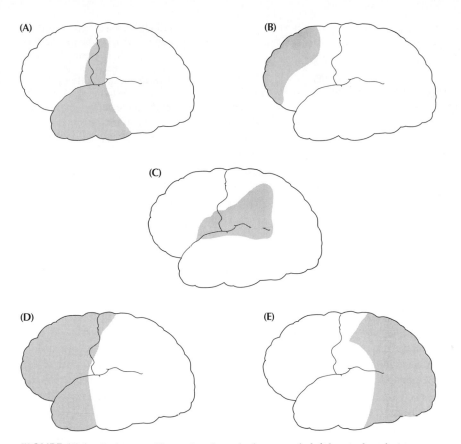

FIGURE 15.1   Brain maps illustrating that whether an early left-hemisphere lesion results in the reorganization of language in the right hemisphere depends on the location of the lesion within the left hemisphere. Lesions that do not encroach on the speech areas (A) and (B) do not result in a shift of language to the right hemisphere, even when the lesion is neighboring one or both of the speech areas. In contrast, even relatively small lesions that include both speech areas (C) result in a complete shift of language. Lesions encroaching only on the anterior speech area (D) or only on the posterior speech area (E) cause a shift only of the functions of the lesioned speech area. Brain map (E) is that of the patient Sho. *(From Rasmussen & Milner, 1977)*

frontal lesions disrupted delayed response in the adults, but not in the juveniles, indicating that the structures mediating delayed response in the younger animals were outside the prefrontal cortex. Thus, during the transition from juvenile to adult, the monkeys acquired or *grew into* the impairment after prefrontal lesions (Goldman, 1974). These findings indicate that in the course of normal development there is a reorganization of the neural structures supporting delayed-response performance.

THE PRICE OF REORGANIZATION AFTER BRAIN LESIONS   One additional aspect of Sho's case was that, although she had been considered a highly intelligent child before her accident, when tested at age 16 she was found to have a full scale IQ of 81, with a verbal IQ of 88 and a performance IQ of 76. This illustrates the negative side of the dramatic recovery of language function after early left-hemisphere lesions: It is achieved at the expense of general intellectual functioning, particularly nonverbal functioning.

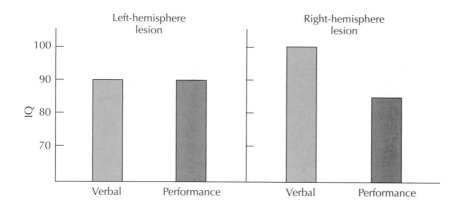

FIGURE 15.2   Verbal and Performance IQs on the Wechsler Adult Intelligence Scale for adults who had early left-hemisphere and early right-hemisphere lesions. After early left-hemisphere lesions, both verbal and performance IQs are depressed in adulthood, whereas after early right-hemisphere lesions, only performance IQ scores are lower. *(From Kolb & Whishaw, 1996, p. 504 [After Teuber, 1975])*

This conclusion is supported by studies of the effects of unilateral lesions on verbal and performance IQ (Figure 15.2). Verbal IQ and performance IQ are not synonymous with left-hemisphere and right-hemisphere functioning, respectively. Nevertheless, they do provide a crude basis for comparing the relative level of functioning of the two hemispheres. The findings reported in Figure 15.2 indicate that the reorganization of language in the right hemisphere following early left-hemisphere damage is achieved at the price of diminished general intellectual functioning. This finding suggests that early lesions do not always result in better recovery of cognitive skills in humans, thereby challenging the generality of the Kennard principle (Teuber, 1975). Teuber and Rudel (1962) conceptualized this effect as **crowding,** suggesting that the impairment in general intellectual functioning is a consequence of the reorganized right hemisphere's dual role as the mediator of both language and the nonverbal functions that it would normally mediate.

In contrast to the reorganization occurring after early left-hemisphere lesions, early damage to the right hemisphere does not appear to result in a complementary reorganization in the left hemisphere. Instead, early damage to the right hemisphere results in selective impairment of right-hemisphere functioning (see Figure 15.2). It thus appears that the preservation of language has priority over the preservation of functions mediated by the right hemisphere. Alternatively, it may be the case that certain right-hemisphere functions are reorganized in the left hemisphere following early right-hemisphere lesions, but that these are less readily identifiable than is language. Although this remains a possibility, such a marker of preserved right-hemisphere function after early right hemisphere damage has yet to be identified.

THE EFFECT OF LESIONS BEFORE AGE 1   Another important exception to the Kennard principle is the finding that very early lesions, before 1 year of age, result in more severe general impairment than do those acquired after age 1 (Riva & Cazzaniga, 1986). Apparently lesions during this very early period interfere profoundly with development, rendering the brain less able to adapt to injury than it is later in childhood.

FOUR PERIODS WITH CHARACTERISTIC RECOVERY PATTERNS   The findings discussed in the preceding sections suggest that, with regard to the capacity for recovery of function, there are four distinct periods within the life span of an individual. During the first year of life, lesions produce extremely profound impairment, to which the system is not able to adapt. From age 1 year to about age 5, interhemispheric reorganization of language function takes place in response to damage to the left hemisphere, resulting in the sparing of language function but a decline in general intelligence. In contrast, right-hemisphere lesions during this period produce effects similar to those seen in adults with right-hemisphere lesions, the left hemisphere not showing a complementary capacity to reorganize in a way that would enable it to take over the mediation of right-hemisphere functioning.

During the third period, from age 5 or 6 years to puberty, the brain continues to maintain significant capacity to reorganize after brain lesions but this appears, at least as far as language is concerned, to be largely intrahemispheric. Finally, after puberty, recovery is less certain: Although there are some dramatic exceptions, lesions sustained in adulthood often result in persistent impairment.

NEURAL MECHANISMS OF RECOVERY OF FUNCTION

The central nervous system does not add neurons to any significant degree after birth. It is also unable to regenerate damaged axons so that they reconnect with their prior targets, as peripheral neurons are able to do, in part because glial cells inhibit such regrowth (Bahr & Bonhoeffer, 1994). For a long time, therefore, it was believed that any modifications of brain structure that might occur in response to injury were destructive, interfering with the intricate structures and orderly interconnections of the fully developed adult brain. However, it has been clear for some time that structural modifications *do* take place in the adult brain and spinal cord in response to injury of tissue (Veraa & Grafstein, 1981). Thus, brain connections are not as anatomically rigid as was once thought. In many cases, it is not definitively established that observed modifications contribute to functional recovery; however, there are many instances in which there is strong circumstantial evidence that observed structural modifications underlie functional recovery. In this section, we examine four processes of structural modification in the central nervous system that appear to be related to recovery of function: rerouting, sprouting, denervation supersensitivity, and regional reorganization of cortical functional representation.

Rerouting

In **rerouting,** a neuron that has lost its target grows to a new target and connects with it. The conditions that make this growth possible are not fully understood; however, **nerve growth factor (NGF),** known to be important in the development of the nervous system, may also play a role in the development of new con-nections after brain injury (Bothwell, 1995; Jessell, 1991). Evidence for this comes from the finding that although cutting the septal neurons that project into the hippocampus normally causes about half the neurons to die, injecting NGF into the neighboring lateral ventricle immediately after transection reduces cell death.

Sprouting

As we have seen, brain lesions not only cause the death of neurons, they also cause the targets of those neurons to lose their input, to be **denervated.** When this happens, neighboring neurons may sprout additional terminal processes to connect with the denervated area. This process is called **sprouting** or **collateral sprouting** (Figure 15.3). Sprouting has been reported as a response to injury in the brain and spinal cord, as well as in the peripheral nervous system. Studies of sprouting in animals (e.g., Lynch, Deadwyler, & Cotman, 1973) indicate that some of the new connections produced by sprouting in the central nervous system are physiologically functional and thus appear to be a mechanism contributing to functional repair after brain lesion (Raisman, 1978; Veraa & Grafstein, 1981). Unfortunately, there is evidence that sprouting may sometimes result in misconnections, so the process is not always functionally adaptive and may even generate abnormal behavior (Scheff & Cotman, 1977; Wall, 1980).

Denervation Supersensitivity

When afferent fibers to a muscle are cut, the muscle becomes hypersensitive to the application of its neurotransmitter. This phenomenon, termed **denervation supersensitivity,** is also seen in the central nervous system and results from the proliferation of receptors on the postsynaptic membrane. Denervation supersensitivity is thus a neurochemical adaptation to injury that helps to compensate for the removal of input to the denervated structure. An example of this compensatory mechanism is the fact that the symptoms of Parkinson's disease do not appear until the vast majority of dopamine-producing neurons have been destroyed by the disease. Supersensitivity is also seen in some types of receptors that are inhibited for a period of time by a drug that blocks them.

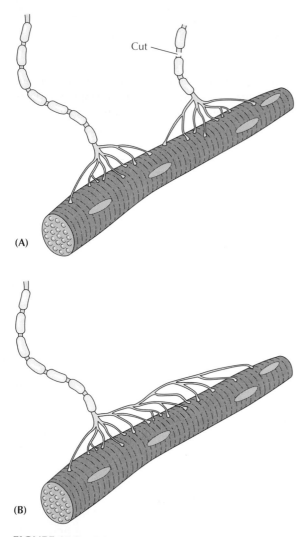

(A)

(B)

FIGURE 15.3   Schematic representation of collateral sprouting in a motor neuron innervating muscle. After one of the motor neurons innervating part of the muscle is cut (*A*), a neighboring neuron undergoes sprouting, providing input to the denervated portion of the muscle (*B*).

The Neural Basis of Cerebral Reorganization

HYPOTHESIS OF TAKEOVER BY UNCOMMIT-TED AREAS   One of the earliest theories of the mechanism of cerebral reorganization in response to brain injury was put forth by Munk (1881). He proposed that there are regions of the brain that are not involved in mediating function; after brain injury, then, these areas can assume the function of the lesioned area. There is no evidence that there are such areas, although this idea has held on in the popular imagination, embodied in the often-heard dictum that we don't use 90% of our brain. The major problem with both Munk's hypothesis and the popular aphorism is that we simply do not have anything close to a sufficient understanding of the brain to be able to determine that some parts of it are not being used.

LASHLEY'S EQUIPOTENTIALITY HYPOTHESIS   As we discussed in chapter 10, Lashley held that different regions of cortex participate equally in the mediation of all complex functions, an idea embodied in his concept of equipotentiality. From this perspective, the mechanism of recovery of function is fairly simple: Cortical areas outside the lesioned area can mediate the functions that were represented in the lesioned area, although the diminished amount of functional tissue involved may render that mediation less efficient (mass action). It is clear, however, that the strongest form of this hypothesis is wrong. Specific cortical regions mediate certain functions that cannot be supported by other areas, although within certain regions, such as Broca's and Wernicke's areas, a kind of equipotentiality may apply.

REGIONAL REORGANIZATION IN THE ADULT BRAIN   We have seen that, in response to lesions during childhood, the brain is able to undergo dramatic changes as it attempts to adapt to injury. We also saw that this reorganization may include, at least in the case of language, the assumption of language function by the right hemisphere when language areas in the left hemisphere are damaged before age 5 or 6. Similarly, animal studies have demonstrated that in utero lesions in the monkey can cause dramatic reorganization of the brain, including its gyral patterns (Goldman-Rakic & Rakic, 1984), and early lesions can cause major alterations in neuroanatomical connectivity (Payne & Cornwell, 1994). These have not been seen in the adult.

Although the brains of infants and children are able to undergo remarkable reorganization, it is clear that the adult brain also is able to adaptively reorganize in response to its own injury and to modification of its input. Evidence for this comes from a study of adult monkeys in whom the thumb area of the motor cortex, as mapped by electrical stimulation, was removed. After an initial period of disuse, the animals gradually recovered the use of the thumb. Subsequent remapping of the motor cortex revealed that areas surrounding the lesion now produced thumb movement when stimulated (Glees & Cole, 1950). More recently, in a similar experiment, evidence emerged that therapy (forced use) of digits enhances the reorganization of their cortical representation after the area representing them in the motor cortex has been removed (Nudo & Grenda, 1992).

Changes in sensory input can also lead to reorganization in the adult. For example, in one study, the somatosensory areas representing the forelimbs and the hind limbs in the rat were mapped, using evoked potential. Then, the sensory pathways from the lower limbs were sectioned. After sectioning, as expected, stimulation of the hind limbs produced no cortical response in the hind limb region, and stimulation of the forelimbs produced a normal response in the forelimb region. After several days, however, it was found that, although stimulation of the hind limbs continued to evoke no response, stimulation of the forelimbs resulted in response in *both* the forelimb and hind limb regions (Wall & Egger, 1971).

These findings are reminiscent of the reorganization seen in V1 of infant monkeys when one eye is occluded during the first month of life and in the somatosensory cortex of infant mice when one or more whiskers are removed (see "Development of the Brain" in chapter 14). The important difference here is that the effect is seen in *adult* rats. Initially, all neurons in V1 receive input from both eyes. Under normal conditions, a competitive process then prunes fibers from the eye that had fewer initial inputs, ultimately yielding that neuron's ocular dominance characteristics. When one eye is occluded, however, this competitive process is short-circuited; input from the unoccluded eye dominates all neurons in V1, while input from the occluded eye drops out. In monkeys this happens only early in life; occluding one eye later in life has no effect on the ocular dominance characteristics of V1 neurons.

What the Wall and Egger experiment and others like it (e.g., Jenkins, Merzenich, & Recanzone, 1990) indicate is that, in at least some cases, an analogous reorganization can occur in adults. Apparently, however, in these instances, the wide distribution of sensory input is retained (rather than dropping out), but the synapses outside the major cortical target area are silent until the normal input to these regions is disrupted. Whatever the mechanism involved, cortical reorganization in adults appears to be an important vehicle for recovery of function. We turn next to a consideration of methods for facilitating recovery of function in people with brain lesions.

THERAPEUTIC APPROACHES TO THE CONSEQUENCES OF BRAIN LESIONS

Systematic therapy for the emotional, cognitive, and behavioral consequences of brain lesions was slower to develop than physical therapy for motor dysfunction. However, as the field of neuropsychology has continued to advance, increasing attention has been devoted to using our accumulating knowledge of brain-behavior relationships to help people with brain lesions lead fuller and more independent lives. In this section, we examine three approaches that are being used to help people with brain lesions: rehabilitation, pharmacological treatment, and brain tissue transplantation. We begin with rehabilitation, an approach that has proved to be highly effective in reducing impairment after brain lesions (Cope, 1995).

Rehabilitation

THE SCOPE OF REHABILITATION   Impairments in the emotional, cognitive, and behavioral domains interact with one another. Therefore, a rehabilitation program that addresses impairments in each of these domains is most likely to foster lasting improvement.

Emotional and Motivational Changes   Cerebral lesions may produce profound emotional, motivational, and personality changes, ranging from depression and apathy to extreme impulsiveness and loss of behavioral control. Premorbid personality characteristics may be radically altered, or, more often, they may be exaggerated in ways that impede adaptive functioning (Lishman, 1973). These changes may result from the primary effects of the lesion, the individual's reaction to the associated cognitive and behavioral impairments, or an interaction of the two factors. Because the success of treatment is influenced by the patient's emotional and motivational functioning, these factors may interfere significantly with efforts directed toward recovery and may ultimately be the patient's most disabling impairment (Lezak, 1987). It is thus extremely important that emotional and motivational issues be addressed vigorously in any rehabilitation program. Psychotherapy is often a useful component in this process.

Cognitive Changes The cognitive impairments seen after cerebral lesions are major targets of strategies aimed at enhancing recovery of function. Therefore, a detailed knowledge of an individual's impairments, as well as his or her relative strengths, is a critical prerequisite for devising a treatment program geared to that individual's specific needs. By providing a detailed profile of an individual's strengths and weaknesses, therefore, a thorough neuropsychological evaluation makes an essential contribution to the formulation of the person's specific treatment program. In addition, reports from a patient's family and friends can provide useful information about how the patient's impairments manifest themselves in the course of daily activities.

One of the most difficult problems faced by people with cerebral lesions is impairment in their ability to realistically evaluate their own cognitive status (Prigatano & Schacter, 1991). In extreme cases this may manifest itself as complete unawareness of impairment. In some cases, the results of neuropsychological assessment can help individuals break through this unawareness by confronting them with objective measures of their performance.

Behavioral Changes Of course, all treatment strategies ultimately attempt to address behavioral change after cerebral lesion. However, there is a growing emphasis on the design of behaviorally based rehabilitation programs that directly address those changes in individual behavior that most concretely affect daily life (O'Hara, 1988). This involves designing behavioral programs geared to training individuals in the performance of specific tasks defined by their particular living situation. Now that we have reviewed the changes that a rehabilitation program needs to address, we turn our attention to strategies of rehabilitation.

INTERVENTION STRATEGIES Remediation is generally approached through one of three strategies: externally focused interventions aimed at changing the environment so that the effect of the dysfunction is minimized, restorative interventions aimed at improving underlying cognitive abilities, and compensatory interventions aimed at teaching alternative and compensatory strategies that reduce the impact of the impairment (Mateer, Kerns, & Eso, 1996).

Externally Focused Interventions **Externally focused interventions** address the problems that follow a brain lesion by modifying the individual's environment. Modifications might include decreasing distractions and organizing working conditions in a way that guides behavior. External cues, such as signs, a checklist, or a computer display, may also be used to guide behavior.

Another way in which the environment may be modified to help those with brain lesions to function more successfully is to alter the demands of the environment so that they do not require the exercise of those functions that are most impaired. This might include modifying the curriculum for a school-age child (D'Amato & Rothlisberg, 1996; Kehle, Clark, & Jenson, 1996), helping the individual's family adjust to the trauma (Conoley & Sheridan, 1996), and finding employment for adults with brain lesions that is geared to their strengths. These modifications can be dispensed with or revised as function is restored. Until that point is reached (if, in fact, it is), a modified environment can make the individual's daily life much less stressful, as well as providing an encouraging sense of success and self-efficacy.

Restorative Interventions **Restorative interventions** attempt to change an individual's cognitive capabilities after a brain lesion. These interventions often take the form of identifying the specific cognitive processes that are impaired and then designing exercises that serve as vehicles for practicing these processes. This **process-specific approach** has mixed results (Sohlberg & Mateer, 1989). However, examples of the usefulness of long-term practice and exercise abound, one of the most publicized being the recovery of the movie actress Patricia Neal. At the age of 39, she suffered a series of strokes that left her unable to speak, read, or write and without the use of one leg. After extensive speech therapy, Neal reached what she considered to be about 80% recovery and, feeling discouraged and exhausted, wanted to stop her rehabilitation. With the insistence of her husband, however, she continued and made further gains. Four years after her strokes she had recovered sufficiently to be able to star in another movie (Griffith, 1970).

Operant conditioning may also prove useful in training an individual to perform certain behaviors. Sometimes behavioral interventions take the form of limiting certain intact behaviors, to force the exercise of impaired function. For example, an animal with a deafferentiated limb (one deprived of sensory input) will act as if the limb is paralyzed and never use it, even though motor control is still possible. However, in an experiment in which the good limb was placed in a hollow ball, allowing the limb full movement but rendering it useless for grasping, the animal began using the deafferentiated limb (Teodoru & Berman, 1980). Similar effects have been seen in human stroke patients, who regain use of a hemiparetic upper limb more rapidly if their good limb is immobilized by placing it in a sling (Taub et al., 1993). Whether analogous methods aimed at restoration of cognitive processes can be devised remains to be investigated.

There is evidence that rats with brain lesions show greater recovery if they are exposed to other rats and to highly enriched and stimulating environments than if they are housed in isolated conditions (Hamm et al., 1996; Rosenzweig, 1980; Rosenzweig, Leiman, & Breedlove, 1996). Although there is some uncertainty as to which variables in the enriched environment are critical for recovery (Rose, 1988), extrapolations from these studies have encouraged an

emphasis on mental and social stimulation as critical components in rehabilitation programs.

Compensatory Interventions   Rather than attempting to restore lost function, compensatory interventions aim at the learning and development of skills that compensate for lost function. In recent years there has been a growing emphasis on therapeutic approaches that foster compensatory behavior. Some of these approaches, termed **alternative strategies**, attempt to utilize ways of processing that remain within the person's cognitive repertoire after a cerebral lesion but that are distinct from the way in which the individual performed the task before the lesion. An example of an alternative strategy is the training of patients with left temporal lobectomy to use interactive visual images to enhance their performance on a verbal paired-associate learning task (M. K. Jones, 1974). As will be recalled from our discussion in chapter 10, patients who have undergone left temporal lobectomy typically do quite poorly on verbal learning tasks. However, after being taught to use visual images, their performance reached the level of normal control subjects who had not been trained in the use of interactive images.

It should be noted that the spontaneous use of alternative strategies potentially confounds attempts to study reorganization of function after cerebral lesions. For example, consider a patient with a left temporal lobectomy who begins on his or her own to employ visual imagery to enhance verbal memory performance. Observing the patient's good performance on verbal memory tasks, one might erroneously conclude that some other region or regions of the brain has taken over the memory function of the left temporal lobe, when in fact the patient is simply using other intact regions of the brain to augment performance on the task.

Like alternative strategies, **compensatory strategies** also utilize the patient's intact functioning to work around impairments. However, compensatory strategies differ from alternative strategies in that they employ special procedures (and, often, special paraphernalia) that generally are not used in everyday life. These include the use of external cues to guide behavior. A dramatically successful example of a compensatory strategy is Glisky and Schacter's (1987) training of a severely amnesic woman to enter data into a computer, also discussed in chapter 10. By means of an elaborate computer-generated cuing procedure that tapped her intact implicit memory, this woman was able to enter data with astonishing skill and accuracy, given the depth of her anterograde amnesia.

Pharmacological Treatments

Amphetamines have been shown to increase the rate of recovery in animals with brain lesions (Feeney & Sutton, 1987), and there is an ongoing search for pharmacological agents that facilitate specific aspects of recovery. Thus far, this search has yet to yield medications that restore cognitive functioning, although it is to be hoped that these may be forthcoming. In addition to the obvious therapeutic value such medications would possess, they would also afford the possibility of furthering our understanding of neurotransmitter and neurotrophic mechanisms involved in recovery of function.

Brain Tissue Transplantation

Brain tissue transplantation typically involves dissecting embryonic tissue from a fetus and placing it in a dish of saline solution. It is then transferred to a test tube and treated to separate neural tissue from surrounding glia and vasculature. The isolated neural tissue is then transferred to a syringe and injected into the appropriate location in the brain of the recipient animal. (Figure 15.4). To survive, the fetal grafts must receive a blood supply, achieve a certain level of normal differentiation and organization, and form appropriate connections with tissue of the host brain. If any of these processes fail, the transplanted tissue may die or cease to influence the host brain. An advantage of embryonic tissue is its tendency to seek out its normal targets; apparently, the developmental mechanisms that direct axons toward their targets (see "Development of the Brain," in chapter 14) continue to be operative in the graft-host system, although erroneous connections are somewhat more likely in the transplant condition.

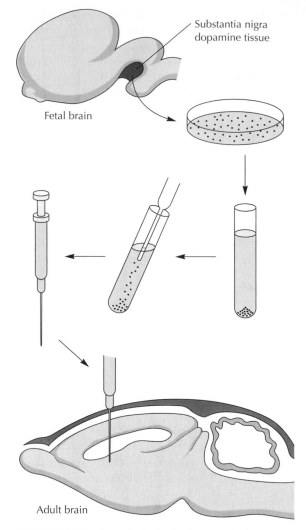

FIGURE 15.4   Steps in the brain tissue transplantation procedure. *(From H. Gleitman, Fridlund, & Reisberg, 1999, p. 65. [After Bjorklund et al., 1983])*

Experimental work with animals has shown some promising results of brain tissue transplants in the treatment of animal models of Parkinson's disease (Fine, 1986) and Alzheimer's disease (Bjorklund & Stenevi, 1984; Gage & Bjorklund, 1986). The mechanisms whereby transplants influence the host brain are not completely understood, but they probably include both the introduction of new functional cells that can release neurotransmitter and other neural factors, and the stimulation and sprouting of remaining host cells.

Transplant surgery for the treatment of Parkinson's disease in humans has been taking place on an experimental basis for several years. Thus far the results are modest at best (Hoffer & van Horne, 1995), although it is hoped that further refinement of the procedure may lead to more successful results in the future. Brain tissue transplantation for the treatment of Alzheimer's disease in humans has not yet been attempted, although some promising results have been obtained in an animal model of the disease in monkeys (Kordower et al., 1994).

SUMMARY

Many cellular and physiological events set in motion by a brain lesion result in the destruction of neurons. Others, such as edema and shock, can produce temporary disruptions of neural tissue, sometimes at sites distant from the site of the lesion itself. This means that the actual consequences of a lesion may not be evident until these acute effects subside, weeks after their onset. Additional recovery of function may or may not occur after the alleviation of these acute effects. Factors favorable to recovery include youth, intelligence, left-handedness, optimism, and being female. Age at the time of lesion is the most important single factor. Thus, children show dramatic recovery of language, typically recovering language completely even after a lesion that severely disrupts it. Before age 5 or 6, this is due to the right hemisphere's taking over of language. Between age 5 or 6 and puberty, this recovery appears to be achieved by intrahemispheric reorganization.

However, a price—in the form of a generalized impairment in intellectual functioning—is paid for the recovery of language after an early left-hemisphere lesion, making the maxim that an early brain lesion is better than a later one not unequivocally valid.

Several possible neural mechanisms of recovery of function have been identified in the adult brain, including rerouting, sprouting, denervation supersensitivity, and regional reorganization. These may contribute importantly to the process of spontaneous recovery of function.

Therapeutic approaches to the consequences of brain lesions that take individual cognitive, behavioral, and emotional changes into account have the greatest chance of helping the person function more adaptively. Our rapidly developing knowledge of the relationship between brain and behavior can be applied to the understanding and treatment of people with brain lesions. Rehabilitation strategies include externally focused interventions, aimed at assisting the individual by modifying the environment; restorative interventions, aimed at recovering lost function; and compensatory interventions, aimed at using residual intact functioning to perform tasks that the brain lesion initially disrupted.

Pharmacological treatment and brain tissue transplantation are active areas of research devoted to discovering new approaches to the treatment of cognitive impairments associated with brain lesions. Although these approaches are still in the experimental stage, some clinical trials are underway. It is to be hoped that continued progress in the development of these methods will yield additional tools for helping those with brain lesions recover from the impairments that have so changed their lives.

Epilogue

SKEPTICISM ABOUT THE POSSIBILITY OF A UNIFIED THEORY OF MIND-BRAIN
The Mind-Brain Problem
Substance Dualism
Property Dualism
Functionalism

THE POSSIBILITY OF INTERTHEORETIC REDUCTION AND A UNIFIED THEORY OF MIND-BRAIN
Intertheoretic Reduction
The Inadequacy of Folk Psychology as a Criterion for the Possibility of Reduction
WHERE ARE WE NOW AND WHERE ARE WE GOING?

We have reached the end of our journey through the domains of current knowledge of neuropsychology. We have examined the relationship between brain and behavior from many perspectives and from a number of different levels of analysis, ranging from the investigation of the individual neuron to the processes mediated by extensive regions of the brain. We have seen that this diversity of approach has begun to yield, if not a coherent picture, at least a decipherable sketch of how the brain works.

Despite current advances, attempts to understand the relationship between the brain and behavior, and, in

particular, between the brain and human experience and consciousness, pose certain difficult philosophical problems. Some of these seem to defy our attempts to achieve a unified theory of brain-behavior and brain-experience relationships. In this epilogue, we step back from the details of our current knowledge and consider some of the philosophical problems inherent in our striving for understanding in this perhaps most enigmatic domain of scientific inquiry. We also consider possible solutions to these problems.

SKEPTICISM ABOUT THE POSSIBILITY OF A UNIFIED THEORY OF MIND-BRAIN

The Mind-Brain Problem

Most of us are materialists when it comes to scientific explanation in the majority of domains. We are quite ready to believe that phenomena as diverse as chemical reactions, changes in the weather, and planetary motion are all, in principle, explainable in terms of the interaction of physical objects. Yet certain features of our experience, certain mental phenomena, seem to defy explanation in terms of physical events (Searle, 1984). They seem to be irreducible to physical events, as if they were another domain entirely. This sense has led to the notion of *mind* as potentially distinct from *body*, creating the problem of how certain mental phenomena and the brain are related. This is the age-old **mind-body,** or **mind-brain, problem.**

Perhaps foremost among the mental phenomena that seem to defy a materialist explanation is **consciousness.** How can a bunch of molecules in our heads—albeit a highly complex and organized arrangement of molecules—know about themselves and even try to understand themselves? Surely this is one of the most astounding and wondrous phenomena in all of nature, perhaps even the most wondrous of all.

A second aspect of mental life that makes the mind-body problem difficult is **intentionality,** a term used by philosophers to denote the feature by which our mental states are directed at, or refer to, objects or states in the world other than themselves. In this context the word *intentionality* refers to "intended meaning or reference," not "intention" in the volitional sense. The problem here is How can the matter in my head be *about* anything? How can molecules *refer* to anything?

A third problem is that of **mental causation.** We all believe that our thoughts, feelings, and intentions influence and direct our behavior. Yet how can mental phenomena cause events in physical systems? How can the mental state of intending to take a step cause the muscles of my legs to execute the necessary motion?

Consciousness, intentionality, and mental causation make the mind-body problem extremely difficult. On the one hand, they seem to defy materialist explanations; on the other hand, it is not obvious how to scientifically investigate the possibility of nonphysical causation.

In the paragraphs that follow, we examine some of the major attempts to resolve the mind-body problem, and the implication of these approaches for neuropsychology and neuroscience more generally. In the process, we explore the place of neuroscience in the larger landscape of attempts to understand human behavior and experience. We will see that three positions regarding the mind-body problem (substance dualism, property dualism, and functionalism) all insist, though for different reasons, that phenomena on the psychological or mental level cannot be reduced to (explained in terms of) phenomena on the neurobiological level. Following an examination of some of the problems with each of these positions, we will argue that, given the current status of attempts to understand the mind-brain, there is a chance that a unified theory of mind-brain may be possible at some future time. We begin with the position that most emphatically repudiates the possibility of such a unified theory, substance dualism.

Substance Dualism

Dualism refers to the notion that mind and body are two separate domains. It is also possible to believe that mind and body constitute one domain, a position termed **monism.** There are two varieties of monist position: either everything is physical (**materialism**) or it is spiritual (**idealism**).

The most emphatic form of dualism, **substance dualism,** holds that there is a distinctly mental dimension that is not reducible to anything physical. From this perspective the universe is made up of two categories of substance: physical substance (matter) and a separate mental substance, or soul, that is not physical. From this point of view, psychological theory is the theory of the states and processes of the mind.

Throughout the history of philosophy, substance dualism has had many eloquent proponents. These include Plato, who, in the *Phaedo* dialogue, has Socrates argue for a world of the mind independent of the body and has him die with the words, "We owe a cock to Asclepius," a reference to the Greek custom of offering a sacrifice to the divine healer Asclepius after recovery from an illness (Hamilton & Cairns, 1964). For Socrates, the death of the material body was a recovery, releasing the nonphysical soul from the bondage of the material body.

Although there were many substance dualists after Plato, none has had a greater influence on the development of science than René Descartes. An avid materialist when it came to understanding the body, Descartes (1644) nevertheless believed that the brain could not be the cause of higher-order cognitive processes. He could not conceive of processes such as language, reasoning, and meaning depending on material processes in the brain. This position has continued to permeate antireductionist arguments. Clearly, from the perspective of the substance dualist, brain function can tell us nothing about higher psychological functioning. This requires, rather, understanding entirely different, nonphysical, principles of causation.

There is something noble, even romantic, about the idea that the mind or soul is not subject to the mundane laws governing the physical universe, that there is an independent spiritual sphere with its own laws. Part of the appeal of this idea is the possibility it offers of the soul's or mind's living on after the death of the body, a comforting idea that is, of course, fundamental to many religions. Substance dualism also persists today in a less explicit form in the body of beliefs known as **folk psychology.** This is the rough-and-ready intuitive psychological lore in terms of which we all tend to explain behavior and experience as the outcome of beliefs, desires, perceptions, expectations, goals, and other mental constructs. In fact, in our everyday thinking we all assume a kind of operational substance dualism, acting as if our mental life follows laws different from those to which the physical world is subject. In addition, it is surprising how many people who consider themselves dedicated materialists in other domains of science nevertheless avow an explicit substance dualism, proclaiming a belief in a spirit or soul that is not caused by brain function. Undoubtedly, many readers of this book share this conviction.

Despite its appeal on several levels, substance dualism presents a number of problems. Foremost among these is the nature of the nonphysical substance that is mind. A related problem can be stated as follows: If higher psychological functions are independent of the brain and yet influence behavior, as substance dualism posits, what is the nature of the interaction between mind and brain that makes this influence possible? Descartes attempted to solve this problem by proposing that "animal spirits" mediate between the two types of substance and that the site of this interaction is the pineal gland. However, because Descartes considered "animal spirits" to be

physical substance, this explanation does not solve the problem of how the nonphysical can affect the physical. Subsequent attempts have been no more successful (Eccles, 1977; Eccles & Robinson, 1984). Another problem with the notion that mind and body are independent is overwhelming evidence that physical events, induced by agents such as drugs or illness, affect psychological functioning. If the two domains were totally independent, such effects should not be seen. Yet another problem with substance dualism is that if higher-order psychological function is the product of evolution, where did the mind-stuff come from?

Substance dualism is not a popular position among neuroscientists, mainly because scientists are generally uncomfortable positing a nonphysical domain with its own laws that cannot be subjected to investigation via the methods of science in any obvious way. There is, however, a more scientifically respectable form of dualism.

Property Dualism

Property dualism abandons the idea that mind is a distinct substance, a soul-stuff radically different from the physical world, yet holds that irreducible, nonphysical properties emerge out of the states and processes of the physical brain. From this perspective, higher-order phenomena on the psychological level are emergent properties with respect to phenomena on the neurobiological level. An **emergent property** is a property inherent in a higher level of explanation that is not reducible to a property of a second, more basic, level of explanation, although it emerges from phenomena at the lower level. For example, a property dualist would argue that the wetness of water cannot be reduced to explanation on the molecular level; a water molecule is not *wet*. Similarly, consciousness would be seen as an emergent property with respect to phenomena on the neuronal and molecular levels. There is no consciousness in the passing of ions across neuronal membranes and the firing of action potentials. Yet out of these processes emerges consciousness. The most important implication of property dualism is that mental states and processes constitute a domain of study autonomous with respect to neuroscience; if phenomena at the psychological level cannot be reduced to more basic levels, then one must study these phenomena at the levels at which they emerge, without resorting to futile attempts at reduction.

From a scientific point of view, property dualism has the virtue of not resorting to nonphysical entities as causal agents, even as it rejects the idea that all psychological phenomena can be reduced to states and processes of the brain. It possesses an alluring plausibility, remaining materialist yet resisting reduction—and, of course, it may also be correct. Consciousness, intentionality, and free will may be emergent properties of our nervous system, irreducible to explanation at the molecular and neuronal levels. However, this is not necessarily the case. As Searle (1984) has argued, just as it is possible to understand water's wetness in terms of the nature of the chemical bonds between water molecules, even though individual water molecules are not *wet*, so it may be possible to understand mental phenomena as features of neuronal systems, even though the individual components of the neural system do not have the attributes of the mental phenomena in question. The principled repudiation of this possibility in the assertion that reduction will *always* be impossible *in principle* is the most problematic aspect of property dualism. It may turn out that even a highly evolved and transformed future psychology will not be reducible to a highly evolved future neurobiology. But this is not a question that can be resolved through logical arguments. It is, rather, an empirical question whose answer depends on further developments in both psychology and neuroscience.

The most sophisticated and seductive antireductionist position remains to be considered, however. We turn next to a discussion of functionalism.

Functionalism

The core of **functionalism** is the idea that mental states are functional states of the brain that stand in the same relation to neural mechanisms as functional states of a computer (its programs) stand to the computer's hardware. Functionalism is entirely materialist in the sense that it holds that mind is dependent on brain. It thus avoids substance dualism's fundamental premise that there are two different universes of phenomena and property dualism's notion of emergent properties that in principle cannot be reduced to a more basic level of explanation. However, functionalism insists that mental states can usefully be described and understood only in terms of their causal roles within the psychological level of explanation. For example, consider the social psychological construct **bystander apathy,** a construct that was generated from data showing that the probability that a person would come to another's assistance is inversely related to the number of other people present. Bystander apathy is a functionalist explanation because it attempts to explain a phenomenon in terms of the relationship between environmental input and behavioral output. It does not deny that some physical events in the brain mediate this relationship, but it posits that understanding those mediating events, in addition to being very difficult, will not in any case contribute to an understanding of psychological phenomena any more than, to use Ulric Neisser's (1966) analogy, understanding how money is transported by armored trucks will help us understand the laws of economics. Thus, although functionalism is materialist, it rejects the possibility of reduction and repudiates the notion that explanation at the neurobiological level contributes to explanation at higher levels. In short, for the functionalist, neurobiology is irrelevant.

Functionalism is the most compelling of the antireductionist positions. Unlike substance dualism, it does not rest on ontological assumptions about the basic distinctness of mind and body (*ontology,* from the Greek *ontos,* "being," is the study of what *is*) and, unlike property dualism, it does not insist on the existence of emergent properties. In other words, it is thoroughly materialist in its foundations. Its repudiation of reduction comes not from ontological assumptions but from the belief that higher-order psychological processes must be understood in terms of relationships between environmental input, internal states, and output, rather than in terms of causal relations between physical states.

There are several arguments supporting this position, but the most compelling rests on the idea that certain phenomena are best understood within a particular level of explanation rather than by reduction. For example, if one wants to understand gas pressure, it could be argued that the best approach is to understand the relationship between a gas's pressure and its mass, volume, and temperature, rather than to attempt to understand pressure in terms of the positions or movements of the gas's molecules, even if it is conceded that events on the molecular level ultimately cause pressure. Analogous positions are omnipresent in experimental psychology. "Yes," the functionalist would say, "the brain causes behavior and experience, but higher-order psychological processes, such as bystander apathy, are best understood in terms of variables on the molar level, on the level of observable input and output."

There is no question that psychology has benefited from the adoption of the functionalist approach, which is alive and well in many domains of psychological inquiry. Even within the domain of neuropsychology, it seems quite possible to attempt to explain many of the disorders discussed in this book in terms of a functional description of how particular brain lesions affect higher-order psychological function under certain input conditions. Yet, in relating dysfunction to brain lesions, we have already begun a reductive process that potentially sheds new light on higher-order function. As we have also seen in the foregoing chapters, explanation on the neuronal and molecular levels can enhance understanding on less basic levels, and vice versa. In the next section, we elaborate further on these points, presenting arguments for both the possibility and the usefulness of reduction as a vehicle for understanding and, ultimately, for developing a unified theory of mind-brain.

THE POSSIBILITY OF INTERTHEORETIC REDUCTION AND A UNIFIED THEORY OF MIND-BRAIN

Intertheoretic Reduction

When one contemplates the possibility that higher-order psychological phenomena could be reduced to neuronal and molecular events, the first reaction is likely to be one of boggled skepticism (Churchland, 1986). How can the experience of consciousness ever be explained in terms of a bunch of membranes with

ions passing through them, the level of explanation examined in chapter 2? In considering the possibility of reduction, however, it is important to recognize that reduction occurs between *theories*, not necessarily between *phenomena as we know them now*. In other words, in reduction, a theory that characterizes one level of phenomenon is reduced to another theory that characterizes a second, more basic, level of phenomenon. For example, theories about the transformation of matter that predated atomic theory have been successfully reduced to atomic theory. This process is termed **intertheoretic reduction,** to emphasize that it is *theories* that are being reduced.

The intertheoretical nature of reduction has important implications for the problem of whether phenomena on the psychological level can be reduced to phenomena on the neurobiological level. The issue now becomes, not whether *mental states and processes as we know them now* can be reduced to *brain states and processes as we know them now*, but, rather, whether some *future theory* of mental states and processes can be reduced to some *future theory* of brain states and processes. This means that the fact that we now find it difficult to imagine how visual experience, decision making, or consciousness could be reduced to phenomena on the neuronal or molecular levels does not preclude the possibility that future coevolution of theories at different levels of explanation will eventually yield newly evolved theories on the psychological level that are reducible to newly evolved theories on a more micro level.

An example of coevolution of theories spawning reductive explanation is seen in current neurobiological-level theories of learning in *Aplysia* (Kandel et al., 1995), discussed in chapter 2. Learning is a multifaceted construct derived from theories of behavior on the molar level that evolved during the early 20th century. We have seen that Kandel and his colleagues have been stunningly successful in reducing theories of certain simple kinds of learning on the molar level to theories of events on the neuronal level. Such a reduction would clearly not have been possible in the middle of the 19th century, before the evolution of the theory of learning and before the evolution of a theory of neurochemical and neurophysiological events on the neuronal level.

To the extent that intertheoretic reduction is possible, it fosters **explanatory unification:** Where there were once two theories, each explaining phenomena on a different level, there is now only one theory, explaining phenomena on a single basic level in a way that also explains phenomena on the more molar level. In the course of this process, specific elements of the molar theory may be explained by specific elements of the more basic reducing theory, a process termed **cross-theoretic identification.** Drawing on our earlier example once again, Kandel's reduction of different constructs of learning theory (e.g., habituation, sensitization, and classical conditioning) to specific neuronal mechanisms exemplifies this process.

But the process of intertheoretic reduction does not always lead to smooth cross-theoretic identifications. In the process of reduction, some or all of the constructs in the reduced theory may be eliminated. An instructive example of this is the problem of understanding what makes living things alive, a problem that challenged and preoccupied 19th-century biology. The leading hypothesis at that time was that living things have some *vital spirit*, qualitatively different from all other forces in nature, that makes them alive. Since that time, biology and chemistry have undergone extensive coevolution. As a result, it is now possible to understand living organisms in terms of biochemical events directed by DNA and enzymes to such an extent that we no longer feel a need for a unique "force" animating living tissue. The molecules of life are truly marvelous in their complexity, but we can now formulate a theory of how they orchestrate the processes of life that is consistent with general theories of chemistry and physics. This reduction simply eliminated the need for a force unique to life, although this needn't diminish our awe of the wondrous complexity and organization of biochemical systems. This elimination also altered some fundamental questions. The problem of the nature of "vital spirits" and how they make things alive was replaced by problems on the biochemical level: how DNA programs and executes the synthesis of proteins and how these proteins facilitate and regulate biochemical processes essential for life. Analogously, as psychology and neuroscience coevolve, many of the seemingly insoluble problems that currently face us, such as the neurobiological mechanisms of consciousness, may ultimately be resolved in a way that entails the elimination of some currently fundamental constructs.

It should be emphasized that coevolution does not imply that theories at two or more levels evolve in isolation until they reach a point at which some form of intertheoretic reduction is possible. On the contrary, during coevolution, theories at one level may correct and extend theories at another level, a process that has been called **theoretic interanimation** (Churchland, 1986). Examples of this cross-fertilization of coevolving theories abound in psychology and neuroscience. To take one example, consider the distinction between procedural and declarative memory, discussed in chapter 10. It must have been known for millennia that motor skills are retained far more permanently than most specific items of information, and experimental psychology recognized this difference early in its history. Nevertheless, when it was shown that H. M. could learn and retain certain motor and perceptual skills despite his severe impairment in the retention of new explicit information (Scoville & Milner, 1957), this indication that different brain regions mediate these two kinds of memory enhanced the validity of the distinction. Subsequent empirical studies of persons with cerebral lesions (Cohen & Squire, 1980) added validity to the distinction between declarative and procedural memory and eventually led to refinements of theoretical formulation embodied in the constructs implicit and explicit memory (Schacter, 1987). This work, in turn, stimulated the experimental investigation of discrete memory systems in normal subjects, further advancing our conceptualization of memory as composed of a number of independent systems.

It is important to recognize that reduction does not require that one first know all about properties on a micro level of explanation before addressing macro properties. Although reduction ultimately results in an explanation of higher-level phenomena in terms of lower-level phenomena, this is not necessarily the order of discovery. In fact, coevolution and fruitful interaction between different levels of explanation (theoretic interanimation) are more likely to lead to a satisfying reduction than are isolated investigations pursued at any one level.

What does all this mean for the study of brain-behavior relationships? We have approached this domain from an almost bewildering range of levels. For example, in the study of the visual system, the system we understand most completely (though hardly *truly* completely), we have found ourselves sometimes being functionalists, describing the relationship between input and output in patients with cerebral lesions and in normal subjects. This included the description of patients with achromatopsia, akinetopsia, and visual agnosia. On the other end of the range of levels of explanation, we have examined the intricate anatomy of the visual pathways and striate and extrastriate cortex. We also examined the results of single unit recording studies in striate and extrastriate cortex in animals, describing how certain cells respond to specific features of stimuli and not to others.

When considering this range of levels of approach, it is tempting to adopt the functionalist position and declare that physiological and anatomical studies cannot meaningfully inform us about the experience of perceiving color, movement, and objects. Indeed, it is tempting to use the metaphor of two construction gangs tunneling from different sides of a mountain and perhaps meeting someday in the distant future, until which time the levels of analysis represented by the two tunnels are so discrepant, so unrelated, that they cannot meaningfully inform each other. This is a beguiling metaphor and one that continues to be employed even by those who take the study of the brain very seriously (Pinker, 1997). What this metaphor leaves out is that the two construction gangs are in communication with each other and this communication sometimes helps each gang identify where it is, what it is seeing, and where it should dig next. Perhaps even more important, the metaphor leaves out the idea of coevolution as a vehicle for eventual reduction. The net effect of these considerations is that the extremely varied levels of analysis within neuroscience may not be the isolated torches scattered in a darkened landscape that they sometimes appear to be. Instead, they may be seen as tentative markers of coevolving approaches that can inform and influence each other now

and that eventually may yield reductions that generate a unified theory of mind-brain.

The Inadequacy of Folk Psychology as a Criterion for the Possibility of Reduction

Despite the foregoing arguments, there remain some experiences that are difficult to reconcile with the possibility of reduction. Folk psychology, that psychological lore that we all intuitively use to explain behavior in terms of internal states such as desires, beliefs, and goals, seems to stubbornly continue to assert itself as the criterion against which the adequacy of reduction must be measured. I am conscious. I have beliefs, desires, goals, and plans. The fancy arguments of the previous section notwithstanding, don't we all retain the intuition that a valid explanation of behavior must be framed in terms of the internal states known to folk psychology rather than in terms of principles of causation governing physical systems on some micro level of explanation?

The problem with this position is that it assumes that our experience of our own mental states is purely observational, unmediated by congitive interpretation. This is, however, not the case. In reality, our observations of our own experience are no more free of interpretative bias than are our observations of the external world. Many or all of the seemingly obvious observations of folk psychology may thus be cognitively mediated distortions of the true state of affairs. As counterintuitive as it sounds, even consciousness itself may be a trick our cognition plays on us, giving us the experience that we are aware when this is in fact false. It may be that the evolution of psychology will yield constructs that supersede consciousness and that can eventually be reduced by newly evolved constructs in neuroscience. Alternatively, consciousness may be retained in a newly evolved psychological theory. In any case, it is certain that the growing interest in investigating the nature and function of consciousness (e.g., Weiskrantz, 1997; Zeki, 1993) will serve to advance our understanding. The important point for our present discussion is that despite the intuitive obviousness of consciousness and other psychological states characterized by folk psychology, it is not necessary that we seek a one-to-one cross-theoretical identification between these psychological states and neurobiological states. What will eventually be reduced in any future unified theory of mind-brain are generalizations from scientific psychology that have undergone major evolution from the characterizations of current folk psychology.

WHERE ARE WE NOW AND WHERE ARE WE GOING?

There is a certain comfort in the possibility that the coevolution of theories at different levels may eventually lead to intertheoretic reduction and a unified theory of mind-brain. This possibility means that findings from vastly different levels of analysis—from unit cell recording, neurochemistry, and neuroanatomy to lesion studies in animals and humans—may all contribute potentially to a unified theory. Nevertheless, this possibility, assuming we accept it, does not prevent us from sometimes being overwhelmed by the enormous diversity of levels of explanation and the data that they generate. Surely, if a unified theory is ever achieved, it will not be soon. We will therefore have to deal with an enormous range of levels of theoretical explanation for some time to come. And, in their day-to-day research efforts, individual investigators will find themselves necessarily adopting and working within a particular level of explanation, temporarily ignoring other levels. The challenge will be to carry out these necessarily circumscribed investigations while at the same time remaining open to, and actively seeking, opportunities to make connections between findings generated by studies utilizing widely disparate levels of explanation.

We have seen many instances of such connections throughout this book. To mention briefly three examples, in chapter 5, we saw that unit recording studies have discovered cells in area V4 of the monkey that are responsive to *perceived color* rather than wavelength. The response characteristics of these cells are thus consistent with color constancy, a construct that emerged from experimental work with normal human subjects. A similar connection was seen in chapter 7, where we found *real position cells* in area V6

of the alert, behaving monkey that respond to the absolute position of an object in space, independent of the animal's point of fixation (see Figure 7.4). It is obvious that we register the spatial location of an object in absolute space, independent of our point of fixation. These neurons in V6 link this phenomenon on the molar level with events at the neuronal level. As a final example, consider Goldman-Rakic's work on the role of prefrontal cortex in working memory. As will be recalled from chapter 10, her work has shown that lesions of the principal sulcus in the monkey disrupt performance on a delayed-response eye-movement task that taps working memory. The deficit was found to be distributed topographically, such that some lesions were associated with memory for targets in the upper visual fields and others were associated with targets in the lower visual fields. There was also a contralateral relationship between side of lesion and the side of space affected (see Figure 10.26). Goldman-Rakic was then able to relate these findings to data on the level of the single neuron by demonstrating the presence of neurons in the principal sulcus that fired during the delay interval when the required movement was in a particular direction but not when it was in other directions (see Figure 10.27). Each of these examples represents a stunning convergence of findings from very different levels of analysis and explanation. Clearly there is much that remains to be understood in each of these domains, but healthy coevolution and interanimation of theoretical levels is under way.

But, although there is room for optimism about the prospects of achieving a unified theory of mind-brain, it must also be acknowledged that there are reasonable grounds for doubting the possibility. To paraphrase Churchland (1986), perhaps the brain is more complicated than it is smart. Perhaps, as Pinker (1997) has suggested, our brains have evolved to solve practical survival-related problems, not to resolve philosophical issues like the mind-body problem or to achieve a unified theory of mind-brain. Whatever its ultimate theoretical yield may be, however, neuropsychology has already provided enormous practical benefit to individuals with cerebral lesions and neurodevelopmental disorders. Despite the development of powerful imaging methods that can detect and localize cerebral lesions far more accurately than is possible with neuropsychological testing, an awareness of the cognitive and emotional consequences of cerebral lesions remains an invaluable tool in the clinical evaluation of psychiatric and medical patients who are not suspected of having an acute cerebral lesion. A certain percentage of these patients have cerebral lesions with early symptoms confined to the cognitive sphere. It is obviously important to identify these individuals and direct them to appropriate evaluation and treatment. Neuropsychological assessment is also the diagnostic method of choice for conditions in which the major symptoms are cognitive in nature and for which no equally reliable diagnostic signs or tests are available to the clinician. Foremost among such disorders is Alzheimer's disease and related dementias.

Even more important than its diagnostic role, however, is neuropsychology's role in delineating the cognitive impairments and residual strengths of people with cerebral lesions—and then using these profiles to design and implement retraining and rehabilitation programs to help individuals achieve their highest possible level of functioning. This unique role of neuropsychology is perhaps the most tangible effect of the basic research in brain-behavior relationships that has been the focus of this book. Future developments in our basic understanding of how the brain works can be expected to yield increasingly powerful and effective methods of helping people recover from the effects of cerebral lesions. We can also expect that future developments in our basic understanding of the relationship between the human brain and behavior will deepen our sense of awe and mystery at the working of this marvelous organ and expand our awareness of how much more there is to learn about it. And, surely, given the rapid pace and stunning nature of recent developments, we must also expect the unexpected— and, indeed, the unimagined.

Glossary

absolute refractory period   The period after an action potential during which another action potential cannot be activated. This is due to the temporary inactivation of Na^+ channels.

acalculia   Inability to perform mathematical operations.

acetylcholine   A major neurotransmitter in the brain. It is found at the junction between motor neurons and muscle. It is also the major neurotransmitter in the parasympathetic nervous system.

achromatopsia   Central (brain-based) color blindness.

action potential   The wave of influx of Na^+ ions into the axon, which is the mechanism by which a signal is communicated down the length of the axon.

active zones   Regions of the presynaptic membrane where neurotransmitter is released.

activity-dependent presynaptic facilitation   A situation in which the magnitude of presynaptic facilitation is dependent upon the activity of the neuron receiving the facilitation.

adenosine triphosphate (ATP)   A molecule important for cellular energy metabolism. Its conversion to adenosine diphosphate (ADP) releases energy. It is also converted to cyclic adenosine monophosphate (cyclic AMP), which serves as a second messenger in a number of capacities, including the activation of postsynaptic potentials by neuropeptides.

adoption studies   A research strategy in which children who are at high risk for a condition and who have been adopted shortly after birth are studied in an effort to identify the effect of having a biological parent with a condition even though one does not grow up with that parent. A higher-than-baseline occurrence of the condition in such children indicates that a genetic factor contributes to the condition.

adrenocorticotrophic hormone (ACTH)   Hormone released by the anterior pituitary that triggers the release of hormones, including cortisol, from the adrenal cortex.

affect   A term often used to mean short-term emotion. The term **mood** is used to designate a long-lasting emotional state, such as depression.

affective aggression   Aggressive behavior that, in contrast to **predatory aggression,** is characterized by display behavior, such as intense vocalizations and threatening postures.

affective disorder   A term that has been replaced by the term **mood disorder.**

affective prosody   Intonation in spoken language that communicates emotion.

afferent   "Toward." Neural input. Thalamic afferents are neurons projecting to the thalamus.

afterpotential   The brief hyperpolarization that precedes the reestablishment of the resting potential after an action potential.

agnosia   Impairment in recognition not due to primary sensory impairment. Agnosias are modality specific.

agoraphobia   Fear of public, unprotected places.

agrammatism   Impairment in the syntactic elements of speech production. Patients with agrammatism make many grammatical errors in their speech.

agraphia   Inability to write. This term may also be used to specify specific disorders of spelling.

akathesia   Motor restlessness.

465

akinesia   Absence of movement.

akinetopsia   Central (brain-based) impairment in the perception of motion.

alexia   Inability to read.

allocentric space   Representations of space in which place is defined by a coordinate system that is independent of the observer.

allocortex   Areas of cortex with fewer than six layers.

alogia   Reduction or absence of verbal expression (i.e., speech).

alternative strategies   Rehabilitation interventions that attempt to utilize the ways of processing that remain within the person's cognitive repertoire after a cerebral lesion, but that are distinct from the way in which the individual performed the task before the lesion.

Alzheimer's disease   The most common form of progressive deterioration of cognitive and emotional functioning (dementia); characterized by neuropathological changes that are detectable only at autopsy.

amacrine cells   Cells forming the inner plexiform layer of the retina, between the inner nuclear layer (bipolar cells) and the ganglion cell layer.

amnesia   Severe loss of memory.

amnesic aphasia   Impairment in word retrieval.

amygdala   Collection of nuclei in the base of the temporal lobe, anterior to the hippocampus. Considered part of the limbic system.

amyloid plaques   *See* **neuritic plaques.**

analogical representation   A representation that captures some of the actual characteristics of that which it represents. For example, a road sign with a curving arrow is an analogical representation of an upcoming curve in the road.

anencephaly   Congenital absence of the cranial vault, with the cerebral hemispheres completely missing or reduced to small masses at the base of the skull.

aneurysm   A blood-filled sac formed by a dilation of the wall of a vein or artery. Bursting of an aneurysm results in cerebral bleeding that destroys brain tissue.

angiography   The process by which a radiopaque (X-ray-absorbing) dye is injected into the cerebral circulation to make the vasculature (veins and arteries) visible on X ray.

anion   A negatively charged ion.

anomia   Inability to come up with a desired word (word-finding problem).

anomic aphasia   Impairment in word retrieval.

anopia   Loss of vision.

anosognosia   Inability to recognize one's illness or bodily defect.

anoxia   Absence or lack of oxygen.

anterior   Term designating the front part of the brain and spinal cord.

anterior commissure   An important fiber tract connecting the two temporal lobes.

anterior pituitary gland   A gland protruding from the base of the hypothalamus that has a major role in the control of endocrine function.

anterograde amnesia   An impairment in the ability to remember new events following some compromise of brain function.

anterograde degeneration   Degeneration of the length of an axon distal to the point of damage. Also called *Wallerian degeneration.*

anterograde topographical amnesia   Impairment in the ability to learn new spatial layouts in the absence of a primary disturbance of spatial processing.

anterograde transport   Axoplasmic transport that conveys materials from the cell body of the neuron to the axon terminal.

antipsychotics   Medications used to treat the symptoms of psychotic disorders. Also called *neuroleptics.*

antisocial personality disorder   A pervasive pattern of behavior characterized by an extreme lack of concern for the immediate or future consequences of one's behavior. Individuals with this disorder tend to be callous, selfish, and irresponsible. They frequently manipulate and exploit others, exhibiting little or no empathy, and they often engage in illegal behavior, without feeling guilt or remorse. In the past the terms *psychopathy* and *sociopathy* have been used to describe this disorder.

anxiolytics   Antianxiety medications.

aphasia Language impairment due to a brain lesion, in the absence of elementary sensory or motor impairment.

apolipoprotein E4 A protein, the gene for the programming of which may represent a risk factor for familial forms of Alzheimer's disease.

apperception Term used by Wundt and other 19th-century psychologists to indicate higher-order perception.

apperceptive agnosia Term coined by Lissauer to designate impairment in visual recognition due to a disruption of perception. It may now be defined as impairment in the organization of visual sensations into percepts in the absence of (commensurately severe) impairment in visual sensory processing.

apraxia A disorder of learned, voluntary movement not due to sensory or elementary motor impairment.

apraxia of speech *See* **kinetic disorder of speech.**

aprosodia Severe impairment in the processing of prosody.

aqueduct of Sylvius The narrow channel, running through the midbrain, that connects the third and fourth ventricles.

arachnoid membrane The middle membrane surrounding the brain (positioned between the dura mater and the pia mater). It consists of two layers of fibrous and elastic tissue. It does not follow the contours of the sulci and gyri of the cortex.

archicortex Areas of cortex that have only one layer. It includes regions of the hippocampus (Ammon's horn and the dentate gyrus).

arcuate fasciculus Fiber tract connecting Wernicke's and Broca's areas.

arousal A state of responsiveness to sensory stimulation.

artificial selection The deliberate control of mating in animals to produce particular characteristics.

aspartate An amino acid neurotransmitter.

Asperger's syndrome A syndrome with many similarities to classical autism but with areas of relatively high functioning. These may include the development of language; the learning of minimal social skills; and, in rare cases, the attainment of significant intellectual achievement.

association Consistent co-occurrence of impairment in two or more functions. Association suggests that the two behavioral or cognitive phenomena are manifestations of one underlying process.

association cortex According to older, sequential models of cortical processing, the areas of cortex (not devoted to sensory or motor function) where higher-order (associative) processes are represented. Because of our growing understanding of the function of these areas, this term is now seen as insufficiently specific and its use is becoming increasingly infrequent.

associative agnosia Term coined by Lissauer to designate impairment in the assignment of meaning to an intact visual percept.

astereognosis Inability to recognize objects by active touch in the absence of elementary sensory impairment; tactual agnosia.

astrocytes Large, star-shaped glia cells that surround the brain's vasculature, forming the blood-brain barrier.

ataxia A general term indicating disruption of muscular coordination.

athetosis Ceaseless occurrence of slow, sinuous, writhing movements performed involuntarily.

atrophy Wasting away; diminution in size.

attention Hypothetical process that allows selective awareness of and/or responsiveness to certain aspects of internal psychological processes or the external environment.

attention deficit disorder (ADD) A disorder characterized by distractibility, impulsivity, restlessness, and difficulty attending to relevant cues in the environment.

attentional dyslexia A word-form dyslexia characterized by an inability to read words and letters when they appear with other written material, co-existing with preserved ability to read isolated words and letters.

atypical antipsychotics A relatively new class of antipsychotic medications, which appear to act by blocking both dopamine and serotonin receptors and which are generally more effective than the classical neuroleptics in treating patients with predominantly negative symptoms. Medications in this category include clozapine, risperidone, and olanzapine.

auditory agnosia　Impairment in the ability to recognize nonspeech sounds in the absence of impairment in elementary auditory function.

auditory association cortex　Area surrounding the auditory cortex that receives projections from the auditory cortex and is involved in higher-order auditory processing.

auditory cortex　Area of cortex in Heschl's gyrus in the lower lip of the Sylvian fissure that receives the major projections from the medial geniculate nucleus of the thalamus.

auditory nerve　The nerve fibers connecting the structures of the inner ear to the cochlear nucleus in the brain stem.

auditory perceptual analysis　The process of perceiving the phonemes of a word.

auditory radiations　Fibers conveying auditory input from the medial geniculate nucleus to the auditory cortex.

auditory temporal acuity　The processes underlying the detection of the elementary acoustic features of a word's sound.

autism　An extremely disabling disorder that almost always begins before age 30 months and typically lasts a lifetime. It is characterized by severe impairment in verbal and nonverbal communication, failure to develop social relationships, and stereotyped and repetitive patterns of behavior.

autistic savants　A subgroup of people with autism, including some who are retarded, who also have a special skill or talent in a specific area, such as music, the ability to memorize, art, or the ability to perform calculations. These special talents within a narrow domain coexist with severely impaired functioning in areas outside the domain of special talent.

autoneurotoxicity　Neuronal responses to insult that further damage neuronal tissue. An example is the excessive release of glutamate by cells in the hippocampus in response to oxygen deprivation. This overexcites hippocampal neurons, causing their death.

autonomic motor system　The component of the autonomic nervous system sending motor output to regulate and control the smooth muscles of internal organs, cardiac muscle, and glands.

autonomic nervous system　The part of the peripheral nervous system that innervates internal organs, blood vessels, and glands and that is not under voluntary control.

autonomic sensory system　The component of the autonomic nervous system that monitors the status of internal structures.

autoradiography　A technique in which radioactive tracer is injected into an area of gray matter and then moved (via axoplasmic transport) to the axon terminals. This allows the identification of the structures that are the targets of the injected neurons.

autoreceptors　Receptors on the presynaptic membrane that bind neurotransmitter and thereby provide the axon with information about the concentration of neurotransmitter in the synapse.

autosomal dominant transmission　Genetic transmission via chromosomes other than the sex chromosomes and requiring the gene from only one parent for the appearance of the trait or disorder in the offspring.

autosomal recessive transmission　Genetic transmission via chromosomes other than the sex chromosomes and requiring two genes, one from each parent, for the occurrence of the trait or disorder in the offspring.

avolition　The apparent absence of motivation.

axial　A plane of section (cut) that divides the brain into upper (superior) and lower (inferior) parts.

axon　The long process (projection or outgrowth) extending from the cell body that passes signals on to the next neuron.

axon hillock　The part of the neuron that forms the junction between the cell body and the axon. This part of the neuron has the lowest threshold for triggering an action potential.

axon terminal　The end of the axon. Also called the terminal *bouton*.

axoplasmic transport   An active process whereby substances within a neuron are moved across its length.

β amyloid precursor protein (APP)   A long chain of amino acids that is cut apart by enzymes to produce β amyloid protein.

β amyloid precursor protein gene (APP gene)   Gene involved in the synthesis of β amyloid precursor protein. Mutations of the APP gene are believed to cause defective forms of β amyloid protein to be produced in at least some cases of familial Alzheimer's disease.

β amyloid protein   The protein that makes up the dense core of neuritic plaques in Alzheimer's disease.

B cones   Cones most sensitive to 419 nanometer (nm) wavelength light.

ballism   Involuntary, violent flinging movements of the extremities.

barrels   Specialized aggregates of cells in mouse sensory cortex, each of which receives input from a single whisker on the contralateral side of the body.

basal ganglia   A large group of gray matter structures deep within the forebrain including the caudate nucleus, putamen, globus pallidus, subthalamic nuclei, and substantia nigra. (The substantia nigra is actually in the midbrain.) This term is an exception to the general rule that collections of neuron cell bodies within the central nervous system are called nuclei, whereas those in the peripheral nervous system are called ganglia.

bilateral   On both sides (of the body).

binding problem   The problem of how the varied aspects of sensory (e.g., visual) input processed in different cortical areas are integrated to yield the coherent percepts and representations that we experience as the external world.

binocular disparity   The difference between the images of an object on the two retinas due to the slightly different location of the two eyes relative to the viewed object. Information regarding binocular disparity is critical for stereoscopic depth perception.

binocular zone   The area of the visual field that projects to the retinas of both eyes.

bipolar cells   Neurons having long processes at both ends, with the cell body at a midpoint. Bipolar cells in the retina connect photoreceptors with ganglion cells, forming the inner nuclear layer of the retina.

bipolar disorder   A disorder characterized by fluctuations between periods of depression and periods of mania, with normal periods interspersed between these two extremes. Formerly called *manic-depressive disorder.*

birth date   The time when a developing neuron loses the capacity for DNA replication.

bizarre behavior   Behavior outside the conventional range of behavior for a given context that does not serve any adaptive purpose.

blind spot   The area within the visual field where stimuli cannot be detected due to the presence of the optic disc.

blindsight   The ability of patients with cortical blindness to have some preserved but unconscious visual function.

blobs   Areas in V1 that stain darkly for the dye for cytochrome oxidase.

blood-brain barrier   A barrier that protects the brain by allowing only certain molecules to pass into it from the general circulation. It is formed by astrocytes (a type of glia) that surround the brain's vasculature.

blunted affect   Diminished or complete absence of emotional expression.

body space   The sense of the body surface as a space on which stimuli can impinge and be localized.

bouton   The end of the axon. Also called the *axon terminal.*

bradykinesia   Slowed movement.

brain abscess   Localized area of pus in the brain formed from disintegrated tissue resulting from infection.

brain hypothesis   The idea that the brain is the biological organ that controls behavior and generates experience.

brain stem   The part of the brain lying between the diencephalon and the spinal cord. It is composed of the midbrain, pons, and medulla.

Broca's aphasia   A central impairment in the ability to program rapid sequences of phonemes to produce fluent speech, in the absence of impairment in the production of individual phonemes.

Broca's area   The area of cortex (in the posterior part of the left inferior frontal gyrus) which, when damaged, results in an aphasia characterized by an impairment in speech production, while language comprehension is relatively intact.

buffers   Specialized temporary storage systems.

bystander apathy   A construct generated from the finding that the probability that a person will come to another's assistance is inversely related to the number of other people present.

calcarine cortex   Region in the occipital lobes that receives the major projections from the lateral geniculate nucleus. Also termed the *primary visual cortex,* or *V1.*

Cannon-Bard theory of emotion   The theory that an emotional stimulus first activates the thalamus, which then simultaneously activates the cortex and the hypothalamus. The quality of subjective emotional experience is the result of activation of the cortex, whereas hypothalamic activation organizes the autonomic and behavioral components of emotion. (Hypothalamic input to the cortex contributes to the perceived intensity, but not the quality, of emotional experience.)

catastrophic reaction   Goldstein's term for the extreme depression he observed after left-hemisphere lesions.

catecholamine hypothesis of attention deficit disorder   The hypothesis that attention deficit disorder is caused by lower-than-normal levels of catecholamines and/or a decrease in their activity level.

catecholamine hypothesis of depression   A refinement of the monoamine hypothesis of depression, which posits that some forms of depression result from a specific abnormality in catecholamine (particularly norepinephrine) activity.

catecholamines   Class of neurotransmitters that includes epinephrine, norepinephrine, and dopamine.

category-specific comprehension impairment   Impairment in the comprehension of words (or drawings) denoting (depicting) instances within certain categories, but not others—for example, the ability to comprehend words denoting living things but not small objects.

cation   A positively charged ion.

cauda equina   "Horse tail." The array of lower spinal nerves as they continue to course caudally beyond the end of the spinal cord before leaving the spinal column.

caudal   In the brain stem and spinal cord, the direction away from the brain.

caudate nucleus   One of the nuclei of the basal ganglia.

cell body   The part of the neuron containing the cell nucleus and many of the organelles that are critical for the functioning of the cell. Also called *soma.*

central disorders of spelling   Disorders of spelling that involve interference with late stages in the spelling process.

central dyslexias   Dyslexias that involve interference with late stages in the reading process, as opposed to **visual word-form dyslexias,** which involve the disruption of earlier stages in the reading process.

central motor aphasia   A disturbance in verbal expression (but not an aphasia in the traditional sense) seen after prefrontal lesions. It is characterized by reduction in spontaneous speech, diminished verbal fluency, and reduction in the volume and scope of narrative expression. Also called *frontal dynamic aphasia* and *prefrontal aphasia.*

central nervous system   The brain and the spinal cord.

central nucleus of the amygdala (ACe)   Specifically involved in the expression of conditioned fear. Damage to ACe results in disruption of every measure of conditioned fear; damage to specific outputs of ACe disrupts specific elements of the fear response.

cerebellar ataxia   Disruptions in the maintenance of posture and the sequential coordination of movement associated with cerebellar dysfunction.

cerebellar peduncles   Massive fiber tracts connecting the cerebellum and forebrain.

cerebellum   The large and intricate structure bulging out of the dorsal surface of the brain at the level of the pons and forming the roof of the fourth ventricle.

cerebral cortex   The massive sheet of neuron cell bodies that forms the outer layer of gray matter surrounding the telencephalon.

cerebral dominance   The idea that one hemisphere is involved in a particular function and the other one is not. This concept was first applied globally to the left hemisphere, because of its representation of language. Now it is recognized that each hemisphere is specialized for certain functions and that the two hemispheres often work in collaboration. The term *complementary hemispheric specialization* has largely supplanted this term.

cerebral hemorrhage   Bleeding in the brain.

cerebral vascular accident (CVA)   Sudden appearance of neurological symptoms resulting from severe interruption of blood flow due to vascular occlusion or hemorrhage. Also called *stroke*.

cerebral ventricles   *See* **ventricles.**

cerebrospinal fluid (CSF)   Fluid that fills the cerebral ventricles and the subarachnoid space. CSF surrounds the brain, providing structural support for it and a measure of protection to it from blows to the head.

cGMP   *See* **cyclic guanosine monophosphate.**

channels   Openings in the neuronal membrane formed by proteins embedded in the lipid bilayer. There are specific channels for specific ions (e.g., K^+, Na^+), each type regulating the permeability (conductance) of the membrane to its particular ion. The degree to which a particular channel type allows its particular ion to pass varies, depending on a number of factors.

chemospecificity hypothesis   The hypothesis that neurons become chemically differentiated at an early stage in their development in such a way that their membranes have distinguishing chemical labels that enable the developing (growing) axons to recognize their targets.

chimeric face   A photograph of a face composed by splitting a photograph of a face down the middle and then splicing together each side with its mirror image.

cholinergic   Pertaining to (the adjectival form of) acetylcholine.

chorea   The ceaseless occurrence of a wide variety of rapid, complex, and jerky movements that may appear to be well coordinated but are involuntary. Choreic movements are seen in a number of different diseases of the nervous system.

choroid plexus   Tufts of capillary vessels in the cerebral ventricles through which CSF enters the ventricle.

chromosome   A structure in the nucleus of each cell that contains the genes. Cells in humans have 46 chromosomes, arranged in 23 pairs. One of these pairs consists of the sex chromosomes. In males, the members of the pair of sex chromosomes are an X-chromosome and a Y-chromosome. In females, both members of the pair of sex chromosomes are X-chromosomes.

chunking   The organization of information into parcels, thereby making possible an increase in the capacity of short-term memory.

cingulate cortex   A long gyrus arching along the superior margin of the corpus callosum on the medial surface of the cerebral hemispheres.

circumlocutory speech   Tendency to "talk around" a word or topic. It is often seen in Wernicke's aphasia.

classical conditioning   A form of learning in which a previously neutral stimulus, the conditioned stimulus (CS), is paired with a stimulus that naturally causes a response, the unconditioned stimulus (US), until the CS also evokes a response (usually similar to that evoked by the US).

cochlear nucleus   The brain-stem nucleus to which the auditory nerve projects.

coextensive single-opponent cells   P ganglion cells that have an undifferentiated receptive field (no center-surround organization) in which the action of B cones is opposed to the combined action of G and R cones.

cognitive arousal theory of emotion   The theory that the quality of subjective emotional experience is the result of a subject's cognitive appraisal or interpretation of the arousal rather than of the arousal per se.

cognitive skill   An efficient, learned method for solving a particular kind of puzzle or problem (often a form of implicit memory).

cogwheel rigidity   A disorder characterized by movement that appears cogwheellike to the examiner when the patient's limb is moved passively.

collateral sprouting   *See* **sprouting.**

color agnosia   Impairment in the association of objects with colors and colors with objects.

color amnesia   Inability to remember the colors of common objects.

color anomia   Inability to name colors, usually associated with aphasia.

color constancy   The tendency of a surface to maintain its color across varying conditions of illumination.

commissural (corticocortical) fibers   Fibers connecting homotopic (corresponding) areas on the left and right sides of the brain.

commissurotomy   Surgical sectioning (cutting) of the corpus callosum.

compensatory interventions   Rehabilitation strategies that utilize an individual's intact functioning to work around an impairment (similar to alternative strategies) but that utilize special procedures (and, often, special paraphernalia) that generally are not used in everyday life.

complementary hemispheric specialization   The idea that each hemisphere is specialized for specific functions (i.e., that neither hemisphere is dominant, but that each has its own areas of specialization of function).

complex cells   Neurons in the cortex with receptive fields consisting of an edge of illumination in a particular orientation in any portion of the visual field to which the cell is responsive. They have been hypothesized to receive input from a number of simple cells.

compulsions   Repetitive behaviors that a person feels a need to perform (often in response to obsessive thoughts) and cannot keep from performing, despite their interference with other aspects of his or her life.

computational neurobiology   An approach that attempts to provide both a rigorous definition of the problems facing the cognitive system in question and a means by which these problems may be solved, without particular reference to explanation of mechanisms on the neuronal or neurological levels.

concentric broad-band cells   P ganglion cells in which R and G cones act together in each area of the receptive field but have opposite action in the two areas. Neurons with these characteristics are also found at higher levels of the visual system.

concentric double-opponent cells   Neurons in which R and G cones act together in each area of the receptive field but have opposite action in the two areas. This makes these neurons highly sensitive to the presence of contrasting colors.

concentric single-opponent cells   P ganglion cells in which one type of cone (e.g., R or G) activates the center of the cell's circular receptive field (exerting an excitatory or an inhibitory effect on the ganglion cell) and the other cone type has the opposite effect on the surround. Neurons with these characteristics are also found at higher levels of the visual system.

conceptual apraxia   Impairment in the use of an object due to disruption of the conceptual knowledge of the relationship between the object and the movements appropriate to it (as opposed to disruption of the programming of the necessary movement, which is intact). This manifests itself as preserved ability to carry out sequences of learned movement, but doing so in ways that do not correspond to the situation, such as picking up a hammer and making movements appropriate for the use of a saw.

concordance rate   The probability that a person in a particular familial relationship with a patient will have the same disorder as the patient.

conditional associative learning   A paired-associate learning task in which subjects are not explicitly told which stimuli are paired with which, but must extract this information through a process of trial and error.

conditioned response   The response evoked by the conditioned stimulus.

conditioned stimulus When a neutral stimulus (one that does not produce a particular response) precedes an unconditioned stimulus on a number of occasions, it may come to evoke a response identical to (or similar to) the response evoked by the unconditioned stimulus. When this learning has occurred, the neutral stimulus has become a conditioned stimulus.

conductance Permeability; the degree to which a membrane allows a particular molecule (or ion) to pass through it.

conduction aphasia Impaired ability to repeat heard language in the absence of impairment in language comprehension and spontaneous language production.

cones Photoreceptors in the retina. There are three different types of cones, each responsive to a different range of wavelengths of light. Together, these three cone types form the first stage of a system that makes color vision possible. Cones are found in the center (fovea) of the retina, the area of highest visual acuity in the visual field.

confabulation The tendency to deny an impairment and act as if it were not present even when doing so entails behavior that is inconsistent with reality.

conformational state The spatial configuration (arrangement) of the atoms in a molecule. Molecules that have the same atoms can have different conformational states, and these different states can have different chemical properties.

consolidation The process of storing information in long-term memory.

constructional apraxia Impairment in copying and drawing. This term is somewhat misleading because it is often applied descriptively to deficits in copying and drawing, even when the underlying impairment is one of spatial processing and not voluntary action.

contextual conditioning Becoming conditioned to the context (environment) in which an unconditioned stimulus is received.

contra coup effect When a blow to the head bruises the brain by causing it to be thrust against the side of the skull opposite the side of the blow.

contralateral On the opposite side.

contrast enhancement The phenomenon in which a darker area that is next to a lighter area appears to have an even darker band along the common border, whereas the lighter area appears to have an even lighter band along the common border. **Lateral inhibition** underlies this effect.

convergent thinking Thinking that hones in on the unique solution to a problem, as opposed to **divergent thinking,** which expands outward from a starting point, generating novel possibilities and ideas.

corollary discharge A hypothetical mechanism by which activity of the motor system is integrated with input to the sensory-perceptual system so that bodily movement (e.g., the moving of the eyes) is not mistaken for movement of the world.

coronal section The plane of section (cut) that divides the brain into anterior and posterior parts. Also called *frontal section.*

corpus callosum The massive fiber tract that forms neural connections between the two cerebral hemispheres.

corpus striatum A collective name for the putamen, globus pallidus, and caudate nucleus.

cortex From the Latin for "bark," the outer layer of a structure. The cerebral cortex is the outer layer of the forebrain.

cortical blindness Blindness due to damage to the cortical visual system, particularly the primary visual cortex (V1).

cortical deafness Deafness due to cortical damage.

cortical dementia A dementia due primarily to lesions in the cerebral cortex.

cortical module A unit (or chunk) of cortex that is necessary and sufficient to process information impinging on one discrete point on a sensory surface.

corticobulbar tract A bundle of fibers carrying information from the forebrain to the brain stem.

corticocortical connections Interconnections between cortical areas.

corticospinal tract A large bundle of fibers carrying information from the forebrain to the spinal cord.

corticotropin releasing hormone (CRH) A hormone released by the hypothalamus that in turn triggers the release of adrenocorticotrophic hormone (ACTH) from the anterior pituitary.

cortisol   A hormone released by the adrenal cortex that is part of the activation of a stress response. In some patients with depression, there appears to be a disruption of the negative feedback loop to the hypothalamus and anterior pituitary that normally shuts down the release of cortisol after it has reached an optimum level. This disruption results in abnormally high levels of cortisol, which exert a widespread influence on cerebral functioning.

cotransmission   A situation in which a small molecule neurotransmitter and a neuropeptide are released by the same neuron.

covert attention   Shifts of attention that occur independently of any overt behavior—for example, visual attention that occurs independently of eye movement.

cranial nerves   The set of 12 pairs of nerves that carries information to and from the brain (as opposed to the spinal cord).

craniotomy   The surgical opening of the skull.

CRH   *See* **corticotropin releasing hormone.**

critical period   The period of time during development during which a particular function must be acquired if it is ever to be acquired. For example, the critical period for language acquisition is between age 2 and puberty. If normal language is not acquired during that period, it will never be acquired.

cross-theoretic identification   The process whereby specific elements of a theory at a more molar (higher) level of analysis come to be satisfactorily explained by specific elements of a more basic (reducing) theory.

crowding   The idea that the reorganization of right-hemisphere function after an early left-hemisphere lesion, and the resulting takeover of language by the right hemisphere, is achieved at the cost of impairment in general intellectual functioning.

CSF   *See* **cerebrospinal fluid.**

CT scan   *See* **X-ray computerized tomography.**

CVA   *See* **cerebral vascular accident.**

cyclic guanosine monophosphate (cGMP)   A molecule synthesized in rods (by the enzyme guany-

lyl cyclase) in darkness (when the cis form of retinal is bound snugly to a site on the opsin component of rhodopsin).

cytoarchitectonics   The study of variations in the characteristics (e.g., thickness, neuron type) of cell layers in different parts of the cerebral cortex.

cytochrome oxidase   An enzyme that, when subjected to a specific stain, can serve as a marker of enhanced metabolic activity in neural tissue.

Dale's law   The principle that a single neuron generally does not release more than one type of small molecule neurotransmitter.

dark current   The influx of Na^+ that occurs in photoreceptors in darkness.

declarative memory   The ability to consciously remember and recount details of events, in contrast to the ability to perform some act or behavior. The term is essentially synonymous with *explicit memory,* although some theoretical distinctions between the two concepts have been drawn by some investigators.

decussation   The crossing-over of fibers from one side of the brain to the other.

deep dyslexia   Impairment in reading along semantic dimensions, as exemplified by reading *leap* for *jump.*

degeneration   Death of neurons or neuron processes.

degrading enzyme   An enzyme that destroys (breaks down) a neurotransmitter. An example is acetylcholinesterase, which breaks down the neurotransmitter acetylcholine.

delayed nonmatching to sample   A task in which a subject is first presented with an object and then, after a delay, presented with the previously seen object and a novel object. The subject must choose the novel object to obtain the reward.

delayed-alternation task   In a typical version of this task, which of two food wells is baited is alternated between trials, but the monkey does not see the baiting. After an interval, during which the food wells remain out of sight, the monkey must choose the well with the food. Success on this task requires that the monkey remember the response that he made on the previous trial.

delayed-response task   In a typical version of this task, a monkey first sees one of two food wells baited. A delay then follows, during which the two food wells are hidden. After the delay, the monkey must choose the correct response.

deletion   Loss of genetic material from a chromosome.

delusions   Beliefs that are not based on reality.

dementia   A group of disorders characterized by progressive deterioration of cognitive and emotional functioning due to brain dysfunction.

demyelination   The destruction or removal of the myelin sheath that normally surrounds neurons.

dendrite   The usually highly branched part of the neuron extending from the cell body that receives signals (binds neurotransmitter) from other neurons.

dendritic spines   Little knobs protruding from dendrites, increasing the surface area of the dendrite. The number of spines on a dendrite is correlated with the number of axonal inputs to the dendrite.

denervation   Loss of neural input to a neural structure or muscle; the state of being deprived of a nerve supply.

denervation supersensitivity   The phenomenon following partial denervation of a structure (neural or muscular) in which the structure becomes hypersensitive to the application of its neurotransmitter.

depolarization   Reduction in membrane potential (decrease in the negativity of the inside of the neuron).

depression   *See* **major depressive disorder.**

dermatome   Area of skin supplied with sensory nerve fibers feeding into a pair of dorsal roots at a particular level of the spinal cord.

developmental dyscalculia   An impairment in carrying out arithmetic operations not due to a known cerebral lesion, general intellectual impairment, lack of opportunity to learn, home environment, or sensory impairment. *See* **language-based dyscalculia** and **spatial dyscalculia.**

developmental dyslexia   A specific disorder of reading not due to a known cerebral lesion (i.e., not acquired dyslexia) and not due to inadequate

intelligence, environmental factors, or sensory handicap.

diaschisis   The temporary disruptive effect that a cerebral lesion may exert on neighboring or even distant neural tissue. This may take the form of swelling, bleeding, or other short-term pathological processes.

diathesis   A predisposition toward some abnormality or disease.

diathesis-stress model   The idea that many disorders are caused by an interaction between a predisposition toward the illness (diathesis) and some form of precipitating environmental stress.

dichaptic studies   Studies that attempt to assess hemispheric specialization by presenting different tactual stimuli to the two hands simultaneously. The accuracy of report for stimuli presented to the two hands is then compared.

dichotic listening   A method in which different stimuli are delivered simultaneously to the two ears, using stereophonic earphones. The accuracy of report for the two ears is then compared.

diencephalic amnesia   Amnesia due to damage to diencephalic structures, particularly the mamillary bodies and the dorsomedial nucleus of the thalamus.

diencephalon   The part of the forebrain between the telencephalon and the midbrain, including the thalamus, hypothalamus, and epithalamus.

diffusion force   The force that tends to equalize the concentration of a particular molecule or ion.

direction vector   A line representing the characteristics of a particular M1 neuron for a particular movement. The line's length represents the relative firing rate of the neuron and its direction represents the cell's preferred direction.

directional tuning   The range of movement over which a particular M1 neuron fires.

direction-selective neurons   Neurons that fire in response to a stimulus moving in a particular direction.

disconnection syndrome hypothesis   The idea that disorders can be understood as the result of damage to specific centers and/or connections between centers. The conceptualization of conduction aphasia (inability to repeat heard language with intact comprehension and spontaneous expression) as a disconnection between Wernicke's area and Broca's area is an example of a disconnection syndrome.

dishabituation method   An experimental method that takes advantage of the fact that infants show an intense interest in viewing novel objects and situations and become bored when repeatedly exposed to familiar objects and situations. Using this method, it is possible to assess various aspects of infant functioning by determining whether the baby considers a given situation to be the same as or different from a previous situation (i.e., familiar or novel).

disorders of spelling assembly   Specific impairments in the sequencing of letters. People with this disorder retrieve the correct letters of a target word but not in the correct order.

dissociable   Capable of being separated (i.e., dissociated). *See* **dissociation of function.**

dissociation apraxia   A proposed category of apraxic disorders characterized by marked dissociations, under different testing conditions, in the ability to execute learned movements. An example of such a dissociation would be impairment in demonstrating the movements involved in using an object when the object is absent, together with preserved ability to demonstrate the use of the object when it is placed in the hand.

dissociation of function   Impairment in one function without impairment in a second function. The two functions are said to be dissociable—for example, vision and hearing are dissociable. *See also* **single dissociation** and **double dissociation.**

dissociative disorders   Disorders in which individuals may remember facts about past traumatic events without experiencing any associated emotion, or even the sense that the events happened to them.

dissolution   The idea put forth by Hughlings-Jackson that lesions to higher brain centers cause a reversal of the evolutionary development of hierarchical organization within the nervous system. This would account for the fact that lesions to higher centers of the nervous system often re-

sult in the release of primitive behaviors (e.g., reflexes) that were previously under the control of those centers.

distal   Remote; located toward the periphery or toward the end of a structure, relative to a point of reference.

distributed processing   The idea that the neural substrate of a psychological process is mediated by a large number of neurons distributed over a wide area (as opposed to by one or a few neurons). Examples of distributed processing are the hypotheses that the activity of a large group of neurons underlies the visual recognition of an object and the movement of a limb.

distributed representation   *See* **distributed processing.**

divergent thinking   Thinking that expands outward from a starting point, generating novel possibilities and ideas, as opposed to **convergent thinking,** which hones in on the unique solution to a problem.

dizygotic twins   Fraternal twins, sharing, on average, 50% of their genes.

dopamine   A small molecule monoamine neurotransmitter.

dopamine theory of schizophrenia   The idea that schizophrenia is caused by dopamine overactivity.

dopamine-serotonin interaction hypothesis of schizophrenia   The hypothesis, generated mainly by the effectiveness of atypical antipsychotics, that the neurochemical abnormality in schizophrenia involves both dopaminergic and serotonergic systems.

dorsal   Term designating the upper part of the brain and the posterior part of the spinal cord.

dorsal hemiretina   The dorsal (upper) half of each retina.

dorsal horn   The dorsal part of the spinal gray matter containing the cell bodies of interneurons that convey input from primary somatosensory neurons to the brain and to motor neurons at the same and other levels of the spinal cord.

dorsal root   Fiber bundles containing the axons of primary sensory neurons as they enter each segment of the dorsal (posterior) spinal cord.

dorsal root ganglion   The concentration of cell bodies of primary sensory neurons forming a protuberance in the spinal nerve near the point where the dorsal root enters the spinal cord.

dorsal simultanagnosia   Impairment in the ability to perceive the parts of objects, including complex parts, that cannot be easily decomposed into constituent parts or for which such decomposition does not aid perception. Faces are an example of such stimuli. This disorder takes its name from its association with bilateral parietal-occipital lesions.

dorsolateral prefrontal syndrome   *See* **dysexecutive syndrome.**

dorsomedial thalamus   Thalamic nucleus providing major input to prefrontal cortex. Lesions of dorsomedial nucleus result in anterograde amnesia.

double dissociation   Two functions are said to constitute a double dissociation if in some cases impairment in function A is seen without impairment in function B and in other cases impairment in function B is seen without impairment in function A. For example, hearing and vision are doubly dissociable.

Down syndrome   A disorder characterized by a number of physical abnormalities and moderate to severe mental retardation. It is associated with a chromosomal abnormality, usually trisomy of chromosome 21.

dualism   The idea that there are two spheres or domains of reality (material and spiritual).

dura mater   The outermost membrane surrounding the brain. It is tough, inelastic, and follows the contour of the skull.

dynamic form   Form in motion.

dysarthria   Impairment in the articulation of speech sounds due to dysfunction of peripheral structures involved in the mechanisms of speech production, such as the face, jaw, tongue, and larynx.

dyscalculia   Impairment in the ability to perform arithmetic operations.

dyseidetic dyslexia   A reading impairment in which a person is able to read words by sound (phonological reading) but not directly from the visual percept (i.e., sight reading). *Compare* **dysphonetic dyslexia.**

dysexecutive syndrome   A syndrome seen after dorsolateral prefrontal lesions that is characterized by impaired attention, diminished drive, reduced awareness, and depressed mood. Impairment in working memory, the temporal integration of behavior, and planning is also seen in this syndrome, as is impairment in the ability to initiate spontaneous and deliberate behavior and to maintain such behavior in a manner necessary for attaining goals. Also called *dorsolateral prefrontal syndrome.*

dysgraphia   Impairment in writing. This term may also be used to specify specific disorders of spelling.

dyskinesia   Generic term for disturbance of movement.

dyslexia   Impairment in the ability to read.

dysmetria   Impairment in moving a limb so that it accurately reaches a target. Seen after cerebellar lesions.

dysphonetic dyslexia   A reading impairment in which a person is able to read words directly from the visual percept (sight reading) but not by sound (phonological decoding). *Compare* **dyseidetic dyslexia.**

dysphoria   Restlessness, malaise.

dysprosodia   Impairment in the ability to produce tonal fluctuations in spoken language.

dyssynergia   The activation of the muscles required for a movement but not in a coordinated, synergistic manner. The result is a decomposition of what would normally be a coordinated movement into individual components. It is seen in association with cerebellar lesions.

dystonia   Abnormality of muscle tone.

echoic memory   Highly accurate but extremely short-lived (milliseconds) auditory representations that are part of normal memory.

ectopic cells   Cells located away from their normal position.

edema   Swelling; the presence of abnormally large amounts of fluid in the intercellular spaces of the body.

EEG   *See* **electroencephalography.**

efferent   "Away from." Neural output. Thalamic efferents are neurons projecting out of the thalamus.

efflux   Movement out.

egocentric space   The perception of spatial location outside the body but relative to it.

eidetic images   Completely veridical (accurate) images. The ability to form eidetic images is very rare.

elaborative encoding   The active organization of information (for later recall) that takes place during or shortly after initial exposure.

elaborative rehearsal   The manipulation, processing, and organization (for later recall) of information that has already been encoded.

electrical self-stimulation   A situation in which an animal receives electrical stimulation to a part of the brain as a consequence of some behavior, such as pressing a bar. Electrical self-stimulation in a number of subcortical areas, particularly the septum, has been shown to be highly rewarding.

electrical synapse   *See* **gap junction channels.**

electrochemical equilibrium   The point at which diffusion force and electrostatic force for a particular ion are equal, so that there is no net movement of the ion from one compartment to the other.

electroconvulsive shock therapy (ECT)   Application of an electrical current across the brain to induce a seizure. Used in the treatment of mood disorders.

electrocorticography (ECo)   The stimulation during surgery of the exposed cortex of a patient (with a low-voltage electrode). The results of this stimulation make possible a functional mapping of the cortex.

electroencephalography (EEG)   A measure of brain electrical activity derived from a bank of electrodes positioned on the scalp.

electrostatic force   The force that manifests itself in like charges repelling and opposite charges attracting.

electrotonic potentials   The graded changes in membrane potential that are the result of passive ion fluxes following the opening of specific membrane channels in response to the binding of neurotransmitter to the postsynaptic membrane. **EPSPs** and **IPSPs** are electrotonic potentials. Also called *graded potentials.*

embolism   A sudden blocking of an artery or vein.

emergent property   A property apparent at a higher level of explanation (analysis) that is not reducible to a property at a second, more basic, level of explanation. From this perspective, the hardness of a rock is an emergent property of the molecules that compose it.

emotional memory   The experience of emotional arousal related to a past event without conscious memory for the past event.

emotional semantics   Cognitive knowledge about the relationship between an event and emotion (e.g., knowing that sadness is a response to loss).

encephalitis   Inflammation of the central nervous system resulting from infection.

encephalopathy   Any degenerative disease of the brain.

encoding   The form in which information is represented in the nervous system. This varies, depending on the aspects or features of the stimulus that serves as the basis for the encoding.

endocranial cast   A cast of the inner surface of the skull. It is possible to get some idea of the features of the brain that the skull contained from such a cast.

endogenous depression   Depression caused by internal factors, presumably biological. This term is not currently in wide use.

engram   The hypothetical (currently unknown) neural substrate (mechanism) of memory.

entorhinal cortex   The cortical region in the medial temporal lobe that occupies the medial bank of the rhinal sulcus. This area provides input to the hippocampus.

environmental dependency syndrome   The tendency of individuals with prefrontal lesions to rely on the environment for cues to regulate their behavior.

epilepsy   *See* **seizures.**

epinephrine   A small molecule monoamine neurotransmitter.

episodic memory   Memory for particular personal experiences.

epithalamus   Part of the diencephalon just superior and posterior to the thalamus, including the pineal body and several other nuclei.

EPSP   *See* **excitatory postsynaptic potential.**

equilibrium potential   The difference in charge between two compartments when a particular ion is in electrochemical equilibrium.

equipotentiality   The idea that all parts of the brain (or all parts of a particular region of the brain, such as the cerebral cortex) contribute equally to complex functions.

ethology   The study of the behavior of animals in their natural environment.

euphoria   In psychiatry, an abnormal or exaggerated sense of well-being that may be accompanied by nervousness, irritability, vulnerability to distraction, and hyperactivity.

event-related potential (ERP)   A method that measures the brief change in EEG activity that occurs in a particular area of the cortex after a specific event.

evoked potential (EP)   The name sometimes given to event-related potential when it is used (often clinically) to assess the integrity of areas of the brain involved in a particular sensory modality, such as vision.

excitatory postsynaptic potential (EPSP)   An instance of a small (a few millivolts), local depolarization of a neuron that occurs as the result of the binding of neurotransmitter to a postsynaptic receptor.

exclusionary attention   The inhibition of attention and responsiveness to features of the environment that are not relevant to our goals. *See also* **selective attention.**

executive function   (1) A group of functions that includes the formulation of goals, the development and execution of strategies to achieve those goals, the monitoring and evaluation of the extent to which these strategies may or may not be contributing to reaching the goals, and the adaptive modification of (or persistence in) behavioral strategies (and possibly also the goals themselves) in light of this evaluation. Lesions to prefrontal cortex disrupt executive function. (2) In the context of working memory, the component that

takes care of the overall coordination of activities in working memory, including which content and processes should be shuffled in and out of the workspace.

exocytosis   The merging of a synaptic vesicle with the presynaptic membrane and the release of neurotransmitter into the synapse.

explanatory unification   The unified view that results when intertheoretic reduction is possible and a wide range of phenomena can be understood in terms of a single theory (in terms of a single level of analysis).

explicit memory   The conscious representation (recollection) of past events.

expressive aphasia   *See* **Broca's aphasia.**

expressive aprosodia   Impairment in the expression of prosody.

expressive gestures   Actions that communicate emotion more directly than symbolic gestures, such as shaking one's fist.

external segment of the globus pallidus   The lateral portion of the globus pallidus.

externally focused interventions   Rehabilitation interventions that address the problems that follow a brain lesion by modifying the individual's environment.

extracellular fluid   Fluid in the spaces between cells.

extrastriate cortex   Areas of cortex outside V1 that are involved in vision. Also called *prestriate cortex.*

facial feedback hypothesis   The hypothesis that the configuration of facial muscles determines or influences subjective emotional experience.

facilitating interneurons   Interneurons that bring about sensitization in *Aplysia* by exerting presynaptic facilitation on sensory neurons via axoaxonal connections

familial Alzheimer's disease   A type of Alzheimer's disease that runs in families and is believed to be hereditary.

fasciculus   A term for a bundle of nerve, muscle, or tendon fibers.

fear conditioning   Classical conditioning in which the conditioned response is fear.

fetal alcohol syndrome   A disorder seen in children of alcoholic mothers that is characterized by facial malformations, intrauterine growth retardation, and neurobehavioral abnormalities.

fiber tract   A large number of axons bundled together and conveying information from one region of the central nervous system to another.

filopodia   Threadlike extensions on the edge of a developing axon's growth cone.

fissure   A particularly deep or prominent groove in the cerebral cortex.

fluent aphasia   *See* **Wernicke's aphasia.**

focal   Pertaining to a relatively circumscribed (limited in size) center or location. Often used in describing the characteristics of a pathological process, as in a focal lesion.

focal seizures   Seizures that begin in a specific location in the brain and then spread.

folk psychology   The everyday psychological conceptual framework in terms of which we all tend to explain behavior and experience as the outcome of beliefs, desires, perceptions, expectations, goals, and other mental constructs.

forebrain   The most rostral part of the brain, including the telencephalon (cerebral hemispheres, basal ganglia, amygdala, and hippocampus) and the diencephalon (thalamus and hypothalamus). Also termed the *prosencephalon.*

foreign language syndrome   Disruption of the production of the tonal aspects of language in a way that produces a distortion of articulation.

formal thought disorder   Disorganization of the form of thinking, typically manifesting itself through an individual's verbal productions.

fovea   The area of the retina that has the highest concentration of cones, resulting in the highest visual acuity. In this area the axons of retinal ganglion cells project away from the other cell layers at an acute angle, producing a kind of indentation in the retina and allowing more light to reach the photoreceptors.

frontal dynamic aphasia   Luria's term for a disturbance in verbal expression (but not an aphasia in the traditional sense) seen after prefrontal lesions. It is characterized by reduction in spontaneous speech, diminished verbal fluency, and reduction in the volume and scope of narrative expression. Also called *central motor aphasia* and *prefrontal aphasia.*

frontal eye fields (FEF)   The regions of the frontal lobes anterior to the premotor area and dorsal to Broca's area involved in the cortical control of purposeful eye movement.

frontal lobes   Area of cortex and underlying white matter in the front part of the forebrain, anterior to the central sulcus.

frontal section   The plane of section (cut) that divides the brain into anterior and posterior parts. Also called *coronal section.*

functional magnetic resonance imaging (fMRI)   An imaging method that takes advantage of the fact that increases in blood flow (and hemoglobin) change the magnetic properties of the blood. Because blood flow is a correlate of neural activity, when MRI is used to detect these changes it becomes a method for measuring brain activity.

functional mapping   The mapping of particular parts of a neural structure to particular behaviors or experiences, using the results of electrical stimulation of the brain, the effects of lesions, or other methods. The homunculi of the motor and sensory cortices are examples.

functional neuroanatomy   The study of the relationship between neuroanatomical structures (and interconnections between them) and function.

functionalism   The idea that mental states are functional states of the brain that stand in the same relation to neural mechanisms as functional states of a computer (its program) stand to the computer's hardware.

G cones   Cones most sensitive to 531 nm wavelength light.

GABA   Gamma-aminobutyric acid, a major inhibitory neurotransmitter in the central nervous system.

ganglion (pl., ganglia)   A concentration of neuron cell bodies outside the central nervous system.

ganglion cell layer   The layer of ganglion cells in the retina.

ganglion cells   Neurons with their cell bodies in the retina that receive input from photoreceptors via retinal bipolar cells. Their axons project to the lateral geniculate nucleus of the thalamus.

gap junction channels   The type of transmission across synapses in which structural connections between two neurons allow a direct current flow between them. This type of transmission is much less common than transmission via the release of neurotransmitter. Also called *electrical synapses*.

gateway theory of memory   The hypothesis that short-term memory is a necessary stage in the process of consolidation of information into long-term memory.

gating   The change in the state of a membrane channel that results in an alteration of the degree to which the channel will allow its particular ion to pass. Changes in channel gating alter the membrane's permeability (conductance) to a particular ion.

gaze-locked cells   Neurons that respond only when a stimulus stimulates a particular area of the retina *and* the animal is gazing in a particular direction. When the animal is fixating a different point, a stimulus falling on the same area of retina that caused the cell to fire during its preferred direction of gaze will not produce a response. Such cells have been found in area V3 and in parietal cortex of the monkey.

gene   The unit of hereditary transmission, located at a particular place on a chromosome. Both members of each pair of chromosomes have corresponding locations containing genes for the same trait. In cases where one member of the gene pair is dominant and the other recessive, the trait coded by the dominant gene will be expressed regardless of the trait coded by the recessive gene. The characteristic coded by a recessive gene will be expressed only if the other member of the gene pair is also recessive.

generalized anxiety disorder (GAD)   An anxiety disorder in which anxiety is not triggered by a stimulus of a particular type. Persons with this disorder have a pervasive feeling of anxiety that is not related to anything in particular.

generator potential   *See* **receptor potential.**

generic memory   Memory for information as such, without memory of the experience during which it was learned. Also called *semantic memory*.

Gerstmann's syndrome   A syndrome consisting of dyscalculia, finger agnosia, agraphia, and impaired right-left discrimination that Gerstman believed was associated with posterior left-hemisphere lesions. The validity of this syndrome has been questioned.

glia   Cells found in the central and peripheral nervous systems. In the central nervous system they provide structural and nutritive support for neurons. Certain types of glia have specialized functions, such as forming the blood-brain barrier. Some types of glia in both the central and peripheral nervous systems surround axons, forming the myelin sheath that increases the speed and efficiency of signal transmission down the axon. Also called *neuroglia*.

glioma   Any brain tumor that arises from glial cells.

gliosis   The reactive proliferation of glial cells in response to the removal of dead neurons by phagocytes. This forms a scar in the area, which may interfere with the functioning of any surviving neurons.

global amnesia   A total devastation of memory, including both semantic and episodic memory.

global aphasia   A syndrome characterized by the combined symptom picture of Broca's aphasia and Wernicke's aphasia.

globus pallidus   One of the nuclei in the basal ganglia.

glutamate   An amino acid neurotransmitter.

glycine   An amino acid neurotransmitter.

graded potential   Electrical potential (depolarization or hyperpolarization) in a neuron or receptor that varies in intensity, as opposed to the **action potential,** which has a constant magnitude. In receptors this is referred to as a generator potential or receptor potential. Also called *electrotonic potential*.

grammar   *See* **syntax.**

grandmother cell   A hypothetical type of neuron that has been proposed to be a component in the neural mechanism underlying visual object recognition. According to this view, such cells have highly specific receptive fields (that register the presence of specific objects) because they are the end point in a converging hierarchy of neurons with progressively more specific receptive fields.

granulovacuolar degeneration   Abnormal areas of cytoplasmic loss filled with granules, seen in neurons in the brains of patients with Alzheimer's disease.

graphic buffer   A hypothetical short-term store for retrieved letter sequences that spell words, analogous to verbal short-term memory.

gray matter   Brain tissue composed of neuron cell bodies.

growth cone   Structure at the end of the developing axon that is involved in guiding the growing axon to its target.

guanylyl cyclase   The enzyme that mediates the synthesis of cyclic guanosine monophosphate in rods in darkness.

gyrus (pl., gyri)   An outfolding on the cerebral cortex.

habituation   A simple form of learning in which an animal learns to suppress a response to a recurring neutral (neither rewarding nor harmful) stimulus that had evoked a response when it was first presented.

hallucinations   Perceptual experiences that are not based on sensory stimuli.

hemianopia   Blindness in one (left or right) visual field.

hemiballism   Involuntary, violent flinging movements of the extremities on one side of the body.

hemiparesis   Impairment in fine-motor behavior and muscular weakness on one side of the body.

hemiplegia   Paralysis on one side of the body.

hemispherectomy   Removal of one cerebral hemisphere.

hemispheric functional asymmetry   *See* **complementary hemispheric specialization.**

hemispheric specialization   *See* **complementary hemispheric specialization.**

Heschl's gyrus   Gyrus on the lower lip of the Sylvian fissure that is roughly equivalent to the primary auditory cortex.

hierarchical organization   The principle that there are different levels of processing, with higher levels controlling lower levels.

hindbrain   The part of the brain stem caudal to the midbrain. It includes the metencephalon (pons and cerebellum) and the myelencephalon (the medulla oblongata).

hippocampus   Cortical structure lying in the anterior and medial part of the temporal lobe.

holism   The idea that the whole brain mediates all functions (in contrast to the idea of localization of function).

homeostasis   The internal biological steady state that every organism must constantly maintain to stay alive.

homonymous hemianopia   Blindness in the same half (left or right) of the visual field in both eyes.

homotopic fields   Corresponding areas in the right and left hemispheres.

horizontal cells   Cells in the retina that form the outer plexiform layer, between the outer nuclear layer (photoreceptors) and the inner nuclear layer (bipolar cells).

horizontal section   The plane of section (cut) that divides the brain into upper (superior) and lower (inferior) parts.

horseradish peroxidase (HRP)   An enzyme that is selectively taken up by axon terminals and then moved by retrograde transport to the cell body. It is used as a marker to identify the origin of the region or regions projecting to a given area.

human V4   An area in humans hypothesized to be analogous to V4 in other species.

human V5   An area in humans hypothesized to be analogous to V5 in other species.

Huntington's chorea   A hereditary disease characterized by chronic progressive chorea and mental deterioration progressing to dementia and terminating in death.

hydrocephalus   A condition characterized by abnormal accumulation of cerebrospinal fluid in one or more cerebral ventricles, resulting in increased intracranial pressure and destruction of brain tissue.

hypergraphia   A tendency to write about one's life in great detail. Some investigators consider this to be a characteristic of patients with temporal-lobe seizures.

hyperkinesia   Unintended and unwanted movements.

hyperpolarization   Increase in membrane potential (increase in the negativity of the inside of the neuron).

hyperprosodia   Disruption in prosody that takes the form of exaggerated variations in the tonal and rhythmic features of spoken language.

hypofrontality   Reduced metabolic activity in prefrontal cortex as measured by functional imaging methods.

hypokinesia   Diminished ability to move the body.

hypothalamus   Collection of nuclei lying below the thalamus and involved in a wide range of functions, particularly autonomic functions. It is considered part of the limbic system.

hypoxia   Low oxygen content; oxygen deprivation.

hypoxic-ischemic encephalopathy   Abnormality of the brain due to oxygen and blood deprivation.

iconic memory   Highly accurate but extremely short-lived (milliseconds) visual representations that are part of normal memory.

idealism   The type of monism that holds that only the spiritual (nonphysical) is real.

ideational apraxia   According to classical terminology, impairment in the ability to perform acts that involve complex sequences of movement, with preserved ability to perform individual movements and actions.

ideational fluency   The ability to creatively generate novel ideas.

ideomotor apraxia   According to classical terminology, impairment in the ability to perform specific learned motor acts not due to paralysis or weakness.

illusions   Distortions in perception that most people would experience under particular stimulus conditions.

imperception   A term (used by Hughlings-Jackson) that Zeki invoked to refer to what is conventionally termed *agnosia*. Zeki felt that this term emphasizes the essential inseparability of perception

and knowing, a central aspect of visual recognition according to Zeki.

implicit memory   The nonconscious representation of past events. In implicit memory, past experience influences present performance without conscious memory of the past experience.

indifference reaction   A descriptive term for the apparent lack of negative emotional response observed in some patients with right-hemisphere lesions.

induction   The process of the formation (differentiation) of new types of cells from undifferentiated embryonic cells.

inferior   Term designating the lower part of the brain. Also designates "below," relative to a reference point.

inferior colliculus   Area in the midbrain that receives auditory projections from the superior olive.

influx   Movement in.

inhibition of return   The tendency of human infants at age 6 months to consistently show a preference for looking at a novel object or a novel location (over an object or location viewed before).

inhibitory postsynaptic potential (IPSP)   An instance of a small (a few millivolts), local hyperpolarization of a neuron that occurs as the result of the binding of neurotransmitter to a postsynaptic receptor.

inner nuclear layer   The layer of the retina composed of bipolar cells.

inner plexiform layer   The layer of cells in the retina between the inner nuclear layer (bipolar cells) and the ganglion cell layer, composed of amacrine cells.

intentionality   In philosophy, intended meaning or reference; the characteristic of our mental state that describes its directedness at or reference to objects or states in the world other than itself.

interblobs   Areas of V1 that stain lightly for the dye for cytochrome oxidase. These areas surround the more darkly staining **blobs** in V1.

interhemispheric specialization of function   Specialization of function between the two hemispheres. The right hemisphere's representation for spatial processing and the left hemisphere's specialization for language exemplify this.

intermediate-term memory   *See* **recent memory.**

internal representation   *See* **representations.**

internal segment of the globus pallidus   The medial portion of the globus pallidus.

interneurons   Neurons neither directly receiving information from the environment (sensory receptors and primary sensory neurons) nor directly causing muscle contractions (motor neurons). The vast majority of neurons in the brains of mammals are interneurons.

interpositus nuclei of the cerebellum   Nuclei in the cerebellum, damage to which has been shown to abolish classical conditioning in animals.

interstripes   Areas in V2 that stain lightly for cytochrome oxidase, lying between the **thin stripes** and the **thick stripes.** They receive input from the interblobs of V1, and neurons in these areas project to V4.

intertheoretic reduction   The reduction of a theory that characterizes one level of phenomenon to another theory that characterizes a second, more basic, level of phenomenon.

intracellular fluid   Fluid within the cell.

intrahemispheric specialization of function   Specialization of function within a hemisphere. The functions of Broca's area and of Wernicke's area exemplify this.

ion   A charged atom or molecule.

ionotropic receptors   Receptors that, when a neurotransmitter binds to them, directly change the gating of an ion channel in the postsynaptic membrane.

ipsilateral   On the same side.

ipsilateral corticocortical fibers   Fibers connecting areas within the same hemisphere.

IPSP   *See* **inhibitory postsynaptic potential.**

ischemia   Deficiency of blood.

isocortex   *See* **neocortex.**

isolation of the speech area   An unusual syndrome characterized by severe impairment in the ability to spontaneously produce and to understand speech, together with preserved ability to repeat heard speech, including sentences. This may be conceptualized as an extreme form of transcortical aphasia.

James-Lange theory of emotion   The theory that subjective emotional experience is the result of feedback from the body (to the cortex) regarding internal state (i.e., peripheral arousal) and the behavior in which it is engaged.

jargon aphasia   Aphasic symptoms characterized by the pervasive use of neologisms. Frequently seen in Wernicke's aphasia.

karyotype   The chromosomal constitution of the nucleus of a cell.

Kennard principle   The principle that the earlier in life a lesion is sustained, the better the recovery.

kinesthesis   Sense of body movement.

kinetic disorder of speech   A central language disturbance in which the ability to organize movements of the speech musculature to produce previously learned phonemes is impaired, even though the speech musculature and the peripheral nerves activating it are intact. This impairment has also been termed *apraxia of speech.*

Klüver-Bucy syndrome   Behavioral changes in monkeys that have undergone bilateral temporal lobectomy. These changes include decreased fear, visual agnosia, oral tendencies, a drive to run about and explore, and changes in sexual behavior.

Korsakoff's disease   A thiamine deficiency disease associated with chronic alcoholism characterized by severe anterograde amnesia, severe retrograde amnesia, and a number of cognitive impairments similar to those seen after frontal-lobe lesions.

kwashiorkor   A syndrome produced by severe protein deficiency characterized by retarded growth, changes in skin and hair pigment, pathological changes in the liver, and mental apathy.

lamellipodia   Flattened sheets between the filopodia at the end of the growth cone.

language-based dyscalculia   A developmental dyscalculia seen in association with spelling and reading difficulty and hypothesized to be similar to the dyscalculia seen after left-hemisphere lesions.

lateral   Term designating that, relative to another structure, a given structure is closer to the side of the brain.

lateral fissure   *See* **Sylvian fissure.**

lateral geniculate nucleus (LGN)   Nucleus of the thalamus, to which information from the retina projects.

lateral inhibition   The process in which adjacent neural elements hold each other in check. This emphasizes borders between areas of different luminance, thereby accentuating contours.

lateral nucleus of the amygdala   The major target of auditory input projected to the amygdala from the medial geniculate nucleus. In fear conditioning, the lateral amygdala receives input activated by the conditioned stimulus.

lateral pathway   In the retina, the indirect pathway from photoreceptor to bipolar cell, via horizontal cells.

laterality studies   Studies that use special techniques to investigate hemispheric specialization in normal subjects.

learning disability   *See* **learning disorder.**

learning disorder   An impairment in a specific domain of cognition, such as reading, mathematics, or spatial processing, not attributable to inadequate general intelligence, lack of opportunity to learn, inadequate home environment, inadequate motivation, or the presence of a handicapping physical condition. Also called *learning disability.*

left-hemisphere hypothesis of schizophrenia   The hypothesis that schizophrenia is caused by an abnormality of the left hemisphere.

lemniscal system   A pathway in the spinal cord that conveys information about touch, proprioception, and body movement to the thalamus.

length constant   The quantification, for a given postsynaptic membrane, of the extent of spread of an EPSP. This depends on the particular characteristics of the membrane.

lesion   A general term meaning any kind of damage or disease.

lesion momentum   The rate of development of a progressive lesion (e.g., a tumor).

LGN   *See* **lateral geniculate nucleus.**

ligand-gated channels   *See* **transmitter-gated channels.**

lightness constancy   The perception of lightness and darkness on the basis of differences in the reflectance of surfaces across varying conditions of light intensity (luminance).

lightness record   The hypothetical comparison by the visual system of the relative reflectance of different objects for short-, middle-, and long-wavelength light.

limb apraxia   An apraxic disorder that affects the limbs, particularly the hands, but does not involve the mouth and tongue.

limbic system   A term that is widely used to denote a number of structures that have been hypothesized to be centrally involved in the neural mediation of emotion.

lipid bilayer   The double layer of lipid molecules that forms the membrane of neurons.

local representation   A representation in which there is a one-to-one correspondence between the entity being represented and the activity of a neuron (or group of neurons) encoding the representation. The grandmother cell is an extreme example of a local representation.

localization of function   The idea that certain functions take place or are mediated by specific regions of the brain.

localization on the body surface   The sense of spatial location on the surface of the body.

location-specific attention-enhanced cells   Neurons in monkey parietal cortex that fire when the animal is covertly attending to (not moving its eyes toward) a location (within the cell's receptive field) where a response-triggering target will appear.

long-term habituation   Habituation that lasts for a relatively long period of time (hours, days, or weeks).

long-term memory   A memory system that stores an enormous amount of information for years or even a lifetime.

long-term potentiation (LTP)   A long-term (minutes to hours) increase in the magnitude of response (slope of depolarization) of a neuron that occurs after prior (often brief) stimulation of that neuron.

loose associations Thinking (as reflected in speech) that moves haphazardly and rapidly from one fragmentary referent to another, so that ideas are touched on fleetingly rather than being logically developed.

lumens Units used to measure luminance (the magnitude of light intensity).

luminance The magnitude of light intensity (measured in units called lumens).

M ganglion cells One of two types of ganglion cells in the retina. They have large receptive fields, are sensitive to low contrast, are not sensitive to wavelength, and respond in transient bursts. They project to neurons in the magnocellular layers of the lateral geniculate.

M1 *See* **motor cortex.**

Mach bands Illusory bands that appear along the common border between areas of differing lightness and darkness. When a darker area is next to a lighter area, an even darker band appears in the dark area along the common border, whereas the lighter area has an even lighter band along the common border. These bands are mediated by **lateral inhibition.**

magnetic resonance imaging (MRI) An imaging process that subjects the brain to a high magnetic field, causing the hydrogen atoms in the brain to line up in parallel. When radio waves are then passed across these atoms, they assume a characteristic pattern that is a function of the number of atoms present. This imaging method is very sensitive to variations in tissue density.

magnetoencephalography (MEG) A technique for measuring small magnetic fields generated by the electrical currents of neurons.

magnocellular layers of the LGN The ventral two layers of the LGN (layers 1 and 2), receiving retinal input from M ganglion cells.

magnocellular-V3 channel The pathway from M retinal ganglion cells to the magnocellular layers of the LGN to layer IVCα of V1 to layer IVB of V1 to the thick stripes of V2 to V3. Processing within

this channel is critical for the perception of the shapes of objects in motion (dynamic form).

magnocellular-V5 channel The pathway from M retinal ganglion cells to the magnocellular layers of the LGN to layer IVCα of V1 to layer IVB of V1 to the thick stripes of V2 to V5. Processing within this channel is critical for the perception of movement.

major depressive disorder A mood disorder characterized by dysphoric (sad, depressed) mood and loss of interest and pleasure in nearly all activities. Associated symptoms may include changes in appetite, sleep disturbance, decreased psychomotor activity, decreased energy, feelings of worthlessness or guilt, difficulty concentrating and making decisions, and thoughts of death (including suicidal thoughts). Also called *unipolar depression.*

malnutritional milieu The idea that malnutrition is seldom found in isolation, usually being accompanied by other environmental and health-related problems.

mamillary bodies Nuclei in the posterior part of the hypothalamus. Their name comes from their breastlike appearance when viewed on the ventral surface of the brain.

mania Episodes characterized by euphoria, hyperactivity, expansiveness, irritable mood, inflated self-esteem, and impaired judgment.

manic-depressive disorder *See* **bipolar disorder.**

marasmus A form of protein-calorie malnutrition mainly occurring in the first year of life, characterized by progressive wasting of subcutaneous fat and muscle.

mass action The idea that the magnitude of a particular deficit is related to the extent of damaged neural tissue (rather than to the location of the damaged tissue).

massively parallel constraint-satisfaction models of object recognition Models that collapse the apparently discrete processes of perception and understanding into a single process by postulating that a stimulus is represented as a specific pattern of activation across a highly interconnected set of units. Activation of one unit activates or inhibits neighboring units (and this unit is activated or inhibited *by* neighboring units) in accordance with the connection strengths and weights between them. At any given time, the network has specific properties, acquired presumably through accumulated visual experience, such that all retinal images consistent with a particular object, regardless of its orientation, lighting, and so forth, will result in a particular pattern of activation of the network.

materialism   The type of monism that holds that only the physical is real.

maturational-lag hypothesis   Explanation of a disorder in terms of a delay of normal development in one or more brain areas or systems.

medial   Term designating that, relative to another structure, a given structure is closer to the midline of the brain.

medial geniculate nucleus   Area of the thalamus that receives auditory input from the inferior colliculus and projects to the auditory cortex.

medial prefrontal cortex   Region of the frontal lobes on the interior surface of the cerebral hemispheres.

medial prefrontal syndrome   The least well defined of the prefrontal syndromes. Lesions of medial prefrontal cortex, including the cingulate gyrus, are associated with impairment in attention.

medial temporal cortex   The entorhinal, perirhinal, and parahippocampal cortices.

medial temporal-lobe amnesia   Amnesia (mainly anterograde but with a retrograde component) involving medial temporal-lobe structures, including the hippocampus, entorhinal cortex, perirhinal cortex, and parahippocampal cortex.

medulla oblongata   Portion of the hindbrain rostral to the spinal cord and caudal to the pons.

membrane potential   The potential difference (difference in charge) between the two sides of a membrane (the inside and the outside of a cell).

memory for emotion   Remembering that in the past one had experienced an emotion, without autonomic arousal at the time of remembering.

meninges   The collective name for the three membranes that surround the brain. From outside in, these are the dura mater, arachnoid membrane, and pia mater.

mental causation   The hypothetical process by which mental processes affect physical objects and events.

mental images   Analogical representations that retain some of the characteristic attributes of sensory experience.

mental module   A relatively independently organized neural representation mediating a particular function. *See also* **modular organization.**

mesencephalon   *See* **midbrain.**

metabolic pump   A biochemical mechanism that actively moves an ion across a membrane in the direction opposite to that dictated by electrochemical forces.

metabotropic receptors   Receptors that, when they bind their neurotransmitter, activate a second messenger.

metamemory   The ability to accurately appraise one's memory capability.

metencephalon   The most rostral part of the hindbrain, including the pons and the cerebellum.

method of loci   A memory-facilitation method in which the subject imagines each to-be-remembered item as interacting with a location along a familiar route.

method of vanishing cues   A method used to train amnesic patients to retain information by exploiting their intact implicit memory. Patients are presented with cues to recall that, over trials, have progressively fewer letters. Using this method, even severely amnesic patients are eventually able to come up with the required information without any cue, although they have no conscious awareness of having been previously exposed to the material.

microcephaly   Abnormal smallness of the head and brain, usually associated with mental retardation.

microglia   A type of glia characterized by small, irregularly shaped cells that invades and removes damaged tissue.

microtubules   Long tubular structures within the axon along which vesicles containing various materials move in the process of axoplasmic transport.

midbrain   The short segment of the brain stem between the forebrain and the hindbrain. It includes the tectum and the tegmentum. Also termed the *mesencephalon*.

migration   The movement of a neuroblast from one area of the developing embryo to another, as part of the normal process of nervous system development.

mind-body problem   The question of how the mind and the body are related—whether they are separate domains (i.e., body and spirit) or aspects of one domain (i.e., all matter or all spirit).

mind-brain problem   *See* **mind-body problem.**

mixed transcortical aphasia   An aphasia characterized by the symptoms of global aphasia (i.e., both spontaneous speech and comprehension are impaired), but the ability to repeat is retained.

modular organization   The idea that different aspects of cognitive or emotional processing are organized relatively independently in different specialized brain regions. The specialization of V4 for color vision and of V5 for the perception of movement are examples of modular organization.

modulation   The capacity to respond flexibly and to varying degrees, taking into account a complex array of factors. Modulation is an essential characteristic of complex nervous systems.

module   Hypothetical unit of modular organization.

monism   The belief that the solution to the mind-body problem is that only one domain (it may be physical or spiritual) is real.

monoamine   A molecule that has a single amine (NH_2). The neurotransmitters epinephrine, norepinephrine, dopamine, and serotonin are monoamines.

monoamine hypothesis of depression   The hypothesis that abnormally low levels of monoamines (norepinephrine, dopamine, and serotonin) play a role in depression.

monoamine oxidase   An enzyme that breaks down monoamine neurotransmitters.

monoamine oxidase inhibitors (MAOs)   A class of drugs that enhances monoamine activity by inhibiting the breakdown of monoamines by monoamine oxidase.

monocular zones   The two peripheral areas of the visual field, each of which, because of the position of the nose, projects to only one retina.

monozygotic twins   Identical twins, sharing 100% of their genes.

mood   The long-term quality of emotional experience.

mood congruity of memory   The tendency of a person to remember information better when in the same or a similar emotional state as when the information was initially encountered.

mood disorders   Disorders that have a long-term disturbance of mood as their prominent feature.

morphological agrammatism   Speech characterized by impairment in the use of function words (i.e., conjunctions, articles, and prepositions) and word endings, together with preservation of correct word order.

morphology   The rules describing how phonemes can be combined into words.

motor aphasia   *See* **Broca's aphasia.**

motor apraxia   Term used by Liepmann to indicate impairment in fine-motor coordination (not due to weakness or paralysis) resulting from a cerebral lesion.

motor cortex   The area of cortex (just anterior to the central sulcus) that is most directly involved in the implementation of movement. Also called *M1*.

motor homunculus   The representation of the body on the precentral gyrus (motor cortex) as revealed by electrical stimulation.

motor learning   The learning of skilled movement. The basal ganglia and the cerebellum are important for motor learning, a form of implicit memory.

motor neurons   Neurons with their cell bodies in the anterior horn of the spinal cord that innervate muscle. They are the last link in the efferent chain from brain to muscle.

motor skill   Learned, coordinated motor control and coordination, as exemplified by throwing a baseball or riding a bike.

motor strip   *See* **motor cortex.**

movement formulas   Liepmann's hypothetical cerebral representation of learned movements, which he believed to be localized in the left hemisphere.

MT   Another term for V5 (taken from "middle temporal," its location in the monkey).

multiple sclerosis (MS)   Disease characterized by patches of demyelination in the central nervous system. This may result in a wide variety of symptoms, depending upon the regions of the brain involved at any given time.

muscarinic acetylcholine receptors   Inhibitory acetylcholine receptors.

myasthenia gravis   A disorder characterized by fatigue and weakness of the motor system due to reduction of acetylcholine at the neuromuscular junction.

myelencephalon   The most caudal part of the hindbrain; the medulla oblongata.

myelin   The lipid sheath formed around certain nerve fibers, serving to enhance the speed and efficiency of neuronal transmission. It is formed by oligodendroglia in the central nervous system and Schwann cells in the peripheral nervous system.

myelination   The formation of myelin around axons.

myelogenetic cycles   A concept that embodies the fact that the axons of neurons in different brain regions undergo the process of myelination at different times during development.

nanometer (nm) 10^{-9} meter

nasal hemiretina   The half of each retina closest to the nose.

natural selection   The central mechanism of change in the theory of evolution whereby individuals with certain characteristics bear and raise to maturity more offspring than individuals with other characteristics, thus leading to the dominance of those characteristics associated with the higher rate of reproduction.

necrosis   Tissue (cell) death.

negative symptoms   Symptoms that take the form of the absence of a function, experience, or behavior that is normally present.

neglect   A disorder in which an individual ignores (neglects) objects and people on one side of space.

neglect dyslexia   A word-form dyslexia in which the initial or terminal part of a word is misread.

neocortex   Six-layer cortex that is thought to have evolved relatively late in evolution. Also called *isocortex*.

neologism   A novel or meaningless word (i.e., a nonword).

neomammalian brain   According to MacLean's triune brain hypothesis, the neocortex. MacLean proposed that this highest level of brain mediates specific emotion based on the perceptions and the interpretations of the immediate world, adding specificity to the expression of general emotion mediated by the paleomammalian brain.

neostriatum   The caudate nucleus and the putamen.

nerve growth factor (NGF)   A molecule that is important for aspects of central nervous system development and that also plays a role in the development of new connections after brain lesions.

neural groove   An elongated groove formed by the folding of the neural plate. The groove eventually deepens, folds over onto itself, and begins to close, forming the neural tube.

neural plate   The pear-shaped sheet of cells that differentiates out of the ectoderm on the dorsal surface of the developing embryo during the third week of gestation. The neural tube, and eventually the entire nervous system, develops from these cells.

neural tube   The tube formed when the neural groove deepens, folds over onto itself, and begins to close. Closure begins in the middle of the neural groove and proceeds both rostrally and caudally, reaching completion at about day 25 of gestation.

neurites   A generic name for the extensions radiating out from the cell body (i.e., dendrites and axon).

neuritic plaques   A particularly important cellular abnormality seen in the cerebral cortex in Alzheimer's disease. Neuritic plaques are areas of incompletely destroyed neurons consisting of a dense core of a protein known as β amyloid, surrounded by degenerating axons and dendrites, together with reactive astrocytes and activated microglia. Eventually the glial cells completely destroy the degenerating neurons and leave a core of β amyloid protein. Also called *senile plaques, amyloid plaques,* or simply *plaques.*

neuroanatomy   The study of the structures of the nervous system and their interconnections.

neuroblasts   Embryonic (immature) nerve cells. These have not yet formed axonal or dendritic processes.

neuroendocrine   A descriptive term for the interaction (interdependence) of the nervous system and the endocrine system.

neuroethology   The study of the relationship between an animal's behavior in its natural environment and the brain.

neurofibrillary tangles   Abnormal proliferation of neurofibrils seen in the neuronal cytoplasm in the brains of persons with Alzheimer's disease.

neurofibrils   Delicate threadlike structures running through the cytoplasm of the cell body of a neuron and extending into the axon and dendrite.

neuroglia   *See* **glia.**

neuroleptics   Medications used to treat the symptoms of psychotic disorders. Also called *antipsychotics.*

neurologist   A physician who specializes in diseases and disorders of the nervous system.

neuromuscular junction   The synapse between motor neuron and muscle.

neuron   An individual nerve cell.

neuron doctrine   Another name for the neuron theory.

neuron theory   The idea that the nervous system is made up of individual cells that are in close proximity to each other but do not form a continuous structure.

neuropeptides   Short chains of amino acids that, like neurotransmitters, are released at the axon terminal. The effects of neuropeptides are typically longer lasting than those of neurotransmitters, suggesting that they may be involved in long-term processes such as learning and memory.

neurotoxin   Any substance that poisons or destroys neurons.

neurotransmitters   The small molecules that are the immediate mechanism by which neurons communicate with each other. They are released into the synapse by the presynaptic membrane and then diffuse across the synapse, eventually binding on receptor sites on the postsynaptic membrane.

neutral stimulus   A stimulus that does not produce a particular response.

nicotinic acetylcholine receptors   Excitatory acetylcholine receptors.

nigrostriatal bundle   A fiber tract projecting from the substantia nigra to the neostriatum.

nodes of Ranvier   Periodic gaps in the myelin sheath that surrounds many axons in the central and peripheral nervous systems.

nonassociative learning   A change in behavioral response that occurs over time in response to a single type of stimulus; includes habituation and sensitization.

nondeclarative memory   *See* **procedural memory.**

nonfluent aphasia   *See* **Broca's aphasia.**

nonverbal affect lexicon   A hypothetical store of information concerning the emotional significance of nonverbal stimuli, such as a facial expression or a gesture.

nonverbal learning disabilities   Learning disorders characterized by difficulties in areas that are not explicitly verbal, including impairment in the domains of perception, spatial processing, and social-emotional processing.

norepinephrine   A small molecule monoamine neurotransmitter.

nucleus (pl., nuclei)   (1) A concentration of neuron cell bodies within the central nervous system. (2) A spheroid body within a cell containing a number of organelles and the cell's complement of DNA.

nucleus basalis   A brain stem system, closely linked to the amygdala, that appears to be important in the mediation of danger-induced cortical arousal.

object permanence   Knowledge that an object exists even when it is no longer present in the immediate environment.

obligatory looking   The inability of human infants age 1–4 months to disengage from stimuli on which they are fixating, particularly when the stimuli include highly contrasting contours.

obsessions   Preoccupying thoughts that involuntarily dominate a person's thinking.

obsessive-compulsive disorder (OCD)   A disorder characterized by the presence of preoccupying, anxiety-producing thoughts (obsessions), often related to a particular theme, and behaviors generated by these thoughts that the individual cannot keep from performing (compulsions).

occipital lobes   The areas of cortex and underlying white matter lying beneath the back part of the skull.

ocular dominance   The phenomenon in which a neuron in V1 will fire at a higher frequency to stimuli presented to one eye than to the other.

ocular dominance column   A perpendicular column of neurons in V1 with similar ocular dominance characteristics.

ocular dominance hypercolumn   A section of visual cortex containing a set of ocular dominance columns that together represent the full range of ocular dominance characteristics.

oculomotor nucleus   One of the cranial nerve nuclei in the midbrain that participates in the control of eye movement. It also mediates the pupillary reflex.

Off-center/On-surround cell   Neurons that fire at their highest frequency when the circular center of their receptive field is not illuminated and the donut-shaped area around it is.

olfaction   The sense of smell.

oligodendrocytes   Glia cells that form the myelin sheath around axons in the central nervous system.

On-center/Off-surround cell   Neurons that fire at their highest frequency when the circular center of their receptive field is illuminated and the donut-shaped area around it is not.

ontology   The science or the study of being.

opsin   The non-light-absorbing component of rhodopsin.

optic aphasia   Impairment in the ability to name seen objects, with preserved ability to demonstrate knowledge of their meaning through nonlinguistic means, such as pantomime.

optic ataxia   Impairment in the ability to point to a stimulus, in the absence of primary visual disorientation or of proprioceptive, kinesthetic, or motor impairment.

optic chiasm   The place where the portion of the optic nerve carrying information from the nasal half of each retina crosses over to the other side of the brain.

optic disc   The area of the retina where ganglion cell axons leave the retina. There are no photoreceptors in this area, so stimuli falling on this area cannot be seen. This results in the blind spot.

optic nerve   The nerve composed of axons of retinal ganglion cells (which convey information from the retina). These axons project to the lateral geniculate nucleus of the thalamus. By convention, after the optic chiasm, these axons are termed the *optic tract.*

optic tract   The term applied to the optic fibers (axons of retinal ganglion cells) posterior to the optic chiasm.

optimum arousal theory of attention deficit disorder   The theory that ADD is caused by higher brain centers not receiving enough input from lower centers. According to this theory, the distractibility, hyperactivity, and risk-taking behaviors often seen in children with ADD are attempts to heighten the level of arousal in these higher centers.

oral apraxia   An impairment in the execution of learned movement (not due to peripheral motor or sensory impairment) that selectively affects the individual's mouth and tongue.

orbital-prefrontal cortex   Area of the frontal lobes on the ventral surface of the cerebral hemispheres. It is named for its proximity to the orbits (the bony cavities that contain the eyeballs). Also called *ventral prefrontal cortex.*

orbital prefrontal syndrome   A syndrome seen after orbital (ventral) prefrontal lesions and characterized by disinhibition of drives and release of behavior from normal regulatory control. Patients with orbital prefrontal lesions often exhibit a disregard for social and ethical conventions and a lack of concern about the impact of their behavior on others.

organic brain syndrome   General term for a disorder due to brain dysfunction.

orientation columns   Columns of neurons in the visual cortex, perpendicular to the cortical surface, each unit of which responds to a bar of illumination of the same orientation.

orientation hypercolumn A section of visual cortex containing a set of orientation columns that together represents the full range of stimulus orientations.

orientation-selective A term referring to the finding that certain cells in the visual cortex have a stimulus at a particular orientation as their receptive field.

outer nuclear layer The layer of cells in the retina composed of photoreceptors.

outer plexiform layer The layer of cells in the retina (between the outer and inner nuclear layers) composed of horizontal cells.

overt attention Attention that is manifested by some overt behavior—for example, anticipatory eye movement in the direction of a soon-to-appear target in response to a cue.

P ganglion cells One of two types of ganglion cells in the retina. They have small receptive fields, respond with sustained discharge, and are sensitive to wavelength. They project to neurons in the parvocellular layers of the lateral geniculate nucleus.

paleocortex Areas of cortex with only two cell layers. This includes olfactory cortex and the parahippocampal gyrus.

paleomammalian brain According to MacLean's triune brain hypothesis, the limbic system. MacLean postulated that the paleomammalian brain adds current and recent experience to the basic drives mediated by the reptilian brain.

panic disorder An anxiety disorder characterized by intermittent but highly intense episodes of anxiety.

Papez circuit The pathway that James Papez proposed to be the neural mechanism whereby subcortical processes mediating body arousal and cortical processes mediating emotional experience influence each other.

paragraphias Errors in writing.

parahippocampal cortex The cortical area in the medial temporal lobe that lies lateral to the perirhinal cortex.

parahippocampal gyrus A gyrus near the hippocampus in the ventral and medial part of the temporal lobe.

parallel processing The idea that information reaches a particular area via many parallel channels, rather than via a single pathway. Parallel-processing models differ from sequential-processing models in holding that different aspects of information are processed simultaneously, rather than being processed in a sequential (linear) manner.

paraphasias Distorted speech productions.

paraplegia Paralysis of the legs resulting from a lesion of the spinal cord.

parietal lobes The area of cortex and underlying white matter lying beneath the parietal bones, at the posterior, superior part of the skull.

Parkinson's disease A disease characterized by hypokinesia, bradykinesia, cogwheel rigidity, and resting tremor resulting from deterioration of dopamine-producing cells in the substantia nigra.

pars opercularis The posterior portion of the inferior frontal gyrus. In the left hemisphere, together with other portions of the pars triangularis, Broca's area.

partial cortical blindness The sparing (or reemergence in the course of recovery) of certain functions after damage to V1.

partial knowledge effect The ability to access information regarding the superordinate category to which an object belongs in the absence of ability to access more specific knowledge about it.

parvocellular layers of the LGN The dorsal four layers of the LGN (layers 3–6), which receive retinal input from P ganglion cells.

parvocellular-blob channel The pathway from P retinal ganglion cells to the parvocellular layers of the LGN to layer IVCβ of V1 to the blobs of V1 to the thin stripes of V2 to V4. Processing in this channel is critical for the construction (perception) of color.

parvocellular-interblob channel The pathway from P retinal ganglion cells to the parvocellular layers of the LGN to layer IVCβ of V1 to the interblobs of V1 to the interstripes of V2 to V4. Processing in this channel is important for the perception of form.

peptide A member of a class of molecules composed of two or more amino acids, but smaller than a protein.

perception   Cognitive processes yielding an internal representation of the external world.

perceptual categorization   *See* **perceptual constancy.**

perceptual constancy   The process by which we recognize an object as equivalent (the same object) despite variations in the characteristics of the proximal stimulus (stimulus on the receptor surface). Also called *perceptual categorization.*

perceptual learning   The development, after repeated exposures, of increasing speed and accuracy on perceptual tasks, such as Gollin's incomplete drawings test and mirror reading.

perceptual representation systems (PRS)   The hypothetical systems that mediate priming. Evidence suggests that they are closely linked to systems mediating perceptual processing.

perceptual skill   The learned development of some aspect of perceptual function, such as reading mirror images of words.

peripheral nervous system   Parts of the nervous system other than the brain stem and spinal cord. This includes the sensory and motor nerves, which are distributed throughout the body and which convey information to and from the brain and spinal cord (peripheral nerves).

perirhinal cortex   The cortical area of the medial temporal lobe that occupies the lateral bank of the rhinal sulcus.

permeability   Conductance. The degree to which a membrane allows a particular molecule (or ion) to pass through it. In neurons, this is determined by the state of the membrane protein channels.

perseveration   Maintenance of a behavior despite continuing feedback that it is not adaptive.

PET   *See* **position emission tomography.**

phagocyte   Any cell that ingests microorganisms or other cells and foreign particles.

phenothiazines   A class of drugs that blocks dopamine receptors and reduces the frequency and magnitude of psychotic symptoms in some individuals with schizophrenia.

phenylalanine hydroxylase   An enzyme that converts phenylalanine to tyrosine. Its alteration in phenylketonuria results in a buildup of phenylalanine, causing mental retardation. *See* **phenylketonuria.**

phenylketonuria (PKU)   A disorder that causes an alteration in the enzyme phenylalanine hydroxylase, which normally converts the amino acid phenylalanine to tyrosine. The resulting buildup of phenylalanine exerts a toxic effect on developing neural tissue, resulting in mental retardation.

phobic disorders   A class of anxiety disorders in which anxiety is related to a particular type of object or situation.

phonemes   The smallest significant sound elements (units) of a language.

phonemic disorder of speech   A central language processing impairment in which the production of individual phonemes is unimpaired but the capacity to program rapid sequences of phonemes to produce fluent speech is disrupted. This is the central impairment in Broca's aphasia.

phonemic jargon   A type of jargon aphasia characterized by speech that contains many nonwords (neologisms).

phonemic paraphasias   Distorted speech productions in which the person cannot come up with a desired (appropriate) phoneme and instead substitutes one with a similar sound (e.g., *mulsuple* for *multiple*).

phonological agraphia   *See* **vocabulary-based spelling.**

phonological buffer   A specific short-term memory store for auditory-verbal material. Also called *phonological store.*

phonological dyslexia   Impaired ability to read by sound (by phonological decoding), with preserved reading by sight vocabulary. Also called *reading by sight vocabulary.*

phonological reading   *See* **surface dyslexia.**

phonological store   A specific short-term store for auditory-verbal material. Also call *phonological buffer.*

photon   The most elementary unit of light energy.

photoreceptors   Cells in the retina sensitive to light.

phototransduction   The process whereby the presence of light is coded (represented) in the form of changes in photoreceptor activity.

phrenology   The theory of localization of function developed by Gall and Spurzheim that attempted to relate specific brain functions to specific protrusions of the skull (which were believed to be indices of brain structure).

pia mater   The innermost membrane surrounding the brain. It follows the contours of the gyri and sulci.

pigmented epithelium   The layer of cells in the back of the eye in which the photoreceptors are embedded.

pineal body   A midline structure in the epithalamus thought to be involved in circadian rhythms.

pituitary gland   *See* **anterior pituitary gland** and **posterior pituitary gland.**

place cell   A type of neuron, typically in the hippocampus, whose receptive field is the presence of the animal in a particular place within the environment.

place field   The place that is the receptive field of a place cell.

planum temporale   An area just posterior to the primary auditory area on the lower lip of the Sylvian fissure in the temporal lobe.

plaques   *See* **neuritic plaques.**

plasticity   The ability of the brain to undergo adaptive change, especially in response to environmental input and to loss of function due to damage.

plexiform layer   The outermost layer of the cerebral cortex, consisting of fibers (axons) connecting different areas of cortex.

pneumoencephalography   The process in which an X ray of the head is taken after the cerebrospinal fluid in the cerebral ventricles is drained and replaced with air. The resulting contrast between the density of brain tissue and the air in the ventricles allows the shape of the ventricles to be visualized on X ray.

point localization threshold   The minimum distance between two successively touched points on the body surface that a person can reliably identify as in different locations.

poliomyelitis   An acute viral disease characterized by destruction of motor neurons and resulting paralysis and muscle atrophy.

polygenic inheritance   Genetic predisposition for a particular trait or disorder transmitted via the interaction of several genes.

pons   Rostral portion of the hindbrain, between the midbrain and the medulla oblongata.

population vector   The sum (in terms of direction and magnitude) of the direction vectors of neurons in M1 associated with a particular movement. The direction of the population vector is very close to the direction of actual movement.

positive symptoms   Symptoms that take the form of the presence of a function, experience, or behavior that is normally absent.

positron emission tomography (PET)   A functional imaging method in which a number of different radioactive tracers can be injected into the cerebral circulation and then very precisely measured by a bank of sensors positioned around the head. This makes possible high resolution measurements of relative metabolic activity in different parts of the brain.

posterior   Term designating the back part of the brain and spinal cord.

posterior commissure   A fiber tract connecting posterior areas of the two hemispheres.

posterior pituitary gland   A part of the brain that protrudes from the hypothalamus (just behind the anterior pituitary). It secretes antidiuretic hormone and ocytocin into the bloodstream.

postsynaptic membrane   The membrane (usually forming the outer surface of the dendrite) containing receptors to which neurotransmitter binds after it is released into the synapse.

potential   Difference in charge (between two compartments). Also called *potential difference.*

pragmatics   The study of the relationship between linguistic meaning and knowledge of the world.

praxicons   Hypothetical neural representations of learned movement in the left parietal lobe. Also called *visuokinesthetic engrams.*

predatory aggression   Aggression that occurs when an animal is killing an animal of another species for food. In contrast to **affective aggression,** it is unaccompanied by vocalizations or by elaborate display behavior and is aimed at vulnerable parts of the prey's body.

preferred direction   The direction of movement being made (or about to be made) that is associated with the maximum firing rate for a particular neuron in M1.

prefrontal aphasia   A disturbance in verbal expression (but not an aphasia in the traditional sense) seen after prefrontal lesions. It is characterized by reduction in spontaneous speech, diminished verbal fluency, and reduction in the volume and scope of narrative expression. Also called *central motor aphasia* and *frontal dynamic aphasia.*

prefrontal cortex   The area of the frontal lobes anterior to the premotor and supplementary motor cortices. It is involved in the higher-order control and regulation of behavior.

prematurity   The condition of an infant born before 37 weeks of gestation or with a birth weight of 5.5 pounds or less.

premotor area (PMA)   The area of cortex just anterior to the motor cortex on the anterior surface of each cerebral hemisphere. It is involved in the co-ordination of sequences of movement.

preparedness theory of phobias   The hypothesis that phobias for certain stimuli (e.g., snakes) were adaptive in the more naturalistic settings in which our early ancestors found themselves and that natural selection has therefore favored the survival of animals that were genetically programmed to fear (or to rapidly learn to fear) these stimuli.

presinilin genes   Genes involved in the synthesis of β amyloid protein, mutations of which cause defective forms of β amyloid protein to be produced in at least some cases of familial Alzheimer's disease.

pressure threshold   The lightest pressure applied to the body surface to which an individual is sensitive.

prestriate cortex   Areas of cortex outside V1 that are involved in vision. Also called *extrastriate cortex.*

presynaptic facilitation   Facilitation that results when axoaxonal inputs increase the magnitude of neurotransmitter release by an axon terminal. A typical mechanism for presynaptic facilitation is increasing Ca^{2+} influx at the presynaptic axon terminal.

presynaptic inhibition   Inhibition that results from axoaxonal inputs that reduce the number of synaptic vesicles releasing neurotransmitter into the synapse (typically by reducing Ca^{2+} influx at the axon terminal).

presynaptic membrane   The membrane (usually forming the outer surface of the axon terminal) from which neurotransmitter is released into the synapse.

primary motor cortex   *See* **motor cortex.** According to the hierarchical sequential model, the area of cortex to which the secondary motor cortex projects.

primary projection area   Area of the brain that receives the major input from another area, most often applied to sensory areas.

primary sensory cortex   The area of cortex receiving the major initial input from sensory centers in lower brain areas. For example, V1 receives the major initial input from the lateral geniculate nucleus of the thalamus.

primary sensory neurons   Neurons that receive input directly from sensory receptors. They are the first link in the afferent chain from sensory receptor to brain.

primary visual cortex   Area in the occipital lobes that receives the primary projection from the lateral geniculate nucleus of the thalamus. Also called *V1.*

primary visual pathway   The pathway from retina to lateral geniculate nucleus to V1.

priming   The facilitating effect of prior experience on perception and other processes, without conscious recollection of the prior experience.

proactive interference   The tendency of previously presented information to interfere with memory for material that is presented later.

procedural memory   Memory for how to do things (ways of doing things) and for certain movements or motor skills, in contrast to **declarative memory** (conscious memory for specific information). Also called *nondeclarative memory* and roughly equivalent to **implicit memory.**

process-specific approach   A restorative intervention approach to rehabilitation that attempts to identify the specific cognitive processes that are impaired in an individual and then designs exercises that serve as vehicles for practicing those processes.

propagation A term frequently used to describe the movement of the action potential down the axon. The term captures the self-generating nature of the positive feedback mechanism underlying this movement.

property dualism The view that mind is not a substance distinct from the physical world (the position of substance dualism) but that, instead, irreducible, nonphysical properties emerge out of the states and processes of the physical brain.

propositional prosody Intonation of spoken language that communicates meaning.

proprioception Body position sense.

prosencephalon *See* **forebrain.**

prosody The tonal aspects of spoken language (resulting from variations in parameters such as emphasis, pitch, rhythm, and timbre).

prosopagnosia Specific impairment in the recognition of faces.

prospective memory The capacity to internally represent future events and utilize these representations to guide problem solving and future behavior.

proximal Located toward the center of a structure, relative to a point of reference.

proximate causes The immediate causes of a syndrome or disorder. For example, in diabetes, the proximate cause of the disorder is insufficient insulin.

pseudodepression A constellation of symptoms, seen after prefrontal lesions, that overlaps with many of the symptoms of major depressive disorder, including depressed mood and apathy.

pseudopsychopathy A syndrome seen after prefrontal lesions that is characterized by an apparent disregard for the effect of one's behavior on others. The syndrome's name comes from it similarity to psychopathy (now termed *antisocial personality disorder*).

psychic inertia Inability to initiate movement or to discontinue movement in progress.

psychometrics The science of measuring human abilities.

psychopathy A term formerly used to describe the disorder affecting individuals who behave in a manner that indicates an extreme lack of concern for the immediate or future consequences of their behavior, particularly its effects on other people. In the past the term *sociopathy* has also been used to describe behavior of this sort. These terms have been largely replaced by the term *antisocial personality disorder*.

psychosurgery Surgical intervention that destroys structures or pathways within the brain in order to modify behavior and/or experience that does not result from a known cerebral lesion.

pure agraphia Selective impairment in the ability to write.

pure alexia Impairment in reading without impairment in other linguistic or perceptual skills.

pure word deafness A selective inability to understand heard speech in the absence of impaired comprehension of linguistic input presented in the visual and tactual modalities.

pure word dumbness A specific impairment in the production of spoken language in the absence of disturbance in other forms of language output, including writing.

putamen One of the nuclei that make up the basal ganglia.

pyramidal cells Neurons that have a pyramid-shaped cell body.

pyramidal decussation The area of the medulla at which corticospinal fibers cross over from one side of the brain stem to the other.

pyramidal tract The pathway from cerebral cortex to spinal cord; important for movement.

quadrantanopia Blindness in one quadrant of the visual field.

quadraplegia Paralysis of the legs and arms resulting from a lesion of the spinal cord.

R cones Cones most sensitive to 559 nm wavelength light.

radiopaque Not permitting the passage of radiant energy, such as X rays.

reactive depression   Depression due to external (interpersonal and social) factors, as opposed to internal (biological) factors.

reading by sight vocabulary   *See* **phonological dyslexia.**

reading by sound   *See* **surface dyslexia.**

real position cells   Neurons that fire in response to a stimulus when the stimulus is in a specific position relative to the monkey regardless of the point being fixated. Such cells are found in area V6 of monkey parietal cortex.

recent memory   A store that maintains information for a time period intermediate between short-term memory (seconds to minutes) and long-term memory (which may last a lifetime). Also called *intermediate-term memory.*

receptive aphasia   *See* **Wernicke's aphasia.**

receptive aprosodia   Impairment in the expression of prosody.

receptive field   The stimulus characteristics that cause an individual neuron to fire maximally or minimally.

receptor   A specialized protein molecule on the postsynaptic membrane that recognizes and binds neurotransmitter. *See also* **sensory receptors.**

receptor blockers   Drugs that diminish the effectiveness of a neurotransmitter by competing for binding sites at its receptors.

receptor potential   Graded depolarization or hyperpolarization that occurs in a sensory receptor in response to stimulation. These have characteristics similar to EPSPs and IPSPs.

recognition memory   Memory that is manifested by discrimination of a previously seen object from one or more objects that had not been seen before.

reentrant connections   Return connections (connections from one structure back to a structure from which it has received input).

reflectance   A measure of the fraction of the light illuminating a surface that the surface reflects.

regeneration   Process by which damaged neurons regrow connections to areas to which they had previously had connections.

regional cerebral blood flow (rCBF)   An imaging method in which a radioactive isotope is inhaled or injected and its distribution is then measured using a bank of sensors arranged symmetrically around the surface of the skull. The radioactive label is a marker of blood flow, which in turn is a correlate of brain metabolic activity.

registration   The initial processing of a stimulus by the nervous system (a prerequisite for further processing, including memory).

relative refractory period   The period after an action potential (and just after the absolute refractory period) when the neuron has an elevated threshold for firing (i.e., greater depolarization at the axon hillock is required). During this period, K$^+$ channels remain open to reestablish the resting potential. Thus, any influx of Na$^+$ is compensated for by an efflux of K$^+$, making depolarization of the neuron more difficult.

release from proactive interference   Reduction in the tendency for earlier-presented material to intrude into memory for more recently presented material when the more recently presented material comes from a different category than the earlier material.

release symptoms   The reemergence or disinhibition, after a cortical lesion, of infantile reflexes that had been under cortical control.

repetition priming   The facilitation of perceptual processing of a stimulus due to prior exposure to the stimulus.

representations   Cognitions (internal symbols) that correspond to, stand for, or represent things or relations between things. *See also* **analogical representation, symbolic representation.**

reptilian brain   According to MacLean's triune brain hypothesis, the brain stem. MacLean postulated that the reptilian brain mediates the most basic elements of survival, such as homeostasis.

rerouting   The process in which a neuron whose target has been lost (due to a lesion) grows to and connects with a new target.

reserpine   A drug used to treat high blood pressure that also decreases monoamine levels. Its association with depression in some individuals has been interpreted as support for the monoamine hypothesis of depression.

resting channels   Channels that are open when the neuron is in the resting (not firing) state.

resting potential   The membrane potential when the neuron is at rest (not firing).

resting tremor   Tremor in the limbs when no movement is being performed (during rest).

restorative interventions   Rehabilitation interventions that attempt to change an individual's cognitive capabilities after a brain lesion.

reticular activating system   Diffuse neural system in the brain stem that strongly influences the arousal level of the cortex.

reticular formation   Multisynaptic (netlike) neural system, extending from the caudal brain stem to the thalamus, that plays an important role in control of the arousal level of the cortex. Sometimes referred to as the *reticular activating system.*

reticular hypothesis   The idea that the nervous system is a continuous structure, a network of tissue that constitutes an exception to the general rule that living tissue is made up of individual units or cells.

retinal   The light-absorbing component of rhodopsin.

retinofugal projections   Neural projections (axons) from the retina to higher brain areas.

retinotopic organization   The mapping of the retinal surface onto the surface of a neural structure, such as V1. Retinotopic mapping onto a neural structure is typically distorted, with retinal locations with higher receptor density mapped onto disproportionately larger areas of the neural structure.

retrieval   The process of gaining access to information stored in memory.

retrieval cue   A stimulus that is perceptually, semantically, or in some other way similar to or related to information that one is trying to recall.

retroactive interference   The tendency of subsequently presented information to interfere with memory for previously presented material.

retrograde amnesia   A disorder involving major loss of previously remembered material.

retrograde degeneration   Degeneration spreading from the point of transection of an axon back to the cell body (as opposed to **anterograde** or **Wallerian degeneration**).

retrograde topographical amnesia   Impairment in the ability to find one's way about in previously known spatial layouts in the absence of primary disturbance of spatial processing.

retrograde transport   The process by which materials within the cell are moved from the axon terminal to the cell body (as distinct from **anterograde transport,** which is in the opposite direction).

reuptake   The reabsorption of neurotransmitter across the presynaptic membrane.

reverse engineering   A term coined by Steven Pinker to refer to the process of figuring out what a machine (or brain or mental module) is designed to do and how it does it (as opposed to forward engineering, which is designing a machine to do something).

rhodopsin   The visual pigment in rods.

rhombencephalon   *See* **hindbrain.**

right-hemisphere hypothesis of emotion   The hypothesis that the right hemisphere is specialized for the interpretation and expression of emotion, regardless of whether the emotion is positive or negative.

rods   Photoreceptors in the retina sensitive to dim light but not to color. They are found in the periphery of the retina.

rostral   In the brain stem and the spinal cord, the direction toward the brain.

rubella   A mild viral infection. Transplacental infection of the fetus in the first trimester may cause developmental abnormalities of the brain, resulting in mental retardation. Abnormalities of the heart, eyes, ears, and bone may also be seen. Also called *German measles.*

S1   *See* **somatosensory cortex.**

saccade   An eye movement in which the eyes jump from one position to the next (rather than moving smoothly).

sagittal section   The plane of section (cut) that divides the brain into right and left parts.

saltatory conduction   The process in myelinated neurons whereby the triggering of an action potential at the axon hillock creates a flow of current down the core of the axon. An intense inward Na^+ movement occurs at breaks in the myelin sheath (nodes of Ranvier), thus preventing the action potential from dissipating. This form of transmission is faster and more metabolically efficient that the continual propagation of an action potential that takes place in unmyelinated neurons.

schemas   The conceptual frameworks or cognitive structures in terms of which information can be organized, interpreted, and remembered.

schizophrenia   A psychotic disorder that may include delusions, hallucinations, disorganized speech, bizarre behavior, and negative symptoms, such as social withdrawal.

Schwann cells   Glia cells that form the myelin sheath around axons in the peripheral nervous system.

scotoma   A small blind spot in the visual field.

script   Knowledge of the behavior that is adaptive in a particular situation, such as eating at a restaurant.

sculpting role of inhibition   The notion that by eliminating elements within the baseline firing sequence of a neuron, inhibition can result in intricate patterns of neural firing that can code psychological processes.

seasonal affective disorder (SAD)   A form of depression that occurs during the winter months, when days are short and nights are long.

second messenger   A response that occurs when neurotransmitter binding to a receptor activates a second molecule, which indirectly alters the gating of membrane channels through the initiation of a sequence of biochemical events. Second messengers can have far-reaching and long-lasting effects on the metabolic state of the neuron. Cyclic adenosine monophosphate (cAMP) is the best understood second messenger.

secondary motor area   According to the sequential hierarchical model, the area of cortex to which tertiary motor cortex projects (i.e., the premotor cortex).

secondary sensory areas   According to the sequential hierarchical model, areas of cortex that receive projections from primary sensory cortex for a given modality.

secondary somatosensory cortex   The area of cortex ventral to the somatosensory cortex that receives input mainly from that structure and projects to posterior parietal areas where higher-order somatosensory and spatial processing takes place.

Seelenblindheit   Literally, "soul-blindness." A 19th-century German term for agnosia.

seizures   Transient disturbances of brain function that may manifest themselves as loss or impairment of consciousness, abnormal motor phenomena, psychic or sensory disturbances, or activation of the autonomic nervous system. Symptoms are due to disturbance of the electrical activity of the brain. Also called *epilepsy*.

selective attention   Focusing of attention on features of the environment that are relevant to goal-directed behavior. *See also* **exclusionary attention.**

selective serotonin reuptake inhibitors (SSRIs)   A class of antidepressant drugs that selectively blocks the reuptake of serotonin. Fluoxetine (Prozac) was the first drug of this class.

semantic dementia   A selective impairment in semantic memory seen in association with dementia.

semantic jargon   A type of jargon aphasia characterized by speech containing real words that are combined inappropriately.

semantic memory   Memory for information whose acquisition is not tied to a particular personal experience (e.g., knowing that the capital of Italy is Rome). Also called *generic memory.*

semantic paraphasias   Distorted speech productions in which the person makes errors that have a semantic similarity to the desired word (e.g., *ship* for *boat*).

semantic processing   The process of assigning meaning to a word.

semantically constrained sentences   Sentences whose meaning is constrained by the words that compose them (e.g., The girl waters the flower).

semantically reversible sentences   Sentences whose meaning is not constrained by the words that compose them (e.g., The lion kills the leopard).

semantics   The study of meaning.

senile plaques   *See* **neuritic plaques.**

sensitization   A simple form of learning in which the vigorousness of a response to a neutral stimulus (one that is neither rewarding nor harmful) increases when it is preceded by a noxious (painful) stimulus.

sensory aphasia   *See* **Wernicke's aphasia.**

sensory homunculus   The orderly mapping of the body surface on the somatosensory cortex (S1) in the postcentral gyrus.

sensory receptors   The first neurons to register the presence of a stimulus.

septum (septal nuclei) Nuclei that lie ventral and medial to the lateral ventricles in the basal forebrain. They are considered part of the limbic system.

sequential processing   The idea that a complex function is composed of a number of more basic processes that are activated in a sequence.

serotonin   A small molecule monoamine neurotransmitter.

serotonin hypothesis of depression   Posits that some forms of depression result from a specific abnormality of serotonin activity; a refinement of the monoamine hypothesis of depression.

sex chromosomes   *See* **chromosomes.**

sex-linked transmission   Any genetic disorder affecting one sex selectively, and thus presumably due to a gene on the sex chromosome.

sexual dimorphism   Differences in structure (or function) between the two sexes of a species.

sexual selection   One of the mechanisms of evolution in which the factors determining who will mate with whom determine the characteristics of the resulting offspring.

shape constancy   The perceptual mechanism whereby we are able to extract the invariant (unchanging) shape of an object from the changing pattern of stimulation impinging on the retina.

short-term habituation   Habituation that lasts for a brief period (minutes).

short-term memory (STM)   A short-duration, limited-capacity memory system that holds information for only a matter of seconds, unless continuous rehearsal takes place. Information in short-term memory is highly vulnerable to the effects of interference.

simple cells   Neurons in V1 (discovered by Hubel and Wiesel) with receptive fields characterized by a bar-shaped stimulus presented at a particular orientation in a particular area of the visual field.

simultanagnosia   Impairment in the ability to perceive and attend to all of the features of an object or a scene at the same time. Individuals with this disorder perceive the individual parts of a complex visual display better than they do the whole. *See also* **ventral simultanagnosia** and **dorsal simultanagnosia.**

single dissociation   Two functions are said to constitute a single dissociation if in some cases impairment in function A is seen without impairment in function B, but impairment in function B is never seen without impairment in function A. For example, understanding heard language and hearing sound are singly dissociable.

single photon emission computerized tomography (SPECT)   A functional imaging method roughly analogous to positron emission tomography (PET) but with less spatial resolution.

single-cell recording   A method that involves inserting an exceedingly small diameter electrode into an individual neuron and measuring that cell's activity (frequency of firing). Also called *unit recording.*

size constancy   The perceptual mechanism whereby we are able to extract the invariant (unchanging) size of an object from the changing pattern of stimulation impinging on the retina.

skull X ray   A simple X ray of the head.

social phobia   Fear of social situations.

sociopathy   *See* **antisocial personality disorder.**

sodium amobarbital test   A procedure in which the barbiturate sodium amobarbital is injected into one hemisphere (via the internal carotid artery), temporarily anesthetizing the hemisphere. During the test, the function of the noninjected hemisphere can be assessed.

sodium-potassium pump   A metabolic pump that transports Na^+ out of the neuron and K^+ into the neuron. This compensates for the slow leak of Na^+ into the neuron (and resulting efflux of K^+) during the resting state.

soma   The cell body.

somatic marker hypothesis   The hypothesis put forth by Damasio that feedback from the body (both autonomic and nonautonomic) about emotional state to ventral prefrontal cortex is a critical component in emotion and, most important, in reasoning. This suggests a close and perhaps inextricable collaboration between what are typically termed cognitive processing and emotional processing.

somatic motor system   Skeletal muscle and the parts of the nervous system that control it.

somatic nervous system   The part of the peripheral nervous system innervating skin, joints, and skeletal muscles.

somatosensory area   *See* **somatosensory cortex.**

somatosensory cortex (S1)   The area of cortex in the postcentral gyrus of each hemisphere that receives and processes sensory information from the contralateral side of the body about touch, temperature, vibration, proprioception, and kinesthesis.

somatosensory system   The system that processes information about the body, including touch, temperature, pain, body position, and body movement.

somesthesis   The generic name for the body senses, including touch, pain, temperature, proprioception, and kinesthesis.

source amnesia   Impairment in the ability to remember the source of information together with preservation of memory for the information itself.

spatial agraphia   Impairment in spelling or writing secondary to an impairment in spatial processing.

spatial dyscalculia   A developmental dyscalculia in which the spatial aspects of calculating, such as lining up numbers, are disrupted. This has been hypothesized to be similar to the dyscalculia seen after right-hemisphere lesions.

spatial summation   The cumulative effect of EPSPs occurring at different locations on the postsynaptic membrane.

special sensory   Term sometimes used to refer to the major sensory modalities other than somesthesis (i.e., vision, audition, smell, and taste).

SPECT   *See* **single photon emission computerized tomography.**

spelling by sound   A central disorder of spelling in which the individual spells according to the most common letter-to-phoneme correspondences in the language.

spelling dyslexia   A word-form dyslexia characterized by an inability to recognize words as coherent visual units.

spinal cord   The part of the central nervous system extending from the medulla rostrally, to the cauda equina caudally. Its exterior portion is white matter, composed of fiber tracts that carry information to and from the brain. Its central portion is gray matter.

spinal reflex   Reflex response mediated by the spinal cord (and obtainable when the spinal cord is disconnected from the brain).

spinal shock   Temporary loss of spinal reflexes after spinal transection.

spinothalamic system   A multisynaptic pathway in the spinal cord that conveys information about pain and temperature to the thalamus.

splenium   The posterior part of the corpus callosum, connecting the posterior regions of the cerebral hemispheres.

split-brain surgery   *See* **commissurotomy.**

sprouting   The processes in which neurons with connections to areas neighboring a denervated area sprout additional terminals that form connections with the denervated area.

staged lesion   An experimental lesion that results from a sequence of smaller lesions performed at intervening intervals (rather than a single lesion performed at one time).

staged-lesion effect   The finding that the effect of a staged lesion on function is much less than the effect of a single lesion of the same size and in the same location.

stereotaxic technique   A method that maps neuroanatomical structures onto a three-dimensional coordinate system, thereby allowing the precise identification of locations within the brain.

stimulus bound   Impairment in the normal ability to inhibit overlearned or automatic responses to a stimulus.

storage   The maintenance of information in the nervous system over time.

strategic retrieval   The organized search for information in memory.

stream of feeling   According to Papez's theory, one of the two streams by means of which conscious feelings may arise. In this stream, input from the thalamus goes first to the hypothalamus and then projects to the cingulate gyrus via the hypothalamus. *See also* **stream of thought.**

stream of thought   According to Papez's theory, one of the two streams by means of which conscious feelings may arise. In this stream, sensory input reaches the cingulate gyrus via the thalamus and other regions of cortex. *See also* **stream of feeling.**

striate cortex   Another name for V1 in the calcarine sulcus of the occipital lobes.

stroke   *See* **cerebral vascular accident.**

study-test modality shift   The phenomenon that priming does not occur if the initial presentation of the words is in a different modality from that used in the later test.

subarachnoid space   The space between the two layers of the arachnoid membrane.

subcallosal gyrus   The area of cortex on the medial aspect of the cerebral hemispheres lying inferior to the anterior part of the corpus callosum.

subcortical dementias   Dementias that primarily affect subcortical structures. These include Huntington's chorea and Parkinson's disease.

subjective contour   The subjective experience of a contour where none is in fact present. The Kanizsa triangle is an example of a figure that elicits the perception of a subjective contour.

subjective organization   Organization imposed on stimuli by the subject.

substance dualism   The most emphatic form of dualism, which holds that there is a distinctly mental domain that is not reducible to anything physical.

substantia nigra   A midbrain nucleus that is a major source of dopamine for the cortex. It is generally considered to be part of the basal ganglia.

subthalamic nuclei   Small nuclei that lie ventral to the thalamus. They are generally considered to be part of the basal ganglia.

subtraction method   The method in which some measure of a control task (that is postulated to differ from the task under investigation in only one critical way) is subtracted from the same measure of the task under investigation. The resulting difference between the two measures is then inferred to reflect the critical difference between the two tasks. This method is used extensively in functional imaging studies.

sulcus (pl., sulci)   Furrows or grooves in the folded surface of the cerebral cortex.

superior   Term designating the upper part of the brain; also designates "above," relative to a reference point.

superior colliculi   Nuclei in the posterior midbrain (tectum) that receive visual input from the retina.

superior olive   Brain-stem nucleus that receives auditory projections from the cochlear nucleus.

supplementary motor area (SMA)   The area on the medial surface of each hemisphere just anterior to the motor cortex. It is involved in the coordination of sequences of movement.

suppression   The phenomenon in which patients with commissurotomy report very few words presented to the left ear in a dichotic listening task (although they are able to report normally words presented to the left ear only).

surface dyslexia   Reading by sound (phonological analysis), following the most common print-to-sound rules of the language, without the ability to read words that do not follow the standard rules (i.e., phonologically irregular words). Also called *phonological reading* or *reading by sound.*

Sylvian fissure   A deep cleft on the lateral surface of the brain, extending posteriorly and upward, and forming the boundary between the temporal and parietal lobes. Also called *lateral fissure.*

symbolic gestures   Actions that communicate meaning symbolically, such as showing the thumbs-up sign or waving good-bye.

symbolic representation   A representation that does not bear any direct relationship to the thing it denotes. Most words are symbolic representations.

symbolic search model of visual recognition   The hypothesis that normal perception entails the generation of an abstract representation of the stimulus, which is then compared with stored visual representations in semantic memory. A match between the abstract representation of the stimulus and the stored visual representation results in recognition.

synapse   The gap between neurons across which neurotransmitter diffuses.

synaptic vesicles   Membrane-bound spheres, found at the synaptic terminal, in which neurotransmitter molecules are stored before their release into the synapse.

syntactic agrammatism   Speech characterized by disruption in word order and word choice, together with intact use of function words (conjunctions, articles, and prepositions) and word endings.

syntax   The rules describing how words can be combined into phrases and sentences.

tachistoscope   An apparatus for rapidly presenting visual stimuli. In laterality studies, different visual stimuli are presented to the two (left and right) visual fields simultaneously. The speed and accuracy of processing of these stimuli are then compared, providing a basis for inferring which hemisphere is more effectively processing the information.

tactile aphasia   Specific impairment in the comprehension of language that is delivered through somatosensory input (i.e., touch).

tactile perception   The perception of stimuli that passively impinge on the body surface (as opposed to **tactual perception,** resulting from active touch).

tactual perception   Active touch. The proprioceptive and kinesthetic sensations resulting from active touch make the recognition of objects and spatial layouts possible.

tardive dyskinesia   A movement disorder that occurs after prolonged use of antipsychotic medication.

tectum   The part of the midbrain dorsal (posterior) to the cerebral aqueduct. It includes the superior and inferior colliculi.

tegmentum   The part of the midbrain that lies ventral to the cerebral aqueduct.

telencephalon   The most rostral part of the forebrain, including the cerebral hemispheres, basal ganglia, the amygdala, and the hippocampus, but not including the diencephalon.

temporal gradient   The characteristic of retrograde amnesia that memory for more recently acquired information is more impaired than is memory for more remote information.

temporal hemiretina   The half of each retina closest to the temple.

temporal integration of behavior   The ability to organize, initiate, and carry out novel patterns of goal-directed behavior over extended time periods.

temporal lobes   Areas of cortex and underlying white matter lying beneath the temporal bone, at the sides of the skull.

temporal memory   Memory for the chronological order of a sequence of stimuli.

temporal summation   The cumulative effect of EPSPs occurring close together in time.

temporal-lobe personality   A pattern of behavior that some investigators believe is characteristic of individuals with temporal-lobe seizures. Features include deepening of emotions, hyperreligiosity (or intense atheism), excessive concern with details, and a tendency to write about one's life in great detail (hypergraphia).

tertiary motor area   According to the sequential hierarchical model, the area in the frontal lobes to which information from the tertiary sensory area projects.

tertiary sensory area   According to the sequential hierarchical model, the area of cortex in which information from each of the secondary sensory areas (visual, auditory, and somatosensory) converges.

tetanic stimulation   High-frequency stimulation.

thalamus   The large, egg-shaped collection of nuclei in the diencephalon in each hemisphere.

theoretic interanimation   The process by which, during coevolution, theories at one level of explanation may extend and correct theories at another level. Theories at different levels of explanation thus do not coevolve in isolation.

theory of mind   An individual is said to have a theory of mind if he or she has the concept or sense that others have mind or consciousness.

thick stripes   Thickly striped areas in V2 defined by the cytochrome oxidase staining technique. Thick stripes receive input from layer IVB of V1 and project to V3 and V5.

thin stripes   Thinly striped areas in V2 defined by the cytochrome oxidase staining technique. Thin stripes receive input from the blobs of V1 and project to V4.

threshold   The magnitude of a stimulus or an event that produces a response.

threshold potential   The critical depolarization that, when achieved at the axon hillock, initiates an action potential.

time constant   The quantification, for a given post-synaptic membrane, of the duration of an EPSP. The time constant depends on the particular characteristics of the membrane.

tonotopic maps   The orderly representation of sound frequency in the auditory cortex.

topographical disorientation   Inability to move about in spatial layouts due to a disruption in the ability to accurately perceive the spatial relationships and distances between landmarks.

topographical memory disorder   Impairment in the ability to learn new spatial layouts (anterograde topographical amnesia) or loss of the ability to move about in previously known spatial layouts (retrograde topographical amnesia), in the absence of a primary disturbance in spatial processing. Also called *topographical amnesia.*

toxin   A poison; a substance that causes damage to an organism.

tract   *See* **fiber tract.**

transcortical aphasia   Aphasia due to damage to cortical areas outside Broca's area and Wernicke's area.

transcortical motor aphasia   An aphasia characterized by the symptoms of Broca's aphasia, with the exception that the ability to repeat heard language is unimpaired.

transcortical sensory aphasia   An aphasia characterized by the symptoms of Wernicke's aphasia, with the exception that the ability to repeat heard language is unimpaired.

transduction   The changing of a specific form of energy into a pattern of neural impulses. It is seen in vision, audition, and somesthesis.

transient global amnesia   A severe but short-lived memory impairment that may result from a transient ischemic attack, trauma, or other causes.

transient ischemia   A short-lived inadequate blood supply to a part of the brain. Also called *transient ischemic attack.*

translocation   The shifting of a segment or fragment of one chromosome into another chromosome.

transmitter-gated channels   Membrane channels that alter their gating in response to the binding of specific neurotransmitters to postsynaptic receptors. Also called *ligand-gated channels.*

transneuronal degeneration   Degeneration extending to neurons that have synaptic connections with a damaged neuron.

trauma   A wound or injury.

traumatic brain injury   Damage to the brain due to injury.

tricyclic antidepressants   A class of antidepressant medications with a three-ringed structure that blocks the reuptake of monoamines (particularly norepinephrine and serotonin). An example is imipramine.

trisomy   The presence of an extra chromosome, so that three chromosomes of a particular type are present instead of two.

trisomy 21   *See* **Down syndrome.**

triune brain hypothesis   A hypothesis put forward by MacLean according to which the brain has undergone three major stages of evolution so that in higher animals there exists a hierarchy of three brains in one: the reptilian brain, comprising the brain stem; the paleomammalian brain, comprising the limbic system; and the neomammalian brain, consisting of the neocortex. *See also* **neomammalian brain, paleomammalian brain,** and **reptilian brain.**

trochlear nucleus   One of the cranial nerve nuclei in the midbrain that participates in the control of eye movement.

Turner's syndrome   A disorder, due to deletion of an X-chromosome, characterized by short stature, undifferentiated gonads, and other variable abnormalities. Impairment in the perception of form and space has also been reported.

twin studies   Studies that investigate the possibility that a genetic factor contributes to a condition by comparing the concordance rates (the probability that a person in a particular familial relationship with a patient also has the condition) between monozygotic (identical) and dizygotic (fraternal) twins. A higher concordance rate for monozygotic twins than for dizygotic twins is evidence for a genetic factor in the condition.

two-point threshold   The closest simultaneous stimulation of two different points on the body surface that a person is able to reliably discriminate from a single point of stimulation.

two-syndrome hypothesis of schizophrenia   The hypothesis that there are two underlying pathological processes in schizophrenia: Type I, associated with normal ventricular size, absence of cortical atrophy, and predominantly positive symptoms; and Type II, associated with enlarged ventricles, cortical atrophy, and predominantly negative symptoms.

Type I schizophrenia   *See* **two-syndrome hypothesis of schizophrenia.**

Type II schizophrenia   *See* **two-syndrome hypothesis of schizophrenia.**

ultimate causes   Remote causes of a disorder. These can be divided into two categories: a predisposition for the disorder (termed *diathesis*) and an environmental component (termed *stress*). For example, in diabetes the diathesis is a genetic factor that predisposes an individual to the disease. This may be triggered by environmental stressors such as obesity.

uncinate fasciculus   The fiber tract connecting temporal and frontal cortex.

unconditioned response   A natural (unlearned) response to an unconditioned stimulus.

unconditioned stimulus   A stimulus that naturally causes a particular response.

unilateral   On one side (of the body).

unipolar depression   *See* **major depressive disorder.**

unit recording   *See* **single-cell recording.**

utilization behavior   The tendency to use objects encountered in the environment without obvious prior intention to do so.

V1   The area in the occipital lobes that receives the major projections from the lateral geniculate nucleus of the thalamus. Also called the *primary visual cortex.*

V2   The area of cortex receiving input from V1 and sending output to V3, V4, and V5.

V3   The area of cortex specialized for the perception of dynamic form (form in motion).

V4   The area of cortex specialized for the perception (construction) of color.

V5   The area of cortex specialized for the perception of movement. Also sometimes referred to as *area MT,* for "middle temporal," its location in the monkey.

valence hypothesis   The hypothesis that the left hemisphere is dominant for positive emotion and the right hemisphere is dominant for negative emotion.

vegetative symptoms   Symptoms of depression that are presumed to be more directly related to brain dysfunction, including disturbances of sleep, changes in appetite, diurnal mood variation, and decrease in sex drive.

ventral   Term designating the lower part of the brain and the anterior part of the spinal cord.

ventral hemiretina   The ventral (lower) half of each retina.

ventral horn   The ventral region of the gray matter within the spinal cord containing the cell bodies of α motor neurons.

ventral prefrontal cortex   The area of the frontal lobes on the ventral surface of the cerebral hemispheres. Also called *orbital prefrontal cortex.*

ventral root   The fiber bundles emerging from the ventral aspect of the spinal cord and containing axons of α motor neurons.

ventral simultanagnosia   Impairment in the ability to rapidly code multiple parts of stimuli, particularly stimuli whose perception requires their decomposition into discrete elements. Printed words are an example of such stimuli. Perception thus proceeds part by part. This impairment derives its name from its association with left inferior temporal-occipital lesions.

ventricular hypothesis   The idea that the cerebral ventricles are the site of (that they mediate) specific psychological processes.

ventricular-brain ratio (VBR)   The ratio of the volume of the cerebral ventricles to overall brain volume.

ventricles   Cavities (filled with cerebrospinal fluid) within the brain. There are four cerebral ventricles: two lateral ventricles (in the telencephalon), the third ventricle (in the diencephalon), and the fourth ventricle (in the hindbrain). Also called *cerebral ventricles.*

verbal fluency   Normal ability to generate words. In spoken language, this manifests itself in an uninterrupted flow of speech.

vertical pathway   In the retina, the direct input from photoreceptor to bipolar cell.

vesicles   Membrane-bound spheres within the neuron containing various materials.

vestibular sense   Sense of position and motion of the head.

vestibular system   Sensory system with receptors in the middle ear that is sensitive to position and movement of the head.

visible spectrum   The band of wavelengths of electromagnetic radiation that humans are able to detect (400–700 nm).

visual acuity   Clarity or clearness of vision as measured in a number of ways, including detecting the presence or absence of light, detecting the presence of a single target, detecting differences in spatial frequency (e.g., number of lines per degree of visual angle), and detecting differences in brightness.

visual agnosia   Impairment in the recognition of aspects of the visual world not due to an impairment in elementary components of vision, such as visual acuity.

visual association cortex   Areas of cortex outside V1 that are involved in vision. These areas are now more frequently referred to as *extrastriate cortex* or *prestriate cortex.*

visual disorientation   The inability to fixate an object (cause a stimulus to fall on the retinal fovea) in the absence of primary visual or primary motor impairment.

visual hemifield   Half (left or right) of the visual field. Typically the terms *right visual field* and *left visual field* are used to mean right and left visual hemifield, respectively.

visual localization   The ability to point to or touch a visual stimulus. Impairment in this ability (termed *optic ataxis*) is defined as impairment in the ability to touch a visual stimulus in the absence of primary visual, primary somatosensory, and primary motor impairment.

visual pigment   A molecule in a photoreceptor that changes its conformation when it absorbs (is activated by) a specific range of wavelengths of light. This is the only light-dependent step in vision. The three types of cones and the rods each have visual pigment with different absorption characteristics.

visual word-form dyslexias   Dyslexias conceptualized as disruptions in the initial processing of a word as a visual unit, as opposed to **central dyslexias,** which involve interference with later stages of the reading process.

visuokinesthetic engrams   Hypothetical neural representations of learned movement in the left parietal lobe. Also termed *praxicons.*

visuospatial agnosia   A term used in the 1950s that embodies the assumption that perceptual impairment could be confined to the domain of visuospatial processing.

visuospatial scratchpad   A hypothesized visuospatial short-term memory store.

vocabulary-based spelling   A central disorder of spelling in which spelling relies on an established vocabulary of word-spelling correspondences, while knowledge of letter-phoneme correspondences is impaired. Also called *phonological agraphia.*

void condition   The condition in which a surface is viewed in isolation (without view of its surround).

voltage-gated channels   Membrane channels that alter their gating in response to changes in voltage.

Wallerian degeneration   Degeneration of the length of an axon distal to the point of damage. Also called *anterograde degeneration*.

Wernicke's aphasia   A central impairment in language characterized by severely impaired comprehension together with hyperfluent (rapid and copious) spontaneous speech that retains the intonation pattern, rhythm, and pronunciation of normal speech but does not make sense. Also called *receptive aphasia* or *sensory aphasia*.

Wernicke's area   The area of cortex in the parietotemporal region of the left hemisphere that, when damaged, results in Wernicke's aphasia (impaired language comprehension and speech that is fluent but not meaningful).

white matter   Brain tissue composed of the axons of neurons.

whole-body movements   Movements involving the entire body, such as standing in the pose of a boxer or walking across a room.

word forms   The hypothetical percepts that result from the grouping of individual letters into higher-order word units.

word salad   A term sometimes applied to the disorganized speech seen in some people with schizophrenia.

word superiority effect   The tendency of normal subjects to recognize a given letter more rapidly and more accurately when it is presented as part of a word than when it is presented as part of a nonword.

working memory (WM)   A part of the memory system that is currently activated. This includes a workspace consisting of (a) several types of specialized temporary storage systems, which at any given time have a specific content, and (b) processes being brought to bear on this content. It also includes (c) the executive function, which takes care of the overall coordination of activities of working memory, regulating both the contents of the workspace and the processes interacting with those contents.

workspace   The component of working memory that consists of several different types of specialized temporary storage systems and processes being applied to their content.

X-ray computerized tomography (CT scan)   The process in which an X-ray beam is aimed through the head and then slowly rotated in an arc around the head to obtain a "shadow" of the brain from all angles.

Young-Helmholtz trichromatic theory of color vision   The theory that color vision is mediated by the three types of cones.

Bibliography _____

Abern, G. L., Schomer, D. L., Kleefield, J., Blume, H., Congrove, G. R., Weintraub, S., & Mesulam, M. M. (1991). Right hemisphere advantage for evaluating emotional facial expressions. *Cortex, 27,* 193–202.

Ackerly, S. S. (1964). A case of paranatal bilateral frontal lobe defect observed for thirty years. In J. M. Warren & K. Akert (Eds.), *The frontal granular cortex and behavior* (pp. 192–218). New York: McGraw-Hill.

Ackerly, S. S., & Benton, A. L. (1947). Report of case of bilateral frontal lobe defect. *Research Publications, Association for Research in Nervous and Mental Disorders, 27,* 479–504.

Adams, P. (Trans.) (1939). *The genuine works of Hippocrates.* Baltimore: Williams and Wilkins.

Adams, R. D., & Victor, M. (Eds.) (1993). *Principles of neurology* (5th ed.). New York: McGraw-Hill.

Adelman, P. K., & Zajonc, R. B. (1989). Facial efference and the experience of emotion. *Annual Review of Psychology, 40,* 249–280.

Adolphs, R., Tranel, D., Damasio, H., & Damasio, A. R. (1995). Fear and the human amygdala. *Journal of Neuroscience, 15,* 587–591.

Aggleton, J. P. (1992). *The amygdala: Neurobiological aspects of emotion, memory and mental dysfunction.* New York: Wiley-Liss.

Aggleton, J. P. and Brown, M. W. (1999). Episodic memory, amnesia, and the hippocampal-anterior thalamic axis. *Behavioral and Brain Sciences, 22,* 425–489.

Akert, K. (1964). Comparative anatomy of the frontal cortex and thalamo-frontal connections. In J. M. Warren & K. Akert (Eds.), *The frontal granular cortex and behavior.* New York: McGraw-Hill.

Albert, M. L. (1973). A simple test of visual neglect. *Neurology, 23,* 658–664.

Albert, M. L., & Bear, D. (1974). Time to understand: A case study in word deafness with reference to the role of time in auditory comprehension. *Brain, 97,* 383–394.

Albert, M. L., Goodglass, H., Helm, N. A., Rubens, A. B., & Alexander, M. P. (1981). *Clinical aspects of dysphasia.* New York: Springer.

Albert, M. S., Butters, N., & Levin, J. (1980). Memory for remote events in chronic alcoholics and alcoholic Korsakoff patients. In H. Begleiter (Ed.), *The biological effects of alcohol* (pp. 719–730). New York: Plenum.

Albin, R. L., Young, A. B., & Penney, J. B. (1989). Functional anatomy of basal ganglia disorders. *Trends in Neuro sciences, 12,* 366–375.

Alford, L. B. (1933). Localization of consciousness and emotion. *American Journal of Psychiatry, 12,* 789–799.

Alivisatos, B. (1992). The role of the frontal cortex in the use of advance information in a mental rotation paradigm. *Neuropsychologia, 30,* 145–159.

Alzheimer, A. (1913). Beitrage sur pathologischen Anatomie der Dementia Praecox. *Allg. Z. Psychiatr. Ihre Grenzgeb., 70,* 810–812.

Amaral, D. G. (1987). Memory: Anatomical organization of the candidate brain regions. In F. Plum (Ed.), *Handbook of physiology: Sect. 1. The nervous system. Vol. 5: Higher functions of the brain* (pp. 211–294). Bethesda, MD: American Physiological Society.

Amaral, D. G., Price, J. L., Pitkämen, A., & Carmichael, S. T. (1992). Anatomical organization of the primate amygdaloid complex. In J. P. Aggleton (Ed.), *The amygdala: Neurobiological aspects of emotion, memory and mental dysfunction* (pp. 1–66). New York: Wiley-Liss.

American Psychiatric Association. (1994). *Diagnostic and statistical manual of mental disorders* (4th ed.). Washington, DC: Author.

Andersen, R. A., Essick, G. K., & Siegel, R. M. (1985). The encoding of spatial location by posterior parietal neurons. *Science, 230,* 456–458.

Andreasen, N. C. (1984). *The broken brain.* New York: Harper and Row.

Andreasen, N. C. (1985). Positive vs. negative schizophrenia: A critical evaluation. *Schizophrenia Bulletin, 11,* 280–289.

Andreasen, N. C. (1988). Brain imaging: Applications in psychiatry. *Science, 239,* 1381–1388.

Andreasen, N. C., & Black, D. W. (1996). *Introductory textbook of psychiatry* (2nd ed.). Washington, DC: American Psychiatric Press.

Andreasen, N. C., Flaum, M., Swayze, V. W., Tyrrell, G., Arndt, S. (1989). Positive and negative symptoms in schizophrenia. *Archives of General Psychiatry, 47,* 615–621.

Andreasen, N. C., Nasrallah, H. A., Dunn, V., Olsen, S. C., Grove, W. M., Ehrheart, J. C., Coffman, J. A., & Crossett, I. H. W. (1986). Structural abnormalities in the frontal system in schizophrenia: A magnetic resonance imaging study. *Archives of General Psychiatry, 43,* 136–144.

Andreasen, N. C., Rezai, K., Alliger, R., Swayze, V. W., Flaum, M., Kirchner, P., Cohen, G., & O'Leary, D. S. (1992). Hypofrontality in neuroleptic-naive patients and in patients with chronic schizophrenia. *Archives of General Psychiatry, 49,* 943–958.

Andreasen, N. C., Swayze, V. W., Flaum, M., O'Leary, D. S., & Alliger, D. S. (1994). The neural mechanisms of mental phenomena. In N. C. Andreasen (Ed.), *Schizophrenia: From mind to molecule* (pp. 49–91). Washington, DC: American Psychiatric Press.

Ansara, A., Geschwind, N., Galaburda, A., Albert, M., & Cartrell, N. (Eds.). (1981). *Sex differences in dyslexia.* Towson, MD: Orton Dyslexia Society.

Ariel, R. N., Golden, C. J., Berg, R. A., Quaife, M. A., Dirksen, J. W., Forsell, T., Wilson, J., & Graber, B. (1983). Regional cerebral blood flow in schizophrenics. *Archives of General Psychiatry, 40,* 258–263.

Armstrong, F. D., Seidel, J. F., & Swales, T. P. (1993). Pediatric HIV infection: A neuropsychological and educational challenge. *Journal of Learning Disabilities, 26*(2), 92–103.

Arnold, M. B. (1960). *Emotion and personality.* New York: Columbia University Press.

Arrigoni, G., & De Renzi, E. (1964). Constructional apraxia and hemispheric locus of lesion. *Cortex, 1,* 170–197.

Asperger, H. (1944). Die "autistichen Psychopathen" im Kindsalter. *Archiv fur Psychiatrie,* 117, 1. Translated in U. Frith (Ed.). (1991). *Autism and Asperger syndrome.* New York: Cambridge University Press.

Bachevalier, J., & Mishkin, M. (1986). Visual recognition impairment follows ventromedial but not dorsolateral prefrontal lesions in monkeys. *Behavioral Brain Research, 20,* 249–261.

Baddeley, A. D. (1986). *Working memory.* Oxford, England: Oxford University Press.

Baddeley, A. D. (1994). Working memory: The interface between memory and cognition. In D. L. Schacter & E. Tulving (Eds.), *Memory systems* (pp. 351–386). Cambridge, MA: MIT Press.

Bahr, M., & Bonhoeffer, F. (1994). Perspectives on axonal regeneration in the mammalian CNS. *Trends in Neurosciences, 17,* 473–478.

Bailey, A. J., Le Couteur, A., Gottesman, I., Bolton, P., Simonoff, E., Yuzda, E., & Rutter, M. (1995). Autism as a strongly genetic disorder: Evidence from a British twin study. *Psychological Medicine, 25,* 63–77.

Bailey, P., von Bonin, G., Davis, E. W., & McCulloch, W. S. (1944). Further observations of associational pathways in the brain of *Mucaca mulatta. Journal of Neuropathology and Experimental Neurology, 3,* 413–415.

Baillargeon, R. (1987). Object permanence in 3½- and 4½-month-old infants. *Developmental Psychology, 23,* 655–664.

Baillargeon, R. (1991). Reasoning about the height and location of a hidden object in 4½- and 6½-month-old infants. *Cognition, 38,* 13–42.

Baillargeon, R. (1995). Physical reasoning in infancy. In M. Gazzaniga (Ed.), *The cognitive neurosciences* (pp. 81–204). Cambridge, MA: MIT Press.

Baillargeon, R., Spelke, E. S., & Wasserman, S. (1985). Object permanence in five-month-old infants. *Cognition, 20,* 191–208.

Balon, R., Jordan, M., Pohl, R., & Yeragami, V. K. (1989). Family history of anxiety disorders in control subjects with lactate-induced panic attacks. *American Journal of Psychiatry, 146,* 1304–1306.

Banich, M. T. (1997). *Neuropsychology.* Boston: Houghton Mifflin.

Bannon, M. J., & Roth, R. H. (1983). Pharmacology of neocortical dopamine neurons. *Pharmacology Review, 35,* 53–68.

Barbas, H., & Mesulam, M.-M. (1981). Organization of afferent input to subdivisions of area 8 in the rhesus monkey. *Journal of Comparative Neurology, 200,* 407–431.

Barbas, H., & Mesulam, M.-M. (1985). Cortical afferent input to the principalis region of the rhesus monkey. *Neuroscience, 15,* 619–637.

Barbieri, C., & De Renzi, E. (1989). Patterns of neglect dissociation. *Behavioral Neurology, 2,* 13–24.

Bard, P. (1929). The central organization of the sympathetic system: As indicated by certain physiological observations. *Archives of Neurology and Psychiatry, 22,* 230–246.

Barkley, R. A. (1990). *Attention deficit hyperactivity disorder: A handbook for diagnosis and treatment* (2nd ed.). New York: Guilford Press.

Baron, I. S., Fennell, E. B., & Voeller, K. K. S. (1995). *Pediatric neuropsychology in the medical setting.* New York: Oxford University Press.

Baron-Cohen, S., Leslie, A. M., & Frith, U. (1985). Does the autistic child have a theory of mind? *Cognition, 21,* 37–46.

Bartlett, F. C. (1932). *Remembering: A study in experimental and social psychology.* Cambridge, England: Cambridge University Press.

Basser, L. S. (1962). Hemiplegia of early onset and the faculty of speech with special reference to the effects of hemispherectomy. *Brain, 85,* 427–460.

Baxter, L. R., Jr., Phelps, M. E., Mazziotta, J. C., Guse, B. H., Schwartz, J. M., & Selin, C. E. (1987). Local cerebral glucose metabolic rates in obsessive-compulsive disorder. *Archives of General Psychiatry, 44,* 211–218.

Baxter, L. R., Jr., Phelps, M. E., Mazziotta, J. C., Schwartz, J. M., Gerner, R. H., Selin, C. E., & Sumida, R. M. (1985). Cerebral metabolic rates for glucose in mood disorders: Studies with positron emission tomography and fluorodeoxyglucose F 18. *Archives of General Psychiatry, 42,* 441–447.

Baxter, L. R., Jr., Schwartz, J. M., Mazziotta, J. C., Phelps, M. E., Pahl, J. J., Guze, B. H., & Fairbanks, L. (1988). Cerebral glucose metabolic rates in nondepressed patients with obsessive-compulsive disorder. *American Journal of Psychiatry, 145,* 1560–1563.

Baxter, L. R., Jr., Schwartz, J. M., Phelps, M. E., Mazziotta, J. C., Guze, B. H., Selin, C. E., Gerner, R. H., & Sumida, R. M. (1989). Reduction of prefrontal glucose metabolism common to three types of depression. *Archives of General Psychiatry, 46,* 243–250.

Bay, E. (1953). Disturbances of visual perception and their examination. *Brain, 76,* 515–530.

Baylis, G. C., Rolls, E. T., & Leonard, C. M. (1985). Selectivity between faces in the responses of a population of neurons in the cortex in the superior temporal sulcus of the monkey. *Brain Research, 342,* 91–102.

Bear, D. (1983). Behavioral symptoms in temporal lobe epilepsy [Letter]. *Archives of General Psychiatry, 40,* 467–468.

Bear, D., Levin, K., Blumer, D. Chetham, D., & Ryder, J. (1982). Interictal behavior in hospitalized temporal lobe epileptics: Relationship to ideopathic psychiatric syndromes. *Journal of Neurology, Neurosurgery, and Psychiatry, 45,* 481–488.

Bear, D. M., & Fedio, O. (1977). Quantitative analysis of interictal behavior in temporal lobe epilepsy. *Archives of Neurology, 34,* 454–567.

Bear, M. F., Connors, B. W., & Paradiso, M. A. (1996). *Neuroscience: Exploring the brain.* Baltimore: Williams and Wilkins.

Beattie, A. D., Moore, M. R., Goldberg, A., Finlayson, M. J. W., Mackie, E. M., Graham, J. S., McLaren, D. A., Murdock, R. M., & Stewart, G. T. (1975). Role of chronic low-level lead exposure in the etiology of mental retardation. *Lancet, 1,* 589.

Beatty, J. (1995). *Principles of behavioral neuroscience.* Madison, WI: Brown and Benchmark.

Bechara, A., Damasio, A. R., & Damasio, H. (1994). Insensitivity to future consequences following damage to human prefrontal cortex. *Cognition, 50,* 7–15.

Bechara, A., Tranel, D., Damasio, H., Adolphs, R., Rockland, C., & Damasio, A. R. (1995). Double dissociation of conditioning and declarative knowledge relative to amygdala and hippocampus in humans. *Science, 269,* 1115–1118.

Bekhterev, V. M. (1900). Demonstration eines Geherns mit Zerstorung der vorderen und inneren Theile der Hirnrinde beider Schlafenlappen. *Neurologisches Zentralblatt, 19,* 990–991.

Beck, A. (1967). *Depression: Causes and treatment.* Philadelphia: University of Pennsylvania Press.

Bellugi, U., Klima, E. S., & Wang, P. P. (1996). Cognitive and neural development: Clues from genetically based syndromes. In D. Madnusson (Ed.), *The lifespan development of individuals: Behavioral, neurobiological, and psychosocial perspectives.* New York: Cambridge University Press.

Benes, F. M., & Bird, E. D. (1987). An analysis of the arrangement of neurons in the cingulate cortex of schizophrenic patients. *Archives of General Psychiatry, 44,* 608–616.

Benes, F. M., Davidson, J., & Bird, E. D. (1986). Quantitative cytoarchitectural studies of the cerebral cortex in schizophrenics. *Archives of General Psychiatry, 43,* 31–35.

Benson, D. F., & Greenberg, J. P. (1969). Visual form agnosia. *Archives of Neurology, 20,* 82–89.

Benton, A. (1982). Spatial thinking in neurological patients: Historical aspects. In M. Potegal (Ed.), *Spatial abilities: Development and physiological foundations.* New York: Academic Press.

Benton, A. (1984). Hemispheric dominance before Broca. *Neuropsychologia, 22,* 807–811.

Benton, A. L. (1961). The fiction of the "Gerstman syndrome." *Journal of Neurology, Neurosurgery and Psychiatry, 24,* 176–181.

Benton, A. L. (1968). Differential behavioral effects in frontal lobe disease. *Neuropsychologia, 6,* 53–60.

Benton, A. L. (1975). Developmental dyslexia: Neurological aspects. In W. J. Friedlander (Ed.), *Advances in neurology* (Vol. 7). New York: Raven Press.

Benton, A. L. (1980). The neuropsychology of face recognition. *American Psychologist, 35,* 176–186.

Benton, A. L. (1985). Reflections on the Gerstman syndrome. In L. Costa & O. Spreen (Eds.), *Studies in neuropsychology: Selected papers of Arthur Benton.* New York: Oxford University Press.

Benton, A. L., Hannay, J., & Varney, N. R. (1975). Visual perception of line direction in patients with unilateral brain disease. *Neurology, 25,* 907–910.

Benton, A. L., & Van Allen, M. W. (1972). Prosopagnosia and facial discrimination. *Journal of Neurological Sciences, 15,* 167–172.

Benton, A. L., Varney, N. R., & Hamsher, K. de S. (1978). Visuo-spatial judgment: A clinical test. *Archives of Neurology* (Chicago), *35,* 364–367.

Berman, K. F., Doran, A. R., Pickar, D., & Weinberger, D. R. (1993). Is the mechanism of prefrontal hypofunction in depression the same as in schizophrenia? Regional cerebral bloodflow during cognitive activation. *British Journal of Psychiatry, 162,* 183–192.

Berman, K. F., & Weinberger, D. R. (1986). Cerebral blood flow studies in schizophrenia. In H. A. Nasralla & D. R. Weinberger (Eds.), *The neurology of schizophrenia* (pp. 277–308). Amsterdam: Elsevier.

Berman, K. F., & Weinberger, D. R. (1992). Regional cerebral blood flow in monozygotic twins concordant and discordant for schizophrenia. *Archives of General Psychiatry, 49,* 927–934.

Berman, K. F., Zec, R. F., & Weinberger, D. R. (1986). Physiological dysfunction in dorsolateral prefrontal cortex in schizophrenia: II. Role of neuroleptic treatment, attention and mental effort. *Archives of General Psychiatry, 43,* 126–135.

Bernstein, A. S., Riedel, J. A., & Graae, F. (1988). Schizophrenia is associated with altered orienting activity. *Journal of Abnormal Psychology, 97,* 3–12.

Berti, A., Maravita, A., Frassinetti, F., & Umilta, C. C. (1995). Unilateral neglect can be affected by stimuli in the neglected field. *Cortex, 31,* 331–343.

Bettelheim, B. (1959). Joey: A mechanical boy. *Scientific American,* March. [Reprinted in R. C. Atkinson (Ed.). (1971). *Contemporary psychology.* San Francisco: W. H. Freeman].

Bettelheim, B. (1967). *The empty fortress: Autism and the birth of the self.* New York: Free Press.

Bianchi, L. (1895). The functions of the frontal lobes. *Brain, 18,* 497–530.

Bianchi, L. (1922). *The mechanism of the brain and the function of the frontal lobes.* New York: Wood.

Biederman, J., Newcom, J., & Sprich, S. (1991). Comorbidity of attention deficit hyperactivity disorder with conduct, depressive, anxiety, and other disorders. *American Journal of Psychiatry, 148,* 564–577.

Bigler, E. D. (1992). The neurobiology and neuropsychology of adult learning disorders. *Journal of Learning Disabilities, 25,* 488–506.

Bisiach, E., Capitani, E., Colombo, A., & Spinnler, H. (1976). Halving a horizontal segment: A study on hemisphere damaged patients with focal lesions. *Archives Swisses de Neurologie Neurochirurgie et de Psychiatre, 118,* 119–206.

Bisiach, E., & Luzzatti, C. (1978). Unilateral neglect in representational space. *Cortex, 14,* 129–133.

Bisiach, E., Luzzatti, C., & Peranni, D. (1979). Unilateral neglect, representational schema and consciousness. *Brain, 102,* 609–618.

Bisiach, E., Nichelli, P., & Spinnler, H. (1976). Hemispheric functional asymmetry in visual discrimination between univariate stimuli: An analysis of sensitivity and response criterion. *Neuropsychologia, 14,* 335–342.

Bjorklund, A., & Stenevi, U. (1984). Intracerebral implants: Neuronal replacement and reconstruction of damaged circuitries. *Annual Review of Neuroscience, 7,* 279–308.

Bjorklund, A., Stenevi, U., Schmidt, R. H., Dunnett, S. B., & Gage, F. H. (1983). Intracerebral grafting of neural suspensions. I. Introduction and general method of preparation. *Acta Physiologica Scandanavica, 522* (Suppl.), 1–8.

Black, D. W., & Andreasen, N. C. (1994). Schizophrenia, schizophreniform disorder, and delusional paranoid disorder. In J. A. Talbott, R. E. Hales, & S. C. Yudofsky (Eds.), *American Psychiatric Press textbook of psychiatry* (pp. 411–463). Washington, DC: American Psychiatric Press.

Black, D. W., & Noyes, R. (1990). Comorbidity in obsessive-compulsive disorder. In J. D. Maser & C. D. Cloninger (Eds.), *Comorbidity in anxiety and mood disorders* (pp. 305–316). Washington, DC: American Psychiatric Press.

Blakemore, C. (1977). *Mechanisms of the mind.* Cambridge, England: Cambridge University Press.

Blanchard, R. J., Blanchard, D. C., & Fial, R. A. (1970). Hippocampal lesions in rats and their effect on activity: Avoidance and aggression. *Journal of Comparative Physiological Psychology, 71*(1), 92–102.

Bleuler, E. (1950). *Dementia praecox, or the group of schizophrenias* (J. Zinkin & N. D. C. Lewis, Trans.). New York: International Universities Press. (Original work published 1911).

Blonder, I. X., Bowers, D., & Heilman, K. M. (1991). The role of the right hemisphere in emotional communication. *Brain, 114,* 1115–1127.

Blum, R. A. (1952). Effects of subtotal lesions of frontal granular cortex on delayed reaction in monkeys. *AMA Archives of Neurology and Psychiatry, 67,* 375–386.

Blumer, D., & Benson, D. F. (1975). Personality changes with frontal and temporal lobe lesions. In D. F. Benson & D. Blumer (Eds.), *Psychiatric aspects of neurological disease.* New York: Grune and Stratton.

Bodamer, J. (1947). Die Prosopagnosie. *Archiv fur Psychiatrie und Zeitschrift fur Neurologie, 179,* 6–54.

Bogerts, B., Meetz, E., & Schonfeldt-Bausch, R. (1985). Basal ganglia and limbic system pathology in schizophrenia: A morphometric study of brain volume and shrinkage. *Archives of General Psychiatry, 42,* 784–791.

Bonin, G. von, & Bailey, P. (1947). *The neocortex of* Macaca mulatta. Urbana: University of Illinois Press.

Bornstein, B. (1963). Prosopagnosia. In L. Halpern (Ed.), *Problems of dynamic neurology* (pp. 283–318). Jerusalem: Hadassah Medical Organization.

Bornstein, B., Stroka, H., & Munitz, H. (1969). Prosopagnosia with animal face agnosia. *Cortex, 5,* 164–169.

Borod, J. C. (1993). Cerebral mechanisms underlying facial, prosodic, and lexical emotional expression: A review of neuropsychological studies and methodological issues. *Neuropsychology, 7,* 445–463.

Borod, J. C., Koff, E., & Buck, R. (1986). The neuropsychology of facial expression in normal and brain-damaged subjects. In P. Blanck, R. Buck, & R. Rosenthal (Eds.), *Nonverbal communication in the clinical context.* University Park: Pennsylvania State University Press.

Borod, J. C., Koff, E., & Caron, H. (1983). Right hemisphere specialization for the expression and appreciation of emotion: A focus on the face. In E. Perecnan (Ed.), *Cognitive processing in the right hemisphere.* New York: Academic Press.

Borod, J. C., Koff, E., Lorch, M. P., & Nicholas, M. (1986). The expression and perception of facial emotion in brain-damaged patients. *Neuropsychologia, 24,* 345–348.

Bothwell, M. (1995). Functional interactions of neurotrophins and neurotrophin receptors. *Annual Review of Neuroscience, 18,* 223–253.

Boucugnani, L. L., & Jones, R. W. (1989). Behaviors analogous to frontal lobe dysfunction in children with attention deficit hyperactivity disorder. *Archives of Clinical Neuropsychology, 4,* 161–174.

Bowers, D., Bauer, R. M., & Heilman, K. M. (1993). The nonverbal affect lexicon: Theoretical perspectives from neuropsychological studies of affect perception. *Neuropsychology, 7,* 433–444.

Bradley, C. (1937). The behavior of children receiving benzedrine. *American Journal of Psychiatry, 94,* 577–585.

Brain, W. R. (1941). Visual disorientation with special reference to lesions in the right cerebral hemisphere. *Brain, 64,* 244–272.

Breasted, J. H. (1930). *The Edwin Smith Surgical Papyrus.* Chicago: University of Chicago Press.

Breiter, H. C., Rauch, S. L., Kwong, K. K., Baker, J. R., Weisskoff, R. M., Kennedy, D. N., Kendrick, A. D., Davis, T. L., Jiang, A. P., Cohen, M. S., Stern, C. E., Belliveau, J. W., Baer, L., O'Sullivan, R. L., Savafe, C. R., Jenike, M. A., & Rosen, B. R. (1996). Functional magnetic resonance imaging of symptom production in obsessive-compulsive disorder. *Archives of General Psychiatry, 53,* 595–606.

Brickner, R. M. (1936). *The intellectual functions of the frontal lobes.* New York: Macmillan.

Bridges, P. K., Goktepe, E. O., & Maratos, J. (1973). A comparative review of patients with obsessional neurosis and with depression treated by psychosurgery. *British Journal of Psychiatry, 123,* 663–674.

Broca, P. (1861a). Loss of speech, chronic softening, and partial destruction of the left anterior lobe of the brain. Translated from *Bulletins de la Societe d'Anthropologie, 2,* 285–288.

Broca, P. (1861b). New observations of aphasia produced by a lesion of the second and third frontal convolutions. Translated from *Bulletin et Manoires de la Societe Anatomique de Paris, 6,* 398–407.

Broca, P. (1878). Anatomie compare de circonvolutions cerebrales. Le grand lobe limbique et la scissure limbique dans le serie des mammiferes. *Review des Anthropologie, 1,* 385–498.

Brodal, A. (1982). *Neurological anatomy.* New York: Oxford University Press.

Brodmann, K. (1912). Neue Ergebnisse uber die vergleichende histologische Lokalisation der Grosshirnrinde mit bisonderer Berucksichtigung des Stirnhirns. *Anatomischer Anzeiger (Suppl.), 41,* 157–216.

Brodmann, K. (1925). *Vergleichende Lokalisationslehre der Grosshirnrinde.* Leipzig, Germany: Barth.

Brown, J. W. (1972). *Aphasia, apraxia and agnosia: Clinical and theoretical aspects.* Springfield, IL: Thomas.

Brown, R. M., Crane, A. M., & Goldman, P. S. (1979). Regional distribution of monoamines in the cerebral cortex and subcortical structures of the rhesus monkey: Concentrations and in vivo synthesis rates. *Brain Research, 168,* 133–150.

Brownell, H. H., Michel, D., Powelson, J., & Gardner H. (1983). Surprise but not coherence: Sensitivity to verbal humor in right hemisphere patients. *Brain and Language, 18,* 20–27.

Brozoski, T., Brown, R. M., Rosvold, H. E., & Goldman, P. S. (1979). Cognitive deficit caused by depletion of dopamine in prefrontal cortex of rhesus monkey. *Science, 205,* 929–931.

Bruce, C. J., & Goldberg, M. E. (1984). Physiology of the frontal eye fields. *Trends in Neurosciences, 7,* 436–441.

Bruce, C. J., & Goldberg, M. E. (1985). Primate frontal eye fields: I. Single neurons discharging before saccades. *Journal of Neurophysiology, 53,* 603–635.

Bruce, C. J., Goldberg, M. E., Bushnell, M. C., & Stanton, G. B. (1985). Primate frontal eye fields: II. Physiological and anatomical correlates of electrically evoked eye movements. *Journal of Neurophysiology, 54,* 714–734.

Bruder, G. E. (1995). Cerebral laterality and psychopathology: Perceptual and event-related potential asymmetries in affective and schizophrenic disorders. In R. J. Davidson & K. Hugdahl (Eds.), *Brain asymmetry.* Cambridge, MA: MIT Press.

Brumbach, R. A. (1983). Personality analysis of epileptics. *Archives of Neurology, 40,* 658–659.

Bruyer, R., Laterre, C., Seron, X., Feyereisne, P., Strypstein, E., Pierrard, E., & Recten, D. (1983). A case of prosopagnosia with some preserved covert remembrance of familiar faces. *Brain and Cognition, 2,* 257–284.

Bryden, M. P. (1988). Does laterality make any difference? Thoughts on the relation between cerebral asymmetry and reading. In D. F. Molfese & S. J. Segalowitz (Eds.), *Brain lateralization in children: Developmental implications.* New York: Guilford Press.

Bryden, M. P., & Ley, R. G. (1983). Right hemisphere involvement in imagery and affect. In Perecman (Ed.), *Cognitive processing in the right hemisphere.* New York: Academic Press.

Bub, D. N., Black, S., & Howell, J. (1989). Word recognition and orthographic context effects in a letter-by-letter reader. *Brain Language, 36,* 357–376.

Buchsbaum, M. S., DeLisi, L. E., Holcomb, H. H., Cappelletti, J., King, A. C., Johnson, J., Hazlett, E., Dowling-Zimmerman, S., Post, R. M., Morihisa, J., Carpenter, W., Cohen, R., Pickar, D., Weinberger, D. R., Margolin, R., & Kessler, R. M. (1984). Anteroposterior gradients in cerebral glucose use in schizophrenia and affective disorders. *Archives of General Psychiatry, 41,* 1159–1166.

Buchsbaum, M. S., Ingvar, D. H., Kessler, R., Watters, R. N., Cappelletti, J., van Kammen, D. P., King, A. C., & Johnson, J. L. (1982). Cerebral glucography with positron tomography. *Archives of General Psychiatry, 39,* 251–259.

Buchsbaum, M. S., Wu, J., DeLisi, L. E., Holcomb, H., Kessler, R., Johnson, K., King, A. C., Hazlett, F., Langston, K., & Post, R. M. (1986). Frontal cortex and basal ganglia metabolic rates assessed by positron emission tomography with [18F]2-deoxyglucose in affective illness. *Journal of Affective Disorders, 10,* 137–152.

Buchtel, H., Campari, F., De Risio, C., & Rota, R. (1978). Hemispheric differences in discriminative reaction time to facial expressions. *Italian Journal of Psychology, 5,* 159–169.

Buckner, R., Paterson, S. E., Ojemann, J. G., Miezin, F. M., Squire, L. R., & Raichle, M. E. (1995). Functional anatomical studies of explicit and implicit memory retrieval tasks. *Journal of Neuroscience, 15,* 19–29.

Buffery, A. W. H. (1976). Sex differences in the neurobiological development of verbal and spatial skills. In R. M. Knights & D. J. Bakker (Eds.), *The neuropsychology of learning disorders: Theoretical approaches.* Baltimore, MD: University Park Press.

Butters, N., & Cermak, L. S. (1986). A case study of forgetting of autobiographical knowledge: Implications for the study of anterograde amnesia. In D. C. Rubin (Ed.), *Autobiographical memory* (pp. 253–272). Cambridge, England: Cambridge University Press.

Butters, N., & Grady, M. (1977). Effect of predistractor delays on the short-term memory performance of patients with Korsakoff's and Huntington's disease. *Neuropsychologia, 15,* 701–706.

Byring, F. K., & Michelson, D. E. (1984). Prevalence of dyslexia in relatives of dyslexic children. *Acta Psychologica Scandinavica, 46,* 105.

Cadoret, R. J., Cummingham, L., Loftus, R., & Edwards, J. (1975). Studies of adoptees from psychiatrically disturbed biological parents: II. Temperament, hyperactive, antisocial and developmental variables. *Journal of Pediatrics, 87,* 301.

Campbell, R. (1978). Asymmetries in interpreting and expressing a posed facial expression. *Cortex, 19,* 327–342.

Cannon, T. D., Mednick, S. A., & Parnas, J. (1990). Antecedents of predominantly negative- and predominantly positive-symptom schizophrenia in a high-risk population. *Archives of General Psychiatry, 47,* 622–632.

Cannon, W. B. (1927). The James-Lange theory of emotion: A critical examination and an alternative theory. *American Journal of Physiology, 39,* 106–124.

Caplan, D., & Waters, G. S. (1990). Short-term memory and language comprehension: A critical review of the neuropsychological literature. In T. Vallar & T. Shallice (Eds.), *Neuropsychological impairment in short-term memory* (pp. 337–389). Cambridge, England: Cambridge University Press.

Caramazza, A., Miceli, G., Silveri, M. C., & Laudanna, A. (1985). Reading mechanisms and the organization of the lexicon: Evidence from acquired dyslexia. *Cognitive Neuropsychology, 2,* 81–114.

Caramazza, A., Miceli, G., Villa, G., & Romani, C. (1987). The role of the graphemic buffer in spelling: Evidence from a case of acquired dysgraphia. *Cognition, 26,* 59–85.

Carlson, A. (1988). The current status of the dopamine hypothesis of schizophrenia. *Neuropsychopharmacology, 1,* 179–203.

Carlson, N. R. (1999). *Physiological psychology.* Boston: Allyn and Bacon.

Carpenter, M. B. (1976). *Human neuroanatomy* (7th ed.). Baltimore: Williams and Wilkins.

Carter, C. S., Mintun, M., Nichols, T., & Cohen, J. D. (1997). Anterior cingulate gyrus dysfunction and selective atten-tion deficits in schizophrenia: $^{15}OH_2O$ PET study during single-trial Stroop task performance. *American Journal of Psychiatry, 154,* 1670–1675.

Casey, J. E., Rourke, B. P., & Picard, E. M. (1991). Syndrome of nonverbal learning disabilities: Age differences in neuropsychological, academic, and socioemotional functioning. *Development and Psychopathology, 3,* 329–345.

Casiro, O. G., Moddeman, D. M., Stanwick, R. S., & Cheang, M. S. (1991). The natural history and predictive value of early language delays in very low birth weight children. *Early Human Development, 26,* 45–50.

Castellucci, V. F., Carew, T. J., & Kandel, E. R. (1978). Cellular analysis of long-term habituation of the gill-withdrawal reflex of *Aplysia californica. Science, 202,* 1306–308.

Cavada, C., & Goldman-Rakic, P. S. (1985). Parieto-prefrontal connections in the monkey: Topographic distribution within the prefrontal cortex of sectors connected with the lateral and medial posterior parietal cortex. *Society for Neuroscience Abstracts, 11,* 323.

Cermak, L. S., & O'Connor, M. (1983). The anterograde and retrograde retrieval ability of a patient with amnesia due to encephalitis. *Neuropsychologia, 21,* 213–234.

Chao, L. L., & Knight, R. T. (1995). Human prefrontal lesions increase distractibility to irrelevant sensory inputs. *NeuroReport, 6,* 1605–1610.

Chedru, F., LeBlanc, M., & Lhemitte, F. (1973). Visual searching in normal and brain damaged subjects: Contributions to the study of unilateral inattention. *Cortex, 9,* 94–111.

Chelune, G. J., Ferguson, W., Koon, R., & Dickey, T. O. (1986). Frontal lobe disinhibition in attention deficit disorder. *Child Psychiatry and Human Development, 16,* 221–234.

Chess, S., Fernandez, F., & Korn, S. J. (1971). *Psychiatric disorders of children with congenital rubella.* New York: Brunner/Mazel.

Chomsky, N. (1959). Review of B. F. Skinner, *Verbal Learning. Language, 35,* 26–58.

Chomsky, N. (1975). *Reflections on language.* New York: Pantheon.

Chomsky, N. (1988). *Language and problems of knowledge: The Manaqua lectures.* Cambridge, MA: MIT Press.

Chomsky, N. (1991). Linguistics and cognitive science: Problems and mysteries. In A. Kasher (Ed.), *The Chomskyan turn.* Cambridge, MA: Blackwell.

Chomsky, N. (1993). *Language and thought.* Wakefield, RI, and London: Moyer Bell.

Chorover, S. L., & Cole, M. (1966). Delayed alternation performance in patients with cerebral lesions. *Neuropsychologia, 4,* 1–7.

Churchland, P. S. (1986). *Neurophilosophy: Toward a unified science of the mind-brain.* Cambridge, MA: MIT Press.

Cicone, M., Wapner, W., & Gardner, H. (1980). Sensitivity to emotional expression and situations in organic patients. *Cortex, 16,* 145–168.

Claparède, E. (1911). Recognition and "me-ness." In D. Rapaport (Ed.). (1951). *Organization and pathology of thought.* New York: Columbia University Press.

Cohen, N. J. (1981). *Neuropsychological evidence for a distinction between procedural and declarative knowledge in human memory and amnesia.* Unpublished doctoral dissertation, University of California, San Diego.

Cohen, N. J. (1984). Evidence for multiple memory systems. In L. R. Squire & N. Butters (Eds.), *Neuropsychology of memory* (pp. 83–103). New York: Guilford Press.

Cohen, N. J. (1997). Memory. In M. T. Banich, *Neuropsychology.* Boston: Houghton Mifflin.

Cohen, N. J., & Corkin, S. (1981). The amnesic patient H. M.: Learning and retention of cognitive skills. *Society for Neuroscience Abstracts, 7,* 517–518.

Cohen, N. J., & Eichenbaum, H. (1993). *Memory, amnesia, and the hippocampal system.* Cambridge, MA: MIT Press.

Cohen, N. J., Eichenbaum, H. E., Deacedo, B. S., & Corkin, S. (1985). Different memory systems underlying acquisition of procedural and declarative knowledge. *Annals of the New York Academy of Sciences, 444,* 54–71.

Cohen, N. J., Ramzy, C., Hu, Z., Tomaso, H., Strupp, J., Erhard, P., Anderson, P., & Ugurbil, K. (1994). Hippocampal activation in fMRI evoked by demand for declarative memory-based binding of multiple streams of information. *Society for Neuroscience Abstracts, 20,* 1290.

Cohen, N. J., & Squire, L. R. (1980). Procedural learning and retention of pattern-analyzing skill in amnesia: Dissociation of knowing how and knowing that. *Science, 210,* 207–209.

Cohen, N. J., & Squire, L. R. (1981). Retrograde amnesia and remote memory impairment. *Neuropsychologia, 19,* 337–356.

Cohen, R. M., Semple, W. E., Gross, M., Nordahl, T. E., King, A. C., Pickar, D., & Post, R. M. (1989). Evidence for common alterations in cerebral glucose metabolism in major affective disorders and schizophrenia. *Neuropsychopharmacology, 2,* 241–254.

Cole, M., & Perez-Cruet, J. (1964). Prosopagnosia. *Neuropsychologia, 2,* 237–246.

Cole, M., Schutta, H. S., & Warrington, E. K. (1962). Visual disorientation in homonymous half fields. *Neurology, 12,* 257–263.

Colombo, A., De Renzi, E., & Faglioni, P. (1976). The occurrence of visual neglect in patients with unilateral cerebral disease. *Cortex, 12,* 221–231.

Comings, D. E., & Comings, B. G. (1984). Tourette's syndrome and attention deficit disorder with hyperactivity: Are they genetically related? *Journal of the American Academy of Child Psychiatry, 23,* 138–146.

Condini, A., Axia, G., Cattelan, C., & D'Urso, M. R. (1991). Development of language in 18 30-month-old HIV-1-infected but not ill children. *AIDS, 5,* 735–739.

Conel, J. (1939–1967). *The postnatal development of the human cerebral cortex* (Vols. 1–8). Cambridge, MA: Harvard University Press.

Conoley, J. C., & Sheridan, J. C. (1996). Pediatric traumatic brain injury: Challenges and interventions for families. *Journal of Learning Disabilities, 29*(6), 662–669.

Cooper, J. R., Bloom, F. E., & Roth, R. H. (1991). *The biochemical basis of neuropharmacology.* New York: Oxford University Press.

Cooper, L. A., & Shepard, R. N. (1973). The time required to prepare for a rotated stimulus. *Memory and Cognition, 1,* 246–250.

Cope, D. N. (1995). The effectiveness of traumatic brain injury rehabilitation: A review. *Brain Injury, 9,* 649–670.

Coplan, J. D., Gorman, J. M., & Klein, D. F. (1992). Serotonin related functions in panic-anxiety: A critical review. *Neuropsychopharmacology, 6,* 189–200.

Corballis, M. C., & Sergent, J. (1988). Imagery in commissurotomized patients. *Neuropsychologia, 26,* 13–26.

Corballis, M. C., & Sergent, J. (1989). Hemispheric specialization for mental rotation. *Cortex, 25,* 15–25.

Corbetta, M., Miezen, F. M., Dobmeyer, S., Shulman, G. L., & Peterson, S. E. (1991). Selective and divided attention during visual discriminations of shape, color, and speed: Functional anatomy by positron emission tomography. *Journal of Neuroscience, 11,* 2383–2402.

Corbetta, M., Miezen, F. M., Schulman, G. L., & Petersen, S. E. (1993). A PET study of visuospatial attention. *Journal of Neuroscience, 13,* 1202–1226.

Corkin, S. (1965). Tactually-guided maze learning in man: Effects of unilateral cortical excisions and bilateral hippocampal lesions. *Neuropsychologia, 3,* 339–351.

Corkin, S. (1968). Acquisition of motor skills after bilateral medial temporal lobe excision. *Neuropsychologia, 6,* 255–265.

Corkin, S. (1984). Lasting consequences of bilateral medial temporal lobectomy: Clinical course and experimental findings in H. M. *Seminars in Neurology, 4,* 249–259.

Corkin, S., Amaral, D., Gonzalez, R., Johnson, K., et al. (1997). H. M.'s medial temporal-lobe lesion: Findings from magnetic resonance imaging. *Journal of Neuroscience, 17,* 3964–3979.

Corkin, S., Milner, B., & Taylor, L. (1973). Bilateral sensory loss after unilateral cerebral lesions in man. *Transactions of the American Neurological Association, 98,* 25–29.

Corsi, P. (1972). *Human memory and the medial temporal region of the brain.* Unpublished doctoral thesis, McGill University, Montreal, Canada.

Corsi, P. (Ed.) (1991). *The enchanted loom: Chapters in the history of neuroscience.* New York: Oxford University Press.

Corton, P. (1994). Constellation of risks and processes seen in search for Alzheimer's clues. *Journal of the American Medical Association, 271,* 88–91.

Costa, E. (1985). Benzodiazepine-GABA interactions: A model to investigate the neurobiology of anxiety. In A. H. Tuma & J. D. Maser (Eds.), *Anxiety and the anxiety disorders.* Hillsdale, NJ: Erlbaum.

Costa, L. D., & Vaughan, H. G. (1962). Performance of patients with localized cerebral lesions: Verbal and perceptual tests. *Journal of Nervous and Mental Disease, 134,* 162–168.

Courchesne, E. (1991a). Chronology of human brain development: Event-related potential, positron emission tomography, myelinogenesis, and synaptogenesis studies. In J. W. Rohrbaugh, R. Parasuraman, & R. Johnson (Eds.), *Event-related brain potentials: Basic issues and applications.* New York: Oxford University Press.

Courchesne, E. (1991b). Neuroanatomic imaging in autism. *Pediatrics, 87,* 781–790.

Cowan, W. M. (1979). The development of the brain. In *The brain: A* Scientific American *book.* New York: W. H. Freeman.

Cox, A., Rutter, M., Newman, S., & Bartak, L. (1975). A comparative study of infantile autism and specific developmental receptive language disorder: II. Parental characteristics. *British Journal of Psychiatry, 126,* 146–159.

Coyle, J. T., Price, D., & Delong, M. R. (1983). Alzheimer's disease: A disorder of cholinergic innervation. *Science, 219,* 1184–1190.

Crary, M. A., & Heilman, K. M. (1988). Letter imagery deficits in a case of pure apraxic agraphia. *Brain and Language, 34,* 147–156.

Critchley, M., & Critchley, E. A. (1978). *Dyslexia defined.* London: Heineman.

Crow, T. J. (1980). Molecular pathology of schizophrenia: More than one disease process. *British Medical Journal, 137,* 383–386.

Crow, T. J. (1982a). The biology of schizophrenia. *Experientia, 38,* 1275–1282.

Crow, T. J. (1982b). Two dimensions of pathology in schizophrenia. *Psychopharmacology Bulletin, 18,* 22–29.

Crow, T. J. (1985). The two syndrome concept: Origins and current status. *Schizophrenia Bulletin, 11,* 471–486.

Crow, T. J., & Johnstone, E. (1987). Schizophrenia: Nature of the disease process and its biological correlates. In F. Plum (Ed.), *Handbook of neurology: The nervous system: Vol. V. Higher functions of the brain* (pp. 843–869). Bethesda, MD: American Physiological Society.

Cummings, J. L. (1993). Frontal-subcortical circuits in human behavior. *Archives of Neurology, 50,* 873–880.

Dalrymple, A. J. C., Kalders, A. S., Jones, R. D., & Watson, R. W. (1994). A central executive deficit in patients with Parkinson's disease. *Journal of Neurology, Neurosurgery and Psychiatry, 57,* 360–367.

Damasio, A. (1999). *The feeling of what happens.* New York: Harcourt.

Damasio, A. R. (1990). Category-related recognition deficits as clues to the neural substrates of knowledge. *Trends in Neuroscience, 13,* 95–98.

Damasio, A. R. (1992). Aphasia. *New England Journal of Medicine, 326,* 531–539.

Damasio, A. R. (1994). *Descartes' error: Emotion, reason and the human brain.* New York: Avon Books.

Damasio, A. R. (1995). On some functions of the human prefrontal cortex. In J. Grafman, K. J. Holyoak, & F. Boller (Eds.), *Structure and functions of the human prefrontal cortex* (pp. 241–251). New York: New York Academy of Sciences.

Damasio, A. R., Damasio, H., & Chui, H. C. (1980). Neglect following damage to the frontal lobe or basal ganglia. *Neuropsychologia, 18,* 123–132.

Damasio, A. R., Damasio, H., & Van Hoesen, G. W. (1982). Prosopagnosia: Anatomic basis and behavioral mechanisms. *Neurology, 32,* 331–341.

Damasio, A. R., Tranel, D., & Damasio, H. (1989). Amnesia caused by *Herpes simplex* encephalitis, infarction in basal forebrain, Alzheimer's disease and anoxia/ischemia. In F. Boller & J Graffman (Eds.), *Handbook of neuropsychology* (Vol. 3, pp. 149–165). Amsterdam: Elsevier.

Damasio, A. R., & Van Hoesen, G. W. (1983). Emotional disturbances associated with lesions of the limbic frontal lobe. In K. M. Heilman & P. Satz (Eds.), *Neuropsychology of human emotion* (pp. 85–110). New York: Guilford Press.

Damasio, H., Grabowski, T., Frank, R., Galaburda, A. M., & Damasio, A. R. (1994). The return of Phineas Gage: The skull of a famous patient yields clues about the brain. *Science, 264,* 1102–1105.

D'Amato, R. C., & Rothlisberg, B. A. (1996). How education should respond to students with traumatic brain injury. *Journal of Learning Disabilities, 29*(6), 670–683.

David, O., Clark, J., & Voeller, K. (1972). Lead and hyperactivity. *Lancet, 2,* 900–903.

Davidson, R. J. (1992). Anterior cerebral asymmetry and the nature of emotion. *Brain and Cognition, 20,* 125–151.

Davis, H. P., & Squire, L. R. (1984). Protein synthesis and memory. *Psychological Bulletin, 96,* 518–559.

Davis, J. M. (1978). Dopamine theory of schizophrenia: A two-factor theory. In L. C. Wynne, R. L. Cromwell, & S. Matthysse (Eds.), *The nature of schizophrenia.* New York: Wiley.

Davis, K. L., Kahn, R. S., Ko, G., & Davidson, M. (1991). Dopamine in schizophrenia: A review and reconceptualization. *American Journal of Psychiatry, 148,* 1474–1486.

Davis, M. (1992a). The role of the amygdala in conditioned fear. In J. P. Aggleton (Ed.), *The amygdala: Neurobiological aspects of emotion, memory and mental dysfunction* (pp. 255–306). New York: Wiley-Liss.

Davis, M. (1992b). The role of the amygdala in fear-potentiated startle: Implications for animal models of anxiety. *Trends in Pharmacological Science, 13,* 35–41.

De Renzi, E. (1985). Methods of limb apraxia examination and their bearing on the interpretation of the disorder. In E. Roy (Ed.), *Neuropsychological studies of apraxia and related disorders* (pp. 45–64). Amsterdam: Elsevier North-Holland.

De Renzi, E. (1986). Current issues in prosopagnosia. In H. D. Ellis, M. A. Jeeves, F. Newcombe, & and A. Young (Eds.), *Aspects of face processing.* Dordrecht, The Netherlands: Martinus Nijhoff.

De Renzi, E., Faglioni, P., Lodesani, M., & Vecchi, A. (1983). Performance of left brain damaged patients on imitation of simple movements and movement sequences: Frontal and parietal injured patients compared. *Cortex, 14,* 41–49.

De Renzi, E., Faglioni, P., & Scotti, G. (1970). Hemispheric contribution to exploration of space through the visual and tactile modality. *Cortex, 6,* 191–203.

De Renzi, E., Faglioni, P., & Scotti, G. (1971). Judgment of spatial orientation in patients with focal brain damage. *Journal of Neurology, Neurosurgery and Psychiatry, 34,* 489–495.

De Renzi, E., Faglioni, P., & Sorgato, P. (1982). Modality specific and supramodal mechanisms of apraxia. *Brain, 105,* 301–312.

De Renzi, E., Liotti, M., & Nichelli, P. (1987). Semantic amnesia with preservation of autobiographic memory: A case study. *Cortex, 23,* 575–597.

De Renzi, E., & Lucchelli, F. (1988). Ideational apraxia. *Brain, 111,* 1173–1188.

De Renzi, E., Motti, F., & Nichelli, P. (1980). Imitating gestures: A quantitative approach to ideomotor apraxia. *Archives of Neurology* (Chicago), *37,* 6–10.

De Renzi, E., Scotti, G., & Spinnler, H. (1969). Perceptual and associative disorders of visual recognition: Relationship to the site of lesion. *Neurology, 19,* 634–642.

De Renzi, E., & Spinnler, H. (1966). Visual recognition in unilateral cerebral disease. *Journal of Nervous and Mental Disorders, 142,* 513–525.

DeArmond, S. J., Fusco, M. M., & Dewey, M. M. (1974). *Structure of the human brain.* New York: Oxford University Press.

Decety, J., Perani, D., Jeannerod, M., Bettinardi, V., Tadary, B., Woods, R., Mazziota, S. C., & Fazio, E. (1994). Mapping motor representations with positron emission tomography. *Nature, 371,* 600–602.

Dee, H. L. (1970). Visuoconstructive and visuoperceptive deficit in patients with unilateral cerebral disease. *Neuropsychologia, 8,* 305–314.

Dejarine, J. (1892). Contribution a l'etude anatomoclinique et clinique des differentes varietes de cecite verbale. *Memoires de la Societe de Biologie, 4,* 61–90.

Dekosky, S. T., Heilman, K. M., Bowers, D., & Valenstein, E. (1980). Recognition and discrimination of emotional faces and pictures. *Brain and Language, 9,* 206–214.

Delis, D. C., Squire, L. R., Bihrle, A., & Massman, P. (1992). Componential analysis of problem-solving ability: Performance of patients with frontal lobe damage and amnesic patients on a new sorting test. *Neuropsychologia, 30,* 683–697.

DeLisi, L. E., Holcomb, H. H., Cohen, R. M., Pickar, D., Carpenter, W., Morihisa, J. M., King, A. C., Kessler, R., & Buchsbaum, M. S. (1985). Positron emission tomography in schizophrenic patients with or without neuroleptic medication. *Journal of Cerebral Blood Flow and Metabolism, 5,* 201–206.

DeLong, G. R. (1992). Autism, amnesia, hippocampus, and learning. *Neuroscience and Biobehavioral Reviews, 16,* 63–70.

DeMyer, M., Pontinis, W., Norton, J., Barton, S., Allen, J., & Steele, R. (1972). Parental practices and innate activity in autistic and brain damaged infants. *Journal of Autism and Childhood Schizophrenia, 2,* 49–66.

Denny-Brown, D. (1951). The frontal lobes and their function. In A. Feiling (Ed.), *Modern trends in neurology.* New York: Hoeber.

Descartes, R. (1644). *The principles of philosophy.* English translation in E. S. Haldane & G. R. T. Ross. (1911). *The philosophical works of Descartes,* 2 vols. (Reprinted 1968. Cambridge, England: Cambridge University Press).

Desimone, R., Albright, T. D., Gross, C. D., & Bruce, C. (1984). Stimulus-selective responses of inferior temporal neurons in the macaque. *Journal of Neuroscience, 4,* 2051–2062.

Desimone, R., Miller, E. K., Chelazzi, L., & Lueschow, A. (1995). Multiple memory systems in the visual cortex. In M. S. Gazzaniga (Ed.), *The cognitive neurosciences* (pp. 475–486). Cambridge, MA: MIT Press.

D'Esposito, M., Detre, J., Alsop, D., Shin, R., Atlas, S., & Grossman, M. (1995). The neural basis of the central executive system of working memory. *Nature, 378,* 279–281.

Diamond, A. (Ed.). (1990). *The development and the neural basis of the higher cognitive processes. Annals of the New York Academy of Sciences.* New York: New York Academy of Sciences.

Diamond, D. M., & Weinberger, N. M. (1986). Classical conditioning rapidly induces changes in frequency receptive fields of single neurons in secondary and ventral ectosylvian cortical fields. *Brain Research, 372,* 357–360.

Dicks, D., Myers, R., & Kling, A. (1969). Uncus and amygdala lesions: Effects on social behavior in the free-ranging rhesus monkey. *Science, 165,* 69–71.

Dimond, S. J., & Farrington, L. (1977). Emotional response to films shown to the right and left hemisphere of the brain measured by heart rate. *Acta Psychologia, 41,* 255–260.

Dimond, S. J., Farrington, L., & Johnson, P. (1976). Differing emotional response from right and left hemispheres. *Nature, 261,* 690–692.

Dobbs, A. R., & Rule, B. G. (1987). Prospective memory and self-reports of memory abilities in older adults. *Canadian Journal of Psychology, 41,* 209–222.

Don, A., & Rourke, B. P. (1995). Fetal alcohol syndrome. In B. P. Rourke (Ed.), *Syndrome of nonverbal learning disabilities.* New York: Guilford Press.

Drake, W. (1968). Clinical and pathological findings in a child with a developmental learning disability. *Journal of Learning Disabilities, 1,* 468–475.

Drevets, W. C., Videen, T. O., Price, J. L., Preskorm, S. H., Carmichael, S. T., & Raichle, M. E. (1992). A functional anatomical study of unipolar depression. *Journal of Neuroscience, 12,* 3628–3641.

Drewe, E. A. (1975). An experimental investigation of Luria's theory on the effects of frontal lobe lesions in man. *Neuropsychologia, 13*, 421–429.

Dubois, B., Boller, F., Pillon, B., & Agid, Y. (1991). Cognitive deficits in Parkinson's disease. In E. Boller & J. Grafman (Eds.), *Handbook of neuropsychology* (Vol. 5, pp. 195–240). New York: Elsevier.

Dudai, Y. (1989). *The neurobiology of memory*. New York: Oxford.

Duman, R. S., Heninger, G. R., & Nestler, E. J. (1997). A molecular and cellular theory of depression. *Archives of General Psychiatry, 54*, 597–606.

Duncan, J. (1986). Disorganization of behavior after frontal lobe damage. *Cognitive Neuropsychology, 3*, 271–290.

Duncan, J., Burgess, P., & Emslie, H. (1995). Fluid intelligence after frontal lobe lesions. *Neuropsychologia, 33*, 261–268.

Duncan, J., Emslie, H., Williams, P., Johnson, R., & Freer, C. (1996). Intelligence and the frontal lobes: The organization of goal-directed behavior. *Cognitive Psychology, 30*, 257–303.

Ebbesson, S. O. E. (1980). The parcellation theory and its relation to inter-specific variability in brain organization, evolutionary and ontogenetic development, and neural plasticity. *Cell and Tissue Research, 213*, 179–212.

Eccles, J. C. (1977). Part II. In K. R. Popper & J. C. Eccles, *The self and its brain* (pp. 225–406). Berlin: Springer.

Eccles, J. C., & Robinson, D. N. (1984). *The wonder of being human*. New York: Free Press.

Edelman, G. (1989). *The remembered present*. New York: Basic Books.

Efron, R. (1968). What is perception? In R. S. Cohen & M. Wartofsky (Eds.), *Normality and pathology in cognitive functions*. New York: Humanities Press.

Efron, R. (1990). *The decline and fall of hemispheric specialization*. Hillsdale, NJ: Erlbaum.

Ehrlichman, H., & Barnett, J. (1983). Right hemisphere specialization for mental imagery: A review of the evidence. *Brain and Cognition, 2*, 39–52.

Eichenbaum, H., & Otto, T. (1992). The hippocampus: What does it do? *Behavioral and Neural Biology, 57*, 2–36.

Eichenbaum, H., Otto, T., & Cohen, N.J. (1994). Two fundamental components of the hippocampal memory system. *Behavioral and Brain Sciences, 17*, 449–518.

Eimas, P. D., Siqueland, E. R., Jusczyk, P., & Vigorito, J. (1971). Speech perception in infants. *Science, 171*, 303–306.

Ekman, P. (1992). Facial expressions of emotion: New findings, new questions. *Psychological Science, 3*, 34–38.

Ekman, P. (1993). Facial expression and emotion. *American Psychologist, 48*, 384–392.

Ekman, P., Levenson, R. W., & Friesen, W. V. (1983). Autonomic nervous system activity distinguishes among emotions. *Science, 221*, 1208–1210.

Erb, J. S., Gwirtsman, H. E., Fuster, J. M., & Richeimer, S. H. (1989). Bulimia associated with frontal lobe lesions. *International Journal of Eating Disorders, 8*, 117–121.

Eslinger, P. J., & Damasio, A. R. (1985). Severe disturbance of higher cognition after bilateral frontal lobe ablation: Patient EVR. *Neurology, 35*, 1731–1741.

Eslinger, P. J., & Grattan, L. M. (1993). Frontal lobe and frontal-striatal substrates for different forms of human cognitive flexibility. *Neuropsychologia, 31*, 17–28.

Etkoff, N. L. (1984). Selective attention to facial identity and facial emotion. *Neuropsychologia, 22*, 281–295.

Ettlinger, G., Warrington, E. K., & Zangwill, O. L. (1957). A further study of visual-spatial agnosia. *Brain, 80*, 335–361.

Evarts, E. V. (1968). Relation of the pyramidal tract activity to force exerted during a voluntary movement. *Journal of Neurophysiology, 31*, 14–27.

Evarts, E. V. (1979). Brain mechanisms of movement. In *The brain* (pp. 98–106). New York: W. H. Freeman.

Everitt, B. J., & Robbins, T. W. (1942). Amygdala-ventral striatal interaction and reward related processes. In J. P. Aggleton (Ed.), *The amygdala: Neurobiological aspects of emotion, memory and mental dysfunction*. New York: Wiley-Liss.

Exner, S. (1881). *Untersuchungen uber die Lokalisation der Funktionen in der Grosshirnrinde des Menschen*. Wien: Braumuller.

Fanselow, M. S. (1994). Neural organization of the defensive behavior system responsible for fear. *Psychonomic Bulletin and Review, 1*, 429–438.

Farah, M. J. (1989). The neural basis of mental imagery. *Trends in Neurosciences, 12*, 395–399.

Farah, M. J. (1990). *Visual agnosia: Disorders of object recognition and what they tell us about normal vision*. Cambridge, MA: MIT Press.

Farah, M. J. (1995). The neural basis of mental imagery. In M. S. Gazzaniga (Ed.), *The cognitive neurosciences* (pp. 963–975). Cambridge, MA: MIT Press.

Farah, M. J., Gazzaniga, M. S., Holtzman, J. D., & Kosslyn, S. M. (1985). A left hemisphere basis for visual mental imagery? *Neuropsychologia, 23*, 115–118.

Farah, M. J., Hammond, K. M., Mehta, Z., & Ratcliff, G. (1989). Category-specificity and modality-specificity in semantic memory. *Neuropsychologia, 27*, 193–200.

Farah, M. J., Levine, D. N., & Calvanio, R. (1988). A case study of mental imagery deficit. *Brain and Cognition, 8*, 147–164.

Farah, M. J., Peronnet, F., Gonon, M., & Giard, M. H. (1988). Electrophysiological evidence for a shared representation medium for visual images and percepts. *Journal of Experimental Physiology (Gen.), 117*, 248–257.

Farah, M. J., Peronnet, F., Weisberg, L., & Monheit, M. A. (1989). Brain activity underlying mental imagery: Event-related potentials during image generation. *Journal of Cognitive Neuroscience, 1*, 302–316.

Farde, L., Wiesel, F.-A., Stone-Elander, S., Halldin, C., Nordstrom, A.-L., Hull, H., & Sedval, G. (1990). D_2 dopamine receptors in neuroleptic-naive schizophrenic patients: A positron emission tomography study with [^{11}C]raclopride. *Archives of General Psychiatry, 47*, 213–219.

Farkas, T., Wolf, A. P., Jaeger, J., Brodie, J. D., Christman, D. R., & Fowler, J. S. (1984). Regional brain glucose metabolism in chronic schizophrenia. *Archives of General Psychiatry, 41,* 292–300.

Farlow, M., Murrell, J., Ghetti, B., Unverzagt, F., Zeldenrust, S., & Benson, M. (1994). Clinical characteristics in a kindred with early-onset Alzheimer's disease and their linkage to a GT change at position 2149 of amyloid precursor protein gene. *Neurology, 44,* 105–111.

Fedio, P., Cox, C. S., Neophytides, A., Camal-Frederick, G., & Chase, T. N. (1979). Neopsychological profile for Huntington's disease: Patients and those at risk. *Archives of Neurology, 23,* 239–356.

Fedio, P., & Martin, A. (1983). Ideative-emotive behavioral characteristics of patients following left and right temporal lobectomy. *Epilepsia, 254,* S117–S130.

Feeney, D. M., & Sutton, R. L. (1987). Pharmacotherapy for recovery of function after brain injury. *CRC Clinical Reviews in Neurology, 3,* 135–197.

Fernell, E., Gillberg, C., & Von Wendt, L. (1991). Autistic symptoms in children with infantile hydrocephalus. *Acta Pediatrica Scandanavica, 80,* 451–457.

Ferrier, D. (1886). *The functions of the brain* (2nd ed.). New York: Putnam.

Ferro, J. M., & Santos, M. E. (1984). Associative visual agnosia: A case study. *Cortex, 20,* 121–134.

Feuchtwanger, E. (1923). Die Funktionen des Stirnhirns: Ihre Pathologie und Psychologie. *Monogr. Gesamtgeb. Neurol., Psychiat. (Berlin), 38,* 4–194.

Fine, A. (1986, August). Transplantation in the central nervous system. *Scientific American,* pp. 52–58.

Finger, S. (1994). *The origins of neuroscience.* New York: Oxford University Press.

Finger, S. (Ed.). (1978). *Recovery from brain damage: Research and theory.* New York: Plenum.

Fisher, J. N., Kennedy, J. L., Caine, E. D., & Shoulson, I. (1983). Dementia in Huntington's disease: A cross-sectional analysis of intellectual decline. In R. Mayeux & W. G. Rosen (Eds.), *The dementias* (pp. 229–238). New York: Raven Press.

Fishman, M. (1975). The brain stem in psychosis. *British Journal of Psychiatry, 126,* 414–422.

Flechsig, P. (1901). Developmental (myelogenetic) localization of the cerebral cortex in the human subject. *Lancet, ii,* 1027–1029.

Fleming, S., Fishman, B., O'Connor, D., & Silverman, D. (1980). *The Egyptian mummy: Secrets and science.* Philadelphia: University of Pennsylvania Museum.

Fletcher, J. M., & Satz, P. (1980). Developmental changes in the neuropsychological correlates of reading achievement: A six-year longitudinal follow-up. *Journal of Clinical Neuropsychology, 2,* 23.

Flor-Henry, P. (1969). Psychoses and temporal lobe epilepsy: A controlled investigation. *Epilepsia, 10,* 363–395.

Flowers, D. L., Wood, F. B., & Naylor, C. E. (1991). Regional cerebral blood flow correlates of language processing in reading disability. *Archives of Neurology, 48,* 637–643.

Flynn, J. P. (1967). The neural basis of aggression in cats. In D. Gloss (Ed.), *Neurophysiology and emotion* (pp. 40–69). New York: Rockefeller University Press.

Folstein, S., & Rutter, M. (1977). Genetic influences and infantile autism. *Nature, 265,* 726.

Folstein, S. E., & Piven, J. (1991). Etiology of autism: Genetic influences. *Pediatrics, 87,* 767–773.

Franz, S. L. (1907). On the function of the cerebrum: The frontal lobes. *Archives of Psychology, 2,* 1–64.

Franzen, E. A., & Myers, R. E. (1973). Neural control of social behavior: Prefrontal and anterior temporal cortex. *Neuropsychologia, 11,* 141–157.

Franzen, G., & Ingvar, D. H. (1975a). Abnormal distribution of cerebral activity in chronic schizophrenia. *Journal of Psychiatric Research, 12,* 199–214.

Franzen, G., & Ingvar, D. H. (1975b). Absence of activation in frontal structures during psychological testing of chronic schizophrenics. *Journal of Neurology, Neurosurgery and Psychiatry, 38,* 1027–1032.

Frauenheim, J. G. (1978). Academic achievement characteristics of adult males who were diagnosed as dyslexic in childhood. *Journal of Learning Disabilities, 11,* 476–483.

Freedman, M., & Oscar-Berman, M. (1986). Bilateral frontal lobe disease and selective delayed response deficits in humans. *Behavioral Neuroscience, 100,* 337–342.

Freeman, W., & Watts, J. W. (1942). *Psychosurgery.* Springfield, IL: Thomas.

Freeman, W., & Watts, J. W. (1948). Thalamic projection to the frontal lobe. *Research Publications, Association for Research in Nervous and Mental Disorders, 27,* 200–209.

Freud, S. (1891). *Zur Aufassung der Aphasien.* Wien: Deuticke.

Freud, S. (1895/1966). *The standard edition of the complete psychological works of Sigmund Freud: Volume I. Pre-psycho-analytic publications and unpublished drafts.* London: Hogarth Press.

Freud, S. (1913/1958). *The standard edition of the complete psychological works of Sigmund Freud: Volume XII. The case of Schreber and papers on technique.* London: Hogarth Press.

Freud, S. (1940/1949). *An outline of psycho-analysis.* New York: Norton.

Freud, S. (1953). *On aphasia* (E. Stengel, Trans.). New York: International Universities Press. (Original work published 1893).

Friedman, R. B., & Alexander, M. P. (1984). Pictures, images and pure alexia: A case study. *Cognitive Neuropsychology, 1,* 9–23.

Frith, U. (1989). *Autism: Explaining the enigma.* New York: Blackwell.

Frith, U. (Ed.). (1991). *Autism and Asperger syndrome.* New York: Cambridge University Press.

Frith, U., Morton, J., & Leslie, J. M. (1991). The cognitive basis of a biological disorder: Autism. *Trends in Neurosciences, 14,* 433–438.

Fritsch, G., & Hitzig, E. (1870). Uber die elektrische Erregbarkeit des Grosshirns. *Arch. Physiol. Wiss. Med. I, 37,* 300–332.

Fuerst, D. R., Fisk, J. L., & Rourke, B. P. (1990). Psychological functioning of learning disabled children: Relationship between WISC verbal IQ-performance IQ-discrepancies and personality subtypes. *Journal of Consulting and Clinical Psychology, 58,* 657–660.

Fulton, J. F. (1950). *Frontal lobotomy and affective behavior.* New York: Norton.

Funahashi, S., Bruce, C. J., & Goldman-Rakic, P. S. (1989). Mnemonic coding of visual space in the monkey's dorsolateral prefrontal cortex. *Journal of Neurophysiology, 61*(2), 331–349.

Funahashi, S., Bruce, C. J., & Goldman-Rakic, P. S. (1991). Neural activity related to saccadic eye movements in the monkey's dorsolateral prefrontal cortex. *Journal of Neurophysiology, 65*(6), 1464–1483.

Fuster, J. M. (1973). Unit activity in prefrontal cortex during delayed-response performance: Neuronal correlates of transient memory. *Journal of Neurophysiology, 36,* 61–78.

Fuster, J. M. (1985). The prefrontal cortex and temporal integration. In A. Peters & E. G. Jones (Eds.), *The cerebral cortex* (Vol. 4, pp. 151–177). New York: Plenum.

Fuster, J. M. (1989). *The prefrontal cortex.* New York: Raven Press.

Fuster, J. M. (1991). Role of prefrontal cortex in delay tasks: Evidence from reversible lesion and unit recording in the monkey. In H. S. Levin, H. M. Eisenberg, & A. L. Benton (Eds.), *Frontal lobe function and dysfunction* (pp. 59–71). New York: Oxford University Press.

Fuster, J. M. (1997). *The prefrontal cortex* (3rd ed.). Philadelphia: Lippincott-Raven.

Fuster, J. M., Bauer, R. H., & Jervey, J. P. (1985). Functional interactions between inferotemporal and prefrontal cortex in a cognitive task. *Brain Research, 330,* 299–307.

Gabrieli, J. D. E., Fleischman, D. A., Keane, M. M., Reminger, S. L., & Morrell, F. (1995). Double dissociation between memory systems underlying explicit and implicit memory in the human brain. *Psychological Science, 6*(2), 76–82.

Gaffan, D. (1974). Recognition impaired and association intact in the memory of monkeys after transection of the fornix. *Journal of Comparative and Physiological Psychology, 86,* 1100–1109.

Gaffan, D., Murray, E. A., & Fabre-Thorpe, M. (1993). Interaction of the amygdala with the frontal lobe in reward memory. *European Journal of Neuroscience, 5,* 968–975.

Gaffan, D., Saunders, R. C., Gaffan, E. A., Harrison, S., Shields, C., & Owen, M. A. (1984). Effects of fornix transection upon associative memory in monkeys: Role of the hippocampus in learned action. *Quarterly Journal of Experimental Psychology: B. Comparative and Physiological Psychology, 36,* 173–221.

Gaffan, E. A., Gaffan, D., & Hodges, J. R. (1991). Amnesia following damage to the left fornix and to other sites. *Brain, 114,* 1297–1313.

Gage, F. H., & Bjorklund, A. (1986). Cholinergic septal grafts into the hippocampal formation improve spatial learning and memory in aged rats by an atropine-sensitive mechanism. *Journal of Neuroscience, 6,* 2837–2847.

Gainotti, G. (1972). Emotional behavior and hemispheric side of the lesion. *Cortex, 8,* 41–55.

Gainotti, G., & Caltagirone, C. (Eds.) (1989). *Emotion and the dual brain.* Berlin: Springer.

Gainotti, G., D'Erme, P., Monteleone, D., & Silveri, M. C. (1986). Mechanisms of unilateral spatial neglect in relation to laterality of cerebral lesions. *Brain, 109,* 599–612.

Gainotti, G., & Tiacci, C. (1970). Patterns of drawing disability in right and left hemisphere patients. *Neuropsychologia, 8,* 289–303.

Galaburda, A. M. (1989). Ordinary and extraordinary brain development: Anatomical variation in developmental dyslexia. *Annals of Dyslexia, 39,* 67–80.

Galaburda, A. M., & Kemper, T. (1979). Cytoarchitectonic abnormalities in developmental dyslexia: A case study. *Annals of Neurology, 6,* 94–100.

Galaburda, A. M., LeMay, M., Kemper, T. L., & Geschwind, N. (1978). Right-left asymmetries in the brain. *Science, 199,* 852–856.

Galaburda, A. M., & Sanides, F. (1980). Cytoarchitectonic organization of the human auditory cortex. *Journal of Comparative Neurology, 190,* 597–610.

Galaburda, A. M., Sherman, G. F., Rosen, G. D., Aboitiz, F., & Geschwind, N. (1985). Developmental dyslexia: Four consecutive patients with cortical anomalies. *Annals of Neurology, 18,* 222–233.

Gallagher, M., & Holland, P. (1994). The amygdala complex. *Proceedings of the National Academy of Sciences, USA, 91,* 771–776.

Galletti, C., & Battaglini, P. P. (1989). Gaze-dependent visual neurons in area V3A of monkey peristriate cortex. *Journal of Neuroscience, 9,* 1112–1125.

Garber, H. J., Ritvo, E. R., Chiu, L. C., & Grisvold, V. J. (1989). A magnetic resonance imaging study of autism: Normal fourth ventricle size and absence of pathology. *American Journal of Psychiatry, 146,* 532–534.

Gardner, H. (1975). *The shattered mind: The person after brain damage.* New York: Knopf.

Gardner, H., King, P. K., Flamm, L., & Silverman, J. (1975). Comprehension and appreciation of humorous material following brain damage. *Brain, 98,* 399–412.

Gardner, R. A., & Gardner, B. T. (1969). Teaching sign language to a chimpanzee. *Science, 165,* 664–672.

Gardner, R. A., & Gardner, B. T. (1975). Early signs of language in child and chimpanzee. *Science, 187,* 752–753.

Gardner, R. A., & Gardner, B. T. (1978). Comparative psychology and language acquisition. *New York Academy of Science, 309,* 37–76.

Garfinkel, B. (1986). Recent developments in attention deficit disorder. *Psychiatric Annals, 16,* 11–15.

Gasparrini, W., Satz, P., Heilman, K., & Cooledge, F. L. (1978). Hemispheric asymmetries of affective processing as determined by the Minnesota Multiphasic Personality Inventory. *Journal of Neurology, Neurosurgery, and Psychiatry, 41,* 470–473.

Gaulin, S. J. C., & FitzGerald, R. W. (1986). Sex differences in spatial ability: An evolutionary hypothesis and text. *American Naturalist, 127,* 74–88.

Gaulin, S. J. C., & FitzGerald, R. W. (1989). Sexual selection in spatial-learning ability. *Animal Behavior, 37,* 322–331.

Gazzaniga, M., Bogen, J., & Sperry, R. (1967). Dyspraxia following diversion of the cerebral commissures. *Archives of Neurology, 16,* 606–612.

Gazzaniga, M. S., & LeDoux, J. E. (1978). *The integrated mind.* New York: Plenum.

Gentile, A. M., & Stamm, J. S. (1972). Supplementary cues and delayed-alternation performance of frontal monkeys. *Journal of Comparative and Physiological Psychology, 80,* 230–237.

George, M. S., Ketter, T. A., Parekh, P. I., Horwitz, B., Herscovitch, P., & Post, R. M. (1995). Brain activity during transient sadness and happiness in healthy women: An in vivo study in humans. *American Journal of Psychiatry, 152,* 341–351.

Georgopoulos, A. P., Kalaska, K. S., Caminiti, R., & Massey, J. T. (1982). On the relations between the directions of two-dimensional arm movements and cell discharge in primate motor cortex. *Journal of Neuroscience, 2,* 1527–1537.

Gershon, E. S., Nurnberger, J. I., Berrettini, W. H., & Goldin, L. R. (1985). Affective disorders: Genetics. In H. I. Kaplan & J. Sadock (Eds.), *Modern synopsis of comprehensive textbook of psychiatry* (4th ed.). Baltimore: Williams and Wilkins.

Gerstman, J. (1927). Fingeragnosie und isolierte Agraphie: Ein neues Syndrom. *Zeitschrift fur Neurologie und Psychiatrie, 108,* 152–177.

Geschwind, N. (1965). Disconnection syndromes in animals and man. *Brain, 88,* 237–294, 585–645.

Geschwind, N. (1975). The apraxias: Neural mechanisms of disorders of learned movements. *Scientific American, 63,* 188–195.

Geschwind, N. (1976). Language and cerebral dominance. In T. N. Chase (Ed.), *Nervous system: Vol. 2. The clinical neurosciences* (pp. 433–439). New York: Raven Press.

Geschwind, N. (1977). Behavioral changes in temporal-lobe epilepsy. *Archives of Neurology, 34,* 453.

Geschwind, N. (1979). Specialization of the human brain. In *The brain: A Scientific American book.* New York: W. H. Freeman.

Geschwind, N. (1982). Why Orton was right. *Annals of Dyslexia, 32,* 13–30.

Geschwind, N., & Galaburda, A. M. (1987). *Cerebral lateralization: Biological mechanisms, associations, and pathology.* Cambridge, MA: MIT Press.

Geschwind, N., & Kaplan, E. (1962). A human cerebral disconnection syndrome. *Neurology, 12,* 675–685.

Geschwind, N., & Levitsky, W. (1968). Human-brain left-right asymmetries in temporal speech region. *Science, 161,* 186–187.

Geschwind, N., Quadfasel, F. A., & Segarra, J. M. (1968). Isolation of the speech area. *Neuropsychologia, 6,* 327–340.

Getzels, J. W., & Jackson, P. W. (1962). *Creativity and intelligence.* New York: Wiley.

Ghent, L. (1956). Perception of overlapping and embedded figures by children of different ages. *American Journal of Psychology, 69,* 575–587.

Ghez, C., & Gordon, J. (1995). Voluntary movement. In E. R. Kandel, J. H. Schwartz, & T. M. Jessell (Eds.), *Essentials of neuroscience and behavior.* Norwalk, CT: Appleton and Lange.

Giedd, J. N., Rapoport, J. L., Kruesi, M. J. P., Parker, C., Shapiro, M. B., Allen, A. J., Leonard, H. L., Kaysen, D., Dickstein, D. P., Marsh, W. L., Kozuch, P. L., Vaituzis, A. C., Hamburger, S. D., & Swedo, S. E. (1995). Sydenham's chorea: Magnetic resonance imaging of the basal ganglia. *Neurology, 45,* 2199–2202.

Gillberg, C. (1992). Subtypes of autism: Are there behavioral phenotypes typical of underlying medical conditions? *Journal of Intellectual Disability Research, 36,* 201–214.

Glees, P., & Cole, J. (1950). Recovery of skilled motor function after small repeated lesions of motor cortex in macaque. *Journal of Neurophysiology, 13,* 137–148.

Gleitman, H. (1995). *Psychology* (4th ed.). New York: Norton.

Gleitman, H., Fridlund, A. J., & Reisberg, D. (1999). *Psychology* (5th ed.). New York: Norton.

Gleitman, L. R. (1995). Language. In H. Gleitman (1995), *Psychology* (4th ed., Ch. 9). New York: Norton.

Glisky, E. L., & Schacter, D. L. (1987). Acquisition of domain-specific knowledge in organic amnesia: Training for computer-related work. *Neuropsychologia, 25,* 893–906.

Glisky, E. L., & Schacter, D. L. (1988). Long-term retention of computer learning by patients with memory disorders. *Neuropsychologia, 26,* 173–178.

Glisky, E. L., & Schacter, D. L. (1989). Extending the limits of complex learning in organic amnesia: Computer training in a vocational domain. *Neuropsychologia, 27,* 107–120.

Glisky, E. L., Schacter, D. L., & Tulving, E. (1986). Computer learning by memory-impaired patients: Acquisition and retention of complex knowledge. *Neuropsychologia, 24,* 313–328.

Gloor, P., Olivier, A., & Quesney, L. F. (1981). The role of the amygdala in the expression of psychic phenomena in temporal lobe seizures. In Y. Ben-Ari (Ed.), *The amygdaloid complex* (pp. 489–498). New York: Elsevier/North-Holland Biomedical Press.

Glosser, G., & Goodglass, H. (1990). Disorders of executive control function among aphasics and other brain-damaged patients. *Journal of Clinical and Experimental Neuropsychology, 12,* 485–501.

Gnadt, J. W., & Andersen, R. A (1988). Memory related motor planning activity in posterior parietal cortex in the macaque. *Experimental Brain Research, 70,* 216–220.

Godwin-Austin, R. B. (1965). A case of visual disorientation. *Journal of Neurology, Neurosurgery and Psychiatry, 28,* 453–458.

Goldberg, E. K., & Costa, L. D. (1981). Hemispheric differences in the acquisition and use of descriptive systems. *Brain and Language, 14,* 144.

Goldberg, T. E., Weinberger, D. R., Berman, K. F., Pliskin, N. H., & Podd, M. H. (1987). Further evidence for dementia of the prefrontal type in schizophrenia? *Archives of General Psychiatry, 44,* 1008–1014.

Goldman, P. S. (1971). Functional development of the prefrontal cortex in early life and the problem of neuronal plasticity. *Experimental Neurology, 32,* 366–387.

Goldman, P. S. (1974). An alternative to developmental plasticity: Heterology of CNS structures in infants and adults. In D. G. Stein, J. J. Rosen, & N. Butters (Eds.), *Plasticity and recovery from brain damage* (pp. 149–174). New York: Academic Press.

Goldman, P. S., & Nauta, W. J. H. (1977). An intricately patterned prefrontal-caudate projection in the rhesus monkey. *Journal of Comparative Neurology, 171,* 369–386.

Goldman, P. S., & Rosvold, H. E. (1970). Localization of function within the dorsolateral prefrontal cortex of the rhesus monkey. *Experimental Neurology, 27,* 291–304.

Goldman, P. S., Rosvold, H. E., Vest, B., & Galkin, T. W. (1971). Analysis of the delayed alternation deficit produced by dorsolateral prefrontal lesions in the rhesus monkey. *Journal of Comparative and Physiological Psychology, 77,* 212–220.

Goldman-Rakic, P. S. (1987). Circuitry of the primate prefrontal cortex and regulation of behavior by representational memory. In F. Plum (Ed.), *Handbook of physiology: The nervous system. Volume 5: Higher functions of the brain* (Part 1, pp. 373–417). Bethesda, MD: American Physiological Society.

Goldman-Rakic, P. S. (1988). Topography of cognition: Parallel distributed networks in primate association cortex. *Annual Review of Neuroscience, 11,* 137–156.

Goldman-Rakic, P. S. (1991). Cortical dysfunction in schizophrenia: The relevance of working memory. In B. J. Carroll & J. E. Barrett (Eds.), *Psychopathology and the brain.* New York: Raven Press.

Goldman-Rakic, P. S. (1992). Working memory and the mind. *Scientific American, 267*(3), 73–79.

Goldman-Rakic, P. S., & Porrino, L. J. (1985). The primate mediodorsal (MD) nucleus and its projections to the frontal lobe. *Journal of Comparative Neurology, 242,* 535–560.

Goldman-Rakic, P. S., & Rakic, P. (1984). Experimental modification of gyral patterns. In N. S. Geschwind & A. M.

Galaburda (Eds.), *Cerebral dominance: The biological foundations.* Cambridge, MA: Harvard University Press.

Goldstein, K. (1939). *The organism: A holistic approach to biology derived from pathological data in man.* New York: American Books.

Goldstein, K. (1948). *Language and language disturbances.* New York: Grune and Stratton.

Goldstein, K. (1949). Frontal lobectomy and impairment of abstract attitude. *Journal of Nervous and Mental Disorders, 110,* 93–111.

Gollin, E. S. (1960). Developmental studies of visual recognition of incomplete objects. *Perceptual and Motor Skills, 11,* 289–298.

Gomori, A. J., & Hawryluk, G. A. (1984). Visual agnosia without alexia. *Neurology, 34,* 947–950.

Goodglass, H., & Kaplan, E. (1963). Disturbance in gesture and pantomime in aphasia. *Brain, 86,* 703–720.

Goodman, R., & Stevenson, J. A. (1989). Twin study of hyperactivity: II. The etiological role of genes, family relationships and perinatal adversity. *Journal of Child Psychology and Psychiatry, 30,* 691–710.

Gordinier, H. C. (1899). A case of brain tumor at the base of the second left frontal convolution. *American Journal of Medical Science, 117,* 526–535.

Gorelick, P. B., & Ross, E. D. (1987). The aprosodias: Further functional-anatomical evidence for the organization of affective language in the right hemisphere. *Journal of Neurology, Neurosurgery and Psychiatry, 50,* 553–560.

Gottesman, I. L., McGuffin, P., & Farmer, A. (1987). Clinical genetics as clues to the "real" genetics of schizophrenia (a decade of modest gain while playing for time). *Schizophrenia Bulletin, 13,* 23–47.

Gottesman, I. L., & Shields, J. (1972). *Schizophrenia and genetics: A twin study vantage point.* New York: Academic Press.

Gottesman, I. L., & Shields, J. (1982). *Schizophrenia: The epigenetic puzzle.* New York: Cambridge University Press.

Grace, A. A. (1991). Phasic versus tonic dopamine release and the modulation of dopamine system responsivity: A hypothesis for the etiology of schizophrenia. *Neuroscience, 41,* 1–24.

Grady, C. L., Haxby, J. V., Horwitz, B., Shapiro, M. B., Rapoport, S. I., Ungerleider, L. G., Mishkin, M., Carson, R. E., & Hersovitch, P. (1992). Dissociation of object and spatial vision in human extrastriate cortex: Age-related changes in activation of regional cerebral blood flow measured with (-sup-l-sup-5O) water and positron emission tomography. *Journal of Cognitive Neuroscience, 4*(1), 23–34.

Graf, P., & Schacter, D. L. (1985). Implicit and explicit memory for new associations in normal subjects and amnesic patients. *Journal of Experimental Psychology: Learning, Memory, and Cognition, 11,* 501–518.

Graf, P., Squire, L. R., & Mandler, G. (1984). The information that amnesic patients do not forget. *Journal of Experimental Psychology: Learning, Memory, and Cognition, 10,* 164–178.

Graff-Radford, N. R., Cooper, W. E., Colsher, P. L., & Dama-sio, A. R. (1986). An unlearned foreign "accent" in a patient with aphasia. *Brain and Language, 28,* 86–94.

Grafman, J. (1989). Plans, actions and mental sets: Managerial knowledge units in the frontal lobes. In E. Perecman (Ed.), *Integrating theory and practice in clinical neuropsychology* (pp. 93–138). Hillsdale, NJ: Erlbaum.

Grafman, J. (1995). Similarities and distinctions among current models of prefrontal cortical functions. In J. Grafman, K. J. Holyoak, & F. Boller (Eds.), *Structures and functions of the human prefrontal cortex* (pp. 337–368). New York: New York Academy of Sciences.

Grafman, J., Passafiume, D., Faglioni, P., & Boller, F. (1982). Calculation disturbances in adults with focal hemispheric damage. *Cortex, 18,* 37–49.

Grafman, J., Sirigu, A., Spector, L., & Hendler, J. (1993). Damage to the prefrontal cortex leads to decomposition of structural event complexes. *Journal of Head Rehabilitation, 8,* 73–87.

Grafman, J., Vance, S. C., Weingartner, H., Salazar, A. M., & Amin, D. (1986). The effects of lateralized frontal lesions on mood regulation. *Brain, 109,* 1127–1148.

Grandin, T., & Scariano, M. (1986). *Emergence: Labeled autistic.* Novato, CA: Arena Press.

Grasby, P. M., Firth, C. D., Friston, K. J., Bench, C., Frackowiak, R. S. J., & Dolan, R. J. (1993). Functional mapping of brain areas implicated in auditory-verbal memory function. *Brain, 116,* 1–20.

Greenberg, N., Scott, M., & Crews, D. (1984). Role of the amygdala in the reproductive and aggressive behavior of the lizard. *Physiology and Behavior, 32,* 147–151.

Greenblatt, M., Arnot, R., & Solomon, H. D. (Eds.) (1950). *Studies in lobotomy.* New York: Grune and Stratton.

Greenough, W. T. (1976). Enduring brain effects of differential experience and training. In M. R. Rosenzweig & E. L. Bennett (Eds.), *Neural mechanisms of learning and memory.* Cambridge, MA: MIT Press.

Griffith, V. E. (1970). *A stroke in the family: A manual of home therapy.* New York: Delacorte.

Gross, C. G., & Weiskrantz, L. (1964). Some changes in behavior produced by lateral frontal lesions in the macaque. In J. M. Warren & K. Akert (Eds.), *The frontal granular cortex and behavior* (pp. 74–101). New York: McGraw-Hill.

Gross-Glenn, K., Duara, R., Barber, W. W., & Loewenstein, D. (1991). Positron emission tomographic studies during serial word-reading by normal and dyslexic subjects. *Journal of Clinical and Experimental Neuropsychology, 13,* 531–544.

Gruzelier, J. H. (1981). Hemispheric imbalances masquerading as paranoid and nonparanoid syndromes. *Schizophrenia Bulletin, 7,* 662–673.

Gruzelier, J. H. (1984). Hemispheric imbalance in schizophrenia. *International Journal of Psychology, 1,* 227–240.

Gruzelier, J. H., & Hammond, N. V. (1980). Lateralized deficits and drug influences on the dichotic listening of schizophrenic patients. *Biological Psychiatry, 15,* 759–779.

Guariglia, C., Padovani, A., Pantono, P., & Pizzamiglio, L. (1993). Unilateral neglect restricted to visual imagery. *Nature, 364,* 235–237.

Guitton, D. (1992). Control of eye-head coordination during orienting gaze shifts. *Trends in Neurosciences, 15,* 174–179.

Guitton, D., Buchtel, H. A., & Douglas, R. M. (1982). Disturbances of voluntary saccadic eye movement mechanisms following discrete unilateral frontal lobe removals. In G. Lennerstrand & E. L. Keller (Eds.), *Functional basis of ocular motility disorders* (pp. 497–499). Oxford, England: Pergamon.

Guitton, D., Buchtel, H. A., & Douglas, R. M. (1985). Frontal lobe lesions in man cause difficulties in suppressing reflexive glances and in generating goal-directed saccades. *Experimental Brain Research, 58,* 455–472.

Gur, R. E. (1978). Left hemisphere dysfunction and left hemisphere overactivation in schizophrenia. *Journal of Abnormal Psychology, 87,* 226–238.

Gur, R. E., Resnick, S. M., Alavi, A., Gur, R. C., Canoff, S., Dann, R., Silver, F. L., Saykin, A. J., Chawluk, J. B., & Kushner, M. (1987). Regional brain function in schizophrenia: I. A positron emission tomography study. *Archives of General Psychiatry, 44,* 119–125.

Gurd, J. M., Bessel, N. J., Bladon, R. A. W., & Banford, J. M. (1988). A case of foreign language syndrome with follow-up clinical neuropsychological and phonetic descriptions. *Neuropsychologia, 26,* 237–251.

Gusella, J. F., Wexler, N. S., Conneally, P. M., Naylor, S. L., Anderson, M. A., Tanzi, R. E., Watkins, P. C., Ottina, K., Wallace, M. R., Sakaguchi, A. Y., Young, A. G., Shoulson, I., Bonilla, E., & Martin, J. B. (1983). A polymorphic DNA marker genetically linked to Huntington's disease. *Nature, 306,* 234–238.

Gwiazda, J., Bauer, J., & Held, R. (1989). From visual acuity to hyperactivity: A 10-year update. *Canadian Journal of Psychology, 43,* 109–120.

Haas, R. H., Townsend, J., Courchesne, E., Lincoln, A. J., Schreibman, L., & Yeung-Courchesne, R. (1996). Neurologic abnormalities in infantile autism. *Journal of Child Neurology, 11,* 84–92.

Halgren, E. (1992). Emotional neurophysiology of the amygdala within the context of human cognition. In J. Aggleton (Ed.), *The amygdala: Neurobiological aspects of emotion, memory and mental dysfunction* (pp. 191–228). New York: Wiley-Liss.

Hall, R. E., Livingston, R. B., & Bloor, C. M. (1977). Orbital cortical influences on cardiovascular dynamics and myocardial structure in conscious monkeys. *Journal of Neurosurgery, 46,* 638–647.

Hallowell, E. M., & Ratey, J. J. (1994). *Driven to distraction.* New York: Pantheon Books.

Hamann, S. B., Stefanacci, L., Squire, L., Adolphs, R., Tranel, D., Damasio, H., & Damasio, R. (1996). Recognizing facial emotion. *Nature, 379,* 497.

Hamilton, E., & Cairns, H. (1964). *The collected dialogues of Plato* (pp. 40–98). New York: Pantheon Books.

Hamm, R. J., Temple, M. D., O'Dell, D. M., Pike, B. R., & Lyeth, B. G. (1996). Exposure to environmental complexity promotes recovery of cognitive function after traumatic brain injury. *Journal of Neurotrauma, 13,* 41–47.

Hannay, H. J., Varney, N., & Benton, A. L. (1976). Visual localization in patients with unilateral brain disease. *Journal of Neurology, Neurosurgery and Psychiatry, 39,* 307–313.

Hansch, E. C., & Pirozolo, F. J. (1980). Task relevant effects on the assessment of cerebral specialization for facial emotion. *Brain and Language, 10,* 51–59.

Happe, F., & Frith, U. (1996). The neuropsychology of autism. *Brain, 119,* 1377–1400.

Hardy, J. (1997). Amyloid, the presinilins and Alzheimer's disease. *Trends in Neurosciences, 4,* 154–159.

Hare, H. D. (1978). A research scale for the assessment of psychopathy in criminal populations. *Personality and Individual Differences, 1,* 111–119.

Harlow, H. F., Davis, R. T., Settlage, P. H., & Meyer, D. R. (1952). Analysis of frontal and posterior association syndromes in brain-damaged monkeys. *Journal of Comparative and Physiological Psychology, 45,* 419–429.

Harlow, J. M. (1848). Passage of an iron rod through the head. *Boston Med. Surg. Journal, 39,* 389–393.

Harlow, J. M. (1868). Recovery from passage of an iron bar through the head. *Publications of the Massachusetts Medical Society, Boston, 2,* 327–346.

Hart, S., & Semple, J. M. (1990). *Neuropsychology and the dementias.* London: Erlbaum.

Hashimoto, T., Tayama, M., Murakawa, K., Yoshimoto, T., Miyazaki, M., Harada, M., & Kurodo, Y. (1995). Development of the brainstem and cerebellum in autistic patients. *Journal of Autism and Developmental Disorders, 25,* 1–18.

Hawkins, R. D., Kandel, E. R., & Siegelbaum, S. A. (1993). Learning to modulate transmitter release: Themes and variations in synaptic plasticity. *Annual Review of Neuroscience, 16,* 625–665.

Haxley, J. V., Horwitz, B., Ungerleider, L. G., Maisog, J. M., Pietrini, P., & Grady, C. L. (1994). The functional organization of human extrastriate cortex: A PET-rCBF study of selective attention to faces and locations. *Journal of Neuroscience, 14*(1), 6336–6353.

Heath, R. C. (1963). Electrical self-stimulation of the brain in man. *American Journal of Psychiatry, 120,* 571–577.

Heaton, R. K., Budde, L. E., & Johnson, K. L. (1978). Neuropsychological test results associated with psychiatric disorders in adults. *Psychological Bulletin, 85,* 141–162.

Heaton, R. K., & Crowley, T. J. (1981). Effects of psychiatric disorders and their somatic treatments on neuropsychological test results. In S. B. Gilskov & G. J. Boll (Eds.), *Handbook of clinical neuropsychology.* New York: Wiley.

Hebb, D. O. (1939). Intelligence in man after large removals of cerebral tissue: Report of four left frontal lobe cases. *Journal of General Psychology, 21,* 73–87.

Hecaen, H. (1964). Mental symptoms associated with tumors of the frontal lobes. In J. M. Warren & K. Akert (Eds.), *The*

frontal granular cortex and behavior (pp. 335–352). New York: McGraw-Hill.

Hecaen, H. (1976). Acquired aphasia in children and the ontogenesis of hemispheric functional specialization. *Brain and Language, 3,* 114–134.

Hecaen, H., & Ajuriaguerra, J. (1956). Agnosie visuelle pour les objets inanimes par lesion unilaterale gauche. *Revue Neurologique, 94,* 222–233.

Hecaen, H., & Albert, M. L. (1978). *Human neuropsychology.* New York: Wiley.

Hecaen, H., Goldblum, M. C., Masure, M. C., & Ramier, A. M. (1974). Une nouvelle observation d'agnosie d'objet: Deficit de l'association ou de la categorisation, specifique de la modalite visuelle. *Neuropsychologia, 12,* 447–464.

Hecaen, H., & Rondot, P. (1985). Apraxia as a disorder of signs. In E. Roy (Ed.), *Neuropsychological studies of apraxia and related disorders* (pp. 75–98). Amsterdam: Elsevier North-Holland.

Hecaen, H., Tzortzis, C., & Romdot, P. (1980). Loss of topographical memory with learning deficits. *Cortex, 16,* 525–542.

Heckers, S. (1997). Neuropathology of schizophrenia: Cortex, thalamus, basal ganglia, and neurotransmitter-specific projection systems. *Schizophrenia Bulletin, 23,* 403–421.

Heilman, K. M. (1973). Ideational apraxia: A redefinition. *Brain, 96,* 861–864.

Heilman, K. M., Bowers, D., & Valenstein, E. (1993). Emotional disorders associated with neurological diseases. In K. M. Heilman & E. Valenstein (Eds.), *Clinical neuropsychology* (3rd ed.). New York: Oxford University Press.

Heilman, K. M., & Rothi, L. J. (1985). Apraxia. In K. M. Heilman & E. Valenstein (Eds.), *Clinical neuropsychology* (pp. 131–150). New York: Oxford University Press.

Heilman, K. M., & Rothi, L. J. (1993). Apraxia. In K. M. Heilman & E. Valenstein (Eds.), *Clinical neuropsychology* (3rd ed.). New York: Oxford University Press.

Heilman, K. M., Rothi, L. J., & Valenstein, E. (1982). Two forms of ideomotor apraxia. *Neurology, 32,* 342–346.

Heilman, K. M., Scholes, R., & Watson, R. T. (1975). Auditory affective agnosia: Disturbed comprehension of affective speech. *Journal of Neurology, Neurosurgery, and Psychiatry, 38,* 69–72.

Heilman, K. M., & Valenstein, E. (1979). Mechanisms underlying hemispatial neglect. *Archives of Neurology, 5,* 166–170.

Heilman, K. M., & Watson, R. T. (1991). Intentional motor disorders. In H. S. Levin, H. M. Eisenberg, & A. L. Benton (Eds.), *Frontal lobe function and dysfunction* (pp. 199–216). New York: Oxford University Press.

Heilman, K. M., Watson, R. T., & Rothi, L. G. (1996, November). *Disorders of higher order motor control.* Presentation at the Annual Meeting of the National Academy of Neuropsychology, New Orleans, LA.

Heindel, W. C., Butters, N., & Salmon, D. P. (1988). Impaired learning of a motor skill in patients with Huntington's disease. *Behavioral Neuroscience, 102,* 141–147.

Heller, W., & Levy, J. (1981). Perception and expression of emotion in right-handers and left-handers. *Neuropsychologia, 10,* 263–272.

Henderson, W. W. (1997). The epidemiology of estrogen replacement therapy in Alzheimer's disease. *Neurology, 48,* S27–S35.

Henik, A., Singh, J., Beckley, R. J., & Rafal, R. D. (1993). Disturbance of automatic word reading in Parkinson's disease. *Cortex, 29,* 589–599.

Henriques, J. B., & Davidson, R. J. (1991). Left frontal hypoactivation in depression. *Journal of Abnormal Psychology, 100,* 535–545.

Heritch, A. J. (1990). Evidence for reduced and dysregulated turnover of dopamine in schizophrenia. *Schizophrenia Bulletin, 16,* 605–615.

Hermelin, B., & O'Connor, N. (1990). Art and accuracy: The drawing ability of idiot-savants. *Journal of Child Psychology and Psychiatry, 31*(2), 217–228.

Hess, W. R. (1954). *Diencephalon: Autonomic and extrapyramidal functions.* New York: Grune and Stratton.

Hillis, A. E., & Caramazza, A. (1991). Category specific memory and comprehension impairment: A double dissociation. *Brain, 114,* 2081–2094.

Hilts, P. (1995). *Memory's ghost: The strange tale of Mr. M and the nature of memory.* New York: Simon and Schuster.

Hinshaw, S. P., Carte, E. T., & Morrison, D. C. (1986). Concurrent prediction of academic achievement in reading disabled children: The rule of neuropsychological and intellectual measures at different ages. *International Journal of Clinical Neuropsychology, 8,* 3–8.

Hinshelwood, J. (1895). Word blindness and visual memory. *Lancet, 2,* 1564.

Hinton, G. E. (1981). A parallel computation that assigns canonical object-based frames of reference. Proceedings of the International Joint Conference on Artificial Intelligence, Vancouver, Canada.

Hiscock, M., Inch, R., Jacek, C., Hiscock-Kalil, C., & Kalil, K. M. (1994). Is there a sex difference in human laterality? I. An exhaustive survey of auditory laterality studies from six neuropsychological journals. *Journal of Clinical and Experimental Neuropsychology, 16,* 423–435.

Hiscock, M., Israelian, M., Inch, R., Jacek, C., & Hiscock-Kalil, C. (1995). Is there a sex difference in human laterality? II. An exhaustive survey of visual laterality studies from six neuropsychological journals. *Journal of Clinical and Experimental Neuropsychology, 17,* 590–610.

Hitzig, E. (1874). *Untersuchung uber das Gehirn.* Berlin: Hirschwald.

Hodges, J. R., Patterson, K., Oxbury, S., & Funnell, E. (1992). Semantic dementia: Progressive fluent aphasia with temporal-lobe atrophy. *Brain, 115,* 1783–1806.

Hodgkinson, S., Mullan, M. J., & Gurling, H. M. (1990). The role of genetic factors in the etiology of the affective disorders. *Behavior Genetics, 20,* 235–250.

Hoff, E. C., Kell, J. E., & Carroll, M. N. (1963). Effects of cortical stimulation and lesions on cardiovascular function. *Physiological Review, 43,* 68–113.

Hoffer, B. J., & van Horne, C. (1995). Survival of dopaminergic neurons in fetal-tissue grafts [Editorial]. *New England Journal of Medicine, 332,* 1163–1164.

Hofstatter, L., Smolik, E. A., & Busch, A. K. (1945). Prefrontal lobotomy in treatment of chronic psychoses. *Archives of Neurology and Neurosurgery, 53,* 125–130.

Holmes, G. (1918). Disturbances of visual orientation. *British Journal of Ophthalmology, 2,* 449–468.

Holmes, G. (1919). Disorders of visual space perception. *British Medical Journal, 2,* 230–233.

Holmes, G. (1931). Mental symptoms associated with brain tumors. *Lancet, 1,* 408–410.

Holroyd, S., Reiss, A. L., & Bryan, R. N. (1991). Autistic features in Joubert syndrome: A genetic disorder with agenesis of the cerebellar vermis. *Biological Psychiatry, 29,* 287–294.

Hooper, S. R., Boyd, T. A., Hynd, G. W., & Rubin, J. (1993). Definitional issues and neuroradiological foundations of severe selective neurodevelopmental disorders. *Archives of Clinical Neuropsychology, 8,* 279–308.

Hooper, S. R., & Willis, W. G. (1989). *Learning disability subtyping: Neuropsychological foundations, conceptual models, and issues in clinical differentiation.* New York: Springer.

Huang, Y.-Y., & Kandel, E. R. (1994). Recruitment of long-lasting protein kinase A dependent long-term potentiation on the CA1 region of hippocampus requires repeated tetanization. *Learning and Memory, 1,* 74–82.

Hubel, D. H. (1979). The brain. In *The brain: A* Scientific American *book.* New York: W. H. Freeman.

Hubel, D. H., & Wiesel, T. N. (1979). Brain mechanisms of vision. In *The brain: A* Scientific American *book.* New York: W. H. Freeman.

Hubel, D. H., Wiesel, T. N., & LeVay, S. (1977). Plasticity of ocular dominance columns in the monkey striate cortex. *Philosophical Transactions of the Royal Society of London, B, 278,* 377–409.

Hubel, D. H., Wiesel, T. N., & Stryker, M. P. (1978). Anatomical demonstration of orientation columns in macaque monkey. *Journal of Comparative Neurology, 177,* 361–379.

Hughlings-Jackson, J. (1864). Clinical remarks on defects of expression (by words, writing, signs, etc.) in diseases of the nervous system. *Lancet, 1,* 604–605.

Hughlings-Jackson, J. (1870). Remarks on non-protrusion of the tongue in some cases of aphasia. *Lancet, 1,* 716. (Reprinted in J. Taylor [Ed.]. [1932]. *Selected writings of John Hughlings-Jackson.* London: Hodder and Stoughton).

Hughlings-Jackson, J. (1874). On the nature of the duality of the brain. *Medical Press and Circular, 17,* 19. Reprinted in *Brain* (1915), *38,* 80–103.

Hughlings-Jackson, J. (1915). On affections of speech from disease of the brain. *Brain, 38,* 107–174.

Humphreys, G. W., & Riddoch, M. J. (1984). Routes to object constancy: Implications from neurological impairments of object constancy. *Quarterly Journal of Experimental Psychology, 26A,* 385–415.

Humphreys, G. W., & Riddoch, M. J. (1987). *To see but not to see: A case study of visual agnosia.* London: Erlbaum.

Humphreys, P., Kaufmann, W. E., & Galaburda, A. M. (1990). Developmental dyslexia in women: Neuropathological findings in three patients. *Archives of Neurology, 28,* 727–738.

Huntington, G. (1872). On chorea. *Medical Surgical Reporter, 26,* 317–321.

Hynd, G. W., & Semrud-Clickeman, M. (1989). Dyslexia and brain morphology. *Psychological Bulletin, 106,* 447–482.

Hynd, G. W., & Willis, W. G. (1987). *Pediatric neuropsychology.* Orlando, FL: Grune and Stratton.

Ilinsky, I. A., Jouandet, M. L., & Goldman-Rakic, P. S. (1985). Organization of the nigrothalamocortical system in the rhesus monkey. *Journal of Comparative Neurology, 236,* 315–330.

Ingvar, D. H. (1979). "Hyperfrontal" distribution of the cerebral gray matter flow in resting wakefulness: On the functional anatomy of the conscious state. *Acta Neurologica Scandanavica, 60,* 12–25.

Ingvar, D. H. (1980). Abnormal distribution of cerebral activity in chronic schizophrenia: A neurophysiological interpretation. In C. Baxter & T. Melmechuk (Eds.), *Schizophrenia* (pp. 107–125). New York: Raven Press.

Ingvar, D. H. (1985). "Memory of the future": A essay on the temporal organization of conscious awareness. *Human Neurobiology, 4,* 127–136.

Ingvar, D. H., & Franzen, G. (1974a). Abnormalities of cerebral blood flow distribution in patients with chronic schizophrenia. *Acta Psychiatrica Scandanavica, 50,* 425–462.

Ingvar, D. H., & Franzen, G. (1974b). Distribution of cerebral activity in chronic schizophrenia. *Lancet, 2,* 1484–1486.

Insel, T. R. (1990). New pharmacologic approaches to obsessive-compulsive disorder. *Journal of Clinical Psychiatry (Suppl.), 51,* 47–51.

Insel, T. R. (1992). Toward a neuroanatomy of obsessive-compulsive disorder. *Archives of General Psychiatry, 49,* 739–740.

Izard, C. E. (1971). *The face of emotion.* New York: Appleton-Century-Crofts.

Izard, C. E. (1992). Basic emotions, relations among emotions, and emotion-cognition relations. *Psychological Review, 99,* 561–565.

Jacobs, L. F., Gaulin, S. J., Sherry, D. F., & Hoffman, G. E. (1990). Evolution of spatial organization: Sex-specific patterns of spatial behavior predict hippocampal size. *Proceedings of the National Academy of Sciences (USA), 87,* 6349–6352.

Jacobsen, C. F. (1936). Studies of cerebral function in primates. *Comparative Psychology Monographs, 13,* 1–68.

Jacobsen, L. K., Giedd, J. N., Gerquin, P. C., Krain, A. L., Hamburger, S. D., Kumra, S., & Rapoport, J. L. (1997). Quantitative morphology of the cerebellum and fourth ventricle in childhood-onset schizophrenia. *American Journal of Psychiatry, 154,* 1663–1669.

Jacobson, R., LeCouteur, A., Howlin, P., & Rutter, M. (1988). Selective subcortical abnormalities in autism. *Psychological Medicine, 18,* 39–48.

James, W. (1884). What is an emotion? *Mind, 9,* 188–205.

James, W. (1950). *Principles of psychology* (Vol. 1). New York: Dover. (Original work published 1890).

Jamison, K. R. (1995). *An unquiet mind.* New York: Vintage Books.

Janowsky, J. S., Shimamura, A. P., & Squire, L. R. (1989). Source memory impairment in patients with frontal lobe lesions. *Neuropsychologia, 27,* 1043–1056.

Jarrell, T. W., Gentile, C. G., Romanski, L. M., McCabe, L. M., & Schneiderman, N. (1987). Involvement of cortical and thalamic auditory radiations in retention of differential bradycardia conditioning to acoustic conditioned stimuli in rabbits. *Brain Research, 412,* 285–294.

Jarvie, H. F. (1954). Frontal lobe lesions causing disinhibition. *Journal of Neurology, Neurosurgery and Psychiatry, 17,* 14–32.

Jaskiw, G., & Kleinman, J. (1988). Postmortem neurochemistry studies in schizophrenia. In S. C. Schultz & C. A. Tamminga (Eds.), *Schizophrenia: A scientific focus.* New York: Oxford University Press.

Jenkins, W. M., Merzenich, M. M., & Recanzone, G. (1990). Neocortical representational dynamics in adult primates: Implications for neuropsychology. *Neuropsychologia, 28,* 573–584.

Jernigan, T. L., Schafer, K., Butters, N., & Cernak, L. S. (1991). Magnetic resonance imaging of alcoholic Korsakoff patients. *Neuropsychopharmacology, 4,* 175–186.

Jessell, T. M. (1991). Reactions of neurons to injury. In E. R. Kandel, J. H. Schwartz, & T. M. Jessell (Eds.), *Principles of neural science* (3rd ed., pp. 258–282). New York: Elsevier.

Jetter, W., Poser, U., Freeman, R. B. J., & Markowitsch, H. J. (1986). A verbal long term memory deficit in frontal lobe damaged patients. *Cortex, 22,* 229–242.

Johnson, D. A., & Roetig-Johnson, K. (1989). Life in the slow lane: Attentional factors after head injury. In D. A. Johnson, D. Uttley, & M. A. Wyke (Eds.), *Children's head injury: Who cares?* London: Taylor and Francis.

Johnson, M. H., Posner, M. I., & Rothbart, M. K. (1991). Components of visual orienting in early infancy: Contingency learning, anticipatory looking and disengaging. *Journal of Cognitive Neuroscience, 3*(4), 335–344.

Johnstone, E. C., Crow, T. J., Frith, C. D., Husband, J., & Kreel, L. (1976). Cortical ventricular size and cognitive impairment in chronic schizophrenia. *Lancet, 2,* 924–926.

Johnstone, E. C., Crow, T. J., Frith, C. D., Stevens, M., Kreel, L., & Husband, J. (1978). The dementia of dementia praecox. *Acta Psychiatrica Scandanavica, 57,* 305–324.

Jones, B., & Mishkin, M. (1972). Limbic lesions and the problem of stimulus-reinforcement associations. *Experimental Neurology, 36,* 362–377.

Jones, K. L. (1977). Fetal alcohol syndrome. In J. L. Rementeria (Ed.), *Drug abuse in pregnancy and neonatal effects*. St. Louis: Mosby.

Jones, M. K. (1974). Imagery as a mnemonic aid after left temporal lobectomy. *Neuropsychologia, 12,* 21–30.

Jones, M. K. (1974). Imaging as a mnemonic aid after left temporal lobectomy. *Neuropsychologia, 12,* 21–30.

Jones-Gotman, M., & Milner, B. (1977). Design fluency: The invention of nonsense drawings after focal cortical lesions. *Neuropsychologia, 15,* 653–674.

Jonides, J., & Baum, D. R. (1978). *Cognitive maps as revealed by distance estimates*. Paper presented at the 18th annual meeting of the Psychonomic Society, Washington, DC.

Jonides, J., Smith, E. E., Keoppe, R. A., Awah, E., Minoshima, S., & Mintun, M. A. (1993). Spatial working memory in humans as revealed by PET. *Nature, 363,* 623–625.

Joynt, R. (1964). Paul Pierre Broca: His contribution to the knowledge of aphasia. *Cortex, 1,* 206–213.

Juraska, J. (1991). Sex differences in "cognitive" regions of the rat brain. *Psychoneuroendocrinology, 16,* 105–119.

Kaczmarek, B. L. J. (1984). Neurolinguistic analysis of verbal utterances in patients with focal lesions of frontal lobes. *Brain and Language, 21,* 52–58.

Kaiserman-Abramoff, I. R., Graybiel, A. M., & Nauta, W. J. H. (1980). The thalamic projection to cortical area 17 in a congenitally anophthalmic mouse strain. *Neuroscience, 5,* 41–52.

Kandel, E. R. (1989). Genes, nerve cells, and the remembrance of things past. *Journal of Neuropsychiatry, 1,* 103–125.

Kandel, E. R., Schwartz, J. H., & Jessell, T. M. (1995). *Essentials of neuroscience and behavior*. Norwalk, CT: Appleton and Lange.

Kanner, L. (1943). Autistic disturbance of affective contact. *Nervous Child, 2,* 217–250.

Kapp, B. S., Frysinger, R. C., Gallagher, M., & Haselton, J. (1979). Amygdala central nucleus lesions: Effect on heart rate conditioning in the rabbit. *Physiology and Behavior, 23,* 1109–1117.

Kapp, B. S., Pascoe, J. P., & Bixler, M. A. (1984). The amygdala: A neuroanatomical systems approach to its contributions to aversive conditioning. In N. Butters & L. R. Squire (Eds.), *Neuropsychology of memory* (pp. 473–488). New York: Guilford Press.

Kapp, B. S., Whalen, P. J., Supple, W. F., & Pascoe, J. P. (1992). Amygdaloid contributions to conditioned arousal and sensory information processing. In J. P. Aggleton (Ed.), *The amygdala: Neurobiological aspects of emotion, memory, and mental dysfunction*. New York: Wiley-Liss.

Kapp, B. S., Wilson, A., Pascoe, J., Supple, W., & Whalen, P. J. (1990). A neuroanatomical systems analysis of conditioned bradycardia in the rabbit. In M. Gabriel & J. Moore (Eds.), *Learning and computational neuroscience: Foundations of adaptive networks* (pp. 53–90). Cambridge, MA: MIT Press.

Kapur, S., & Remington, G. (1996). Serotonin-dopamine interaction and its relevance to schizophrenia. *American Journal of Psychiatry, 153,* 466–476.

Karmath, H. O., & Wallesch, C. W. (1992). Inflexibility of mental planning: A characteristic disorder with prefrontal lobe lesions? *Neuropsychologia, 30,* 1011–1016.

Karmath, H. O., Wallesch, C. W., & Zimmerman, P. (1991). Mental planning and anticipatory processes with acute and chronic frontal lobe lesions: A comparison of maze performance in routine and nonroutine situations. *Neuropsychologia, 29,* 271–290.

Karni, A., Meyer, G., Jezzard, A., Adams, M., Turner, R., & Ungerleider, L. G. (1995). Functional MRI evidence for adult motor cortex plasticity during motor skill learning. *Nature, 377,* 155–158.

Karpov, B. A., Luria, A. R., & Yarbuss, A. L. (1968). Disturbances of the structure of active perception in lesions of the posterior and anterior regions of the brain. *Neuropsychologia, 6,* 157–166.

Karten, H. J., & Shimizu, T. (1991). Are visual hierarchies in the brains of the beholders? Constancy and variability in the visual systems of birds and mammals. In P. Bagnoli & W. Hodos (Eds.), *The changing visual system* (pp. 51–59). New York: Plenum.

Keane, M. M., Clarke, H., & Corkin, S. (1992). Impaired perceptual priming and intact conceptual priming in a patient with bilateral posterior cerebral lesions. *Society for Neuroscience Abstracts, 18,* 386.

Kehle, T. J., Clark, E., & Jenson, W. R. (1996). Interventions for students with traumatic brain injury: Managing behavioral disturbances. *Journal of Learning Disabilities, 29*(6), 633–642.

Kelly, G. (1955). *A theory of personality: The psychology of personal constructs*. New York: Norton.

Kendler, K. S., & Greenberg, A. M. (1984). An independent analysis of the Danish adoption study of schizophrenia: IV. The relationship between psychiatric disorders as defined by *DSM-III* in the relatives and the adoptees. *Archives of General Psychiatry, 41,* 555–564.

Kennard, M. A. (1936). Age and other factors in motor recovery from precentral lesions in monkeys. *Journal of Neurophysiology, 1,* 477–496.

Kennard, M. A. (1942). Cortical reorganization of motor function. *Archives of Neurological Psychiatry, 48,* 227–240.

Kent, R. D., & Rosenbek, J. C. (1982). Prosodic disturbance and neurological lesion. *Brain and Language, 15,* 259–291.

Kertesz, A., Ferro, J. M., & Shewon, C. M. (1984). Apraxia and aphasia: The functional anatomical basis for their dissociation. *Neurology, 30,* 40–47.

Kety, S. S. (1983). Mental illness in the biological and adoptive relatives of schizophrenic adoptees: Findings relevant to genetic and environmental factors in etiology. *Journal of American Psychiatry, 140,* 720–727.

Kievit, J., & Kuypers, H. G. J. M. (1977). Subcortical afferents to the frontal lobe in the rhesus monkey studied by means of retrograde horseradish peroxidase transport. *Brain Research, 85,* 261–266.

Kim, J. J., & Fanselow, M. S. (1992). Modality-specific retrograde amnesia of fear. *Science, 256,* 675–677.

Kim, S. G., Ugurbil, K., & Strick, P. L. (1994). Activation of cellular output during cognitive processing. *Science, 265,* 949–951.

Kimble, D. P., Bagshaw, M. H., & Pribram, K. H. (1965). The GSR of monkeys during orientation and habituation after selective partial ablations of the cingulate and frontal cortex. *Neuropsychologia, 3,* 121–128.

Kimura, D. (1980). Neuromotor mechanisms in the evolution of human communication. In H. D. Steklis & M. J. Raleigh (Eds.), *Neurobiology of social communication in primates: An evolutionary perspective.* New York: Academic Press.

Kimura, D. (1981). Neural mechanisms of manual signing. *Sign Language Studies, 33,* 291–312.

Kimura, D. (1982). Left hemisphere control of oral and brachial movements and their relationship to communication. *Philosophical Transactions of the Royal Society of London, Series B, 298,* 135–149.

Kimura, D., & Archibald, Y. (1974). Motor functions of the left hemisphere. *Brain, 97,* 337–350.

King, F. L., & Kimura, D. (1972). Left-ear superiority in dichotic perception of social nonverbal sounds. *Canadian Journal of Psychology, 26,* 111–116.

Kinsbourne, M. (1973). Minimal brain dysfunction as a neurodevelopmental lag. *Annals of the New York Academy of Sciences, 205,* 268.

Klages, W. (1954). Frontale and diencephale Antriebsschwache. *Arch. Psychiatr. Z. Neurol., 191,* 365–387.

Klein, M. C., Sayre, J. W., & Kotok, D. (1974). Lead poisoning: Current status of the problem facing pediatricians. *American Journal of Diseases of Children, 127,* 805–807.

Klein, R., & Harper, J. (1956). The problem of agnosia in the light of a case of pure word deafness. *Journal of Mental Science, 102,* 112–120.

Kleist, K. (1934). *Gehirnpathologie.* Leipzig, Germany: Barth.

Klüver, H., & Bucy, P. C. (1937). "Psychic blindness" and other symptoms following bilateral temporal lobe lobectomy in rhesus monkeys. *Annual Review of Physiology, 119,* 342–343.

Klüver, H., & Bucy, P. C. (1939). Preliminary analysis of functions of the temporal lobes in monkeys. *Archives of Neurology and Psychiatry, 42,* 979–1000.

Knight, R. T. (1984). Decreased response to novel stimuli after prefrontal lesions in man. *Electroencephalography and Clinical Neurophysiology, 59,* 9–20.

Knight, R. T., Hillyard, S. A., Woods, D. L., & Neville, H. J. (1980). The effects of frontal and temporal-parietal lesions on the auditory evoked potential in man. *Electroencephalography and Clinical Neurophysiology, 50,* 112–124.

Knight, R. T., Hillyard, S. A., Woods, D. L., & Neville, H. J. (1981). The effects of frontal cortex lesions on event-related potentials during auditory selective attention. *Electroencephalography and Clinical Neurophysiology, 52,* 571–582.

Kojima, S., & Goldman-Rakic, P. S. (1984). Functional analysis of spatially discriminative neurons in prefrontal cortex of the rhesus monkey. *Brain Research, 291,* 229–240.

Kolb, B., & Milner, B. (1981a). Observations on spontaneous facial expression after focal cerebral excisions and after intracarotid injection of sodium amytal. *Neuropsychologia, 19,* 505–519.

Kolb, B., & Milner, B. (1981b). Performance of complex arm and facial movements after focal brain lesions. *Neuropsychologia, 19,* 491–503.

Kolb, B., & Taylor, L. (1981). Affective behavior in patients with localized cortical excisions: Role of lesion site and side. *Science, 214,* 89–91.

Kolb, B., & Taylor, L. (1988). Facial expression and the neocortex. *Society for Neuroscience Abstracts, 14,* 219.

Kolb, B., & Whishaw, I. Q. (1983). Performance of schizophrenic patients on tests sensitive to left and right frontal, temporal, or parietal function in neurological patients. *Journal of Nervous and Mental Disease, 171,* 435–443.

Kolb, B., & Whishaw, I. Q. (1996). *Fundamentals of human neuropsychology.* New York: W. H. Freeman.

Kolb, J. E., & Heaton, R. K. (1975). Lateralized neurologic deficits and psychopathology in a Turner syndrome patient. *Archives of General Psychiatry, 32,* 1198–2000.

Konorski, J. (1967). *Integrative activity of the brain.* Chicago: University of Chicago Press.

Konow, A., & Pribram, K. H. (1970). Error recognition and utilization produced by injury to the frontal cortex in man. *Neuropsychologia, 8,* 489–491.

Konstantareas, M. M., Homatidis, S., & Busch, J. (1989). Cognitive, communication, and social differences between autistic boys and girls. *Journal of Applied Developmental Psychology, 10,* 411–424.

Kordower, J. H., Winn, S. R., Liu, Y. T., Mufson, E. J., Sladek, J. R., Jr., Hammang, J. R., Baetge, E. E., & Emerich, D. E. (1994). The aged monkey basal forebrain: Rescue and sprouting of axotomized basal forebrain neurons after grafts of encapsulated cells secreting human nerve growth factor. *Proceedings of the National Academy of Sciences of the United States, 91,* 10898–10902.

Kosslyn, S. M. (1988). Aspects of the cognitive neuroscience of mental imagery. *Science, 240,* 1621–1626.

Kosslyn, S. M., Ball, T. M., & Reisser, B. J. (1978). Visual images preserve metric spatial information: Evidence from studies of image scanning. *Journal of Experimental Psychology: Human Perception and Performance, 4,* 1–20.

Kosslyn, S. M., & Koenig, O. (1992). *Wet mind: The new cognitive neuroscience.* New York: Macmillan.

Kotter, R., & Meyer, N. (1992). The limbic system: A review of its empirical foundation. *Behavioral Brain Research, 52,* 105–127.

Kovelman, J. A., & Scheibel, A. B. (1984). The neurobiological correlates of schizophrenia. *Biological Psychiatry, 19*(12), 1601–1621.

Kraepelin, E. (1919). *Dementia praecox and paraphrenia* (R. M. Barclay, Trans.). New York: Robert E. Krieger.

Kraepelin, E. (1921). *Clinical psychiatry: A textbook for teachers and physicians* (A. R. Desfendorf, Trans.). New York: Macmillan.

Kramer, P. D. (1993). *Listening to Prozac.* New York: Viking.

Kuljis, R. O., & Rakic, P. (1990). Hypercolumns in primate visual cortex develop in the absence of cues from photoreceptors. *Proceedings of the National Academy of Sciences USA, 87,* 5303–5306.

LaBar, K. S., LeDoux, J. E., Spencer, D. D., & Phelps, E. A. (1995). Impaired fear conditioning following unilateral temporal lobectomy in humans. *Journal of Neuroscience, 15,* 6846–6855.

Ladavas, E. (1987). Is the hemispatial deficit produced by right parietal lobe damage associated with retinal or gravitational coordinates? *Brain, 110,* 167–180.

Ladavas, E., Umilta, C., & Ricci-Bitti, P. E. (1980). Evidence for sex differences in right hemisphere dominance for emotions. *Neuropsychologia, 18,* 361–367.

Laeng, B. (1994). Lateralization of categorical and coordinate spatial functions: A study of unilateral stroke patients. *Journal of Cognitive Neuroscience, 6,* 189–203.

Laeng, P., & Peters, M. (1995). Cerebral lateralization for the processing of spatial coordinates in left- and right-handers. *Neuropsychologia, 33,* 421–439.

Landis, T., Assal, G., & Perret, E. (1979). Opposite cerebral hemispheric superiorities for visual associative processing of emotional facial expressions and objects. *Nature, 278,* 739–740.

Lange, C. G. (1887). *Uber Gemuthsbewegungen.* Liepzig: T. Thomas.

Lansdell, H. (1964). Sex differences in hemispheric asymmetry of the human brain. *Nature, 203,* 550.

Lashley, K. S. (1950). In search of the engram. *Symposia of the Society for Experimental Biology, 4,* 454–482.

Layman, S., & Greene, E. (1988). The effect of stroke on object recognition. *Brain and Cognition, 7,* 87–114.

Lazarus, R. S. (1966). *Psychological stress and the coping process.* New York: McGraw-Hill.

Lecours, A. R. (1975). Myelogenetic correlates of the development of speech and language. In E. H. Lenneberg & E. Lenneberg (Eds.), *Foundations of language development* (Vol. 1). New York: Academic Press.

LeDoux, J. (1996). *The emotional brain.* New York: Simon and Schuster.

LeDoux, J. E. (1987). Emotion. In F. Plum (Ed.), *Handbook of physiology: Sect. 1. The nervous system. Vol. 5. Higher functions of the brain* (pp. 419–460). Bethesda, MD: American Physiological Society.

LeDoux, J. E. (1990). Information flow from sensation to emotion: Plasticity in the neural computation of stim-ulus value. In M. Gabriel & J. Moore (Eds.), *Learning and computational neuroscience.* Cambridge, MA: MIT Press.

LeDoux, J. E. (1991). Emotion and the limbic system concept. *Concepts in Neuroscience, 2,* 169–199.

LeDoux, J. E. (1993a). Emotional memory systems in the brain. *Behavioral Brain Research, 58,* 69–79.

LeDoux, J. E. (1993b). *Emotional networks in the brain.* In M. Lewis & J. M. Haveland (Eds.), *Handbook of emotions* (pp. 109–118). New York: Guilford Press.

LeDoux, J. E. (1994). Emotion, memory and the brain. *Scientific American, 270,* 32–39.

LeDoux, J. E. (1995a). Emotion: Clues from the brain. *Annual Review of Psychology, 46,* 209–235.

LeDoux, J. E. (1995b). In search of an emotional system in the brain: Leaping from fear to emotion and consciousness. In M. S. Gazzaniga (Ed.), *The cognitive neurosciences.* Cambridge, MA: MIT Press.

LeDoux, J. E. (1996). *The emotional brain.* New York: Simon and Schuster.

LeDoux, J. E., Cicchetti, P., Xagoraris, A., & Romanski, L. M. (1990). The lateral amygdaloid nucleus: Sensory interface of the amygdala in fear conditioning. *Journal of Neuroscience, 10,* 1062–1069.

LeDoux, J. E., Farb, C. F., & Ruggiero, D. A. (1990). Topographic organization of neurons in the acoustic thalamus that project to the amygdala. *Journal of Neuroscience, 10,* 1043–1054.

LeDoux, J. E., Sakaguchi, A., Iwata, J., & Reis, D. J. (1986). Interruption of projections from the medial geniculate body to an archineocortical field disrupts the classical conditioning of emotional responses to acoustic stimuli in the rat. *Neuroscience, 17,* 615–627.

LcDoux, J. E., Sakaguchi, A., & Reis, D. J. (1984). Subcortical efferent projections of the medial geniculate nucleus mediate emotional responses conditioned by acoustic stimuli. *Journal of Neuroscience, 4*(3), 683–698.

Lees, A. J., & Smith, E. (1983). Cognitive decline in the early stages of Parkinson's disease. *Brain, 106,* 257–270.

Lehmkuhl, G., Poeck, K., & Williams, K. (1983). Ideomotor apraxia and aphasia: An examination of types and manifestations of apraxic symptoms. *Neuropsychologia, 21,* 199–212.

LeMay, M. (1984). Radiological, developmental and fossil asymmetries. In N. Geschwind & A. M. Galaburda (Eds.), *Cerebral dominance: The biological foundations.* Cambridge, MA: Harvard University Press.

Lenneberg, E. H. (1967). *Biological foundations of language.* New York: Wiley.

Leonard, H. L., Swedo, S. E., Rapoport, J. L., Koby, E. V., Lenane, M. C., Cheslow, D. L., & Hamburger, S. D. (1989). Treatment of obsessive-compulsive disorder with clomipramine and desipramine in children and adolescents: A double-blind crossover comparison. *Archives of General Psychiatry, 46,* 1088–1092.

Levenson, R. W. (1992). Autonomic nervous system differences among emotions. *Psychological Science, 3,* 23–27.

Leventhal, H., & Scherer, K. (1987). The relationship to emotion and cognition: A functional approach to a semantic controversy. *Cognition and Emotion, 1,* 3–28.

Levin, H. S., & Eisenberg, H. M. (1979). Neuropsychological impairment after closed head injury in children and adolescents. *Journal of Pediatric Psychology, 4,* 389–402.

Levin, S. (1984a). Frontal lobe dysfunctions in schizophrenia: I. Eye movement impairments. *Journal of Psychiatric Research, 18,* 27–55.

Levin, S. (1984b). Frontal lobe dysfunctions in schizophrenia: II. Impairment of psychological and brain function. *Journal of Psychiatric Research, 18,* 57–72.

Levin, S., Holzman, P. S., Rosenberg, S. J., & Lipton, R. B. (1981). Saccadic eye movements in psychotic patients. *Psychiatric Research, 5,* 47–58.

Levine, D. N., & Calvanio, R. (1989). Prosopagnosia: A deficit in visual configural processing. *Brain and Cognition, 10,* 149–170.

Levine, D. N., Warach, J., & Farah, M. J. (1985). Two visual systems in mental imagery: Dissociation of "what" and "where" in imagery disorders due to posterior cerebral lesions. *Neurology, 35,* 1010–1018.

Levy, J., Heller, W., Banich, M. T., & Burton, L. A. (1983). Asymmetry of perception in freeviewing of chimeric faces. *Brain and Cognition, 2,* 404–419.

Ley, R. G., & Bryden, M. P. (1982). A dissociation of right and left hemispheric effects for recognizing emotional tone and verbal content. *Brain and Cognition, 1,* 3–9.

Lezak, M. D. (1982). The problem of assessing executive function. *International Journal of Psychology, 17,* 281–297.

Lezak, M. D. (1983). *Neuropsychological assessment* (2nd ed.). New York: Oxford University Press.

Lezak, M. D. (1987). Relationship between personality disorders, social disturbances, and physical disability following traumatic brain injury. *Journal of Head Trauma Rehabilitation, 2,* 57–69.

Lezak, M. D. (1995). *Neuropsychological assessment* (3rd ed.). New York: Oxford University Press.

Lhermitte, F. (1986). Human anatomy and the frontal lobes: Part II. Patient behavior in complex and social situations: The "Environmental Dependency Syndrome." *Annals of Neurology, 19,* 335–343.

Lhermitte, F., Pillon, B., & Serdaru, M. (1986). Human anatomy and the frontal lobes: Part I. Imitation and utilization behavior: A neuropsychological study of 75 patients. *Annals of Neurology, 19,* 326–334.

Licht, R., Kok, A., Bakker, D. J., & Bouma, A. (1986). Hemispheric distribution of ERP components and word naming in preschool children. *Brain and Language, 27,* 101–116.

Lichtheim, L. (1885). On aphasia. *Brain, 7,* 433–484. (Reprinted and translated from Uber Aphasie, *Deutsches Arkiv fur Klinisches Midizin, 36,* 204–268).

Liepmann, H. (1900). Das Krankheitsbild der Apraxie (motorische Asymbolie). *Monatschrift fur Psychiatrie und Neurologie, 8,* 15–44, 102–132, 182–197. (Reprinted in D. A. Rottenberg & F. H. Hochberg [Eds.], *Neurological classics in modern translation* [pp. 155–183]. New York: Macmillan).

Liepmann, H. (1905). The left hemisphere and action. (Republished in 1908 in *Drei Aufsatze aus dem Apraxiegebiet.* Berlin: Karger. Translated in 1980 by D. Kimura, *Translations from Liepmann's essays on apraxia* [Research Bulletin No. 506]. Department of Psychology, University of Western Ontario, London, Ontario, Canada).

Lingjaerde, O. (1993). The biochemistry of depression. A survey of monoaminergic, neuroendocrinological, and biorhythmic disturbances in endogenous depression. *Acta Psychiatrica Scandinavica Supplementum, 302,* 36–51.

Lipman, J. (1975). *Calder's universe.* New York: Viking.

Lippert, W. W., & Senter, R. J. (1966). Electrodermal response in the sociopath. *Psychonomic Science, 4,* 25–26.

Lishman, W. A. (1968). Brain damage in relation to psychiatric disability after injury. *British Journal of Psychiatry, 114,* 373–410.

Lishman, W. A. (1973). The psychiatric sequelae of head injury: A review. *Psychological Medicine, 3,* 304–318.

Lissauer, H. (1890). Ein Fall von Seelenblindheit nebst einem Beitrag zur Theorie derselben. *Archiv fur Psychiatrie und Nervenkrankheiten, 21,* 222–270. (Edited and reprinted in translation by Jackson, M. [1988]. Lissauer on agnosia. *Cognitive Neuropsychology, 5,* 155–192).

Loftus, E. F. (1975). Leading questions and the eyewitness report. *Cognitive Psychology, 7,* 560–572.

Loftus, E. F., & Zanni, G. (1975). The influence of the wording of a question. *Bulletin of the Psychonomic Society, 5,* 86–88.

Lord-Maes, J., & Obrzut, J. E. (1996). Neuropsychological consequences of traumatic brain injury in children and adolescents. *Journal of Learning Disabilities, 29*(6), 609–617.

Lorenz, K. Z. (1966). *On aggression.* London: Methuen.

Lou, H. C., Henrikson, L., & Bruhn, P. (1984). Focal cerebral hypoprofusion in children with dysphasia and/or attention deficit disorder. *Archives of Neurology, 41,* 825.

Lou, H. C., Henrikson, L., Bruhn, P., Borner, H., & Nielsen, J. B. (1989). Striatal dysfunction in attention deficit and hyperkinetic disorder. *Archives of Neurology, 46,* 48–52.

Lucey, J. V., Costa, D. C., Busatto, G., Pilowsky, L. S., Marks, I. M., Ell, P. J., & Kerwin, R. W. (1997). Caudate regional cerebral blood flow in obsessive-compulsive disorder, panic disorder and healthy controls on single positron emission computerized tomography. *Psychiatry Research: Neuroimaging, 74,* 25–33.

Luciana, M., Depue, R. A., Arbisi, P., & Leon, A. (1992). Facilitation of working memory in humans by a D2 dopamine receptor agonist. *Journal of Cognitive Neuroscience, 4,* 58–68.

Luria, A. R. (1966). *Higher cortical functions in man.* New York: Basic Books.

Luria, A. R. (1970). *Traumatic aphasia.* The Hague: Mouton.

Luria, A. R. (1973). *The working brain*. New York: Basic Books.

Luria, A. R., & Homskaya, E. D. (1964). Disturbance in the regulative role of speech with frontal lobe lesions. In J. M. Warren & K. Akert (Eds.), *The frontal granular cortex and behavior* (pp. 353–371). New York: McGraw-Hill.

Luria, A. R., Karpov, B. A., & Yarbuss, A. L. (1966). Disturbances of active visual perception with lesions of the frontal lobes. *Cortex, 2*, 202–212.

Lynch, G. S., Deadwyler, S., & Cotman, C. W. (1973). Postlesion axonal growth produces permanent functional connections. *Science, 180*, 1364–1366.

MacLay, A. V. P. (1980). Positive and negative schizophrenic symptoms and the role of dopamine. *British Journal of Psychiatry, 137*, 379–386.

MacLean, P. D. (1949). Psychosomatic disease and the visceral brain: Recent developments bearing on the Papez theory of emotion. *Psychosomatic Medicine, 11*, 338–353.

MacLean, P. D. (1952). Some psychiatric implications of physiological studies on frontotemporal portion of limbic system (visceral brain). *Electroencephalography and Clinical Neurophysiology, 4*, 407–418.

MacLean, P. D. (1954). Studies on limbic system (visceral brain) and their bearing on psychosomatic problems. In E. Wittkower & R. Cleghord (Eds.), Recent developments in psychosomatic medicine. London: Pitman.

MacLean, P. D. (1970). The triune brain: Emotion and the scientific bias. In F. O. Schmitt (Ed.) *The neurosciences: Third study program* (pp. 336–348). New York: Rockefeller University Press.

Mair, W. G. P., Warrington, E. K., & Weiskrantz, L. (1979). Memory disorder in Korsakoff psychosis: A neuropathological and neuropsychological investigation of two cases. *Brain, 102*, 749–783.

Malmo, H. P. (1974). On frontal lobe functions: Psychiatric patient controls. *Cortex, 10*, 231–237.

Marie, P. (1906). La troisieme circonvolution frontale gauche ne joue aucun role spécial dans la fonction du langage. *Semaine Médicale, 26*, 241–247. In M. F. Cole & M. Cole (Eds./Trans.). (1971). *Piere Marie papers on speech disorders* (pp. 111–133). New York: Hafner.

Mark, V. H., & Ervin, F. R. (1970). *Violence and the brain*. New York: Harper and Row.

Mark, V. H., Sweet, W. H., & Ervin, F. R. (1972). The effect of amygdalectomy on violent behavior in patients with temporal lobe epilepsy. In E. Hitchcock, L. Laitinen, & K. Vernet (Eds.), *Psychosurgery*. Springfield, IL: Thomas.

Markowitsch, H. J., Emmans, D., Irle, E., Streicher, M., & Preilowski, B. (1985). Cortical and subcortical afferent connections of the primate's temporal pole: A study of rhesus monkeys, squirrel monkeys, and marmosets. *Journal of Comparative Neurology, 242*, 425–458.

Marlowe, M., Cossairt, A. Moon, C., Errara, J., MacNeel, A., Peak, R., Ray, J., & Schroeder, C. (1984). Main and interaction effects of metallic toxins on classroom behavior. *Journal of Abnormal Child Psychology, 13*, 185–198.

Martin, A., Wiggs, C. L., Ungeleider, L. G., & Haxby, J. V. (1996). Neural correlates of category-specific knowledge. *Nature, 379*, 649–652.

Martin, P., & Albers, P. (1995). Cerebellum and schizophrenia: A review. *Schizophrenia Bulletin, 21*, 241–251.

Martineau, J., Barthelemy, C., Herault, J., & Jouve, J. (1991). Monoamines in autistic children: A study of age-related changes. *Brain Dysfunction, 4*, 141–146.

Martinez, M., Campion, D., Babron, M. C., & Clergetdarpous, F. (1993). Is a single genetic mutation at the same locus responsible for all affected cases in a large Alzheimer pedigree (Fad4)? *Genetic Epidemiology, 10*, 431–435.

Martinot, J. L., Hardy, P., Feline, A., Huret, J.-D., Mazoyer, B., Attar-Levy, D., Pappata, S., & Syrota, S. (1990). Left prefrontal glucose hypometabolism in the depressed state: A confirmation. *American Journal of Psychiatry, 147*, 1313–1317.

Masdeu, J. (1980). Aphasia after infarction of the left supplementary motor area. *Neurology, 30*, 359.

Mateer, C., & Kimura, D. (1977). The impairment in nonverbal oral movements in aphasia. *Brain and Language, 4*, 262–276.

Mateer, C. A., Kerns, K. A., & Eso, K. L. (1996). Management of attention and memory disorders following traumatic brain injury. *Journal of Learning Disabilities, 29*(6), 618–632.

Matelli, M., Camarda, R., Glickstein, M., & Rizzolatti, G. (1984). Afferent and efferent projections of the inferior area 6 of the macaque monkey. *Brain Research, 310*, 388–392.

Mathew, R. J., Duncan, G. C., Weinman, M. L., & Barr, D. L. (1982). Regional cerebral blood flow in schizophrenia. *Archives of General Psychiatry, 39*, 1121–1130.

McAdoo, G., & DeMyer, M. K. (1978). Personality characteristics of parents. In M. Rutter & E. Schopher (Eds.), *Autism*. New York: Plenum.

McBride, H. C. G. (1975). The isolation syndrome in childhood: Part I. The syndrome and its diagnosis. *Developmental Medicine and Child Neurology, 17*, 198–219.

McCarthy, R. A., & Warrington, E. K. (1984). A two route model of speech production: Evidence from aphasia. *Brain, 107*, 463–485.

McCarthy, R. A., & Warrington, E. K. (1986). Visual associative agnosia: A clinico-anatomical study of a single case. *Journal of Neurology, Neurosurgery and Psychiatry, 49*, 1233–1240.

McCarthy, R. A., & Warrington, E. K. (1990). *Cognitive neuropsychology: A clinical introduction*. San Diego: Academic Press.

McFie, J., Piercy, M. F., & Zangwill, O. L. (1950). Visual spatial agnosia associated with lesions of the right cerebral hemisphere. *Brain, 73*, 167–190.

McFie, J., & Zangwill, O. L. (1960). Visual-constructive disabilities associated with lesions of the left cerebral hemisphere. *Brain, 82*, 243–259.

McGaugh, J. L., & Herz, M. J. (1972). *Memory consolidation*. San Francisco: Albion.

McGeer, P. L., & Rogers, J. (1992). Anti-inflammatory agents as a therapeutic approach to Alzheimer's disease. *Neurology, 42*, 447–449.

McGlone, J. (1980). Sex differences in human brain asymmetry: A critical survey. *Behavioral and Brain Sciences, 3*(2), 215–263.

McGlynn, S. C., & Schacter, D. L. (1989). Unawareness of deficits in neuropsychological syndromes. *Journal of Clinical and Experimental Neuropsychology, 11,* 143–205.

McHenry, L. C. (1969). *Garrison's history of neurology.* Springfield, IL: Thomas.

McMahon, R. C. (1980). Genetic etiology in the hyperactive child syndrome: A critical review. *American Journal of Orthopsychiatry, 50,* 145–150.

Meacham, J. A., & Leiman, B. (1982). Remembering to perform future actions. In U. Neisser (Ed.), *Memory observed: Remembering in natural contexts* (pp. 327–336). San Francisco: W. H. Freeman.

Meador, K. J., Watson, R. T., Bowers, D., & Heilman, K. H. (1986). Hypermetria with hemispatial and limb motor neglect. *Brain, 109,* 293–305.

Meesters, Y., Jansen, J. H. C., Beersma, D. G. M., Bouhuys, A. L., & Van den Hoofdaker, R. H. (1995). Light therapy for seasonal affective disorder: The effects of timing. *British Journal of Psychiatry, 166,* 607–612.

Megens, A. A., & Kennis, L. E. (1996). Risperidone and related 5HT2/D_2 antagonists: A new type of antipsychotic agent? *Progress in Medical Chemistry, 33,* 185–232.

Mehta, Z., Newcombe, F., & Damasio, H. (1987). A left hemisphere contribution to visuospatial processing. *Cortex, 23,* 447–461.

Meltzer, H. Y. (1986). Lithium mechanisms in bipolar illness and altered intracellular calcium functions. *Biological Psychiatry, 21,* 492–510.

Mendez, M. F. (1988). Visuoperceptual function in visual agnosia. *Neurology, 38,* 1754–1759.

Mercer, B., Wapner, W., Gardner, H., & Benson, D. F. (1977). A study of confabulation. *Archives of Neurology, 34,* 429–433.

Merzenich, M. M., Recanzone, G. H., Jenkins, W. M., & Grajski, K. A. (1990). Adaptive mechanisms in cortical network underlying cortical contributions to learning and nondeclarative memory. In *Cold Spring Harbor Symposium on Quantitative Biology. Vol. 55: The brain.* New York: Cold Spring Harbor Laboratory.

Mesulam, M. M. (1981). A cortical network for directed attention and unilateral neglect. *Archives of Neurology, 10,* 309–325.

Mesulam, M. M. (1985). Patterns in behavioral neuroanatomy. In M. M. Mesulam (Ed.), *Principles of behavioral neurology.* Philadelphia: Davis.

Meunier, M., Bachevalier, J., Mishkin, M., & Murray, E. A. (1993). Effects on visual recognition of combined and separate ablations of the entorhinal and perirhinal cortex in rhesus monkeys. *Journal of Neuroscience, 13,* 5418–5432.

Meyer, A. (1974). The frontal lobe syndrome, the aphasias and related conditions: A contribution to the history of cortical localization. *Brain, 97,* 565–600.

Mialet, J. P., & Pichot, P. (1981). Eye-tracking patterns in schizophrenia. *Archives of General Psychiatry, 38,* 183–186.

Miller, G. A. (1956). The magic number seven plus or minus two: Some limits in our capacity for processing information. *Psychological Review, 63,* 81–97.

Miller, K. F., Delgado, P. L., Salomon, R. M., Berman, R., Krystal, J. H., Heninger, G. R., & Charney, D. S. (1996). Clinical and biochemical effects of catecholamine depletion on antidepressant-induced remission of depression. *Archives of General Psychiatry, 53,* 117–128.

Miller, L. A. (1992). Impulsivity, risk-taking, and the ability to synthesize fragmented information after frontal lobectomy. *Neuropsychologia, 31,* 69–79.

Milner, B. (1963). Effects of different brain lesions on card sorting. *Archives of Neurology, 9,* 90–100.

Milner, B. (1964). Some effects of frontal lobectomy in man. In J. M. Warren & K. Akert (Eds.), *The frontal granular cortex and behavior* (pp. 313–334). New York: McGraw-Hill.

Milner, B. (1965a). Memory disturbance after bilateral hippocampal lesions in man. In P. M. Milner & S. E. Glickman (Eds.), *Cognitive processes and brain.* Princeton, NJ: Van Nostrand.

Milner, B. (1965b). Visually-guided maze learning in man: Effects of bilateral hippocampal, bilateral frontal and unilateral cerebral lesions. *Neuropsychologia, 3,* 317–338.

Milner, B. (1968). Visual recognition and recall after right temporal-lobe excision in man. *Neuropsychologia, 6,* 191–209.

Milner, B. (1970). Memory and the medial temporal region of the brain. In K. H. Pribram & D. E. Broadbent (Eds.), *Biological bases of memory* (pp. 29–50). New York: Academic Press.

Milner, B. (1971). Interhemispheric differences in the localization of psychological processes in man. *British Medical Bulletin, 27,* 272–277.

Milner, B. (1975). Psychological aspects of focal epilepsy and its neurosurgical management. In D. R. Pampura, J. K. Penry, & R. D. Walter (Eds.), *Advances in neurology* (Vol. 8). New York: Raven Press.

Milner, B. (1982). Some cognitive effects of frontal-lobe lesions in man. *Philosophical Transactions of the Royal Society of London, B, 298,* 211–226.

Milner, B., Branch, C., & Rasmussen, T. (1964). Observations on cerebral dominance. In A. V. S. de Rueck & M. O'Connor (Eds.), *Disorders of language.* London: Churchill.

Milner, B., Corkin, S., & Teuber, H.-L. (1968). Further analysis of the hippocampal amnesic syndrome: Fourteen-year follow-up study of H. M. *Neuropsychologia, 6,* 215–234.

Milner, B., Corsi, P., & Leonard, G. (1991). Frontal-lobe contributions to recency judgments. *Neuropsychologia, 29,* 601–618.

Milner, B., & Kolb, B. (1985). Performance of complex arm movements and facial-movement sequences after cerebral commissurotomy. *Neuropsychologia, 23,* 791–799.

Milner, B., & Petrides, M. (1984). Behavioral effects of frontal-lobe lesions in man. *Trends in Neurosciences, 7*, 403–407.

Milner, B., Petrides, M., & Smith, M. L. (1986). Frontal lobes and the temporal organization of memory. *Human Neurobiology, 4*, 137–142.

Milner, B., & Taylor, L. (1972). Right-hemisphere superiority in tactile pattern recognition after cerebral commissurotomy: Evidence for nonverbal memory. *Neuropsychologia, 10*, 1–15.

Milner, B., Taylor, L., & Sperry, R. (1968). Lateralized suppression of dichotically presented digits after commissural section in man. *Science, 161*, 184–185.

Milner, B., & Teuber, H.-L. (1968). Alterations of perception and memory in man: Reflection on methods. In L. Weiskrantz (Ed.), *Analysis of behavior change* (pp. 353–355). New York: Harper and Row.

Mink, J. W., & Thach, W. T. (1993). Basal ganglia intrinsic circuits and their role in behavior. *Current Opinions in Neurobiology, 3*, 950–957.

Mishkin, M. (1964). Perseveration of central sets after frontal lesions in monkeys. In J. M. Warren & K. Akert (Eds.), *The frontal granular cortex and behavior* (pp. 219–241). New York: McGraw-Hill.

Mishkin, M. (1966). Visual mechanisms beyond the striate cortex. In R. Russell (Ed.), *Frontiers of physiological psychology*. New York: Academic Press.

Mishkin, M. (1978). Memory in monkeys severely impaired by combined but not separate removal of amygdala and hippocampus. *Nature, 273*, 297–298.

Mishkin, M. (1982). A memory system in the monkey. *Philosophical Transactions of the Royal Society of London, Series B, 298*, 85–95.

Mishkin, M., & Manning, F. J. (1978). Non-spatial memory after selective prefrontal lesions in monkeys. *Brain Research, 143*, 313–323.

Mishkin, M., Ungerleider, L., & Macko, K. (1983). Object vision and spatial vision: Two cortical pathways. *Trends in Neurosciences, 6*, 414–417.

Mishkin, M., Vest, B., Waxler, M., & Rosvold, H. A. (1969). A reexamination of the effects of frontal lesions in object alternation. *Neuropsychologia, 7*, 357–363.

Miyakawa, T., Sumiyoshi, S., Deshimaru, M., Suzuki, T., Tomonari, H., Yasuoka, F., & Tatetsu, S. (1972). Electron microscopic study in schizophrenia. *Acta Neuropathologica, 20*, 67–77.

Monrad-Krohn, G. H. (1947). Dysprosody of altered "melody of language." *Brain, 70*, 405–415.

Morgan, M., & LeDoux, J. E. (1995). Differential contribution of dorsal and ventral medial prefrontal cortex to acquisition and extinction of conditioned fear. *Behavioral Neuroscience, 109*, 681–688.

Morgan, M., Romanski, L. M., & LeDoux, J. E. (1993). Extinction of emotional learning: Contribution of medial prefrontal cortex. *Neuroscience Letters, 163*, 109–113.

Morgan, W. P. (1896). A case of congenital word blindness. *British Medical Journal, 2*, 1378.

Morihisa, J. M., Duffy, F. H., & Wyatt, R. J. (1983). Brain electrical activity mapping (BEAM) in schizophrenic patients. *Archives of General Psychiatry, 40*, 719–728.

Morrison, J. R., & Stewart, M. A. (1971). A family study of the hyperactive child syndrome. *Biological Psychiatry, 3*, 189–195.

Moscovitch, M., & Olds, J. (1982). Asymmetries in spontaneous facial expressions and their possible relation to hemispheric specialization. *Neuropsychologia, 20*, 71–82.

Mountcastle, V. B., Motter, B. C., Steinmetz, M. A., & Duffy, C. J. (1984). Looking and seeing: The visual functions of the parietal lobe. In G. M. Edelman, W. E. Gall, & W. M. Cowan (Eds.), *Dynamic aspects of neocortical function* (pp. 159–193). New York: Wiley.

Mungas, D. (1982). Interictal behavioral abnormality in temporal lobe epilepsy. *Archives of General Psychiatry, 39*, 108–111.

Mungas, D. (1983). Behavioral symptoms in temporal lobe epilepsy [Letter]. *Archives of General Psychiatry, 40*, 468–469.

Munk, H. (1881). *Uber die Funktionen der Grosshirndrinde. Gesammelte Mittielungen aus den Jahren.* 1877–1880. Berlin: August Hershwald.

Murray, E. A. (1992). Medial temporal lobe structures contributing to recognition memory: The amygdaloid complex versus the rhinal cortex. In J. P. Aggleton (Ed.), *The amygdala: Neurobiological aspects of emotion, memory and mental dysfunction.* New York: Wiley-Liss.

Murray, E. A., Gaffan, D., & Mishkin, M. (1993). Neural substrates of visual stimulus-stimulus association in rhesus monkeys. *Journal of Neuroscience, 13*, 4549–4561.

Myers, R. E. (1955). Interocular transfer of pattern discrimination in cats following section of crossed optic fibers. *Journal of Comparative and Physiological Psychology, 48*, 470–473.

Myers, R. E., Swett, C., & Miller, M. (1973). Loss of social group affinity following prefrontal lesions in free-ranging macaques. *Brain Research, 64*, 257–269.

Myers, S. (1972). Role of peripheral and anterior temporal cortex in social behavior and affect in monkeys. *Acta Neurobiologiae Experimentalis, 32*, 567–579.

Myklebust, H. R. (1975). Nonverbal learning disabilities: Assessment and intervention. In H. R. Myklebust (Ed.), *Progress in learning disabilities* (Vol. 3). New York: Grune and Stratton.

Nadel, L., & Willner, J. (1980). Context and conditioning: A place for space. *Physiological Psychology, 8*, 218–228.

Nauta, W. J. H. (1971). The problem of the frontal lobe: A reinterpretation. *Journal of Psychiatric Research, 8*, 167–187.

Nauta, W. J. H., & Feirtag, M. (1979). The organization of the brain. In *The brain: A* Scientific American *book.* New York: W. H. Freeman.

Nauta, W. J. H., & Feirtag, M. (1986). *Fundamental neuroanatomy.* New York: W. H. Freeman.

Nauta, W. J. H., & Karten, H. J. (1970). A general profile of the vertebrate brain, with sidelights on the ancestry of the cerebral cortex. In F. O. Schmitt (Ed.), *The neurosciences: Second study program* (pp. 7–26). New York: Rockefeller University Press.

Neisser, U. (1966). *Cognitive psychology.* New York: Appleton-Century-Crofts.

Netter, F. (1974). *The CIBA collection of medical illustrations: Vol. 1. Nervous system.* Summit, NJ: CIBA.

Newcombe, F. (1969). *Missile wounds of the brain: A study of psychological deficits.* London: Oxford University Press.

Newcombe, F. (1979). The processing of visual information in prosopagnosia and acquired dyslexia: Functional versus physiological interpretation. In D. J. Oborne, M. M. Gruneberg, & J. R. Eiser (Eds.), *Research in Psychology and Medicine* (Vol. 1, pp. 315–322). London: Academic Press.

Nicoll, R. A., Kauer, J. A., & Malenka, R. C. (1988). The current excitement in long-term potentiation. *Neuron, 1,* 97–103.

Nielsen, J. S. (1937). Unilateral cerebral dominance as related to mind blindness. *Archives of Neurology and Psychiatry, 38,* 108–135.

Nielsen, J. S. (1946). *Agnosia, apraxia, aphasia: Their value in cerebral localization* (2nd ed.). New York: Harper (Hoeber).

Nieto, D., & Escobar, A. (1972). Major psychoses. In J. Minkler (Ed.), *Pathology of the nervous system.* New York: McGraw-Hill.

Niki, H., & Watanabe, M. (1976). Prefrontal unit activity and delayed response: Relation to cue location versus direction of response. *Brain Research, 105,* 79–88.

Nobler, M. S., Sackeim, H. A., Porhovnik, I., Moeller, J. R., Mukherjee, S., Schnur, D. B., Prudic, J., & Devanand, D. P. (1994). Regional cerebral blood flow in mood disorders: III. Treatment and clinical response. *Archives of General Psychiatry, 51,* 884–897.

Nordahl, T. E., Benkelfat, C., Semple, W. E., Gross, M., King, A. C., & Cohen, R. M. (1989). Cerebral glucose metabolic rates in obsessive compulsive disorder. *Neuropsychopharmacology, 2,* 23–28.

Norman, D., & Shallice, T. (1986). Attention to action: Willed and autonomic control of behavior. In R. J. Davidson, G. E. Schwartz, & D. Shapiro (Eds.), *Consciousness and self-regulation* (Vol. 4). New York: Plenum.

Northcutt, R. G., & Kaas, J. H. (1995). The emergence and evolution of mammalian neocortex. *Trends in Neuroscience, 18,* 373–379.

Nudo, R. J., & Grenda, R. (1992). Reorganization of distal forelimb representation in primary motor cortex of adult squirrel monkeys following focal ischemic infarct. *Society for Neuroscience Abstracts, 18,* Part 1, 216.

Nuechterlein, K. H., & Dawson, M. E. (1984). Information processing and attentional functioning in the developmental course of schizophrenic disorders. *Schizophrenia Bulletin, 10,* 160–203.

Ogden, J. A. (1987). The "neglected" left hemisphere and its contribution to visuospatial neglect. In M. Jeannerod (Ed.), *Neurophysiological and neuropsychological aspects of spatial neglect* (pp. 215–233). Amsterdam: Elsevier North-Holland.

O'Hara, C. (1988). Emotional adjustment following minor head injury. *Cognitive Rehabilitation, 6,* 26–33.

Ojemann, G. A., Blick, K. I., & Ward, A. A., Jr. (1971). Improvement and disturbance of short term verbal memory with human ventromedial thalamic stimulation. *Brain, 94,* 225–240.

O'Keefe, J., & Dostrovsky, J. (1971). The hippocampus as a spatial map: Preliminary evidence from unit activity in the freely moving rat. *Brain Research, 34,* 171–175.

O'Keefe, J., & Nadel, L. (1978). *The hippocampus as a cognitive map.* New York: Clarendon Press.

Olavarria, J., & Van Sluyters, R. C. (1984). Callosal connections of the posterior neocortex in normal-eyed, congenitally anophthalmic and neonatally enucleated mice. *Journal of Comparative Neurology, 230,* 249–268.

Olds, J., & Milner, P. (1954). Positive reinforcement produced by electrical stimulation of the septal area and other regions of the rat brain. *Comparative and Physiological Psychology, 47,* 419–427.

Olton, D., Becker, J. T., & Handleman, G. E. (1979). Hippocampus, space and memory. *Behavioral and Brain Sciences, 2,* 313–365.

Ono, T., & Nishijo, H. (1992). Neurophysiological basis of the Klüver-Bucy syndrome: Responses of monkey amygdaloid neurons to biologically significant objects. In J. P. Aggleton (Ed.), *The amygdala: Neurobiological aspects of emotion, memory, and mental dysfunction* (pp. 167–190). New York: Wiley-Liss.

Ornitz, E. M. (1973). Childhood autism. A review of the experimental and medical literature (Medical Progress). *California Medicine, 118,* 21–47.

Ornitz, E. M. (1978). Biological homogeneity or heterogeneity? In M. Rutter & E. Schopher (Eds.), *Autism: A reappraisal of concepts and treatment.* New York: Plenum.

Orton, S. (1925). Word-blindness in school children. *Archives of Neurology and Psychiatry, 14,* 582.

Orton, S. (1937). *Reading, writing and speech problems in children.* New York: Norton.

Oscar-Berman, M., McNamara, P., & Freedman, M. (1991). Delayed-response tasks: Parallels between experimental ablation studies and findings in patients with frontal lesions. In H. S. Levin, H. M. Eisenberg, & A. L. Benton (Eds.), *Frontal lobe function and dysfunction* (pp. 230–255). New York: Oxford University Press.

Owen, A. M., Roberts, A. C., Polkey, C. E., Sahakian, B. J., & Robbins, T. W. (1991). Extradimensional versus intradimensional set shifting performance following frontal lobe excisions, temporal lobe excisions or amygdalo-hippocampectomy in man. *Neuropsychologia, 29,* 993–1006.

Owen, M. J., & Mullen, J. M. (1990). Molecular genetic studies of manic-depression and schizophrenia. *Trends in Neurosciences, 13,* 29–31.

Oxbury, J. M., Campbell, D. C., & Oxbury, S. M. (1974). Unilateral spatial neglect and impairments of spatial analysis and visual perception. *Brain, 97,* 551–564.

Pandya, D. N., & Kuypers, H. G. J. M. (1969). Cortico-cortical connections in the rhesus monkey. *Brain Research, 13,* 13–36.

Pandya, D. N., & Seltzer, B. (1982). Intrinsic connections and architectonics of posterior parietal cortex in the rhesus monkey. *Journal of Comparative Neurology, 204,* 196–210.

Papez, J. (1937). A proposed mechanism of emotion. *Archives of Neurology and Psychiatry, 38,* 725–744.

Pardo, J. V., Pardo, P. J., & Raichle, M. E. (1993). Neural correlates of self-induced dysphoria. *American Journal of Psychiatry, 150,* 713–719.

Park, S. (1995). Spatial working memory function in schizophrenia. In M. Spitzer & B. A. Maher (Eds.), *Experimental psychopathology.* New York: Cambridge University Press.

Park, S., & Holzman, P. S. (1992). Schizophrenics show spatial working memory deficits. *Archives of General Psychiatry, 49,* 975–982.

Parkin, A. J., & Leng, N. R. C. (1993). *Neuropsychology of the amnesic syndrome.* Hillsdale, NJ: Erlbaum.

Pascual-Leone, A., Grafman, J., Clark, K., Stewart, M., Massaquoi, S., Lou, J., & Hallet, M. (1993). Procedural learning in Parkinson's disease and cerebellar degeneration. *Annals of Neurology, 34,* 594–602.

Passingham, R. E. (1972). Visual discrimination learning after selective prefrontal ablations in monkeys (*Macaca mulatta*). *Neuropsychologia, 10,* 27–39.

Passingham, R. E. (1975). Delayed matching after selective prefrontal lesions in monkeys (*Macaca mulatta*). *Brain Research, 92,* 89–102.

Passingham, R. E. (1985a). Cortical mechanisms and cues for action. *Philosophical Transactions of the Royal Society of London, B, 308,* 101–111.

Passingham, R. E. (1985b). Memory of monkeys (*Macaca mulatta*) with lesions in prefrontal cortex. *Behavioral Neuroscience, 99,* 3–21.

Passingham, R. E. (1993). *The temporal lobe and voluntary action.* Oxford, England: Oxford University Press.

Paterson, A., & Zangwill, O. L. (1944). Disorders of visual space perception associated with lesions of the right cerebral hemisphere. *Brain, 67,* 331–358.

Paterson, A., & Zangwill, O. L. (1945). A case of topographical disorientation associated with a unilateral cerebral lesion. *Brain, 68,* 188–211.

Patterson, K. E., & Kay, J. (1982). Letter-by-letter reading: Psychological description of a neurological syndrome. *Quarterly Journal of Experimental Psychology, 34A,* 411–441.

Patterson, K. E., Marshall, J. C., & Coltheart, M. (1985). *Surface dyslexia: Neuropsychological and cognitive studies of phonological reading.* Hove, London: Erlbaum.

Pavlov, I. (1927). *Conditioned reflexes.* New York: Dover.

Payne, B. R., & Cornwell, P. (1994). System-wide repercussions of damage to the immature visual cortex. *Trends in Neurosciences, 17*(3), 126–130.

Penfield, W., & Evans, J. (1935). The frontal lobe in man: A clinical study of maximum removals. *Brain, 68,* 115–133.

Penfield, W., & Jaspers, H. (1954). *Epilepsy and the functional anatomy of the human brain.* Boston: Little, Brown.

Penfield, W., & Milner, B. (1958). Memory deficit produced by bilateral lesions of the hippocampal zone. *AMA Archives of Neurology and Psychiatry, 79,* 475–497.

Penfield, W., & Perot, P. (1963). The brain's record of auditory and visual experience. *Brain, 86,* 595–696.

Penfield, W., & Rasmussen, T. (1950). *The cerebral cortex of man.* New York: Macmillan.

Penfield, W., & Roberts, L. (1959). *Speech and brain mechanisms.* Princeton, NJ: Princeton University Press.

Penney, J. B., Jr., & Young, A. B. (1981). GABA as the pallido-thalamic neurotransmitter: Implications for basal ganglia function. *Brain Research, 207,* 195–199.

Perenin, M. T., & Vighetto, A. (1983). Optic ataxia: A specific disorder of visuomotor coordination. In A. Hein & M. Jeannerod (Eds.), *Spatially oriented behavior* (pp. 305–326). New York: Springer.

Perenin, M. T., & Vighetto, A. (1988). Optic ataxia: A specific disruption of visuomotor mechanisms. *Brain, 111,* 643–674.

Perret, E. (1974). The left frontal lobe of man and suppression of habitual responses in verbal categorical behavior. *Neuropsychologia, 12,* 323–330.

Perrett, D., Rolls, E. T., & Caan, W. (1982). Visual neurons responsive to faces in the monkey visual cortex. *Experimental Brain Research, 47,* 329–342.

Perria, L., Rossalini, G., & Rossi, G. F. (1961). Determination of the side of cerebral dominance with amobarbital. *Archives of Neurology, 4,* 173–181.

Petrides, M. (1985). Deficits in conditioned associative learning tasks after frontal- and temporal-lobe lesions in man. *Neuropsychologia, 23,* 601–614.

Petrides, M. (1990). Nonspatial conditioned learning impaired in patients with unilateral frontal but not unilateral temporal lobe excisions. *Neuropsychologia, 28,* 137–149.

Petrides, M. (1994a). Frontal lobes and behavior. *Current Opinions in Neurobiology, 4,* 207–211.

Petrides, M. (1994b). Frontal lobe and working memory: Evidence from investigations of the effect of cortical excisions in nonhuman primates. In F. Boller & J. Grafman (Eds.), *Handbook of neuropsychology* (Vol. 9, pp. 59–82). New York: Elsevier.

Petrides, M., Alivsatos, B., Meyers, E., & Evans, A. C. (1993). Functional activation of the human frontal cortex during the performance of verbal working memory tasks. *Proceedings of the National Academy of Sciences USA, 90,* 878–882.

Petrides, M., & Iversen, S. D. (1976). Cross-modal matching and the primate frontal cortex. *Science, 192,* 1023–1024.

Petrides, M., & Milner, B. (1982). Deficits on subject-ordered tasks after frontal- and temporal-lobe lesions in man. *Neuropsychologia, 20,* 249–262.

Petrides, M., & Pandya, D. N. (1984). Projections to the frontal cortex from the posterior parietal region in the rhesus monkey. *Journal of Comparative Neurology, 228,* 105–116.

Phillips, R. G., & LeDoux, J. E. (1992). Differential contribution of amygdala and hippocampus to cued and contextual fear conditioning. *Behavioral Neuroscience, 106,* 274–285.

Piaget, J. (1952). *The origins of intelligence in children.* New York: International Universities Press.

Piccinelli, M., Pini, S., Bellantuono, C., & Wilkinson, G. (1995). Efficacy of drug treatment in obsessive-compulsive disorder: A meta-analytic review. *British Journal of Psychiatry, 166,* 424–443.

Piercy, M., Hecaen, H., & Ajuriaguerra, J. (1960). Constructional apraxia associated with unilateral cerebral lesions— Left and right sided cases combined. *Brain, 83,* 225–242.

Pierot-Deseilligny, C., Rivaud, S., Gaymard, B., & Agid, Y. (1991). Cortical control of memory-guided saccades in man. *Experimental Brain Research, 83,* 607–617.

Pigarev, I. N., Rizzolatti, G., & Scandolara, C. (1979). Neurons responding to visual stimuli in the frontal lobe of macaque monkeys. *Neuroscience Letters, 12,* 207–212.

Pinker, S. (1994). *The language instinct.* New York: Morrow.

Pinker, S. (1995). *Language is a human instinct.* In J. Brockman (Ed.), *The third culture.* New York: Simon and Schuster.

Pinker, S. (1997). *How the mind works.* New York: Norton.

Pitkämen, A., Stefanacci, L., Farb, C. R., Go, C.-G., LeDoux, J. E., & Amaral, D. G. (1995). Intrinsic connections of the rat amygdaloid complex: Projections originating in the lateral nucleus. *Journal of Comparative Neurology, 356,* 288–310.

Piven, J., Berthier, M. L., Starkstein, S. E., & Nehme, E., Pearlson, G., Folstein, S. (1990). Magnetic resonance imaging evidence for a defect of cerebral cortical development in autism. *American Journal of Psychiatry, 147*(6), 731–739.

Pizzamiglio, L., Zoccolotti, P., Mannucari, A., & Cesaroni, R. (1983). Independence of face identity and facial expression recognition mechanisms: Relation to sex and cognitive style. *Brain and Cognition, 2,* 176–188.

Poeck, K. (1969). Pathophysiology of emotional disorders associated with brain damage. In P. J. Vinken & G. W. Bruyn (Eds.), *Handbook of Neurology* (Vol. 3). New York: American Elsevier.

Poeck, K., & Lehmkuhl, G. (1980). Das Syndrom der ideatorischen Apraxie und seine Localisation. *Nervenarzt, 51,* 217–225.

Pohl, W. (1973). Dissociation of spatial discrimination deficits following frontal and parietal lesions in monkeys. *Journal of Comparative and Physiological Psychology, 82,* 227–239.

Poizner, H., Klima, E. S., & Bellugi, U. (1987). *What the hands reveal about the brain.* Cambridge, MA: MIT Press.

Porac, C., & Coren, S. (1981). *Lateral preference and human behavior.* New York: Springer.

Porrino, L. J., Crane, A. M., & Goldman-Rakic, P. S. (1981). Direct and indirect pathways from the amygdala to the frontal lobe in rhesus monkeys. *Journal of Comparative Neurology, 198,* 121–136.

Porrino, L. J., & Goldman-Rakic, P. S. (1982). Brain stem innervation of the prefrontal and anterior cingulate cortex in the rhesus monkey revealed by retrograde transport of HRP. *Journal of Comparative Neurology, 205,* 63–76.

Posner, M., & Peterson, S. (1990). The attention system of the human brain. *Annual Review of Neuroscience, 13,* 25–42.

Posner, M. I., Cohen, Y., & Rafal, R. D. (1982). Neural systems control of spatial orienting. *Philosophical Transactions of the Royal Society of London, Series B, 298,* 60–70.

Posner, M. I., & Raichle, M. E. (1994). *Images of mind.* New York: W. H. Freeman.

Posner, M. I., Walker, J. A., Friedrich, F. J., & Rafal, R. D. (1984). Effects of parietal injury on covert orienting of attention. *Journal of Neuroscience, 4,* 1863–1874.

Povenelli, D. J., & Preuss, T. M. (1995). Theory of mind: Evolutionary history of a cognitive specialization. *Trends in Neuroscience, 18,* 418–424.

Premack, D. (1976). *Intelligence in ape and man.* Hillsdale, NJ: Erlbaum.

Preuss, T. M. (1995). Do rats have prefrontal cortex? The Rose-Woolsey-Akert program reconsidered. *Journal of Cognitive Neuroscience, 7,* 1–24.

Pribram, K. H. (1954). Toward a science of neuropsychology (method and data). In R. A. Patton (Ed.), *Current trends in neuropsychology and the behavioral sciences.* Pittsburgh, PA: University of Pittsburgh Press.

Pribram, K. H. (1973). Primate frontal cortex-Executive of the brain. In K. H. Pribram & A. R. Luria (Eds.), *Psychophysiology of the frontal lobes* (pp. 293–314). New York: Academic Press.

Pribram, K. H., Chow, K., & Semmes, J. (1953). Limit and organization of the cortical projection from the medial thalamic nucleus in the monkey. *Journal of Comparative Neurology, 98,* 433–448.

Pribram, K. H., & Mishkin, M. (1956). Analysis of the effects of frontal lesions in monkeys: III. Object alternation. *Journal of Comparative and Physiological Psychology, 49,* 41–45.

Pribram, K. H., & Tubbs, W. E. (1967). Short-term memory, parsing, and primate frontal cortex. *Science, 156,* 1765–1767.

Price, D. L., & Sisodia, S. S. (1992). Alzheimer's disease: Neural and molecular basis. In L. R. Squire (Ed.), *Encyclopedia of learning and memory* (pp. 22–25). New York: Macmillan.

Price, J. L., Russchen, F. T., & Amaral, D. G. (1987). The limbic region: II. The amygdaloid complex. In A. Bjorklund, T. Hokfelt, & L. W. Swanson (Eds.), *Handbook of clinical neuroanatomy:Vol. 5. Integrated systems in the CNS, Part 1* (pp. 279–388). Amsterdam: Elsevier.

Prigatano, G. P., Altman, I. M., & O'Brian, K. P. (1990). Behavioral limitations that traumatic-brain-injured patients tend to underestimate. *Clinical Neuropsychologist, 4,* 163–176.

Prigatano, G. P., & Schacter, D. L. (Eds.). (1991). *Awareness of deficit after brain injury: Clinical and theoretical issues.* New York: Oxford University Press.

Quay, H. C. (1965). Psychopathic personality as pathological stimulation seeking. *American Journal of Psychiatry, 122,* 180–183.

Raine, A., Buchsbaum, M. S., Stanley, J., Lottenberg, S., Abel, L., & Stoddard, J. (1994). Selective reductions in prefrontal glucose metabolism in murderers. *Biological Psychiatry, 36,* 365–373.

Rains, G. D., & Milner, B. (1994a). Right-hippocampal contralateral-hand effect in the recall of spatial location in the tactual modality. *Neuropsychologia, 32,* 1233–1242.

Rains, G. D., & Milner, B. (1994b). Verbal recall and recognition as a function of depth of encoding in patients with unilateral temporal lobectomy. *Neuropsychologia, 32,* 1243–1256.

Raisman, G. (1978). What hope for repair of the brain? *Annals of Neurology, 3,* 101–106.

Rakic, P. (1988a). Defects of neuronal migration and pathogenesis of cortical malformations. *Progress in Brain Research, 73,* 15–37.

Rakic, P. (1988b). Specification of cerebral cortical areas. *Science, 241,* 170–176.

Rakic, P. (1995). Corticogenesis in human and nonhuman primates. In M. S. Gazzaniga (Ed.), *The cognitive neurosciences* (pp. 127–145). Cambridge, MA: MIT Press.

Rasmussen, S. A. (1993). Genetic studies of obsessive-compulsive disorders. *Annals of Clinical Psychiatry, 5,* 241–247.

Rasmussen, T., & Milner, B. (1975). Clinical and surgical studies of the cerebral speech areas in man. In K. J. Zulch, O. Creutzfeldt, & G. C. Galbraith (Eds.), *Cerebral localization.* Berlin: Springer.

Rasmussen, T., & Milner, B. (1977). The role of early left brain injury in determining lateralization of cerebral speech functions. *Annals of the New York Academy of Sciences, 299,* 355–369.

Ratcliff, G. (1979). Spatial thought, mental rotation and the right cerebral hemisphere. *Neuropsychologia, 17,* 49–54.

Ratcliff, G., & Newcombe, F. (1982). Object recognition: Some deductions from the clinical evidence. In A. W. Ellis (Ed.), *Normality and pathology in cognitive functions.* New York: Academic Press.

Reep, R. (1984). Relationship between prefrontal and limbic cortex: A comparative anatomical review. *Brain, Behavior and Evolution, 25,* 5–80.

Rees, W. L. (1973). The value and limitations of psychosurgery in the treatment of psychiatric illness. *Psychiatria Neurologia Neurochirurgia, 76,* 323–324.

Reitan, R. M., & Davison, L. A. (1974). *Clinical neuropsychology: Current status and application.* New York: Wiley.

Reynolds, O. (1996). Causes and outcome of perinatal brain injury. In D. Magnusson (Ed.), *The lifespan development of individuals: Behavioral, neurobiological, and psychosocial perspectives.* New York: Cambridge University Press.

Riddoch, G. (1935). Visual disorientation in homonymous half-fields. *Brain, 58,* 376–382.

Riddoch, M. J., & Humphreys, G. W. (1986). Neurological impairments of object constancy: The effect of orientation and size disparities. *Cognitive Neuropsychology, 3,* 207–224.

Riddoch, M. J., & Humphreys, G. W. (1987). A case of integrative visual agnosia. *Brain, 110,* 1431–1462.

Riva, D., & Cazzaniga, L. (1986). Late effects of unilateral brain lesions sustained before and after age one. *Neuropsychologia, 24,* 423–428.

Roberts, G. W. (1990). Schizophrenia: The cellular biology of a functional psychosis. *Trends in Neurosciences, 12*(6), 207–211.

Robinson, D., Wu, H. W., Munne, R. A., Ashtam, M., Alvir, J. M. M., Lerner, G., Koreen, A., Cole, K., & Rogers, B. (1995). Reduced caudate nucleus volume in obsessive-compulsive disorder. *Archives of General Psychiatry, 52,* 393–398.

Robinson, R. G., & Benson, D. F. (1981). Depression in aphasic patients: Frequency, severity, and clinical pathological correlation. *Brain and Language, 14,* 282–291.

Robinson, R. G., Kubos, K. L., Starr, L. B., Rao, K., & Price, T. R. (1984). Mood disorders in stroke patients: Importance of location of lesion. *Brain, 107,* 81–93.

Roediger, H. L., III, & McDermott, K. B. (1993). Implicit memory in normal human subjects. In H. Spinnler & F. Boller (Eds.), *Handbook of neuropsychology* (pp. 63–131). Amsterdam: Elsevier.

Rogers, J., Kirby, L. C., Hempelman, S. R., Beery, D. L., McGeer, P. L., Kaszniak, A. W., Zalinshi, J., Cofield, M., Mansukhani, L., Wilson, P., & Kogan, F. (1993). Clinical-trial of indomethacin in Alzheimers-disease. *Neurology, 43,* 1609–1611.

Roland, P. E., & Friberg, L. (1985). Localization of cortical areas activated by thinking. *Journal of Neurophysiology, 53,* 1219–1243.

Roland, P. E., Larsen, B., Larsen, N. A., & Skinhut, E. (1980). Supplementary motor areas and other cortical areas in organization of voluntary movement in man. *Journal of Neurophysiology, 43,* 118–136.

Rolls, E. T. (1984). Neurons in the temporal lobe and amygdala of the monkey with responses selective for faces. *Human Neurobiology, 3,* 209–222.

Rolls, E. T. (1992). Neurophysiology and the functions of the primate amygdala. In J. P. Aggleton (Ed.), *The amygdala: Neurobiological aspects of emotion, memory, and mental dysfunction* (pp. 143–165). New York: Wiley-Liss.

Rolls, E. T. (1995). A theory of emotion and consciousness and its application to understanding the neural basis of emotion. In M. S. Gazzaniga (Ed.), *The cognitive neurosciences.* Cambridge, MA: MIT Press.

Rose, F. D. (1988). Environmental enrichment and recovery of function following brain damage in the rat. *Medical Science Research, 16,* 257–263.

Rose, J. E., & Woolsey, N. (1948). The orbitofrontal cortex and its connections with the mediodorsal nucleus in the rabbit, sheep and cat. *Research Publications, Association for Research in Nervous and Mental Disorders, 27,* 210–232.

Rosen, G. D., Sherman, G. F., & Galaburda, A. M. (1986). Biological interactions in dyslexia. In J. E. Obrzut & G. W. Hynd (Eds.), *Child neuropsychology* (Vol. 1). New York: Academic Press.

Rosenthal, N. E., Sack, D. A., Gillin, C., Lewy, A. J., Goodwin, F. K., Davenport, Y., Mueller, P. S., Newsome, D. A., & Wehr, T. A. (1984). Seasonal affective disorder: A description of the syndrome and preliminary findings with light therapy. *Archives of General Psychiatry, 41,* 72–80.

Rosenthal, N. E., Sack, D. A., James, S. P., Parry, B. L., Mendelson, W. B., Tamarkin, L., & Wehr, T. A. (1985). Seasonal affective disorder and phototherapy. *Annals of the New York Academy of Sciences, 453,* 260–269.

Rosenzweig, M. C. (1977). Effects of environmental enrichment and impoverishment on learning and on brain values in rodents. In A. Oliverio (Ed.), *Genetics, environment and intelligence.* Amsterdam: Elsevier North-Holland.

Rosenzweig, M. R. (1980). Animal models for effects of brain lesions and for rehabilitation. In P. Bach-y-Rita (Ed.), *Recovery of function: Theoretical considerations for brain injury rehabilitation.* Bern: Hans Huber.

Rosenzweig, M. R., Bennett, E. L., & Diamond, M. C. (1972). Brain changes in response to experience. *Scientific American, 226,* 22–29.

Rosenzweig, M. R., & Leiman, A.(1982). *Physiological psychology.* Lexington, MA: Heath.

Rosenzweig, M. R., & Leiman, A. L. (1989). *Physiological psychology* (2nd ed.). New York: McGraw-Hill.

Rosenzweig, M. R., Leiman, A. K., & Breedlove, S. M. (1996). *Biological psychology.* Sunderland, MA: Sinauer.

Ross, E. D. (1981). The aprosodias: Functional-anatomical organization of the affective components of language in the right hemisphere. *Archives of Neurology, 38,* 561–569.

Ross, E. D., & Mesulam, M. M. (1979). Dominant language functions of the right hemisphere? Prosody and emotional gesturing. *Archives of Neurology, 36,* 144–148.

Ross-Russell, R. W., & Bharucha, N. (1984). Visual localization in patients with occipital infarction. *Journal of Neurology, Neurosurgery and Psychiatry, 47,* 153–158.

Rothi, L. J., & Heilman, K. M. (1996). Liepmann 1900 and 1905: A definition of apraxia and a model of praxis. In C. Cole, C.-W. Wallesch, Y. Joanette, & A. R. Lecours (Eds.), *Classic cases in neuropsychology.* Hove, UK: Erlbaum (UK) Taylor & Francis, Psychology Press.

Rourke, B. P. (1978). Neuropsychological research in reading retardation. In A. L. Benton & D. Pearl (Eds.), *Dyslexia: An appraisal of current knowledge.* New York: Oxford University Press.

Rourke, B. P. (1989). *Nonverbal learning disabilities: The syndrome and the model.* New York: Guilford Press.

Rourke, B. P. (1993). Arithmetic disabilities, specific and otherwise. *Journal of Learning Disabilities, 26,* 214–226.

Rourke, B. P. (1995). The NLD syndrome and the white matter model. In B. P. Rourke (Ed.), *Syndrome of nonverbal learning disabilities.* New York: Guilford Press.

Rourke, B. P., Del Dotto, J. E., Rourke, S. B., & Casey, J. E. (1990). Nonverbal learning disabilities: The syndrome and a case study. *Journal of School Psychology, 28,* 361–385.

Rourke, B. P., & Finlayson, M. A. J. (1978). Neuropsychological significance of variations in patterns of academic performance: Verbal and visual-spatial abilities. *Journal of Abnormal Child Psychology, 6,* 121–133.

Rourke, B. P., & Fuerst, D. R. (1992). Psychosocial dimensions of learning disability subtypes: Neuropsychological studies in the Windsor laboratory. *School Psychology Review, 21,* 361–374.

Rourke, B. P., & Strang, J. D. (1981). Subtypes of reading and arithmetic disabilities: A neuropsychological analysis. In M. Rutter (Ed.), *Behavioral syndromes of brain dysfunction in children.* New York: Guilford Press.

Rubens, A. B., & Benson, D. F. (1971). Associative visual agnosia. *Archives of Neurology* (Chicago), *24,* 305–316.

Rubin, R. T., Ananth, J., Villanueva-Myer, J., Trajmar, P. G., & Mena, I. (1995). Regional ^{133}Xenon cerebral blood flow and 99mTcHm-Pao uptake in patients with obsessive-compulsive disorder before and during treatment. *Biological Psychiatry, 38,* 429–437.

Rubin, R. T., Holm, S., Friberg, L., Videbech, P., Andersen, H. S., Bendsen, B. B., Stromso, N., Larsen, J. K., Lassen, N. A., & Hemmingsen, R. (1991). Altered modulation of prefrontal and subcortical brain activity in newly diagnosed schizophrenia and schizophrenifrom disorder. *Archives of General Psychiatry, 48,* 987–995.

Rubin, R. T., Villanueva-Myer, J., Ananth, J., Trajmar, P. G., & Mena, I. (1992). Regional xenon 133 cerebral blood flow and cerebral technetium 99m HMPAO uptake in unmedicated patients with obsessive compulsive disorder and matched normal control subjects: Determination of high-resolution single-photon emission computed tomography. *Archives of General Psychiatry, 49,* 695–702.

Rumbaugh, D. M. (Ed.) (1977). *Language learning in a chimpanzee: The Lena Project.* New York: Academic Press.

Russchen, F. T., Amaral, D. G., & Price, J. L. (1985). The source and termination of afferent fibers to the mediodorsal nucleus of the thalamus in the monkey, *Macaca fascicularis. Journal of Comparative Neurology, 242,* 1–27.

Rutter, M. (1978). The influence of organic and emotional factors in the origins, nature and outcome of child psychosis. *Developmental Medicine and Child Neurology, 7,* 518.

Rylander, G. (1939). *Personality changes after operations on the frontal lobes.* London: Oxford University Press.

Sackheim, H. A., Greenberg, M. S., Weiman, A. L., Gur, R. C., Hungerbuhler, J. P., & Geschwind, N. (1982). Hemispheric asymmetry in the expression of positive and negative emotions: Neurological evidence. *Archives of Neurology, 39*, 210–218.

Sackheim, H. A, & Gur, R. C. (1978). Lateral intensity of emotional expression. *Neuropsychologia, 16*, 473–482.

Sackheim, H. A., Gur, R. C., & Saucy, M. C. (1978). Emotion is expressed more intensely on the left side of the face. *Science, 202*, 434.

Sacks, O. (1985). *The man who mistook his wife for a hat and other clinical tales*. New York: Summit Books.

Sacks, O. (1995). *An anthropologist on Mars*. New York: Knopf.

Sacks, O., & Wasserman, R. (1987, November 19). The case of the colorblind artist. *New York Review of Books*, 25–34.

Safer, D. J. (1973). A familial factor in minimal brain dysfunction. *Behavioral Genetics, 3*, 175.

Safer, M. A., & Leventhal, H. (1977). Ear differences in evaluating emotional tones of voice and verbal content. *Journal of Experimental Psychology: Human Perception and Performance, 3*, 75–82.

Sakai, K., & Miyashita, Y. (1991). Neural organization for long-term memory of paired associates. *Nature, 354*, 152–155.

Salzman, C. D., Britten, K. H., & Newsome, W. T. (1990). Cortical microstimulation influences perceptual judgement of motion direction. *Nature, 346*, 174–177.

Salzman, C. D., Murasugi, C. M., Britten, K. H., & Newsome, W. T. (1992). Microstimulation in visual area MT: Effects on direction discrimination performance. *Journal of Neuroscience, 12*, 2331–2355.

Sarason, I. G., & Sarason, B. R. (1999). *Abnormal psychology* (9th ed.). Upper Saddle River, NJ: Prentice-Hall.

Sarazin, F. F. (1982). Evidence for the involvement of orbitofrontal cortex in memory function: An interference effect. *Journal of Comparative and Physiological Psychology, 96*, 913–925.

Satz, P. (1972). Pathological left-handedness: An exploratory model. *Cortex, 8*, 121.

Satz, P., & Soper, H. V. (1986). Left-handedness, dyslexia, and autoimmune disorder: A critique. *Journal of Clinical and Experimental Neuropsychology, 8*, 453.

Savage-Rumbaugh, E. S. (1987). A new look at ape language: Comprehension of vocal speech and syntax. *Nebraska Symposium on Motivation, 35*, 201–255.

Savage-Rumbaugh, E. S., McDonald, D., Sevcik, R., Hopkins, W., & Rubert, E. (1986). Spontaneous symbol acquisition and communicative use by pygmie chimpanzees. *Journal of Experimental Psychology: General, 115*, 211–235.

Savander, V., Go, C.-G., LeDoux, J. E., & Pitkämen, A. (1995). Intrinsic connections of the rat amygdaloid complex: Projections originating in the basal nucleus. *Journal of Comparative Neurology, 361*, 345–368.

Saxon, L. (1980). Neural induction: Past, present, and future. In R. K. Hunt (Ed.), *Neural development: Part I. Current topics in developmental biology* (Vol. 15). New York: Academic Press.

Schachter, S., & Singer, J. E. (1962). Cognitive, social, and physiological determinants of emotional state. *Psychological Review, 69*, 379–399.

Schacter, D. L. (1987). Implicit memory: History and current status. *Journal of Experimental Psychology: Learning, Memory, and Cognition, 13*, 501–518.

Schacter, D. L. (1991). Unawareness of deficits and unawareness of knowledge in patients with memory disorders. In G. P. Prigatano & D. L. Schacter (Eds.), *Awareness of deficit after brain injury: Clinical and theoretic issues* (pp. 127–151). New York: Oxford University Press.

Schacter, D. L. (1995). Implicit memory: A new frontier for cognitive neuroscience. In M. Gazzaniga (Ed.), *The cognitive neurosciences*. Cambridge, MA: MIT Press.

Schacter, D. L. (1996). *Searching for memory*. New York: HarperCollins.

Schacter, D. L., Chin, C. Y. P., & Ochsner, K. N. (1993). Implicit memory: A selective review. *Annual Review of Neuroscience, 16*, 159–182.

Schacter, D. L., & Graf, P. (1986). Effects of elaborative processing on implicit and explicit memory for new associations. *Journal of Experimental Psychology: Learning, Memory, and Cognition, 12*(3), 432–444.

Schank, R. (1982). *Dynamic memory: A theory of reminding and learning in computers and people*. Cambridge, England: Cambridge University Press.

Scheff, S. W., Bernardo, L. S., & Cotman, C. W. (1978). Effect of serial lesions on sprouting in the dentate gyrus: Onset and decline of the catalytic effect. *Brain Research, 150*, 45–53.

Scheff, S. W., & Cotman, C. W. (1977). Recovery of spontaneous alternation following lesions of the entorhinal cortex in adult rats: Possible correlation to axon sprouting. *Behavioral Biology, 21*, 286–293.

Scheibel, A. B. (1984). A dendritic correlate of human speech. In Geschwind, N., & Galaburda, A. M. (Eds.) *Cerebral dominance: The biological foundations*. Cambridge, MA: Harvard University Press.

Scheibel, A. B., & Kovelman, J. A. (1980). Disorientation of the hippocampal pyramidal cell and its processes in the schizophrenic patient. *Behavioral Psychiatry, 16*, 101–102.

Scherer, K. R. (1984). On the nature and function of emotion: A component process approach. In K. R. Scherer & P. Ekman (Eds.), *Approaches to emotion*. Hillsdale, NJ: Erlbaum.

Scherer, K. R. (1993). Neuroscience projections to current debates in emotion psychology. *Cognition and Emotion, 7*, 1–41.

Schmitt, J. J., Hartje, W., & Willmes, K. (1997). Hemispheric asymmetry in the recognition of emotional attitude conveyed by facial expression, prosody, and propositional speech. *Cortex, 33*, 65–81.

Schwartz, B. E., Halgren, E., Fuster, J. M., Simpkins, E., Gee, M., & Mandelkern, M. (1995). Cortical metabolic activation in humans during a visual memory task. *Cerebral Cortex, 5*, 205–214.

Schwartz, M. L., & Goldman-Rakic, P. S. (1984). Callosal and intrahemispheric connectivity of prefrontal association cortex in the rhesus monkey: Relation between intraparietal and principal sulcal cortex. *Journal of Comparative Neurology, 226,* 403–420.

Scoville, W. B., & Milner, B. (1957). Loss of recent memory after bilateral hippocampal lesions. *Journal of Neurology, Neurosurgery, and Psychiatry, 20,* 11–21.

Searle, J. (1984). *Mind, brain and science.* Cambridge, MA: Harvard University Press.

Sedvall, G. (1990). PET imaging of dopamine receptors in human basal ganglia: Relevance to mental illness. *Trends in Neurosciences, 13*(7), 302–308.

Seidenberg, M. S., & Pettito, L. A. (1979). Signing behavior in apes: A critical review. *Cognition, 7,* 177–215.

Seil, F. J., Leiman, A. L., & Kelly, J. (1976). Neuroelectric blocking factors in multiple sclerosis and normal brain sera. *Archives of Neurology, 33,* 418–422.

Selden, N. R. W., Everitt, B. J., Jarrard, L. E., & Robbins, T. W. (1991). Complementary roles for the amygdala and hippocampus in aversive conditioning to explicit and contextual cues. *Neuroscience, 42*(2), 335–350.

Semmes, J. (1968). Hemispheric specialization: A possible clue to mechanism. *Neuropsychologia, 6,* 11–26.

Semrud-Clickeman, M., & Hynd, G. W. (1991). Specific nonverbal and social-skills deficits in children with learning disabilities. In J. E. Obrzut & G. W. Hynd (Eds.), *Neuropsychological foundations of learning disabilities.* San Diego: Academic Press.

Shader, R. I., & Greenblatt, D. J. (1995). The psychopharmacology of acute anxiety. In F. E. Bloom & D. Kupfer (Eds.), *Psychopharmacology: The fourth generation of progress* (pp. 1341–1348). New York: Raven Press.

Shallice, T. (1982). Specific impairment in planning. *Philosophical Transactions of the Royal Society of London, B, 289,* 199–209.

Shallice, T. (1988). *From neuropsychology to neural structure.* Cambridge, England: Cambridge University Press.

Shallice, T., & Evans, M. E. (1978). The involvement of the frontal lobe in cognitive estimation. *Cortex, 12,* 294–303.

Shallice, T., & Warrington, E. K. (1977). Auditory-verbal short term memory impairment and spontaneous speech. *Brain and Language, 4,* 479–491.

Shapley, R. (1995). Parallel neural pathways and visual function. In Gazzaniga, M. S. (Ed.), *The cognitive neurosciences.* Cambridge, MA: MIT Press.

Shaywitz, B. A., Shaywitz, S. E., Pugh, K. R., Constable, R. T., Skudlarski, P., Fulbright, R. K., Bronen, R. A., Fletcher, J. M., Shankweiler, D. P., Katz, L., & Gore, J. C. (1995). Sex differences in the functional organization of the brain for language. *Nature, 373,* 607–609.

Shaywitz, S. E., & Shaywitz, B. A. (1991). Introduction to the special series on attention deficit disorder. *Journal of Learning Disabilities, 24,* 68–71.

Shepard, R. N., & Cooper, L. A. (1982). *Mental images and their transformations.* Cambridge, MA: MIT Press.

Sheppard, G., Gruzelier, J., Manchanda, R., Hirsch, S. R., Wise, R., Frackowiak, R., & James, T. (1983). 15O positron emission tomographic scanning in predominantly never-treated acute schizophrenic patients. *Lancet, 2,* 1448–1452.

Sherry, D. F., Jacobs, L., & Gaulin, J. (1992). Spatial memory and adaptive specialization of the hippocampus. *Trends in Neurosciences, 15,* 298–303.

Sherry, D. F., & Vaccarino, A. L. (1989). Hippocampus and memory for food caches in black-capped chickadees. *Behavioral Neuroscience, 103,* 308–318.

Sherry, D. F., Vaccaromp, A. L., Buckenham, K., & Herz, R. S. (1989). The hippocampal complex of food-storing birds. *Brain Behavior and Evolution, 34,* 308–317.

Shimamura, A. (1995). Memory and frontal lobe function. In M. S. Gazzaniga (Ed.), *The cognitive neurosciences.* Cambridge: MIT Press.

Shimamura, A., Janowsky, J. S., & Squire, L. R. (1990). Memory for the temporal order of events in patients with frontal lobe lesions and amnesic patients. *Neuropsychologia, 28,* 803–813.

Shimamura, A., Jernigan, T. L., & Squire, L. R. (1988). Korsakoff's syndrome: Radiological (CT) findings and neuropsychological correlates. *Journal of Neuroscience, 8,* 4400–4410.

Shuttleworth, E. C., Syring, V., & Allen, N. (1982). Further observations on the nature of prosopagnosia. *Brain and Cognition, 1,* 302–332.

Sidman, R. L., & Sidman, M. S. (1965). *Neuroanatomy: A programmed text.* Boston: Little, Brown.

Siever, L. J., Davis, K. L., & Gorman, L. K. (1991). Pathogenesis of mood disorders. In Davis, K., Klar, H., & Coyle, J. T. (Eds.), *Foundations of psychiatry.* Philadelphia: Saunders.

Silberman, E. K. (1983). Behavioral symptoms in temporal lobe epilepsy [Letter]. *Archives of General Psychiatry, 40,* 468.

Silberman, E. K., & Weingartner, H. (1986). Hemispheric lateralization of function related to emotion. *Brain and Cognition, 5,* 322–353.

Silva, A. J., Paylor, R., Wehner, J. M., & Tonegawa, S. (1992). Impaired spatial learning in (α-calcium-calmodulin kinase II mutant mice. *Science, 257,* 206–211.

Silva, A. J., Stevens, C. F., Tonegawa, S., & Wang, Y. (1992). Deficient hippocampal long-term potentiation in (α-calcium-calmodulin kinase II mutant mice. *Science, 257,* 201–206.

Simon, H., Scatton, B., & LeMoal, M. (1980). Dopaminergic A10 neurons are involved in cognitive functions. *Nature (London), 286,* 150–151.

Singer, J. E., Westphal, M., & Niswander, K. R. (1968). Sex differences in the incidence of neonatal abnormalities and abnormal performance of early childhood. *Child Development, 39,* 103–112.

Skinner, B. F. (1965). *Science and human behavior.* New York: Macmillan.

Slater, B., & Shields, J. (1969). Genetical aspects of anxiety. *British Journal of Psychiatry Special Publication No. 3: Studies of Anxiety.* Ashford, Kent: Headley.

Smith, A., & Sugar, O. (1975). Development of above normal language and intelligence 21 years after hemispherectomy. *Neurology, 25,* 813–818.

Smith, M. L., & Milner, B. (1981). The role of the right hippocampus in the recall of spatial location. *Neuropsychologia, 19,* 781–793.

Smith, M. L., & Milner, B. (1984). Differential effects of frontal-lobe lesions on cognitive estimation and spatial memory. *Neuropsychologia, 22,* 697–705.

Snyder, S. H. (1976). The dopamine hypothesis of schizophrenia. *American Journal of Psychiatry, 133,* 197–202.

Sohlberg, M. M., & Mateer, C. A. (1989). *Introduction to cognitive rehabilitation: Theory and practice.* New York: Guilford Press.

Sperry, R. W. (1961). Cerebral organization and behavior. *Science, 133,* 1749–1757.

Sperry, R. W. (1968). Plasticity of neuronal maturation. *Developmental Biology (Suppl.), 2,* 36.

Sperry, R. W. (1971). How a developing brain gets itself properly wired for adaptive function. In E. Tobach, L. R. Aronson, & E. Shaw (Eds.), *The biopsychology of development.* New York: Academic Press.

Spitz, R., & Wolf, K. M. (1946). Anaclitic depression: An inquiry into the genesis of psychiatric conditions in early childhood. *Psychoanalytic Study of the Child, 2,* 313–342.

Spreen, O. (1988a). *Learning disabled children growing up.* New York: Oxford University Press.

Spreen, O. (1988b). Prognosis of learning disability. *Journal of Counseling and Clinical Psychology, 56,* 836–842.

Spreen, O., Risser, A. H., & Edgell, D. (1995). *Developmental neuropsychology.* New York: Oxford University Press.

Squire, L. R. (1987). *Memory and the brain.* New York: Oxford University Press.

Squire, L. R., & Cohen, N. J. (1979). Memory and amnesia: Resistance to disruption develops for years after learning. *Behavioral and Neural Biology, 25,* 115–125.

Squire, L. R., & Cohen, N. J. (1982). Remote memory, retrograde amnesia, and the neurobiology of memory. In L. S. Cermak (Ed.), *Human memory and amnesia.* Hillsdale, NJ: Erlbaum.

Squire, L. R., & Cohen, N. J. (1984). Human memory and amnesia. In G. Lynch, J. L. McGaugh, & N. M. Weinberger (Eds.), *Neurobiology of learning and memory.* New York: Guilford Press.

Squire, L. R., Cohen, N. J., & Nadel, L. (1984). The medial temporal region and memory consolidation: A new hypothesis. In H. Eingartner & E. Parker (Eds.), *Memory consolidation.* Hillsdale, NJ: Erlbaum.

Squire, L. R., Ojemann, J. G., Miezin, F. M., Peterson, S. E., Videen, T. O., & Raichle, M. E. (1992). Activation of the hippocampus in normal humans: A functional anatomical study of memory. *Proceedings of the National Academy of Sciences, USA, 89,* 1837–1841.

Squire, L. R., & Zola-Morgan, S. (1991). The medial temporal lobe memory system. *Science, 253,* 1380–1386.

St. George-Hislop, P. H., Tanzi, R. E., Polinsky, R. J., Haines, J. L., Nee, L., Watkins, P. C., Meyers, R. H., Feldman, R. G., Pollen, D., Drachman, D., Growdon, J., Bruni, A., Foncin, J.-F., Salmon, D., Frommelt, P., Amaducci, L., Sorbi, S., Piacentini, S., Stewart, G. D., Hobbs, W. J., Conneally, P. M., & Gusella, J. F. (1987). The genetic defect causing familial Alzheimer's disease maps on chromosome 21. *Science I, 235,* 885–890.

Stamm, J. S., & Kreder, S. V. (1979). Minimal brain dysfunction: Psychological and neuropsychological disorders in hyperkinetic children. In M. S. Gazzaniga (Ed.), *Neuropsychology.* New York: Plenum Press.

Starkstein, S. E., & Robinson, R. G. (1991). The role of the frontal lobes in affective disorder following stroke. In H. S. Levin, H. M. Eisenberg, & A. L. Benton (Eds.), *Frontal lobe function and dysfunction* (pp. 288–303). New York: Oxford University Press.

Stein, M. B., & Uhde, T. W. (1995). The biology of anxiety disorders. *American Psychiatric Press textbook of psychopharmacology.* Washington, DC: American Psychiatric Press.

Steinmetz, J. E., & Thompson, R. F. (1991). Brain substrates of aversive classical conditioning. In J. I. Madden (Ed.), *Neurobiology of learning emotion and affect* (pp. 97–120). New York: Raven Press.

Stevens, A., & Coupe, P. (1978). Distortion in judged spatial relations. *Cognitive Psychology, 10,* 422–437.

Stevens, J. R. (1982). Neuropathology of schizophrenia. *Archives of General Psychiatry, 39,* 1131–1139.

Stinson, D., & Thompson, C. (1990). Clinical experience with phototherapy. *Journal of Affective Disorders, 18,* 129–135.

Strauss, E., & Moscovitch, M. (1981). Perception of facial expression. *Brain and Language, 13,* 308–332.

Stuss, D. T. (1991a). Interference effects on memory function in postleukotomy patients: An attentional perspective. In H. S. Levin, H. M. Eisenberg, & A. L. Benton (Eds.), *Frontal lobe function and dysfunction* (pp. 157–172). New York: Oxford University Press.

Stuss, D. T. (1991b). Self, awareness, and the frontal lobes: A neuropsychological perspective. In J. Strauss & G. R. Goethals (Eds.), *The self: Interdisciplinary approaches.* New York: Springer.

Stuss, D. T., & Benson, D. F. (1986). *The frontal lobes.* New York: Raven Press.

Stuss, D. T., & Gow, C. A. (1992). "Frontal dysfunction" after traumatic brain injury. *Neuropsychiatry, Neuropsychology, and Behavioral Neurology, 5,* 272–282.

Stuss, D. T., Kaplan, E. F., Benson, D. F., Weir, W. S., Chiulli, S., & Sarazin, F. F. (1982). Evidence for the involvement of orbitofrontal cortex in monkey functions: An interference effect. *Journal of Comparative and Physiological Psychology, 96,* 913–925.

Styron, W. (1990). *Darkness visible: A memoir of madness.* New York: Random House.

Suberi, M., & McKeever, W. F. (1977). Differential right hemispheric memory storage of emotional and non-emotional faces. *Neuropsychologia, 15,* 757–768.

Sutherland, R. J., & Rudy, J. W. (1989). Configural association theory: The role of the hippocampal formation in learning, memory, and amnesia. *Psychobiology, 17,* 129–144.

Swanson, L. W. (1983). The hippocampus and the concept of the limbic system. In W. Seifert (Ed.), *Neurobiology of the hippocampus* (pp. 3–19). London: Academic Press.

Swedo, S. E., Pietrini, P., Leonard, H. L., Shapiro, M. B., Rettew, D. C., Goldberger, E. L., Rapoport, S. I., Rapoport, J. L., & Grady, C. L. (1992). Cerebral glucose metabolism in childhood-onset obsessive-compulsive disorder: Revisualization during pharmacotherapy. *Archives of General Psychiatry, 49,* 690–694.

Swedo, S. E., Shapiro, M. B., Grady, C. L., Cheslow, D. L., Leonard, H. L., Kumar, A., Friedland, R., Rapoport, S. I., & Rapoport, J. L. (1989). Cerebral glucose metabolism in childhood-onset obsessive-compulsive disorder. *Archives of General Psychiatry, 46,* 518–523.

Szasz, T. (1961). *The myth of mental illness.* New York: Harper and Row.

Tanabe, T., Iino, M., Ooshima, Y., & Takagi, S. F. (1975). Neurophysiological studies on the prefrontal olfactory center in the monkey. In D. A. Denton & J. P. Coghlan (Eds.), *Olfaction and taste* (pp. 309–312). New York: Academic Press.

Tarr, R. S. (1977). The role of the amygdala in the intraspecies aggressive behavior of the iguanid lizard. *Physiology and Behavior, 18,* 1153–1158.

Tatetsu, S. (1964). A contribution to the morphological background of schizophrenia. *Acta Neuropathologica, 3,* 558–571.

Taub, E., Miller, N. E., Novack, T. A., Cook, E. W., Fleming, W. C., Nepomuceno, C. S., Connell, J. S., & Crago, J. E. (1993). Technique to improve chronic motor deficit after stroke. *Archives of Physical Medicine and Rehabilitation, 74,* 347–354.

Taylor, A. E., Saint-Cry, J. A., & Lang, A. E. (1986). Frontal lobe dysfunction in Parkinson's disease: The cortical focus of neostriatal outflow. *Brain, 109,* 845–883.

Taylor, A. M., & Warrington, E. K. (1971). Visual agnosia: A single case report. *Cortex, 7,* 152–161.

Taylor, A. M., & Warrington, E. K. (1973). Visual discrimination in patients with localized cerebral lesions. *Cortex, 9,* 82–93.

Taylor, G. (1987). Workshop on learning disabilities. Annual Meeting of the International Neuropsychological Society.

Taylor, L. B. (1969). Localization of cerebral lesions by psychological testing. *Clinical Neurosurgery, 16,* 269–287.

Taylor, M. A., & Abrams, R. (1984). Cognitive impairment in schizophrenia. *American Journal of Psychiatry, 141,* 196–201.

Teodoru, T. E., & Berman, A. J. (1980). The role of attempted movements in recovery from lateral dorsal rhizotomy. *Society for Neuroscience Abstracts, G,* 25.

Terrace, H. S. (1979). *Nim.* New York: Knopf.

Terry, R. D., & Davis, P. (1980). Dementia of the Alzheimer type. *Annual Review of Neuroscience, 3,* 77–96.

Terzian, H. (1964). Behavioral and EEG effects of intracarotid sodium amytal injection. *Acta Neurochirurgica, 12,* 230–239.

Teuber, H. L. (1964). The riddle of frontal lobe function in man. In J. M. Warren & K. Akert (Eds.), *The frontal granular cortex and behavior* (pp. 410–477). New York: McGraw-Hill.

Teuber, H. L. (1966). The frontal lobes and their functions: Further observations on rodents, carnivores, subhuman primates, and man. *International Journal of Neurology, 5,* 282–300.

Teuber, H. L. (1972). Unity and diversity of frontal lobe functions. *Acta Neurobiologiae Experimentalis, 32,* 615–656.

Teuber, H. L. (1975). Recovery of function after brain injury in man. In *Outcomes of severe damage to the nervous system, CIBA Foundation Symposium 34.* Amsterdam: Elsevier North-Holland.

Teuber, H. L., & Mishkin, M. (1954). Judgment of visual and postural vertical after brain injury. *Journal of Psychology, 38,* 161–175.

Teuber, H. L., & Rudel, R. G. (1962). Behavior after cerebral lesions in children and adults. *Developmental Medicine and Child Neurology, 3,* 3–20.

Thompson, R. F. (1990). Neural mechanisms of classical conditioning in mammals. *Philosophical Transactions of the Royal Society of London (Biology), 329,* 161–170.

Thorpe, S. J., Rolls, E. T., & Maddison, S. (1983). The orbitofrontal cortex: Neuronal activity in the behaving monkey. *Experimental Brain Research, 49,* 93–115.

Tinbergen, N. (1951). *The study of aggression.* Oxford, England: Clarendon.

Tognola, C., & Vignolo, L. A. (1980). Brain lesions associated with oral apraxia in stroke patients: A clinical neuroradiological investigation with the CT scan. *Neuropsychologia, 18,* 257–271.

Tomkins, S. S. (1962). *Affect, imagery, consciousness.* New York: Springer.

Torgersen, S. (1986). Genetic factors in moderately severe and mild affective disorders. *Archives of General Psychiatry, 43,* 222–226.

Tsai, L. K., Nasralla, H. A., & Jacoby, C. G. (1983). Hemispheric asymmetries on computed tomographic scans in schizophrenia and mania. *Archives of General Psychiatry, 40,* 1286–1289.

Tsuang, M. T., Gilbertson, M. W., & Faraone, S. V. (1991). The genetics of schizophrenia. *Schizophrenia Research, 4,* 157–171.

Tucker, D. M. (1981). Lateral brain function, emotion, and conceptualization. *Psychological Bulletin, 89,* 19–46.

Tucker, D. M., Watson, R. T., & Heilman, K. M. (1977). The discrimination and evocation of affectively entoned speech in patients with right parietal disease. *Neurology, 27,* 947–958.

Tulving, E. (1972). Episodic and semantic memory. In E. Tulving & W. Donaldson (Eds.), *Organization of memory*. New York: Academic Press.

Tulving, E. (1995). Organization of memory: Quo vadis? In M. Gazzaniga (Ed.), *The cognitive neurosciences*. Cambridge, MA: MIT Press.

Tulving, E., Kapur, S. Craik, F. I. M., Moskovitch, M., & Houle, S. (1994). Hemispheric encoding/retrieval asymmetry in episodic memory: Positron emission tomography finding. *Proceedings of the National Academy of Sciences, 91*, 2016–2020.

Tulving, E., Schacter, D. L., McLachlan, D. R., & Moscovitch, M. (1988). Priming and semantic autobiographical knowledge: A case study of retrograde amnesia. *Brain and Cognition, 8*, 3–20.

Tulving, E., Schacter, D. L., & Stark, H. (1982). Priming effects in word-fragment completion are independent of recognition memory. *Journal of Experimental Psychology: Learning, Memory, and Cognition, 8*, 336–342.

Tyler, R. H. (1969). Disorders of visual scanning with frontal lobe lesions. In S. Locke (Ed.), *Modern neurology* (pp. 381–393). Boston: Little, Brown.

Uylings, H. B. M., & van Eden, C. G. (1990). Qualitative and quantitative comparison of the prefrontal cortex in rat and in primates, including humans. *Progress in Brain Research, 85*, 31–62.

Valenstein, E. S. (1986). *Great and desperate cures*. New York: Basic Books.

Valenstein, E. S. (1990). The prefrontal area and psychosurgery. *Progress in Brain Research, 85*, 257–303.

Valins, S. (1966). Cognitive effects of false heart-rate feedback. *Journal of Personality and Social Psychology, 4*, 400–408.

Vallar, G., & Baddeley, A. (1984). Phonological short-term store, phonological processing, and sentence comprehension: A neuropsychological case study. *Cognitive Neuropsychology, 1*, 121–141.

Vallar, G., Guariglia, C., Nico, D., & Bisiach, E. (1995). Spatial hemineglect in back space. *Brain, 118*, 467–472.

Van Cantfort, E., & Rimpau, J. (1982). Sign language studies with children and chimpanzees. *Sign Language Studies, 34*, 15–72.

Van Hoesen, G. W. (1982). The hippocampal gyrus: New observations concerning its connections in the monkey. *Trends in Neuroscience, 5*, 345–350.

Van Hoesen, G. W., & Damasio, A. R. (1987). Neural correlates of cognitive impairments in Alzheimer's disease. In *Handbook of physiology* (Vol. 5, pp. 871–898). Bethesda, MD: American Physiological Association.

Van Hoesen, G. W., & Pandya, D. N. (1975). Some connections of the entorhinal (area 28) and perirhinal (area 25) cortices of the rhesus monkey: I. Temporal lobe afferents. *Brain Research, 95*, 1–24.

Van Hoesen, G. W., Pandya, D. N., & Butters, N. (1975). Some connections of the entorhinal (area 28) and perirhinal

(area 25) cortices of the rhesus monkey: II. Frontal lobe afferents. *Brain Research, 95*, 25–38.

Van Tol, H. H. M., Bunzow, J. R., Hong-Chan, G., Sunahara, R. K., Seeman, P., Niznik, H. B., & Civelli, O. (1991). Cloning the gene for a human dopamine D_4 receptor with high affinity for the antipsychotic clozapine. *Nature, 350*, 614–619.

Vendrell, P., Junque, C., Pujol, J., Jurado, M. A., Molet, J., & Grafman, J. (1995). The role of prefrontal regions in the Stroop task. *Neuropsychologia, 33*, 341–352.

Veraa, R. P., & Grafstein, B. (1981). Cellular mechanisms for recovery from nervous system injury: A conference report. *Experimental Neurology, 71*, 6–75.

Verfaellie, M., & Heilman, K. M. (1987). Response preparation and response inhibition after lesions of the medial frontal lobe. *Archives of Neurology, 44*, 1265–1271.

Vernon, M. D. (1971). *Reading and its difficulties*. Cambridge, England: Cambridge University Press.

Vessie, P. R. (1932). On the transmission of Huntington's chorea for 300 years: The Bures family group. *Journal of Nervous and Mental Disorders, 76*, 533–565.

Victor, M., Adams, R. D., & Collins, G. H. (1989). *The Wernicke-Korsakoff syndrome and related neurologic disorders due to alcoholism and malnutrition* (2nd ed.). Philadelphia: Davis.

Von Cramon, D. Y., Hebel, N., & Schuri, U. (1985). A contribution to the anatomical basis of thalamic amnesia. *Brain, 198*, 993–1008.

von Monakow, C. V. (1911). Lokalization der Hirnfunktionen. *Joyrnal fur Psychologie und Neurologie, 17*, 185–200. (Reprinted in G. von Bonin. [1960]. *The cerebral cortex*. Springfield, IL: Thomas).

von Senden, M. (1932). *Space and sight: The perception of space and shape in the completely blind before and after operation*. (Reprint. Glencoe, IL: Free Press, 1960).

Waber, D. P. (1979). Neuropsychological aspects of Turner's syndrome. *Developmental Medicine and Child Neurology, 21*, 58–70.

Wada, J. A., Clarke, R., & Hamm, A. (1975). Cerebral hemispheric asymmetry in humans: Cortical speech zones in 100 adult and 100 infant brains. *Archives of Neurology, 32*, 239–246.

Walker, A. E. (1940). Cytoarchitectural study of the prefrontal area of the macaque monkey. *Journal of Comparative Neurology, 73*, 59–86.

Wall, P. D. (1980). Mechanisms of plasticity of connection following damage of adult mammalian nervous system. In P. Bach-y-Rita (Ed.), *Recovery of function: Theoretical considerations of brain injury rehabilitation*. Bern: Hans Huber.

Wall, P. D., & Egger, M. D. (1971). Formation of new connections in adult rat brains after partial deafferentiation. *Nature, 232*, 542–545.

Wapner, W., Hamby, S., & Gardner, H. (1981). The role of the right hemisphere in the apprehension of complex linguistic materials. *Brain and Language, 14*, 15–33.

Wapner, W., Judd, T., & Gardner, H. (1978). Visual agnosia in an artist. *Cortex, 14,* 343–364.

Warrington, E. K. (1975). The selective impairment of semantic memory. *Quarterly Journal of Experimental Psychology, 27,* 187–199.

Warrington, E. K. (1982). Neuropsychological studies of object recognition. *Philosophical Transactions of the Royal Society of London, Series B, 298,* 15–33.

Warrington, E. K. (1985). Agnosia: The impairment of object recognition. In P. J. Vinkin, G. W. Bruyan, & H. L. Klewans (Eds.). *Handbook of clinical neurology.* Amsterdam: Elsevier.

Warrington, E. K. (1986). Visual deficits associated with occipital lobe lesions in man. *Experimental Brain Research Supplementum, 11,* 247–261.

Warrington, E. K. (1992, February). *Visual agnosia.* Presentation to the 20th Annual Meeting of the International Neuropsychological Society, San Diego, CA.

Warrington, E. K., & James, M. (1967a). Disorders of visual perception in patients with localized cerebral lesions. *Neuropsychologia, 5,* 253–266.

Warrington, E. K., & James, M. (1967b). An experimental investigation of facial recognition in patients with unilateral cerebral lesions. *Cortex, 3,* 317–326.

Warrington, E. K., & James, M. (1988). Visual apperceptive agnosia: A clinico-anatomical study of three cases. *Cortex, 24,* 13–32.

Warrington, E. K., James, M., & Kinsbourne, M. (1966). Drawing disability in relation to the laterality of cerebral lesion. *Brain, 89,* 53–82.

Warrington, E. K., & Rabin, P. (1970). Perceptual matching in patients with cerebral lesions. *Neuropsychologia, 8,* 475–487.

Warrington, E. K., & Shallice, T. (1972). Neuropsychological evidence of visual storage in short-term memory tasks. *Quarterly Journal of Experimental Psychology, 24,* 30–40.

Warrington, E. K., & Shallice, T. (1980). Word-form dyslexia. *Brain, 103,* 99–112.

Warrington, E. K., & Shallice, T. (1984). Category specific semantic impairment. *Brain, 107,* 829–854.

Warrington, E. K., & Taylor, A. M. (1973). Contribution of the right parietal lobe to object recognition. *Cortex, 9,* 152–164.

Warrington, E. K., & Weiskrantz, L. (1968). A new method of testing long term retention with special reference to amnesic patients. *Nature, 217,* 972–974.

Warrington, E. K., & Weiskrantz, L. (1970). The amnesic syndrome: Consolidation or retrieval? *Nature, 228,* 628–630.

Warrington, E. K., & Weiskrantz, L. (1974). The effect of prior learning on subsequent retention in amnesic patients. *Neuropsychologia, 20,* 233–248.

Watanabe, T., & Niki, H. (1985). Hippocampal unit activity and delayed response in the monkey. *Brain Research, 325,* 241–254.

Watson, J. B. (1913). Psychology as the behaviorist views it. *Psychological Review, 20,* 158–177.

Watson, R. T., & Heilman, K. M. (1983). Callosal apraxia. *Brain, 106,* 391–403.

Waxler, M., & Rosvold, H. E. (1970). Delayed alternation in monkeys after removal of the hippocampus. *Neuropsychologia, 8,* 137–146.

Waxman, S. G., & Geschwind, N. (1974). Hypergraphia in temporal lobe epilepsy. *Neurology, 24,* 629–636.

Weddell, R. A., Milner, J. D., & Trevarthen, C. (1990). Voluntary emotional facial expressions in patients with focal cerebral lesions. *Neuropsychologia, 28,* 49–60.

Weinberger, D. R. (1995). Schizophrenia: From neuropathology to neurodevelopment. *Nature, 346,* 552–557.

Weinberger, D. R., Berman, K. F., & Illowsky, B. P. (1988). Physiological dysfunction of dorsolateral prefrontal cortex in schizophrenia: III. A new cohort and evidence for a monoaminergic mechanism. *Archives of General Psychiatry, 45,* 609–615.

Weinberger, D. R., Berman, K. F., Suddath, R. L., & Torrey, E. F. (1992). Evidence for dysfunction of a prefrontal-limbic network in schizophrenia: An MRI and regional cerebral blood flow study of discordant monozygotic twins. *American Journal of Psychiatry, 149,* 890–897.

Weinberger, D. R., Berman, K. F., & Zec, R. F. (1986). Physiological dysfunction of dorsolateral prefrontal cortex in schizophrenia: I. Regional cerebral blood flow (rCBF) evidence. *Archives of General Psychiatry, 43,* 114–125.

Weinberger, D. R., Torrey, E. F., Neophytudes, A. N., & Wyatt, R. J. (1979). Structural abnormalities in the cerebral cortex of chronic schizophrenic patients. *Archives of General Psychiatry, 36,* 935–939.

Weinberger, N. M. (1995). Retuning the brain by fear conditioning. In M. S. Gazzaniga (Ed.), *The cognitive neurosciences* (pp. 1071–1090). Cambridge, MA: MIT Press.

Weinrich, M., & Weis, S. (1982). The premotor cortex of the monkey. *Journal of Neuroscience, 2,* 1329–1345.

Weiskrantz, L. (1986). *Blindsight: A case study and implications.* Oxford: Oxford University Press.

Weiskrantz, L. (1997). *Consciousness lost and found.* Oxford: Oxford University Press.

Weiskrantz, L., & Warrington, E. K. (1979). Conditioning in amnesic patients. *Neuropsychologia, 17,* 187–194.

Weissman, M. (1985). The epidemiology of anxiety disorders: Rates, risks, and familial patterns. In A. H. Tuma & J. D. Maser (Eds.), *Anxiety and the anxiety disorders* (pp. 275–296). Hillsdale, NJ: Erlbaum.

Wender, P. H. (1971). *Minimal brain dysfunction in children.* New York: Wiley Interscience Series.

Wender, P. H., Kety, S. S., Rosenthal, D., Schulsinger, F., & Ortmann, J. (1986). Psychiatric disorders in the biological relatives of adopted individuals with affective disorders. *Archives of General Psychiatry, 43,* 923–929.

Wernicke, C. (1874). The aphasic symptom-complex: A psychological study on an anatomical basis. [Der aphasische Symptomencomplex: Eine Psychologische Studie auf Anatimischer Basis. Breslau.] Translated in *Boston Studies in Philosophy of Science, 4,* 34–97.

Wexler, N. S. (1979). Perceptual-motor, cognitive, and emotional characteristics of patients at risk for Huntington's disease. *Advances in Neurology, 23,* 257–272.

Whitely, A. M., & Warrington, E. K. (1977). Prosopagnosia: A clinical, psychological and anatomical study of three patients. *Journal of Neurology, Neurosurgery and Psychiatry, 40,* 395–403.

Wilkins, A. J., Shallice, T., & McCarthy, R. (1987). Frontal lesions and sustained attention. *Neuropsychologia, 25,* 359–365.

Willerman, L. (1973). Activity level and hyperactivity in twins. *Child Development, 44,* 288–293.

Wilson, F. A. W., Brown, M. W., & Riches, I. P. (1986). Sensory and motor related unit activity in the monkey hippocampal formation. *Society for Neuroscience Abstracts, 12,* 556.

Wilson, F. A. W., Scalaidhe, S. P. O., & Goldman-Rakic, P. S. (1993). Dissociation of object and spatial processing domains in primate prefrontal cortex. *Science, 260,* 1955–1958.

Wilson, M. A., & McNaughton, B. L. (1993). Dynamics of the hippocampal ensemble code for space. *Science, 261,* 1055–1058.

Wing, L. (1991). The relationship between Asperger's syndrome and Kanner's autism. In U. Frith (Ed.), *Autism and Asperger syndrome.* New York: Cambridge University Press.

Winn, P. (1994). Schizophrenia research moves to the prefrontal cortex. *Trends in Neurosciences, 17,* 265–268.

Winner, E., & Gardner, H. (1977). The comprehension of metaphor in brain-damaged patients. *Brain, 100,* 719–727.

Winslow, J. T., & Insel, T. R. (1990). Neurobiology of obsessive-compulsive disorder: A possible role for serotonin. *Journal of Clinical Psychiatry (Suppl.), 51,* 27–31.

Wirz-Justice, A., Graw, P., Kraeuchi, K., Gisin, B., Jochum, A., Arendt, J., Fisch, H.-U., Buddeberg, C., & Poeldinger, W. (1993). Light therapy in seasonal affective disorder is independent of time of day or circadian phase. *Archives of General Psychiatry, 50,* 929–937.

Witelson, S. F. (1976). Abnormal right hemispheric specialization in developmental dyslexia. In R. Knights & D. Bakker (Eds.), *The neuropsychology of learning disorders.* Baltimore, MD: University Park Press.

Witelson, S. F. (1977). Early hemisphere specialization and interhemispheric plasticity, an empirical and theoretical review. In S. J. Segalowitz & F. A. Gruber (Eds.), *Language development and neurological theory.* New York: Academic Press.

Witelson, S. F. (1985). On hemisphere specialization and cerebral plasticity from birth. Mark II. In C. Best (Ed.), *Hemispheric function and collaboration in the child.* New York: Academic Press.

Wolkin, A., Jaeger, J., Brodie, J. D., Wolf, A. P., Fowler, J., Rotrosen, J., Gomez-Mont, F., & Cancro, R. (1985). Persistence of cerebral metabolic abnormalities in chronic schizophrenia as determined by positron emission tomography. *American Journal of Psychiatry, 142,* 564–571.

Wong, D. F., Wagner, H. N., Tune, L. E., Dannals, R. F., Pearlson, G. D., Links, J. M., Tamminga, C. A., Broussolle, E. P., Ravert, H. T., & Wilson, A. A. (1986). Positron emission tomography reveals elevated D2 dopamine receptors in drug-naive schizophrenics. *Science, 234,* 1558–1563.

Wood, A. J., & Goodwin, G. M. (1987). A review of the biochemical and the neuropharmacological actions of lithium. *Psychological Medicine, 17,* 579–600.

Woods, B. T. (1980). The restricted effects of right hemisphere lesions after age one: Wechsler test data. *Neuropsychologia, 18,* 65–70.

Woods, B. T., & Teuber, H.-L. (1978). Changing patterns of childhood aphasia. *Annals of Neurology, 3,* 273–280.

Woolsey, T. A., Durham, D., Harris, R., Simons, D. J., & Valentino, K. (1981). Somatosensory development. In R. N. Aslin, J. R. Alberts, & M. R. Peterson (Eds.), *Development of perception: Psychological perspectives: Vol. 1. Audition, somatic perception and chemical senses.* New York: Academic Press.

World Health Organization. (1961). *Public health aspects of low birth weight.* Report of the Expert Committee on Maternal Care and Child Care. Geneva: Author.

Wu, J. C., Gillin, J. C., Buchsbaum, M. S., Hershey, T., Johnson, J. C., & Bunney, W. E. (1992). Effect of sleep deprivation on brain metabolism of depressed patients. *American Journal of Psychiatry, 149,* 538–543.

Wurtz, R. H., Goldberg, M. E., & Robinson, D. L. (1982). Brain mechanisms of visual attention. *Scientific American, 246,* 124–135.

Yakovlev, P. I., & Lecours, A. R. (1967). The myelogenic cycles of regional maturation of the brain. In A. Minkowski (Ed.), *The regional development of the brain in early life.* Oxford, England: Blackwell Scientific.

Yarita, H., Iino, M., Tanabe, T., Kogure, S., & Takagi, S. F. (1980). A transthalamic olfactory pathway to the orbitofrontal cortex in the monkey. *Journal of Neurophysiology, 43,* 69–85.

Young, A. W. (1988). Functional organization of visual recognition. In L. Weiskrantz (Ed.), *Thought without language.* Oxford: Oxford University Press.

Yu-Huan, H., Ying-Quan, Q., & Gui-Qing, Z. (1990). Crossed aphasia in Chinese: A clinical survey. *Brain and Language, 39,* 347–356.

Yule, M., & Rutter, M. (1976). Epidemiology and social implications of specific reading retardation. In R. M. Knights & D. J. Bakkar (Eds.), *The neuropsychology of learning disorders.* Baltimore, MD: University Park Press.

Zaidel, E. (1976). Auditory vocabulary of the right hemisphere after brain bisection or hemidecortication. *Cortex, 12,* 191–211.

Zametkin, A. J., Nordahl, T. E., Gross, M., King, A. C., Semple, W. E., Rumsey, J., Hamburger, S., & Cohen, R. (1990). Cerebral glucose metabolism in adults with hyperactivity of childhood onset. *New England Journal of Medicine, 323,* 1361–1366.

Zangwill, O. (1960). *Cerebral dominance and its relation to psychological function.* Edinburgh: Oliver and Boyd.

Zangwill, O. (1962). Dyslexia in relation to cerebral dominance. In J. Money (Ed.), *Reading disability.* Baltimore, MD: Johns Hopkins University Press.

Zangwill, O. L. (1954). Agraphia due to a left parietal glioma in a left handed man. *Brain, 77,* 510–520.

Zangwill, O. L. (1960). La probleme de l'apraxie ideatoire. *Revue Neurologique* (Paris), *102,* 595–603.

Zangwill, O. L. (1966). Psychological deficits associated with frontal lobe lesions. *International Journal of Neurology, 5,* 395–402.

Zeki, S. (1992, September). The visual image in mind and brain. *Scientific American,* pp. 69–76.

Zeki, S. (1993). *A vision of the brain.* Oxford: Blackwell Scientific.

Zeki, S., Watson, J. D. G., Lueck, C. J., Friston, K. J., Kennard, C., & Frackowiak, R. S. J. (1991). A direct demonstration of functional specialization in human visual cortex. *Journal of Neuroscience, 11,* 641–649.

Zigmond, M. J., Bloom, F. E., Landis, S. C., Roberts, J. L., & Squire, L. R. (1999). *Fundamental neuroscience.* San Diego: Academic Press.

Zihl, J., Von Cramon, D., & Mai, N. (1983). Selective disturbance of movement vision after bilateral brain damage. *Brain, 106,* 313–340.

Zohar, J., Insel, T., Zohar-Kadouch, R. C., Hill, J. L., & Murphy, D. (1986). Serotonergic responsivity in obsessive-compulsive disorder. Effects of chronic clomipramine treatment. *Archives of General Psychiatry, 45,* 167–172.

Zola-Morgan, S., & Squire, L. (1985). Medial temporal lesions in monkeys impair memory on a variety of tasks sensitive to amnesia. *Behavioral Neuroscience, 99,* 22–34.

Zola-Morgan, S., Squire, L. R., & Amaral, D. G. (1986). Human amnesia and the medial temporal region: Enduring memory impairment following a bilateral lesion limited to field CA1 of the hippocampus. *Journal of Neuroscience, 6*(10), 2950–2967.

Zola-Morgan, S., Squire, L. R., & Amaral, D. G. (1989). Lesions of the amygdala that spare adjacent cortical regions do not impair memory or exacerbate the impairment following lesions of the hippocampal formation. *Journal of Neuroscience, 9,* 1922–1936.

Zola-Morgan, S., Squire, L. R., Amaral, D. G., & Suzuki, W. A. (1989). Lesions of perirhinal and parahippocampal cortex that spare the amygdala and hippocampal formation produce severe memory impairment. *Journal of Neuroscience, 9,* 4355–4370.

Zorilla, L. T. E., & Cannon T. D. (1995). Structural brain abnormalities in schizophrenia: Distribution, etiology, and implications. In S. A. Mednick (Ed.), *Neural development in schizophrenia: Theory and research.* New York: Plenum.

Credits

Chapter 1 **Fig. 1.3** From J. R. Breasted, *The Edwin Smith Surgical Papyrus.* Copyright © 1930 University of Chicago Press. Reprinted by permission of the publisher.
Chapter 2 **Figs. 2.2, 2.8, 2.9, 2.10, 2.14, 2.15, 2.16** From Kandel, E. R., J. H. Schwartz, and T. M. Jessell, *Essentials of Neural Science and Behavior.* Copyright © 1995 Appleton & Lange. Reprinted by permission of the McGraw-Hill Companies. **Fig. 2.17** Reprinted from *Neuron,* Volume 1, R. A. Nicoll, J. A. Kauer, and R. C. Malenka, "The Current Excitement in Long-Term Potentiation," pp. 96–103. Copyright © 1998 Elsevier Science. With permission from Elsevier Science.
Chapter 3 **Figs. 3.11, 3.12** From *Fundamental Neuroanatomy* by W. H. W. Nauta and M. Feirtag. Copyright © 1986 by W. H. Freeman and Company. Reprinted with permission from the publisher. **Fig. 3.14** From F. Netter, *The CIBA Collection of Medical Illustrations, Volume I: Nervous System.* Copyright © 1999 Icon Learning Systems, LLC, a subsidiary of Havas MediMedia USA, Inc. Reprinted with permission from ICON Learning Systems, LLC, illustrated by Frank H. Netter, MD. All rights reserved. **Fig. 3.22** From Jackson Beatty, "The Major Nuclei of the Hypothalamus," *Principles of Neuroscience,* Brown & Benchmark, 1995, p. 128. With permission from the author. **Fig. 3.23A** From Kandel, E. R., J. H. Schwartz, and T. M. Jessell, *Essentials of Neural Science and Behavior.* Copyright © 1995 Appleton & Lange. Reprinted by permission of the McGraw-Hill Companies.
Chapter 4 **Fig. 4.1** From M. Bear, B. Connors, and M. Paradiso, *Neuroscience: Exploring the Brain.* Copyright © 1996 Lippincott Williams & Wilkins. Reproduced by permission. **Fig. 4.6** From Kandel, E. R., J. H. Schwartz, and T. M. Jessell, *Essentials of Neural Science and Behavior.* Copyright © 1995 Appleton & Lange. Reprinted by permission of the McGraw-Hill Companies. **Fig. 4.8** From Penfield, W. and Jaspers, H., *Epilepsy and the Functional Anatomy of the Human Brain,* Lippincott Williams & Wilkins, 1954. Reprinted with permission.
Chapter 5 **Fig. 5.3** From M. Bear, B. Connors, and M. Paradiso, *Neuroscience: Exploring the Brain.* Copyright © 1996 Lippincott Williams & Wilkins. Reproduced by per-

mission. **Fig. 5.4** From H. J. A. Dartnell, J. K. Bowmaker, and J. D. Mollon, "Microspectrophotometry of Human Photoreceptors," J. D. Mollon and L. T. Sharpe (eds.), *Colorvision Physiology and Psychophysics.* Copyright © 1983 Academic Press. Reprinted by permission of the publisher. **Fig. 5.6** From S. W. Kuffler, "Discharge Patterns and Functional Organization of Mammalian Retina," *Journal of Neurophysiology,* 16, 1953, pp. 37–68. Reproduced by permission of the publisher. **Fig. 5.7** From M. Bear, B. Connors, and M. Paradiso, *Neuroscience: Exploring the Brain,* © 1996 Lippincott Williams & Wilkins. Reproduced by permission. **Figs. 5.8, 5.9, 5.11, 5.12** From Kandel, E. R., J. H. Schwartz, and T. M. Jessell, *Essentials of Neural Science and Behavior.* Copyright © 1995 Appleton & Lange. Reprinted by permission of the McGraw-Hill Companies. **Fig. 5.10** From Tom N. Cornsweet, *Visual Perception.* Copyright © 1970 by Harcourt, Inc. Reproduced by permission of the publisher. **Fig. 5.14** From B. Curtis, "The Visual System," B. A. Curtis, S. Jacobson, and E. M. Marcus (eds.), *An Introduction to the Neurosciences,* Philadelphia and Toronto: W. B. Saunders, 1972. Reprinted by permission of the author. **Fig. 5.15** From *Eye, Brain, and Vision* by David H. Hubel, Scientific American Library, 1988. Used with permission of W. H. Freeman and Company. **Fig. 5.16** From M. S. Livingstone and D. H. Hubel, "Anatomy and Physiology of a Color System in the Primate Cortex," *Journal of Neuroscience,* 4, 309–356. Copyright © 1984 by the Society for Neuroscience. Reprinted by permission of the publisher. **Fig. 5.18** From D. H. Hubel and T. N. Wiesel, "Receptive Fields, Binocular Interaction and Functional Architecture in the Cat's Visual Cortex," *Journal of Physiology,* 1962, 160, pp. 106–154. Copyright © 1962 by The Journal of Physiology. Reprinted with permission of the publisher and the author. **Figs. 5.19, 5.20** From Kandel, E. R., J. H. Schwartz, and T. M. Jessell, *Essentials of Neural Science and Behavior.* Copyright © 1995 Appleton & Lange. Reprinted by permission of the McGraw-Hill Companies. **Figs. 5.22, 5.23** From D. H. Hubel and T. N. Wiesel, "Receptive Fields, Binocular Interaction and Functional Architecture in the Cat's Visual Cortex," *Journal of Physiology,* 1962, 160, pp. 106–154. Copyright © 1962 by The Journal of Physiology. Reprinted with

in Conditional Associative-Learning Tasks After Frontal and Temporal Lobe Lesions in Man," pp. 601–614. Copyright © 1985 Elsevier Science. With permission from Elsevier Science. **Chapter 8** **Figs. 8.2, 8.3** From Rosaleen A. McCarthy and Elizabeth K. Warrington, *Cognitive Neuropsychology: A Clinical Introduction.* Copyright © 1990 by Academic Press. Reproduced by permission of the publisher. **Fig. 8.4** From *Neuropsycholgical Assessment* by Muriel Lezak. Copyright © 1976 by Oxford University Press, Inc. Used by permission of Oxford University Press, Inc. **Fig. 8.5** From M. J. Farah, *Visual Agnosia: Disorders of Object Recognition and What They Tell Us About Normal Vision.* Copyright © 1990 The MIT Press. Reprinted by permission of the publisher. **Fig. 8.6** From E. DeRenzi, G. Scotti, and H. Spinnler, "Perceptual and Associative Disorders of Visual Recognition: Relationship to the Site of Lesion," *Neurology,* 1969, 19, pp. 634–642. Reprinted with permission of Lippincott Williams & Wilkins. **Fig. 8.7** From R. A. McCarthy and E. K. Warrington, *Cognitive Neuropsychology: A Clinical Introduction.* Copyright © 1990 by Academic Press. Reproduced by permission of the publisher. **Fig. 8.10** From R. A. McCarthy and E. K. Warrington, "Visual Associative Agnosia: A Clinico-Anatomical Study of a Single Case," *Journal of Neurology, Neurosurgery and Psychiatry,* 1986, 49, 1233–1240. Reprinted by permission of the author. **Fig. 8.11** From E. K. Warrington and M. James, "Visual Apperceptive Agnosia: A Clinico-Anatomical Study of Three Cases," *Cortex,* 1988, 24, pp. 13–34. Reprinted by permission of the author. **Fig. 8.13** From R. A. McCarthy and E. K. Warrington, "Visual Associative Agnosia: A Clinico-Anatomical Study of a Single Case," *Journal of Neurology, Neurosurgery and Psychiatry,* 1986, 49, 1233–1240. Copyright © 1986 BMJ Publishing Group. Reprinted by permission of the publisher and the author. **Fig. 8.15a** From Rosaleen A. McCarthy and Elizabeth K. Warrington, *Cognitive Neuropsychology: A Clinical Introduction.* Copyright © 1990 by Academic Press. Reproduced by permission of the publisher. **Fig. 8.15 b, c** From M. J. Farah, *Visual Agnosia: Disorders of Object Recognition and What They Tell Us About Normal Vision.* Copyright © 1990 The MIT Press. Reprinted by permission of the publisher. **Fig. 8.16** From D. F. Benson and J. P. Greenberg, "Visual Form Agnosia: A Specific Defect in Visual Discrimination," *Archives of Neurology,* 1969, Vol. 20, pp. 82–89. **Fig. 8.17** G. W. Humphreys & M. J. Riddoch, *To See But Not to See,* Psychology Press, Taylor & Francis Group, 1987. Reprinted with permission from the publisher. **Fig. 8.18** From M. J. Farah, *Visual Agnosia: Disorders of Object Recognition and What They Tell Us About Normal Vision.* Copyright © 1990 The MIT Press. Reprinted by permission of the publisher. **Fig. 8.21** From S. Zeki, *A Vision of the Brain,* Oxford: Blackwell Scientific Publications, 1993, p. 263. Reprinted by permission of Blackwell Science, Ltd. **Fig. 8.22** From S. Zeki, *A Vision of the Brain,* Oxford: Blackwell Scientific Publica-

tions, 1993, p. 324. Reprinted by permission of Blackwell Science, Ltd and by kind permissions of Semir Zeki, Professor of Neurobiology, UCL. **Chapter 9** **Fig. 9.2** From E. V. Evarts, "Brain Mechanisms of Movement, " *Scientific American,* September 1979. Copyright © 1979 by Bunji Tagawa. Used by permission of Ikuyo Tagawa Garber, Executrix of the Estate of Bunji Tagawa. **Fig. 9.3** From E. V. Evarts, "Relation of the Pyramidal Tract Activity to Force Exerted During Voluntary Movement," *Journal of Neurophysiology,* 31, 1968, pp. 14–27. **Fig. 9.4** From E. V. Evarts, "Relation of the Pyramidal Tract Activity to Force Exerted During Voluntary Movement," *Journal of Neurophysiology,* 31, 1995, pp. 14–27. Reproduced by permission of the publisher. **Figs. 9.5, 9.6** From A. P. Georgopoulos, K. S. Kalaska, R. Caminiti and J. T. Massey, "On the Relations Between the Directions of Two-dimensional Arm Movements and the Cell Discharge of the Primate Motor Cortex," *Journal of Neuroscience,* 2, 1996, pp. 1147–1537. Copyright © 1996 by the Society for Neuroscience. Reprinted by permission of the publisher. **Fig. 9.9** From P. E. Roland, B. Larsen, N. A. Larsen, and E. Skinhut, "Supplementary Motor Areas and Other Cortical Areas in Organization of Voluntary Movement in Man," *Journal of Neurophysiology,* 43, 1980, pp. 118–136. Reproduced by permission of the publisher. **Figs. 9.10, 9.11** From Kandel, E. R., J. H. Schwartz, and T. M. Jessell, *Essentials of Neural Science and Behavior.* Copyright © 1995 Appleton & Lange. Reprinted by permission of the McGraw-Hill Companies. **Fig. 9.13** Reprinted from *Current Opinion in Neurobiology,* Vol. 3, J. W. Mink and W. T. Thatch, "Basal Ganglia Intrinsic Circuits and Their Behavior," p. 952, Copyright © 1993 Elsevier Science. With permission from Elsevier Science. **Figs. 9.15, 9.16, 9.17** From N. Geschwind and E. Kaplan, "Cerebral Disconnection Syndrome," *Neurology,* 12, 1962, p. 677. Reprinted with permission of Lippincott Williams & Wilkins. **Fig. 9.19** From Frontal Lobe Function and Dysfunction, edited by Harvey S. Levine, H. M. Eisenberg. Copyright © 1991 by Oxford University Press, Inc. Used by permission of Oxford University Press, Inc. **Chapter 10** **Fig. 10.3** From W. B. Scoville and B. Milner, "Loss of Recent Memory After Bilateral Hippocampal Lesions," *Journal of Neurology, Neurosurgery, and Psychiatry,* 1957, 20, pp. 11–21. Copyright © 1957 by the BMJ Publishing Group. Reproduced by permission of the publisher. **Fig. 10.4** From M. Bear, B. Connors, and M. Paradiso, *Neuroscience: Exploring the Brain.* Copyright © 1996 Lippincott Williams & Wilkins. Reproduced by permission. **Fig. 10.6** From B. Milner, "Memory and the Medial Temporal Region of the Brain," *Biological Bases of Memory,* edited by K. H. Pribram and D. E. Broadbent. Copyright © 1970 by Academic Press. Reproduced by permission of the publisher. **Fig. 10.7** Philip Corsi, "Human Memory and the Medial Temporal Region of the Brain," doctoral dissertation, 1972. Used with permission. **Fig. 10.8** From B. Milner,

Index _____

Boldface page numbers indicate pages in the text where the term appears in boldface. A page number followed by (fig.) *indicates a figure. A page number followed by* (table) *indicates a table. A page number followed by* n *indicates a footnote.*

absolute refractory period, **30**
acetylcholine, **32**
    antagonists and agonists for, 34n
    corelease of, 33
    enzymatic degradation of, 33
    Loewi's discovery of, 20
    substances reducing/facilitating
        release of, 31, 32
achromatopsia, 15, 83, **116**, 186
action potential, **28**, 29–30, 30(fig.)
active zones, **31**
activity-dependent presynaptic
    facilitation, **40**
adoption studies, **384**
adrenocorticotrophic hormone
    (ACTH), **395**
affect, **324**
affective aggression, 307–308, 307(fig.)
affective disorders. *See* mood disorders
affective prosody, **325,** 327
afferent, **47**
afterpotential, **30**
age, as factor in functional recovery
        after brain damage, 445–449,
        447(fig.), 448(fig.)
aggression
    amygdala's role, 311–312
    predatory vs. affective, 307–308,
        307(fig.)
agnosias, **60**
    visuospatial, **165**–166, 168
    See also visual agnosia
agonists, 34n
agoraphobia, **398**
agrammatism, **133, 143**
agraphia, **12, 149**
    alexia without, 12–13, 136
    phonological, **149**–150

pure, **150**
    spatial, **150**
    spelling disorders as, 149
Akelaitis, 87
akinesia, **241**
akinetopsia, **118**–119
Alcmaeon of Croton, 4
alcohol, cerebellum's sensitivity to, 240
alexia, **12, 136**
    without agraphia, 12–13, 136, 137
    pure, **205,** 211–212, 213, 214
    See also dyslexias
Alford, L.B., 324
Alivisatos, B., 358
allocentric space, **159**–160, 164–171
    complex spatial tasks, 166(fig.),
        167–168, 169(fig.)
    hemispheric specialization for
        spatial processing, 166–167,
        166(fig.)
    orientation discrimination, 167,
        167(fig.)
    relative spatial location, 167
    spatial analysis, 165–166
    topographical orientation and
        memory, 168, 170
    two-pathway hypothesis for object
        recognition and spatial
        processing, 170–171, 171(fig.)
allocortex, **53**
alogia, **383**
alternative strategies, **453**
Alzheimer, Alois, 381, 382, 401
Alzheimer's disease, 401–405
    brain tissue transplantation, 454, 455
    Frederick (golfer) case, 258, 260
    genetic factors, 403, 405
    neurochemical abnormalities, 401

physostigmine to lessen symptoms,
        33
    prevalence, 401
    semantic and episodic memory
        impairment, 282
    structural abnormalities, 401–403,
        402(figs.), 403(fig.), 404(figs.)
amacrine cells, **96**
amnesia
    anterograde, **63, 263,** 263(fig.)
    anterograde topographical, **170**
    diencephalic, 271–274, 274(fig.)
    famous patient (H. M.), 256,
        261–265, 262(fig.), 268, 270,
        276–277, 276(fig.)
    global, **282**
    medial temporal-lobe, **264**–265,
        268–270, 273–274, 274(fig.)
    preserved aspects of memory,
        275–281
    retrograde, **263,** 263(fig.), 264–265,
        271, 271(fig.)
    retrograde topographical, **170**
    source, **272,** 349
    thalamic, 273
amnestic aphasia, **141**
amphetamines
    neurotransmitter release facilitated
        by, 32
    norepinephrine reuptake blocked
        by, 34
amygdala, **61**
    emotional role, 63, 311–312, 312(fig.),
        323–324, 323(fig.), 329–335
    fear conditioning role, 317–319,
        318(fig.), 321–322, 322(fig.)
    influences on cortex, 330–332,
        330(fig.), 331(fig.)

amygdala *(continued)*
  integration of cortex and, 332–335, 333(fig.), 335(fig.)
  removal or lesions of, memory impairment after, 268, 270
analogical representations, **158**
Andreasen, N. C., 388, 407
anencephaly, **428**
angiography, **75**, 75(fig.)
anomia, **133**
anomic aphasia, **141**
anoxic episodes, **429**
antagonists, 34n
anterior commissure, 54(fig.), **55**
anterior nucleus of thalamus, **61**
anterior pituitary gland, **66**
anterior position, **46**, 46(fig.), 47
anterograde amnesia, **63, 263**, 263(fig.)
anterograde degeneration, **443**
anterograde topographical amnesia, **170**
anterograde transport, **73**–74, 73(fig.)
antidepressants
  monoamine oxidase inhibitors, **33, 395**
  selective serotonin reuptake inhibitors (SSRIs), **34, 395**
  tricyclic, **34, 395**
antipsychotics, **384**
  atypical, **385**
antisocial personality disorder, **400**
anxiety disorders, 398–400
  generalized anxiety disorder (GAD), **398**, 399
  neurochemical factors, 398–399
  obsessive-compulsive disorder (OCD), **398**, 400
  panic disorder, **398**, 399–400
  phobias, **398**, 399
anxiolytics, **398**–399
aotonomic sensory, **47**
apathy
  bystander, **459**
  following prefrontal lesions, 347–348
aphasias, **9**, 131–136
  anomic (amnestic), **141**
  Broca's, **9**, 84, 132–134, 143
  central motor, **350**
  conduction, **11**, 135, 135(fig.), 136, 144
  disconnection syndrome hypothesis, 136–138, 137(fig.)
  double dissociability of, 84

factors affecting recovery from, 444–445
  frontal dynamic, **350**
  global, 135
  jargon, **134**, 143
  optic, **215**–216
  prefrontal, **350**
  tactile, **136**, 138
  transcortical, **135**–136, 135(fig.)
  Wernicke's, 10, 84, 134–135, 143
Aplysia californica, 460
  classical conditioning, 39–41, 40(fig.)
  habituation, 37–38, 37(fig.)
  sensitization, 38, 39(fig.)
apolipoprotein E4, **405**
apperception, **197**
apperceptive agnosia, 197, **199**–203, 208(fig.), 211
  tests for detecting, 200(figs.), 201(figs.), 202(figs.), 209(fig.)
apraxias, **13**, 150, 167, 227
  conceptual, **249**
  constructional, **167**–168, 251
  dissociation, **247**
  early studies, 243–244
  empirical classification, 245–250
  ideational, **244**, 244(fig.)
  ideomotor, **244**, 244(fig.)
  Liepmann's classification, 244, 244(fig.)
  limb, **246**
  motor, **244**, 244(fig.)
  oral, **246**
  Ravel's symptoms, 226
  of speech, **132**, 132n, 143
aprosodia, **133**, 152
arachnoid membrane, **48**–49, 50(fig.)
archicortex, **53**
arcuate convexity, **364**
arcuate fasciculus, **55**, 56(fig.)
arcuate sulcus, **364**
Aristotle, 4
arousal
  cognitive arousal theory of emotion, **303**, 303(fig.)
  disturbed, following prefrontal lesions, 347
  theories of, with attention deficit disorder (ADD), 437
arteriography, **75**, 75(fig.)
aspartate, **32**
Asperger, N., 438
Asperger's syndrome, 438–439
associated impairments, 84–85, 86

association cortex, **17, 60**
associative agnosia, 197, **203**–211, 208(fig.), 221
  perceptual impairment, 207–211, 209(fig.), 210(fig.), 211(fig.)
  stimuli for detecting, 204(fig.), 205(fig.), 206(fig.)
astrocytes, **21**, 22(fig.)
athetosis, **242**
atropine, 35
attention
  covert, **179**
  exclusionary, **358**, 359–360
  impairment of, with schizophrenia, 392, 392(fig.)
  neglect as disorder of, 177–182, 178(fig.), 180(fig.), 181(figs.)
  overt, **179**
  selective, **358**–359
attentional dyslexia, **146**
attention deficit disorder (ADD), **435**–438
  genetic factors, 436–437
  theories of, 436–438
atypical antipsychotics, **385**
Auburtin, Ernest, 8
auditory association cortex (AII), **59**
auditory cortex, 59
  conditioned fear role, 319–320, 320(fig.)
auditory nerve, **59**
auditory pathway, conditioned fear role, 316–317, 317(fig.), 320, 320(fig.)
auditory perceptual analysis, **138**, 139
auditory radiations, **59**
auditory temporal acuity, **138**–139
auditory word comprehension, 138–141, 139(fig.), 140(table), 141(table)
autism, 438–440
  genetic factors, 439
  theories of, 438, 439
autistic savants, **438**
autonomic motor system, **47**
autonomic nervous system (ANS), **47**
autonomonic sensory system, **47**
autoradiography, **74**
autoreceptors, **34**
autosomal dominant transmission, **428**
autosomal recessive transmission, **428**
avolition, **383**
axial sections, **47**, 48(fig.)
axon hillock, 21(fig.), **28**–29

axons, **21,** 21(fig.)
  growth of, in brain development,
    416–417, 416(fig.)
axon terminal, **21, 73**
axoplasmic transport, **73**–74, 73(fig.)

Baillargeon, R., 424, 424(fig.)
ballism, **242**
Bard, Philip, theory of emotion, 306,
    306(fig.)
Barkley, R. A., 437
barrels, **419**
Bartholow, R., 81
Bartlett, Frederic, 261
basal ganglia, **48, 51, 60**–61, 62(fig.)
  disorders from lesions of, 241–242
  looping connections, 240–241, 241(fig.)
  voluntary movement role, **229,**
    240–243, 240(fig.), 241(fig.),
    242(fig.)
basolateral nuclei (nuclear group), **317**
Bauer, J., 421
Bay, Eberhard, 15, 197
B cones, **96,** 97(fig.), 104
Bear, D., 328
behavior
  bizarre, **383**
  stimulus bound, **359**
  temporal integration of, **355,** 358
  utilization, **359**
Bekhterev, V. M., 261
Benedikt, 149
Benton's line-orientation task, 167,
    167(fig.)
Berger, Hans, 80
Berlin, 431
β amyloid, **403**
β amyloid precursor protein (APP),
    403–405
bilateral structure/connections, **47**
binding problem, **125**
binocular disparity, **118**
binocular zone, **106,** 106(fig.)
bipolar cells, **96**
bipolar disorder, **397**–398, 397(fig.)
  genetic factors, 398
  prevalence, 397
birth date, **413**
Bisiach, E., 182, 186
bizarre behavior, **383**
black widow spider venom,
    neurotransmitter release
    facilitated by, 32
Bleuler, Eugen, 382

blindness
  color, 15, 83, 98, 116, 186
  cortical, **59,** 67–68, **198**–199
  psychic, **310**
  sight restoration with, 223–224
blindsight, **68,** 126–127
blind spot, **106**
blobs, **110**
Block-Tapping Test, 267, 267(fig.)
blood-brain barrier, **21,** 444
blunted affect, **383**
Bodamer, J., 212
body space, **159,** 160–161
Borod, J. C., 328
botulism, as result of reduced
    neurotransmitter release, 31
Bouillaud, Jean Baptiste, 8
bouton, **21,** 73
Bradley, C., 436
bradykinesia, **241**
brain
  ancient Egyptian views, 2–4
  ancient Greek views, 4–5
  biological preparedness for
    language, 130–131
  hierarchical functioning, 13–15
  inaccuracy of early depictions, 6
  major divisions, 48, 49(fig.),
    49(table)
  terminology for directions/positions
    in, 46–47, 46(fig.)
  terminology for sections cut
    through, 47, 48(fig.)
  triune brain hypothesis, 313–**314,**
    314(fig.)
brain damage, 442–455
  effects of, 442–444
  factors affecting functional recovery
    after, 444–449
  neural mechanisms of functional
    recovery after, 449–451
  as reversal of evolutionary
    development, 15
  therapeutic approaches to, 451–455
brain development, 411–440
  causes of abnormality, 427–430
  cellular processes, 412–420
  developmental disorders (*see*
    developmental disorders)
  executive function development,
    422–425, 424(fig.), 425(fig.)
  language development, 425–427
  visual acuity development, 421–422,
    422(fig.)

visual orienting development, 422,
    423(fig.)
brain functioning
  hierarchical view, 13–15
  holistic view, 7–8, 13
  localization, 5–7, 13
brain hypothesis, 2–5
brain stem
  regions of, **48,** 49(table), 66–68,
    67(fig.)
  terminology for directions in, 46
brain tissue transplantation, 454–455,
    454(fig.)
Broca, Paul, 8–10
  Broca's aphasia, 9, 84, 132–134, 143
  Broca's area, **9,** 10(fig.), 133–134,
    137(fig.), 138, 151
  great limbic lobe, 61, 312
  hemispheric dominance concept,
    9–10, 13
  patient Leborgne ("Tan"), 9, 9(fig.),
    13
Brodmann, Korbinian, 381
  area 17, 55, 58, 94
  cytoarchitectonic map, 55, 55(fig.)
  macaque and human prefrontal
    cortexes, 343, 343(fig.)
Buchtel, H., 359
Bucy, Paul, 310
buffers, **284**–285
bystander apathy, **459**

caffeine, effect on second messenger
    activity, 36
calcarine sulcus, 54(fig.), 58
calcitonin gene-related peptide
    (CGRP), corelease of, 33
calcium (Ca^{2+}), neurotransmitter
    release modulated by, 29n, 31
Cannon, Walter, theory of emotion,
    306, 306(fig.)
case study approach, 15, 16
catastrophic reaction, **324**
catecholamine hypothesis
  attention deficit disorder (ADD), **436**
  depression, 395
catecholamines, substances
    reducing/facilitating release of,
    31, 32
category specificity, **140**
category specificity effects, **205**–206,
    206(fig.), 212–214
cauda equina, **69**
caudal direction, **46**–47, 46(fig.)

caudate nucleus, **60,** 61, **240**
cell bodies, **21**
cell membranes
  ion movement through, 24–25,
    25(figs.)
  in neurons, 23, 24(fig.)
  resting potential of, 25–27
central disorders of spelling, **149**–150
central dyslexias, **146,** 148
central motor aphasia, **350**
central nervous system (CNS),
  overview of, 47–51
central nucleus, **317**
central sulcus, **57**
central visual processing, 94, 109,
  115(fig.)
cerebellar ataxia, **240**
cerebellar peduncles, **68**
cerebellum, **48,** 49(table), 68–69
  alcohol sensitivity, 240
  looping connections, 240–241,
    241(fig.)
  voluntary movement role, **229,**
    238–240
cerebral cortex, **8, 48, 50**
  amygdala influences on, 330–332,
    330(fig.), 331(fig.)
  emotional role, 324–335
  functional divisions, 55–60, 57(fig.),
    58(fig.)
  integration of amygdala and,
    332–335, 333(fig.), 335(fig.)
  long-term memory storage, 292–296
  Rolando's drawing of, 6, 6(fig.)
  sequential-hierarchical processing,
    60, 61(fig.), 94, 109
  structure, 51–55, 52(fig.), 53(fig.),
    54(fig.), 55(fig.), 56(fig.)
  visual processing, 94, 109, 115(fig.)
cerebral dominance for language, **9**
cerebral hemispheres
  dominance of, evidence for, 9–10
  imbalance between, as factor in
    clinical depression, 324
  lobes of, 52–53, 52(fig.)
  See also left hemisphere; right
    hemisphere
cerebral hemispheric anatomical
    asymmetries
  handedness, 153–154, 154n
  language, 131, 153–154, 153(fig.),
    154(fig.), 155, 155(fig.)
cerebral hemispheric functional
    asymmetry, **12**
  handedness, 154, 154n

cerebral hemispheric specialization
  complementary, 11–**12**
  for emotions, 324–328, 328(fig.)
  handedness and, 89, 89(tables),
    90(table)
  intrahemispheric, **9**–10
  for mental imagery, 187–188
  reorganization of, after brain
    damage in children, 446–448,
    447(fig.), 448(fig.)
  for spatial processing, 166–167,
    166(fig.)
cerebral ventricles, 49–50, 51(fig.)
  enlarged, with Alzheimer's disease,
    401, 403(fig.)
  enlarged, with schizophrenia,
    385–386, 386(figs.), 387–388
  ventricular-brain ratio (VBR), **386,**
    386(fig.)
  ventricular hypothesis, **5,** 5(fig.)
cerebrospinal fluids (CSF), **49,** 50
chemospecificity hypothesis, **418**–419,
    418(fig.)
chimeric face, **327**–328, 328(fig.)
chorea, **242**
choroid plexus, **50**
chromosomal deletion, **428**
chromosomal disorders, **428**
chunking, **259**
Churchland, P. S., 463
cingulate fasciculus, **55,** 56(fig.)
cingulate gyrus, **61,** 63, 312
  Papez circuit theory of emotion,
    308–310, 309(fig.), 310(fig.)
circumlocutory speech, **134**
Claparède, E., 275–276
classical conditioning, 39–41, 40(fig.),
    257, 316
  preserved in amnesic patients,
    277–278
  See also fear conditioning
clinical depression. See major
    depressive disorder
cocaine, norepinephrine reuptake
    blocked by, 34
cochlear nucleus, **59**
coextensive single-opponent cells, **104**
cognition. See thinking
cognitive arousal theory of emotion,
    303, 303(fig.)
cognitive neuroscience, 304
cognitive skills, **257**
  learning of, preserved in amnesic
    patients, 278–279, 278(fig.),
    279(fig.)

cogwheel rigidity, **241**
collateral sprouting, **449,** 450(fig.)
color anomia, **140**
color blindness
  central, 15, 83, 116, 186
  cones associated with, 98
color constancy, **114**
color opponent cells, **104,** 105(fig.)
color vision
  Young-Helmholtz trichromatic
    theory, 97–**98**
  See also color blindness
commissurotomy, 86–89, 88(fig.)
  complex spatial task behavior after,
    168, 169(fig.)
compensatory strategies, **453**–454
complementary hemispheric
    specialization, 11–12
complex cells, **117,** 117(fig.)
compulsions, **398**
computational neurobiology, **217**
computation by constraint satisfaction,
    217
computerized tomography (CT),
    75–76, 76(fig.)
concentric broadband cells, **104**
concentric double-opponent receptive
    fields, **110,** 113(fig.), 114–116
concentric single-opponent cells, **104,**
    105(fig.)
conceptual apraxias, **249**
concordance rate, **384**
conditional associative learning, **189**
conditioned response, **39,** 316
conditioned stimulus, **39, 316**
conditioning
  contextual, **320**–321
  fear, **316**–322
  See also classical conditioning
conductance, **23,** 24
conduction aphasia, **11,** 135, 135(fig.),
    136, 144
cones, **96,** 96(fig.)
  B cones, **96,** 97(fig.), 104
  G cones, **96,** 97(fig.), 104
  phototransduction in, 97–98
  R cones, **96,** 97(fig.), 98(fig.), 104
confabulation, **272**
conformational state, **23**
connectionism, **217**
consciousness, **457**
consolidation, **264**–265, 274–275
constructional apraxias, **167**–168,
    251
contextual conditioning, **320**–321

Continuous Performance Test, 392, 392(fig.), 437
contra coup effect, **4**
contralateral side, **4, 47**
contrast enhancement, **103**
convergent thinking, **352**
Cooper, L. A., 358
Corbetta, M., 181
corollary discharge, **360**
coronal sections, **47,** 48(fig.)
corpus callosum, **12,** 54(fig.), **55,** 56(fig.)
  See also commissurotomy
corpus striatum, **61**
Corsi, Philip, 265–267
Corsi Block-Tapping Task 267, 267(fig.)
cortex. *See* cerebral cortex
cortical atrophy
  Alzheimer's disease, 401, 402(fig.), 403(fig.)
  with schizophrenia, 386–388, 387(fig.)
cortical blindness, **59,** 67–68, **198**
  partial, 198–199
cortical commissural fibers, **55,** 56(fig.)
cortical deafness, **59**
cortical dementia, 401–405
cortical modules, **124**
cortical retina, 94, 109
corticobulbar tract, **67**
corticocortical connections, **55,** 56(fig.)
corticomedial nuclei (nuclear group), **317**
corticospinal tract, **67**
corticotropin releasing hormone (CRH), **395**
cortisol, **395**–396
cotransmission, **33**
covert attention, **179**
craniotomy, **2**
Creutzfeldt-Jacob disease, 401
critical period, **131**
cross-theoretic identification, **461**
crowding, **448**
Crow, Timothy, 387
curare, 34n, 35
cyclic guanosine monophosphate (cGMP), **97**
cytoarchitectonics, **53,** 55, 55(fig.)
  of prefrontal cortex, 343, 343(fig.)
  See also Brodmann, Korbinian
cytochrome oxidase, 74, **110**
cytoplasm, **23**

Dale's law, **33**
Damasio, H., 364

dark current, **97**
Dax, Marc, 9
deafness
  cortical, **59**
  pure word, **136,** 137–138
declarative memory, **257**–258, 258n
decussation, **68**
deep dyslexia, **148, 431**
degrading enzymes, **33**
Dejarine, Joseph Jules, 1, 12–13, 137, 215
delayed-alternation tasks, **285**
delayed nonmatching to sample (DNMS) tasks, **269**
delayed-response tasks, **285**–286, 286(fig.)
  ocular analogue of, 286–287, 287(fig.), 288(fig.), 289(fig.)
deletion, chromosomal, **428**
Delis, D. C., 352
delusions, **383**
dementias, 401–407
  cortical, 401–405
  dementia praecox (*see* schizophrenia)
  semantic, **282**
  subcortical, 405–407
  See also specific diseases
dendrites, **21,** 21(fig.), 417, 417(fig.)
dendritic spines, **292,** 293(fig.)
denervation, **449**
denervation supersensitivity, **449**
depolarization, **25,** 28–29
depression
  antidepressants, 33, 34, 395
  bipolar disorder, **397**–398, 397(fig.)
  major depressive disorder, **394**–397, 396(fig.)
  pseudodepression, **348**
  seasonal affective disorder (SAD), 397, **397**
De Renzi, E., 200, 204
Descartes, René, 7, 8, 457–458
developmental disorders, 427–440
  attention deficit disorder (ADD), 435–438
  autism, 438–440
  with known causes, 427–430
  learning disorders, 430–435, 430(fig.)
developmental dyslexia, **431**–434, 433(fig.)
  genetic factors, 434
  metabolic abnormalities, 434
  neuroanatomical abnormalities, 433–434, 433(fig.)
  theories of, 431–432, 434

Diagnostic and Statistical Manual of Mental Disorders (DSM-IV) (American Psychiatric Association), 383, 407
Diamond, D. M., 424–425, 425(fig.)
diaschisis, **86, 443**
diathesis, **409**
dichotic listening, **88**
diencephalic amnesia, 271–274, 274(fig.)
diencephalon, **48,** 49(table), 63–66
diffusion force, **24**
digit span, **261**
dihaptic tasks, **91**
directional tuning, **234**
direction selectivity, **118**
direction vector, **234,** 235(fig.)
disconnection model, 11, 135, 135(fig.)
  language disorders, 136–138, 137(fig.)
  visual agnosia, 215–216, 215(fig.)
disconnection syndromes, **11,** 12–13
  See also disconnection model
dishabituation, **424**
dishabituation method, **423**
disinhibition, following prefrontal lesions, 348
disorders of spelling assembly, **150**
dissociation apraxias, **247**
dissociation of function, **83**–86, 84(fig.), 85(fig.)
  auditory word comprehension, 139–141, 140(table), 141(table)
  spelling, 149–150
  word retrieval, 141–142, 141(table), 142(table)
  See also double dissociation
dissociative disorders, **323**
dissolution, **15**
distributed representation, **38, 217**
divergent thinking, **351**–352
Donders, F. C., 78
dopamine, **32,** 33(fig.)
dopamine hypothesis of schizophrenia, **35, 384**–385
dopamine-serotonin interaction hypothesis of schizophrenia, **385**
dorsal hemiretina, **106**
dorsal horn, **70**
dorsal position, **46**–47, 46(fig.)
dorsal root, **70**
dorsal root ganglia, **70**
dorsolateral prefrontal cortex, **342,** 342(fig.)
dorsolateral prefrontal syndrome, 362
Dostrovsky, 172

double dissociation, **84,** 84(fig.), 85,
    85(fig.), 85n, 86
  auditory comprehension and
      naming, 139–140, 142
  disorders of object recognition and
      spatial location, 170–171, 171(fig.)
  dyslexia as, 90–91, 148
  speech production, 144
  See also dissociation of function
Douglas, R. M., 359
Down syndrome (trisomy 21), **428**
Drevets, W. C., 396
dualism, **6–7, 457**
  property dualism, 458–459
  substance dualism, 7, **457**–458
Duncan, J., 364
dura mater, **48,** 50(fig.)
dynamic form, **119**
dysarthria, **132, 143**
dyscalculia, **434**–435
dyseidetic dyslexia, **90**
dysexecutive syndrome, **362**
dysgraphia, **133**
dyslexias, 90–91, **146**
  attentional, **146**
  categories of, 146, 148, 148(table)
  central, **146,** 148
  deep, **148,** 431
  developmental, **431**–434, 433(fig.)
  dyseidetic, **90**
  dysphonetic, **90**
  neglect, **146**
  phonological, **148,** 148(table), **431**
  spelling, **146**
  surface, **148,** 148(table), **431**
  visual word-form, **146**
  See also alexia
dysmetria, **240**
dysphonetic dyslexia, **90**
dysprosodia, **133**
dyssynergia, **240**

Ebers Papyrus, 132
Eccles, John, 256
echoic memory, **258**
ectopic cells, **433**
Edelman, Gerald, 256
edema, **443**
Edgell, D., 427
Edwin Smith Surgical Papyrus, 2–4,
    3(fig.)
efferent, **47**
Efron, Robert, 91
Efron Squares Test, 198, 198(fig.),
    199–200

Eggar, M. D., 451
egocentric space, **159,** 161–164
Egyptians, ancient, views of brain, 2–4,
    2(fig.)
eidetic images, **158**
elaborative encoding, **297**
elaborative rehearsal, **297**
electrical self-stimulation, **312**–313,
    313(fig.)
electrical synapses, **23,** 43(fig.)
electrochemical equilibrium, **24,** 25(fig.)
electrocorticography (ECo), **81**–83,
    82(fig.)
electroencephalography (EEG), **80**–81,
    81(fig.)
electrostatic force, **24**
electrotonic potentials, **29**
emergent property, **458**
emotion, 302–337
  amygdala role, 63, 311–312, 312(fig.),
      323–324, 323(fig.), 329–335
  Cannon-Bard theory, 306, 306(fig.)
  cognition vs., neural basis of,
      336–337
  cognitive arousal theory, **303,**
      303(fig.)
  components of, 304
  conscious experience of, 336–337
  cortex role, 324–335
  difficulties in studying, 303–304
  higher-order mediation of, 329–335
  hippocampal role, 323–324, 323(fig.)
  hypothalamus role, 63, 306–308,
      307(figs.), 314–315
  impaired, following prefrontal
      lesions, 347–348
  intuitive theory, 305, 305(fig.)
  James-Lange theory, 305–306,
      305(fig.)
  Klüver-Bucy syndrome, 310–312
  limbic structures role, 63
  limbic system conceptualization,
      312–315, 313(fig.)
  memory of, vs. emotional memory,
      323–324, 323(fig.)
  mood, 324–325
  neural basis of fear, 316–322
  Papez circuit theory, 308–310,
      309(fig.), 310(fig.)
  in speech, 152
  temporal lobes role, 328–329
emotional memory, **323**
emotional perseveration, **334**
emotional semantics, **327**
Empedocles, 4

encoding, **260,** 274
  elaborative, **297**
endogenous depression, **395**
engram, **291**
environmental dependency syndrome,
    359
epinephrine, **32**
episodic memory, **257**
  lost with global amnesia, 282
  selective impairments of, 282
equilibrium potential, 24–**25**
equipotentiality, **8**
etiologies, **384**
euphoria, following prefrontal lesions,
    348
Evans, 353
Evarts, Edward, 230–231
event-related potentials (ERPs), **81,**
    81(fig.)
evoked potential, **81**
evolution
  hierarchical functioning of brain,
      14–15
  human language, 154–155, 155(fig.)
  triune brain hypothesis, 313–**314,**
      314(fig.)
excitation, postsynaptic, 32(fig.)
excitatory postsynaptic potentials
    (EPSPs), **27,** 28–29
exclusionary attention, **358,** 359–360
executive function, **259,** 284, 289–290,
    355
  development of, 422–425, 424(fig.),
      425(fig.)
  impaired, following prefrontal
      lesions, 353–358
Exner, S., 149
exocytosis, 31
explanatory unification, **461**
explicit memory, **257,** 258, 258n,
    294–295
expressive aprosodia, **152**
expressive gestures, **245**
externally focused interventions, **452**
extinction behavior, as example of
    cortex-amygdala integration, 334
extracellular fluid, **23**
extrastriate cortex, **59, 94**
eyes. *See* vision

facial expressions
  execution of, 327–328, 328(fig.)
  perception of, 325
facial feedback hypothesis, **306**
facilitating interneurons, **38**

Farah, M. J., 185, 185(fig.), 207, 214, 220
fear, decreased, with Klüver-Bucy
    syndrome, 310
fear conditioning, **316**–322
    amygdala role, 317–319, 318(fig.),
        321–322, 322(fig.)
    auditory cortex role, 319–320,
        320(fig.)
    auditory pathway role, 316–317,
        317(fig.), 320, 320(fig.)
    categories of response, 319(fig.)
    contextual conditioning
        accompanying, 320–321
Fedio, P., 328, 329
feelings. *See* emotion
fetal alcohol syndrome, **429**
fiber tracts, **50**, 73
filopodia, **417**
fissures, **53**
5-hydroxyindoleacetic acid, **395**
Flechsig, Paul, 197, 420
Flor-Henry, P., 393
Flourens, Marie-Jean-Pierre, 7–8
Flynn, J. P., 307
folk psychology, **458**, 462–463
Folstein, S. E., 439
forebrain (prosencephalon), **48**,
    49(fig.), 49(table)
    structures of, 51–66
foreign language syndrome, **152**
formal thought disorder, **383**
fornix, **63**
fourth ventricle, **50**, 51(fig.)
fovea, **106**
Franzen, E. A., 389
Frederick (golfer with Alzheimer's
    disease), 258, 260
Freud, Sigmund
    On Aphasia, 13
    Project for a Scientific Psychology, 381
    Schreber case study, 381
    term *agnosia* coined by, 196–197, 203
Friberg, 185
Fritsch, Gustav, 10, 81
frontal dynamic aphasia, **350**
frontal eye fields (FEF), **364**, 373–374
frontal granular cortex. *See* prefrontal
    cortex
frontal lobes, **52**, 52(fig.)
    organization-related memory role,
        296–298
    spatial processing role, 188–190,
        189(fig.), 190(figs.), 191(fig.)
    working memory role, 285–290
frontal sections, **47**, 48(fig.)

functional imaging methods, 78–80
    functional magnetic resonance
        imaging (fMRI), **79**
    interpretation problems, 79–80
    positron emission tomography
        (PET), **78**, 79(fig.)
    single photon emission
        computerized tomography
        (SPECT), **78**–79
    subtraction method, **78**, 79–80
functionalism, **459**–460
functional magnetic resonance
    imaging (fMRI), **79**
functional map, **57**
functional neuroanatomy, **45**
Fuster, Joaquin, 251, 367, 377, 393, 396

Gaffan, D., 269
Gage, Phineas, 341–342, 341(fig.)
Galaburda, A. M., 153, 432, 433
Galen, 5, 442
Gall, Franz Josef, 7, 8, 132
Galletti, C., 164
gamma-aminobutyric acid (GABA),
    27, 32
ganglia, **51**
    See also basal ganglia; retinal
        ganglion cells
gap junction channels, **23**, 43(fig.)
gap junctions, **43**
gating, **23**, 35–36
gaze-locked cells, **163**, 163(fig.)
G cones, **96**, 97(fig.), 104
gender
    and developmental dyslexia, 432
    and functional recovery after brain
        damage, 444
generalized anxiety disorder (GAD),
    398, 399
general paresis, **381**–382
generator potentials, **42**
genetic factors
    Alzheimer's disease, 403, 405
    attention deficit disorder (ADD),
        436–437
    autism, 439
    bipolar disorder, 398
    developmental disorders, 427–428
    developmental dyslexia, 434
    Huntington's chorea (disease), 306
    major depression, 397
    obsessive-compulsive disorder
        (OCD), 400
    panic disorder, 400
    schizophrenia, 384

Georgopoulos, Apostolos, 234
Gerstman, J., 149
Gerstman syndrome, 149n, **435**
Geschwind, Norman
    apraxia patient, 246–249, 247(fig.),
        248(figs.)
    disconnection model, 11, 215
    hemispheric anatomical asymmetry,
        153–154
    hypothesis on gender's relationship
        to dyslexia, 432
    left hemisphere role in voluntary
        movement, 250
    transcortical aphasia case, 136
gestures, symbolic vs. expressive, **245**
Ghent, L., Overlapping Figures Test,
    200, 201(fig.)
Gleitman, H., 380
glia, **21**–22, 22(fig.)
    membrane potential of, 25, 26(fig.)
gliosis, **443**
Glisky, E. L., 454
global amnesia, **282**
global aphasia, 135
globus pallidus, **60**–61, **240**
glutamate, **32**
glycine, **32**
goal-directed behavior
    impaired regulation of, following
        prefrontal lesions, 340–342,
        353–362
    as manifestation of intelligence, 340
Goldman-Rakic, P. S.
    on prefrontal cortex role in working
        memory, 286–287, 288(fig.),
        289(fig.), 463
    on regulation of behavior by
        representational knowledge,
        364, 366, 367, 373, 377
Goldstein, K., 324
Golgi, Camillo, 20
Gollin incomplete figures test, 200–201,
    201(fig.), 203, 277, 277(fig.)
Goltz, Friedrich, 13
Grafe, P., 223
grammar, **129**
Grandin, Temple, 438–439
grandmother cells, **125**, **217**
granulovacular degeneration, **403**
graphic buffer, **150**
gray matter, **50**–51, 51(fig.)
    in spinal cord, 69, 70
Greeks, ancient, views of brain, 4–5
group studies, 16
growth cone, **416**, 416(fig.)

guanylyl cyclase, 97
Guitton, D., 359, 371
Gwiazda, J., 421
gyri, 6, 6(fig.), 53, 53(fig.), 54(fig.)

habituation, 37–38, 37(fig.), 423–424
hallucinations, 383
handedness
    developmental dyslexia, 432
    hemispheric anatomical
        asymmetries, 153–154, 154n
    hemispheric specialization, 89,
        89(tables), 90(table)
    recovery from aphasia, 444–445
Harlow, J. M., 341, 342
hearing. See auditory cortex
heavy metals, effect on second
        messenger activity, 36
Hecaen, H., 160
Heilman, K. M., 249
Held, R., 421
Helmholtz, Hermann von, 98
hemianopia, 58, 107
hemiballism, 242
hemiparesis, 236
hemiplegia, 57
hemispheres. See cerebral hemispheres
Henschen, 94, 109
Heschl's gyrus, 59
Hess, W. R., 307
hierarchical functioning of brain, 13–15
    as evolutionary development, 14–15
    Hughlings-Jackson's concept of,
        13–14
hierarchical processing, 94
    See also sequential-hierarchical
        processing
hindbrain (rhombecephalon), 48,
    49(fig.), 49(table), 68
Hinshelwood, J., 431
hippocampus, 61
    connections between prefrontal
        cortex and, 370–371, 370(fig.)
    contextual conditioning role, 321
    cortical input to, 271(fig.)
    explicit memory role, 294–295
    impaired memory after removal or
        lesions of, 265–267, 266(fig.),
        268–269, 270
    as limbic system structure, 312
    long-term potentiation (LTP), 41–42,
        41(fig)
    spatial processing role, 171–176,
        172(fig.), 173(figs.), 174(fig.),
        175(fig.)

Hippocrates, 4–5, 132
Hitzig, Eduard, 10, 81
H. M. (amnesia patient), 261–265,
    262(fig.)
    author's meeting with, 256
    lesions of, 268, 270
    motor learning by, 276–277, 276(fig.)
holism, 7
    Flourens's experiment, 7–8
    Goltz's view, 13
    localization vs., 13–15
Holmes, G., 162
homeostasis, 65
homonymous hemianopia, 58, 107
homotopic fields, 55
horizontal cells, 96
horizontal sections, 47, 48(fig.)
horseradish perioxidase (HRP)
        method, 74
Hubel, David, 110, 117, 120, 123, 124,
    419
Hughlings-Jackson, John
    apraxia case description, 243, 246
    brain involvement in language, 136
    hierarchy concept, 13–15
    imperception, 221
    on positive and negative symptoms,
        383
    right hemisphere's specialization for
        visual imagery, 12, 160
human immunodeficiency virus
    (HIV), 429
human V4, 115, 116, 116(fig.)
human V5, 115(fig.), 119, 119(fig.)
humor, comprehension of, 325–326
Huntington, George, 405
Huntington's chorea (disease), 242,
    405–406
    biochemical and structural
        abnormalities, 406
    genetic factors, 306
    motor learning impairment, 277
    prefrontal dysfunction hypothesis,
        406
hydrocephalus, 50
hypergraphia, 328
hyperkinesia, 242
hypermetamorphosis, 310–311
hyperpolarization, 27, 28, 29
    afterpotential as, 30
hyperprosodia, 133
hypofrontality, 389
hypokinesia, 241, 242
hypothalamus, 61, 64(fig.), 65–66,
    66(fig.)

emotional role, 63, 306–308,
    307(figs.), 314–315
hypoxic-ischemic encephalopathy, 428

iconic memory, 258
idealism, 6, 457
ideational apraxias, 244, 244(fig.)
ideational fluency, 351–352
ideomotor apraxias, 244, 244(fig.)
illusions, 383
imipramine, 34
impairments
    associated, 84–85, 86
    dissociation of function, 83–86
imperception, 221
implicit memory, 257, 258, 258n
    intact in amnesic patients, 276–281
    storage of, 295
indifference reaction, 324
induction, 412–413, 412(fig.)
inferior colliculus, 59, 68
inferior longitudinal fasciculus, 55,
    56(fig.)
inferior position, 46, 46(fig.)
inferior prefrontal convexity, 364,
    374–375
inferotemporal cortex (TE), long-term
        memory role, 294
Ingvar, D. H., 389
inhibition
    postsynaptic, 32(fig.)
    presynaptic, 31, 32(fig.), 40
    of return, 422, 423(fig.)
    sculpting role, 27, 28(fig.)
inhibitory postsynaptic potentials
    (IPSPs), 27, 28, 29
inner nuclear layer, 96
inner plexiform layer, 96
intelligence
    and functional recovery after brain
        damage, 445
    goal-directed behavior as
        manifestation of, 340
    impaired, following prefrontal
        lesions, 350
intentionality, 457
interblobs, 110
intermediate-term memory, 260
interneurons, 19
    facilitating, 38
interstripes, 114
intertheoretic reduction, 460–462
intracellular fluid, 23
intrahemispheric specialization of
        function, 9–10

ionotropic receptors, **35**
ions, **23**
   movement of potassium and
      sodium, 25–27
   physical forces influencing
      movement of, 24–25
ipsilateral corticocortical fibers, **55,**
   56(fig.)
ipsilateral side, **4, 47**
isocortex, **53**
isolation of the speech area, **136**

Jacobsen, C. F., 285, 286, 365, 366
James, William, 336
   intelligence as viewed by, 340
   Principles of Psychology, 19
   theory of emotion, 305–306, 305(fig.)
   types of memory, 264, 282
Jamison, Kay Redfield, 398
jargon aphasia, **134,** 143
Joubert syndrome, **440**
Joynt, R., 9

Kandel, E. R., 37, 460
Kanizsa triangle, 220–221, 221(fig.)
Kanner, L., 438
Kaplan, E., apraxia patient, 246–249,
   247(fig.), 248(figs.), 250
Karpov, B. A., 358
karyotype, **428**
Kemper, T. L., 433
Kennard principle, **445**–446
Kimura, Doreen, 250–251
kinesthesis, **57, 159,** 161
kinetic disorder of speech, **132,** 132n, **143**
Klüver, Heinrich, 310
Klüver-Bucy syndrome, **310**–312
Kolb, B., 325
Kornetsky, 436
Korsakoff's disease, 265, **271**–273,
   271(fig.), 297, 298
Koskinas, 55
Kosslyn, S. M., 186
Kraepelin, Emil
   important research from laboratory
      of, 381–382
   work on schizophrenia, 381, 383,
      388
Krafft-Ebbing, Richard von, 381–382
Kuffler, Steven, 99, 108, 110
Kussmall, 431
kwashiorkor, **429**

lamellipodia, **417**
Land, Erwin, 114

Lange, Carl, theory of emotion,
   305–306, 305(fig.)
language, 128–155
   cerebral dominance, **9**
   characteristics of, 129–130
   components of function in, 138–150
   development of, in infants/children,
      130–131, 425–427
   and hemispheric anatomical
      asymmetries, 153–154, 153(fig.),
      154(fig.), 155, 155(fig.)
   human, evolution of, 154–155,
      155(fig.)
   impaired, following prefrontal
      lesions, 350–351
   left hemisphere role, 9–10, 11, 12
   mental representations underlying,
      157–158
   right hemisphere role, 151–153
   sequential processing, **10**–11, 11(fig.)
   Wernicke's area role, 139, 139(fig.),
      150–151
language-based dyscalculia, **435**
language disorders. *See* aphasias
Lashley, Karl, 8, 292, 296
lateral geniculate nucleus (LGN), **58,**
   64, 107–109, 108(fig.)
   magnocellular layers, 118–120
   projections to visual cortex, 109–110,
      110(fig.), 111(table), 112(figs.)
   receptive field characteristics of
      neurons, 108–109, 111(table)
lateral inhibition, **102**–103
laterality studies, **91**
lateral pathways, **101,** 103(fig.)
lateral position, **46,** 46(fig.)
lateral sections, **47,** 48(fig.)
lateral ventricles, **50,** 51(fig.)
lead, effect on second messenger
   activity, 36
learning
   habituation, 37–38, 37(fig.)
   long-term potentiation (LTP), 41–**42,**
      41(fig.)
   and multiple memory systems,
      290–291, 291(table)
   neuronal mechanisms, 37–42
   nonassociative, **257**
   preserved in amnesic patients,
      276–279, 276(fig.), 277(fig.),
      278(figs.), 279(fig.)
   sensitization, **38,** 39(fig.)
   See also classical conditioning
learning disabilities. *See* learning
   disorders

learning disorders, **430**–435
   developmental dyscalculia, 434–435
   developmental dyslexia, **431**–434,
      433(fig.)
   nonverbal learning disabilities, 435
   Taylor's model for identifying, 430,
      430(fig.)
Leborgne ("Tan"), 9, 9(fig.), 13
left-handedness. *See* handedness
left hemisphere
   dominance of, 11, 12
   emotional role, 324, 326, 327–328,
      328(fig.)
   language role, 9–10, 11, 12
   schizophrenia as functional
      abnormality of, 393
   spatial processing role, 159, 166(fig.),
      167, 168, 169(fig.)
   speech specialization, 131, 154n
Leibniz, Gottfried, 197
lemniscal system, **57**
length constant, **28**
Leonardo da Vinci, 5–6, 5(fig.)
lesion methods, 83–86
   hippocampus role in spatial
      processing, 172–174, 173(figs.)
   staged-lesion effect, **445**
lesion momentum, **443**
lesions, 7
   See also brain damage
Levitsky, W., 153–154
Lichtheim, L., 135–136, 135(fig.),
   139–140
Liepmann, Hugo, 13, 215, 250
   apraxia classification, 244, 244(fig.)
   early studies of apraxias, 243–244
ligand-gated channels, **23**
lightness constancy, **101**
lightness record, **114**
limb apraxias, **246**
limbic system, **48, 61**–63, 62(fig.), 63(fig.)
   connections of, 64(fig.)
   MacLean's conceptualization,
      312–315, 313(fig.)
line-cancellation task, 177(fig.)
linguistic disorders of spelling,
   149–150
lipid bilayer, **23,** 24(fig.)
Lissauer, Heinrich, 196, 203, 206
localization on the body surface, **159**
localization of function, **5**
   history of views about, 5–7
   holism vs., 13–15
   and lesion method, 86
   mapmakers, 13

local representation, **217**
Loewi, Otto, 20
Loftus, Elizabeth, 261
long-term habituation, **37**
long-term memory, **260**
  neural representation, 291–296
  as separate from short-term
    memory, 264
long-term potentiation (LTP), 41–**42**,
  41(fig.)
loose associations, **383**
LSD, 34
lumens, **99**
luminance, **99**
Luria, Aleksandr, 358
  cortical processing model, 60,
    61(fig.), 94
Luzzatti, C., 182, 186

M1. *See* motor cortex (M1)
Mach bands, **103**, 104(fig.)
MacLean, Paul, 61
  limbic system conceptualization,
    312–315, 313(fig.)
  triune brain hypothesis, 313–314,
    314(fig.), 315
magnetic resonance imaging (MRI), **76**,
  77(fig.)
  functional magnetic resonance
    imaging (fMRI), **78**–79
magnetoencephalography (MEG), **83**
magnocellular layers, **108**
magnocellular-V3 channel, 119–120
magnocellular-V5 channel, 118–119,
  119(fig.)
maintenance, **261**, 274–275
major depressive disorder, **394**–397,
  396(fig.)
  catecholamine hypothesis, **395**
  endocrine dysfunction, 395–396
  endogenous depression, **395**
  genetic factors, 397
  hemispheric imbalance, 324
  monoamine hypothesis, **395**
  prevalence, 395
  reactive depression, **395**
  serotonin hypothesis, **395**
malnutritional milieu, **429**
mamillary bodies, **61**
mania, **397**
manic-depressive disorder. *See* bipolar
  disorder
The Man Who Mistook His Wife for a Hat
  (Sacks), 195
mapmakers, 13

marasmus, **429**
Marie, Pierre, 13
Martin, A., 329
mass action, **8**
massively parallel constraint-
  satisfaction models, **217**
  of visual agnosia, 217–220
master area hypothesis of vision,
  125–126
materialism, **6**, **457**
McCarthy, R. A., 204
  speech production model, 144,
    144(fig.), 145
  word retrieval model, 142,
    142(fig.)
McFie, J., 160
medial geniculate nucleus, 59, **64**
medial position, **46**, 46(fig.)
medial prefrontal cortex, **342**, 342(fig.),
  364
medial prefrontal syndrome,
  362–363
medial temporal-lobe amnesia,
  264–265, 268–270, 273–274,
  274(fig.)
  See also H. M. (amnesia patient)
medulla. *See* medulla oblongata
  (myelencephalon)
medulla oblongata (myelencephalon),
  48, 49(table), 68
membrane potential, **25**, 26(fig.)
memory, 256–298
  categories of, 257–260, 258(fig.)
  component processes, 260–261,
    274–275
  emotional, vs. memory of emotion,
    323–324, 323(fig.)
  frontal lobes role, 285–290, 296–298
  impaired, after temporal-lobe
    lesions, 265–270
  impaired, following prefrontal
    lesions, 349–350
  impairments of, 281–290
  long-term potentiation (LTP)
    role, 42
  metamemory, **272**, 349–350
  mood congruity, **324**
  multiple systems, 290–291,
    291(table)
  and other cognitive domains, 261
  preserved with amnesia, 275–281
  prospective, **354**
  protein synthesis and, 295, 296(fig.)
  recognition, **269**–270
  topographical, 170

  See also amnesia; *specific categories of*
    memory
memory of emotion, **323**–324, 323(fig.)
meninges, **48**–49, 50(fig.)
mental causation, **457**
mental imagery
  hemispheric specialization, 187–188
  in spatial processing, 184–188,
    185(fig.), 186(fig.), 187(fig.)
mental neuroscience, 304
mesencephalon. *See* midbrain
  (mesencephalon)
metabolic pumps, **26**
metabotropic receptors, **36**
metamemory, **272**, 349–350
metencephalon, 48, 49(table)
method of loci, **281**
method of vanishing cues, **281**
M ganglion cells, **104**, 108, 109, 110(fig.)
microcephaly, **428**
microglia, **21**
microtubules, **73**
midbrain (mesencephalon), **48**, 49(fig.),
  49(table), 67–68
migration, neuronal, 188, 189(fig.),
  190(fig.), **413**, 415(fig.), 416,
  416(fig.)
Milner, Brenda, 261, 265, 297, 312
mind-body problem, **6**–7, 456–464,
  457
  folk psychology approach, **458**,
    462–463
  functionalism approach, **459**–460
  intertheoretic reduction and, **460**,
    462
  potential for unified theory, 460–464
  property dualism approach, 458–459
  substance dualism approach, 7,
    457–458
mind-brain problem. *See* mind-body
  problem
Mirror Drawing Task, 276, 276(fig.)
Mirror Reading Task, 277, 278(fig.)
Mishkin, M., 170, 171, 270
mixed transcortical aphasia, 135–136
Miyashita, Y., 294
modular organization, **17**
modulation, **19**
monamines, **32**
Mondrian field, 114, 115
monism, **6**, **457**
monoamine hypothesis of depression,
  395
monoamine oxidase inhibitors, **33**, **395**
monocular zones, **106**, 106(fig.)

mood, 324–325
  as factor in functional recovery after brain damage, 445
mood congruity of memory, **324**
mood disorders, 394–398
  bipolar disorder, 397–398, 397(fig.)
  major depressive disorder, 394–397, 396(fig.)
  seasonal affective disorder (SAD), **397**
Morgan, W. P., 431
morphological agrammatism, **143**
morphology, **129**
Morris Water Maze, 296
motor apraxias, **244,** 244(fig.)
motor cortex (M1), **10, 57,** 58(fig.)
  voluntary movement role, **229,** 230–235, 231(fig.), 232(fig.), 233(fig.), 234(fig.), 235(fig.)
motor homunculus, **57,** 58(fig.)
motor learning, preserved in amnesic patients, 276–277, 276(fig.)
motor neurons, **19**
motor skill, **257**
motor strip. *See* motor cortex (M1)
Mountcastle, Vernon, 99
movement
  reflex vs. voluntary, 231, 231(fig.), 232(fig.)
  whole-body movements, **246**
  See also voluntary movement
movement disorders. *See* Huntington's chorea (disease); Parkinson's disease
movement formulas, **243**
multiple sclerosis, 22
Munk, Herman, 196, 450
muscular dystrophy, 228
myasthenia gravis, 228
myelencephalon. *See* medulla oblongata (myelencephalon)
myelin, **22**
  transmission speed and efficiency influenced by, 30–31
myelination, **420,** 421(fig.)
myelogenetic cycles, **420,** 421(fig.)
Myklebust, H. R., 435

nasal hemiretina, **104,** 106(fig.)
Nauta, Walle, 60
necrosis, **443**
neglect (neglect syndrome), **176**–184, 176(fig.), 177(fig.)
  as attention disorder, 177–182, 178(fig.), 180(fig.), 181(figs.)

as internal space representation disruption, 182–184, 182(fig.), 183(fig.)
neglect dyslexia, **146**
Neisser, Ulric, 459
Nemesius, 5
neocortex, **53**
neologisms, **134**
neomammalian brain, **314**
neostriatum, **61, 240**
nerve growth factor (NGF), **449**
nervous system
  adaptivity of, 19
  "doorbell," 19–20
  theories on basic structure, 20
neural groove, **413**
neural plate, **412**
neural tube, **413**
neurites, **21**
neuritic plaques, **403**
neuroanatomy, **45**
  functional, **45**
neuroblasts, **413**
  proliferation of, 413, 414(fig.)
neuroethology, **174**
  studies on hippocampus role in spatial processing, 175–176, 175(fig.)
neurofibrillary tangles, **403**
neuroglia. *See* glia
neuroleptics, **384**
neuronal migration, **413,** 415(fig.), 416, 416(fig.)
neuronal transmission
  chemical, at synapses, 22–24, 34(fig.), 42–43
  electrical, 43–44
neuron doctrine. *See* neuron hypothesis
neuron hypothesis, **20**
neurons
  cell membranes in, 23, 24(fig.)
  components of, 20–21, 21(fig.)
  discovery of, 20
  human number of, 19
  motor, **19**
  primary sensory, **19**
  types of, 19
  See also interneurons
neuropeptides, **33**
  prolonged effect of, 34–35
neurophysiological methods, 80–83
  electrocorticography (ECo), **81**–83, 82(fig.)

electroencephalography (EEG), **80**–81, 81(fig.)
  event-related potentials (ERPs), **81,** 81(fig.)
  single-cell recording, **80**
neurotransmitter release, 31–33, 32(fig.)
  effect on postsynaptic membranes, 27
  substances reducing/facilitating, 31–32
neurotransmitters, **20**
  antagonists and agonists, 34n
  categories of, 32–33
  enzymatic degradation, 33
  neuronal transmission role, 22–23
  responses to receptors binding to, 35–36
  reuptake of, 33–34
  See also specific neurotransmitters
neutral stimulus, **39, 316**
Newcombe, F., 210
Newsome, William, 119
nicotine, effect on second messenger activity, 36
nigrostriatal bundle, **242**
Nissl, Franz, 381
nodes of Ranvier, 21(fig.), **22,** 31
Noguchi, Hideyo, 382
nonassociative learning, **257**
nondeclarative memory, **257**–258, 258n
nonverbal affect lexicon, **327**
nonverbal learning disabilities, **435**
norepinephrine, **32,** 33(fig.), 34
nuclei
  as concentrations of cell bodies, 50–51
  as part of cells, **21**
nucleus basalis, **331**
nutritional disorders, 429

object agnosia, 205–206, 206(fig.), 212, 214
object permanence, **423**–424, 424(fig.)
object recognition
  massively parallel constraint-satisfaction models, 217–220
  two-pathway hypothesis for, and spatial processing, 170–171, 171(fig.)
  See also visual agnosia
obligatory looking, **422**
obsessions, **398**
obsessive-compulsive disorder (OCD), **398,** 400
occipital lobes, **52,** 52(fig.)

occulomotor nucleus, **68**

ocular dominance columns, **120,** 121(fig.), 122(figs.), 123–124

ocular dominance hypercolumn, **124**

OFF-center/ON-surround receptive fields, **99,** 100(fig.), 102–103, 103(fig.)

Ogle, 149

O'Keefe, J., 172

Olds, J., 312

olfactory cortex, 59

oligodendrocytes, **22,** 22(fig.)

On Aphasia (Freud), 13

ON-center/OFF-surround receptive fields, **99,** 100(fig.), 102, 103(fig.)

opsin, **97**

optic aphasia, **215**–216

optic ataxia, **162**

optic chiasm, 107, 107(fig.)

optic disc, **106**

optic nerve, **106**

optic tract, **107**

optimum arousal theory of attention deficit disorder (ADD), **437**

oral apaxias, **246**

orbital prefrontal cortex, **342,** 342(fig.), **364,** 365(fig.), 375–377, 376(fig.)

orbital prefrontal syndrome, 362–363

organelles, **21**

orientation columns, **120**–124, 121(fig.), 123(figs.)

orientation hypercolumn, **124**

orientation selectivity, **110**

Orton, S., 431

outer nuclear layer, **96**

outer plexiform layer, **96**

Overlapping Figures Test, 200, 201(fig.), 207

overt attention, **179**

Owen, A. M., 362

paleocortex, **53**

paleomammalian brain, **314**

panic disorder, **398,** 399–400

Papez, James, circuit theory of emotion, 308–310, 309(fig.), 310(fig.)

paragraphias, 133

parahippocampal cortex, **174**

parahippocampal gyrus, **61,** 312

parallel distributed processing, **16**–17, **94,** 217

parallel hierarchical processing, **94**

paraphasias, 133

paraplegia, 229

parietal lobes, **52,** 52(fig.)

connections between prefrontal cortex and, 368–369, 369(fig.)

left, voluntary movement role, **229,** 250–251

See also apraxias

Parkinson's disease, 241–242, 406–407

brain tissue transplantation, 454, 455

pars operacularis, **144**

partial cortical blindness, **198**–199, 198(fig.), 199(figs.)

partial knowledge, **140**

partial knowledge effects, **204**

parvocellular-blob channel, **110**

parvocellular-interblob channel, **110,** **116**–118

parvocellular layers, **108**

Paterson, A., 160, 166

Pavlov, Ivan, 316

Penfield, Wilder, 81–82, 235, 292

perceptual categorization (constancy), **217**

perceptual learning, preserved in amnesic patients, 277, 277(fig.), 278(fig.)

perceptual representation system (PRS), **281**

perceptual skill, **257**

peripheral nervous system (PNS), **47**

perirhinal cortex, **174**

permeability, **23,** 24

perseveration, **133,** 334, 361, 367, 371

Wisconsin Card Sorting Test, 334, 334(fig.)

personality, as factor in functional recovery after brain damage, 445

Petrides, M., 189, 297, 298

P ganglion cells, **104,** 105(fig.), 108, 109, 110(fig.)

phenothiazines, **35**

phenylalanine hydroxylase, **428**

phenylketonuria (PKU), **428**

phobic disorders, **398**–400

phonemes, **129,** 131

phonemic disorder of speech, **132,** 143

phonemic jargon aphasia, **143**

phonemic paraphasia, **133**

phonological agraphia, **149**–150

phonological buffer, **285**

phonological dyslexia, **148,** 148(table), **431**

phonological reading. *See* surface dyslexia

phonological store, **285**

photon, **97**

photoreceptors, **95,** 96–97, 96(fig.), 97(fig.), 98(fig.)

phototransduction, **97**

phrenology, **7,** 7(fig.)

physostigmine, 33, 34n

Piaget, Jean, 423

pia mater, **49,** 50(fig.)

Pick's disease, 401

pigmented epithelium, **96**

Pinker, S., 463

Piven, J., 439

place cells, **172,** 172(fig.)

place fields, **172,** 172(fig.)

planum temporale, **131,** 153–154, **153,** 153(fig.)

plasticity, **419**

Plato, 4, 457

plexiform layer, **53**

pneumoencephalography, **75,** 75(fig.)

point localization thresholds, **160**–161, 161n

poliomyelitis, 228

polygenic inheritance, **428**

pons, **48,** 68

population vector, **234,** 235(fig.)

positron emission tomography (PET), **78,** 79(fig.)

Posner, M. I., 139, 144, 145, 146, 177, 181

postcentral gyrus, **57,** 160

posterior commissure, 54(fig.), **55**

posterior pituitary gland, **66**

posterior position, **46,** 46(fig.), 47

postsynaptic excitation, 32(fig.)

excitatory postsynaptic potentials (EPSPs), **27,** 28–29

postsynaptic inhibition, 32(fig.)

postsynaptic membranes, **22**

effect of neurotransmitter release on, 27

potassium

movement of ions, 25–27

sodium-potassium pump, **26**–27

pragmatics, **130**

praxicons, **249**

precentral gyrus, **57**

predatory aggression, **307**–308, 307(fig.)

predisposition, **409**

preferred direction, **234**

prefrontal aphasias, **350**

prefrontal cortex, **57,** 229, 339–377

anatomy of, 342–343, 342(fig.), 343(fig.)

connections between other brain regions and, 343–344, 344(fig.),

370–377, 370(fig.), 372(fig.), 373(fig.), 376(fig.)
dysfunction of, with Huntington's chorea, 406
dysfunction of, with schizophrenia, 392–393, 393–394
impaired functions after lesions of, 345, 347–362
inventiveness and, 351–352, 351(fig.)
as limbic system structure, 313
Phineas Gage injury case, 341–342, 341(fig.)
regulation of goal-directed behavior role, 340–342
syndromes following lesions of, 362–363
theories of functioning of, 363–377
visual search and, 354–355, 355(fig.)
voluntary movement role, **229,** 251, 252(fig.)
working memory role, 287
working model of function of, 345–347, 346(fig.)
prematurity, **428**
premotor area (PMA), **57**
voluntary movement role, **229,** 235–238, 236(fig.), 237(fig.), 239(fig.)
preparedness theory of phobias, **399**
presinilin genes, **405**
prestriate cortex, **59,** 94
presynaptic facilitation, **31,** 32(fig.)
activity-dependent, **40**
presynaptic inhibition, **31,** 32(fig.)
presynaptic membranes, **22**
active zones, **31**
primary auditory cortex (AI), **59**
primary sensory cortex, **17**
primary sensory neurons, **19**
primary visual cortex (V1), 55, **58, 94,** 110
See also cortical blindness
primary visual pathway. *See* primary visual cortex (V1)
priming, **257**
in amnesic patients, 279–281, 280(fig.)
principal sulcus, **364**
specialized for visuospatial delayed response in monkeys, 367–373
Principles of Psychology (James), 19
proactive interference (PI), **272**
procedural memory, **257**–258, 258n
process-specific approach, **453**
Project for a Scientific Psychology (Freud), 381

property dualism, 458–459
propositional prosody, **325**
proprioception, **57, 159,** 161
prosencephalon. *See* forebrain (prosencephalon)
prosody, **133, 152**
affective, **325,** 327
propositional, **325**
prosopagnosia, **205,** 211–212, 212–213, 214
prospective memory, **354**
proximate causes, **408**
pseudodepression, **348**
pseudopsychopathy, **348**
psychic blindness, **310**
psychic inertia, **348**
psychic neuroscience, 304
psychometric approach to neuropsychology, 15–16
psychopathology, 379–408
anxiety disorders, 398–400
defining, 380–382
dementing diseases, 401–407
mood disorders, **394**–398
schizophrenic disorders, 382–394
sociopathy, **400**
unsolved problems, 407–408
See also specific diseases
psychopathy, **400**
pupillary reflex, **68**
pure agraphia, **150**
pure alexia, **205,** 211–212, 213, 214
pure word deafness, **136,** 137–138
pure word dumbness, **136,** 138
putamen, 60–61, **240**
pyramidal decussation, **68**

Quadfasel, F. A., 136
quadriplegia, **229**

rage, sham, **307,** 307(fig.)
Raichle, M. E., 139, 144, 145, 146, 181
Rakic, P., 420
Ramón y Cajal, Santiago, 20
Ranvier, Louis Antoine, 22
nodes of Ranvier, 21(fig.), **22**
Ratcliff, G., 188, 210, 211
Ravel, Maurice, 226
R cones, **96,** 97(fig.), 98(fig.), 104
reactive depression, **395**
reading, two-route model of, 148, 149(fig.)
reading by sight vocabulary. *See* phonological dyslexia
reading by sound. *See* surface dyslexia

real-position cells, **164,** 164(fig.)
recent memory, **260**
receptive aphasia. *See* Wernicke's aphasia
receptive aprosodia, **152**
receptive fields, **80, 98**–103, 100(fig.)
characteristics of, 99, 104, 108–109, 111(table), 116–118
concentric double-opponent, **110,** 113(fig.), 114–116
types of, 99, 100(fig.)
receptor blockers, **35**
receptor potentials, **42**
receptors, **22**
ionotropic, **35**
metabotropic, **36**
responses to neurotransmitters binding to, 35–36
recognition memory, **269**–270
Recurring Digits Test, 266, 267, 267(fig.)
reduced verbal fluency, **133**
reduction, intertheoretic, **460**–462
reentrant connections, **126,** 126(fig.)
reflectance, **99,** 101, 101(fig.)
refractory period
absolute, **30**
relative, **30**
regional cerebral blood flow (rCBF) method, **78**
registration, **260,** 274
rehabilitation, as approach to brain damage, 451–454
relative refractory period, **30**
release from proactive interference, **272**
release symptoms, **15**
The Remembered Present (Edelman), 256
Remembering (Bartlett), 261
repetition priming, **279**
reptilian brain, **314**
rerouting, 449
reserpine, **395**
effect on neurotransmitter release, 31
response
conditioned, **39**
unconditioned, **39**
resting channels, **23**
resting potential, **25**
resting tremor, **241**
restorative interventions, **452**–453
reticular formation, 68
reticular hypothesis, **20**
retina, **95**–104
cortical, 94, 109
neural processing within, 98–104

retina *(continued)*
photoreceptors, **95,** 96–97, 96(fig.),
97(fig.), 98(fig.)
phototransduction in, 97–98
receptive field characteristics of
neurons, 99, 111(table)
structural overview, 95–96, 95(fig.),
104, 106, 106(fig.)
retinal, **97,** 97n
retinal ganglion cells
ganglion cell layer, **96**
receptive fields, 98–103, 111(table)
types of, 103–104
retinofugal projections, 104, 106–110
retinotopical organization, **94**
retrieval, **261**
strategic, **297**
word, 141–142, 141(table), 142(fig.),
142(table)
retrieval cue, **275**
retrograde amnesia, **263,** 263(fig.), 271,
271(fig.)
and consolidation process, 264–265,
274–275
retrograde degeneration, **443**
retrograde topographical amnesia,
170
retrograde transport, **74**
reuptake, **33**–34
rhinal cortex, memory role of, 268, 270
rhodopsin, **97**
rhombecephalon. *See* hindbrain
(rhombecephalon)
right hemisphere
emotional role, 324–328, 328(fig.)
language role, 151–153
spatial processing role, 165(fig.),
166–167, 166(fig.), 168, 169(fig.)
spatial processing specialization,
159, 160
specialized functioning, 11–12, 160
Risser, A. H., 427
rods, **96,** 96(fig.), 97(fig.)
phototransduction in, 97
Roland, Per, 185, 237
Rolando, Luigi, 6, 6(fig.)
Rolls, E. T., 364
rooting reflex, 15
Rosenzweig, Mark, 292
rostral direction, **46**–47, 46(fig.)
rubella, **429**
Rutter, M., 439

S1. *See* somatosensory cortex (S1)
Sacks, Oliver, 83n

achromatopsia artist account, 83,
116, 186
aprosodia patient, 152
associative agnosia account, 221
sight restored in blind patient, 223
visual agnosia case (Dr. P), 195–196,
203
saggital sections, **47,** 48(fig.)
Sakai, K., 294
saltatory conduction, **31**
Schacter, Daniel
cognitive arousal theory of emotion,
303, 303(fig.)
golfer with Alzheimer's disease, 258
patients with memory impairments,
281, 282, 454
Scheibel, A. B., 153
schemas, **261**
schizophrenia, 382–394
cerebellar atrophy, 388
cortical atrophy, 386–388, 387(fig.)
dopamine hypothesis, **35,** 384–385
dopamine-serotonin interaction
hypothesis, **385**
enlarged ventricles, 385–386,
386(figs.), 387–388
genetic factors, 384
Kraepelin's work, 381, 383, 388
left-hemisphere hypothesis, 393
multiple etiologies, 383–384
neurological abnormalities, 391–392
neuropsychological dysfunction,
392–393, 392(fig.)
prefrontal dysfunction hypothesis,
393–394
prevalence, 382
structural abnormalities, 385–391
symptoms, 383
two-syndrome hypothesis, 387–388
Type I and Type II, **387**–388
Schreber case study (Freud), 381
Schwann cells, **22,** 22(fig.)
Scotti, G., 200, 204
Scoville, William, 261
scripts, **364**
Searl, J., 459
seasonal affective disorder (SAD),
397
secondary motor area, **60,** 61(fig.)
secondary sensory area, **60**
secondary somatosensory cortex (SII),
57, 161
second messengers, **36**
Seelenblindheit, **196**
Segarra, J. M., 136

seizures
commissurotomy, 86–87
sodium amobarbital test in surgery,
89–90
surgical removal of portion of
cortex, 82
selective attention, **358**–359
selective serotonin reuptake inhibitors
(SSRIs), **34,** 395
semantically constrained sentences, **143**
semantically reversible sentences, **143**
semantic dementia, **282**
semantic jargon aphasia, **143**
semantic memory, **257**
loss of, in global amnesia, 282
selective impairments of, 282–283
semantic paraphasia, **133**
semantic processing, **138,** 139–141,
140(table), 141(table)
semantics, **130**
sensitization, **38,** 39(fig.)
sensory association area, **60**
sensory homunculus, **57, 160,** 160(fig.)
sensory receptors, **19**
sentence comprehension and
production, 142–143
septum, **61**–62, 63, 312–313
sequential-hierarchical processing
by visual brain, 94
Luria's model of, 60, 61(fig.), 94
sequential processing, **94**
of language, **10**–11, 11(fig.)
serotonin, **32**
antidepressants blocking reuptake
of, 34
dopamine-serotonin interaction
hypothesis of schizophrenia,
385
LSD slowing release of, 34
selective serotonin reuptake
inhibitors (SSRIs), **34,** 395
serotonin hypothesis of depression,
395
sex-linked transmission, **428**
sex. *See* gender
Shallice, T., 353
sham rage, **307,** 307(fig.)
shape constancy, **203**
Shepard, R. N., 358
Sherrington, Sir Charles, 20, 228
Sherry, D. F., 173
shock, **443**
short-term habituation, **37**
short-term memory, **258**–259
gateway theory, 283–284

selective impairments of, 283–284, 284(figs.), 285(fig.)

separate system for, 264, 284, 284(fig.)

sight. *See* vision

SII. *See* secondary somatosensory cortex (SII)

simple cells, **110**

simultanagnosia, **214**

Singer, J. E., cognitive arousal theory of emotion, 303, 303(fig.)

single-cell recording, **80**

single dissociation, **84,** 84(fig.), 85, 85(fig.), 86

single photon emission computerized tomography (SPECT), **78**–79

Skinner, B. F., 130

smell, olfactory cortex, 59

Snellen Chart, 198

social behavior, impact of prefrontal lesions on, 348–349

social phobia, **398**

social withdrawal, **383**

sociopathy, **400**

Socrates, 457

sodium, movement of ions, 25–27

sodium amobarbital test, **89**–90, 89(tables), 90(table)

sodium-potassium pump, **26**–27

Sokoloff, Louis, 120

soma, **21**

somatic motor system, **47**

somatic nervous system, **47**

somatosensory cortex (S1), **57**–58

body space processing, 160, 160(fig.)

voluntary movement role, **229,** 237, 238(fig.)

somatosensory system, **47**

source amnesia, **272,** 349

spatial agraphia, **150**

spatial dyscalculia, **435**

spatial processing, 157–191

allocentric space, **159**–160, 164–171

body space, **159,** 160–161

egocentric space, **159,** 161–164

frontal lobes role, 188–190, 189(fig.), 190(figs.), 191(fig.)

hemispheric specialization, 159, 160, 166–167, 166(fig.)

hippocampus role, 171–176, 172(fig.), 173(fig.), 174(figs.), 175(fig.)

mental imagery involved in, 184–188, 185(fig.), 186(fig.), 187(fig.)

mental representations of space, 158

neglect, **176**–184, 176(fig.), 177(fig.)

problems in studying, 158–159

and two-pathway hypothesis for object recognition, 170–171, 171(fig.)

spatial summation, **28**

specialization of function

complementary hemispheric specialization, 11–12

Dejarine case providing evidence for, 1, 12–13

discovery of motor cortex, 10

experimental evidence of, 8

intrahemispheric, **9**–10

within visual cortex, 110, 112–120, 124–125

See also cerebral hemispheric specialization

special sensory modalities, **47**

speech production, 143–146, 144(fig.)

brain activation pattern, 144–146, 145(fig.), 146(fig.), 147(figs.)

spelling, 148–150

linguistic (central) disorders, **149**–150

by sound, **149**

two-route model, 150, 150(fig.)

spelling dyslexia, **146**

Sperry, Roger, 87–88

chemospecificity hypothesis, 418–419, 418(fig.)

spinal cord, **69**–70, 69(fig.)

terminology for directions in, 46

spinal nerves, 69

spinal shock, **443**

Spinnler, H., 200, 204

spinothalamic system, 57

splenium, **12**

split-brain surgery. *See* commissurotomy

Spreen, O., 427

sprouting, **449,** 450(fig.)

Spurzheim, Johann Casper, 7, 7(fig.)

staged-lesion effect, **445**

statistical analysis, 16

Steinthal, 243

stereotaxic technique, **307**

stimulus

conditioned, **39**

neutral, **39**

unconditioned, **39**

stimulus bound behavior, **359**

storage, **261,** 274–275

strategic retrieval, **297**

stream of feeling, **308**

stream of thought, **308**

Street Completion Test, 200(fig.)

stress, **409**

striate cortex. *See* visual association cortex

Stroop Test, **359,** 367, 406, 424

structural imaging methods, 74–76

angiography, 75, 75(fig.)

computerized tomography (CT), **75**–76, 76(fig.)

magnetic resonance imaging (MRI), **76,** 77(fig.)

pneumoencephalography, **75,** 75(fig.)

skull X rays, **74**–75, 74(fig.)

study-test modality shift, **280**

stylus maze, 264, 264(fig.)

Styron, William, 395

subarachnoid space, **49,** 50(fig.)

subcallosal gyrus, **61**

subcortical dementia, 405–407

subjective contour, **220**–221

substance dualism, 7, **457**–458

substantia nigra, **61,** 67, **240**

subthalamic nucleus, **61,** 240

subtraction method, **78,** 79–80

sulci, 6, 6(fig.), **53,** 53(fig.), 54(fig.)

superior colliculus, 67–68

superior longitudinal fasciculus, **55,** 56(fig.)

superior occipitofrontal fasciculus, **55,** 56(fig.)

superior olive, **59**

superior position, **46,** 46(fig.)

superior prefrontal convexity, **364**

supplementary motor area (SMA), **57**

voluntary movement role, **229,** 235–238, 236(fig.), 238(fig.)

suppression, **88**

surface dyslexia, **148,** 148(table), **431**

symbolic gestures, **245**

symbolic representations, **157**–158

symbolic search model of visual agnosia, **216**–217, 216(fig.)

symptoms

positive and negative, 347–348, 383

release, **15**

vegetative, **395**

synapses, **20,** 23(fig.)

discovery of, 20

methods for regulating neurotransmitter quantity, 33–35

naming, 23n

transmission at, 22–24, 34(fig.), 42–43

synaptic vesicles, **22**

syntactic agrammatism, **143**
syntax, **129**
syphilis, 381–**382**

tactile aphasia, **136**, 138
tactual perception, **161**
taste, cortical representation for, 60
Taylor, A. M., 201, 203, 325
Taylor, G., model for identifying
    learning disorders, 430, 430(fig.)
tectum, **67**
tegmentum, **67**, 68
telencephalon, **48**, 49(table)
temporal gradient, **265**
temporal hemiretina, **104**, 106(fig.)
temporal integration of behavior, **355**,
    358
temporal-lobe personality, **328**
temporal lobes, **52**, 52(fig.)
    dysfunction of, with schizophrenia,
        392–393
    emotional role, 328–329
    lesions of, impaired memory after,
        265–270, 268(fig.)
temporal summation, **29**
terminology
    for directions/positions in brain,
        46–47
    Greek or Latin derivation, 45–46
    for sections cut through brain, 47,
        48(fig.)
tertiary motor area, **60**
tertiary sensory area, **60**, 61(fig.)
tetanic stimulation (tetanus), 31,
    41(fig.), **42**
Teuber, H. L., 354, 372
thalamic amnesia, **273**
thalamus, 63–65, 64(fig.)
    anterior nucleus, **61**
    lateral geniculate nucleus (LGN), **64**,
        107–109, 108(fig.)
theoretic interanimation, **461**
theory of mind, **438**
thick stripes, **114**
thinking
    convergent, **352**
    divergent, 351–**352**
    feeling vs., neural basis of, 336–337
    impaired, following prefrontal
        lesions, 351–353, 351(fig.)
thin stripes, **114**
third ventricles, **50**, 51(fig.)
threshold potential, **29**
time constant, **29**
tonotopic maps, **59**

topographical disorientation, **168**, 170
topographical memory, 170
topographical memory disorder
    (amnesia), **170**
Tower of Hanoi puzzle, 278–279,
    278(fig.), 279(fig.)
Tower of London Test, 353–354,
    354(fig.), 371
tracts, **50**, 73
transcortical aphasias, **135**–136,
    135(fig.), 139–140, 144
transduction, **59**
translocation, **428**
transmitter-gated channels, **23**
transneuronal degeneration, **443**
transplantation, 454, 455, 455(fig.)
trepanning, 2, 2(fig.)
tricyclic antidepressants, **34**, **395**
trisomy, **428**
triune brain hypothesis, 313–**314**,
    314(fig.)
trochlear nucleus, **68**
Trousseau, Armand, 133
Tulving, Endel, 257, 281, 291
Turner's syndrome, **428**
twin studies, **384**
Type I schizophrenia, **387**
Type II schizophrenia, **387**

ultimate causes, **408**
uncinate fasciculus, **55**, 56(fig.)
unconditioned response, **39**, 316
unconditioned stimulus, **39**, 316
Uneven Lighting Test, 201, 202(fig.)
unilateral structure/connections, 47
unipolar depression. *See* major
    depressive disorder
Unusual Views Test, 201–203, 202(fig.),
    207
Uses of Objects Test, 352
utilization behavior, **359**

V1. *See* primary visual cortex (V1)
Vaccarino, A. L., 173
valence hypothesis, **324**
vegetative symptoms, **395**
ventral hemiretina, **106**
ventral horn, **70**
ventral position, 46–47, 46(fig.)
ventral prefrontal cortex. *See* orbital
    prefrontal cortex
ventral root, **70**
ventricles. *See* cerebral ventricles
ventricular-brain ratio (VBR), **386**,
    386(fig.)

ventricular hypothesis, **5**, 5(fig.)
ventrolateral nucleus of the thalamus
    (VL), **241**
vertical pathways, **101**, 102, 102(fig.),
    103(fig.)
vesicles, **73**
vestibular function, **68**
Vinci, Leonardo da. *See* Leonardo da
    Vinci
visible spectrum, **96**
vision
    amygdala role, 330, 330(fig.)
    color, Young-Helmholtz trichromatic
        theory, 97–98
    construction of representation,
        125–127
    cross-sectional diagram of eye,
        95(fig.)
    deficits of, visual pathways
        associated with, 107, 108(fig.)
    integration problem, 125
    master area hypothesis, 125–126
visual acuity, **198**
    development of, 421–422, 422(fig.)
visual agnosia, **15**, **94**, **195**
    apperceptive agnosia, 197, **199**–203,
        200(figs.), 201(figs.), 202(figs.),
        208(fig.), 209(fig.), 211
    associative agnosia, 197, **203**–211,
        204(fig.), 205(fig.), 206(fig.),
        208(fig.), 209(fig.), 210(fig.),
        211(fig.), 221
    Bay's critique of, 15
    category specificity effects, **205**–206,
        206(fig.), 212–214
    classical model summarized,
        206–207, 207(fig.), 208(fig.)
    disconnection model, 215–216,
        215(fig.)
    early studies of, 196–198
    with Klüver-Bucy syndrome, 310
    massively parallel constraint-
        satisfaction models, 217–220
    vs. partial cortical blindness,
        198–199, 198(fig.), 199(figs.)
    Sacks's case description, 195–196, 203
    symbolic search model, 216–217,
        216(fig.)
    Zeki's conceptualization, 220–222,
        221(fig.), 222(fig.), 223(figs.)
visual association cortex, **59**, **94**, 109
visual cortex, 58–59, 115(fig.)
    microanatomy of, 120–124
    projections from LGN to, 109–110,
        110(fig.), 111(table), 112(figs.)

specialization of function within, 110, 112–120, 124–125
visual disorientation, **161**–164
visual hemifield, **106**
visual localization, 161(fig.), **162**–164
visual orienting, development of, 422, 423(fig.)
visual pigment, **96**–97
visual recognition. *See* visual agnosia
visual word-form dyslexias, **146**
visuokinesthetic engrams, **249**
visuospatial agnosia, **165**–166, 168
visuospatial scratchpad, **285**
vocabulary-based spelling, **149**–150
void condition, **114**
voltage-gated channels, **23**
voluntary movement, 226–252
   cerebellum role, **229**, 238–240
   clarification of term, 227
   components of, 227–228
   elementary disorders, 228–229
   higher-order control of (overview), 229–230, 229(fig.)
   motor cortex (M1) role, **229**, 230–235, 231(fig.), 232(fig.), 233(fig.), 234(fig.), 235(fig.)
   parietal lobes role, **229**, 250–251
   prefrontal cortex role, **229**, 251, 252(fig.)
   premotor area (PMA) role, **229**, 235–238, 236(fig.), 237(fig.), 239(fig.)
   reflex movement vs., 231, 231(fig.), 232(fig.)
   somatosensory area (S1) role, **229**, 237, 238(fig.)
   supplementary motor area (SMA) role, **229**, 235–238, 236(fig.), 238(fig.)
   See also apraxias

von Economo, 55
von Senden, M., 223

Walker, A. E., 343, 343(fig.), 365(fig.)
Wall, P. D., 451
Wallerian degeneration, **443**
Warrington, E. K., 203, 212, 277
   partial cortical blindness impairments, 198–199
   speech production model, 144, 144(fig.), 145
   visual impairment tests, 201, 204
   word retrieval model, 142, 142(fig.)
Watson, John, 130, 381
Wechsler Adult Intelligence Scale
   Arithmetic and Digit Span subtests, 350
   Block Design Subtest, 158
Weiskrantz, L., 277
Wernicke, Carl, 10–13
   conduction aphasia, 11, 135
   disconnection syndrome hypothesis, 11, 135, 135(fig.), 215
   sequential processing concept, 10–11, 11(fig.)
   Wernicke's aphasia, 10, 84, 134–135, 143
   Wernicke's area, **10**, 10(fig.), 137–138, 137(fig.), 139, 139(fig.), 150–151
white matter, 50, 51(fig.)
   in spinal cord, 69–70
whole-body movements, **246**
Wiesel, Torsten, 110, 117, 120, 123, 124, 419
Wisconsin Card Sorting Test, 362
   attention deficit disorder, 437
   conceptual thinking, 352–353
   Parkinson's disease, 407
   perseveration, 334, 334(fig.), 361, 367, 371

schizophrenia, 390, 391(fig.)
Wong-Riley, Margaret, 110
word forms, **213**
word retrieval, 141–142, 141(table), 142(fig.), 142(table)
word salad, **383**
word superiority effect, **213**
The Working Brain (Luria), 94
working memory, **259**–260, 259(fig.), 260(fig.), 289(fig.)
   buffers component, 284–285, 284–290
   emotional, 334–335, 336
   frontal lobes role, 285–290
   impaired, following prefrontal lesions, 350
workspace, **259**, 284
writing, 150
Wundt, Wilhelm, 78, 197

X rays, skull, 74–75, 74(fig.)

Yarbuss, A. L., 358
Young, Thomas, 97, 98
Young-Helmholtz trichromatic theory of color vision, 97–**98**

Zaidel, E., 152
Zangwill, O., 160, 166, 432
Zeki, Semir, 116, 208
   critique of two-pathway hypothesis for object recognition and spatial processing, 171
   reentrant hypothesis, 126, 163, 222
   visual agnosia conceptualization, 207, 220, 220–222, 221, 221(fig.), 222(fig.), 223(figs.)
Zola-Morgan, S., 270